JOHN LOCKE

AN ESSAY CONCERNING HUMAN UNDERSTANDING

EDITED WITH A FOREWORD
BY
PETER H. NIDDITCH

CLARENDON PRESS · OXFORD

Oxford University Press, Walton Street, Oxford OX2 6DP
Oxford New York Toronto
Delhi Bombay Calcutta Madras Karachi
Petaling Jaya Singapore Hong Kong Tokyo
Nairobi Dar es Salaam Cape Town
Melbourne Auckland
and associated companies in
Berlin Ibadan

Oxford is a trade mark of Oxford University Press

The text of Locke's Essay is reprinted (with corrections) from the Clarendon Edition, first Published 1975.

First Published 1975
Reprinted 1979, 1987
First issued as a paperback 1979
Reprinted 1982, 1984, 1985, 1987, 1988

British Library Cataloguing in Publication Data
Locke, John
An essay concerning human understanding.
Clarendon edn.
I. Knowledge, Theory of
I. Title II. Nidditch, Peter Harold
121 B1290 79–40403
ISBN 0–19–824386–3
ISBN 0–19–824595–5 (Pbk)

Printed in Hong Kong

Michael Smith
Spring '90
(Empiricism
330)

AN ESSAY CONCERNING HUMAN UNDERSTANDING

questions:
difference between
Volition
Will
Liberty
?

Why no clear + distinct idea of substance?

Tom Hebert

665-1264

CONTENTS

FOREWORD

To prejudg other mens notions before we have looked into them is not to shew their darkness but to put out our own eyes. LOCKE

The Present Edition

THIS edition of the *Essay* contains a complete, critically established, and unmodernized text (including the author's index) that aims at being historically faithful to Locke's final intentions. The text is supplemented by footnotes detailing alterations of wording and others of significance in the early, authorized printings of the book. The text pages are reproduced from my full historico-critical edition of the *Essay* in the Clarendon Edition of the Works of John Locke; although the introduction, the glossary, and the other editorial material in that volume are omitted here for reasons of economy and compactness, it has been possible in the new format to insert this short foreword, which offers information and suggestions complementary to discussions the philosophical reader is likely to encounter elsewhere.

The Ascendancy of the Essay

The *Essay* has long been recognized as one of the great works of English literature of the seventeenth century, and one of the epoch-making works in the history of philosophy. It has been one of the most repeatedly reprinted, widely disseminated and read, and profoundly influential books of the past three centuries, since its initial publication in December 1689. In particular, it has been and continues to be actively studied by philosophers and students of philosophy the world over; the reasons for this are naturally complex, but two focal points may be singled out.

(1) The *Essay* gained for itself a unique standing as the most thorough and plausible formulation of empiricism—a viewpoint that it caused to become an enduring powerful force. Philosophical terms ending in 'ism', e.g. 'empiricism', and their cognates and various other class or type terms are dangerous to apply because they may, and commonly do, conceal historical differences and even divergences; it may therefore be misleading to use them without definite clarification, and it may be impossible to give a

satisfactory short account of the meaning of such a term because imprecision may be the price of brief comprehensiveness. The ordinary needs and habits of communication, however, override these difficulties to a great extent. The empiricism of Hobbes (1588–1679), Locke (1632–1704), and Hume (1711–76) should be seen as a compound of several doctrines, not all of them exclusively epistemological. Among them are, as a first approximation: that our natural powers operate in a social and physical environment that we seek to adapt ourselves to, and that the variable functioning of these powers in that environment is the agency by which we get and retain all our ideas, knowledge, and habits of mind; that our capacities of conscious sense-experience and of feeling pleasure or discomfort are primary natural powers; that the abuse of language, especially in scholastic systems and indulgent speculative hypotheses, is a troublesome source of errors and of obstacles to intellectual improvement and moral and social stability; that religious fervour is contemptible and sectarian strife is deplorable; and that although science, which proceeds by reasoning about propositions whose terms represent existent ideas or realities, deserves our respect, its scope for attaining conclusive success is extremely limited at best. A marked difference between Hume's empiricism and Hobbes's and Locke's is his low estimation of the power of reason; Hume's assertion that reason 'can never pretend to any other office than to serve and obey' the passions would have been abhorrent to Hobbes and Locke.

The *Essay* presents, for the first time, a systematic, detailed, reasoned, and wide-ranging philosophy of mind and cognition whose thrust, so far as it is in line with the future rather than the past, is empiricist. It must be acknowledged that it was Hobbes among British philosophers—concurrently with the Frenchman Gassendi (1592–1655)—who first produced in the modern era, especially in his *Leviathan* and *De Corpore*, a philosophy of mind and cognition that built on empiricist principles. A characteristic declaration of Hobbes's empiricism (and nominalism) is:

No Discourse whatsoever, can End in absolute knowledge of Fact, past, or to come. For, as for the knowledge of Fact, it is originally, Sense; and ever after, Memory. And for the knowledge of Consequence, which I have said before is called Science, it is not Absolute, but Conditionall. No man can know by Discourse, that this, or that, is, has been, or will be; which is to know absolutely: but onely, that if This be, That is; if This has been, That has been; if This shall be, That shall be: which is to know conditionally; and that not the consequence of one thing to another; but of one name of a thing, to another name of the same thing (*Leviathan*, I. vii).

Nevertheless, that Hobbes was a forerunner does not detract from Locke's achievement and role. Hobbes did not manage to write a book that could begin to match the quickly won and lasting popularity of Locke's major work. His masterpiece, *Leviathan*, differs from the *Essay* in not being chiefly concerned with questions in the philosophy of mind and cognition, and it is these that have been largely dominant since the sixteenth century. Hobbes did not undertake a systematic tracing of our ideas to their empirical origins; this was pioneered by Locke, who deployed in the process an original concept of experience divided into external ('sensation') and internal ('reflection'). Also, in contrast with Locke's emphatic dualism of mind and body, his moderate theism, and his ultimately libertarian account of action (II. xxi. 47–8), Hobbes's reduction of everything to bodies and motions, his suspected atheism, and his strict determinism were—along with his extreme egoism in ethics—repugnant to his contemporaries and to the next century and beyond; and his theory of matter was soon overtaken by that of Boyle (1627–91), from which Locke's derives. An additional, different sort of reason may be conjectured: Hobbes's name in his own period and in the next century did not, unlike that of the author of the *Essay*, resound with opposition to authoritarianism, with the vindication of toleration (i.e. religious freedom), and with other liberal values, with which the generality of advancing philosophers and educationists associated themselves.

(2) The *Essay* is rich in philosophical matter; this makes it a much sought-after quarry—both a source and a target. As a glance through the Contents (pp. 17 ff.) or the book itself reveals, it grapples with fundamental questions in the philosophy of mind and cognition, and with some in the philosophy of language, the philosophy of logic, the philosophy of religion, and moral philosophy; and it touches on numerous other topics. The book is written in a broadly intelligible style (cf. 9(6–11) (i.e. page 9, lines 6–11), 10(10–11)), and the gist of its teachings and the outlines of its arguments are tolerably clear. So what it says about, for example, innateness, experience, sense-perception, self-knowledge, qualities, memory, space, time, number, infinity, freedom and

necessity, universals, substance, causality, personal identity, truth and falsity, meaning, knowledge, probability, belief, and the role of logical principles, is often found a convenient starting-point for further consideration by practising philosophers. But to the critically minded, even if they find the tenor of his work attractive, Locke's statements, assumptions, and arguments, amidst the rambling rose (and rows) of the *Essay*, are a continual provocation; this comes about especially through his simplicities and conflations, the ambiguities of key terms and hence of key assertions, and inner tensions and clashes in his thought: these sometimes make him resemble Bunyan's Mr. Facing-bothways, Mr. Two-tongues, and the 'Water-man, looking one way, and Rowing another'. On the other hand, the divisions and oppositions in his thought (e.g. between his perceptual idealism and realism, his naturalism and supernaturalism, and his factual claim that 'Number applies it self to . . . every thing' (II. xvi. 1) and his nominalist claim that 'Names [are] necessary to Numbers' (II. xvi. 5)) may well have been creative: without them, he might not have been driven to pursue his problems as persistently and devotedly as he did in preparing the *Essay* over many years—and then, after its publication, recurrently touching it up and writing additions for it—in order to resolve them with full explicitness and coherence. Of course, he did not succeed. But has any other philosopher succeeded better, or been of more widespread service to his fellows?

Locke's Life and Works

Locke's biography, besides its intrinsic interest, affords essential knowledge of the context in which the *Essay* was produced, and of its place among his works.

John Locke (29 August 1632–28 October 1704) was the son of John Locke senior (1606–61), an attorney and small land-owner, and Agnes Locke (*née* Keene) (1597–1654). He was born and brought up in a district of Somerset that was within ten miles of Bristol. One permanently formative part of his upbringing was his induction into his parents' determined Protestant faith; this led him in his manhood to be contemptuous and distrustful of religious enthusiasts, Catholics, and atheists. From the age of fourteen he was educated at Westminster School, which he later described as being a 'very severe schoole' because of the flogging practices there.

(In his *Some Thoughts Concerning Education* he counselled strongly against the punishment of children as a means of correcting or guiding them; kind firmness should suffice.) From Westminster, where he received a thorough grounding in Latin and Greek, Locke went in 1652 to Christ Church, Oxford, where, after following the usual Arts course (in Classical studies, grammar, rhetoric, logic, geometry, and moral philosophy) with limited interest and with distaste for the disputatious exercises, he graduated B.A. in 1656. He shortly afterwards became a senior Student of his college and retained this status, with rooms and emoluments, until Charles II (1630–85) personally required his expulsion in 1684, in the wake of Shaftesbury's final fall. It was perhaps in the late 1650s that Locke first read, and was refreshed by, Descartes (1596–1650). About this time or a little later he began to take an interest in physical science, and then in medicine where he became a close associate of Sydenham (1624–89), the distinguished physician with notable empirical leanings. He was acquainted with Boyle, the chemist and physicist (whose liberal views on toleration Locke found persuasive) and probably with other originators of the budding Royal Society, of which he became a Fellow in 1668. He lectured on Greek and rhetoric and performed supervisory duties for his college until 1665, when he left the confines of the academic world, henceforth to mix at home and abroad with persons of rank, affairs, and fortune, and with distinguished virtuosi, physicians, and scholars.

In the winter of 1665–6 he was abroad for the first time, as secretary to Charles II's ambassador to the Elector of Brandenburg at Cleves, where, as he wrote to Boyle, the Calvinists, Lutherans, Catholics, and Anabaptists 'quietly permit one another to choose their way to heaven'. He returned home, his future course still uncertain. He desired to get exemption from the usual obligation of a Student to take holy orders, and to be allowed to remain a layman by qualifying as a physician with a higher degree, and so, without waiting to fulfil the conditions for graduating M.B. first (he obtained this degree in 1675), he made a bid for the degree of Doctor of Medicine; after a failure, he gained his exemption in 1667, but not the degree.

A chance encounter had occurred in 1666 that proved to be the decisive turning-point in Locke's life: he met Lord Ashley (1621–83; created Earl of Shaftesbury, 1672), at that time Chancellor of the Exchequer, who used his influence to get Locke granted the latter's desired exemption from holy orders. Ashley soon invited Locke to take up residence at his London house, where Locke lived, from 1667 to 1675, as confidant and medical adviser. Locke was responsible in 1668 for a life-saving surgical operation on Ashley, who remained duly grateful. He subsequently became Secretary to the Lords Proprietors of Carolina (of whom Ashley was the most important) and to the Council of Trade and Plantations (of which Ashley was the President), and, during his patron's Lord Chancellorship, his Secretary for Presentations. These private and public roles were congenial to him. This was the happy period when the *Essay* was initially engendered, shaped, and developed. Without Ashley, there would have been no *Essay*. Ashley's powerful personality, keen mind, and forward-looking outlook probably did much to strengthen and extend Locke's maturing liberalism, not least by adding an economic dimension to it.

In November 1673 Shaftesbury (as Ashley had become) was dismissed by the King from the Lord Chancellorship; his other offices were then terminated, and the Council of Trade and Plantations was abolished. Locke must have been dismayed by all this; he was a man who (in Sydenham's description) had more than 'naturall tenderness and delicacy of sence', i.e. was hypersensitive. The upset and Locke's resulting fear—those were harsh days of royal retribution—contributed to the return of his asthmatic cough, from which he often suffered till his death.

There was an introverted, valetudinarian component in Locke's nature—which may have aided his self-preservation. He was a careful, cautious man, possessed of a good sense of business and method. Almost until he died he kept, with minute exactness, running accounts of all monies he received, spent, lent, or owed. He shied away from drinking parties and other hectic forms of social life, and from emotionality, high spirits, the dramatic, and even the aesthetic. He never married, and remained, it seems, completely continent; but he liked the attentions of lady admirers. He had many loyal friends, and got on especially well with some of his friends' children. His preference was for undisturbing circumstances and friendly surroundings where he could be active and industrious while maintaining an independence, calmness, self-control, and deliberation in all things; but from time to time unruly events and people unfortunately intruded.

Locke's finances were much improved by an annuity to which Shaftesbury substantially contributed. With Shaftesbury's consent he went abroad, to France (where he had been for a few weeks' holiday in 1672); he stayed there, with bases first at Montpellier and then at Paris, from November 1675 till the end of April 1679, when he returned to England, as it happened promptly on Shaftesbury's resumption of public office. He occupied those years with travel, acting as a tutor-companion, diverse reading, translating (some of the *Essais de morale* of Pierre Nicole (1625–95)), social visits, and numerous scientific, medical, philosophical, and other intellectual interchanges; and with writing up his Journal that he commenced on his departure, filling it with records of books, medical and scientific notes, descriptions of his travels, money accounts, other memoranda, and a variety of philosophical sketches, many of them substantial and mostly on themes to be found in the *Essay* for which the sketches, after revision, were perhaps designed. It was during this period that he became a friend of the future Earl of Pembroke (1656–1733) to whom the *Essay* is dedicated. (Pembroke achieved a remarkable double: he is also the dedicatee of Berkeley's *Principles of Human Knowledge* (1710).)

When Locke returned from France in 1679, English politics were disturbed, and continued to be so for another ten years, by the consequences of the Catholicism of Charles II's younger brother James (1633–1701), the heir apparent. To many citizens—Locke among them—a papist King meant monarchical despotism, the forced conversion of the nation to a Catholic kingdom, its subservience to foreign powers, and persecution. A number of politicians, with Shaftesbury and his party, the Whigs, in the vanguard, wanted, even desperately, to get James's succession excluded by Act of Parliament. Charles, while an avowed Anglican, had shown that he was not without Catholic sympathies, and on his deathbed he entered the Church of Rome. Further, he saw that a victory for his opponents would affect his own powers. He stood by his brother. The Whigs lost that battle. Shaftesbury, in 1681, now in poor health, was committed to the Tower of London (where he had already spent a year in 1677–8) on a charge of high treason; he had a moment of triumph when he was acquitted by the grand jury, but, fearing revenge for the indignities he had inflicted on the King in recent years, he soon fled to Holland in November 1682 and died in Amsterdam a couple of months later.

Locke, who, although he had not returned to Shaftesbury's employment in 1679, had actively continued his association with him, liked and admired him both as a statesman concerned with liberty and toleration and for his personal qualities. Shaftesbury's body was brought back to England for burial; Locke attended the funeral.

We have only sporadic pieces of Locke's philosophical writing during the years 1679–83, when perhaps his principal literary activity was harnessed to politics and toleration. This was interrupted in August 1683. By this time a number of Whigs—peers, publicists, and ordinary followers—had been arrested and Locke, as a known Shaftesburian, planned his removal to Holland (tolerant, and convenient for keeping in touch with friends in England), where he arrived on 7 September into a second exile that was to last longer than his first, French one. It was during his stay in Holland that his decades of reading, thinking, note-making, and drafting leaped towards momentous and manifold authorship. He further drafted and rewrote material for the *Essay*, getting this into final shape; he also made an abridgement of the book which, appearing in French translation in a scholarly periodical in 1688, at once brought international attention to the *Essay*. He wrote his *Epistola de Tolerantia* (*Letter on Toleration*), and possibly worked on the *Two Treatises of Government*. His *Some Thoughts Concerning Education* was mostly composed from letters of this period that he sent to his friend and agent Edward Clarke (*c.* 1650–1710) about the upbringing of the latter's son Edward.

Charles II died in 1685 and James became King, speedily arousing hostility and agitations because some steps and policies of his were markedly Catholic. William of Orange (1650–1702) and his wife Mary (1662–94), who were James's nephew and daughter, and Protestants, became joint King and Queen of England, after James had been compelled by events to withdraw to France in December 1688. William had landed in England in November 1688; Mary, like Locke, waited in Holland until all was settled, when they sailed, in February 1689, in the same yacht to Greenwich.

After his return to England Locke lodged in London, which he continued to visit fairly frequently until 1700 from an estate called Oates, near High Laver (about twenty-five miles from London) in Essex, where from Christmas 1690 he stayed for periods as a paying guest, and then from 1692 settled as a resident in the house of Sir Francis Masham, M.P. (1645–1722) and his second wife, Damaris (1659–1708), a daughter of the Cambridge Platonist, Ralph Cudworth (1617–88): it was probably Damaris who invited Locke to make his home at Oates, and it was she who looked after him in his last days.

Within a week of Locke's arrival in London in 1689 he was offered the post of English ambassador to the Elector of Brandenburg (the future King Frederick I of Prussia). But he resolved, after the dangers, discomforts, and interruptions of so many years, to remain in England; and he never left it again. He declined the King's offer on the grounds of 'that weak and broken constitution of my health which has soe long threatend my life', his inexperience in diplomatic business, and the disability from his being 'the soberest man in the Kingdom' who knew 'noe such rack in the world to draw out mens thoughts as a well managed Bottle'. The only occupation as a public servant he then accepted was as a Commissioner of Appeals in Excise; later he held the demanding and more important office of a Commissioner of the Board of Trade until 1700. From 1689 he took an active interest in parliamentary affairs and contributed significantly towards the liberation of printing and publishing from the constraints of the Licensing Act.

Locke's refusal of a diplomatic appointment had been motivated not merely by considerations of his health and convenience. He had plans as an author that he was determined to accomplish. He urgently wanted to see the *Essay* and the *Two Treatises of Government* properly in print; the manuscripts of these were in their almost final state. The completed manuscript of his *Epistola de Tolerantia* had been left behind for printing in the care of his closest Dutch friend van Limborch (1643–1712), a scholar and theologian belonging to the heterodox Remonstrant sect of Dutch Calvinists who believed (as Locke did) that the sovereignty of God is compatible with man's freedom and does not entail predestination; the book was published in Gouda in Spring 1689, and an English translation (by another hand) in London six months later. That Locke's first published book was on toleration and his next to appear, about mid November 1689 (only about a month before the *Essay*), was the *Two Treatises*, with its insistence that the authority of rulers is limited and conditioned by individuals' rights and the sake of 'the Publick Good', is symbolic of Locke's moral priorities, which are largely influential in the *Essay* too.

He was already disposed towards the priority of the moral when a young man: his earliest surviving systematic writings, left unpublished, were on questions of toleration, political power, and natural law. He had, in one way or another, been working towards the *Epistola* for nearly thirty years, the *Essay* for nearly twenty years, and the *Two Treatises* for a decade; the results of all these prolonged efforts, made in days of light and shadow, suddenly emerged into public view in 1689, which was indeed Locke's *annus mirabilis*.

The *Essay* bore the author's name, as the already published abridgement had done; the other two books remained anonymous until after his death, when his acknowledgement of their authorship in his last will became known. Whether the anonymity of these and some of his other books was due solely to a wish to appear unegotistically concerned with principles or was in some degree motivated by self-protection against personal attacks by opponents is a matter of conjecture.

Although Locke was approaching sixty, his energy for writing books was far from waning. Two additional pieces on toleration soon followed (1690, 1692; these and other book dates below are those on the title-page of the first printing); three on monetary matters (1692, 1695, 1695); *Some Thoughts Concerning Education* (1693); and *The Reasonableness of Christianity* (1695), and two defences of it (1695, 1697), which represented Christianity, on the historical basis of scripture, in a latitudinarian spirit. Locke was certainly unorthodox; he was also devout.

The last years of the 1690s were taken up with a lot of work relating to the *Essay* again. Locke wrote three successive replies—the first two of moderate length, the third of 120,000 words—to criticisms of the *Essay* made by Edward Stillingfleet, Bishop of Worcester (1635–99). He had carefully revised the *Essay* for the second edition (1694: see 11 (1 ff.)), substantially altering one chapter (II. xxi) and adding another (II. xxvii); he now renewed this task for the fourth edition (1700), and added two more chapters (II. xxxiii and IV. xix). He actively supervised a French translation, and took some interest in the preparation of a Latin translation (1700, 1701, respectively).

Locke's last completed book was the studious *Paraphrase and Notes on the Epistles of St. Paul*; this was published posthumously (1705–7), as was a collection of other *Posthumous Works* (1706), of which the most substantial item was 'Of the Conduct of the Understanding', edited from an extensive and heavily amended manuscript which Locke had for some years been trying to finalize for incorporating as a very long additional chapter into the *Essay*.

Objectives of the Essay

During the seventeenth century educated opinion in England—to some extent paralleled on the Continent—drifted from an admiring preoccupation with the history, literature, and language of the ancient world, especially Rome, and from Christian theology and ritual, logical formality, scholastic thought, and authoritarianism, towards, in various degrees of proximity, a confidence in the superiority of modern novelties and modern powers, reasonable religion and secular values, personal expression and plain style, a critical appeal to reason and the rule of sensible evidence, and individualistic, egalitarian freedom of practice, thought, and judgement. The *Essay* had this distinction, that in it Locke was a firm spokesman for all these currents at once, in association with an elaborated philosophy of mind and cognition. His progressive predecessors and contemporaries, such as Gilbert (1540–1603), Bacon (1561–1626), Hobbes, Descartes, Spinoza (1632–77), and Bayle (1647–1706), favoured only some of them while opposing others, or did not connect them with a general philosophy suited to propelling them further. The propagation of these currents was a significant part of Locke's purpose in the book, whose prefatory Epistles immediately reveal his attitude in regard to several of them.

Thus, he upheld novelty and the independence of individual judgement by saying that 'The Imputation of Novelty, is a terrible charge amongst those, who judge of Men's Heads, as they do of their Perukes, by the Fashion; and can allow none to be right, but the received Doctrines' (4(1–3)), and that the quest of the *Essay* 'is the Entertainment of those, who let loose their own Thoughts, and follow them in writing' (6(25–6)). He stressed the vital role of the search and application of experienced fact in the accumulation and testing of truth; it is 'Trial and Examination must give [Truth] price, and not any antick Fashion' (4(8–9): 'antick' = 'antique', 'antiquated'). He returned to these themes repeatedly; and with striking rhetoric near the end of the book (IV. xix. 2, xx. 11, 17; cf. 552 (15 ff.)) he launched attacks on both those who dictate opinions and those who submissively follow them, and derided the suffering of 'the learned Professor' whose 'Authority . . . [is] overturned by an upstart Novelist' (714(9–14): 'Novelist' = 'innovator').

He also, influentially, complimented the attainments of the commonwealth of learning of his age, with its 'Master-Builders, whose mighty Designs, in advancing the Sciences, will leave lasting Monuments to the Admiration of Posterity' (9(35–7)), and blamed the 'learned but frivolous use of uncouth, affected, or unintelligible Terms, introduced into the Sciences' and 'Vague and insignificant Forms of Speech, and Abuse of Language, [which] have so long passed for Mysteries of Science' (10(7–12)) for the earlier lack of progress. These and other remarks of his soon, and have often since, struck readers as implying that the only profitable intellectual pathway to the knowledge of things is through observational, experimental, and mathematical methods, the only alternative being idle, verbal speculation. And on top of this Locke seemed to boost the branches of learning that use those methods, by describing in very modest terms his philosophical tasks, of analysing the understanding and the pathology and purgation of language, as if they were merely subservient to the smooth advancement of such knowledge (6(6–8), 9(33–4), 10(3–5)). But his turns of phrase here were an ironic masking of his priority of concern with conduct over scientific inquisitiveness (cf., e.g., 645(20)–646(17)). Accordingly, a philosophical inquiry into the nature and grounds of certainty was required above all to determine the application and scope of certainty in the most important cases, namely in religion and ethics.

A passage in the Epistle to the Reader (7(16 ff.)) narrates the origin of Locke's engagement with his philosophical tasks: some friends of his at a meeting in his apartment found themselves in difficulties on all sides in the course of their discussion on a subject very remote from that of the understanding; whereupon—Locke now involving himself—'it came into my Thoughts, that we took a wrong course; and that, before we set our selves upon Enquiries of that Nature, it was necessary to examine our own Abilities, and see, what Objects our Understandings were, or were not fitted to deal with'. A partial hint of the subject of the discussion was provided in I. i. 6–7, where after postulating that 'Our Business here is not to know all things, but those which concern our Conduct' (46(31–2); cf. 'Morality and Divinity, those parts of Knowledge, that Men are most concern'd to be clear in' (11(13–14)) and '*Morality* is *the proper Science, and Business of Mankind in general*' (646(12–13)); see also, e.g., 302(10 ff.)), a view he shared with Nicole, he went on to explain that 'This was that which gave the first *Rise* to this Essay concerning the Understanding. For I thought that the first Step towards satisfying several Enquiries, the Mind of Man was very apt to run into, was, to take a Survey of our own Understandings, examine our own Powers, and see to what Things they were adapted. Till that was done I suspected we began at the wrong end', this common mistake resulting in the multiplication of irresolvable disputes and in complete scepticism (46(37)–47(16)). This throws light on the programme he had just stated: it is 'my *Purpose* to enquire into the Original, Certainty, and Extent of humane Knowledge; together, with the Grounds and Degrees of Belief, Opinion, and Assent . . . It is therefore worth while, to search out the *Bounds* between Opinion and Knowledge; and examine by what Measures, in things, whereof we have no certain Knowledge, we ought to regulate our Assent, and moderate our Perswasions' (43(14–16), 44(17–20)).

He readily assumed, because of his presupposed identification of what is in the mind and what may be consciously perceived (e.g. 50(39)–51(2)), that an adequate ophthalmology of the eye of the understanding (cf. 43(4–7)) can be discovered by a process of self-examination. But Locke did not regard this as being an *a priori* science that could be completed and made certain once and for all, as Kant (1724–1804) was later to do in respect of his articulation of reason in the first *Critique*. Locke conceded his fallibility (e.g. at 7(10) and 11(10–25); cf. 682(13–15)), admitting (too much for Kantian and post-Kantian tastes) the limitations and imperfections of his subject—the natural philosophy of mind and cognition, and semantics (cf. IV. xxi. 2, 4).

Locke's friend James Tyrrell (1642–1718), whose interests and views regarding politics and toleration were closely similar to Locke's, was present at the original meeting in Locke's apartment; he annotated the passage on the history of the *Essay* in the Epistle to the Reader, and recorded in his copy that the discussion had been about 'the Principles of morality, and reveald Religion'. These were not neglected in the *Essay*; but Locke's version of those principles underlay his text much more than they were his main explicit topics. His direct treatment of those principles here was occasional, and clearer in what it denied than what it affirmed. The innateness of moral principles was controverted in I. iii; the thesis that moral science is capable of demonstration, as well as mathematics is, was adumbrated more than once (516(21 ff.), 549(17 ff.), 643 (26 ff.)), although never worked out, despite repeated requests by another friend, the Irishman William Molyneux (1656–98); and an account of moral conditions and relations was included in II. xx–xxi and xxviii. 4–16. These last passages supplied all that Locke wanted to state in the *Essay* about the norms of conduct. The source of the highest of these norms is the divine law, 'whether promulgated to [Men] by the light of Nature, or the voice of Revelation. . . . by comparing them to this Law, it is, that Men judge of the most considerable *Moral Good* or *Evil* of their Actions; that is, whether as *Duties, or Sins*, they are like to procure them happiness, or misery, from the hands of the ALMIGHTY' (352(15–26)). Locke was brief about this supreme matter because he, in part rightly and in part to avoid spoiling his case by the inclusion of controversial details, presumed his readers' awareness of the content of the moral life entailed by his references to 'the light of Nature', i.e. reason, which is 'natural *Revelation*' (698(25)), and to supernatural revelation in the Bible.

Revealed religion was discussed in two chapters (IV. xviii, xix), in which he restricted it, obliquely, to the Christian scriptures by his distrust and contempt of other pretensions to revelation, and rationalistically emphasized (e.g. at 692(29 ff.)) that no supposed revealed proposition can contradict our knowledge or reason. There had been anticipations of this distrust, contempt, and rationalism earlier in the Restoration by, amongst others, Joseph Glanvill (1636–80) in his essays on 'The Usefulness of Real Philosophy to Religion', 'The Agreement of Reason and Religion', and 'Anti-fanatical Religion and Free Philosophy'; and prior to the Restoration by Hobbes (*Leviathan*, III. xxxii). Those attitudes and standards prefigured the militant deism and atheism of the eighteenth century, which adopted them against the Christian scriptures too. Locke renewed his inquiry into the principles of revealed religion in his *Reasonableness of Christianity*. In this, as is clear from its first paragraph, he advocated a historical empiricism, plainness of sense, and the rejection of systems of divinity with their 'learned, artificial, and forced senses' of expressions, in the understanding of the scriptures, which were for him, with his simple faith, designed by God 'for the instruction of the illiterate bulk of Mankind in the way to Salvation; and therefore generally and in necessary points to be understood in the plain direct meaning of the words and phrases, such as they may be supposed to have had in the mouths of the Speakers, who used them according to the Language of that Time and Country wherein they lived'. The considerations adduced here are analogous to or identical with fundamental grounds he utilized in the *Essay*. Locke did not labour to support them: they were what he built on and around.

Human Understanding

It has frequently happened to great philosophers that they have been in the grip of contrastive pairs of fundamental convictions, valuations, or orientations, and hence commonly that what they have constructed is itself riddled with inner clashes and tensions; thus Plato's conceptions of the soul as movement and life, and as allied to the Ideas which are unmoving and lifeless, were scarcely harmonious notions of reality, any more than were his conceptions that each Idea is a supreme reality and that the Ideas are sortally related in a hierarchical way; and underlying Kant's bifurcation of 'the starry heavens above and the moral law within' were his opposing principles about the regulated world of empirical appearances and the free world of spiritual values. Locke likewise was torn or driven in contrary directions. His committed anti-scepticism was at odds with his chief epistemological stance, which was agnostic. His restriction of our proper business to knowledge of matters of conduct was, as perhaps he recognized and excused (at 6(10–13)), curious in an author of a large epistemological book that was distinctly reticent, yet not agnostic, about our knowledge of such matters. His perceptual realism pulled against the idealism bound up with ways in which he persistently used the term 'idea' to stand for 'whatsoever is the Object of the Understanding when a Man thinks' (47(29–30)), and against his corpuscularian conception of the nature of material things, together with his doctrine of secondary versus primary qualities. His rationalistic canon that 'Reason must be our last Judge and Guide in every Thing' (704(20–1)) was not readily convergent with his empiricist or his Christian convictions.

These illustrations should be complemented by another observation. In his constructive efforts Locke had to reconcile with one another his repudiation of sophistical speculation and the abuse of language, his wish to be instructive, and his urbane concern that his philosophical output be fit and able to be 'brought into well-bred Company, and polite Conversation' (10(10–11): 'polite' = 'civilized'). The latter consideration imparts a new twist to the cause of plain simplicity of utterance advocated a generation or two earlier by preachers and by spokesmen linked with the Royal Society, with the aims—which Locke also shared—of securely effecting moral or scientific improvement. One symptom of his not always successful struggle is that he entitled the book an 'Essay' which suggested a personal, informal, descriptive work catering widely for the ordinary educated reader; and yet within the text he sometimes called it a 'Treatise' (e.g. at 3(12, 26), 6(9)), which connoted a more ponderous, systematic, and learned book (cf. 12(13–19)).

One of the consequences of Locke's determination to be informal in the *Essay* was that he did not make clear near the beginning what he meant by the 'human understanding', and it was not until he reached II. vi. 2, after numerous, apparently synonymous references to 'the Mind' and 'the Understanding', that he turned, in passing, to elucidate these terms and the relation between their designations. He distinguished, following tradition, between the 'two great and principal Actions of the Mind', which are perception or thinking, and volition. The understanding—the term corresponded to the Latin *intellectus*, 'intellect'—is the mind's faculty, power, or ability to think; volition is the mind's faculty, power, or ability to will. Locke showed, at II. xxi. 6, 20, that he was aware of some problems about the meaning and use of 'faculty'; but he did not dwell on them. The term 'the Mind' is usually applied in the *Essay* to represent only the understanding. Further, this intellectual faculty is not uniform, but is exercised in a variety of ways, among them contemplating, remembering, distinguishing, comparing, compounding, abstracting, reasoning, judging, knowing, and believing (II. ix ff. and IV).

With a stab at Descartes's school, Locke excluded the passions, e.g. desire, love, hatred, and anger, from the faculty of volition

(249(29 ff.)). He described desire, feeling, and emotion as variants of pleasure or pain, which are states of the understanding. Not surprisingly in view of his medical interests, he assigned an important place in the life of the mind to the passions, especially to what he called uneasiness, 'All pain of the body of what sort soever, and disquiet of the mind' (251(4–5)). It is uneasiness alone that determines the will (II. xxi. 29, 31, 33 ff.); nevertheless, as Locke insisted in 'Of the Conduct of the Understanding' with Socratic intellectualism, the will 'never fails in its Obedience to the Dictates of the Understanding' (cf. 237 (6)). Hence a man's thoughts bear a responsible precedence in him as a cognitive and as an active agent. But neither the understanding nor the will are more than powers: 'it is the Mind that operates, and exerts these Powers; it is the Man that does the Action, . . . or is able to do' (243(5–6)).

Why was the title of the *Essay* chosen to refer to 'human understanding'? The epithet 'human' made clear that the book was about man and not about the understanding belonging to God, angelic spirits (cf. e.g. 557(27)–558(19)), or 'intellectual corporeal Beings, infinitely different from those of our little spot of Earth' elsewhere in the universe (555(20–32); cf. 191(20–7)). The term 'understanding' was more appropriate than 'mind' or 'soul' partly because Locke's inquiry was principally epistemological and partly because it was directly concerned just with conscious perceptions or thoughts, and these are precisely the extension of the understanding; mentality outside the understanding is pertinent only inasmuch as it gives rise to acts or objects of the understanding; e.g. the discussion of the will, liberty, and necessity in II. xxi is relevant to the subject of the understanding inasmuch as the latter has ideas of them.

Locke classified the understanding's acts of perception into three types; only the last two match our usual sense of 'to understand'. There are perceptions of '*Ideas* in our Minds', of the signification of signs, and of 'the Connexion or Repugnancy, Agreement or Disagreement' between our ideas (236(21–7)); he took stock of these three sorts chiefly in Books II, III, and IV, respectively. He first investigated the origin of the ideas in our minds. He maintained that the individual's experience in 'Observation employ'd either about *external, sensible Objects; or about the internal Operations*' of its own '*perceived and reflected on*' by itself is that which supplies it '*with all the materials of thinking*' (II. i. 2; cf., e.g., II. xi. 14–17, II. xii. 1–2), a principle he pursued through Book II in reference not only to ideas thus plausibly derived from sense-experience or reflection, but also to ideas, e.g. of space, time, number, infinity, and causality, which were a much sterner test of his hypothesis, this being, he trusted, all the more strongly confirmed by his empirical accounting of them. His assumptions, arguments, and conclusions in this connection were soon disputed, notably by Leibniz (1646–1714), first in personal communications to Locke and then in his long *Nouveaux essais sur l'entendement humain.* Perhaps Leibniz's most effective criticism resulted from deploying his doctrine of subconscious thought, the very possibility of which Locke had repeatedly rejected out of hand. Locke denied that we were born into the world with any completed or incorrigible knowledge, or with any of its conceptual constituents; whether pertaining to the nature of things or to our conduct, an elimination he sought to justify in the main run of chapters of Book I, whose concluding chapter, against innate ideas (as distinct from innate principles, which he had already dealt with), afforded a suitable transition to Book II (cf. also I. ii. 15).

Locke's epistemology is notoriously a 'way of ideas': 'Having *Ideas*, and Perception [are] the same thing' (108(9–10)); ''Tis evident, the Mind knows not Things immediately, but only by the intervention of the *Ideas* it has of them' (563(27–8); cf., e.g., Descartes, Third Meditation, and the Port-Royal *Logic*, I. i–v). What exactly these intervening 'ideas' are, and whether experience can be satisfactorily resolved into them or so-called ideas of other sorts, are among Locke's immediate difficulties. Our general knowledge of things has two branches in his account—which runs in two divergent directions. He has a conventionalist (apriorist) view of knowledge regarding our human concepts of the essences of things: 'Truths belonging to Essences of Things, (that is, to abstract *Ideas*) are eternal, and are to be found out by the contemplation only of those Essences' (562(12–14)). But he has at the same time an empiricist (aposteriorist) view of other aspects of the knowledge of things. First, the existence of things is to be known only from experience (562(14–15); 553(2–4), 631(14 ff.)). Secondly, the knowledge of the coexistences of qualities of a (sort of) substance is limited by our mind's inabilities to conceive connections and depends on experience, since we neither know the real Constitution of the minute Parts, on which their Qualities do depend; nor, did we know them, could we discover any necessary *connexion* between them, and any of the *secondary Qualities*: which is necessary to be done, before we can certainly know their *necessary co-existence*. . . . Our Knowledge in all these Enquiries, reaches very little farther than our Experience. . . . we are left only to the assistance of our Senses, to make known to us, what Qualities [Substances] contain. For of all the Qualities that are *co-existent* in any Subject, without this dependence and evident connexion of their *Ideas* one with another, we cannot know certainly any two to *co-exist* any farther, than Experience, by our Senses, informs us (546(2–24)).

For this and related reasons he maintains that inquiries into the nature of things have exceedingly limited prospects of attaining the status of strict science (cf. IV. iii, and *Some Thoughts Concerning Education*, §§ 301–7).

Since Locke, epistemology and the philosophy of science (and the philosophy of mathematics) have strained at the problem of the conflict between conventionalism and empiricism in respect of general knowledge, either by eliminating one of the alternatives—conventionalism at the cost of certainty, or even rational probability; empiricism at the cost of meaningfulness, verifiability, or innovation—or by trying to show how they can be reconciled. This is one of many Lockian problems which have continued to attract philosophers' vigorous, and, happily, increasingly rigorous attention.

The Present Text and Notes

The present text is based on the original fourth edition of the *Essay*; readings in the other early authorized editions are adopted, in appropriate form, where necessary, and recorded otherwise in the textual notes. Occasionally, readings from other early editions, especially the French translation by Pierre Coste (1668–1747), are also cited. Full information about textual methods is given in the Clarendon Locke edition (pp. xxxvii ff.), which also includes numerous details in a separate register of apparently trifling alterations of punctuation, spelling, capitalization, italicization, etc., in the early printings.

The editorial symbols and abbreviations, with their meanings, used in the textual notes are the following:

1	the first edition (1690)
2	the second edition (1694)
3	the third edition (1695)
4	the fourth edition (1700)
5	the fifth edition (1706)
6	the sixth edition (1710)
W	*The Works of John Locke* (1st edn., 1714)
Coste	Coste's translation (1st edn., 1700)
$\mathbf{Coste_2}$	Coste's translation (2nd edn., 1729)
er	Errata (page in **1**, **2**, **4**, or **5**; indicated by e.g. '**2er**')
1T.er	manuscript additions to the Errata page in Tyrrell's copy of **1** (British Library, C. 122, f. 14)
add.	added
edit.	editorial
om.	omitted
]	end of quoted expression from the text
/	end-of-line marker
|	separation sign between successive annotations of a quoted expression from the text
[ ]	editorial insertion

Grindleford, January 1978 P.H.N.

AN

ESSAY

CONCERNING

Humane Understanding.

In Four BOOKS.

[1-]Written by *JOHN LOCKE*, Gent.[-1]

[2-]*The Fourth*[3] *Edition, with large Additions.*[-2]

[4-]ECCLES. XI. 5.
As thou knoweſt not what is the way of the Spirit, nor how the bones do grow in the Womb of her that is with Child: even ſo thou knoweſt not the works of God, who maketh all things.[-4]

Quam bellum eſt velle confiteri potius neſcire quod neſcias, quam iſta effutientem nauſeare, atque ipſum ſibi diſplicere! Cic. de Natur. Deor. *l.* 1.

LONDON:
[5-]Printed for *Awnſham* and *John Churchil*,[6] at the *Black-Swan*[7] in *Pater-Noſter-Row*; and *Samuel Manſhip*, at the *Ship* in *Cornhill*, near the *Royal-Exchange*,[8],[-5] MDCC.[9]

[*The apparatus to this page is overleaf.*]

TITLE-PAGE

[1–1] Written . . . Gent.] *add.* **2–5** [2–2] *The . . . Additions.*] *add.* **2, 4–5** | *The Third* EDITION. **3** [3] *Fourth*] **4** | *Fifth* **5** | *Third* **3** | *Second* **2** [4–4] ECCLES. . . . *things.*] *add.* **4–5** [5–5] Printed . . . *Royal-Exchange,*] **2–5** | Printed by *Eliz. Holt,* for **Thomas Bassett,** at the *George* in *Fleetstreet,* near St. *Dunstan*'s Church. **1**. (*Concerning other issues of* **1** *and* **2**, *v. pp. xvii and xxv above.*) [6] *Churchil*] **2–4** | *Churchill* **5** [7] *Black-Swan*] **4** | *Black Swan* **2–3, 5** [8] *Royal-Exchange*] **4** | *Royal Exchange* **2–3, 5** [9] MDCC.] **4** | MDCCVI. **5** | 1695. **3** | MDCXCIV. **2** | MDCXC. **1**

TO THE

RIGHT HONOURABLE

THOMAS

EARL OF

Pembroke and **Montgomery,**

Baron Herbert *of* Cardiff, *Lord* Ross *of* Kendal, Par, Fitzhugh, Marmion, *St.* Quintin, *and* Shurland; *Lord President of his Majesties most Honourable Privy-Council, and Lord Lieutenant of the County of* Wilts, *and of* South Wales.

My LORD,

THIS Treatise, which is grown up under your Lordship's Eye, and has ventured into the World by your Order, does now, by a natural kind of Right, come to your Lordship for that Protection, which you several years since promised it. 'Tis not that I think any Name, how great soever, set at the beginning of a Book, will be able to cover the Faults are to be found in it. Things in print must stand and fall by their own Worth, or the Reader's Fancy. But there being nothing more to be desired for Truth, than a fair unprejudiced Hearing, no body is more likely to procure me that, than your Lordship, who are allowed to have got so intimate an Acquaintance with her, in her more retired recesses. Your Lordship is known to have so far advanced your Speculations in the most abstract and general Knowledge of Things, beyond the ordinary reach, or common Methods, that your Allowance, and Approbation of the Design of this Treatise, will at least preserve it from being condemned without reading; and will prevail to have those Parts a little weighed, which might otherwise, perhaps, be thought to deserve no Consideration, for being somewhat out of the common road.

(6–9) *Lord . . . and*] **4–5** | *Lord* Ross *of* Kendal, Par, Marmion, *St.* Quintin *and* Shurland; *Lord Privy-Seal*, **2–3** | *&c.* **1** (10) *and of* South Wales.] **4–5** | *and of* South-Wales; *and one of Their Majesties most Honourable Privy-Council.* **2–3** | *and One of Their Majesties most Honourable Privy Council.* **1** (17) in it] **1er–5** | it **1**

The Imputation of Novelty, is a terrible charge amongst those, who judge of Men's Heads, as they do of their Perukes, by the Fashion; and can allow none to be right, but the received Doctrines. Truth scarce ever yet carried it by Vote any where at its first appearance: New Opinions are always suspected, and usually opposed, without any other Reason, but because they are not already common. But Truth, like Gold, is not the less so, for being newly brought out of the Mine. 'Tis Trial and Examination must give it price, and not any antick Fashion: And though it be not yet current by the publick stamp; yet it may, for all that, be as old as Nature, and is certainly not the less genuine. Your Lordship can give great and convincing Instances of this, whenever you please to oblige the Publick with some of those large and comprehensive Discoveries, you have made, of Truths, hitherto unknown, unless to some few, to whom your Lordship has been pleased not wholly to conceal them. This alone were a sufficient Reason, were there no other, why I should Dedicate this *Essay* to your Lordship; and its having some little Correspondence with some parts of that nobler and vast System of the Sciences, your Lordship has made, so new, exact, and instructive a Draught of, I think it Glory enough, if your Lordship permit me to boast, that here and there I have fallen into some Thoughts not wholly different from yours. If your Lordship think fit, that, by your encouragement, this should appear in the World, I hope it may be a Reason, some time or other, to lead your Lordship farther; and you will allow me to say, That you here give the World an earnest of something, that, if they can bear with this, will be truly worth their expectation. This, my Lord, shews what a Present I here make to your Lordship; just such as the poor Man does to his Rich and Great Neighbour, by whom the Basket of Flowers, or Fruit, is not ill taken, though he has more plenty of his own growth, and in much greater perfection. Worthless Things receive a Value, when they are made the Offerings of Respect, Esteem, and Gratitude: These you have given me so mighty and peculiar Reasons to have, in the highest degree, for your Lordship, that if they can add a price to what they go along with, proportionable to their own Greatness, I can with Confidence brag, I here make your Lordship the richest Present, you ever received. This I am sure, I am under the greatest Obligation to seek all occasions to acknowledge a long Train of Favors, I have received from your

(17) *Essay*] **2–5** | piece **1**

Lordship; Favors, though great and important in themselves, yet made much more so by the Forwardness, Concern, and Kindness, and other obliging Circumstances, that never failed to accompany them. To all this you are pleased to add that, which gives yet more weight and relish to all the rest: You vouchsafe to continue me in some degrees of your Esteem, and allow me a place in your good Thoughts, I had almost said Friendship. This, my Lord, your Words and Actions so constantly shew on all occasions, even to others when I am absent, that it is not Vanity in me to mention, what every body knows: But it would be want of good Manners not to acknowledge what so many are Witnesses of, and every day tell me, I am indebted to your Lordship for. I wish they could as easily assist my Gratitude, as they convince me of the great and growing Engagements it has to your Lordship. This I am sure, I should write of the *Understanding* without having any, if I were not extremely sensible of them, and did not lay hold on this Opportunity to testifie to the World, how much I am obliged to be, and how much I am,

Dorset Court 24th
of *May* 1689.

My Lord,
Your Lordship's
Most Humble, and
Most Obedient Servant,

JOHN LOCKE.

(10) good] *add.* **4–5** (16) extremely] **2–5** | certainly **1**. *In some, but not all, copies of the Holt issue of* **1**, 'certainly' *was altered in ink by the printers to* 'extreamly' (*or this word differently spelt*). (19) *Dorset Court* 24th of *May* 1689.] *add.* **4–5** (*not in* **Coste**). (*Cf. p. xv above.*)

THE

EPISTLE

TO THE

READER

Reader,

I *Here put into thy Hands, what has been the diversion of some of my idle and heavy Hours: If it has the good luck to prove so of any of thine, and thou hast but half so much Pleasure in reading, as I had in writing it, thou wilt as little think thy Money, as I do my Pains, ill bestowed. Mistake not this, for a Commendation of my Work; nor conclude, because I was pleased with the doing of it, that therefore I am fondly taken with it now it is done. He that hawks at Larks and Sparrows, has no less Sport, though a much less considerable Quarry, than he that flies at nobler Game: And he is little acquainted with the Subject of this Treatise, the* UNDERSTANDING, *who does not know, that as it is the most elevated Faculty of the Soul, so it is employed with a greater, and more constant Delight than any of the other. Its searches after Truth, are a sort of Hawking and Hunting, wherein the very pursuit makes a great part of the Pleasure. Every step the Mind takes in its Progress towards Knowledge, makes some Discovery, which is not only new, but the best too, for the time at least.*

For the Understanding, like the Eye, judging of Objects, only by its own Sight, cannot but be pleased with what it discovers, having less regret for what has scaped it, because it is unknown. Thus he who has raised himself above the Alms-Basket, and not content to live lazily on scraps of begg'd Opinions, sets his own Thoughts on work, to find and follow Truth, will (whatever he lights on) not miss the Hunter's Satisfaction; every moment of his Pursuit, will reward his Pains with some Delight; and he will have Reason to think his time not ill spent, even when he cannot much boast of any great Acquisition.

This, Reader, is the Entertainment of those, who let loose their own Thoughts, and follow them in writing; which thou oughtest not to envy

(14) *some*] *add.* **2–5**. *In some, but not all, copies of the Holt issue of* **1**, 'some' *was inserted in ink by the printers.*

them, since they afford thee an Opportunity of the like Diversion, if thou wilt make use of thy own Thoughts in reading. 'Tis to them, if they are thy own, that I referr my self: But if they are taken upon Trust from others, 'tis no great Matter what they are, they not following Truth, but some meaner Consideration: and 'tis not worth while to be concerned, what he says or thinks, who says or thinks only as he is directed by another. If thou judgest for thy self, I know thou wilt judge candidly; and then I shall not be harmed or offended, whatever be thy Censure. For though it be certain, that there is nothing in this Treatise of the Truth whereof I am not fully persuaded; yet I consider my self as liable to Mistakes, as I can think thee; and know, that this Book must stand or fall with thee, not by any Opinion I have of it, but thy own. If thou findest little in it new or instructive to thee, thou art not to blame me for it. It was not meant for those, that had already mastered this Subject, and made a through Acquaintance with their own Understandings; but for my own Information, and the Satisfaction of a few Friends, who acknowledged themselves not to have sufficiently considered it. Were it fit to trouble thee with the History of this Essay, I should tell thee that five or six Friends meeting at my Chamber, and discoursing on a Subject very remote from this, found themselves quickly at a stand, by the Difficulties that rose on every side. After we had a while puzzled our selves, without coming any nearer a Resolution of those Doubts which perplexed us, it came into my Thoughts, that we took a wrong course; and that, before we set our selves upon Enquiries of that Nature, it was necessary to examine our own Abilities, and see, what Objects our Understandings were, or were not fitted to deal with. This I proposed to the Company, who all readily assented; and thereupon it was agreed, that this should be our first Enquiry. Some hasty and undigested Thoughts, on a Subject I had never before considered, which I set down against our next Meeting, gave the first entrance into this Discourse, which having been thus begun by Chance, was continued by Intreaty; written by incoherent parcels; and, after long intervals of neglect, resum'd again, as my Humour or Occasions permitted; and at last, in a retirement, where an Attendance on my Health gave me leisure, it was brought into that order, thou now seest it.

This discontinued way of writing may have occasioned, besides others, two contrary Faults, viz. *that too little, and too much may be said in it. If thou findest any thing wanting, I shall be glad, that what I have writ, gives thee any Desire, that I should have gone farther: If it seems too much to thee, thou must blame the Subject; for when I first put Pen to Paper, I thought all I should have to say on this Matter, would have been contained in one sheet of*

(9) *the . . . persuaded*] **2–5** | *whose Truth I am not persuaded* **1**

Paper; but the farther I went, the larger Prospect I had: New Discoveries led me still on, and so it grew insensibly to the bulk it now appears in. I will not deny, but possibly it might be reduced to a narrower compass than it is; and that some Parts of it might be contracted: the way it has been writ in, by catches, and many long intervals of Interruption, being apt to cause some Repetitions. But to confess the Truth, I am now too lazie, or too busie to make it shorter.

I am not ignorant how little I herein consult my own Reputation, when I knowingly let it go with a Fault, so apt to disgust the most judicious, who are always the nicest, Readers. But they who know Sloth is apt to content it self with any Excuse, will pardon me, if mine has prevailed on me, where, I think, I have a very good one. I will not therefore alledge in my Defence, that the same Notion, having different Respects, may be convenient or necessary, to prove or illustrate several Parts of the same Discourse; and that so it has happened in many Parts of this: But waving that, I shall frankly avow, that I have sometimes dwelt long upon the same Argument, and expressed it different ways, with a quite different Design. I pretend not to publish this Essay for the Information of Men of large Thoughts and quick Apprehensions; to such Masters of Knowledge I profess my self a Scholar, and therefore warn them before-hand not to expect any thing here, but what being spun out of my own course Thoughts, is fitted to Men of my own size, to whom, perhaps, it will not be unacceptable, that I have taken some Pains, to make plain and familiar to their Thoughts some Truths, which established Prejudice, or the Abstractness of the Ideas *themselves, might render difficult. Some Objects had need be turned on every side; and when the Notion is new, as I confess some of these are to me; or out of the ordinary Road, as I suspect they will appear to others, 'tis not one simple view of it, that will gain it admittance into every Understanding, or fix it there with a clear and lasting Impression. There are few, I believe, who have not observed in themselves or others, That what in one way of proposing was very obscure, another way of expressing it, has made very clear and intelligible: Though afterward the Mind found little difference in the Phrases, and wondered why one failed to be understood more than the other. But every thing does not hit alike upon every Man's Imagination. We have our Understandings no less different than our Palates; and he that thinks the same Truth shall be equally relished by every one in the same dress, may as well hope to feast every one with the same sort of Cookery: The Meat may be the same, and the Nourishment good, yet every one not be able to receive it with that Seasoning; and it must be dressed another way, if you will have it go down with some, even of strong Constitutions. The Truth is, those who advised me to publish it, advised me,* for this Reason, to publish it as it is: and since I have been brought to let it go abroad, I desire it should be understood by whoever gives himself the Pains to read it. I have so little Affection to be in Print, that if I were not flattered, this Essay might be of some use to others, as I think, it has been to me, I should have confined it to the view of some Friends, who gave the first Occasion to it. My appearing therefore in Print, being on purpose to be as useful as I may, I think it necessary to make, what I have to say, as easie and intelligible to all sorts of Readers as I can. And I had much rather the speculative and quick-sighted should complain of my being in some parts tedious, than that any one, not accustomed to abstract Speculations, or prepossessed with different Notions, should mistake, or not comprehend my meaning.

It will possibly be censured as a great piece of Vanity, or Insolence in me, to pretend to instruct this our knowing Age, it amounting to little less, when I own, that I publish this Essay with hopes it may be useful to others. But if it may be permitted to speak freely of those, who with a feigned Modesty condemn as useless, what they themselves Write, methinks it savours much more of Vanity or Insolence, to publish a Book for any other end; and he fails very much of that Respect he owes the Publick, who prints, and consequently expects Men should read that, wherein he intends not they should meet with any thing of Use to themselves or others: and should nothing else be found allowable in this Treatise, yet my Design will not cease to be so; and the Goodness of my intention ought to be some Excuse for the Worthlessness of my Present. 'Tis that chiefly which secures me from the Fear of Censure, which I expect not to escape more than better Writers. Men's Principles, Notions, and Relishes are so different, that it is hard to find a Book which pleases or displeases all Men. I acknowledge the Age we live in, is not the least knowing, and therefore not the most easie to be satisfied. If I have not the good luck to please, yet no Body ought to be offended with me. I plainly tell all my Readers, except half a dozen, this Treatise was not at first intended for them; and therefore they need not be at the Trouble to be of that number. But yet if any one thinks fit to be angry, and rail at it, he may do it securely: For I shall find some better way of spending my time, than in such kind of Conversation. I shall always have the satisfaction to have aimed sincerely at Truth and Usefulness, though in one of the meanest ways. The Commonwealth of Learning, is not at this time without Master-Builders, whose mighty Designs, in advancing the Sciences, will leave lasting Monuments to the Admiration of Posterity; But every one must not hope to be a Boyle, or a Sydenham; and

(3) *Affection*] **4–5** | *Affectation* **1–3** (14) *this Essay*] **2–5** | *it* **1** (27–8) *satisfied . . . ought*] **2–5** | *satisfied; which if I have not the good luck to doe, no Body yet ought* **1** (31) *to*] **1–4**; *om.* **5**

in an Age that produces such Masters, as the Great —— Huygenius, *and the incomparable Mr.* Newton, *with some other of that Strain; 'tis Ambition enough to be employed as an Under-Labourer in clearing Ground a little, and removing some of the Rubbish, that lies in the way to Knowledge; which certainly had been very much more advanced in the World, if the Endeavours of ingenious and industrious Men had not been much cumbred with the learned but frivolous use of uncouth, affected, or unintelligible Terms, introduced into the Sciences, and there made an Art of, to that Degree, that Philosophy, which is nothing but the true Knowledge of Things, was thought unfit, or uncapable to be brought into well-bred Company, and polite Conversation. Vague and insignificant Forms of Speech, and Abuse of Language, have so long passed for Mysteries of Science; And hard or misapply'd Words, with little or no meaning, have, by Prescription, such a Right to be mistaken for deep Learning, and heighth of Speculation, that it will not be easie to persuade, either those who speak, or those who hear them, that they are but the Covers of Ignorance, and hindrance of true Knowledge. To break in upon the Sanctuary of Vanity and Ignorance, will be, I suppose, some Service to Humane Understanding: Though so few are apt to think, they deceive, or are deceived in the Use of Words; or that the Language of the Sect they are of, has any Faults in it, which ought to be examined or corrected, that I hope I shall be pardon'd, if I have in the Third Book dwelt long on this Subject; and endeavoured to make it so plain, that neither the inveterateness of the Mischief, nor the prevalency of the Fashion, shall be any Excuse for those, who will not take Care about the meaning of their own Words, and will not suffer the Significancy of their Expressions to be enquired into.*

I have been told that a short Epitome of this Treatise, which was printed 1688, *was by some condemned without reading, because innate* Ideas *were denied in it; they too hastily concluding, that if innate* Ideas *were not supposed, there would be little left, either of the Notion or Proof of Spirits. If any one take the like Offence at the Entrance of this Treatise, I shall desire him to read it through: and then I hope he will be convinced, that the taking away false Foundations, is not to the prejudice, but advantage of Truth; which is never injur'd or endanger'd so much, as when mixed with, or built on, Falshood. In the Second Edition, I added as followeth:*

(4) *Ground*] **4–5** | *the Ground* **1–3** (*likewise* **Coste**) (17) *the*] **5** | *this* **1–4** (28) 1688] **4–5** | *about two Years since* **1–3** (35) *In . . . followeth:*] *add.* **5**. *Instead of this and the remainder of the* Epistle, **1** *concludes here with this paragraph: 'One thing more I must advertise my Reader of, and that is, That the Summary of each Section is printed in Italick Characters, whereby the Reader may find the Contents almost as well as if it had been printed in the Margin by the side, if a little allowance be made for the Grammatical Construction, which in the Text*

The Bookseller will not forgive me, if I say nothing of this Second Edition, which he has promised, by the correctness of it, shall make amends for the many Faults committed in the former. He desires too, that it should be known, that it has one whole new Chapter concerning Identity, and many additions, and amendments in other places. These I must inform my Reader are not all new matter, but most of them either farther confirmation of what I had said, or Explications to prevent others being mistaken in the sence of what was formerly printed, and not any variation in me from it; I must only except the alterations I have made in Book 2. Chap. 21.

What I had there Writ concerning Liberty and the Will, I thought deserv'd as accurate a review, as I was capable of: Those Subjects having in all Ages exercised the learned part of the World, with Questions and Difficulties, that have not a little perplex'd Morality and Divinity, those parts of Knowledge, that Men are most concern'd to be clear in. Upon a closer inspection into the working of Men's Minds, and a stricter examination of those motives and views, they are turn'd by, I have found reason somewhat to alter the thoughts I formerly had concerning that, which gives the last determination to the Will in all voluntary actions. This I cannot forbear to acknowledge to the World, with as much freedom and readiness, as I at first published, what then seem'd to me to be right, thinking my self more concern'd to quit and renounce any Opinion of my own, than oppose that of another, when Truth appears against it. For 'tis Truth alone I seek, and that will always be welcome to me, when or from whencesoever it comes.

But what forwardness soever I have to resign any Opinion I have, or to recede from any thing I have Writ, upon the first evidence of any error in it; yet this I must own, that I have not had the good luck to receive any light from those Exceptions, I have met with in print against any part of my Book, nor have, from any thing has been urg'd against it, found reason to alter my Sense, in any of the Points have been question'd. Whether the Subject, I have in hand, requires often more thought and attention, than Cursory Readers, at least such as are prepossessed, are willing to allow? Or whether any obscurity in my expressions casts a cloud over it, and these notions are made difficult to others apprehension in my way of treating them? So it is, that my meaning, I find, is often mistaken, and I have not the good luck to be every where rightly understood. There are so many Instances of this, that I think it Justice to my

it self could not always be so ordered, as to make perfect Propositions, which yet by the Words printed in Italick, may be easily guessed at.'

(1–35) *The . . . understood.*] **2–5** (1) *Second*] **4–5** | *New* **2–3** (*likewise* **Coste**) (35)–12(12) *There . . . understood.*] *add.* **5**. *In* **2–4**, *five paragraphs followed 'every where rightly understood.', which in* **5** *were placed instead in a footnote at II. xxviii. 11 (see pp. 354–5 below).*

Reader and my self, to conclude, that either my Book is plainly enough written to be rightly understood by those, who peruse it with that Attention and Indifferency, which every one, who will give himself the Pains to read, ought to imploy in reading; or else that I have writ mine so obscurely, that it is in vain to go about to mend it. Which ever of these be that Truth, 'tis my self only am affected thereby, and therefore I shall be far from troubling my Reader with what I think might be said, in answer to those several Objections I have met with, to Passages here and there of my Book. Since I perswade my self, that he who thinks them of Moment enough to be concerned, whether they are true or false, will be able to see, that what is said, is either not well founded, or else not contrary to my Doctrine, when I and my Opposer come both to be well understood.

If any, careful that none of their good thoughts should be lost, have publish'd their censures of my Essay, *with this honour done to it, that they will not suffer it to be an* Essay, *I leave it to the publick to value the obligation they have to their critical Pens, and shall not wast my Reader's time, in so idle or ill natur'd an employment of mine, as to lessen the satisfaction any one has in himself, or gives to others in so hasty a confutation of what I have Written.*

The Booksellers preparing for the fourth Edition of my Essay, *gave me notice of it, that I might, if I had leisure, make any additions or alterations I should think fit. Whereupon I thought it convenient to advertise the Reader, that besides several corrections I had made here and there, there was one alteration which it was necessary to mention, because it ran through the whole Book, and is of consequence to be rightly understood. What I thereupon said, was this:*

Clear and distinct Ideas *are terms, which though familiar and frequent in Men's Mouths, I have reason to think every one, who uses, does not perfectly understand. And possibly 'tis but here and there one, who gives*

(5–6) *self . . . far*] **W** | *self,* **5–6** (12) *v.* 11(35), n. (13–19) *If . . . Written.*] **2–5** (13) *any*] **5** | *any other Authors* **2–4** (16) *Reader's*] **5** | *Readers* **2–4** (19) *Residue of* Epistle *not in* **2–3**, *which instead conclude: 'Besides what is already mentioned, this Second Edition has the Summaries of the several §§. not only Printed, as before, in a Table by themselves, but in the Margent too. And at the end there is now an* Index *added. These two, with a great number of short additions, amendments, and alterations are advantages of this Edition, which the Bookseller hopes will make it sell. For as to the larger additions and alterations, I have obliged him, and he has promised me to print them by themselves, so that the former Edition may not be wholly lost to those who have it, but by the inserting in their proper places the passages that will be reprinted alone, to that purpose, the former Book may be made as little defective as is possible.'* **Coste** *adds paragraph: 'C'est là ce que je jugeai nécessaire de dire sur la seconde Edition de cet Ouvrage, et voici ce que je suis obligé d'ajoûter présentement.'* (20–5) *The . . . understood.*] **4–5** (20) *the*] **5** | *this* **4** (21) *leisure,*] **5** | *leisure* **4** (22) *I thought it*] **5** | *it may be* **4** (23) *had*] **5** | *have* **4** *was*] **5** | *is* **4** (24) *it was*] **5** | *I think* **4** *mention*] **5** | *mention here* **4** *ran*] **5** | *runs* **4** (25–6) *What . . . this:*] *add.* **5** (27)–14(14) Clear . . . *Impression.*] **4–5**

himself the trouble to consider them so far as to know what he himself, or others precisely mean by them; I have therefore in most places chose to put determinate or determined, instead of clear and distinct, as more likely to direct Men's thoughts to my meaning in this matter. By those denominations, I mean some object in the Mind, and consequently determined, i.e. such as it is there seen and perceived to be. This I think may fitly be called a determinate or determin'd Idea, when such as it is at any time objectively in the Mind, and so determined there, it is annex'd, and without variation determined to a name or articulate sound, which is to be steadily the sign of that very same object of the Mind, or determinate Idea.

To explain this a little more particularly. By determinate, when applied to a simple Idea, I mean that simple appearance, which the Mind has in its view, or perceives in it self, when that Idea is said to be in it: By determined, when applied to a complex Idea, I mean such an one as consists of a determinate number of certain simple or less complex Ideas, joyn'd in such a proportion and situation, as the Mind has before its view, and sees in it self when that Idea is present in it, or should be present in it, when a Man gives a name to it. I say should be: because it is not every one, nor perhaps any one, who is so careful of his Language, as to use no Word, till he views in his Mind the precise determined Idea, which he resolves to make it the sign of. The want of this is the cause of no small obscurity and confusion in Men's thoughts and discourses.

I know there are not Words enough in any Language to answer all the variety of Ideas, that enter into Men's discourses and reasonings. But this hinders not, but that when any one uses any term, he may have in his Mind a determined Idea, which he makes it the sign of, and to which he should keep it steadily annex'd during that present discourse. Where he does not, or cannot do this, he in vain pretends to clear or distinct Ideas: 'Tis plain his are not so: and therefore there can be expected nothing but obscurity and confusion, where such terms are made use of, which have not such a precise determination.

Upon this Ground I have thought determined Ideas a way of speaking less liable to mistake, than clear and distinct: and where Men have got such determined Ideas of all, that they reason, enquire, or argue about, they will find a great part of their Doubts and Disputes at an end. The greatest part of the Questions and Controversies that perplex Mankind depending on the doubtful and uncertain use of Words, or (which is the same) indetermined Ideas, which they are made to stand for. I have made choice of these

(4) By] **5** | And by **4** (6) there] **5** | there, **4** (12) simple Idea] edit. | simple Idea **4–5**

terms to signifie, 1. *Some immediate object of the Mind, which it perceives and has before it distinct from the sound it uses as a sign of it.* 2. *That this Idea thus* determined, *i.e. which the Mind has in it self, and knows, and sees there be* determined *without any change to that name, and that name* determined *to that precise Idea. If Men had such* determined *Ideas in their enquiries and discourses, they would both discern how far their own enquiries and discourses went, and avoid the greatest part of the Disputes and Wranglings they have with others.*

Besides this the Bookseller will think it necessary I should advertise the Reader, that there is an addition of two Chapters wholly new; the one of the Association of Ideas, *the other* of Enthusiasm. *These with some other larger additions never before printed, he has engaged to print by themselves after the same manner, and for the same purpose as was done when this* Essay *had the Second Impression.*

In this fifth Edition, there is very little added or altered; the greatest part of what is new, is contained in the 21 *Chapter of the second Book, which any one, if he thinks it worth the while, may, with a very little Labour, transcribe into the Margent of the former Edition.*

(14) *v.* 12(27), n. (15–18) *In . . . Edition.*] *add.* **5** (15) *altered;*] *edit.* | *altered,* **5**

THE

CONTENTS[1]

BOOK I

Of Innate Notions.

BOOK II

Of Ideas.

BOOK III

Of Words.

[1] *This Table (which is not included in* **Coste** *or in* **W**), *and the following Table with summaries of sections of chapters, preceded the main text of the* Essay *in* **2–5**, *but were placed after it in* **1**. [2] *Relations*] **1–3, 5** (*likewise* **Coste**) | *Relation* **4** [3–3] *Of . . . Diversity.*] *add.* **2–5**. *The chapters here numbered 28, . . ., 32 in* **2–5** *are numbered 27, . . ., 31, respectively, in* **1**. [4–4] 33. . . . *Ideas.*] *add.* **4–5** [5] 7. *Of Particles.*] *edit.*; *om.* **1–5**

BOOK IV

Of Knowledge and Opinion.

CHAPTER

[1] *The chapters here numbered 8, . . ., 11 are in the Table in* **1–5** *numbered 7, . . ., 10, respectively (cf. p. 15, n. 5).* [2] 19. *Of Enthusiasm.*] *add.* **4–5**. *The chapters here numbered 20, 21 in* **4–5** *are numbered 19, 20, respectively, in* **1–3.**

THE

CONTENTS

BOOK I

CHAPTER I

Introduction.

CHAPTER II

No innate speculative Principles.

[1]–[1] *What . . . for.*] **2–5** | *Apology for* Idea. **1**

CHAPTER III

No innate practical Principles.

SECTION

CHAPTER IV

Other Considerations about innate Principles, both Speculative and Practical.

SECTION

BOOK II

CHAPTER I

Of Ideas in general.[4]

SECTION

[1] *no*] *add.* **2–5** [2–2] *No . . . introduc'd.*] *add.* **2–5** [3] *Sections here numbered 21, . . ., 25 in* **2–5** *are numbered 20, . . ., 24, respectively, in* **1**. [4] *Cf. heading in text, ad loc.* [5] *Minds*] **2–5** | *Minds about sensible Ideas,* **1** [6] *Reflection later*] **2–5** | *Reflexion had later* **1** [7] *for this*] **2–5** | *for, First, it* **1** [8] *It*] **2–5** | *Secondly, It* **1** [9] *If*] **2–5** | *Thirdly, If* **1** [10] *Impossible*] **2–5** | *Fourthly, Impossible* **1** [11] *That*] **2–5** | *Fifthly, That* **1** [12] *Upon this*] **2–5** | *Sixthly, Upon their* **1** [13] *On*] **2–5** | *Seventhly, On* **1** [14] *If*] **2–5** | *Eightly, If* **1** [15] *How*] **2–5** | *Ninthly, How* **1** [16] *That*] **2–5** | *Tenthly, That* **1**

CHAPTER II

Of simple Ideas.

CHAPTER III

Of Ideas of one Sense.

CHAPTER IV

Of Solidity

CHAPTER V

Of simple Ideas by more than one Sense.

CHAPTER VI

Of simple Ideas of Reflection.

CHAPTER VII

Of Simple Ideas, both of Sensation and Reflection.

CHAPTER VIII

Other Considerations concerning simple Ideas.

CHAPTER IX

Of Perception.

[1] *What it is*] **1–3** (*likewise* **Coste**) | *What is it* **4–5** [2] *Reflection*] *Reflexion* **1–3** (*Reflection* **2–3**) | *the Reflection* **4–5**

CHAPTER X

Of Retention.

SECTION

CHAPTER XI

Of Discerning, etc.

SECTION

CHAPTER XII

Of Complex Ideas.

SECTION

CHAPTER XIII

Of Space, and its simple Modes.

SECTION

[1] 10.] **2–5** | 9. **1**

CHAPTER XIV

Of Duration.

SECTION

CHAPTER XV

Of Duration and Expansion considered together.

SECTION

CHAPTER XVI

Of Number.

SECTION

[1] *This entry for § 24 is in* **1–5** *(but not in* **Coste**), *although they contain no § 24 in the text of Ch. xiv.* [2] *§§ 28–32 in Ch. xiv in* **1–5** [3] *Bodies*] **2–5** | *Body* **1**

CHAPTER XVII

Of Infinity.

SECTION

CHAPTER XVIII

Of other simple Modes.

SECTION

CHAPTER XIX

Of the Modes of Thinking.

SECTION

CHAPTER XX

Of Modes of Pleasure and Pain.

SECTION

[1] 4. *Modes of Colours.*] *edit.* (*likewise* **Coste**) | 7. *Modes of Colours.* [*placed after* '*Modes of Tastes*'] **1–5** [2] 5, 6. *Modes of Tastes.*] *edit.* | 4. [5. **1**] *Modes of Tastes.* **1–5.** (**Coste** '5, 6. *Modes des Saveurs et des Odeurs.*') (*Tastes* **1**, *Trastes* **2–5**) [3] 7. *Why . . . Names.*] *edit.* (*likewise* **Coste**) | 8. *Why . . . Names.* **1–5**

CHAPTER XXI

Of Power.

[1] *These*] **1–4** | *The* **5** [2] *Passions*] **1–3** (*likewise* **Coste**) | *Passion* **4–5** [3] *Relatives*] **2–5** | *Relation* **1** (*likewise* **Coste**) [4] 8.] **2–5** | 8–12. **1** [5] *Understanding*] **2–5** | *the Understanding* **1** [6] 12. *Liberty what.*] *add.* **2–5** [7] *belongs*] **2–5** | *belong* **1** [8] 25, 26, 27.] **2–5** | 25–28. **1**

[9–9] *v. p.* 25, *left-hand column, ad fin.*
28. *Volition what . . . wrong Judgment.*] **2–5** |
29. *The greater apparent Good determines the Will.*
30–32. *This is a Perfection of humane Nature.*
33. *And takes not away Liberty.*
34, 35. *Why Men chuse differently.*
36. *Why they chuse amiss.*
38. *From the different appearance of Good.*
39. *And judging amiss on these Appearances.*
40–42. *First, in comparing present and future.*
43. *Secondly, In thinking wrong of the greatness or certainty of the Consequence of any Action.*
44. *Causes of wrong Judgment, Ignorance, Inadvertency, Sloth, Passion, Fashion,* etc.
45. *Preference of Vice to Vertue, a manifest wrong Judgment.*
47. *Recapitulation.* **1**

[10] *any*] **2–4** | *a* **5** [11] *Uneasiness*] **2–3, 5** | *uneasiness* **4** [12] *determines*] **2–3, 5** | *determins* **4**

CHAPTER XXII

Of Mixed Modes.

SECTION

CHAPTER XXIII

Of the complex Ideas of Substances.

SECTION

[1] *all*] *add.* **4–5** (*not in* **Coste**) [2] *Thinking,*] **5** | *Thinking* **1–4** [3] *Idea*] **1–4** | *Ideas* **5**

CHAPTER XXIV

Of collective Ideas of Substances.

SECTION

CHAPTER XXV

Of Relation.

SECTION

CHAPTER XXVI

Of Cause and[3] *Effect, and other Relations.*

SECTION

[1] *Relations*] **1–3** (*likewise* **Coste**) | *Relation* **4–5** (*see Glossary, s.v.*) [2] *than*] **1–3, 5** | *then* **4** [3] *and*] *edit.* (*likewise* **Coste**) | *of* **1–5**

CHAPTER XXVII

[1]-*Of Identity and Diversity.*

CHAPTER XXVIII

Of other Relations.

CHAPTER XXIX

Of Clear and Distinct, Obscure and Confused Ideas.

[1-1] *Of . . . Identity.*] *add.* **2–5**. *Chapters numbered xxvii, . . ., xxxi in* **1** *are numbered xxviii, . . ., xxxii, respectively, in* **2–5**. [2] *Good*] **1–3, 5** | *good* **4** [3] *these*] **1–4** | *the* **5** [4] *ordinarily*] **5** (*likewise in margin ad loc.* **2–5**) | *ordinary* **1–4** [5] *Relation,*] **1–3, 5** | *Relation*/ **4** [6] *to, be*] **1–3, 5** (*likewise* **Coste**) | *to be,* **4** [7] *and*] **1–4** | *and some* **5**

CHAPTER XXX

Of Real and Fantastical Ideas.

SECTION

CHAPTER XXXI

Of Adequate and Inadequate Ideas.

SECTION

CHAPTER XXXII

Of true and false Ideas.

SECTION

[1] *and*] **1–3** (*likewise* **Coste**) | *or* **4–5**

[2] *Instances*] **2–5** | *Instance* **1** (*likewise* **Coste**)

[2]CHAPTER XXXIII

Of the Association of Ideas.

SECTION

BOOK III

CHAPTER I

Of Words or Language in general.

SECTION

CHAPTER II

Of the Signification of Words.

SECTION

[1–1] *Ideas . . . false*] **2–5** | *Ideas of Substances are false, when the Combination is made of simple Ideas that do never co-exist; or has in it the negation of any one that does constantly coexist* **1**
[2–2] CHAPTER XXXIII . . . *different Sects.*] *add.* **4–5** [3] *Effect*] *edit.* | *Offices* **4** | *Effects* **5.** (**Coste** '14. Cinquiéme exemple . . . 15. Autres exemples. 16. Exemple .. .')

CHAPTER III

Of general Terms.

SECTION

CHAPTER IV

Of the Names of simple Ideas.

SECTION

CHAPTER V

Of the Names of mixed Modes and Relations.

SECTION

CHAPTER VI

Of the Names of Substances.

SECTION

[1] *instance*] **1–3** (*likewise* **Coste**) | *instances* **4–5** [2] *Not by substantial Forms.*] **2–5** | *Distinguishing them by substantial Forms, not pretended to but in this part of the World.* [*paragraph-break*] *Substances distinguished into Species, by their obvious appearances before substantial Forms were thought of.* **1** [3] 26, 27.] *edit.* (*likewise* **Coste**) | 26. **1–5**. *The entries in the Table of Contents in* **1–5** *for* §§ *27–51 are, generally, wrongly applied—to the immediately preceding section (e.g. the entry for* § *28 is numbered* '27.'); *the Table in*

CHAPTER VII

Of Particles.

SECTION

CHAPTER VIII

Of Abstract and Concrete Terms.

SECTION

CHAPTER IX

Of the Imperfection of Words.

SECTION

1–5 *lists separate entries numbered* 27., . . ., 42.; 43., 44. (*together*); 45., 46. (*together*); 48., 49., 50. (*each separately*). *Also, in* **2–5**, *these entries, so numbered, are incompatible with at least some of the marginal summaries in the body of the* Essay. *The present edition here adopts (as in* **Coste**) *the arrangement of the marginal summaries first given in* **4**.

[1] *The Table of Contents in* **1–5** *lists separate entries (numbered* 35. *and* 36.) *for these §§ 36 and 37: 'Though Nature make the Similitude.' and 'And continues it in the races of Things.', respectively.* [2] *imperfect*] **1–4** | *perfect* **5**

CHAPTER X

Of the Abuse of Words.

SECTION

[1] *Names . . . referr'd.*] *add.* **2–5** [2] *clear*] *add.* **2–5** [3] *benefits*] **2–5** | *benefited* **1** [4] *destroys*] **2–5** | *destroy'd* **1** [5] *Fourthly,*] **2–5** | *Fourthly, Abuse,* **1** [6] *Fifthly,*] **2–5** | *Fifthly, Abuse* **1** [7] *Abuse*] **1–3, 5** | *abuse* **4** [8] *Sixthly,*] **2–5** | *Sixthly, Abuse,* **1**

CHAPTER XI

Of the Remedies of the foregoing Imperfections[1] *and Abuses.*

BOOK IV

CHAPTER I

Of Knowledge in general.

CHAPTER II

Of the Degrees of our Knowledge.

[1] *Imperfections*] **4–5** | *Imperfection* **1–3** [2] *To have*] **5** | *to have* **2–4** | *Have* **1** [3] *By*] **4–5** | *by* **2–3** | *Remedy,* **1** [4–4] *When . . . explain'd*] **2–5** | *Where it ought to be explained, when varied* **1** [5] *Relative*] **1–4** | *Relation* **5**

CHAPTER III

Of the Extent[1] *of Humane Knowledge.*

SECTION

CHAPTER IV

Of the Reality of our Knowledge.

SECTION

[1] *Extent*] **1–2, 5** | *extent* **3–4** [2] *their*] **1–3** | *the* **4–5** [3] *God's,*] **1** | *God's* / **2–5**
[4] *it*] **1–3** (*likewise* **Coste**) | *its* **4–5**

CHAPTER V

Of Truth in general.

SECTION

CHAPTER VI

Of universal Propositions, their Truth and Certainty.

SECTION

[1] *excepted*] **2–5** | *except of Substances* **1**
[2] *separating*] **1–3, 5** | *seperating* **4**
[3] *joining*] **1–3 5,** | *joyning* **4**
[4] *all chimerical*] *edit.* | *alchimerical* **1–5**
[5] *Answered,*] **5** | *Answered* **1–4**
[6] *Qualities,*] **1–3** | *Qualities* **4–5**

CHAPTER VII

Of Maxims.

CHAPTER VIII

Of trifling Propositions.

CHAPTER IX

Of our Knowledge of Existence.

[1] *Using*] **1, 5** | *using* **2–4**

CHAPTER X

Of the Existence of a GOD.

CHAPTER XI

Of the Knowledge of the Existence of other Things.

CHAPTER XII

Of the Improvement of our Knowledge.

[1] *cogitative*] **1–3, 5** | *Cogitative* **4**

CHAPTER XIII

Some other Considerations concerning our Knowledge.

CHAPTER XIV

Of Judgment.

CHAPTER XV

Of Probability.

CHAPTER XVI

Of the Degrees of Assent.

[1] *Knowledge*] **1, 5** | *knowledge* **2–4**   [2] *Instance in numbers.*] *edit.* (*likewise* **Coste**) | *Instances in number.* **2–5** | *Instances in Numbers.* **1**. (**Coste** *adds* 'Et dans la Religion naturelle.')

CHAPTER XVII

Of Reason.

SECTION

CHAPTER XVIII

Of Faith and Reason, and their distinct Provinces.

SECTION

[1] *Testimony,*] **1–3, 5** | *Testimony* **4**
[2] *farther removed*] **2–5** | *more their removed* **1**
[3] *For*] **1–3, 5** | *for* **4**

CHAPTER XIX

[2–]*Of Enthusiasm.*

CHAPTER XX

Of wrong Assent, or Errour.

CHAPTER XXI

Division of the Sciences.

[1] *hearkened*] **1, 5** | *hearkned* **2–4**   [2–2] *Of . . . Revelation.*] *add.* **4–5**. *The Chapters numbered xx and xxi in* **4–5** *are numbered xix and xx, respectively, in* **1–3**.

BOOK I

CHAPTER I[1]

Introduction.

§ 1. SINCE it is the *Understanding* that sets Man above the rest of sensible Beings, and gives him all the Advantage and Dominion, which he has over them; it is certainly a Subject, even for its Nobleness, worth our Labour to enquire into. The Understanding, like the Eye, whilst it makes us see, and perceive all other Things, takes no notice of it self: And it requires Art and Pains to set it at a distance, and make it its own Object. But whatever be the Difficulties, that lie in the way of this Enquiry; whatever it be, that keeps us so much in the Dark to our selves; sure I am, that all the Light we can let in upon our own Minds; all the Acquaintance we can make with our own Understandings, will not only be very pleasant; but bring us great Advantage, in directing our Thoughts in the search of other Things.

§ 2. This, therefore, being my *Purpose* to enquire into the Original, Certainty, and Extent of humane Knowledge; together, with the Grounds and Degrees of Belief, Opinion, and Assent; I shall not at present meddle with the Physical Consideration of the Mind; or trouble my self to examine, wherein its Essence consists, or by what Motions of our Spirits, or Alterations of our Bodies, we come to have any Sensation by our Organs, or any *Ideas* in our Understandings; and whether those *Ideas* do in their Formation, any, or all of them, depend on Matter, or no. These are Speculations, which, however curious and entertaining, I shall decline, as lying out of my Way, in the Design I am now upon. It shall suffice to my present Purpose, to

§ 1. *An Enquiry into the Understanding pleasant and useful.*[2] § 2. *Design.*

---

[1] In **1–5**, 'OF Humane Understanding' is printed above 'BOOK I. CHAP. I.', separated by a rule.

Coste *treats this Chapter as an introduction to the whole following work* ('AVANT-PROPOS. Dessein de l'Auteur dans cet Ouvrage.') *and makes Bk. I begin with the original Ch. ii, with a consequent renumbering of the original Chs. iii and iv as Chs. ii and iii.*

[2] *This marginal summary, in common with all subsequent marginal summaries unless an editorial indication to the contrary is given, add.* **2–5**.

consider the discerning Faculties of a Man, as they are employ'd about the Objects, which they have to do with: and I shall imagine I have not wholly misimploy'd my self in the Thoughts I shall have on this Occasion, if, in this Historical, plain Method, I can give any Account of the Ways, whereby our Understandings come to attain those Notions of Things we have, and can set down any Measures of the Certainty of our Knowledge, or the Grounds of those Perswasions, which are to be found amongst Men, so various, different, and wholly contradictory; and yet asserted some where or other with such Assurance, and Confidence, that he that shall take a view of the Opinions of Mankind, observe their Opposition, and at the same time, consider the Fondness, and Devotion wherewith they are embrac'd; the Resolution, and Eagerness, wherewith they are maintain'd, may perhaps have Reason to suspect, That either there is no such thing as Truth at all; or that Mankind hath no sufficient Means to attain a certain Knowledge of it.

§ 3. It is therefore worth while, to search out the *Bounds* between Opinion and Knowledge; and examine by what Measures, in things, whereof we have no certain Knowledge, we ought to regulate our Assent, and moderate our Perswasions. In Order whereunto, I shall pursue this following Method.

First, I shall enquire into the *Original* of those *Ideas*, Notions, or whatever else you please to call them, which a Man observes, and is conscious to himself he has in his Mind; and the ways whereby the Understanding comes to be furnished with them.

Secondly, I shall endeavour to shew, what *Knowledge* the Understanding hath by those *Ideas*; and the Certainty, Evidence, and Extent of it.

Thirdly, I shall make some Enquiry into the Nature and Grounds of *Faith*, or *Opinion*: whereby I mean that Assent, which we give to any Proposition as true, of whose Truth yet we have no certain Knowledge: And here we shall have Occasion to examine the Reasons and Degrees of *Assent*.

§ 4. If by this Enquiry into the Nature of the Understanding, I can discover the Powers thereof; *how far* they reach; to what things they are in any Degree proportionate; and where they fail us, I suppose it may be of use, to prevail with the busy Mind of Man, to

§ 3. *Method.* § 4. *Useful to know the extent of our Comprehension.*

---

(35) *how*] **1T.er, 2–5** | at *how* **1** what] **1er–5** | which **1**

be more cautious in meddling with things exceeding its Comprehension; to stop, when it is at the utmost Extent of its Tether; and to sit down in a quiet Ignorance of those Things, which, upon Examination, are found to be beyond the reach of our Capacities. We should not then perhaps be so forward, out of an Affectation of an universal Knowledge, to raise Questions, and perplex our selves and others with Disputes about Things, to which our Understandings are not suited; and of which we cannot frame in our Minds any clear or distinct Perceptions, or whereof (as it has perhaps too often happen'd) we have not any Notions at all. If we can find out, how far the Understanding can extend its view; how far it has Faculties to attain Certainty; and in what Cases it can only judge and guess, we may learn to content our selves with what is attainable by us in this State.

§ 5. For though the *Comprehension* of our Understandings, comes exceeding short of the vast Extent of Things; yet, we shall have Cause enough to magnify the bountiful Author of our Being, for that Portion and Degree of Knowledge, he has bestowed on us, so far above all the rest of the Inhabitants of this our Mansion. Men have Reason to be well satisfied with what God hath thought fit for them, since he has given them (as St. *Peter* says,) πάντα πρὸς ζωὴν καὶ εὐσέβειαν, Whatsoever is necessary for the Conveniences of Life, and Information of Vertue;* and has put within the reach of their Discovery the comfortable Provision for this Life and the Way that leads to a better. How short soever their Knowledge may come of an universal, or perfect Comprehension of whatsoever is, it yet secures their great Concernments, that they have Light enough to lead them to the Knowledge of their Maker, and the sight of their own Duties. Men may find Matter sufficient to busy their Heads, and employ their Hands with Variety, Delight, and Satisfaction; if they will not boldly quarrel with their own Constitution, and throw away the Blessings their Hands are fill'd with, because they are not big enough to grasp every thing. We shall not have much Reason to complain of the narrowness of our Minds, if we will but employ

§ 5. *Our Capacity suited to our State and Concerns.*

(21) St.] **1–3, 5** | S. **4** says,)] *edit.* | says, **1–5** (22) Conveniences] **1–4** | Conveniencies **5** (24) the . . . Life] **2–5** | the Provisions, that may support, or sweeten this Life, **1** (28) sight] **2–5** | Discovery **1**

* 2 Pet. 1: 3.

them about what may be of use to us; for of that they are very capable: And it will be an unpardonable, as well as Childish Peevishness, if we undervalue the Advantages of our Knowledge, and neglect to improve it to the ends for which it was given us, because there are some Things that are set out of the reach of it. It will be no Excuse to an idle and untoward Servant, who would not attend his Business by Candle-light, to plead that he had not broad Sun-shine. The Candle, that is set up in us, shines bright enough for all our Purposes. The Discoveries we can make with this, ought to satisfy us: And we shall then use our Understandings right, when we entertain all Objects in that Way and Proportion, that they are suited to our Faculties; and upon those Grounds, they are capable of being propos'd to us; and not peremptorily, or intemperately require Demonstration, and demand Certainty, where Probability only is to be had, and which is sufficient to govern all our Concernments. If we will disbelieve every thing, because we cannot certainly know all things; we shall do much-what as wisely as he, who would not use his Legs, but sit still and perish, because he had no Wings to fly.

§ 6. When we know our own *Strength*, we shall the better know what to undertake with hopes of Success: And when we have well survey'd the *Powers* of our own Minds, and made some Estimate what we may expect from them, we shall not be inclined either to sit still, and not set our Thoughts on work at all, in Despair of knowing any thing; nor on the other side question every thing, and disclaim all Knowledge, because some Things are not to be understood. 'Tis of great use to the Sailor to know the length of his Line, though he cannot with it fathom all the depths of the Ocean. 'Tis well he knows, that it is long enough to reach the bottom, at such Places, as are necessary to direct his Voyage, and caution him against running upon Shoals, that may ruin him. Our Business here is not to know all things, but those which concern our Conduct. If we can find out those Measures, whereby a rational Creature put in that State, which Man is in, in this World, may, and ought to govern his Opinions, and Actions depending thereon, we need not be troubled, that some other things escape our Knowledge.

§ 7. This was that which gave the first *Rise* to this Essay con-

§ 6. *Knowledge of our Capacity a cure of Scepticism and Idleness.* § 7. *Occasion of this Essay.*

(9) **Coste$_2$** *adds a reference, in a marginal note, to* Prov. 20: 27. (36) escape] **4–5** | scape **1–3**

cerning the Understanding. For I thought that the first Step towards satisfying several Enquiries, the Mind of Man was very apt to run into, was, to take a Survey of our own Understandings, examine our own Powers, and see to what Things they were adapted. Till that was done I suspected we began at the wrong end, and in vain sought for Satisfaction in a quiet and secure Possession of Truths, that most concern'd us, whilst we let loose our Thoughts into the vast Ocean of *Being*, as if all that boundless Extent, were the natural, and undoubted Possession of our Understandings, wherein there was nothing exempt from its Decisions, or that escaped its Comprehension. Thus Men, extending their Enquiries beyond their Capacities, and letting their Thoughts wander into those depths, where they can find no sure Footing; 'tis no Wonder, that they raise Questions, and multiply Disputes, which never coming to any clear Resolution, are proper only to continue and increase their Doubts, and to confirm them at last in perfect Scepticism. Whereas were the Capacities of our Understandings well considered, the Extent of our Knowledge once discovered, and the Horizon found, which sets the Bounds between the enlightned and dark Parts of Things; between what is, and what is not comprehensible by us, Men would perhaps with less scruple acquiesce in the avow'd Ignorance of the one, and imploy their Thoughts and Discourse, with more Advantage and Satisfaction in the other.

§ 8. Thus much I thought necessary to say concerning the Occasion of this Enquiry into humane Understanding. But, before I proceed on to what I have thought on this Subject, I must here in the Entrance beg pardon of my Reader, for the frequent use of the Word *Idea*, which he will find in the following Treatise. It being that Term, which, I think, serves best to stand for whatsoever is the Object of the Understanding when a Man thinks, I have used it to express whatever is meant by *Phantasm*, *Notion*, *Species*, or whatever it is, which the Mind can be employ'd about in thinking; and I could not avoid frequently using it.

§ 8. *What* Idea *stands for.*

---

(6) secure] **1–4** | sure **5**. (**Coste** 'la possession tranquille et assurée') (33) **5** *adds, in a footnote, quotations from the Bishop of Worcester's* Answer to Mr Locke's First Letter, *p. 93, Locke's* Second Letter to the Bishop of Worcester, *pp. 63, etc., and Locke's* Third Letter to the Bishop of Worcester, *pp. 353, etc.*; *prefaced by* 'This modest Apology of our Author could not procure him the free use of the Word *Idea*. But great offence has been taken at it, and it has been censured as of dangerous Consequence: To which you may here see what he Answers'.

I presume it will be easily granted me, that there are such *Ideas* in Men's Minds; every one is conscious of them in himself, and Men's Words and Actions will satisfy him, that they are in others.

Our first Enquiry then shall be, how they come into the Mind.

CHAPTER II

No innate Principles in the Mind.

§ 1. It is an established Opinion amongst some Men, That there are in the Understanding certain *innate Principles*; some primary Notions, *Κοιναὶ ἔννοιαι*, Characters, as it were stamped upon the Mind of Man, which the Soul receives in its very first Being; and brings into the World with it. It would be sufficient to convince unprejudiced Readers of the falseness of this Supposition, if I should only shew (as I hope I shall in the following Parts of this Discourse) how Men, barely by the Use of their natural Faculties, may attain to all the Knowledge they have, without the help of any innate Impressions; and may arrive at Certainty, without any such Original Notions or Principles. For I imagine any one will easily grant, That it would be impertinent to suppose, the *Ideas* of Colours innate in a Creature, to whom God hath given Sight, and a Power to receive them by the Eyes from external Objects: and no less unreasonable would it be to attribute several Truths, to the Impressions of Nature, and innate Characters, when we may observe in our selves Faculties, fit to attain as easie and certain Knowledge of them, as if they were Originally imprinted on the Mind.

But because a Man is not permitted without Censure to follow his own Thoughts in the search of Truth, when they lead him ever so little out of the common Road: I shall set down the Reasons, that made me doubt of the Truth of that Opinion, as an Excuse for my Mistake, if I be in one, which I leave to be consider'd by those, who, with me, dispose themselves to embrace Truth, where-ever they find it.

§ 1. *The way shewn how we come by any Knowledge, sufficient to prove it not innate.*

---

(2) [*2nd*] Men's] **2–4** | Mens **1er, 5** | a Man's **1** (15) Original] **1–3, 5** | original **4**

§ 2. There is nothing more commonly taken for granted, than that there are certain Principles both *Speculative* and *Practical* (for they speak of both) universally agreed upon by all Mankind: which therefore they argue, must needs be the constant Impressions, which the Souls of Men receive in their first Beings, and which they bring into the World with them, as necessarily and really as they do any of their inherent Faculties.

§ 3. This Argument, drawn from *Universal Consent*, has this Misfortune in it, That if it were true in matter of Fact, that there were certain Truths, wherein all Mankind agreed, it would not prove them innate, if there can be any other way shewn, how Men may come to that Universal Agreement, in the things they do consent in; which I presume may be done.

§ 4. But, which is worse, this Argument of Universal Consent, which is made use of, to prove innate Principles, seems to me a Demonstration that there are none such: Because there are none to which all Mankind give an Universal Assent. I shall begin with the Speculative, and instance in those magnified Principles of Demonstration, *Whatsoever is, is*; and *'Tis impossible for the same thing to be, and not to be,* which of all others I think have the most allow'd Title to innate. These have so setled a Reputation of Maxims universally received, that 'twill, no doubt, be thought strange, if any one should seem to question it. But yet I take liberty to say, That these Propositions are so far from having an universal Assent, that there are a great Part of Mankind, to whom they are not so much as known.

§ 5. For, first 'tis evident, that all *Children, and Ideots, have not* the least Apprehension or Thought of them: and the want of that is enough to destroy that universal Assent, which must needs be the necessary concomitant of all innate Truths: it seeming to me near a Contradiction, to say, that there are Truths imprinted on the Soul, which it perceives or understands not; imprinting, if it signify any thing, being nothing else, but the making certain Truths to be perceived. For to imprint any thing on the Mind without the

§ 2. *General Assent the great Argument.* § 3. *Universal Consent proves nothing innate.* § 4. What is, is; *and* It is impossible for the same thing to be, and not to be, *not universally assented to.* § 5. *Not on the Mind naturally imprinted, because not known to Children, Ideots,* etc.

(4) the] **1–4**; *om.* **5** (18–19) Demonstration,] *edit.* | Demonstration. **2–4** | Demonstration: **5** | Demonstration **1**

Mind's perceiving it, seems to me hardly intelligible. If therefore Children and *Ideots* have Souls, have Minds, with those Impressions upon them, they must unavoidably perceive them, and necessarily know and assent to these Truths, which since they do not, it is evident that there are no such Impressions. For if they are not Notions naturally imprinted, How can they be innate? And if they are Notions imprinted, How can they be unknown? To say a Notion is imprinted on the Mind, and yet at the same time to say, that the mind is ignorant of it, and never yet took notice of it, is to make this Impression nothing. No Proposition can be said to be in the Mind, which it never yet knew, which it was never yet conscious of. For if any one may; then, by the same Reason, all Propositions that are true, and the Mind is capable ever of assenting to, may be said to be in the Mind, and to be imprinted: Since if any one can be said to be in the Mind, which it never yet knew, it must be only because it is capable of knowing it; and so the Mind is of all Truths it ever shall know. Nay, thus Truths may be imprinted on the Mind, which it never did, nor ever shall know: for a Man may live long, and die at last in Ignorance of many Truths, which his Mind was capable of knowing, and that with Certainty. So that if the Capacity of knowing be the natural Impression contended for, all the Truths a Man ever comes to know, will, by this Account, be, every one of them, innate; and this great Point will amount to no more, but only to a very improper way of speaking; which whilst it pretends to assert the contrary, says nothing different from those, who deny innate Principles. For no Body, I think, ever denied, that the Mind was capable of knowing several Truths. The Capacity, they say, is innate, the Knowledge acquired. But then to what end such contest for certain innate Maxims? If Truths can be imprinted on the Understanding without being perceived, I can see no difference there can be, between any Truths the Mind is capable of knowing in respect of their Original: They must all be innate, or all adventitious: In vain shall a Man go about to distinguish them. He therefore that talks of innate Notions in the Understanding, cannot (if he intend thereby any distinct sort of Truths) mean such Truths to be in the Understanding, as it never perceived, and is yet wholly ignorant of. For if these Words (*to be in the Understanding*) have any Propriety, they signify to be understood. So that, to be in the Understanding, and, not to be understood; to be in the Mind, and, never to be

(36) wholly] **3–5** | fully **1–2**

perceived, is all one, as to say, any thing is, and is not, in the Mind or Understanding. If therefore these two Propositions, *Whatsoever is, is*; and, *It is impossible for the same thing to be, and not to be*, are by Nature imprinted, Children cannot be ignorant of them: Infants, and all that have Souls must necessarily have them in their Understandings, know the Truth of them, and assent to it.

§ 6. To avoid this, 'tis usually answered, that all Men know and *assent* to them, *when they come to the use of Reason*, and this is enough to prove them innate. I answer,

§ 7. Doubtful Expressions, that have scarce any signification, go for clear Reasons to those, who being prepossessed, take not the pains to examine even what they themselves say. For to apply this Answer with any tolerable Sence to our present Purpose, it must signify one of these two things; either, That as soon as Men come to the use of Reason, these supposed native Inscriptions come to be known, and observed by them: Or else, that the Use and Exercise of Men's Reasons assists them in the Discovery of these Principles, and certainly makes them known to them.

§ 8. If they mean that by the *Use of Reason* Men may discover these Principles; and that this is sufficient to prove them innate; their way of arguing will stand thus, (*viz.*) That whatever Truths Reason can certainly discover to us, and make us firmly assent to, those are all naturally imprinted on the Mind; since that universal Assent, which is made the Mark of them, amounts to no more but this; That by the use of Reason, we are capable to come to a certain Knowledge of, and assent to them; and by this Means there will be no difference between the Maxims of the Mathematicians, and Theorems they deduce from them: All must be equally allow'd innate, they being all Discoveries made by the use of Reason, and Truths that a rational Creature may certainly come to know, if he apply his Thoughts rightly that Way.

§ 9. But how can these Men think the *Use of Reason* necessary to discover Principles that are supposed innate, when Reason (if we may believe them) is nothing else, but the Faculty of deducing unknown Truths from Principles or Propositions, that are already

§§ 6, 7. *That Men know them when they come to the use of Reason, answered.* § 8. *If Reason discovered them, that would not prove them innate.* §§ 9–11. *'Tis false that Reason discovers them.*

---

(17) assists] **2–5** | assist **1** (18) makes] **2er–5** | make **1–2** to them.] **Coste** *adds* 'Or ceux à qui j'ai à faire, ne sçauroient montrer par aucune de ces deux choses qu'il y ait des Principes *innez*.' (32) these] **4–5** | those **1–3**

known? That certainly can never be thought innate, which we have need of Reason to discover, unless as I have said, we will have all the certain Truths, that Reason ever teaches us, to be innate. We may as well think the use of Reason necessary to make our Eyes discover visible Objects, as that there should be need of Reason, or the Exercise thereof, to make the Understanding see, what is Originally engraven in it, and cannot be in the Understanding, before it be perceived by it. So that to make Reason discover those Truths thus imprinted, is to say, that the use of Reason discovers to a Man, what he knew before; and if Men have these innate, impressed Truths Originally, and before the use of Reason, and yet are always ignorant of them, till they come to the use of Reason, 'tis in effect to say, that Men know, and know them not at the same time.

§ 10. 'Twill here perhaps be said, That Mathematical Demonstrations, and other Truths, that are not innate, are not assented to, as soon as propos'd, wherein they are distinguish'd from these Maxims, and other innate Truths. I shall have occasion to speak of Assent upon the first proposing, more particularly by and by. I shall here only, and that very readily, allow, That these Maxims, and Mathematical Demonstrations are in this different; That the one has need of Reason using of Proofs, to make them out, and to gain our Assent; but the other, as soon as understood, are, without any the least reasoning, embraced and assented to. But I withal beg leave to observe, That it lays open the Weakness of this Subterfuge, which requires the *Use of Reason* for the Discovery of these general Truths: Since it must be confessed, that in their Discovery, there is no Use made of reasoning at all. And I think those who give this Answer, will not be forward to affirm, That the Knowledge of this Maxim, *That it is impossible for the same thing to be, and not to be*, is a deduction of our Reason. For this would be to destroy that Bounty of Nature, they seem so fond of, whilst they make the Knowledge of those Principles to depend on the labour of our Thoughts. For all Reasoning is search, and casting about, and requires Pains and Application. And how can it with any tolerable Sence be suppos'd, that what was imprinted by Nature, as the Foundation and Guide of our Reason, should need the Use of Reason to discover it?

§ 11. Those who will take the Pains to reflect with a little attention on the Operations of the Understanding, will find, that this ready Assent of the Mind to some Truths, depends not, either on

(10) these] **1–4** | those **5** (39)–53(1) not . . . or] **2–5** | not either on native Inscription, nor **1**

native Inscription, or the *Use of Reason*; but on a Faculty of the Mind quite distinct from both of them as we shall see hereafter. Reason therefore, having nothing to do in procuring our Assent to these Maxims, if by saying, that *Men know and assent to them, when they come to the Use of Reason*, be meant, That the use of Reason assists us in the Knowledge of these Maxims, it is utterly false; and were it true, would prove them not to be innate.

§ 12. If by knowing and assenting to them, *when we come to the use of Reason* be meant, that this is the time, when they come to be taken notice of by the Mind; and that as soon as Children come to the use of Reason, they come also to know and assent to these Maxims; this also is false, and frivolous. *First*, It is false. Because it is evident, these Maxims are not in the Mind so early as the use of Reason: and therefore the coming to the use of Reason is falsly assigned, as the time of their Discovery. How many instances of the use of Reason may we observe in Children, a long time before they have any Knowledge of this Maxim, *That it is impossible for the same thing to be, and not to be*? and a great part of illiterate People, and Savages, pass many Years, even of their rational Age, without ever thinking on this, and the like general Propositions. I grant Men come not to the Knowledge of these general and more abstract Truths, which are thought innate, till they come to the use of Reason; and I add, nor then neither. Which is so, because till after they come to the use of Reason, those general abstract *Ideas* are not framed in the Mind, about which those general Maxims are, which are mistaken for innate Principles, but are indeed Discoveries made, and Verities introduced, and brought into the Mind by the same Way, and discovered by the same Steps, as several other Propositions, which no Body was ever so extravagant as to suppose innate. This I hope to make plain in the sequel of this Discourse. I allow therefore a Necessity, that Men should come to the use of Reason, before they get the Knowledge of those general Truths: but deny, that Men's coming to the use of Reason is the time of their Discovery.

§ 13. In the mean time, it is observable, that this saying, that Men know, and assent to these Maxims, *when they come to the use of*

§ 12. *The coming to the use of Reason, not the time we come to know these Maxims.* § 13. *By this, they are not distinguished from other knowable Truths.*

(1) *v.* 52(39), n. (16) a] **1–4**; *om.* **5** (19) Age] **1T.er, 2–5** | Ages **1**
(22) innate,] **2–5** | innate / **1** (27), and] **2–5** | and **1** (32) get] **1–2, 4–5** | get to **3**

Reason, amounts in reality of Fact to no more but this, That they are never known, nor taken notice of before the use of Reason, but may possibly be assented to sometime after, during a Man's Life; but when, is uncertain: And so may all other knowable Truths, as well as these, which therefore have no Advantage, nor distinction from others, by this Note of being known when we come to the use of Reason; nor are thereby proved to be innate, but quite the contrary.

§ 14. But *Secondly*, were it true, that the precise time of their being known, and assented to, were, when Men come to the *Use of Reason*; neither would that prove them innate. This way of arguing is as frivolous, as the Supposition of it self is false. For by what kind of Logick will it appear, that any Notion is Originally by Nature imprinted in the Mind in its first Constitution, because it comes first to be observed, and assented to, when a Faculty of the Mind, which has quite a distinct Province, begins to exert it self? And therefore, the coming to the use of Speech, if it were supposed the time, that these Maxims are first assented to (which it may be with as much Truth, as the time when Men come to the use of Reason) would be as good a Proof that they were innate, as to say, they are innate because Men assent to them, when they come to the use of Reason. I agree then with these Men of innate Principles, that there is no Knowledge of these general and self-evident Maxims in the Mind, till it comes to the Exercise of Reason: but I deny that the coming to the use of Reason, is the precise time when they are first taken notice of; and, if that were the precise time, I deny that it would prove them innate. All that can with any Truth be meant by this Proposition, That Men *assent to them when they come to the use of Reason*, is no more but this, That the making of general abstract *Ideas*, and the Understanding of general Names, being a Concomitant of the rational Faculty, and growing up with it, Children commonly get not those general *Ideas*, nor learn the Names that stand for them, till having for a good while exercised their Reason about familiar and more particular *Ideas*, they are by their ordinary Discourse and Actions with others, acknowledged to be capable of rational Conversation. If assenting to these Maxims, when Men come to the use of Reason, can be true in any other Sence, I desire it

§ 14. *If coming to the use of Reason were the time of their discovery, it would not prove them innate.*

(3) after,] **2–5** | after **1** (11) [*1st*] as] **1–4** | so **5** (25) and . . . [*2nd*] that] **4–5** | and that if it were, **3** | and that if it were, that **1–2**

may be shewn; or at least, how in this, or any other Sence it proves them innate.

§ 15. The Senses at first let in particular *Ideas*, and furnish the yet empty Cabinet: And the Mind by degrees growing familiar with some of them, they are lodged in the Memory, and Names got to them. Afterwards the Mind proceeding farther, abstracts them, and by Degrees learns the use of general Names. In this manner the Mind comes to be furnish'd with *Ideas* and Language, the Materials about which to exercise its discursive Faculty: And the use of Reason becomes daily more visible, as these Materials, that give it Employment, increase. But though the having of general *Ideas*, and the use of general Words and Reason usually grow together: yet, I see not, how this any way proves them innate. The Knowledge of some Truths, I confess, is very early in the Mind; but in a way that shews them not to be innate. For, if we will observe, we shall find it still to be about *Ideas*, not innate, but acquired: It being about those first, which are imprinted by external Things, with which Infants have earliest to do, and which make the most frequent Impressions on their Senses. In *Ideas* thus got, the Mind discovers, That some agree, and others differ, probably as soon as it has any use of Memory; as soon as it is able, to retain and receive distinct *Ideas*. But whether it be then, or no, this is certain, it does so long before it has the use of Words; or comes to that, which we commonly call the *use of Reason*. For a Child knows as certainly, before it can speak, the difference between the *Ideas* of Sweet and Bitter (*i.e.* That Sweet is not Bitter) as it knows afterwards (when it comes to speak) That Worm-wood and Sugar-plumbs, are not the same thing.

§ 16. A Child knows not that Three and Four are equal to Seven, till he comes to be able to count to Seven, and has got the Name and *Idea* of Equality: and then upon the explaining those Words, he presently assents to, or rather perceives the Truth of that Proposition. But neither does he then readily assent, because it is an innate Truth, nor was his Assent wanting, till then, because he wanted the *Use of Reason*; but the Truth of it appears to him, as soon as he has setled in his Mind the clear and distinct *Ideas*, that these Names stand for: And then, he knows the Truth of that Proposition,

§§ 15, 16. *The steps by which the Mind attains several Truths.*

---

(7) In] **2–5** | By **1** (18) and which] **1–4** | which **5** (19) In . . . discovers] **Coste** 'C'est en reflêchissant sur ces idées . . . que l'Esprit juge' (30) the] **1–4**; *om.* **5**

upon the same Grounds, and by the same means, that he knew before, That a Rod and Cherry are not the same thing; and upon the same Grounds also, that he may come to know afterwards, *That it is impossible for the same thing to be, and not to be*, as shall be more fully shewn hereafter. So that the later it is before any one comes to have those general *Ideas*, about which those Maxims are; or to know the Signification of those general Terms, that stand for them; or to put together in his Mind, the *Ideas* they stand for: the later also will it be, before he comes to assent to those Maxims, whose Terms, with the *Ideas* they stand for, being no more innate, than those of a Cat or a Weesel, he must stay till Time and Observation have acquainted him with them; and then he will be in a Capacity to know the Truth of these Maxims, upon the first Occasion, that shall make him put together those *Ideas* in his Mind, and observe, whether they agree or disagree, according as is expressed in those Propositions. And therefore it is, That a Man knows that Eighteen and Nineteen, are equal to Thirty Seven, by the same self-Evidence, that he knows One and Two to be equal to Three: Yet, a Child knows this, not so soon as the other; not for want of the use of Reason: but because the *Ideas* the Words Eighteen, Nineteen, and Thirty seven stand for, are not so soon got, as those, which are signify'd by One, Two, and Three.

§ 17. This Evasion therefore of general Assent, when Men come to the use of Reason, failing as it does, and leaving no difference between those supposed-innate, and other Truths, that are afterwards acquired and learnt, Men have endeavoured to secure an universal Assent to those they call Maxims, by saying, they are generally *assented to, as soon as proposed*, and the Terms they are propos'd in, understood: Seeing all Men, even Children, as soon as they hear and understand the Terms, assent to these Propositions, they think it is sufficient to prove them innate. For since Men never fail, after they have once understood the Words, to acknowledge them for undoubted Truths, they would inferr, That certainly these Propositions were first lodged in the Understanding, which, without any teaching, the Mind at very first Proposal, immediately closes with, and assents to, and after that never doubts again.

§ 17. *Assenting as soon as proposed and understood, proves them not innate.*

(4–5) shall be more fully shewn] **4–5** | we shall more fully shew **1–3** (19) this] **2–5** | that **1** (25) other] **Coste** 'plusieurs autres'

§ 18. In Answer to this, I demand whether ready *assent*, given to a Proposition *upon first hearing*, and understanding the Terms, be a certain mark of an innate Principle? If it be not, such a general assent is in vain urged as a Proof of them: If it be said, that it is a mark of innate, they must then allow all such Propositions to be innate, which are generally assented to as soon as heard, whereby they will find themselves plentifully stored with innate Principles. For upon the same ground (*viz.*) of Assent at first hearing and understanding the Terms, That Men would have those Maxims pass for innate, they must also admit several Propositions about Numbers, to be innate: And thus, *That One and Two are equal to Three*, *That Two and Two are equal to Four*, and a multitude of other the like Propositions in Numbers, that every Body assents to, at first hearing, and understanding the Terms, must have a place amongst these innate Axioms. Nor is this the Prerogative of Numbers alone, and Propositions made about several of them: But even natural Philosophy, and all the other Sciences afford Propositions, which are sure to meet with Assent, as soon as they are understood. *That two Bodies cannot be in the same place*, is a Truth, that no Body any more sticks at, than at this Maxim, *That it is impossible for the same thing to be, and not to be*; *That White is not Black*, *That a Square is not a Circle*, *That Yellowness is not Sweetness*: These, and a Million of other such Propositions, as many at least, as we have distinct *Ideas*, every Man in his Wits, at first hearing, and knowing what the Names stand for, must necessarily assent to. If then these Men will be true to their own Rule, and have *Assent at first hearing and understanding the Terms*, to be a mark of innate, they must allow, not only as many innate Propositions, as Men have distinct *Ideas*; but as many as Men can make Propositions, wherein different *Ideas* are denied one of another. Since every Proposition, wherein one different *Idea* is denied of another, will as certainly find Assent at first hearing and understanding the Terms, as this general one, *It is impossible for the same to be, and not to be*; or that which is the Foundation of it, and is the easier understood of the two, *The same is not different*: By which Account, they will have Legions of innate Propositions of this one sort, without mentioning any other.

§ 18. *If such an Assent be a mark of innate, then that One and Two are equal to Three; that Sweetness is not Bitterness; and a thousand the like must be innate.*

---

(11) innate: And thus,] **2–5** | innate, **1** (20) this] **2–5** | that **1** (26) then] **1–4**; *om.* **5** (36) Propositions] **1–3, 5** (*likewise* **Coste**) | Proposition **4**

But since no Proposition can be innate, unless the *Ideas*, about which it is, be innate, This will be, to suppose all our *Ideas* of Colours, Sounds, Tastes, Figures, *etc.* innate; than which there cannot be any thing more opposite to Reason and Experience. Universal and ready assent, upon hearing and understanding the Terms, is (I grant) a mark of self-evidence: but self-evidence, depending not on innate Impressions, but on something else (as we shall shew hereafter) belongs to several Propositions, which no Body was yet so extravagant, as to pretend to be innate.

§ 19. Nor let it be said, That those more particular self-evident Propositions, which are assented to at first hearing, as, *That One and Two are equal to Three*; *That Green is not Red*, etc. are received as the Consequences of those more universal Propositions, which are look'd on as innate Principles: since any one, who will but take the Pains to observe what passes in the Understanding, will certainly find, That these, and the like less general Propositions, are certainly known and firmly assented to, by those, who are utterly ignorant of those more general Maxims; and so, being earlier in the Mind than those (as they are called) first Principles, cannot owe to them the Assent, wherewith they are received at first hearing.

§ 20. If it be said, that these Propositions, *viz. Two and Two are equal to Four*; *Red is not Blue*, etc. are not general Maxims, nor of any great use. I answer, That makes nothing to the Argument of universal assent, upon hearing and understanding. For if that be the certain mark of innate, whatever Proposition can be found, that receives general assent, as soon as heard and understood, that must be admitted for an innate Proposition, as well as this Maxim, *That it is impossible for the same thing to be, and not to be*, they being upon this Ground equal. And as to the difference of being more general, that makes this Maxim more remote from being innate; those general and abstract *Ideas*, being more strangers to our first Apprehensions, than those of more particular self-evident Propositions; and therefore, 'tis longer before they are admitted and assented to by the growing Understanding. And as to the usefulness of these magnified Maxims, that perhaps will not be found so great as is generally conceived, when it comes in its due place to be more fully considered.

§ 19. *Such less general Propositions known before these universal Maxims.* § 20. *One and One, equal to Two*, etc. *not general nor useful*, *answered.*

---

(1) Proposition] **1–3**, **5** (*likewise* **Coste**) | Propositions **4** (3) Figures] **1–4** | Figure **5** (36) in] **1–4** | to **5** (*l. below* 36: § 19.) *In* **Coste** *this summary is applied to* §§ *19 and 20.*

§ 21. But we have not yet done with *assenting to Propositions at first hearing and understanding their Terms*; 'tis fit we first take notice, That this, instead of being a mark, that they are innate, is a proof of the contrary: Since it supposes, that several, who understand and know other things, are ignorant of these Principles, till they are propos'd to them; and that one may be unacquainted with these Truths, till he hears them from others. For if they were innate, What need they be propos'd, in order to gaining assent; when, by being in the Understanding, by a natural and original Impression (if there were any such) they could not but be known before? Or, doth the proposing them, print them clearer in the Mind, than Nature did? If so, then the Consequence will be, That a Man knows them better, after he has been thus taught them, than he did before. Whence it will follow, That these Principles may be made more evident to us by other's teaching, than Nature has made them by Impression: which will ill agree with the Opinion of innate Principles, and give but little Authority to them; but on the contrary, makes them unfit to be the foundations of all our other Knowledge, as they are pretended to be. This cannot be deny'd, that Men grow first acquainted with many of these self-evident Truths, upon their being proposed: But it is clear, that whosoever does so, finds in himself, That he then begins to know a Proposition, which he knew not before; and which from thenceforth he never questions: not because it was innate; but, because the consideration of the Nature of the things contained in those Words, would not suffer him to think otherwise, how, or whensoever he is brought to reflect on them. And if whatever is assented to at first hearing, and understanding the terms, must pass for an innate Principle, every well grounded Observation drawn from particulars into a general Rule, must be innate. When yet it is certain, that not all, but only sagacious Heads light at first on these Observations, and reduce them into general Propositions, not innate, but collected from a preceding acquaintance, and reflection on particular instances. These, when observing Men have made them, unobserving Men, when they are propos'd to them, cannot refuse their assent to.

§ 22. If it be said, The Understanding hath an *implicit Knowledge*

§ 21. *These Maxims not being known sometimes till proposed, proves them not innate.* § 22. *Implicitly known before proposing, signifies that the Mind is capable of understanding them, or else signifies nothing.*

(27–35) And . . . to.] *add.* **2–5**

of these Principles, but not an explicit, before this first hearing, (as they must, who will say, That they are in the Understanding before they are known) it will be hard to conceive what is meant by a Principle imprinted on the Understanding Implicitly; unless it be this, That the Mind is capable of understanding and assenting firmly to such Propositions. And thus all Mathematical Demonstrations, as well as first Principles, must be received as native Impressions on the Mind: which, I fear they will scarce allow them to be, who find it harder to demonstrate a Proposition, than assent to it, when demonstrated. And few Mathematicians will be forward to believe, That all the Diagrams they have drawn, were but Copies of those innate Characters, which Nature had ingraven upon their Minds.

§ 23. There is I fear this farther weakness in the foregoing Argument, which would perswade us, That therefore those Maxims are to be thought innate, which Men *admit at first hearing*, because they assent to Propositions, which they are not taught, nor do receive from the force of any Argument or Demonstration, but a bare Explication or Understanding of the Terms. Under which, there seems to me to lie this fallacy; That Men are supposed not to be *taught*, nor to *learn* any thing *de novo*; when in truth, they are taught, and do learn something they were ignorant of before. For first it is evident, they have learned the Terms and their Signification: neither of which was born with them. But this is not all the acquired Knowledge in the case: The *Ideas* themselves, about which the Proposition is, are not born with them, no more than their Names, but got afterwards. So, that in all Propositions that are assented to, at first hearing; the Terms of the Proposition, their standing for such *Ideas*, and the *Ideas* themselves that they stand for, being neither of them innate, I would fain know what there is remaining in such Propositions, that is innate. For I would gladly have any one name that Proposition, whose Terms or *Ideas* were either of them innate. We by degrees get *Ideas* and Names, and learn their appropriated connexion one with another; and then to Propositions, made in such Terms, whose signification we have learnt, and wherein the Agreement or Disagreement we can perceive in our *Ideas*, when put together, is expressed, we at first

§ 23. *The Argument of assenting on first hearing, is upon a false supposition of no precedent teaching.*

(27) hearing;] **3–5** | hearing **1–2**

hearing assent; though to other Propositions, in themselves as certain and evident, but which are concerning *Ideas*, not so soon or so easily got, we are at the same time no way capable of assenting. For though a Child quickly assent to this Proposition, *That an Apple is not Fire*; when, by familiar Acquaintance, he has got the *Ideas* of those two different things distinctly imprinted on his Mind, and has learnt that the Names *Apple* and *Fire* stand for them: yet, it will be some years after, perhaps, before the same Child will assent to this Proposition, *That it is impossible for the same thing to be, and not to be*. Because, that though, perhaps, the Words are as easie to be learnt: yet the signification of them, being more large, comprehensive, and abstract, than of the Names annexed to those sensible things, the Child hath to do with, it is longer before he learns their precise meaning, and it requires more time plainly to form in his Mind those general *Ideas*, they stand for. Till that be done, you will in vain endeavour to make any Child assent to a Proposition, made up of such general Terms: but as soon as ever he has got those *Ideas*, and learn'd their Names, he forwardly closes with the one, as well as the other of the forementioned Propositions; and with both for the same Reason; (*viz.*) because he finds the *Ideas* he has in his Mind, to agree or disagree, according as the Words standing for them, are affirmed, or denied one of another in the Proposition. But if Propositions be brought to him in Words, which stand for *Ideas* he has not yet in his Mind: to such Propositions, however evidently true or false in themselves, he affords neither assent nor dissent, but is ignorant. For Words being but empty sounds, any farther than they are signs of our *Ideas*, we cannot but assent to them, as they correspond to those *Ideas* we have, but no farther than that. But the shewing by what Steps and Ways Knowledge comes into our Minds, and the grounds of several degrees of assent, being the Business of the following Discourse, it may suffice to have only touched on it here, as one Reason, that made me doubt of those innate Principles.

§ 24. To conclude this Argument of universal Consent, I agree with these Defenders of innate Principles, That if they are *innate, they must needs have universal assent*. For that a Truth should be innate, and yet not assented to, is to me as unintelligible, as for a

§ 24. *Not innate, because not universally assented to.*

(2–3) or so] **4–5** | nor **1–3** (30) [*1st*] the] **1–4**; *om.* **5**

Man to know a Truth, and be ignorant of it at the same time. But then, by these Men's own Confession, they cannot be innate; since they are not assented to, by those who understand not the Terms, nor by a great part of those who do understand them, but have yet never heard, nor thought of those Propositions; which, I think, is at least one half of Mankind. But were the Number far less, it would be enough to destroy universal assent, and thereby shew these Propositions not to be innate, if Children alone were ignorant of them.

§ 25. But that I may not be accused, to argue from the thoughts of Infants, which are unknown to us, and to conclude, from what passes in their Understandings, before they express it; I say next, That these two general Propositions are not the Truths, that *first possess the Minds* of Children; nor are antecedent to all acquired, and adventitious Notions: which if they were innate, they must needs be. Whether we can determine it or no, it matters not, there is certainly a time, when Children begin to think, and their Words and Actions do assure us, that they do so. When therefore they are capable of Thought, of Knowledge, of Assent, can it rationally be supposed, they can be ignorant of those Notions that Nature has imprinted, were there any such? Can it be imagin'd, with any appearance of Reason, That they perceive the Impressions from things without; and be at the same time ignorant of those Characters, which Nature it self has taken care to stamp within? Can they receive and assent to adventitious Notions, and be ignorant of those, which are supposed woven into the very Principles of their Being, and imprinted there in indelible Characters, to be the Foundation, and Guide of all their acquired Knowledge, and future Reasonings? This would be, to make Nature take Pains to no Purpose; Or, at least, to write very ill; since its Characters could not be read by those Eyes, which saw other things very well: and those are very ill supposed the clearest parts of Truth, and the Foundations of all our Knowledge, which are not first known, and without which, the undoubted Knowledge of several other things may be had. The Child certainly knows, that the *Nurse* that feeds it, is neither the *Cat* it plays with, nor the *Blackmoor* it is afraid of; That the *Wormseed* or *Mustard* it refuses, is not the *Apple* or *Sugar* it cries for: this it is

§ 25. *These Maxims not the first known.*

---

(12) **Coste** *adds a marginal note expressing them; they are the italicized sentences at* 57 (33–5).

certainly and undoubtedly assured of: But will any one say, it is by Virtue of this Principle, *That it is impossible for the same thing to be, and not to be*, that it so firmly assents to these, and other parts of its Knowledge? Or that the Child has any Notion or Apprehension of that Proposition at an Age, wherein yet 'tis plain, it knows a great many other Truths? He that will say, Children join these general abstract Speculations with their sucking Bottles, and their Rattles, may, perhaps, with Justice be thought to have more Passion and Zeal for his Opinion; but less Sincerity and Truth, than one of that Age.

§ 26. Though therefore there be several general Propositions, that meet with constant and ready assent, as soon as proposed to Men grown up, who have attained the use of more general and abstract *Ideas*, and Names standing for them: yet they not being to be found in those of tender Years, who nevertheless know other things, they cannot pretend to universal assent of intelligent Persons, and so by no means can be supposed innate: It being impossible, that any Truth which is innate (if there were any such) should be unknown, at least to any one, who knows any thing else. Since, if they are innate Truths, they must be innate thoughts: there being nothing a Truth in the Mind, that it has never thought on. Whereby it is evident, if there be any *innate Truths*, they *must necessarily be the first of any thought on*; the first that appear there.

§ 27. That the general Maxims, we are discoursing of, are not known to Children, *Ideots*, and a great part of Mankind, we have already sufficiently proved: whereby it is evident, they have not an universal assent, nor are general Impressions. But there is this farther Argument in it against their being innate: That these Characters, if they were native and original Impressions, *should appear fairest and clearest in* those Persons, in whom yet we find no Footsteps of them: And 'tis, in my Opinion, a strong Presumption, that they are not innate; since they are least known to those, in whom, if they were innate, they must needs exert themselves with most Force and Vigour. For *Children*, *Ideots*, *Savages*, and *illiterate* People, being of all others the least corrupted by Custom, or borrowed Opinions; Learning, and Education, having not cast their Native thoughts into new Moulds; nor by super-inducing foreign

§ 26. *And so not innate.* § 27. *Not innate, because they appear least, where what is innate shews it self clearest.*

(*l. below* 37: § 27.) *In* **Coste**, *this summary is applied to* §§ *27 and 28.*

and studied Doctrines, confounded those fair Characters Nature had written there; one might reasonably imagine, that in their Minds these innate Notions should lie open fairly to every one's view, as 'tis certain the thoughts of Children do. It might very well be expected, that these Principles should be perfectly known to Naturals; which being stamped immediately on the Soul (as these Men suppose) can have no dependence on the Constitutions, or Organs of the Body, the only confessed difference between them and others. One would think, according to these Men's Principles, That all these native Beams of Light (were there any such) should in those, who have no Reserves, no Arts of Concealment, shine out in their full Lustre, and leave us in no more doubt of their being there, than we are of their love of Pleasure, and abhorrence of Pain. But alas, amongst *Children*, *Ideots*, *Savages*, and the grosly *Illiterate*, what general Maxims are to be found? What universal Principles of Knowledge? Their Notions are few and narrow, borrowed only from those Objects, they have had most to do with, and which have made upon their Senses the frequentest and strongest Impressions. A Child knows his Nurse, and his Cradle, and by degrees the Playthings of a little more advanced Age: And a young Savage has, perhaps, his Head fill'd with Love and Hunting, according to the fashion of his Tribe. But he that from a Child untaught, or a wild Inhabitant of the Woods, will expect these abstract Maxims, and reputed Principles of Sciences, will I fear, find himself mistaken. Such kind of general Propositions, are seldom mentioned in the Huts of *Indians*: much less are they to be found in the thoughts of *Children*, or any Impressions of them on the Minds of *Naturals*. They are the Language and Business of the Schools, and Academies of learned Nations, accustomed to that sort of Conversation, or Learning, where Disputes are frequent: These Maxims being suited to artificial Argumentation, and useful for Conviction; but not much conducing to the discovery of Truth, or advancement of Knowledge. But of their small use for the improvement of Knowledge, I shall have occasion to speak more at large, *l*. 4. *c*. 7.

§ 28. I know not how absurd this may seem to the Masters of Demonstration: And probably, it will hardly down with any Body

§28. *Recapitulation.*

(10) these] **2–5** | the **1** (18) Impressions] **2–5** | Impression **1** (23–4) and reputed] **2–5** | or the **1** (28) Language and Business] **2–5** | Discourses **1**

at first Hearing. I must therefore beg a little truce with prejudice, and the forbearance of censure till I have been heard out in the sequel of this Discourse, being very willing to submit to better Judgments. And since I impartially search after Truth, I shall not be sorry to be convinced, that I have been too fond of my own Notions; which I confess we are all apt to be, when Application and Study have warmed our Heads with them.

Upon the whole matter, I cannot see any ground, to think these two famed speculative Maxims innate: since they are not universally assented to; and the assent they so generally find, is no other, than what several Propositions, not allowed to be innate, equally partake in with them: And since the assent that is given them, is produced another way, and comes not from natural Inscription, as I doubt not but to make appear in the following Discourse. And if *these first Principles* of Knowledge and Science, *are* found *not* to be *innate, no other speculative Maxims can* (I suppose) *with better Right pretend to be so.*

CHAPTER III

No innate practical Principles.

§ 1. IF those speculative Maxims, whereof we discoursed in the fore-going Chapter, have not an actual universal assent from all Mankind, as we there proved, it is much more visible concerning *practical Principles*, that they *come short of an universal Reception*: and I think it will be hard to instance any one moral Rule, which can pretend to so general and ready an assent as, *What is, is*, or to be so manifest a Truth as this, *That it is impossible for the same thing to be, and not to be*. Whereby it is evident, That they are farther removed from a title to be innate; and the doubt of their being native Impressions on the Mind, is stronger against these moral Principles than the other. Not that it brings their Truth at all in question. They are equally true, though not equally evident. Those speculative

§ 1. *No moral Principles so clear and so generally received, as the forementioned speculative Maxims.*

(1–2) a . . . heard] **2–5** | you a little to lay by your prejudice, and suspend your censure, till you have heard me **1** (10) and] **2–5** | Since **1** (12) that] *add.* **2–5**

Maxims carry their own Evidence with them: But moral Principles require Reasoning and Discourse, and some Exercise of the Mind, to discover the certainty of their Truth. They lie not open as natural Characters ingraven on the Mind; which if any such were, they must needs be visible by themselves, and by their own light be certain and known to every Body. But this is no Derogation to their Truth and Certainty, no more than it is to the Truth or Certainty, of the Three Angles of a Triangle being equal to two right ones, because it is not so evident, as *The whole is bigger than a part*; nor so apt to be assented to at first hearing. It may suffice, that these moral Rules are capable of Demonstration: and therefore it is our own faults, if we come not to a certain Knowledge of them. But the Ignorance wherein many Men are of them, and the slowness of assent, wherewith others receive them, are manifest Proofs, that they are not innate, and such as offer themselves to their view without searching.

§ 2. Whether there be any such moral Principles, wherein all Men do agree, I appeal to any, who have been but moderately conversant in the History of Mankind, and look'd abroad beyond the Smoak of their own Chimneys. Where is that practical Truth, that is universally received without doubt or question, as it must be if innate? *Justice*, and keeping of Contracts, is that which *most Men seem to agree in*. This is a Principle, which is thought to extend it self to the Dens of Thieves, and the Confederacies of the greatest Villains; and they who have gone farthest towards the putting off of Humanity it self, keep Faith and Rules of Justice one with another. I grant that Outlaws themselves do this one amongst another: but 'tis without receiving these as the innate Laws of Nature. They practise them as Rules of convenience within their own Communities: But it is impossible to conceive, that he imbraces Justice as a practical Principle, who acts fairly with his Fellow High-way-men, and at the same time plunders, or kills the next honest Man he meets with. Justice and Truth are the common ties of Society; and therefore, even Outlaws and Robbers, who break with all the World besides, must keep Faith and Rules of Equity amongst themselves, or else they cannot hold together. But

§ 2. *Faith and Justice not owned as Principles by all Men.*

---

(18) but] **1–2, 4–5**; *om.* **3** (*likewise* **Coste**) (24–5) Confederacies of the greatest Villains] **2–5** | Troops of Robbers **1** (34) Robbers] **2–5** | Villains **1**

will any one say, That those that live by Fraud and Rapine, have innate Principles of Truth and Justice which they allow and assent to?

§ 3. Perhaps it will be urged, That the *tacit assent of their Minds agrees to what their Practice contradicts*. I answer, *First*, I have always thought the Actions of Men the best Interpreters of their thoughts. But since it is certain, that most Men's Practice, and some Men's open Professions, have either questioned or denied these Principles, it is impossible to establish an universal consent (though we should look for it only amongst grown Men) without which, it is impossible to conclude them innate. *Secondly*, 'Tis very strange and unreasonable, to suppose innate practical Principles, that terminate only in Contemplation. Practical Principles derived from Nature, are there for Operation, and must produce Conformity of Action, not barely speculative assent to their truth, or else they are in vain distinguish'd from speculative Maxims. Nature, I confess, has put into Man a desire of Happiness, and an aversion to Misery: These indeed are innate practical Principles, which (as practical Principles ought) do continue constantly to operate and influence all our Actions, without ceasing: These may be observ'd in all Persons and all Ages, steady and universal; but these are Inclinations of the Appetite to good, not Impressions of truth on the Understanding. I deny not, that there are natural tendencies imprinted on the Minds of Men; and that, from the very first instances of Sense and Perception, there are some things, that are grateful, and others unwelcome to them; some things that they incline to, and others that they fly: But this makes nothing for innate Characters on the Mind, which are to be the Principles of Knowledge, regulating our Practice. Such natural Impressions on the Understanding, are so far from being confirm'd hereby, that this is an Argument against them; since if there were certain Characters, imprinted by Nature on the Understanding, as the Principles of Knowledge, we could not but perceive them constantly operate in us, and influence our Knowledge, as we do those others on the Will and Appetite; which never cease to be the constant Springs and Motives of all our Actions, to which, we perpetually feel them strongly impelling us.

§ 3. Obj. *Though Men deny them in their Practice, yet they admit them in their Thoughts, answered.*

(21–2) Inclinations . . . truth] **2–5** | Inclinations of the Will and Appetite, not Impressions and Characters **1** (35) Springs] **1er–5** | Spring **1**

§ 4. Another Reason that makes me doubt of any innate practical Principles, is, That I think, *there cannot any one moral Rule be propos'd, whereof a Man may not justly demand a Reason*: which would be perfectly ridiculous and absurd, if they were innate, or so much as self-evident; which every innate Principle must needs be, and not need any Proof to ascertain its Truth, nor want any Reason to gain it Approbation. He would be thought void of common Sense, who asked on the one side, or on the other side went about to give a Reason, *Why it is impossible for the same thing to be, and not to be*. It carries its own Light and Evidence with it, and needs no other Proof: He that understands the Terms, assents to it for its own sake, or else nothing will ever be able to prevail with him to do it. But should that most unshaken Rule of Morality, and Foundation of all social Virtue, *That one should do as he would be done unto*, be propos'd to one, who never heard it before, but yet is of capacity to understand its meaning; Might he not without any absurdity ask a Reason why? And were not he that propos'd it, bound to make out the Truth and Reasonableness of it to him? Which plainly shews it not to be innate; for if it were, it could neither want nor receive any Proof: but must needs (at least, as soon as heard and understood) be received and assented to, as an unquestionable Truth, which a Man can by no means doubt of. So that the truth of all these moral Rules, plainly depends upon some other antecedent to them, and from which they must be deduced, which could not be, if either they were innate, or so much as self-evident.

§ 5. That Men should keep their Compacts, is certainly a great and undeniable Rule in Morality: But yet, if a Christian, who has the view of Happiness and Misery in another Life, be asked why a Man must keep his Word, he will *give* this as a *Reason*: Because God, who has the Power of eternal Life and Death, requires it of us. But if an *Hobbist* be asked why; he will answer: Because the Publick requires it, and the *Leviathan* will punish you, if you do not. And if one of the old *Heathen* Philosophers had been asked, he would have answer'd: Because it was dishonest, below the Dignity of a Man, and opposite to Vertue, the highest Perfection of humane Nature, to do otherwise.

§ 6. Hence naturally flows the great variety of Opinions, con-

§ 4. *Moral Rules need a Proof*, ergo *not innate*. § 5. *Instance in keeping Compacts*. § 6. *Vertue generally approved, not because innate, but because profitable.*

(8) about] **1–4**; *om.* **5** (35) , to do otherwise] *add.* **2er–5**

cerning Moral Rules, which are to be found amongst Men, according to the different sorts of Happiness, they have a Prospect of, or propose to themselves: Which could not be, if practical Principles were innate, and imprinted in our Minds immediately by the Hand of God. I grant the existence of God, is so many ways manifest, and the Obedience we owe him, so congruous to the Light of Reason, that a great part of Mankind give Testimony to the Law of Nature: But yet I think it must be allowed, That several Moral Rules, may receive, from Mankind, a very general Approbation, without either knowing, or admitting the true ground of Morality; which can only be the Will and Law of a God, who sees Men in the dark, has in his Hand Rewards and Punishments, and Power enough to call to account the Proudest Offender. For God, having, by an inseparable connexion, joined *Virtue* and publick Happiness together; and made the Practice thereof, necessary to the preservation of Society, and visibly *beneficial* to all, with whom the Virtuous Man has to do; it is no wonder, that every one should, not only allow, but recommend, and magnifie those Rules to others, from whose observance of them, he is sure to reap Advantage to himself. He may, out of Interest, as well as Conviction, cry up that for Sacred; which if once trampled on, and prophaned, he himself cannot be safe nor secure. This, though it takes nothing from the Moral and Eternal Obligation, which these Rules evidently have; yet it shews, that the outward acknowledgment Men pay to them in their Words, proves not that they are innate Principles: Nay, it proves not so much, as, that Men assent to them inwardly in their own Minds, as the inviolable Rules of their own Practice: Since we find that self-interest and the Conveniences of this Life, make many Men, own an outward Profession and Approbation of them, whose Actions sufficiently prove, that they very little consider the Law-giver, that prescribed these Rules; nor the Hell he has ordain'd for the Punishment of those that transgress them.

§ 7. For, if we will not in Civility allow too much Sincerity to the Professions of most *Men*, but think their Actions to be the Interpreters of their Thoughts, we shall find, that they have *no* such

§ 7. *Men's Actions convince us, that the Rule of Vertue is not their internal Principle.*

(1) Rules] **1–3, 5** | rules **4** (11) Will and] *add.* **2–5** (11–12) has . . . Punishments,] *add.* **2–5** (12–13) Power enough to call to account] **2–5** | and has Power enough to punish **1** (28) Conveniences] **1, 4–5** | Conveniencies **2–3** (*l. below* 35: § 7.) *Marginal summary not in* **Coste**, *which applies the summary for* § *6 also to* § *7.*

internal Veneration for these Rules, nor so *full a Perswasion of their Certainty* and Obligation. The great Principle of Morality, *To do as one would be done to*, is more commended, than practised. But the Breach of this Rule cannot be a greater Vice, than to teach others, That it is no Moral Rule, nor Obligatory, would be thought Madness, and contrary to that Interest Men sacrifice to, when they break it themselves. Perhaps *Conscience* will be urged as checking us for such Breaches, and so the internal Obligation and Establishment of the Rule be preserved.

§ 8. To which, I answer, That I doubt not, but without being written on their Hearts, many Men, may, by the same way that they come to the Knowledge of other things, come to assent to several Moral Rules, and be convinced of their Obligation. Others also may come to be of the same Mind, from their Education, Company, and Customs of their Country; which, *Perswasion however got, will serve to set Conscience on work*, which is nothing else, but our own Opinion or Judgment of the Moral Rectitude or Pravity of our own Actions. And if Conscience be a Proof of innate Principles, contraries may be innate Principles: Since some Men, with the same bent of Conscience, prosecute what others avoid.

§ 9. But I cannot see how any *Men*, should ever *transgress* those *Moral Rules, with Confidence*, and *Serenity*, were they innate, and stamped upon their Minds. View but an Army at the sacking of a Town, and see what Observation, or Sense of Moral Principles, or what touch of Conscience, for all the Outrages they do. *Robberies, Murders, Rapes*, are the Sports of Men set at Liberty from Punishment and Censure. Have there not been whole Nations, and those of the most civilized People, amongst whom, the exposing their Children, and leaving them in the Fields, to perish by Want or wild Beasts, has been the Practice, as little condemned or scrupled, as the begetting them? Do they not still, in some Countries, put them into the same Graves with their Mothers, if they die in Child-birth; Or dispatch them, if a pretended Astrologer declares them to have unhappy Stars? And are there not Places, where at a certain Age, they kill, or expose their Parents without any remorse

§ 8. *Conscience no proof of any innate Moral Rule.* § 9. *Instances of Enormities practised without remorse.*

(17) or Judgment . . . Pravity] *add.* **4–5**. (*Not in* **Coste**) (24) Observation] **2–5** | Observations **1**

at all? In a Part of *Asia*, the Sick, when their Case comes to be thought desperate, are carried out and laid on the Earth, before they are dead, and left there, exposed to Wind and Weather, to perish without Assistance or Pity. (α) It is familiar amongst the *Mengrelians*, a People professing Christianity, to bury their Children alive without scruple. (β) There are Places where they eat their own Children. (γ) The *Caribes* were wont to geld their Children, on purpose to fat and eat them. (δ) And *Garcilasso de la Vega* tells us of a People in *Peru*, which were wont to fat and eat the Children they got on their female Captives, whom they kept as Concubines for that purpose; and when they were past Breeding the Mothers themselves were kill'd too and eaten. (ϵ) The Vertues, whereby the *Tououpinambos* believed they merited Paradise, were Revenge, and eating abundance of their Enemies. (ζ) They have not so much as a Name for God, *Lery*, *pag.* 216. No Acknowledgment of any God, no Religion, no Worship, *pag.* 231. The Saints, who are canonized amongst the *Turks*, lead Lives, which one cannot with Modesty relate. A remarkable Passage to this purpose, out of the Voyage of *Baumgarten*, which is a Book, not every Day to be met with, I shall set down at large, in the Language it is published in. *Ibi (sc. prope* Belbes *in* Ægypto) *vidimus sanctum unum Saracenicun inter arenarum cumulos, ita ut ex utero matris prodiit nudum sedentem. Mos est, ut didicimus* Mahometistis, *ut eos, qui amentes et sine ratione sunt, pro sanctis colant et venerentur. Insuper et eos qui cum diu vitam egerint inquinatissimam, voluntariam demum pænitentiam et paupertatem, sanctitate venerandos deputant. Ejusmodi verò genus hominum libertatem quandam effrænem habent, domos quas volunt intrandi, edendi, bibendi, et quod majus est, concumbendi; ex quo concubitu, si proles secuta fuerit, sancta similiter habetur. Iis ergo hominibus, dum vivunt, magnos exhibent honores; mortuis verò vel templa vel monumenta extruunt amplissima, eosque contingere ac sepelire maximæ fortunæ ducunt loco. Audivimus hæc dicta et dicenda per*

(α) *Gruber* apud *Thevenot*, *part* 4. *p.* 23.
(β) *Lambert* apud *Thevenot*, *p.* 38.
(γ) *Vossius* de Nili Origine *c.* 18, 19.
(δ) *P. Mart. Dec.* 1.
(ϵ) Hist. des Incas, *l.* 1. *c.* 12.
(ζ) *Lery*, *c.* 16.

---

(9) the] **4–5** | their **1–3** (10) whom] **4–5** | which **1–3** (11–12) ; and . . . eaten] *add.* **4–5** (14–15) They . . . 216.] **1–3, 5er**; *om.* **4.** (*Not in* **Coste**) (14) a] **1–3** | the **5er** (15) *pag.*] **1–3** | *p.* **5er** (15–16) No . . . 231.] *not in* **Coste**. (16) *pag.*] **1–3** | *page.* **4** | *page* **5** (*l. below* 31) 23] **1–2** | 13 **3–5**

interpretem à Mucrelo nostro. Insuper sanctum illum, quem eo loci vidimus, publicitus apprimè commendari, eum esse Hominem sanctum, divinum ac integritate præcipuum; eo quod, nec fœminarum unquam esset, nec puerorum, sed tantummodo asellarum concubitor atque mularum. Peregr. Baumgarten, l. 2. c. 1. p. 73. More of the same Kind, concerning these precious Saints amongst the *Turks*, may be seen in *Pietro della Valle*, in his Letter of the 25*th of January*, 1616. Where then are those innate Principles, of Justice, Piety, Gratitude, Equity, Chastity? Or, where is that universal Consent, that assures us there are such inbred Rules? Murders in Duels, when Fashion has made them honourable, are committed without remorse of Conscience: Nay, in many Places, Innocence in this Case is the greatest Ignominy. And if we look abroad, to take a view of Men, as they are, we shall find, that they have remorse in one Place, for doing or omitting that, which others, in another Place, think they merit by.

§ 10. He that will carefully peruse the History of Mankind, and look abroad into the several Tribes of Men, and with indifferency survey their Actions, will be able to satisfy himself, That there is scarce that Principle of Morality to be named, or *Rule* of *Vertue* to be thought on (those only excepted, that are absolutely necessary to hold Society together, which commonly too are neglected betwixt distinct Societies) which is not, somewhere or other, *slighted* and condemned by the general Fashion of *whole Societies* of Men, governed by practical Opinions, and Rules of living quite opposite to others.

§ 11. Here, perhaps, 'twill be objected, that it is no Argument, that the *Rule* is *not known*, *because* it is *broken*. I grant the Objection good, where Men, though they transgress, yet disown not the Law; where fear of Shame, Censure, or Punishment, carries the Mark of some awe it has upon them. But it is impossible to conceive, that a *whole Nation* of Men should all *publickly reject* and renounce, what every one of them, certainly and infallibly, knew to be a Law: For so they must, who have it naturally imprinted on their Minds. 'Tis possible, Men may sometimes own *Rules of Morality*, which, in their private Thoughts, they do not believe to be true, only to keep themselves in Reputation, and esteem amongst those, who are

§ 10. *Men have contrary practical Principles.* §§ 11–13. *Whole Nations reject several Moral Rules.*

(5–7) More . . . 1616.] *add.* **5** (13) look] **5** | will look **1–4**. (**Coste** 'si nous nous jettons les yeux') (14) remorse] **2–5** | a remorse **1**

persuaded of their Obligation. But 'tis not to be imagin'd, That a whole Society of Men, should, publickly and professedly, disown, and cast off a Rule, which they could not, in their own Minds, but be infallibly certain, was a Law; nor be ignorant, That all Men, they should have to do with, knew it to be such: And therefore must every one of them apprehend from others, all the Contempt and Abhorrence due to one, who professes himself void of Humanity; and one, who confounding the known and natural measures of Right and Wrong, cannot but be look'd on, as the professed Enemy of their Peace and Happiness. Whatever practical Principle is innate, cannot but be known to every one, to be just and good. It is therefore little less than a contradiction, to suppose, That whole Nations of Men should both in their Professions, and Practice unanimously and universally give the Lye to what, by the most invincible Evidence, every one of them knew to be true, right, and good. This is enough to satisfy us, That no practical Rule, which is any where universally, and with publick Approbation, or Allowance, transgressed, can be supposed innate. But I have something farther to add, in Answer to this Objection.

§ 12. The breaking of a Rule, say you, is no Argument, that it is unknown. I grant it: But the *generally allowed breach of it any where*, I say, *is a Proof, that it is not innate*. For Example, Let us take any of these Rules, which being the most obvious deductions of Humane Reason, and conformable to the natural Inclination of the greatest part of Men, fewest People have had the Impudence to deny, or Inconsideration to doubt of. If any can be thought to be naturally imprinted, none, I think, can have a fairer Pretence to be innate, than this; *Parents preserve and cherish your Children.* When therefore you say, That this is an innate Rule, What do you mean? Either, that it is an innate Principle; which upon all Occasions, excites and directs the Actions of all Men: Or else, that it is a Truth, which all Men have imprinted on their Minds, and which therefore they know, and assent to. But in neither of these Senses is it innate. *First*, That it is not a Principle, which influences all Men's Actions, is, what I have proved by the Examples before cited: Nor need we seek so far as *Mingrelia* or *Peru*, to find instances of such as neglect, abuse, nay and destroy their Children; or look on it only as the more than Brutality of some savage and barbarous Nations, when we remember, that it was a familiar, and uncondemned Practice amongst the

(30) it] **1–4**; *om.* **5**

Greeks and *Romans*, to expose, without pity or remorse, their innocent Infants. *Secondly*, That it is an innate Truth, known to all Men, is also false. For, *Parents preserve your Children*, is so far from an innate Truth, that it is no Truth at all; it being a Command, and not a Proposition, and so not capable of Truth or Falshood. To make it capable of being assented to as true, it must be reduced to some such Proposition as this: *It is the Duty of Parents to preserve their Children.* But what Duty is, cannot be understood without a Law; nor a Law be known, or supposed without a Law-maker, or without Reward and Punishment: So that it is impossible, that this, or any other practical Principle should be innate; *i.e.* be imprinted on the Mind as a Duty, without supposing the *Ideas* of God, of Law, of Obligation, of Punishment, of a Life after this, innate. For that Punishment follows not, in this Life, the breach of this Rule; and consequently, that it has not the Force of a Law in Countries, where the generally allow'd Practice runs counter to it, is in it self evident. But these *Ideas* (which must be all of them innate, if any thing as a Duty be so) are so far from being innate, that 'tis not every studious or thinking Man, much less every one that is born, in whom they are to be found clear and distinct: And that one of them, which of all others seems most likely to be innate, is not so, (I mean the *Idea* of God) I think, in the next Chapter, will appear very evident to any considering Man.

§ 13. From what has been said, I think we may safely conclude, That, *whatever practical Rule is, in any Place, generally, and with allowance, broken, cannot be supposed innate*, it being impossible, that Men should, without Shame or Fear, confidently and serenely break a Rule, which they could not but evidently know, that God had set up, and would certainly punish the breach of (which they must if it were innate) to a degree to make it a very ill Bargain to the Transgressor. Without such a Knowledge as this, a Man can never be certain, that any thing is his Duty. Ignorance or Doubt of the Law; hopes to escape the Knowledge or Power of the Law-maker, or the like, may make Men give way to a present Appetite: But let any one see the Fault, and the Rod by it, and with the Transgression, a Fire ready to punish it; a Pleasure tempting, and the Hand of the Almighty visibly held up, and prepared to take Vengeance (for this must be the Case, where any Duty is imprinted on the Mind) and then tell me, whether it be possible, for People, with such a Prospect, such a certain Knowledge as this, wantonly, and without scruple, to offend against a Law, which they carry about them in indelible Characters, and that stares them in the Face, whilst they are breaking it? Whether Men, at the same time that they feel in themselves the imprinted Edicts of an Omnipotent Law-maker, can, with assurance and gaity, slight and trample under Foot his most sacred Injunctions? And lastly, Whether it be possible, that whilst a Man thus openly bids defiance to this innate Law, and supreme Law-giver, all the By-standers; yea even the Governors and Rulers of the People, full of the same Sense, both of the Law and Law-maker, should silently connive, without testifying their dislike, or laying the least blame on it? Principles of Actions indeed there are lodged in Men's Appetites, but these are so far from being innate Moral Principles, that if they were left to their full swing, they would carry Men to the over-turning of all Morality. Moral Laws are set as a curb and restraint to these exorbitant Desires, which they cannot be but by Rewards and Punishments, that will over-balance the satisfaction any one shall propose to himself in the breach of the Law. If therefore any thing be imprinted on the Mind of all Men as a Law, all Men must have a certain and unavoidable knowledge, that certain, and unavoidable punishment will attend the breach of it. For if Men can be ignorant or doubtful of what is innate, innate Principles are insisted on, and urged to no purpose; Truth and Certainty (the things pretended) are not at all secured by them: But Men are in the same uncertain, floating estate with, as without them. An evident indubitable knowledge of unavoidable punishment, great enough to make the transgression very uneligible, must accompany an innate Law: Unless with an innate Law, they can suppose an innate Gospel too. I would not be here mistaken, as if, because I deny an innate Law, I thought there were none but positive Laws. There is a great deal of difference between an innate Law, and a Law of Nature; between something imprinted on our Minds in their very original, and something that we being ignorant of may attain to the knowledge of, by the use and due application of our natural Faculties. And I think they equally forsake the Truth, who running into the contrary extreams, either affirm an innate Law, or deny that there is a Law, knowable by the light of Nature; *i.e.* without the help of positive Revelation.

(32) their] **1–3, W** | this **4–5.** (**Coste** 'une verité gravée originairement dans l'Ame') (32–4) being . . . Faculties] **4–5** | may attain to the knowledge of, by our natural Faculties from natural Principles **1–3** (36) affirm] **1–2, 4–5** | affirms **3**

§ 14. The difference there is amongst Men in their practical Principles, is so evident, that, I think, I need say no more to evince, that it will be impossible to find any innate Moral Rules, by this mark of general assent: And 'tis enough to make one suspect, that the supposition of such innate Principles, is but an Opinion taken up at pleasure; since those who talk so confidently of them, are so sparing to *tell* us, *which they are*. This might with Justice be expected from those Men, who lay stress upon this Opinion: and it gives occasion to distrust either their Knowledge or Charity, who declaring, That God has imprinted on the Minds of Men, the foundations of Knowledge, and the Rules of Living, are yet so little favourable to the Information of their Neighbours, or the Quiet of Mankind, as not to point out to them, which they are, in the variety Men are distracted with. But in truth, were there any such innate Principles, there would be no need to teach them. Did Men find such innate Propositions stamped on their Minds, they would easily be able to distinguish them from other Truths, that they afterwards learned, and deduced from them; and there would be nothing more easy, than to know what, and how many they were. There could be no more doubt about their number, than there is about the number of our Fingers; and 'tis like then, every System would be ready to give them us by tale. But since no body, that I know, has ventured yet to give a Catalogue of them, they cannot blame those who doubt of these innate Principles; since even they who require Men to believe, that there are such innate Propositions, do not tell us what they are. 'Tis easy to foresee, that if different Men of different Sects should go about to give us a List of those innate practical Principles, they would set down only such as suited their distinct Hypotheses, and were fit to support the Doctrines of their particular Schools or Churches: A plain evidence, that there are no such innate Truths. Nay, a great part of Men are so far from finding any such innate Moral Principles in themselves, that by denying freedom to Mankind; and thereby making Men no other than bare Machins, they take away not only innate, but all Moral Rules whatsoever, and leave not a possibility to believe any such, to those who cannot conceive, how any thing can be capable of a Law, that is not a free Agent: And upon that ground, they must

§ 14. *Those who maintain innate practical Principles, tell us not what they are.*

---

(29) Hypotheses] **1–4, W** | Hypothesis **5**

necessarily reject all Principles of Vertue, who cannot *put Morality and Mechanism together*; which are not very easy to be reconciled, or made consistent.

§ 15. When I had writ this, being informed, that my Lord *Herbert* had in his Books *de Veritate*, assigned these innate Principles, I presently consulted him, hoping to find, in a Man of so great Parts, something that might satisfy me in this point, and put an end to my Enquiry. In his Chapter *de Instinctu naturali*, *p.* 76. *edit.* 1656. I met with these six Marks of his *notitiæ Communes*, 1. *Prioritas*. 2. *Independentia*. 3. *Universalitas*. 4. *Certitudo*. 5. *Necessitas*, i.e. as he explains it, *faciunt ad hominis conservationem*. 6. *Modus conformationis*, i.e. *Assensus nullâ interpositâ morâ*. And at the latter end of his little Treatise, *De Religione Laici*, he says this of these innate Principles: *Adeo ut non uniuscujusvis Religionis confinio arctentur quæ ubique vigent veritates. Sunt enim in ipsâ mente cœlitùs descriptæ nullisque traditionibus, sive scriptis, sive non scriptis, obnoxiæ*, p. 3. And, *Veritates nostræ Catholicæ, quæ tanquam indubia Dei effata in foro interiori descripta*. Thus having given the Marks of the innate Principles or common Notions, and asserted their being imprinted on the Minds of Men by the Hand of God, he proceeds to set them down; and they are these: 1. *Esse aliquod supremum numen*. 2. *Numen illud coli debere*. 3. *Virtutem cum pietate conjunctam optimam esse rationem cultûs divini*. 4. *Resipiscendum esse à peccatis*. 5. *Dari præmium vel pœnam post hanc vitam transactam*. Though I allow these to be clear Truths, and such as, if rightly explained, a rational Creature can hardly avoid giving his assent to: yet I think he is far from proving them innate Impressions *in Foro interiori descriptæ*. For I must take leave to observe,

§ 16. First, That these Five Propositions are either not all, or more than all, those common Notions writ on our Minds by the finger of God, if it were reasonable to believe any at all to be so written. Since there are other Propositions, which even by his own Rules, have as just a pretence to such an Original, and may be as well admitted for innate Principles, as, at least, some of these Five he enumerates, *viz. Do as thou wouldst be done unto*: And, perhaps, some hundreds of others, when well considered.

§ 17. Secondly, That all his Marks are not to be found in each of his Five Propositions, *viz.* his First, Second, and Third Marks, agree

§§ 15–19. *Lord* Herbert's *innate Principles examined.*

(20) proceeds] **2–5** | proceeds at last **1** (24) Though I allow these] **5** | These, though I allow them **1–4** (28) not] *add.* **1T.er, 2–5**

perfectly to neither of them; and the First, Second, Third, Fourth, and Sixth Marks, agree but ill to his Third, Fourth, and Fifth Propositions. For, besides that, we are assured from History, of many Men, nay, whole Nations who doubt or disbelieve some or all of them, I cannot see how the Third, *viz. That Vertue join'd with Piety, is the best Worship of God*, can be an innate Principle, when the name, or sound *Vertue*, is so hard to be understood; liable to so much uncertainty in its signification; and the thing it stands for, so much contended about, and difficult to be known. And therefore this can be but a very uncertain Rule of Humane Practice, and serve but very little to the conduct of our Lives, and is therefore very unfit to be assigned as an innate practical Principle.

§ 18. For let us consider this Proposition as to its meaning, (for it is the sence, and not sound, that is, and must be the Principle or common Notion) *viz. Vertue is the best Worship of God*; i.e. is most acceptable to him; which if *Vertue* be taken, as most commonly it is, for those Actions, which according to the different Opinions of several Countries, are accounted laudable, will be a Proposition so far from being certain, that it will not be true. If *Vertue* be taken for Actions conformable to God's Will, or to the Rule prescribed by God, which is the true and only measure of Vertue, when Vertue is used to signifie what is in its own nature right and good; then this Proposition, *That Vertue is the best Worship of God*, will be most true and certain, but of very little use in humane Life: since it will amount to no more but this, *viz. That God is pleased with the doing of what he Commands*; which a Man may certainly know to be true, without knowing what it is, that God doth command; and so be as far from any Rule or Principle of his Actions, as he was before: And I think very few will take a Proposition which amounts to no more than this, *viz.* That God is pleased with the doing of what he himself commands, for an innate Moral Principle writ on the Minds of all Men, (however true and certain it may be) since it teaches so little. Whosoever does so, will have reason to think hundreds of Propositions, innate Principles, since there are many, which have as good a title, as this, to be received for such, which no body yet ever put into that rank of innate Principles.

§ 19. Nor is the Fourth Proposition (*viz.*) *Men must repent of their Sins*, much more instructive, till what those Actions are, that are

(5) *Vertue*] **1–3, 5** | *Virtue* **4** (21–2) , when . . . good] *add.* **2–5**
(28) Principle] **1–4** | Principles **5** (34) , which] **2–5** | who **1**

meant by Sins, be set down. For the word *Peccata*, or *Sins*, being put, as it usually is, to signifie in general ill Actions, that will draw on punishment upon the Doers; What great Principle of Morality can that be, to tell us we should be sorry, and cease to do that, which will bring mischief upon us, without knowing what those particular Actions are, that will do so? Indeed, this is a very true Proposition, and fit to be inculcated on, and received by those, who are supposed, to have been taught, what Actions in all kinds are *sins*; but neither this, nor the former, can be imagined to be innate Principles; nor to be of any use, if they were innate, unless the particular measures and bounds of all Vertues and Vices, were engraven in Men's Minds, and were innate Principles also, which, I think, is very much to be doubted. And therefore, I imagine, it will scarce seem possible, that God should engrave Principles in Mens Minds, in words of uncertain signification, such as *Vertues* and *Sins*, which amongst different Men, stand for different things: Nay, it cannot be supposed to be in words at all, which, being in most of these Principles very general names cannot be understood, but by knowing the particulars comprehended under them. And in the practical instances, the measures must be taken from the knowledge of the Actions themselves, and the Rules of them abstracted from words, and antecedent to the knowledge of Names; which Rules a Man must know, what Language soever he chance to learn, whether English or Japan, or if he should learn no Language at all, or never should understand the use of Words, as happens in the case of Dumb and Deaf Men. When it shall be made out, that Men ignorant of Words, or untaught by the Laws and Customs of their Country, know that it is part of the Worship of God, Not to kill another Man; Not to know more Women than one; Not to procure Abortion; Not to expose their Children; Not to take from another what is his, though we want it our selves, but on the contrary, relieve and supply his wants; And whenever we have done the contrary, we ought to repent, be sorry, and resolve to do so no more: When, I say, all Men shall be proved actually to know, and allow all these and a thousand other such Rules, all which come under these two general words made use of above, *viz. Virtutes et Peccata*, *Vertues* and *Sins*, there will be more reason for admitting these, and the like, for common Notions, and practical Principles:

(9) *sins*] **1er–5** | *sin* **1** (15) as] **5** | as are **1–4** (17–18) which, . . . names] **2–5** | (which . . . names) **1** (28) know] *add.* **4er–5**. (*Not in* **Coste**)

yet after all, universal Consent (were there any in Moral Principles) to Truths, the knowledge whereof may be attained otherwise, would scarce prove them to be innate; which is all I contend for.

§ 20. Nor will it be of much moment here, to offer that very ready, but not very material Answer, (*viz.*) That the *innate Principles* of Morality, *may*, *by Education, and Custom*, and the general Opinion of those, amongst whom we converse, *be darkned*, and at last *quite worn out* of the Minds of Men. Which assertion of theirs, if true, quite takes away the Argument of universal Consent, by which this Opinion of innate Principles is endeavoured to be proved: unless those Men will think it reasonable, that their private Perswasions, or that of their Party, should pass for universal Consent; a thing not unfrequently done, when Men presuming themselves to be the only Masters of right Reason, cast by the Votes and Opinions of the rest of Mankind, as not worthy the reckoning. And then their Argument stands thus: The Principles which all mankind allow for true, are innate; those that Men of right Reason admit, are the Principles allowed by all mankind; we and those of our mind, are Men of reason; therefore we agreeing, our Principles are innate: which is a very pretty way of arguing, and a short cut to Infallibility. For otherwise it will be very hard to understand, how there be some Principles, which all Men do acknowledge, and agree in; and yet there are none of those *Principles*, which are *not by depraved Custom, and ill Education, blotted out* of the minds of many Men: Which is to say, That all Men admit, but yet many Men do deny, and dissent from them. And indeed the supposition of such first Principles, will serve us to very little purpose; and we shall be as much at a loss with, as without them, if they may by any humane Power, such as is the Will of our Teachers, or Opinions of our Companions, be altered or lost in us: and notwithstanding all this boast of first Principles, and innate Light, we shall be as much in the dark and uncertainty, as if there were no such thing at all: It being all one to have no Rule, and one that will warp any way; or amongst various and contrary Rules, not to know which is the right. But concerning innate Principles, I desire these Men to say, whether they can, or cannot, by Education and Custom, be blurr'd and blotted out: If

§ 20. Obj. *Innate Principles may be corrupted, answered.*

---

(2) may] **5** | might **1–4**. (**Coste** 'qu'on peut') (11) their] **5** | their own **1–4**
(19) reason] **2–5** | right Reason **1**

they cannot, we must find them in all Mankind alike, and they must be clear in every body: And if they may suffer variation from adventitious Notions, we must then find them clearest and most perspicuous, nearest the Fountain, in Children and illiterate People, who have received least impression from foreign Opinions. Let them take which side they please, they will certainly find it inconsistent with visible matter of fact, and daily observation.

§ 21. I easily grant, that there are great numbers of *Opinions*, which, by Men of different Countries, Educations, and Tempers, are received and *embraced as first and unquestionable Principles*; *many whereof*, both for their absurdity, as well as oppositions one to another, *it is impossible should be true*. But yet all those Propositions, how remote soever from Reason, are so sacred somewhere or other, that Men even of Good Understanding in other matters, will sooner part with their Lives, and whatever is dearest to them, than suffer themselves to doubt, or others to question, the truth of them.

§ 22. This, however strange it may seem, is that which every days Experience confirms; and will not, perhaps, appear so wonderful, if we consider the *ways*, and steps *by which* it is brought about; and how really it may come to pass, that *Doctrines*, that have been derived from no better original, than the Superstition of a Nurse, or the Authority of an old Woman; may, by length of time, and consent of Neighbours, *grow up to the dignity of Principles* in Religion or Morality. For such, who are careful (as they call it) to principle Children well, (and few there be who have not a set of those Principles for them, which they believe in) instil into the unwary, and, as yet, unprejudiced Understanding, (for white Paper receives any Characters) those Doctrines they would have them retain and profess. These being taught them as soon as they have any apprehension; and still as they grow up, confirmed to them, either by the open Profession, or tacit Consent, of all they have to do with; or at least by those, of whose Wisdom, Knowledge, and Piety, they have an Opinion, who never suffer those Propositions to be otherwise mentioned, but as the Basis and Foundation, on which they build

§ 21. *Contrary Principles in the World.* §§ 22–6. *How Men commonly come by their Principles.*

---

(11) *Principles*;] **1–3, 5** | *Principles*: **4** (13) *be*] **1–3, 5** | *be* **4**

their Religion or Manners, come, by these means, to have the reputation of unquestionable, self-evident, and innate Truths.

§ 23. To which we may add, That when *Men*, so instructed, are grown up, and reflect on their own Minds, they cannot find any thing more ancient there, than those Opinions, which were taught them, before their Memory began to keep a Register of their Actions, or date the time, when any new thing appeared to them; and therefore make no scruple to *conclude, That those Propositions, of whose knowledge they can find in themselves no original, were certainly the impress of God and Nature* upon their Minds; and not taught them by any one else. These they entertain and submit to, as many do to their Parents, with Veneration; not because it is natural; nor do Children do it, where they are not so taught; but because, having been always so educated, and having no remembrance of the beginning of this Respect, they think it is natural.

§ 24. This will appear very likely, and almost unavoidable to come to pass, if we consider the Nature of Mankind, and the Constitution of Humane Affairs: Wherein *most Men cannot live, without employing their time in the daily Labours of their Callings; nor be at quiet in their Minds, without some Foundation or Principles to rest their Thoughts on.* There is scarce any one so floating and superficial in his Understanding, who hath not some reverenced Propositions, which are to him the Principles on which he bottoms his Reasonings; and by which he judgeth of Truth and Falshood, Right and Wrong; which some, wanting skill and leisure, and others the inclination, and some being taught, that they ought not, to examine; there are few to be found, who are not exposed by their Ignorance, Laziness, Education, or Precipitancy, to *take them upon trust.*

§ 25. This is evidently the case of all Children and young Folk; and Custom, a greater power than Nature, seldom failing to make them worship for Divine, what she hath inured them to bow their Minds, and submit their Understandings to, it is no wonder, that grown *Men*, either perplexed in the necessary affairs of Life, or hot in the pursuit of Pleasures, should *not* seriously sit down to *examine their own Tenets*; especially when one of their Principles is, That Principles ought not to be questioned. And had Men leisure, parts, and will, Who is there almost, that dare shake the foundations of all

(1) their] **5** | either their **1–4** (18) Affairs:] **1–3** | Affairs; **4–5**. (**Coste** *has full stop.*) (22) who] **2–5** | that **1** (26) that they] **2–5** | They **1** (37) dare shake] **5** | dares shake **4** | dares to shake **1–3**

his past Thoughts and Actions, and endure to bring upon himself, the shame of having been a long time wholly in mistake and error? Who is there, hardy enough to contend with the reproach, which is every where prepared for those, who dare venture to dissent from the received Opinions of their Country or Party? And where is the Man to be found, that can patiently prepare himself to bear the name of Whimsical, Sceptical, or Atheist, which he is sure to meet with, who does in the least scruple any of the common Opinions? And he will be much more *afraid to question those Principles*, when he shall think them, as most Men do, the Standards set up by God in his Mind, to be the Rule and Touchstone of all other Opinions. And what can hinder him from thinking them sacred, when he finds them the earliest of all his own Thoughts, and the most reverenced by others?

§ 26. It is easy to imagine, *how* by these means it comes to pass, that *Men* worship the Idols that have been set up in their Minds; grow fond of the Notions they have been long acquainted with there; and *stamp the Characters of Divinity, upon Absurdities and Errors*, become zealous Votaries to Bulls and Monkeys; and contend too, fight, and die in defence of their Opinions. *Dum solos credit habendos esse Deos, quos ipse colit.** For since the reasoning Faculties of the Soul, which are almost constantly, though not always warily nor wisely employ'd, would not know how to move, for want of a foundation and footing, in most Men, who through laziness or avocation, do not; or for want of time, or true helps, or for other causes, cannot, penetrate into the Principles of Knowledge, and trace Truth to its fountain and original, 'tis natural for them, and almost unavoidable, to take up with some borrowed Principles; which being reputed and presumed to be the evident proofs of other things, are thought not to need any other proof themselves. Whoever shall receive any of these into his Mind, and entertain them there, with the reverence usually paid to Principles, never venturing to examine them; but accustoming himself to believe them, because they are to be believed, may take up from his Education, and the fashions of his

(15) *In* **Coste**, § 26 *has a separate marginal summary*: 'Comment les hommes viennent pour l'ordinaire à se faire des Principes.' (16) [*2nd*] that] *add.* **5** (19) contend] **2–5** | contented **1** (25) [*2nd*] for] *add.* **2–5** (31) his Mind] **4er–5** | their minds **2–4** | their thoughts **1** (31–3) and . . . them] **2–5** | without due examination, but believe them **1** (33) himself] **4er–5** | themselves **2–4**

* Juvenal, *Satires*, XV, 37–8.

Country, any absurdity for innate Principles; and by long poring on the same Objects, so dim his sight, as to take Monsters lodged in his own brain, for the Images of the Deity, and the Workmanship of his Hands.

§ 27. By this progress, how many there are, who arrive at Principles, which they believe innate, may be easily observed, in the variety of opposite Principles, held, and contended for, by all sorts and degrees of Men. And he that shall deny this to be the method, wherein most Men proceed to the assurance they have, of the truth and evidence of their Principles, will, perhaps, find it a hard matter, any other way to account for the contrary Tenets, which are firmly believed, confidently asserted, and which great numbers are ready at any time to seal with their Blood. And, indeed, if it be the privilege of innate Principles, to be received upon their own Authority, without examination, I know not what may not be believed, or how any one's *Principles* can be questioned. If they may, and *ought to be examined*, and tried, I desire to know how first and innate Principles can be tried; or at least it is reasonable to demand the marks and characters, whereby the genuine, innate Principles, may be distinguished from others; that so, amidst the great variety of Pretenders, I may be kept from mistakes, in so material a point as this. When this is done, I shall be ready to embrace such welcome, and useful, Propositions; and till then I may with modesty doubt, since I fear universal Consent, which is the only one produced, will scarce prove a sufficient mark to direct my Choice, and assure me of any innate Principles. From what has been said, I think it is past doubt, that there are no practical Principles wherein all Men agree; and therefore none innate.

CHAPTER IV

Other Considerations concerning innate Principles, both speculative and practical.

§ 1. HAD those, who would perswade us, that there are innate Principles, not taken them together in gross; but considered,

§ 27. *Principles must be examined.* § 1. *Principles not innate, unless their* Ideas *be innate.*

(9) truth] **2–5** | unalterable truth **1** (17) desire] **1, 3–5** | desired **2** (26) is] **1–4**; *om.* **5**

separately, the parts, out of which those Propositions are made, they would not, perhaps, have been so forward to believe they were innate. Since, if the *Ideas*, which made up those Truths, were not, it was impossible, that the Propositions, made up of them, should be innate, or our Knowledge of them be born with us. For if the *Ideas* be not *innate*, there was a time, when the Mind was without those Principles; and then, they will not be innate, but be derived from some other Original. For, where the *Ideas* themselves are not, there can be no Knowledge, no Assent, no Mental, or Verbal Propositions about them.

§ 2. If we will attentively consider new born *Children*, we shall have little Reason, to think, that they bring many *Ideas* into the World with them. For, bating, perhaps, some faint *Ideas*, of Hunger, and Thirst, and Warmth, and some Pains, which they may *have* felt in the Womb, there is *not* the least appearance of any setled *Ideas* at all in them; especially of *Ideas, answering the Terms, which make up those universal Propositions*, that are esteemed innate Principles. One may perceive how, by degrees, afterwards, *Ideas* come into their Minds; and that they get no more, nor no other, than what Experience, and the Observation of things, that come in their way, furnish them with; which might be enough to satisfy us, that they are not Original Characters, stamped on the Mind.

§ 3. *It is impossible for the same thing to be, and not to be*, is certainly (if there be any such) an innate Principle. But can any one think, or will any one say, that *Impossibility* and *Identity*, are two innate *Ideas*? Are they such as all Mankind have, and bring into the World with them? And are they those, that are the first in Children, and antecedent to all acquired ones? If they are innate, they must needs be so. Hath a Child an *Idea* of *Impossibility* and *Identity*, before it has of *White* or *Black*; *Sweet* or *Bitter*? And is it from the Knowledge of this Principle, that it concludes, that Wormwood rubb'd on the Nipple, hath not the same Taste, that it used to receive from thence? Is it the actual Knowledge of *impossibile est idem esse, et non esse*, that makes a Child distinguish between its Mother and a Stranger; or, that makes it fond of the one, and fly the other? Or does the Mind regulate it self, and its assent by *Ideas*, that it never yet had? Or the

§§ 2, 3. Ideas, *especially those belonging to Principles, not born with Children.*

(11) attentively] **4–5** | attently **1–3** (25) two] **1–3** | too **4–5** (32) hath] **4–5** | is **1–3** (*l. below* 36) *In* **Coste**, *§ 3 has the marginal summary* 'Preuve de la même verité.'

Understanding draw Conclusions from Principles, which it never yet knew or understood? The Names *Impossibility* and *Identity*, stand for two *Ideas*, so *far from being innate*, or born with us, that I think it requires great Care and Attention, to form them right in our Understandings. They are so far from being brought into the World with us; so remote from the thoughts of Infancy and Childhood, that, I believe, upon Examination, it will be found, that many grown Men want them.

§ 4. If *Identity* (to instance in that alone) be a native Impression; and consequently so clear and obvious to us, that we must needs know it even from our Cradles; I would gladly be resolved, by one of Seven, or Seventy Years old, Whether a Man, being a Creature, consisting of Soul and Body, be the same Man, when his Body is changed? Whether *Euphorbus* and *Pythagoras*, having had the same Soul, were the same Man, though they lived several Ages asunder? Nay, Whether the Cock too, which had the same Soul, were not the same with both of them? Whereby, perhaps, it will appear, that our *Idea of sameness*, is *not* so settled and clear, as to deserve to be thought *innate* in us. For if those innate *Ideas*, are not clear and distinct, so as to be universally known, and naturally agreed on, they cannot be the Subjects of universal, and undoubted Truths; but will be the unavoidable Occasion of perpetual Uncertainty. For, I suppose, every one's *Idea* of *Identity*, will not be the same, that *Pythagoras*, and Thousands others of his Followers, have: And which then shall be the true? Which innate? Or are there two different *Ideas* of *Identity*, both innate?

§ 5. Nor let any one think, that the Questions, I have here proposed, about the *Identity* of Man, are bare, empty Speculations; which if they were, would be enough to shew, That there was in the Understandings of Men *no innate* Idea *of* Identity. He, that shall, with a little Attention, reflect on the Resurrection, and consider, that Divine Justice shall bring to Judgment, at the last Day, the very same Persons, to be happy or miserable in the other, who did well or ill in this Life, will find it, perhaps, not easy to resolve with himself, what makes the same Man, or wherein *Identity* consists: And will not be forward to think he, and every one, even Children themselves, have naturally a clear *Idea* of it.

§§ 4, 5. *Identity an* Idea *not innate.*

---

(21) the] **1–4**; *om.* **5**

§ 6. Let us examine that Principle of Mathematicks, *viz. That the whole is bigger than a part.* This, I take it, is reckon'd amongst innate Principles. I am sure it has as good a Title, as any, to be thought so; which yet, no Body can think it to be, when he considers the *Ideas* it comprehends in it, *Whole* and *Part*, are perfectly Relative; but the Positive *Ideas*, to which they properly and immediately belong, are Extension and Number, of which alone, *Whole* and *Part*, are Relations. So that if *Whole* and *Part* are innate *Ideas*, Extension and Number must be so too, it being impossible to have an *Idea* of a Relation, without having any at all of the thing to which it belongs, and in which it is founded. Now, Whether the Minds of Men have naturally imprinted on them the *Ideas* of Extension and Number, I leave to be considered by those, who are the Patrons of innate Principles.

§ 7. That *God is to be worshipped*, is, without doubt, as great a Truth as any can enter into the mind of Man, and deserves the first place amongst all practical Principles. But yet, it can by no means be thought innate, unless the *Ideas* of *God*, and *Worship*, are innate. That the *Idea*, the Term *Worship* stands for, is not in the Understanding of Children, and a Character stamped on the Mind in its first Original, I think, will be easily granted, by any one, that considers how few there be, amongst grown Men, who have a clear and distinct Notion of it. And, I suppose, there cannot be any thing more ridiculous, than to say, that Children have this practical Principle innate, *That God is to be worshipped*; and yet, that they know not what that Worship of God is, which is their Duty. But to pass by this.

§ 8. If any *Idea* can be imagin'd *innate*, the *Idea of God* may, of all others, for many Reasons, be thought so; since it is hard to conceive, how there should be innate Moral Principles, without an innate *Idea* of a *Deity*: Without a Notion of a Law-maker, it is impossible to have a Notion of a Law, and an Obligation to observe it. Besides the Atheists, taken notice of amongst the Ancients, and left branded upon the Records of History, hath not Navigation discovered, in these latter Ages, whole Nations, at the Bay of *Soldania* (α), in *Brasil* (β), in *Boranday* (γ), and the *Caribee* Islands, *etc.* amongst whom there was to be found no Notion of a

§ 6. *Whole and Part not innate* Ideas. § 7. Idea *of Worship not innate.* §§ 8–11. Idea *of* GOD *not innate.*

(α) Rhoe apud *Thevenot*, *p.* 2. (β) *Jo. de Lery*, *c.* 16.
(γ) *Martiniere* $\frac{201}{322}$. *Terry* $\frac{17}{545}$ & $\frac{23}{545}$. *Ovington* $\frac{489}{606}$.

(34) in *Boranday* (γ),] *add.* **4–5**. (*Not in* **Coste**) (*4 ll. below* 35: (γ)) *Note add.* **4–5**

God, no Religion. *Nicolàus del Techo in literis, ex Paraquaria de Caaiguarum conversione*, has these Words (δ), *Reperi eam gentem nullum nomen habere, quod Deum, et Hominis animam significet, nulla sacra habet, nulla Idola*. These are Instances of Nations where uncultivated Nature has been left to it self, without the help of Letters, and Discipline, and the Improvements of Arts and Sciences. But there are others to be found, who have enjoy'd these in a very great measure, who yet, for want of a due application of their thoughts this way, want the *Idea*, and Knowledge of God. 'Twill I doubt not be a Surprise to others, as it was to me, to find the *Siamites* of this number. But for this, let them consult the King of *France*'s late Envoy thither (ϵ), who gives no better account of the *Chineses* themselves (ζ). And if we will not believe *La Loubere*, the Missionaries of *China*, even the Jesuits themselves, the great Encomiasts of the *Chineses*, do all to a Man agree and will convince us that the Sect of the *Litterati*, or *Learned*, keeping to the old Religion of *China*, and the ruling Party there, are all of them *Atheist*. Vid. *Navarette* in the Collection of Voyages, Vol. the First, and *Historia cultus Sinensium*. And, perhaps, if we should, with attention, mind the Lives, and Discourses of People not so far off, we should have too much Reason to fear, that many, in more civilized Countries, have no very strong, and clear Impressions of a Deity upon their Minds; and that the Complaints of Atheism, made from the Pulpit, are not without Reason. And though only some profligate Wretches own it too barefacedly now; yet, perhaps, we should hear, more than we do, of it, from others, did not the fear of the Magistrate's Sword, or their Neighbour's Censure, tie up Peoples Tongues; which, were the Apprehensions of Punishment, or Shame taken away, would as openly proclaim their *Atheism*, as their Lives do.

(δ) Relatio triplex de rebus Indicis Caaiguarum $\frac{43}{70}$.
(ϵ) La Loubere du Royaume de Siam. *T*. 1. *c*. 9. *sect*. 15. & *c*. 20. *sect*. 22. & *c*. 22. *sect*. 6.
(ζ) *Ib*. *T*. 1. *c*. 20. *sect*. 4. & *c*. 23.

---

(1) , no Religion] *add*. **4–5**. (*Not in* **Coste**) (2) *conversione*, has these Words (δ),] **4–5** | *conversione*, has these words (γ), **2–3** | *conversione haec habet*. **1** (4) *Idola*.] **2–5** | *Idola. Relatio triplex de rebus Indicis Caaiguarum* $\frac{43}{70}$. **1** (4–12) These . . . themselves (ζ).] *add*. **4–5**. (*Not in* **Coste**) (4) These] **5er** | There **4–5** (12–18) And . . . *Sinensium*.] *add*. **5** (23) Pulpit] **2–5** | Pulpits **1** (29) **5** *adds, in a footnote, a quotation from Locke's* Third Letter to the Bishop of Worcester, *pp*. 447, *etc*.; *prefaced by* 'On this Reasoning of the Author against Innate *Ideas*, great blame hath been laid; because it seems to invalidate an Argument commonly used to prove the Being of a God, *viz*. *Universal Consent*: To which our Author Answers,'. (*l. below* 29) *Note* (δ) *in* **4–5** *is marked* (γ) *in* **2–3**. (*2 ll. below* 29) *Note* (ϵ) *add*. **4–5** (*3 ll. below* 29) *Note* (ζ) *add*. **4–5**

§ 9. But had all Mankind, every where, a *Notion of a God*, (whereof yet History tells us the contrary) it would *not* from thence follow, that the *Idea* of him was *innate*. For, though no Nation were to be found without a Name, and some few dark Notions of him; yet that would not prove them to be natural Impressions on the Mind, no more than the Names of Fire, or the Sun, Heat, or Number, do prove the *Ideas* they stand for, to be innate, because the Names of those things, and the *Ideas* of them, are so universally received, and known amongst Mankind. Nor, on the contrary, is the want of such a Name, or the absence of such a Notion out of Men's Minds, any Argument against the Being of a God, any more, than it would be a Proof, that there was no Load-stone in the World, because a great part of Mankind, had neither a Notion of any such thing, nor a Name for it; or be any shew of Argument to prove, that there are no distinct and various species of Angels, or intelligent Beings above us, because we have no *Ideas* of such distinct species, or names for them: For Men, being furnished with Words, by the common Language of their own Countries, can scarce avoid having some kind of *Ideas* of those things, whose Names, those they converse with, have occasion frequently to mention to them: and if it carry with it the Notion of Excellency, Greatness, or something extraordinary; if Apprehension and Concernment accompany it; if the Fear of absolute and irresistible Power set it on upon the Mind, the *Idea* is likely to sink the deeper, and spread the farther; especially if it be such an *Idea*, as is agreeable to the common light of Reason, and naturally deducible from every part of our Knowledge, as that of a God is. For the visible marks of extraordinary Wisdom and Power, appear so plainly in all the Works of the Creation, that a rational Creature, who will but seriously reflect on them, cannot miss the discovery of a *Deity*: And the influence, that the discovery of such a Being must necessarily have on the Minds of all, that have but once heard of it, is so great, and carries such a weight of Thought and Communication with it, that it seems stranger to me, that a whole Nation of Men should be any where found so brutish, as to want the Notion of a God; than that they should be without any Notion of Numbers, or Fire.

§ 10. The Name of God being once mentioned in any part of the World, to express a superior, powerful, wise, invisible Being, the

(16–17) species, or names for them:] **2–5** | species. **1** (24) [*1st*] the] *add.* **2–5**

suitableness of such a Notion to the Principles of common Reason, and the Interest Men will always have to mention it often, must necessarily spread it far and wide; and continue it down to all Generations: though yet the *general reception of this Name, and some imperfect and unsteady Notions, conveyed thereby* to the unthinking part of Mankind, *prove not the* Idea *to be innate*; but only that they, who made the Discovery, had made a right use of their Reason, thought maturely of the Causes of things, and traced them to their Original; from whom other less considering People, having once received so important a Notion, it could not easily be lost again.

§ 11. This is all could be inferr'd from the Notion of a *God*, were it to be found universally in all the Tribes of Mankind, and generally acknowledged, by Men grown to maturity in all Countries. For the generality of the acknowledging of a God, as I imagine, is extended no farther than that; which if it be sufficient to prove the *Idea of God, innate*, will as well prove the *Idea* of Fire, innate; since, I think, it may truly be said, That there is not a Person in the World, who has a Notion of a *God*, who has not also the *Idea* of Fire. I doubt not, but if a Colony of young Children should be placed in an Island, where no Fire was, they would certainly neither have any Notion of such a thing, nor Name for it, how generally soever it were received, and known in all the World besides; and, perhaps too, their Apprehensions would be as far removed from any Name, or Notion of a God, till some one amongst them had imployed his Thoughts, to enquire into the Constitution and Causes of things, which would easily lead him to the Notion of a *God*; which having once taught to others, Reason, and the natural Propensity of their own Thoughts, would afterwards propagate, and continue amongst them.

§ 12. Indeed it is urged, That it is *suitable to the goodness of God, to imprint, upon the Minds of Men, Characters and Notions of himself*, and not to leave them in the dark, and doubt, in so grand a Concernment; and also by that means, to secure to himself the Homage and Veneration, due from so intelligent a Creature as Man; and therefore he has done it.

This Argument, if it be of any Force, will prove much more than

§ 12. *Suitable to* GOD'*s Goodness, that all Men should have an* Idea *of Him, therefore naturally imprinted by Him*; *answer'd.*

---

(31) to] *add.* 5

those, who use it in this case, expect from it. For if we may conclude, that *God* hath done for Men, all that Men shall judge is best for them, because it is suitable to his goodness so to do, it will prove, not only, that God has imprinted on the Minds of Men an *Idea* of himself; but that he hath plainly stamp'd there, in fair Characters, all that Men ought to know, or believe of him, all that they ought to do in obedience to his Will; and that he hath given them a Will and Affections conformable to it. This, no doubt, every one will think it better for Men, than that they should, in the dark, grope after Knowledge, as St. *Paul* tells us all Nations did after God, *Acts* XVII. 27. than that their Wills should clash with their Understandings, and their Appetites cross their Duty. The *Romanists* say, 'Tis best for Men, and so, suitable to the goodness of God, that there should be an infallible Judge of Controversies on Earth ; and therefore there is one: and I, by the same Reason, say, 'Tis better for Men that every Man himself should be infallible. I leave them to consider, whether by the force of this Argument they shall think, that every Man is so. I think it a very good Argument, to say, the infinitely wise God hath made it so: And therefore it is best. But it *seems to me a little too much Confidence of our own Wisdom, to say, I think it best, and therefore God hath made it so*; and in the matter in Hand, it will be in vain to argue from such a Topick, that God hath done so, when certain Experience shews us, that he hath not. But the Goodness of God hath not been wanting to Men without such Original Impressions of Knowledge, or *Ideas* stamped on the Mind: since he hath furnished Man with those Faculties, which will serve for the sufficient discovery of all things requisite to the end of such a Being; and I doubt not but to shew, that a Man by the right use of his natural Abilities, may, without any innate Principles, attain the Knowledge of a God, and other things that concern him. God having endued Man with those Faculties of knowing which he hath, was no more obliged by his Goodness, to implant those innate Notions in his Mind, than that having given him Reason, Hands, and Materials, he should build him Bridges, or Houses; which some People in the World, however of good parts, do either totally want, or are but ill provided of, as well as others are wholly without *Ideas of*

(8) Affections] **2er–5** | Affection **1–2** (12–18) The . . . so] *not in* **Coste**. (14) there] **1–3, 5** (*likewise* **Coste**) | their **4** (18) it] **1–2, 4–5** | it is **3** (*likewise* **Coste**) (34) Houses;] **1–3, W** | Houses **4** | Houses, **5**. (**Coste** *has a full stop.*) (35) parts,] **1–3, 5** | parts **4**

God, and Principles of Morality; or at least have but very ill ones. The reason in both cases being, That they never employ'd their Parts, Faculties, and Powers, industriously that way, but contented themselves with the Opinions, Fashions, and Things of their Country, as they found them, without looking any farther. Had you or I been born at the Bay of *Soldania*, possibly our Thoughts, and Notions, had not exceeded those brutish ones of the *Hotentots* that inhabit there: And had the *Virginia* King *Apochancana*, been educated in *England*, he had, perhaps, been as knowing a Divine, and as good a Mathematician, as any in it. The difference between him, and a more improved *English*-man, lying barely in this, That the exercise of his Faculties was bounded within the Ways, Modes, and Notions of his own Country, and never directed to any other, or farther Enquiries: And if he had not any *Idea* of a God, it was only because he pursued not those Thoughts, that would have led him to it.

§ 13. I grant, That *if* there were *any Ideas* to be found *imprinted* on the Minds of Men, we have reason to expect, *it should be the Notion of his Maker*, as a mark GOD set on his own Workmanship, to mind Man of his dependance and Duty; and that herein should appear the first instances of humane Knowledge. But how late is it before any such notion is discoverable in Children? And when we find it there, How much more does it resemble the Opinion, and Notion of the Teacher, than represent the True God? He that shall observe in Children, the progress whereby their Minds attain the knowledge they have, will think, that the Objects they do first, and most familiarly converse with, are those that make the first impressions on their Understandings: Nor will he find the least footsteps of any other. It is easie to take notice, how their Thoughts enlarge themselves, only as they come to be acquainted with a greater variety of sensible Objects, to retain the *Ideas* of them in their memories; and to get the skill to compound and enlarge them, and several ways put them together. How by these means they come to frame in their minds an *Idea* Men have of a Deity, I shall hereafter shew.

§ 14. Can it be thought, that the *Ideas* Men have of God, are the Characters, and Marks of Himself, engraven in their minds by his own finger, when we see, that in the same Country, under one and

§§ 13–16. Ideas *of* GOD *various in different Men.*

(9) educated] **1–3, 5** | Educated **4** (12) [*1st*] the] **1–3**; *om.* **4–5**. (**Coste** 'l'exercice') (34) Men have] *add.* **5**

the same Name, *Men have far different*, nay, often *contrary and inconsistent Ideas*, and conceptions *of him*? Their agreeing in a Name, or Sound, will scarce prove an innate Notion of Him.

§ 15. What true or tolerable Notion of a *Deity*, could they have, who acknowledged, and worshipped hundreds? Every Deity, that they owned above one, was an infallible evidence of their ignorance of Him, and a proof, that they had no true Notion of God, where Unity, Infinity, and Eternity, were excluded. To which if we add their gross Conceptions of Corporeity, expressed in their Images, and Representations of their Deities; the Amours, Marriages, Copulations, Lusts, Quarrels, and other mean Qualities, attributed by them to their gods; we shall have little reason to think, that the heathen World, *i.e.* the greatest part of mankind, had such *Ideas* of God in their minds, as he himself, out of care, that they should not be mistaken about him, was Author of. And this universality of consent, so much argued, if it prove any native impressions, 'twill be only this: That God imprinted on the minds of all Men, speaking the same Language, a Name for Himself, but not any *Idea*: Since those People, who agreed in the Name, had at the same time, far different apprehensions about the thing signified. If they say, That the variety of Deities worshipped by the heathen World, were but figurative ways of expressing the several Attributes of that incomprehensible Being, or several parts of his Providence: I answer, What they might be in their original, I will not here enquire; but that they were so in the Thoughts of the Vulgar, I think no body will affirm: And he that will consult the Voyage of the Bishop of *Beryte*, c. 13. (not to mention other Testimonies) will find, that the Theology of the *Siamites*, professedly owns a plurality of Gods: Or, as the *Abbé de Choisy* more judiciously remarks, in his Journal *du Voiage de Siam*, $\frac{107}{177}$, it consists properly in acknowledging no God at all.

§ 15 [*bis*]. If it be said, That *wise Men* of all Nations came to *have true Conceptions* of the Unity and Infinity *of the Deity*, I grant it. But then this,

First, Excludes universality of Consent in any thing, but the name, for those wise Men being very few, perhaps one of a thousand, this universality is very narrow.

(8) were] **1er–5** | were always **1** (28) a] *add.* **4–5** (29) *Abbé*] **1–3** (*likewise* **Coste**) | *Abbe* **4–5** (32) *In* **1–5**, *this section is numbered 15, as is the preceding one; in* **Coste**, *it is numbered 16.*

Secondly, It seems to me plainly to prove, That the truest and best Notions Men had of God, were not imprinted, but acquired by thought and meditation, and a right use of their Faculties: since the wise and considerate Men of the World, by a right and careful employment of their Thoughts and Reason, attained true Notions in this, as well as other things; whilst the lazy and inconsiderate part of Men, making the far greater number, took up their Notions, by chance, from common Tradition and vulgar Conceptions, without much beating their Heads about them. And if it be a reason to think *the notion of God innate*, because all wise Men had it, Vertue too must be thought innate; for that also wise Men have always had.

§ 16. This was evidently the case of all *Gentilism*: Nor hath even amongst *Jews*, *Christians*, and *Mahometans*, who acknowledge but One God, this Doctrine, and the care is taken in those Nations to teach Men, to have true Notions of a GOD, prevailed so far, as to make Men to have the same, and true *Ideas* of Him. How many, even amongst us, will be found upon enquiry, to fancy him in the shape of a Man, sitting in Heaven; and to have many other absurd and unfit conceptions of him? Christians, as well as Turks, have had whole Sects owning, and contending earnestly for it, That the Deity was corporeal and of humane shape: And though we find few amongst us, who profess themselves *Anthropomorphites*, (though some I have met with, that own it) yet, I believe, he that will make it his business, may find amongst the ignorant, and uninstructed Christians, many of that Opinion. Talk but with Country-people, almost of any Age; or young People, almost of any condition, and you shall find, that though the Name of GOD be frequently in their mouths; yet the notions they apply this Name to, are so odd, low, and pitiful, that no body can imagine, they were taught by a rational Man; much less, that they were Characters writ by the finger of God Himself. Nor do I see how it derogates more from the Goodness of God, that he has given us minds unfurnished with these *Ideas* of Himself, than that he hath sent us into the World, with Bodies uncloathed; and that there is no Art or Skill born with us. For being fitted with Faculties to attain these, it is want of Industry, and Consideration in us, and not of Bounty in Him, if we have them not. 'Tis as certain, that there is a God, as that the opposite Angles,

(8) Conceptions,] **1–3, 5** | Conceptions **4** (10) too] *add.* **2–5** (12) *This section is treated in* **Coste** *as a paragraph in the section there numbered 16* (*v.* 93(32), n.). (21) few] **5** | few now **1–4** (26) People . . . condition] **2–5** | people almost any where **1** (30) Characters] **1er–5** | the Characters **1**

made by the intersection of two strait Lines, are equal. There was never any rational Creature, that set himself sincerely to examine the truth of these Propositions, that could fail to assent to them: Though yet it be past doubt, that there are many Men, who having not applied their Thoughts that way, are ignorant both of the one and the other. If any one think fit to call this (which is the utmost of its extent) universal Consent, such an one I easily allow: But such an universal Consent as this, proves not the *Idea* of *God*, no more than it does the *Idea* of such Angles, *innate*.

§ 17. Since then though the knowledge of a *GOD*, be the most natural discovery of humane Reason, yet *the Idea of him*, is *not innate*, as, I think, is evident from what has been said; I imagine there will be scarce any other *Idea* found, that can pretend to it: since if God had set any impression, any character on the Understanding of Men, it is most reasonable to expect it should have been some clear and uniform *Idea* of Himself, as far as our weak Capacities were capable to receive so incomprehensible and infinite an Object. But our minds being, at first, void of that *Idea*, which we are most concerned to have, it *is a strong presumption against all other innate Characters*. I must own, as far as I can observe, I can find none, and would be glad to be informed by any other.

§ 18. I confess, there is another *Idea*, which would be of general use for Mankind to have, as it is of general talk as if they had it; and that is the *Idea of Substance*, which we neither have, nor can have, by *Sensation* or *Reflection*. If Nature took care to provide us any *Ideas*, we might well expect it should be such, as by our own Faculties we cannot procure to our selves: But we see on the contrary, that since by those ways, whereby other *Ideas* are brought into our Minds, this is not, We have no such *clear Idea* at all, and therefore signify nothing by the word *Substance*, but only an uncertain supposition of we know not what; (*i.e.* of something whereof we have no particular distinct positive) *Idea*, which we take to be the *substratum*, or support, of those *Ideas* we do know.

§ 19. Whatever then we talk of innate, either *speculative*, or

§ 17. *If the* Idea *of* GOD *be not innate, no other can be supposed innate.* § 18. Idea *of Substance not innate.* § 19. *No Propositions can be innate, since no* Ideas *are innate.*

---

(4) it] **1–4**; *om.* **5** (14) set . . . character] **2–5** | left any natural impressions **1** (15–16) clear and uniform *Idea*] **2–5** | Characters **1** (28) whereby] **1–3, 5** | where by **4** (31–2) particular distinct positive] *add.* **4–5**

practical Principles, it may, with as much probability, be said, That a Man hath 100 *l.* sterling in his Pocket, and yet denied, that he hath there either Penny, Shilling, Crown, or any other Coin, out of which the Sum is to be made up; as to think, that certain Propositions are innate, when the *Ideas* about which they are, can by no means be supposed to be so. The general reception and assent that is given, doth *not* at all prove, that the *Ideas* expressed in them, are *innate*: For in many cases, however the *Ideas* came there, the assent to Words expressing the agreement, or disagreement, of such *Ideas*, will necessarily follow. Every one that hath a true *Idea* of *God*, and *Worship*, will assent to this Proposition, That God is to be worshiped, when expressed, in a Language he understands: And every rational Man, that hath not thought on it to day, may be ready to assent to this Proposition to morrow; and yet millions of Men may be well supposed to want one, or both, of those *Ideas* to day. For if we will allow Savages, and most Country-people, to have *Ideas* of *God* and *Worship* (which conversation with them, will not make one forward to believe) yet I think, few Children can be supposed to have those *Ideas*, which therefore they must begin to have sometime or other; and then they will also begin to assent to that Proposition, and make very little question of it ever after. But such an assent upon hearing, no more proves the *Ideas* to be innate, than it does, That one born blind (with Cataracts, which will be couched to morrow) had the innate *Ideas* of the Sun, or Light, or Saffron, or Yellow; because when his Sight is cleared, he will certainly assent to this Proposition, That the Sun is lucid, or that Saffron is yellow: And therefore if such an assent upon hearing cannot prove the *Ideas* innate, it can much less the Propositions made up of those *Ideas*. If they have any innate *Ideas*, I would be glad to be told, what, and how many they are.

§ 20. To which let me add: If there be any innate *Ideas*, any *Ideas*, in the mind, which the mind does not actually think on; they must be lodg'd in the memory, and from thence must be brought into view by Remembrance; *i.e.* must be known, when they are remembred, to have been perceptions in the mind before, unless Remembrance can be without Remembrance. For to remember is to

§ 20. *No innate* Ideas *in the memory.*

---

(2) denied,] **4–5** | deny **1–3** (3) there] **1–4**; *om.* **5** (15) of] **1–3**; *om.* **4–5** (31)–98(25) *The whole of this section add.* **2–5**

perceive any thing with memory, or with a consciousness, that it was known or perceived before: without this, whatever *Idea* comes into the mind is new, and not remembred: This consciousness of its having been in the mind before, being that, which distinguishes Remembring from all other ways of Thinking. Whatever *Idea* was never perceived by the mind, was never in the mind. Whatever *Idea* is in the mind, is either an actual perception, or else having been an actual perception, is so in the mind, that by the memory it can be made an actual perception again. Whenever there is the actual perception of an *Idea* without memory, the *Idea* appears perfectly new and unknown before to the Understanding: Whenever the memory brings any *Idea* into actual view, it is with a consciousness, that it had been there before, and was not wholly a Stranger to the mind. Whether this be not so, I appeal to every ones observation: And then I desire an instance of an *Idea*, pretended to be innate, which (before any impression of it by ways hereafter to be mentioned) any one could revive and remember as an *Idea*, he had formerly known; without which consciousness of a former perception there is no remembrance; and whatever *Idea* comes into the mind without that consciousness is not remembred, or comes not out of the memory, nor can be said to be in the mind before that appearance. For what is not either actually in view, or in the memory, is in the mind no way at all, and is all one as if it never had been there. Suppose a Child had the use of his Eyes till he knows and distinguishes Colours; but then Cataracts shut the Windows, and he is forty or fifty years perfectly in the dark; and in that time perfectly loses all memory of the *Ideas* of colours, he once had. This was the case of a blind Man I once talked with, who lost his sight by the small Pox when he was a Child, and had no more notion of colours, than one born Blind. I ask whether any one can say this Man had then any *Ideas* of colours in his mind, any more than one born Blind? And I think no body will say, that either of them had in his mind any *Idea* of colours at all. His cataracts are couch'd, and then he has the *Ideas* (which he remembers not) of colours, *de novo*, by his restor'd sight, convey'd to his mind, and that without any consciousness of a former acquaintance. And these now he can revive, and call to mind in the dark. In this case all these *Ideas* of colours, which when out of view can be reviv'd with a consciousness

(10) an] **5** | any **2–4** (15) [*2nd*] an] **5** | any **2–4** (16) hereafter] **2–3, 5** | here after **4**

of a former acquaintance, being thus in the memory, are said to be in the mind. The use I make of this is, that whatever *Idea* being not actually in view, is in the mind, is there only by being in the memory; and if it be not in the memory, it is not in the mind; and if it be in the memory, it cannot by the memory be brought into actual view, without a perception that it comes out of the memory, which is this, that it had been known before, and is now remembred. If therefore there be any innate *Ideas*, they must be in the memory, or else no where in the mind; and if they be in the memory, they can be reviv'd without any impression from without, and whenever they are brought into the mind, they are remembred, *i.e.* they bring with them a perception of their not being wholly new to it. This being a constant, and distinguishing difference between what is, and what is not in the memory, or in the mind; that what is not in the memory, whenever it appears there, appears perfectly new, and unknown before; and what is in the memory, or in the mind, whenever it is suggested by the memory, appears not to be new, but the mind finds it in it self, and knows it was there before. By this it may be tried, whether there be any innate *Ideas* in the mind before impression from *Sensation* or *Reflection*. I would fain meet with the Man, who when he came to the use of reason, or at any other time remembred any of them: And to whom, after he was born, they were never new. If any one will say, there are *Ideas* in the mind, that are not in the memory; I desire him to explain himself, and make what he says intelligible.

§ 21. Besides what I have already said, there is another Reason, why I doubt, that neither these, nor any other Principles are innate. I that am fully perswaded, that the infinitely Wise GOD made all Things in perfect Wisdom, cannot satisfy my self, why he should be supposed to print upon the minds of Men, some universal *Principles*; whereof those *that* are pretended innate, and *concern Speculation, are of no great use; and those that concern Practice, not self-evident*; *and neither of them distinguishable from some other Truths, not allowed to be innate*. For to what purpose should Characters be graven on the Mind, by the Finger of God, which are not clearer there, than those, which are afterwards introduced, or cannot be distinguish'd from them? If any one thinks there are such innate *Ideas* and

§ 21. *Principles not innate, because of little use, or little certainty.*

(3) mind, is there] **2er, 4–5** | mind, there **3** | mind **2** (14) mind;] **2–3, 5** | mind: **4** (18) [*2nd*] it] **2–4** | its **5** (25) *v.* 96(31), n. (26) 21] **2–5** | 20 **1**

Propositions, which by their clearness and usefulness, are distinguishable from all that is adventitious in the mind, and acquired, it will not be a hard matter for him to tell us, which they are; and then every one will be a fit Judge, whether they be so, or no. Since if there be such innate *Ideas* and Impressions, plainly different from all our other perceptions and knowledge, every one will find it true in himself. Of the evidence of these supposed innate Maxims, I have spoken already; of their usefulness, I shall have occasion to speak more hereafter.

§ 22. To conclude, some *Ideas* forwardly offer themselves to all Men's Understandings; and some sorts of Truths result from any *Ideas*, as soon as the mind puts them into Propositions: Other Truths require a train of *Ideas* placed in order, a due comparing of them, and deductions made with attention, before they can be discovered, and assented to. Some of the first sort, because of their general and easy reception, have been mistaken for innate: But the truth is, *Ideas* and Notions are no more born with us, than Arts and Sciences; though some of them, indeed, offer themselves to our Faculties, more readily than others; and therefore are more generally received: Though that too, be according as the Organs of our Bodies, and Powers of our Minds, happen to be employ'd; *God having fitted Men with faculties and means, to discover, receive, and retain Truths, accordingly as they are employ'd.* The great difference that is to be found in the Notions of Mankind, is, from the different use they put their Faculties to, whilst some (and those the most) taking things upon trust, misimploy their power of Assent, by lazily enslaving their Minds, to the Dictates and Dominion of others, in Doctrines, which it is their duty carefully to examine; and not blindly, with an implicit faith, to swallow: Others employing their Thoughts only about some few things, grow acquainted sufficiently with them, attain great degrees of knowledge in them, and are ignorant of all other, having never let their Thoughts loose, in the search of other Enquiries. Thus, that the three Angles of a Triangle are equal to two Right ones, is a Truth, as certain as any thing can be; and I think more evident, than many of those Propositions, that go for Principles; and yet there are millions, however expert in other things, who know not this at all, because they never set their

§ 22. *Difference of Men's Discoveries depends upon the different application of their Faculties.*

---

(6) our] **1–4**; *om.* **5** (10) 22] **2–5** | 21 **1** (11) and] **1–4**; *om.* **5** (22) *receive*] **2–5** | *observe* **1** (24) Notions] **1er–5** | Notion **1** (37) who] *add.* **2–5**

Thoughts on work about such Angles: And he that certainly knows this Proposition, may yet be utterly ignorant of the truth of other Propositions, in Mathematicks it self, which are as clear and evident as this; because, in his search of those mathematical Truths, he stopp'd his Thoughts short, and went not so far. The same may happen concerning the notions we have of the Being of a Deity; for though there be no Truth, which a Man may more evidently make out to himself, than the Existence of a God, yet he that shall content himself with things, as he finds them, in this World, as they minister to his Pleasures and Passions, and not make enquiry a little farther into their Causes, Ends, and admirable Contrivances, and pursue the thoughts thereof with diligence and attention, may live long without any notion of such a Being: And if any Person hath, by talk, put such a Notion into his head, he may, perhaps, believe it: But if he hath never *examined* it, his knowledge of it will be no perfecter, than his, who having been told, that the three Angles of a Triangle are equal to two Right ones, takes it upon trust, without examining the demonstration; and may yield his assent as to a probable Opinion, but hath no knowledge of the truth of it; which yet his Faculties, if carefully employ'd, were able to make clear and evident to him. But this only by the by, to shew how much our *knowledge depends upon the right use of those Powers Nature hath bestowed upon us*, and how little upon such innate Principles, as are in vain supposed to be in all Mankind for their direction; which all Men could not but know, if they were there, or else they would be there to no purpose: And which since all Men do not know, nor can distinguish from other adventitious truths, we may well conclude there are no such.

§ 23. What censure, doubting thus of innate Principles, may deserve from Men, who will be apt to call it, pulling up the old foundations of Knowledge and Certainty, I cannot tell: I perswade my self, at least, that the way I have pursued, being conformable to Truth, lays those foundations surer. This I am certain, I have not made it my business, either to quit, or follow any Authority in the ensuing Discourse: Truth has been my only aim; and where-ever that has appeared to lead, my Thoughts have impartially followed,

§ 23. *Men must think and know for themselves.*

---

(18) to] **1–4**; *om.* **5** (23) such innate Principles, as] **2–5** | those innate Principles, which **1** (25) not but] **1–4** | but not **5** (26–8) : And . . . such] *add.* **2–5** (29) 23] **2–5** | 22 **1** (31) foundations] **2–5** | foundation **1**

without minding, whether the footsteps of any other lay that way, or no. Not that I want a due respect to other Mens Opinions; but after all, the *greatest reverence is due to Truth*; and, I hope, it will not be thought arrogance, to say, That, perhaps, we should make greater progress in the discovery of rational and contemplative *Knowledge*, if we *sought* it in the Fountain, *in the consideration of Things themselves*; and made use rather of our own Thoughts, than other Mens to find it. For, I think, we may as rationally hope to see with other Mens Eyes, as to know by other Mens Understandings. So much as we our selves consider and comprehend of Truth and Reason, so much we possess of real and true Knowledge. The floating of other Mens Opinions in our brains makes us not one jot the more knowing, though they happen to be true. What in them was Science, is in us but Opiniatrety, whilst we give up our Assent only to reverend Names, and do not, as they did, employ our own Reason to *understand* those *Truths*, which gave them reputation. *Aristotle* was certainly a knowing Man, but no body ever thought him so, because he blindly embraced, and confidently vented the Opinions of another. And if the taking up of another's Principles, without examining them, made not him a Philosopher, I suppose it will hardly make any body else so. In the Sciences, every one has so much, as he really knows and comprehends: What he believes only, and takes upon trust, are but shreads; which however well in the whole piece, make no considerable addition to his stock, who gathers them. Such borrowed Wealth, like Fairy-money, though it were Gold in the hand from which he received it, will be but Leaves and Dust when it comes to use.

§ 24. When Men have found some general Propositions that could not be doubted of, as soon as understood, it was, I know, *a short and easy way to conclude them innate*. This being once received, it eased the lazy from the pains of search, and stopp'd the enquiry of the doubtful, concerning all that was once stiled innate: And it was of no small advantage to those who affected to be Masters and Teachers, to make this the Principle of *Principles*, That Principles must not be questioned: For having once established this Tenet, That there are innate Principles, it put their Followers upon a

§ 24. *Whence the Opinion of innate Principles.*

(20–1) will hardly make any body] **2–5** | can make no body **1** (28) 24] **2–5** | 23 **1**

necessity of receiving some Doctrines as such; which was to take them off from the use of their own Reason and Judgment, and put them upon believing and taking them upon trust, without farther examination: In which posture of blind Credulity, they might be more easily governed by, and made useful to some sort of Men, who had the skill and office to principle and guide them. Nor is it a small power it gives one Man over another, to have the Authority to be the Dictator of Principles, and Teacher of unquestionable Truths; and to make a Man swallow that for an innate Principle, which may serve to his purpose, who teacheth them. Whereas had they examined the ways, whereby Men came to the knowledge of many universal *Truths*, they would have found them to result in the minds of Men, from the being of things themselves, when duly considered; and that they were discovered by the application of those Faculties, that were fitted by Nature to receive and judge of them, when duly employ'd about them.

§ 25. *To shew how the Understanding proceeds herein, is the design of the following Discourse*; which I shall proceed to, when I have first premised, that hitherto to clear my way to those foundations, which, I conceive are the only true ones, whereon to establish those Notions we can have of our own Knowledge, it hath been necessary for me to give an account of the Reasons I had to doubt of innate Principles: And since the Arguments which are against them, do, some of them, rise from common received Opinions, I have been forced to take several things for granted, which is hardly avoidable to any one, whose Task it is to shew the falshood, or improbability, of any Tenet; it happening in Controversial Discourses, as it does in assaulting of Towns; where, if the ground be but firm, whereon the Batteries are erected, there is no farther enquiry of whom it is borrowed, nor whom it belongs to, so it affords but a fit rise for the present purpose. But in the future part of this Discourse, designing to raise an Edifice uniform, and consistent with it self, as far as my own Experience and Observation will assist me, I hope, to erect it on such a Basis, that I shall not need to shore it up with props and buttresses, leaning on borrowed or begg'd foundations: Or at least,

§ 25. *Conclusion.*

---

(17) 25] **2–5** | 24 **1** (22) give] **2–5** | give you **1** (33–4) to . . . that] **2–5** | to lay the foundation so, that the rest will easily depend upon it: And **1** (*l. below* 35) *In* **Coste**, 'Conclusion du Premier Livre.' *is in the Table of Contents, but* 'Conclusion.' *is the marginal summary.*

if mine prove a Castle in the Air, I will endeavour it shall be all of a piece, and hang together. Wherein I warn the Reader not to expect undeniable cogent demonstrations, unless I may be allow'd the Privilege, not seldom assumed by others, to take my Principles for granted; and then, I doubt not, but I can demonstrate too. All that I shall say for the Principles I proceed on, is, that I can only *appeal* to Mens own unprejudiced *Experience*, and Observation, whether they be true, or no; and this is enough for a Man who professes no more, than to lay down candidly and freely his own Conjectures, concerning a Subject lying somewhat in the dark, without any other design, than an unbias'd enquiry after Truth.

(2) I warn the Reader] **2–5** | I tell you before-hand, you are **1** (3–4) I . . . others] **2–5** | you will suffer me, as others have done **1** (7) Observation] **2–5** | Observations **1** (10) lying somewhat in the dark] **2–5** | not very obvious **1**

BOOK II

CHAPTER I

Of Ideas *in general, and their Original.*

§ 1. EVERY Man being conscious to himself, That he thinks, and that which his Mind is employ'd about whilst thinking, being the *Ideas*, that are there, 'tis past doubt, that Men have in their Minds several *Ideas*, such as are those expressed by the words, *Whiteness, Hardness, Sweetness, Thinking, Motion, Man, Elephant, Army, Drunkenness,* and others: It is in the first place then to be enquired, How he comes by them? I know it is a received Doctrine, That Men have native *Ideas*, and original Characters stamped upon their Minds, in their very first Being. This Opinion I have at large examined already; and, I suppose, what I have said in the fore-going Book, will be much more easily admitted, when I have shewn, whence the Understanding may get all the *Ideas* it has, and by what ways and degrees they may come into the Mind; for which I shall appeal to every one's own Observation and Experience.

§ 2. Let us then suppose the Mind to be, as we say, white Paper, void of all Characters, without any *Ideas*; How comes it to be furnished? Whence comes it by that vast store, which the busy and boundless Fancy of Man has painted on it, with an almost endless variety? Whence has it all the materials of Reason and Knowledge? To this I answer, in one word, From *Experience*: In that, all our Knowledge is founded; and from that it ultimately derives it self. Our Observation employ'd either about *external, sensible Objects; or about the internal Operations of our Minds, perceived and reflected on by our selves, is that, which supplies our Understandings with all the materials of thinking.* These two are the Fountains of Knowledge, from whence all the *Ideas* we have, or can naturally have, do spring.

§ 1. Idea *is the Object of Thinking.* § 2. *All* Ideas *come from Sensation or Reflection.*

(*l. above* 1) **Coste** *adds, before full stop,* '; et où l'on examine par occasion si l'Ame de l'Homme pense toûjours'. (2) employ'd] **1–4** | apply'd **5** (11) shewn] **2–5** | shewed **1**

§ 3. First, *Our Senses*, conversant about particular sensible Objects, do *convey into the Mind*, several distinct *Perceptions* of things, according to those various ways, wherein those Objects do affect them: And thus we come by those *Ideas*, we have of *Yellow*, *White*, *Heat*, *Cold*, *Soft*, *Hard*, *Bitter*, *Sweet*, and all those which we call sensible qualities, which when I say the senses convey into the mind, I mean, they from external Objects convey into the mind what produces there those *Perceptions*. This great Source, of most of the *Ideas* we have, depending wholly upon our Senses, and derived by them to the Understanding, I call *SENSATION*.

§ 4. Secondly, The other Fountain, from which Experience furnisheth the Understanding with *Ideas*, is the *Perception of the Operations of our own Minds* within us, as it is employ'd about the *Ideas* it has got; which Operations, when the Soul comes to reflect on, and consider, do furnish the Understanding with another set of *Ideas*, which could not be had from things without: and such are, *Perception*, *Thinking*, *Doubting*, *Believing*, *Reasoning*, *Knowing*, *Willing*, and all the different actings of our own Minds; which we being conscious of, and observing in our selves, do from these receive into our Understandings, as distinct *Ideas*, as we do from Bodies affecting our Senses. This Source of *Ideas*, every Man has wholly in himself: And though it be not Sense, as having nothing to do with external Objects; yet it is very like it, and might properly enough be call'd internal Sense. But as I call the other *Sensation*, so I call this *REFLECTION*, the *Ideas* it affords being such only, as the Mind gets by reflecting on its own Operations within it self. By *REFLECTION* then, in the following part of this Discourse, I would be understood to mean, that notice which the Mind takes of its own Operations, and the manner of them, by reason whereof, there come to be *Ideas* of these Operations in the Understanding. These two, I say, *viz.* External, Material things, as the Objects of *SENSATION*; and the Operations of our own Minds within, as the Objects of *REFLECTION*, are, to me, the only Originals, from whence all our *Ideas* take their beginnings. The term *Operations* here, I use in a large sence, as comprehending not barely the Actions of the Mind about

§ 3. *The Objects of Sensation one Source of* Ideas. § 4. *The Operations of our Minds, the other Source of them.*

(6–8) , which . . . *Perceptions*] *add.* **2–5** (10) the] **4–5** | our **1–3** (20) Understandings] **4–5** | Understanding **1–3**

its *Ideas*, but some sort of Passions arising sometimes from them, such as is the satisfaction or uneasiness arising from any thought.

§ 5. The Understanding seems to me, not to have the least glimmering of any *Ideas*, which it doth not receive from one of these two. *External Objects furnish the Mind with the* Ideas *of sensible qualities*, which are all those different perceptions they produce in us: And the *Mind furnishes the Understanding with* Ideas *of its own Operations*. These, when we have taken a full survey of them, and their several Modes, Combinations, and Relations, we shall find to contain all our whole stock of *Ideas*; and that we have nothing in our Minds, which did not come in, one of these two ways. Let any one examine his own Thoughts, and throughly search into his Understanding, and then let him tell me, Whether all the original *Ideas* he has there, are any other than of the Objects of his *Senses*; or of the Operations of his Mind, considered as Objects of his *Reflection*: and how great a mass of Knowledge soever he imagines to be lodged there, he will, upon taking a strict view, see, that he has *not any* Idea *in his Mind, but what one of these two have imprinted*; though, perhaps, with infinite variety compounded and enlarged by the Understanding, as we shall see hereafter.

§ 6. He that attentively considers the state of a *Child*, at his first coming into the World, will have little reason to think him stored with plenty of *Ideas*, that are to be the matter of his future Knowledge. 'Tis by degrees he comes to be furnished with them: And though the *Ideas* of obvious and familiar qualities, imprint themselves, before the Memory begins to keep a Register of Time and Order, yet 'tis often so late, before some unusual qualities come in the way, that there are few Men that cannot recollect the beginning of their acquaintance with them: And if it were worth while, no doubt a Child might be so ordered, as to have but a very few, even of the ordinary *Ideas*, till he were grown up to a Man. But all that are born into the World being surrounded with Bodies, that perpetually and diversly affect them, variety of *Ideas*, whether care be taken about it or no, are imprinted on the Minds of Children. *Light*, and *Colours*, are busie at hand every where, when the Eye is but

§ 5. *All our* Ideas *are of the one or the other of these.* § 6. *Observable in Children.*

(6) produce] **2–5** | produced **1** (7) *Paragraph break here in* **5**, *not in* **1–4**. (9) Modes, Combinations, and Relations] **4–5** | modes, and the Compositions made out of them **1–3** (14) *Senses*;] **4–5** | *Senses*, **1–3** (18) *these*] **2–5** | *those* **1** (31–2) all . . . World] *add.* **4–5** (33) them] **4–5** | us **1–3** (35) at] **5** | and at **1–4**

open; *Sounds*, and some *tangible Qualities* fail not to solicite their proper Senses, and force an entrance to the Mind; but yet, I think, it will be granted easily, That if a Child were kept in a place, where he never saw any other but Black and White, till he were a Man, he would have no more *Ideas* of Scarlet or Green, than he that from his Childhood never tasted an Oyster, or a Pine-Apple, has of those particular Relishes.

§ 7. Men then come to be furnished with fewer or more simple *Ideas* from without, according as the *Objects*, they converse with, afford greater or less variety; and from the Operation of their Minds within, according as they more or less *reflect* on them. For, though he that contemplates the Operations of his Mind, cannot but have plain and clear *Ideas* of them; yet unless he turn his Thoughts that way, and considers them *attentively*, he will no more have clear and distinct *Ideas* of all the *Operations of his Mind*, and all that may be observed therein, than he will have all the particular *Ideas* of any Landscape, or of the Parts and Motions of a Clock, who will not turn his Eyes to it, and with attention heed all the Parts of it. The Picture, or Clock may be so placed, that they may come in his way every day; but yet he will have but a confused *Idea* of all the Parts they are made up of, till he *applies himself with attention*, to consider them each in particular.

§ 8. And hence we see the Reason, why 'tis pretty late, before most Children get *Ideas* of the Operations of their own Minds; and some have not any very clear, or perfect *Ideas* of the greatest part of them all their Lives. Because, though they pass there continually; yet like floating Visions, they make not deep Impressions enough, to leave in the Mind clear distinct lasting *Ideas*, till the Understanding turns inwards upon it self, *reflects* on its own *Operations*, and makes them the Object of its own Contemplation. Children, when they come first into it, are surrounded with a world of new things, which, by a constant solicitation of their senses, draw the mind constantly to them, forward to take notice of new, and apt to be

§ 7. *Men are differently furnished with these, according to the different Objects they converse with.* § 8. Ideas *of Reflexion later, because they need Attention.*

---

(10) less] **1er–5** | lesser **1** (28) clear distinct] **2–5** | clear and distinct, **1** (',' *om.* **1T.er**) (29) turns] **2–5** | turn **1** it] **4–5** | its **1–3** *reflects*] **2–5** | and *reflect* **1** (30) makes] **2–5** | make **1** (30)–108(4) Children . . . without] **2–5** | Whereas Children at their first coming into the World, seek particularly after nothing, but what may ease their Hunger, or other Pain: but take all other Objects as they come, are generally pleased with all new ones, that are not painful **1**

delighted with the variety of changing Objects. Thus the first Years are usually imploy'd and diverted in looking abroad. Men's Business in them is to acquaint themselves with what is to be found without; and so growing up in a constant attention to outward Sensations, seldom make any considerable Reflection on what passes within them, till they come to be of riper Years; and some scarce ever at all.

§ 9. To ask, *at what time a Man has first any* Ideas, is to ask, when he begins to perceive; having *Ideas*, and Perception being the same thing. I know it is an Opinion, that the Soul always thinks, and that it has the actual Perception of *Ideas* in it self constantly, as long as it exists; and that actual thinking is as inseparable from the Soul, as actual Extension is from the Body; which if true, to enquire after the beginning of a Man's *Ideas*, is the same, as to enquire after the beginning of his Soul. For by this Account, Soul and its *Ideas*, as Body and its Extension, will begin to exist both at the same time.

§ 10. But whether the Soul be supposed to exist antecedent to, or coeval with, or some time after the first Rudiments of Organisation, or the beginnings of Life in the Body, I leave to be disputed by those, who have better thought of that matter. I confess my self, to have one of those dull Souls, that doth not perceive it self always to contemplate *Ideas*, nor can conceive it any more necessary for the *Soul always to think*, than for the Body always to move; the perception of *Ideas* being (as I conceive) to the Soul, what motion is to the Body, not its Essence, but one of its Operations: And therefore, though thinking be supposed never so much the proper Action of the Soul; yet it is not necessary, to suppose, that it should be always thinking, always in Action. That, perhaps, is the Privilege of the infinite Author and Preserver of things, *who never slumbers nor sleeps*;* but is not competent to any finite Being, at least not to the Soul of Man. We know certainly by Experience, that we sometimes think,

§ 9. *The Soul begins to have* Ideas, *when it begins to perceive.* § 10. *The Soul thinks not always; for this wants Proofs.*

(2–3) . Men's . . . acquaint] **4er–5** | , and acquainting **2–4** (4) *v.* 107(30), n. (9) perceive; . . . *Ideas*,] **5** | perceive, . . . *Ideas* **1–4** (10) **Coste** 'Je sai bien qu'il y a une Opinion qui pose'; **Coste**$_2$ 'Je sai bien que certains Philosophes assurent' *and appends a note* 'Les Cartesiens' *on* 'certains Philosophes'. (11) [*2nd*] it] **3–5** | its **1–2** (15, 16) its] *add.* **2–5** (18) of] **1–4** | or **5** (22) *Ideas*] **2–5** | its *Ideas* **1** (23); the] **5** | : the **1–4** (25) one of its Operations] **2–5** | Operation **1** (29) of]**4–5** | of all **1–3** (*likewise* **Coste**)

* Ps. 121: 4.

and thence draw this infallible Consequence, That there is something in us, that has a Power to think: But whether that Substance perpetually thinks, or no, we can be no farther assured, than Experience informs us. For to say, that actual thinking is essential to the Soul, and inseparable from it, is to beg, what is in Question, and not to prove it by Reason; which is necessary to be done, if it be not a self-evident Proposition. But whether this, *That the Soul always thinks*, be a self-evident Proposition, that every Body assents to at first hearing, I appeal to Mankind. 'Tis doubted whether I thought all last night, or no; the Question being about a matter of fact, 'tis begging it, to bring, as a proof for it, an Hypothesis, which is the very thing in dispute: by which way one may prove any thing, and 'tis but supposing that all watches, whilst the balance beats, think, and 'tis sufficiently proved, and past doubt, that my watch thought all last night. But he, that would not deceive himself, ought to build his Hypothesis on matter of fact, and make it out by sensible experience, and not presume on matter of fact, because of his Hypothesis, that is, because he supposes it to be so: which way of proving, amounts to this, That I must necessarily think all last night, because another supposes I always think, though I my self cannot perceive, that I always do so.

But Men in love with their Opinions, may not only suppose what is in question, but alledge wrong matter of fact. How else could any one make it an *inference* of mine, *that a thing is not, because we are not sensible of it in our sleep*. I do not say there is no Soul in a Man, because he is not sensible of it in his sleep; But I do say, he cannot think at any time waking or sleeping, without being sensible of it. Our being sensible of it is not necessary to any thing, but to our thoughts; and to them it is; and to them it will always be necessary, till we can think without being conscious of it.

§ 11. I grant that the Soul in a waking Man is never without thought, because it is the condition of being awake: But whether

§ 11. *It is not always conscious of it.*

(6) Reason] **2–5** | Reasons **1** (9–30) 'Tis . . . it.] *add.* **2–5** (23–5) but . . . *sleep.*] **Coste** 'mais encore de faire dire à ceux qui ne sont pas de leur avis, toute autre chose que ce qu'ils ont dit effectivement. C'est ce que j'ai éprouvé dans cette occasion; car il s'est trouvé un Auteur qui ayant lû la prémiére Edition de cet Ouvrage, et n'étant pas satisfait de ce que je viens d'avancer contre l'opinion de ceux qui soûtiennent que l'*Ame pense toûjours*, me fait dire, qu'*une chose cesse d'exister parce que nous ne sentons pas qu'elle existe pendant nôtre sommeil*. Etrange conséquence qu'on ne peut m'attribuer sans avoir l'Esprit rempli d'une aveugle préoccupation!'

sleeping without dreaming be not an Affection of the whole Man, Mind as well as Body, may be worth a waking Man's Consideration; it being hard to conceive, that any thing should think, and not be conscious of it. If the *Soul* doth *think in a sleeping Man*, without being conscious of it, I ask, whether, during such thinking, it has any Pleasure or Pain, or be capable of Happiness or Misery? I am sure the Man is not, no more than the Bed or Earth he lies on. For to be happy or miserable without being conscious of it, seems to me utterly inconsistent and impossible. Or if it be possible, that the Soul can, whilst the Body is sleeping, have its Thinking, Enjoyments, and Concerns, its Pleasure or Pain apart, which the Man is not conscious of, nor partakes in: It is certain, that *Socrates* asleep, and *Socrates* awake, is not the same Person; but his Soul when he sleeps, and *Socrates* the Man consisting of Body and Soul when he is waking, are two Persons: Since waking *Socrates*, has no Knowledge of, or Concernment for that Happiness, or Misery of his Soul, which it enjoys alone by it self whilst he sleeps, without perceiving any thing of it; no more than he has for the Happiness, or Misery of a Man in the *Indies*, whom he knows not. For if we take wholly away all Consciousness of our Actions and Sensations, especially of Pleasure and Pain, and the concernment that accompanies it, it will be hard to know wherein to place personal Identity.

§ 12. The Soul, during sound Sleep, thinks, say these Men. *Whilst it thinks* and perceives, it is capable certainly of those of Delight or Trouble, as well as any other Perceptions; and *it must necessarily be conscious of its own Perceptions*. But it has all this apart: The sleeping Man, 'tis plain, is conscious of nothing of all this. Let us suppose then the Soul of *Castor*, whilst he is sleeping, retired from his Body, which is no impossible Supposition for the Men I have here to do with, who so liberally allow Life, without a thinking Soul to all other Animals. These Men cannot then judge it impossible, or a contradiction, That the Body should live without the Soul; nor that the Soul should subsist and think, or have Perception, even Perception of Happiness or Misery, without the Body. Let us then, as I say, suppose the Soul of *Castor* separated, during his Sleep, from

§ 12. *If a sleeping Man thinks without knowing it, the sleeping and waking Man are two Persons.*

---

(8) me] **1–2, 4–5** | be **3** (12) in:] **5** | in. **3–4** | in, **1–2** (14) sleeps] **1–3, 5** | Sleeps 4 (31) it] **2–5** | it is **1** (33) should . . . have] **2–5** | subsists and thinks, or has **1**

his Body, to think apart. Let us suppose too, that it chuses for its Scene of Thinking, the Body of another Man, *v.g. Pollux*, who is sleeping without a Soul: For if *Castor*'s Soul can think whilst *Castor* is asleep, what *Castor* is never conscious of, 'tis no matter what Place it chuses to think in. We have here then the Bodies of two Men with only one Soul between them, which we will suppose to sleep and wake by turns; and the Soul still thinking in the waking Man, whereof the sleeping Man is never conscious, has never the least Perception. I ask then, Whether *Castor* and *Pollux*, thus, with only one Soul between them, which thinks and perceives in one, what the other is never conscious of, nor is concerned for, are not two as distinct Persons, as *Castor* and *Hercules*; or, as *Socrates* and *Plato* were? And whether one of them might not be very happy, and the other very miserable? Just by the same Reason, they make the Soul and the Man two Persons, who make the Soul think apart, what the Man is not conscious of. For, I suppose, no body will make Identity of Persons, to consist in the Soul's being united to the very same numerical Particles of matter: For if that be necessary to Identity, 'twill be impossible, in that constant flux of the Particles of our Bodies, that any Man should be the same Person, two days, or two moments together.

§ 13. Thus, methinks, every drowsy Nod shakes their Doctrine, who teach, That the Soul is always thinking. Those, at least, who do at any time *sleep without dreaming*, can never be convinced, That their Thoughts are sometimes for four hours busy without their knowing of it; and if they are taken in the very act, waked in the middle of that sleeping contemplation, can give no manner of account of it.

§ 14. 'Twill perhaps be said, That the *Soul thinks*, even *in* the soundest *Sleep, but the Memory retains it not*. That the Soul in a sleeping Man should be this moment busy a thinking, and the next moment in a waking Man, not remember, nor be able to recollect one jot of all those Thoughts, is very hard to be conceived, and would need some better Proof than bare Assertion, to make it be believed. For who can without any more ado, but being barely told so, imagine, That the greatest part of Men, do, during all their Lives, for several hours every day, think of something, which if they were asked, even in the middle of these Thoughts, they could

§ 13. *Impossible to convince those that sleep without dreaming, that they think.* § 14. ***That Men dream without remembring it, in vain urged.***

remember nothing at all of? Most Men, I think, pass a great part of their Sleep without dreaming. I once knew a Man, that was bred a Scholar, and had no bad Memory, who told me, he had never dream'd in his Life, till he had that Fever, he was then newly recovered of, which was about the Five or Six and Twentieth Year of his Age. I suppose the World affords more such Instances: At least every one's Acquaintance will furnish him with Examples enough of such, as pass most of their Nights without dreaming.

§ 15. *To think often, and never to retain it so much as one moment, is a very useless sort of thinking*: and the Soul in such a state of thinking, does very little, if at all, excel that of a Looking-glass, which constantly receives variety of Images, or *Ideas*, but retains none; they disappear and vanish, and there remain no footsteps of them; the Looking-glass is never the better for such *Ideas*, nor the Soul for such Thoughts. Perhaps it will be said, that in a waking Man, the materials of the Body are employ'd, and made use of, in thinking; and that the memory of Thoughts, is retained by the impressions that are made on the Brain, and the traces there left after such thinking; but that in the *thinking of the Soul*, which is not perceived *in a sleeping Man*, there the Soul thinks apart, and *making no use* of the Organs of *the Body*, *leaves no impressions on it*, *and consequently no memory* of such Thoughts. Not to mention again the absurdity of two distinct Persons, which follows from this Supposition, I answer farther, That whatever *Ideas* the Mind can receive, and contemplate without the help of the Body, it is reasonable to conclude, it can retain without the help of the Body too, or else the Soul, or any separate Spirit, will have but little advantage by thinking. If it has no memory of its own Thoughts; if it cannot lay them up for its use, and be able to recal them upon occasion; if it cannot reflect upon what is past, and make use of its former Experiences, Reasonings, and Contemplations, to what purpose does it think? They, who make the Soul a thinking Thing at this rate, will not make it a much more noble Being, than those do, whom they condemn, for allowing it to be nothing but the subtilest parts of Matter. Characters drawn on Dust, that the first breath of wind effaces; or Impressions made on a heap of Atoms, or animal Spirits, are altogether

§ 15. *Upon this Hypothesis, the Thoughts of a sleeping Man ought to be most rational.*

(28) lay them up] **4** | lay up them **5** | record them **1–3** (29) occasion] **5** | any occasion **1–4**. (**Coste** 'dans l'occasion') (32) at . . . rate,] **2–4** | , at . . . rate, **5** | , at . . . rate **1**

as useful, and render the Subject as noble, as the Thoughts of a Soul that perish in thinking; that once out of sight, are gone for ever, and leave no memory of themselves behind them. Nature never makes excellent things, for mean or no uses: and it is hardly to be conceived, that our infinitely wise Creator, should make so admirable a Faculty, as the power of Thinking, that Faculty which comes nearest the Excellency of his own incomprehensible Being, to be so idlely and uselesly employ'd, at least ¼ part of its time here, as to think constantly, without remembring any of those Thoughts, without doing any good to it self or others, or being any way useful to any other part of the Creation. If we will examine it, we shall not find, I suppose, the motion of dull and sensless matter, any where in the Universe, made so little use of, and so wholly thrown away.

§ 16. 'Tis true, we have sometimes instances of Perception, whilst we are *asleep*, and retain the memory of those *Thoughts*: but how *extravagant* and incoherent for the most part they are; how little conformable to the Perfection and Order of a rational Being, those who are acquainted with Dreams, need not be told. This I would willingly be satisfied in, Whether the Soul, when it thinks thus apart, and as it were separate from the Body, acts less rationally than when conjointly with it, or no: If its separate Thoughts be less rational, then these Men must say, That the Soul owes the perfection of rational thinking to the Body: If it does not, 'tis a wonder that our Dreams should be, for the most part, so frivolous and irrational; and that the Soul should retain none of its more rational Soliloquies and Meditations.

§ 17. Those who so confidently tell us, That the Soul always actually thinks, I would they would also tell us, what those *Ideas* are, that are in the Soul of a Child, before, or just at the union with the Body, before it hath received any by *Sensation*. The *Dreams* of sleeping Men, *are*, as I take it, all *made up of the waking Man's* Ideas, though, for the most part, oddly put together. 'Tis strange, if the Soul has *Ideas* of its own, that it derived not from *Sensation* or *Reflection*, (as it must have, if it thought before it received any impressions from the Body) that it should never, in its private

§ 16. *On this Hypothesis the Soul must have* Ideas *not derived from Sensation or Reflexion, of which there is no appearance.* § 17. *If I think when I know it not, no body else can know it.*

---

(10) it] **4–5** | its **1–3** (21) than] **1T.er, 2–5** | then, **1** (22) then] **1–3, 5** (*likewise* **Coste**) | than **4**

thinking, (so private, that the Man himself perceives it not) retain any of them, the very moment it wakes out of them, and then make the Man glad with new discoveries. Who can find it reasonable, that the Soul should, in its retirement, during sleep, have so many hours thoughts, and yet never light on any of those *Ideas* it borrowed not from *Sensation* or *Reflection*, or at least preserve the memory of none, but such, which being occasioned from the Body, must needs be less natural to a Spirit? 'Tis strange, the Soul should never once in a Man's whole life, recal over any of its pure, native Thoughts, and those *Ideas* it had before it borrowed any thing from the Body; never bring into the waking Man's view, any other *Ideas*, but what have a tangue of the Cask, and manifestly derive their Original from that union. If it always thinks, and so had *Ideas* before it was united, or before it received any from the Body, 'tis not to be supposed, but that during sleep, it recollects its native *Ideas*, and during that retirement from communicating with the Body, whilst it thinks by it self, the *Ideas*, it is busied about, should be, sometimes at least, those more natural and congenial ones which it had in it self, underived from the Body or its own Operations about them: which since the waking Man never remembers, we must from this Hypothesis conclude, either that the Soul remembers something that the Man does not; or else that Memory belongs only to such *Ideas*, as are derived from the Body, or the Minds Operations about them.

§ 18. I would be glad also to learn from these Men, who so confidently pronounce, that the humane Soul, or which is all one, that a Man always thinks, how they come to know it; nay, *how they come to know, that they themselves think, when they themselves do not perceive it.* This, I am afraid, is to be sure, without proofs; and to know, without perceiving: 'Tis, I suspect, a confused Notion, taken up to serve an Hypothesis; and none of those clear Truths, that either their own Evidence forces us to admit, or common Experience makes it impudence to deny. For the most that can be said of it, is, That 'tis possible the Soul may always think, but not always

§ 18. *How knows any one that the Soul always thinks? For if it be not a self-evident Proposition, it needs proof.*

---

(3) reasonable] **5** | reason **1–4** (12) and] *add.* **4–5** (17) , sometimes at least,] **1T.er, 2–5** | sometimes, at least **1** (18) which it had] **4–5** | it had **1T.er, 2–3** | had **1** (21–3) either . . . them] **2–5** | that Memory belongs only to *Ideas*, derived from the Body, and the Operations of the Mind about them, or else that the Soul remembers something that the Man does not **1** (28) This,] **1–3, W** | This **4–5** (31) forces] **4–5** | force **1–3**

retain it in memory: And, I say, it is as possible, that the Soul may not always think; and much more probable, that it should sometimes not think, than that it should often think, and that a long while together, and not be conscious to it self the next moment after, that it had thought.

§ 19. To suppose the Soul to think, and the Man not to perceive it, is, as has been said, to make two Persons in one Man: And if one considers well these Men's way of speaking, one should be led into a suspicion, that they do so. For they who tell us, that the Soul always thinks, do never, that I remember, say, That a Man always thinks. Can the Soul think, and not the Man? Or a Man think, and not be conscious of it? This, perhaps, would be suspected of *Jargon* in others. If they say, The Man thinks always, but is not always conscious of it; they may as well say, His Body is extended, without having parts. For 'tis altogether as intelligible to say, that a body is extended without parts, as that any thing *thinks without being conscious of it*, or perceiving, that it does so. They who talk thus, may, with as much reason, if it be necessary to their Hypothesis, say, That a Man is always hungry, but that he does not always feel it: Whereas hunger consists in that very sensation, as thinking consists in being conscious that one thinks. If they say, That a Man is always conscious to himself of thinking; I ask, How they know it? Consciousness is the perception of what passes in a Man's own mind. Can another Man perceive, that I am conscious of any thing, when I perceive it not my self? No Man's Knowledge here, can go beyond his Experience. Wake a Man out of a sound sleep, and ask him, What he was that moment thinking on. If he himself be conscious of nothing he then thought on, he must be a notable Diviner of Thoughts, that can assure him, that he was thinking: May he not with more reason assure him, he was not asleep? This is something beyond Philosophy; and it cannot be less than Revelation, that discovers to another, Thoughts in my mind, when I can find none there my self: And they must needs have a penetrating sight, who can certainly see, that I think, when I cannot perceive

§ 19. *That a Man should be busie in thinking, and yet not retain it the next moment, very improbable.*

---

(6) not to perceive] **W** | not perceive **1–4** | to perceive **5** (8) considers] **4–5** | consider **1–3** should] **5** | shall **1–4** (15) a body] **2–5** | any thing **1** (17) , or] **2–5** | ; without **1** (*l. below* 34) *Marginal summary not in* **Coste,** *which applies the summary for* § *18 also to* § *19.*

it my self, and when I declare, that I do not; and yet can see, that Dogs or Elephants do not think, when they give all the demonstration of it imaginable, except only telling us, that they do so. This some may suspect to be a step beyond the *Rosecrucians*; it seeming easier to make ones self invisible to others, than to make another's thoughts visible to me, which are not visible to himself. But 'tis but defining the Soul to be a substance, that always thinks, and the business is done. If such a definition be of any Authority, I know not what it can serve for, but to make many Men suspect, That they have no Souls at all, since they find a good part of their Lives pass away without thinking. For no Definitions, that I know, no Suppositions of any Sect, are of force enough to destroy constant Experience; and, perhaps, 'tis the affectation of knowing beyond what we perceive, that makes so much useless dispute, and noise, in the World.

§ 20. I see no Reason therefore to believe, that the *Soul thinks before the Senses have furnish'd it with Ideas* to think on; and as those are increased, and retained; so it comes, by Exercise, to improve its Faculty of thinking in the several parts of it, as well as afterwards, by compounding those *Ideas*, and reflecting on its own Operations, it increases its Stock as well as Facility, in remembring, imagining, reasoning, and other modes of thinking.

§ 21. He that will suffer himself, to be informed by Observation and Experience, and not make his own Hypothesis the Rule of Nature, will find few Signs of a Soul accustomed to much thinking in a new born Child, and much fewer of any Reasoning at all. And yet it is hard to imagine, that the rational Soul should think so much, and not reason at all. And he that will consider, that Infants, newly come into the World, spend the greatest part of their time in Sleep, and are seldom awake, but when either Hunger calls for the Teat, or some Pain, (the most importunate of all Sensations) or some other violent Impression on the Body, forces the mind to perceive, and

§§ 20–3. *No* Ideas *but from Sensation or Reflection, evident, if we observe Children.*

---

(1) when I declare, that] **2–5** | declare, That **1** (2) Dogs or Elephants] **2–5** | a Dog, or an Elephant, **1** when] **2–5** | though **1** (3) so.] **Coste₂** *adds in a footnote*: 'Il paroît visiblement par cet endroit, que c'est à Des Cartes et à ses Disciples qu'en veut M. Locke dans tout ce Chapitre.' (8) a] **1–4**; *om.* **5** (32) Impression on the Body] **4–5** | *Idea* **1–3** (*l. below* 32) **Coste** *has separate marginal summaries for §§ 20 and 21, they being, respectively*, 'L'Ame n'a aucune idée que par Sensation ou par Reflexion.' *and* 'C'est ce que nous pouvons observer évidemment dans les Enfans.'

attend to it. He, I say, who considers this, will, perhaps, find Reason to imagine, That a *Fœtus in the Mother's Womb, differs not much from the State of a Vegetable*; but passes the greatest part of its time without Perception or Thought, doing very little, but sleep in a Place, where it needs not seek for Food, and is surrounded with Liquor, always equally soft, and near of the same Temper; where the Eyes have no Light, and the Ears, so shut up, are not very susceptible of Sounds; and where there is little or no variety, or change of Objects, to move the Senses.

§ 22. Follow a *Child* from its Birth, and observe the alterations that time makes, and you shall find, as the Mind by the Senses comes more and more to be furnished with *Ideas*, it comes to be more and more awake; thinks more, the more it has matter to think on. After some time, it begins to know the Objects, which being most familiar with it, have made lasting Impressions. Thus it comes, by degrees, to know the Persons it daily converses with, and distinguish them from Strangers; which are Instances and Effects of its coming to retain and distinguish the *Ideas* the Senses convey to it: And so we may observe, how the Mind, *by degrees*, improves in these, and *advances* to the Exercise of those other Faculties of *Enlarging*, *Compounding*, and *Abstracting* its *Ideas*, and of reasoning about them, and reflecting upon all these, of which, I shall have occasion to speak more hereafter.

§ 23. If it shall be demanded then, *When a Man begins to have any Ideas?* I think, the true Answer is, When he first has any *Sensation*. For since there appear not to be any *Ideas* in the Mind, before the Senses have conveyed any in, I conceive that *Ideas* in the Understanding, are coeval with *Sensation*; which is such an Impression or Motion, made in some part of the Body, as produces some Perception in the Understanding. 'Tis about these Impressions made on our Senses by outward Objects, that the Mind seems first to employ it self in such Operations as we call *Perception*, *Remembring*, *Consideration*, *Reasoning*, etc.

§ 24. In time, the Mind comes to reflect on its own *Operations*, about the *Ideas* got by *Sensation*, and thereby stores it self with a new

§ 24. *The original of all our Knowledge.*

(29–30) produces some Perception] **4–5** | makes it be taken notice of **1–3** (30–33) 'Tis . . . etc.] *add.* **5** (34)–118(2) In . . . *Impressions*] **5** | The *Impressions* then, **1–4** (*l. below* 35) *The original of all our Knowledge.*] **4–5** | *No Ideas but from Sensation or Reflection, evident, if we observe Children.* **2–3**

set of *Ideas*, which I call *Ideas of Reflection*. These are the *Impressions* that are made on our *Senses* by outward Objects, that are extrinsical to the Mind; and *its own Operations*, proceeding from Powers intrinsical and proper to it self, which when reflected on by it self, become also Objects of its contemplation, are, as I have said, *the Original of all Knowledge*. Thus the first Capacity of Humane Intellect, is, That the mind is fitted to receive the Impressions made on it; either, through the *Senses*, by outward Objects; or by its own Operations, when it *reflects* on them. This is the first step a Man makes towards the Discovery of any thing, and the Groundwork, whereon to build all those Notions, which ever he shall have naturally in this World. All those sublime Thoughts, which towre above the Clouds, and reach as high as Heaven it self, take their Rise and Footing here: In all that great Extent wherein the mind wanders, in those remote Speculations, it may seem to be elevated with, it stirs not one jot beyond those *Ideas*, which *Sense* or *Reflection*, have offered for its Contemplation.

§ 25. In this Part, the *Understanding* is meerly *passive*; and whether or no, it will have these Beginnings, and as it were materials of Knowledge, is not in its own Power. For the Objects of our Senses, do, many of them, obtrude their particular *Ideas* upon our minds, whether we will or no: And the Operations of our minds, will not let us be without, at least some obscure Notions of them. No Man, can be wholly ignorant of what he does, when he thinks. These *simple Ideas*, when offered to the mind, *the Understanding can* no more refuse to have, nor alter, when they are imprinted, nor blot them out, and make new ones in it self, than a mirror can refuse, alter, or obliterate the Images or *Ideas*, which, the Objects set before it, do therein produce. As the Bodies that surround us, do diversly affect our Organs, the mind is forced to receive the Impressions; and cannot avoid the Perception of those *Ideas* that are annexed to them.

§ 25. *In the reception of simple* Ideas, *the Understanding is for the most part passive.*

---

(2) *v.* 117(34), n. (3) Mind;] **5** | Mind, **1–4** (3–6) proceeding . . . Thus] **5** | about the [these **1–3**] Impressions, *reflected* on by it [its **1–3**] self, as proper Objects to be contemplated by it, *are*, I conceive, *the Original of all Knowledge*; and **1–4** (13) it] **4–5** | its **1–3** (27) in] **1–4**; *om.* **5** (*l. below* 31) *for the most part*] **4–5** | *most of all* **2–3**

CHAPTER II

Of simple Ideas.

§ 1. THE better to understand the Nature, Manner, and Extent of our Knowledge, one thing is carefully to be observed, concerning the *Ideas* we have; and that is, That *some* of them are *simple*, and *some complex.*

Though the Qualities that affect our Senses, are, in the things themselves, so united and blended, that there is no separation, no distance between them; yet 'tis plain, the *Ideas* they produce in the Mind, enter by the Senses simple and unmixed. For though the Sight and Touch often take in from the same Object, at the same time, different *Ideas*; as a Man sees at once Motion and Colour; the Hand feels Softness and Warmth in the same piece of Wax: Yet the simple *Ideas* thus united in the same Subject, are as perfectly distinct, as those that come in by different Senses. The coldness and hardness, which a Man feels in a piece of *Ice*, being as distinct *Ideas* in the Mind, as the Smell and Whiteness of a Lily; or as the taste of Sugar, and smell of a Rose: And there is nothing can be plainer to a Man, than the clear and distinct Perception he has of those simple *Ideas*; which being each in it self uncompounded, contains in it nothing but *one uniform Appearance*, or Conception in the mind, and is not distinguishable into different *Ideas.*

§ 2. These simple *Ideas*, the Materials of all our Knowledge, are suggested and furnished to the Mind, only by those two ways above mentioned, *viz. Sensation* and *Reflection.* When the Understanding is once stored with these simple *Ideas*, it has the Power to repeat, compare, and unite them even to an almost infinite Variety, and so can make at Pleasure new complex *Ideas.* But it is not in the Power of the most exalted Wit, or enlarged Understanding, by any quickness or

§ 1. *Uncompounded Appearances.* §§ 2, 3. *The mind can neither make nor destroy them.*

---

(11) feels] **1–4** | feel **5** (23) **5** *adds, in a footnote, quotation from Locke's* First Letter to the Bishop of Worcester, *pp. 35, etc.*; *prefaced by* 'Against this, that the Materials of all our Knowledge, are suggested and furnished to the Mind only by Sensation and Reflection, the Bishop of *Worcester* makes Use of the Idea of *Substance* in these Words: *If the Idea of Substance be grounded upon plain and evident Reason, then we must allow an Idea of Substance, which comes not in by Sensation, or Reflection, so we may be certain of something which we have not by those* Ideas. To which our Author answers: ...'

variety of Thought, to *invent or frame one new simple* Idea in the mind, not taken in by the ways before mentioned: nor can any force of the Understanding, *destroy* those that are there. The Dominion of Man, in this little World of his own Understanding, being muchwhat the same, as it is in the great World of visible things; wherein his Power, however managed by Art and Skill, reaches no farther, than to compound and divide the Materials, that are made to his Hand; but can do nothing towards the making the least Particle of new Matter, or destroying one Atome of what is already in Being. The same inability, will every one find in himself, who shall go about to fashion in his Understanding any simple *Idea*, not received in by his Senses, from external Objects; or by reflection from the Operations of his own mind about them. I would have any one try to fancy any Taste, which had never affected his Palate; or frame the *Idea* of a Scent, he had never smelt: And when he can do this, I will also conclude, that a blind Man hath *Ideas* of Colours, and a deaf Man true distinct Notions of Sounds.

§ 3. This is the Reason why, though we cannot believe it impossible to God, to make a Creature with other Organs, and more ways to convey into the Understanding the notice of Corporeal things, than those five, as they are usually counted, which he has given to Man: Yet I think, it is *not possible*, for any one *to imagine* any other *Qualities* in Bodies, howsoever constituted, whereby they can be taken notice of, besides Sounds, Tastes, Smells, visible and tangible Qualities. And had Mankind been made with but four Senses, the Qualities then, which are the Object of the Fifth Sense, had been as far from our Notice, Imagination, and Conception, as now any *belonging to a Sixth, Seventh, or Eighth Sense*, can possibly be: which, whether yet some other Creatures, in some other Parts of this vast, and stupendious Universe, may not have, will be a great Presumption to deny. He that will not set himself proudly at the top of all things; but will consider the Immensity of this Fabrick, and the great variety, that is to be found in this little and inconsiderable part of it, which he has to do with, may be apt to think, that in other Mansions of it, there may be other, and different intelligent Beings, of whose Faculties, he has as little Knowledge or Apprehension, as a Worm shut up in one drawer of a Cabinet, hath of the Senses or Understanding of a Man; Such Variety and Excellency, being suitable to the Wisdom and Power of the Maker.

(12) ; or by reflection] **4–5** |, or **1–3**

I have here followed the common Opinion of Man's having but five Senses; though, perhaps, there may be justly counted more; but either Supposition serves equally to my present purpose.

CHAPTER III

Of Ideas *of one Sense.*

§ 1. THE better to conceive the *Ideas*, we receive from Sensation, it may not be amiss for us to consider them, in reference to the different ways, whereby they make their Approaches to our minds, and make themselves perceivable by us.

First then, There are some, which come into our minds *by one Sense* only.

Secondly, There are others, that convey themselves into the mind *by more Senses than one.*

Thirdly, Others that are had from *Reflection* only.

Fourthly, There are some that make themselves way, and are suggested to the mind *by all the ways of Sensation and Reflection.*

We shall consider them apart under these several Heads.

First, There are *some* Ideas, *which have admittance only through one Sense*, which is peculiarly adapted to receive them. Thus Light and Colours, as white, red, yellow, blue; with their several Degrees or Shades, and Mixtures, as Green, Scarlet, Purple, Sea-green, and the rest, come in only by the Eyes: All kinds of Noises, Sounds, and Tones only by the Ears: The several Tastes and Smells, by the Nose and Palate. And if these Organs, or the Nerves which are the Conduits, to convey them from without to their Audience in the Brain, the mind's Presence-room (as I may so call it) are any of them so disordered, as not to perform their Functions, they have no Postern to be admitted by; no other way to bring themselves into view, and be perceived by the Understanding.

§ 1. *Division of simple* Ideas. § 1 (16). Ideas *of one Sense.*

---

(1) Opinion] **1, 3–5** | Opinions **2** (20) kinds] **1–4** | kind **5** (*l. below* 27) *Division of simple* Ideas.] **4–5** | *As Colours of Seeing, Sounds of Hearing.* **2–3** Ideas *of one Sense.*] **4**; *not in* **2–3, 5**

The most considerable of those, belonging to the Touch, are Heat and Cold, and Solidity; all the rest, consisting almost wholly in the sensible Configuration, as smooth and rough; or else more, or less firm adhesion of the Parts, as hard and soft, tough and brittle, are obvious enough.

§ 2. I think, it will be needless to enumerate all the particular *simple Ideas*, belonging to each Sense. Nor indeed is it possible, if we would, there being a great many *more* of them belonging to most of the Senses, *than we have Names for*. The variety of Smells, which are as many almost, if not more than Species of Bodies in the World, do most of them want Names. *Sweet* and *Stinking* commonly serve our turn for these *Ideas*, which in effect, is little more than to call them pleasing or displeasing; though the smell of a Rose, and Violet, both sweet, are certainly very distinct *Ideas*. Nor are the different Tastes that by our Palates we receive *Ideas* of, much better provided with Names. Sweet, Bitter, Sowr, Harsh, and Salt, are almost all the Epithets we have to denominate that numberless variety of Relishes, which are to be found distinct, not only in almost every sort of Creatures, but in the different Parts of the same Plant, Fruit, or Animal. The same may be said of Colours and Sounds. I shall therefore in the account of simple *Ideas*, I am here giving, content my self to set down only such, as are most material to our present Purpose, or are in themselves less apt to be taken notice of, though they are very frequently the Ingredients of our complex *Ideas*, amongst which, I think, I may well account Solidity; which therefore I shall treat of in the next Chapter.

CHAPTER IV

Of Solidity.

§ 1. THE *Idea* of *Solidity* we receive by our Touch; and it arises from the resistance which we find in Body, to the entrance of any other

§ 2. *Few simple* Ideas *have Names.*
§ 1. *We receive this* Idea *from touch.*

(15) by . . . of] **4–5** | are in Nature **1–3** (16) Bitter, Sowr, Harsh,] **4–5** | Bitter and Sowre, Harsh **1–3** (16–17) the Epithets] *add.* **4–5** (17) that numberless] **4–5** | all the **1–3** (19) , Fruit,] *add.* **4–5** (20) Colours and Sounds] **4–5** | Colour and Sound **1–3** (28) which] *add.* **4–5** (*l. below* 28: §2.) **2–4**; *om.* **5**

Body into the Place it possesses, till it has left it. There is no *Idea*, which we receive more constantly from Sensation, than *Solidity*. Whether we move, or rest, in what Posture soever we are, we always feel something under us, that supports us, and hinders our farther sinking downwards; and the Bodies which we daily handle, make us perceive, that whilst they remain between them, they do by an insurmountable Force, hinder the approach of the parts of our Hands that press them. That which thus hinders the approach of two Bodies, when they are moving one towards another, I call *Solidity*. I will not dispute, whether this acceptation of the Word *solid* be nearer to its Original Signification, than that which Mathematicians use it in: It suffices, that I think, the common Notion of Solidity will allow, if not justifie, this use of it; but if any one think it better to call it *Impenetrability*, he has my Consent. Only I have thought the Term *Solidity*, the more proper to express this *Idea*, not only because of its vulgar use in that Sense; but also, because it carries something more of positive in it, than *Impenetrability*, which is negative, and is, perhaps, more a consequence of *Solidity*, than *Solidity* it self. This of all other, seems the *Idea* most intimately connected with, and essential to Body, so as no where else to be found or imagin'd, but only in matter: and though our Senses take no notice of it, but in masses of matter, of a bulk sufficient to cause a Sensation in us; Yet the Mind, having once got this *Idea* from such grosser sensible Bodies, traces it farther; and considers it, as well as Figure, in the minutest Particle of Matter, that can exist; and finds it inseparably inherent in Body, where-ever, or however modified.

§ 2. This is the *Idea* belongs to Body, whereby we conceive it *to fill space*. The *Idea* of which filling of space, is, That where we imagine any space taken up by a solid Substance, we conceive it so to possess it, that it excludes all other solid Substances; and, will for ever hinder any two other Bodies, that move towards one another in a strait Line, from coming to touch one another, unless it removes from between them in a Line, not parallel to that which they move in. This *Idea* of it the Bodies, which we ordinarily handle, sufficiently furnish us with.

§ 2. *Solidity fills Space.*

---

(5) which] *add.* **4–5** (18) negative,] **5** | negative; **1–4** (21) and] **4–5** | which **1–3** (22) it] *add.* **4–5** (32) removes] **4–5** | remove **1–3** (33) which] *add.* **4–5** (34) , which] *add.* **4–5** (',' *om.* **5**)

§ 3. This Resistance, whereby it keeps other Bodies out of the space which it possesses, is so great, That no force, how great soever, can surmount it. All the Bodies in the World, pressing a drop of Water on all sides, will never be able to overcome the Resistance, which it will make, as soft as it is, to their approaching one another, till it be removed out of their way: whereby our *Idea of Solidity* is *distinguished* both *from pure space*, which is capable neither of Resistance nor Motion; and from the ordinary *Idea of Hardness*. For a Man may conceive two Bodies at a distance, so as they may approach one another, without touching or displacing any solid thing, till their Superficies come to meet: whereby, I think, we have the clear *Idea* of Space without *Solidity*. For (not to go so far as annihilation of any particular Body) I ask, Whether a Man cannot have the *Idea* of the motion of one single Body alone, without any other succeeding immediately into its Place? I think, 'tis evident he can: the *Idea* of Motion in one Body, no more including the *Idea* of Motion in another, than the *Idea* of a square Figure in one Body includes the *Idea* of a square Figure in another. I do not ask, Whether Bodies do so exist, that the motion of one Body cannot really be without the motion of another. To determine this either way, is to beg the Question for, or against a *Vacuum*. But my Question is, Whether one cannot have the *Idea* of one Body moved, whilst others are at rest? And, I think, this no one will deny: If so, then the Place it deserted, gives us the *Idea* of pure Space without Solidity, whereinto another Body may enter, without either Resistance or Protrusion of any thing. When the Sucker in a Pump is drawn, the space it filled in the Tube is certainly the same, whether any other Body follows the motion of the Sucker or no: nor does it imply a contradiction, That upon the motion of one Body, another, that is only contiguous to it, should not follow it. The necessity of such a motion, is built only on the Supposition, That the World is full; but not on the distinct *Ideas* of Space and Solidity: which are as different, as Resistance and not Resistance, Protrusion and not Protrusion. And that Men have *Ideas* of Space without Body, their very Disputes about a *Vacuum* plainly demonstrate, as is shewed in another Place.

§ 3. *Distinct from Space.*

(2) which] *add.* **4–5** (4–5) , which] *add.* **4–5** (',' *om.* **5**) (8) from] *add.* **4–5** (15) Place?] **4–5** | Place; which, **2–3** | Place? which, **1** (36) Place.] **1–4** | Place. As **5**

§ 4. *Solidity* is hereby also *differenced from Hardness*, in that Solidity consists in repletion, and so an utter Exclusion of other Bodies out of the space it possesses; but Hardness, in a firm Cohesion of the parts of Matter, making up masses of a sensible bulk, so that the whole does not easily change its Figure. And indeed, Hard and Soft are Names that we give to things, only in relation to the Constitutions of our own Bodies; that being generally call'd hard by us, which will put us to Pain, sooner than change Figure by the pressure of any part of our Bodies; and that, on the contrary, soft, which changes the Situation of its parts upon an easie, and unpainful touch.

But this Difficulty of changing the Situation of the sensible parts amongst themselves, or of the Figure of the whole, gives no more Solidity to the hardest Body in the World, than to the softest; nor is an Adamant one jot more solid than Water. For though the two flat sides of two pieces of Marble, will more easily approach each other, between which there is nothing but Water or Air, than if there be a Diamond between them: yet it is not, that the parts of the Diamond are more solid than those of Water, or resist more; but because the parts of Water, being more easily separable from each other, they will by a side-motion be more easily removed, and give way to the approach of the two pieces of Marble: But if they could be kept from making Place, by that side-motion, they would eternally hinder the approach of these two pieces of Marble, as much as the Diamond; and 'twould be as impossible by any force, to surmount their Resistance, as to surmount the Resistance of the parts of a Diamond. The softest Body in the World will as invincibly resist the coming together of any two other Bodies, if it be not put out of the way, but remain between them, as the hardest, that can be found, or imagined. He that shall fill a yielding soft Body well with Air or Water, will quickly find its Resistance: And he that thinks, that nothing but Bodies, that are hard, can keep his Hands from approaching one another, may be pleased to make a trial, with the Air inclosed in a Football. The Experiment, I have been told was made at *Florence*, with a hollow Globe of Gold fill'd with

§ 4. *From Hardness.*

---

(6) Names . . . relation] **4–5** | , as apprehended by us, only relative Terms, **1–3** (7) own] *add.* **4–5** (18) a Diamond] **2–5** | an Adamant **1** (19) Diamond] **2–5** | Adamant **1** (33) a trial] **2–5** | an Experiment **1** (34)–126(8) The . . . it.] *add.* **2–5**

Water, and exactly closed, farther shews the solidity of so soft a body as Water. For the golden Globe thus filled, being put into a Press, which was driven by the extreme force of skrews, the water made it self way through the pores of that very close metal, and finding no room for a nearer approach of its Particles within, got to the outside, where it rose like a dew, and so fell in drops, before the sides of the Globe could be made to yield to the violent compression of the Engine, that squeezed it.

§ 5. By this *Idea* of Solidity, is the Extension of Body distinguished from the Extension of Space. The Extension of Body being nothing, but the cohesion or continuity of solid, separable, moveable Parts; and the Extension of Space, the continuity of unsolid, inseparable, and immoveable Parts. *Upon the Solidity of Bodies* also *depends their mutual Impulse, Resistance, and Protrusion.* Of pure Space then, and Solidity, there are several (amongst which, I confess my self one) who persuade themselves, they have clear and distinct *Ideas*; and that they can think on Space, without any thing in it, that resists, or is protruded by Body. This is the *Idea* of pure Space, which they think they have as clear, as any *Idea* they can have of the Extension of Body: the *Idea* of the distance, between the opposite Parts of a concave Superficies, being equally as clear, without, as with the *Idea* of any solid Parts between: and on the other side, they persuade themselves, That they have, distinct from that of pure Space, the *Idea* of something that fills Space, that can be protruded by the impulse of other Bodies, or resist their Motion. If there be others, that have not these two *Ideas* distinct but confound them, and make but one of them, I know not, how Men, who have the same *Idea*, under different Names, or different *Ideas*, under the same Name, can, in that case, talk with one another, any more than a Man, who not being blind, or deaf, has distinct *Ideas* of the Colour of Scarlet, and the sound of a Trumpet, could discourse concerning Scarlet-Colour with the blind Man, I mention in another Place, who fancied, that the *Idea* of Scarlet was like the sound of a Trumpet.

§ 6. If any one asks me, *What this Solidity is*, I send him to his Senses to inform him: Let him put a Flint, or a Foot-ball between

§ 5. *On Solidity depends Impulse, Resistance, and Protrusion.* § 6. *What it is.*

---

(3) by] **5** | with **2–4** (8) *v.* 125(34), n. (14) *Impulse*] *edit.* | *impulse* **1–5** (18–20) Body . . . Body:] **4–5** | Body; whereof they think they have as clear an *Idea*, as of the Extension of Body, **1–3** (22–3) they . . . Space,] **4–5** | That they have **1–3** (34) asks] **4–5** | ask **1–3** (*l. below* 35: § 5.) *Marginal summary not in* **Coste** *here, but only in his Table of Contents.*

his Hands; and then endeavour to join them, and he will know. If he thinks this not a sufficient Explication of Solidity, what it is, and wherein it consists; I promise to tell him, what it is, and wherein it consists, when he tells me what thinking is, or wherein it consists; or explain to me, what Extension or Motion is, which, perhaps, seems much easier. The simple *Ideas* we have are such, as experience teaches them us; but if beyond that, we endeavour, by Words, to make them clearer in the Mind, we shall succeed no better, than if we went about to clear up the Darkness of a blind Man's mind, by talking; and to discourse into him the *Ideas* of Light and Colours. The Reason of this, I shall shew, in another Place.

CHAPTER V

Of simple Ideas *of divers Senses.*

THE *Ideas* we get by more than one Sense, are of *Space*, or *Extension*, *Figure*, *Rest*, and *Motion*: For these make perceivable impressions, both on the Eyes and Touch; and we can receive and convey into our Minds the *Ideas* of the Extension, Figure, Motion, and Rest of Bodies, both by seeing and feeling. But having occasion to speak more at large of these in another place, I here only enumerate them.

CHAPTER VI

Of simple Ideas *of Reflection.*

§ 1. THE Mind receiving the *Ideas*, mentioned in the foregoing Chapters, from without, when it turns its view inward upon it self, and observes its own Actions about those *Ideas* it has, takes from thence other *Ideas*, which are as capable to be the Objects of its Contemplation, as any of those it received from foreign things.

§ 1. *Are the Operations of the Mind about its other* Ideas.

---

(6) we have are] **4–5** | are **3** | we have **1–2** (15) [*2nd*] the] **1–4** | our **5** (19) Chapters] **2er–5** | Chapter **1–2** [*2nd*] it] **4–5** | its **1–3** (22) as] **1er–5** | as of **1**

§ 2. The two great and principal Actions of the Mind, which are most frequently considered, and which are so frequent, that every one that pleases, may take notice of 'em in himself, are these two:

Perception, or *Thinking*, and
Volition, or *Willing*.

The Power of Thinking is called the *Understanding*, and the Power of Volition is called the *Will*, and these two Powers or Abilities in the Mind are denominated *Faculties*. Of some of the Modes of these simple *Ideas* of Reflection, such as are *Remembrance*, *Discerning*, *Reasoning*, *Judging*, *Knowledge*, *Faith*, etc. I shall have occasion to speak hereafter.

CHAPTER VII

Of simple Ideas *of both Sensation and Reflection.*

§ 1. THERE be other simple *Ideas*, which convey themselves into the Mind, by all the ways of Sensation and Reflection, *viz.*

Pleasure, or *Delight*, and its opposite.
Pain, or *Uneasiness*.
Power.
Existence.
Unity.

§ 2. *Delight*, or *Uneasiness*, one or other of them join themselves to almost all our *Ideas*, both of Sensation and Reflection: And there is scarce any affection of our Senses from without, any retired thought of our Mind within, which is not able to produce in us *pleasure* or *pain*. By *Pleasure* and *Pain*, I would be understood to signifie, whatsoever delights or molests us; whether it arises from the thoughts of our Minds, or any thing operating on our Bodies. For whether we call it Satisfaction, Delight, Pleasure, Happiness, *etc.* on the one side; or Uneasiness, Trouble, Pain, Torment, Anguish, Misery, *etc.*

§ 2. *The* Idea *of Perception, and* Idea *of Willing, we have from Reflection.*
§§ 1–6. *Pleasure and Pain.*

---

(3) 'em] *add.* **4–5** (6–8) The . . . *Faculties.*] **2–5** | The power in the Mind of producing these Actions we denominate Faculties, and are called the *Understanding*, and the *Will*. **1**

on the other, they are still but different degrees of the same thing, and belong to the *Ideas* of *Pleasure* and *Pain*, Delight or Uneasiness; which are the Names I shall most commonly use for those two sorts of *Ideas*.

§ 3. The infinite Wise Author of our being, having given us the power over several parts of our Bodies, to move or keep them at rest, as we think fit; and also by the motion of them, to move our selves, and other contiguous Bodies, in which consists all the Actions of our Body: Having also given a power to our Minds, in several Instances, to chuse, amongst its *Ideas*, which it will think on, and to pursue the enquiry of this or that Subject with consideration and attention, to excite us to these Actions of thinking and motion, that we are capable of, has been pleased to join to several Thoughts, and several Sensations, a *perception of Delight*. If this were wholly separated from all our outward Sensations, and inward Thoughts, we should have no reason to preferr one Thought or Action, to another; Negligence, to Attention; or Motion, to Rest. And so we should neither stir our Bodies, nor employ our Minds; but let our Thoughts (if I may so call it) run a drift, without any direction or design; and suffer the *Ideas* of our Minds, like unregarded shadows, to make their appearances there, as it happen'd, without attending to them. In which state Man, however furnished with the Faculties of Understanding and Will, would be a very idle unactive Creature, and pass his time only in a lazy lethargick Dream. It has therefore pleased our Wise Creator, to annex to several Objects, and to the *Ideas* which we receive from them, as also to several of our Thoughts, a concomitant pleasure, and that in several Objects, to several degrees, that those Faculties which he had endowed us with, might not remain wholly idle, and unemploy'd by us.

§ 4. *Pain* has the same efficacy and use to set us on work, that Pleasure has, we being as ready to employ our Faculties to avoid that, as to pursue this: Only this is worth our consideration, That *Pain is often produced by the same Objects and* Ideas, *that produce Pleasure in us*. This their near Conjunction, which makes us often feel pain in the sensations where we expected pleasure, gives us new occasion of admiring the Wisdom and Goodness of our Maker, who

(5) infinite] **4–5** | infinitely **1–3** (8) other] **1–4** | our **5** (9) Having] **2–5** | He having **1** (13) has] **2–5** | he has **1** (14) If this] **2–5** | This if it **1** were] **1–4** | where **5** (21) their] **1, 4–5** | there **2–3** (25–6) to the *Ideas* which] **4–5** | the *Ideas* **1–3** (28) which] *add.* **4–5** (32) [*1st*] this] **2–5** | the other **1** (33) *Pain is*] **4–5** | *Pain* is **2–3** | it is **1**

designing the preservation of our Being, has annexed Pain to the application of many things to our Bodies, to warn us of the harm that they will do; and as advices to withdraw from them. But he, not designing our preservation barely, but the preservation of every part and organ in its perfection, hath, in many cases, annexed pain to those very *Ideas*, which delight us. Thus Heat, that is very agreeable to us in one degree, by a little greater increase of it, proves no ordinary torment: and the most pleasant of all sensible Objects, Light it self, if there be too much of it, if increased beyond a due proportion to our Eyes, causes a very painful sensation. Which is wisely and favourably so ordered by Nature, that when any Object does, by the vehemency of its operation, disorder the instruments of Sensation, whose Structures cannot but be very nice and delicate, we might by the pain, be warned to withdraw, before the Organ be quite put out of order, and so be unfitted for its proper Functions for the future. The consideration of those Objects that produce it, may well perswade us, That this is the end or use of pain. For though great light be insufferable to our Eyes, yet the highest degree of darkness does not at all disease them: because that causing no disorderly motion in it, leaves that curious Organ unharm'd, in its natural state. But yet excess of Cold, as well as Heat, pains us: because it is equally destructive to that temper, which is necessary to the preservation of life, and the exercise of the several functions of the Body, and which consists in a moderate degree of warmth; or, if you please, a motion of the insensible parts of our Bodies, confin'd within certain bounds.

§ 5. Beyond all this, we may find another reason *why* God hath scattered up and down *several degrees of Pleasure and Pain, in all the things that environ and affect us*; and blended them together, in almost all that our Thoughts and Senses have to do with; that we finding imperfection, dissatisfaction, and want of complete happiness, in all the Enjoyments which the Creatures can afford us, might be led to seek it in the enjoyment of him, *with whom there is fullness of joy, and at whose right hand are pleasures for evermore.**

§ 6. Though what I have here said, may not, perhaps, make the *Ideas of Pleasure and Pain* clearer to us, than our own Experience does,

(3) that] *add.* **4–5** (12) vehemency] **4–5** | vehemence **1–3** (20) [*1st*] that] **1–4** | the **5** (24) and] *add.* **4–5** (31) complete] **2–3** | compleate **4** | compleat **1, 5** (32) which] **4–5** | of **1**. (*Neither in* **2–3**)

* Ps. 16: 11.

which is the only way that we are capable of having them; yet the consideration of the Reason, why they are annexed to so many other *Ideas*, serving to give us due sentiments of the Wisdom and Goodness of the Soveraign Disposer of all Things, may not be unsuitable to the main end of these enquiries: The knowledge and veneration of Him, being the chief end of all our Thoughts, and the proper business of all Understandings.

§ 7. *Existence* and *Unity*, are two other *Ideas*, that are suggested to the Understanding, by every Object without, and every *Idea* within. When *Ideas* are in our Minds, we consider them as being actually there, as well as we consider things to be actually without us; which is, that they exist, or have *Existence*: And whatever we can consider as one thing, whether a real Being, or *Idea*, suggests to the Understanding, the *Idea* of *Unity*.

§ 8. *Power* also is another of those simple *Ideas*, which we receive from *Sensation and Reflection*. For observing in our selves, that we can, at pleasure, move several parts of our Bodies, which were at rest; the effects also, that natural Bodies are able to produce in one another, occurring every moment to our Senses, we both these ways get the *Idea* of *Power*.

§ 9. Besides these, there is another *Idea*, which though suggested by our Senses, yet is more constantly offered us, by what passes in our own Minds; and that is the *Idea* of *Succession*. For if we look immediately into our selves, and reflect on what is observable there, we shall find our *Ideas* always, whilst we are awake, or have any thought, passing in train, one going, and another coming, without intermission.

§ 10. These, if they are not all, are at least (as I think) the most considerable of those *simple Ideas* which the Mind has, and out of which is made all its other knowledge; all which it receives only by the two forementioned ways of *Sensation* and *Reflection*.

Nor let any one think these too narrow bounds for the capacious Mind of Man to expatiate in, which takes its flight farther than the Stars, and cannot be confined by the limits of the World; that extends its thoughts often, even beyond the utmost expansion of

§ 7. *Existence and Unity.* § 8. *Power.* § 9. *Succession.* § 10. *Simple* Ideas *the Materials of all our Knowledge.*

---

(16) selves,] **5** | selves, that we do, and can think; and **1–4** (23) look] **5** | will look **1–4** (26) thought,] **1T.er, 2–4** | thought **1, 5** (30) is] **4–5** | are **1–3** (35) often,] **2–5** | often **1**

Matter, and makes excursions into that incomprehensible *Inane*. I grant all this, but desire any one to assign any *simple Idea*, which is not *received from* one of *those Inlets* before-mentioned, or any *complex Idea* not *made out of those simple ones*. Nor will it be so strange, to think these few simple *Ideas* sufficient to employ the quickest Thought, or largest Capacity; and to furnish the Materials of all that various Knowledge, and more various Fancies and Opinions of all Mankind, if we consider how many Words may be made out of the various composition of 24 Letters; or if going one step farther, we will but reflect on the variety of combinations may be made, with barely one of the above-mentioned *Ideas*, *viz.* Number, whose stock is inexhaustible, and truly infinite: And what a large and immense field, doth Extension alone afford the Mathematicians?

CHAPTER VIII

Some farther Considerations concerning our simple Ideas.

§ 1. CONCERNING the simple *Ideas* of Sensation 'tis to be considered, That whatsoever is so constituted in Nature, as to be able, by affecting our Senses, to cause any perception in the Mind, doth thereby produce in the Understanding a simple *Idea*; which, whatever be the external cause of it, when it comes to be taken notice of, by our discerning Faculty, it is by the Mind looked on and considered there, to be a real *positive Idea* in the Understanding, as much as any other whatsoever; though, perhaps, the cause of it be but a privation in the subject.

§ 2. Thus the *Idea* of Heat and Cold, Light and Darkness, White and Black, Motion and Rest, are equally clear and *positive Ideas* in the Mind; though, perhaps, some of *the causes* which produce them, are barely *privations* in those Subjects, from whence our Senses derive those *Ideas*. These the Understanding, in its view of them, considers all as distinct positive *Ideas*, without taking notice of the Causes that produce them: which is an enquiry not belonging to the *Idea*, as it is in the Understanding; but to the nature of the things

§§ 1–6. *Positive* Ideas *from privative Causes.*

(2–3) is not *received*] **4–5** | it *received not* **1–3** (11) the above-mentioned] **2–5** | these **1** (13) Extension] **1er–5** | Excursion **1** (17) thereby] **1–2, 4–5** | hereby **3**

existing without us. These are two very different things, and carefully to be distinguished; it being one thing to perceive, and know the *Idea* of White or Black, and quite another to examine what kind of particles they must be, and how ranged in the Superficies, to make any Object appear White or Black.

§ 3. A Painter or Dyer, who never enquired into their causes, hath the *Ideas* of White and Black, and other Colours, as clearly, perfectly, and distinctly in his Understanding, and perhaps more distinctly, than the Philosopher, who hath busied himself in considering their Natures, and thinks he knows how far either of them is in its cause positive or privative; and the *Idea of Black* is no less *positive* in his Mind, than that of White, *however the cause* of that Colour in the external Object, may *be only a privation.*

§ 4. If it were the design of my present Undertaking, to enquire into the natural Causes and manner of Perception, I should offer this as a reason *why a privative cause might*, in some cases at least, *produce a positive Idea*, *viz.* That all Sensation being produced in us, only by different degrees and modes of Motion in our animal Spirits, variously agitated by external Objects, the abatement of any former motion, must as necessarily produce a new sensation, as the variation or increase of it; and so introduce a new *Idea*, which depends only on a different motion of the animal Spirits in that Organ.

§ 5. But whether this be so, or no, I will not here determine, but appeal to every one's own Experience, whether the shadow of a Man, though it consists of nothing but the absence of Light (and the more the absence of Light is, the more discernible is the shadow) does not, when a Man looks on it, cause as clear and positive an *Idea* in his mind, as a Man himself, though covered over with clear Sun-shine? And the Picture of a Shadow, is a positive thing. Indeed, we have *negative Names*, which stand not directly for positive *Ideas*, but for their absence, such as *Insipid*, *silence*, *Nihil*, etc. which Words denote positive *Ideas*; *v.g. Tast*, *Sound*, *Being*, with a signification of their absence.

§ 6. And thus one may truly be said to see Darkness. For supposing a hole perfectly dark, from whence no light is reflected,

(25) every one's] **1–3, 5** | ever ones **4** (30) And] **1–3, 5** | and **4** thing.] **1–3, 4er, 5** | thing **4** (33–4) which . . . absence.] **4–5** | to which there be no positive *Ideas*; but they consist wholly in negation of some certain *Ideas*, as *Silence*, *Invisible*; but these *signifie* not any *Ideas* in the Mind, but their *absence.* **1–3**

'tis certain one may see the Figure of it, or it may be Painted; or whether the Ink, I write with, makes any other *Idea*, is a Question. The privative causes I have here assigned of positive *Ideas*, are according to the common Opinion; but in truth it will be hard to determine, whether there be really any *Ideas* from a privative cause, till it be determined, *Whether Rest be any more a privation than Motion.*

§ 7. To discover the nature of our *Ideas* the better, and to discourse of them intelligibly, it will be convenient to distinguish them, as they are *Ideas* or Perceptions in our Minds; and as they are modifications of matter in the Bodies that cause such Perceptions in us: that so we *may not* think (as perhaps usually is done) that they are exactly the Images and *Resemblances* of something inherent in the subject; most of those of Sensation being in the Mind no more the likeness of something existing without us, than the Names, that stand for them, are the likeness of our *Ideas*, which yet upon hearing, they are apt to excite in us.

§ 8. Whatsoever the Mind perceives in it self, or is the immediate object of Perception, Thought, or Understanding, that I call *Idea*; and the Power to produce any *Idea* in our mind, I call *Quality* of the Subject wherein that power is. Thus a Snow-ball having the power to produce in us the *Ideas* of *White*, *Cold*, and *Round*, the Powers to produce those *Ideas* in us, as they are in the Snow-ball, I call *Qualities*; and as they are Sensations, or Perceptions, in our Understandings, I call them *Ideas*: which *Ideas*, if I speak of sometimes, as in the things themselves, I would be understood to mean those Qualities in the Objects which produce them in us.

§ 9. Qualities thus considered in Bodies are, First such as are utterly inseparable from the Body, in what estate soever it be; such as in all the alterations and changes it suffers, all the force can be used upon it, it constantly keeps; and such as Sense constantly finds in every particle of Matter, which has bulk enough to be

§§ 7, 8. Ideas *in the Mind, Qualities in Bodies.* §§ 9, 10. *Primary and Secondary Qualities.*

(1) [*2nd*] or] **4–5** | and **1–3** (2) makes] **4–5** | make **1–3** (3) privative] **1–3, 5er** (*likewise* **Coste**) | private **4–5** (10) modifications of matter] *add.* **2–5** (15) them,] **1–3** | them **4–5** (27)–135(14) Qualities . . . produce] **4–5** | Concerning these *Qualities*, we may, I think, observe these *primary* ones in Bodies, that produce **1–3** (27) **Coste** 'Cela posé, l'on doit distinguer dans les Corps deux sortes de Qualitez.' (28) inseparable] **5** (*and v. next note*) | inseperable **4** (28)–135(13) such . . . certain Number.] *This passage preceded by* 'These, which I call *original* or *primary Qualities* of Body, are wholly inseparable from it; and' *constitutes* § *10 in* **1–3**. (*l. below* 31: §§ 9, 10.) *and Secondary*] **2–3** (*likewise* **Coste**); *om.* **4–5**, *but in their Table of Contents.*

perceived, and the Mind finds inseparable from every particle of Matter, though less than to make it self singly be perceived by our Senses. *v.g.* Take a grain of Wheat, divide it into two parts, each part has still *Solidity*, *Extension*, *Figure*, and *Mobility*; divide it again, and it retains still the same qualities; and so divide it on, till the parts become insensible, they must retain still each of them all those qualities. For division (which is all that a Mill, or Pestel, or any other Body, does upon another, in reducing it to insensible parts) can never take away either Solidity, Extension, Figure, or Mobility from any Body, but only makes two, or more distinct separate masses of Matter, of that which was but one before, all which distinct masses, reckon'd as so many distinct Bodies, after division make a certain Number. These I call *original* or *primary Qualities* of Body, which I think we may observe to produce simple *Ideas* in us, *viz.* Solidity, Extension, Figure, Motion, or Rest, and Number.

§ 10. 2*dly*, Such *Qualities*, which in truth are nothing in the Objects themselves, but Powers to produce various Sensations in us by their *primary Qualities*, *i.e.* by the Bulk, Figure, Texture, and Motion of their insensible parts, as Colours, Sounds, Tasts, *etc.* These I call *secondary Qualities*. To these might be added a third sort which are allowed to be barely Powers though they are as much real Qualities in the Subject, as those which I to comply with the common way of speaking call *Qualities*, but for distinction *secondary Qualities*. For the power in Fire to produce a new Colour, or consistency in Wax or Clay by its primary Qualities, is as much a quality in Fire, as the power it has to produce in me a new *Idea* or Sensation of warmth or burning, which I felt not before, by the same primary Qualities, *viz.* The Bulk, Texture, and Motion of its insensible parts.

§ 11. The next thing to be consider'd, is how *Bodies* produce

§§ 11, 12. *How primary Qualities produce their* Ideas.

(10–13) two . . . a] **2–5** | two distinct Bodies, or more, of one, which altogether after division have their **1** (13, 14) *v.* 134(27, 28), nn. (15–16) Figure . . . Number] **4–5** | Motion or Rest, Number and Figure **1–3**. (**Coste** 'la figure, le nombre, le mouvement ou le repos') (15) Rest,] **1–3, 5** | Rest **4** (17–30) 2*dly* . . . parts.] **4–5** (17) 2*dly*,] **5** | 2*dly*. **4** (29) Texture,] *edit.* | Texture/ **4–5** (31)–136(2) produce . . . in.] **4–5** | *operate* one upon another, and that is manifestly *by impulse*, and nothing else. It being impossible to conceive, that Body should operate on what it does not touch, (which is all one as to imagine it can operate where it is not) or when it does touch, operate any other [other *om.* **2–3**] way than by [without **2–3** | than by **1**] Motion. **1–3** (**Coste** *like* **2–3**)

Ideas in us, and that is manifestly *by impulse*, the only way which we can conceive Bodies operate in.

§ 12. If then external Objects be not united to our Minds, when they produce *Ideas* in it; and yet we perceive *these original Qualities* in such of them as singly fall under our Senses, 'tis evident, that some motion must be thence continued by our Nerves, or animal Spirits, by some parts of our Bodies, to the Brains or the seat of Sensation, there *to produce in our Minds the particular* Ideas *we have of them.* And since the Extension, Figure, Number, and Motion of Bodies of an observable bigness, may be perceived at a distance *by* the sight, 'tis evident some singly imperceptible Bodies must come from them to the Eyes, and thereby convey to the Brain some *Motion*, which produces these *Ideas*, which we have of them in us.

§ 13. After the same manner, that the *Ideas* of these original Qualities are produced in us, we may conceive, that the *Ideas of secondary Qualities* are also *produced*, viz. *by the operation of insensible particles on our Senses.* For it being manifest, that there are Bodies, and good store of Bodies, each whereof is so small, that we cannot, by any of our Senses, discover either their bulk, figure, or motion, as is evident in the Particles of the Air and Water, and other extremely smaller than those, perhaps, as much smaller than the Particles of Air, or Water, as the Particles of Air or Water, are smaller than Pease or Hail-stones. Let us suppose at present, that the different Motions and Figures, Bulk, and Number of such Particles, affecting the several Organs of our Senses, produce in us those different Sensations, which we have from the Colours and Smells of Bodies, *v.g.* that a Violet, by the impulse of such insensible particles of matter of peculiar figures, and bulks, and in different degrees and modifications of their Motions, causes the *Ideas* of the blue Colour, and sweet Scent of that Flower to be produced in our Minds. It being no more impossible, to conceive, that God should annex such *Ideas* to such Motions, with which they have no similitude; than that he should annex the *Idea* of Pain to the motion of a piece of

§§ 13, 14. *How Secondary.*

(2) *v.* 135(31), n. (3) then] **4–5** | then Bodies cannot operate at a distance; if **1–3** (*likewise* **Coste**) (7) Brains or] **2–5** (Brains, **5**) | Brains, **1** (13) , which] *add.* **4–5** (18) is] **1–4** | are **5** (19) Senses,] **1–3** | Senses **4–5** (21) [*2nd*] smaller] **4–5** | less **1–3** (24) Bulk,] **1–3** | Bulk/ **4–5** (27–30) that . . . be] **2–5** | a Violet, by which impulse of those insensible Particles of Matter of different figures and bulks, and in a different Degree and Modification, we may have the *Ideas* of the blue Colour, and sweet Scent of a Violet **1** (31) impossible] **1er–5** | conceived impossible **1**

Steel dividing our Flesh, with which that *Idea* hath no resemblance.

§ 14. What I have said concerning *Colours* and *Smells*, may be understood also of *Tastes* and *Sounds*, *and other the like sensible Qualities*; which, whatever reality we, by mistake, attribute to them, are in truth nothing in the Objects themselves, but Powers to produce various Sensations in us, and *depend on those primary Qualities, viz.* Bulk, Figure, Texture, and Motion of parts; as I have said.

§ 15. From whence I think it is easie to draw this Observation, That the *Ideas of primary Qualities* of Bodies, *are Resemblances* of them, and their Patterns do really exist in the Bodies themselves; but the *Ideas, produced* in us *by* these *Secondary Qualities, have no resemblance* of them at all. There is nothing like our *Ideas*, existing in the Bodies themselves. They are in the Bodies, we denominate from them, only a Power to produce those Sensations in us: And what is Sweet, Blue, or Warm in *Idea*, is but the certain Bulk, Figure, and Motion of the insensible Parts in the Bodies themselves, which we call so.

§ 16. *Flame* is denominated *Hot* and *Light*; *Snow White* and *Cold*; and *Manna White* and *Sweet*, from the *Ideas* they produce in us. Which Qualities are commonly thought to be the same in those Bodies, that those *Ideas* are in us, the one the perfect resemblance of the other, as they are in a Mirror; and it would by most Men be judged very extravagant, if one should say otherwise. And yet he, that will consider, that *the same Fire*, that at one distance *produces* in us the Sensation of *Warmth*, does at a nearer approach, produce in us the far different Sensation of *Pain*, ought to bethink himself, what Reason he has to say, That his *Idea* of *Warmth*, which was produced in him by the Fire, is actually *in the Fire*; and his *Idea* of *Pain*, which the same Fire produced in him the same way, is *not* in the *Fire*. Why is Whiteness and Coldness in Snow, and Pain not, when it produces the one and the other *Idea* in us; and can do neither, but by the Bulk, Figure, Number, and Motion of its solid Parts?

§ 17. The particular *Bulk, Number, Figure, and Motion of the parts of Fire, or Snow, are really in them*, whether any ones Senses perceive them or no: and therefore they may be called *real Qualities*, because

§§ 15–22. Ideas *of primary Qualities are resemblances*; *of secondary, not.*

---

(7) *depend*] **1–3** | depend **4–5** (8) Texture,] **1–3** | Texture **4–5** as I have said] **4–5** | and therefore *I call* them *Secundary Qualities* **1–3** (17) Parts . . . we] **2–5** (',' *not in* **2–3**) | Parts, in the Bodies themselves we **1** (28) Fire] **1–3, 5** | Fier **4** (35) because] *add.* **4–5**

they really exist in those Bodies. But *Light*, *Heat*, *Whiteness*, or *Coldness*, *are no more really in them*, *than Sickness or Pain is in* Manna. Take away the Sensation of them; let not the Eyes see Light, or Colours, nor the Ears hear Sounds; let the Palate not Taste, nor the Nose Smell, and all Colours, Tastes, Odors, and Sounds, as they are such particular *Ideas*, vanish and cease, and are reduced to their Causes, *i.e.* Bulk, Figure, and Motion of Parts.

§ 18. A piece of *Manna* of a sensible Bulk, is able to produce in us the *Idea* of a round or square Figure; and, by being removed from one place to another, the *Idea* of Motion. This *Idea* of Motion represents it, as it really is in the *Manna* moving: A Circle or Square are the same, whether in *Idea* or Existence; in the Mind, or in the *Manna*: And this, both *Motion and Figure are really in the Manna*, whether we take notice of them or no: This every Body is ready to agree to. Besides, *Manna* by the Bulk, Figure, Texture, and Motion of its Parts, has a Power to produce the Sensations of Sickness, and sometimes of acute Pains, or Gripings in us. That these *Ideas* of *Sickness and Pain are not in the* Manna, but Effects of its Operations on us, and are no where when we feel them not: This also every one readily agrees to. And yet Men are hardly to be brought to think, that *Sweetness and Whiteness are not really in Manna*; which are but the effects of the operations of *Manna*, by the motion, size, and figure of its Particles on the Eyes and Palate; as the Pain and Sickness caused by *Manna*, are confessedly nothing, but the effects of its operations on the Stomach and Guts, by the size, motion, and figure of its insensible parts; (for by nothing else can a Body operate, as has been proved:) As if it could not operate on the Eyes and Palate, and thereby produce in the Mind particular distinct *Ideas*, which in it self it has not, as well as we allow it can operate on the Guts and Stomach, and thereby produce distinct *Ideas*, which in it self it has not. These *Ideas* being all effects of the operations of *Manna*, on several parts of our Bodies, by the size, figure, number, and motion of its parts, why those produced by the Eyes and Palate, should rather be thought to be really in the *Manna*, than those produced by the Stomach and Guts; or why the Pain and Sickness, *Ideas* that are the effects of *Manna*, should be thought to be no-where, when they are not felt; and yet the Sweetness and Whiteness, effects of the same *Manna* on other parts of the Body, by ways equally as

(9) *Idea*] **2–5** | *Ideas* **1** (22) size] **Coste** 'la situation' (25) size] **Coste** 'la contexture' (32) size] **Coste** 'la situation' (38) equally] **2–5** | equal **1**

unknown, should be thought to exist in the *Manna*, when they are not seen nor tasted, would need some Reason to explain.

§ 19. Let us consider the red and white colours in *Porphyre*: Hinder light but from striking on it, and its Colours Vanish; it no longer produces any such *Ideas* in us: Upon the return of Light, it produces these appearances on us again. Can any one think any real alterations are made in the *Porphyre*, by the presence or absence of Light; and that those *Ideas* of whiteness and redness, are really in *Porphyre* in the light, when 'tis plain *it has no colour in the dark*? It has, indeed, such a Configuration of Particles, both Night and Day, as are apt by the Rays of Light rebounding from some parts of that hard Stone, to produce in us the *Idea* of redness, and from others the *Idea* of whiteness: But whiteness or redness are not in it at any time, but such a texture, that hath the power to produce such a sensation in us.

§ 20. Pound an Almond, and the clear white *Colour* will be altered into a dirty one, and the sweet *Taste* into an oily one. What real Alteration can the beating of the Pestle make in any Body, but an Alteration of the *Texture* of it?

§ 21. *Ideas* being thus distinguished and understood, we may be able to give an Account, how the same Water, at the same time, may produce the *Idea* of Cold by one Hand, and of Heat by the other: Whereas it is impossible, that the same Water, if those *Ideas* were really in it, should at the same time be both Hot and Cold. For if we imagine *Warmth*, as it is *in our Hands*, to be *nothing but a certain sort and degree of Motion in the minute Particles of our Nerves, or animal Spirits*, we may understand, how it is possible, that the same Water may at the same time produce the Sensation of Heat in one Hand, and Cold in the other; which yet Figure never does, that never producing the *Idea* of a square by one Hand, which has produced the *Idea* of a Globe by another. But if the Sensation of Heat and Cold, be nothing but the increase or diminution of the motion of the minute Parts of our Bodies, caused by the Corpuscles of any other Body, it is easie to be understood, That if that motion be greater in one Hand, than in the other; if a Body be applied to the two Hands, which has in its minute Particles a greater motion, than in those of one of the Hands, and a less, than in those of the other, it will increase the motion of the one Hand, and lessen it in the other, and so cause the different Sensations of Heat and Cold, that depend thereon.

§ 22. I have in what just goes before, been engaged in Physical Enquiries a little farther than, perhaps, I intended. But it being necessary, to make the Nature of Sensation a little understood, and to make the *difference between the Qualities in Bodies, and the* Ideas *produced by them in the Mind*, to be distinctly conceived, without which it were impossible to discourse intelligibly of them; I hope, I shall be pardoned this little Excursion into Natural Philosophy, it being necessary in our present Enquiry, to distinguish the *primary*, and *real Qualities* of Bodies, which are always in them, (*viz.* Solidity, Extension, Figure, Number, and Motion, or Rest; and are sometimes perceived by us, *viz.* when the Bodies they are in, are big enough singly to be discerned) from those *secondary* and *imputed Qualities*, which are but the Powers of several Combinations of those primary ones, when they operate, without being distinctly discerned; whereby we also may come to know what *Ideas* are, and what are not Resemblances of something really existing in the Bodies, we denominate from them.

§ 23. The *Qualities* then that are in *Bodies* rightly considered, are of *Three sorts.*

First, The *Bulk*, *Figure*, *Number*, *Situation*, and *Motion, or Rest* of their solid Parts; those are in them, whether we perceive them or no; and when they are of that size, that we can discover them, we have by these an *Idea* of the thing, as it is in it self, as is plain in artificial things. These I call *primary Qualities.*

Secondly, The *Power* that is in any Body, *by* Reason of *its* insensible *primary Qualities*, to operate after a peculiar manner on any of our Senses, and thereby *produce in us* the *different Ideas* of several Colours, Sounds, Smells, Tasts, *etc.* These are usually called sensible Qualities.

Thirdly, The *Power* that is in any Body, *by* Reason of the particular Constitution of *its primary Qualities*, *to* make such a *change* in the *Bulk*, *Figure*, *Texture*, *and Motion of another Body*, as to make it operate on our Senses, differently from what it did before. Thus the

§ 23. *Three sorts of Qualities in Bodies.*

---

(6) impossible] **1–3, 5** | Impossible **4** (21) those] **4–5** | these **1–3** (25) *by*] **1–3** | by **4–5** (*l. below* 33) *This marginal summary, in* **4–5**, *replaces* 'Ideas *of primary Qualities are resemblances*; *of secondary, not.*' *that is in* **2–3.**

Sun has a Power to make Wax white, and Fire to make Lead fluid. These are usually called Powers.

The First of these, as has been said, I think, may be properly called *real Original*, or *primary Qualities*, because they are in the things themselves, whether they are perceived or no: and upon their different Modifications it is, that the secondary Qualities depend.

The other two, are only Powers to act differently upon other things, which Powers result from the different Modifications of those primary Qualities.

§ 24. But though *these two later sorts of Qualities are Powers barely*, and nothing but Powers, relating to several other Bodies, and resulting from the different Modifications of the Original Qualities; yet they are generally otherwise thought of. For *the Second sort, viz.* The Powers to produce several *Ideas* in us by our Senses, *are looked upon as real Qualities, in the things* thus affecting us: But *the Third sort are call'd, and esteemed barely Powers. v.g.* the *Idea* of Heat, or Light, which we receive by our Eyes, or touch from the Sun, are commonly thought *real Qualities*, existing in the Sun, and something more than mere Powers in it. But when we consider the Sun, in reference to Wax, which it melts or blanches, we look upon the Whiteness and Softness produced in the Wax, not as Qualities in the Sun, but Effects produced by *Powers* in it: Whereas, if rightly considered, these Qualities of Light and Warmth, which are Perceptions in me when I am warmed, or enlightned by the Sun, are no otherwise in the Sun, than the changes made in the Wax, when it is blanched or melted, are in the Sun. They are all of them equally Powers in the Sun, depending on its primary Qualities; whereby it is able in the one case, so to alter the Bulk, Figure, Texture, or Motion of some of the insensible parts of my Eyes, or Hands, as thereby to produce in me the *Idea* of Light or Heat; and in the other, it is able so to alter the Bulk, Figure, Texture, or Motion of the insensible Parts of the Wax, as to make them fit to produce in me the distinct *Ideas* of White and Fluid.

§§ 24, 25. *The* 1st. *are Resemblances. The* 2d. *thought Resemblances, but are not. The* 3d. *neither are nor are thought so.*

---

(2) These . . . Powers.] *add.* **4–5**. (*Not in* **Coste**) are] *edit.* | *are* **4–5** (16) *Powers.*] **1–3** | *Powers,* **4–5** (19) mere] **2–5** (meer **5**) | barely **1** (22) it: Whereas] **2–5** | it: whilst yet we look on Light and Warmth to be *real Qualities*, something more than bare Powers in the Sun. Whereas **1** (30) *Idea* of Light] **5** | *Ideas* of Light **4** | *Ideas* of Light, **1–3** (*l. below* 33) *This marginal summary, in* **4–5**, *replaces* '*Reason of our mistake in this.*' *that is in* **2–3**.

§ 25. The Reason, *Why the one are ordinarily taken for real Qualities, and the other only for bare Powers*, seems to be, because the *Ideas* we have of distinct Colours, Sounds, *etc.* containing nothing at all in them, of Bulk, Figure, or Motion, we are not apt to think them the Effects of these primary Qualities, which appear not to our Senses to operate in their Production; and with which, they have not any apparent Congruity, or conceivable Connexion. Hence it is, that we are so forward to imagine, that those *Ideas* are the resemblances of something really existing in the Objects themselves: Since Sensation discovers nothing of Bulk, Figure, or Motion of parts in their Production; nor can Reason shew, how Bodies by their Bulk, Figure, and Motion, should produce in the Mind the *Ideas* of Blue, or Yellow, *etc.* But in the other Case, in the Operations of Bodies, changing the Qualities one of another, we plainly discover, that the Quality produced, hath commonly no resemblance with any thing in the thing producing it; wherefore we look on it as a bare Effect of Power. For though receiving the *Idea* of Heat, or Light, from the Sun, we are apt to think, 'tis a Perception and Resemblance of such a Quality in the Sun: yet when we see Wax, or a fair Face, receive change of Colour from the Sun, we cannot imagine, that to be the Reception or Resemblance of any thing in the Sun, because we find not those different Colours in the Sun it self. For our Senses, being able to observe a likeness, or unlikeness of sensible Qualities in two different external Objects, we forwardly enough conclude the Production of any sensible Quality in any Subject, to be an Effect of bare Power, and not the Communication of any Quality, which was really in the efficient, when we find no such sensible Quality in the thing that produced it. But our Senses, not being able to discover any unlikeness between the *Idea* produced in us, and the Quality of the Object producing it, we are apt to imagine, that our *Ideas* are resemblances of something in the Objects, and not the Effects of certain Powers, placed in the Modification of their primary Qualities, with which primary Qualities the *Ideas* produced in us have no resemblance.

§ 26. To conclude, beside those before mentioned *primary Qualities* in Bodies, *viz.* Bulk, Figure, Extension, Number, and

§ 26. *Secondary Qualities two-fold; First, Immediately perceivable; Secondly, Mediately perceivable.*

(5) Effects] **2–5** | Effect **1** (12) Motion] **2–5** | Motions **1**

Motion of their solid Parts; all the rest, whereby we take notice of Bodies, and distinguish them one from another, are nothing else, but several Powers in them, depending on those primary Qualities; whereby they are fitted, either by immediately operating on our Bodies, to produce several different *Ideas* in us; or else by operating on other Bodies, so to change their primary Qualities, as to render them capable of producing *Ideas* in us, different from what before they did. The former of these, I think, may be called *Secondary Qualities, immediately perceivable*: The latter, *Secondary Qualities, mediately perceivable.*

CHAPTER IX

Of Perception.

§ 1. *PERCEPTION*, as it is the first faculty of the Mind, exercised about our *Ideas*; so it is the first and simplest *Idea* we have from Reflection, and is by some called Thinking in general. Though Thinking, in the propriety of the *English* Tongue, signifies that sort of operation of the Mind about its *Ideas*, wherein the Mind is active; where it with some degree of voluntary attention, considers any thing. For in bare naked *Perception*, the Mind is, for the most part, only passive; and what it perceives, it cannot avoid perceiving.

§ 2. *What Perception is*, every one will know better by reflecting on what he does himself, when he sees, hears, feels, *etc.* or thinks, than by any discourse of mine. Whoever reflects on what passes in his own Mind, cannot miss it: And if he does not reflect, all the Words in the World, cannot make him have any notion of it.

§ 3. This is certain, That whatever alterations are made in the Body, if they reach not the Mind; whatever impressions are made on the outward parts, if they are not taken notice of within, there is no Perception. Fire may burn our Bodies, with no other effect, than it does a Billet, unless the motion be continued to the Brain, and there the sence of Heat, or *Idea* of Pain, be produced in the Mind, wherein consists *actual Perception.*

§ 1. *It is the first simple* Idea *of Reflection.* §§ 2–4. *Perception is only when the Mind receives the Impression.*

---

(8) think,] **1–3, 5** | think **4** (9) latter] **2–5** | later **1** (21) in] **2–5** | in himself in **1**

§ 4. How often may a Man observe in himself, that whilst his Mind is intently employ'd in the contemplation of some Objects; and curiously surveying some *Ideas* that are there, it takes no notice of impressions of sounding Bodies, made upon the Organ of Hearing, with the same alteration, that uses to be for the producing the *Idea* of a Sound? A sufficient impulse there may be on the Organ; but it not reaching the observation of the Mind, there follows no perception: And though the motion, that uses to produce the *Idea* of Sound, be made in the Ear, yet no sound is heard. Want of Sensation in this case, is not through any defect in the Organ, or that the Man's Ears are less affected, than at other times, when he does hear: but that which uses to produce the *Idea*, though conveyed in by the usual Organ, not being taken notice of in the Understanding, and so imprinting no *Idea* on the Mind, there follows no Sensation. *So that where-ever there is Sense*, or *Perception*, *there some* Idea *is actually produced, and present in the Understanding.*

§ 5. Therefore I doubt not but *Children*, by the exercise of their Senses about Objects, that affect them *in the Womb*, *receive some few Ideas*, before they are born, as the unavoidable effects, either of the Bodies that environ them, or else of those Wants or Diseases they suffer; amongst which, (if one may conjecture concerning things not very capable of examination) I think the *Ideas* of Hunger and Warmth are two: which probably are some of the first that Children have, and which they scarce ever part with again.

§ 6. But though it be reasonable to imagine, that *Children* receive some *Ideas* before they come into the World, yet these simple *Ideas* are *far from* those *innate Principles*, which some contend for, and we above have rejected. These here mentioned, being the effects of Sensation, are only from some Affections of the Body, which happen to them there, and so depend on something exterior to the Mind; no otherwise differing in their manner of production from other *Ideas* derived from Sense, but only in the precedency of Time: Whereas those innate Principles are supposed to be of quite another nature; not coming into the Mind by any accidental alterations in, or operations on the Body; but, as it were, original Characters

§§ 5, 6. *Children, tho' they have* Ideas, *in the Womb, have none innate.*

(4–5) made . . . alteration] **2–5** | which are brought in, though the same alteration be made upon the Organ of Hearing **1** (6) a] **1–4**; *om.* **5** (11) the Man's] **2–5** | his **1** (14) and . . . Mind,] *add.* **2–5** (33) of quite] **1–4** | quite of **5** (34) any] **2–5** | the **1**

impressed upon it, in the very first moment of its Being and Constitution.

§ 7. As there are some *Ideas*, which we may reasonably suppose may be introduced into the Minds of Children in the Womb, subservient to the necessities of their Life, and Being there: So after they are born, *those Ideas* are the *earliest imprinted, which happen to be the sensible Qualities, which first occur* to them; amongst which, Light is not the least considerable, nor of the weakest efficacy. And how covetous the Mind is, to be furnished with all such *Ideas*, as have no pain accompanying them, may be a little guess'd, by what is observable in Children new-born, who always turn their Eyes to that part, from whence the Light comes, lay them how you please. But the *Ideas* that are most familiar at first, being various, according to the divers circumstances of Childrens first entertainment in the World, the order, wherein the several *Ideas* come at first into the Mind, is very various, and uncertain also; neither is it much material to know it.

§ 8. We are farther to consider concerning Perception, that the *Ideas we receive by sensation, are often* in grown People *alter'd by the Judgment*, without our taking notice of it. When we set before our Eyes a round Globe, of any uniform colour, *v.g.* Gold, Alabaster, or Jet, 'tis certain, that the *Idea* thereby imprinted in our Mind, is of a flat Circle variously shadow'd, with several degrees of Light and Brightness coming to our Eyes. But we having by use been accustomed to perceive, what kind of appearance convex Bodies are wont to make in us; what alterations are made in the reflections of Light, by the difference of the sensible Figures of Bodies, the Judgment presently, by an habitual custom, alters the Appearances into their Causes: So that from that, which truly is variety of shadow or colour, collecting the Figure, it makes it pass for a mark of Figure, and frames to it self the perception of a convex Figure, and an uniform Colour; when the *Idea* we receive from thence, is only a Plain variously colour'd, as is evident in Painting. To which purpose I shall here insert a Problem of that very Ingenious and Studious promoter of real Knowledge, the Learned and Worthy Mr. *Molineux*, which he was pleased to

§ 7. *Which* Ideas *first is not evident.* §§ 8–10. Ideas *of Sensation often changed by the Judgment.*

(5) necessities] **2–5** | necessity **1** (33)–146(25) To . . . *convinced.*] *add.* **2–5**

send me in a Letter some Months since; and it is this: *Suppose a Man born blind, and now adult, and taught by his touch to distinguish between a Cube, and a Sphere of the same metal, and nighly of the same bigness, so as to tell, when he felt one and t'other, which is the Cube, which the Sphere. Suppose then the Cube and Sphere placed on a Table, and the Blind Man to be made to see. Quære, Whether by his sight, before he touch'd them, he could now distinguish, and tell, which is the Globe, which the Cube.* To which the acute and judicious Proposer answers: *Not. For though he has obtain'd the experience of, how a Globe, how a Cube affects his touch; yet he has not yet attained the Experience, that what affects his touch so or so, must affect his sight so or so; Or that a protuberant angle in the Cube, that pressed his hand unequally, shall appear to his eye, as it does in the Cube.* I agree with this thinking Gent. whom I am proud to call my Friend, in his answer to this his Problem; and am of opinion, that the Blind Man, at first sight, would not be able with certainty to say, which was the Globe, which the Cube, whilst he only saw them: though he could unerringly name them by his touch, and certainly distinguish them by the difference of their Figures felt. This I have set down, and leave with my Reader, as an occasion for him to consider, how much he may be beholding to experience, improvement, and acquired notions, where he thinks, he has not the least use of, or help from them: And the rather, because this observing Gent. farther adds, that *having upon the occasion of my Book, proposed this to divers very ingenious Men, he hardly ever met with one, that at first gave the answer to it, which he thinks true, till by hearing his reasons they were convinced.*

§ 9. But this is not, I think, usual in any of our *Ideas*, but those received by *Sight*: Because Sight, the most comprehensive of all our Senses, conveying to our Minds the *Ideas* of Light and Colours, which are peculiar only to that Sense; and also the far different *Ideas* of Space, Figure, and Motion, the several varieties whereof change the appearances of its proper Object, *viz.* Light and Colours, we bring our selves by use, to judge of the one by the other. This in many cases, by a settled habit, in things whereof we have frequent experience, is performed so constantly, and so quick, that we take that for the Perception of our Sensation, which is an *Idea* formed by our Judgment; so that one, *viz.* that of Sensation, serves only to excite the other, and is scarce taken notice of it self; as a Man who

(13) whom] **4–5** | whom though I have never had the happiness to see, **2–3** (*likewise* **Coste**) (25) *v.* 145(33), n. (28) the] **2–5** | the far different **1** (29–30) the . . . *Ideas*] *add.* **2–5** (31) Object] **2–5** | Objects **1** (32) we . . . selves] **2–5** | it accustoms it self **1** (35) is] **2–5** | is but **1**

reads or hears with attention and understanding, takes little notice of the Characters, or Sounds, but of the *Ideas*, that are excited in him by them.

§ 10. Nor need we wonder, that this is done with so little notice, if we consider, how very *quick* the *actions of the Mind* are performed: For as it self is thought to take up no space, to have no extension; so its actions seem to require no time, but many of them seem to be crouded into an Instant. I speak this in comparison to the Actions of the Body. Any one may easily observe this in his own Thoughts, who will take the pains to reflect on them. How, as it were in an instant, do our Minds, with one glance, see all the parts of a demonstration, which may very well be called a long one, if we consider the time it will require to put it into words, and step by step shew it another? Secondly, we shall not be so much surprized, that this is done in us with so little notice, if we consider, how the facility which we get of doing things, by a custom of doing, makes them often pass in us without our notice. *Habits*, especially such as are begun very early, come, at last, to *produce actions in us, which often escape our observation.* How frequently do we, in a day, cover our Eyes with our Eye-lids, without perceiving that we are at all in the dark? Men, that by custom have got the use of a By-word, do almost in every sentence, pronounce sounds, which, though taken notice of by others, they themselves neither hear, nor observe. And therefore 'tis not so strange, that our Mind should often change the *Idea* of its Sensation, into that of its Judgment, and make one serve only to excite the other, without our taking notice of it.

§ 11. This faculty of *Perception*, seems to me to be that, which *puts the distinction betwixt the animal Kingdom, and the inferior parts of Nature.* For however Vegetables have, many of them, some degrees of Motion, and upon the different application of other Bodies to them, do very briskly alter their Figures and Motions, and so have obtained the name of sensitive Plants, from a motion, which has some resemblance to that, which in Animals follows upon Sensation: Yet, I suppose, it is all bare Mechanism; and no otherwise produced, than the turning of a wild Oat-beard, by the insinuation of the

§§ 11–14. *Perception puts the difference between Animals and inferior Beings.*

---

(1) or] **2–5** | and **1** (6) is . . . have] **4–5** | takes up no space, has **1–3** (11) do] **2–5** | does **1** (16) which] *add.* **4–5** (19) *escape*] **4–5** | *scape* **1–3** (21) By-word] **Coste** *adds a linguistic note.*

Particles of Moisture; or the short'ning of a Rope, by the affusion of Water. All which is done without any Sensation in the Subject, or the having or receiving any *Ideas*.

§ 12. *Perception*, I believe, is, in some degree, *in all sorts of Animals*; though in some, possibly, the Avenues, provided by Nature for the reception of Sensations are so few, and the Perception, they are received with, so obscure and dull, that it comes extremely short of the quickness and variety of Sensations, which is in other Animals: but yet it is sufficient for, and wisely adapted to, the state and condition of that sort of Animals, who are thus made: So that the Wisdom and Goodness of the Maker plainly appears in all the Parts of this stupendious Fabrick, and all the several degrees and ranks of Creatures in it.

§ 13. We may, I think, from the Make of an *Oyster*, or *Cockle*, reasonably conclude, that it has not so many, nor so quick Senses, as a Man, or several other Animals; nor if it had, would it, in that state and incapacity of transferring it self from one place to another, be better'd by them. What good would Sight and Hearing do to a Creature, that cannot move it self to, or from the Objects, wherein at a distance it perceives Good or Evil? And would not quickness of Sensation, be an Inconvenience to an Animal, that must lie still, where Chance has once placed it; and there receive the afflux of colder or warmer, clean or foul Water, as it happens to come to it?

§ 14. But yet, I cannot but think, there is some small dull Perception, whereby they are distinguished from perfect Insensibility. And that this may be so, we have plain instances, even in Mankind it self. Take one, in whom decrepid old Age has blotted out the Memory of his past Knowledge, and clearly wiped out the *Ideas* his Mind was formerly stored with; and has, by destroying his Sight, Hearing, and Smell quite, and his Taste to a great degree, stopp'd up almost all the Passages for new ones to enter; or, if there be some of the Inlets yet half open, the Impressions made are scarce perceived, or not at all retained. How far such an one (notwithstanding all that is boasted of innate Principles) is in his Knowledge, and intellectual Faculties, above the Condition of a Cockle, or an Oyster, I leave to be considered. And if a Man had passed Sixty Years in such a State, as 'tis possible he might, as well as three Days, I

(5–6) , provided . . . few] **2–5** (receptions **3**) | provided for the reception of Sensations, are so few by Nature **1** (10) made] **2–5** | constituted by Nature **1** (22) receive] **4er–5** | receives **1–4**

wonder what difference there would have been, in any intellectual Perfections, between him, and the lowest degree of Animals.

§ 15. *Perception* then being *the first step and degree towards Knowledge, and the inlet of all the Materials of it*, the fewer Senses any Man, as well as any other Creature, hath; and the fewer and duller the Impressions are, that are made by them; and the duller the Faculties are, that are employed about them, the more remote are they from that Knowledge, which is to be found in some Men. But this being in great variety of Degrees, (as may be perceived amongst Men,) cannot certainly be discovered in the several Species of Animals, much less in their particular Individuals. It suffices me only to have remarked here, that Perception is the first Operation of all our intellectual Faculties, and the inlet of all Knowledge into our Minds. And I am apt too to imagine, That it is Perception in the lowest degree of it, which puts the Boundaries between Animals, and the inferior ranks of Creatures. But this I mention only as my conjecture by the by, it being indifferent to the Matter in Hand, which way the Learned shall determine of it.

CHAPTER X

Of Retention.

§ 1. THE next Faculty of the Mind, whereby it makes a farther Progress towards Knowledge, is that which I call *Retention*, or the keeping of those simple *Ideas*, which from Sensation or Reflection it hath received. This is done two ways. First, by keeping the *Idea*, which is brought into it, for some time actually in view, which is called *Contemplation*.

§ 2. The other way of Retention is the Power to revive again in our Minds those *Ideas*, which after imprinting have disappeared, or have been as it were laid aside out of Sight: And thus we do, when

§ 15. *Perception the inlet of Knowledge.*
§ 1. *Contemplation.* § 2. *Memory.*

(2) degree] **2–5** | degrees **1** (3) *The section index* '§ 15.' *add.* **2–5** (20) which I call *Retention*,] **4–5** | I call *Retention*; **1–3** (22) received . . . First,] **4–5** | received, which is done two ways; First, either **1–3** (25) other way of Retention] **4–5** | other, **1–3** (*l. below* 27) *Knowledge*] **2–4** | *the Knowledge* **5**

we conceive Heat or Light, Yellow or Sweet, the Object being removed. This is *Memory*, which is as it were the Store-house of our *Ideas*. For the narrow Mind of Man, not being capable of having many *Ideas* under View and Consideration at once, it was necessary to have a Repository, to lay up those *Ideas*, which at another time it might have use of. But our *Ideas* being nothing, but actual Perceptions in the Mind, which cease to be any thing, when there is no perception of them, this *laying up* of our *Ideas* in the Repository of the Memory, signifies no more but this, that the Mind has a Power, in many cases, to revive Perceptions, which it has once had, with this additional Perception annexed to them, that it has had them before. And in this Sense it is, that our *Ideas* are said to be in our Memories, when indeed, they are actually no where, but only there is an ability in the Mind, when it will, to revive them again; and as it were paint them anew on it self, though some with more, some with less difficulty; some more lively, and others more obscurely. And thus it is, by the Assistance of this Faculty, that we are said to have all those *Ideas* in our Understandings, which though we do not actually contemplate, yet we can bring in sight, and make appear again, and be the Objects of our Thoughts, without the help of those sensible Qualities, which first imprinted them there.

§ 3. *Attention* and *Repetition help* much to the fixing any *Ideas* in *the Memory*: But those, which naturally at first make the deepest, and most lasting Impression, are those, which are accompanied with *Pleasure* or *Pain*. The great Business of the Senses, being to make us take notice of what hurts, or advantages the Body, it is wisely ordered by Nature (as has been shewn) that Pain should accompany the Reception of several *Ideas*; which supplying the Place of Consideration and Reasoning in Children, and acting quicker than Consideration in grown Men, makes both the Young and Old avoid painful Objects, with that haste, which is necessary for their Preservation; and in both settles in the Memory a caution for the Future.

§ 4. Concerning the several *degrees of* lasting, wherewith *Ideas* are

§ 3. *Attention, Repetition, Pleasure, and Pain fix* Ideas. §§ 4, 5. Ideas *fade in the Memory.*

---

(2) removed. This] **4–5** | removed; and this **1–3** (*likewise* **Coste**) (6–16) But . . . obscurely.] *add.* **2–5** (10) which] *add.* **4–5** (17) this Faculty] **2–5** | the Memory **1** (18) Understandings,] **2–5** | Understanding; **1** (',' **1er**) (22) *the*] **2–5** | *our* **1** (34) Concerning] **4–5** | But concerning **1–3**

imprinted on the *Memory*, we may observe, That some of them have been produced in the Understanding, by an Object affecting the Senses once only, and no more than once: Others, that have more than once offer'd themselves to the Senses, have yet been little taken notice of; the Mind, either heedless, as in Children, or otherwise employ'd, as in Men, intent only on one thing, not setting the stamp deep into it self. And in some, where they are set on with care and repeated impressions, either through the temper of the Body, or some other default, the Memory is very weak: In all these cases, *Ideas* in the Mind quickly fade, and often vanish quite out of the Understanding, leaving no more footsteps or remaining Characters of themselves, than Shadows do flying over Fields of Corn; and the Mind is as void of them, as if they never had been there.

§ 5. Thus many of those *Ideas*, which were produced in the Minds of Children, in the beginning of their Sensation (some of which, perhaps, as of some Pleasures and Pains, were before they were born, and others in their Infancy) if in the future Course of their Lives, they are not repeated again, are quite lost, without the least glimpse remaining of them. This may be observed in those, who by some Mischance have lost their sight, when they were very Young; in whom the *Ideas* of Colours, having been but slightly taken notice of, and ceasing to be repeated, do quite wear out; so that some years after, there is no more Notion, nor Memory of Colours left in their Minds, than in those of People born blind. The Memory in some Men, 'tis true, is very tenacious, even to a Miracle: But yet there seems to be a constant decay of all our *Ideas*, even of those which are struck deepest, and in Minds the most retentive; so that if they be not sometimes renewed by repeated Exercise of the Senses, or Reflection on those kind of Objects, which at first occasioned them, the Print wears out, and at last there remains nothing to be seen. Thus the *Ideas*, as well as Children, of our Youth, often die before us: And our Minds represent to us those Tombs, to which we are approaching; where though the Brass and Marble remain, yet the

(1–12) That . . . than] **2–5** | First, That some of them being produced in the Understanding, either by the Objects affecting the Senses once barely, and no more, especially if the Mind then otherwise imployed, took but little notice of it, and set not on the stamp deep into it self; or else, when through the Temper of the Body, or otherwise, the Memory is very weak, such *Ideas* quickly fade, and vanish quite out of the Understanding, and leave it as clear without any Foot-steps, or remaining Characters, as **1** (25) , even] **2–5** | even, **1** (26) [*2nd*] of] *add.* **2–5** (27) Minds] **2–5** | the Minds **1** (29) on] **2–5** | about **1** (31) Children,] **2, 4–5** | Children **1, 3**

Inscriptions are effaced by time, and the Imagery moulders away. *The Pictures drawn in our Minds, are laid in fading Colours*; and if not sometimes refreshed, vanish and disappear. How much the Constitution of our Bodies, and the make of our animal Spirits, are concerned in this; and whether the Temper of the Brain make this difference, that in some it retains the Characters drawn on it like Marble, in others like Free-stone, and in others little better than Sand, I shall not here enquire, though it may seem probable, that the Constitution of the Body does sometimes influence the Memory; since we oftentimes find a Disease quite strip the Mind of all its *Ideas*, and the flames of a Fever, in a few days, calcine all those Images to dust and confusion, which seem'd to be as lasting, as if graved in Marble.

§ 6. But concerning the *Ideas* themselves, it is easie to remark, That those that are *oftenest refreshed* (amongst which are those that are conveyed into the Mind by more ways than one) by a frequent return of the Objects or Actions that produce them, *fix themselves best in the Memory*, and remain clearest and longest there; and therefore those, which are of the original Qualities of Bodies, *viz.* *Solidity*, *Extension*, *Figure*, *Motion*, and *Rest*, and those that almost constantly affect our Bodies, as *Heat* and *Cold*; and those which are the Affections of all kinds of Beings, as *Existence*, *Duration*, and *Number*, which almost every Object that affects our Senses, every Thought which imploys our Minds, bring along with them: These, I say, and the like *Ideas*, are seldom quite lost, whilst the Mind retains any *Ideas* at all.

§ 7. In this secondary Perception, as I may so call it, or viewing again the *Ideas*, that are lodg'd *in* the *Memory*, *the Mind is oftentimes more than barely passive*, the appearance of those dormant Pictures, depending sometimes on the Will. The Mind very often sets it self on work in search of some hidden *Idea*, and turns, as it were, the Eye of the Soul upon it; though sometimes too they start up in our Minds of their own accord, and offer themselves to the Understanding; and very often are rouzed and tumbled out of their dark

§ 6. *Constantly repeated* Ideas *can scarce be lost.* § 7. *In remembring the Mind is often active.*

---

(4) , and . . . Spirits,] *add.* **4–5** (5) the Brain] **4–5** | the Spirits and Brain **1–3** (6) in some it retains] **4–5** | some retain **1–3** (7) in . . . in] **4–5** | others like free Stone, and **1–3** than] **1–3** | then **4–5** (11) calcine] **2–5** | calcines **1** (13) graved] **5** | carved **1–4**. (**Coste** 'si elles eussent été gravées') (22) kinds] **2–5** | kind **1** (*l. below* 34: § 7.) *In* **Coste**, § 7 *comes under the same marginal summary as* § 6.

Cells, into open Day-light, by some turbulent and tempestuous Passion; our Affections bringing *Ideas* to our Memory, which had otherwise lain quiet and unregarded. This farther is to be observed, concerning *Ideas* lodg'd in the Memory, and upon occasion revived by the Mind, that they are not only (as the Word *revive* imports) none of them new ones; but also that the Mind takes notice of them, as of a former Impression, and renews its acquaintance with them, as with *Ideas* it had known before. So that though *Ideas* formerly imprinted are not all constantly in view, yet in remembrance they are constantly known to be such, as have been formerly imprinted, *i.e.* in view, and taken notice of before by the Understanding.

§ 8. *Memory*, in an intellectual Creature, is necessary in the next degree to Perception. It is of so great moment, that where it is wanting, all the rest of our Faculties are in a great measure useless: And we in our Thoughts, Reasonings, and Knowledge, could not proceed beyond present Objects, were it not for the assistance of our Memories, wherein there may be *two defects*.

First, That it *loses the Idea* quite, and so far it produces perfect Ignorance. For since we can know nothing farther, than we have the *Idea* of it, when that is gone, we are in perfect *ignorance*.

Secondly, That it moves slowly, and *retrieves not the Ideas*, that it has, and are laid up in store, *quick enough* to serve the Mind upon occasions. This, if it be to a great degree, is *Stupidity*; and he, who through this default in his Memory, has not the *Ideas*, that are really preserved there, ready at hand, when need and occasion calls for them, were almost as good be without them quite, since they serve him to little purpose. The dull Man, who loses the opportunity, whilst he is seeking in his Mind for those *Ideas*, that should serve his turn, is not much more happy in his Knowledge, than one that is perfectly ignorant. 'Tis the business therefore of the Memory to furnish to the Mind those dormant *Ideas*, which it has present occasion for, and in the having them ready at hand on all occasions, consists that which we call *Invention*, *Fancy*, and quickness of Parts.

§ 9. These are defects, we may observe, in the Memory of one Man compared with another. There is another defect, which we may

§§ 8, 9. *Two defects in the Memory, Oblivion and Slowness.*

(3–11) This . . . Understanding.] *add.* **2–5** (12) intellectual] **Coste** 'raisonnable' (20) *Idea* . . . is] **2–5** | *Ideas* of it, when they are **1** (32) and] **1–4**; *om.* **5** (34)–154(29) These . . . ours.] *add.* **2–5**, *with* § *9 in* **1** *consequently becoming* § *10 in* **2–5**

conceive to be in the memory of Man in general, compared with some superiour created intellectual Beings, which in this faculty may so far excel Man, that they may have constantly in view the whole Scene of all their former actions, wherein no one of the thoughts they have ever had, may slip out of their sight. The omniscience of God, who knows all things past, present, and to come, and to whom the thoughts of Men's hearts always lie open, may satisfie us of the possibility of this. For who can doubt, but God may communicate to those glorious Spirits, his immediate Attendants, any of his Perfections, in what proportion he pleases, as far as created finite Beings can be capable. 'Tis reported of that prodigy of Parts, Monsieur *Pascal*, that, till the decay of his health had impaired his memory, he forgot nothing of what he had done, read, or thought in any part of his rational Age. This is a privilege so little known to most Men, that it seems almost incredible to those, who, after the ordinary way, measure all others by themselves: But yet, when considered, may help us to enlarge our thoughts towards greater Perfections of it in superior ranks of Spirits. For this of Mr. *Pascal* was still with the narrowness, that humane Minds are confin'd to here, of having great variety of *Ideas* only by succession, not all at once: Whereas the several degrees of Angels may probably have larger views, and some of them be endowed with capacities able to retain together, and constantly set before them, as in one Picture, all their past knowledge at once. This, we may conceive, would be no small advantage to the knowledge of a thinking Man; if all his past thoughts, and reasonings could be always present to him. And therefore we may suppose it one of those ways, wherein the knowledge of separate Spirits may exceedingly surpass ours.

§ 10. This faculty of laying up, and retaining the *Ideas*, that are brought into the Mind, several *other Animals* seem to have, to a great degree, as well as Man. For to pass by other Instances, Birds learning of Tunes, and the endeavours one may observe in them, to hit the Notes right, put it past doubt with me, that they have Perception, and retain *Ideas* in their Memories, and use them for Patterns. For it seems to me impossible, that they should endeavour to conform their Voices to Notes (as 'tis plain they do) of which they

§ 10. *Brutes have Memory.*

---

(4) Scene **2, 4** | Sence **3** | sense **5**. (**Coste** 'sentiment') (20) by] **5** | in **2–4**
(29, 30) *v.* 153(34), n.

had no *Ideas*. For though I should grant Sound may mechanically cause a certain motion of the animal Spirits, in the Brains of those Birds, whilst the Tune is actually playing; and that motion may be continued on to the Muscles of the Wings, and so the Bird mechanically be driven away by certain noises, because this may tend to the Birds Preservation: yet that can never be supposed a Reason, why it should cause mechanically, either whilst the Tune was playing, much less after it has ceased, such a motion in the Organs of the Bird's Voice, as should conform it to the Notes of a foreign Sound, which imitation can be of no use to the Bird's Preservation. But which is more, it cannot with any appearance of Reason, be supposed (much less proved) that Birds, without Sense and Memory, can approach their Notes, nearer and nearer by degrees, to a Tune play'd yesterday; which if they have no *Idea* of in their Memory, is now no-where, nor can be a Pattern for them to imitate, or which any repeated Essays can bring them nearer to. Since there is no reason why the sound of a Pipe should leave traces in their Brains, which not at first, but by their after-endeavours, should produce the like Sounds; and why the Sounds they make themselves, should not make traces which they should follow, as well as those of the Pipe, is impossible to conceive.

CHAPTER XI

Of Discerning, and other Operations of the Mind.

§ 1. ANOTHER Faculty, we may take notice of in our Minds, is that of *Discerning* and distinguishing between the several *Ideas* it has. It is not enough to have a confused Perception of something in general: Unless the Mind had a distinct Perception of different Objects, and their Qualities, it would be capable of very little Knowledge; though the Bodies that affect us, were as busie about us, as they are now, and the Mind were continually employ'd in thinking. On this faculty of Distinguishing one thing from another, depends the *evidence and certainty* of several, even very general Propositions, which have passed for innate Truths; because Men over-looking the true cause, why those Propositions find universal

§ 1. *No Knowledge without it.*

assent, impute it wholly to native uniform Impressions; whereas it in truth *depends upon this clear discerning Faculty* of the Mind, whereby it perceives two *Ideas* to be the same, or different. But of this more hereafter.

§ 2. How much the imperfection of accurately discriminating *Ideas* one from another lies, either in the dulness, or faults of the Organs of Sense; or want of acuteness, exercise, or attention in the Understanding; or hastiness and precipitancy, natural to some Tempers, I will not here examine: It suffices to take notice, that this is one of the Operations, that the Mind may reflect on, and observe in it self. It is of that consequence to its other Knowledge, that so far as this faculty is in it self dull, or not rightly made use of, for the distinguishing one thing from another; so far our Notions are confused, and our Reason and Judgment disturbed or misled. If in having our *Ideas* in the Memory ready at hand, consists quickness of parts; in this of having them unconfused, and being able nicely to distinguish one thing from another, where there is but the least difference, consists, in a great measure, the exactness of Judgment, and clearness of Reason, which is to be observed in one Man above another. And hence, perhaps, may be given some Reason of that common Observation, That Men who have a great deal of Wit, and prompt Memories, have not always the clearest Judgment, or deepest Reason. For *Wit* lying most in the assemblage of *Ideas*, and putting those together with quickness and variety, wherein can be found any resemblance or congruity, thereby to make up pleasant Pictures, and agreeable Visions in the Fancy: *Judgment*, on the contrary, lies quite on the other side, in separating carefully, one from another, *Ideas*, wherein can be found the least difference, thereby to avoid being misled by Similitude, and by affinity to take one thing for another. This is a way of proceeding quite contrary to Metaphor and Allusion, wherein, for the most part, lies that entertainment and pleasantry of Wit, which strikes so lively on the Fancy, and therefore so acceptable to all People; because its Beauty appears at first sight, and there is required no labour of thought, to examine what Truth or Reason there is in it. The Mind without looking any farther, rests satisfied

§ 2. *The difference of Wit and Judgment.*

---

(28) , one from another, *Ideas*,] **2–5** (one . . . another *Ideas*, **2–3**) | *Ideas* one from another, **1** (33–4) Fancy, . . . People;] **4–5** | Fancy; . . . People, **1–3**

with the agreeableness of the Picture, and the gayety of the Fancy: And it is a kind of an affront to go about to examine it, by the severe Rules of Truth, and good Reason; whereby it appears, that it consists in something, that is not perfectly conformable to them.

§ 3. To the well distinguishing our *Ideas*, it chiefly contributes, that they be *clear and determinate*: And when they are so, it *will not breed any confusion* or mistake about them, though the Senses should (as sometimes they do) convey them from the same Object differently, on different occasions, and so seem to err. For though a Man in a Fever should from Sugar have a bitter taste, which at another time would produce a sweet one; yet the *Idea* of Bitter in that Man's Mind, would be as clear and distinct from the *Idea* of Sweet, as if he had tasted only Gall. Nor does it make any more confusion between the two *Ideas* of Sweet and Bitter, that the same sort of Body produces at one time one, and at another time another *Idea*, by the taste, than it makes a confusion in the two *Ideas* of White and Sweet, or White and Round, that the same piece of Sugar produces them both in the Mind at the same time. And the *Ideas* of Orange-colour and Azure, that are produced in the Mind by the same parcel of the infusion of *Lignum Nephriticum*, are no less distinct *Ideas*, than those of the same Colours, taken from two very different Bodies.

§ 4. The *COMPARING* them one with another, in respect of Extent, Degrees, Time, Place, or any other Circumstances, is another operation of the Mind about its *Ideas*, and is that upon which depends all that large tribe of *Ideas*, comprehended under *Relation*; which of how vast an extent it is, I shall have occasion to consider hereafter.

§ 5. How far Brutes partake in this faculty, is not easie to determine; I imagine they have it not in any great degree: For though they probably have several *Ideas* distinct enough, yet it seems to me to be the Prerogative of Humane Understanding, when it has sufficiently distinguished any *Ideas*, so as to perceive them to be perfectly different, and so consequently two, to cast about and consider in what circumstances they are capable to be compared. And therefore, I think, *Beasts compare* not their *Ideas*, farther than

§ 3. *Clearness alone hinders Confusion.* § 4. *Comparing.* § 5. *Brutes compare, but imperfectly.*

(1) agreeableness] **4–5** | pleasantness **1–3** (6) that] **1–4**; *om.* **5** (16) the] **1–4**; *om.* **5** (33) two] **1–3, 4er–5** (*likewise* **Coste**) | too **4** (*l. below* 35: § 3.) *This marginal summary not in* **Coste**, *which applies that for* § *2 also to* § *3.*

some sensible Circumstances annexed to the Objects themselves. The other power of Comparing, which may be observed in Men, belonging to general *Ideas*, and useful only to abstract Reasonings, we may probably conjecture Beasts have not.

§ 6. The next Operation we may observe in the Mind about its *Ideas*, is *COMPOSITION*; whereby it puts together several of those simple ones it has received from Sensation and Reflection, and combines them into complex ones. Under this of Composition, may be reckon'd also that of *ENLARGING*; wherein though the Composition does not so much appear as in more complex ones, yet it is nevertheless a putting several *Ideas* together, though of the same kind. Thus by adding several Unites together, we make the *Idea* of a dozen; and putting together the repeated *Ideas* of several Perches, we frame that of Furlong.

§ 7. In this also, I suppose, *Brutes* come far short of Men. For though they take in, and retain together several Combinations of simple *Ideas*, as possibly the Shape, Smell, and Voice of his Master, make up the complex *Idea* a Dog has of him; or rather are so many distinct Marks whereby he knows him: yet, I *do not* think they do of themselves ever compound them, and *make complex* Ideas. And perhaps even where we think they have complex *Ideas*, 'tis only one simple one that directs them in the knowledge of several things, which possibly they distinguish less by their Sight, than we imagine. For I have been credibly informed, that a Bitch will nurse, play with, and be fond of young Foxes, as much as, and in place of her Puppies, if you can but get them once to suck her so long, that her Milk may go through them. And those animals, which have a numerous brood of young ones at once, appear not to have any knowledge of their number; for though they are mightily concerned for any of their Young, that are taken from them whilst they are in sight or hearing, yet if one or two of them be stollen from them in their absence, or without noise, they appear not to miss them; or to have any sense, that their number is lessen'd.

§ 8. When Children have, by repeated Sensations, got *Ideas* fixed in their Memories, they begin, by degrees, to learn the use of Signs.

§ 6. *Compounding*. § 7. *Brutes compound but little*. § 8. *Naming*.

---

(13) putting] **1–3** | puting **4–5** (14) Furlong] **4–5** | a Furlong **1–3** (15) Men] **5** (*likewise* **Coste**) | Man **1–4** (18) the] **5** | a **1–4** (20) Ideas.] **5** | *Ideas*. **4** | *Ideas*: **1–3** (27–33) And . . . lessen'd.] *add*. **2–5**

And when they have got the skill to apply the Organs of Speech to the framing of articulate Sounds, they begin to make *Use of Words*, to signifie their *Ideas* to others: These verbal Signs they sometimes borrow from others, and sometimes make themselves, as one may observe among the new and unusual Names Children often give to things in their first use of Language.

§ 9. The use of Words then being to stand as outward Marks of our internal *Ideas*, and those *Ideas* being taken from particular things, if every particular *Idea* that we take in, should have a distinct Name, Names must be endless. To prevent this, the Mind makes the particular *Ideas*, received from particular Objects, to become general; which is done by considering them as they are in the Mind such Appearances, separate from all other Existences, and the circumstances of real Existence, as Time, Place, or any other concomitant *Ideas*. This is called *ABSTRACTION*, whereby *Ideas* taken from particular Beings, become general Representatives of all of the same kind; and their Names general Names, applicable to whatever exists conformable to such abstract *Ideas*. Such precise, naked Appearances in the Mind, without considering, how, whence, or with what others they came there, the Understanding lays up (with Names commonly annexed to them) as the Standards to rank real Existences into sorts, as they agree with these Patterns, and to *denominate* them accordingly. Thus the same Colour being observed to day in Chalk or Snow, which the Mind yesterday received from Milk, it considers that Appearance alone, makes it a representative of all of that kind; and having given it the name *Whiteness*, it by that sound signifies the same quality wheresoever to be imagin'd or met with; and thus Universals, whether *Ideas* or Terms, are made.

§ 10. If it may be doubted, Whether *Beasts* compound and enlarge their *Ideas* that way, to any degree: This, I think, I may be positive in, That the power of *Abstracting* is not at all in them; and that the having of general *Ideas*, is that which puts a perfect distinction betwixt Man and Brutes; and is an Excellency which the Faculties of Brutes do by no means attain to. For it is evident, we observe no

§ 9. *Abstraction.* §§ 10, 11. *Brutes abstract not.*

(3) others: These verbal Signs] **4–5** | others; which words **1–3** (9) that] *add.* **4–5** (13, 22) Existences] **4–5** | Existencies **1–3** (27) quality] **2–5** | quali-/ **1**

foot-steps in them, of making use of general signs for universal *Ideas*; from which we have reason to imagine, that they have not the faculty of abstracting, or making general *Ideas*, since they have no use of Words, or any other general Signs.

§ 11. Nor can it be imputed to their want of fit Organs, to frame articulate Sounds, that they have no use, or knowledge of general Words; since many of them, we find, can fashion such Sounds, and pronounce Words distinctly enough, but never with any such application. And on the other side, Men, who through some defect in the Organs, want words, yet fail not to express their universal *Ideas* by signs, which serve them instead of general words, a faculty which we see Beasts come short in. And therefore I think we may suppose, That 'tis in this, that the Species of *Brutes* are discriminated from Man; and 'tis that proper difference wherein they are wholly separated, and which at last widens to so vast a distance. For if they have any *Ideas* at all, and are not bare Machins (as some would have them) we cannot deny them to have some Reason. It seems as evident to me, that they do some of them in certain Instances reason, as that they have sence; but it is only in particular *Ideas*, just as they receiv'd them from their Senses. They are the best of them tied up within those narrow bounds, and *have not* (as I think) the faculty to enlarge them by any kind of *Abstraction*.

§ 12. How far *Idiots* are concerned in the want or weakness of any, or all of the foregoing Faculties, an exact observation of their several ways of faltering, would no doubt discover. For those who either perceive but dully, or retain the *Ideas* that come into their Minds but ill, who cannot readily excite or compound them, will have little matter to think on. Those who cannot distinguish, compare, and abstract, would hardly be able to understand, and make use of Language, or judge, or reason to any tolerable degree: but only a little, and imperfectly, about things present, and very familiar to their Senses. And indeed, any of the forementioned Faculties, if wanting, or out of order, produce suitable defects in Men's Understandings and Knowledge.

§ 13. In fine, the defect in *Naturals* seems to proceed from want of quickness, activity, and motion, in the intellectual Faculties, where-

§§ 12, 13. *Idiots and mad Men.*

---

(18) some . . . Instances] *add.* **4–5** (*l. below* 36) *In* **Coste**, *the marginal summary for* § *12 is* 'Défaut des Imbecilles.', *the marginal summary for* § *12 in* **2–5** *being applied to* § *13* (*and* § *14*) *instead.*

by they are deprived of Reason: Whereas *mad Men*, on the other side, seem to suffer by the other Extreme. For they do not appear to me to have lost the Faculty of Reasoning: but having joined together some *Ideas* very wrongly, they mistake them for Truths; and they err as Men do, that argue right from wrong Principles. For by the violence of their Imaginations, having taken their Fancies for Realities, they make right deductions from them. Thus you shall find a distracted Man fancying himself a King, with a right inference, require suitable Attendance, Respect, and Obedience: Others who have thought themselves made of Glass, have used the caution necessary to preserve such brittle Bodies. Hence it comes to pass, that a Man, who is very sober, and of a right Understanding in all other things, may in one particular be as frantick, as any in *Bedlam*; if either by any sudden very strong impression, or long fixing his Fancy upon one sort of Thoughts, incoherent *Ideas* have been cemented together so powerfully, as to remain united. But there are degrees of Madness, as of Folly; the disorderly jumbling *Ideas* together, is in some more, and some less. In short, herein seems to lie the difference between Idiots and mad Men, That mad Men put wrong *Ideas* together, and so make wrong Propositions, but argue and reason right from them: But Idiots make very few or no Propositions, and reason scarce at all.

§ 14. These, I think, are the first Faculties and Operations of the Mind, which it makes use of in Understanding; and though they are exercised about all its *Ideas* in general; yet the Instances, I have hitherto given, have been chiefly in simple *Ideas*; and I have subjoined the explication of these Faculties of the Mind, to that of simple *Ideas*, before I come to what I have to say, concerning complex ones, for these following Reasons:

First, Because several of these Faculties being exercised at first principally about simple *Ideas*, we might, by following Nature in its ordinary method, trace and discover them in their rise, progress, and gradual improvements.

Secondly, Because observing the Faculties of the Mind, how they operate about simple *Ideas*, which are usually in most Men's Minds

§ 14. *Method.*

---

(7) deductions] **2–5** | deduction **1** (9) require] **1T.er, 2–5** | requires **1** (24) and] **2–5** | which **1** (34) [*2nd*] the] **2–5** | our **1** (*l. below* 35) *In* **Coste,** *§ 14 comes under the same marginal summary as that for § 13 (v. p. 160, last n.)*

much more clear, precise, and distinct, than complex ones, we may the better examine and learn how the Mind abstracts, denominates, compares, and exercises its other Operations, about those which are complex, wherein we are much more liable to mistake.

Thirdly, Because these very Operations of the Mind about *Ideas*, receiv'd from *Sensation*, are themselves, when reflected on, another set of *Ideas*, derived from that other source of our Knowledge, which I call *Reflection*; and therefore fit to be considered in this place, after the simple *Ideas* of *Sensation*. Of Compounding, Comparing, Abstracting, *etc.* I have but just spoken, having occasion to treat of them more at large in other places.

§ 15. And thus I have given a short, and, I think, true *History of the first beginnings of Humane Knowledge*; whence the Mind has its first Objects, and by what steps it makes its Progress to the laying in, and storing up those *Ideas*, out of which is to be framed all the Knowledge it is capable of; wherein I must appeal to Experience and Observation, whether I am in the right: The best way to come to Truth, being to examine Things as really they are, and not to conclude they are, as we fancy of our selves, or have been taught by others to imagine.

§ 16. To deal truly, *this is the only way*, that I can discover, *whereby* the *Ideas* of things *are brought into the Understanding*: If other Men have either innate *Ideas*, or infused Principles, they have reason to enjoy them; and if they are sure of it, it is impossible for others to deny them the privilege that they have above their Neighbours. I can speak but of what I find in my self, and is agreeable to those Notions; which, if we will examine the whole course of Men in their several Ages, Countries, and Educations, seem to depend on these foundations which I have laid, and to correspond with this Method, in all the parts and degrees thereof.

§ 17. I pretend not to teach, but to enquire; and therefore cannot but confess here again, That external and internal Sensation, are the only passages that I can find, of Knowledge, to the Understanding. These alone, as far as I can discover, are the Windows by

§ 15. *These are the beginnings of humane Knowledge.* § 16. *Appeal to Experience.*
§ 17. *Dark room.*

(19–20) by others to imagine] **4–5** | to imagine by others **1–3** (25) that] *add.* **4–5** above] **1–4** | about **5** (28) seem] **1er–5** | seems **1** these] **1–4** | those **5** (29) which] *add.* **4–5** Method,] **4–5** | Method **1–3** (33) that] *add.* **4–5** (*l. below* 34: § 15.) *beginnings*] **2–4** | *Beginning* **5** which light is let into this *dark Room*. For, methinks, the *Understanding* is not much unlike a Closet wholly shut from light, with only some little openings left, to let in external visible Resemblances, or *Ideas* of things without; would the Pictures coming into such a dark Room but stay there, and lie so orderly as to be found upon occasion, it would very much resemble the Understanding of a Man, in reference to all Objects of sight, and the *Ideas* of them.

These are my Guesses concerning the means whereby the Understanding comes to have, and retain simple *Ideas*, and the modes of them, with some other operations about them. I proceed now to examine some of these simple *Ideas*, and their Modes, a little more particularly.

CHAPTER XII

Of Complex Ideas.

§ 1. WE have hitherto considered those *Ideas*, in the reception whereof, the Mind is only passive, which are those simple ones received from *Sensation* and *Reflection* before-mentioned, whereof the Mind cannot make any one to it self, nor have any *Idea* which does not wholly consist of them. But as the Mind is wholly Passive in the reception of all its simple *Ideas*, so it exerts several acts of its own, whereby out of its simple *Ideas*, as the Materials and Foundations of the rest, the other are framed. The Acts of the Mind wherein it exerts its Power over its simple *Ideas* are chiefly these three, 1. Combining several simple *Ideas* into one compound one, and thus all Complex *Ideas* are made. 2. The 2*d*. is bringing two *Ideas*, whether simple or complex, together; and setting them by one another, so as to take a view of them at once, without uniting them into one; by which way it gets all its *Ideas* of Relations. 3. The 3*d*. is separating them from all other *Ideas* that accompany them in their real existence; this is called *Abstraction*: And thus all its General *Ideas* are made. This shews Man's Power and its way of Operation to be muchwhat the same in the Material and Intellectual World. For the

§ 1. *Made by the Mind out of simple ones.*

---

(3) openings] **1–3** (*likewise* **Coste**) | opening/ **4–5** (4–5) would . . . Room] **4–5** | which would they **1–3** (7) sight] **1er–5** | sights **1** (11) Modes,] **4–5** | Modes **1–3** (16) [*1st*] any] **1–4**; *om.* **5** (17)–164(5) But . . . places.] *add.* **4–5** (30) World] **4** | Word **5**

Materials in both being such as he has no power over, either to make or destroy, all that Man can do is either to unite them together, or to set them by one another, or wholly separate them. I shall here begin with the first of these in the consideration of Complex *Ideas*, and come to the other two in their due places. As simple *Ideas* are observed to exist in several Combinations united together; so the Mind has a power to consider several of them united together, as one *Idea*; and that not only as they are united in external Objects, but as it self has join'd them. *Ideas* thus made up of several simple ones put together, I call *Complex*; such as are *Beauty, Gratitude, a Man, an Army, the Universe*; which though complicated of various simple *Ideas*, or *complex Ideas* made up of simple ones, yet are, when the Mind pleases, considered each by it self, as one entire thing, and signified by one name.

§ 2. In this faculty of repeating and joining together its *Ideas*, the Mind has great power in varying and multiplying the Objects of its Thoughts, infinitely beyond what *Sensation* or *Reflection* furnished it with: But all this still confined to those simple *Ideas*, which it received from those two Sources, and which are the ultimate Materials of all its Compositions. For simple *Ideas* are all from things themselves; and of these *the Mind can* have no more, nor other than what are suggested to it. It can have no other *Ideas* of sensible Qualities, than what come from without by the Senses; nor any *Ideas* of other kind of Operations of a thinking Substance, than what it finds in it self: but when it has once got these simple *Ideas*, it is not confined barely to Observation, and what offers it self from without; it can, by its own power, put together those *Ideas* it has, and *make new complex ones*, which it never received so united.

§ 3. *Complex Ideas*, however compounded and decompounded, though their number be infinite, and the variety endless, wherewith they fill, and entertain the Thoughts of Men; yet, I think, they may be all reduced under these three Heads.

1. *Modes.*
2. *Substances.*
3. *Relations.*

§ 2. *Made voluntarily.* § 3. *Are either Modes, Substances, or Relations.*

(3) another,] **5** | another/ **4** (5) *v.* 163(17), n. As] **4–5** | But as these **1–3**
(20) simple *Ideas*] **2–5** | these [those **1er**], they **1** (21) of these] *add.* **2–5**
(21–2) than what] **2–5** | simple *Ideas*, than as they **1** (25) these] **2–5** | those **1**

§ 4. First, *Modes* I call such complex *Ideas*, which however compounded, contain not in them the supposition of subsisting by themselves, but are considered as Dependences on, or Affections of Substances; such are the *Ideas* signified by the Words *Triangle*, *Gratitude*, *Murther*, *etc.* And if in this I use the word *Mode*, in somewhat a different sence from its ordinary signification, I beg pardon; it being unavoidable in Discourses, differing from the ordinary received Notions, either to make new Words, or to use old Words in somewhat a new signification, the latter whereof, in our present case, is perhaps the more tolerable of the two.

§ 5. Of these *Modes*, there are two sorts, which deserve distinct consideration. First, There are some which are only variations, or different combinations of the same simple *Idea*, without the mixture of any other, as a dozen, or score; which are nothing but the *Ideas* of so many distinct Unites added together, and these I call *simple Modes*, as being contained within the bounds of one simple *Idea*. Secondly, There are others compounded of simple *Ideas* of several kinds, put together to make one complex one; *v.g. Beauty*, consisting of a certain composition of Colour and Figure, causing delight in the Beholder; *Theft*, which being the concealed change of the possession of any thing, without the consent of the Proprietor, contains, as is visible, a combination of several *Ideas* of several kinds; and these I call *mixed Modes*.

§ 6. Secondly, The *Ideas of Substances* are such combinations of simple *Ideas*, as are taken to represent distinct particular things subsisting by themselves; in which the supposed, or confused *Idea* of Substance, such as it is, is always the first and chief. Thus if to Substance be joined the simple *Idea* of a certain dull whitish colour, with certain degrees of Weight, Hardness, Ductility, and Fusibility, we have the *Idea* of *Lead*; and a combination of the *Ideas* of a certain sort of Figure, with the powers of Motion, Thought, and Reasoning, joined to Substance, make the ordinary *Idea* of *a Man*. Now of Substances also, there are two sorts of *Ideas*; one of single Substances, as they exist separately, as of *a Man*, or *a Sheep*; the other of several of those put together, as an *Army* of Men, or *Flock* of Sheep; which *collective* Ideas *of* several *Substances* thus put

§ 4. *Modes.* § 5. *Simple and mixed Modes.* § 6. *Substances Single or Collective.*

---

(9) , the latter whereof,] **2–5** | ; which **1**

together, are as much each of them one single *Idea*, as that of a Man, or an Unite.

§ 7. Thirdly, The last sort of complex *Ideas*, is that we call *Relation*, which consists in the consideration and comparing one *Idea* with another: Of these several kinds we shall treat in their order.

§ 8. If we will trace the progress of our Minds, and with attention observe how it repeats, adds together, and unites its simple *Ideas* received from Sensation or Reflection, it will lead us farther than at first, perhaps, we should have imagined. And, I believe, we shall find, if we warily observe the Originals of our Notions, that even *the most abstruse* Ideas, how remote soever they may seem from Sense, or from any operation of our own Minds, are yet only such, as the Understanding frames to it self, by repeating and joining together *Ideas*, that it had either from Objects of Sense, or from its own operations about them: So that those even large *and abstract* Ideas *are derived from Sensation, or Reflection*, being no other than what the Mind, by the ordinary use of its own Faculties, employed about *Ideas*, received from Objects of Sense, or from the Operations it observes in it self about them, may, and does attain unto. This I shall endeavour to shew in the *Ideas* we have of *Space*, *Time*, and *Infinity*, and some few other, that seem the most remote from those Originals.

CHAPTER XIII

Of simple Modes; and first, of the simple Modes of Space.

§ 1. THOUGH in the foregoing part, I have often mentioned simple *Ideas*, which are truly the Materials of all our Knowledge; yet having treated of them there, rather in the way that they come into the Mind, than as distinguished from others more compounded, it will not be, perhaps, amiss to take a view of some of them again under this Consideration, and examine those different *Modifications of the same* Idea; which the Mind either finds in things existing, or is able

§ 7. *Relation.* § 8. *The abstrusest* Ideas *from the two Sources.*
§ 1. *Simple Modes.*

---

(13) from] *add.* **4–5** (15) [*2nd*] from] *add.* **4–5** (19) [*2nd*] from] *add.* **4–5**

to make within it self, without the help of any extrinsical Object, or any foreign Suggestion.

Those *Modifications of any one simple* Idea, (which, as has been said, *I call simple Modes*) are as perfectly different and distinct *Ideas* in the Mind, as those of the greatest distance or contrariety. For the *Idea* of *Two*, is as distinct from that of *One*, as *Blueness* from *Heat*, or either of them from any Number: and yet it is made up only of that simple *Idea* of an Unite repeated; and Repetitions of this kind joined together, make those distinct *simple Modes*, of a *Dozen*, a *Gross*, a *Million*.

§ 2. I shall begin with the *simple Idea of Space*. I have shewed above, *c*.4. that we get the *Idea* of Space, both by our Sight, and Touch; which, I think, is so evident, that it would be as needless, to go to prove, that Men perceive, by their Sight, a distance between Bodies of different Colours, or between the parts of the same Body; as that they see Colours themselves: Nor is it less obvious, that they can do so in the Dark by Feeling and Touch.

§ 3. This Space considered barely in length between any two Beings, without considering any thing else between them, is called *Distance*: If considered in Length, Breadth, and Thickness, I think, it may be called *Capacity*: The term Extension is usually applied to it, in what manner soever considered.

§ 4. Each different distance is a different Modification of Space, and *each* Idea *of any different distance, or Space, is a simple Mode of this* Idea. Men for the use, and by the custom of measuring, settle in their Minds the *Ideas* of certain stated lengths, such as are an *Inch*, *Foot*, *Yard*, *Fathom*, *Mile*, *Diameter of the Earth*, etc. which are so many distinct *Ideas* made up only of Space. When any such stated lengths or measures of Space are made familiar to Men's Thoughts, they

§ 2. Idea *of Space*. § 3. *Space and Extension*. § 4. *Immensity*.

---

(6) that of *One*] **4–5** | that of *Three* **2–3** | *Three* **1** (7) it is] **4–5** | they are **1–3** (8) Repetitions of this kind] **4–5** | these Repetitions **1–3** (20–1) The . . . considered.] **4–5** | When considered between the extremities of Matter, which fills the Capacity of Space with something solid, tangible, and movable, it is properly called *Extension*. And so Extension is an *Idea* belonging to Body only; but *Space* may, as is evident, be considered without it. At least, I think it most intelligible, and the best way to avoid Confusion, if we use the Word *Extension* for an Affection of Matter, or the distance of the Extremities of particular solid Bodies; and *Space* in the more general Signification for distance, with or without solid Matter possessing it. **1–3** (24)–168(1) Men . . . can,] **2–5** | Men having by accustoming themselves to stated lengths of Space, which they use for measuring of other distances, as *a Foot*, *a Yard*, *or a Fathom*, *a League*, *or Diametre of the Earth*, made those *Ideas* familiar to their Thoughts, can **1** (*l. below* 28: § 3.) *In* **Coste**, *§ 3 comes under the same marginal summary as § 2.*

can, in their Minds, repeat them as often as they will, without mixing or joining to them the *Idea* of Body, or any thing else; and frame to themselves the *Ideas* of long, square, or cubick, *Feet*, *Yards*, or *Fathoms*, here amongst the Bodies of the Universe, or else beyond the utmost Bounds of all Bodies; and by adding these still one to another, enlarge their *Idea* of Space as much as they please. This Power of repeating, or doubling any *Idea* we have of any distance, and adding it to the former as often as we will, without being ever able to come to any stop or stint, let us enlarge it as much as we will, is that, which gives us the *Idea* of *Immensity*.

§ 5. There is another Modification of this *Idea*, which is nothing but the Relation which the Parts of the Termination of Extension, or circumscribed Space have amongst themselves. This the Touch discovers in sensible Bodies, whose Extremities come within our reach; and the Eye takes both from Bodies and Colours, whose Boundaries are within its view: Where observing how the Extremities terminate, either in streight Lines, which meet at discernible Angles; or in crooked Lines, wherein no Angles can be perceived, by considering these as they relate to one another, in all Parts of the Extremities of any Body or Space, it has that *Idea* we call *Figure*, which affords to the Mind infinite Variety. For besides the vast Number of different Figures, that do really exist in the coherent masses of Matter, the Stock, that the Mind has in its Power, by varying the *Idea* of Space; and thereby making still new Compositions, by repeating its own *Ideas*, and joining them as it pleases, is perfectly inexhaustible: And so it can multiply Figures *in infinitum*.

§ 6. For the Mind, having a Power to repeat the *Idea* of any length directly stretched out, and join it to another in the same Direction, which is to double the length of that streight Line; or else join it to another with what Inclination it thinks fit, and so make what sort of Angle it pleases: And being able also to shorten any Line it imagines, by taking from it $\frac{1}{2}$ or $\frac{1}{4}$, or what part it pleases, without being able to come to an end of any such Divisions, it can make an

§§ 5, 6. *Figure.*

(1) *v.* 167(24), n. (11) *Idea*] **4–5** | *Idea* of Space **1–3** (*likewise* **Coste**) (12) which] **4–5** | of **1–3** (12–13) Extension, or circumscribed Space have] **4–5** | Capacity, or Extension **1–3**. (**Coste** 'qui n'est autre chose que la relation qui est entre les parties qui terminent l'étenduë.') (33) $\frac{1}{2}$ or $\frac{1}{4}$] **1–4** | one half, or one fourth **5**

Angle of any bigness: So also the Lines that are its sides, of what length it pleases, which joining again to other Lines of different lengths, and at different Angles, till it has wholly inclosed any Space, it is evident that it can multiply *Figures* both in their Shape, and Capacity, *in infinitum*, all which are but so many different *simple Modes of Space*.

The same that it can do with streight Lines, it can do also with crooked, or crooked and streight together; and the same it can do in Lines, it can also in Superficies, by which we may be led into farther Thoughts of the endless Variety of *Figures*, that the Mind has a Power to make, and thereby to multiply the *simple Modes* of Space.

§ 7. Another *Idea* coming under this Head, and belonging to this Tribe, is that we call *Place*. As in simple Space, we consider the relation of Distance between any two Bodies, or Points; so in our *Idea* of *Place*, we consider the relation of Distance betwixt any thing, and any two or more Points, which are considered, as keeping the same distance one with another, and so considered as at rest; for when we find any thing at the same distance now, which it was Yesterday from any two or more Points, which have not since changed their distance one with another, and with which we then compared it, we say it hath kept the same *Place*: But if it hath sensibly altered its distance with either of those Points, we say it hath changed its Place: Though vulgarly speaking in the common Notion of *Place*, we do not always exactly observe the distance from precise Points; but from larger Portions of sensible Objects, to which we consider the thing placed to bear Relation, and its distance from which we have some Reason to observe.

§ 8. Thus a Company of Chess-men, standing on the same squares of the Chess-board, where we left them, we say they are all in the *same Place*, or unmoved; though, perhaps, the Chess-board hath been in the mean time carried out of one Room into another, because we compared them only to the Parts of the Chess-board, which keep the same distance one with another. The Chess-board, we also say, is in the *same Place* it was, if it remain in the same part of the Cabin, though, perhaps, the Ship which it is in, sails all the

§§ 7–10. *Place.*

(1) sides,] **2–5** | sides **1** (17) considered] **1–3, 5** | consider'd **4** (9) it] **1–3, 5** | in **4** (24) its] **1–4** | it **5** (26) from] *add.* **2–5** (28) distance] **2–5** | distance, **1** (36) which] *add.* **4–5**

while: and the Ship is said to be in the *same Place*, supposing it kept the same distance with the Parts of the neighbouring Land; though, perhaps, the Earth hath turned round; and so both Chess-men, and Board, and Ship, have every one *changed Place* in respect of remoter Bodies, which have kept the same distance one with another. But yet the distance from certain Parts of the Board, being that which determines the Place of the Chess-men; and the distance from the fixed parts of the Cabin (with which we made the Comparison) being that which determined the Place of the Chess-board, and the fixed parts of the Earth, that by which we determined the Place of the Ship, these things may be said properly to be in the *same Place*, in those respects: Though their distance from some other things, which in this matter we did not consider, being varied, they have undoubtedly *changed Place* in that respect; and we our selves shall think so, when we have occasion to compare them with those other.

§ 9. But this Modification of Distance, we call *Place*, being made by Men, for their common use, that by it they might be able to design the particular Position of Things, where they had occasion for such Designation, Men consider and determine of this *Place*, by reference to those adjacent things, which best served to their present Purpose, without considering other things, which to another Purpose would better *determine the Place* of the same thing. Thus in the Chess-board, the use of the *Designation of* the *Place* of each Chess-man, being determined only within that chequer'd piece of Wood, 'twould cross that Purpose, to measure it by any thing else: But when these very Chess-men are put up in a Bag, if any one should ask, where the black King is, it would be proper to *determine the Place* by the parts of the Room it was in, and not by the Chess-board; there being another use of *designing the Place* it is now in, than when in Play it was on the Chess-board, and so must be determined by other Bodies. So if any one should ask, in what Place are the Verses, which report the Story of *Nisus* and *Eurialus*, 'twould be very improper to determine this Place, by saying, they were in such a part of the Earth, or in *Bodley*'s Library: But the right Designation of the place, would be by the parts of *Virgil*'s Works; and the proper Answer would be, That these Verses were about the middle of the Ninth Book of his *Æneids*; And that they have been always constantly in the same Place ever since *Virgil* was printed: Which is true, though the Book it self hath moved a Thousand times, the use of the *Idea* of Place here, being to know only, in what part of the Book that Story is; that so upon occasion, we may know where to find it, and have recourse to it for our use.

§ 10. That our *Idea* of Place, is nothing else, but such a relative Position of any thing, as I have before mentioned, I think, is plain, and will be easily admitted, when we consider, that we can have no *Idea* of the Place of the Universe, though we can of all the parts of it; because beyond that, we have not the *Idea* of any fixed, distinct, particular Beings, in reference to which, we can imagine it to have any relation of distance; but all beyond it is one uniform Space or Expansion, wherein the Mind finds no variety, no marks. For to say that the World is somewhere, means no more, than that it does exist; this though a Phrase, borrowed from Place, signifying only its Existence, not Location; and when one can find out, and frame in his Mind clearly and distinctly the Place of the Universe, he will be able to tell us, whether it moves or stands still in the undistinguishable *Inane* of infinite Space; though it be true, that the Word Place, has sometimes a more confused Sense, and stands for that Space, which any Body takes up; and so the Universe is in a Place. The *Idea* therefore of *Place*, we have by the same means, that we get the *Idea* of Space, (whereof this is but a particular limited Consideration) *viz.* by our Sight and Touch; by either of which we receive into our Minds the *Ideas* of Extension or Distance.

§ 11. There are some that would persuade us, that *Body and Extension are the same thing*; who either change the Signification of Words, which I would not suspect them of, they having so severely condemned the Philosophy of others, because it hath been too much placed in the uncertain meaning, or deceitful obscurity of doubtful or insignificant Terms. If therefore they mean by *Body and Extension the same*, that other People do, *viz.* by *Body* something that is solid, and extended, whose parts are separable and movable different ways; and by Extension, only the Space that lies between the Extremities of those solid coherent Parts, and which is possessed by them, they confound very different *Ideas* one with another. For I appeal to every Man's own Thoughts, whether the *Idea* of Space be

§§ 11–14. *Extension and Body not the same.*

(12) than] **5** | but **1–4** (20–3) The . . . Distance.] **4–5**; *this forms* § *11 in* **1–3**. (24)–172(34) There . . . *Space.*] **4–5**; *this forms* § *12 in* **1–3**. (24) some] **Coste**$_2$ *adds in a footnote* 'Les Cartesiens'. (27) others] **Coste** 'la Philosophie qui étoit en vogue avant eux'; *and* **Coste**$_2$ *adds, in a note, a reference to* 'La Philosophie Scholastique'. (*l. below* 35) *In* **1–3**, *this marginal summary is applied to their* §§ *11–14*.

not as distinct from that of Solidity, as it is from the *Idea* of Scarlet-Colour? 'Tis true, Solidity cannot exist without Extension, neither can Scarlet-Colour exist without Extension; but this hinders not, but that they are distinct *Ideas*. Many *Ideas* require others as necessary to their Existence or Conception, which yet are very distinct *Ideas*. Motion can neither be, nor be conceived without Space; and yet Motion is not Space, nor Space Motion: Space can exist without it, and they are very distinct *Ideas*; and so, I think, are those of Space and Solidity. Solidity is so inseparable an *Idea* from Body, that upon that depends its filling of Space, its Contact, Impulse, and Communication of Motion upon Impulse. And if it be a Reason to prove, that Spirit is different from Body, because Thinking includes not the *Idea* of Extension in it; the same Reason will be as valid, I suppose, to prove, that *Space is not Body*, because it includes not the *Idea* of Solidity in it; *Space and Solidity* being *as distinct Ideas*, as Thinking and Extension, and as wholly separable in the Mind one from another. *Body* then and *Extension*, 'tis evident, are two distinct *Ideas*. For,

§ 12. *First*, *Extension* includes no Solidity, nor resistance to the Motion of *Body*, as Body does.

§ 13. *Secondly*, The Parts of pure Space are inseparable one from the other; so that the Continuity cannot be separated, neither really, nor mentally. For I demand of any one, to remove any part of it from another, with which it is continued, even so much as in Thought. To divide and separate actually, is, as I think, by removing the parts one from another, to make two Superficies, where before there was a Continuity: And to divide mentally, is to make in the Mind two Superficies, where before there was a Continuity, and consider them as removed one from the other; which can only be done in things considered by the Mind, as capable of being separated; and by separation, of acquiring new distinct Superficies, which they then have not, but are capable of: But neither of these ways of Separation, whether real or mental, is, as I think, compatible to pure *Space*.

'Tis true, a Man may consider so much of such a *Space*, as is answerable or commensurate to a Foot, without considering the rest; which is indeed a partial Consideration, but not so much as mental Separation, or Division; since a Man can no more mentally divide, without considering two Superficies, separate one from the

(34) *v.* 171(24), n. (35)–173(7) 'Tis . . . separately.] **4–5**; *this forms* § *13 in* **1–3**.

other, than he can actually divide, without making two Superficies disjoin'd one from the other: But a partial consideration is not separating. A Man may consider Light in the Sun, without its Heat; or Mobility in Body without its Extension, without thinking of their separation. One is only a partial Consideration, terminating in one alone; and the other is a Consideration of both, as existing separately.

§ 14. *Thirdly*, The parts of pure *Space*, are immovable, which follows from their inseparability; *Motion* being nothing but change of distance between any two things: But this cannot be between Parts that are inseparable; which therefore must needs be at perpetual rest one amongst another.

Thus the determined *Idea* of simple *Space* distinguishes it plainly, and sufficiently from *Body*; since its Parts are inseparable, immovable, and without resistance to the Motion of Body.

§ 15. If any one ask me, *What* this *Space*, I speak of, *is*? I will tell him, when he tells me what his *Extension* is. For to say, as is usually done, That Extension is to have *partes extra partes*, is to say only, That *Extension* is *Extension*: For what am I the better informed in the nature of *Extension*, when I am told, That *Extension is to have parts that are extended*, *exterior to parts that are extended*, i.e. *Extension* consists of extended Parts? As if one asking, What a Fibre was; I should answer him, That it was a thing made up of several Fibres: Would he hereby be enabled to understand what a Fibre was, better than he did before? Or rather, would he not have reason to think, that my design was to make sport with him, rather than seriously to instruct him?

§ 16. Those who contend that *Space and Body* are *the same*, bring this *Dilemma*. Either this *Space* is something or nothing; if nothing be between two Bodies, they must necessarily touch; if it be allowed to be something, they ask, whether it be Body or Spirit? To which I answer by another Question, Who told them, that there was, or could be nothing, but solid Beings, which could not think; and thinking Beings that were not extended? Which is all they mean by the terms *Body* and *Spirit*.

§ 15. *The definition of Extension explains it not.* § 16. *Division of Beings into Bodies and Spirits proves not Space and Body the same.*

---

(7) *v.* 172(35), n. (13) determined] **4–5** | clear and distinct **1–3** (*l. below* 35: § 15.) *This marginal summary for* § 15 *in* **4–5** *replaces* 'Substance which we know not, no proof against Space without Body'. *for* §§ 15–17 *in* **2–3**. (*l. below* 35: § 16.) *This marginal summary for* § 16, *in* **4–5** *but not in* **2–3**.

§ 17. If it be demanded (as usually it is) whether this *Space* void of *Body*, be *Substance* or *Accident*, I shall readily answer, I know not: nor shall be ashamed to own my Ignorance, till they that ask, shew me a clear distinct *Idea* of *Substance*.

§ 18. I endeavour, as much as I can, to deliver my self from those Fallacies, which we are apt to put upon our selves, by taking Words for Things. It helps not our Ignorance, to feign a Knowledge, where we have none, by making a noise with Sounds, without clear and distinct Significations. Names made at pleasure, neither alter the nature of things, nor make us understand them, but as they are signs of, and stand for determined *Ideas*. And I desire those who lay so much stress on the sound of these two Syllables, *Substance*, to consider, whether applying it, as they do, to the infinite incomprehensible GOD, to finite Spirit, and to Body, it be in the same sense; and whether it stands for the same *Idea*, when each of those three so different Beings are called *Substances*? If so, whether it will not thence follow, That God, Spirits, and Body, agreeing in the same common nature of *Substance*, differ not any otherwise than in a bare different modification of that *Substance*; as a Tree and a Pebble, being in the same sense Body, and agreeing in the common nature of Body, differ only in a bare modification of that common matter; which will be a very harsh Doctrine. If they say, That they apply it to God, finite Spirits, and Matter, in three different significations, and that it stands for one *Idea*, when GOD is said to be a *Substance*; for another, when the Soul is called *Substance*; and for a third, when a Body is called so. If the name *Substance*, stands for three several distinct *Ideas*, they would do well to make known those distinct *Ideas*, or at least to give three distinct names to them, to prevent in so important a Notion, the Confusion and Errors, that will naturally follow from the promiscuous use of so doubtful a term; which is so far from being suspected to have three distinct, that in ordinary use it has scarce one clear distinct signification: And if they can thus make three distinct *Ideas* of *Substance*, what hinders, why another may not make a fourth?

§§ 17, 18. *Substance which we know not, no proof against Space without Body.*

---

(11) determined] **4–5** | clear and distinct **1–3** (14) Spirit] **5** | Spirits **1–4** (15) stands] **4–5** | stand **1–3** (18) any] *add.* **2–5** (20) Body] **1er–5** | bodied **1** (31) in ordinary use] *add.* **4–5** (*l. below* 34) *In* **4–5**, *this marginal summary is for* §§ *17–18; in* **2–3**, *it is for* §§ *15–17, that for* § *18 being* 'Substance and Accidents of little use in Philosophy.'

§ 19. They who first ran into the Notion of *Accidents*, as a sort of real Beings, that needed something to inhere in, were forced to find out the word *Substance*, to support them. Had the poor *Indian* Philosopher (who imagined that the Earth also wanted something to bear it up) but thought of this word *Substance*, he needed not to have been at the trouble to find an Elephant to support it, and a Tortoise to support his Elephant: The word *Substance* would have done it effectually. And he that enquired, might have taken it for as good an Answer from an *Indian* Philosopher, That *Substance*, without knowing what it is, is that which supports the Earth, as we take it for a sufficient Answer, and good Doctrine, from our *European* Philosophers, That *Substance* without knowing what it is, is that which supports *Accidents*. So that of *Substance*, we have no *Idea* of what it is, but only a confused obscure one of what it does.

§ 20. Whatever a learned Man may do here, an intelligent *American*, who enquired into the Nature of Things, would scarce take it for a satisfactory Account, if desiring to learn our Architecture, he should be told, That a Pillar was a thing supported by a *Basis*, and a *Basis* something that supported a Pillar. Would he not think himself mocked, instead of taught, with such an account as this? And a Stranger to them would be very liberally instructed in the nature of Books, and the things they contained, if he should be told, that all learned Books consisted of Paper and Letters, and that Letters were things inhering in Paper, and Paper a thing that held forth Letters; a notable way of having clear *Ideas* of Letters and Paper. But were the Latin words *Inhærentia* and *Substantia*, put into the plain English ones that answer them, and were called *Sticking on*, and *Under-propping*, they would better discover to us the very great clearness there is in the Doctrine of *Substance and Accidents*, and shew of what use they are in deciding of Questions in Philosophy.

§ 21. But to return to our *Idea* of *Space*. If *Body* be not supposed infinite, which, I think, no one will affirm, I would ask, Whether, if God placed a Man at the extremity of corporeal Beings, he could not stretch his Hand beyond his Body? If he could, then he would put

§§ 19, 20. *Substance and Accidents of little use in Philosophy.* § 21. *A* Vacuum *beyond the utmost bounds of Body.*

---

(23) Letters] **1–4** | Letter **5** (31) *Idea*] **2–5** | *Ideas* **1** (*l. below* 34: §§ 19, 20.) *This marginal summary is for* §§ *19–20 in* **4–5**; *but in* **2–3** *it is for* §§ *18–19, that for* § *20 being* 'A *Vacuum* beyond the utmost bounds of Body.' (*l. below* 34: § 21.) *A . . . Body.*] **4–5** | *The Power of annihilation proves a* Vacuum. **2–3**

his Arm, where there was before *Space* without *Body*; and if there he spread his Fingers, there would still be *Space* between them without *Body*: If he could not stretch out his Hand, it must be because of some external hindrance; (for we suppose him alive, with such a power of moving the parts of his Body, that he hath now, which is not in it self impossible, if God so pleased to have it; or at least it is not impossible for God so to move him:) And then I ask, Whether that which hinders his Hand from moving outwards, be Substance or Accident, Something or Nothing? And when they have resolved that, they will be able to resolve themselves, what that is, which is or may be between two Bodies at a distance, that is not Body, has no Solidity. In the mean time, the Argument is at least as good, That where nothing hinders, (as beyond the utmost bounds of all Bodies) a *Body* put into motion may move on, as where there is nothing between, there two Bodies must necessarily touch. For pure *Space* between, is sufficient to take away the necessity of mutual Contact; but bare *Space* in the way, is not sufficient to stop Motion. The truth is, these Men must either own, that they think Body infinite, though they are loth to speak it out, or else affirm, that *Space* is not *Body*. For I would fain meet with that thinking Man, that can, in his Thoughts, set any bounds to Space, more than he can to Duration; or by thinking, hope to arrive at the end of either: And therefore if his *Idea* of Eternity be infinite, so is his *Idea* of Immensity; they are both finite or infinite alike.

§ 21 [*bis*]. Farther, those who assert the impossibility of *Space* existing without *Matter*, must not only make Body infinite, but must also deny a power in God to annihilate any part of Matter. No one, I suppose, will deny, that God can put an end to all motion that is in Matter, and fix all the Bodies of the Universe in a perfect quiet and rest, and continue them so as long as he pleases. Whoever then will allow, that God can, during such a general rest, annihilate either this Book, or the Body of him that reads it, must necessarily admit the possibility of a *Vacuum*. For it is evident, that the Space, that was filled by the parts of the annihilated Body, will still remain, and be a Space without Body. For the circumambient Bodies being in perfect rest, are a Wall of Adamant, and in that state make it a

§ 21 [*bis*]. *The Power of annihilation proves a* Vacuum.

(1) he] **1, 3–5** | be **2** (25)–177(20) In **1–5**, *this section is numbered 21, as is the preceding one; in* **Coste**, *this section is numbered 22, with a consequent re-numbering of the following sections.*

perfect impossibility for any other Body to get into that Space. And indeed the necessary motion of one Particle of Matter, into the place from whence another Particle of Matter is removed, is but a consequence from the supposition of Plenitude; which will therefore need some better proof, than a supposed matter of fact, which Experiment can never make out; our own clear and distinct *Ideas* plainly satisfying us, that there is no necessary connexion between *Space* and *Solidity*, since we can conceive the one without the other. And those who dispute for or against a *Vacuum*, do thereby confess, they have distinct *Ideas* of *Vacuum* and *Plenum*, i.e. that they have an *Idea* of Extension void of Solidity, though they deny its existence; or else they dispute about nothing at all. For they who so much alter the signification of Words, as to call *Extension Body*, and consequently make the whole Essence of Body, to be nothing but pure Extension without Solidity, must talk absurdly, whenever they speak of *Vacuum*, since it is impossible for Extension to be without Extension. For *Vacuum*, whether we affirm or deny its existence, signifies Space without Body, whose very existence no one can deny to be possible, who will not make Matter infinite, and take from God a power to annihilate any Particle of it.

§ 22. But not to go so far as beyond the utmost bounds of Body in the Universe, nor appeal to God's Omnipotency to find a *Vacuum*, the *motion* of Bodies, that are in our view and neighbourhood, seem to me plainly to evince it. For I desire any one so to divide a solid Body, of any dimension he pleases, as to make it possible for the solid Parts to move up and down freely every way within the bounds of that Superficies, if there be not left in it a void space, as big as the least part into which he has divided the said solid Body. And if where the least Particle of the Body divided, is as big as a Mustard-seed, a void Space equal to the bulk of a Mustard-seed, be requisite to make room for the free motion of the Parts of the divided Body within the bounds of its Superficies, where the Particles of Matter are 100,000,000 less than a Mustard-seed, there must also be a space void of solid Matter, as big as 100,000,000 part of a Mustard-seed; for if it holds in one, it will hold in the other, and so on *in infinitum*. And let this void Space be as little as it will, it

§ 22. *Motion proves a* Vacuum.

---

(20) *v.* 176(25), n. (24) plainly] **1T.er, 2–5** | plain **1** (35) holds] **4** (**Coste** 'si ce Vuide proportionnel est nécessaire dans le prémier cas') | hold **1–3, 5**

destroys the Hypothesis of *Plenitude*. For if there can be a Space void of Body, equal to the smallest separate Particle of Matter now existing in Nature, 'tis still Space without Body; and makes as great a difference between Space and Body, as if it were Μέγα χάσμα, a distance as wide as any in Nature. And therefore if we suppose not the void Space necessary to Motion, equal to the least parcel of the divided solid Matter, but to $\frac{1}{10}$ or $\frac{1}{1000}$ of it, the same consequence will always follow of Space without Matter.

§ 23. But the Question being here, whether the *Idea of Space* or *Extension*, be *the same with the Idea of Body*, it is not necessary to prove the real existence of a *Vacuum*, but the *Idea* of it; which 'tis plain Men have, when they enquire and dispute, whether there be a *Vacuum* or no? For if they had not the *Idea* of Space without Body, they could not make a question about its existence: And if their *Idea* of Body did not include in it something more than the bare *Idea* of Space, they could have no doubt about the plenitude of the World; and 'twould be as absurd to demand, whether there were Space without Body, as whether there were Space without Space, or Body without Body, since these were but different Names of the same *Idea*.

§ 24. 'Tis true, the *Idea* of *Extension* joins it self so inseparably with all visible, and most tangible Qualities, that it suffers us to see no one, or feel very few external Objects, without taking in impressions of Extension too. This readiness of Extension to make it self be taken notice of so constantly with other *Ideas*, has been the occasion, I guess, that some have made the whole essence of *Body*, to consist in Extension; which is not much to be wond'red at, since some have had their Minds, by their Eyes and Touch, (the busiest of all our Senses) so filled with the *Idea* of Extension, and as it were wholly possessed with it, that they allowed no existence to any thing, that had not Extension. I shall not now argue with those Men, who take the measure and possibility of all Being, only from their narrow and gross Imaginations: but having here to do only with those, who conclude the essence of Body to be *Extension*, because, they say, they cannot imagine any sensible Quality of any Body without Extension, I shall desire them to consider, That had they reflected on their *Ideas* of Tastes and Smells, as much as on those of Sight and Touch; nay, had they examined their *Ideas* of Hunger and Thirst,

§ 23. *The* Ideas *of Space and Body distinct.* §§ 24, 25. *Extension being inseparable from Body, proves it not the same.*

and several other Pains, they would have found, that they included in them no *Idea* of Extension at all, which is but an affection of Body, as well as the rest discoverable by our Senses, which are scarce acute enough to look into the pure Essences of Things.

§ 25. If those *Ideas*, which are constantly joined to all others, must therefore be concluded to be the Essence of those Things, which have constantly those *Ideas* joined to them, and are inseparable from them; then Unity is without doubt the essence of every thing. For there is not any Object of Sensation or Reflection, which does not carry with it the *Idea* of one: But the weakness of this kind of Argument, we have already shewn sufficiently.

§ 26. To conclude, whatever Men shall think concerning the existence of a *Vacuum*, this is plain to me, That we have as clear an *Idea of Space distinct from Solidity*, as we have of Solidity distinct from Motion, or Motion from Space. We have not any two more distinct *Ideas*, and we can as easily conceive space without Solidity, as we can conceive Body or Space without Motion, though it be never so certain, that neither Body nor Motion can exist without Space. But whether any one will take Space to be only a relation resulting from the Existence of other Beings at a distance; or whether they will think the Words of the most knowing King *Solomon*, *The Heaven, and the Heaven of Heavens, cannot contain Thee*;* or those more emphatical ones of the inspired Philosopher St. *Paul*, *In Him we live, move, and have our Being*,** are to be understood in a literal sence, I leave every one to consider; only our *Idea* of *Space* is, I think, such as I have mentioned, and distinct from that of *Body*. For whether we consider in Matter it self, the distance of its coherent solid parts, and call it, in respect of those solid parts, *Extension*; or whether considering it, as lying between the extremities of any Body in its several dimensions, we call it *Length*, *Breadth*, and *Thickness*; or else considering it as lying between any two Bodies, or positive Beings, without any consideration, whether there be any Matter or no between, we call it *Distance*. However named or considered, it is always the same uniform simple *Idea* of *Space*, taken from Objects, about which our Senses have been conversant, whereof having

§ 26. Ideas *of Space and Solidity distinct.*

(4) Essences] **2–5** | Essence **1**   (17) or Space] *add.* **2–5**

* 1 Kgs. 8: 27; 2 Chr. 2: 6 and 6: 18.
** Acts 17: 28.

setled *Ideas* in our Minds, we can revive, repeat, and add them one to another as often as we will, and consider the Space or Distance so imagined, either as filled with solid parts, so that another Body cannot come there, without displacing and thrusting out the Body that was there before; or else as void of Solidity, so that a Body of equal dimensions to that empty or pure Space, may be placed in it without the removing or expulsion of any thing that was there. But to avoid Confusion in Discourses concerning this Matter, it were possibly to be wished that the Name *Extension* were applied only to Matter, or the distance of the Extremities of particular Bodies, and the Term *Expansion* to Space in general, with or without solid Matter possessing it, so as to say *Space* is *expanded*, and *Body extended*. But in this every one has his liberty; I propose it only for the more clear and distinct way of speaking.

§ 27. The knowing precisely what our Words stand for, would, I imagine, in this, as well as a great many other cases, quickly end the dispute. For I am apt to think, that Men, when they come to examine them, find their simple *Ideas* all generally to agree, though in discourse with one another, they perhaps confound one another with different Names. I imagine, that *Men* who abstract their Thoughts, and do well examine the *Ideas* of their own Minds, *cannot much differ in thinking*; however, they may perplex themselves with words, according to the way of speaking of the several Schools, or Sects, they have been bred up in: Though amongst unthinking Men, who examine not scrupulously and carefully their own *Ideas*, and strip them not from the marks Men use for them, but confound them with words, there must be endless dispute, wrangling, and jargon; especially if they be learned bookish Men, devoted to some Sect, and accustomed to the Language of it; and have learned to talk after others. But if it should happen, that any two thinking Men should really have different *Ideas*, I do not see how they could discourse or argue one with another. Here I must not be mistaken, to think that every floating Imagination in Men's Brains, is presently of that sort of *Ideas* I speak of. 'Tis not easie for the Mind to put off those confused Notions and Prejudices it has imbibed from Custom, Inadvertency, and common Conversation:

§ 27. *Men differ little in clear simple* Ideas.

(7–14) But . . . speaking.] *add.* **4–5** (24) , or Sects,] **2–4** | or Sects **5** | , or Sects **1** (31) *Ideas*,] **2–5** | *Ideas*, different Notions, **1** (32) discourse] **2–5** | discourse, **1** it requires pains and assiduity to examine its *Ideas*, till it resolves them into those clear and distinct simple ones, out of which they are compounded; and to see which, amongst its simple ones, have or have not a necessary connexion and dependence one upon another: Till a Man doth this in the primary and original Notions of Things, he builds upon floating and uncertain Principles, and will often find himself at a loss.

CHAPTER XIV

Of Duration, and its simple Modes.

§ 1. THERE is another sort of Distance, or Length, the *Idea* whereof we get not from the permanent parts of Space, but from the fleeting and perpetually perishing parts of Succession. This we call *Duration*, the simple Modes whereof are any different lengths of it, whereof we have distinct *Ideas*, as *Hours*, *Days*, *Years*, etc. *Time*, and *Eternity*.

§ 2. The Answer of a great Man, to one who asked what Time was *Si non rogas intelligo*,* (which amounts to this; the more I set my self to think of it, the less I understand it;) might perhaps perswade one, That *Time*, which reveals all other things, is it self not to be discovered. *Duration*, *Time*, and *Eternity*, are, not without reason, thought to have something very abstruse in their nature. But however remote these may seem from our Comprehension, yet if we trace them right to their Originals, I doubt not but one of those Sources of all our Knowledge, *viz. Sensation* and *Reflection*, will be able to furnish us with these *Ideas*, as clear and distinct as many other, which are thought much less obscure; and we shall find, that the *Idea* of Eternity it self is derived from the same common Original with the rest of our *Ideas*.

§ 3. To understand *Time* and *Eternity* aright, we ought with attention to consider what *Idea* it is we have of *Duration*, and how

§ 1. *Duration is fleeting Extension.* §§ 2–4. *Its* Idea *from Reflection on the train of our* Ideas.

(15) *Si* . . ., (which] **3–5** | (*Si* . . ., which **1–2** (16) understand] **1er–5** | understood **1** (18) are, not] **1–4** | are not, **5** (20) these] **3–5** | this **1–2** (23) these] **3–5** | those **1–2** (24) other] **2–5** | others **1**

* St. Augustine, *Confessions*, XI, xiv.

we came by it. 'Tis evident to any one who will but observe what passes in his own Mind, that there is a train of *Ideas*, which constantly succeed one another in his Understanding, as long as he is awake. *Reflection* on these appearances of several *Ideas* one after another in our Minds, is that which furnishes us with the *Idea* of *Succession*: And the distance between any parts of that Succession, or between the appearance of any two *Ideas* in our Minds, is that we call *Duration*. For whilst we are thinking, or whilst we receive successively several *Ideas* in our Minds, we know that we do exist; and so we call the Existence, or the Continuation of the Existence of our selves, or any thing else, Commensurate to the succession of any *Ideas* in our Minds, the *Duration* of our selves, or any such other thing co-existing with our Thinking.

§ 4. That we have our notion of *Succession and Duration* from this Original, *viz.* from Reflection on the train of *Ideas*, which we find to appear one after another in our own Minds, seems plain to me, in that we have no perception of *Duration*, but by considering the train of *Ideas*, that take their turns in our Understandings. When that succession of *Ideas* ceases, our perception of Duration ceases with it; which every one clearly experiments in himself, whilst he sleeps soundly, whether an hour, or a day; a month, or a year; of which Duration of things, whilst he sleeps, or thinks not, he has no perception at all, but it is quite lost to him; and the moment wherein he leaves off to think, till the moment he begins to think again, seems to him to have no distance. And so I doubt not but it would be to a waking Man, if it were possible for him to keep only one *Idea* in his Mind, without variation, and the succession of others: And we see, that one who fixes his Thoughts very intently on one thing, so as to take but little notice of the succession of *Ideas* that pass in his Mind, whilst he is taken up with that earnest Contemplation, lets slip out of his Account a good part of that Duration, and thinks that time shorter than it is. But if sleep commonly unites the distant parts of Duration, it is, because during that time we have no Succession of *Ideas* in our Minds. For if a Man, during his Sleep, dreams, and variety of *Ideas* make themselves perceptible in his Mind one after another, he hath then, during such a dreaming, a Sense of *Duration*, and of the length of it. By which it is to me very clear, that Men derive their *Ideas* of Duration, from their

(5) the] *add.* **1er–5** (25) seems] **5** (*likewise* **Coste**) | seem **1–4** (33) unites] **4–5** | unite **1–3** (35) dreams] **4–5** | dream **1–3** (37) [*1st*] a] *add.* **4–5**

Reflection on the train of the Ideas, they observe to succeed one another in their own Understandings, without which Observation they can have no Notion of *Duration*, whatever may happen in the World.

§ 5. Indeed a Man having from reflecting on the Succession and Number of his own Thoughts, got the Notion or *Idea* of *Duration*, he can apply that Notion to things, which exist while he does not think; as he, that has got the *Idea* of Extension from Bodies by his Sight or Touch, can apply it to distances, where no Body is seen or felt. And therefore, though a Man has no Perception of the length of Duration, which past whilst he slept or thought not: yet having observed the Revolution of Days and Nights, and found the length of their Duration to be in Appearance regular and constant, he can, upon the supposition, that that Revolution has proceeded after the same manner, whilst he was asleep or thought not, as it used to do at other times, he can, I say, imagine and make allowance for the length of *Duration*, whilst he slept. But if *Adam* and *Eve* (when they were alone in the World) instead of their ordinary Nights Sleep, had passed the whole 24 hours in one continued Sleep, the Duration of that 24 hours had been irrecoverably lost to them, and been for ever left out of their Account of time.

§ 6. Thus *by reflecting on the appearing of various* Ideas, *one after another in our Understandings, we get the Notion of Succession*; which if any one should think, we did rather get from our Observation of Motion by our Senses, he will, perhaps, be of my Mind, when he considers, that even Motion produces in his Mind an *Idea* of Succession, no otherwise than as it produces there a continued train of distinguishable *Ideas*. For a Man looking upon a Body really moving, perceives yet no Motion at all, unless that Motion produces a constant train *of successive* Ideas. *v.g.* a Man becalmed at Sea, out of sight of Land, in a fair Day, may look on the Sun, or Sea, or Ship, a whole hour together, and perceive no Motion at all in either; though it be certain, that two, and perhaps all of them, have moved, during that time, a great way: But as soon as he perceives either of them to have changed distance with some other Body, as

§ 5. *The* Idea *of Duration applicable to Things whilst we sleep.* §§ 6–8. *The* Idea *of Succession not from Motion.*

---

(7) while] **2–5** | whilst **1** (10) has] **4–5** | have **1–3** (11) past] **1–4** | passed **5** (19) the whole] **4–5** | that, and the following **1–3**

soon as this Motion produces any new *Idea* in him, then he perceives, that there has been Motion. But where-ever a Man is, with all things at rest about him, without perceiving any Motion at all; if during this hour of quiet he has been thinking, he will perceive the various *Ideas* of his own Thoughts in his own Mind, appearing one after another, and thereby observe and find Succession, where he could observe no Motion.

§ 7. And this, I think, is the Reason, *why Motions very slow*, though they are constant, *are not perceived* by us; because in their remove from one sensible part towards another, their change of distance is so slow, that it causes no new *Ideas* in us, but a good while one after another: And so not causing a constant train of new *Ideas*, to follow one another immediately in our Minds, we have no Perception of Motion; which consisting in a constant Succession, we cannot perceive that Succession, without a constant Succession of varying *Ideas* arising from it.

§ 8. On the contrary, *things that move* so swift, as not to affect the Senses distinctly with several distinguishable distances of their Motion, and so cause not any train of *Ideas* in the Mind, *are not* also *perceived* to move. For any thing, that moves round about in a Circle, in less time than our *Ideas* are wont to succeed one another in our Minds, is not perceived to move; but seems to be a perfect, entire Circle of that Matter, or Colour, and not a part of a Circle in Motion.

§ 9. Hence I leave it to others to judge, whether it be not probable that our *Ideas* do, whilst we are awake, succeed one another in our Minds at certain distances, not much unlike the Images in the inside of a Lanthorn, turned round by the Heat of a Candle. This Appearance of theirs in train, though, perhaps, it may be sometimes faster, and sometimes slower; yet, I guess, varies not very much in a waking Man: There seem to be *certain Bounds to the quickness and slowness of the Succession of* those *Ideas* one to another in our Minds, beyond which they can neither delay nor hasten.

§ 10. The Reason I have for this odd conjecture is, from observing that in the Impressions made upon any of our Senses, we can but to a certain degree perceive any Succession; which if exceeding quick, the Sense of Succession is lost, even in Cases where it is

§§ 9–11. *The train of* Ideas *has a certain degree of quickness.*

---

(20) to move] *add.* **5**

evident, that there is a real Succession. Let a Cannon-Bullet pass through a Room, and in its way take with it any Limb, or fleshy Parts of a Man; 'tis as clear as any Demonstration can be, that it must strike successively the two sides of the Room: 'Tis also evident, that it must touch one part of the Flesh first, and another after; and so in Succession: And yet I believe, no Body, who ever felt the pain of such a shot, or heard the blow against the two distant Walls, could perceive any Succession, either in the pain, or sound of so swift a stroke. Such a part of Duration as this, wherein we perceive no Succession, is that which we may call an *Instant*; and is *that which takes up the time of only one Idea* in our Minds, without the Succession of another, wherein therefore we perceive no Succession at all.

§ 11. This also happens, *where the Motion is* so *slow*, as not to supply a constant train of fresh *Ideas* to the Senses, as fast as the Mind is capable of receiving new ones into it; and so other *Ideas* of our own Thoughts, having room to come into our Minds, between those offered to our Senses by the moving Body, *there the Sense of Motion is lost*; and the Body, though it really moves, yet not changing perceivable distance with some other Bodies, as fast as the *Ideas* of our own Minds do naturally follow one another in train, the thing seems to stand still, as is evident in the Hands of Clocks, and Shadows of Sun-dials, and other constant, but slow Motions, where though after certain Intervals, we perceive by the change of distance, that it hath moved, yet the Motion it self we perceive not.

§ 12. So that to me it seems, that *the constant and regular Succession of Ideas* in a waking Man, *is*, as it were, *the Measure* and Standard *of all other Successions*, whereof if any one either exceeds the pace of our *Ideas*; as where two sounds or pains, *etc.* take up in their Succession the Duration of but one *Idea*; or else where any Motion or Succession is so slow, as that it keeps not pace with the *Ideas* in our Minds, or the quickness, in which they take their turns; as when any one, or more *Ideas* in their ordinary course come into our Mind between those, which are offered to the sight, by the different perceptible distances of a Body in Motion, or between Sounds, or Smells,

§ 12. *This train the measure of other Successions.*

---

(2) fleshy] **1–3, 5** | fleshly **4.** (**Coste** 'emporte quelque membre du Corps d'un homme') (19) moves] **4–5** | move **1–3** (27) *is*] **4–5** | *are* **1–3** (28) *Successions*] **4–5** | *Succession* **1–3** (28–9) whereof . . . *Ideas*;] **4–5** | which if it either exceeds their pace, **1–3** (35) , or Smells,] **1–2, 4** | or Smells **5** |, or Smells **3**

following one another, there also the Sense of a constant continued Succession is lost, and we perceive it not, but with certain gaps of rest between.

§ 13. If it be so, that the *Ideas* of our Minds, whilst we have any there, do constantly change, and shift in a continual Succession, it would be impossible, may any one say, for a Man to think long of any one thing: By which if it be meant, that a Man may *have one self-same single* Idea *a long time alone in his Mind, without any variation at all*, I think, in matter of Fact it is *not possible*, for which (not knowing how the *Ideas* of our Minds are framed, of what Materials they are made, whence they have their Light, and how they come to make their Appearances,) I can give no other Reason but Experience: and I would have any one try, whether he can keep one unvaried single *Idea* in his Mind, without any other, for any considerable time together.

§ 14. For Trial, let him take any Figure, any Degree of Light or Whiteness, or what other he pleases; and he will, I suppose, find it difficult to keep all other *Ideas* out of his Mind: But that some, either of another kind, or various Consideration of that *Idea* (each of which Considerations is a new *Idea*) will constantly succeed one another in his Thoughts, let him be as wary as he can.

§ 15. All that is in a Man's Power in this Case, I think, is only to mind and observe what the *Ideas* are, that take their turns *in* his Understanding; or else, to direct the sort, and call in such as he hath a desire or use of: but hinder the *constant Succession* of fresh ones, I think he cannot, though he may commonly chuse, whether he will heedfully observe and consider them.

§ 16. Whether these several *Ideas* in a Man's Mind be made by certain Motions, I will not here dispute: But this I am sure, that they include no *Idea* of Motion in their Appearance; and if a Man had not the *Idea* of Motion otherwise, I think he would have none at all, which is enough to my present Purpose; and sufficiently shews, that the notice we take of the *Ideas* of our own Minds, appearing there one after another, is that, which gives us the *Idea* of Succession and Duration, without which we should have no such *Ideas* at all. 'Tis *not* then, *Motion*, but the constant train of *Ideas* in our Minds, whilst

§§ 13–15. *The Mind cannot fix long on one invariable* Idea. § 16. Ideas, *however made, include no sense of Motion.*

---

(20) Considerations] **2–5** | Consideration **1** (27) observe] **4–5** | observe, **1–3**

we are waking, *that furnishes us with the* Idea *of Duration*, whereof Motion no otherwise gives us any Perception, than as it causes in our Minds a constant Succession of *Ideas*, as I have before shewed: and we have as clear an *Idea* of Succession, and Duration by the train of other *Ideas* succeeding one another in our Minds, without the *Idea* of any Motion, as by the train of *Ideas* caused by the uninterrupted sensible change of distance between two Bodies, which we have from Motion; and therefore we should as well have the *Idea* of Duration, were there no Sense of Motion at all.

§ 17. Having thus got the *Idea* of Duration, the next thing natural for the Mind to do, is to get some *measure of* this common *Duration*, whereby it might judge of its different lengths, and consider the distinct Order, wherein several things exist, without which a great part of our Knowledge would be confused, and a great part of History be rendered very useless. This Consideration of Duration, as set out by certain Periods, and marked by certain Measures or *Epochs*, is that, I think, which most properly we call *Time*.

§ 18. In the measuring of Extension, there is nothing more required, but the Application of the Standard or Measure we make use of, to the thing of whose Extension we would be informed. But in the measuring of Duration, this cannot be done, because no two different parts of Succession can be put together to measure one another: And nothing being a *measure of Duration*, but Duration; as nothing is of Extension, but Extension, we cannot keep by us any standing unvarying measure of Duration, which consists in a constant fleeting Succession, as we can of certain lengths of Extension, as Inches, Feet, Yards, *etc.* marked out in permanent parcels of Matter. Nothing then could serve well for a convenient measure of Time, but what has divided the whole length of its Duration into apparently equal Portions, by constantly repeated Periods. What Portions of Duration are not distinguished, or considered as distinguished and measured by such Periods, come not so properly under the Notion of Time, as appears by such Phrases as these, *viz. before all time*, and *when time shall be no more*.

§ 17. *Time is Duration set out by Measures.* § 18. *A good measure of Time must divide its whole Duration into equal periods.*

(5) other] *add.* **2–5** (6) caused by] **2–5** | of **1** (7) sensible] *add.* **2–5** (27) parcels] **4–5** | parts **1–3**. (**Coste** 'parties') (34) and] **1–2** (*likewise* **Coste**) | *and* **3–5**

§ 19. The diurnal, and annual *Revolutions of the Sun*, as having been from the beginning of Nature, constant, regular, and universally observable by all Mankind, and supposed equal to one another, have been with Reason *made use of for the measure of Duration.* But the distinction of Days and Years, having depended on the motion of the Sun, it has brought this mistake with it, that it has been thought, that Motion and Duration were the measure one of another. For Men in the *measuring of the length of time*, having been accustomed to the *Ideas* of Minutes, Hours, Days, Months, Years, *etc.* which they found themselves upon any mention of Time or Duration presently to think on, all which Portions of Time, were measured out by the motion of those heavenly Bodies, they were apt to confound time and motion; or at least to think, that they had a necessary Connexion one with another: whereas any constant periodical Appearance, or Alteration of *Ideas* in seemingly equidistant Spaces of Duration, if constant and universally observable, would have as well distinguished the intervals of Time, as those that have been made use of. For supposing the Sun, which some have taken to be a Fire, had been lighted up at the same distance of time that it now every Day comes about to the same Meridian, and then gone out again about twelve hours after, and that in the Space of an annual Revolution, it had sensibly increased in Brightness and Heat, and so decreased again; would not such regular Appearances serve to measure out the distances of Duration to all that could observe it, as well without as with Motion? For if the Appearances were constant, universally observable, and in equidistant Periods, they would serve Mankind for measure of time as well, were the Motion away.

§ 20. For the freezing of Water, or the blowing of a Plant, returning at equidistant Periods in all parts of the Earth, would as well serve Men to reckon their Years by, as the Motions of the Sun: and in effect we see, that some People in *America* counted their Years by the coming of certain Birds amongst them at their certain Seasons, and leaving them at others. For a Fit of an Ague; the Sense

§ 19. *The Revolutions of the Sun and Moon the properest Measures of Time.* § 20. *But not by their motion, but periodical appearances.*

(12) those heavenly Bodies] **2–5** | the Heavens **1** (25) Motion?] **3, 5** (*likewise* **Coste**) | Motion **1–2, 4** (34)–189(2) For . . . Periods,] **2–5** | For *any* Idea *returning constantly at equidistant Periods*, as a Fit of an Ague; the Sense of Hunger, or Thirst; a Smell, or a Taste; **1**

of Hunger, or Thirst; a Smell, or a Taste; or any other *Idea* returning constantly at equidistant Periods, and making it self universally be taken notice of, *would* not fail to *measure* out the course of Succession, and distinguish the distances of *Time*. Thus we see that Men born blind, count Time well enough by Years, whose Revolutions yet they cannot distinguish by Motions, that they perceive not: And I ask, whether a blind Man, who distinguished his Years, either by heat of Summer, or cold of Winter; by the Smell of any Flower of the Spring, or taste of any Fruit of the Autumn, would not have a better measure of Time, than the *Romans* had before the Reformation of their *Calendar* by *Julius Cæsar*, or many other People, whose Years, notwithstanding the motion of the Sun, which they pretend to make use of, are very irregular: and it adds no small difficulty to Chronology, that the exact lengths of the Years that several Nations counted by, are hard to be known, they differing very much one from another, and, I think, I may say all of them, from the precise motion of the Sun: and if the Sun moved from the Creation to the Flood constantly in the Æquator, and so equally dispersed its light and heat to all the habitable Parts of the Earth, in Days all of the same length, without its annual variations to the Tropicks, as a late ingenious Author supposes, I do not think it very easie to imagine, that (notwithstanding the motion of the Sun) Men should in the *Antediluvian* World, from the beginning count by years, or measure their time by Periods that had no sensible marks very obvious to distinguish them by.

§ 21. But, perhaps, it will be said without a regular Motion, such as of the Sun, or some other, how could it ever be known that such Periods were equal? To which I answer, the Equality of any other returning appearances might be known by the same way, that that of Days was known, or presumed to be so at first, which was only by judging of them by the train of *Ideas* had passed in Men's Minds in the Intervals, by which train of *Ideas* discovering inequality in the natural days, but none in the artificial days, the artificial days, or Νυχθήμερα were guessed to be equal, which was sufficient to make

§ 21. *No two parts of Duration can be certainly known to be equal.*

---

(2) *v.* 188(34), n. (4) Thus] **4–5** | And **1–3** (8) or] **4–5** | and **1–3** (*likewise* **Coste**) (19) its] **4–5** | his **1–3** (21) supposes] **Coste** *adds a marginal note citing Burnet*, Telluris Theoria Sacra. (32–4) by . . . guessed] **2–5** | whereby they guessed them **1** (33) [*2nd*] the artificial days,] *add.* **4–5**

them serve for a measure: tho' exacter search has since discovered inequality in the diurnal Revolutions of the Sun, and we know not whether the Annual also be not unequal: These yet by their presum'd and apparent Equality, serve as well to reckon time by, (though not to measure the parts of Duration exactly) as if they could be proved to be exactly equal. We must therefore carefully distinguish betwixt Duration it self, and the measures we make use of to judge of its length. Duration in it self is to be considered, as going on in one constant, equal, uniform Course: but none of the measures of it, which we make use of, can be known to do so; nor can we be assured, that their assigned Parts or Periods are equal in Duration one to another; for two successive lengths of Duration, however measured, can never be demonstrated to be equal. The Motion of the Sun, which the World used so long, and so confidently for an exact measure of Duration, has, as I said, been found in its several parts unequal: and though Men have of late made use of a Pendulum, as a more steady and regular Motion, than that of the Sun or (to speak more truly) of the Earth; yet if any one should be asked how he certainly knows, that the two successive swings of a Pendulum are equal, it would be very hard to satisfie himself, that they are infallibly so: since we cannot be sure, that the Cause of that Motion which is unknown to us, shall always operate equally; and we are sure, that the Medium in which the Pendulum moves, is not constantly the same: either of which varying, may alter the Equality of such Periods, and thereby destroy the certainty and exactness of the measure by Motion, as well as any other Periods of other Appearances, the Notion of Duration still remaining clear, though our measures of it cannot any of them be demonstrated to be exact. Since then no two Portions of Succession can be brought together, it is impossible ever certainly to know their Equality. All that we can do for a measure of Time, is to take such as have continual successive Appearances at seemingly equidistant Periods; *of* which *seeming Equality, we have no other measure, but* such as *the train of our own Ideas* have lodged in our Memories, with the concurrence of other probable Reasons, to perswade us of their Equality.

(1) exacter search has since] **4–5** | since exacter search has **1–3** (3) : These] **2–5** | . Those **1** (10) which] *add.* **4–5** (13–15) The . . . Duration,] **2–5** | That which the World used so long, and so confidently for an exact measure of Duration, the motion of the Sun **1** (18) or (to] **1–3** | (or to **4–5**. (**Coste** ', ou, pour mieux dire,')

§ 22. One thing seems strange to me, that whilst all Men manifestly measured Time by the motion of the great and visible Bodies of the World, *Time* yet should be *defined* to be the *measure of Motion*: whereas 'tis obvious to every one, who reflects ever so little on it, that, to measure Motion, Space is as necessary to be considered as Time; and those who look a little farther, will find also the bulk of the thing moved necessary to be taken into the Computation, by any one who will estimate or measure Motion, so as to judge right of it. Nor, indeed, does Motion any otherwise conduce to the measuring of Duration, than as it constantly brings about the return of certain sensible *Ideas*, in seeming equidistant Periods. For if the Motion of the Sun, were as unequal as of a Ship driven by unsteady Winds, sometimes very slow, and at others, irregularly very swift; or if being constantly equally swift, it yet was not circular, and produced not the same Appearances, it would not at all help us to measure time, any more than the seeming unequal motion of a Comet does.

§ 23. *Minutes, Hours, Days, and Years*, are then *no* more *necessary to Time* or Duration, than Inches, Feet, Yards, and Miles, marked out in any Matter, are to Extension. For though we in this part of the Universe, by the constant use of them, as of Periods set out by the Revolutions of the Sun, or as known parts of such Periods, have fixed the *Ideas* of such Lengths of Duration in our Minds, which we apply to all parts of Time, whose Lengths we would consider; yet there may be other parts of the Universe, where they no more use these measures of ours, than in *Japan* they do our Inches, Feet, or Miles: but yet something Analogous to them, there must be. For without some regular periodical returns, we could not measure our selves, or signifie to others, the length of any Duration, though at the same time the World were as full of Motion, as it is now, but no part of it disposed into regular and apparently equidistant Revolutions. But the different measures that may be made use of for the account of Time, do not at all alter the notion of Duration, which is the thing to be measured, no more than the different standards of a

§ 22. *Time not the measure of Motion.* § 23. *Minutes, Hours, and Years, not necessary measures of Duration.*

---

(4) , who] **2–5** | that **1** (21) [*2nd*] of] *add.* **2–5** (22) as] *add.* **2–5** such Periods] **2–5** | them **1** (26) these] **3–5** | those **1–2** (29) others,] **2–5** | others **1** (31) apparently] **3–5** | apparent **1–2**

Foot, and a Cubit alter the notion of Extension, to those, who make use of those different Measures.

§ 24. The Mind having once got such a measure of Time, as the annual Revolution of the Sun, can apply that measure to Duration, wherein that measure it self did not exist, and with which in the reality of its being, it had nothing to do: For should one say, That *Abraham* was born in the 2712 year of the *Julian* Period, it is altogether as intelligible, as reckoning from the beginning of the World, though there were so far back no motion of the Sun, nor any other motion at all. For though the *Julian* Period be supposed to begin several hundred years, before there were really either Days, Nights, or Years, marked out by any Revolutions of the Sun, yet we reckon as right, and thereby measure Durations as well, as if really at that time the Sun had existed, and kept the same ordinary motion it doth now. The *Idea of Duration equal to an annual Revolution of the Sun*, is as easily *applicable* in our Thoughts *to Duration, where no Sun nor Motion was*, as the *Idea* of a Foot or Yard taken from Bodies here, can be applied in our Thoughts to Distances, beyond the Confines of the World, where are no Bodies at all.

§ 25. For supposing it were 5639 Miles, or millions of Miles, from this place to the remotest Body of the Universe, (for being finite, it must be at a certain distance,) as we suppose it to be 5639 years, from this time to the first existence of any Body in the beginning of the World, *we can*, in our Thoughts, *apply this measure of a Year to Duration before the Creation*, or beyond the Duration of Bodies or Motion, as we can this measure of a Mile to Space beyond the utmost Bodies; and by the one measure Duration, where there was no Motion, as well as by the other measure Space in our Thoughts, where there is no Body.

§ 26. If it be objected to me here, That in this way of explaining of Time, I have beg'd what I should not, *viz.* That the World is neither eternal, nor infinite; I answer, That to my present purpose, it is not needful, in this place, to make use of Arguments, to evince the World to be finite, both in Duration and Extension: But it being at least as conceivable as the contrary, I have certainly the

§§ 24–6. *Our measure of Time applicable to Duration before Time.*

---

(3) *This and the following sections of this chapter are numbered 25, 26, and so on, in* **1–5**, *which contain no section numbered 24 although their Table of Contents lists § 24 and gives its contents as* 'The measure of Time two ways applied.' *The present re-numbering follows* **Coste**.

liberty to suppose it, as well as any one hath to suppose the contrary; and I doubt not but that *every one* that will go about it, may easily *conceive* in his Mind *the beginning of Motion, though not of all Duration*; and so may come to a stop, and *non ultra* in his Consideration of Motion: so also in his Thoughts he may set limits to Body, and the Extension belonging to it, but not to Space where no Body is, the utmost bounds of Space and Duration being beyond the reach of Thought, as well as the utmost bounds of Number are beyond the largest comprehension of the Mind, and all for the same reason, as we shall see in another place.

§ 27. By the same means therefore, and from the same Original that we come to have *the Idea of* Time, we have also that *Idea* which we call *Eternity*; *viz.* having got the *Idea* of Succession and Duration, be reflecting on the Train of our own *Ideas*, caused in us either by the natural appearances of those *Ideas* coming constantly of themselves into our waking Thoughts, or else caused by external Objects successively affecting our Senses; and having from the Revolutions of the Sun got the *Ideas* of certain lengths of Duration, we can, in our Thoughts, add such lengths of Duration to one another, as often as we please, and apply them, so added, to Durations past or to come: And this we can continue to do on, without bounds or limits, and proceed *in infinitum*, and apply thus the length of the annual motion of the Sun to Duration, supposed before the Sun's, or any other Motion had its being; which is no more difficult or absurd, than to apply the Notion I have of the moving of a Shadow, one Hour to day upon the Sun-dial, to the Duration of something last night; *v.g.* The burning of a Candle, which is now absolutely separate from all actual motion, and it is as impossible for the Duration of that Flame for an hour last Night, to co-exist with any Motion that now is, or forever shall be, as for any part of Duration, that was before the beginning of the World, to co-exist with the motion of the Sun now. But yet this hinders not, but that having the *Idea* of the length of the Motion of the Shadow on a Dial between the Marks of two Hours, I can as distinctly measure in my Thoughts the Duration of that Candle-light last night, as I can the Duration of any thing, that does now exist: And it is no more than to think,

§§ 27–31. *Eternity*.

(8) Thought] **1T.er, 2–5** | Thoughts **1** (28) as] *add.* **2–5** (35) Candle-light] **4–5** | Candle **1–3** (*likewise* **Coste**) (35–6) the Duration of] *add.* **2–5** (*l. below* 36) **Coste** 'Comment nous vient l'Idée de l'*Eternité*.'

that had the Sun shone then on the Dial, and moved after the same rate it doth now, the shadow on the Dial would have passed from one Hour-line to another, whilst that Flame of the Candle lasted.

§ 28. The notion of an Hour, Day, or Year, being only the *Idea* I have of the length of certain periodical regular Motions, neither of which Motions do ever all at once exist, but only in the *Ideas* I have of them in my Memory derived from my Senses or Reflection, I can with the same ease, and for the same reason, apply it in my Thoughts to Duration antecedent to all manner of Motion, as well as to any thing, that is but a Minute, or a Day, antecedent to the Motion, that at this very moment the Sun is in. All things past are equally and perfectly at rest; and to this way of consideration of them, are all one, whether they were before the beginning of the World, or but yesterday; *the measuring of* any *Duration* by some motion, *depending* not at all *on* the real co-existence of that thing to that motion, or any other Periods of Revolution, but the having *a clear Idea of the length of some* periodical known Motion, or other intervals of *Duration* in my Mind, and *applying that to the Duration of the thing I would measure.*

§ 29. Hence we see, that some Men imagine the Duration of the World from its first existence, to this present year 1689. to have been 5639 years, or equal to 5639 annual Revolutions of the Sun, and others a great deal more; as the *Ægyptians* of old, who in the time of *Alexander* counted 23000 years, from the Reign of the Sun; and the *Chineses* now, who account the World 3,269,000 years old, or more; which longer duration of the World, according to their Computation, though I should not believe to be true, yet I can equally imagine it with them, and as truly understand, and say one is longer than the other, as I understand, that *Methusalem*'s life was longer than *Enoch*'s: And if the common reckoning of 5639 should be true, (as it may be, as well as any other assigned,) it hinders not at all my imagining what others mean, when they make the World 1000 years older, since every one may with the same Facility imagine (I do not say believe) the World to be 50000 years old, as 5639; and may as well conceive the duration of 50000 years, as 5639. Whereby it appears, that *to the measuring the duration of any thing by Time*, it is not requisite, that that thing should be

(1) [*2nd*] the] **1–2, 4–5** | a **3** (*likewise* **Coste**) (2) doth now] **1–2, 4–5** | now doth **3** (8) it] *add.* **1er–5** (9) Duration] **2–5** | Duration, **1** (10) the] **2–5** | this present **1** (33) 1000] **5** | a 1000 **1–4**

co-existent to the Motion we measure by, or any other periodical Revolution; but *it suffices* to this purpose, *that we have the Idea of the length of any regular periodical Appearances*, which we can in our Minds apply to Duration, with which the Motion or Appearance never co-existed.

§ 30. For as in the History of the Creation delivered by *Moses*, I can imagine that Light existed three days before the Sun was, or had any motion, barely by thinking, that the duration of Light before the Sun was created, was so long as (if the Sun had moved then, as it doth now,) would have been equal to three of his diurnal Revolutions; so by the same way I can have an *Idea* of the *Chaos*, or Angels, being created before there was either Light, or any continued motion, a Minute, an Hour, a Day, a Year, or 1000 Years. For if I can but consider *Duration* equal to one Minute, before either the Being or Motion of any Body, I can add one Minute more till I come to 60; And by the same way of adding Minutes, Hours, or Years, (*i.e.* such or such parts of the Sun's revolution, or any other period whereof I have the *Idea*,) proceed *in infinitum*, and suppose a duration exceeding as many such periods as I can reckon, let me add whilst I will, which I think is the notion we have of *Eternity*, of whose infinity we have no other notion, than we have of the infinity of Number, to which we can add for ever without end.

§ 31. And thus I think it is plain, that *from* those two Fountains of all Knowledge before mentioned, (*viz.*) *Reflection and Sensation, we get the Ideas of Duration*, and the measures of it.

For *First*, By observing what passes in our Minds, how our *Ideas* there in train constantly some vanish, and others begin to appear, we come by the *Idea* of *Succession*.

Secondly, By observing a distance in the parts of this Succession, we get the *Idea* of *Duration*.

Thirdly, By Sensation observing certain appearances, at certain regular and seeming equidistant periods, we get the *Ideas* of certain Lengths or *Measures of Duration*, as Minutes, Hours, Days, Years, *etc.*

Fourthly, By being able to repeat those Measures of Time, or *Ideas* of stated length of Duration in our Minds, as often as we will, we can come to *imagine Duration, where nothing does really endure or*

(6) **Coste** *has the marginal summary* 'De l'idée de l'*Eternité*.' *for the final two sections of this chapter*. (15) Minute more] **5** (**Coste** 'une minute de plus, & encore une autre,') | more Minute **1–4** (18) , and] **2–5** | . And **1**

exist; and thus we imagine to morrow, next year, or seven years hence.

Fifthly, By being able to repeat any such *Idea* of any length of Time, as of a Minute, a Year, or an Age, as often as we will in our own Thoughts, and add them one to another, without ever coming to the end of such addition, any nearer than we can to the end of Number, to which we can always add, we come by the *Idea* of *Eternity*, as the future eternal Duration of our Souls, as well as the Eternity of that infinite Being, which must necessarily have always existed.

Sixthly, By considering any part of infinite Duration, as set out by periodical Measures, we come by the *Idea* of what we call *Time* in general.

CHAPTER XV

Of Duration and Expansion, considered together.

§ 1. THOUGH we have in the precedent Chapters dwelt pretty long on the Considerations of Space and Duration; yet they being *Ideas* of general concernment, that have something very abstruse and peculiar in their Nature, the comparing them one with another may, perhaps, be of use for their illustration; and we may have the more clear and distinct conception of them, by taking a view of them together. Distance or Space, in its simple abstract conception, to avoid confusion, I call *Expansion*, to distinguish it from *Extension*, which by some is used to express this distance only as it is in the solid parts of Matter, and so includes, or at least intimates the *Idea* of Body: Whereas the *Idea* of pure Distance includes no such thing. I prefer also the Word *Expansion* to *Space*, because *Space* is often applied to Distance of fleeting successive parts, which never exist together, as well as to those which are permanent. In both these, (*viz.*) *Expansion* and *Duration*, the Mind has this common *Idea* of continued Lengths, capable of greater, or less quantities: For a Man has as clear an *Idea* of the difference of the length of an Hour, and a Day, as of an Inch and a Foot.

§ 2. The *Mind*, having got the *Idea* of the length of any part of *Expansion*, let it be a Span, or a Pace, or what length you will, *can*, as

§ 1. *Both capable of greater and less.* § 2. *Expansion not bounded by Matter.*

has been said, repeat that *Idea*; and so adding it to the former, *enlarge its Idea of Length*, and make it equal to two Spans, or two Paces, and so as often as it will, till it equals the distance of any parts of the Earth one from another, and increase thus, till it amounts to the distance of the Sun, or remotest Star. By such a progression as this, setting out from the place where it is, or any other place, it can proceed and pass beyond all those lengths, and find nothing to stop its going on, either in, or without Body. 'Tis true, we can easily in our Thoughts come to the end of solid Extension; the extremity and bounds of all Body, we have no difficulty to arrive at: But when the Mind is there, it finds nothing to hinder its progress into this endless Expansion; of that it can neither find nor conceive any end. Nor let any one say, That beyond the bounds of Body, there is nothing at all, unless he will confine GOD within the limits of Matter. *Solomon*, whose Understanding was filled and enlarged with Wisdom, seems to have other Thoughts, when he says, *Heaven, and the Heaven of Heavens, cannot contain Thee*:* And he, I think, very much magnifies to himself the Capacity of his own Understanding, who persuades himself, that he can extend his Thoughts farther than GOD exists, or imagine any Expansion where he is not.

§ 3. Just so is it in Duration. *The Mind having got the Idea of any length of Duration, can double, multiply, and enlarge it*, not only beyond its own, but beyond the existence of all corporeal Beings, and all the measures of Time, taken from the great Bodies of the World, and their Motions. But yet every one easily admits, That though we make Duration boundless, as certainly it is, we cannot yet extend it beyond all being. GOD, every one easily allows, fills Eternity; and 'tis hard to find a Reason, why any one should doubt, that he likewise fills Immensity: His infinite Being is certainly as boundless one way as another; and methinks it ascribes a little too much to Matter, to say, where there is no Body, there is nothing.

§ 4. Hence, I think, we may learn the Reason, *why every one* familiarly, and without the least hesitation, speaks of, and supposes Eternity, and sticks not to *ascribe Infinity to Duration*; *but* 'tis *with more doubting* and reserve, that many *admit*, or suppose *the*

§ 3. *Nor Duration by Motion.* § 4. *Why Men more easily admit infinite Duration, than infinite Expansion.*

(16) says] **Coste** 'lorsqu'il dit en parlant à Dieu'

* 1 Kgs. 8: 27; 2 Chr. 2: 6 and 6: 18.

Infinity of Space. The reason whereof seems to me to be this, That Duration and Extension being used as names of affections belonging to other Beings, we easily conceive in GOD infinite Duration, and we cannot avoid doing so: but not attributing to him Extension, but only to Matter, which is finite, we are apter to doubt of the existence of Expansion without Matter; of which alone we commonly suppose it an Attribute. And therefore when Men pursue their Thoughts of Space, they are apt to stop at the confines of Body: as if Space were there at an end too, and reached no farther. Or if their *Ideas* upon consideration carry them farther, yet they term what is beyond the limits of the Universe, imaginary Space: as if it were nothing, because there is no Body existing in it. Whereas Duration, antecedent to all Body, and to the motions, which it is measured by, they never term imaginary: because it is never supposed void of some other real existence. And if the names of things may at all direct our Thoughts towards the Originals of Mens *Ideas*, (as I am apt to think they may very much,) one may have occasion to think by the name *Duration*, that the continuation of Existence, with a kind of Resistance to any destructive force, and the continuation of Solidity, (which is apt to be confounded with, and if we will look into the minute atomical parts of Matter, is little different from Hardness,) were thought to have some Analogy, and gave occasion to Words, so near of kin as *Durare* and *Durum esse*. And that *durare* is applied to the *Idea* of Hardness, as well as that of Existence we see in *Horace*, *Epod*. 16. *ferro duravit sæcula*. But be that as it will, this is certain, That whoever pursues his own Thoughts, will find them sometimes lanch out beyond the extent of Body, into the Infinity of Space or Expansion; the *Idea* whereof is distinct and separate from Body, and all other things: which may (to those who please) be a subject of farther meditation.

§ 5. *Time* in general is to *Duration*, as *Place* to *Expansion*. They are so much of those boundless Oceans of Eternity and Immensity, as is set out and distinguished from the rest, as it were by Land-marks; and so are made use of, to denote the Position of finite real Beings, in respect one to another, in those uniform infinite Oceans of Duration and Space. These rightly considered, are nothing but *Ideas* of deter-

§ 5. *Time to Duration is as Place to Expansion.*

---

(13) [*2nd*] to] *add.* **4–5** , which] *add.* **4–5** (21) atomical] **1–4** | anatomical **5**
(23–5) And . . . *sæcula.*] *add.* **4–5** (25) *Epod.*] *edit.* | *Epod* **4** | *Epod*, **5**

minate Distances, from certain known points fixed in distinguishable sensible things, and supposed to keep the same distance one from another. From such points fixed in sensible Beings we reckon, and from them we measure out Portions of those infinite Quantities; which so considered, are that which we call *Time* and *Place*. For Duration and Space being in themselves uniform and boundless, the Order and Position of things, without such known setled Points, would be lost in them; and all things would lie jumbled in an incurable Confusion.

§ 6. *Time* and *Place* taken thus, for determinate distinguishable Portions of those infinite Abysses of Space and Duration, set out, or supposed to be distinguished from the rest, by marks, and known Boundaries, have each of them a two-fold Acceptation.

First, *Time* in general is commonly taken for so much of infinite Duration, as is measured out by, and co-existent with the Existence, and Motions of the great Bodies of the Universe, as far as we know any thing of them: and in this Sense, Time begins and ends with the frame of this sensible World, as in these Phrases before mentioned, *before all time*, or *when time shall be no more*. *Place* likewise is taken sometimes for that Portion of infinite Space, which is possessed by, and comprehended within the Material World; and is thereby distinguished from the rest of Expansion; though this may more properly be called *Extension*, than Place. Within these two are confined, and by the observable Parts of them are measured and determined the particular Time or Duration, and the particular Extension and Place, of all corporeal Beings.

§ 7. *Secondly*, Sometimes the word *Time* is used *in a larger sense*, and is applied to Parts of that infinite Duration, not that were really distinguished and measured out by this real Existence, and periodical Motions of Bodies that were appointed from the Beginning to be for Signs, and for Seasons, and for Days, and Years,* and are accordingly our measures of time; but such other portions too of that infinite uniform Duration, which we upon any occasion do suppose

§ 6. *Time and Place are taken for so much of either, as are set out by the Existence and Motion of Bodies.* § 7. *Sometimes for so much of either, as we design by measures taken from the bulk or motion of Bodies.*

---

(4) out] **1–4** | our **5** (18) before mentioned] **1–3** | beforementioned **4** | before-mentioned **5** (23) Within] **4–5** | Within, **1–3**

---

* Gen. 1: 14.

equal to certain lengths of measured Time; and so consider them as bounded and determined. For if we should suppose the Creation, or Fall of the Angels, was at the Beginning of the *Julian* Period, we should speak properly enough, and should be understood, if we said, 'tis a longer time since the Creation of Angels, than the Creation of the World, by 764 years: Whereby we would mark out so much of that undistinguished Duration, as we suppose equal to, and would have admitted, 764 annual Revolutions of the Sun, moving at the rate it now does. And thus likewise, we sometimes speak of Place, Distance, or Bulk in the great *Inane* beyond the Confines of the World, when we consider so much of that Space, as is equal to, or capable to receive a Body of any assigned Dimensions, as a Cubick-foot; or do suppose a Point in it, at such a certain distance from any part of the Universe.

§ 8. *Where* and *when* are Questions belonging to all finite Existences, and are by us always reckoned from some known Parts of this sensible World, and from some certain Epochs marked out to us by the Motions observable in it. Without some such fixed Parts or Periods, the Order of things would be lost, to our finite Understandings, in the boundless invariable Oceans of Duration and Expansion; which comprehend in them all finite Beings, and in their full Extent, belong only to the Deity. And therefore we are not to wonder, that we comprehend them not, and do so often find our Thoughts at a loss, when we would consider them, either abstractly in themselves, or as any way attributed to the first incomprehensible Being. But when applied to any particular finite Beings, the Extension of any Body is so much of that infinite Space, as the bulk of that Body takes up. And Place is the Position of any Body, when considered at a certain distance from some other. As the *Idea* of the particular *Duration* of any thing, is an *Idea* of that Portion of infinite *Duration*, which passes during the Existence of that thing; so the time *when* the thing existed, is the *Idea* of that Space of Duration, which passed between some known and fixed Period of Duration, and the Being of that thing. One shews the distance of the Extremities of the Bulk, or Existence of the same thing, as that it is a Foot Square, or lasted two Years; the other shews the distance of

§ 8. *They belong to all Beings.*

---

(10) of] *add.* **2–5** (*l. below* 36) *all Beings*] **Coste** 'tous les Etres finis'

it in Place, or Existence from other fixed points of Space or Duration; as that it was in the middle of *Lincolns-Inn*-Fields, or the first degree of *Taurus*, and in the year of our Lord, 1671. or the 1000 year of the *Julian* Period: All which distances, we measure by preconceived *Ideas* of certain lengths of Space and Duration, as Inches, Feet, Miles, and Degrees, and in the other Minutes, Days, and Years, *etc.*

§ 9. There is one thing more, wherein *Space and Duration* have a great Conformity, and that is, though they are justly reckoned amongst our *simple Ideas*: Yet none of the distinct *Ideas* we have of either is without all manner of *Composition*, it is the very nature of

§ 9. *All the parts of Extension are Extension; and all the parts of Duration, are Duration.*

---

(1) Space or Duration] **4–5** | Duration or Space **1–3** (6) Days,] **3, 5** | Days **2, 4** | days **1** (10) *Composition*] **5** *adds, in a footnote:*

'It has been objected to Mr. *Locke*, that if Space consists of Parts, as 'tis confessed in this Place, he should not have reckoned it in the Number of Simple *Ideas*; because it seems to be inconsistent with what he says elsewhere, That a Simple *Idea* is *uncompounded, and contains in it nothing but one uniform Appearance, or Conception of the Mind, and is not distinguishable into different* Ideas, pag. [119]. 'Tis farther objected, That Mr. *Locke* has not given in the 2d [2d *edit.* | 11th **5**] Chapter of the 2d Book, where he begins to speak of *Simple Ideas*, an exact Definition of what he understands by the Word *Simple Ideas*. To these Difficulties, Mr. *Locke* answers thus: To begin with the last, he declares, That he has not treated his Subject in an Order perfectly Scholastick, having not had much Familiarity with those sort of Books during the Writing of his, and not remembring at all the Method in which they are written; and therefore his Readers ought not to expect Definitions regularly placed at the Beginning of each new Subject. Mr. *Locke* contents himself to imploy the principal Terms that he uses, so that from his Use of them the Reader may easily comprehend what he means by them. But with Respect to the Term *Simple Idea*, he has had the good Luck to define that in the Place cited in the Objection; and therefore there is no Reason to supply that Defect. The Question then is to know, Whether the *Idea* of *Extension* agrees with this Definition? Which will effectually agree to it, if it be understood in the Sense which Mr. *Locke* had principally in his View; for that Composition which he designed to exclude in that Definition, was a Composition of different *Ideas* in the Mind, and not a Composition of the same kind in a Thing whose Essence consists in having Parts of the same kind, where you can never come to a Part intirely exempted from this Composition. So that if the *Idea* of *Extension* consists in having *Partes extra Partes*, (as the Schools speak,) 'tis always, in the Sense of Mr. *Locke*, a *Simple Idea*; because the *Idea* of having *Partes extra Partes*, cannot be resolved into two other *Ideas*. For the remainder of the Objection made to Mr. *Locke*, with Respect to the Nature of Extension, Mr. *Locke* was aware of it, as may be seen in § 9. Ch. 15. of the 2d Book, where he says, That the least Portion of Space or Extension, whereof we have a clear and distinct *Idea*, may perhaps be the fittest to be consider'd by us as a *Simple Idea* of that kind, out of which our complex Modes of Space and Extension are made up. So that, according to Mr. *Locke*, it may very fitly be call'd a *Simple Idea*, since it is the least *Idea* of Space that the Mind can form to it self, and that cannot be divided by the Mind into any less whereof it has in it self any determined Perception. From whence it follows, that it is to the Mind one *Simple Idea*; and that is sufficient to take away this Objection; for 'tis not the Design of Mr. *Locke*, in this Place, to discourse of any thing but concerning the *Ideas* of the Mind. But if this is not sufficient to clear the Difficulty, Mr. *Locke* hath nothing more to add, but that if the *Idea* of Extension is so peculiar, that it cannot exactly agree with the Definition

both of them to consist of Parts: But their Parts being all of the same kind, and without the mixture of any other *Idea*, hinder them not from having a Place amongst simple *Ideas*. Could the Mind, as in Number, come to so small a part of Extension or Duration, as excluded Divisibility, that would be, as it were, the indivisible Unite, or *Idea*; by repetition of which, it would make its more inlarged *Ideas* of Extension and Duration. But since the Mind is not able to frame an *Idea* of any Space, without Parts; instead thereof it makes use of the common Measures, which by familiar use, in each Country, have imprinted themselves on the Memory (as Inches, and Feet; or Cubits, and Parasangs; and so Seconds, Minutes, Hours, Days, and Years in Duration:) The Mind makes use, I say, of such *Ideas* as these, as simple ones: and these are the component Parts of larger *Ideas*, which the Mind, upon Occasion, makes by the addition of such known Lengths, which it is acquainted with. On the other side, the ordinary smallest measure we have of either, is look'd on as an Unite in Number, when the Mind by division would reduce them into less Fractions. Though on both sides, both in addition and division, either of Space or Duration, when the *Idea* under Consideration becomes very big, or very small, its precise Bulk becomes very obscure and confused; and it is the Number of its repeated additions, or divisions, that alone remains clear and distinct, as will easily appear to any one, who will let his Thoughts loose in the vast Expansion of Space, or Divisibility of Matter. Every part of Duration is Duration too; and every part of Extension is Extension, both of them capable of addition or division *in infinitum*. But the least Portions of either of them, whereof we have clear and distinct *Ideas*, may perhaps be fittest to be considered by us, as the simple *Ideas* of that kind, out of which our complex modes of Space, Extension, and Duration, are made up, and into which they can again be distinctly

that he has given of those *Simple Ideas*, so that it differs in some manner from all others of that kind, he thinks 'tis better to leave it there expos'd to this Difficulty, than to make a new Division in his Favour. 'Tis enough for Mr. *Locke* that his Meaning can be understood. 'Tis very common to observe intelligible Discourses spoiled by too much Subtilty in nice Divisions. We ought to [to *add.* **W**] put things together, as well as we can, *Doctrinæ Causa*; but, after all, several Things will not be bundled up together under our Terms and Ways of Speaking.'

This passage is not in **Coste**, *but is in* **Coste**$_2$, *where it begins* 'C'est M. Barbeyrac, à présent Professeur en droit à Groningue, qui me communiqua ces Objections dans une Lettre que je fis voir à M. Locke. Et voici la réponse que M. Locke me dicta peu de jours après.'

(16) is] **W**; *not in* **1–5**. (**Coste** 'est regardée') (20) its precise Bulk] **2–5** | the *Idea* of its precise Bulk **1**

resolved. Such a small part in Duration, may be called a *Moment*, and is the time of one *Idea* in our Minds, in the train of their ordinary Succession there. The other, wanting a proper Name, I know not whether I may be allowed to call *a sensible Point*, meaning thereby the least Particle of Matter or Space we can discern, which is ordinarily about a Minute, and to the sharpest eyes seldom less than thirty Seconds of a Circle, whereof the Eye is the centre.

§ 10. Expansion, and Duration have this farther Agreement, that though they are both considered by us as having Parts; yet *their Parts* are *not separable* one from another, no not even in Thought: Though the parts of Bodies, from whence we take our measure of the one; and the parts of Motion, or rather the succession of *Ideas* in our Minds, from whence we take the measure of the other, may be interrupted and separated; as the one is often by Rest, and the other is by Sleep, which we call rest too.

§ 11. But yet there is this manifest difference between them, That the *Ideas* of Length, which we have of *Expansion, are turned every way*, and so make Figure, and Breadth, and Thickness; but *Duration is but as it were the length of one streight Line*, extended *in infinitum*, not capable of Multiplicity, Variation, or Figure; but is one common measure of all Existence whatsoever, wherein all things whilst they exist, equally partake. For this present moment is common to all things, that are now in being, and equally comprehends that part of their Existence, as much as if they were all but one single Being; and we may truly say, they all exist in the same moment of Time. Whether Angels and Spirits have any Analogy to this, in respect of Expansion, is beyond my Comprehension: and, perhaps, for us, who have Understandings and Comprehensions, suited to our own Preservation, and the ends of our own Being, but not to the reality and extent of all other Beings, 'tis near as hard to conceive any Existence, or to have an *Idea* of any real Being, with a perfect Negation of all manner of Expansion; as it is, to have the *Idea* of any real Existence, with a perfect Negation of all manner of Duration: And therefore what Spirits have to do with Space, or how they communicate in it, we know not. All that we know is, that Bodies do each singly possess its proper Portion of it, according to the

§ 10. *Their parts inseparable.* § 11. *Duration is as a Line, Expansion as a Solid.*

(6–7) Minute . . . Seconds] **2–5** | Second **1** (17) which] *add.* **4–5**

extent of its solid Parts; and thereby exclude all other Bodies from having any share in that particular portion of Space, whilst it remains there.

§ 12. *Duration*, and Time which is a part of it, *is the Idea* we have *of perishing distance, of which no two parts exist together*, but follow each other in Succession; as *Expansion is the* Idea *of lasting distance, all whose parts exist together*, and are not capable of Succession. And therefore though we cannot conceive any Duration without Succession, nor can put it together in our Thoughts, that any Being does now exist to Morrow, or possess at once more than the present moment of Duration; yet we can conceive the eternal Duration of the Almighty far different from that of Man, or any other finite Being. Because Man comprehends not in his Knowledge, or Power, all past and future things: His Thoughts are but of yesterday, and he knows not what to morrow will bring forth.* What is once passed, he can never recal; and what is yet to come, he cannot make present. What I say of Man, I say of all finite Beings, who though they may far exceed Man in Knowledge and Power, yet are no more than the meanest Creature, in comparison with God himself. Finite of any Magnitude, holds not any proportion to infinite. God's infinite Duration being accompanied with infinite Knowledge, and infinite Power, he sees all things past and to come; and they are no more distant from his Knowledge, no farther removed from his sight, than the present: They all lie under the same view: And there is nothing, which he cannot make exist each moment he pleases. For the Existence of all things, depending upon his good Pleasure; all things exist every moment, that he thinks fit to have them exist. To conclude, Expansion and Duration do mutually imbrace, and comprehend each other; every part of Space, being in every part of Duration; and every part of Duration, in every part of Expansion. Such a Combination of two distinct *Ideas*, is, I suppose, scarce to be found in all that great Variety, we do or can conceive, and may afford Matter to farther Speculation.

§ 12. *Duration has never two parts together, Expansion altogether.*

---

* *This is an amalgam of* Job 8: 9 *and* Prov. 27: 1.

CHAPTER XVI

Of Number.

§ 1. AMONGST all the *Ideas* we have, as there is none suggested to the Mind by more ways, so there is none more simple, than that *of Unity*, or One: it has no shadow of Variety or Composition in it: every Object our Senses are employed about; every *Idea* in our Understandings; every Thought of our Minds brings this *Idea* along with it. And therefore it is the most intimate to our Thoughts, as well as it is, in its Agreement to all other things, the most universal *Idea* we have. For Number applies it self to Men, Angels, Actions, Thoughts, every thing that either doth exist, or can be imagined.

§ 2. By repeating this *Idea* in our Minds, and adding the Repetitions together, we come by the *complex* Ideas *of the Modes of it.* Thus by adding one to one, we have the complex *Idea* of a Couple; by putting twelve Unites together, we have the complex *Idea* of a dozen; and so of a Score, or a Million, or any other Number.

§ 3. *The simple modes of Number are of all other the most distinct*; every the least Variation, which is an unite, making each Combination, as clearly different from that, which approacheth nearest to it, as the most remote; two being as distinct from one, as Two hundred; and the *Idea* of Two, as distinct from the *Idea* of Three, as the Magnitude of the whole Earth, is from that of a Mite. This is not so in other simple Modes, in which it is not so easie, nor, perhaps, possible for us to distinguish betwixt two approaching *Ideas*, which yet are really different. For who will undertake to find a difference between the white of this Paper, and that of the next degree to it: Or can form distinct *Ideas* of every the least excess in Extension?

§ 4. The Clearness and *Distinctness of each mode of Number* from all others, even those that approach nearest, makes me apt to think, that Demonstrations in Numbers, if they are not more evident and exact, than in Extension, yet they are more general in their use, and

§ 1. *Number the simplest and most universal* Idea. § 2. *Its Modes made by Addition.* § 3. *Each Mode distinct.* § 4. *Therefore Demonstrations in Numbers the most precise.*

---

(3) [*2nd*] or] **4er, 5** (*likewise* **Coste**) | nor **1–4** (13) a Couple] **5** | two **1–4** (15) so] **1–4**; *om.* **5** (20) [*1st*] *Idea*] *edit.* (*likewise* **Coste**) | *Ideas* **1–5**

more determinate in their Application. Because the *Ideas* of Numbers are more precise, and distinguishable than in Extension; where every Equality and Excess are not so easie to be observed, or measured; because our Thoughts cannot in Space arrive at any determined smallness beyond which it cannot go, as an Unite; and therefore the quantity or proportion of any the least Excess cannot be discovered, which is clear otherwise in Number, where, as has been said, 91 is as distinguishable from 90, as from 9000, though 91 be the next immediate Excess to 90. But it is not so in Extension, where whatsoever is more than just a Foot, or an Inch, is not distinguishable from the Standard of a Foot, or an Inch; and in Lines which appear of an equal length, one may be longer than the other by innumerable Parts: Nor can any one assign an Angle, which shall be the next biggest to a right one.

§ 5. By the repeating, as has been said, of the *Idea* of an Unite, and joining it to another Unite, we make thereof one collective *Idea*, marked by the Name *Two*. And whosoever can do this, and proceed on, still adding one more to the last collective *Idea*, which he had of any Number, and give a Name to it, may count, or have *Ideas* for several Collections of Unites, distinguished one from another, as far as he hath a Series of Names for following Numbers, and a Memory to retain that Series, with their several Names: All *Numeration* being but still the adding of one Unite more, and giving to the whole together, as comprehended in one *Idea*, a new or distinct Name or Sign, whereby to know it from those before and after, and distinguish it from every smaller or greater multitude of Unites. So that he, that can add one to one, and so to two, and so go on with his Tale, taking still with him the distinct Names belonging to every Progression; and so again by substracting an Unite from each Collection retreat and lessen them, is capable of all the *Ideas* of Numbers, within the compass of his Language, or for which he hath names, though not, perhaps, of more. For the several simple Modes of Numbers, being in our Minds, but so many Combinations of Unites, which have no variety, nor are capable of any other difference, but more or less, Names or Marks for each distinct Combination, seem more necessary, than in any other sort of *Ideas*.

§ 5. *Names necessary to Numbers.*

---

(4) measured;] **4–5** | measured, **1–3** (*likewise* **Coste**) (5) as] **4–5** | as in **1–3**
(18) , which] *add.* **4–5** (20) Unites,] **1** *catchword*, **2–5** | Unites **1**

For without such Names or Marks, we can hardly well make use of Numbers in reckoning, especially where the Combination is made up of any great multitude of Unites, which put together without a Name or Mark, to distinguish that precise Collection, will hardly be kept from being a heap in Confusion.

§ 6. This, I think, to be the reason why some *Americans*, I have spoken with, (who were otherwise of quick and rational Parts enough,) could not, as we do, by any means count to 1000; nor had any distinct *Idea* of that Number, though they could reckon very well to 20. Because their Language being scanty, and accommodated only to the few necessaries of a needy simple Life, unacquainted either with Trade or Mathematicks, had no Words in it to stand for 1000; so that when they were discoursed with of those greater Numbers, they would shew the Hairs of their Head, to express a great multitude, which they could not number; which inability, I suppose, proceeded from their want of Names. The *Tououpinambos* had no Names for Numbers above 5; any Number beyond that, they made out by shewing their Fingers, and the Fingers of others who were present [(*a*)]: And I doubt not but we our selves might distinctly number in Words, a great deal farther than we usually do, would we find out but some fit denominations to signifie them by; whereas in the way we take now to name them by Millions of Millions of Millions, *etc.* it is hard to go beyond eighteen, or at most four and twenty decimal Progressions, without confusion. But to shew how much *distinct Names conduce to our well reckoning*, or having useful *Ideas* of Numbers, let us set all these following Figures in one continued Line, as the Marks of one Number: *v.g.*

Nonilions.	*Octilions.*	*Septilions.*	*Sextilions.*	*Quintilions.*	*Quatrilions.*	*Trilions.*	*Bilions.*	*Milions.*	*Unites.*
857324.	162486.	345896.	437916.	423147.	248106.	235421.	261734.	368149.	623137.

The ordinary way of naming this Number in *English*, will be the often repeating of Millions, of Millions, of Millions, of Millions, of Millions, of Millions, of Millions, of Millions, (which is the denomination of the second six Figures.) In which way, it will be very hard

§ 6. *Names necessary to Numbers.*

[(*a*)] *Histoire d'un Voiage fait en la Terre du Bresil, par Jean de Lery*, c. 20. $\frac{307}{382}$.

(23) *etc.*] *add.* **2–5** (28) *Quintilions*] **1–3** (*likewise* **Coste**) | *Quintrilions* **4–5** (30) *English*] **Coste** *adds a linguistic footnote.* (33) the] *add.* **1er–5** the second six Figures] **Coste** 'la seconde *sizaine*, 368149' (*l. below* 33) **Coste** 'Autre raison pour établir cette nécessité.' (*2 ll. below* 33) *This reference is in margin in* **2–5**, *but in text after* 'present:' *in* **1**.

to have any distinguishing Notions of this Number: But whether, by giving every six Figures a new and orderly denomination, these, and perhaps a great many more Figures, in progression, might not easily be counted distinctly, and *Ideas* of them both got more easily to our selves, and more plainly signified to others, I leave it to be considered. This I mention only to shew how necessary distinct Names are to Numbering, without pretending to introduce new ones of my invention.

§ 7. Thus Children, either for want of Names to mark the several Progressions of Numbers, or not having yet the faculty to collect scattered *Ideas* into complex ones, and range them in a regular Order, and so retain them in their Memories, as is necessary to reckoning, do not begin to number very early, nor proceed in it very far or steadily, till a good while after they are well furnished with good store of other *Ideas*; and one may often observe them discourse and reason pretty well, and have very clear conceptions of several other things, before they can tell 20. And some, through the default of their Memories, who cannot retain the several Combinations of Numbers, with their Names annexed in their distinct orders, and the dependence of so long a train of numeral Progressions, and their relation one to another, are not able all their life-time, to reckon, or regularly go over any moderate Series of Numbers. For he that will count Twenty, or have any *Idea* of that Number, must know that Nineteen went before, with the distinct Name or Sign of every one of them, as they stand marked in their order; for where-ever this fails, a gap is made, the Chain breaks, and the Progress in numbering can go no farther. So that *to reckon right, it is required*, 1. That the Mind distinguish carefully two *Ideas*, which are different one from another only by the addition or subtraction of one Unite. 2. That it retain in Memory the Names, or Marks, of the several Combinations from an Unite to that Number; and that not confusedly, and at random, but in that exact order, that the Numbers follow one another: in either of which, if it trips, the whole business of Numbering will be disturbed, and there will remain only the confused *Idea* of multitude, but the *Ideas* necessary to distinct numeration, will not be attained to.

§ 7. *Why Children number not earlier.*

---

(11) in] **1T.er, 2–5** | to **1** (16) discourse] **1er–5** | in discourse **1**

§ 8. This farther is observable in *Number*, That it is that, which the Mind makes use of in *measuring all things*, that by us are measurable, which principally are *Expansion* and *Duration*; and our *Idea* of Infinity, even when applied to those, seems to be nothing, but the Infinity of Number. For what else are our *Ideas* of Eternity and Immensity, but the repeated additions of certain *Ideas* of imagined parts of Duration, and Expansion with the Infinity of Number, in which we can come to no end of Addition? For such an inexhaustible stock, Number, of all other our *Ideas*, most clearly furnishes us with, as is obvious to every one. For let a Man collect into one Sum, as great a Number as he pleases, this Multitude, how great soever, lessens not one jot the power of adding to it, or brings him any nearer the end of the inexhaustible stock of Number, where still there remains as much to be added, as if none were taken out. And this endless *addition* or *addibility* (if any one like the word better) of Numbers, so apparent to the Mind, is that, I think, which gives us the clearest and most distinct *Idea* of Infinity: of which more in the following Chapter.

CHAPTER XVII

Of Infinity.

§ 1. HE that would know what kind of *Idea* it is to which we give the name of *Infinity*, cannot do it better, than by considering to what Infinity is by the Mind more immediately attributed, and then how the Mind comes to frame it.

Finite, and *Infinite*, seem to me to be looked upon by the Mind, as the *Modes of Quantity*, and to be attributed primarily in their first designation only to those things, which have parts, and are capable of increase or diminution, by the addition or subtraction of any the least part: and such are the *Ideas* of Space, Duration, and Number, which we have considered in the foregoing Chapters.

§ 8. *Number measures all Measurables.*
§ 1. *Infinity, in its original intention, attributed to Space, Duration, and Number.*

---

(3) and] **1–3** (*likewise* **Coste**) | *and* **4–5** (7) Duration, and Expansion] **2–5** (Expansion, **5**) | Space and Expansion, or Duration, **1** (15) *addition* . . . better)] **4–5** | addition **1–3** (*likewise* **Coste**)

'Tis true, that we cannot but be assured, That the Great GOD, of whom, and from whom are all things, is incomprehensibly Infinite: but yet, when we apply to that first and supreme Being, our *Idea* of Infinite, in our weak and narrow Thoughts, we do it primarily in respect of his Duration and Ubiquity; and, I think, more figuratively to his Power, Wisdom, and Goodness, and other Attributes, which are properly inexhaustible and incomprehensible, *etc.* For when we call them Infinite, we have no other *Idea* of this Infinity, but what carries with it some reflection on, and intimation of that Number or Extent of the Acts or Objects of God's Power, Wisdom, and Goodness, which can never be supposed so great, or so many, which these Attributes will not always surmount and exceed, let us multiply them in our Thoughts, as far as we can, with all the infinity of endless number. I do not pretend to say how these Attributes are in GOD, who is infinitely beyond the reach of our narrow Capacities: They do, without doubt, contain in them all possible perfection: but this, I say, is our way of conceiving them, and these our *Ideas* of their Infinity.

§ 2. Finite then, and Infinite, being by the Mind look'd on as modifications of Expansion and Duration, the next thing to be considered is, *How the Mind comes by* them. As for the *Idea of Finite*, there is no great difficulty. The obvious portions of Extension, that affect our Senses, carry with them into the Mind the *Idea* of Finite: and the ordinary periods of Succession, whereby we measure Time and Duration, as Hours, Days, and Years, are bounded Lengths. The difficulty is, how we come by those boundless *Ideas* of *Eternity* and *Immensity*, since the Objects, which we converse with, come so much short of any approach or proportion to that Largeness.

§ 3. Every one, that has any *Idea* of any stated lengths of Space, as a Foot, finds, that he can repeat that *Idea*; and joining it to the former, make the *Idea* of two Foot; and by the addition of a third, three Foot; and so on, without ever coming to an end of his additions, whether of the same *Idea* of a Foot, or if he pleases of doubling it, or any other *Idea* he has of any length, as a Mile, or

§ 2. *The* Idea *of Finite easily got.* § 3. *How we come by the* Idea *of Infinity.*

(9) intimation] **2–5** | imitation **1** (13) , as far as we can,] *add.* **5** (23–5) Finite: . . . Duration,] **4–5** | Finite, . . . Duration; **1–3** (27) , which] *add.* **4–5** (33) pleases] **4–5** | please **1–3** (*l. below* 34: § 2.) *This marginal summary, in* **4–5**, *replaces that in* **2–3** *which is* '*How we come by the* Idea *of Infinity.*' (*l. below* 34: § 3.) *In* **Coste,** § *3 comes under the same marginal summary as* § *2.*

Diameter of the Earth, or of the *Orbis Magnus*: for whichsoever of these he takes, and how often soever he doubles, or any otherwise multiplies it, he finds, that after he has continued this doubling in his Thoughts, and enlarged his *Idea*, as much as he pleases, he has no more reason to stop, nor is one jot nearer the end of such Addition, than he was at first setting out; the power of enlarging his *Idea* of Space by farther Additions, remaining still the same, he hence takes *the Idea of infinite Space.*

§ 4. This, I think, is the way, whereby the Mind gets the *Idea of infinite Space.* 'Tis a quite different Consideration to examine, whether the Mind has the *Idea* of such a *boundless Space actually existing*, since our *Ideas* are not always Proofs of the Existence of Things; but yet, since this comes here in our way, I suppose I may say, that we are apt to think, that Space in it self is actually boundless, to which Imagination, the *Idea* of Space or Expansion of it self naturally leads us. For it being considered by us, either as the Extension of Body, or as existing by it self, without any solid Matter taking it up, (for of such a void Space, we have not only the *Idea*, but I have proved, as I think, from the Motion of Body, its necessary existence,) it is impossible the Mind should be ever able to find or suppose any end of it, or be stopp'd any where in its progress in this Space, how far soever it extends its Thoughts. Any Bounds made with Body, even Adamantine Walls, are so far from putting a stop to the Mind in its farther progress in Space and Extension, that it rather facilitates and enlarges it: For so far as that Body reaches, so far no one can doubt of Extension; and when we are come to the utmost extremity of Body, what is there, that can there put a stop, and satisfie the Mind, that it is at the end of Space, when it perceives it is not; nay, when it is satisfied that Body it self can move into it? For if it be necessary for the motion of Body, that there should be an empty Space, though never so little, here amongst Bodies; and it be possible for Body to move in or through that empty Space; nay, it is impossible for any particle of Matter to move but into an empty Space, the same possibility of a Body's moving into a void Space, beyond the utmost Bounds of Body, as well as into a void Space interspersed amongst

§ 4. *Our* Idea *of Space boundless.*

(1) whichsoever] **5** | which-ever **1–4** (15) it] **W** | its **1–5** (19) from] **1–2, 4–5** | for **3** (*likewise* **Coste**) (28) perceives] **2–5** | perceive **1** (31) little,] **4–5** | little **1–3**

Bodies, will always remain clear and evident, the *Idea* of empty pure Space, whether within, or beyond the confines of all Bodies, being exactly the same, differing not in Nature, though in Bulk; and there being nothing to hinder Body from moving into it: So that where-ever the Mind places it self by any thought, either amongst, or remote from all Bodies, it can, in this uniform *Idea* of Space, no-where find any bounds, any end; and so must necessarily conclude it by the very Nature and *Idea* of each part of it, to be actually infinite.

§ 5. As, by the power we find in our selves of repeating, as often as we will, any *Idea* of Space, we get the *Idea* of Immensity; so, by being able to repeat the *Idea* of any length of Duration, we have in our Minds, with all the endless addition of Number, we come by the *Idea* of *Eternity*. For we find in our selves, we can no more come to an end of such repeated *Ideas*, than we can come to the end of Number, which every one perceives he cannot. But here again 'tis another question, quite different from our having an *Idea* of Eternity, to know whether there were *any real Being*, whose Duration has been *eternal*. And as to this I say, He that considers something now existing, must necessarily come to something eternal. But having spoke of this in another place, I shall say here no more of it, but proceed on to some other Considerations of our *Idea* of Infinity.

§ 6. If it be so, that our *Idea* of Infinity be got from the Power, we observe in our selves, of repeating without end our own *Ideas*; It may be demanded, *Why we do not attribute Infinity to other Ideas, as well as those of Space and Duration*; since they may be as easily, and as often repeated in our Minds as the other; and yet no body ever thinks of infinite sweetness, or infinite whiteness, though he can repeat the *Idea* of Sweet or White, as frequently as those of a Yard, or a Day? To which I answer, All the *Ideas*, that are considered as having parts, and are capable of increase by the addition of any equal or less parts, afford us by their repetition the *Idea* of Infinity; because with this endless repetition, there is continued an enlargement, of which there can be no end. But in other *Ideas* it is not so; for to the largest *Idea* of Extension or Duration, that I at present have, the addition of any the least part makes an increase; but to the perfectest *Idea* I have of the whitest Whiteness, if I add another

§ 5. *And so of Duration.* § 6. *Why other* Ideas *are not capable of Infinity.*

---

(7) bounds,] **1–3, 5** | bounds; **4** (19) And . . . say,] *add.* **4–5**

of a less or equal whiteness, (and of a whiter than I have, I cannot add the *Idea*,) it makes no increase, and enlarges not my *Idea* at all; and therefore the different *Ideas* of Whiteness, *etc.* are called Degrees. For those *Ideas*, that consist of Parts, are capable of being augmented by every addition of the least part; but if you take the *Idea* of White, which one parcel of Snow yielded yesterday to your Sight, and another *Idea* of White from another parcel of Snow you see to day, and put them together in your Mind, they embody, as it were, and run into one, and the *Idea* of Whiteness is not at all increased; and if we add a less degree of Whiteness to a greater, we are so far from increasing, that we diminish it. Those *Ideas* that consist not of Parts, cannot be augmented to what proportion Men please, or be stretched beyond what they have received by their Senses; but Space, Duration, and Number, being capable of increase by repetition, leave in the Mind an *Idea* of an endless room for more; nor can we conceive any where a stop to a farther Addition or Progression, and so those *Ideas* alone lead our Minds towards the Thought of Infinity.

§ 7. Though our *Idea* of Infinity arise from the contemplation of Quantity, and the endless increase the Mind is able to make in Quantity, by the repeated additions of what Portions thereof it pleases; yet I guess we cause great confusion in our Thoughts, when we join Infinity to any supposed *Idea* of Quantity the Mind can be thought to have, and so discourse or reason about an infinite quantity, (*viz.*) an infinite Space, or an infinite Duration: For *our Idea of Infinity* being, as I think, *an endless growing Idea*, but the *Idea* of any Quantity the Mind has, being at that time terminated in that *Idea*, (for be it as great as it will, it can be no greater than it is,) to join Infinity to it is to adjust a standing measure to a growing bulk; and therefore I think it is not an insignificant subtilty, if I say, that we are carefully to distinguish between the *Idea* of the Infinity of Space, and the *Idea* of a Space infinite: The first is nothing but a supposed endless Progression of the Mind, over what repeated *Ideas* of Space it pleases; but to have actually in the Mind the *Idea* of a Space infinite, is to suppose the Mind already passed over, and actually to have a view of all those repeated *Ideas* of Space, which an

§ 7. *Difference between infinity of Space, and Space infinite.*

---

(6) your] **2–5** | our **1** (25), (*viz.*)] **5** |, as **1–4** (as **1**)

endless repetition can never totally represent to it, which carries in it a plain contradiction.

§ 8. This, perhaps, will be a little plainer, if we consider it in Numbers. The infinity of Numbers, to the end of whose addition every one perceives there is no approach, easily appears to any one that reflects on it: But how clear soever this *Idea* of the Infinity of Number be, there is nothing yet more evident, than the absurdity of the actual *Idea* of an Infinite Number. Whatsoever positive *Ideas* we have in our Minds of any Space, Duration, or Number, let them be never so great, they are still finite; but when we suppose an inexhaustible remainder, from which we remove all bounds, and wherein we allow the Mind an endless progression of Thought, without ever compleating the *Idea*, there we have our *Idea* of Infinity; which though it seems to be pretty clear, when we consider nothing else in it, but the Negation of an end, yet when we would frame in our Minds the *Idea* of an infinite Space or Duration, that *Idea* is very obscure, and confused, because it is made up of two Parts, very different, if not inconsistent. For let a Man frame in his mind an *Idea* of any Space or Number, as great as he will; 'tis plain, the mind rests and terminates in that *Idea*, which is contrary to the *Idea of Infinity*, which *consists in a supposed endless Progression*. And therefore, I think, it is, that we are so easily confounded, when we come to argue, and reason about infinite Space or Duration, *etc.* Because the parts of such an *Idea*, not being perceived to be, as they are, inconsistent, the one side or other always perplexes, whatever Consequences we draw from the other, as an *Idea* of Motion not passing on, would perplex any one, who should argue from such an *Idea*, which is not better than an *Idea* of motion at rest; and such another seems to me to be the *Idea* of a Space, or (which is the same thing) a Number infinite, *i.e.* of a Space or Number, which the Mind actually has, and so views, and terminates in; and of a Space or Number, which in a constant and endless inlarging, and Progression, it can in Thought never attain to. For how large soever an *Idea* of Space I have in my Mind, it is no larger than it is that Instant, that I have it, though I be capable the next instant to double it; and so on *in infinitum*: For that alone is infinite, which has

§ 8. *We have no* Idea *of infinite Space.*

(8) . Whatsoever] **2–5** | , whatsoever **1** (14) seems] **4–5** | seem **1–3** (32–3) inlarging, and Progression] **2–5** | Progression, and enlarging **1** (33) , it can] **1er–5** | it, can **1**

no Bounds; and that the *Idea* of Infinity, in which our Thoughts can find none.

§ 9. But of all other *Ideas*, it is *Number*, as I have said, which, I think, *furnishes us with the clearest and most distinct* Idea *of Infinity*, we are capable of. For even in Space and Duration, when the Mind pursues the *Idea* of Infinity, it there makes use of the *Ideas* and Repetitions of Numbers, as of millions of millions of Miles, or Years, which are so many distinct *Ideas*, kept best by Number from running into a confused heap, wherein the Mind loses it self; and when it has added together as many millions, *etc.* as it pleases, of known lengths of Space or Duration, the clearest *Idea*, it can get of Infinity, is the confused incomprehensible remainder of endless addible Numbers, which affords no prospect of Stop or Boundary.

§ 10. It will, perhaps, give us a little farther light into the *Idea* we have *of Infinity*, and discover to us, that it *is nothing but the Infinity of Number applied to determinate parts*, of which we have in our Minds the distinct *Ideas*, if we consider that Number is not generally thought by us infinite, whereas Duration and Extension are apt to be so; which arises from hence, That in Number we are at one end as it were: for there being in Number nothing less than an Unite, we there stop, and are at an end; but in addition, or increase of Number, we can set no Bounds: and so it is like a Line, whereof one end terminating with us, the other is extended still forwards beyond all that we can conceive; but in Space and Duration it is otherwise. For in Duration, we consider it, as if this Line of Number were extended both ways to an unconceivable, undeterminate, and infinite length; which is evident to any one, that will but reflect on what Consideration he hath of Eternity; which, I suppose, he will find to be nothing else, but the turning this Infinity of Number both ways, *à parte ante*, and *à parte post*, as they speak. For when we would consider Eternity, *à parte ante*, what do we but, beginning from our selves, and the present time we are in, repeat in our Minds the *Ideas* of Years, or Ages, or any other assignable Portion of Duration past, with a prospect of proceeding, in such Addition, with all the Infinity of Number; and when we would consider

§ 9. *Number affords us the clearest* Idea *of Infinity.* §§ 10, 11. *Our different conception of the Infinity of Number, Duration, and Expansion.*

---

(1) Bounds; . . . Infinity,] **1T.er, 2–5** | Bounds, . . . Infinity; **1** (6) use] **2–5** | uses **1** (8) so] **4–5** | as so **1–3** (18) are] **1er–5** | is **1** (25) Number] **1–3, 5** | Number, **4** (32) repeat] **2–5** | we repeat **1**

Eternity, *à parte post*, we just after the same rate begin from our selves, and reckon by multiplied Periods yet to come, still extending that Line of Number, as before; and these two being put together, are that infinite Duration we call *Eternity*; which, as we turn our view either way forwards or backwards, appears infinite, because we still turn that way the infinite end of Number, *i.e.* the Power still of adding more.

§ 11. The same happens also in Space, wherein conceiving our selves to be as it were in the Centre, we do on all sides pursue those indeterminable Lines of Number; and reckoning any way from our selves, a Yard, Mile, Diameter of the Earth, or *Orbis magnus*, by the infinity of Number, we add others to them, as often as we will; and having no more Reason to set Bounds to those repeated *Ideas*, than we have to set Bounds to Number, we have that indeterminable *Idea of Immensity*.

§ 12. And since in any bulk of Matter, our Thoughts can never arrive at the utmost *Divisibility*, therefore there is an apparent Infinity to us also in that, which has the Infinity also of Number, but with this difference, That in the former Considerations of the Infinity of Space and Duration, we only use Addition of Numbers; whereas this is like the division of an Unite into its Fractions, wherein the Mind also can proceed *in infinitum*, as well as in the former Additions, it being indeed but the Addition still of new Numbers: though in the Addition of the one, we can have no more the positive *Idea* of a Space infinitely great, than in the Division of the other, we can have the *Idea* of a Body infinitely little; our *Idea* of Infinity being, as I may so say, a growing and fugitive *Idea*, still in a boundless Progression, that can stop no where.

§ 13. Though it be hard, I think, to find any one so absurd, as to say, he has the positive *Idea* of an actual infinite Number; the Infinity whereof lies only in a Power still of adding any Combination of Unites to any former Number, and that as long, and as much as one will; the like also being in the Infinity of Space and Duration, which Power leaves always to the Mind room for endless Additions; yet there be those, who imagine they have *positive* Ideas *of infinite* Duration and Space. It would, I think, be enough to destroy any

§ 12. *Infinite Divisibility.* §§ 13, 14. *No positive* Idea *of Infinite.*

(2) , still] **1T.er, 2–5** | still, **1** (4–5) , as . . . backwards] **2–5** | every way we consider **1** (8) **Coste** *has a distinctive marginal summary for* § *11*: 'Comment nous concevons l'Infinité de l'Espace.' (28) stop] **2–5** | step **1**

such positive *Idea* of infinite, to ask him that has it, whether he could add to it or no; which would easily shew the mistake of such a positive *Idea.* We can, I think, have no positive *Idea* of any Space or Duration, which is not made up of, and commensurate to repeated Numbers of Feet or Yards, or Days and Years, which are the common measures, whereof we have the *Ideas* in our Minds, and whereby we judge of the greatness of these sort of quantities. And therefore, since an *Idea* of infinite Space or Duration must needs be made up of infinite Parts, it can have no other Infinity, than that of Number capable still of farther Addition; but not an actual positive *Idea* of a Number infinite. For, I think, it is evident, that the Addition of finite things together (as are all lengths, whereof we have the positive *Ideas*) can never otherwise produce the *Idea* of infinite, than as Number does; which consisting of Additions of finite Unites one to another, suggests the *Idea* of Infinite, only by a Power, we find we have of still increasing the Sum, and adding more of the same kind, without coming one jot nearer the end of such Progression.

§ 14. They who would prove their *Idea of Infinite to be positive*, seem to me to do it by a pleasant Argument, taken from the Negation of an end; which being negative, the Negation of it is positive. He that considers, that the end is in Body but the extremity or superficies of that Body, will not, perhaps, be forward to grant, that the end is a bare negative: And he that perceives the end of his Pen is black or white, will be apt to think, that the end is something more than a pure Negation. Nor is it, when applied to Duration, the bare Negation of Existence, but more properly the last moment of it. But if they will have the end to be nothing but the bare Negation of Existence, I am sure they cannot deny, but that the beginning is the first instant of Being, and is not by any Body conceived to be a bare Negation; and therefore by their own Argument, the *Idea* of Eternal, *à parte ante*, or of a Duration without a beginning, is but a negative *Idea.*

§ 15. The *Idea* of Infinite, has, I confess, something of positive in all those things we apply to it. When we would think of infinite Space or Duration, we at first step usually make some very large *Idea*, as, perhaps, of Millions of Ages, or Miles, which possibly we double and multiply several times. All that we thus amass together in our Thoughts, is positive, and the assemblage of a great number

§ 15. *What is positive, what negative in our* Idea *of Infinite.*

of positive *Ideas* of Space or Duration. But what still remains beyond this, we have no more a positive distinct notion of, than a Mariner has of the depth of the Sea, where having let down a large portion of his Sounding-line, he reaches no bottom: Whereby he knows the depth to be so many fathoms, and more; but how much that more is, he hath no distinct notion at all: And could he always supply new Line, and find the Plummet always sink, without ever stopping, he would be something in the posture of the Mind reaching after a compleat and positive *Idea* of Infinity. In which case, let this Line be 10, or 10000 fathoms long, it equally discovers what is beyond it; and gives only this confused, and comparative *Idea*, That this is not all, but one may yet go farther. So much as the Mind comprehends of any Space, it has a positive *Idea* of: But in endeavouring to make it Infinite, it being always enlarging, always advancing, the *Idea* is still imperfect and incompleat. So much Space as the Mind takes a view of, in its contemplation of Greatness, is a clear Picture, and positive in the Understanding: But Infinite is still greater. 1. Then *the Idea of so much is positive* and clear. 2. *The Idea of Greater is also clear, but it* is but a *comparative Idea*. 3. *The Idea of so much greater, as cannot be comprehended*, and this *is plain Negative*; Not Positive. For he has no positive clear *Idea* of the largeness of any Extension, (which is that sought for in the *Idea* of Infinite,) that has not a comprehensive *Idea* of the Dimensions of it: And such, no body, I think, pretends to, in what is infinite. For to say a Man has a positive clear *Idea* of any Quantity, without knowing how great it is, is as reasonable as to say, He has the positive clear *Idea* of the number of the Sands on the Sea-shore, who knows not how many they be; but only that they are more than Twenty. For just such a perfect and positive *Idea* has he of an infinite Space or Duration, who says it is larger than the Extent or Duration of 10, 100, 1000, or any other number of Miles, or Years, whereof he has, or can have, a positive *Idea*; which is all the *Idea*, I think, we have of Infinite. So that what lies beyond our positive *Idea* towards Infinity, lies in Obscurity; and has the indeterminate confusion of a Negative *Idea*, wherein I know, I neither do nor can comprehend all I would, it being too large for a finite and narrow Capacity: And that cannot but be very far from a positive compleat *Idea*, wherein the greatest part, of

(4) his] **1–2, 4–5**; *om.* **3** bottom:] **4–5** | bottom, **1–3** (13–14) endeavouring to make it Infinite] **4–5** | this thought of Infinity **1–3** (17–18) 1. Then] **Coste** 'D'où j'infére, 1.' (29) an infinite Space] **4–5** | Infinity, when he applies it to Space **1–3**

what I would comprehend, is left out, under the undeterminate intimation of being still greater. For to say, that having in any quantity measured so much, or gone so far, you are not yet at the end, is only to say, that that Quantity is greater. So that the Negation of an end in any Quantity, is, in other words, only to say, That it is bigger: And a total negation of an end, is but the carrying this Bigger still with you, in all the Progressions your Thoughts shall make in Quantity; and adding this *Idea* of still greater, to all the *Ideas* you have, or can be supposed to have of Quantity. Now whether such an *Idea* as that, be positive, I leave any one to consider.

§ 16. I ask those who say they have a *positive* Idea *of Eternity*, whether their *Idea* of Duration includes in it Succession, or not? If it does not, they ought to shew the difference of their Notion of Duration, when applied to an eternal Being, and to a finite: Since, perhaps, there may be others, as well as I, who will own to them their Weakness of Understanding in this point; and acknowledge, That the Notion they have of Duration, forces them to conceive, That whatever has Duration, is of a longer continuance to day, than it was yesterday. If to avoid Succession in eternal Existence, they recur to the *Punctum Stans* of the Schools, I suppose, they will thereby very little mend the matter, or help us to a more clear and positive *Idea* of infinite Duration, there being nothing more inconceivable to me, than Duration without Succession. Besides, that *Punctum Stans*, if it signify any thing, being not *Quantum*, finite or infinite, cannot belong to it. But if our weak Apprehensions cannot separate Succession from any Duration whatsoever, our *Idea* of Eternity can be nothing but of infinite Succession of Moments of Duration, wherein any thing does exist; and whether any one has, or can have, a positive *Idea* of an actual infinite Number, I leave him to consider, till his infinite Number be so great, that he himself can add no more to it; and as long as he can increase it, I doubt, he himself will think the *Idea*, he hath of it, a little too scanty for positive Infinity.

§ 17. I think it unavoidable for every considering rational

§§ 16, 17. *We have no positive* Idea *of an infinite Duration.*

---

(9) . Now] **4–5** | ; and **1–3**   (14) does] **4–5** | do **1–3**   (18) Notion] **2–5** | Notions **1**   forces] **2–5** | force **1**   (25) *Quantum*] **Coste** *adds marginal note* '*Non est quantum*, disent les Scholastiques.'   (*l. below* 35) *In* **2–3**, *marginal summary for* § *16 is* '*What is positive, what negative in our* Idea *of Infinite.*' *and for* § *17 is* '*No positive* Idea *of Infinite.*'

Creature, that will but examine his own, or any other Existence, to have the Notion of an eternal wise Being, who had no beginning: And such an *Idea* of infinite Duration, I am sure I have. But this *Negation of a Beginning*, being but the Negation of a positive thing, *scarce gives* me *a positive* Idea *of Infinity*; which whenever I endeavour to extend my Thoughts to, I confess my self at a loss, and find I cannot attain any clear comprehension of it.

§ 18. He that thinks he has a positive *Idea* of infinite Space, will, when he considers it, find that he can *no* more have a *positive Idea* of the greatest, than he has *of the least Space*. For in this latter, which seems the easier of the two, and more within our comprehension, we are capable only of a comparative *Idea* of Smalness, which will always be less than any one, whereof we have the positive *Idea*. All our positive *Ideas* of any Quantity, whether great or little, have always bounds; though our comparative *Idea*, whereby we can always add to the one, and take from the other, hath no bounds. For that which remains either great or little, not being comprehended in that positive *Idea*, which we have, lies in obscurity: And we have no other *Idea* of it, but of the power of enlarging the one, and diminishing the other, without ceasing. A Pestle and Mortar will as soon bring any Particle of Matter to Indivisibility, as the acutest Thought of a Mathematician: And a Surveyor may, as soon with his Chain, measure out infinite *Space*, as a Philosopher, by the quickest flight of Mind, reach it; or by thinking comprehend it, which is to have a positive *Idea* of it. He that thinks on a Cube of an Inch diameter, has a clear and positive *Idea* of it in his mind, and so can frame one of $\frac{1}{2}$ a $\frac{1}{4}$ $\frac{1}{8}$, and so on till he has the *Idea* in his Thoughts of something very little: but yet reaches not the *Idea* of that incomprehensible Littleness, which Division can produce. What remains of Smalness, is as far from his Thoughts, as when he first began; and therefore he never comes at all to have a clear and positive *Idea* of that Smalness, which is consequent to infinite Divisibility.

§ 19. Every one that looks towards Infinity, does, as I have said, at first glance make some very large *Idea* of that which he applies it

§ 18. *No positive* Idea *of infinite Space.* § 19. *What is positive, what negative, in our* Idea *of Infinite.*

(13) . All] **4–5** | ; for all **1–3** A] **4–5** | For a **1–3** (**Coste** 'd'extrêmement petit') *infinite Space*] **4–5** | *Infinite* **2–3** (18) , which] *add.* **4–5** (20) other,] **4–5** | other **1–3** (28) very little:] **4–5** | very very little, **1–3**. (35) which] *add.* **4–5** (*l. below* 35: § 18.)

to, let it be Space, or Duration; and possibly he wearies his Thoughts, by multiplying in his mind that first large *Idea*: But yet by that he comes no nearer to the having a *positive clear Idea* of what remains, to make up a positive Infinite, than the Country-fellow had of the Water, which was yet to come, and pass the Channel of the River where he stood:

> *Rusticus expectat dum transeat amnis, at ille*
> *Labitur, et labetur in omne volubilis ævum.**

§ 20. There are some I have met with, that put so much difference between infinite Duration, and infinite Space, that they persuade themselves, that they have *a positive* Idea *of Eternity*; *but* that they *have not*, nor can have any *Idea of infinite Space*. The reason of which mistake, I suppose to be this, That finding by a due Contemplation of Causes and Effects, that it is necessary to admit some Eternal Being, and so to consider the real existence of that Being, as taking up, and commensurate to their *Idea* of Eternity: But on the other side, not finding it necessary, but on the contrary apparently absurd, that Body should be infinite, they forwardly conclude, they can have no *Idea* of infinite Space, because they can have no *Idea* of infinite Matter. Which Consequence, I conceive, is very ill collected; because the Existence of Matter is no ways necessary to the Existence of Space, no more than the Existence of Motion, or the Sun, is necessary to Duration, though Duration uses to be measured by it: And I doubt not but a Man may have the *Idea* of 10000 Miles square, without any Body so big, as well as the *Idea* of 10000 Years, without any Body so old. It seems as easy to me to have the *Idea* of Space empty of Body, as to think of the Capacity of a Bushel without Corn, or the hollow of a Nutshel without a Kernel in it: It being no more necessary, that there should be existing a solid Body infinitely extended, because we have an *Idea* of the Infinity of Space, than it is necessary that the World should be eternal, because we have an *Idea* of infinite Duration: And why should we think our *Idea* of infinite Space, requires the real existence of Matter to support it,

§ 20. *Some think they have a positive* Idea *of Eternity, and not Space.*

(1) he] *add.* **4–5** (3) to the] *add.* **2–5** (8) *in*] **4–5** | *per* **1–3**
(20–1) collected . . . is] **4–5** | collected, the Existence of Matter being **1–3**
(27) a] **2–5** | his **1** (29) no] **1–4**; *om.* **5** (30) an] **3–5** | any **1–2**

* Horace, *Epistles*, I, ii, 42–3.

when we find, that we have as clear an *Idea* of infinite Duration to come, as we have of infinite Duration past? Though, I suppose, no body thinks it conceivable, that any thing does, or has existed in that future Duration. Nor is it possible to join our *Idea* of future Duration, with present or past Existence, any more than it is possible to make the *Ideas* of yesterday, to day, and to morrow to be the same; or bring Ages past and future together, and make them contemporary. But if these Men are of the Mind, That they have clearer *Ideas* of infinite Duration, than of infinite Space, because it is past doubt, that GOD has existed from all Eternity, but there is no real Matter co-extended with infinite Space: Yet those Philosophers who are of Opinion, That infinite Space is possessed by GOD's infinite Omnipresence, as well as infinite Duration by his eternal Existence, must be allowed to have as clear an *Idea* of infinite Space, as of infinite Duration; though neither of them, I think, has any *positive* Idea *of Infinity* in either case. For whatsoever positive *Ideas* a Man has in his Mind of any Quantity, he can repeat it, and add it to the former, as easy as he can add together the *Ideas* of two Days, or two Paces, which are positive *Ideas* of Lengths he has in his Mind, and so on, as long as he pleases: whereby, if a Man had a positive *Idea* of infinite, either Duration, or Space, he could add two Infinites together; nay, make one Infinite infinitely bigger than another, Absurdities too gross to be confuted.

§ 21. But yet if after all this, there be Men, who persuade themselves, that they have clear positive comprehensive *Ideas* of Infinity, 'tis fit they enjoy their privilege: And I should be very glad (with some others, that I know, who acknowledge they have none such,) to be better informed by their Communication. For I have been hitherto apt to think, that the great and *inextricable Difficulties*, which perpetually involve all Discourses *concerning Infinity*, whether of Space, Duration, or Divisibility, have been the certain *marks of a defect in our* Ideas *of Infinity*, and the disproportion the Nature thereof has to the Comprehension of our narrow Capacities. For whilst Men talk and dispute of infinite Space or Duration, as if they had as compleat and positive *Ideas* of them, as they have of the Names they use for them, or as they have of a Yard, or an Hour, or

§ 21. *Supposed positive* Ideas *of Infinity cause of Mistakes.*

(1) that] *add.* **4–5** (14) an] *add.* **1er–5** (20) pleases:] **4–5** | please; **1–3** (35) them] **4–5** | it **1–3** (36) Names . . . have] **4–5** | Name they use for it, or **1–3** (Name, **2–3**) [*2nd*] or] **2–5** | or of **1**

any other determinate Quantity, it is no wonder, if the incomprehensible Nature of the thing, they discourse of, or reason about, leads them into Perplexities and Contradictions; and their Minds be overlaid by an Object too large and mighty, to be surveyed and managed by them.

§ 22. If I have dwelt pretty long on the Considerations of Duration, Space, and Number; and what arises from the Contemplation of them, Infinity, 'tis possibly no more, than the matter requires, there being few simple *Ideas*, whose Modes give more exercise to the Thoughts of Men, than these do. I pretend not to treat of them in their full Latitude: it suffices to my Design, to shew, how the Mind receives them, such as they are, from *Sensation* and *Reflection*; And how even the *Idea* we have of *Infinity*, how remote soever it may seem to be from any Object of Sense, or Operation of our Mind, has nevertheless, as all our other *Ideas*, its Original there. Some Mathematicians, perhaps, of advanced Speculations, may have other ways to introduce into their Minds *Ideas* of Infinity: But this hinders not, but that they themselves, as well as all other Men, got the first *Ideas*, which they had of Infinity, from Sensation and Reflection, in the method we have here set down.

CHAPTER XVIII

Of other Simple Modes.

§ 1. THOUGH I have in the foregoing Chapters, shewn how from simple *Ideas* taken in by Sensation, the Mind comes to extend it self even to Infinity. Which however it may, of all others, seem most remote from any sensible Perception, yet at last hath nothing in it, but what is made out of simple *Ideas*: received into the Mind by the Senses, and afterwards there put together, by the Faculty the Mind has to repeat its own *Ideas*. Though, I say, these might be instances enough of simple Modes of the simple *Ideas* of Sensation; and suffice to shew, how the mind comes by them: yet I shall for Methods sake,

§ 22. *All these* Ideas *from Sensation and Reflection.*
§§ 1, 2. *Modes of Motion.*

(3) leads] **4–5** | lead **1–3** (19) , which] *add.* **4–5** (23) it] **4–5** | its **1–3** (29) enough of] **1er–5** | of enough **1** (*l. below* 30) *In* **Coste**, *§ 22 comes under the same marginal summary as § 21.*

though briefly, give an account of some few more, and then proceed to more complex *Ideas*.

§ 2. To *slide*, *roll*, *tumble*, *walk*, *creep*, *run*, *dance*, *leap*, *skip*, and abundance others, that might be named, are Words, which are no sooner heard, but every one, who understands English, has presently in his Mind distinct *Ideas*, which are all but the different modifications of Motion. *Modes of Motion* answer those of Extension: *Swift* and *Slow* are two different *Ideas* of Motion, the measures whereof are made of the distances of Time and Space put together, so they are complex *Ideas* comprehending Time and Space with Motion.

§ 3. The like variety have we in Sounds. Every articulate word is a different *modification of Sound*: by which we see, that from the sense of Hearing by such modifications, the mind may be furnished with distinct *Ideas*, to almost an infinite Number. Sounds also, besides the distinct cries of Birds and Beasts, are modified by diversity of Notes of different length put together, which make that complex *Idea* call'd a *Tune*, which a Musician may have in his mind, when he hears or makes no Sound at all, by reflecting on the *Ideas* of those Sounds, so put together silently in his own Fancy.

§ 4. Those of Colours are also very various: Some we take notice of, as the different degrees, or as they are termed, *Shades of the same Colour*. But since we very seldom make assemblages of Colours, either for Use or Delight, but Figure is taken in also, and has its part in it, as in Painting, Weaving, Needle-works, *etc.* those which are taken notice of, do most commonly belong to mixed Modes, as being made up of *Ideas* of divers kinds, *viz.* Figure and Colour, such as *Beauty*, *Rainbow*, etc.

§ 5. All *compounded Tastes and Smells*, are also Modes made up of these simple *Ideas* of those Senses. But they being such, as generally we have no names for, are less taken notice of, and cannot be set down in writing; and therefore must be left without enumeration, to the Thoughts and Experience of my Reader.

§ 6. In general it may be observed, that those *simple Modes, which are considered but as different degrees of the same simple* Idea; though they are in themselves many of them very distinct *Ideas*; yet *have*

§ 3. *Modes of Sounds.* § 4. *Modes of Colours.* §§ 5, 6. *Modes of Tastes.*

---

(4) others,] **4–5** | other **1–3** (20) are also] **4–5** | might also be **1–3** (24) those] **4–5** | Those **1–3** (34) Idea;] **2–5** (, **5**) | *Idea*; **1** (*l. below* 35: § 4.) *Modes of Colours.*] *add.* **4–5** (*l. below* 35: §§ 5, 6.) *In* **2–3**, § *6 has marginal summary* '*Modes of Colours.*'

ordinarily no distinct Names, nor are much taken notice of, as distinct *Ideas*, where the difference is but very small between them. Whether Men have neglected these modes, and given no Names to them, as wanting measures nicely to distinguish them; or because when they were so distinguished, that Knowledge would not be of general, or necessary use, I leave it to the Thoughts of others; it is sufficient to my purpose to shew, that all our simple *Ideas* come to our Minds only by Sensation and Reflection; and that when the Mind has them, it can variously repeat and compound them, and so make new complex *Ideas*. But though White, Red, or Sweet, *etc.* have not been modified, or made into complex *Ideas*, by several Combinations, so as to be named, and thereby ranked into Species; yet some others of the simple *Ideas*, *viz.* those of Unity, Duration, Motion, *etc.* above instanced in, as also Power and Thinking have been thus modified to a great variety of complex *Ideas*, with Names belonging to them.

§ 7. *The Reason whereof*, I suppose, has been this, That the great Concernment of Men being with Men one amongst another, the Knowledge of Men, and their Actions, and the signifying of them to one another, was most necessary; and therefore they made *Ideas* of Actions very nicely modified, and gave those complex *Ideas* names, that they might the more easily record, and discourse of those things, they were daily conversant in, without long Ambages and Circumlocutions; and that the things they were continually to give and receive information about, might be the easier and quicker understood. That this is so, and that Men in framing different complex *Ideas*, and giving them Names, have been much governed by the end of Speech in general (which is a very short and expedite way of conveying their Thoughts one to another) is evident in the Names, which in several Arts have been found out, and applied to several complex *Ideas* of modified Actions, belonging to their several Trades, for dispatch sake, in their Direction or Discourses about them. Which *Ideas* are not generally framed in the minds of Men not conversant about these Operations. And thence the words that stand for them, by the greatest part of Men of the same Language, are not understood. *v.g. Coltshire*, *Drilling*, *Filtration*, *Cohobation*, are words standing for certain complex *Ideas*, which

§ 7. *Why some Modes have, and others have not Names.*

(7) [*1st*] our] **1er–5** | these **1** (35) *v.g.*] **Coste** *gives different, French examples* 'frisser, amalgamer, sublimation, cohobation', *indicating in marginal notes that the first of these is a term in printing and the others are terms in chemistry.*

being seldom in the minds of any but those few, whose particular Imployments do at every turn suggest them to their Thoughts, those names of them are not generally understood but by Smiths, and Chymists; who having framed the complex *Ideas*, which these words stand for, and having given names to them, or received them from others, upon hearing of these names in communication readily conceive those *Ideas* in their Minds; as by *Cohobation* all the simple *Ideas* of Distilling, and the pouring the Liquor, distilled from any thing, back upon the remaining Matter, and distilling it again. Thus we see, that there are great varieties of simple *Ideas*, as of Tastes and Smells, which have no Names; and of Modes many more. Which either not having been generally enough observed, or else not being of any great use to be taken notice of in the Affairs and Converse of Men, they have not had names given to them, and so pass not for Species. This we shall have occasion hereafter to consider more at large, when we come to speak of Words.

CHAPTER XIX

Of the Modes of Thinking.

§ 1. WHEN the Mind turns its view inwards upon it self, and contemplates its own Actions, *Thinking* is the first that occurs. In it the Mind observes a great variety of Modifications, and from thence receives distinct *Ideas*. Thus the Perception, which actually accompanies, and is annexed to any impression on the Body, made by an external Object, being distinct from all other Modifications of *thinking*, furnishes the mind with a distinct *Idea*, which we call *Sensation*; which is, as it were, the actual entrance of any *Idea* into the Understanding by the Senses. The same *Idea*, when it again recurs without the operation of the like Object on the external Sensory, is

§§ 1, 2. *Sensation*, *Remembrance*, *Contemplation*, etc.

(1–2) seldom . . . Thoughts,] **4–5** | not in the Minds of every body, they having no use of them, **1–3** (3) Smiths] **Coste** 'imprimeurs' (6) others,] **2–5** | others **1** communication] **2–4** | communication, **1, 5** (11) more.] **4–5** | more; **1–3** (15) . This] **4–5** | , which **1–3** (17) it self] **W** | its self **1–5** (18–20) . In . . . Perception] **4–5** | ; wherein it observes a great variety of Modifications, and thereof frames to it self distinct *Ideas*. Thus the Perception, or Thought **1–3**. (**Coste** '. . . Modifications, qui luy fournissent différentes idées distinctes. Ainsi, la perception ou pensée') (20–1) accompanies] **1er–5** | accompany **1** (22–3) being . . . *Idea*] **4–5** | it frames a distinct *Idea* of **1–3** (26) external] **2–5** | eternal **1**

Remembrance: If it be sought after by the mind, and with pain and endeavour found, and brought again in view, 'tis *Recollection*: If it be held there long under attentive Consideration, 'tis *Contemplation*: When *Ideas* float in our mind, without any reflection or regard of the Understanding, it is that, which the *French* call *Reverie*; our Language has scarce a name for it: When the *Ideas* that offer themselves, (for as I have observed in another place, whilst we are awake, there will always be a train of *Ideas* succeeding one another in our minds,) are taken notice of, and, as it were, registred in the Memory, it is *Attention*: When the mind with great earnestness, and of choice, fixes its view on any *Idea*, considers it on all sides, and will not be called off by the ordinary sollicitation of other *Ideas*, it is that we call *Intention*, or *Study*: Sleep, without dreaming, is rest from all these. And *Dreaming* it self, is the having of *Ideas*, (whilst the outward Senses are stopp'd, so that they receive not outward Objects with their usual quickness,) in the mind, not suggested by any external Objects, or known occasion; nor under any Choice or Conduct of the Understanding at all: And whether that, which we call *Extasy*, be not dreaming with the Eyes open, I leave to be examined.

§ 2. These are some few instances of those various *Modes of thinking*, which the Mind may observe in it self, and so have as distinct *Ideas* of, as it hath of *White* and *Red*, a *Square* or a *Circle*. I do not pretend to enumerate them all, nor to treat at large of this set of *Ideas*, which are got from *Reflection*: That would be to make a Volume. It suffices to my present purpose, to have shewn here, by some few Examples, of what sort these *Ideas* are, and how the mind comes by them; especially since I shall have occasion hereafter to treat more at large of *Reasoning*, *Judging*, *Volition*, and *Knowledge*, which are some of the most considerable Operations of the mind, and *Modes of thinking*.

§ 3. But, perhaps, it may not be an unpardonable Digression, nor wholly impertinent to our present Design, if we reflect here upon *the different State of the Mind in thinking*, which those instances of Attention, *Resvery*, and Dreaming, *etc.* before mentioned, naturally enough suggest. That there are *Ideas*, some or other, always present

§ 3. *The various attention of the Mind in Thinking.*

---

(10) choice] **1T.er, 2–5** | a choice **1** (12) sollicitation] **1–3, 5** | so-/licitation **4** (14) having] **4–5** | perception **1–3** (21) have] **4–5** | frame **1–3** (22) hath] **4–5** | does **1–3** (24) : That] **4–5** | , that **1–3** (26) these] **4–5** | those **1–3**

in the mind of a waking Man, every one's Experience convinces him; though the mind employs it self about them with several degrees of Attention. Sometimes the mind fixes it self with so much earnestness on the Contemplation of some Objects, that it turns their *Ideas* on all sides; remarks their Relations and Circumstances; and views every part so nicely, and with such intention, that it shuts out all other Thoughts, and takes no notice of the ordinary Impressions made then on the Senses, which at another Season would produce very sensible Perceptions: At other times, it barely observes the train of *Ideas*, that succeed in the Understanding, without directing, and pursuing any of them: And at other times, it lets them pass almost quite unregarded, as faint shadows, that make no Impression.

§ 4. This difference of *Intention*, and *Remission* of the mind in thinking, with a great variety of Degrees, between earnest Study, and very near minding nothing at all, Every one, I think, has experimented in himself. Trace it a little farther, and you find the mind in Sleep, retired as it were from the Senses, and out of the reach of those Motions made on the Organs of Sense, which at other times produce very vivid and sensible *Ideas*. I need not, for this, instance in those, who sleep out whole stormy Nights, without hearing the Thunder, or seeing the Lightning, or feeling the shaking of the House, which are sensible enough to those, who are waking. But in this retirement of the mind from the Senses, it often retains a yet more loose and incoherent manner of *thinking*, which we call *Dreaming*: And last of all sound Sleep closes the Scene quite, and puts an end to all Appearances. This I think almost every one has Experience of in himself, and his own Observation without difficulty leads him thus far. That which I would farther conclude from hence is, That since the mind can sensibly put on, at several times, several degrees of *Thinking*; and be sometimes even in a waking Man so remiss, as to have Thoughts dim and obscure to that degree, that they are very little removed from none at all; and at last in the dark retirements of sound Sleep, loses the sight perfectly of all *Ideas* whatsoever: Since, I say, this is evidently so in Matter of Fact, and constant Experience, I ask, whether it be not probable, that *thinking is the Action, and not the Essence of the Soul*? Since the

§ 4. *Hence 'tis probable that Thinking is the Action, not Essence of the Soul.*

(24) waking] **1–2, 4–5** | walking **3** (*l. below* 37) *'tis*] *add.* **4–5**

Operations of Agents will easily admit of intention and remission; but the Essences of things, are not conceived capable of any such variation. But this by the bye.

CHAPTER XX

Of Modes of Pleasure and Pain.

§ 1. AMONGST the simple *Ideas*, which we receive both from *Sensation* and *Reflection*, *Pain* and *Pleasure* are two very considerable ones. For as in the Body, there is Sensation barely in it self, or accompanied with *Pain* or *Pleasure*; so the Thought, or Perception of the Mind is simply so, or else accompanied also with *Pleasure* or *Pain*, Delight or Trouble, call it how you please. These like other simple *Ideas* cannot be described, nor their Names defined; the way of knowing them is, as of the simple *Ideas* of the Senses, only by Experience. For to define them by the Presence of Good or Evil, is no otherwise to make them known to us, than by making us reflect on what we feel in our selves, upon the several and various Operations of Good and Evil upon our Minds, as they are differently applied to, or considered by us.

§ 2. Things then are Good or Evil, only in reference to Pleasure or Pain. That we call *Good*, which *is apt to cause or increase Pleasure, or diminish Pain in us; or else to procure, or preserve us the possession of any other Good, or absence of any Evil.* And on the contrary we name that *Evil*, which *is apt to produce or increase any Pain, or diminish any Pleasure in us; or else to procure us any Evil, or deprive us of any Good.* By Pleasure and Pain, I must be understood to mean of Body or Mind, as they are commonly distinguished; though in truth, they be only different Constitutions of the Mind, sometimes occasioned by disorder in the Body, sometimes by Thoughts of the Mind.

§ 3. *Pleasure* and *Pain*, and that which causes them, Good and Evil, are the hinges on which our *Passions* turn: and if we reflect on our selves, and observe how these, under various Considerations, operate in us; what Modifications or Tempers of Mind, what

§ 1. *Pleasure and Pain simple* Ideas. § 2. *Good and Evil what.* § 3. *Our Passions moved by Good and Evil.*

(1–2) ; but] **1–3, 5** | . But **4** (6) it self] **W** | its self **1–5** (29) and observe] *add.* **4–5**

internal Sensations, (if I may so call them,) they produce in us, we may thence form to our selves the *Ideas* of our *Passions.*

§ 4. Thus any one reflecting upon the thought he has of the Delight, which any present, or absent thing is apt to produce in him, has the *Idea* we call *Love.* For when a Man declares in Autumn, when he is eating them, or in Spring, when there are none, that he *loves* Grapes, it is no more, but that the taste of Grapes delights him; let an alteration of Health or Constitution destroy the delight of their Taste, and he then can be said to *love* Grapes no longer.

§ 5. On the contrary, the Thought of the Pain, which any thing present or absent is apt to produce in us, is what we call *Hatred.* Were it my business here, to enquire any farther, than into the bare *Ideas* of our Passions, as they depend on different Modifications of Pleasure and Pain, I should remark, that our *Love* and *Hatred* of inanimate insensible Beings, is commonly founded on that Pleasure and Pain which we receive from their use and application any way to our Senses, though with their Destruction: But *Hatred* or *Love,* to Beings capable of Happiness or Misery, is often the Uneasiness or Delight, which we find in our selves arising from a consideration of their very Being, or Happiness. Thus the Being and Welfare of a Man's Children or Friends, producing constant Delight in him, he is said constantly to *love* them. But it suffices to note, that our *Ideas* of *Love* and *Hatred,* are but the Dispositions of the Mind, in respect of Pleasure and Pain in general, however caused in us.

§ 6. The uneasiness a Man finds in himself upon the absence of any thing, whose present enjoyment carries the *Idea* of Delight with it, is that we call *Desire,* which is greater or less, as that uneasiness is more or less vehement. Where by the bye it may perhaps be of some use to remark, that the chief if not only spur to humane Industry and Action is uneasiness. For whatever good is propos'd, if its absence carries no displeasure nor pain with it; if a Man be easie and content without it, there is no desire of it, nor endeavour after it; there is no more but a bare *Velleity,* the term used to signifie the lowest degree of Desire, and that which is next to none at all, when there is so little uneasiness in the absence of any thing, that it

§ 4. *Love.* § 5. *Hatred.* § 6. *Desire.*

---

(16) which] *add.* **4–5** (17) *Hatred* or *Love,*] **4–5** | *Love* and *Hatred* **2–3** | Love and Hatred **1** (18) Uneasiness] **4–5** | Pain **1–3** (19) , which . . . of] **4–5** | we have in **1–3** (, we **2–3**) (25) uneasiness] **Coste** *adds a footnote, on the absence of a satisfactory French equivalent of this word.* (28)–231(6) Where . . . place.] *add.* **2–5**

carries a Man no farther than some faint wishes for it, without any more effectual or vigorous use of the means to attain it. *Desire* also is stopp'd or abated by the Opinion of the impossibility or unattainableness of the good propos'd, as far as the uneasiness is cured or allay'd by that consideration. This might carry our thoughts farther were it seasonable in this place.

§ 7. *Joy* is a delight of the Mind, from the consideration of the present or assured approaching possession of a Good; and we are then possessed of any Good, when we have it so in our power, that we can use it when we please. Thus a Man almost starved, has *Joy* at the arrival of Relief, even before he has the pleasure of using it: and a Father, in whom the very well-being of his Children causes delight, is always, as long as his Children are in such a State, in the possession of that Good; for he needs but to reflect on it to have that pleasure.

§ 8. *Sorrow* is uneasiness in the Mind, upon the thought of a Good lost, which might have been enjoy'd longer; or the sense of a present Evil.

§ 9. *Hope* is that pleasure in the Mind, which every one finds in himself, upon the thought of a probable future enjoyment of a thing, which is apt to delight him.

§ 10. *Fear* is an uneasiness of the Mind, upon the thought of future Evil likely to befal us.

§ 11. *Despair* is the thought of the unattainableness of any Good, which works differently in Mens Minds, sometimes producing uneasiness or pain, sometimes rest and indolency.

§ 12. *Anger* is uneasiness or discomposure of the Mind, upon the receit of any Injury, with a present purpose of Revenge.

§ 13. *Envy* is an uneasiness of Mind, caused by the consideration of a Good we desire, obtained by one, we think should not have had it before us.

§ 14. These two last, *Envy* and *Anger*, not being caused by Pain and Pleasure simply in themselves, but having in them some mixed Considerations of our selves and others, are not therefore to be found in all Men, because those other parts of valuing their Merits,

§ 7. *Joy.* § 8. *Sorrow.* § 9. *Hope.* § 10. *Fear.* § 11. *Despair.* § 12. *Anger.* § 13. *Envy.* § 14. *What Passions all Men have.*

---

(6) *v.* 230(28), n. (13) a State] **2–5** | an estate **1** (20) probable] **1–3** (*likewise* **Coste**) | profitable **4–5**

or intending Revenge, is wanting in them: But all the rest terminated purely in Pain and Pleasure, are, I think, to be found in all Men. For we *love*, *desire*, *rejoice*, and *hope*, only in respect of Pleasure; we *hate*, *fear*, and *grieve* only in respect of Pain ultimately: In fine all these Passions are moved by things, only as they appear to be the Causes of Pleasure and Pain, or to have Pleasure or Pain some way or other annexed to them. Thus we extend our Hatred usually to the subject, (at least if a sensible or voluntary Agent,) which has produced Pain in us, because the fear it leaves is a constant pain: But we do not so constantly love what has done us good; because Pleasure operates not so strongly on us, as Pain; and because we are not so ready to have hope, it will do so again. But this by the bye.

§ 15. By *Pleasure* and *Pain*, Delight and Uneasiness, I must all along be understood (as I have above intimated) to mean, not only bodily Pain and Pleasure, but whatsoever *Delight* or *Uneasiness* is felt by us, whether arising from any grateful, or unacceptable Sensation or Reflection.

§ 16. 'Tis farther to be considered, That in reference to the Passions, the removal or *lessening of a Pain is* considered, and operates as a *Pleasure*: And the loss or diminishing of a Pleasure, as a Pain.

§ 17. The Passions too have most of them in most Persons operations on the Body, and cause various changes in it: Which not being always sensible, do not make a necessary part of the *Idea* of each Passion. For *Shame*, which is an uneasiness of the Mind, upon the thought of having done something, which is indecent, or will lessen the valued Esteem, which others have for us, has not always blushing accompanying it.

§ 18. I would not be mistaken here, as if I meant this as a Discourse of the *Passions*; they are *many more than those* I have here named: And those I have taken notice of, would each of them require a much larger, and more accurate Discourse. I have only mentioned these here, as so many instances of Modes of Pleasure and Pain resulting in our Minds, from various Considerations of Good and

§§ 15, 16. *Pleasure and Pain what.* § 17. *Shame.* § 18. *These instances to shew how our* Ideas *of the Passions are got from Sensation and Reflection.*

(1–2) terminated] **4–5** | terminating **1–3** (4) *hate*, *fear*, and *grieve*] **2–5** | hate and fear, and are sad **1** : In fine all] **4–5** | ; and **1–3** (5) things, only] **2–5** | things only, **1** (6) [*1st*] or] **4–5** | and **1–3**. (**Coste** 'en sorte que') (27) the . . . us] **4–5** | the Esteem we value **1–3** (*2 ll. below* 34) *Sensation*] **2–3**, **5** | *Sensation*, **4**

Evil. I might, perhaps, have instanced in other Modes of Pleasure and Pain more simple than these, as the Pain of *Hunger* and *Thirst*, and the Pleasure of Eating and Drinking to remove them; The pain of tender Eyes, and the pleasure of Musick; Pain from captious uninstructive wrangling, and the pleasure of rational conversation with a Friend, or of well directed study in the search and discovery of Truth. But the Passions being of much more concernment to us, I rather made choice to instance in them, and shew how the *Ideas* we have of them, are derived from Sensation and Reflection.

CHAPTER XXI

Of Power.

§ 1. THE Mind, being every day informed, by the Senses, of the alteration of those simple *Ideas*, it observes in things without; and taking notice how one comes to an end, and ceases to be, and another begins to exist, which was not before; reflecting also on what passes within it self, and observing a constant change of its *Ideas*, sometimes by the impression of outward Objects on the Senses, and sometimes by the Determination of its own choice; and concluding from what it has so constantly observed to have been, that the like Changes will for the future be made, in the same things, by like Agents, and by the like ways, considers in one thing the possibility of having any of its simple *Ideas* changed, and in another the possibility of making that change; and so comes by that *Idea* which we call *Power*. Thus we say, Fire has a *power* to melt Gold, *i.e.* to destroy the consistency of its insensible parts, and consequently its hardness, and make it fluid; and Gold has a *power* to be melted; That the Sun has a *power* to blanch Wax, and Wax a *power* to be blanched by the Sun, whereby the Yellowness is destroy'd, and Whiteness made to exist in its room. In which, and the like Cases, the *Power* we consider is in reference to the change of perceivable *Ideas*. For we cannot observe any alteration to be made in, or

§ 1. *This* Idea *how got.*

(3–7) to . . . Truth] **2–5** | , when one is so: The pain of the Head-ach, or pleasure of rational Conversation with one's Friend, or discovering of a speculative Truth upon study **1**

operation upon any thing, but by the observable change of its sensible *Ideas*; nor conceive any alteration to be made, but by conceiving a Change of some of its *Ideas*.

§ 2. *Power* thus considered is twofold, *viz.* as able to make, or able to receive any change: The one may be called *Active*, and the other *Passive Power*. Whether Matter be not wholly destitute of *active Power*, as its Author GOD is truly above all *passive Power*; and whether the intermediate state of created Spirits be not that alone, which is capable of both *active* and *passive Power*, may be worth consideration. I shall not now enter into that Enquiry, my present Business being not to search into the original of Power, but how we come by the *Idea* of it. But since *active Powers* make so great a part of our complex *Ideas* of natural Substances, (as we shall see hereafter,) and I mention them as such, according to common apprehension; yet they being not, perhaps, so truly *active Powers*, as our hasty Thoughts are apt to represent them, I judge it not amiss, by this intimation, to direct our Minds to the consideration of GOD and Spirits, for the clearest *Idea* of *active Power*.

§ 3. I confess *Power includes in it some kind of relation*, (a relation to Action or Change,) as indeed which of our *Ideas*, of what kind soever, when attentively considered, does not? For our *Ideas* of Extension, Duration, and Number, do they not all contain in them a secret relation of the Parts? Figure and Motion have something relative in them much more visibly: And sensible Qualities, as Colours and Smells, *etc.* what are they but the *Powers* of different Bodies, in relation to our Perception, *etc.* And if considered in the things themselves, do they not depend on the Bulk, Figure, Texture, and Motion of the Parts? All which include some kind of relation in them. Our *Idea* therefore of *Power*, I think, may well have a place amongst other simple *Ideas*, and be considered as one of them, being one of those, that make a principal Ingredient in our complex *Ideas* of Substances, as we shall hereafter have occasion to observe.

§ 4. We are abundantly furnished with the *Idea* of *passive Power*, by almost all sorts of sensible things. In most of them we cannot

§ 2. *Power active and passive.* § 3. *Power includes Relation.* § 4. *The clearest* Idea *of active Power had from Spirit.*

---

(31) make] **4–5** | makes **1–3** (32) observe] **4–5** | shew **1–3** (*likewise* **Coste**) (33)–235(1) We . . . Substances] **4–5** | Of passive Power, all sensible things abundantly furnish us with *Ideas*; whose sensible Qualities and Beings we find **1–3**

avoid observing their sensible Qualities, nay their very Substances to be in a continual flux: And therefore with reason we look on them as liable still to the same Change. Nor have we of *active Power* (which is the more proper signification of the word *Power*) fewer instances. Since whatever Change is observed, the Mind must collect a Power somewhere, able to make that Change, as well as a possibility in the thing it self to receive it. But yet, if we will consider it attentively, Bodies, by our Senses, do not afford us so clear and distinct an *Idea* of *active Power*, as we have from reflection on the Operations of our Minds. For all *Power* relating to Action, and there being but two sorts of Action, whereof we have any *Idea*, *viz.* Thinking and Motion, let us consider whence we have the clearest *Ideas* of the *Powers*, which produce these Actions. 1. Of Thinking, Body affords us no *Idea* at all, it is only from Reflection that we have that: 2. Neither have we from Body any *Idea* of the beginning of Motion. A Body at rest affords us no *Idea* of any *active Power* to move; and when it is set in motion it self, that Motion is rather a Passion, than an Action in it. For when the Ball obeys the stroke of a Billiard-stick, it is not any action of the Ball, but bare passion: Also when by impulse it sets another Ball in motion, that lay in its way, it only communicates the motion it had received from another, and loses in it self so much, as the other received; which gives us but a very obscure *Idea* of an *active Power* of moving in Body, whilst we observe it only to transfer, but not produce any motion. For it is but a very obscure *Idea* of *Power*, which reaches not the Production of the Action, but the Continuation of the Passion. For so is motion in a Body impelled by another: The continuation of the Alteration made in it from rest to motion being little more an Action, than the continuation of the Alteration of its Figure by the same blow is an Action. The *Idea* of the beginning of motion, we have only from reflection on what passes in our selves, where we find by Experience, that barely by willing it, barely by a thought of the Mind, we can move the parts of our Bodies, which were before at rest. So that it seems to me, we have from the observation of the operation of Bodies by our Senses, but a very imperfect obscure *Idea* of *active Power*, since they afford us not any *Idea* in themselves of the *Power* to begin any Action, either motion or thought. But if, from the Impulse Bodies are observed to make one upon another, any one

(1) *v.* 234(33), n. (15) that: 2. Neither] **4–5** | that; neither **1–3** (17) [*2nd*] it] **4–5** | its **1–3**

thinks he has a clear *Idea* of *Power*, it serves as well to my purpose, *Sensation* being one of those ways, whereby the mind comes by its *Ideas*: Only I thought it worth while to consider here by the way, whether the mind doth not receive its *Idea* of *active Power* clearer from reflection on its own Operations, than it doth from any external Sensation.

§ 5. This at least I think evident, That we find in our selves a *Power* to begin or forbear, continue or end several actions of our minds, and motions of our Bodies, barely by a thought or preference of the mind ordering, or as it were commanding the doing or not doing such or such a particular action. This *Power* which the mind has, thus to order the consideration of any *Idea*, or the forbearing to consider it; or to prefer the motion of any part of the body to its rest, and *vice versâ* in any particular instance is that which we call the *Will*. The actual exercise of that power, by directing any particular action, or its forbearance is that which we call *Volition* or *Willing*. The forbearance or performance of that action, consequent to such order or command of the mind is called *Voluntary*. And whatsoever action is performed without such a thought of the mind is called *Involuntary*. The power of Perception is that which we call the *Understanding*. Perception, which we make the act of the Understanding, is of three sorts: 1. The Perception of *Ideas* in our Minds. 2. The Perception of the signification of Signs. 3. The Perception of the Connexion or Repugnancy, Agreement or Disagreement, that there is between any of our *Ideas*. All these are attributed to the *Understanding*, or perceptive Power, though it be the two latter only that use allows us to say we understand.

§ 6. These Powers of the Mind, *viz.* of *Perceiving*, and of *Preferring*, are usually call'd by another Name: And the ordinary way of Speaking is, That the *Understanding* and *Will* are two *Faculties* of the mind; a word proper enough, if it be used as all Words should be,

§ 5. *Will and Understanding, two Powers.* § 6. *Faculties.*

(8) several actions] **2–5** | several, Thoughts **1** (9–11) a . . . action] **2–5** | the choice or preference of our Minds **1** (11–12) which . . . order] **2–5** | the Mind has to prefer **1** (12–13) or the forbearing to consider] **2–5** | to the not considering **1** (14) and . . . instance] *add.* **2–5** that which] **4–5** | that **2–3** | that, I think, **1** (15–20) . The . . . *Involuntary*] **2–5** | ; and the actual preferring one to another, is that we call *Volition*, or *Willing* **1** (17) or performance] **2–4**; *om.* **5** (20) which] *add.* **4–5** (24) Connexion or Repugnancy,] *add.* **4–5** (25), that . . . *Ideas*] **4–5** | of any distinct *Ideas* **1–3** (27) the . . . understand] **4–5** | to the two latter, that in strictness of Speech, the act of Understanding is usually applied **1–3** (*l. below* 31: § 6.) *In* **Coste**, § *6 comes under the same marginal summary as* §5.

so as not to breed any confusion in Mens Thoughts, by being supposed (as I suspect it has been) to stand for some real Beings in the Soul, that performed those Actions of Understanding and Volition. For when we say the *Will* is the commanding and superior Faculty of the Soul; that it is, or is not free; that it determines the inferior Faculties; that it follows the Dictates of the *Understanding*, etc. though these, and the like Expressions, by those that carefully attend to their own *Ideas*, and conduct their Thoughts more by the evidence of Things, than the sound of Words, may be understood in a clear and distinct sense: Yet I suspect, I say, that this way of Speaking of *Faculties*, has misled many into a confused Notion of so many distinct Agents in us, which had their several Provinces and Authorities, and did command, obey, and perform several Actions, as so many distinct Beings; which has been no small occasion of wrangling, obscurity, and uncertainty in Questions relating to them.

§ 7. Every one, I think, finds in himself a *Power* to begin or forbear, continue or put an end to several Actions in himself. From the consideration of the extent of this power of the mind over the actions of the Man, which every one finds in himself, arise the *Ideas* of *Liberty* and *Necessity*.

§ 8. All the Actions, that we have any *Idea* of, reducing themselves, as has been said, to these two, *viz.* Thinking and Motion, so far as a Man has a power to think, or not to think; to move, or not to move, according to the preference or direction of his own mind, so far is a Man *Free*. Where-ever any performance or forbearance are not equally in a Man's power; where-ever doing or not doing, will not equally follow upon the preference of his mind directing it, there he is not *Free*, though perhaps the Action may be voluntary. So that the *Idea* of *Liberty*, is the *Idea* of a Power in any Agent to do or forbear any particular Action, according to the determination or thought of the mind, whereby either of them is preferr'd to the other; where either of them is not in the Power of the Agent to be

§ 7. *Whence the* Ideas *of Liberty and Necessity.* § 8. *Liberty what.*

(17–20) From ... *Necessity.*] **2–5** | The power the Mind has at any time to prefer any particular one of those Actions to its forbearance, or *Vice versa*, is that Faculty which, as I have said, we call the *Will*; the actual exercise of that Power we call *Volition*; and the forbearance or performance of that Action, consequent to such a preference of the Mind, is call'd *Voluntary*. Hence we have the *Ideas* of *Liberty* and *Necessity*, which arise from the consideration of the extent of this Power of the Mind over the Actions, not only of the Mind, but the whole Agent, the whole Man. **1** (18) this] **5** | the **2–4** (24) or ... mind] **2–5** | of his own choice **1** (27) directing it] *add.* **5** (30) particular] *add.* **5**. (**Coste** 'une certaine action')

produced by him according to his *Volition*, there he is not at *Liberty*, that Agent is under *Necessity*. So that *Liberty* cannot be, where there is no Thought, no Volition, no Will; but there may be Thought, there may be Will, there may be Volition, where there is no *Liberty*. A little Consideration of an obvious instance or two may make this clear.

§ 9. A Tennis-ball, whether in motion by the stroke of a Racket, or lying still at rest, is not by any one taken to be a *free Agent*. If we enquire into the Reason, we shall find it is, because we conceive not a Tennis-ball to think, and consequently not to have any Volition, or preference of Motion to rest, or *vice versâ*; and therefore has not *Liberty*, is not a free Agent; but all its both Motion and Rest, come under our *Idea* of *Necessary*, and are so call'd. Likewise a Man falling into the Water, (a Bridge breaking under him,) has not herein liberty, is not a free Agent. For though he has Volition, though he prefers his not falling to falling; yet the forbearance of that Motion not being in his Power, the Stop or Cessation of that Motion follows not upon his Volition; and therefore therein he is not *free*. So a Man striking himself, or his Friend, by a Convulsive motion of his Arm, which it is not in his Power, by Volition or the direction of his Mind to stop, or forbear; no Body thinks he has in this *Liberty*; every one pities him, as acting by Necessity and Constraint.

§ 10. Again, suppose a Man be carried, whilst fast asleep, into a Room, where is a Person he longs to see and speak with; and be there locked fast in, beyond his Power to get out: he awakes, and is glad to find himself in so desirable Company, which he stays willingly in, *i.e.* preferrs his stay to going away. I ask, Is not this stay voluntary? I think, no Body will doubt it: and yet being locked fast in, 'tis evident he is not at liberty not to stay, he has not freedom to be gone. So that *Liberty is not an* Idea *belonging to Volition*, or preferring; but to the Person having the Power of doing, or forbearing to do, according as the Mind shall chuse or direct. Our *Idea* of Liberty reaches as far as that Power, and no farther. For whereever restraint comes to check that Power, or compulsion takes away that Indifferency of Ability on either side to act, or to forbear acting, there *liberty*, and our Notion of it, presently ceases.

§ 9. *Supposes the Understanding, and Will.* § 10. *Belongs not to Volition.*

---

(1) *Volition . . . Liberty*] **2–5** | preference, there is not *Liberty* **1** (19) it] *add.* **2–5** (19–20) , by . . . or] **2–5** | upon his Preference or Volition to **1** (31) or direct] *add.* **2–5** (33) takes] **2–5** | , takes **1** (34) of . . . acting,] **5** | to act, or not to act, [; **1–3**] **1–4**

§ 11. We have instances enough, and often more than enough in our own Bodies. A Man's Heart beats, and the Blood circulates, which 'tis not in his Power by any Thought or Volition to stop; and therefore in respect of these Motions, where rest depends not on his choice, nor would follow the determination of his Mind, if it should preferr it, he is not a *free Agent*. Convulsive Motions agitate his Legs, so that though he *wills* it never so much, he cannot by any power of his Mind stop their Motion, (as in that odd Disease called *Chorea Sancti Viti*,) but he is perpetually dancing: He is not at Liberty in this Action, but under as much Necessity of moving, as a Stone that falls, or a Tennis-ball struck with a Racket. On the other side, a Palsie or the Stocks hinder his Legs from obeying the determination of his Mind, if it would thereby transferr his Body to another Place. In all these there is want of *Freedom*, though the sitting still even of a Paralytick, whilst he preferrs it to a removal, is truly voluntary. *Voluntary* then *is not opposed to Necessary*; *but to Involuntary*. For a Man may preferr what he can do, to what he cannot do; the State he is in, to its absence or change, though Necessity has made it in it self unalterable.

§ 12. As it is in the motions of the Body, so it is in the Thoughts of our Minds; where any one is such, that we have power to take it up, or lay it by, according to the preference of the Mind, there we are *at liberty*. A waking Man being under the necessity of having some *Ideas* constantly in his Mind, is not at *liberty* to think, or not to think; no more than he is at *liberty*, whether his Body shall touch any other, or no: But whether he will remove his Contemplation from one *Idea* to another, is many times in his choice; and then he is in respect of his *Ideas*, as much at *liberty*, as he is in respect of Bodies he rests on: He can at pleasure remove himself from one to another. But yet some *Ideas* to the Mind, like some Motions to the Body, are such, as in certain circumstances it cannot avoid, nor obtain their absence by the utmost effort it can use. A Man on the Rack, is not at *liberty* to lay by the *Idea* of pain, and divert himself with other Contemplations: and sometimes a boisterous Passion hurries our Thoughts, as a Hurricane does our Bodies, without leaving us the

§ 11. *Voluntary opposed to involuntary, not to Necessary*. § 12. *Liberty what*.

---

(12) or the Stocks] **4–5** | or Stocks **1–3**. (**Coste** *omits this phrase*.) (15) [*2nd*] a] *add*. **2–5** (33) divert himself with] **4–5** | entertain **1–3** (*l. below* 35: § 11.) *In* **Coste**, § *11 comes under the same marginal summary as* § *10*.

liberty of thinking on other things, which we would rather chuse. But as soon as the Mind regains the power to stop or continue, begin or forbear any of these Motions of the Body without, or Thoughts within, according as it thinks fit to preferr either to the other, we then consider the Man as a *free Agent* again.

§ 13. Where-ever Thought is wholly wanting, or the power to act or forbear according to the direction of Thought, there *Necessity* takes place. This in an Agent capable of Volition, when the beginning or continuation of any Action is contrary to that preference of his Mind, is called *Compulsion*; when the hind'ring or stopping any Action is contrary to his Volition, it is called *Restraint*. Agents that have no Thought, no Volition at all, are in every thing *necessary* Agents.

§ 14. If this be so, (as I imagine it is,) I leave it to be considered, whether it may not help to put an end to that long agitated, and, I think, unreasonable, because unintelligible, Question, *viz. Whether Man's Will be free, or no*. For if I mistake not, it follows, from what I have said, that the Question it self is altogether improper; and it is as insignificant to ask, whether Man's *Will* be free, as to ask, whether his Sleep be Swift, or his Vertue square: *Liberty* being as little applicable to the *Will*, as swiftness of Motion is to Sleep, or squareness to Vertue. Every one would laugh at the absurdity of such a Question, as either of these: because it is obvious, that the modifications of motion belong not to sleep, nor the difference of Figure to Vertue: and when any one well considers it, I think he will as plainly perceive, that *Liberty*, which is but a power, belongs only to Agents, and cannot be an attribute or modification of the *Will*, which is also but a Power.

§ 15. Such is the difficulty of explaining, and giving clear notions of internal Actions by sounds, that I must here warn my Reader that *Ordering, Directing, Chusing, Preferring*, etc. which I have made use of, will not distinctly enough express *Volition*, unless he will reflect on what he himself does, when he *wills*. For Example, *Preferring* which seems perhaps best to express the Act of *Volition*, does

§ 13. *Necessity what.* § 14. *Liberty belongs not to the Will.* § 15. *Volition.*

(5) we then] **2–5** | then we **1** (7) according . . . Thought] *add.* **2–5**
(11) **Coste** *uses 'Cohibition' for 'Restraint' here, and adds a linguistic note on it.*
(29)–241(2) Such . . . it?] *add.* **2–5** (*l. below* 34: § 14.) *In* **2–3**, *§§ 15–20 come under the same marginal summary as* § 14. *belongs*] **3–5** | *belong* **2**

it not precisely. For though a Man would preferr flying to walking, yet who can say he ever *wills* it? *Volition*, 'tis plain, is an Act of the Mind knowingly exerting that Dominion it takes it self to have over any part of the Man, by imploying it in, or witholding it from any particular Action. And what is the *Will*, but the Faculty to do this? And is that Faculty any thing more in effect, than a Power, the power of the Mind to determine its thought, to the producing, continuing, or stopping any Action, as far as it depends on us? For can it be denied, that whatever Agent has a power to think on its own Actions, and to preferr their doing or omission either to other, has that Faculty call'd *Will*. *Will* then is nothing but such a power. *Liberty*, on the other side, is the power a Man has to do or forbear doing any particular Action, according as its doing or forbearance has the actual preference in the Mind, which is the same thing as to say, according as he himself *wills* it.

§ 16. 'Tis plain then, That the *Will* is nothing but one Power or Ability, and *Freedom* another Power or Ability: So that to ask, whether the *Will has Freedom*, is to ask, whether one Power has another Power, one Ability another Ability; a Question at first sight too grosly absurd to make a Dispute, or need an Answer. For who is it that sees not, that *Powers* belong only to *Agents*, and *are Attributes only of Substances, and not of Powers* themselves? So that this way of putting the Question, *viz.* whether the *Will be free*, is in effect to ask, whether the *Will* be a Substance, an Agent, or at least to suppose it, since Freedom can properly be attributed to nothing else. If Freedom can with any propriety of Speech be applied to Power, it may be attributed to the Power, that is in a Man, to produce, or forbear producing Motion in parts of his Body, by choice or preference; which is that which denominates him free, and is Freedom it self. But if any one should ask, whether Freedom were free, he would be suspected, not to understand well what he said; and he would be thought to deserve *Midas*'s Ears, who knowing that Rich was a denomination from the possession of Riches, should demand whether Riches themselves were rich.

§§ 16–19. *Powers belong to Agents.*

---

(2) *v.* 240(29), n. (2–5) an . . . Action] **2–5** | nothing but the actual choosing or preferring forbearance to the doing, or doing to the forbearance, of any particular Action in our power, that we think on **1** (7–8) [*1st*] the . . . depends] **2–5** | preferring any Action to its Forbearance, or *vice versâ*, as far as it appears to depend **1** (27) that] *add.* **4–5**

§ 17. However the *name Faculty*, which Men have given to this Power call'd the *Will*, and whereby they have been led into a way of talking of the Will as acting, may, by an appropriation that disguises its true sense, serve a little to palliate the absurdity; yet the *Will* in truth, signifies nothing but a Power, or Ability, to prefer or chuse: And when the *Will*, under the name of a *Faculty*, is considered, as it is, barely as an ability to do something, the absurdity, in saying it is free, or not free, will easily discover it self. For if it be reasonable to suppose and talk of *Faculties*, as distinct Beings, that can act, (as we do, when we say the *Will* orders, and the *Will* is free,) 'tis fit that we should make a speaking *Faculty*, and a walking *Faculty*, and a dancing *Faculty*, by which those Actions are produced, which are but several Modes of Motion; as well as we make the *Will* and *Understanding* to be *Faculties*, by which the Actions of Chusing and Perceiving are produced, which are but several Modes of Thinking: And we may as properly say, that 'tis the singing *Faculty* sings, and the dancing *Faculty* dances; as that the *Will* chuses, or that the Understanding conceives; or, as is usual, that the *Will* directs the Understanding, or the Understanding obeys, or obeys not the *Will*: It being altogether as proper and intelligible to say, that the power of Speaking directs the power of Singing, or the power of Singing obeys or disobeys the power of Speaking.

§ 18. This way of talking, nevertheless, has prevailed, and, as I guess, produced great confusion. For these being all different Powers in the Mind, or in the Man, to do several Actions, he exerts them as he thinks fit: But the power to do one Action, is not operated on by the power of doing another Action. For the power of Thinking operates not on the power of Chusing, nor the power of Chusing on the power of Thinking; no more than the power of Dancing operates on the power of Singing, or the power of Singing on the power of Dancing, as any one, who reflects on it, will easily perceive: And yet this is it which we say, when we thus speak, that *the Will operates on the Understanding, or the Understanding on the Will*.

§ 19. I grant, that this or that actual Thought may be the occasion of Volition, or exercising the power a Man has to chuse;

(2–4) whereby . . . serve] **4–5** | so talked of it as acting, may by this appropriated term, seem **1–3** (6) : And . . . is] **4–5** | ; and when **1–3** (7–8) the . . . self] **4–5** | it will easily discover the absurdity, in saying it is free, or not free **1–3** (13) make] **4–5** | do **1–3** (32–3) , who . . . this] **4–5** | may easily perceive, who will but consider; and yet that **1–3** or the actual choice of the Mind, the cause of actual thinking on this or that thing: As the actual singing of such a Tune, may be the occasion of dancing such a Dance, and the actual dancing of such a Dance, the occasion of singing such a Tune. But in all these, it is not one *power* that operates on another: But it is the Mind that operates, and exerts these Powers; it is the Man that does the Action, it is the Agent that has power, or is able to do. For *Powers* are Relations, not Agents: And *that which has the power, or not the power to operate, is that alone, which is, or is not free,* and not the Power it self: For Freedom, or not Freedom, can belong to nothing, but what has, or has not a power to act.

§ 20. The attributing to *Faculties*, that which belonged not to them, has given occasion to this way of talking: but the introducing into Discourses concerning the Mind, with the name of *Faculties*, a Notion of their operating, has, I suppose, as little advanced our Knowledge in that part of our selves, as the great use and mention of the like invention of *Faculties*, in the operations of the Body, has helped us in the knowledge of Physick. Not that I deny there are *Faculties* both in the Body and Mind: they both of them have their *powers* of Operating, else neither the one nor the other could operate. For nothing can operate, that is not able to operate; and that is not able to operate, that has no *power* to operate. Nor do I deny, that those Words, and the like, are to have their place in the common use of Languages, that have made them currant. It looks like too much affectation wholly to lay them by: and Philosophy it self, though it likes not a gaudy dress, yet when it appears in publick, must have so much Complacency, as to be cloathed in the ordinary Fashion and Language of the Country, so far as it can consist with Truth and Perspicuity. But the fault has been, that Faculties have been spoken of, and represented, as so many distinct Agents. For it being asked, what it was that digested the Meat in our Stomachs? It was a ready, and very satisfactory Answer, to say, That it was the *digestive Faculty*. What was it that made any thing come out of the Body? The *expulsive Faculty*. What moved? The *Motive Faculty*: And so in the Mind, the *intellectual*

§ 20. *Liberty belongs not to the Will.*

(5–8) : But . . . [*1st*] *that*] **4–5** | ; [, **2–3**] for Powers [*Powers* **2–3**] are Relations, not Agents: but [But **2–3**] it is the Mind, or the Man, that operates, and exerts these Powers; that does the Action, he has power, or is able to do. *That* **1–3**. (**Coste** *is closer to* **1–3**.)

Faculty, or the Understanding, understood; and the *elective Faculty*, or the Will, willed or commanded: which is in short to say, That the ability to digest, digested; and the ability to move, moved; and the ability to understand, understood. For *Faculty*, *Ability*, and *Power*, I think, are but different names of the same things: Which ways of speaking, when put into more intelligible Words, will, I think, amount to thus much; That Digestion is performed by something that is able to digest; Motion by something able to move; and Understanding by something able to understand. And in truth it would be very strange, if it should be otherwise; as strange as it would be for a Man to be free without being able to be free.

§ 21. To return then to the Enquiry about Liberty, I think *the Question is not proper, whether the Will be free, but whether a Man be free.* Thus, I think,

1. That so far as any one can, by the direction or choice of his Mind, preferring the existence of any Action, to the non-existence of that Action, and, *vice versâ*, make it to exist, or not exist, so far he is *free*. For if I can, by a thought, directing the motion of my Finger, make it move, when it was at rest, or *vice versâ*, 'tis evident, that in respect of that, I am free: and if I can, by a like thought of my Mind, preferring one to the other, produce either words, or silence, I am at liberty to speak, or hold my peace: and *as far as this Power reaches, of acting, or not acting, by the determination of his own Thought preferring either, so far is a Man free.* For how can we think any one freer than to have the power to do what he will? And so far as any one can, by preferring any Action to its not being, or Rest to any Action, produce that Action or Rest, so far can he do what he will. For such a preferring of Action to its absence, is the *willing* of it: and we can scarce tell how to imagine any *Being* freer, than to be able to do what he *wills*. So that in respect of Actions, within the reach of such a power in him, a Man seems as free, as 'tis possible for Freedom to make him.

§ 22. But the inquisitive Mind of Man, willing to shift off from himself, as far as he can, all thoughts of guilt, though it be by putting himself into a worse state, than that of fatal Necessity, is

§ 21. *But to the Agent or Man.* §§ 22–4. *In respect of willing, a Man is not free.*

(15–16) the . . . preferring] **2–5** | choice, or preference of **1** (18–19) a . . . rest] **2–5** | the preference of the motion of my Finger to its rest, make it move **1** (30) *wills*.] **2–5** | will: **1** (34) thoughts] **1–2**, **4–5** | thoughte **3** (**Coste** 'la pensée')

not content with this: Freedom, unless it reaches farther than this, will not serve the turn: And it passes for a good Plea, that a Man is not free at all, if he be not as free to will, as he is to act, what he wills. Concerning a Man's Liberty there yet therefore is raised this farther Question, *Whether a Man be free to will*; which, I think, is what is meant, when it is disputed, Whether the *will* be free. And as to that I imagine,

§ 23. 2. That *Willing*, or *Volition* being an Action, and Freedom consisting in a power of acting, or not acting, *a Man in respect of willing, or the Act of Volition, when any Action in his power is once proposed to his Thoughts, as presently to be done, cannot be free.* The reason whereof is very manifest: For it being unavoidable that the Action depending on his *Will*, should exist, or not exist; and its existence, or not existence, following perfectly the determination, and preference of his Will, he cannot avoid willing the existence, or not existence, of that Action; it is absolutely necessary that he *will* the one, or the other, *i.e. prefer* the one to the other: since one of them must necessarily follow; and that which does follow, follows by the choice and determination of his Mind, that is, by his *willing it*: for if he did not *will* it, it would not be. So that in respect of the act of *willing*, a Man in such a case is not free: Liberty consisting in a power to act, or not to act, which, in regard of Volition, a Man, upon such a proposal, has not. For it is unavoidably necessary to prefer the doing, or forbearance, of an Action in a Man's power, which is once so proposed to his thoughts; a Man must necessarily *will* the one, or the other of them, upon which preference, or volition, the action, or its forbearance, certainly follows, and is truly

(1–2) : Freedom . . . that] **4–5** | ; will have this to be no freedom, unless it reaches farther: but is ready to say, **1** (6) what is] **2–5** | that **1** (8) *Volition*] **5** | Chusing [Choosing **1–3**] **1–4** (10) , *or . . . when*] *add.* **5** *is*] *add.* **5** (11) *as . . . done*,] *add.* **5** (21) in such a case] **W** | in such Case **5**. (*Not in* **1–4**) (22–3) , upon such a proposal,] *add.* **5** (23) not.] **Coste** *adds a footnote*: 'Pour bien entrer dans le sens de l'Auteur, il faut toûjours avoir dans l'Esprit ce qu'il entend par *Volition*, et *Volonté*, comme il l'a expliqué cy-dessus §. 5 et §. 15. Cela soit dit une fois pour toutes.' (23)–246(5) . For . . . once.] **4–5** | : it being necessary, and unavoidable (any Action in his power being once thought on) to prefer either its doing, or forbearance, upon which preference, the Action, or its forbearance certainly follows, and is truly voluntary. **1–3**. *In* **1–4**, § *23 goes on* '[Besides, to make a Man free after this manner, by making the Action of *willing* to depend on his *Will*, **4**] [So that to make a Man free in this sense, **1–3**] there must be another antecedent *Will*, to determine the Acts of this *Will*, and another to determine that, and so *in infinitum*: For [for **1**] where-ever one stops, the Actions of the last *Will* [Will **1**] cannot be free: Nor is any Being, as far as I can comprehend Beings above me, capable of such a freedom of *Will* [Will **1**], that it can forbear to *Will*, *i.e.* to prefer the Being [being **1–3**], or not Being [being **1–3**] of any thing in its power, which it has once considered as such.' (25) so] *add.* **5** voluntary: But the act of volition, or preferring one of the two, being that which he cannot avoid, a Man in respect of that act of *willing*, is under a necessity, and so cannot be free; unless Necessity and Freedom can consist together, and a Man can be Free and Bound at once.

§ 24. This then is evident, That in all proposals of present Action, *a Man is not at liberty to will, or not to will, because he cannot forbear willing*: Liberty consisting in a power to act, or to forbear acting, and in that only. For a Man that sits still, is said yet to be at liberty, because he can walk if he *wills* it. A Man that walks is at liberty also, not because he walks, or moves; but because he can stand still if he *wills* it. But if a Man sitting still has not a power to remove himself, he is not at liberty; so likewise a Man falling down a precipice, though in motion, is not at liberty, because he cannot stop that motion, if he would. This being so, 'tis plain that a Man that is walking, to whom it is proposed to give off walking, is not at liberty, whether he *will* determine himself to walk, or give off walking, or no: He must necessarily prefer one, or t'other of them; walking or not walking: and so it is in regard of all other Actions in our power so proposed, which are the far greater number. For considering the vast number of voluntary Actions, that succeed one another every moment that we are awake, in the course of our Lives, there are but few of them that are thought on or proposed to the *Will*, 'till the time they are to be done: And in all such Actions, as I have shewn, the Mind in respect of *willing* has not a power to act, or not to act, wherein consists Liberty: The Mind in that case has not a power to forbear *willing*; it cannot avoid some determination concerning them, let the Consideration be as short, the Thought as quick, as it will, it either leaves the Man in the state he was before thinking, or changes it; continues the Action, or puts an end to it. Whereby it is manifest, that it orders and directs one in preference to, or with neglect of the other, and thereby either the continuation, or change becomes unavoidably voluntary.

(2–3) act of *willing*,] **5** | action **4** (5) *v.* 245(23), n. (6–7) That . . . *a*] **5** | *A* **1–4** (7–8) , *because he cannot* [*cannot* **W** | *can* **5**] *forbear willing*:] **5** | *any thing in his power, that he once considers of*: **1–4** (8) to forbear acting] **5** | not to act **1–4** (10–12) A . . . it.] **1–4**; *om.* **5** (10) also,] **4** | in that respect: **1–3** (13) so likewise] **4–5** | nor **1–3** (15) . This . . . that] **4–5** | : But **1–3** (17) *will* . . . walking] **4–5** | will *will* **1, 3** (*likewise* **Coste**) | *will* **2** (19–25) [*2nd*] so . . . *willing*] **5** | ; they being once proposed, the Mind **1–4** (25) has not] **1–3** (had **3**), **5** (*likewise* **Coste**) | has **4** (26) The Mind in that case] **4–5** | It **1–3** (27) some] **1–2, 4–5** | same **3** (30) ; continues . . . [*2nd*] it] *add.* **2–5** (31) , that] *add.* **4–5** (31–2) orders . . . other] **2–5** | prefers one to the other **1** (32) with] *add.* **4–5**

§ 25. Since then it is plain, that in most cases a Man is not at liberty, whether he will *Will*, or no; the next thing demanded is, *Whether a Man be at liberty to will which of the two he pleases, Motion or Rest*. This Question carries the absurdity of it so manifestly in it self, that one might thereby sufficiently be convinced, that Liberty concerns not the Will. For to ask, whether a Man be at liberty to will either Motion, or Rest; Speaking, or Silence; which he pleases, is to ask, whether a Man can *will*, what he *wills*; or be pleased with what he is pleased with. A Question, which, I think, needs no answer: and they, who can make a Question of it, must suppose one Will to determine the Acts of another, and another to determinate that; and so on *in infinitum*.

§ 26. To avoid these, and the like absurdities, nothing can be of greater use, than to establish in our Minds determined *Ideas* of the things under Consideration. If the *Ideas* of Liberty, and Volition, were well fixed in our Understandings, and carried along with us in our Minds, as they ought, through all the Questions that are raised about them, I suppose, a great part of the Difficulties, that perplex Men's Thoughts, and entangle their Understandings, would be much easier resolved; and we should perceive where the confused signification of terms, or where the nature of the thing caused the obscurity.

§ 27. *First* then, it is carefully to be remembred, That *Freedom consists in the dependence of the Existence, or not Existence of any Action, upon our Volition of it, and not in the dependence of any Action, or its contrary, on our preference*. A Man standing on a cliff, is at liberty to leap twenty yards downwards into the Sea, not because he has a power to do the contrary Action, which is to leap twenty yards upwards, for that he cannot do: but he is therefore free, because he has a power to leap, or not to leap. But if a greater force than his, either holds him fast, or tumbles him down, he is no longer free in that case: Because the doing, or forbearance of that particular

§§ 25, 26. *The Will determined by something without it.* § 27. *Freedom.*

---

(1) that in most cases] *add.* **5** (2) no;] **5** | no; (for when [an action **2–4** | a thing **1**] in his power is proposed to his Thoughts, he cannot forbear Volition, he must determine one way or other;) **1–4** demanded] **5** | to be demanded **1–4** (6) Will] **5** | Will in any case **1–4** (12) *infinitum*] **5** | *infinitum*, an absurdity before taken notice of **1–4** (14) determined *Ideas*] **4–5** | clear and steady Notions **1–3**. (**Coste** 'Idées distinctes et déterminées') (17) that] *add.* **5** (31) holds] **4–5** | hold **1–3** tumbles] **4–5** | tumble **1–3** (*l. below* 32: § 27.) *In* **2–3**, *§ 27 comes under the same marginal summary as that for §§ 25–6.*

Action, is no longer in his power. He that is a close Prisoner, in a Room twenty foot-square, being at the North-side of his Chamber, is at liberty to walk twenty foot Southward, because he can walk, or not walk it: But is not, at the same time, at liberty, to do the contrary; *i.e.* to walk twenty foot Northward.

In this then consists Freedom, (*viz.*) in our being able to act, or not to act, according as we shall chuse, or *will.*

§ 28. *Secondly*, We must remember, that *Volition*, or *Willing*, is an act of the Mind directing its thought to the production of any Action, and thereby exerting its power to produce it. To avoid multiplying of words, I would crave leave here, under the word *Action*, to comprehend the forbearance too of any Action proposed; *sitting still*, or *holding one's peace*, when *walking* or *speaking* are propos'd, though mere forbearances, requiring as much the determination of the *Will*, and being often as weighty in their consequences, as the contrary Actions, may, on that consideration, well enough pass for Actions too: But this I say, that I may not be mistaken, if for brevity's sake I speak thus.

§ 28. *Volition what.*

---

(8) *Secondly*] **1, 5** | Secondly **2–4**. *From here in* **2–5**, §§ *28–60* (*until* 'God the righteous Judge') *are different from contents of* **1** *and replace* §§ *28–38* (*until* 'God the righteous Judge') *of* **1**; *much of this material in* **1** *is, however, used in* **2–5**: § *29 in* **1** *corresponds to* §§ *41–2 in* **2–5**; § *30, to* § *48*; § *31, to* § *49*; §§ *32–3, to* § *50*; § *34, to* § *54*; § *35, to* § *55*; § *36, to* § *56*; § *37, to* §§ *58–9. That material in* **1** *runs in full as follows*:

'§ 28. *Secondly*, In the next place we must remember, that *Volition* or *Willing*, regarding only what is in our power, *is* nothing but the *preferring* the doing of any thing, to the not doing of it; Action to Rest, *et contra.* Well, but what is this *Preferring*? It *is* nothing but the *being pleased more with the one, than the other.* Is then a Man indifferent to be pleased, or not pleased, more with one thing than another? Is it in his choice, whether he will, or will not be better pleased with one thing than another? And to this, I think, every one's Experience is ready to make answer, No. From whence it follows,

§ 29. *Thirdly*, That the Will, or Preference, is determined by something without it self: Let us see then what it is determined by. If willing be but the being better pleased, as has been shewn, it is easie to know what 'tis determines the Will, what 'tis pleases best: every one knows 'tis Happiness, or that which makes any part of Happiness, or contributes to it; and that is it we call *Good.* Happiness and Misery are the names of two extremes, the utmost bounds whereof we know not: 'tis what *Eye hath not seen, Ear hath not heard, nor hath entred into the Heart of Man to conceive.* But of some degrees of both, we have very lively impressions made by several instances of Delight and Joy on the one side, and Torment and Sorrow on the other: which, for shortness sake, I shall comprehend under the names of Pleasure and Pain, there being pleasure and pain of the Mind, as well as the Body: *With Him is fulness of Joy, and Pleasures for evermore*: Or to speak truly, they are all of the Mind; though some have their rise in the Mind from Thought, others in the Body from Motion. Happiness then is the utmost Pleasure we are capable of, and Misery the utmost Pain. Now because Pleasure and Pain are produced in us, by the operation of certain Objects, either on our Minds, or our Bodies; and in different degrees: therefore

§ 29. *Thirdly*, The *Will* being nothing but a power in the Mind to direct the operative Faculties of a Man to motion or rest, as far as they depend on such direction. To the Question, what is it determines the Will? The true and proper Answer is, The mind. For that which determines the general power of directing, to this or that particular direction, is nothing but the Agent it self Exercising the power it has, that particular way. If this Answer satisfies not, 'tis plain the meaning of the Question, *what determines the Will?* is this, What moves the mind, in every particular instance, to determine its general power of directing, to this or that particular Motion or Rest? And to this I answer, The motive, for continuing in the same State or Action, is only the present satisfaction in it; The motive to change, is always some *uneasiness*: nothing setting us upon the change of State, or upon any new Action, but some *uneasiness*. This is the great motive that works on the Mind to put it upon Action, which for shortness sake we will call *determining of the Will*, which I shall more at large explain.

§ 30. But in the way to it, it will be necessary to premise, that though I have above endeavoured to express the Act of *Volition*, by *chusing*, *preferring*, and the like Terms, that signify *Desire* as well as *Volition*, for want of other words to mark that Act of the mind, whose proper Name is *Willing* or *Volition*; yet it being a very simple Act, whosoever desires to understand what it is, will better find it by reflecting on his own mind, and observing what it does, when it *wills*, than by any variety of articulate sounds whatsoever. This Caution of being careful not to be misled by Expressions, that do not enough keep up the difference between the *Will*, and several Acts of the mind, that are quite distinct from it, I think the more necessary: Because I find the Will often confounded with several of the Affections, especially *Desire*; and one put for the other, and that by Men, who would not willingly be thought, not to have had very

§ 29. *What determines the Will.* § 30. *Will and Desire must not be confounded.*

---

what has an aptness to produce pleasure in us, is that we labour for, and is that we call *Good*; and what is apt to produce pain in us, we avoid and call *Evil*, for no other reason, but for its aptness to produce Pleasure and Pain in us, wherein consists our happiness or misery. Farther, because the degrees of Pleasure and Pain have also justly a preference; though what is apt to produce any degree of Pleasure, be in it

(1) *Thirdly*] **5** | Thirdly **2–4** (7) satisfies] **4–5** | satisfie **2–3** (13) *uneasiness*] **5** | uneasiness **2–4**. (**Coste** *adds a note on* 'inquiétude' *with a cross-reference to his note at II. xx. 6.*) (14) *uneasiness*] **5** | uneasiness **2–4** (31) Men] **Coste**[2] *adds in a note*: 'M. Locke en vouloit ici au P. *Malebranche*.'

distinct notions of things, and not to have writ very clearly about them. This, I imagine, has been no small occasion of obscurity and mistake in this matter; and therefore is, as much as may be, to be avoided. For he, that shall turn his thoughts inwards upon what passes in his mind, when he *wills*, shall see, that the *will* or power of *Volition* is conversant about nothing, but our own Actions; terminates there; and reaches no farther; and that *Volition* is nothing, but that particular determination of the mind, whereby, barely by a thought, the mind endeavours to give rise, continuation, or stop to any Action, which it takes to be in its power. This well considered plainly shews, that the *Will* is perfectly distinguished from *Desire*, which in the very same Action may have a quite contrary tendency from that which our *Wills* sets us upon. A Man, whom I cannot deny, may oblige me to use persuasions to another, which at the same time I am speaking, I may wish may not prevail on him. In this case, 'tis plain the *Will* and *Desire* run counter. I will the Action, that tends one way, whilst my desire tends another, and that the direct contrary. A Man, who by a violent Fit of the Gout in his Limbs, finds a doziness in his Head, or a want of appetite in his Stomach removed, desires to be eased too of the pain of his Feet or Hands (for where-ever there is pain there is a desire to be rid of it) though yet, whilst he apprehends, that the removal of the pain may translate the noxious humour to a more vital part, his will is never determin'd to any one Action, that may serve to remove this pain. Whence it is evident, that *desiring* and *willing* are two distinct Acts of the mind; and consequently that the *Will*, which is but the power of *Volition*, is much more distinct from *Desire*.

§ 31. To return then to the Enquiry, *what is it that determines the Will in regard to our Actions?* And that upon second thoughts I am apt to imagine is not, as is generally supposed, the greater good in view: But some (and for the most part the most pressing) *uneasiness*

§ 31. *Uneasiness determines the Will.*

---

self good; and what is apt to produce any degree of Pain, be evil; yet it often happens, that we do not call it so, when it comes in competition with a greater of its sort. So that if we will rightly estimate what we call *Good* and *Evil*, we shall find it lies much in comparison: For the cause of every less degree of Pain, as well as every greater degree of Pleasure, has the nature of Good, and *vice versâ*, and is that which deter-

(3) is, . . . be,] **4–5** | as much as may be **2–3** (6–7) but . . . nothing,] **2–4**; *om.* **5** (10–11) . This . . . that] **4–5** | : Whereby **2–3** (14) persuasions] **2, 4–5** | persuasion **3** (26) ; and consequently that] **4–5** | : and so **2–3** (27) , is] *add.* **4–5** (28–9) *is . . . Actions?*] **5** | *it is . . . Actions.* **2–4**

a Man is at present under. This is that which successively determines the *Will*, and sets us upon those Actions, we perform. This *Uneasiness* we may call, as it is, *Desire*; which is an *uneasiness* of the Mind for want of some absent good. All pain of the body of what sort soever, and disquiet of the mind, is *uneasiness*: And with this is always join'd Desire, equal to the pain or *uneasiness* felt; and is scarce distinguishable from it. For *desire* being nothing but an *uneasiness* in the want of an absent good, in reference to any pain felt, ease is that absent good; and till that ease be attained, we may call it *desire*, no body feeling pain, that he wishes not to be eased of, with a desire equal to that pain, and inseparable from it. Besides this desire of ease from pain, there is another of absent positive good, and here also the desire and *uneasiness* is equal. As much as we desire any absent good, so much are we in pain for it. But here all absent good does not, according to the greatness it has, or is acknowledg'd to have, cause pain equal to that greatness; as all pain causes desire equal to it self: Because the absence of good is not always a pain, as the presence of pain is. And therefore absent good may be looked on, and considered without *desire*. But so much as there is any where of *desire*, so much there is of *uneasiness*.

§ 32. That *Desire* is a state of uneasiness, every one who reflects on himself, will quickly find. Who is there, that has not felt in *Desire*, what the Wise-man says of Hope, (which is not much different from it) that it being *deferr'd makes the Heart sick*,* and that still proportionable to the greatness of the *Desire*, which sometimes raises the *uneasiness* to that pitch, that it makes People cry out, *Give me Children*, give me the thing desir'd, *or I die*?** Life it self, and all its Enjoyments, is a burden cannot be born under the lasting and unremoved pressure of such an *uneasiness*.

§ 32. *Desire is uneasiness.*

---

mines our Choice, and challenges our Preference. *Good* then, *the greater Good is that alone which determines the Will.*

§ 30. This is not an imperfection in Man, it is the highest perfection of intellectual Natures: it is so far from being a restraint or diminution of Freedom, that it is the very improvement and benefit of it: 'tis not an Abridgment, 'tis the end and use

(2) This] **4–5** | This, **2–3** (3) *uneasiness*] **5** | uneasiness **2–4** (9) [*1st*] ease] **Coste** *adds a note on* 'quiétude'. (15) acknowledg'd] **4–5** | acknowledg'd, and confess'd **2–3** (23) *Desire*] **5** | Desire **2–4** (25) proportionable] **4–5** | proportionably **2–3** *Desire*,] **5** | Desire, **4** | Desire **2–3** (27) *die*?] **5** (*likewise* **Coste**) | *die:* **2–4**

---

* Prov. 13: 12. ** Gen. 30: 1.

§ 33. Good and Evil, present and absent, 'tis true, work upon the mind: But that which immediately determines the *Will*, from time to time, to every voluntary Action, is the *uneasiness* of *desire*, fixed on some absent good, either negative, as indolency to one in pain; or positive, as enjoyment of pleasure. That it is this *uneasiness*, that determines the *Will* to the successive voluntary actions, whereof the greatest part of our Lives is made up, and by which we are conducted through different courses to different ends, I shall endeavour to shew both from Experience, and the reason of the thing.

§ 34. When a Man is perfectly content with the State he is in, which is when he is perfectly without any *uneasiness*, what industry, what action, what *Will* is there left, but to continue in it? of this every Man's observation will satisfy him. And thus we see our All-wise Maker, suitable to our constitution and frame, and knowing what it is that determines the *Will*, has put into Man the *uneasiness* of hunger and thirst, and other natural desires, that return at their Seasons, to move and determine their *Wills*, for the preservation of themselves, and the continuation of their Species. For I think we may conclude, that, if the bare contemplation of these good ends, to which we are carried by these several *uneasinesses*, had been sufficient to determine the *will*, and set us on work, we should have had none of these natural pains, and perhaps in this World, little or no pain at all. *It is better to marry than to burn*, says St. *Paul*;* where we may see, what it is, that chiefly drives Men into the enjoyments of a conjugal life. A little burning felt pushes us more powerfully, than greater pleasures in prospect draw or allure.

§ 35. It seems so establish'd and settled a maxim by the general consent of all Mankind, That good, the greater good, determines the will, that I do not at all wonder, that when I first publish'd my

§ 33. *The uneasiness of Desire determines the Will.* § 34. *This the spring of Action.* § 35. *The greatest positive good determines not the will, but uneasiness.*

---

of our Liberty: and the farther we are removed from such a determination to Good, the nearer we are to Misery and Slavery. A perfect Indifferency in the Will, or Power of Preferring, not determinable by the Good or Evil, that is thought to attend its Choice, would be so far from being an advantage and excellency of any intellectual Nature, that it would be as great an imperfection, as the want of Indifferency to act,

(24) *Paul*;] **5** (*likewise* **Coste**) | *Paul*, **2–4** where] **4–5** | whereby **2–3** (*likewise* **Coste**)

---

* 1 Cor. 7: 9.

thoughts on this Subject, I took it for granted; and I imagine, that by a great many I shall be thought more excusable, for having then done so, than that now I have ventur'd to recede from so received an Opinion. But yet upon a stricter enquiry, I am forced to conclude, that *good*, the *greater good*, though apprehended and acknowledged to be so, does not determine the *will*, until our desire, raised proportionably to it, makes us *uneasy* in the want of it. Convince a Man never so much, that plenty has its advantages over poverty; make him see and own, that the handsome conveniencies of life are better than nasty penury: yet as long as he is content with the latter, and finds no *uneasiness* in it, he moves not; his *will* never is determin'd to any action, that shall bring him out of it. Let a Man be never so well perswaded of the advantages of virtue, that it is as necessary to a Man, who has any great aims in this World, or hopes in the next, as food to life: yet till he *hungers and thirsts after righteousness*;* till he feels an *uneasiness* in the want of it, his *will* will not be determin'd to any action in pursuit of this confessed greater good; but any other *uneasinesses* he feels in himself, shall take place, and carry his *will* to other actions. On the other side, let a Drunkard see, that his Health decays, his Estate wastes; Discredit and Diseases, and the want of all things, even of his beloved Drink, attends him in the course he follows: yet the returns of *uneasiness* to miss his Companions; the habitual thirst after his Cups, at the usual time, drives him to the Tavern, though he has in his view the loss of health and plenty, and perhaps of the joys of another life: the least of which is no inconsiderable good, but such as he confesses, is far greater, than the tickling of his palate with a glass of Wine, or the idle chat of a soaking Club. 'Tis not for want of viewing the greater good: for he sees, and acknowledges it, and in the intervals of his drinking hours, will take resolutions to pursue the greater good; but when the *uneasiness* to miss his accustomed delight returns, the

or not to act, till determined by the Will, would be an imperfection on the other side. A Man is at liberty to lift up his Hand to his Head, or let it rest quiet: He is perfectly indifferent to either; and it would be an imperfection in him, if he wanted that Power, if he were deprived of that Indifferency. But it would be as great an imperfection, if he had the same Indifferency, whether he would prefer the lifting up his Hand, or its remaining in rest, when it would save his Head or Eyes from a blow he sees coming: *'tis* as much *a perfection, that the power of Preferring should be determined*

(7) *uneasy*] **5** | uneasy **2–4**　(18) *uneasinesses*] **5** | *uneasiness* **4** | uneasiness **2–3**
(24) has] **4–5** | have **2–3**　(26) as] **4–5** | as, **2–3**

* Matt. 5: 6.

greater acknowledged good loses its hold, and the present *uneasiness* determines the *will* to the accustomed action; which thereby gets stronger footing to prevail against the next occasion, though he at the same time makes secret promises to himself, that he will do so no more; this is the last time he will act against the attainment of those greater goods. And thus he is, from time to time, in the State of that unhappy Complainer, *Video meliora proboque, Deteriora sequor*:* which Sentence, allowed for true, and made good by constant Experience, may this, and possibly no other, way be easily made intelligible.

§ 36. If we enquire into the reason of what Experience makes so evident in fact, and examine why 'tis *uneasiness* alone operates on the *will*, and determines it in its choice, we shall find, that we being capable but of one determination of the will to one action at once, the present *uneasiness*, that we are under, does naturally determine the will, in order to that happiness which we all aim at in all our actions: For as much as whilst we are under any *uneasiness*, we cannot apprehend our selves happy, or in the way to it. Pain and *uneasiness* being, by every one, concluded, and felt, to be inconsistent with happiness; spoiling the relish, even of those good things which we have: a little pain serving to marr all the pleasure we rejoyced in. And therefore that, which of course determines the choice of our *will* to the next action, will always be the removing of pain, as long as we have any left, as the first and necessary step towards happiness.

§ 37. Another reason why 'tis *uneasiness* alone determines the will, may be this. Because that alone is present, and 'tis against the nature of things, that what is absent should operate, where it is not. It may be said, that absent good may by contemplation be brought home to the mind, and made present. The *Idea* of it indeed may be in the mind, and view'd as present there: but nothing will be in the

§ 36. *Because the removal of uneasiness is the first step to happiness.* § 37. *Because uneasiness alone is present.*

---

by Good, as that the power of Acting should be determined by the Will; and the certainer such determination is, the greater is the perfection.

§ 31. If we look upon those *superiour Beings* above us, who enjoy perfect Happiness, we shall have reason to judge they are more steadily *determined in their choice of Good* than we: and yet we have no reason to think they are less happy, or less free,

(3) against] **4–5** | again **2–3** (16, 20) which] *add.* **4–5** (18) *uneasiness*] **5** | uneasiness **2–4**

---

* Ovid, *Metamorphoses*, VII, 20–1.

mind as a present good, able to counter-balance the removal of any *uneasiness*, which we are under, till it raises our desire, and the *uneasiness* of that has the prevalency in determining the *will*. Till then the *Idea* in the mind of whatever good, is there only like other *Ideas*, the object of bare unactive speculation; but operates not on the will, nor sets us on work: the reason whereof I shall shew by and by. How many are to be found, that have had lively representations set before their minds of the unspeakable joys of Heaven, which they acknowledge both possible and probable too, who yet would be content to take up with their happiness here? and so the prevailing *uneasinesses* of their desires, let loose after the enjoyments of this life, take their turns in the determining their *wills*, and all that while they take not one step, are not one jot moved, towards the good things of another life considered as never so great.

§ 38. Were the *will* determin'd by the views of good, as it appears in Contemplation greater or less to the understanding, which is the State of all absent good, and that, which in the received Opinion the *will* is supposed to move to, and to be moved by, I do not see how it could ever get loose from the infinite eternal Joys of Heaven, once propos'd and consider'd as possible. For all absent good, by which alone barely propos'd, and coming in view, the *will* is thought to be determin'd, and so to set us on action, being only possible, but not infallibly certain, 'tis unavoidable, that the infinitely greater possible good should regularly and constantly determine the *will* in all the successive actions it directs; and then we should keep constantly and steadily in our course towards Heaven, without ever standing still, or directing our actions to any other end: The eternal condition of a future state infinitely out-weighing the Expectation of Riches, or Honour, or any other worldly pleasure, which we can propose to our selves, though we should grant these the more probable to be attain'd: For nothing future is

§ 38. *Because all who allow the joys of Heaven possible, pursue them not.*

---

than we are. And if it were fit for such poor finite Creatures as we are, to pronounce what infinite Wisdom and Goodness could do, I think we might say, That God himself cannot choose what is not good; the Freedom of the Almighty hinders not his being determined by what is best.

§ 32. But to consider this mistaken part of Liberty right, Would any one be a Changeling, because he is less determined, by wise Considerations, than a wise Man? Is it worth the Name of Freedom to be at liberty to play the Fool, and draw Shame and Misery upon a Man's self? If want of restraint to chuse, or to do the

(2) , which] *add.* **4–5** (13) , towards] **4–5** | toward **2–3** (30) which] *add.* **4–5**

yet in possession, and so the expectation even of these may deceive us. If it were so, that the greater good in view determines the *will*, so great a good once propos'd could not but seize the *will*, and hold it fast to the pursuit of this infinitely greatest good, without ever letting it go again: For the *will* having a power over, and directing the thoughts, as well as other actions, would, if it were so, hold the contemplation of the mind fixed to that good.

This would be the state of the mind, and regular tendency of the *will* in all its determinations, were it determin'd by that, which is consider'd, and in view the greater good; but that it is not so is visible in Experience. The infinitely greatest confessed good being often neglected, to satisfy the successive *uneasiness* of our desires pursuing trifles. But though the greatest allowed, even everlasting unspeakable good, which has sometimes moved, and affected the mind, does not stedfastly hold the *will*, yet we see any very great, and prevailing *uneasiness*, having once laid hold on the *will*, lets it not go; by which we may be convinced, what it is that determines the *will*. Thus any vehement pain of the Body; the ungovernable passion of a Man violently in love; or the impatient desire of revenge, keeps the *will* steady and intent; and the *will* thus determined never lets the Understanding lay by the object, but all the thoughts of the Mind, and powers of the Body are uninterruptedly employ'd that way, by the determinations of the *will*, influenced by that topping *uneasiness*, as long as it lasts; whereby it seems to me evident, that the will, or power of setting us upon one action in preference to all other, is determin'd in us, by *uneasiness*: and whether this be not so, I desire every one to observe in himself.

§ 39. I have hitherto chiefly instanced in the *uneasiness* of desire, as that which determines the *will*. Because that is the chief, and most sensible; and the *will* seldom orders any action, nor is there any voluntary action performed, without some *desire* accompanying

§ 38(8). *But any great uneasiness is never neglected.* § 39. *Desire accompanies all uneasiness.*

---

worse, be Liberty, true Liberty, mad Men and Fools are the only Free-men: but yet, I think, no Body would chuse to be mad for the sake of such Liberty, but he that is mad already.

§ 33. But though the preference of the Mind be always determined by the appearance of Good, greater Good; yet the Person who has the Power, in which

(3) could not] **4–5** | cannot **2–3** (6) , would, if it were so,] **4–5** | will **2–3** (10) good; but] **5** | good. But **2–4** (12) *uneasiness*] **5** | *uneasinesses* **2–4** (15) *will*] **5** | will **2–4** (23) determinations] **5** | determination **2–4** (24) *uneasiness*] **5** | uneasiness **2–4** (26) *uneasiness*:] **5** | uneasiness: **2–4** (; **2–3**) (31) , without] **4–5** | without **2–3**

it; which I think is the reason why the *will* and *desire* are so often confounded. But yet we are not to look upon the *uneasiness* which makes up, or at least accompanies most of the other Passions, as wholly excluded in the case. *Aversion*, *Fear*, *Anger*, *Envy*, *Shame*, etc. have each their *uneasiness* too, and thereby influence the *will*. These Passions are scarce any of them in life and practice, simple, and alone, and wholly unmixed with others; though usually in discourse and contemplation, that carries the name, which operates strongest, and appears most in the present state of the mind. Nay there is, I think, scarce any of the Passions to be found without *desire* join'd with it. I am sure, where-ever there is *uneasiness* there is *desire*: For we constantly desire happiness; and whatever we feel of *uneasiness*, so much, 'tis certain, we want of happiness; even in our own Opinion, let our state and condition otherwise be what it will. Besides, the present moment not being our eternity, whatever our enjoyment be, we look beyond the present, and desire goes with our foresight, and that still carries the *will* with it. So that even in *joy* it self, that which keeps up the action, whereon the enjoyment depends, is the desire to continue it, and fear to lose it: And whenever a greater *uneasiness* than that takes place in the mind, the *will* presently is by that determin'd to some new action, and the present delight neglected.

§ 40. But we being in this World beset with sundry *uneasinesses*, distracted with different *desires*, the next enquiry naturally will be, which of them has the precedency in determining the *will* to the next action? and to that the answer is, that ordinarily, which is the most pressing of those, that are judged capable of being then removed. For the *will* being the power of directing our operative faculties to some action, for some end, cannot at any time be moved towards what is judg'd at that time unattainable: That would be to suppose an intelligent being designedly to act for an end, only to

§ 40. *The most pressing uneasiness naturally determines the will.*

alone consists liberty to act, or not to act according to such preference, is nevertheless free, such determination abridges not that Power. He that has his Chains knocked off, and the Prison-doors set open to him, is perfectly at liberty, because he may either go or stay, as he best likes; though his preference be determined to stay by the darkness of the Night, or illness of the Weather, or want of other Lodging. He ceases not to be free; though that which at that time appears to him the greater

(2) *uneasiness*] **4–5** | uneasinesses, **2–3** (5) *uneasiness*] **5** | *uneasinesses* **2–4** (12) *uneasiness*] **5** | uneasiness **2–4** (15) Besides,] **5** (*likewise* **Coste**) | Besides **2–4** (30) : That] **4–5** | ; for that **2–3**

lose its labour; for so it is to act, for what is judg'd not attainable; and therefore very great *uneasinesses* move not the *will*, when they are judg'd not capable of a Cure: They, in that case, put us not upon endeavours. But these set a-part, the most important and urgent *uneasiness*, we at that time feel, is that, which ordinarily determines the *will* successively, in that train of voluntary actions, which make up our lives. The greatest present *uneasiness* is the spur to action, that is constantly felt; and for the most part determines the *will* in its choice of the next action. For this we must carry along with us, that the proper and only object of the *will* is some action of ours, and nothing else. For we producing nothing, by our *willing* it, but some action in our power, 'tis there the *will* terminates, and reaches no farther.

§ 41. If it be farther asked, what 'tis moves *desire*? I answer happiness and that alone. *Happiness* and *Misery* are the names of two extremes, the utmost bounds whereof we know not; 'tis what *Eye hath not seen, Ear hath not heard, nor hath it entred into the Heart of Man to conceive.** But of some degrees of both, we have very lively impressions, made by several instances of Delight and Joy on the one side; and Torment and Sorrow on the other; which, for shortness sake, I shall comprehend under the names of Pleasure and Pain, there being pleasure and pain of the Mind, as well as the Body: *With him is fullness of Joy, and Pleasure for evermore*:** Or to speak truly, they are all of the Mind; though some have their rise in the Mind from Thought, others in the Body from certain modifications of Motion.

§ 42. *Happiness* then in its full extent is the utmost Pleasure we are capable of, and *Misery* the utmost Pain: And the lowest degree of what can be called *Happiness*, is so much ease from all Pain, and so much present Pleasure, as without which any one cannot be content. Now because Pleasure and Pain are produced in us, by the

§ 41. *All desire happiness.* § 42. *Happiness what.*

Good absolutely determines his preference, and makes him stay in his Prison. I have rather made use of the Word *Preference* than *Choice*, to express the act of Volition, because choice is of a more doubtful signification, and bordering more upon Desire,

(3) They, in that case,] **4–5** | Those therefore **2–3** (8) felt] **5** | most felt **2–4** (17) *it*] *add.* **4–5** (22–3) **Coste** *omits this quotation.* (23) *Pleasure*] **5** | *pleasure* **4** | *Pleasures* **2–3** (25) certain modifications of] *add.* **4–5** (28) so much ease from] **4–5** | the being eas'd of **2–3** (29) so much present Pleasure] **4–5** | enjoying so much Pleasure **2–3**

* 1 Cor. 2: 9. ** Ps. 16: 11.

operation of certain Objects, either on our Minds or our Bodies; and in different degrees: therefore what has an aptness to produce Pleasure in us, is that we call *Good*, and what is apt to produce Pain in us, we call *Evil*, for no other reason, but for its aptness to produce Pleasure and Pain in us, wherein consists our *Happiness* and *Misery*. Farther, though what is apt to produce any degree of Pleasure, be in it self *good*; and what is apt to produce any degree of Pain, be *evil*; yet it often happens, that we do not call it so, when it comes in competition with a greater of its sort; because when they come in competition the degrees also of Pleasure and Pain have justly a preference. So that if we will rightly estimate what we call *Good* and *Evil*, we shall find it lies much in comparison: For the cause of every less degree of Pain, as well as every greater degree of Pleasure has the nature of *good*, and *vice versâ*.

§ 43. Though this be that, which is called *good* and *evil*; and all good be the proper object of *Desire* in general; yet all good, even seen, and confessed to be so, does not necessarily move every particular Man's *desire*; but only that part, or so much of it, as is consider'd, and taken to make a necessary part of his happiness. All other good however great in reality, or appearance, excites not a Man's *desires*, who looks not on it to make a part of that happiness, wherewith he, in his present thoughts, can satisfie himself. *Happiness*, under this view, every one constantly pursues, and *desires* what makes any part of it: Other things, acknowledged to be good, he can look upon without *desire*; pass by, and be content without. There is no Body, I think, so sensless as to deny, that there is pleasure in Knowledge: And for the pleasures of Sense, they have too many followers to let it be question'd whether Men are taken with them or no. Now let one Man place his satisfaction in sensual Pleasures, another in the delight of Knowledge: Though each of them cannot but confess, there is great Pleasure in what the other

§ 43. *What good is desired, what not?*

---

and so is referred to things remote; whereas Volition, or the Act of Willing, signifies nothing properly, but the actual producing of something that is voluntary.

§ 34. The next thing to be considered is, If our Wills be determined by Good, *How it comes to pass that Men's Wills carry them so contrarily*, and consequently some of them to what is Evil? And to this I say, that the various and contrary choices, that

(6) Farther,] **4–5** | Farther, because the degrees of Pleasure and Pain have also justly a preference; **2–3** (9–11) ; because . . . preference] *add.* **4–5** (22–3) *Happiness*] **5** | Happiness **2–4** (',' *add.* **4–5**) (26–9) There . . . Now] *add.* **4–5** (*l. below* 31) *In* **Coste,** *§ 43 comes under the same marginal summary as § 42.*

pursues; yet neither of them making the other's delight a part of his happiness, their *desires* are not moved, but each is satisfied without what the other enjoys, and so his will is not determined to the pursuit of it. But yet as soon as the studious Man's hunger and thirst makes him *uneasie*, he whose *will* was never determined to any pursuit of good chear, poinant Sauces, or delicious Wine by the pleasant tast he has found in them, is, by the uneasiness of Hunger and Thirst, presently determined to Eating and Drinking; though possibly with great indifferency, what wholesome Food comes in his way. And on the other side, the Epicure buckles to study, when shame, or the desire to recommend himself to his Mistress, shall make him *uneasie* in the want of any sort of Knowledge. Thus, how much soever Men are in earnest, and constant in pursuit of happiness; yet they may have a clear view of good, great and confessed good, without being concern'd for it, or moved by it, if they think they can make up their happiness without it. Though, as to pain, that they are always concern'd for; they can feel no *uneasiness* without being moved. And therefore being *uneasie* in the want of whatever is judged necessary to their Happiness, as soon as any good appears to make a part of their portion of happiness, they begin to *desire* it.

§ 44. This, I think, any one may observe in himself, and others, that the *greater visible good* does not always raise Men's *desires* in proportion to the greatness, it appears, and is acknowledged to have: Though every little trouble moves us, and sets us on work to get rid of it. The reason whereof is evident from the nature of our *happiness* and *misery* it self. All present pain, whatever it be, makes a part of our present *misery*: But all absent good does not at any time make a necessary part of our present *happiness*, nor the absence of it make a part of our *misery*. If it did, we should be constantly and infinitely miserable; there being infinite degrees of happiness, which

§ 44. *Why the greatest good is not always desired.*

Men make in the World, doe not argue, that they do not all chuse Good; but that the same thing is not good to every Man. Were all the Concerns of Man terminated in this Life; why one pursued Study and Knowledge, and another Hawking and Hunting; why one chose Luxury and Debauchery, and another Sobriety and Riches, would not be, because every one of these did not pursue his own Happiness; but

(1) pursues;] **4–5** | pursues; (For I think there is no Body so sensless as to deny, that there is Pleasure in knowledge; and also Pleasure in the taste of good Meats and Drinks:) **2–3** (5) *will*] **5** | will **2–4** (6) or] **2–4**; *om.* **5** (17) *uneasiness*] **5** | uneasiness **2–4** (18) *uneasie*] **5** | uneasie **2–4**. (**Coste** *adds a note on* '*inquiéts*'.)

are not in our possession. All *uneasiness* therefore being removed, a moderate portion of good serves at present to content Men; and some few degrees of Pleasure in a succession of ordinary Enjoyments make up a happiness, wherein they can be satisfied. If this were not so, there could be no room for those indifferent, and visibly trifling actions; to which our *wills* are so often determined; and wherein we voluntarily wast so much of our Lives; which remissness could by no means consist with a constant determination of *will* or *desire* to the greatest apparent good. That this is so, I think, few People need go far from home to be convinced. And indeed in this life there are not many, whose happiness reaches so far, as to afford them a constant train of moderate mean Pleasures, without any mixture of *uneasiness*; and yet they could be content to stay here for ever: Though they cannot deny, but that it is possible, there may be a state of eternal durable Joys after this life, far surpassing all the good is to be found here. Nay they cannot but see, that it is more possible, than the attainment, and continuation of that pittance of Honour, Riches, or Pleasure, which they pursue; and for which they neglect that eternal State: But yet in full view of this difference, satisfied of the possibility of a perfect, secure, and lasting happiness in a future State, and under a clear conviction, that it is not to be had here, whilst they bound their happiness within some little enjoyment, or aim of this life, and exclude the joys of Heaven from making any necessary part of it, their desires are not moved by this greater apparent good, nor their *wills* determin'd to any action, or endeavour for its attainment.

§ 45. The ordinary necessities of our lives, fill a great part of them with the *uneasiness* of *Hunger*, *Thirst*, *Heat*, *Cold*, *Weariness* with labour, and *Sleepiness* in their constant returns, *etc.* To which, if besides accidental harms, we add the fantastical *uneasiness*, (as itch after *Honour*, *Power*, or *Riches*, etc.) which acquir'd habits by Fashion,

§ 45. *Why not being desired, it moves not the will.*

---

because their Happiness lay in different things: And therefore 'twas a right Answer of the Physician to his Patient, that had sore Eyes. If you have more Pleasure in the Taste of Wine, than in the use of your Sight, Wine is good for you: but if the Pleasure of Seeing be greater to you, than that of Drinking, Wine is naught.

§ 35. The Mind has a different relish, as well as the Palate; and you will as fruitlesly endeavour to delight all Men with Riches or Glory, (which yet some Men place

(3) some] **5** | a **2–4** (3–4) Pleasure in a succession of ordinary Enjoyments] **5** | succeeding Pleasures **2–4** (13) *uneasiness*] **5** | uneasiness **2–4** (22) here,] **2–4** | here **5** (28) *uneasiness*] **5** | uneasinesses **2–4** (29) *Sleepiness*] **4–5** | *Sleepishness* **2–3** (30) *uneasiness*,] **5** | uneasinesses **2–4** (31) etc.] **2–3** | *etc.* **4–5**

Example, and Education have setled in us, and a thousand other irregular desires, which custom has made natural to us, we shall find, that a very little part of our life is so vacant from these *uneasinesses*, as to leave us free to the attraction of remoter absent good. We are seldom at ease, and free enough from the sollicitation of our natural or adopted desires, but a constant succession of *uneasinesses* out of that stock, which natural wants, or acquired habits have heaped up, take the *will* in their turns; and no sooner is one action dispatch'd, which by such a determination of the *will* we are set upon, but another *uneasiness* is ready to set us on work. For the removing of the pains we feel, and are at present pressed with, being the getting out of misery, and consequently the first thing to be done in order to happiness, absent good, though thought on, confessed, and appearing to be good, not making any part of this unhappiness in its absence, is jostled out, to make way for the removal of those *uneasinesses* we feel, till due, and repeated Contemplation has brought it nearer to our Mind, given some relish of it, and raised in us some desire; which then beginning to make a part of our present *uneasiness*, stands upon fair terms with the rest, to be satisfied, and so according to its greatness, and pressure, comes in its turn to determine the *will*.

§ 46. And thus, by a due consideration and examining any good proposed, it is in our power, to raise our desires, in a due proportion to the value of that good, whereby in its turn, and place, it may come to work upon the *will*, and be pursued. For good, though appearing, and allowed never so great, yet till it has raised desires in our Minds, and thereby made us *uneasie* in its want, it reaches not our *wills*; we are not within the Sphere of its activity; our *wills* being under the determination only of those *uneasinesses*, which are present to us, which, (whilst we have any) are always sollicting, and ready at hand to give the *will* its next determination. The balancing,

§ 46. *Due consideration raises desire.*

---

their Happiness in,) as you would to satisfie all Men's Hunger with Cheese or Lobsters; which, though very agreeable and delicious fare to some, are to others extremely nauseous and offensive: And many People would with Reason prefer the griping of an hungry Belly, to those Dishes, which are a Feast to others. Hence it was, I think, that the Philosophers of old did in vain enquire, whether *Summum bonum* consisted in Riches, or bodily Delights, or Virtue, or Contemplation: And

(1) Example,] **5** | Example **2–4** (8) turns;] **5** | turns, **2–4** (11) with,] **4–5** | with **2–3** (19) rest,] **5** | rest **2–4** (*l. below* 31) **Coste** 'Deux considerations excitent le desir en nous.'

when there is any in the Mind, being only, which desire shall be next satisfied, which *uneasiness* first removed. Whereby it comes to pass, that as long as any *uneasiness*, any desire remains in our Mind, there is no room for *good*, barely as such, to come at the *will*, or at all to determine it. Because, as has been said, the first step in our endeavours after happiness being to get wholly out of the confines of misery, and to feel no part of it, the *will* can be at leisure for nothing else, till every *uneasiness* we feel be perfectly removed: which in the multitude of wants, and desires, we are beset with in this imperfect State, we are not like to be ever freed from in this World.

§ 47. There being in us a great many *uneasinesses* always sollicîting, and ready to determine the *will*, it is natural, as I have said, that the greatest, and most pressing should determine the *will* to the next action; and so it does for the most part, but not always. For the mind having in most cases, as is evident in Experience, a power to *suspend* the execution and satisfaction of any of its desires, and so all, one after another, is at liberty to consider the objects of them; examine them on all sides, and weigh them with others. In this lies the liberty Man has; and from the not using of it right comes all that variety of mistakes, errors, and faults which we run into, in the conduct of our lives, and our endeavours after happiness; whilst we precipitate the determination of our *wills*, and engage too soon before due *Examination*. To prevent this we have a power to *suspend* the prosecution of this or that desire, as every one daily may Experiment in himself. This seems to me the source of all liberty; in this seems to consist that, which is (as I think improperly) call'd *Free will*. For during this *suspension* of any desire, before the *will* be determined to action, and the action (which follows that determination) done, we have opportunity to examine, view, and judge, of the good or evil of what we are going to do; and when, upon due

§ 47. *The power to suspend the prosecution of any desire makes way for consideration.*

---

they might have as reasonably disputed, whether the best Relish were to be found in Apples, Plumbs, or Nuts; and have divided themselves into Sects upon it. For as pleasant Tastes depend not on the things themselves, but their agreeableness to this or that particular Palate, wherein there is great variety: So the greatest Happiness consists, in the having those things which produce the greatest Pleasure, and the absence of those which cause any disturbance, any pain, which to different Men are very different things. If therefore Men in this Life only have hope; if in this Life they can only enjoy, 'tis not strange, nor unreasonable, they should seek their

(12) *uneasinesses*] **5** | uneasinesses **2–4** (21) faults which] **4–5** | faults, **2–3**

Examination, we have judg'd, we have done our duty, all that we can, or ought to do, in pursuit of our happiness; and 'tis not a fault, but a perfection of our nature to desire, will, and act according to the last result of a fair *Examination*.

§ 48. This is so far from being a restraint or diminution of *Freedom*, that it is the very improvement and benefit of it: 'tis not an Abridgment, 'tis the end and use of our *Liberty*; and the farther we are removed from such a determination, the nearer we are to Misery and Slavery. A perfect Indifferency in the Mind, not determinable by its last judgment of the Good or Evil, that is thought to attend its Choice, would be so far from being an advantage and excellency of any intellectual Nature, that it would be as great an imperfection, as the want of Indifferency to act, or not to act, till determined by the *Will*, would be an imperfection on the other side. A Man is at liberty to lift up his Hand to his Head, or let it rest quiet: He is perfectly indifferent in either; and it would be an imperfection in him, if he wanted that Power, if he were deprived of that Indifferency. But it would be as great an imperfection, if he had the same indifferency, whether he would prefer the lifting up his Hand, or its remaining in rest, when it would save his Head or Eyes from a blow he sees coming: '*tis* as much *a perfection, that desire or the power of Preferring should be determined by Good*, as that the power of Acting should be determined by the *Will*, and the certainer such determination is, the greater is the perfection. Nay were we determined by any thing but the last result of our own Minds, judging of the good or evil of any action, we were not free, the very end of our Freedom being, that we might attain the good we chuse. And therefore every Man is put under a necessity by his constitution, as an intelligent Being, to be determined in *willing* by his own Thought and Judgment, what is best for him to do: else he would be under the determination of some other than himself, which is want of Liberty.

§ 48. *To be determined by our own judgment is no restraint to Liberty.*

Happiness by avoiding all things that disease them here, and by preferring all that delight them; wherein it will be no wonder to find variety and difference. For if there be no Prospect beyond the Grave, the inference is certainly right, *Let us eat and drink*, let us enjoy what we delight in, *for to morrow we shall die*. This, I think, may serve to shew us the Reason, why, though all Men's Wills are determined by Good,

(3) according] **4–5** | accordingly **2–3** (9) Mind,] **4–5** | Mind, or Power of Preferring, **2–3** (16) in] **4–5** | to **2–3** (19) whether] **2–4** | whither **5** (26) free,] *edit.* | free. **2–5** (26)–265(7) the [*edit.* | The **5**] . . . admitted.] *add.* **5**

And to deny, that a Man's *will*, in every determination, follows his own Judgment, is to say, that a Man *wills* and acts for an end that he would not have at the time that he *wills* and acts for it. For if he prefers it in his present Thoughts before any other, 'tis plain he then thinks better of it, and would have it before any other, unless he can have, and not have it; *will* and not *will* it at the same time; a Contradiction too manifest to be admitted.

§ 49. If we look upon those *superiour Beings* above us, who enjoy perfect Happiness, we shall have reason to judge that they are more steadily *determined in their choice of Good* than we; and yet we have no reason to think they are less happy, or less free, than we are. And if it were fit for such poor finite Creatures as we are, to pronounce what infinite Wisdom and Goodness could do, I think, we might say, That God himself cannot choose what is not good; the Freedom of the Almighty hinders not his being determined by what is best.

§ 50. But to give a right view of this mistaken part of Liberty, let me ask, Would any one be a Changeling, because he is less determined, by wise Considerations, than a wise Man? Is it worth the Name of *Freedom* to be at liberty to play the Fool, and draw Shame and Misery upon a Man's self? If to break loose from the conduct of Reason, and to want that restraint of Examination and Judgment, which keeps us from chusing or doing the worse, be *Liberty*, true Liberty, mad Men and Fools are the only Freemen: But yet, I think, no Body would chuse to be mad for the sake of such *Liberty*, but he that is mad already. The constant desire of Happiness, and the constraint it puts upon us to act for it, no Body, I think, accounts an abridgment of *Liberty*, or at least an abridgment of *Liberty* to be complain'd of. God Almighty himself is under the necessity of being happy; and the more any intelligent Being is so, the nearer is its approach to infinite perfection and happiness. That in this state of Ignorance we short-sighted Creatures might

§ 49. *The freest Agents are so determined.* § 50. *A constant determination to a pursuit of happiness no abridgment of Liberty.*

---

yet they are not determined by the same Object. Men may chuse different things, and yet all chuse right, supposing them only like a Company of poor Insects, whereof some are Bees, delighted with Flowers, and their sweetness; others Scarabes, delighted with other kind of Viands; which having enjoyed for a Season, they should cease to be, and exist no more for ever.

§ 36. This sufficiently discovers to us, why Men in this World prefer different

(7) *v.* 264(26), n. (9) that] *add.* **4–5** (16) give a right view of] **4–5** | consider **2–3** Liberty,] **5** | Liberty **2–4** (17) let me ask] **4–5** | right **2–3**

not mistake true felicity, we are endowed with a power to suspend any particular desire, and keep it from determining the *will*, and engaging us in action. This is *standing still*, where we are not sufficiently assured of the way: Examination is *consulting a guide*. The determination of the *will* upon enquiry is *following the direction of that Guide*: And he that has a power to act, or not to act according as such determination directs, is a *free Agent*; such determination abridges not that Power wherein Liberty consists. He that has his Chains knocked off, and the Prison-doors set open to him, is perfectly at *liberty*, because he may either go or stay, as he best likes; though his preference be determined to stay, by the darkness of the Night, or illness of the Weather, or want of other Lodging. He ceases not to be free; though the desire of some convenience to be had there, absolutely determines his preference, and makes him stay in his Prison.

§ 51. As therefore the highest perfection of intellectual nature, lies in a careful and constant pursuit of true and solid happiness; so the care of our selves, that we mistake not imaginary for real happiness, is the necessary foundation of our *liberty*. The stronger ties, we have, to an unalterable pursuit of happiness in general, which is our greatest good, and which as such our desires always follow, the more are we free from any necessary determination of our *will* to any particular action, and from a necessary compliance with our desire, set upon any particular, and then appearing preferable good, till we have duly examin'd, whether it has a tendency to, or be inconsistent with our real happiness; and therefore till we are as much inform'd upon this enquiry, as the weight of the matter, and the nature of the case demands, we are by the necessity of prefering and pursuing true happiness as our greatest good, obliged to suspend the satisfaction of our desire in particular cases.

§ 52. This is the hinge on which turns the *liberty* of intellectual Beings in their constant endeavours after, and a steady prosecution

§ 51. *The necessity of pursuing true happiness the foundation of Liberty.* § 52. *The reason of it.*

---

things, and pursue Happiness by contrary Courses: But yet since Men are always determined by Good, the greater Good; and are constant, and in earnest, in matter of Happiness and Misery, the Question still remains, *How Men come often to prefer the*

(19) *liberty.* The] **4–5** | liberty, and the **2–3** (23) and] **4–5** | or **2–3** (25) preferable] **5** | greater **2–4**. (**Coste** 'le plus important') (26) inconsistent] **2–4** | inconstant **5** (26–7) therefore] *add.* **5** (30) desire] **5** | desires **2–4** (32) a] *add.* **5**

of true felicity, that they can *suspend* this prosecution in particular cases, till they have looked before them, and informed themselves, whether that particular thing, which is then proposed, or desired, lie in the way to their main end, and make a real part of that which is their greatest good. For the inclination, and tendency of their nature to happiness is an obligation, and motive to them, to take care not to mistake, or miss it; and so necessarily puts them upon caution, deliberation, and wariness, in the direction of their particular actions, which are the means to obtain it. Whatever necessity determines to the pursuit of real Bliss, the same necessity, with the same force establishes *suspence*, *deliberation*, and scrutiny of each successive desire, whether the satisfaction of it, does not interfere with our true happiness, and mislead us from it. This as seems to me is the great privilege of finite intellectual Beings; and I desire it may be well consider'd, whether the great inlet, and exercise of all the *liberty* Men have, are capable of, or can be useful to them, and that whereon depends the turn of their actions, does not lie in this, that they can *suspend* their desires, and stop them from determining their *wills* to any action, till they have duly and fairly *examin'd* the good and evil of it, as far forth as the weight of the thing requires. This we are able to do; and when we have done it, we have done our duty, and all that is in our power; and indeed all that needs. For, since the *will* supposes knowledge to guide its choice, all that we can do, is to hold our *wills* undetermined, till we have *examin'd* the good and evil of what we desire. What follows after that, follows in a chain of Consequences linked one to another, all depending on the last determination of the Judgment, which whether it shall be upon an hasty and precipitate view, or upon a due and mature *Examination*, is in our power; Experience shewing us, that in most cases we are able to suspend the present satisfaction of any desire.

§ 53. But if any extreme disturbance (as sometimes it happens) possesses our whole Mind, as when the pain of the Rack, an

§ 53. *Government of our Passions the right improvement of Liberty.*

---

worse to the better; and to chuse that, which by their own Confession has made them miserable?

§ 37. To this I answer, That *as to present Happiness, or Misery*; *present Pleasure or Pain, when that alone comes in Consideration, a Man never chuses amiss*: he knows what best pleases him, and that, he actually prefers. Things in their present enjoyment, are

(28–9) view . . . *Examination*,] **4–5** | , or due and mature Examination **2–3**
(29) shewing] **4er–5** | she wings **4** | she-wing **2–3**

impetuous *uneasiness*, as of Love, Anger, or any other violent Passion, running away with us, allows us not the liberty of thought, and we are not Masters enough of our own Minds to consider throughly, and examine fairly; God, who knows our frailty, pities our weakness, and requires of us no more than we are able to do, and sees what was, and what was not in our power, will judge as a kind and merciful Father. But the forbearance of a too hasty compliance with our desires, the moderation and restraint of our Passions, so that our Understandings may be *free* to examine, and reason unbiassed give its judgment, being that, whereon a right direction of our conduct to true Happiness depends; 'tis in this we should employ our chief care and endeavours. In this we should take pains to suit the relish of our Minds to the true intrinsick good or ill, that is in things; and not permit an allow'd or supposed possible great and weighty good to slip out of our thoughts, without leaving any relish, any desire of it self there, till, by a due consideration of its true worth, we have formed appetites in our Minds suitable to it, and made our selves uneasie in the want of it, or in the fear of losing it. And how much this is in every ones power, every one by making resolutions to himself, such as he may keep, is easie for every one to try. Nor let any one say, he cannot govern his Passions, nor hinder them from breaking out, and carrying him into action; for what he can do before a Prince, or a great Man, he can do alone, or in the presence of God, if he will.

§ 54. From what has been said, it is easie to give an account, how it comes to pass, that though all Men desire Happiness, yet their *wills carry them so contrarily*, and consequently some of them to what is Evil. And to this I say, that the various and contrary choices, that Men make in the World, do not argue, that they do not all pursue Good; but that the same thing is not good to every Man alike. This variety of pursuits shews, that every one does not place his happiness in the same thing, or chuse the same way to it. Were all the

§§ 54, 55. *How Men come to pursue different courses.*

---

what they seem: the apparent and real good, are, in this case, always the same. For the Pain or Pleasure being just so great, and no greater, than it is felt, the present Good or Evil is really so much as it appears. And therefore were every Action of ours concluded within it self, and drew no Consequences after it, we should undoubtedly always will nothing but Good; always infallibly prefer the best. Were the

(1) *uneasiness*] **5** | uneasiness **2–4** (24) God,] **4–5** | God **2–3** (25) an] **2–4**; *om.* **5** (30–1) . This . . . not] **4–5** | ; nor does every one **2–3**

Concerns of Man terminated in this Life, why one followed Study and Knowledge, and another Hawking and Hunting; why one chose Luxury and Debauchery, and another Sobriety and Riches, would not be, because every one of these did not aim at his own happiness; but because their *Happiness* was placed in different things. And therefore 'twas a right Answer of the Physician to his Patient, that had sore Eyes. If you have more Pleasure in the Taste of Wine, than in the use of your Sight, Wine is good for you; but if the Pleasure of Seeing be greater to you, than that of Drinking, Wine is naught.

§ 55. The Mind has a different relish, as well as the Palate; and you will as fruitlesly endeavour to delight all Men with Riches or Glory, (which yet some Men place their Happiness in,) as you would to satisfy all Men's Hunger with Cheese or Lobsters; which, though very agreeable and delicious fare to some, are to others extremely nauseous and offensive: And many People would with Reason preferr the griping of an hungry Belly, to those Dishes, which are a Feast to others. Hence it was, I think, that the Philosophers of old did in vain enquire, whether *Summum bonum* consisted in Riches, or bodily Delights, or Virtue, or Contemplation: And they might have as reasonably disputed, whether the best Relish were to be found in Apples, Plumbs, or Nuts; and have divided themselves into Sects upon it. For as pleasant Tastes depend not on the things themselves, but their agreeableness to this or that particular Palate, wherein there is great variety: So the greatest Happiness consists, in the having those things, which produce the greatest Pleasure; and in the absence of those, which cause any disturbance, any pain. Now these, to different Men, are very different things. If therefore Men in this Life only have hope; if in this Life they can only enjoy, 'tis not strange, nor unreasonable, that they should seek their Happiness by avoiding all things, that disease them here, and by pursuing all that delight them; wherein

pains of honest Industry, and of starving with Hunger and Cold set together before us, no Body would be in doubt which to chuse: were the satisfaction of a Lust, and the Joys of Heaven offered at once to any one's present Possession, he would not balance, or err in the choice, and determination of his Will. But since our voluntary Actions carry not all the Happiness, and Misery, that depend on them, along with them in their present performance; but are the precedent Causes of Good and Evil, which they draw after them, and bring upon us, when they themselves are passed,

(15) fare] **2–4** | Fair **5** (27) in] *add.* **4–5** (28) . Now these] **5** | ; now these, **4** | , which **2–3** (31) [*1st*] that] *add.* **4–5** (32) pursuing] **4–5** | preferring **2–3**

it will be no wonder to find variety and difference. For if there be no Prospect beyond the Grave, the inference is certainly right, *Let us eat and drink*, let us enjoy what we delight in, *for to morrow we shall die.** This, I think, may serve to shew us the Reason, why, though all Men's desires tend to Happiness, yet they are not moved by the same Object. Men may chuse different things, and yet all chuse right, supposing them only like a Company of poor Insects, whereof some are Bees, delighted with Flowers, and their sweetness; others, Beetles, delighted with other kind of Viands; which having enjoyed for a season, they should cease to be, and exist no more for ever.

§ 56. These things duly weigh'd, will give us, as I think, a clear view into the state of humane Liberty. Liberty 'tis plain consists in a Power to do, or not to do; to do, or forbear doing as we *will*. This cannot be deny'd. But this seeming to comprehend only the actions of a Man consecutive to volition, it is farther enquired, whether he be at Liberty to *will*, or no? and to this it has been answered, that in most cases a Man is not at Liberty to forbear the act of volition; he must exert an act of his *will*, whereby the action proposed, is made to exist, or not to exist. But yet there is a case wherein a Man is at Liberty in respect of *willing*, and that is the chusing of a remote Good as an end to be pursued. Here a Man may suspend the act of his choice from being determined for or against the thing proposed, till he has examined, whether it be really of a nature in it self and consequences to make him happy, or no. For when he has once chosen it, and thereby it is become a part of his Happiness, it raises desire, and that proportionably gives him *uneasiness*, which determines his *will*, and sets him at work in pursuit of his choice on all occasions that offer. And here we may see how it comes to pass, that a Man may justly incur punishment, though it be certain that in all the particular actions that he *wills*,

§§ 56, 57. *How Men come to chuse ill.*

---

and cease to be; *that which has the Preference*, and makes us will the doing or omitting any Action in our Power, *is the greater Good*, appearing to result from that choice in all its Consequences, as far as at present they are represented to our view.

§ 38. So that, *that which determines the choice* of the Will, and obtains the preference, *is still Good, the greater Good*: But it is also only Good *that appears*; that which carries

(12)–271(18) These . . . Reason] **5** | This sufficiently discovers to us **2–4**
(25) it] **W** | its **5** (28) *uneasiness*] *edit.* | Uneasiness **5**

* Isa. 22: 13; 1 Cor. 15: 32.

he does, and necessarily does will that, which he then judges to be good. For though his *will* be always determined by that, which is judg'd good by his Understanding, yet it excuses him not: Because, by a too hasty choice of his own making, he has imposed on himself wrong measures of good and evil; which however false and fallacious, have the same influence on all his future conduct, as if they were true and right. He has vitiated his own Palate, and must be answerable to himself for the sickness and death that follows from it. The eternal Law and Nature of things must not be alter'd to comply with his ill-order'd choice. If the neglect or abuse of the Liberty he had, to examine what would really and truly make for his Happiness, misleads him, the miscarriages that follow on it, must be imputed to his own election. He had a Power to suspend his determination: It was given him, that he might examine, and take care of his own Happiness, and look that he were not deceived. And he could never judge, that it was better to be deceived, than not, in a matter of so great and near concernment.

What has been said, may also discover to us the Reason, why Men in this World prefer different things, and pursue Happiness by contrary Courses. But yet since Men are always constant, and in earnest, in matter of Happiness and Misery, the Question still remains, *How Men come often to prefer the worse to the better*; and to chuse that, which, by their own Confession, has made them miserable.

§ 57. To account for the various and contrary ways Men take, though all aim at being happy, we must consider, whence the various *uneasinesses*, that determine the will in the preference of each voluntary action, have their rise.

1. Some of them come from causes not in our power, such as are often the pains of the Body from want, disease, or outward injuries, as the rack, *etc.* which when present, and violent, operate for the most part forcibly on the *will*, and turn the courses of Men's lives

§ 57(29). *From bodily pains.*

---

with it the Expectation of Addition to our Happiness, by the increase of our Pleasures, either in Degrees, Sorts, or Duration, or by the preventing, lessening, or shortning of pain. Thus the Temptation of a pleasant Taste, brings a Surfeit, a Disease, and, perhaps, Death too, on one, who looks no farther than that apparent Good, than the present Pleasure; who sees not the remote and concealed Evil: and

(18) *v.* 270(12), n. (32) *will*] **5** | will **2–4** (*l. below* 32) *pains*] **2–3** | *pain* **4–5**. (*In* **2–3**, *this marginal summary faces the first paragraph, and not subsection* 1, *of* § 57.) (*3 ll. below* 32) Pleasures] Pleasure **1T.er**

from Virtue, Piety, and Religion, and what before they judged to lead to happiness; every one not endeavouring, or through disuse, not being able by the contemplation of remote, and future good, to raise in himself desires of them strong enough to counter-balance the uneasiness, he feels in those bodily torments; and to keep his *will* steady in the choice of those actions, which lead to future Happiness. A neighbour Country has been of late a Tragical Theatre, from which we might fetch instances, if there needed any, and the World did not in all Countries and Ages furnish examples enough to confirm that received observation, *Necessitas cogit ad Turpia*, and therefore there is great reason for us to pray *Lead us not into Temptation.**

2. Other *uneasinesses* arise from our desires of absent good; which desires always bear proportion to, and depend on the judgment we make, and the relish we have of any absent good; in both which we are apt to be variously misled, and that by our own fault.

§ 58. In the first place, I shall consider the wrong judgments Men make of future Good and Evil, whereby their desires are misled. For as to present Happiness and Misery, when that alone comes in consideration, and the consequences are quite removed, *a Man never chuses amiss*; he knows what best pleases him, and that, he actually prefers. Things in their present enjoyment are what they seem; the apparent and real good are, in this case, always the same. For the Pain or Pleasure being just so great, and no greater, than it is felt, the present Good or Evil is really so much as it appears. And therefore were every Action of ours concluded within it self, and drew no Consequences after it, we should undoubtedly never err in our choice of good; we should always infallibly prefer the best. Were the pains of honest Industry, and of starving with Hunger and Cold set together before us, no Body would be in doubt which to chuse: were the satisfaction of a Lust, and the Joys of Heaven

§ 57 (13). *From wrong desires arising from wrong judgment.* §§ 58, 59. *Our judgment of present Good or Evil always right.*

---

the hopes of easing or preventing some greater pain, sweetens another Man's Draught, and makes that willingly be swallowed, which in it self is nauseous and unpleasant. Both these Men were moved to what they did by the appearance of

(2) through disuse,] *add.* **5** (6) *will*] **5** | will **2–4** (7–8) A . . . any] *om.* **Coste**

---

* Matt. 6: 13; Luke 11: 4.

offered at once to any one's present Possession, he would not balance, or err in the determination of his choice.

§ 59. But since our voluntary Actions carry not all the Happiness and Misery, that depend on them, along with them in their present performance; but are the precedent Causes of Good and Evil, which they draw after them, and bring upon us, when they themselves are passed, and cease to be; our desires look beyond our present enjoyments, and carry the Mind out to absent *good*, according to the necessity which we think there is of it, to the making or increase of our Happiness. 'Tis our opinion of such a necessity that gives it its attraction: without that we are not moved by absent *good*. For in this narrow scantling of capacity, which we are accustomed to, and sensible of here, wherein we enjoy but one pleasure at once, which, when all uneasiness is away, is, whilst it lasts, sufficient to make us think our selves happy, 'tis not all remote, and even apparent good, that affects us. Because the indolency and enjoyment we have, sufficing for our present Happiness, we desire not to venture the change: Since we judge that we are happy already, being content, and that is enough. For who is content is happy. But as soon as any new uneasiness comes in, this Happiness is disturb'd, and we are set afresh on work in the pursuit of Happiness.

§ 60. Their aptness therefore to conclude, that they can be happy without it, is one great occasion, that Men often are not raised to the desire of the greatest absent *good*. For whilst such thoughts possess them, the Joys of a future State move them not; they have little concern or uneasiness about them; and the *will*, free from the determination of such desires, is left to the pursuit of nearer satisfactions, and to the removal of those uneasinesses which it then feels in its want of, and longings after them. Change but a Man's view of these things; let him see, that Virtue and Religion are necessary to his Happiness; let him look into the future State of Bliss or Misery, and see there God the righteous Judge, ready to *render to every Man according to his Deeds*; *To them who by patient*

§ 60. *From a wrong judgment of what makes a necessary part of their happiness.*

Good, though the one found Ease and Health, and the other a Disease and Destruction: and therefore to him that looks beyond this World, and is fully persuaded, that God the righteous Judge,'

(9) which] *add.* **4–5** it,] **4–5** | them **2–3** (10–11) 'Tis . . . *good.*] *add.* **4–5** (not *add.* **4er–5**) (12) which] *add.* **4–5** (15) , 'tis] **4–5** | . 'Tis **2–3** (18) judge that] **4–5** | judge, **2–3** already,] **5** (*likewise* **Coste**) | already **2–4** (28) to] *add.* **4–5** which] *add.* **4–5** (32) ready to] **2–5** | will **1**

*continuance in well-doing, seek for Glory, and Honour, and Immortality, Eternal Life; but unto every Soul that doth Evil, Indignation and Wrath, Tribulation and Anguish:** To him, I say, who hath a prospect of the different State of perfect Happiness or Misery, that attends all Men after this Life, depending on their Behaviour here, the measures of Good and Evil, that govern his choice, are mightily changed. For since nothing of Pleasure and Pain in this Life, can bear any proportion to endless Happiness, or exquisite Misery of an immortal Soul hereafter, Actions in his Power will have their preference, not according to the transient Pleasure, or Pain that accompanies, or follows them here; but as they serve to secure that perfect durable Happiness hereafter.

§ 61. But to account more particularly for the Misery, that Men often bring on themselves, notwithstanding that they do all in earnest pursue Happiness, we must consider, how *Things* come to be *represented* to our desires, *under deceitful appearances*: and that is *by the Judgment* pronouncing wrongly concerning them. To see how far this reaches, and what are the Causes of wrong Judgment, we must remember, that things are judged good or bad in a double sense.

First, *That which is properly good or bad, is nothing but barely Pleasure or Pain.*

Secondly, But because not only present Pleasure and Pain, but that also which is apt by its efficacy, or consequences, to bring it upon us at a distance, is a proper Object of our desires, and apt to move a Creature, that has foresight; therefore *things* also *that draw after them Pleasure and Pain, are considered as Good and Evil.*

§ 62. The *wrong Judgment* that *misleads us*, and makes the Will often fasten on the worse side, lies in misreporting upon the various Comparisons of these. The *wrong Judgment* I am here speaking of, is not what one Man may think of the determination of another; but what every Man himself must confess to be wrong. For since I lay it for a certain ground, that every intelligent Being really seeks

§§ 61, 62. *A more particular account of wrong judgments.*

---

(13) §§ *61–4 in* **2–5** *correspond, respectively, to* §§ *39–42 in* **1**. But . . . particularly] **2–5** | He that will account **1** (14) notwithstanding] **1–3** | notwithstand **4–5** (15) we] **2–5** | and always prefer the greater apparent Good, **1** (16) desires] **2–5** | choice **1** (24) is . . . move] **2–5** | cannot but move the Will, and determine the choice of **1**

---

* Rom. 2: 6–9.

Happiness, which consists in the enjoyment of Pleasure, without any considerable mixture of uneasiness; 'tis impossible any one should willingly put into his own draught any bitter ingredient, or leave out any thing in his power, that would tend to his satisfaction, and the compleating of his Happiness, but only by a *wrong Judgment.* I shall not here speak of that mistake, which is the consequence of invincible Error, which scarce deserves the Name of *wrong Judgment*; but of that *wrong Judgment*, which every Man himself must confess to be so.

§ 63. I. Therefore, as to present Pleasure and Pain, the Mind, as has been said, never mistakes that which is really good or evil; that, which is the greater Pleasure, or the greater Pain, is really just as it appears. But though present Pleasure and Pain shew their difference and degrees so plainly, as not to leave room for mistake; yet *when we compare present Pleasure or Pain with future,* (which is usually the case in the most important determinations of the Will) *we often make wrong Judgments* of them, taking our measures of them in different positions of distance. Objects, near our view, are apt to be thought greater, than those of a larger size, that are more remote: And so it is with Pleasures and Pains, the present is apt to carry it, and those at a distance have the disadvantage in the Comparison. Thus most Men, like spend-thrift Heirs, are apt to judge a little in Hand better than a great deal to come; and so for small Matters in Possession, part with great ones in Reversion. But that this is a *wrong Judgment* every one must allow, let his Pleasure consist in whatever it will: since that which is future, will certainly come to be present; and then, having the same advantage of nearness, will shew it self in its full dimensions, and discover his wilful mistake, who judged of it by unequal measures. Were the Pleasure of Drinking accompanied, the very moment a Man takes off his Glass, with that sick Stomack, and aking Head, which, in some Men, are sure to follow not many hours after, I think no body, whatever Pleasure he had in his Cups, would, on these Conditions, ever let Wine touch his Lips; which yet he daily swallows, and the evil side

§ 63. *In comparing present and future.*

(1–2) which . . . uneasiness] **2–5** | and would enjoy all the pleasures he could, and suffer no pain **1** (2) considerable] *add.* **4–5** (4–5) would . . . Happiness] **4–5** | he could desire, or would . . . Happiness **2–3** | could add to its sweetness **1** (5) a] **1–4**; *om.* **5** (11) said] **Coste** *adds a marginal reference to* § *58 of this chapter.* (12) just] **2–5** | just, **1** (15–16) (which . . . Will)] *add.* **2–5** (28) it] **4–5** | its **1–3** (34) daily] **3–5** | gaily **1–2**

comes to be chosen only by the fallacy of a little difference in time. But if Pleasure or Pain can be so lessened only by a few hours removal, how much more will it be so, by a farther distance, to a Man, that will not by a right judgment do what time will, *i.e.* bring it home upon himself, and consider it as present, and there take its true dimensions? This is the way we usually impose on our selves, in respect of bare Pleasure and Pain, or the true degrees of Happiness or Misery: The future loses its just proportion, and what is present, obtains the preference as the greater. I mention not here the *wrong Judgment*, whereby the absent are not only lessened, but reduced to perfect nothing; when Men enjoy what they can in present, and make sure of that, concluding amiss, That no evil will thence follow. For that lies not in comparing the greatness of future Good and Evil, which is that we are here speaking of; but in another sort of *wrong Judgment*, which is concerning Good or Evil, as it is considered to be the cause and procurement of Pleasure or Pain, that will follow from it.

§ 64. *The cause of our judging amiss*, when we compare our present Pleasure or Pain with future, seems to me to be *the weak and narrow Constitution of our Minds*. We cannot well enjoy two Pleasures at once, much less any Pleasure almost, whilst Pain possesses us. The present Pleasure, if it be not very languid, and almost none at all, fills our narrow Souls, and so takes up the whole Mind, that it scarce leaves any thought of things absent: Or if among our Pleasures there are some, which are not strong enough, to exclude the consideration of things at a distance; yet we have so great an abhorrence of Pain, that a little of it extinguishes all our Pleasures: A little bitter mingled in our Cup, leaves no relish of the sweet. Hence it comes, that, at any rate, we desire to be rid of the present Evil, which we are apt to think nothing absent can equal; because under the present Pain we find not our selves capable of any the least degree of Happiness. Mens daily complaints are a loud proof

§§ 64, 65. *Causes of this.*

---

(2) hours] **1–4** | Hour **5** (4) by a right judgment] **4–5** | (by a due consideration, **1–3**. (**Coste** 'un juste examen de la chose même') (5) himself, and] **4–5** | himself) **1–3** (20) *Constitution*] **2–5** | *Constitutions* **1** (23) the whole Mind] **2–5** | all our Minds **1** (24–5) among . . . which] **4–5** | many of our Pleasures **1–3** (28–9) . Hence] **4–5** | : [; **2–3**] and hence **1–3** (*likewise* **Coste**) (30–1) because . . . Pain] **4–5** | since while the Pain remains, **1–3** (32)–277 (1) Mens . . . other] **4–5** | Hence we see the present Pain, any one suffers, is always **1–3**

of this: The Pain that any one actually feels, is still of all other the worst; and 'tis with anguish they cry out, *Any rather than this; nothing can be so intolerable as what I now suffer.* And therefore our whole Endeavours and Thoughts are intent, to get rid of the present Evil, before all things, as the first necessary condition to our Happiness, let what will follow. Nothing, as we passionately think, can exceed, or almost equal, the uneasiness that sits so heavy upon us. And because the abstinence from a present Pleasure, that offers it self, is a Pain, nay, oftentimes a very great one, the desire being inflamed by a near and tempting Object; 'tis no wonder that that operates after the same manner Pain does, and lessens in our Thoughts, what is future; and so forces us, as it were, blindfold into its embraces.

§ 65. Add to this, that absent good, or which is the same thing, future pleasure, especially if of a sort which we are unacquainted with, seldom is able to counter-balance any uneasiness, either of pain or desire, which is present. For its greatness being no more, than what shall be really tasted when enjoyed, Men are apt enough to lessen that, to make it give place to any present desire; and conclude with themselves, that when it comes to trial, it may possibly not answer the report, or opinion, that generally passes of it, they having often found, that not only what others have magnified, but even what they themselves have enjoyed with great pleasure and delight at one time, has proved insipid or nauseous at another; and therefore they see nothing in it, for which they should forego a present enjoyment. But that this is a *false* way of *judging*, when apply'd to the Happiness of another life, they must confess, unless they will say, God cannot make those happy he designs to be so. For that being intended for a State of Happiness, it must certainly be agreeable to every one's wish and desire: Could we suppose their relishes as different there as they are here, yet the Manna in Heaven will suit every one's Palate. Thus much of the *wrong Judgment* we make of present and future Pleasure and Pain, when they are compared together, and so the absent considered as future.

(1) *v.* 276(32), n. (2) *Any*] **4–5** | *Any other* **1–3** (*likewise* **Coste**) (5) condition to our] **2–5** | step towards **1** (7–8) uneasiness . . . us.] **4–5** | Pain we feel: **1–3** (9) Pain,] **2–5** (; **2–3**) | sort of Pain; **1** (9–10) the . . . Object;] *add.* **2–5** (13) *In* **1**, *this section concludes with what is, in* **2–5**, *the concluding sentence* 'Thus . . . future.' *of* § 65. (14–32) Add . . . Palate.] **2–5** (15) which] *add.* **4–5** (21) possibly] **2–4** | possible **5** (30) : Could we] **4–5** | ; though we could **2–3** (32–5) Thus . . . future.] **2–5**; *cf.* (13), n.

§ 66. II. *As to things good or bad in their Consequences*, and by the aptness is in them to procure us good or evil in the future, *we judge amiss several ways.*

1. When we *judge* that so much evil does not really depend on them, as in truth there does.

2. When we *judge*, that though the Consequence be of that moment, yet it is not of that certainty, but that it may otherwise fall out; or else by some means be avoided, as by industry, address, change, repentance, *etc.* That these are *wrong* ways of *judging*, were easy to shew in every particular, if I would examine them at large singly: But I shall only mention this in general, *viz.* That it is a very wrong, and irrational way of proceeding, to venture a greater Good, for a less, upon uncertain guesses, and before a due examination be made, proportionable to the weightiness of the matter, and the concernment it is to us not to mistake. This, I think, every one must confess, especially if he considers the usual *Causes* of this *wrong Judgment*, whereof these following are some.

§ 67. I. *Ignorance*: He that judges without informing himself to the utmost that he is capable, cannot acquit himself of *judging amiss.*

II. *Inadvertency*: When a Man overlooks even that, which he does know. This is an affected and present Ignorance, which misleads our Judgments, as much as the other. Judging is, as it were, balancing an account, and determining on which side the odds lies. If therefore either side be hudled up in haste, and several of the Sums, that should have gone into the reckoning, be overlook'd, and left out, this Precipitancy causes as *wrong* a *Judgment*, as if it were a perfect Ignorance. That which most commonly causes this, is the prevalency of some present Pleasure or Pain, heightned by our feeble passionate Nature, most strongly wrought on by what is present. To check this Precipitancy, our Understanding and Reason was given us, if we will make a right use of it, to search, and see, and then judge thereupon. Without Liberty the Understanding would be to no purpose: And without Understanding, Liberty (if it could be) would signify nothing. If a Man sees, what would do

§ 66. *In considering consequences of actions.* § 67. *Causes of this.*

---

(1) §§ *66–7 in* **2–5** *correspond, respectively, to* §§ *43–4 in* **1**. (9) That] **4–5** | But that **1–3** (13) Good] **2–5** | Good and Evil **1** (13–15) [*2nd*] a . . . mistake] **2–5** | due, and through examination, as far as a Man's knowledge can, by any endeavours or assistance, attain **1** (28) or Pain] *add.* **2–5** (32)–279(11) Without . . . requires.] *add.* **4–5**

him good or harm, what would make him happy or miserable, without being able to move himself one step towards or from it, what is he the better for seeing? And he that is at liberty to ramble in perfect darkness, what is his liberty better than if he were driven up and down, as a bubble by the force of the wind? The being acted by a blind impulse from without, or from within, is little odds. The first therefore and great use of Liberty, is to hinder blind Precipitancy; the principal exercise of Freedom is to stand still, open the eyes, look about, and take a view of the consequence of what we are going to do, as much as the weight of the matter requires. How much sloth and negligence, heat and passion, the prevalency of fashion, or acquired indispositions, do severally contribute on occasion, to these *wrong Judgments*, I shall not here farther enquire. I shall only add one other false Judgment, which I think necessary to mention, because perhaps it is little taken notice of, though of great influence.

§ 68. All Men desire Happiness, that's past doubt: but, as has been already observed, when they are rid of pain, they are apt to take up with any pleasure at hand, or that custom has endear'd to them; to rest satisfied in that; and so being happy, till some new desire by making them uneasy, disturbs that happiness, and shews them, that they are not so, they look no farther; nor is the will determined to any action in pursuit of any other known or apparent good. For since we find, that we cannot enjoy all sorts of good, but one excludes another; we do not fix our desires on every apparent greater good, unless it be judged to be necessary to our happiness: If we think we can be happy without it, it moves us not. This is another occasion to Men of *judging wrong*, when they take not that to be necessary to their Happiness, which really is so. This mistake misleads us both in the choice of the good we aim at, and very often in the means to it, when it is a remote good. But, which way ever it be, either by placing it where really it is not, or by neglecting the means, as not necessary to it, when a Man misses his great end Happiness, he will acknowledge he judg'd not right. That which contributes to this mistake is the real or suppos'd unpleasantness of the actions, which are the way to this end; it seeming so

§ 68. *Wrong Judgment of what is necessary to our happiness.*

---

(11) *v.* 278(32), n. much] **1, 4–5** | much, **2–3** (14–16) [*1st*] I . . . influence.] *add.* **2–5** (17)–281(10) All . . . so?] *add.* **2–5** (23) known] **4er–5** | knowledge **2–4** (*likewise* **Coste**) (24) that] *add.* **4–5**

preposterous a thing to Men, to make themselves unhappy in order to Happiness, that they do not easily bring themselves to it.

§ 69. The last enquiry therefore concerning this matter is, Whether it be in a Man's power to change the pleasantness, and unpleasantness, that accompanies any sort of action? and to that, it is plain in many cases he can. Men may and should correct their palates, and give a relish to what either has, or they suppose has none. The relish of the mind is as various as that of the Body, and like that too may be alter'd; and 'tis a mistake to think, that Men cannot change the displeasingness, or indifferency, that is in actions, into pleasure and desire, if they will do but what is in their power. A due consideration will do it in some cases; and practice, application, and custom in most. Bread or Tobacco may be neglected, where they are shewn to be useful to health, because of an in-indifferency or disrelish to them; reason and consideration at first recommends, and begins their trial, and use finds, or custom makes them pleasant. That this is so in Vertue too, is very certain. Actions are pleasing or displeasing, either in themselves, or consider'd as a means to a greater and more desirable end. The eating of a well-season'd dish, suited to a Man's palate, may move the Mind by the delight it self, that accompanies the eating, without reference to any other end: To which the consideration of the pleasure there is in health and strength (to which that meat is subservient) may add a new Gusto, able to make us swallow an ill relish'd potion. In the latter of these, any action is rendred more or less pleasing, only by the contemplation of the end, and the being more or less perswaded of its tendency to it, or necessary connexion with it: But the pleasure of the action it self is best acquir'd, or increased, by use and practice. Trials often reconcile us to that, which at a distance we looked on with aversion; and by repetition wears us into a liking, of what possibly, in the first essay, displeased us. Habits have powerful charms, and put so strong attractions of easiness and pleasure into what we accustom our selves to, that we cannot forbear to do, or at least be easy in the omission of actions, which habitual practice has suited, and thereby recommends to us. Though this be very visible, and every one's Experience shews him he can do; yet it is a part, in the conduct of Men towards their Happiness, neglected to a degree, that it will be possibly entertain'd as a Paradox, if it be said, that Men can make things or actions more or less pleasing to themselves;

§ 69. *We can change the agreeableness or disagreeableness in things.*

and thereby remedy that, to which one may justly impute a great deal of their wandering. Fashion and the common Opinion having settled wrong Notions, and education and custom ill habits, the just values of things are misplaced, and the palates of Men corrupted. Pains should be taken to rectify these; and contrary habits change our pleasures, and give a relish to that, which is necessary, or conducive to our Happiness. This every one must confess he can do, and when Happiness is lost, and misery overtakes him, he will confess, he did amiss in neglecting it; and condemn himself for it: And I ask every one whether he has not often done so?

§ 70. I shall not now enlarge any farther on the *wrong Judgments*, and neglect of what is in their power, whereby Men mislead themselves. This would make a Volume, and is not my business. But whatever false notions, or shameful neglect of what is in their power, may put Men out of their way to Happiness, and distract them, as we see, into so different courses of life, this yet is certain, that Morality, established upon its true Foundations, cannot but determine the Choice in any one, that will but consider: and he that will not be so far a rational Creature, as to reflect seriously upon infinite Happiness and Misery, must needs condemn himself, as not making that use of his Understanding he should. The Rewards and Punishments of another Life, which the Almighty has established, as the Enforcements of his Law, are of weight enough to determine the Choice, against whatever Pleasure or Pain this Life can shew, when the eternal State is considered but in its bare possibility, which no Body can make any doubt of. He that will allow exquisite and endless Happiness to be but the possible consequence of a good Life here, and the contrary state the possible Reward of a bad one, must own himself to judge very much amiss, if he does not conclude, That a vertuous Life, with the certain expectation of everlasting Bliss, which may come, is to be preferred to a vicious one, with the fear of that dreadful state of Misery, which 'tis very possible may overtake the guilty; or at best the terrible uncertain hope of Annihilation. This is evidently so, though the vertuous Life here had

§ 70. *Preference of Vice to Vertue a manifest wrong Judgment.*

(10) *v.* 279(17), n. (11) § *70 in* **2–5** *corresponds to* § *45 in* **1**. (11–17) I . . . that] **2–5** | This, I think, is certain, That the choice of the Will is every-where determined by the greater apparent Good, however it may be wrong represented by the Understanding; and it would be impossible Men should pursue so different Courses as they do in the World, had they not different Measures of Good and Evil. But yet **1** (25) but] *add.* **4–5** (26) make any doubt of] **2–5** | deny **1** (28) and] **5** | or **1–4**

nothing but Pain, and the vicious continual pleasure: which yet is for the most part quite otherwise, and wicked Men have not much the odds to brag of, even in their present possession; nay, all things rightly considered, have, I think even the worse part here. But when infinite Happiness is put in one Scale, against infinite Misery in the other; if the worst, that comes to the pious Man, if he mistakes, be the best that the wicked can attain to, if he be in the right, Who can without madness run the venture? Who in his Wits would chuse to come within a possibility of infinite Misery, which if he miss, there is yet nothing to be got by that hazard? Whereas on the other side, the sober Man ventures nothing against infinite Happiness to be got, if his Expectation comes to pass. If the good Man be in the right, he is eternally happy; if he mistakes, he is not miserable, he feels nothing. On the other side, if the wicked be in the right, he is not happy; if he mistakes, he is infinitely miserable. Must it not be a most manifest wrong Judgment, that does not presently see, to which side, in this case, the preference is to be given? I have foreborn to mention any thing of the certainty, or probability of a future State, designing here to shew the *wrong Judgment*, that any one must allow, he makes upon his own Principles laid how he pleases, who prefers the short pleasures of a vicious Life upon any consideration, whilst he knows, and cannot but be certain, that a future Life is at least possible.

§ 71. To conclude this enquiry into humane Liberty, which as it stood before, I my self from the beginning fearing, and a very judicious Friend of mine, since the publication suspecting, to have some mistake in it, though he could not particularly shew it me, I was put upon a stricter review of this Chapter. Wherein lighting upon a very easy, and scarce observable slip I had made, in putting one seemingly indifferent word for another, that discovery open'd to me this present view, which here in this second Edition, I submit to the learned World, and which in short is this: *Liberty* is a power to act or not to act according as the Mind directs. A power to direct the operative faculties to motion or rest in particular instances, is that which we call the *Will*. That which in the train of

§§ 71–3. *Recapitulation.*

---

(6) mistakes] **4–5** | mistake **1–3** (13) mistakes] **4–5** | mistake **1–3** (15) mistakes] **4–5** | mistake **1–3** (24)–283(16) To . . . *Judgment.*] *add.* **2–5** (*l. below* 35) *Recapitulation.*] **4–5**; *in* **2–3** *and* **Coste**, *§§ 71–3 come under the same marginal summary as § 70.*

our voluntary actions determines the *Will* to any change of operation, is some present uneasiness, which is, or at least is always accompanied with that of *Desire*. Desire is always moved by Evil, to fly it: Because a total freedom from pain always makes a necessary part of our Happiness: But every *Good*, nay every *greater Good* does not constantly move *Desire*, because it may not make, or may not be taken to make any necessary part of our Happiness. For all that we desire is only to be Happy. But though this general *Desire* of Happiness operates constantly and invariably, yet the satisfaction of any particular *desire* can be suspended from determining the *will* to any subservient action, till we have maturely examin'd, whether the particular apparent good, which we then desire, makes a part of our real Happiness, or be consistent or inconsistent with it. The result of our judgment upon that Examination is what ultimately determines the Man, who could not be *free* if his *will* were determin'd by any thing, but his own *desire* guided by his own *Judgment*. I know that Liberty by some, is placed in an *indifferency* of the Man, antecedent to the determination of his *Will*. I wish they, who lay so much stress on such an *antecedent indifferency*, as they call it, had told us plainly, whether this supposed *indifferency* be antecedent to the Thought and Judgment of the Understanding, as well as to the decree of the *Will*. For it is pretty hard to state it between them; *i.e.* immediately after the Judgment of the Understanding, and before the determination of the *Will*, because the determination of the *Will* immediately follows the Judgment of the Understanding; and to place Liberty in an *indifferency*, antecedent to the Thought and Judgment of the Understanding, seems to me to place Liberty in a state of darkness, wherein we can neither see nor say any thing of it; at least it places it in a subject incapable of it, no Agent being allowed capable of Liberty, but in consequence of Thought and Judgment. I am not nice about Phrases, and therefore consent to say with those that love to speak so, that Liberty is plac'd in *indifferency*; but 'tis in an *indifferency* that remains after the Judgment of the Understanding; yea, even after the determination of the *Will*: And that is an indifferency not of the Man, (for after he has once judg'd which is best, *viz.* to do, or forbear, he is no longer indifferent,) but an *indifferency* of the operative Powers of the Man, which remaining equally able to operate, or to forbear operating

(3) . Desire] *add.* **2er–5** (12) , which . . . makes] **4–5** | we then desire make **2–3** (16) *v.* 282(24), n. (16)–284(21) I . . . imaginary.] *add.* **5**

after, as before the decree of the *Will*, are in a state, which, if one pleases, may be called *indifferency*; and as far as this *indifferency* reaches, a Man is free, and no farther. *v.g.* I have the Ability to move my Hand, or to let it rest, that operative Power is indifferent to move, or not to move my Hand: I am then in that respect perfectly free. My *Will* determines that operative Power to rest, I am yet free, because the *indifferency* of that my operative Power to act, or not to act, still remains; the Power of moving my Hand, is not at all impair'd by the determination of my *Will*, which at present orders rest; the *indifferency* of that Power to act, or not to act, is just as it was before, as will appear, if the *Will* puts it to the trial, by ordering the contrary. But if during the rest of my Hand, it be seized by a sudden Palsy, the *indifferency* of that operative Power is gone, and with it my Liberty: I have no longer Freedom in that respect, but am under a Necessity of letting my Hand rest. On the other side, if my Hand be put into motion by a Convulsion, the *indifferency* of that operative Faculty is taken away by that motion, and my Liberty in that case is lost: For I am under a Necessity of having my Hand move. I have added this, to shew in what sort of *indifferency* Liberty seems to me to consist, and not in any other, real or imaginary.

§ 72. True notions concerning the nature and extent of *Liberty* are of so great importance, that I hope I shall be pardon'd this Digression, which my attempt to explain it, has led me into. The *Ideas* of *Will*, *Volition*, *Liberty*, and *Necessity*, in this Chapter of Power, came naturally in my way. In the former Edition of this Treatise, I gave an account of my thoughts concerning them,

(21) *v.* 283(16), 2nd n. (22) § 72 *in* **2–5** *replaces the section numbered 46 in* **1**: '§ 46. Under this simple *Idea* of Power, I have taken occasion to explain our *Ideas* of *Will*, *Volition*, *Liberty*, and *Necessity*; which having a greater mixture in them, than belongs barely to simple Modes, might perhaps, be better placed amongst the more complex. For *Will*, for example, contains in it the *Idea* of a Power to prefer the doing, to the not doing any particular Action (*et vice versâ*) which it has thought on; which preference is truly a Mode of Thinking, and so the *Idea* which the word *Will* stands for, is a complex and mixed one, made up of the simple *Ideas* of Power, and a certain Mode of Thinking: and the *Idea* of *Liberty* is yet more complex, being made up of the *Idea* of a Power to act, or not to act, in conformity to Volition. But I hoped this transgression, against the method I have proposed to my self, will be forgiven me, if I have quitted it a little, to explain some *Ideas* of great importance; such as are those of the *Will*, *Liberty*, and *Necessity*, in this place, where they, as it were, offered themselves, and sprang up from their proper roots. Besides, having before largely enough instanced in several simple Modes, to shew what I meant by them, and how the Mind got them, (for I intend not to enumerate all the particular *Ideas* of each sort,) these of *Will*, *Liberty*, and *Necessity*, may serve as instances of mixed Modes, which are that sort of *Ideas* I purpose next to treat of.'

according to the light I then had: And now as a Lover of Truth, and not a Worshipper of my own Doctrines, I own some change of my Opinion, which I think I have discover'd ground for. In what I first writ, I with an unbiassed indifferency followed Truth, whither I thought she led me. But neither being so vain as to fancy Infallibility, nor so disingenuous as to dissemble my mistakes for fear of blemishing my reputation, I have with the same sincere design for truth only, not been asham'd to publish what a severer enquiry has suggested. It is not impossible, but that some may think my former notions right, and some (as I have already found) these later; and some neither. I shall not at all wonder at this variety in Men's Opinions: Impartial deductions of reason in controverted points being so very rare, and exact ones in abstract notions not so very easy, especially if of any length. And therefore, I should think my self not a little beholding to any one, who would upon these or any other grounds fairly clear this subject of *Liberty* from any difficulties that may yet remain.

Before I close this Chapter, it may perhaps be to our purpose, and help to give us clearer conceptions about *power*, if we make our thoughts take a little more exact survey of *Action*. I have said above, that we have *Ideas* but of two sorts of *Action*, viz. *Motion* and *Thinking*. These, in truth, though called and counted *Actions*, yet, if nearly considered, will not be found to be always perfectly so. For, if I mistake not, there are instances of both kinds, which, upon due consideration, will be found rather *Passions* than *Actions*, and consequently so far the effects barely of passive Powers in those subjects, which yet on their account are thought *Agents*. For in these instances, the substance that hath motion, or thought, receives the impression whereby it is put into that *Action* purely from without, and so acts merely by the capacity it has to receive such an impression from some external Agent; and such a *Power* is not properly an *Active Power*, but a mere passive capacity in the subject. Sometimes the Substance, or Agent, puts it self into *Action* by its own Power, and this is properly *Active Power*. Whatsoever modification a substance has, whereby it produces any effect, that is called *Action*; *v.g.* a solid substance by motion operates on, or alters the sensible *Ideas* of another substance, and therefore this modification

(17) *Paragraph break here in* **5**, *not in* **4**. (18)–286(23) Before . . . *Power*.] *add.* **4–5** (20) above] **Coste** *adds marginal reference to* § *4*. (23) nearly] **5** | nearly, **4** (31) Agent;] **5** | Agent, **4** (36) *Action*;] **5** | *Action*: **4**

of motion we call Action. But yet this motion in that solid substance is, when rightly considered, but a passion, if it received it only from some external Agent. So that the *Active Power* of motion is in no substance which cannot begin motion in it self, or in another substance when at rest. So likewise in *Thinking*, a Power to receive *Ideas*, or Thoughts, from the operation of any external substance, is called a *Power* of thinking: But this is but a *Passive Power*, or Capacity. But to be able to bring into view *Ideas* out of sight, at one's own choice, and to compare which of them one thinks fit, this is an *Active Power*. This reflection may be of some use to preserve us from mistakes about *Powers* and *Actions*, which Grammar, and the common frame of Languages, may be apt to lead us into: Since what is signified by *Verbs* that Grammarians call *Active*, does not always signify *Action*; *v.g.* this Proposition, I see the Moon, or a Star, or I feel the heat of the Sun, though expressed by a *Verb Active*, does not signify any *Action* in me whereby I operate on those Substances; but the reception of the *Ideas* of light, roundness, and heat, wherein I am not active but barely passive, and cannot in that position of my Eyes, or Body, avoid receiving them. But when I turn my Eyes another way, or remove my Body out of the Sun-beams, I am properly active; because of my own choice, by a power within my self, I put my self into that Motion. Such an *Action* is the product of *Active Power*.

§ 73. And thus I have, in a short draught, given a view of our *original Ideas*, from whence all the rest are derived, and of which they are made up; which if I would consider, as a Philosopher, and examine on what Causes they depend, and of what they are made, I believe they all might be reduced to these very few primary, and original ones, *viz.*

Extension,
Solidity,
Mobility, or the Power of being moved;

which by our Senses we receive from Body:

Perceptivity, or the Power of perception, or thinking;
Motivity, or the Power of moving;

which by reflection we receive from our Minds. I crave leave to

(17) roundness,] *edit.* | roundness **4–5** (23) *v.* 285(18), n. (24) § 73, *in* **2–5**, *corresponds to* § 47, *in* **1**. (32) , or . . . moved] *add.* **4–5** (34–5) *Perceptivity* . . . moving] **4–5** | *Thinking*, and the / *Power of Moving* **1–3** (36)–287(2) I . . . æquivocal.] *add.* **4–5**. (**Coste** *further adds a linguistic footnote.*)

make use of these two new Words, to avoid the danger of being mistaken in the use of those which are æquivocal. To which if we add

Existence,
Duration,
Number;

which belong both to the one, and the other, we have, perhaps, all the Original *Ideas* on which the rest depend. For by these, I imagine, might be explained the nature of Colours, Sounds, Tastes, Smells, and all other *Ideas* we have, if we had but Faculties acute enough to perceive the severally modified Extensions, and Motions, of these minute Bodies, which produce those several Sensations in us. But my present purpose being only to enquire into the Knowledge the Mind has of Things, by those *Ideas*, and Appearances, which *God* has fitted it to receive from them, and how the Mind comes by that Knowledge; rather than into their Causes, or manner of Production, I shall not, contrary to the Design of this Essay, set my self to enquire philosophically into the peculiar Constitution of Bodies, and the Configuration of Parts, whereby they have the power to produce in us the *Ideas* of their sensible Qualities: I shall not enter any farther into that Disquisition; it sufficing to my purpose to observe, That Gold, or Saffron, has a power to produce in us the *Idea* of Yellow; and Snow, or Milk, the *Idea* of White; which we can only have by our Sight, without examining the Texture of the Parts of those Bodies, or the particular Figures, or Motion of the Particles, which rebound from them, to cause in us that particular Sensation: though when we go beyond the bare *Ideas* in our Minds, and would enquire into their Causes, we cannot conceive any thing else, to be in any sensible Object, whereby it produces different *Ideas* in us, but the different Bulk, Figure, Number, Texture, and Motion of its insensible Parts.

(2) *v.* 286(36), n. (13) only to enquire] **4–5** | to enquire only **1–3**
(14) , which] *add.* **2–5** (24) only have] **4–5** | have only **1–3**

CHAPTER XXII

Of Mixed Modes.

§ 1. HAVING treated of *Simple Modes* in the foregoing Chapters, and given several instances of some of the most considerable of them, to shew what they are, and how we come by them; we are now in the next place to consider those we call *Mixed Modes*, such are the Complex *Ideas*, we mark by the names *Obligation*, *Drunkenness*, a *Lye*, etc. which consisting of several Combinations of simple *Ideas* of different kinds, I have called *Mixed Modes*, to distinguish them from the more simple Modes, which consist only of simple *Ideas* of the same kind. These mixed Modes being also such Combinations of simple *Ideas*, as are not looked upon to be the characteristical Marks of any real Beings that have a steady existence, but scattered and independent *Ideas*, put together by the Mind, are thereby distinguished from the complex *Ideas* of Substances.

§ 2. That the Mind, in respect of its simple *Ideas*, is wholly passive, and receives them all from the Existence and Operations of Things, such as Sensation or Reflection offers them, without being able to make any one *Idea*, Experience shews us. But if we attentively consider these *Ideas* I call *mixed Modes*, we are now speaking of, we shall find their Original quite different. *The Mind* often *exercises an active Power in the making these* several *Combinations*. For it being once furnished with simple *Ideas*, it can put them together in several Compositions, and so make variety of complex *Ideas*, without examining whether they exist so together in Nature. And hence, I think, it is, that these *Ideas* are called *Notions*: as if they had their Original, and constant Existence, more in the Thoughts of Men, than in the reality of things; and to form such *Ideas*, it sufficed, that the Mind put the parts of them together, and that they were consistent in the Understanding, without considering whether they had any real Being: though I do not deny, but several

§ 1. *Mixed Modes what.* § 2. *Made by the Mind.*

(5) mark] **1T.er, 2–5** | make **1** (7) distinguish] **1–4** | distinguished **5** (8) consist] **2er–5** | consists **1–2** (10) be the] **1–4** | be/ **5.** (**Coste** 'qu'on ne regarde pas comme des marques caracteristiques') (16) Reflection] **1–3, 5** | reflection **4** (17) *Idea*,] **1er–5** | *Idea* **1** (19) often] **2–5** | here often **1** (20) *the*] **1–4**; *om.* **5** (24) these *Ideas*] **2–5** | these sort of *Ideas* **1** (27) put] **1–4** | puts **5**

of them might be taken from Observation, and the Existence of several simple *Ideas* so combined, as they are put together in the Understanding. For the Man who first framed the *Idea* of *Hypocrisy*, might have either taken it at first from the observation of one, who made shew of good Qualities which he had not; or else have framed that *Idea* in his Mind, without having any such pattern to fashion it by. For it is evident, that in the beginning of Languages and Societies of Men, several of those complex *Ideas*, which were consequent to the Constitutions established amongst them, must needs have been in the Minds of Men, before they existed any where else; and that many names that stood for such complex *Ideas*, were in use, and so those *Ideas* framed, before the Combinations they stood for, ever existed.

§ 3. Indeed, now that Languages are made, and abound with words standing for such Combinations, *an usual way of getting these complex* Ideas, *is by the explication of those terms that stand for them.* For consisting of a company of simple *Ideas* combined, they may by words, standing for those simple *Ideas*, be represented to the Mind of one who understands those words, though that complex Combination of simple *Ideas* were never offered to his Mind by the real existence of things. Thus a Man may come to have the *Idea* of *Sacrilege*, or *Murther*, by enumerating to him the simple *Ideas* which these words stand for, without ever seeing either of them committed.

§ 4. Every *mixed Mode* consisting of many distinct simple *Ideas*, it seems reasonable to enquire, *whence it has its Unity*; and how such a precise multitude comes to make but one *Idea*, since that Combination does not always exist together in Nature. To which I answer it is plain, it has its Unity from an Act of the Mind combining those several simple *Ideas* together, and considering them as one complex one, consisting of those parts; and the mark of this Union, or that which is looked on generally to compleat it, is one name given to that Combination. For 'tis by their names, that Men commonly regulate their account of their distinct Species of mixed Modes, seldom allowing or considering any number of simple *Ideas*, to make

§ 3. *Sometimes got by the Explication of their Names.* § 4. *The Name ties the Parts of the mixed Modes into one* Idea.

(7) Languages] **2–5** | Languages, **1** (15) such Combinations] **2–5** | them **1** (23) which] *add.* **4–5** (26) seems reasonable to enquire] **4–5** | may be well enquired **1–3** (28–9) . [?**5**] To . . . Unity] **4–5** | : And this, it is plain, it has **1–3** (*l. below* 35: § 4.) [*2nd*] *the*] **2–4**; *om.* **5**

one complex one, but such Collections as there be names for. Thus, though the killing of an old Man be as fit in Nature to be united into one complex *Idea*, as the killing a Man's Father; yet, there being no name standing precisely for the one, as there is the name of *Parricide* to mark the other, it is not taken for a particular complex *Idea*, nor a distinct Species of Actions, from that of killing a young Man, or any other Man.

§ 5. If we should enquire a little farther, to see *what it is, that occasions Men to make several Combinations of simple* Ideas *into distinct, and, as it were, settled Modes*, and neglect others, which in the Nature of Things themselves, have as much an aptness to be combined, and make distinct *Ideas*, we shall find the reason of it to be the end of Language; which being to mark, or communicate Men's Thoughts to one another, with all the dispatch that may be, they usually make such Collections of *Ideas* into complex Modes, and affix names to them, as they have frequent use of in their way of Living and Conversation, leaving others, which they have but seldom an occasion to mention, loose and without names, that tie them together: they rather chusing to enumerate (when they have need) such *Ideas* as make them up, by the particular names, that stand for them, than to trouble their Memories, by multiplying of complex *Ideas* with names to them, which they shall seldom or never have any occasion to make use of.

§ 6. This shews us *how it comes to pass that there are in every Language many particular words, which cannot be rendred by any one single word of another*. For the several Fashions, Customs, and Manners of one Nation, making several Combinations of *Ideas* familiar and necessary in one, which another people have had never any occasion to make, or, perhaps, so much as take notice of, Names come of course to be annexed to them, to avoid long Periphrases in things of daily Conversation; and so they become so many distinct complex *Ideas* in their Minds. Thus ὀστρακισμός amongst the *Greeks*, and *Proscriptio* amongst the *Romans*, were words which other Languages

§ 5. *The Cause of making mixed Modes.* § 6. *Why Words in one Language, have none answering in another.*

(24) shews us] **2–5** | gives us the Reason **1** (25) *many particular*] *add.* **2–5** *one single word*] **2–5** | *words* **1** (28) have] *add.* **5** (*likewise* **Coste**) (30) Periphrases] **1–3, 5** (*likewise* **Coste**) | Paraphrases **4, 4er** (32) ὀστρακισμός] *edit.* | ὀϛρακισμὸς **1–5** (33)–291(2) were . . . Nations.] **4–5** | stood for complex *Ideas*, which were not in the Minds of other People, nor had therefore any names in other Languages that answered them. **1–3**

had no names that exactly answered; because they stood for complex *Ideas*, which were not in the Minds of the Men of other Nations. Where there was no such Custom, there was no notion of any such Actions; no use of such Combinations of *Ideas*, as were united, and, as it were, tied together by those terms: and therefore in other Countries there were no names for them.

§ 7. Hence also we may see the Reason, *Why Languages constantly change*, take up new, and lay by old terms. Because change of Customs and Opinions bringing with it new Combinations of *Ideas*, which it is necessary frequently to think on, and talk about, new names, to avoid long descriptions, are annexed to them; and so they become new Species of complex Modes. What a number of different *Ideas* are by this means wrapped up in one short sound, and how much of our Time and Breath is thereby saved, any one will see, who will but take the pains to enumerate all the *Ideas*, that either *Reprieve* or *Appeal* stand for; and instead of either of those Names use a Periphrasis, to make any one understand their meaning.

§ 8. Though I shall have occasion to consider this more at large, when I come to treat of Words, and their Use: yet I could not avoid to take thus much notice here of the names of *mixed Modes*, which being fleeting, and transient Combinations of simple *Ideas*, which have but a short existence any where, but in the Minds of Men, and there too have no longer any existence, than whilst they are thought on, *have not so much any where the appearance of a constant and lasting existence, as in their Names*: which are therefore, in these sort of *Ideas*, very apt to be taken for the *Ideas* themselves. For if we should enquire where the *Idea* of a *Triumph*, or *Apotheosis* exists, it is evident, they could neither of them exist altogether any where in the things themselves, being Actions that required time to their performance, and so could never all exist together: and as to the Minds of Men, where the *Ideas* of these Actions are supposed to be lodged, they have there too a very uncertain existence; and therefore we are apt to annex them to the Names, that excite them in us.

§ 9. There are therefore *three ways whereby we get the complex* Ideas *of mixed Modes*. 1. By Experience and *Observation* of things themselves.

§ 7. *And Languages change.* § 8. *Mixed Modes, where they exist.* § 9. *How we get the* Ideas *of mixed Modes.*

(2) *v.* 290(33), n. (9) it] **4–5** | them **1–3** (11) names,] **4–5** | names **1–3**
(19) Words] **Coste** *adds marginal reference to Book III.* Use:] **1–3, 5** | Use. **4**
(34) *the*] **5** | *these* **1–4**

Thus by seeing two Men wrestle, or fence, we get the *Idea* of wrestling or fencing. 2. By *Invention*, or voluntary putting together of several simple *Ideas* in our own Minds: So he that first invented Printing, or Etching, had an *Idea* of it in his Mind, before it ever existed. 3. Which is the most usual way, by *explaining the names* of Actions we never saw, or Notions we cannot see; and by enumerating, and thereby, as it were, setting before our Imaginations all those *Ideas* which go to the making them up, and are the constituent parts of them. For having by *Sensation* and *Reflection* stored our Minds with simple *Ideas*, and by use got the Names, that stand for them, we can by those Names represent to another any complex *Idea*, we would have him conceive; so that it has in it no simple *Idea*, but what he knows, and has, with us, the same name for. For all our complex *Ideas* are ultimately resolvable into simple *Ideas*, of which they are compounded, and originally made up, though perhaps their immediate Ingredients, as I may so say, are also complex *Ideas*. Thus the *mixed Mode*, which the word *Lye* stands for, is made of these simple *Ideas*: 1. Articulate Sounds. 2. Certain *Ideas* in the Mind of the Speaker. 3. Those words the signs of those *Ideas*. 4. Those signs put together by affirmation or negation, otherwise than the *Ideas* they stand for, are in the mind of the Speaker. I think I need not go any farther in the Analysis of that complex *Idea*, we call a *Lye*: What I have said is enough to shew, that it is made up of simple *Ideas*: And it could not but be an offensive tediousness to my Reader, to trouble him with a more minute enumeration of every particular simple *Idea*, that goes to this complex one; which, from what has been said, he cannot but be able to make out to himself. The same may be done in all our complex *Ideas* whatsoever; which however compounded, and decompounded, may at last be resolved into simple *Ideas*, which are all the Materials of Knowledge or Thought we have or can have. Nor shall we have reason to fear, that the Mind is hereby stinted to too scanty a number of *Ideas*, if we consider, what an inexhaustible stock of simple Modes, Number, and Figure alone affords us. How far then *mixed Modes*, which admit of the various Combinations of different simple *Ideas*, and their infinite Modes, are from being few and scanty, we may easily imagine. So that before we have done, we shall see, that, no Body need be afraid, he shall not have scope, and compass enough for his

(12) would] **2–5** | could **1** (13) *Idea*] **1–4** | *Ideas* **5** (38) need] **1–3, 5** | needs **4** not] *add.* **1T.er, 2–5**

Thoughts to range in, though they be, as I pretend, confined only to simple *Ideas* received from Sensation or Reflection, and their several Combinations.

§ 10. It is worth our observing *which of all our simple* Ideas *have been most modified, and had most mixed Modes made out of them, with names given to them*: And those have been these three; Thinking, and Motion, (which are the two *Ideas* which comprehend in them all Action,) and Power, from whence these Actions are conceived to flow. These simple *Ideas*, I say, of Thinking, Motion, and Power, have been those, which have been most modified; and out of whose Modifications have been made most complex Modes, with names to them. For Action being the great business of Mankind, and the whole matter about which all Laws are conversant, it is no wonder, that the several Modes of Thinking and Motion, should be taken notice of, the *Ideas* of them observed, and laid up in the memory, and have Names assigned to them; without which, Laws could be but ill made, or Vice and Disorder repressed. Nor could any Communication be well had amongst Men, without such complex *Ideas*, with Names to them: and therefore Men have setled Names, and supposed setled *Ideas* in their Minds, of modes of Actions distinguished by their Causes, Means, Objects, Ends, Instruments, Time, Place, and other circumstances; and also of their Powers fitted for those Actions: *v.g.* Boldness is the Power to speak or do what we intend, before others, without fear or disorder; and the *Greeks* call the confidence of speaking by a peculiar name παῤῥησία: Which power or ability in Man, of doing any thing, when it has been acquired by frequent doing the same thing, is that *Idea*, we name *Habit*; when it is forward, and ready upon every occasion, to break into Action, we *call* it *Disposition*: Thus *Testiness* is a disposition or aptness to be angry.

To conclude, Let us examine any *Modes of Action*, v.g. *Consideration* and *Assent*, which are Actions of the Mind; *Running* and *Speaking*, which are Actions of the Body; *Revenge* and *Murther*, which are Actions of both together, and we shall find them but so many *Collections of simple Ideas*, which together make up the complex ones signified by those Names.

§ 10. *Motion, Thinking, and Power, have been most modified.*

(15) observed,] **4–5** | observed **1–3** (17) Disorder] **5** (*likewise* **Coste**) | Disorders **1–4** (23–4) what we intend,] *add.* **2–5** (27) is that *Idea*,] **1T.er** (*without* ‘,’), **2–5** | is, that the *Idea* **1** (*l. below* 36) *Thinking*,] **5** | *Thinking* **2–4**

§ 11. *Power* being the Source from whence all Action proceeds, the Substances wherein these Powers are, when they exert this Power into Act, are called *Causes*; and the Substances which thereupon are produced, or the simple *Ideas* which are introduced into any subject by the exerting of that Power, are called *Effects*. The *efficacy* whereby the new Substance or *Idea* is produced, is called, in the subject exerting that Power, *Action*; but in the subject, wherein any simple *Idea* is changed or produced, it is called *Passion*: Which efficacy however various, and the effects almost infinite; yet we can, I think, conceive it, in intellectual Agents, to be nothing else but Modes of Thinking, and Willing; in corporeal Agents, nothing else but Modifications of Motion. I say, I think we cannot conceive it to be any other but these two: For whatever sort of Action, besides these, produces any effects, I confess my self to have no Notion, nor *Idea* of; and so it is quite remote from my Thoughts, Apprehensions, and Knowledge; and as much in the dark to me as five other Senses, or as the *Ideas* of Colours to a blind Man: And therefore *many words, which seem to express some Action*, signify nothing of the Action, or *Modus Operandi* at all, *but* barely *the effect*, with some circumstances of the Subject wrought on, or Cause operating; *v.g.* Creation, Annihilation, contain in them no *Idea* of the Action or Manner, whereby they are produced, but barely of the Cause, and the thing done. And when a Country-man says, the Cold freezes Water, though the word Freezing seems to import some *Action*, yet truly it signifies nothing, but the effect, *viz.* that Water, that was before fluid, is become hard and consistent, without containing any *Idea* of the Action whereby it is done.

§ 12. I think I shall not need to remark here, that though Power and Action make the greatest part of mixed Modes, marked by Names, and familiar in the Minds and Mouths of Men; yet other simple *Ideas*, and their several Combinations, are *not* excluded; much less, I think, will it be *necessary* for me *to enumerate all the mixed Modes*, which have been settled, with Names to them. That would be to make a Dictionary of the greatest part of the Words made use of in Divinity, Ethicks, Law, and Politicks, and several other Sciences. All, that is requisite to my present design, is to shew, what sort of

§ 11. *Several Words seeming to signify Action, signify but the Effect.* § 12. *Mixed Modes, made also of other* Ideas.

(10–11) it, . . . Willing;] **1er–5** | it . . . Willing, **1** (15) it is] **2er, 4–5** | it is they are **3** | they are **1–2** (16) [*2nd*] and] **2er–5** | and are **1–2** (17) as] *add.* **4–5** (20) Cause] **1–3, 5** | cause **4** (24) seems] **4–5** | seem **1–3**

Ideas those are which I call *Mixed Modes*; how the Mind comes by them; and that they are Compositions, made up of simple *Ideas* got from Sensation and Reflection, which, I suppose, I have done.

CHAPTER XXIII

Of our Complex Ideas *of Substances.*

§ 1. THE Mind being, as I have declared, furnished with a great number of the simple *Ideas*, conveyed in by the *Senses*, as they are found in exteriour things, or by *Reflection* on its own Operations, takes notice also, that a certain number of these simple *Ideas* go constantly together; which being presumed to belong to one thing, and Words being suited to common apprehensions, and made use of for quick dispatch, are called so united in one subject, by one name; which by inadvertency we are apt afterward to talk of and consider as one simple *Idea*, which indeed is a complication of many *Ideas* together; Because, as I have said, not imagining how these simple *Ideas* can subsist by themselves, we accustom our selves, to suppose some *Substratum*, wherein they do subsist, and from which they do result, which therefore we call *Substance*.

§ 2. So that if any one will examine himself concerning his *Notion of pure Substance in general*, he will find he has no other *Idea* of it at all, but only a Supposition of he knows not what support of such Qualities, which are capable of producing simple *Ideas* in us; which Qualities are commonly called Accidents. If any one should be asked, what is the subject wherein Colour or Weight inheres, he would have nothing to say, but the solid extended parts: And if he were demanded, what is it, that that Solidity and Extension

§ 1. Ideas *of Substances how made.* § 2. *Our* Idea *of Substance in general.*

---

(1) are which] **4–5** | are, **1–3** (12) simple] **1T.er, 2–5** | single **1** (13) together;] **4** | together: **1–3, 5** (16) **5** *adds, in a footnote, quotations from the Bishop of Worcester's* Discourse in Vindication of the Trinity, *p. 236, and Locke's* Letter to the Bishop of Worcester, *pp. 27, etc.*; *prefaced by* 'This Section, which was intended only to shew how the Individuals of distinct Species of Substances came to be look'd upon as simple *Ideas*, and so to have simple Names, *viz.* from the supposed simple *Substratum* or *Substance*, which was look'd upon as the thing it self in which inhere, and from which resulted that Complication of *Ideas* by which it was represented to us, hath been mistaken for an Account of the *Idea* of Substance in general; and as such hath been reprehended in these Words: . . . To which Objection of the Bishop of *Worcester*, our Author answers thus:' (21) . If] **4–5** | : And if **1–3**

inhere in, he would not be in a much better case, than the *Indian* before mentioned; who, saying that the World was supported by a great Elephant, was asked, what the Elephant rested on; to which his answer was, a great Tortoise: But being again pressed to know what gave support to the broad-back'd Tortoise, replied, something, he knew not what. And thus here, as in all other cases, where we use Words without having clear and distinct *Ideas*, we talk like Children; who, being questioned, what such a thing is, which they know not, readily give this satisfactory answer, That it is *something*; which in truth signifies no more, when so used, either by Children or Men, but that they know not what; and that the thing they pretend to know, and talk of, is what they have no distinct *Idea* of at all, and so are perfectly ignorant of it, and in the dark. The *Idea* then we have, to which we give the general name Substance, being nothing, but the supposed, but unknown support of those Qualities, we find existing, which we imagine cannot subsist, *sine re substante*, without something to support them, we call that Support *Substantia*; which, according to the true import of the Word, is in plain *English*, *standing under*, or *upholding*.

§ 3. An obscure and relative *Idea* of Substance in general being thus made, we come to have the *Ideas of particular sorts of Substances*, by collecting such Combinations of simple *Ideas*, as are by Experience and Observation of Men's Senses taken notice of to exist together, and are therefore supposed to flow from the particular internal Constitution, or unknown Essence of that Substance. Thus we come to have the *Ideas* of a Man, Horse, Gold, Water, *etc.* of which Substances, whether any one has any other clear *Idea*, farther than of certain simple *Ideas* coexisting together, I appeal to every one's own Experience. 'Tis the ordinary Qualities, observable in Iron, or a Diamond, put together, that make the true complex *Idea* of those Substances, which a Smith, or a Jeweller, commonly knows better

§ 3. *Of the sorts of Substances.*

---

(2) mentioned] **Coste** *adds marginal reference to II. xiii. 19.* (4) was, a] **5** | was a **4** | was, A **1–3** (9) it is *something*] **4–5** | it is something **1er**, **2–3** | is something **1** (11) know] **2–5** | knew **1** (19) **5** *adds, in a footnote, quotations from Locke's* Letter to the Bishop of Worcester, *pp. 6, etc., and his* Third Letter to the Bishop of Worcester, *p. 381*; *prefaced by* 'From this Paragraph, there hath been raised an Objection by the Bishop of *Worcester*, as if our Author's Doctrine here concerning *Ideas*, *had almost discarded Substance out of the World*. His Words in this second Paragraph being brought to prove, that he is one of the *Gentlemen of this new way of Reasoning, that have almost discarded Substance out of the reasonable part of the World*. **To which our Author replies:'**

than a Philosopher; who, whatever substantial forms he may talk of, has no other *Idea* of those Substances, than what is framed by a collection of those simple *Ideas* which are to be found in them; only we must take notice, that our complex *Ideas* of Substances, besides all these simple *Ideas* they are made up of, have always the confused *Idea* of *something* to which they belong, and in which they subsist: and therefore when we speak of any sort of Substance, we say it is a *thing* having such or such Qualities, as Body is a *thing* that is extended, figured, and capable of Motion; a Spirit a *thing* capable of thinking; and so Hardness, Friability, and Power to draw Iron, we say, are Qualities to be found in a Loadstone. These, and the like fashions of speaking intimate, that the Substance is supposed always *something* besides the Extension, Figure, Solidity, Motion, Thinking, or other observable *Ideas*, though we know not what it is.

§ 4. Hence when we talk or think of any particular sort of corporeal Substances, as *Horse*, *Stone*, *etc.* though the *Idea*, we have of either of them, be but the Complication, or Collection of those several simple *Ideas* of sensible Qualities, which we use to find united in the thing called *Horse* or *Stone*, yet because we cannot conceive, how they should subsist alone, nor one in another, we suppose them existing in, and supported by some common subject; *which Support we denote by the name Substance*, though it be certain, we have no clear, or distinct *Idea* of that *thing* we suppose a Support.

§ 5. The same happens concerning the Operations of the Mind, *viz.* Thinking, Reasoning, Fearing, *etc.* which we concluding not to subsist of themselves, nor apprehending how they can belong to Body, or be produced by it, we are apt to think these the Actions of some other *Substance*, which we call *Spirit*; whereby yet it is evident, that having no other *Idea* or Notion, of Matter, but *something* wherein those many sensible Qualities, which affect our Senses, do subsist; by supposing a Substance, wherein *Thinking*, *Knowing*, *Doubting*, and a power of Moving, *etc.* do subsist, *We have as clear a Notion of the Substance of Spirit, as we have of Body*; the one being supposed to be (without knowing what it is) the *Substratum* to those simple *Ideas* we have from without; and the other supposed (with a like ignorance of what it is) to be the *Substratum* to those

§ 4. *No clear* Idea *of Substance in general.* § 5. *As clear an* Idea *of Spirit, as Body.*

---

(3) which] *add.* **4–5** (21) existing] **2–5** | to exist **1** (33) *Substance*] **4–5** | *Nature, or Substance* **1–3**

Operations, which we experiment in our selves within. 'Tis plain then, that the *Idea* of corporeal *Substance* in Matter is as remote from our Conceptions, and Apprehensions, as that of Spiritual *Substance*, or *Spirit*; and therefore from our not having any notion of the *Substance* of Spirit, we can no more conclude its non-Existence, than we can, for the same reason, deny the Existence of Body: It being as rational to affirm, there is no Body, because we have no clear and distinct *Idea* of the *Substance* of Matter; as to say, there is no Spirit, because we have no clear and distinct *Idea* of the *Substance* of a Spirit.

§ 6. Whatever therefore be the secret and abstract Nature of *Substance* in general, all *the* Ideas *we have of particular distinct sorts of Substances*, are nothing but several Combinations of simple *Ideas*, co-existing in such, though unknown, Cause of their Union, as makes the whole subsist of itself. 'Tis by such Combinations of simple *Ideas* and nothing else, that we represent particular sorts of *Substances* to our selves; such are the *Ideas* we have of their several species in our Minds; and such only do we, by their specifick Names, signify to others, *v.g. Man*, *Horse*, *Sun*, *Water*, *Iron*, upon hearing which Words, every one who understands the Language, frames in his Mind a Combination of those several simple *Ideas*, which he has usually observed, or fancied to exist together under that denomination; all which he supposes to rest in, and be, as it were, adherent to that unknown common Subject, which inheres not in any thing else. Though in the mean time it be manifest, and every one upon Enquiry into his own thoughts, will find that he has no other *Idea* of any *Substance*, *v.g.* let it be *Gold*, *Horse*, *Iron*, *Man*, *Vitriol*, *Bread*, but what he has barely of those sensible Qualities, which he supposes to inhere, with a supposition of such a *Substratum*, as gives as it were a support to those Qualities, or simple *Ideas*, which he has observed to exist united together. Thus the *Idea* of the *Sun*, What is it, but an aggregate of those several simple *Ideas*, Bright, Hot, Roundish, having a constant regular motion, at a

§ 6. *Of the sorts of Substances.*

(7–8) have . . . distinct] **4–5** ('clear and distinct' *not in* **Coste**) | cannot know its Essence, as 'tis called, or have no **1–3** (9–10) have . . . Spirit] **4–5** ('clear and distinct' *not in* **Coste**) | know not its Essence, or have no *Idea* of a Spiritual Substance **1–3** (11) secret and] *not in* **Coste** (12) *sorts of*] *add.* **4–5** (16–17) sorts of *Substances*] **4–5** | Substances **1–3** (18) species] **4–5** | sorts **1–3** (29) inhere,] **2–5** | inhere **1** (32) the *Sun*] **4–5** | the Sun **1T.er, 2–3** | Sun **1** those] **4–5** | these **1–3**

certain distance from us, and, perhaps, some other: as he who thinks and discourses of the *Sun*, has been more or less accurate, in observing those sensible Qualities, *Ideas*, or Properties, which are in that thing, which he calls the *Sun*.

§ 7. For he has the perfectest *Idea* of any of the particular sorts of *Substance*, who has gathered, and put together, most of those simple *Ideas*, which do exist in it, among which are to be reckoned its active Powers, and passive Capacities; which though not simple *Ideas*, yet, in this respect, for brevity's sake, may conveniently enough be reckoned amongst them. Thus the power of drawing Iron, is one of the *Ideas* of the Complex one of that substance we call a *Load-stone*, and a Power to be so drawn is a part of the Complex one we call *Iron*; which Powers pass for inherent Qualities in those Subjects. Because every *Substance* being as apt, by the Powers we observe in it, to change some sensible Qualities in other Subjects, as it is to produce in us those simple *Ideas*, which we receive immediately from it, does, by those new sensible Qualities introduced into other Subjects, discover to us those Powers, which do thereby mediately affect our Senses, as regularly, as its sensible Qualities do it immediately, *v.g.* we immediately by our Senses perceive in *Fire* its Heat and Colour; which are, if rightly considered, nothing but Powers in it, to produce those *Ideas* in us: We also by our Senses perceive the colour and brittleness of *Charcoal*, whereby we come by the Knowledge of another Power in Fire, which it has to change the colour and consistency of Wood. By the former Fire immediately, by the latter it mediately discovers to us these several Powers, which therefore we look upon to be a part of the Qualities of Fire, and so make them a part of the complex *Ideas* of it. For all those Powers, that we take Cognizance of, terminating only in the alteration of some sensible Qualities, in those Subjects, on which they operate, and so making them exhibit to us new sensible *Ideas*, therefore it is, that I have reckoned these Powers amongst the simple *Ideas*, which make the complex ones of the sorts of *Substances*; though these Powers, considered in themselves, are truly complex *Ideas*. And in this looser sence, I crave leave to be understood, when I

§ 7. *Powers a great part of our complex* Ideas *of Substances.*

---

(4) *Sun.*] **4–5** | Sun. **1–3** | Sun? **1T.er** (5–6) [*2nd*] of . . . *Substance*] **4–5** | particular Substance **1–3** (8) not] **4–5** | not strictly **1–3** (16) which] *add.* **4–5** (26) latter] **2–5** | later **1** (*l. below* 35) *Powers*] **2–4** | *Power* **5**

name any of these *Potentialities amongst the simple Ideas*, which we recollect in our Minds, when we think *of particular Substances*. For the Powers that are severally in them, are necessary to be considered, if we will have true distinct Notions of the several sorts of Substances.

§ 8. Nor are we to wonder, that *Powers make a great part of our complex* Ideas *of Substances*; since their secondary Qualities are those, which in most of them serve principally to distinguish Substances one from another, and commonly make a considerable part of the complex *Idea* of the several sorts of them. For our Senses failing us, in the discovery of the Bulk, Texture, and Figure of the minute parts of Bodies, on which their real Constitutions and Differences depend, we are fain to make use of their secondary Qualities, as the characteristical Notes and Marks, whereby to frame *Ideas* of them in our Minds, and distinguish them one from another. All which secondary Qualities, as has been shewn, are nothing but bare Powers. For the Colour and Taste of *Opium*, are, as well as its soporifick or anodyne Virtues, meer Powers depending on its primary Qualities, whereby it is fitted to produce different Operations, on different parts of our Bodies.

§ 9. *The* Ideas *that make our complex ones of corporeal Substances*, are of these three sorts. *First*, The *Ideas* of the primary Qualities of things, which are discovered by our Senses, and are in them even when we perceive them not, such are the Bulk, Figure, Number, Situation, and Motion of the parts of Bodies, which are really in them, whether we take notice of them or no. *Secondly*, The sensible secondary Qualities, which depending on these, are nothing but the Powers, those Substances have to produce several *Ideas* in us by our Senses; which *Ideas* are not in the things themselves, otherwise than as any thing is in its Cause. *Thirdly*, The aptness we consider in any Substance, to give or receive such alterations of primary Qualities, as that the Substance so altered, should produce in us different *Ideas* from what it did before, these are called active and passive Powers: All which Powers, as far as we have any Notice or Notion of them, terminate only in sensible simple *Ideas*. For whatever

§ 8. *And why.* § 9. *Three sorts of* Ideas *make our complex ones of Substances.*

(4) the several sorts of] *add.* **4–5**. (*Not in* **Coste**) (7) Qualities] **Coste** *adds marginal reference to II. viii.* (12) parts] **1–2, 4–5** | part **3** (16) shewn] **Coste** *adds marginal reference to II. viii. 13.* (21) '§ 9.' *add.* **2–5** (26) take notice of] **4–5** | perceive **1–3** (*likewise* **Coste**)

alteration a *Load-stone* has the Power to make in the minute Particles of Iron, we should have no Notion of any Power it had at all to operate on Iron, did not its sensible Motion discover it; and I doubt not, but there are a thousand Changes, that Bodies we daily handle, have a Power to cause in one another, which we never suspect, because they never appear in sensible effects.

§ 10. *Powers* therefore, justly *make a great part of our complex* Ideas *of Substances.* He, that will examine his complex *Idea* of Gold, will find several of its *Ideas*, that make it up, to be only Powers, as the Power of being melted, but of not spending it self in the Fire; of being dissolved in *Aqua Regia*, are *Ideas*, as necessary to make up our complex *Idea* of Gold, as its Colour and Weight: which if duly considered, are also nothing but different Powers. For to speak truly, Yellowness is not actually in Gold; but is a Power in Gold, to produce that *Idea* in us by our Eyes, when placed in a due Light: and the Heat, which we cannot leave out of our *Idea* of the Sun, is no more really in the Sun, than the white Colour it introduces into Wax. These are both equally Powers in the Sun, operating, by the Motion and Figure of its insensible Parts, so on a Man, as to make him have the *Idea* of Heat; and so on Wax, as to make it capable to produce in a Man the *Idea* of White.

§ 11. Had we Senses acute enough to discern the minute particles of Bodies, and the real Constitution on which their sensible Qualities depend, I doubt not but they would produce quite different *Ideas* in us; and that which is now the yellow Colour of Gold, would then disappear, and instead of it we should see an admirable Texture of parts of a certain Size and Figure. This Microscopes plainly discover to us: for what to our naked Eyes produces a certain Colour, is by thus augmenting the acuteness of our Senses, discovered to be quite a different thing; and the thus altering, as it were, the proportion of the Bulk of the minute parts of a coloured Object to our usual Sight, produces different *Ideas*, from what it did before. Thus Sand, or pounded Glass, which is opaque,

§ 10. *Powers make a great part of our complex* Ideas *of Substances.* § 11. *The now secondary Qualities of Bodies would disappear, if we could discover the primary ones of their minute Parts.*

---

(3) it;] **1–3, 5** | it, **4** (10) not spending it self] **4–5** | keeping its weight **1–3** (17) into] **2–5** | in **1** (19) Parts,] **2–3, 5** | Parts **4** | Parts; **1** (*l. below* 33: § 10.) **4–5**. *In* **2–3**, *the marginal summary for* § *10 is the same as that for* § *11 in* **4–5**, *whereas in* **Coste** § *10 comes under the same marginal summary as that for* § *9.*

and white to the naked Eye, is pellucid in a Microscope; and a Hair seen this way, loses its former Colour, and is in a great measure pellucid, with a mixture of some bright sparkling Colours, such as appear from the refraction of Diamonds, and other pellucid Bodies. Blood to the naked Eye appears all red; but by a good Microscope, wherein its lesser parts appear, shews only some few Globules of Red, swimming in a pellucid Liquor; and how these red Globules would appear, if Glasses could be found, that yet could magnify them 1000, or 10000 times more, is uncertain.

§ 12. The infinite wise Contriver of us, and all things about us, hath fitted our Senses, Faculties, and Organs, to the conveniences of Life, and the Business we have to do here. We are able, by our Senses, to know, and distinguish things; and to examine them so far, as to apply them to our Uses, and several ways to accommodate the Exigences of this Life. We have insight enough into their admirable Contrivances, and wonderful Effects, to admire, and magnify the Wisdom, Power, and Goodness of their Author. Such a Knowledge as this, which is suited to our present Condition, we want not Faculties to attain. But it appears not, that God intended, we should have a perfect, clear, and adequate Knowledge of them: that perhaps is not in the Comprehension of any finite Being. We are furnished with Faculties (dull and weak as they are) to discover enough in the Creatures, to lead us to the Knowledge of the Creator, and the Knowledge of our Duty; and we are fitted well enough with Abilities, to provide for the Conveniences of living: These are our Business in this World. But were our Senses alter'd, and made much quicker and acuter, the appearance and outward Scheme of things would have quite another Face to us; and I am apt to think, would be inconsistent with our Being, or at least well-being in this part of the Universe, which we inhabit. He that considers, how little our Constitution is able to bear a remove into parts of this Air, not much higher than that we commonly breath in, will have reason to be satisfied, that in this Globe of Earth allotted for our Mansion, the all-wise Architect has suited our Organs, and the Bodies, that are to affect them, one to another. If our Sense of Hearing were but 1000 times quicker than it is, how would a perpetual noise distract

§ 12. *Our Faculties of Discovery suited to our State.*

---

(4) appear] **1–2, 4–5** | appears **3** (10) infinite] **2–5** | infinitely **1** (14) [*3rd*] to] *add.* **4–5** (23) Creatures] **1–2, 4–5** | Creature **3** (*likewise* **Coste**) (30) , which] *add.* **4–5** (35) them,] **2–5** | them **1**

us. And we should in the quietest Retirement, be less able to sleep or meditate, than in the middle of a Sea-fight. Nay, if that most instructive of our Senses, Seeing, were in any Man 1000, or 100000 times more acute than it is now by the best Microscope, things several millions of times less than the smallest Object of his sight now, would then be visible to his naked Eyes, and so he would come nearer the Discovery of the Texture and Motion of the minute Parts of corporeal things; and in many of them, probably get *Ideas* of their internal Constitutions: But then he would be in a quite different World from other People: Nothing would appear the same to him, and others: The visible *Ideas* of every thing would be different. So that I doubt, Whether he, and the rest of Men, could discourse concerning the Objects of Sight; or have any Communication about Colours, their appearances being so wholly different. And, perhaps, such a quickness and tenderness of Sight could not endure bright Sun-shine, or so much as open Day-light; nor take in but a very small part of any Object at once, and that too only at a very near distance. And if by the help of such Microscopical Eyes, (if I may so call them,) a Man could penetrate farther than ordinary into the secret Composition, and radical Texture of Bodies, he would not make any great advantage by the change, if such an acute Sight would not serve to conduct him to the Market and Exchange; If he could not see things, he was to avoid, at a convenient distance; nor distinguish things he had to do with, by those sensible Qualities others do. He that was sharp-sighted enough to see the Configuration of the minute Particles of the Spring of a Clock, and observe upon what peculiar Structure and Impulse its elastick Motion depends, would no doubt discover something very admirable: But if Eyes so framed, could not view at once the Hand, and the Characters of the Hour-plate, and thereby at a distance see what a-Clock it was, their Owner could not be much benefited by that acuteness; which, whilst it discovered the secret contrivance of the Parts of the Machin, made him lose its use.

§ 13. And here give me leave to propose an extravagant conjecture of mine, *viz.* That since we have some Reason, (if there be any Credit to be given to the report of things, that our Philosophy

§ 13. *Conjecture about Spirits.*

(1) us.] **4–5** | us? **1–3** (4) times] *add.* **4–5**. (**Coste** 'dix mille fois') (5–6) things . . . [*2nd*] would] **4–5** | he would see things 1000 or 100000 less than he does now, and so **1–3** (23) , at] **1er–5** | at **1** (24) ; nor] **1–4** | , nor **5**

cannot account for,) to imagine, that Spirits can assume to themselves Bodies of different Bulk, Figure, and Conformation of Parts. Whether one great advantage some of them have over us, may not lie in this, that they can so frame, and shape to themselves Organs of Sensation or Perception, as to suit them to their present Design, and the Circumstances of the Object they would consider. For how much would that Man exceed all others in Knowledge, who had but the Faculty so to alter the Structure of his Eyes, that one Sense, as to make it capable of all the several degrees of Vision, which the assistance of Glasses (casually at first light on) has taught us to conceive? What wonders would he discover, who could so fit his Eye to all sorts of Objects, as to see, when he pleased, the Figure and Motion of the minute Particles in the Blood, and other juices of Animals, as distinctly, as he does, at other times, the shape and motion of the Animals themselves. But to us in our present State, unalterable Organs, so contrived, as to discover the Figure and Motion of the minute parts of Bodies, whereon depend those sensible Qualities, we now observe in them, would, perhaps, be of no advantage. God has no doubt made us so, as is best for us in our present Condition. He hath fitted us for the Neighbourhood of the Bodies, that surround us, and we have to do with: And though we cannot by the Faculties we have, attain to a perfect Knowledge of Things; yet they will serve us well enough for those ends abovementioned, which are our great Concernment. I beg my Reader's Pardon, for laying before him so wild a Fancy, concerning the ways of Perception in Beings above us: But how extravagant soever it be, I doubt whether we can imagine any thing about the Knowledge of Angels, but after this manner, some way or other, in proportion to what we find and observe in our selves. And though we cannot but allow, that the infinite Power and Wisdom of God, may frame Creatures with a thousand other Faculties, and ways of perceiving things without them, than what we have: Yet our Thoughts can go no farther than our own, so impossible it is for us to enlarge our very Guesses, beyond the *Ideas* received from our own Sensation and Reflection. The Supposition at least, that Angels do sometimes assume Bodies, needs not startle us, since some of the most ancient, and most learned Fathers of the Church, seemed to believe, that they had Bodies: And this is certain, that their state and way of Existence is unknown to us.

(26) Perception] **1er–5** | Conception **1** (36) needs] **4–5** | need **1–3**

§ 14. But to return to the Matter in hand, the *Ideas* we have of Substances, and the ways we come by them; I say *our specifick* Ideas *of Substances* are nothing else but *a Collection of a certain number of simple* Ideas, *considered as united in one thing*. These *Ideas* of Substances, though they are commonly called simple Apprehensions, and the Names of them simple Terms; yet in effect, are complex and compounded. Thus the *Idea* which an *English*-man signifies by the Name *Swan* is white Colour, long Neck, red Beak, black Legs, and whole Feet, and all these of a certain size, with a power of swimming in the Water, and making a certain kind of Noise, and, perhaps, to a Man, who has long observed those kind of Birds, some other Properties, which all terminate in sensible simple *Ideas*, all united in one common subject.

§ 15. Besides the complex *Ideas* we have of material sensible Substances, of which I have last spoken, by the simple *Ideas* we have taken from those Operations of our own Minds, which we experiment daily in our selves, as Thinking, Understanding, Willing, Knowing, and Power of beginning Motion, *etc.* co-existing in some Substance, we are able to frame *the complex* Idea *of an immaterial Spirit*. And thus by putting together the *Ideas* of Thinking, Perceiving, Liberty, and Power of moving themselves and other things, we have as clear a perception, and notion of immaterial Substances, as we have of material. For putting together the *Ideas* of Thinking and Willing, or the Power of moving or quieting corporeal Motion, joined to Substance, of which we have no distinct *Idea*, we have the *Idea* of an immaterial Spirit; and by putting together the *Ideas* of coherent solid parts, and a power of being moved, joined with Substance, of which likewise we have no positive *Idea*, we have the *Idea* of Matter. The one is as clear and distinct an *Idea*, as the other: The *Idea* of Thinking, and moving a Body, being as clear and distinct *Ideas*, as the *Ideas* of Extension, Solidity, and being moved. For our *Idea* of Substance, is equally obscure, or none at all, in both; it is but a supposed, I know not what, to support those *Ideas*, we call Accidents. It is for want of reflection, that we are apt to think, that

§ 14. *Complex* Ideas *of Substances.* § 15. Idea *of spiritual Substances, as clear as of bodily Substances.*

---

(2) *specifick*] *add.* **4–5** (7) signifies] **2–5** | signified **1** (12–13) , all . . . subject] *add.* **4–5** (16) which] *add.* **2–5** (19) *an immaterial*] **4–5** | *a* **1–3** (26) an immaterial] *add.* **4–5** (34)–306(8) It . . . Being.] *add.* **4–5**

our Senses shew us nothing but material things. Every act of sensation, when duly considered, gives us an equal view of both parts of nature, the Corporeal and Spiritual. For whilst I know, by seeing or hearing, *etc.* that there is some Corporeal Being without me, the Object of that sensation, I do more certainly know, that there is some Spiritual Being within me, that sees and hears. This I must be convinced cannot be the action of bare insensible matter; nor ever could be without an immaterial thinking Being.

§ 16. By the complex *Idea* of extended, figured, coloured, and all other sensible Qualities, which is all that we know of it, we are as far from the *Idea* of the Substance of Body, as if we knew nothing at all: *Nor* after all the acquaintance and familiarity, which we imagine we *have* with Matter, and the many Qualities *Men* assure themselves they perceive and know in Bodies, will it, perhaps, upon examination be found, that they have any *more, or clearer, primary* Ideas *belonging to Body, than they have belonging to immaterial Spirit.*

§ 17. *The primary* Ideas *we have peculiar to Body*, as contradistinguished to Spirit, *are the cohesion of solid*, and consequently separable *parts, and a power of communicating Motion by impulse.* These, I think, are the original *Ideas* proper and peculiar to Body: for Figure is but the consequence of finite Extension.

§ 18. *The* Ideas *we have* belonging, and *peculiar to Spirit, are Thinking, and Will*, or a power of putting Body into motion by Thought, and, which is consequent to it, Liberty. For as Body cannot but communicate its Motion by impulse, to another Body, which it meets with at rest; so the Mind can put Bodies into Motion, or forbear to do so, as it pleases. The *Ideas* of Existence, Duration, and Mobility, are common to them both.

§ 19. There is no reason why it should be thought strange, that I make *Mobility belong to Spirit*: For having no other *Idea* of Motion, but change of distance, with other Beings, that are considered as at rest; and finding that Spirits, as well as Bodies, cannot operate, but where they are; and that Spirits do operate at several times in several places, I cannot but attribute change of place to all finite Spirits: (for of the infinite Spirit, I speak not here.) For my Soul being a real Being, as well as my Body, is certainly as capable of

§ 16. *No* Idea *of abstract Substance.* § 17. *The Cohesion of solid Parts, and impulse, the primary* Ideas *of Body.* § 18. *Thinking and Motivity, the primary* Ideas *of Spirit.* §§ 19–21. *Spirits capable of Motion.*

(8) *v.* 305(34), n. (16) *immaterial*] *add.* **4–5** (33) in] **2–5** |, at **1**

changing distance with any other Body, or Being, as Body it self; and so is capable of Motion. And if a Mathematician can consider a certain distance, or a change of that distance between two Points; one may certainly conceive a distance, and a change of distance between two Spirits; and so conceive their Motion, their approach, or removal, one from another.

§ 20. Every one finds in himself, that his Soul can think, will, and operate on his Body, in the place where that is; but cannot operate on a Body, or in a place, an hundred Miles distant from it. No Body can imagine, that his Soul can think, or move a Body at *Oxford*, whilst he is at *London*; and cannot but know, that being united to his Body, it constantly changes place all the whole Journey, between *Oxford* and *London*, as the Coach, or Horse does, that carries him; and, I think, may be said to be truly all that while in motion: Or if that will not be allowed to afford us a clear *Idea* enough of its motion, its being separated from the Body in death, I think, will: For to consider it as going out of the Body, or leaving it, and yet to have no *Idea* of its motion, seems to me impossible.

§ 21. If it be said by any one, that it cannot change place, because it hath none, for Spirits are not *in Loco*, but *Ubi*; I suppose that way of talking, will not now be of much weight to many, in an Age, that is not much disposed to admire, or suffer themselves to be deceived, by such unintelligible ways of speaking. But if any one thinks there is any sense in that distinction, and that it is applicable to our present purpose, I desire him to put it into intelligible *English*; and then from thence draw a reason to shew that immaterial Spirits are not capable of Motion. Indeed, Motion cannot be attributed to GOD, not because he is an immaterial, but because he is an Infinite Spirit.

§ 22. Let us *compare* then our complex *Idea* of an immaterial Spirit, with our complex *Idea* of Body, and see whether there be any more obscurity in one, than in the other, and in which most. Our *Idea* of Body, as I think, is an extended solid Substance, capable of communicating Motion by impulse: and our *Idea* of our Soul, as an

§ 22. Idea *of Soul and Body compared.*

---

(1) distance] **2–5** | of distance **1** (9) [*2nd*] a] *add.* **2–5** (17) as . . . leaving] **2–5** | , to go out of the Body, or leave **1** (20) *in*] **1–3** | in **4–5** (20) *in . . . Ubi*] **Coste** *adds a linguistic note on these Latin expressions.* (24) that it is] *add.* **4–5** (25) *English*] **5** | English **1–4** (26) immaterial] *add.* **4–5** (27) Indeed,] **1–3** | Indeed **4–5** attributed] **1–4** | attribute **5** (28) an immaterial] **4–5** | a Spirit **1–3** (29) an immaterial] *add.* **4–5**. (*Not in* **Coste**) (33)–308(1) Soul . . . Spirit,] **4–5** | Souls, **1–3**

immaterial Spirit, is of a Substance that thinks, and has a power of exciting Motion in Body, by Will, or Thought. These, I think, are *our complex* Ideas *of Soul and Body, as contra-distinguished*; and now let us examine which has most obscurity in it, and difficulty to be apprehended. I know that People, whose Thoughts are immersed in Matter, and have so subjected their Minds to their Senses, that they seldom reflect on any thing beyond them, are apt to say, they cannot comprehend a thinking thing, which, perhaps, is true: But I affirm, when they consider it well, they can no more comprehend an extended thing.

§ 23. If any one says, he knows not what 'tis thinks in him; he means he knows not what the substance is of that thinking thing: No more, say I, knows he what the substance is of that solid thing. Farther, if he says he knows not how he thinks; I answer, Neither knows he how he is extended; how the solid parts of Body are united, or cohere together to make Extension. For though the pressure of the Particles of Air, may account for the *cohesion of several parts of Matter*, that are grosser than the Particles of Air, and have Pores less than the Corpuscles of Air; yet the weight, or pressure of the Air, will not explain, nor can be a cause of the coherence of the Particles of Air themselves. And if the pressure of the Æther, or any subtiler Matter than the Air, may unite, and hold fast together the parts of a Particle of Air, as well as other Bodies; yet it cannot make Bonds for it self, and hold together the parts, that make up every the least corpuscle of that *materia subtilis*. So that that Hypothesis, how ingeniously soever explained, by shewing, that the parts of sensible Bodies are held together, by the pressure of other external insensible Bodies, reaches not the parts of the Æther it self; and by how much the more evident it proves, that the parts of other Bodies are held together, by the external pressure of the Æther, and can have no other conceivable cause of their cohesion and union, by so much the more it leaves us in the dark, concerning the cohesion of the parts of the Corpuscles of the Æther it self: which we can neither conceive without parts, they being Bodies, and divisible; nor yet how their parts cohere, they wanting that cause of cohesion, which is given of the cohesion of the parts of all other Bodies.

§§ 23–7. *Cohesion of solid parts in Body, as hard to be conceived as Thinking in a Soul.*

(1) *v.* 307(33), n.   (11) one says] **1–3** | ones say **4** | one say **5**

§ 24. But in truth, *the pressure of any ambient Fluid*, how great soever, *can be no* intelligible *cause of the cohesion of the solid parts of Matter*. For though such a pressure may hinder the avulsion of two polished Superficies, one from another in a Line perpendicular to them, as in the Experiment of two polished Marbles: Yet it can never, in the least, hinder the separation by a Motion, in a Line parallel to those Surfaces. Because the ambient fluid, having a full liberty to succeed in each point of Space, deserted by a lateral motion, resists such a motion of Bodies so joined, no more, than it would resist the motion of that Body, were it on all sides environed by that Fluid, and touched no other Body: And therefore, if there were no other cause of cohesion, all parts of Bodies must be easily separable by such a lateral sliding motion. For if the pressure of the Æther be the adequate cause of cohesion, where-ever that cause operates not, there can be no cohesion. And since it cannot operate against such a lateral separation, (as has been shewed,) therefore in every imaginary plain, intersecting any mass of Matter, there could be no more cohesion, than of two polished Surfaces, which will always, notwithstanding any imaginable pressure of a Fluid, easily slide one from another. So that, perhaps, how clear an *Idea* soever we think we have of the Extension of Body, which is nothing but the cohesion of solid parts, he that shall well consider it in his Mind, may have reason to conclude, That 'tis *as easie* for him *to have a clear* Idea, *how the Soul thinks*, *as how Body is extended*. For since Body is no farther, nor otherwise extended, than by the union and cohesion of its solid parts, we shall very ill comprehend the *extension* of Body, without understanding wherein consists the union and cohesion of its parts; which seems to me as incomprehensible, as the manner of Thinking, and how it is performed.

§ 25. I allow, it is usual for most People to wonder, how any one should find a difficulty in what they think, they every day observe. Do we not see, will they be ready to say, the parts of Bodies stick firmly together? Is there any thing more common? And what doubt can there be made of it? And the like, I say, concerning *Thinking*, and *voluntary Motion*: Do we not every moment experiment it in our selves; and therefore can it be doubted? The matter of Fact is clear, I confess; but when we would a little nearer look into it, and consider how it is done, there, I think, we are at a loss, both in the

(7) those Surfaces] **4–5** | those Superficies **2–3** | these Superficies **1** (18) Surfaces,] **4–5** | Superficies; **1–3** (20) another.] **4–5** | another: **1–3**

one, and the other; and can as little understand how the parts of Body cohere, as how we our selves perceive, or move. I would have any one intelligibly explain to me, how the parts of Gold, or Brass, (that but now in fusion were as loose from one another, as the Particles of Water, or the Sands of an Hour-glass,) come in a few moments to be so united, and adhere so strongly one to another, that the utmost force of Mens arms cannot separate them: A considering Man will, I suppose, be here at a loss, to satisfie his own, or another Man's Understanding.

§ 26. The little Bodies that compose that Fluid, we call *Water*, are so extremely small, that I have never heard of any one, who by a Microscope, (and yet I have heard of some, that have magnified to 10000; nay, to much above 100,000 times,) pretended to perceive their distinct Bulk, Figure, or Motion: And the Particles of *Water* are also so perfectly loose one from another, that the least force sensibly separates them. Nay, if we consider their perpetual motion, we must allow them to have no cohesion one with another; and yet let but a sharp cold come, and they unite, they consolidate, these little Atoms cohere, and are not, without great force, separable. He that could find the Bonds, that tie these heaps of loose little Bodies together so firmly; he that could make known the Cement, that makes them stick so fast one to another, would discover a great, and yet unknown Secret: And yet when that was done, would he be far enough from making the extension of Body (which is the cohesion of its solid parts) intelligible, till he could shew wherein consisted the union, or consolidation of the parts of those Bonds, or of that Cement, or of the least Particle of Matter that exists. Whereby it appears that this primary and supposed obvious Quality of Body, will be found, when examined, to be as incomprehensible, as any thing belonging to our Minds, and *a solid extended Substance, as hard to be conceived, as a thinking immaterial one*, whatever difficulties some would raise against it.

§ 27. For to extend our Thoughts a little farther, that pressure, which is brought to explain the cohesion of Bodies, is as unintelligible, as the cohesion it self. For if Matter be considered, as no doubt it is, finite, let any one send his Contemplation to the Extremities of the Universe, and there see what conceivable Hoops, what Bond he can imagine to hold this mass of Matter, in so close a

(31) *immaterial*] *add.* **4–5.** (*Not in* **Coste**) (37) the] *add.* **2–5** (38) imagine] **1–3, 5** | imagin 4

pressure together, from whence Steel has its firmness, and the parts of a Diamond their hardness and indissolubility. If Matter be finite, it must have its Extremes; and there must be something to hinder it from scattering asunder. If to avoid this difficulty, any one will throw himself into the Supposition and Abyss of infinite Matter, let him consider, what light he thereby brings to the *cohesion* of Body; and whether he be ever the nearer making it intelligible, by resolving it into a Supposition, the most absurd and most incomprehensible of all other: So far is our Extension of Body, (which is nothing but the cohesion of solid parts,) from being clearer, or more distinct, when we would enquire into the Nature, Cause, or Manner of it, than the *Idea* of Thinking.

§ 28. Another *Idea* we have of Body, is the power of *communication of Motion by impulse*; and of our Souls, the power of *exciting of Motion by Thought*. These *Ideas*, the one of Body, the other of our Minds, every days experience clearly furnishes us with: But if here again we enquire how this is done, we *are equally in the dark*. For in the communication of Motion by impulse, wherein as much Motion is lost to one Body, as is got to the other, which is the ordinariest case, we can have no other conception, but of the passing of Motion out of one Body into another; which, I think, is as obscure and unconceivable, as how our Minds move or stop our Bodies by Thought; which we every moment find they do. The increase of Motion by impulse, which is observed or believed sometimes to happen, is yet harder to be understood. We have by daily experience clear evidence of Motion produced both by impulse, and by thought; but the manner how, hardly comes within our comprehension; we are equally at a loss in both. So that however we consider Motion, and its communication either from Body or Spirit, *the* Idea *which belongs to Spirit, is at least as clear, as that, that belongs to Body*. And if we consider the active power of Moving, or, as I may call it, *Motivity*, it is much clearer in Spirit than Body; since two Bodies, placed by one another at rest, will never afford us the *Idea* of a power in the one to move the other, but by a borrowed motion: whereas the Mind, every day, affords us *Ideas* of an active power of moving of Bodies; and therefore it is worth our consideration, whether active power be not

§§ 28, 29. *Communication of Motion by Impulse, or by Thought, equally intelligible.*

(4) asunder] **1–3, 5** | a sunder **4** (29) from] **2–5** | in **1** (34) motion] **Coste** *adds marginal reference to II. xxi. 4.* (*l. below* 36) *intelligible*] **Coste** '*inintelligible*'

the proper attribute of Spirits, and passive power of Matter. Hence may be conjectured, that created Spirits are not totally separate from Matter, because they are both active and passive. Pure Spirit, *viz.* God, is only active; pure Matter is only passive; those Beings that are both active and passive we may judge to partake of both. But be that as it will, I think, we have as many, and as clear *Ideas* belonging to Spirit, as we have belonging to Body, the Substance of each being equally unknown to us; and the *Idea* of Thinking in Spirit, as clear as of Extension in Body; and the communication of Motion by Thought, which we attribute to Spirit, is as evident, as that by impulse, which we ascribe to Body. Constant Experience makes us sensible of both of these, though our narrow Understandings can comprehend neither. For when the Mind would look beyond those original *Ideas* we have from Sensation or Reflection, and penetrate into their Causes, and manner of production, we find still it discovers nothing but its own short-sightedness.

§ 29. To conclude, Sensation convinces us, that there are solid extended Substances; and Reflection, that there are thinking ones: Experience assures us of the Existence of such Beings; and that the one hath a power to move Body by impulse, the other by thought; this we cannot doubt of. Experience, I say, every moment furnishes us with the clear *Ideas*, both of the one, and the other. But beyond these *Ideas*, as received from their proper Sources, our Faculties will not reach. If we would enquire farther into their Nature, Causes, and Manner, we perceive not the Nature of Extension, clearer than we do of Thinking. If we would explain them any farther, one is as easie as the other; and there is no more difficulty, to conceive how a Substance we know not, should by thought set Body into motion, than how a Substance we know not, should by impulse set Body into motion. So that we are no more able to discover, wherein the *Ideas* belonging to Body consist, than those belonging to Spirit. From whence it seems probable to me, that the simple *Ideas* we receive from Sensation and Reflection, are the Boundaries of our Thoughts; beyond which, the Mind, whatever efforts it would make, is not able to advance one jot; nor can it make any discoveries, when it would prie into the Nature and hidden Causes of those *Ideas*.

§ 30. So that, in short, *the Idea* we have *of Spirit*, *compared with the*

§ 30. Ideas *of Body and Spirit compared.*

(1–5) Hence . . . both.] *add.* **4–5** (14) those] **4–5** | these **1–3**

Idea we have *of Body*, stands thus: The substance of Spirit is unknown to us; and so is the substance of Body, equally unknown to us: Two primary Qualities, or Properties of Body, *viz.* solid coherent parts, and impulse, we have distinct clear *Ideas* of: So likewise we know, and have distinct clear *Ideas* of two primary Qualities, or Properties of Spirit, *viz.* Thinking, and a power of Action; *i.e.* a power of beginning, or stopping several Thoughts or Motions. We have also the *Ideas* of several Qualities inherent in Bodies, and have the clear distinct *Ideas* of them: which Qualities, are but the various modifications of the Extension of cohering solid Parts, and their motion. We have likewise the *Ideas* of the several modes of Thinking, *viz.* Believing, Doubting, Intending, Fearing, Hoping; all which, are but the several modes of Thinking. We have also the *Ideas* of Willing, and Moving the Body consequent to it, and with the Body it self too; for, as has been shewed, Spirit is capable of Motion.

§ 31. Lastly, if this Notion of immaterial Spirit may have, perhaps, some difficulties in it, not easie to be explained, we have therefore no more reason to deny, or doubt the existence of such Spirits, than we have to deny, or doubt the existence of Body; because the notion of Body is cumbred with some difficulties very hard, and, perhaps, impossible to be explained, or understood by us. For I would fain have instanced any thing in our notion of Spirit more perplexed, or nearer a Contradiction, than the very notion of Body includes in it; the divisibility *in infinitum* of any finite Extension, involving us, whether we grant or deny it, in consequences impossible to be explicated, or made in our apprehensions consistent; Consequences that carry greater difficulty, and more apparent absurdity, than any thing can follow from the Notion of an immaterial knowing substance.

§ 32. Which we are not at all to wonder at, since we having but some few superficial *Ideas* of things, discovered to us only by the Senses from without, or by the Mind, reflecting on what it experiments in it self within, have no Knowledge beyond that, much less of the internal Constitution, and true Nature of things, being destitute of Faculties to attain it. And therefore experimenting and

§ 31. *The Notion of Spirit involves no more difficulty in it than that of Body.* § 32. *We know nothing beyond our simple* Ideas.

(3) , or] **1–3, 5** | or **4** (4) impulse,] **1–3, 5** | impulse **4** (6) [*2nd*] of] *add.* **1er-5** (15) shewed] **Coste** *adds marginal reference to* §§ *19–21 of this chapter.* (16) immaterial] *add.* **4–5.** (*Not in* **Coste**) (18) therefore] **4–5** | thereby **1–3** such] *add.* **4–5** (26–7) in our apprehensions] *add.* **3–5.**

discovering in our selves Knowledge, and the power of voluntary Motion, as certainly as we experiment, or discover in things without us, the cohesion and separation of solid Parts, which is the Extension and Motion of Bodies; *we have as much Reason to be satisfied with our Notion of immaterial Spirit, as with our Notion of Body; and the Existence of the one, as well as the other.* For it being no more a contradiction, that Thinking should exist, separate, and independent from Solidity; than it is a contradiction, that Solidity should exist, separate, and independent from Thinking, they being both but simple *Ideas*, independent one from another; and having as clear and distinct *Ideas* in us of Thinking, as of Solidity, I know not, why we may not as well allow a thinking thing without Solidity, *i.e. immaterial*, to exist; as a solid thing without Thinking, *i.e. Matter*, to exist; especially since it is no harder to conceive how Thinking should exist without Matter, than how Matter should think. For whensoever we would proceed beyond these simple *Ideas*, we have from Sensation and Reflection, and dive farther into the Nature of Things, we fall presently into Darkness and Obscurity, Perplexedness and Difficulties; and can discover nothing farther, but our own Blindness and Ignorance. But which ever of these complex *Ideas* be clearest, that of Body, or immaterial Spirit, this is evident, that the simple *Ideas* that make them up, are no other than what we have received from Sensation or Reflection; and so is it of all our other *Ideas* of Substances, even of God himself.

§ 33. For if we examine the *Idea* we have of the incomprehensible supreme Being, we shall find, that we come by it the same way; and that the complex *Ideas* we have both of God, and separate Spirits, are made up of the simple *Ideas* we receive from *Reflection*; *v.g.* having from what we experiment in our selves, got the *Ideas* of Existence and Duration; of Knowledge and Power; of Pleasure and Happiness; and of several other Qualities and Powers, which it is better to have, than to be without; when we would frame an *Idea* the most suitable we can to the supreme Being, we enlarge every one of these with our *Idea* of Infinity; and so putting them together, make our complex *Idea of God*. For that the Mind has such a power of enlarg-

§§ 33–5. Idea *of God.*

---

(5) *immaterial*] *add.* **4–5** (13) , to] **1–3** | to **4–5** (21) immaterial] *add.* **4–5**. (*Not in* **Coste**) (28) *Reflection*;] **1–3**, **5** | *Reflection*, **4** (34) Infinity] **Coste** *adds marginal reference to II. xvii.*

ing some of its *Ideas*, received from Sensation and Reflection, has been already shewed.

§ 34. If I find, that I know some few things, and some of them, or all, perhaps, imperfectly, I can frame an *Idea* of knowing twice as many; which I can double again, as often as I can add to Number, and thus enlarge my *Idea* of Knowledge, by extending its Comprehension to all things existing, or possible: The same also I can do of knowing them more perfectly; *i.e.* all their Qualities, Powers, Causes, Consequences, and Relations, *etc.* till all be perfectly known, that is in them, or can any way relate to them, and thus frame the *Idea* of infinite or boundless Knowledge: The same may also be done of Power, till we come to that we call infinite; and also of the Duration of Existence, without beginning or end; and so frame the *Idea* of an eternal Being: The Degrees or Extent, wherein we ascribe Existence, Power, Wisdom, and all other Perfection, (which we can have any *Ideas* of) to that Sovereign Being, which we call God, being all boundless and infinite, we frame the best *Idea* of him our Minds are capable of; all which is done, I say, by enlarging those simple *Ideas*, we have taken from the Operations of our own Minds, by Reflection; or by our Senses, from exterior things, to that vastness, to which Infinity can extend them.

§ 35. For it is Infinity, which, joined to our *Ideas* of Existence, Power, Knowledge, *etc.* makes that complex *Idea*, whereby we represent to our selves the best we can, the supreme Being. For though in his own Essence, (which certainly we do not know, not knowing the real Essence of a Peble, or a Fly, or of our own selves,) God be simple and uncompounded; yet, I think, I may say we have no other *Idea* of him, but a complex one of Existence, Knowledge, Power, Happiness, *etc.* infinite and eternal: which are all distinct *Ideas*, and some of them being relative, are again compounded of others; all which being, as has been shewn, originally got from *Sensation* and *Reflection*, go to make up the *Idea* or Notion we have of God.

§ 36. This farther is to be observed, that there is no *Idea* we attribute to God, bating Infinity, which is not also a part of our complex *Idea* of other Spirits. Because being capable of no other simple *Ideas*, belonging to any thing but Body, but those which by

§ 36. No Ideas *in our Complex one of Spirits, but those got from Sensation or Reflection.*

---

(2) Shewed] **Coste** *adds marginal reference to II. xi. 6 etc.* (14–18) Being: . . . of;] **1–4** | Being. . . . of: **5**

Reflection we receive from the Operation of our own Minds, we can attribute to Spirits no other, but what we receive from thence: And all the difference we can put between them in our Contemplation of Spirits, is only in the several Extents and Degrees of their Knowledge, Power, Duration, Happiness, *etc.* For that in our *Ideas*, as well *of Spirits*, as of other things, we are *restrained to those we receive from Sensation and Reflection*, is evident from hence, that in our *Ideas* of Spirits, how much soever advanced in Perfection, beyond those of Bodies, even to that of Infinite, we cannot yet have any *Idea* of the manner, wherein they discover their Thoughts one to another: Though we must necessarily conclude, that separate Spirits, which are Beings that have perfecter Knowledge, and greater Happiness than we, must needs have also a perfecter way of communicating their Thoughts, than we have, who are fain to make use of corporeal Signs, and particularly Sounds, which are therefore of most general use, as being the best, and quickest we are capable of. But of immediate Communication, having no Experiment in our selves, and consequently, no Notion of it at all, we have no *Idea*, how Spirits, which use not Words, can with quickness; or much less, how Spirits that have no Bodies, can be Masters of their own Thoughts, and communicate or conceal them at Pleasure, though we cannot but necessarily suppose they have such a Power.

§ 37. And thus we have seen, *what kind of* Ideas *we have of Substances of all kinds*, wherein they consist, and how we come by them. From whence, I think, it is very evident.

First, That all our *Ideas* of the several sorts of Substances, are nothing but Collections of simple *Ideas*, with a Supposition of something, to which they belong, and in which they subsist; though of this supposed something, we have no clear distinct *Idea* at all.

Secondly, That all the simple *Ideas*, that thus united in one common *Substratum* make up our complex *Ideas* of the several sorts of Substances, are no other but such, as we have received from *Sensation* or *Reflection*. So that even in those, which we think, we are

§ 37. *Recapitulation.*

(11) separate] *add.* **4–5** (15) particularly] **1–3** (*likewise* **Coste**) | particular **4–5** (30–2) simple . . . other] **4–5** | complex *Ideas* we have of Substances, are made up of no other simple *Ideas*, **1–3** (31–2) the several sorts of Substances] *edit.* | several sorts of the Substances **4–5.** (**Coste** 'les *Idées complexes* que nous avons de différentes sortes de substances')

most intimately acquainted with, and come nearest the Comprehension of, our most enlarged Conceptions, cannot reach beyond those simple *Ideas*. And even in those, which seem most remote from all we have to do with, and do infinitely surpass any thing, we can perceive in our selves by *Reflection*, or discover by *Sensation* in other things, we can attain to nothing, but those simple *Ideas*, which we originally received from *Sensation* or *Reflection*, as is evident in the complex *Ideas* we have of Angels, and particularly of God himself.

Thirdly, That most of the simple *Ideas*, that make up our complex *Ideas* of Substances, when truly considered, are only Powers, however we are apt to take them for positive Qualities; *v.g.* the greatest part of the *Ideas*, that make our complex *Idea* of *Gold*, are Yellowness, great Weight, Ductility, Fusibility, and Solubility, in *Aqua Regia*, *etc.* all united together in an unknown *Substratum*; all which *Ideas*, are nothing else, but so many relations to other Substances; and are not really in the Gold, considered barely in it self, though they depend on those real, and primary Qualities of its internal constitution, whereby it has a fitness, differently to operate, and be operated on by several other Substances.

CHAPTER XXIV

Of Collective Ideas *of Substances.*

§ 1. BESIDES these complex *Ideas* of several single Substances, as of Man, Horse, Gold, Violet, Apple, *etc.* the Mind hath also *complex collective Ideas* of Substances; which I so call, because such *Ideas* are made up of many particular Substances considered together, as united into one *Idea*, and which so joined, are looked on as one; *v.g.* the *Idea* of such a collection of Men as make an Army, though consisting of a great number of distinct Substances, is as much one *Idea*, as the *Idea of a Man*: And the great collective *Idea* of all Bodies whatsoever signified by the name World, is as much one *Idea*, as the *Idea* of any the least Particle of Matter in it; it sufficing,

§ 1. *One* Idea.

(2) of,] **1–3** | of **4–5** (6) those] **4–5** | these **1–3** (17) , considered barely in] *add.* **4–5**

to the unity of any *Idea*, that it be considered as one Representation, or Picture, though made up of never so many Particulars.

§ 2. These collective *Ideas* of Substances, the Mind makes by its power of Composition, and uniting severally either simple or complex *Ideas* into one, as it does, by the same Faculty make the complex *Ideas* of particular Substances, consisting of an aggregate of divers simple *Ideas*, united in one Substance: And as the Mind by putting together the repeated *Ideas* of Unity, makes the collective Mode, or complex *Idea* of any number, as a Score, or a Gross, *etc.* So by putting together several particular Substances, it makes collective *Ideas* of Substances, as a Troop, an Army, a Swarm, a City, a Fleet; each of which, every one finds, that he represents to his own Mind, by one *Idea*, in one view; and so under that Notion considers those several Things as perfectly one, as one Ship, or one Atom. Nor is it harder to conceive, how an Army of ten Thousand Men, should make one *Idea*, than how a Man should make one *Idea*; it being as easie to the Mind, to unite into one, the *Idea* of a great number of Men, and consider it as one; as it is to unite into one particular, all the distinct *Ideas*, that make up the composition of a Man, and consider them altogether as one.

§ 3. Amongst such kind of collective *Ideas*, are to be counted most part of artificial Things, at least such of them as are made up of distinct Substances: And, in truth, if we consider all these collective *Ideas* aright, as *ARMY*, *Constellation*, *Universe*; as they are united into so many single *Ideas*, they are but the artificial Draughts of the Mind, bringing things very remote, and independent on one another, into one view, the better to contemplate, and discourse of them, united into one conception, and signified by one name. For there are no Things so remote, nor so contrary, which the Mind cannot, by this art of Composition, bring into one *Idea*, as is visible in that signified by the name *Universe*.

§ 2. *Made by the Power of composing in the Mind.* § 3. *All artificial Things are collective* Ideas.

---

(1) *Idea*,] **1–3, 5** | *Idea* **4** (14) those several Things] **4–5** | the Things themselves **1–3** (26–7) on one another] **2–5** | one from another **1**

CHAPTER XXV

Of Relation.

§ 1. BESIDES the *Ideas*, whether simple or complex, that the Mind has of Things, as they are in themselves, there are others it gets from their comparison one with another. The Understanding, in the consideration of any thing, is not confined to that precise Object: It can carry any *Idea*, as it were, beyond it self, or, at least, look beyond it, to see how it stands in conformity to any other. When the Mind so considers one thing, that it does, as it were, bring it to, and set it by another, and carry its view from one to t'other: This is, as the Words import, *Relation* and *Respect*; and the Denominations given to positive Things, intimating that Respect, and serving as Marks to lead the Thoughts beyond the Subject it self denominated, to something distinct from it, are what we call *Relatives*; and the Things so brought together, *Related*. Thus when the Mind considers *Cajus*, as such a positive Being, it takes nothing into that *Idea*, but what really exists in *Cajus*; *v.g.* when I consider him, as a Man, I have nothing in my Mind, but the complex *Idea* of the Species, Man. So likewise, when I say *Cajus* is a white Man, I have nothing but the bare consideration of Man, who hath that white Colour. But when I give *Cajus* the name *Husband*, I intimate some other Person: and when I give him the name *Whiter*, I intimate some other thing: in both cases my Thought is led to something beyond *Cajus*, and there are two things brought into consideration. And since any *Idea*, whether simple, or complex, may be the occasion, why the Mind thus brings two things together, and, as it were, takes a view of them at once, though still considered as distinct: therefore any of our *Ideas*, may be the foundation of Relation. As in the above-mentioned instance, the Contract, and Ceremony of Marriage with *Sempronia*, is the occasion of the Denomination, or Relation of Husband; and the colour White, the occasion why he is said whiter than Free-stone.

§ 2. These, and the like *Relations*, *expressed by relative terms*, *that*

§ 1. *Relation what.* § 2. *Relations without correlative Terms, not easily perceived.*

---

(5) *Idea*] **1er–5** | *Ideas* **1** (13) *Related*] **Coste** '*sujets de la Relation*', *with a marginal note* '*Relata.*' (21) thing] **Coste** *adds* 'par exemple l'*yvoire*'. thing: [; **2–3**] . . . cases] **1er–5** | thing . . . cases: **1** (30) Free-stone] **Coste** 'l'*yvoire*'

have others answering them, with a reciprocal intimation, as Father, and Son; Bigger, and Less; Cause, and Effect, *are very obvious* to every one, and every Body, at first sight, perceives the Relation. For Father, and Son; Husband and Wife, and such other correlative terms, seem so nearly to belong one to another, and, through Custom, do so readily chime, and answer one another in Peoples Memories, that upon the naming of either of them, the Thoughts are presently carried beyond the Thing so named; and no body over-looks, or doubts of a Relation, where it is so plainly intimated. But where Languages have failed to give correlative Names, there the Relation is not always so easily taken notice of. *Concubine* is no doubt, a relative Name, as well as Wife: But in Languages where this, and the like Words, have not a correlative term, there People are not so apt to take them to be so, as wanting that evident Mark of Relation, which is between Correlatives, which seem to explain one another, and not to be able to exist but together. Hence it is, that many of those Names, which duly considered, do include evident Relations, have been called External Denominations. But all Names, that are more than empty sounds, must signify some *Idea*, which is either in the thing to which the name is applied; and then it is positive, and is looked on as united to, and existing in the Thing to which the Denomination is given: or else it arises from the respect the Mind finds in it, to something distinct from it, with which it considers it; and then it includes a Relation.

§ 3. Another sort of *relative terms* there is, which are not looked on to be either relative, or so much as external Denominations: *which* yet, under the form and appearance of signifying something absolute in the Subject do conceal a tacit, though less observable, Relation. Such are the *seemingly positive* terms of *Old*, *Great*, *Imperfect*, etc. whereof I shall have occasion to speak more at large in the following Chapters.

§ 4. This farther may be observed, That the *Ideas* of Relation, may be the same in Men, who have far different *Ideas* of the Things that are related, or that are thus compared. *v.g.* Those who have far different *Ideas* of a *Man*, may yet agree in the notion of a *Father*: which is a notion superinduced to the Substance, or Man, and refers only to an act of that thing called Man; whereby he con-

§ 3. *Some seemingly absolute Terms contain Relations.* § 4. *Relation different from the Things related.*

(26) : *which*] **4** | ; *which* **1–3, 5** (37) he] **4–5** (**Coste** 'cet homme') | it **1–3**

tributed to the Generation of one of his own kind, let Man be what it will.

§ 5. *The nature* therefore *of Relation*, consists in the referring, or comparing two things, one to another; from which comparison, one or both comes to be denominated. And if either of those things be removed, or cease to be, the Relation ceases, and the Denomination consequent to it, though the other receive in it self no alteration at all. *v.g. Cajus*, whom I consider to day as a Father, ceases to be so to morrow, only by the death of his Son, without any alteration made in himself. Nay, barely by the Mind's changing the Object, to which it compares any thing, the same thing is capable of having contrary Denominations, at the same time. *v.g. Cajus*, compared to several Persons, may truly be said to be Older, and Younger; Stronger and Weaker, *etc.*

§ 6. Whatsoever doth, or can exist, or be considered as one thing, is positive: and so not only simple *Ideas*, and Substances, but Modes also are positive Beings; though the parts, of which they consist, are very often relative one to another; but the whole together considered as one thing, and producing in us the complex *Idea* of one thing; which *Idea* is in our Minds, as one Picture, though an aggregate of divers parts; and under one name, it is a positive or absolute Thing, or *Idea*. Thus a Triangle, though the parts thereof, compared one to another, be *relative*, yet the *Idea* of the whole, is a positive absolute *Idea*. The same may be said of a Family, a Tune, *etc.* for there can be no Relation, but betwixt two Things, considered as two Things. There must always be in relation two *Ideas*, or Things, either in themselves really separate, or considered as distinct, and then a ground or occasion for their comparison.

§ 7. Concerning Relation in general, these things may be considered:

First, That there is *no one thing*, whether simple *Idea*, Substance, Mode, or Relation, or Name of either of them, *which is not capable of almost an infinite number of* Considerations, in reference to other things: and therefore this makes no small part of Men's Thoughts and Words. *v.g.* One single Man may at once be concerned in, and sustain all these following *Relations*, and many more, *viz.* Father,

§ 5. *Change of Relation may be without any Change in the Subject.* § 6. *Relation only betwixt two Things.* § 7. *All Things capable of Relation.*

(18) ; but [But **4**]] **2–5** | : but **1** (28) a] *add.* **2–5**.

Brother, Son, Grandfather, Grandson, Father-in-Law, Son-in-Law, Husband, Friend, Enemy, Subject, General, Judge, Patron, Client, Professor, European, English-man, Islander, Servant, Master, Possessor, Captain, Superior, Inferior, Bigger, Less, Older, Younger, Contemporary, Like, Unlike, *etc.* to an almost infinite number: he being capable of as many Relations, as there can be occasions of comparing him to other things, in any manner of agreement, disagreement, or respect whatsoever: For, as I said, *Relation* is a way of comparing, or considering two things together; and giving one, or both of them, some appellation from that Comparison, and sometimes giving even the Relation it self a Name.

§ 8. *Secondly*, This farther may be considered concerning *Relation*, That though it be not contained in the real existence of Things, but something extraneous, and superinduced: yet the *Ideas* which relative Words stand for, are often clearer, and more distinct, than of those Substances to which they do belong. The Notion we have of a Father, or Brother, is a great deal clearer, and more distinct, than that we have of a Man: Or, if you will, *Paternity* is a thing whereof 'tis easier to have a clear *Idea*, than of *Humanity*: And I can much easier conceive what a Friend is, than what GOD. Because the knowledge of one Action, or one simple *Idea*, is oftentimes sufficient to give me the Notion of a Relation: but to the knowing of any substantial Being, an accurate collection of sundry *Ideas* is necessary. A Man, if he compares two things together, can hardly be supposed not to know what it is, wherein he compares them: So that when he compares any Things together, he cannot but have a very clear *Idea* of that Relation. *The Ideas* then of *Relations are capable* at least *of being more perfect and distinct in our Minds, than those of Substances.* Because it is commonly hard to know all the simple *Ideas*, which are really in any Substance, but for the most part easie enough to know the simple *Ideas* that make up any Relation I think on, or have a Name for. *v.g.* Comparing two Men, in reference to one common Parent, it is very easy to frame the *Ideas* of Brothers, without having yet the perfect *Idea* of a Man. For significant relative Words, as well as others, standing only for *Ideas*; and those

§ 8. *The* Ideas *of Relations clearer often, than of the Subjects related.*

---

(1) Grandfather, Grandson] **1–3** | Grand- / father, Grand-son **4–5** (3) Islander] **2–5** | Islanders **1** (7–8) in . . . whatsoever] **2–5** | with which he may agree, or disagree, or have any respect **1** (24) compares] **4–5** | compare **1–3**

being all either simple, or made up of simple ones, it suffices for the knowing the precise *Idea* the relative term stands for, to have a clear conception of that, which is the foundation of the Relation; which may be done without having a perfect and clear *Idea* of the thing it is attributed to. Thus having the Notion, that one laid the Egg, out of which the other was hatched, I have a clear *Idea* of the Relation of *Dam* and *Chick*, between the two Cassiowaries in St. *James*'s Park; though, perhaps, I have but a very obscure and imperfect *Idea* of those Birds themselves.

§ 9. *Thirdly*, Though there be a great number of Considerations, wherein Things may be compared one with another, and so a multitude of *Relations*: yet they *all terminate in*, and are concerned about those *simple Ideas*, either of Sensation or Reflection; which I think to be the whole Materials of all our Knowledge. To clear this, I shall shew it in the most considerable Relations, that we have any notion of; and in some that seem to be the most remote from *Sense* or *Reflection*: which yet will appear to have their *Ideas* from thence, and leave it past doubt, that the Notions we have of them, are but certain simple *Ideas*, and so originally derived from Sense or Reflection.

§ 10. *Fourthly*, That *Relation* being the considering of one thing with another, which is extrinsical to it, it is evident, that all Words, that necessarily lead the Mind to any other *Ideas*, than are supposed really to exist in that thing, to which the Word is applied, are *relative Words. v.g.* A *Man Black*, *Merry*, *Thoughtful*, *Thirsty*, *Angry*, *Extended*; these, and the like, are all absolute, because they neither signify nor intimate any thing, but what does, or is supposed really to exist in the Man thus denominated: But *Father*, *Brother*, *King*, *Husband*, *Blacker*, *Merrier*, *etc.* are Words, which, together with the thing they denominate, imply also something else separate, and exterior to the existence of that thing.

§ 11. Having laid down these Premises concerning *Relation* in general, I shall now proceed to shew, in some instances, how all the *Ideas* we have of *Relation*, are made up, as the others are, only of simple *Ideas*; and that they all, how refined, or remote from Sense

§ 9. *Relations all terminate in simple* Ideas. § 10. *Terms leading the Mind beyond the Subject denominated, are Relative.* § 11. *Conclusion.*

---

(16) in] *add.* **4–5** (18) leave it past doubt,] *add.* **4–5** (23) lead] **4–5** | infer, and lead **1–3** (30) separate,] **4–5** | separate **1–3** (*2 ll. below* 35: § 10.) *Relative*] **2, 4–5** | Related **3**

soever they seem, terminate at last in simple *Ideas.* I shall begin with the most comprehensive Relation, wherein all things that do, or can exist, are concerned, and that is the Relation of *Cause* and *Effect*. The *Idea* whereof, how derived from the two Fountains of all our Knowledge, *Sensation* and *Reflection*, I shall in the next place consider.

CHAPTER XXVI

Of Cause and Effect, and other Relations.

§ 1. In the notice, that our Senses take of the constant Vicissitude of Things, we cannot but observe, that several particular, both Qualities, and Substances begin to exist; and that they receive this their Existence, from the due Application and Operation of some other Being. From this Observation, we get our *Ideas* of *Cause* and *Effect*. That which produces any simple or complex *Idea*, we denote by the general Name *Cause*; and that which is produced, *Effect*. Thus finding, that in that Substance which we call Wax, Fluidity, which is a simple *Idea*, that was not in it before, is constantly produced by the Application of a certain degree of Heat, we call the simple *Idea* of Heat, in relation to Fluidity in Wax, the Cause of it, and Fluidity the Effect. So also finding that the Substance, Wood, which is a certain Collection of simple *Ideas*, so called, by the Application of Fire, is turned into another Substance, called Ashes; *i.e.* another complex *Idea*, consisting of a Collection of simple *Ideas*, quite different from that complex *Idea*, which we call Wood; we consider Fire, in relation to Ashes, as Cause, and the Ashes, as Effect. So that whatever is considered by us, to conduce or operate, to the producing any particular simple *Idea*, or Collection of simple *Ideas*, whether Substance, or Mode, which did not before exist, hath thereby in our Minds the relation of a Cause, and so is denominated by us.

§ 2. Having thus, from what our Senses are able to discover, in the Operations of Bodies on one another, got the Notion of *Cause*

§ 1. *Whence their* Ideas *got.* § 2. *Creation, Generation, making Alteration.*

(19–20) , by . . . is turned] **4–5** | , is by . . . turned **3** | , will by . . . be turned **1–2** (*but* **2er** 'is turned')

and *Effect*; *viz.* That a *Cause* is that which makes any other thing, either simple *Idea*, Substance, or Mode, begin to be; and an *Effect* is that, which had its Beginning from some other thing. The Mind finds no great difficulty, to distinguish the several Originals of things into two sorts.

First, When the thing is wholly made new, so that no part thereof did ever exist before; as when a new Particle of Matter doth begin to exist, *in rerum natura*, which had before no Being, and this we call *Creation*.

Secondly, When a thing is made up of Particles, which did all of them before exist, but that very thing, so constituted of pre-existing Particles, which considered altogether make up such a Collection of simple *Ideas*, had not any *Existence* before, as this Man, this Egg, Rose, or Cherry, *etc.* And this, when referred to a Substance, produced in the ordinary course of Nature, by an internal Principle, but set on work by, and received from some external Agent, or Cause, and working by insensible ways, which we perceive not, we call *Generation*; when the Cause is extrinsical, and the Effect produced by a sensible Separation, or *juxta* Position of discernible Parts, we call it *Making*; and such are all artificial things. When any simple *Idea* is produced, which was not in that Subject before, we call it *Alteration*. Thus a Man is generated, a Picture made, and either of them altered, when any new sensible Quality, or simple *Idea*, is produced in either of them, which was not there before; and the things thus made to exist, which were not there before, are *Effects*; and those things, which operated to the Existence, *Causes*. In which, and all other Cases, we may observe, that the Notion of *Cause* and *Effect*, has its rise from *Ideas*, received by Sensation or Reflection; and that this Relation, how comprehensive soever, terminates at last in them. For to have the *Idea* of *Cause* and *Effect*, it suffices to consider any simple *Idea*, or Substance, as beginning to exist, by the Operation of some other, without knowing the manner of that Operation.

§ 3. *Time* and *Place* are also the Foundations of very large Relations, and all finite Beings at least are concerned in them. But having already shewn in another Place, how we get these *Ideas*, it may suffice here to intimate, that most of the Denominations of

§§ 3, 4. *Relations of Time.*

(35) Beings] **1er–5** | Beings, **1**   (36) get] **2–5** | got **1**

things, received from time, are only Relations; thus, when any one says, that Queen *Elizabeth* lived sixty nine, and reigned forty five years; these Words import only the Relation of that Duration to some other, and means no more but this, That the Duration of her Existence was equal to sixty nine, and the Duration of her Government to forty five Annual Revolutions of the Sun; and so are all Words, answering, *how long*. Again, *William* the Conqueror invaded *England* about the year 1070. which means this; That taking the Duration from our Saviour's Time, till now, for one entire great length of time, it shews at what distance this Invasion was from the two Extremes: and so do all Words of time, answering to the Question *when*, which shew only the distance of any point of time, from the Period of a longer Duration, from which we measure, and to which we thereby consider it, as related.

§ 4. There are yet besides those, other Words of time, that ordinarily are thought to stand for positive *Ideas*, which yet will, when considered, be found to be relative, such as are *Young*, *Old*, etc. which include, and intimate the Relation any thing has, to a certain length of Duration, whereof we have the *Idea* in our Minds. Thus having setled in our Thoughts the *Idea* of the ordinary Duration of a Man to be seventy years, when we say a Man is *Young*, we mean, that his Age is yet but a small part of that which usually Men attain to: And when we denominate him *Old*, we mean, that his Duration is run out almost to the end of that which Men do not usually exceed. And so 'tis but comparing the particular Age, or Duration of this or that Man, to the *Idea* of that Duration which we have in our Minds, as ordinarily belonging to that sort of Animals: Which is plain, in the application of these Names to other Things; for a Man is called Young at Twenty years, and very Young at Seven years old: But yet a Horse we call Old at Twenty, and a Dog at Seven years; because in each of these, we compare their Age to different *Ideas* of Duration which are settled in our Minds, as belonging to these several sorts of Animals, in the ordinary course of Nature. But the Sun, and Stars, though they have outlasted several Generations of Men, we call not old, because we do not know what period GOD hath set to that sort of Beings. This Term belonging properly to those Things, which we can observe in the ordinary course of Things, by a natural decay to come to an end, in a certain period of time; and so have in our Minds, as it were, a Standard, to

(18) thing] **2–5** | things **1**

which we can compare the several parts of their Duration; and by the relation they bear thereunto, call them Young, or Old; which we cannot therefore do to a Ruby, or a Diamond, things whose usual periods we know not.

§ 5. The *Relation* also that things have to one another, in their *Places* and Distances, is very obvious to observe; as Above, Below, a Mile distant from *Charing-cross*, in *England*, and in *London*. But as in Duration, so in *Extension* and Bulk, there are some *Ideas* that are relative, which we signify by Names, that are thought positive; as *Great, and Little, are* truly *Relations*. For here also having, by observation, settled in our Minds the *Ideas* of the Bigness of several Species of Things, from those we have been most accustomed to, we make them, as it were, the Standards whereby to denominate the Bulk of others. Thus we call a great Apple, such a one as is bigger than the ordinary sort of those we have been used to; and a little Horse, such a one as comes not up to the size of that *Idea*, which we have in our Minds, to belong ordinarily to Horses: And that will be a great Horse to a *Welsh*-man, which is but a little one to a *Fleming*; they two having from the different Breed of their Countries, taken several siz'd *Ideas* to which they compare, and in relation to which they denominate their Great, and their Little.

§ 6. So likewise *Weak and Strong, are* but *relative Denominations* of Power, compared to some *Idea* we have, at that time, of greater or less Power. Thus when we say a Weak Man, we mean one that has not so much Strength, or Power to move, as usually Men have, or usually those of his size have; which is a comparing his Strength to the *Idea* we have of the usual Strength of Men, or Men of such a size. The like when we say the Creatures are all weak Things; Weak, there, is but a relative term, signifying the disproportion there is in the Power of GOD, and the Creatures. And so abundance of Words, in ordinary Speech, stand only for Relations, (and, perhaps, the greatest part,) which at first sight, seem to have no such signification: *v.g.* The Ship has necessary Stores. *Necessary*, and *Stores*, are both relative Words: one having a relation to the accomplishing the Voyage intended, and the other to future use. All which Relations, how they are confined to, and terminate in *Ideas*

§ 5. *Relations of Place and Extension.* § 6. *Absolute Terms often stand for Relations.*

(14) [*2nd*] a] **4–5** | an **1–3** (16) a] **4–5** | an **1–3** (23) *Idea*] **1–4** | *Ideas* **5**
(35) Voyage] **2–5** | thing **1**

derived from *Sensation*, or *Reflection*, is too obvious to need any Explication.

CHAPTER XXVII[1]

Of Identity and Diversity.

§ 1. ANOTHER occasion, the mind often takes of comparing, is the very Being of things, when considering any thing as existing at any determin'd time and place, we compare it with it self existing at another time, and thereon form the *Ideas* of *Identity* and *Diversity*. When we see any thing to be in any place in any instant of time, we are sure, (be it what it will) that it is that very thing, and not another, which at that same time exists in another place, how like and undistinguishable soever it may be in all other respects: And in this consists *Identity*, when the *Ideas* it is attributed to vary not at all from what they were that moment, wherein we consider their former existence, and to which we compare the present. For we never finding, nor conceiving it possible, that two things of the same kind should exist in the same place at the same time, we rightly conclude, that whatever exists any where at any time, excludes all of the same kind, and is there it self alone. When therefore we demand, whether any thing be the same or no, it refers always to something that existed such a time in such a place, which 'twas certain, at that instant, was the same with it self and no other: From whence it follows, that one thing cannot have two beginnings of Existence, nor two things one beginning, it being impossible for two things of the same kind, to be or exist in the same instant, in the very same place; or one and the same thing in different places. That therefore that had one beginning is the same thing, and that which had a different beginning in time and place from that, is not the same but divers. That which has made the Difficulty about this Relation, has been the little care and attention used in having precise Notions of the things to which it is attributed.

§ 1. *Wherein Identity consists.*

---

[1] *The whole of this Chapter xxvii add.* **2–5**, *with a consequent re-numbering in* **2–5** *of the following chapters of Book II.*

§ 2. We have the *Ideas* but of three sorts of Substances; 1. God. 2. Finite Intelligences. 3. *Bodies*. First, God is without beginning, eternal, unalterable, and every where; and therefore concerning his Identity, there can be no doubt. Secondly, Finite Spirits having had each its determinate time and place of beginning to exist, the relation to that time and place will always determine to each of them its Identity as long as it exists.

Thirdly, The same will hold of every Particle of Matter, to which no Addition or Substraction of Matter being made, it is the same. For though these three sorts of Substances, as we term them, do not exclude one another out of the same place; yet we cannot conceive but that they must necessarily each of them exclude any of the same kind out of the same place: Or else the Notions and Names of Identity and Diversity would be in vain, and there could be no such distinction of Substances, or any thing else one from another. For Example, could two Bodies be in the same place at the same time; then those two parcels of Matter must be one and the same, take them great or little; nay, all Bodies must be one and the same. For by the same reason that two particles of Matter may be in one place, all Bodies may be in one place: Which, when it can be supposed, takes away the distinction of Identity and Diversity, of one and more, and renders it ridiculous. But it being a contradiction, that two or more should be one, Identity and Diversity are relations and ways of comparing well founded, and of use to the Understanding. All other things being but Modes or Relations ultimately terminated in Substances, the Identity and Diversity of each particular Existence of them too will be by the same way determined: Only as to things whose Existence is in succession, such as are the Actions of finite Beings, *v.g. Motion* and *Thought*, both which consist in a continued train of Succession, concerning their Diversity there can be no question: Because each perishing the moment it begins, they cannot exist in different times, or in different places, as permanent Beings can at different times exist in distant places; and therefore no motion or thought considered as at different times can be the same, each part thereof having a different beginning of Existence.

§ 2. *Identity of Substances.* § 2(20). *Identity of Modes.*

(*l. below* 36: § 2(20).) *In* **2–4**, *this faces in the margin* 'Which, when it can be supposed, . . .'; *in* **5** *it faces ll.* 19–20; *in* **Coste**, *it faces* 'All other things . . .' (*l.* 25), *which begins a new paragraph in* § 2.

§ 3. From what has been said, 'tis easy to discover, what is so much enquired after, the *principium Individuationis*, and that 'tis plain is Existence it self, which determines a Being of any sort to a particular time and place incommunicable to two Beings of the same kind. This though it seems easier to conceive in simple Substances or Modes; yet when reflected on, is not more difficult in compounded ones, if care be taken to what it is applied; *v.g.* Let us suppose an Atom, *i.e.* a continued body under one immutable Superficies, existing in a determined time and place: 'tis evident, that, considered in any instant of its Existence, it is, in that instant, the same with it self. For being, at that instant, what it is, and nothing else, it is the same, and so must continue, as long as its Existence is continued: for so long it will be the same, and no other. In like manner, if two or more Atoms be joined together into the same Mass, every one of those Atoms will be the same, by the foregoing Rule: And whilst they exist united together, the Mass, consisting of the same Atoms, must be the same Mass, or the same Body, let the parts be never so differently jumbled: But if one of these Atoms be taken away, or one new one added, it is no longer the same Mass, or the same Body. In the state of living Creatures, their Identity depends not on a Mass of the same Particles; but on something else. For in them the variation of great parcels of Matter alters not the Identity: An Oak, growing from a Plant to a great Tree, and then lopp'd, is still the same Oak: And a Colt grown up to a Horse, sometimes fat, sometimes lean, is all the while the same Horse: though, in both these Cases, there may be a manifest change of the parts: So that truly they are not either of them the same Masses of Matter, though they be truly one of them the same Oak, and the other the same Horse. The reason whereof is, that in these two cases of a Mass of Matter, and a living Body, *Identity* is not applied to the same thing.

§ 4. We must therefore consider wherein an Oak differs from a Mass of Matter, and that seems to me to be in this; that the one is only the Cohesion of Particles of Matter any how united, the other such a disposition of them as constitutes the parts of an Oak; and

§ 3. Principium Individuationis. § 4. *Identity of Vegetables.*

(3) a Being of any sort] **4–5** | any sort of Being **2–3** (11) instant,] **2–3** | instant **4–5** (17–18) or the same Body,] *add.* **4–5** (19) no longer] **4–5** | not **2–3** (20) , or the same Body] *add.* **4–5** (26) may] *add.* **4–5**. (*Not in* **Coste**) (28) Masses] **2, 4–5** | Mass **3** (*likewise* **Coste**)

such an Organization of those parts, as is fit to receive, and distribute nourishment, so as to continue, and frame the Wood, Bark, and Leaves, *etc.* of an Oak, in which consists the vegetable Life. That being then one Plant, which has such an Organization of Parts in one coherent Body, partaking of one Common Life, it continues to be the same Plant, as long as it partakes of the same Life, though that Life be communicated to new Particles of Matter vitally united to the living Plant, in a like continued Organization, conformable to that sort of Plants. For this Organization being at any one instant in any one Collection of *Matter*, is in that particular concrete distinguished from all other, and is that individual Life, which existing constantly from that moment both forwards and backwards in the same continuity of insensibly succeeding Parts united to the living Body of the Plant, it has that Identity, which makes the same Plant, and all the parts of it, parts of the same Plant, during all the time that they exist united in that continued Organization, which is fit to convey that Common Life to all the Parts so united.

§ 5. The Case is not so much different in *Brutes*, but that any one may hence see what makes an Animal, and continues it the same. Something we have like this in Machines, and may serve to illustrate it. For Example, what is a Watch? 'Tis plain 'tis nothing but a fit Organization, or Construction of Parts, to a certain end, which, when a sufficient force is added to it, it is capable to attain. If we would suppose this Machine one continued Body, all whose organized Parts were repair'd, increas'd or diminish'd, by a constant Addition or Separation of insensible Parts, with one Common Life, we should have something very much like the Body of an Animal, with this difference, That in an Animal the fitness of the Organization, and the Motion wherein Life consists, begin together, the Motion coming from within; but in Machines the force, coming sensibly from without, is often away, when the Organ is in order, and well fitted to receive it.

§ 6. This also shews wherein the Identity of the same *Man* consists; *viz.* in nothing but a participation of the same continued Life,

§ 5. *Identity of Animals.* § 6. *Identity of Man.*

(14) [*1st*] the] **4–5** | the same **2–3** (15) and . . . Plant,] *add.* **4–5** (16) they exist] **4er–5** (*likewise* **Coste**) | they exist, **4** | it exists, one Body, **2–3** (29) in an Animal] *add.* **4–5** (30) , and] **4–5** | and **2–3**

by constantly fleeting Particles of Matter, in succession vitally united to the same organized Body. He that shall place the *Identity* of Man in any thing else, but like that of other Animals in one fitly organized Body taken in any one instant, and from thence continued under one Organization of Life in several successively fleeting Particles of Matter, united to it, will find it hard, to make an *Embryo*, one of Years, mad, and sober, the same Man, by any Supposition, that will not make it possible for *Seth*, *Ismael*, *Socrates*, *Pilate*, St. *Austin*, and *Cæsar Borgia* to be the same Man. For if the *Identity* of Soul alone makes the same Man, and there be nothing in the Nature of Matter, why the same individual Spirit may not be united to different Bodies, it will be possible, that those Men, living in distant Ages, and of different Tempers, may have been the same Man: Which way of speaking must be from a very strange use of the Word *Man*, applied to an *Idea*, out of which Body and Shape is excluded: And that way of speaking would agree yet worse with the Notions of those Philosophers, who allow of Transmigration, and are of Opinion that the Souls of Men may, for their Miscarriages, be detruded into the Bodies of Beasts, as fit Habitations with Organs suited to the satisfaction of their Brutal Inclinations. But yet I think no body, could he be sure that the Soul of *Heliogabalus* were in one of his Hogs, would yet say that Hog were a *Man* or *Heliogabalus*.

§ 7. 'Tis not therefore Unity of Substance that comprehends all sorts of *Identity*, or will determine it in every Case: But to conceive, and judge of it aright, we must consider what *Idea* the Word it is applied to stands for: It being one thing to be the same *Substance*, another the same *Man*, and a third the same *Person*, if *Person*, *Man*, and *Substance*, are three Names standing for three different *Ideas*; for such as is the *Idea* belonging to that Name, such must be the *Identity*: Which if it had been a little more carefully attended to, would possibly have prevented a great deal of that Confusion, which often occurs about this Matter, with no small seeming Difficulties; especially concerning *Personal Identity*, which therefore we shall in the next place a little consider.

§ 8. An Animal is a living organized Body; and consequently, the same Animal, as we have observed, is the same continued Life

§ 7. *Identity suited to the* Idea. § 8. *Same Man.*

---

(19) Habitations with] **4–5** | Habitations with, and **3** | Habitants and **2**
(27) , if] **4–5** | . If **2–3**

communicated to different Particles of Matter, as they happen successively to be united to that organiz'd living Body. And whatever is talked of other definitions, ingenuous observation puts it past doubt, that the *Idea* in our Minds, of which the Sound *Man* in our Mouths is the Sign, is nothing else but of an Animal of such a certain Form: Since I think I may be confident, that whoever should see a Creature of his own Shape and Make, though it had no more reason all its Life, than a *Cat* or a *Parrot*, would call him still a *Man*; or whoever should hear a *Cat* or a *Parrot* discourse, reason, and philosophize, would call or think it nothing but a *Cat* or a *Parrot*; and say, the one was a dull irrational *Man*, and the other a very intelligent rational *Parrot*. A Relation we have in an Author of great note is sufficient to countenance the supposition of a rational *Parrot*. His Words(α) are,

"I had a mind to know from *Prince Maurice*'s own Mouth, the account of a common, but much credited Story, that I had heard so often from many others, of an old *Parrot* he had in *Brasil*, during his Government there, that spoke, and asked, and answered common Questions like a reasonable Creature; so that those of his Train there, generally concluded it to be Witchery or Possession; and one of his Chaplains, who lived long afterwards in *Holland*, would never from that time endure a *Parrot*, but said, they all had a Devil in them. I had heard many particulars of this Story, and assevered by People hard to be discredited, which made me ask *Prince Maurice* what there was of it. He said, with his usual plainess, and dryness in talk, there was something true, but a great deal false, of what had been reported. I desired to know of him, what there was of the first; he told me short and coldly, that he had heard of such an old *Parrot* when he came to *Brasil*, and though he believed nothing of it, and 'twas a good way off, yet he had so much Curiosity as to send for it, that 'twas a very great and a very old one; and when it came first into the Room where the Prince was, with a great many *Dutch-men* about him, it said presently, *What a company of white Men are here?* They asked it what he thought that Man was, pointing at the Prince? It answered, *Some General or other*; when they brought it

(α) *Memoires of what past in* Christendom *from* 1672. to 1679. p. $\frac{57}{392}$.

(2–6) . And . . . Form:] **5** | : and that our Notion of a *Man*, whatever is talked of other definitions, is but of a particular sort of Animal, I doubt not. **2–4** (9–10) discourse . . . philosophize] **5** | Discourse, Reason and Philosophize **4** | discourse Reason and Philosophize **2–3** (*likewise* **Coste**) (12)–335(3) A . . . *Parrots*?] *add.* **4–5**. (*Not in* **Coste**, *but in* **Coste$_2$**.) (*l. below* 35) [*Memoires* . . ., by Sir William Temple]

close to him, he asked it, *D'ou venes vous?* it answered, *De Marinnan.* The Prince, *A qui estes vous?* The Parrot, *A un Portugais.* Prince, *Que fais tu la?* Parrot, *Je garde les poulles.* The Prince laughed and said, *Vous gardez les poulles?* The Parrot answered, *Ouy, moy et je scay bien faire*; and made the Chuck four or five times that People use to make to Chickens when they call them.† I set down the Words of this worthy Dialogue in *French*, just as Prince *Maurice* said them to me. I asked him in what Language the *Parrot* spoke, and he said, in *Brasilian*; I asked whether he understood *Brasilian*; he said No, but he had taken care to have two Interpreters by him, the one a *Dutch-man*, that spoke *Brasilian*, and the other a *Brasilian*, that spoke *Dutch*; that he asked them separately and privately, and both of them agreed in telling him just the same thing that the *Parrot* said. I could not but tell this odd Story, because it is so much out of the way, and from the first hand, and what may pass for a good one; for I dare say this Prince, at least, believed himself in all he told me, having ever passed for a very honest and pious Man; I leave it to Naturalists to reason, and to other Men to believe as they please upon it; however, it is not, perhaps, amiss to relieve or enliven a busie Scene sometimes with such digressions, whether to the purpose or no."

I have taken care that the Reader should have the Story at large in the Authors own Words, because he seems to me not to have thought it incredible; for it cannot be imagined that so able a Man as he, who had sufficiency enough to warrant all the Testimonies he gives of himself, should take so much pains, in a place where it had nothing to do, to pin so close, not only on a Man whom he mentions as his Friend, but on a Prince in whom he acknowledges very great Honesty and Piety, a Story which if he himself thought incredible, he could not but also think ridiculous. The Prince, 'tis plain, who vouches this Story, and our Author who relates it from him, both of them call this Talker a *Parrot*; and I ask any one else who thinks such a Story fit to be told, whether if this *Parrot*, and all of its kind, had always talked as we have a Princes word for it, this one did,

† *Whence come ye? It answered, From* Marinnan. *The* Prince, *To whom do you belong? The* Parrot, *To a* Portugeze. Prince, *What do you there?* Parrot, *I look after the Chickens. The* Prince laughed and said, *You look after the Chickens? The* Parrot answered, *Yes I, and I know well enough how to do it.*

(1) it,] **5** | it; **4** (22) *In* **4–5**, *the marginal sectional summary 'Same Man.' is repeated facing the beginning of this paragraph.* (*2 ll. below* 34) Portugeze.] **5** | Portugez **4**

whether, I say, they would not have passed for a race of *rational Animals*, but yet whether for all that, they would have been allowed to be Men and not *Parrots*? For I presume 'tis not the *Idea* of a thinking or rational Being alone, that makes the *Idea* of a *Man* in most Peoples Sense; but of a Body so and so shaped joined to it; and if that be the *Idea* of a *Man*, the same successive Body not shifted all at once, must as well as the same immaterial Spirit go to the making of the same *Man*.

§ 9. This being premised to find wherein *personal Identity* consists, we must consider what *Person* stands for; which, I think, is a thinking intelligent Being, that has reason and reflection, and can consider it self as it self, the same thinking thing in different times and places; which it does only by that consciousness, which is inseparable from thinking, and as it seems to me essential to it: It being impossible for any one to perceive, without perceiving, that he does perceive. When we see, hear, smell, taste, feel, meditate, or will any thing, we know that we do so. Thus it is always as to our present Sensations and Perceptions: And by this every one is to himself, that which he calls *self*: It not being considered in this case, whether the same *self* be continued in the same, or divers Substances. For since consciousness always accompanies thinking, and 'tis that, that makes every one to be, what he calls *self*; and thereby distinguishes himself from all other thinking things, in this alone consists *personal Identity*, *i.e.* the sameness of a rational Being: And as far as this consciousness can be extended backwards to any past Action or Thought, so far reaches the Identity of that *Person*; it is the same *self* now it was then; and 'tis by the same *self* with this present one that now reflects on it, that that Action was done.

§ 10. But it is farther enquir'd whether it be the same Identical Substance. This few would think they had reason to doubt of, if these Perceptions, with their consciousness, always remain'd present in the Mind, whereby the same thinking thing would be always consciously present, and, as would be thought, evidently the same to it self. But that which seems to make the difficulty is this, that this consciousness, being interrupted always by forgetfulness, there being no moment of our Lives wherein we have the

§ 9. *Personal Identity.* § 10. *Consciousness makes Personal Identity.*

---

(3) *v.* 333(12), n. (20, 21) **Coste** *adds linguistic footnotes on* '*self*' *and* 'consciousness'.
(22) to] *add.* **4–5**

whole train of all our past Actions before our Eyes in one view: But even the best Memories losing the sight of one part whilst they are viewing another; and we sometimes, and that the greatest part of our Lives, not reflecting on our past selves, being intent on our present Thoughts, and in sound sleep, having no Thoughts at all, or at least none with that consciousness, which remarks our waking Thoughts. I say, in all these cases, our consciousness being interrupted, and we losing the sight of our past *selves*, doubts are raised whether we are the same thinking thing; *i.e.* the same substance or no. Which however reasonable, or unreasonable, concerns not *personal Identity* at all. The Question being what makes the same *Person*, and not whether it be the same Identical Substance, which always thinks in the same *Person*, which in this case matters not at all. Different Substances, by the same consciousness (where they do partake in it) being united into one Person; as well as different Bodies, by the same Life are united into one Animal, whose *Identity* is preserved, in that change of Substances, by the unity of one continued Life. For it being the same consciousness that makes a Man be himself to himself, *personal Identity* depends on that only, whether it be annexed only to one individual Substance, or can be continued in a succession of several Substances. For as far as any intelligent Being can repeat the *Idea* of any past Action with the same consciousness it had of it at first, and with the same consciousness it has of any present Action; so far it is the same *personal self*. For it is by the consciousness it has of its present Thoughts and Actions, that it is *self* to it *self* now, and so will be the same *self* as far as the same consciousness can extend to Actions past or to come; and would be by distance of Time, or change of Substance, no more two *Persons* than a Man be two Men, by wearing other Cloaths to Day than he did Yesterday, with a long or short sleep between: The same consciousness uniting those distant Actions into the same *Person*, whatever Substances contributed to their Production.

§ 11. That this is so, we have some kind of Evidence in our very Bodies, all whose Particles, whilst vitally united to this same thinking conscious self, so that we feel when they are touch'd, and are affected by, and conscious of good or harm that happens to them, are a part of our *selves*: *i.e.* of our thinking conscious *self*. Thus

§ 11. *Personal Identity in change of Substances.*

(10) not] **2–3** (*likewise* **Coste**) | no **4–5** (29) Cloaths] **4–5** | Cloths **2–3**
(32) *Person*,] **4–5** | *Person* **2–3**

the Limbs of his Body is to every one a part of *himself*: He sympathizes and is concerned for them. Cut off an hand, and thereby separate it from that consciousness, we had of its Heat, Cold, and other Affections; and it is then no longer a part of that which is *himself*, any more than the remotest part of Matter. Thus we see the *Substance*, whereof *personal self* consisted at one time, may be varied at another, without the change of personal *Identity*: There being no Question about the same Person, though the Limbs, which but now were a part of it, be cut off.

§ 12. But the Question is, whether if the same Substance, which thinks, be changed, it can be the same Person, or remaining the same, it can be different Persons.

And to this I answer first, this can be no Question at all to those, who place Thought in a purely material, animal, Constitution, void of an immaterial Substance. For, whether their Supposition be true or no, 'tis plain they conceive personal Identity preserved in something else than Identity of Substance; as animal Identity is preserved in Identity of Life, and not of Substance. And therefore those, who place thinking in an immaterial Substance only, before they can come to deal with these Men, must shew why personal Identity cannot be preserved in the change of immaterial Substances, or variety of particular immaterial Substances, as well as animal Identity is preserved in the change of material Substances, or variety of particular Bodies: Unless they will say, 'tis one immaterial Spirit, that makes the same Life in Brutes; as it is one immaterial Spirit that makes the same Person in Men, which the *Cartesians* at least will not admit, for fear of making Brutes thinking things too.

§ 13. But next, as to the first part of the Question, Whether if the same thinking Substance (supposing immaterial Substances only to think) be changed, it can be the same Person. I answer, that cannot be resolv'd, but by those, who know what kind of Substances they are, that do think; and whether the consciousness of past Actions can be transferr'd from one thinking Substance to another. I grant, were the same Consciousness the same individual Action, it could not: But it being but a present representation of a past Action, why it may not be possible, that that may be represented to the Mind to have been, which really never was, will remain to be shewn. And

§§ 12–15. *Whether in the change of thinking Substances.*

(15) an immaterial Substance] **4–5** | Spirit **2–3** (22) immaterial Substances,] **4–5** | Spirits **2–3**

therefore how far the consciousness of past Actions is annexed to any individual Agent, so that another cannot possibly have it, will be hard for us to determine, till we know what kind of Action it is, that cannot be done without a reflex Act of Perception accompanying it, and how perform'd by thinking Substances, who cannot think without being conscious of it. But that which we call the *same consciousness*, not being the same individual Act, why one intellectual Substance may not have represented to it, as done by it self, what it never did, and was perhaps done by some other Agent, why I say such a representation may not possibly be without reality of Matter of Fact, as well as several representations in Dreams are, which yet, whilst dreaming, we take for true, will be difficult to conclude from the Nature of things. And that it never is so, will by us, till we have clearer views of the Nature of thinking Substances, be best resolv'd into the Goodness of God, who as far as the Happiness or Misery of any of his sensible Creatures is concerned in it, will not by a fatal Error of theirs transfer from one to another, that consciousness, which draws Reward or Punishment with it. How far this may be an Argument against those who would place Thinking in a System of fleeting animal Spirits, I leave to be considered. But yet to return to the Question before us, it must be allowed, That if the same consciousness (which, as has been shewn, is quite a different thing from the same numerical Figure or Motion in Body) can be transferr'd from one thinking Substance to another, it will be possible, that two thinking Substances may make but one Person. For the same consciousness being preserv'd, whether in the same or different Substances, the personal Identity is preserv'd.

§ 14. As to the second part of the Question, Whether the same immaterial Substance remaining, there may be two distinct Persons; which Question seems to me to be built on this, Whether the same immaterial Being, being conscious of the Actions of its past Duration, may be wholly stripp'd of all the consciousness of its past Existence, and lose it beyond the power of ever retrieving again: And so as it were beginning a new Account from a new Period, have a consciousness that cannot reach beyond this new State. All those who hold pre-existence, are evidently of this Mind, since they allow the Soul to have no remaining consciousness of what it did in that pre-existent State, either wholly separate from

(3) is,] **2–4** | is; **5** (4) without] **2er–5** | with **2** (18) with] **4–5** | after **2–3**. (**Coste** 'entraîne après luy') (29) , there] **3–5** | there, **2**

Body, or informing any other Body; and if they should not, 'tis plain Experience would be against them. So that personal Identity reaching no farther than consciousness reaches, a pre-existent Spirit not having continued so many Ages in a state of Silence, must needs make different Persons. Suppose a Christian *Platonist* or *Pythagorean*, should upon God's having ended all his Works of Creation the Seventh Day, think his Soul hath existed ever since; and should imagine it has revolved in several Humane Bodies, as I once met with one, who was perswaded his had been the Soul of *Socrates* (how reasonably I will not dispute. This I know, that in the Post he fill'd, which was no inconsiderable one, he passed for a very rational Man, and the Press has shewn, that he wanted not Parts or Learning) would any one say, that he, being not conscious of any of *Socrates*'s Actions or Thoughts, could be the same Person with *Socrates*? Let any one reflect upon himself, and conclude, that he has in himself an immaterial Spirit, which is that which thinks in him, and in the constant change of his Body keeps him the same; and is that which he calls himself: Let him also suppose it to be the same Soul, that was in *Nestor* or *Thersites*, at the Siege of *Troy*, (For Souls being, as far as we know any thing of them in their Nature, indifferent to any parcel of Matter, the Supposition has no apparent absurdity in it) which it may have been, as well as it is now, the Soul of any other Man: But he, now having no consciousness of any of the Actions either of *Nestor* or *Thersites*, does, or can he, conceive himself the same Person with either of them? Can he be concerned in either of their Actions? Attribute them to himself, or think them his own more than the Actions of any other Man, that ever existed? So that this consciousness not reaching to any of the Actions of either of those Men, he is no more one *self* with either of them, than if the Soul or immaterial Spirit, that now informs him, had been created, and began to exist, when it began to inform his present Body, though it were never so true, that the same Spirit that informed *Nestor*'s or *Thersites*'s Body, were numerically the same that now informs his. For this would no more make him the same Person with *Nestor*, than if some of the Particles of Matter, that were once a part of *Nestor*, were now a part of this Man, the same immaterial Substance without the same consciousness, no more making the same Person by being united to any Body, than the same Particle of

(38)–340(2) the . . . Person.] **Coste** 'les mêmes particules de matiére unies à quelque Corps sans une *con-science* commune, peuvent faire la même personne.'

Matter without consciousness united to any Body, makes the same Person. But let him once find himself conscious of any of the Actions of *Nestor*, he then finds himself the same Person with *Nestor*.

§ 15. And thus we may be able without any difficulty to conceive, the same Person at the Resurrection, though in a Body not exactly in make or parts the same which he had here, the same consciousness going along with the Soul that inhabits it. But yet the Soul alone in the change of Bodies, would scarce to any one, but to him that makes the Soul the *Man*, be enough to make the same *Man*. For should the Soul of a Prince, carrying with it the consciousness of the Prince's past Life, enter and inform the Body of a Cobler as soon as deserted by his own Soul, every one sees, he would be the same Person with the Prince, accountable only for the Prince's Actions: But who would say it was the same Man? The Body too goes to the making the Man, and would, I guess, to every Body determine the Man in this case, wherein the Soul, with all its Princely Thoughts about it, would not make another Man: But he would be the same Cobler to every one besides himself. I know that in the ordinary way of speaking, the same Person, and the same Man, stand for one and the same thing. And indeed every one will always have a liberty to speak, as he pleases, and to apply what articulate Sounds to what *Ideas* he thinks fit, and change them as often as he pleases. But yet when we will enquire, what makes the same *Spirit*, *Man*, or *Person*, we must fix the *Ideas* of *Spirit*, *Man*, or *Person*, in our Minds; and having resolved with our selves what we mean by them, it will not be hard to determine, in either of them, or the like, when it is the *same*, and when not.

§ 16. But though the same immaterial Substance, or Soul does not alone, where-ever it be, and in whatsoever State, make the same Man; yet 'tis plain consciousness, as far as ever it can be extended, should it be to Ages past, unites Existences, and Actions, very remote in time, into the same Person, as well as it does the Existence and Actions of the immediately preceding moment: So that whatever has the consciousness of present and past Actions, is the same Person to whom they both belong. Had I the same consciousness,

§ 16. *Consciousness makes the same Person.*

---

(5) , the . . . Resurrection] **4–5** | at the Resurrection the same Person **2–3** (6) which] *add.* **4–5** (17–18) he . . . besides] **4–5** | it would to every one be the same Cobler beside **2–3** (24) [*2nd*] *Spirit*] **2er–5** | *Spirits* **2** (29) -ever] *v. Register* (31) Actions,] **4–5** | Actions **2–3** (*l. below* 35) *makes*] **2–3** | *make* **4–5**

that I saw the Ark and *Noah*'s Flood, as that I saw an overflowing of the *Thames* last Winter, or as that I write now, I could no more doubt that I, that write this now, that saw the *Thames* overflow'd last Winter, and that view'd the Flood at the general Deluge, was the same *self*, place that *self* in what Substance you please, than that I that write this am the same *my self* now whilst I write (whether I consist of all the same Substance, material or immaterial, or no) that I was Yesterday. For as to this point of being the same *self*, it matters not whether this present *self* be made up of the same or other Substances, I being as much concern'd, and as justly accountable for any Action was done a thousand Years since, appropriated to me now by this self-consciousness, as I am, for what I did the last moment.

§ 17. *Self* is that conscious thinking thing, (whatever Substance, made up of whether Spiritual, or Material, Simple, or Compounded, it matters not) which is sensible, or conscious of Pleasure and Pain, capable of Happiness or Misery, and so is concern'd for it *self*, as far as that consciousness extends. Thus every one finds, that whilst comprehended under that consciousness, the little Finger is as much a part of it *self*, as what is most so. Upon separation of this little Finger, should this consciousness go along with the little Finger, and leave the rest of the Body, 'tis evident the little Finger would be the *Person*, the *same Person*; and *self* then would have nothing to do with the rest of the Body. As in this case it is the consciousness that goes along with the Substance, when one part is separated from another, which makes the same *Person*, and constitutes this inseparable *self*: so it is in reference to Substances remote in time. That with which the *consciousness* of this present thinking thing can join it self, makes the same *Person*, and is one *self* with it, and with nothing else; and so attributes to it *self*, and owns all the Actions of that thing, as its own, as far as that consciousness reaches, and no farther; as every one who reflects will perceive.

§ 18. In this *personal Identity* is founded all the Right and Justice of Reward and Punishment; Happiness and Misery, being that, for

§ 17. *Self depends on Consciousness.* §§ 18–20. *Object of Reward and Punishment.*

(1) [*2nd*] that] *add.* **3–5** (12) self-consciousness] **Coste** *adds a marginal linguistic note.* (14) Substance, /] **2–3, 5** | Substance / **4** (23) *self*] **2–3** (*likewise* **Coste**) | self **4–5** (26) separated] **2–3** (*likewise* **Coste**) | separate **4–5** (27) Substances] **2–4** | Substance **5** (27–32) : so . . . time. That . . . farther;] **4–5** | . So . . . time, that . . . farther, **2–3** (34) Punishment;] **4–5** | Punishment, **2–3** (*l. below* 34: §§ 18–20.) *Punishment.*] **2–3** | *Punishments* **4–5**

which every one is concerned for *himself*, not mattering what becomes of any Substance, not joined to, or affected with that consciousness. For as it is evident in the instance I gave but now, if the consciousness went along with the little Finger, when it was cut off, that would be the same *self* which was concerned for the whole Body Yesterday, as making a part of it *self*, whose Actions then it cannot but admit as its own now. Though if the same Body should still live, and immediately from the separation of the little Finger have its own peculiar consciousness, whereof the little Finger knew nothing, it would not at all be concerned for it, as a part of it *self*, or could own any of its Actions, or have any of them imputed to him.

§ 19. This may shew us wherein *personal Identity* consists, not in the Identity of Substance, but, as I have said, in the Identity of *consciousness*, wherein, if *Socrates* and the present Mayor of *Quinborough* agree, they are the same Person: If the same *Socrates* waking and sleeping do not partake of the same *consciousness*, *Socrates* waking and sleeping is not the same Person. And to punish *Socrates* waking, for what sleeping *Socrates* thought, and waking *Socrates* was never conscious of, would be no more of Right, than to punish one Twin for what his Brother-Twin did, whereof he knew nothing, because their outsides were so like, that they could not be distinguished; for such Twins have been seen.

§ 20. But yet possibly it will still be objected, suppose I wholly lose the memory of some parts of my Life, beyond a possibility of retrieving them, so that perhaps I shall never be conscious of them again; yet am I not the same Person, that did those Actions, had those Thoughts, that I was once conscious of, though I have now forgot them? To which I answer, that we must here take notice what the Word *I* is applied to, which in this case is the Man only. And the same Man being presumed to be the same Person, *I* is easily here supposed to stand also for the same Person. But if it be possible for the same Man to have distinct incommunicable consciousness at different times, it is past doubt the same Man would at different times make different Persons; which, we see, is the Sense of Mankind in the solemnest Declaration of their Opinions, Humane Laws not punishing the *Mad Man* for the *Sober Man*'s Actions, nor the *Sober Man* for what the *Mad Man* did, thereby making them two Persons; which is somewhat explained by our

(14) Mayor of *Quinborough*] **Coste** 'Roy de *Mogol*' (23) I] *add.* **2er–5**
(30) , *I*] **3–5** | *I*, **2**

way of speaking in *English*, when we say such an one *is not himself*, or is *besides himself*; in which Phrases it is insinuated, as if those who now, or, at least, first used them, thought, that *self* was changed, the *self* same Person was no longer in that Man.

§ 21. But yet 'tis hard to conceive, that *Socrates* the same individual Man should be two Persons. To help us a little in this, we must consider what is meant by *Socrates*, or the same individual *Man*.

First, It must be either the same individual, immaterial, thinking Substance: In short, the same numerical Soul, and nothing else.

Secondly, Or the same Animal, without any regard to an immaterial Soul.

Thirdly, Or the same immaterial Spirit united to the same Animal.

Now take which of these Suppositions you please, it is impossible to make personal Identity to consist in any thing but consciousness; or reach any farther than that does.

For by the First of them, it must be allowed possible that a Man born of different Women, and in distant times, may be the same Man. A way of speaking, which whoever admits, must allow it possible, for the same Man to be two distinct Persons, as any two that have lived in different Ages without the knowledge of one anothers Thoughts.

By the Second and Third, *Socrates* in this Life, and after it, cannot be the same Man any way, but by the same consciousness; and so making *Humane Identity* to consist in the same thing wherein we place *Personal Identity*, there will be no difficulty to allow the same Man to be the same Person. But then they who place *Humane Identity* in consciousness only, and not in something else, must consider how they will make the Infant *Socrates* the same Man with *Socrates* after the Resurrection. But whatsoever to some Men makes a *Man*, and consequently the same individual Man, wherein perhaps few are agreed, personal Identity can by us be placed in nothing but consciousness (which is that alone which makes what we call *self*) without involving us in great Absurdities.

§ 22. But is not a Man Drunk and Sober the same Person, why else is he punish'd for the Fact he commits when Drunk, though he be never afterwards conscious of it? Just as much the same Person, as a Man that walks, and does other things in his sleep, is the same Person, and is answerable for any mischief he shall do in it. Humane

§§ 21, 22. *Difference between Identity of Man and Person.*

(2) , as] **4–5** | as **2–3** (9) Substance:] **2–3, 5** | Substance; **4**

Laws punish both with a Justice suitable to their way of Knowledge: Because in these cases, they cannot distinguish certainly what is real, what counterfeit; and so the ignorance in Drunkenness or Sleep is not admitted as a plea. For though punishment be annexed to personality, and personality to consciousness, and the Drunkard perhaps be not conscious of what he did; yet Humane Judicatures justly punish him; because the Fact is proved against him, but want of consciousness cannot be proved for him. But in the great Day, wherein the Secrets of all Hearts shall be laid open, it may be reasonable to think, no one shall be made to answer for what he knows nothing of; but shall receive his Doom, his Conscience accusing or excusing him.

§ 23. Nothing but consciousness can unite remote Existences into the same Person, the Identity of Substance will not do it. For whatever Substance there is, however framed, without consciousness, there is no Person: And a Carcase may be a Person, as well as any sort of Substance be so without consciousness.

Could we suppose two distinct incommunicable consciousnesses acting the same Body, the one constantly by Day, the other by Night; and on the other side the same consciousness acting by Intervals two distinct Bodies: I ask in the first case, Whether the *Day* and the *Night-man* would not be two as distinct Persons, as *Socrates* and *Plato*; and whether in the second case, there would not be one Person in two distinct Bodies, as much as one Man is the same in two distinct clothings. Nor is it at all material to say, that this same, and this distinct *consciousness* in the cases above-mentioned, is owing to the same and distinct immaterial Substances, bringing it with them to those Bodies, which whether true or no, alters not the case: Since 'tis evident the *personal Identity* would equally be determined by the consciousness, whether that consciousness were annexed to some individual immaterial Substance or no. For granting that the thinking Substance in Man must be necessarily suppos'd immaterial, 'tis evident, that immaterial thinking thing may sometimes part with its past consciousness, and be restored to it again, as appears in the forgetfulness Men often have of their past Actions, and the Mind many times recovers the memory of a

§§ 23–5. *Consciousness alone makes self.*

(4–8) For . . . him.] *add.* **2er–5** (6) be] **4–5** | is **2er–3** (7) justly] **2er, 4–5**; *om.* **3** (*likewise* **Coste**) (11) [*2nd*] his] **4–5** | his own **2–3** (15) consciousness,] **4–5** | consciousness **2–3** (31–2) granting that] **4–5** | though **2–3**

past consciousness, which it had lost for twenty Years together. Make these intervals of Memory and Forgetfulness to take their turns regularly by Day and Night, and you have two Persons with the same immaterial Spirit, as much as in the former instance two Persons with the same Body. So that *self* is not determined by Identity or Diversity of Substance, which it cannot be sure of, but only by Identity of consciousness.

§ 24. Indeed it may conceive the Substance whereof it is now made up, to have existed formerly, united in the same conscious Being: But consciousness removed, that Substance is no more it *self*, or makes no more a part of it, than any other Substance, as is evident in the instance, we have already given, of a Limb cut off, of whose Heat, or Cold, or other Affections, having no longer any consciousness, it is no more of a Man's self than any other Matter of the Universe. In like manner it will be in reference to any immaterial Substance, which is void of that consciousness whereby I am my *self* to my *self*: If there be any part of its Existence, which I cannot upon recollection join with that present consciousness, whereby I am now my *self*, it is in that part of its Existence no more my *self*, than any other immaterial Being. For whatsoever any Substance has thought or done, which I cannot recollect, and by my consciousness make my own Thought and Action, it will no more belong to me, whether a part of me thought or did it, than if it had been thought or done by any other immaterial Being any where existing.

§ 25. I agree the more probable Opinion is, that this consciousness is annexed to, and the Affection of one individual immaterial Substance.

But let Men according to their divers Hypotheses resolve of that as they please. This every intelligent Being, sensible of Happiness or Misery, must grant, that there is something that is *himself*, that he is concerned for, and would have happy; that this *self* has existed in a continued Duration more than one instant, and therefore 'tis possible may exist, as it has done, Months and Years to come, without any certain bounds to be set to its duration; and may be the same *self*, by the same consciousness, continued on for the future. And thus, by this consciousness, he finds himself to be the *same self* which did such or such an Action some Years since, by

(3) two] **4–5** | the two **2–3** (17) : If . . . which] **4–5** | ; so that **2–3** (18) join] **4–5** | join any part of its Existence **2–3** (22) it] *add.* **4–5** (28) Hypotheses] **3–5** | Hypothesis **2** (29) every] **2er–5** | very **2**

which he comes to be happy or miserable now. In all which account of *self*, the same numerical Substance is not considered, as making the same *self*: But the same continued consciousness, in which several Substances may have been united, and again separated from it, which, whilst they continued in a vital union with that, wherein this consciousness then resided, made a part of that same *self*. Thus any part of our Bodies vitally united to that, which is conscious in us, makes a part of our *selves*: But upon separation from the vital union, by which that consciousness is communicated, that, which a moment since was part of our *selves*, is now no more so, than a part of another Man's *self* is a part of me; and 'tis not impossible, but in a little time may become a real part of another Person. And so we have the same numerical Substance become a part of two different Persons; and the same Person preserved under the change of various Substances. Could we suppose any Spirit wholly stripp'd of all its memory or consciousness of past Actions, as we find our Minds always are of a great part of ours, and sometimes of them all, the union or separation of such a Spiritual Substance would make no variation of personal Identity, any more than that of any Particle of Matter does. Any Substance vitally united to the present thinking Being, is a part of that very *same self* which now is: Any thing united to it by a consciousness of former Actions makes also a part of the *same self*, which is the same both then and now.

§ 26. *Person*, as I take it, is the name for this *self*. Where-ever a Man finds, what he calls *himself*, there I think another may say is the same *Person*. It is a Forensick Term appropriating Actions and their Merit; and so belongs only to intelligent Agents capable of a Law, and Happiness and Misery. This personality extends it *self* beyond present Existence to what is past, only by consciousness, whereby it becomes concerned and accountable, owns and imputes to it *self* past Actions, just upon the same ground, and for the same reason, that it does the present. All which is founded in a concern for Happiness the unavoidable concomitant of consciousness, that which is conscious of Pleasure and Pain, desiring, that that *self*, that is conscious, should be happy. And therefore whatever past Actions it cannot reconcile or appropriate to that present *self* by consciousness, it can be no more concerned in, than if they had never been done: And to receive Pleasure or Pain; *i.e.* Reward or Punishment,

§§ 26, 27. *Person a Forensick Term.*

(19) Particle] **4–5** | Particles **2–3** (28) [*2nd*] and] **4–5** | or **2–3** (*likewise* **Coste**)

on the account of any such Action, is all one, as to be made happy or miserable in its first being, without any demerit at all. For supposing a Man punish'd now, for what he had done in another Life, whereof he could be made to have no consciousness at all, what difference is there between that Punishment, and being created miserable? And therefore conformable to this, the Apostle tells us, that at the Great Day, when every one shall *receive according to his doings, the secrets of all Hearts shall be laid open.** The Sentence shall be justified by the consciousness all Persons shall have, that they *themselves* in what Bodies soever they appear, or what Substances soever that consciousness adheres to, are the *same*, that committed those Actions, and deserve that Punishment for them.

§ 27. I am apt enough to think I have in treating of this Subject made some Suppositions that will look strange to some Readers, and possibly they are so in themselves. But yet I think, they are such, as are pardonable in this ignorance we are in of the Nature of that thinking thing, that is in us, and which we look on as our *selves*. Did we know what it was, or how it was tied to a certain System of fleeting Animal Spirits; or whether it could, or could not perform its Operations of Thinking and Memory out of a Body organized as ours is; and whether it has pleased God, that no one such Spirit shall ever be united to any but one such Body, upon the right Constitution of whose Organs its Memory should depend, we might see the Absurdity of some of those Suppositions I have made. But taking, as we ordinarily now do, (in the dark concerning these Matters) the Soul of a Man, for an immaterial Substance, independent from Matter, and indifferent alike to it all, there can from the Nature of things, be no Absurdity at all, to suppose, that the same Soul may, at different times be united to different Bodies, and with them make up, for that time, one Man; As well as we suppose a part of a Sheep's Body yesterday should be a part of a Man's Body tomorrow, and in that union make a vital part of *Melibœus* himself as well as it did of his Ram.

§ 28. To conclude, whatever Substance begins to exist, it must, during its Existence, necessarily be the same: Whatever Compositions of Substances begin to exist, during the union of those

§ 28. *The difficulty from ill use of Names.*

(6–7), that] *add.* **4–5** (25) these] **2er–5** | those **2** (*l. below* 35) *In* **Coste**, *§§ 28, 29 come under the same marginal summary as that for §§ 26, 27.*

---

* *cf.* 1 Cor. 14: 25 *and* 2 Cor. 5: 10.

Substances, the concrete must be the same: Whatsoever Mode begins to exist, during its Existence, it is the same: And so if the Composition be of distinct Substances, and different Modes, the same Rule holds. Whereby it will appear, that the difficulty or obscurity, that has been about this Matter, rather rises from the Names ill used, than from any obscurity in things themselves. For whatever makes the specifick *Idea*, to which the name is applied, if that *Idea* be steadily kept to, the distinction of any thing into the same, and divers will easily be conceived, and there can arise no doubt about it.

§ 29. For supposing a rational Spirit be the *Idea* of a *Man*, 'tis easie to know, what is the *same Man*, *viz.* the *same Spirit*, whether separate or in a Body will be the *same Man*. Supposing a rational Spirit vitally united to a Body of a certain conformation of Parts to make a *Man*, whilst that rational Spirit, with that vital conformation of Parts, though continued in a fleeting successive Body, remains, it will be the *same Man*. But if to any one the *Idea* of a *Man* be, but the vital union of Parts in a certain shape; as long as that vital union and shape remains, in a concrete no otherwise the same, but by a continued succession of fleeting Particles, it will be the same *Man*. For whatever be the composition whereof the complex *Idea* is made, whenever Existence makes it one particular thing under any denomination, the same Existence continued, preserves it the same individual under the same denomination.

CHAPTER XXVIII

Of other Relations.

§ 1. Besides the before-mentioned occasions of Time, Place, and Causality of comparing, or referring Things one to another, there are, as I have said, infinite others, some whereof I shall mention.

§ 29. *Continued Existence makes Identity.* § 1. *Proportional.*

(19–20) remains, . . . Particles,] **4–5** | remains . . . Particles **2–3** (24) **5** *adds, in a footnote, quotations from Locke's* Third Letter to the Bishop of Worcester, *pp. 165, etc.*; *prefaced by* 'The Doctrine of Identity and Diversity, contained in this Chapter, the Bishop of *Worcester* pretends to be inconsistent with the Doctrine of the Christian Faith, concerning the Resurrection of the Dead. His Way of arguing from it, is this: He says, *The Reason of believing the Resurrection of the same Body upon Mr.* Locke's *Grounds, is from the* Idea *of Identity*. To which our Author answers:' (*l. below* 24) XXVIII] **2–5** | XXVII **1** (*l. above* 25) *Relations*] **Coste** *adds* ', *et sur tout, des Relations Morales*' (26) Causality] **1–4** | Casualty **5**

First, The first I shall name, is some one simple *Idea*; which being capable of Parts or Degrees, affords an occasion of comparing the Subjects wherein it is to one another, in respect of that simple *Idea*, *v.g. Whiter*, *Sweeter*, *Bigger*, *Equal*, *More*, etc. These Relations depending on the Equality and Excess of the same simple *Idea*, in several Subjects, may be called, if one will, *Proportional*; and that these are only conversant about those simple *Ideas* received from Sensation or Reflection, is so evident, that nothing need be said to evince it.

§ 2. *Secondly*, Another occasion of comparing Things together, or considering one thing, so as to include in that Consideration some other thing, is the Circumstances of their origin or beginning; which being not afterwards to be altered, make the Relations, depending thereon, as lasting as the Subjects to which they belong; *v.g. Father* and *Son*, *Brothers*, *Cousin-Germans*, etc. which have their Relations by one Community of Blood, wherein they partake in several degrees; *Country-men*, *i.e.* those who were born in the same Country, or Tract of Ground; and these I call *natural Relations*: Wherein we may observe, that Mankind have fitted their Notions and Words to the use of common Life, and not to the truth and extent of Things. For 'tis certain, that in reality, the Relation is the same, betwixt the Begetter, and the Begotten, in the several Races of other Animals, as well as Men: But yet 'tis seldom said, This Bull is the Grandfather of such a Calf; or that two Pidgeons are Cousin-Germains. It is very convenient, that by distinct Names, these Relations should be observed, and marked out in Mankind, there being occasion, both in Laws, and other Communications one with another, to mention and take notice of Men, under these Relations: From whence also arise the Obligations of several Duties amongst Men: Whereas in Brutes, Men having very little or no cause to mind these Relations, they have not thought fit to give them distinct and peculiar Names. This, by the way, may give us some light into the different state and growth of Languages, which being suited only to the convenience of Communication, are proportioned to the Notions Men have, and the commerce of Thoughts familiar amongst them; and not to the reality or extent of Things, nor to the various Respects might be found among them;

§ 2. *Natural.*

---

(31) these] **2–5** | those **1**

nor the different abstract Considerations might be framed about them. Where they had no philosophical Notions, there they had no Terms to express them: And 'tis no wonder Men should have framed no Names for those Things, they found no occasion to discourse of. From whence it is easy to imagine, why, as in some Countries, they may not have so much as the Name for a Horse; and in others, where they are more careful of the Pedigrees of their Horses, than of their own, that there they may have not only Names for particular Horses, but also of their several Relations of Kindred one to another.

§ 3. *Thirdly*, Sometimes the foundation of considering Things, with reference to one another, is some act, whereby any one comes by a Moral Right, Power, or Obligation to do something. Thus a *General* is one, that hath power to command an Army; and an Army under a General, is a Collection of armed Men, obliged to obey one Man. A *Citizen*, or a *Burgher*, is one who has a Right to certain Privileges in this or that place. All this sort depending upon Men's Wills, or Agreement in Society, I call *Instituted*, or *Voluntary*; and may be distinguished from the natural, in that they are most, if not all of them, some way or other alterable, and separable from the Persons, to whom they have sometimes belonged, though neither of the Substances, so related, be destroy'd. Now though these are all reciprocal, as well as the rest; and contain in them a reference of two things, one to the other: yet because one of the two things often wants a relative Name, importing that reference, Men usually take no notice of it, and the Relation is commonly over-look'd, *v.g.* A *Patron* and *Client*, are easily allow'd to be Relations: but a *Constable*, or *Dictator*, are not so readily, at first hearing, considered as such. Because there is no peculiar Name for those who are under the Command of a Dictator, or Constable, expressing a Relation to either of them; though it be certain, that either of them hath a certain Power over some others; and so is so far related to them, as well as a Patron is to his Client, or General to his Army.

§ 4. *Fourthly*, There is another sort of Relation, which is the Conformity, or Disagreement, Men's voluntary Actions have to a Rule, to which they are referred, and by which they are judged of: which, I think, may be called *Moral Relation*; as being that, which

§ 3. *Instituted.* § 4. *Moral.*

(1) nor] **4–5** | or **1–3** (6) a] **4–5** | an **1–3**

denominates our Moral Actions, and deserves well to be examined, there being no part of Knowledge wherein we should be more careful to get determined *Ideas*, and avoid, as much as may be, Obscurity and Confusion. Humane Actions, when with their various Ends, Objects, Manners, and Circumstances, they are framed into distinct complex *Ideas*, are, as has been shewn, so many *mixed Modes*, a great part whereof have Names annexed to them. Thus supposing Gratitude to be a readiness to acknowledge and return Kindness received; Polygamy to be the having more Wives than one at once: when we frame these Notions thus in our Minds, we have there so many determined *Ideas* of mixed Modes. But this is not all that concerns our Actions; it is not enough to have determined *Ideas* of them, and to know what Names belong to such and such Combinations of *Ideas*. We have a farther and greater Concernment, and that is, to know whether such Actions so made up, are morally good, or bad.

§ 5. Good and Evil, as hath been shewn, B.II.Ch.XX. § 2. and Ch.XXI. § 42. are nothing but Pleasure or Pain, or that which occasions, or procures Pleasure or Pain to us. *Morally Good and Evil* then, is only the Conformity or Disagreement of our voluntary Actions to some Law, whereby Good or Evil is drawn on us, from the Will and Power of the Law-maker; which Good and Evil, Pleasure or Pain, attending our observance, or breach of the Law, by the Decree of the Law-maker, is that we call *Reward* and *Punishment*.

§ 6. Of these *Moral Rules*, or Laws, to which Men generally refer, and by which they judge of the Rectitude or Pravity of their Actions, there seem to me to be *three sorts*, with their three different Enforcements, or Rewards and Punishments. For since it would be utterly in vain, to suppose a Rule set to the free Actions of Man, without annexing to it some Enforcement of Good and Evil, to determine his Will, we must, where-ever we suppose a Law, suppose also some Reward or Punishment annexed to that Law. It would be in vain for one intelligent Being, to set a Rule to the Actions of

§ 5. *Moral Good and Evil.* § 6. *Moral Rules.*

(3) determined] **4–5** | clear and distinct **1–3** (6) are . . . shewn] **2–5** | they are, as has been shewed **1** (11) determined] **4–5** | clear and distinct **1–3** (12) that concerns] **2er–5** | concerning **1–2** (12–13) determined] **4–5** | clear and distinct **1–3** (14) *Ideas.*] **4–5** | *Ideas*, as make up the complex *Idea* belonging to such a Name. [: **2–3**] **1–3** (17–18) hath . . . § 42.] **4–5** | has been shewed [shewn **2–3**] in another place, **1–3** (32) Law] **4–5** | Rule **1–3**

another, if he had it not in his Power, to reward the compliance with, and punish deviation from his Rule, by some Good and Evil, that is not the natural product and consequence of the Action it self. For that being a natural Convenience, or Inconvenience, would operate of it self without a Law. This, if I mistake not, is the true nature of all *Law*, properly so called.

§ 7. The *Laws* that Men generally refer their Actions to, to judge of their Rectitude, or Obliquity, seem to me to be these three. 1. The *Divine* Law. 2. The *Civil* Law. 3. The Law of *Opinion* or *Reputation*, if I may so call it. By the Relation they bear to the first of these, Men judge whether their Actions are Sins, or Duties; by the second, whether they be Criminal, or Innocent; and by the third, whether they be Vertues or Vices.

§ 8. *First*, The *Divine* Law, whereby I mean, that Law which God has set to the actions of Men, whether promulgated to them by the light of Nature, or the voice of Revelation. That God has given a Rule whereby Men should govern themselves, I think there is no body so brutish as to deny. He has a Right to do it, we are his Creatures: He has Goodness and Wisdom to direct our Actions to that which is best: and he has Power to enforce it by Rewards and Punishments, of infinite weight and duration, in another Life: for no body can take us out of his hands. This is the only true touchstone of *moral Rectitude*; and by comparing them to this Law, it is, that Men judge of the most considerable *Moral Good* or *Evil* of their Actions; that is, whether as *Duties, or Sins*, they are like to procure them happiness, or misery, from the hands of the ALMIGHTY.

§ 9. *Secondly*, The *Civil* Law, the Rule set by the Commonwealth, to the Actions of those, who belong to it, is another Rule, to which Men refer their Actions, to judge whether they be *criminal*, or no. This Law no body over-looks: the Rewards and Punishments, that enforce it, being ready at hand, and suitable to the Power that makes it: which is the force of the Commonwealth, engaged to protect the Lives, Liberties, and Possessions, of those who live according to its

§ 7. *Laws.* § 8. *Divine Law, the measure of Sin and Duty.* § 9. *Civil Law, the measure of Crimes and Innocence.*

(1–2) the . . . punish] **2–5** | and punish the compliance with, or **1** (9–10) [*3rd*] Law . . . *Reputation*] **2–5** | *philosophical* Law **1** (11) Men judge whether their] **2–5** | we judge whether our **1** (14–17) The . . . themselves] **2–5** | That GOD has given a Law to Mankind **1** (20) it by Rewards] **4–5** | it by Reward **2–3** | by Reward **1** (22–3) This . . . and] *add.* **2–5** (27) *Secondly*,] *add.* **2–5** (32) engaged] **2–5** | which is engaged **1**

Laws, and has power to take away Life, Liberty, or Goods, from him, who disobeys; which is the punishment of Offences committed against this Law.

§ 10. *Thirdly*, The *Law of Opinion or Reputation.* Vertue and Vice are Names pretended, and supposed every where to stand for actions in their own nature right and wrong: And as far as they really are so applied, they so far are co-incident with the *divine Law* abovementioned. But yet, whatever is pretended, this is visible, that these Names, *Vertue* and *Vice*, in the particular instances of their application, through the several Nations and Societies of Men in the World, are constantly attributed only to such actions, as in each Country and Society are in reputation or discredit. Nor is it to be thought strange, that Men every where should give the Name of *Vertue* to those actions, which amongst them are judged praise worthy; and call that *Vice*, which they account blamable: Since otherwise they would condemn themselves, if they should think any thing *Right*, to which they allow'd not Commendation; any thing *Wrong*, which they let pass without Blame. Thus the measure of what is every where called and esteemed *Vertue* and *Vice* is this approbation or dislike, praise or blame, which by a secret and tacit consent establishes it self in the several Societies, Tribes, and Clubs of Men in the World: whereby several actions come to find Credit or Disgrace amongst them, according to the Judgment, Maxims, or Fashions of that place. For though Men uniting into politick Societies, have resigned up to the publick the disposing of all their Force, so that they cannot employ it against any Fellow-Citizen, any farther than the Law of the Country directs: yet they retain still the power of Thinking well or ill; approving or disapproving of the actions of those whom they live amongst, and

§§ 10, 11. *Philosophical Law, the measure of Vertue and Vice.*

(4–18) The . . . Thus] **2–5** | The third, which I call the *philosophical Law*, not because Philosophers make it, but because they have most busied themselves to enquire after it, and talk about it, is the Law of *Vertue*, and *Vice*; which though it be more talked of, possibly, than either of the other, yet how it comes to be established with such Authority as it has, to distinguish and denominate the Actions of Men; and what are the true measures of it, perhaps, is not so generally taken notice of. To comprehend this aright, we must consider, that Men uniting into Politick Societies, though they have resigned up to the Publick the disposing of all their force; so that they cannot employ it against any fellow-Citizen, any farther than the Law of their Country directs: yet they retain still the Power of Thinking well or ill; approving or disapproving the Actions of those they live amongst, and converse with. If therefore we examine it right, we shall find, that **1**. (Cf. (24)–354(2).) (9) Names, *Vertue*] **4–5** | names of *Vertue* **2–3** (24)–354(2) For . . . *Vice*.] *add.* **2–5** (29) whom] *add.* **4–5**

converse with: And by this approbation and dislike they establish amongst themselves, what they will call *Vertue* and *Vice*.

§ 11. That this is the common *measure of Vertue and Vice*, will appear to any one, who considers, that though that passes for *Vice* in one Country, which is counted a *Vertue*, or at least not *Vice*, in another; yet every-where *Vertue* and Praise, *Vice* and Blame, go together. *Vertue* is every-where that, which is thought Praise-worthy; and nothing else but that, which has the allowance of publick Esteem, is called *Vertue*.† *Vertue* and Praise are so united

† Our Author, in his Preface to the 4th Edition, taking Notice how apt Men have been to mistake him, added what here follows. "Of this the ingenious Author of the *Discourse concerning the nature of Man*, has given me a late instance to mention no other. For the civility of his expressions, and the candor that belongs to his order, forbid me to think, that he would have closed his Preface with an insinuation, as if in what I had said Book 2. Chap. 28. concerning the third Rule, which Men referr their actions to, I went about to make *Vertue Vice* and *Vice Vertue*, unless he had mistaken my meaning; which he could not have done, if he had but given himself the trouble to consider, what the argument was I was then upon, and what was the chief design of that Chapter, plainly enough set down in the fourth Section and those following. For I was there, not laying down moral Rules, but shewing the original and nature of moral *Ideas*, and enumerating the Rules Men make use of in moral Relations, whether those Rules were true or false: and pursuant thereunto I tell, what has everywhere that denomination, which in the language of that place answers to *Vertue* and *Vice* in ours, which *alters not the nature of things*, though Men generally do judge of, and denominate their actions according to the esteem and fashion of the Place or Sect they are of.

If he had been at the pains to reflect on what I had said B.I. c. III, §.18. and in this present Chapter, §. 13, 14, 15, and 20. he would have known, what I think of the eternal and unalterable nature of right and wrong, and what I call *Vertue* and *Vice*: And if he had observed, that in the place he quotes, I only report as matter of fact, what others call *Vertue* and *Vice*, he would not have found it liable to any great Exception. For I think I am not much out, in saying, that one of the Rules made use of in the World for a ground or measure of a moral Relation, is that esteem and reputation, which several sorts of actions find variously in the several Societies of Men, according to which they are there called *Vertues* or *Vices*: And whatever authority the Learned Mr. *Lowde* places in his *Old English Dictionary*, I dare say it no where tells him (if I should appeal to it) that the same action is not in credit, call'd and counted a *Vertue* in one place, which being in disrepute, passes for, and under the name of *Vice* in another. The taking notice that Men bestow the names of *Vertue* and *Vice*, according to this Rule of Reputation is all I have done, or can be laid to my charge to have done, towards the making *Vice Vertue*, and *Vertue Vice*. But the good Man does well, and as becomes his calling, to be watchful in such points, and to take the allarm, even at Expressions which standing alone by themselves might sound ill and be suspected.

'Tis to this Zeal, allowable in his Function, that I forgive his citing, as he does, these words of mine in § 11 of this Chapter. *The Exhortations of inspired Teachers have*

(2) *v*. 353(24), n. (5) , or at least not *Vice*,] *add*. **4–5** (9) called] *add*. **2–5** † (1–2) Our . . . follows.] **5** † (2–88) Of . . . to.] **2–5**. (*See* 11(35), n.) † (2) "Of] **5** | Of **2–4** † (6) Chap. 28.] **5** (*likewise* **Coste**) | Chap. 27. **2–4** † (10) Section] **5** (*likewise* **Coste**) | §. **2–4** † (14–15) has . . . ours] **5** (*likewise* **Coste**) | is every where called *Vertue* and *Vice* **2–4** † (18–19) B.I. . . . Chapter,] **5** | p. 23. §.18. and p. 160. **2–4** † (37) in § 11 of this Chapter] **5** | , p. 159 **2–4**

that they are called often by the same Name. *Sunt sua præmia Laudi*, says *Virgil*;* and so *Cicero*, *Nihil habet natura præstantius*, *quam Hone-*

not feared to appeal to common repute, *whatsoever things are lovely*, *whatsoever things are of good report*, *if there be any Vertue*, *if there be any Praise*, etc. Philippians 4. 8. Without taking notice of those immediately preceding, which introduce them, and run thus. *Whereby in the corruption of manners the true boundaries of the Law of Nature*, *which ought to be the Rule of Vertue and Vice*, *were pretty well preserv'd: So that even the Exhortations of inspired Teachers*, etc. By which words, and the rest of that Section it is plain, that I brought that passage of St. *Paul*, not to prove, that the general measure of what Men called *Vertue* and *Vice*, throughout the World, was the Reputation and fashion of each particular Society within it self; but to shew, that though it were so, yet, for reasons I there give, Men, in that way of denominating their actions, did not for the most part much vary from the Law of Nature, which is that standing and unalterable Rule, by which they ought to judge of the moral rectitude and pravity of their actions, and accordingly denominate them *Vertues* or *Vices*. Had Mr. *Lowde* considered this, he would have found it little to his purpose, to have quoted that passage in a sence, I used it not; and would I imagine have spared the Explication he subjoins to it, as not very necessary. But I hope this second Edition will give him satisfaction in the point, and that this matter is now so expressed as to shew him there was no cause of scruple.

Though I am forced to differ from him in those apprehensions, he has expressed, in the latter end of his Preface, concerning what I had said about *Vertue* and *Vice*; yet we are better agreed than he thinks, in what he says in his 3d. Chapter p. 78. Concerning *Natural Inscription* and *Innate Notions*. I shall not deny him the Privilege, he claims p. 52. to state the question as he pleases, especially when he states it so, as to leave nothing in it, contrary to what I have said: For according to him, *Innate Notions*, *being conditional things*, *depending upon the concurrence of several other circumstances in order to the Soul's exerting them*; all that he says for *innate*, *imprinted*, *impressed Notions* (for of *innate Ideas* he says nothing at all) amounts at last only to this, That there are certain Propositions, which though the Soul, from the beginning, or when a Man is born, does not know; yet by *assistance from the outward Senses and the help of some previous Cultivation*, it may afterwards come certainly to know the truth of; which is no more than what I have affirm'd in my first Book. For I suppose by the *Soul's exerting* them, he means its beginning to know them, or else the Soul's *Exerting of Notions* will be to me a very unintelligible expression, and I think at best is a very unfit one in this case, it misleading Men's thoughts by an insinuation, as if these Notions were in the Mind before the *Soul exerts them*, i.e. before they are known; whereas truly before they are known, there is nothing of them in the mind, but a capacity to know them, when the *concurrence of those circumstances*, which this ingenious Author thinks necessary, *in order to the Soul's exerting them*, brings them into our Knowledge.

P. 52. I find him express it thus, *These natural Notions are not so imprinted upon the Soul*, *as that they naturally and necessarily exert themselves* (*even in Children and Ideots*) *without any assistance from the outward Senses*, *or without the help of some previous cultivation*. Here he says they *exert themselves*, as p. 78. that the *Soul exerts them*. When he has explain'd to himself or others, what he means by *the Soul's exerting Innate Notions*, or their *exerting themselves*, and what that *previous cultivation and circumstances in order* to their being *exerted* are, he will I suppose find, there is so little of controversie between him and me in the point, bating that he calls that *exerting of Notions*, which I in a more vulgar stile call *knowing*, that I have reason to think he brought in my name upon this occasion only, out of the pleasure he has to speak civilly of me, which I must gratefully acknowledge he has done every where he mentions me, not without conferring on me, as some others have done, a title I have no right to."

† (43) Section] **5** (*likewise* **Coste**) | § **2–4** † (45) called] **2–4** | call **5** (*likewise* **Coste**) † (71) case] *add.* **3–5** † (88) to."] *edit.* | to. **2–5**

* *Aeneid*, I, 461.

statem, quam Laudem, quam Dignitatem, quam Decus, which he tells you, are all Names for the same thing, *Tusc. l.2* This is the Language of the Heathen Philosophers, who well understood wherein their Notions of *Vertue* and *Vice* consisted. And though, perhaps, by the different Temper, Education, Fashion, Maxims, or Interest of different sorts of Men it fell out, that what was thought Praiseworthy in one Place, escaped not censure in another; and so in different Societies, *Vertues* and *Vices* were changed: Yet, as to the Main, they for the most part kept the same every where. For since nothing can be more natural, than to encourage with Esteem and Reputation that, wherein every one finds his Advantage; and to blame and discountenance the contrary: 'tis no Wonder, that Esteem and Discredit, Vertue and Vice, should in a great measure every-where correspond with the unchangeable Rule of Right and Wrong, which the Law of God hath established; there being nothing, that so directly, and visibly secures, and advances the general Good of Mankind in this World, as Obedience to the Laws, he has set them, and nothing that breeds such Mischiefs and Confusion, as the neglect of them. And therefore Men, without renouncing all Sense and Reason, and their own Interest, which they are so constantly true to, could not generally mistake, in placing their Commendation and Blame on that side, that really deserved it not. Nay, even those Men, whose Practice was otherwise, failed not to give their Approbation right, few being depraved to that Degree, as not to condemn, at least in others, the Faults they themselves were guilty of: whereby even in the Corruption of Manners, the true Boundaries of the Law of Nature, which ought to be the Rule of Vertue and Vice, were pretty well preserved. So that even the Exhortations of inspired Teachers have not feared to appeal to common Repute. *Whatsoever is lovely, whatsoever is of good report, if there be any Vertue, if there be any praise*, etc. Philippians, 4.8.

§ 12. If any one shall imagine, that I have forgot my own Notion of a Law, when I make *the Law*, whereby Men judge *of Vertue and Vice*, to be nothing else, but the Consent of private Men, who have not Authority enough to make a Law: Especially wanting that, which is so necessary, and essential to a Law, a Power to inforce it: I think, I may say, that he, who imagines Commendation and Disgrace, not to be strong Motives on Men, to accommodate themselves to the Opinions and Rules of those, with whom they

§ 12. *Its Inforcements, Commendation, and Discredit.*

converse, seems little skill'd in the Nature, or History of Mankind: the greatest part whereof he shall find to govern themselves chiefly, if not solely, by this Law of Fashion; and so they do that, which keeps them in Reputation with their Company, little regard the Laws of God, or the Magistrate. The Penalties that attend the breach of God's Laws, some, nay, perhaps, most Men seldom seriously reflect on: and amongst those that do, many, whilst they break the Law, entertain Thoughts of future reconciliation, and making their Peace for such Breaches. And as to the Punishments, due from the Laws of the Commonwealth, they frequently flatter themselves with the hopes of Impunity. But no Man scapes the Punishment of their Censure and Dislike, who offends against the Fashion and Opinion of the Company he keeps, and would recommend himself to. Nor is there one of ten thousand, who is stiff and insensible enough, to bear up under the constant Dislike, and Condemnation of his own Club. He must be of a strange, and unusual Constitution, who can content himself, to live in constant Disgrace and Disrepute with his own particular Society. Solitude many Men have sought, and been reconciled to: But no Body, that has the least Thought, or Sense of a Man about him, can live in Society, under the constant Dislike, and ill Opinion of his Familiars, and those he converses with. This is a Burthen too heavy for humane Sufferance: And he must be made up of irreconcilable Contradictions, who can take Pleasure in Company, and yet be insensible of Contempt and Disgrace from his Companions.

§ 13. These Three then, *First*, The Law of God. *Secondly*, The Law of politick Societies. *Thirdly*, The Law of Fashion, or private Censure, are those, to which Men variously compare their Actions: And 'tis by their Conformity to one of these Laws, that they take their measures, when they would judge of their Moral Rectitude, and denominate their Actions good or bad.

§ 14. Whether the Rule, to which, as to a Touch-stone, we bring our voluntary Actions, to examine them by, and try their Goodness, and accordingly to name them; which is, as it were, the Mark

§ 13. *These three Laws the Rules of moral Good and Evil.* §§ 14, 15. *Morality is the Relation of Actions to these Rules.*

---

(20) Thought] **2–5** | Thoughts **1**. (**Coste** 'quelque sentiment de sa propre nature') (*l. below* 34: §§ 14, 15.) *In* **Coste**, § *14 comes under the same marginal summary as that for* § *13, the summary for* § *14 in* **2–5** *being there applied to* § *15.*

of the value we set upon them: Whether, I say, we take that Rule from the Fashion of the Country, or the Will of a Law-maker, the Mind is easily able to observe the Relation any Action hath to it; and to judge, whether the Action agrees, or disagrees with the Rule: and so hath a Notion of *Moral Goodness or Evil*, which is either Conformity, or not Conformity of any Action to that Rule: And therefore, is often called Moral Rectitude. This Rule being nothing but a Collection of several simple *Ideas*, the Conformity thereto is but so ordering the Action, that the simple *Ideas*, belonging to it, may correspond to those, which the Law requires. And thus we see, how Moral Beings and Notions, are founded on, and terminated in these simple *Ideas*, we have received from Sensation or Reflection. For Example, let us consider the complex *Idea*, we signify by the Word Murther: and when we have taken it asunder, and examined all the Particulars, we shall find them to amount to a Collection of simple *Ideas*, derived from Reflection or Sensation, *viz. First*, From Reflection on the Operations of our own Minds, we have the *Ideas* of Willing, Considering, Purposing before-hand, Malice, or wishing Ill to another; and also of Life, or Perception, and Self-motion. *Secondly*, From Sensation, we have the Collection of those simple sensible *Ideas* which are to be found in a Man, and of some Action, whereby we put an end to Perception, and Motion in the Man; all which simple *Ideas*, are comprehended in the Word Murther. This Collection of simple *Ideas*, being found by me to agree or disagree, with the Esteem of the Country I have been bred in; and to be held by most Men there, worthy Praise, or Blame, I call the Action vertuous or vitious: If I have the Will of a supreme, invisible Law-maker for my Rule: then, as I supposed the Action commanded, or forbidden by God, I call it Good or Evil, Sin or Duty: and if I compare it to the civil Law, the Rule made by the Legislative of the Country, I call it lawful, or unlawful, a Crime, or no Crime. So that whencesoever we take the Rule of Moral Actions; or by what Standard soever we frame in our Minds the *Ideas* of Vertues or Vices, they consist only, and are made up of Collections of simple *Ideas*, which we originally received from Sense or Reflection: and their Rectitude, or Obliquity, consists in the Agreement, or Disagreement, with those Patterns prescribed by some Law.

(12) Reflection] **4–5** | Reflection, besides which, we have nothing at all in our Understandings, to employ our Thoughts about **1–3** (20) those] **4–5** | the **1–3** (*likewise* **Coste**) (21) which . . . in] **4–5** | of **1–3** (22) Perception] **4–5** | that Perception **1–3** (30) [*1st*] the] *add.* **2–5** (36) , or . . ., or] **4** | or . . . or **1–3, 5**

§ 15. To conceive rightly of *Moral Actions*, we must take notice of them, under this two-fold Consideration. *First*, As they are in themselves each made up of such a Collection of simple *Ideas*. Thus *Drunkenness*, or *Lying*, signify such or such a Collection of simple *Ideas*, which I call mixed Modes: and in this Sense, they are as much *positive absolute Ideas*, as the drinking of a Horse, or speaking of a Parrot. *Secondly*, Our Actions are considered, as Good, Bad, *or* Indifferent; and in this respect, they are *Relative*, it being their Conformity to, or Disagreement with some Rule, that makes them to be regular or irregular, Good or Bad: and so, as far as they are compared with a Rule, and thereupon denominated, they come under Relation. Thus the challenging, and fighting with a Man, as it is a certain positive Mode, or particular sort of Action, by particular *Ideas*, distinguished from all others, is called *Duelling*: which, when considered, in relation to the Law of God, will deserve the Name Sin; to the Law of Fashion, in some Countries, Valour and Vertue; and to the municipal Laws of some Governments, a capital Crime. In this Case, when the positive Mode has one Name, and another Name as it stands in relation to the Law, the distinction may as easily be observed, as it is in Substances, where one Name, *v.g. Man*, is used to signify the thing, another, *v.g. Father*, to signify the Relation.

§ 16. But because, very frequently the positive *Idea* of the Action, and its Moral Relation, are comprehended together under one Name, and the same Word made use of, to express both the Mode or Action, and its Moral Rectitude or Obliquity: therefore the Relation it self is less taken notice of; and there is often no *distinction* made *between the positive Idea* of the Action, *and the reference it has to a Rule*. By which confusion, of these two distinct Considerations, under one Term, those who yield too easily to the Impressions of Sounds, and are forward to take Names for Things, are often misled in their Judgment of Actions. Thus the taking from another what is his, without his Knowledge or Allowance, is properly called *Stealing*: but that Name, being commonly understood to signify also the Moral pravity of the Action, and to denote its contrariety to the Law, Men are apt to condemn, whatever they hear called Stealing, as an ill Action, disagreeing with the Rule of Right. And

§ 16. *The denominations of Actions often mislead us.*

---

(1) rightly] **1er–5** | a Right **1** (29) *a Rule*] **2–5** (*rule* **2–3**) | *rule* **1**

yet the private taking away his Sword from a Mad-man, to prevent his doing Mischief, though it be properly denominated *Stealing*, as the Name of such a *mixed Mode*: yet when compared to the Law of God; and considered in its relation to that supreme Rule, it is no Sin, or Transgression, though the Name *Stealing* ordinarily carries such an intimation with it.

§ 17. And thus much for the Relation of humane Actions to a Law, which therefore I call *Moral Relations*.

'Twould make a Volume, to go over all sorts of *Relations*: 'tis not therefore to be expected, that I should here mention them all. It suffices to our present purpose, to shew by these, what the *Ideas* are, we have *of* this comprehensive Consideration, call'd *Relation*. Which is so *various*, and the Occasions of it so *many*, (as many as there can be of comparing things one to another,) that it is not very easy to reduce it to Rules, or under just Heads. Those I have mentioned, I think, are some of the most considerable, and such, as may serve to let us see, from whence we get our *Ideas* of Relations, and wherein they are founded. But before I quit this Argument, from what has been said, give me leave to observe,

§ 18. *First*, That it is evident, That *all Relation terminates in*, and is ultimately founded on those *simple Ideas*, we have *got from Sensation, or Reflection*: So that all that we have in our Thoughts our selves, (if we think of any thing, or have any meaning,) or would signify to others, when we use Words, standing for Relations, is nothing but some simple *Ideas*, or Collections of simple *Ideas*, compared one with another. This is so manifest in that sort called *proportional*, that nothing can be more. For when a Man says, Honey is sweeter than Wax, it is plain, that his Thoughts in this Relation, terminate in this simple *Idea*, Sweetness, which is equally true of all the rest; though, where they are compounded, or decompounded, the simple *Ideas*, they are made up of, are, perhaps, seldom taken notice of: *v.g.* when the Word Father is mentioned: *First*, There is meant that particular Species, or collective *Idea*, signified by the Word Man; *Secondly*, Those sensible simple *Ideas*, signified by the Word Generation; And, *Thirdly*, The Effects of it, and all the simple *Ideas*, signified by the Word Child. So the Word Friend, being taken

§ 17. *Relations innumerable.* § 18. *All Relations terminate in simple* Ideas.

---

(4) and] **4–5** | when **1–3** (32) Father] **1–4** | Farther **5** (33) Species,] **1er–5** (',' *not in* **1er–3**) | of Species **1** (*l. below* 36: § 18.) *Relations terminate*] **2, 4–5** | *Relation terminates* **3**

for a Man, who loves, and is ready to do good to another, has all those following *Ideas* to the making of it up. *First*, all the simple *Ideas*, comprehended in the Word Man, or intelligent Being. *Secondly*, The *Idea* of Love. *Thirdly*, The *Idea* of Readiness, or Disposition. *Fourthly*, The *Idea* of Action, which is any kind of Thought, or Motion. *Fifthly*, The *Idea* of Good, which signifies any thing that may advance his Happiness; and terminates at last, if examined, in particular simple *Ideas*, of which the Word *Good* in general, signifies any one, but if removed from all simple *Ideas* quite, it signifies nothing at all. And thus also, all Moral Words terminate at last, though, perhaps, more remotely, in a Collection of simple *Ideas*: the immediate signification of Relative Words, being very often other supposed known Relations; which, if traced one to another, still end in simple *Ideas*.

§ 19. *Secondly*, That in Relations, we have for the most part, if not always, *as clear a Notion of the Relation, as we have of those simple* Ideas, *wherein it is founded*: Agreement or Disagreement, whereon Relation depends, being Things, whereof we have commonly as clear *Ideas*, as of any other whatsoever; it being but the distinguishing simple *Ideas*, or their Degrees one from another, without which, we could have no distinct Knowledge at all. For if I have a clear *Idea* of Sweetness, Light, or Extension, I have too, of equal or more, or less, of each of these: If I know what it is for one Man to be born of a Woman, *viz. Sempronia*, I know what it is for another Man to be born of the same Woman, *Sempronia*; and so have as clear a Notion of Brothers, as of Births, and, perhaps, clearer. For if I believed, that *Sempronia* digged *Titus* out of the Parsley-Bed, (as they use to tell Children,) and thereby became his Mother; and that afterwards in the same manner, she digged *Cajus* out of the Parsley-Bed, I had as clear a Notion of the Relation of Brothers between them, as if I had all the Skill of a Midwife; the Notion that the same Woman contributed, as Mother, equally to their Births, (though I were ignorant or mistaken in the manner of it,) being that on which I grounded the Relation; and that they agreed in that Circumstance of Birth, let it be what it will. The comparing them then in their descent from the same Person, without knowing the particular Circumstances of that descent, is enough to found my Notion of

§ 19. *We have ordinarily as clear (or clearer) Notion of the Relation, as of its Foundation.*

(5–6) , or] **1–4, W** | of **5** (16) [*1st*] *of*] **1–4, W** | *for* **5** (29–30) Parsley-Bed] **Coste** *adds a marginal note on the corresponding phrase in French.* (33) or] **4–5** | , or **1–3**

their having, or not having the Relation of Brothers. But though the *Ideas* of particular *Relations*, are capable of being as clear and distinct in the Minds of those, who will duly consider them, as those of mixed Modes, and more determinate, than those of Substances; yet the Names belonging to *Relation*, are often of as doubtful, and incertain Signification, as those of Substances, or mixed Modes; and much more than those of simple *Ideas*. Because Relative Words, being the Marks of this Comparison, which is made only by Men's Thoughts, and is an *Idea* only in Men's Minds, Men frequently apply them to different Comparisons of Things, according to their own Imaginations, which do not always correspond with those of others using the same Names.

§ 20. *Thirdly*, That in these I call *Moral Relations*, I have a true Notion of Relation, by comparing the Action with the Rule, whether the Rule be true, or false. For if I measure any thing by a Yard, I know, whether the thing I measure be longer, or shorter, than that supposed Yard, though, perhaps, the Yard I measure by, be not exactly the Standard: Which, indeed, is another Enquiry. For though the Rule be erroneous, and I mistaken in it; yet the agreement, or disagreement observable in that which I compare with it, makes me perceive the Relation. Though measuring by a wrong Rule, I shall thereby be brought to judge amiss of its moral Rectitude; because I have tried it by that, which is not the true Rule; but I am not mistaken in the Relation which that Action bears to that Rule I compare it to, which is agreement, or disagreement.

CHAPTER XXIX

Of Clear and Obscure, Distinct and Confused Ideas.

§ 1. HAVING shewn the Original of our *Ideas*, and taken a view of their several sorts; considered the difference between the simple

§ 20. *The Notion of the Relation is the same, whether the Rule any Action is compared to be true or false.*
§ 1. Ideas *some clear and distinct, others obscure and confused.*

(19) mistaken] **2–5** | mistake **1** (20) observable in] **4–5** | of **1–3** (21) makes . . . Relation] **4–5** | is evidently known by me; wherein consists my knowledge of Relation **1–3** (24) I] *add.* **4–5** which] *add.* **4–5** (27) shewn] **2–5** | shewed **1** (27)–363(2) taken . . . Relations] **2–5** | considered the several sorts of them, as Simple and Complex; and shewed the difference in Complex ones, betwixt those of Modes, Relations, and Substances **1** (*l. below* 26) XXIX] **2–5** | XXVIII **1**

and the complex; and observed how the complex ones are divided into those of Modes, Substances, and Relations, all which, I think, is necessary to be done by any one, who would acquaint himself throughly with the progress of the Mind, in its Apprehension and Knowledge of Things, it will, perhaps, be thought I have dwelt long enough upon the Examination of *Ideas*. I must, nevertheless, crave leave to offer some few other Considerations concerning them. The first is, That some are *clear*, and others *obscure*; some *distinct*, and others *confused*.

§ 2. The Perception of the Mind, being most aptly explained by Words relating to the Sight, we shall best understand what is meant by *Clear*, and *Obscure* in our *Ideas*, by reflecting on what we call *Clear* and *Obscure* in the Objects of Sight. Light being that which discovers to us visible Objects, we give the name of *Obscure*, to that, which is not placed in a Light sufficient to discover minutely to us the Figure and Colours, which are observable in it, and which, in a better Light, would be discernable. In like manner, our *simple Ideas* are *clear*, when they are such as the Objects themselves, from whence they were taken, did or might, in a well-ordered Sensation or Perception, present them. Whilst the Memory retains them thus, and can produce them to the Mind, when-ever it has occasion to consider them, they are *clear Ideas*. So far as they either want any thing of that original Exactness, or have lost any of their first Freshness, and are, as it were, faded or tarnished by Time, so far are they *obscure*. *Complex Ideas*, as they are made up of Simple ones; so they are *clear*, when the *Ideas* that go to their Composition, are clear; and the Number and Order of those Simple *Ideas*, that are the Ingredients of any Complex one, is determinate and certain.

§ 3. The *cause of Obscurity* in simple *Ideas*, seems to be either dull Organs; or very slight and transient Impressions made by the Objects; or else a weakness in the Memory, not able to retain them as received. For to return again to visible Objects, to help us to apprehend this matter. If the Organs, or Faculties of Perception, like Wax over-hardned with Cold, will not receive the Impression of the Seal, from the usual impulse wont to imprint it; or, like Wax of a temper too soft, will not hold it well, when well imprinted; or

§ 2. *Clear and Obscure, explained by Sight.* § 3. *Causes of Obscurity.*

(2) , and] *edit.* | and **2–5** *v.* 362(27), n. (10) The] *add.* **2–5** (17) In like manner,] **4–5** | Thus **1–3** (19) or might] *add.* **4–5** (21) them] **4–5** | them so, **1–3** (*likewise* **Coste**)

else supposing the Wax of a temper fit, but the Seal not applied with a sufficient force, to make a clear Impression: In any of these cases, the print left by the Seal, will be *obscure*. This, I suppose, needs no application to make it plainer.

§ 4. As a *clear Idea* is that whereof the Mind has such a full and evident perception, as it does receive from an outward Object operating duly on a well-disposed Organ, so a *distinct Idea* is that wherein the Mind perceives a difference from all other; and a *confused Idea* is such an one, as is not sufficiently distinguishable from another, from which it ought to be different.

§ 5. If no *Idea* be *confused*, but such as is not sufficiently distinguishable from another, from which it should be different, it will be hard, may any one say, to find any where a *confused Idea*. For let any *Idea* be as it will, it can be no other but such as the Mind perceives it to be; and that very perception, sufficiently distinguishes it from all other *Ideas*, which cannot be other, *i.e.* different, without being perceived to be so. No *Idea* therefore can be undistinguishable from another, from which it ought to be different, unless you would have it different from it self: for from all other, it is evidently different.

§ 6. To remove this difficulty, and to help us to conceive aright, what it is, that makes the *confusion*, *Ideas* are at any time chargeable with, we must consider, that Things ranked under distinct Names, are supposed different enough to be distinguished, that so each sort, by its peculiar Name, may be marked, and discoursed of apart, upon any occasion: And there is nothing more evident, than that the greatest part of different Names, are supposed to stand for different Things. Now every *Idea* a Man has, being visibly what it is, and distinct from all other *Ideas* but it self, that which makes it *confused* is, when it is such, that it may as well be called by another Name, as that which it is expressed by, the difference which keeps the Things (to be ranked under those two different Names) distinct, and makes some of them belong rather to the one, and some of them to the other of those Names, being left out; and so the

§ 4. *Distinct and Confused, what.* § 5. *Objection.* § 6. *Confusion of* Ideas, *is in reference to their Names.*

---

(5) such] *add.* **4–5** (6–7) as . . . Organ,] *add.* **4–5** (8) perceives] **1–4** | perceive **5** (23–5) ranked . . . may] **2–5** | are supposed different enough to have different Names, whereby to **1** (31) keeps] **1T.er, 2–5** | keep **1** (33) some of] *add.* **2–5** (33–4) [*2nd*] and . . . Names] **2–5** | than the other of them **1**

distinction, which was intended to be kept up by those different Names, is quite lost.

§ 7. The *Defaults which* usually *occasion* this *Confusion*, I think, are chiefly these following.

First, When any complex *Idea* (for 'tis complex *Ideas* that are most liable to confusion) is made up of *too small a number of simple Ideas*, and such only as are common to other Things, whereby the differences, that make it deserve a different Name, are left out. Thus he, that has an *Idea* made up of barely the simple ones of a Beast with Spots, has but a confused *Idea* of a Leopard, it not being thereby sufficiently distinguished from a Lynx, and several other sorts of Beasts that are spotted. So that such an *Idea*, though it hath the peculiar Name Leopard, is not distinguishable from those designed by the Names Lynx, or Panther, and may as well come under the Name Lynx, as Leopard. How much the custom of defining of Words by general terms, contributes to make the *Ideas* we would express by them, confused and undetermined, I leave others to consider. This is evident, that confused *Ideas* are such as render the Use of Words uncertain, and take away the benefit of distinct Names. When the *Ideas*, for which we use different terms, have not a difference answerable to their distinct Names, and so cannot be distinguished by them, there it is that they are truly confused.

§ 8. *Secondly*, Another default, which makes our *Ideas* confused, is, when though the particulars that make up any *Idea*, are in number enough; yet they are so *jumbled together*, that it is not easily discernable, whether it more belongs to the Name that is given it, than to any other. There is nothing properer to make us conceive this Confusion, than a sort of Pictures usually shewn, as surprizing Pieces of Art, wherein the Colours, as they are laid by the Pencil on the Table it self, mark out very odd and unusual Figures, and have no discernable order in their Position. This Draught, thus made up of parts, wherein no Symmetry nor Order appears, is, in it self, no more a confused Thing, than the Picture of a cloudy Sky; wherein though there be as little order of Colours, or Figures to be found, yet no body thinks it a confused Picture. What is it then, that makes it be thought confused, since the want of Symmetry does not? As it

§ 7. *Defaults which make Confusion.* § 7(5). *First, complex* Ideas *made up of too few simple ones.* § 8. *Secondly, Or its simple ones jumbled disorderly together.*

(8) it] **1–4, W** | it, **5** (20) use] **2–5** | used **1**

is plain it does not: for another Draught made, barely in imitation of this, could not be called confused. I answer, That which makes it be thought confused, is the applying it to some Name, to which it does no more discernibly belong, than to some other. *v.g.* When it is said to be the Picture of a Man, or *Cæsar*, then any one with reason counts it confused: because it is not discernible, in that state, to belong more to the name Man, or *Cæsar*, than to the name Baboon, or *Pompey*: which are supposed to stand for different *Ideas*, from those signified by Man, or *Cæsar*. But when a cylindrical Mirrour, placed right, hath reduced those irregular Lines on the Table, into their due order and proportion, then the Confusion ceases, and the Eye presently sees, that it is a Man, or *Cæsar*; *i.e.* that it belongs to those Names; and that it is sufficiently distinguishable from a Baboon, or *Pompey*; *i.e.* from the *Ideas* signified by those Names. Just thus it is with our *Ideas*, which are, as it were, the Pictures of Things. No one of these mental Draughts, however the parts are put together, can be called confused, (for they are plainly discernible as they are,) till it be ranked under some ordinary Name, to which it cannot be discerned to belong, any more than it does to some other Name, of an allowed different signification.

§ 9. *Thirdly*, A third defect that frequently gives the name of Confused, to our *Ideas*, is when any one of them is *uncertain, and undetermined.* Thus we may observe Men, who not forbearing to use the ordinary Words of their Language, till they have learn'd their precise signification, change the *Idea*, they make this or that term stand for, almost as often as they use it. He that does this, out of uncertainty of what he should leave out, or put into his *Idea* of *Church*, or *Idolatry*, every time he thinks of either, and holds not steady to any one precise Combination of *Ideas*, that makes it up, is said to have a confused *Idea* of Idolatry, or the Church: Though this be still for the same reason that the former, *viz.* Because a mutable *Idea* (if we will allow it to be one *Idea*) cannot belong to one Name, rather than another; and so loses the distinction, that distinct Names are designed for.

§ 10. By what has been said, we may observe how much *Names*, as supposed steady signs of Things, and by their difference to stand

§ 9. *Thirdly, Or are mutable and undetermined.* § 10. *Confusion without reference to Names, hardly conceivable.*

(5) then] **1–2, 4–5** | than **3**

for, and keep Things distinct, that in themselves are different, are the *occasion of denominating* Ideas *distinct or confused*, by a secret and unobserved reference, the Mind makes of its *Ideas* to such Names. This, perhaps, will be fuller understood, after what I say of Words, in the Third Book, has been read and considered. But without taking notice of such a reference of *Ideas* to distinct Names, as the signs of distinct Things, it will be hard to say what a *confused Idea* is. And therefore when a Man designs, by any Name, a sort of Things, or any one particular Thing, distinct from all others, the complex *Idea* he annexes to that Name, is the more distinct, the more particular the *Ideas* are, and the greater and more determinate the number and order of them is, whereof it is made up. For the more it has of these, the more has it still of the perceivable differences, whereby it is kept separate and distinct from all *Ideas* belonging to other Names, even those that approach nearest to it, and thereby all confusion with them is avoided.

§ 11. *Confusion*, making it a difficulty to separate two Things that should be separated, *concerns always two Ideas*; and those most, which most approach one another. Whenever therefore we suspect any *Idea* to be *confused*, we must examine what other it is in danger to be confounded with, or which it cannot easily be separated from, and that will always be found an *Idea* belonging to another Name, and so should be a different Thing, from which yet it is not sufficiently distinct: being either the same with it, or making a part of it, or, at least, as properly call'd by that Name, as the other it is ranked under; and so keeps not that difference from that other *Idea*, which the different Names import.

§ 12. This, I think, is the *confusion* proper to *Ideas*; which still carries with it a secret reference to Names. At least if there be any other confusion of *Ideas*, this is that which most of all disorders Men's Thoughts and Discourses: *Ideas*, as ranked under Names, being those that for the most part Men reason of within themselves, and always those which they commune about, with others. And therefore where there are supposed two different *Ideas*, marked by two different Names, which are not as distinguishable as the Sounds that stand for them, there never fails to be *confusion*: And where any

§ 11. *Confusion concerns always two* Ideas. § 12. *Causes of Confusion.*

---

(2) *of*] **2–5** | *if* **1** (33) commune] **2–5** | communicate **1** (*l. below* 36: § 11.) *In* **Coste**, *this marginal summary is applied to* §§ *11 and 12.*

Ideas are distinct, as the *Ideas* of those two Sounds they are marked by, there can be between them no *confusion. The way to prevent it*, is to collect and unite into our complex *Idea*, as precisely as is possible, all those Ingredients, whereby it is differenced from others; and to them so united in a determinate number and order, apply steadily the same Name. But this neither accommodating Men's ease or vanity, or serving any design, but that of naked Truth, which is not always the thing aimed at, such exactness, is rather to be wished, than hoped for. And since the loose application of Names, to undetermined, variable, and almost no *Ideas*, serves both to cover our own Ignorance, as well as to perplex and confound others, which goes for Learning and Superiority in Knowledge, it is no wonder that most Men should use it themselves, whilst they complain of it in others. Though, I think, no small part of the *confusion*, to be found in the Notions of Men, might by care and ingenuity, be avoided; yet I am far from concluding it every-where wilful. Some *Ideas* are so complex, and made up of so many parts, that the Memory does not easily retain the very same precise Combination of simple *Ideas*, under one Name: much less are we able constantly to divine for what precise complex *Idea* such a Name stands in another Man's use of it. From the first of these, follows *confusion* in a Man's own Reasonings and Opinions within himself; from the latter, frequent *confusion* in discoursing and arguing with others. But having more at large treated of Words, their Defects and Abuses in the following Book, I shall here say no more of it.

§ 13. Our *complex Ideas* being made up of Collections, and so variety of simple ones, *may* accordingly *be very clear and distinct in one part, and very obscure and confused in another*. In a Man who speaks of a *Chiliaëdron*, or a Body of a thousand sides, the *Idea* of the Figure may be very confused, though that of the Number be very distinct; so that he being able to discourse, and demonstrate concerning that part of his complex *Idea*, which depends upon the Number of a Thousand, he is apt to think, he has a distinct *Idea* of a *Chiliaëdron*; though it be plain, he has no precise *Idea* of its Figure, so as to distinguish it, by that, from one that has but 999 sides: The not

§ 13. *Complex* Ideas *may be distinct in one part, and confused in another.*

---

(4) it] **1–2, 4–5** | is **3** (9–10) undetermined, variable] **4–5** | uncertain **1–3** (14) Though] **4–5** | Though yet **1–3** (16) concluding] **4–5** | thinking **1–3** (25) here] **1–4** | hear **5**

observing whereof, causes no small Error in Men's Thoughts, and Confusion in their Discourses.

§ 14. He that thinks he has a distinct *Idea* of the Figure of a *Chiliaë-dron*, let him for Trial's-sake take another parcel of the same uniform Matter, *viz.* Gold, or Wax, of an equal Bulk, and make it into a Figure of 999 sides. He will, I doubt not, be able to distinguish these two *Ideas* one from another by the Number of sides; and reason, and argue distinctly about them, whilst he keeps his Thoughts and Reasoning to that part only of these *Ideas*, which is contained in their Numbers; as that the sides of the one, could be divided into two equal Numbers; and of the other, not, *etc.* But when he goes about to distinguish them by their Figure, he will there be presently at a loss, and not be able, I think, to frame in his Mind two *Ideas*, one of them distinct from the other, by the bare Figure of these two pieces of Gold; as he could, if the same parcels of Gold were made one into a Cube, the other a Figure of five sides. In which incomplete *Ideas*, we are very apt to impose on our selves, and wrangle with others, especially where they have particular and familiar Names. For being satisfied in that part of the *Idea*, which we have clear; and the Name which is familiar to us, being applied to the whole, containing that part also, which is imperfect and obscure, we are apt to use it for that confused part, and draw deductions from it, in the obscure part of its Signification, as confidently, as we do from the other.

§ 15. Having frequently in our Mouths the Name *Eternity*, we are apt to think, we have a positive comprehensive *Idea* of it, which is as much as to say, that there is no part of that Duration, which is not clearly contained in our *Idea*. 'Tis true, that he that thinks so, may have a clear *Idea* of Duration; he may also have a very clear *Idea* of a very great length of Duration; he may also have a clear *Idea* of the Comparison of that great one, with still a greater: But it not being possible for him to include in his *Idea* of any Duration, let it be as great as it will, the whole Extent together of a Duration, where he supposes no end, that part of his *Idea*, which is still beyond the Bounds of that large Duration, he represents to his own Thoughts, is very obscure and undetermined. And hence it is, that in Disputes and Reasonings concerning Eternity, or any other *Infinite*, we are very apt to blunder, and involve our selves in manifest Absurdities.

§ 14. *This if not heeded, causes Confusion in our Arguings.* § 15. *Instance in Eternity.*

(36) very] **1–4**; *om.* **5**

§ 16. In Matter, we have no clear *Ideas* of the smalness of Parts, much beyond the smallest, that occur to any of our Senses: and therefore when we talk of the divisibility of Matter *in infinitum*, though we have clear *Ideas* of Division and Divisibility, and have also clear *Ideas* of Parts, made out of a whole, by Division; yet we have but very obscure, and confused *Ideas* of Corpuscles, or minute Bodies, so to be divided, when by former Divisions, they are reduced to a smalness, much exceeding the perception of any of our Senses; and so all that we have clear, and distinct *Ideas* of, is of what Division in general, or abstractly is, and the Relation of *Totum* and *Pars*: But of the bulk of the Body, to be thus infinitely divided after certain Progressions, I think, we have no clear, nor distinct *Idea* at all. For I ask any one, Whether taking the smallest Atom of Dust he ever saw, he has any distinct *Idea*, (bating still the Number which concerns not Extension,) betwixt the 100 000, and the 1000 000 part of it. Or if he think he can refine his *Ideas* to that Degree, without losing sight of them, let him add ten Cyphers to each of those Numbers. Such a degree of smalness is not unreasonable to be supposed, since a Division carried on so far brings it no nearer the end of infinite Division, than the first Division into two halfs does. I must confess for my part, I have no clear, distinct *Ideas* of the different Bulk, or Extension of those Bodies, having but a very obscure one of either of them. So that, I think, when we talk of Division of Bodies *in infinitum*, our *Idea* of their distinct Bulks, which is the Subject and Foundation of Division, comes after a little progression, to be confounded, and almost lost in Obscurity. For that *Idea*, which is to represent only Bigness, must be very obscure and confused, which we cannot distinguish from one ten times as big, but only by Number: so that we have clear, distinct *Ideas*, we may say of Ten and One, but no distinct *Ideas* of two such Extensions. 'Tis plain from hence, that when we talk of infinite Divisibility of Body, or Extension, our distinct and clear *Ideas* are only of Numbers: but the clear, distinct *Ideas* of Extension, after some Progress of Division, is quite lost; and of such minute Parts, we have no distinct *Ideas* at all; but it returns, as all our *Ideas* of Infinite do, at last

§ 16. *Divisibility of Matter.*

(12) *Idea*] **4–5** | *Ideas* **1–3** (16) think] **1–4** | thinks **5** (18–20) . Such . . . does] **4–5** | ; for that will bring it no nearer the end of infinite Division than the first half does **1–3** (24) Bulks] **4–5** | Bulks or Extension **1–3** (25) Division] **4–5** | Divisions **1–3** after a little progression,] *add.* **4–5**

to that of Number always to be added; but thereby never amounts to any distinct *Idea* of actual, infinite Parts. We have, 'tis true, a clear *Idea* of Division, as often as we will think of it; but thereby we have no more a clear *Idea* of infinite Parts in Matter, than we have a clear *Idea* of an infinite Number, by being able still to add new Numbers to any assigned Number we have: endless Divisibility giving us no more a clear and distinct *Idea* of actually infinite Parts, than endless Addibility (if I may so speak) gives us a clear and distinct *Idea* of an actually infinite Number. They both being only in a Power still of increasing the Number, be it already as great as it will. So that of what remains to be added, (wherein consists the Infinity,) we have but an obscure, imperfect, and confused *Idea*; from or about which we can argue, or reason with no Certainty or Clearness, no more than we can in Arithmetick, about a Number of which we have no such distinct *Idea*, as we have of 4 or 100; but only this relative obscure one, that compared to any other, it is still bigger: and we have no more a clear, positive *Idea* of it, when we say or conceive it is bigger, or more than 400,000,000, than if we should say, it is bigger than 40, or 4: 400,000,000, having no nearer a proportion to the end of Addition, or Number, than 4. For he that adds only 4 to 4, and so proceeds, shall as soon come to the end of all Addition, as he that adds 400,000,000, to 400,000,000. And so likewise in Eternity, he that has an *Idea* of but four Years, has as much a positive complete *Idea* of Eternity, as he that has one of 400,000,000 of Years: For what remains of Eternity beyond either of these two Numbers of Years, is as clear to the one as the other; *i.e.* neither of them has any clear positive *Idea* of it at all. For he that adds only 4 Years to 4, and so on, shall as soon reach Eternity, as he that adds 400,000,000 of Years, and so on; or if he please, doubles the Increase as often as he will: The remaining Abyss being still as far beyond the end of all these Progressions, as it is from the length of a Day, or an Hour. For nothing finite bears any proportion to infinite; and therefore our *Ideas*, which are all finite, cannot bear any. Thus it is also in our *Idea* of *Extension*, when we increase it by Addition, as well as when we diminish it by Division, and would enlarge our Thoughts to infinite Space. After a few doublings of those *Ideas* of Extension, which are the largest we are accustomed to have, we lose the clear distinct *Idea* of that Space: it becomes a confusedly great one, with a Surplus of still greater; about which,

(8) gives] **1–4** | give **5** (19) 400,000,000] **2–5** | 4000,000,000 **1**

when we would argue, or reason, we shall always find our selves at a loss; confused *Ideas*, in our Arguings and Deductions from that part of them which is confused, always leading us into confusion.

CHAPTER XXX

Of Real and Fantastical Ideas.

§ 1. BESIDES what we have already mentioned, concerning *Ideas*, other Considerations belong to them, in reference to things from whence they are taken, or which they may be supposed to represent; and thus, I think, they may come under a threefold distinction; and are,

First, Either real, or fantastical.
Secondly, Adequate, or inadequate.
Thirdly, True, or false.

First, By *real Ideas*, I mean such as have a Foundation in Nature; such as have a Conformity with the real Being, and Existence of Things, or with their Archetypes. *Fantastical or Chimerical*, I call such as have no Foundation in Nature, nor have any Conformity with that reality of Being, to which they are tacitly referr'd, as to their Archetypes. If we examine the several sorts of *Ideas* before-mentioned, we shall find, that,

§ 2. *First*, Our *simple* Ideas *are all real*, all agree to the reality of things. Not that they are all of them the Images, or Representations of what does exist, the contrary whereof, in all but the primary Qualities of Bodies, hath been already shewed. But though Whiteness and Coldness are no more in Snow, than Pain is; yet those *Ideas* of Whiteness, and Coldness, Pain, *etc.* being in us the Effects of Powers in Things without us, ordained by our Maker, to produce in us such Sensations; they are real *Ideas* in us, whereby we distinguish the Qualities, that are really in things themselves. For these several Appearances, being designed to be the Marks,

§ 1. *Real* Ideas *are conformable to their Archetypes.* § 2. *Simple* Ideas *all real.*

(2–3) that . . . confused] **4–5** | them **1–3** (*l. below* 3) XXX] **2–5** | XXIX **1**
(22) shewed] **Coste** *adds marginal reference to II. viii. 9, 10 to end of that chapter.*

whereby we are to know, and distinguish Things, which we have to do with; our *Ideas* do as well serve us to that purpose, and are as real distinguishing Characters, whether they be only constant Effects, or else exact Resemblances of something in the things themselves: the reality lying in that steady correspondence, they have with the distinct Constitutions of real Beings. But whether they answer to those Constitutions, as to Causes, or Patterns, it matters not; it suffices, that they are constantly produced by them. And thus our simple *Ideas* are all real and true, because they answer and agree to those Powers of Things, which produce them in our Minds, that being all that is requisite to make them real, and not fictions at Pleasure. For in simple *Ideas*, (as has been shewn,) the Mind is wholly confined to the Operation of things upon it; and can make to it self no simple *Idea*, more than what it has received.

§ 3. Though the Mind be wholly passive, in respect of its simple *Ideas*: Yet, I think, we may say, it is not so, in respect of its complex *Ideas*: For those being Combinations of simple *Ideas*, put together, and united under one general Name; 'tis plain, that the Mind of Man uses some kind of Liberty, in forming those complex *Ideas*: How else comes it to pass, that one Man's *Idea* of Gold, or Justice, is different from anothers? But because he has put in, or left out of his, some simple *Idea*, which the other has not. The Question then is, Which of these are real, and which barely imaginary Combinations: what Collections agree to the reality of Things, and what not? And to this I say, That

§ 4. *Secondly*, *Mixed Modes and Relations*, having no other *reality*, but what they have in the Minds of Men, there is nothing more required to those kind of *Ideas*, to make them *real*, but that they be so framed, that there be a possibility of existing conformable to them. These *Ideas*, being themselves Archetypes, cannot differ from their Archetypes, and so *cannot be chimerical*, unless any one will jumble together in them inconsistent *Ideas*. Indeed, as any of them have the Names of a known Language assigned to them, by which, he that has them in his Mind, would signify them to others, so bare Possibility of existing is not enough; they must have a

§ 3. *Complex* Ideas *are voluntary Combinations.* § 4. *Mixed Modes made of consistent* Ideas *are real.*

---

(1) , which] *add.* **4–5** (7) those] **2–5** | these **1** (12) fictions] **2–5** | fictious **1** shewn] **2–5** | shewed **1** (35) bare] **1T.er, 2–5** | barely **1**

Conformity to the ordinary Signification of the Name, that is given them, that they may not be thought fantastical: as if a Man would give the Name of Justice to that *Idea*, which common use calls Liberality. But this Fantasticalness relates more to Propriety of Speech, than Reality of *Ideas*. For a Man to be undisturbed in Danger, sedately to consider what is fittest to be done, and to execute it steadily, is a mixed Mode, or a complex *Idea* of an Action which may exist. But to be undisturbed in Danger, without using ones Reason or Industry, is what is also possible to be; and so is as real an *Idea* as the other. Though the first of these having the Name *Courage* given to it, may, in respect of that Name, be a right or wrong *Idea*: But the other, whilst it has not a common received Name of any known Language assigned to it, is not capable of any Deformity, being made with no reference to any thing but it self.

§ 5. *Thirdly*, Our *complex* Ideas *of Substances*, being made all of them in reference to Things existing without us, and intended to be Representations of Substances, as they really are, are no farther *real*, than as they are such Combinations of simple *Ideas*, as are really united, and co-exist in Things without us. On the contrary, those are *fantastical*, which are made up of such Collections of simple *Ideas*, as were really never united, never were found together in any Substance; *v.g.* a rational Creature, consisting of a Horse's Head, joined to a body of humane shape, or such as the *Centaurs* are described: Or, a Body, yellow, very malleable, fusible, and fixed; but lighter than common Water: Or, an uniform, unorganized Body, consisting as to Sense, all of similar Parts, with Perception and voluntary Motion joined to it. Whether such Substances, as these, can possibly exist, or no, 'tis probable we do not know: But be that as it will, these *Ideas* of Substances, being made conformable to no Pattern existing, that we know; and consisting of such Collections of *Ideas*, as no Substance ever shewed us united together, they ought to pass with us for barely imaginary: But much more are those complex *Ideas* so, which contain in them any Inconsistency or Contradiction of their Parts.

§ 5. Ideas *of Substances are real, when they agree with the Existence of Things.*

(6) sedately] **2–5** | but sedately **1** or Deformity **1** it] **4–5** | its **1–3** (14) Deformity] **1T.er, 2–5** | Rectitude (18) [*2nd*] as] **2–5** | that **1** (33) so] *add.* **1er–5**

CHAPTER XXXI

Of Adequate and Inadequate Ideas.

§ 1. Of our real *Ideas* some are Adequate, and some are Inadequate. Those I call *Adequate*, which perfectly represent those Archetypes, which the Mind supposes them taken from; which it intends them to stand for, and to which it refers them. *Inadequate Ideas* are such, which are but a partial, or incomplete representation of those Archetypes to which they are referred. Upon which account it is plain,

§ 2. *First*, That *all our simple* Ideas *are adequate*. Because being nothing but the effects of certain Powers in Things, fitted and ordained by GOD, to produce such Sensations in us, they cannot but be correspondent, and adequate to those Powers: And we are sure they agree to the reality of Things. For if Sugar produce in us the *Ideas*, which we call Whiteness, and Sweetness, we are sure there is a power in Sugar to produce those *Ideas* in our Minds, or else they could not have been produced by it. And so each Sensation answering the Power, that operates on any of our Senses, the *Idea* so produced, is a real *Idea*, (and not a fiction of the Mind, which has no power to produce any simple *Idea*;) and cannot but be adequate, since it ought only to answer that power: and so all simple *Ideas* are adequate. 'Tis true, the Things producing in us these simple *Ideas*, are but few of them denominated by us, as if they were only the causes of them; but as if those *Ideas* were real Beings in them. For though Fire be call'd painful to the Touch, whereby is signified the power of producing in us the *Idea* of Pain; yet it is denominated also Light, and Hot; as if Light and Heat, were really something in the Fire, more than a power to excite these *Ideas* in us; and therefore are called *Qualities* in, or of the Fire. But these being nothing, in

§ 1. *Adequate* Ideas, *are such as perfectly represent their Archetypes.* § 2. *Simple* Ideas *all adequate.*

(*2 ll. above* 1) XXXI] **2–5** | XXX **1** (1) *In* **Coste**, 'Entre nos Idées réelles quelques-unes sont *completes* et quelques autres *incompletes*.'; *notes are there appended on the italicized epithets*, 'En Latin *adæquatæ*.' and '*Inadæquatæ*.', *respectively*. (15) by it] *add.* **4–5** (17–18) (and ... *Idea*;)] **5** | and ... *Idea*; **4er** (*likewise* **Coste**) | (and not a fiction of the Mind,) which ... *Idea*; **1–4**. (**Coste** *adds* 'comme nous l'avons déja prouvé') (23) painful] **Coste** *adds a linguistic marginal note.* is] **4–5** | it **1–3**

truth, but powers to excite such *Ideas* in us, I must, in that sense, be understood, when I speak of secondary *Qualities*, as being in Things; or of their *Ideas*, as being in the Objects, that excite them in us. Such ways of speaking, though accommodated to the vulgar Notions, without which, one cannot be well understood; yet truly signify nothing, but those Powers, which are in Things, to excite certain Sensations or *Ideas* in us. Since were there no fit Organs to receive the impressions Fire makes on the Sight and Touch; nor a Mind joined to those Organs to receive the *Ideas* of Light and Heat, by those impressions from the Fire, or the Sun, there would yet be no more Light, or Heat in the World, than there would be Pain if there were no sensible Creature to feel it, though the Sun should continue just as it is now, and Mount *Ætna* flame higher than ever it did. Solidity, and Extension, and the termination of it, Figure, with Motion and Rest, whereof we have the *Ideas*, would be really in the World as they are, whether there were any sensible Being to perceive them, or no: And therefore those we have reason to look on, as the real modifications of Matter; and such as are the exciting Causes of all our various Sensations from Bodies. But this being an Enquiry not belonging to this place, I shall enter no farther into it, but proceed to shew, what complex *Ideas* are *adequate*, and what not.

§ 3. *Secondly*, Our *complex* Ideas *of Modes*, being voluntary Collections of simple *Ideas*, which the Mind puts together, without reference to any real Archetypes, or standing Patterns, existing any where, *are*, and cannot but be *adequate Ideas*. Because they not being intended for Copies of Things really existing, but for Archetypes made by the Mind, to rank and denominate Things by, cannot want any thing; they having each of them that combination of *Ideas*, and thereby that perfection which the Mind intended they should: So that the Mind acquiesces in them, and can find nothing wanting. Thus by having the *Idea* of a Figure, with three sides meeting at three Angles, I have a complete *Idea*, wherein I require nothing else to make it perfect. That the Mind is satisfied with the perfection of this its *Idea*, is plain, in that it does not conceive, that any Understanding hath, or can have a more compleat or perfect *Idea* of that thing it signifies by the word *Triangle*,

§ 3. *Modes are all adequate.*

---

(11) Pain] **4** | Pain, **1–3, 5** (29) which] *add.* **4–5** (32) sides] **4–5** | sides, **1–3**

supposing it to exist, than it self has in that complex *Idea* of three Sides, and three Angles: in which is contained all that is, or can be essential to it, or necessary to complete it, where-ever or however it exists. But in our *Ideas* of *Substances*, it is otherwise. For there desiring to copy Things, as they really do exist; and to represent to our selves that Constitution, on which all their Properties depend, we perceive our *Ideas* attain not that Perfection we intend: We find they still want something, we should be glad were in them; and so are all *inadequate*. But *mixed Modes* and *Relations*, being Archetypes without Patterns, and so having nothing to represent but themselves, cannot but be adequate, every thing being so to it self. He that at first put together the *Idea* of Danger perceived, absence of disorder from Fear, sedate consideration of what was justly to be done, and executing of that without disturbance, or being deterred by the danger of it, had certainly in his Mind that complex *Idea* made up of that Combination: and intending it to be nothing else, but what it is; nor to have in it any other simple *Ideas*, but what it hath, it could not also but be an *adequate Idea*: and laying this up in his Memory, with the name *Courage* annexed to it, to signifie it to others, and denominate from thence any Action he should observe to agree with it, had thereby a Standard to measure and denominate Actions by, as they agreed to it. This *Idea* thus made, and laid up for a Pattern, must necessarily be *adequate*, being referred to nothing else but it self, nor made by any other Original, but the Good-liking and Will of him, that first made this Combination.

§ 4. Indeed, another coming after, and in Conversation learning from him the word *Courage*, may make an *Idea*, to which he gives that name *Courage*, different from what the first Author applied it to, and has in his Mind, when he uses it. And in this case, if he designs, that his *Idea* in Thinking, should be conformable to the other's *Idea*, as the Name he uses in speaking, is conformable in sound to his, from whom he learned it, his *Idea* may be very wrong and *inadequate*. Because in this case, making the other Man's *Idea* the pattern of his *Idea* in thinking, as the other Man's Word, or Sound, is the pattern of his in speaking, his *Idea* is so far defective and *inadequate*, as it is distant from the Archetype and Pattern he referrs it to, and intends to express and signify by the name he uses for it, which name he would have to be a sign of the other Man's *Idea*, (to which, in its proper use, it is primarily annexed,) and of his

§§ 4, 5. *Modes in reference to settled Names, may be inadequate.*

own, as agreeing to it: to which if his own does not exactly correspond, it is faulty and inadequate.

§ 5. Therefore these *complex* Ideas *of Modes*, when they are referred by the Mind, and intended to correspond to the *Ideas* in the Mind of some other intelligent Being, expressed by the Names we apply to them, they *may be* very deficient, wrong, and *inadequate*. Because they agree not to that, which the Mind designs to be their Archetype, and Pattern: In which respect only, any *Idea* of *Modes* can be wrong, imperfect, or *inadequate*. And on this account, our *Ideas* of *mixed Modes* are the most liable to be faulty of any other; but this refers more to proper Speaking, than knowing right.

§ 6. *Thirdly*, What *Ideas we have of Substances*, I have above shewed: Now those *Ideas* have in the Mind a double reference: 1. Sometimes they are referred to a supposed real Essence of each Species of Things. 2. Sometimes they are only design'd to be Pictures and Representations in the Mind, of Things that do exist, by *Ideas* of those qualities that are discoverable in them. In both which ways, these Copies of those Originals, and Archetypes, *are* imperfect and *inadequate*.

First, It is usual for Men to make the Names of Substances, stand for Things, as supposed to have certain real Essences, whereby they are of this or that Species: And Names standing for nothing but the *Ideas*, that are in Men's Minds, they must consequently referr their *Ideas* to such real Essences, as to their Archetypes. That Men (especially such as have been bred up in the Learning taught in this part of the World) do suppose certain specifick Essences of Substances, which each Individual in its several kind is made conformable to, and partakes of, is so far from needing proof, that it will be thought strange, if any one should do otherwise. And thus they ordinarily apply the specifick Names, they rank particular Substances under, to Things, as distinguished by such specifick real Essences. Who is there almost, who would not take it amiss, if it should be doubted, whether he call'd himself Man, with any other meaning, than as having the real Essence of a Man? And yet if you demand, what those real Essences are, 'tis plain Men are ignorant, and know them not. From whence it follows, that the *Ideas* they

§§ 6, 7. Ideas *of Substances, as referr'd to real Essences not adequate.*

---

(12) shewed] **Coste** *adds marginal reference to II. xxiii.* (16–17) of those qualities] *add.* **2–5** (18) those] **2–5** | their **1** (27) kind] **1–4** | kinds **5**

have in their Minds, being referred to real Essences as to Archetypes which are unknown, must be so far from being *adequate*, that they cannot be supposed to be any representation of them at all. The complex *Ideas* we have of Substances, are, as it has been shewn, certain Collections of simple *Ideas*, that have been observed or supposed constantly to exist together. But such a complex *Idea* cannot be the real Essence of any Substance; for then the Properties we discover in that Body, would depend on that complex *Idea*, and be deducible from it, and their necessary connexion with it be known; as all Properties of a Triangle depend on, and as far as they are discoverable, are deducible from the complex *Idea* of three Lines, including a Space. But it is plain, that in our complex *Ideas* of Substances, are not contained such *Ideas*, on which all the other Qualities, that are to be found in them, do depend. The common *Idea* Men have of *Iron*, is a Body of a certain Colour, Weight, and Hardness; and a Property that they look on as belonging to it, is malleableness. But yet this Property has no necessary connexion with that complex *Idea*, or any part of it: And there is no more reason to think, that malleableness depends on that Colour, Weight, and Hardness, than that that Colour, or that Weight depends on its malleableness. And yet, though we know nothing of these real Essences, there is nothing more ordinary, than that Men should attribute the sorts of Things to such Essences. The particular parcel of Matter which makes the Ring I have on my Finger, is forwardly, by most Men, supposed to have a real Essence, whereby it is *Gold*; and from whence those Qualities flow, which I find in it, *viz.* its peculiar Colour, Weight, Hardness, Fusibility, Fixedness, and change of Colour upon a slight touch of Mercury, *etc.* This Essence, from which all these Properties flow, when I enquire into it, and search after it, I plainly perceive I cannot discover: the farthest I can go, is only to presume, that it being nothing but Body, its real Essence, or internal Constitution, on which these Qualities depend, can be nothing but the Figure, Size, and Connexion of its solid Parts; of neither of which, I having any distinct perception at all, I can have no *Idea* of its Essence, which is the cause that it has that particular shining yellowness; a greater weight than any thing I know of the same bulk; and a fitness to have its Colour

(1) [*2nd*] to] *add.* **4–5** (4) it has been shewn] **4–5** | has been shewn **2–3** | has been shewed **1.** (**Coste** 'j'ai déja montré') (18) or] **5** (*likewise* **Coste**) | nor **1–4** (35) Essence] **4–5** | real Essence **1–3** (*likewise* **Coste**)

changed by the touch of Quicksilver. If any one will say, that the real Essence, and internal Constitution, on which these Properties depend, is not the Figure, Size, and Arangement or Connexion of its solid Parts, but something else, call'd its particular *form*; I am farther from having any *Idea* of its real Essence, than I was before. For I have an *Idea* of Figure, Size, and Situation of solid Parts in general, though I have none of the particular Figure, Size, or putting together of Parts, whereby the Qualities above-mentioned are produced; which Qualities I find in that particular parcel of Matter, that is on my Finger, and not in another parcel of Matter, with which I cut the Pen I write with. But when I am told, that something besides the Figure, Size, and Posture of the solid Parts of that Body, is its Essence, something called *substantial form*, of that, I confess, I have no *Idea* at all, but only of the sound *Form*; which is far enough from an *Idea* of its real Essence, or Constitution. The like ignorance as I have of the real Essence of this particular Substance, I have also of the real Essence of all other natural ones: Of which Essences, I confess, I have no distinct *Ideas* at all; and I am apt to suppose others, when they examine their own Knowledge, will find in themselves, in this one point, the same sort of ignorance.

§ 7. Now then, when Men apply to this particular parcel of Matter on my Finger, a general Name already in use, and denominate it *Gold*, Do they not ordinarily, or are they not understood to give it that Name as belonging to a particular Species of Bodies, having a real internal Essence; by having of which Essence, this particular Substance comes to be of that Species, and to be called by that Name? If it be so, as it is plain it is, the name, by which Things are marked, as having that Essence, must be referred primarily to that Essence; and consequently the *Idea* to which that name is given, must be referred also to that Essence, and be intended to represent it. Which Essence, since they, who so use the Names, know not, their Ideas *of Substances* must be *all inadequate* in that respect, as not containing in them that real Essence, which the Mind intends they should.

§ 8. *Secondly*, Those who, neglecting that useless Supposition of unknown real Essences, whereby they are distinguished, endeavour to copy the Substances, that exist in the World, by putting

§§ 8–11. Ideas *of Substances, as Collections of their Qualities, are all inadequate.*

(5) before.] **1–3** | before, **4** | before; **5** (7) putting] **1–3, 5** | puting **4**
(32) not,] **1er–5** | not **1** (34) Mind] **1–4** | Minds **5**

together the *Ideas* of those sensible Qualities, which are found co-existing in them, though they come much nearer a likeness of them, than those who imagine, they know not what real specifick Essences: yet they arrive not at perfectly adequate *Ideas* of those Substances, they would thus copy into their Minds: nor do those Copies, exactly, and fully, contain all that is to be found in their Archetypes. Because those Qualities, and Powers of Substances, whereof we make their complex *Ideas*, are so many and various, that no Man's complex *Idea* contains them all. That our abstract *Ideas* of Substances, do not contain in them all the simple *Ideas*, that are united in the Things themselves, is evident, in that Men do rarely put into their complex *Idea* of any Substance, all the simple *Ideas* they do know to exist in it. Because endeavouring to make the signification of their specifick Names as clear, and as little cumbersome as they can, they make their specifick *Ideas* of the sorts of Substances, for the most part, of a few of those simple *Ideas* which are to be found in them: But these having no original precedency, or right to be put in, and make the specifick *Idea*, more than others that are left out, 'tis plain, that both these ways, *our* Ideas *of Substances* are deficient, and *inadequate*. The simple *Ideas* whereof we make our complex ones of Substances, are all of them (bating only the Figure and Bulk of some sorts) Powers; which being Relations to other Substances, we can never be sure that we know all the Powers, that are in any one Body, till we have tried what Changes it is fitted to give to, or receive from other Substances, in their several ways of application: which being impossible to be tried upon any one Body, much less upon all, it is impossible we should have adequate *Ideas* of any Substance, made up of a Collection of all its Properties.

§ 9. Whosoever first light on a parcel of that sort of Substance, we denote by the word *Gold*, could not rationally take the Bulk and Figure he observed in that lump, to depend on its real Essence, or internal Constitution. Therefore those never went into his *Idea* of that Species of Body; but its peculiar Colour, perhaps, and Weight, were the first he abstracted from it, to make the complex *Idea* of that Species. Which both are but Powers; the one to affect our Eyes, after such a manner, and to produce in us that *Idea*, we call Yellow; and the other to force upwards any other Body of equal bulk, they being put into a pair of equal Scales, one against another. Another,

(22) Powers;] **1–3** (*likewise* **Coste**) | Powers **4** | Powers, **5** (23) that] *add.* **4–5**
(31) , or] **4–5** | ; on its **1–3**

perhaps, added to these, the *Ideas* of Fusibility, and Fixedness, two other passive Powers, in relation to the operation of Fire upon it; Another, its Ductility, and Solubility in *Aqua Regia*, two other Powers, relating to the operation of other Bodies, in changing its outward Figure or Separation of it, into insensible Parts. These, or part of these, put together, usually make the complex *Idea* in Men's Minds, of that sort of Body we call *Gold*.

§ 10. But no one, who hath considered the Properties of Bodies in general, or this sort in particular, can doubt, that this, call'd *Gold*, has infinite other Properties, not contained in that complex *Idea*. Some, who have examined this Species more accurately, could, I believe, enumerate ten times as many Properties in *Gold*, all of them as inseparable from its internal Constitution, as its Colour, or Weight: And 'tis probable, if any one knew all the Properties, that are by divers Men known of this Metal, there would an hundred times as many *Ideas*, go to the complex *Idea* of *Gold*, as any one Man yet has in his; and yet, perhaps, that not be the thousandth part of what is to be discovered in it. The changes that that one Body is apt to receive, and make in other Bodies, upon a due application, exceeding far, not only what we know, but what we are apt to imagine. Which will not appear so much a Paradox to any one, who will but consider, how far Men are yet from knowing all the Properties of that one, no very compound Figure, a *Triangle*, though it be no small numbers, that are already by Mathematicians discovered of it.

§ 11. So that *all our complex* Ideas *of Substances are* imperfect and *inadequate*. Which would be so also in mathematical Figures, if we were to have our complex *Ideas* of them, only by collecting their Properties, in reference to other Figures. How uncertain, and imperfect, would our *Ideas* be of an *Ellipsis*, if we had no other *Idea* of it, but some few of its Properties? Whereas having in our plain *Idea*, the whole Essence of that Figure, we from thence discover those Properties, and demonstratively see how they flow, and are inseparable from it.

§ 12. Thus the Mind has three sorts of abstract *Ideas*, or nominal Essences:

§ 12. *Simple* Ideas *ἔκτυπα, and adequate.*

(5) insensible] **2–5** | sensible **1** (17) , perhaps, that not] **4–5** | that not, perhaps, **1–3**. (**Coste** 'ce ne seroit peut-être pas') (24) though] **1–4** | thought **5** numbers] **1–2, 4** | number **3, 5** (*likewise* **Coste**)

First, *Simple* Ideas, which *are* *ἔκτυπα*, or *Copies*; but yet certainly *adequate*. Because being intended to express nothing but the power in Things to produce in the Mind such a Sensation, that Sensation, when it is produced, cannot but be the Effect of that Power. So the Paper I write on, having the Power, in the Light, (I speak according to the common Notion of Light,) to produce in me the Sensation, which I call White, it cannot but be the Effect of such a Power, in something without the Mind; since the Mind has not the Power to produce any such *Idea* in it self, and being meant for nothing else but the Effect of such a Power, that simple *Idea* is real and *adequate*: the Sensation of White, in my Mind, being the Effect of that Power, which is in the Paper to produce it, is perfectly *adequate* to that Power; or else, that Power would produce a different *Idea*.

§ 13. *Secondly*, The *complex* Ideas *of Substances are Ectypes*, *Copies* too; but not perfect ones, not *adequate*: which is very evident to the Mind, in that it plainly perceives, that whatever Collection of simple *Ideas* it makes of any Substance that exists, it cannot be sure, that it exactly answers all that are in that Substance. Since not having tried all the Operations of all other Substances upon it, and found all the Alterations it would receive from, or cause in other Substances, it cannot have an exact *adequate* Collection of all its active and passive Capacities; and so *not* have an *adequate* complex *Idea* of the Powers of any Substance, existing, and its Relations, which is that sort of complex *Idea* of Substances we have. And, after all, if we could have, and actually had, in our complex *Idea*, an exact Collection of all the secondary Qualities, or Powers of any Substance, we should not yet thereby have an *Idea* of the Essence of that Thing. For since the Powers, or Qualities, that are observable by us, are not the real Essence of that Substance, but depend on it, and flow from it, any Collection whatsoever of these Qualities, cannot be the real Essence of that Thing. Whereby it is plain, that our *Ideas* of Substances are not *adequate*; are not what the Mind intends them to be. Besides, a Man has no *Idea* of Substance in general, nor knows what Substance is in it self.

§ 14. *Thirdly*, *Complex* Ideas *of Modes and Relations*, *are* Originals,

§ 13. Ideas *of Substances are ἔκτυπα, inadequate.* § 14. Ideas *of Modes and Relations are Archetypes, and cannot but be adequate.*

(9) it] **4–5** | its **1–3** (12) *adequate*] **Coste** *adds a linguistic footnote.* (14) '§ 13.' *add.* **2–5** *are*] **1–3, 5** (*likewise* **Coste**) | *or* **4** (*l. below* 35: § 14.) Ideas] **2–3, 5** | Idea **4**

and *Archetypes*; are not Copies, nor made after the Pattern of any real Existence, to which the Mind intends them to be conformable, and exactly to answer. These being such Collections of simple *Ideas*, that the Mind it self puts together, and such Collections, that each of them contains in it precisely all that the Mind intends it should, they are Archetypes and Essences of Modes that may exist; and so are designed only for, and belong only to such Modes, as when they do exist, have an exact conformity with those complex *Ideas*. The *Ideas* therefore of Modes and Relations, cannot but be *adequate*.

CHAPTER XXXII

Of True and False Ideas.

§ 1. THOUGH Truth and Falshood belong, in Propriety of Speech, only to Propositions; yet *Ideas* are oftentimes termed *true or false* (as what Words are there, that are not used with great Latitude, and with some deviation from their strict and proper Significations?) Though, I think, that when *Ideas* themselves are termed true or false, there is still some secret or tacit Proposition, which is the Foundation of that Denomination: as we shall see, if we examine the particular Occasions, wherein they come to be called true or false. In all which, we shall find some kind of Affirmation, or Negation, which is the Reason of that Denomination. For our *Ideas*, being nothing but bare Appearances or Perceptions in our Minds, cannot properly and simply in themselves be said to be *true* or *false*, no more than a single Name of any thing, can be said to be *true* or *false*.

§ 2. Indeed, both *Ideas* and Words, *may* be said to be *true in a metaphysical Sense* of the Word Truth; as all other Things, that any way exist, are said to be true; *i.e.* really to be such as they exist. Though in Things called *true*, even in that Sense, there is, perhaps, a secret reference to our *Ideas*, look'd upon as the Standards of that Truth, which amounts to a mental Proposition, though it be usually not taken notice of.

§ 3. But 'tis not in that metaphysical Sense of Truth, which we enquire here, when we examine, whether our *Ideas* are capable of

§ 1. *Truth and Falshood properly belong to Propositions.* § 2. *Metaphysical Truth contains a tacit Proposition.* § 3. *No* Idea *as an appearance in the Mind true or false.*

(*l. below* 9) XXXII] **2–5** | XXXI **1**

being *true* or *false*; but in the more ordinary Acceptation of those Words: And so I say, that the *Ideas* in our Minds, being only so many Perceptions, or Appearances there, none of them are *false*. The *Idea* of a Centaur, having no more Falshood in it, when it appears in our Minds; than the Name Centaur has Falshood in it, when it is pronounced by our Mouths, or written on Paper. For Truth or Falshood, lying always in some Affirmation, or Negation, Mental or Verbal, our *Ideas are not capable* any of them *of being false*, till the Mind passes some Judgment on them; that is, affirms or denies something of them.

§ 4. When-ever the Mind refers any of its *Ideas* to any thing extraneous to them, they are then *capable to be called true or false*. Because the Mind in such a reference, makes a tacit Supposition of their Conformity to that Thing: which Supposition, as it happens to be *true* or *false*; so the *Ideas* themselves come to be denominated. The most usual Cases wherein this happens, are these following:

§ 5. *First*, When the Mind supposes any *Idea* it has, *conformable to* that in *other Men's* Minds called by the same common Name; *v.g.* when the Mind intends, or judges its *Ideas* of *Justice*, *Temperance*, *Religion*, to be the same, with what other Men give those Names to.

Secondly, When the Mind supposes any *Idea* it has in it self, to be *conformable to some real Existence*. Thus the two *Ideas*, of a Man, and a Centaur, supposed to be the *Ideas* of real Substances, are the one *true*, and the other *false*; the one having a Conformity to what has really existed; the other not.

Thirdly, When the Mind *refers* any of its *Ideas to* that *real* Constitution, and *Essence* of any thing, whereon all its Properties depend: and thus the greatest part, if not all our *Ideas* of Substances, are *false*.

§ 6. These Suppositions, the Mind is very apt tacitly to make concerning its own *Ideas*. But yet if we will examine it, we shall find it is chiefly, if not only concerning its abstract complex *Ideas*. For the natural tendency of the Mind being towards Knowledge; and finding that, if it should proceed by, and dwell upon only particular Things, its Progress would be very slow, and its Work endless: Therefore to shorten its way to Knowledge, and make each

§ 4. Ideas *referred to any thing may be true or false.* § 5. *Other Men's* Ideas, *real Existence, and supposed real Essences, are what Men usually refer their* Ideas *to.* §§ 6–8. *The cause of such references.*

---

(33) that,] *add.* **4–5**

Perception the more comprehensive; the first Thing it does, as the Foundation of the easier enlarging its Knowledge, either by Contemplation of the things themselves, that it would know; or conference with others about them, is to bind them into Bundles, and rank them so into sorts, that what Knowledge it gets of any of them, it may thereby with assurance extend to all of that sort; and so advance by larger steps in that, which is its great Business, Knowledge. This, as I have elsewhere shewed, is the Reason, why we collect Things under comprehensive *Ideas*, with Names annexed to them into *Genera* and *Species*; *i.e.* into kinds, and sorts.

§ 7. If therefore we will warily attend to the Motions of the Mind, and observe what Course it usually takes in its way to Knowledge, we shall, I think, find, that the Mind having got any *Idea*, which it thinks it may have use of, either in Contemplation or Discourse, the first Thing it does, is to abstract it, and then get a Name to it; and so lay it up in its Store-house, the Memory, as containing the Essence of a sort of Things, of which that Name is always to be the Mark. Hence it is, that we may often observe, that when any one sees a new Thing of a kind that he knows not, he presently asks, what it is, meaning by that Enquiry nothing but the Name. As if the Name carried with it the Knowledge of the Species, or the Essence of it; whereof it is indeed used as the Mark, and is generally supposed annexed to it.

§ 8. But this abstract *Idea*, being something in the Mind between the thing that exists, and the Name that is given to it; it is in our *Ideas*, that both the Rightness of our Knowledge, and the Propriety or Intelligibleness of our Speaking consists. And hence it is, that Men are so forward to suppose, that the abstract *Ideas* they have in their Minds, are such, as agree to the Things existing without them, to which they are referr'd; and are the same also, to which the Names they give them, do by the Use and Propriety of that Language belong. For without this *double Conformity of* their *Ideas*, they find, they should both think amiss of Things in themselves, and talk of them unintelligibly to others.

§ 9. *First* then, I say, That *when the Truth of our* Ideas *is judged of, by the Conformity they have to the* Ideas *which other Men have, and commonly signify by the same Name, they may be any of them false.* But yet *simple* Ideas are *least* of all *liable to be so mistaken.* Because a Man by his

§ 9. *Simple* Ideas *may be false in reference to others of the same Name, but are least liable to be so.*

Senses and every Day's Observation, may easily satisfy himself, what the simple *Ideas* are, which their several Names, that are in common use stand for, they being but few in Number, and such, as if he doubts or mistakes in, he may easily rectify by the Objects they are to be found in. Therefore it is seldom, that any one mistakes in his Names of simple *Ideas*; or applies the Name *Red*, to the *Idea* of Green; or the Name Sweet, to the *Idea* Bitter: Much less are Men apt to confound the Names of *Ideas*, belonging to different Senses; and call a Colour, by the Name of a Taste, *etc.* whereby it is evident, that the simple *Ideas*, they call by any Name, are commonly the same, that others have and mean, when they use the same Names.

§ 10. *Complex* Ideas *are much more liable to be false in this respect; and the complex* Ideas *of mixed Modes, much more than those of Substances*: Because in Substances, (especially those, which the common and unborrowed Names of any Language are applied to,) some remarkable sensible Qualities, serving ordinarily to distinguish one sort from another, easily preserve those, who take any Care in the use of their Words, from applying them to sorts of Substances, to which they do not at all belong. But in mixed Modes, we are much more uncertain, it being not so easy to determine of several Actions; whether they are to be called *Justice*, or *Cruelty*; *Liberality*, or *Prodigality*. And so in referring our *Ideas* to those of other Men, call'd by the same Names, ours may be *false*; and the *Idea* in our Minds, which we express by the word *Justice*, may, perhaps, be that, which ought to have another Name.

§ 11. But whether or no our *Ideas* of mixed Modes are more liable than any sort, to be different from those of other Men, which are marked by the same Names: This at least is certain, That *this sort of Falshood is much more familiarly attributed to* our *Ideas* of *mixed Modes, than to any other*. When a Man is thought to have a false *Idea* of *Justice*, or *Gratitude*, or *Glory*, it is for no other Reason, but that his agrees not with the *Ideas*, which each of those Names are the Signs of in other Men.

§ 12. *The Reason whereof* seems to me to be this, That the abstract *Ideas* of mixed Modes, being Men's voluntary Combinations of such

§ 10. Ideas *of mixed Modes most liable to be false in this sense.* § 11. *Or at least to be thought false.* § 12. *And why.*

---

(8) of *Ideas*] *add.* **4–5**. (*Not in* **Coste**) (23) Names] **1er–5** | Name **1** (23–4) [*2nd*] the . . . *Justice*] **2–5** | our *Idea* we call Justice **1** (28) Names] **1er–5** | Name **1** (34) '§ 12.' *add.* **2–5**

a precise Collection of simple *Ideas*; and so the Essence of each Species, being made by Men alone, whereof we have no other sensible Standard, existing any where, but the Name it self, or the definition of that Name: We have nothing else to refer these our *Ideas* of mixed Modes to as a Standard, to which we would conform them, but the *Ideas* of those, who are thought to use those Names in their most proper Significations; and so as our *Ideas* conform, or differ from them, they pass for true or false. And thus much concerning the *Truth* and *Falshood* of our *Ideas*, in reference to their Names.

§ 13. *Secondly*, As to the *Truth and Falshood of our* Ideas, *in reference* to the *real Existence* of Things, when that is made the Standard of their Truth, none of them can be termed false, but only our complex *Ideas* of Substances.

§ 14. *First*, Our simple *Ideas*, being barely such Perceptions, as God has fitted us to receive, and given Power to external Objects to produce in us by established Laws, and Ways, suitable to his Wisdom and Goodness, though incomprehensible to us, their Truth consists in nothing else, but in such Appearances, as are produced in us, and must be suitable to those Powers, he has placed in external Objects, or else they could not be produced in us: And thus answering those Powers, they are what they should be, *true Ideas*. Nor do they become liable to any Imputation of *Falshood*, if the Mind (as in most Men I believe it does) judges these *Ideas* to be in the Things themselves. For God in his Wisdom, having set them as Marks of Distinction in Things, whereby we may be able to discern one Thing from another; and so chuse any of them for our uses, as we have Occasion, it alters not the Nature of our simple *Idea*, whether we think, that the *Idea* of Blue, be in the Violet it self, or in our Mind only; and only the Power of producing it by the Texture of its Parts, reflecting the Particles of Light, after a certain Manner, to be in the Violet it self. For that Texture in the Object, by a regular and constant operation, producing the same *Idea* of Blue in us, it serves us to distinguish, by our Eyes, that from any other Thing, whether that distinguishing Mark, as it is really in the *Violet*, be only a peculiar Texture of Parts, or else that very

§ 13. *As referred to real Existences, none of our* Ideas *can be false, but those of Substances.*
§ 14. *First, Simple* Ideas *in this sense not false, and why.*

(5) a Standard] **2er–5** | Standards **1–2** (33) by . . . operation] **4–5** | operating regularly and constantly **1–3**

Colour, the *Idea* whereof (which is in us) is the exact resemblance. And it is equally from that Appearance, to be denominated *Blue*, whether it be that real Colour, or only a peculiar Texture in it, that causes in us that *Idea*: Since the Name *Blue* notes properly nothing, but that Mark of Distinction, that is in a *Violet*, discernible only by our Eyes, whatever it consists in, that being beyond our Capacities distinctly to know, and, perhaps, would be of less use to us, if we had Faculties to discern.

§ 15. Neither would it carry any Imputation of *Falshood* to our simple *Ideas*, *if* by the different Structure of our Organs, it were so ordered, That *the same Object should produce in several Men's Minds different* Ideas at the same time; *v.g.* if the *Idea*, that a *Violet* produced in one Man's Mind by his Eyes, were the same that a *Marigold* produced in another Man's, and *vice versâ*. For since this could never be known: because one Man's Mind could not pass into another Man's Body, to perceive, what Appearances were produced by those Organs; neither the *Ideas* hereby, nor the Names, would be at all confounded, or any *Falshood* be in either. For all Things, that had the Texture of a *Violet*, producing constantly the *Idea*, which he called *Blue*; and those which had the Texture of a *Marigold*, producing constantly the *Idea*, which he as constantly called *Yellow*, whatever those Appearances were in his Mind; he would be able as regularly to distinguish Things for his Use by those Appearances, and understand, and signify those distinctions, marked by the Names *Blue* and *Yellow*, as if the Appearances, or *Ideas* in his Mind, received from those two Flowers, were exactly the same, with the *Ideas* in other Men's Minds. I am nevertheless very apt to think, that the sensible *Ideas*, produced by any Object in different Men's Minds, are most commonly very near and undiscernibly alike. For which Opinion, I think, there might be many Reasons offered: but that being besides my present Business, I shall not trouble my Reader with them; but only mind him, that the contrary Supposition, if it could be proved, is of little use, either for the Improvement of our Knowledge, or Conveniency of Life; and so we need not trouble our selves to examine it.

§ 15. *Though one Man's* Idea *of Blue, should be different from anothers.*

---

(7) us] **Coste** *adds marginal reference to II. xxiii. 12.* (8) *In § 14*, 'Violet' *and* 'Blue', *in italic or in roman, are given by* **Coste** *as 'souci'* [*'marigold'*] *and 'jaune'* [*'yellow'*], *respectively.* (20) *Blue*] **Coste** *'bleuâtre'* (25) *Blue*] **Coste** *'bleu'* (*l. below* 35) *Though*] **2, 4–5** | *The* **3**

§ 16. From what has been said concerning our simple *Ideas*, I think it evident, That our *simple* Ideas *can none of them be false, in respect of Things* existing without us. For the Truth of these Appearances, or Perceptions in our Minds, consisting, as has been said, only in their being answerable to the Powers in external Objects, to produce by our Senses such Appearances in us: and each of them being in the Mind, such as it is, suitable to the Power that produced it, and which alone it represents, it cannot upon that Account, or as referr'd to such a Pattern, be *false*. *Blue* or *Yellow*, *Bitter* or *Sweet*, can never be false *Ideas*, these Perceptions in the Mind, are just such as they are there, answering the Powers appointed by God to produce them; and so are truly, what they are, and are intended to be. Indeed the Names may be misapply'd: but that in this respect, makes no Falshood in the *Ideas*: As if a Man ignorant in the *English* Tongue, should call *Purple*, *Scarlet*.

§ 17. *Secondly, Neither can* our *complex* Ideas *of Modes, in reference to the Essence of any Thing really existing, be false*. Because whatever complex *Idea* I have of any Mode, it hath no reference to any Pattern existing, and made by Nature: it is not supposed to contain in it any other *Ideas*, than what it hath; nor to represent any thing, but such a Complication of *Ideas*, as it does. Thus when I have the *Idea* of such an Action of a Man, who forbears to afford himself such Meat, Drink, and Cloathing, and other Conveniencies of Life, as his Riches and Estate will be sufficient to supply, and his station requires, I have no *false Idea*; but such an one as represents an Action, either as I find, or imagine it; and so is capable of neither *Truth*, or *Falshood*. But when I give the name *Frugality*, or *Vertue*, to this Action, then it may be called a *false Idea*, if thereby it be supposed to agree with that *Idea*, to which, in propriety of Speech, the name of *Frugality* doth belong; or to be conformable to that Law, which is the Standard of Vertue and Vice.

§ 18. *Thirdly*, Our complex *Ideas of Substances, being all referred to Patterns in Things themselves, may be false*. That they are all *false*, when looked upon as the Representations of the unknown Essences of Things, is so evident, that there needs nothing to be said of it. I shall therefore pass over that chimerical Supposition, and consider them as Collections of simple *Ideas* in the Mind, taken from Com-

§ 16. *First, Simple* Ideas *in this sense not false, and why.* § 17. *Secondly, Modes not false.*
§ 18. *Thirdly,* Ideas *of Substances when false.*

(23) Conveniencies] **1–3, 5** | Conveniences **4** (25) an one] *add.* **4–5**

binations of simple *Ideas* existing together constantly in Things, of which Patterns, they are the supposed Copies: And in this reference of them, to the existence of Things, they *are false* Ideas. 1. *When* they put together simple *Ideas*, which in the real Existence of Things, have no union: as when to the Shape, and Size, that exist together in a Horse, is joined, in the same complex *Idea*, the power of Barking like a Dog: Which three *Ideas*, however put together into one in the Mind, were never united in Nature: and this therefore may be called a *false Idea* of an Horse. 2. *Ideas* of Substances are, in this respect, also *false*, when from any Collection of simple *Ideas*, that do always exist together, there is separated, by a direct Negation, any other simple *Idea*, which is constantly joined with them. Thus if to Extension, Solidity, Fusibility, the peculiar Weightiness, and yellow Colour of Gold, any one join in his Thoughts the Negation of a greater degree of fixedness, than is in Lead or Copper, he may be said to have a false complex *Idea*, as well as when he joins to those other simple ones, the *Idea* of perfect absolute Fixedness. For either way, the complex *Idea* of Gold being made up of such simple ones, as have no union in Nature, may be termed false. But if he leave out of this his complex *Idea*, that of Fixedness quite, without either actually joining to, or separating of it from the rest in his Mind, it is, I think, to be looked on, as an inadequate and imperfect *Idea*, rather than a *false* one: since though it contains not all the simple *Ideas*, that are united in Nature, yet it puts none together, but what do really exist together.

§ 19. Though in compliance with the ordinary way of Speaking, I have shewed in what sense, and upon what ground our *Ideas* may be sometimes called *true*, or *false*; yet if we will look a little nearer into the matter in all cases, where any *Idea* is call'd *true*, or *false*, it is from some Judgment that the Mind makes, or is supposed to make, that is *true*, or *false*. For *Truth, or Falshood*, being *never without some Affirmation, or Negation*, Express, or Tacit, it is not to be found, but where signs are joined or separated, according to the agreement, or disagreement, of the Things they stand for. The signs we chiefly use, are either *Ideas*, or Words, wherewith we make either mental, or verbal Propositions. *Truth* lies in so joining, or separating these Representatives, as the Things they stand for, do, in themselves, agree, or disagree: and *Falshood* in the contrary, as shall be more fully shewed hereafter.

§ 19. *Truth or Falshood always supposes affirmation or negation.*

§ 20. Any *Idea* then which we have in our Minds, whether conformable, or not, to the existence of Things, or to any *Ideas* in the Minds of other Men, cannot properly for this alone be called *false*. For these Representations, if they have nothing in them, but what is really existing in Things without, cannot be thought *false*, being exact Representations of something: nor yet if they have any thing in them, differing from the reality of Things, can they properly be said to be false Representations, or *Ideas* of Things, they do not represent. But the mistake and *falshood is*,

§ 21. *First, When the Mind* having any *Idea, it judges* and concludes *it the same, that is in other Men's Minds, signified by the same name*; or that it is conformable to the ordinary received signification, or definition of that Word, when indeed it is not: Which is the most usual mistake in mixed Modes, though other *Ideas* also are liable to it.

§ 22. *Secondly*, When it having a complex *Idea* made up of such a Collection of simple ones, as Nature never puts together, *it judges it to agree to a Species of Creatures really existing*; as when it joins the weight of Tin, to the colour, fusibility, and fixedness of Gold.

§ 23. *Thirdly*, When in its complex *Idea*, it has united a certain number of simple *Ideas*, that do really exist together in some sorts of Creatures, but has also left out others, as much inseparable, *it judges this to be a perfect complete* Idea, *of a sort of things which really it is not*; *v.g.* having joined the *Ideas* of substance, yellow, malleable, most heavy, and fusible, it takes that complex *Idea* to be the complete *Idea* of Gold, when yet its peculiar fixedness and solubility in *Aqua Regia* are as inseparable from those other *Ideas*, or Qualities of that Body, as they are one from another.

§ 24. *Fourthly*, The Mistake is yet greater, *when I judge, that this complex* Idea, *contains in it the real Essence of any Body existing*; when at least it contains but some few of those Properties, which flow from its real Essence and Constitution. I say, only some few of those Properties; for those Properties consisting mostly in the active and

§ 20. Ideas *in themselves neither true nor false.* § 21. *But are false, First, When judged agreeable to another Man's* Idea *without being so.* § 22. *Secondly, When judged to agree to real Existence, when they do not.* § 23. *Thirdly, When judged adequate without being so.* § 24. *Fourthly, When judged to represent the real Essence.*

---

(1) which] *add.* **4–5** (4) Representations] **1–4** | Representation **5** (*l. below* 33: § 21.) *In* **Coste**, *the summaries for* §§ *21–4 are* 'En quel cas elles sont fausses. Prémier cas.', 'Second cas.', 'Troisiéme cas.', 'Quatriéme cas.', *respectively*.

passive Powers, it has, in reference to other Things, all that are vulgarly known of any one Body, and of which the complex *Idea* of that kind of Things is usually made, are but a very few, in comparison of what a Man, that has several ways tried and examined it, knows of that one sort of Things; and all that the most expert Man knows, are but few, in comparison of what are really in that Body, and depend on its internal or essential Constitution. The essence of a Triangle, lies in a very little compass, consists in a very few *Ideas*; three Lines including a Space, make up that Essence: But the Properties that flow from this Essence, are more than can be easily known, or enumerated. So I imagine it is in Substances, their real Essences lie in a little compass; though the Properties flowing from that internal Constitution, are endless.

§ 25. To conclude, a Man having no notion of any Thing without him, but by the *Idea* he has of it in his Mind (which *Idea*, he has a power to call by what Name he pleases) he may, indeed, make an *Idea* neither answering the reality of Things, nor agreeing to the *Ideas* commonly signified by other Peoples Words; but cannot make a wrong, or *false Idea* of a Thing, which is no otherwise known to him, but by the *Idea* he has of it. *v.g.* When I frame an *Idea* of the Legs, Arms, and Body of a Man, and join to this a Horse's Head and Neck, I do not make a *false Idea* of any thing; because it represents nothing without me. But when I call it a *Man*, or *Tartar*, and imagine it either to represent some real Being without me, or to be the same *Idea*, that others call by the same name; in either of these cases, I may err. And upon this account it is, that it comes to be termed a *false Idea*; though, indeed, the *falshood* lie not in the *Idea*, but in that tacit mental Proposition, wherein a conformity and resemblance is attributed to it, which it has not. But yet, if having framed such an *Idea* in my Mind, without thinking, either that Existence, or the name *Man* or *Tartar*, belongs to it, I will call it *Man*, or *Tartar*, I may be justly thought fantastical in the Naming; but not erroneous in my Judgment; nor the *Idea* any way *false*.

§ 26. Upon the whole matter, I think, That our *Ideas*, as they are considered by the Mind, either in reference to the proper signification of their Names; or in reference to the reality of Things, *may*

§ 25. Ideas *when false.* § 26. *More properly to be called Right or Wrong.*

---

(9) including a Space] **4–5** | meeting at three Angles **1–3** (11–12), their . . . lie] **2–5** | their . . . lie, **1** (27) lie] **1–4** | lies **5** (*l. below* 36: § 25.) **Coste** 'Cinquiéme cas.' *in Table of Contents but not in text.*

very fitly *be called right, or wrong* Ideas, according as they agree, or disagree to those Patterns to which they are referred. But if any one had rather call them *true*, or *false*, 'tis fit he use a liberty which every one has, to call Things by those Names he thinks best; though in propriety of Speech, *Truth*, or *Falshood*, will, I think, scarce agree to them, but as they, some way or other, virtually contain in them some mental Proposition. The *Ideas* that are in a Man's Mind, simply considered, cannot be wrong, unless complex ones, wherein inconsistent parts are jumbled together. All other *Ideas* are in themselves right; and the knowledge about them right and true Knowledge: but when we come to refer them to any thing, as to their Patterns and Archetypes, then they are capable of being wrong, as far as they disagree with such Archetypes.

CHAPTER XXXIII

Of the Association of Ideas.

§ 1. THERE is scarce any one that does not observe something that seems odd to him, and is in it self really Extravagant in the Opinions, Reasonings, and Actions of other Men. The least flaw of this kind, if at all different from his own, every one is quick-sighted enough to espie in another, and will by the Authority of Reason forwardly condemn, though he be guilty of much greater Unreasonableness in his own Tenets and Conduct, which he never perceives, and will very hardly, if at all, be convinced of.

§ 2. This proceeds not wholly from Self-love, though that has often a great hand in it. Men of fair Minds, and not given up to the over weening of Self-flattery, are frequently guilty of it; and in many Cases one with amazement hears the Arguings, and is astonish'd at the Obstinacy of a worthy Man, who yields not to the Evidence of Reason, though laid before him as clear as Day-light.

§ 3. This sort of Unreasonableness is usually imputed to Education and Prejudice, and for the most part truly enough, though

§ 1. *Something unreasonable in most Men.* § 2. *Not wholly from Self-love.* § 3. *Nor from Education.*

---

(1) *right, or wrong*] **Coste** *adds a linguistic footnote.* (13) *This chapter (and Book II) concludes in* **1–3** *with a further section,* § 27, *which is omitted here in* **4–5** *but is the concluding section,* § 19, *of the next chapter, added in* **4–5**. (*l. below* 13) *This chapter add.* **4–5**.

that reaches not the bottom of the Disease, nor shews distinctly enough whence it rises, or wherein it lies. Education is often rightly assigned for the Cause, and Prejudice is a good general Name for the thing it self: But yet, I think, he ought to look a little farther who would trace this sort of Madness to the root it springs from, and so explain it, as to shew whence this flaw has its Original in very sober and rational Minds, and wherein it consists.

§ 4. I shall be pardon'd for calling it by so harsh a name as *Madness*, when it is considered, that opposition to Reason deserves that Name, and is really Madness; and there is scarce a Man so free from it, but that if he should always on all occasions argue or do as in some cases he constantly does, would not be thought fitter for *Bedlam*, than Civil Conversation. I do not here mean when he is under the power of an unruly Passion, but in the steady calm course of his Life. That which will yet more apologize for this harsh Name, and ungrateful Imputation on the greatest part of Mankind is, that enquiring a little by the bye into the Nature of Madness, *B.*2. *c.*11. §13. I found it to spring from the very same Root, and to depend on the very same Cause we are here speaking of. This consideration of the thing it self, at a time when I thought not the least on the Subject which I am now treating of, suggested it to me. And if this be a Weakness to which all Men are so liable; if this be a Taint which so universally infects Mankind, the greater care should be taken to lay it open under its due Name, thereby to excite the greater care in its Prevention and Cure.

§ 5. Some of our *Ideas* have a natural Correspondence and Connexion one with another: It is the Office and Excellency of our Reason to trace these, and hold them together in that Union and Correspondence which is founded in their peculiar Beings. Besides this there is another Connexion of *Ideas* wholly owing to Chance or Custom; *Ideas* that in themselves are not at all of kin, come to be so united in some Mens Minds, that 'tis very hard to separate them, they always keep in company, and the one no sooner at any time comes into the Understanding but its Associate appears with it; and if they are more than two which are thus united, the whole gang always inseparable shew themselves together.

§ 4. *A degree of Madness.* § 5. *From a wrong connexion of* Ideas.

(21) suggested] **5** | suggest'd **4** (31) Custom;] **5** | Custom, **4** (*l. below* 36: § 4.) **Coste** 'Pourquoy on luy donne le nom de *folie?*'

§ 6. This strong Combination of *Ideas*, not ally'd by Nature, the Mind makes in it self either voluntarily, or by chance, and hence it comes in different Men to be very different, according to their different Inclinations, Educations, Interests, *etc.* Custom settles habits of Thinking in the Understanding, as well as of Determining in the Will, and of Motions in the Body; all which seems to be but Trains of Motion in the Animal Spirits, which once set a going continue on in the same steps they have been used to, which by often treading are worn into a smooth path, and the Motion in it becomes easy and as it were Natural. As far as we can comprehend Thinking, thus *Ideas* seem to be produced in our Minds; or if they are not, this may serve to explain their following one another in an habitual train, when once they are put into that tract, as well as it does to explain such Motions of the Body. A Musician used to any Tune will find that let it but once begin in his Head, the *Ideas* of the several Notes of it will follow one another orderly in his Understanding without any care or attention, as regularly as his Fingers move orderly over the Keys of the Organ to play out the Tune he has begun, though his unattentive Thoughts be elsewhere a wandering. Whether the natural cause of these *Ideas*, as well as of that regular Dancing of his Fingers be the Motion of his Animal Spirits, I will not determine, how probable soever by this Instance it appears to be so: But this may help us a little to conceive of Intellectual Habits, and of the tying together of *Ideas*.

§ 7. That there are such Associations of them made by Custom in the Minds of most Men, I think no Body will question who has well consider'd himself or others; and to this, perhaps, might be justly attributed most of the Sympathies and Antipathies observable in Men, which work as strongly, and produce as regular Effects as if they were Natural, and are therefore called so, though they at first had no other Original but the accidental Connexion of two *Ideas*, which either the strength of the first Impression, or future Indulgence so united, that they always afterwards kept company together in that Man's Mind, as if they were but one *Idea*. I say most of the Antipathies, I do not say all, for some of them are truly Natural, depend upon our original Constitution, and are born with

§ 6. *This Connexion how made.* §§ 7, 8. *Some Antipathies an effect of it.*

(8) on] **4**; *om.* **5** (11) Minds;] **5** | Minds, **4** (22) Spirits,] **5** | Spirits: **4** determine,] **5** | determine **4**

us; but a great part of those which are counted Natural, would have been known to be from unheeded, though, perhaps, early Impressions, or wanton Phancies at first, which would have been acknowledged the Original of them if they had been warily observed. A grown Person surfeiting with Honey, no sooner hears the Name of it, but his Phancy immediately carries Sickness and Qualms to his Stomach, and he cannot bear the very *Idea* of it; other *Ideas* of Dislike and Sickness, and Vomiting presently accompany it, and he is disturb'd, but he knows from whence to date this Weakness, and can tell how he got this Indisposition: Had this happen'd to him, by an over dose of Honey, when a Child, all the same Effects would have followed, but the Cause would have been mistaken, and the Antipathy counted Natural.

§ 8. I mention this not out of any great necessity there is in this present Argument, to distinguish nicely between Natural and Acquired Antipathies, but I take notice of it for another purpose, (*viz.*) that those who have Children, or the charge of their Education, would think it worth their while diligently to watch, and carefully to prevent the undue Connexion of *Ideas* in the Minds of young People. This is the time most susceptible of lasting Impressions, and though those relating to the Health of the Body, are by discreet People minded and fenced against, yet I am apt to doubt, that those which relate more peculiarly to the Mind, and terminate in the Understanding, or Passions, have been much less heeded than the thing deserves; nay, those relating purely to the Understanding have, as I suspect, been by most Men wholly over-look'd.

§ 9. This wrong Connexion in our Minds of *Ideas* in themselves, loose and independent one of another, has such an influence, and is of so great force to set us awry in our Actions, as well Moral as Natural, Passions, Reasonings, and Notions themselves, that, perhaps, there is not any one thing that deserves more to be looked after.

§ 10. The *Ideas* of *Goblines* and *Sprights* have really no more to do with Darkness than Light; yet let but a foolish Maid inculcate these

§ 9. *A great cause of Errors.* §§ 10–12. *Instances.*

---

(14) *In* **Coste**, § *8 has a separate marginal summary*: 'Combien il importe de prévenir de bonne heure cette bizarre connexion d'Idées.'; *this is applied also to* § *9.* (16) purpose,] **5** | purpose **4** (25) deserves; nay,] **5** | deserves, nay / **4** (28) another,] **5** | another **4** (34) Light;] **5** | Light, **4** (*l. below* 34: §§ 10–12.) *In* **Coste**, 'Exemple de cette liaison d'idées.', 'Autre exemple.', *and* 'Troisiéme exemple.' *are the marginal summaries for* §§ *10, 11, and 12, respectively.*

often on the Mind of a Child, and raise them there together, possibly he shall never be able to separate them again so long as he lives, but Darkness shall ever afterwards bring with it those frightful *Ideas*, and they shall be so joined that he can no more bear the one than the other.

§ 11. A Man receives a sensible Injury from another, thinks on the Man and that Action over and over, and by ruminating on them strongly, or much in his Mind, so cements those two *Ideas* together, that he makes them almost one; never thinks on the Man, but the Pain and Displeasure he suffered comes into his Mind with it, so that he scarce distinguishes them, but has as much an aversion for the one as the other. Thus Hatreds are often begotten from slight and almost innocent Occasions, and Quarrels propagated and continued in the World.

§ 12. A Man has suffered Pain or Sickness in any Place, he saw his Friend die in such a Room; though these have in Nature nothing to do one with another, yet when the *Idea* of the Place occurs to his Mind, it brings (the Impression being once made) that of the Pain and Displeasure with it, he confounds them in his Mind, and can as little bear the one as the other.

§ 13. When this Combination is settled and whilst it lasts, it is not in the power of Reason to help us, and relieve us from the Effects of it. *Ideas* in our Minds, when they are there, will operate according to their Natures and Circumstances; and here we see the cause why Time cures certain Affections, which Reason, though in the right, and allow'd to be so, has not power over, nor is able against them to prevail with those who are apt to hearken to it in other cases. The Death of a Child, that was the daily delight of his Mother's Eyes, and joy of her Soul, rends from her Heart the whole comfort of her Life, and gives her all the torment imaginable; use the Consolations of Reason in this case, and you were as good preach Ease to one on the Rack, and hope to allay, by rational Discourses, the Pain of his Joints tearing asunder. Till time has by disuse separated the sense of that Enjoyment and its loss from the *Idea* of the Child returning to her Memory, all Representations, though never so reasonable, are in vain; and therefore some in whom the

§ 13. *Why Time cures some Disorders in the Mind which Reason cannot.*

---

(8) Mind,] **5** | Mind **4** (16) Room;] **5** | Room, **4** (29) Mother's] **5** | Mothers **4** (*l. below* 36) **Coste** 'Quatriéme exemple.'

union between these *Ideas* is never dissolved, spend their Lives in Mourning, and carry an incurable Sorrow to their Graves.

§ 14. A Friend of mine knew one perfectly cured of Madness by a very harsh and offensive Operation. The Gentleman, who was thus recovered, with great sense of Gratitude and Acknowledgment, owned the Cure all his Life after, as the greatest Obligation he could have received; but whatever Gratitude and Reason suggested to him, he could never bear the sight of the Operator: That Image brought back with it the *Idea* of that Agony which he suffer'd from his Hands, which was too mighty and intolerable for him to endure.

§ 15. Many Children imputing the Pain they endured at School to their Books they were corrected for, so joyn those *Ideas* together, that a Book becomes their Aversion, and they are never reconciled to the study and use of them all their Lives after; and thus Reading becomes a torment to them, which otherwise possibly they might have made the great Pleasure of their Lives. There are Rooms convenient enough, that some Men cannot Study in, and fashions of Vessels, which though never so clean and commodious they cannot Drink out of, and that by reason of some accidental *Ideas* which are annex'd to them, and make them offensive; and who is there that hath not observed some Man to flag at the appearance, or in the company of some certain Person not otherwise superior to him, but because having once on some occasion got the Ascendant, the *Idea* of Authority and Distance goes along with that of the Person, and he that has been thus subjected is not able to separate them.

§ 16. Instances of this kind are so plentiful every where, that if I add one more, it is only for the pleasant oddness of it. It is of a young Gentleman, who having learnt to Dance, and that to great Perfection, there happened to stand an old Trunk in the Room where he learnt. The *Idea* of this remarkable piece of Houshold-stuff, had so mixed it self with the turns and steps of all his Dances, that though in that Chamber he could Dance excellently well, yet it was only whilst that Trunk was there, nor could he perform well in any other place, unless that, or some such other Trunk had its due position in the Room. If this Story shall be suspected to be dressed

§§ 14–16. *Farther Instances of the effect of the Association of* Ideas.

(*l. below* 35) *In* **Coste**, *each of* §§ *14, 15, and 16 has a separate marginal summary*: 'Cinquiéme exemple bien remarquable.', 'Autres exemples.' *and* 'Exemple qu'on ajoûte pour son singularité.', *respectively*.

up with some comical Circumstances, a little beyond precise Nature; I answer for my self, that I had it some Years since from a very sober and worthy Man, upon his own knowledge, as I report it; and I dare say, there are very few inquisitive Persons, who read this, who have not met with Accounts, if not Examples of this Nature, that may parallel, or at least justify this.

§ 17. Intellectual Habits and Defects this way contracted are not less frequent and powerful, though less observed. Let the *Ideas* of Being and Matter be strongly joined either by Education or much Thought, whilst these are still combined in the Mind, what Notions, what Reasonings, will there be about separate Spirits? Let custom from the very Childhood have join'd Figure and Shape to the *Idea* of God, and what Absurdities will that Mind be liable to about the Deity?

Let the *Idea* of Infallibility be inseparably join'd to any Person, and these two constantly together possess the Mind, and then one Body in two Places at once, shall unexamined be swallowed for a certain Truth, by an implicit Faith, when ever that imagin'd infallible Person dictates and demands assent without enquiry.

§ 18. Some such wrong and unnatural Combinations of *Ideas* will be found to establish the Irreconcilable opposition between different Sects of Philosophy and Religion; for we cannot imagine every one of their Followers to impose wilfully on himself, and knowingly refuse Truth offer'd by plain Reason. Interest, though it does a great deal in the case, yet cannot be thought to work whole Societies of Men to so universal a Perverseness, as that every one of them to a Man should knowingly maintain Falshood: Some at least must be allow'd to do what all pretend to, *i.e.* to pursue Truth sincerely; and therefore there must be something that blinds their Understandings, and makes them not see the falshood of what they embrace for real Truth. That which thus captivates their Reasons, and leads Men of Sincerity blindfold from common Sence, will, when examin'd, be found to be what we are speaking of: some independent *Ideas*, of no alliance to one another, are by Education, Custom, and the constant din of their Party, so coupled in their Minds, that they always appear there together, and they can no more separate them in their Thoughts, than if they were but one

§ 17. *Its influence on intellectual habits.* § 18. *Observable in different Sects.*

(15–19) Let . . . enquiry.] *Not in* **Coste** (24) Interest,] **5** | Interest **4**

Idea, and they operate as if they were so. This gives Sence to *Jargon*, Demonstration to Absurdities, and Consistency to Nonsense, and is the foundation of the greatest, I had almost said, of all the Errors in the World; or if it does not reach so far, it is at least the most dangerous one, since so far as it obtains, it hinders Men from seeing and examining. When two things in themselves disjoin'd, appear to the sight constantly united; if the Eye sees these things rivetted which are loose, where will you begin to rectify the mistakes that follow in two *Ideas*, that they have been accustom'd so to join in their Minds, as to substitute one for the other, and, as I am apt to think, often without perceiving it themselves? This, whilst they are under the deceit of it, makes them uncapable of Conviction, and they applaud themselves as zealous Champions for Truth, when indeed they are contending for Error; and the confusion of two different *Ideas*, which a customary connexion of them in their Minds hath to them made in effect but one, fills their Heads with false Views, and their Reasonings with false Consequences.

§ 19. Having thus given an account of the original, sorts, and extent of our *Ideas*, with several other Considerations, about these (I know not whether I may say) Instruments, or Materials, of our Knowledge, the method I at first proposed to my self, would now require, that I should immediately proceed to shew, what use the Understanding makes of them, and what Knowledge we have by them. This was that, which, in the first general view I had of this Subject, was all that I thought I should have to do: but upon a nearer approach, I find, that there is so close a connexion between *Ideas* and Words; and our abstract *Ideas*, and general Words, have so constant a relation one to another, that it is impossible to speak clearly and distinctly of our Knowledge, which all consists in Propositions, without considering, first, the Nature, Use, and Signification of Language; which therefore must be the business of the next Book.

§ 19. *Conclusion.*

---

(5) obtains,] **5** | obtains **4** (6) disjoin'd,] **5** | disjoin'd **4** (12) it,] **5** | it. **4**
(18) *This section is § 27 of Book II, Chapter xxxi in* **1** *and Chapter xxxii in* **2–3**.

BOOK III

CHAPTER I

Of Words or Language in General.

§ 1. GOD having designed Man for a sociable Creature, made him not only with an inclination, and under a necessity to have fellowship with those of his own kind; but furnished him also with Language, which was to be the great Instrument, and common Tye of Society. *Man* therefore had by Nature his Organs so fashioned, as to be *fit to frame articulate Sounds*, which we call Words. But this was not enough to produce Language; for Parrots, and several other Birds, will be taught to make articulate Sounds distinct enough, which yet, by no means, are capable of Language.

§ 2. Besides articulate Sounds therefore, it was farther necessary, that he should be *able to use these Sounds, as Signs of internal Conceptions*; and to make them stand as marks for the *Ideas* within his own Mind, whereby they might be made known to others, and the Thoughts of Men's Minds be conveyed from one to another.

§ 3. But neither was this sufficient to make Words so useful as they ought to be. It is not enough for the perfection of Language, that Sounds can be made signs of *Ideas*, unless those *signs* can be so made use of, as *to comprehend several particular Things*: For the multiplication of Words would have perplexed their Use, had every particular thing need of a distinct name to be signified by. To remedy this inconvenience, Language had yet a farther improvement in the use of general Terms, whereby one word was made to mark a multitude of particular existences: Which advantageous use of Sounds was obtain'd only by the difference of the *Ideas* they were made signs of. Those names becoming general, which are made to stand for general *Ideas*, and those remaining particular, where the *Ideas* they are used for are particular.

§ 1. *Man fitted to form articulate Sounds.* § 2. *To make them signs of* Ideas. §§ 3, 4. *To make general Signs.*

(20–7) To . . . particular.] *add.* **2–5**

§ 4. Besides these Names which stand for *Ideas*, there be other words which Men make use of, not to signify any *Idea*, but the want or absence of some *Ideas* simple or complex, or all *Ideas* together; such as are *Nihil* in Latin, and in English, *Ignorance* and *Barrenness*. All which negative or privative Words, cannot be said properly to belong to, or signify no *Ideas*: for then they would be perfectly insignificant Sounds; but they relate to positive *Ideas*, and signify their absence.

§ 5. It may also lead us a little towards the Original of all our Notions and Knowledge, if we remark, how great a dependance our *Words* have on common sensible *Ideas*; and how those, which are made use of to stand for Actions and Notions quite removed from sense, *have their rise from thence, and from obvious sensible* Ideas *are transferred to more abstruse significations*, and made to stand for *Ideas* that come not under the cognizance of our senses; *v.g.* to *Imagine*, *Apprehend*, *Comprehend*, *Adhere*, *Conceive*, *Instill*, *Disgust*, *Disturbance*, *Tranquillity*, etc. are all Words taken from the Operations of sensible Things, and applied to certain Modes of Thinking. *Spirit*, in its primary signification, is Breath; *Angel*, a Messenger: And I doubt not, but if we could trace them to their sources, we should find, in all Languages, the names, which stand for Things that fall not under our Senses, to have had their first rise from sensible *Ideas*. By which we may give some kind of guess, what kind of Notions they were, and whence derived, which filled their Minds, who were the first Beginners of Languages; and how Nature, even in the naming of Things, unawares suggested to Men the Originals and Principles of all their Knowledge: whilst, to give Names, that might make known to others any Operations they felt in themselves, or any other *Ideas*, that came not under their Senses, they were fain to borrow Words from ordinary known *Ideas* of Sensation, by that means to make others the more easily to conceive those Operations they experimented in themselves, which made no outward sensible appearances; and then when they had got known and agreed Names, to signify those internal Operations of their own Minds,

§ 5. *Words ultimately derived from such as signify sensible* Ideas.

---

(1) Besides] **2–5** | *Words* then are made to be signs of our *Ideas*, and *are general or particular*, *as the Ideas they stand for are general or particular*. But besides **1** (1–2) other words] **2–5** | others **1** (2) Men] **2–5** | Men have found and **1** (4) *Nihil* in Latin] **2–5** | the Latin words, *Nihil* **1** (13–15) *rise* . . . senses] **2–5** | *Original*, and are transferred *from obvious sensible Ideas* **1** (20) sources] **2–5** | Originals **1**

they were sufficiently furnished to make known by Words, all their other *Ideas*; since they could consist of nothing, but either of outward sensible Perceptions, or of the inward Operations of their Minds about them; we having, as has been proved, no *Ideas* at all, but what originally come either from sensible Objects without, or what we feel within our selves, from the inward Workings of our own Spirits, which we are conscious to our selves of within.

§ 6. But to understand better the use and force of Language, as subservient to Instruction and Knowledge, it will be convenient to consider,

First, To what it is that Names, in the use of Language, are immediately applied.

Secondly, Since all (except proper) Names are general, and so stand not particularly for this or that single Thing; but for sorts and ranks of Things, it will be necessary to consider, in the next place, what the Sorts and Kinds, or, if you rather like the Latin Names, *what the Species and Genera of Things* are; wherein they consist; and how they come to be made. These being (as they ought) well looked into, we shall the better come to find the right use of Words; the natural Advantages and Defects of Language; and the remedies that ought to be used, to avoid the inconveniencies of obscurity or uncertainty in the signification of Words, without which, it is impossible to discourse with any clearness, or order, concerning Knowledge: Which being conversant about Propositions, and those most commonly universal ones, has greater connexion with Words, than perhaps is suspected.

These Considerations therefore, shall be the matter of the following Chapters.

CHAPTER II

Of the Signification of Words.

§ 1. MAN, though he have great variety of Thoughts, and such, from which others, as well as himself, might receive Profit and

§ 6. *Distribution.*
§ 1. *Words are sensible Signs necessary for Communication.*

(17–18) are; . . . consist;] **4er–5** | are, . . . consist, **1–4** (22) Words,] **4–5** | Words: **1–3** (*l. below* 30) **Coste** 'Division générale de ce Troisiéme Livre.'

Delight; yet they are all within his own Breast, invisible, and hidden from others, nor can of themselves be made appear. The Comfort, and Advantage of Society, not being to be had without Communication of Thoughts, it was necessary, that Man should find out some external sensible Signs, whereby those invisible *Ideas*, which his thoughts are made up of, might be made known to others. For this purpose, nothing was so fit, either for Plenty or Quickness, as those articulate Sounds, which with so much Ease and Variety, he found himself able to make. Thus we may conceive how *Words*, which were by Nature so well adapted to that purpose, come to be made use of by Men, as *the Signs of* their *Ideas*; not by any natural connexion, that there is between particular articulate Sounds and certain *Ideas*, for then there would be but one Language amongst all Men; but by a voluntary Imposition, whereby such a Word is made arbitrarily the Mark of such an *Idea*. The use then of Words, is to be sensible Marks of *Ideas*; and the *Ideas* they stand for, are their proper and immediate Signification.

§ 2. The use Men have of these Marks, being either to record their own Thoughts for the Assistance of their own Memory; or as it were, to bring out their *Ideas*, and lay them before the view of others: *Words in their primary or immediate Signification, stand for nothing, but the* Ideas *in the Mind of him that uses them*, how imperfectly soever, or carelesly those *Ideas* are collected from the Things, which they are supposed to represent. When a Man speaks to another, it is, that he may be understood; and the end of Speech is, that those Sounds, as Marks, may make known his *Ideas* to the Hearer. That then which Words are the Marks of, are the *Ideas* of the Speaker: Nor can any one apply them, as Marks, immediately to any thing else, but the *Ideas*, that he himself hath: For this would be to make them Signs of his own Conceptions, and yet apply them to other *Ideas*; which would be to make them Signs, and not Signs of his *Ideas* at the same time; and so in effect, to have no Signification at all. Words being voluntary Signs, they cannot be voluntary Signs imposed by him on Things he knows not. That would be

§§ 2, 3. *Words are the sensible Signs of his* Ideas *who uses them.*

(2) Comfort] **4–5** | Comfort therefore **1–3** (*likewise* **Coste**) (6) his . . . of] **4–5** | possess his Mind in so great variety **1–3** (7) this] **4–5** | which **1–3** (13) Sounds] **4–5** | Sounds, **1–3** (19) Thoughts] **4–5** | *Ideas* **1–3** (20) out their *Ideas*] **4–5** | them out **1–3** (21) others:] **4er–5** | others. **1–4** *or*] **5** | *and* **1–4** (25) Speech] **1T.er, 2–5** | the Speech **1** (30) Conceptions] **1er–5** | Conception **1**

to make them Signs of nothing, Sounds without Signification. A Man cannot make his Words the Signs either of Qualities in Things, or of Conceptions in the Mind of another, whereof he has none in his own. Till he has some *Ideas* of his own, he cannot suppose them to correspond with the Conceptions of another Man; nor can he use any Signs for them: For thus they would be the Signs of he knows not what, which is in Truth to be the Signs of nothing. But when he represents to himself other Men's *Ideas*, by some of his own, if he consent to give them the same Names, that other Men do, 'tis still to his own *Ideas*; to *Ideas* that he has, and not to *Ideas* that he has not.

§ 3. This is so necessary in the use of Language, that in this respect, the Knowing, and the Ignorant; the Learned, and Unlearned, use the *Words* they speak (with any meaning) all alike. They, *in every Man's Mouth, stand for the* Ideas *he has*, and which he would express by them. A Child having taken notice of nothing in the Metal he hears called Gold, but the bright shining yellow colour, he applies the Word Gold only to his own *Idea* of that Colour, and nothing else; and therefore calls the same Colour in a Peacocks Tail, Gold. Another that hath better observed, adds to shining yellow, great Weight: And then the Sound Gold, when he uses it, stands for a complex *Idea* of a shining Yellow and very weighty Substance. Another adds to those Qualities, Fusibility: and then the Word Gold to him signifies a Body, bright, yellow, fusible, and very heavy. Another adds Malleability. Each of these uses equally the Word Gold, when they have Occasion to express the *Idea*, which they have apply'd it to: But it is evident, that each can apply it only to his own *Idea*; nor can he make it stand, as a Sign of such a complex *Idea*, as he has not.

§ 4. But though Words, as they are used by Men, can properly and immediately signify nothing but the *Ideas*, that are in the Mind of the Speaker; yet they in their Thoughts give them a secret reference to two other things.

First, they suppose their Words to be Marks of the Ideas *in the Minds also of other Men, with whom they communicate*: For else they should talk in vain, and could not be understood, if the Sounds they applied to one *Idea*, were such, as by the Hearer, were applied to another,

§ 4. *Words often secretly referred, First, to the* Ideas *in other Mens Minds.*

---

(6) thus they] **4–5** | it **1–3** (7) Signs] **2–5** | Sign **1** (26) which] *add.* **4–5** (30–1) [*2nd*] the . . . Speaker] **2–5** | their Minds **1** (*l. below* 36) *other*] **2–3, 5** | *others* **4**
In **Coste**, *§§ 4–6 come under the same marginal summary as that for §§ 2, 3.*

which is to speak two Languages. But in this, Men stand not usually to examine, whether the *Idea* they, and those they discourse with have in their Minds, be the same: But think it enough, that they use the Word, as they imagine, in the common Acceptation of that Language; in which case they suppose, that the *Idea*, they make it a Sign of, is precisely the same, to which the Understanding Men of that Country apply that Name.

§ 5. *Secondly*, Because *Men* would not be thought to talk *barely* of their own Imaginations, but of Things as really they are; therefore they *often suppose their Words to stand also for the reality of Things*. But this relating more particularly to Substances, and their Names, as perhaps the former does to simple *Ideas* and Modes, we shall speak of these two different ways of applying Words more at large, when we come to treat of the Names of mixed Modes, and Substances, in particular: Though give me leave here to say, that it is a perverting the use of Words, and brings unavoidable Obscurity and Confusion into their Signification, whenever we make them stand for any thing, but those *Ideas* we have in our own Minds.

§ 6. Concerning Words also it is farther to be considered. *First*, That they being immediately the Signs of Mens *Ideas*; and, by that means, the Instruments whereby Men communicate their Conceptions, and express to one another those Thoughts and Imaginations, they have within their own Breasts, *there comes by constant use*, to be such *a Connexion between certain Sounds, and the* Ideas *they stand for*, that the Names heard, almost as readily excite certain *Ideas*, as if the Objects themselves, which are apt to produce them, did actually affect the Senses. Which is manifestly so in all obvious sensible Qualities; and in all Substances, that frequently, and familiarly occur to us.

§ 7. *Secondly*, That though the proper and immediate Signification of Words, are *Ideas* in the Mind of the Speaker; yet because by familiar use from our Cradles, we come to learn certain articulate Sounds very perfectly, and have them readily on our Tongues, and always at hand in our Memories; but yet are not always careful to examine, or settle their Significations perfectly, it *often* happens that *Men*, even when they would apply themselves to an attentive

§ 5. *Secondly, To the reality of Things*. § 6. *Words by use readily excite* Ideas. § 7. *Words often used without signification*.

(2) those] **2–5** | he **1** (3) have in their Minds] *add.* **2–5** (5) case] **1–4**; *om.* **5** (19) it] **2–5** | this **1** (34) always . . . in] *add.* **2–5**

Consideration, do *set their Thoughts more on Words than Things.* Nay, because Words are many of them learn'd, before the *Ideas* are known for which they stand: Therefore some, not only Children, but Men, speak several Words, no otherwise than Parrots do, only because they have learn'd them, and have been accustomed to those Sounds. But so far as Words are of Use and Signification, so far is there a constant connexion between the Sound and the *Idea*; and a Designation, that the one stand for the other: without which Application of them, they are nothing but so much insignificant Noise.

§ 8. *Words* by long and familiar use, as has been said, come to excite in Men certain *Ideas*, so constantly and readily, that they are apt to suppose a natural connexion between them. But that they *signify* only Men's peculiar *Ideas*, and that *by a perfectly arbitrary Imposition*, is evident, in that they often fail to excite in others (even that use the same Language) the same *Ideas*, we take them to be the Signs of: And every Man has so inviolable a Liberty, to make Words stand for what *Ideas* he pleases, that no one hath the Power to make others have the same *Ideas* in their Minds, that he has, when they use the same Words, that he does. And therefore the great *Augustus* himself, in the Possession of that Power which ruled the World, acknowledged, he could not make a new Latin Word: which was as much as to say, that he could not arbitrarily appoint, what *Idea* any Sound should be a Sign of, in the Mouths and common Language of his Subjects. 'Tis true, common use, by a tacit Consent, appropriates certain Sounds to certain *Ideas* in all Languages, which so far limits the signification of that Sound, that unless a Man applies it to the same *Idea*, he does not speak properly: And let me add, that unless a Man's Words excite the same *Ideas* in the Hearer, which he makes them stand for in speaking, he does not speak intelligibly. But whatever be the consequence of any Man's using of Words differently, either from their general Meaning, or the particular Sense of the Person to whom he addresses them, this is certain, their signification, in his use of them, is limited to his *Ideas*, and they can be Signs of nothing else.

§§ 8–11. *Their Signification perfectly arbitrary.*

---

(27) does not] **4–5** | cannot **1–3** (28) let me add] **4–5** | it is also true **1–3** (29) does not] **4–5** | cannot **1–3** (30–2) consequence . . . Person] **4–5** | consequence of any Man's use of Words different either from their Publick use, or that of the Persons **2–3** | consequences of his use of any Words, different either from the Publick, or that Person **1** (**1T.er** 'persons')

CHAPTER III

Of General Terms.

§ 1. ALL Things, that exist, being Particulars, it may perhaps be thought reasonable, that Words, which ought to be conformed to Things, should be so too, I mean in their Signification: but yet we find the quite contrary. The far *greatest part of Words*, that make all Languages, *are general Terms*: which has not been the Effect of Neglect, or Chance, but of Reason, and Necessity.

§ 2. First, *It is impossible, that every particular Thing should have a distinct peculiar Name*. For the signification and use of Words, depending on that connexion, which the Mind makes between its *Ideas*, and the Sounds it uses as Signs of them, it is necessary, in the Application of Names to things, that the Mind should have distinct *Ideas* of the Things, and retain also the particular Name that belongs to every one, with its peculiar appropriation to that *Idea*. But it is beyond the Power of humane Capacity to frame and retain distinct *Ideas* of all the particular Things we meet with: every Bird, and Beast Men saw; every Tree, and Plant, that affected the Senses, could not find a place in the most capacious Understanding. If it be looked on, as an instance of a prodigious Memory, That some Generals have been able to call every Soldier in their Army, by his proper Name: We may easily find a Reason, why Men have never attempted to give Names to each Sheep in their Flock, or Crow that flies over their Heads; much less to call every Leaf of Plants, or Grain of Sand that came in their way, by a peculiar Name.

§ 3. *Secondly*, If it were possible, *it would yet be useless*; because it would not serve to the chief end of Language. Men would in vain heap up Names of particular Things, that would not serve them to communicate their Thoughts. Men learn Names, and use them in Talk with others, only that they may be understood: which is then only done, when by Use or Consent, the Sound I make by the Organs of Speech, excites in another Man's Mind, who hears it, the *Idea* I apply it to in mine, when I speak it. This cannot be done by

§ 1. *The greatest part of Words general.* § 2. *For every particular thing to have a name is impossible.* §§ 3, 4. *And useless.*

(19) their] **1–2, 4–5** | the **3** (22) Leaf] **1–3, 5** | leaf **4**

Names, applied to particular Things, whereof I alone having the *Ideas* in my mind, the Names of them could not be significant, or intelligible to another, who was not acquainted with all those very particular Things, which had fallen under my Notice.

§ 4. *Thirdly*, But yet granting this also feasible; (which I think is not,) yet *a distinct Name for every particular Thing, would not be of any great use for the improvement of Knowledge*: which though founded in particular Things, enlarges it self by general Views; to which, Things reduced into sorts under general Names, are properly subservient. These, with the Names belonging to them, come within some compass, and do not multiply every Moment, beyond what, either the Mind can contain, or Use requires. And therefore in these Men have for the most part stopp'd: but yet not so, as to hinder themselves from distinguishing particular Things, by appropriated Names, where Convenience demands it. And therefore in their own Species, which they have most to do with, and wherein they have often occasion to mention particular Persons; they make use of proper Names, and there distinct Individuals have distinct Denominations.

§ 5. Besides Persons, Countries also, Cities, Rivers, Mountains, and other the like Distinctions of Place, have usually found peculiar Names, and that for the same Reason; they being such as Men have often an Occasion to mark particularly, and, as it were, set before others in their Discourses with them. And I doubt not, but if we had Reason to mention particular Horses, as often as we have to mention particular Men, we should have *proper Names* for the one, as familiar as for the other; and *Bucephalus* would be a Word as much in use, as *Alexander*. And therefore we see that amongst Jockeys, Horses have their proper Names to be known and distinguished by, as commonly as their Servants: Because amongst them, there is often Occasion to mention this or that particular Horse, when he is out of Sight.

§ 6. The next thing to be considered is, *how general Words come to be made*. For since all things that exist are only particulars, how come we by general Terms, or where find we those general Natures they are supposed to stand for? Words become general, by being

§ 5. *What things have proper names.* §§ 6–8. *How general Words are made.*

---

(6) *Thing*] **1–4** | *Things* **5** (13) Men] **4** | Men, **5** | , Men **1–3** (18) they . . . there] **4–5** | there they make use of proper Names, and **1–3**. (**Coste** *om.* 'there')

made the signs of general *Ideas*: and *Ideas* become general, by separating from them the circumstances of Time, and Place, and any other *Ideas*, that may determine them to this or that particular Existence. By this way of abstraction they are made capable of representing more Individuals than one; each of which, having in it a conformity to that abstract *Idea*, is (as we call it) of that sort.

§ 7. But to deduce this a little more distinctly, it will not perhaps be amiss, to trace our Notions, and Names, from their beginning, and observe by what degrees we proceed, and by what steps we enlarge our *Ideas* from our first Infancy. There is nothing more evident, than that the *Ideas* of the Persons Children converse with, (to instance in them alone,) are like the Persons themselves, only particular. The *Ideas* of the Nurse, and the Mother, are well framed in their Minds; and, like Pictures of them there, represent only those Individuals. The Names they first give to them, are confined to these Individuals; and the Names of *Nurse* and *Mamma*, the Child uses, determine themselves to those Persons. Afterwards, when time and a larger Acquaintance has made them observe, that there are a great many other Things in the World, that in some common agreements of Shape, and several other Qualities, resemble their Father and Mother, and those Persons they have been used to, they frame an *Idea*, which they find those many Particulars do partake in; and to that they give, with others, the name *Man*, for Example. And *thus they come to have a general Name*, and a general *Idea*. Wherein they make nothing new, but only leave out of the complex *Idea* they had of *Peter* and *James*, *Mary* and *Jane*, that which is peculiar to each, and retain only what is common to them all.

§ 8. By the same way, that they come by the general Name and *Idea* of *Man*, they easily *advance to more general Names* and Notions. For observing, that several Things that differ from their *Idea* of *Man*, and cannot therefore be comprehended under that Name, have yet certain Qualities, wherein they agree with *Man*, by retaining only those Qualities, and uniting them into one *Idea*, they have again another and a more general *Idea*; to which having given a Name, they make a term of a more comprehensive extension: Which new *Idea* is made, not by any new addition, but only, as before, by leaving out the shape, and some other Properties

(2) [*each*] and] **4–5** | or **1–3** (12) alone,] **1–3** | alone **4–5** (15) give] **1–4** | gave **5** (21) Mother,] **4–5** | Mother: **1–3** (27) common] **1–2, 4–5** | commonly **3**

signified by the name *Man*, and retaining only a Body, with Life, Sense, and spontaneous Motion, comprehended under the Name *Animal*.

§ 9. That this is the *way*, *whereby Men first formed general* Ideas, *and general Names to them*, I think, is so evident, that there needs no other proof of it, but the considering of a Man's self, or others, and the ordinary proceedings of their Minds in Knowledge: And he that thinks general Natures or Notions, are any thing else but such abstract and partial *Ideas* of more complex ones, taken at first from particular Existences, will, I fear, be at a loss where to find them. For let any one reflect, and then tell me, wherein does his *Idea* of *Man* differ from that of *Peter*, and *Paul*; or his *Idea* of *Horse*, from that of *Bucephalus*, but in the leaving out something, that is peculiar to each Individual; and retaining so much of those particular complex *Ideas*, of several particular Existences, as they are found to agree in? Of the complex *Ideas*, signified by the names *Man*, and *Horse*, leaving out but those particulars wherein they differ, and retaining only those wherein they agree, and of those, making a new distinct complex *Idea*, and giving the name *Animal* to it, one has a more general term, that comprehends, with Man, several other Creatures. Leave out of the *Idea* of *Animal*, Sense and spontaneous Motion, and the remaining complex *Idea*, made up of the remaining simple ones of Body, Life, and Nourishment, becomes a more general one, under the more comprehensive term, *Vivens*. And not to dwell longer upon this particular, so evident in it self, by the same way the Mind proceeds to *Body*, *Substance*, and at last to *Being*, *Thing*, and such universal terms, which stand for any of our *Ideas* whatsoever. To conclude, this whole *mystery* of *Genera* and *Species*, which make such a noise in the Schools, and are, with Justice, so little regarded out of them, is nothing else but abstract *Ideas*, more or less comprehensive, with names annexed to them. In all which, this is constant and unvariable, That every more general term, stands for such an *Idea*, as is but a part of any of those contained under it.

§ 10. This may shew us the reason, *why*, *in the defining of Words*, which is nothing but declaring their signification, *we make use of the Genus*, or next general Word that comprehends it. Which is not out

§ 9. *General Natures are nothing but abstract* Ideas. § 10. *Why the* Genus *is ordinarily made use of in Definitions.*

(11) and then tell me,] *add.* **4–5** (12) *Man*] **4–5** | a Man, **1–3** *Horse*] **4–5** an Horse **1–3** (21) [*1st*] of] *add.* **4–5** Sense] **4–5** | Sense, **1–3**

of necessity, but only to save the labour of enumerating the several simple *Ideas*, which the next general Word, or *Genus*, stands for; or, perhaps, sometimes the shame of not being able to do it. But though defining by *Genus* and *Differentia*, (I crave leave to use these terms of Art, though originally Latin, since they most properly suit those Notions they are applied to;) I say, though defining by the *Genus* be the shortest way; yet, I think, it may be doubted, whether it be the best. This I am sure, it is not the only, and so not absolutely necessary. For Definition being nothing but making another understand by Words, what *Idea*, the term defined stands for, a definition is best made by enumerating those simple *Ideas* that are combined in the signification of the term Defined: and if instead of such an enumeration, Men have accustomed themselves to use the next general term, it has not been out of necessity, or for greater clearness; but for quickness and dispatch sake. For, I think, that to one who desired to know what *Idea* the word *Man* stood for; if it should be said, that *Man* was a solid extended Substance, having Life, Sense, spontaneous Motion, and the Faculty of Reasoning, I doubt not but the meaning of the term *Man*, would be as well understood, and the *Idea* it stands for be at least as clearly made known, as when it is defined to be a *rational Animal*; which by the several definitions of *Animal*, *Vivens*, and *Corpus*, resolves it self into those enumerated *Ideas*. I have in explaining the term *Man*, followed here the ordinary Definition of the Schools: which though, perhaps, not the most exact, yet serves well enough to my present purpose. And one may in this instance, see what gave occasion to the Rule, that a Definition must consist of *Genus*, and *Differentia*: and it suffices to shew us the little necessity there is of such a Rule, or advantage in the strict observing of it. For Definitions, as has been said, being only the explaining of one Word, by several others, so that the meaning, or *Idea* it stands for, may be certainly known, Languages are not always so made, according to the Rules of Logick, that every term can have its signification, exactly and clearly expressed by two others. Experience sufficiently satisfies us to the contrary; or else those who have made this Rule, have done ill, that they have given us so few Definitions conformable to it. But of Definitions, more in the next Chapter.

(17) *Man*] **4–5** | a Man **1–3** (21) is] **1–3, 5** | it **4** (22) it] **1–3, 5** | its **4**
(25) serves] **1–2, 4–5** | it serves **3** (26) the] **4–5** | that **1–3** (*likewise* **Coste**)
(27) *Genus*] **4–5** | its *Genus* **1–3**

§ 11. To return to general Words, it is plain, by what has been said, That *General and Universal*, belong not to the real existence of Things; but *are the Inventions and Creatures of the Understanding*, made by it for its own use, *and concern only Signs*, whether Words, or *Ideas*. Words are general, as has been said, when used, for Signs of general *Ideas*; and so are applicable indifferently to many particular Things; And *Ideas* are general, when they are set up, as the Representatives of many particular Things: but universality belongs not to things themselves, which are all of them particular in their Existence, even those Words, and *Ideas*, which in their signification, are general. When therefore we quit Particulars, the Generals that rest, are only Creatures of our own making, their general Nature being nothing but the Capacity they are put into by the Understanding, of signifying or representing many particulars. For the signification they have, is nothing but a relation, that by the mind of Man is added to them.

§ 12. The next thing therefore to be considered, is, *What kind of signification it is, that general Words have.* For as it is evident, that they do not signify barely one particular thing; for then they would not be general Terms, but proper Names: so on the other side, 'tis as evident, they do not signify a plurality; for Man and Men would then signify the same; and the distinction of numbers (as Grammarians call them) would be superfluous and useless. That then which general Words signify, is a sort of Things; and each of them does that, by being a sign of an abstract *Idea* in the mind, to which *Idea*, as Things existing are found to agree, so they come to be ranked under that name; or, which is all one, be of that sort. Whereby it is evident, that the *Essences of* the *sorts, or* (if the Latin word pleases better) *Species* of Things, are nothing else but these abstract *Ideas*. For the having the Essence of any Species, being that which makes any thing to be of that Species, and the conformity to the *Idea*, to which the name is annexed, being that which gives a right to that name, the having the Essence, and the having that Conformity, must needs be the same thing: Since to be of any

§ 11. *General and universal are Creatures of the Understanding.* § 12. *Abstract* Ideas *are the Essences of the* Genera *and* Species.

---

(7) *Ideas*] **1–3** | *Ideas*, **4–5** (11) Particulars] **Coste** *adds marginal note* 'Mots, idées ou choses.' (16) them] **5** *adds, in a footnote, a quotation from Locke's* First Letter to the Bishop of Worcester, *pp. 189, etc.* (20) Names:] **1–3** | Names, **4** | Names; **5** (24–5) each . . . that] **4–5** | that each of them does **1–3**

Species, and to have a right to the name of that Species, is all one. As for Example, to be a *Man*, or of the Species *Man*, and to have a right to the name *Man*, is the same thing. Again, to be a *Man*, or of the Species *Man*, and have the Essence of a *Man*, is the same thing. Now since nothing can be a *Man*, or have a right to the name *Man*, but what has a conformity to the abstract *Idea* the name *Man* stands for; nor any thing be a Man, or have a right to be of the Species *Man*, but what has the Essence of that Species, it follows, that the abstract *Idea*, for which the name stands, and the Essence of the Species, is one and the same. From whence it is easy to observe, that the essences of the sorts of things, and consequently the sorting of Things, is the Workmanship of the Understanding, since it is the Understanding that abstracts and makes those general *Ideas*.

§ 13. I would not here be thought to forget, much less to deny, that Nature in the Production of Things, makes several of them alike: there is nothing more obvious, especially in the Races of Animals, and all Things propagated by Seed. But yet, I think, we may say, the *sorting* of them under Names, *is the Workmanship of the Understanding, taking occasion from the similitude* it observes amongst them, to make abstract general *Ideas*, and set them up in the mind, with Names annexed to them, as Patterns, or Forms, (for in that sence the word Form has a very proper signification,) to which, as particular Things existing are found to agree, so they come to be of that Species, have that Denomination, or are put into that *Classis*. For when we say, this is a *Man*, that a *Horse*; this *Justice*, that *Cruelty*; this a *Watch*, that a *Jack*; what do we else but rank Things under different specifick Names, as agreeing to those abstract *Ideas*, of which we have made those Names the signs? And what are the Essences of those Species, set out and marked by Names, but those abstract *Ideas* in the mind; which are, as it were, the bonds between particular Things that exist and the Names they are to be ranked under? And when general Names have any connexion with particular Beings, these abstract *Ideas* are the *Medium* that unites them: so that the Essences of Species, as distinguished and denominated by us, neither are, nor can be any thing but those

§ 13. *They are the Workmanship of the Understanding, but have their foundation in the similitude of things.*

(2) [*2nd*] a] **1–4**; *om.* **5** (4) [*1st*] the] **1–4** | the same **5** (5) to] **1–4** | to / to **5** (7) be of] **1–4**; *om.* **5** (12) Things] **1–4** | This **5** (12–13) , since . . . Understanding] **1–4**; *om.* **5** (29) [*2nd*] those] **2–5** | these **1** (31) exist] **2er–4** | exist, **1–2**, **5**

precise abstract *Ideas* we have in our minds. And therefore the supposed real Essences of Substances, if different from our abstract *Ideas*, cannot be the Essences of the Species we rank Things into. For two Species may be one, as rationally, as two different Essences be the Essence of one Species: And I demand, what are the alterations may, or may not be made in a *Horse*, or *Lead*, without making either of them to be of another Species? In determining the Species of Things by our abstract *Ideas*, this is easy to resolve: but if any one will regulate himself herein, by supposed real Essences, he will, I suppose, be at a loss: and he will never be able to know when any thing precisely ceases to be of the Species of a *Horse*, or *Lead*.

§ 14. Nor will any one wonder, that I say these *Essences*, or abstract *Ideas*, (which are the measures of Names, and the boundaries of Species) are *the Workmanship of the Understanding*, who considers, that at least the complex ones are often, in several Men, different Collections of simple *Ideas*: and therefore that is *Covetousness* to one Man, which is not so to another. Nay, even in Substances, where their abstract *Ideas* seem to be taken from the Things themselves, they are not constantly the same; no not in that Species, which is most familiar to us, and with which we have the most intimate acquaintance: It having been more than once doubted, whether the *Fœtus* born of a Woman were a *Man*, even so far, as that it hath been debated, whether it were, or were not to be nourished and baptized: which could not be, if the abstract *Idea* or Essence, to which the Name Man belonged, were of Nature's making; and were not the uncertain and various Collection of simple *Ideas*, which the Understanding puts together, and then abstracting it, affixed a name to it. So that in truth *every distinct abstract* Idea, *is a distinct Essence*: and the names that stand for such distinct *Ideas*, are the names of Things essentially different. Thus a Circle is as essentially different from an Oval, as a Sheep from a Goat: and Rain is as essentially different from Snow, as Water from Earth; that abstract *Idea* which is the Essence of one, being impossible to be communicated to the other. And thus any two abstract *Ideas*, that in any part vary one from another, with two distinct names annexed to them, constitute two

§ 14. *Each distinct abstract* Idea *is a distinct Essence.*

---

(6) made] **1–4**; *om.* **5** (7) In] **2–5** | By **1** (11) a *Horse*, or *Lead*] **4–5** | an Horse, or Lead **1–3** (13) Names] **1–4** | Name **5** (32) Earth;] **1–3** (*likewise* **Coste**) | Earth, **4–5**

distinct sorts, or, if you please, *Species*, as essentially different, as any two the most remote, or opposite in the World.

§ 15. But since the *Essences* of Things are Thought, by some, (and not without reason,) to be wholly unknown; it may not be amiss to consider the *several significations of the Word Essence*.

First, *Essence* may be taken for the very being of any thing, whereby it is, what it is. And thus the real internal, but generally in Substances, unknown Constitution of Things, whereon their discoverable Qualities depend, may be called their *Essence*. This is the proper original signification of the Word, as is evident from the formation of it; *Essentia*, in its primary notation signifying properly *Being*. And in this sense it is still used, when we speak of the *Essence* of particular things, without giving them any Name.

Secondly, The Learning and Disputes of the Schools, having been much busied about *Genus* and *Species*, the Word *Essence* has almost lost its primary signification; and instead of the real Constitution of things, has been almost wholly applied to the artificial Constitution of *Genus* and *Species*. 'Tis true, there is ordinarily supposed a real Constitution of the sorts of Things; and 'tis past doubt, there must be some real Constitution, on which any Collection of simple *Ideas* co-existing, must depend. But it being evident, that Things are ranked under Names into sorts or *Species*, only as they agree to certain abstract *Ideas*, to which we have annexed those Names, the *Essence* of each *Genus*, or Sort, comes to be nothing but that abstract *Idea*, which the General, or *Sortal* (if I may have leave so to call it from *Sort*, as I do *General* from *Genus*,) Name stands for. And this we shall find to be that, which the Word *Essence* imports, in its most familiar use. These two sorts of *Essences*, I suppose, may not unfitly be termed, the one the *Real*, the other the *Nominal Essence*.

§ 16. *Between the Nominal Essence, and the Name*, there is so *near* a *Connexion*, that the Name of any sort of Things cannot be attributed to any particular Being, but what has this *Essence*, whereby it answers that abstract *Idea*, whereof that Name is the Sign.

§ 17. Concerning the real Essences of corporeal Substances, (to mention those only,) there are, if I mistake not, two Opinions. The

§ 15. *Real and nominal Essence.* § 16. *Constant Connection between the Name and nominal Essence.* § 17. *Supposition that Species are distinguished by their real Essences useless.*

---

(12) *Being*] **Coste** *adds a marginal note* 'Ab *esse essentia*.' (28) *Essences*] **4–5** | Essence **1–3**

one is of those, who using the Word *Essence*, for they know not what, suppose a certain number of those Essences, according to which, all natural things are made, and wherein they do exactly every one of them partake, and so become of this or that *Species*. The other, and more rational Opinion, is of those, who look on all natural Things to have a real, but unknown Constitution of their insensible Parts, from which flow those sensible Qualities, which serve us to distinguish them one from another, according as we have Occasion to rank them into sorts, under common Denominations. The former of these Opinions, which supposes these *Essences*, as a certain number of Forms or Molds, wherein all natural Things, that exist, are cast, and do equally partake, has, I imagine, very much perplexed the Knowledge of natural Things. The frequent Productions of Monsters, in all the Species of Animals, and of Changelings, and other strange Issues of humane Birth, carry with them difficulties, not possible to consist with this *Hypothesis*: Since it is as impossible, that two Things, partaking exactly of the same real *Essence*, should have different Properties, as that two Figures partaking in the same real *Essence* of a Circle, should have different Properties. But were there no other reason against it, yet the *supposition of Essences, that cannot be known*; and the making them nevertheless to be that, which distinguishes the Species of Things, *is* so *wholly useless*, and unserviceable to any part of our Knowledge, that that alone were sufficient, to make us lay it by; and content our selves with such *Essences* of the Sorts or Species of Things, as come within the reach of our Knowledge: which, when seriously considered, will be found, as I have said, to be nothing else, but those abstract complex *Ideas*, to which we have annexed distinct general Names.

§ 18. *Essences* being thus distinguished into *Nominal and Real*, we may farther observe, that *in* the Species of *simple* Ideas *and Modes*, they *are always the same*: But *in Substances, always quite different*. Thus a Figure including a Space between three Lines, is the real, as well as nominal *Essence* of a Triangle; it being not only the abstract *Idea* to which the general Name is annexed, but the very *Essentia*, or Being, of the thing it self, that Foundation from which all its Properties flow, and to which they are all inseparably annexed. But it is far

§ 18. *Real and nominal Essence the same in simple* Ideas *and Modes, different in Substances.*

---

(16) as] *add.* **2–5** (21) the . . . nevertheless] **2–5** | yet the making them **1**
(29) being] *add.* **2–5** (30) farther] *add.* **2–5**

otherwise concerning that parcel of Matter, which makes the Ring on my Finger, wherein these two *Essences* are apparently different. For it is the real Constitution of its insensible Parts, on which depend all those Properties of Colour, Weight, Fusibility, Fixedness, *etc.* which are to be found in it. Which Constitution we know not; and so having no particular *Idea* of, have no Name that is the Sign of it. But yet it is its Colour, Weight, Fusibility, and Fixedness, *etc.* which makes it to be *Gold*, or gives it a right to that Name, which is therefore its nominal *Essence*. Since nothing can be call'd *Gold*, but what has a Conformity of Qualities to that abstract complex *Idea*, to which that Name is annexed. But this Distinction of *Essences*, belonging particularly to Substances, we shall, when we come to consider their Names, have an occasion to treat of more fully.

§ 19. That such *abstract* Ideas, *with Names to them*, as we have been speaking of, *are Essences*, may farther appear by what we are told concerning *Essences*, *viz.* that they are all ingenerable, and incorruptible. Which cannot be true of the real Constitutions of Things, which begin and perish with them. All Things, that exist, besides their Author, are all liable to Change; especially those Things we are acquainted with, and have ranked into Bands, under distinct Names or Ensigns. Thus that, which was Grass to Day, is to Morrow the Flesh of a Sheep; and within few days after, becomes part of a Man: In all which, and the like Changes, 'tis evident, their real *Essence*, *i.e.* that Constitution, whereon the Properties of these several things depended, is destroy'd, and perishes with them. But *Essences* being taken for *Ideas*, established in the Mind, with Names annexed to them, they are supposed to remain steadily the same, whatever mutations the particular Substances are liable to. For whatever becomes of *Alexander* and *Bucephalus*, the *Ideas* to which *Man* and *Horse* are annexed, are supposed nevertheless to remain the same; and so the *Essences* of those Species are preserved whole and undestroy'd, whatever Changes happen to any, or all of the Individuals of those *Species*. By this means the *Essence* of a *Species* rests safe and entire, without the existence of so much as one Individual of that kind. For were there now no Circle existing any where in the

§ 19. *Essences ingenerable and incorruptible.*

(5–7) which . . . *etc.*] **1–4**; *om.* **5** (17) Constitutions] **2–5** | Constitution **1** (18) exist] **4–5** | exist in Nature **1–3** (24) *i.e.*] *add.* **4–5** (27) they] **1–2**, **4–5**; *om.* **3** (30) remain] **1–4** | remain in **5** (31–2) whole and] *add.* **2–5**

World, (as, perhaps, that Figure exists not any where exactly marked out,) yet the *Idea* annexed to that Name would not cease to be what it is; nor cease to be as a pattern, to determine which of the particular Figures we meet with, have, or have not a Right to the Name *Circle*, and so to shew which of them, by having that Essence, was of that *Species*. And though there neither were, nor had been in Nature such a Beast as an *Unicorn*, nor such a Fish as a *Mermaid*; yet supposing those Names to stand for complex abstract *Ideas*, that contained no inconsistency in them; the *Essence* of a *Mermaid* is as intelligible, as that of a *Man*; and the *Idea* of an *Unicorn*, as certain, steady, and permanent, as that of a Horse. From what has been said, it is evident, that the Doctrine of the Immutability of *Essences*, proves them to be only abstract *Ideas*; and is founded on the Relation, established between them, and certain Sounds as Signs of them; and will always be true, as long as the same Name can have the same signification.

§ 20. To conclude, this is that, which in short I would say, (*viz.*) that all the great Business of *Genera* and *Species*, and their *Essences*, amounts to no more but this, That Men making abstract *Ideas*, and settling them in their Minds, with names annexed to them, do thereby enable themselves to consider Things, and discourse of them, as it were in bundles, for the easier and readier improvement, and communication of their Knowledge, which would advance but slowly, were their Words and Thoughts confined only to Particulars.

CHAPTER IV

Of the Names of simple Ideas.

§ 1. THOUGH all Words, as I have shewn, signify nothing immediately, but the *Ideas* in the Mind of the Speaker; yet upon a nearer survey, we shall find that the *Names of simple* Ideas, *mixed Modes*, (under which I comprise Relations too,) *and natural*

§ 20. *Recapitulation.*
§ 1. *Names of simple* Ideas, *Modes, and Substances, have each something peculiar.*

---

(3) nor cease] **4–5** | and **1–3** (*likewise* **Coste**) (5) to . . . them,] *add.* **4–5** (6) was] **4–5** | were **1–3** (11) a] **4–5** | an **1–3** (26) shewn] **2–5** | shewed **1**

Substances, have each of them something peculiar, and different from the other. For Example:

§ 2. *First*, The *Names of simple* Ideas *and Substances*, with the abstract *Ideas* in the Mind, which they immediately signify, *intimate* also *some real Existence*, from which was derived their original pattern. But the *Names of mixed Modes, terminate in the* Idea that is in the Mind, and lead not the Thoughts any farther, as we shall see more at large in the following Chapter.

§ 3. *Secondly*, The *Names of simple* Ideas *and Modes, signify always the real, as well as nominal Essence of their Species*. But *the Names of natural Substances, signify* rarely, if ever, any thing but *barely the nominal Essences* of those Species, as we shall shew in the Chapter, that treats of the Names of Substances in particular.

§ 4. *Thirdly*, The *Names of simple* Ideas *are not capable of any definitions*; the Names of all complex *Ideas* are. It has not, that I know, hitherto been taken notice of by any Body, what Words are, and what are not capable of being defined: the want whereof is (as I am apt to think) not seldom the occasion of great wrangling, and obscurity in Men's Discourses, whilst some demand definitions of Terms, that cannot be defined; and others think, they ought to rest satisfied, in an Explication made by a more general Word, and its Restriction, (or to speak in Terms of Art by a Genus and Difference,) when even after such Definition made according to rule, those who hear it, have often no more a clear Conception of the meaning of the Word, than they had before. This at least, I think, that the shewing what Words are, and what are not capable of Definitions, and wherein consists a good Definition, is not wholly besides our present purpose; and perhaps, will afford so much Light to the Nature of these Signs, and our *Ideas*, as to deserve a more particular Consideration.

§ 5. I will not here trouble my self, to prove that all Terms are not definable from that Progress, *in infinitum*, which it will visibly lead us into, if we should allow, that all Names could be defined. For if the Terms of one Definition, were still to be defined by

§ 2. *First, Names of simple* Ideas *and Substances, intimate real Existence.* § 3. *Secondly, Names of simple* Ideas *and Modes signify always both real and nominal Essence.* § 4. *Thirdly, Names of simple* Ideas *undefinable.* § 5. *If all were definable, 'twould be a process* in infinitum.

---

(2) other] **2–5** | others **1** (*likewise* **Coste**) (15) *definitions*] **2–5** | *definition* **1**
(23–4) such . . . rule] **5** | that regular Definition, **1–4**. (',' *after* 'rule' *not in* **5**)

another, Where at last should we stop? But I shall from the Nature of our *Ideas*, and the Signification of our Words shew, *why some Names can, and others cannot be defined*, and which they are.

§ 6. I think, it is agreed, that *a Definition is* nothing else, but *the shewing the meaning of one Word by several other not synonymous Terms.* The meaning of Words, being only the *Ideas* they are made to stand for by him that uses them; the meaning of any Term is then shewed, or the Word is defined when by other Words, the *Idea* it is made the Sign of, and annexed to in the Mind of the Speaker, is as it were represented, or set before the view of another; and thus its Signification ascertained: This is the only use and end of Definitions; and therefore the only measure of what is, or is not a good Definition.

§ 7. This being premised, I say, that *the Names of Simple* Ideas, and those only, *are incapable of being defined.* The reason whereof is this, That the several Terms of a Definition, signifying several *Ideas*, they can altogether by no means represent an *Idea*, which has no Composition at all: And therefore a Definition, which is properly nothing but the shewing the meaning of one Word by several others not signifying each the same thing, can in the Names of simple *Ideas* have no Place.

§ 8. The not observing this difference in our *Ideas*, and their Names, has produced that eminent trifling in the Schools, which is so easy to be observed, in the definitions they give us of some few of these simple *Ideas*. For as to the greatest part of them, even those Masters of Definitions, were fain to leave them untouch'd, meerly by the impossibility they found in it. What more exquisite *Jargon* could the Wit of Man invent, than this Definition, *The Act of a being in Power, as far forth as in Power*, which would puzzle any rational Man, to whom it was not already known by its famous absurdity, to guess what Word it could ever be supposed to be the Explication of. If *Tully* asking a *Dutchman* what *Beweeginge* was, should have received this Explication in his own Language, that it was *Actus entis in potentia quatenus in potentia*;* I ask whether any one

§ 6. *What a Definition is.* § 7. *Simple* Ideas *why undefinable.* §§ 8, 9. *Instances Motion.*

---

(9) made . . . to] **2–5** | annexed to, and made the Sign of, **1** (17) has] **5** | hath **1–4** (*l. below* 34: §§ 8, 9.) *Instances*] **Coste** 'Exemple'

---

* E.g., Thomas Aquinas, *In III Phys.*, Lect. 2, § 285 (*on* Aristotle, *Physics*, 201a10)

can imagine he could thereby have understood what the Word *Beweeginge* signified, or have guessed what *Idea* a *Dutchman* ordinarily had in his Mind, and would signify to another, when he used that sound.

§ 9. Nor have the Modern Philosophers, who have endeavoured to throw off the *Jargon* of the Schools, and speak intelligibly, much better succeeded in defining simple *Ideas*, whether by explaining their Causes, or any otherwise. The *Atomists*, who define Motion to be a *passage from one place to another*, What do they more than put one synonymous Word for another? For what is *Passage* other than *Motion*? And if they were asked what Passage was, How would they better define it than by *Motion*? For is it not at least as proper and significant, to say, *Passage is a Motion from one place to another*, as to say, *Motion is a passage*, etc. This is to translate, and not to define, when we change two Words of the same Signification one for another; which when one is better understood than the other, may serve to discover what *Idea* the unknown stands for; but is very far from a *Definition*, unless we will say, every English Word in the Dictionary, is the definition of the Latin Word it answers, and that Motion is a definition of *Motus*. *Nor will the successive Application of the parts of the* Superficies *of one Body, to those of another*, which the *Cartesians* give us, prove a much better definition of Motion, when well examined.

§ 10. *The Act of Perspicuous, as far forth as perspicuous*, is another Peripatetick definition of a simple *Idea*; which though not more absurd than the former of *Motion*, yet betrays its Uselessness and Insignificancy more plainly, because Experience will easily convince any one, that it cannot make the meaning of the Word *Light* (which it pretends to define) at all understood by a blind Man: but the definition of *Motion* appears not at first sight so useless, because it scapes this way of Trial. For this simple *Idea*, entring by the Touch as well as Sight; 'tis impossible to shew an Example of any one, who has no other way to get the *Idea* of *Motion*, but barely by the definition of that Name. Those who tell us, that *Light* is a great number of little Globules, striking briskly on the bottom of the Eye, speak more intelligibly than the Schools: but yet these

§ 10. *Light*.

---

(32) Sight] **1–3** | sight **4–5** (34) Those who] **4–5** | When the *Cartesians* **1–3**
(36) speak more] **4–5** | they speak a little more **1–3**

Words never so well understood, would make the *Idea*, the Word *Light* stands for, no more known to a Man that understands it not before, than if one should tell him, that *Light* was nothing but a Company of little Tennis-balls, which Fairies all day long struck with Rackets against some Men's Fore-heads, whilst they passed by others. For granting this explication of the thing to be true; yet the *Idea* of the cause of *Light*, if we had it never so exact, would no more give us the *Idea* of *Light* it self, as it is such a particular perception in us, than the *Idea* of the Figure and Motion of a sharp piece of Steel, would give us the *Idea* of that Pain, which it is able to cause in us. For the cause of any Sensation, and the Sensation it self, in all the simple *Ideas* of one Sense, are two *Ideas*; and two *Ideas* so different, and distant one from another, that no two can be more so. And therefore should *Des Cartes*'s Globules strike never so long on the *retina* of a Man, who was blind by a *Guttâ Serenâ*, he would thereby never have any *Idea* of *Light*, or any thing approaching to it, though he understood what little Globules were, and what striking on another Body was, never so well. And therefore the *Cartesians* very well distinguish between that Light which is the Cause of that Sensation in us, and the *Idea* which is produced in us by it, and is that which is properly Light.

§ 11. *Simple Ideas*, as has been shewn, *are only* to be *got by* those *impressions* Objects themselves make on our Minds, by the proper Inlets appointed to each sort. If they are not received this way, all the *Words* in the World, *made use of to explain, or define any of their Names, will never be able to produce in us the* Idea *it stands for*. For Words being Sounds, can produce in us no other simple *Ideas*, than of those very Sounds; nor excite any in us, but by that voluntary connexion, which is known to be between them, and those simple *Ideas*, which common Use has made them Signs of. He that thinks otherwise, let him try if any Words can give him the taste of a Pine-Apple, and make him have the true *Idea* of the Relish of that celebrated delicious Fruit. So far as he is told it has a resemblance with any Tastes, whereof he has the *Ideas* already in his Memory, imprinted there by sensible Objects not Strangers to his Palate, so far

§ 11. *Simple* Ideas *why undefinable, farther explained.*

---

(4) struck] **4–5** | strook **1–3** (6) this] **4–5** | his **1–3** (18–21) And . . . Light.] *add.* **4–5** (22) shewn] **2–5** | shewed **1** (31–2) Pine-Apple] **Coste** *adds a marginal note on* 'Ananas'.

may he approach that resemblance in his Mind. But this is not giving us that *Idea* by a *Definition*, but exciting in us other simple *Ideas*, by their known Names; which will be still very different from the true taste of that Fruit it self. In Light and Colours, and all other simple *Ideas*, it is the same thing: for the signification of Sounds, is not natural, but only imposed and arbitrary. And no definition of *Light*, or *Redness*, is more fitted, or able to produce either of those *Ideas* in us, than the sound *Light*, or *Red*, by it self. For to hope to produce an *Idea* of Light, or Colour, by a Sound, however formed, is to expect that Sounds should be visible, or Colours audible; and to make the Ears do the Office of all the other Senses. Which is all one as to say, that we might Taste, Smell, and See by the Ears: a sort of Philosophy worthy only of *Sanco Panca*, who had the Faculty to see *Dulcinea* by Hearsay. And therefore he that has not before received into his Mind, by the proper Inlet, the simple *Idea* which any Word stands for, can never come to know the signification of that Word, by any other Words, or Sounds, whatsoever put together, according to any Rules of Definition. The only way is, by applying to his Senses the proper Object; and so producing that *Idea* in him, for which he has learn'd the name already. A studious blind Man, who had mightily beat his Head about visible Objects, and made use of the explication of his Books and Friends, to understand those names of Light, and Colours, which often came in his way; bragg'd one day, That he now understood what *Scarlet* signified. Upon which his Friend demanding, what *Scarlet* was? the blind Man answered, It was like the Sound of a Trumpet. Just such an Understanding of the name of any other simple *Idea* will he have, who hopes to get it only from a Definition, or other Words made use of to explain it.

§ 12. The case is quite otherwise *in complex Ideas*; which consisting of several simple ones, it is in the power of Words, standing for the several *Ideas*, that make that Composition, to imprint complex *Ideas* in the Mind, which were never there before, and so make their Names be understood. In such Collections of *Ideas*, passing under one name, *Definitions*, or the teaching the signification of one word, by several others, has place, and *may make us understand the Names* of Things, which never came within the reach of our Senses; and frame

§§ 12, 13. *The contrary shewed in complex* Ideas *by instances of a Statue and Rainbow.*

---

(4) taste] **2–5** | Tastes **1** (11) [*3rd*] the] *add.* **4–5**

Ideas suitable to those in other Men's Minds, when they use those Names: provided that none of the terms of the Definition stand for any such simple *Ideas*, which he to whom the Explication is made, has never yet had in his Thoughts. Thus the word *Statue* may be explained to a blind Man by other words, when *Picture* cannot, his Senses having given him the *Idea* of Figure, but not of Colours, which therefore Words cannot excite in him. This gain'd the Prize to the Painter, against the Statuary; each of which contending for the excellency of his Art, and the Statuary bragging, that his was to be preferred, because it reached farther, and even those who had lost their Eyes, could yet perceive the excellency of it. The Painter agreed to refer himself to the Judgment of a blind Man; who being brought where there was a Statue made by the one, and a Picture drawn by the other; he was first led to the Statue, in which he traced with his Hands, all the Lineaments of the Face and Body; and with great admiration, applauded the Skill of the Work-man. But being led to the Picture, and having his Hands laid upon it, was told, That now he touched the Head, and then the Forehead, Eyes, Nose, *etc.* as his Hand moved over the parts of the Picture on the Cloth, without finding any the least distinction: Whereupon he cried out, that certainly that must needs be a very admirable and divine piece of Workmanship, which could represent to them all those Parts, where he could neither feel nor perceive any thing.

§ 13. He that should use the word *Rainbow*, to one who knew all those Colours, but yet had never seen that *Phænomenon*, would, by enumerating the Figure, Largeness, Position, and Order of the Colours, so well define that word, that it might be perfectly understood. But yet that *Definition*, how exact and perfect soever, would never make a blind Man understand it; because several of the simple *Ideas* that make that complex one, being such as he never received by Sensation and Experience, no words are able to excite them in his Mind.

§ 14. Simple *Ideas*, as has been shewed, can only be got by Experience, from those Objects, which are proper to produce in us those Perceptions. *When* by this means we have our Minds stored with them, and know the Names for them, then *we are in a condition to define*, and by *Definition* to understand the Names of complex

§ 14. *The Names of complex* Ideas *when to be made intelligible by Words.*

---

(4) Thoughts] **1–4** | Thought **5**. (**Coste** 'dans l'Esprit')

Ideas, that are made up of them. But when any term stands for a simple *Idea*, that a Man has never yet had in his Mind, it is impossible, by any Words, to make known its meaning to him. When any term stands for an *Idea* a Man is acquainted with, but is ignorant, that that term is the sign of it, there another name, of the same *Idea* which he has been accustomed to, may make him understand its meaning. But in no case whatsoever, is any name, of any simple *Idea*, capable of a *Definition.*

§ 15. *Fourthly*, But though the Names of *simple Ideas*, have not the help of *Definition* to determine their signification; yet that hinders not but that they *are generally less doubtful and uncertain, than those of mixed Modes and Substances.* Because they standing only for one simple Perception, Men, for the most part, easily and perfectly agree in their signification: And there is little room for mistake and wrangling about their meaning. He that knows once, that Whiteness is the Name of that Colour he has observed in Snow, or Milk, will not be apt to misapply that Word, as long as he retains that *Idea*; which when he has quite lost, he is not apt to mistake the meaning of it, but perceives he understands it not. There is neither a multiplicity of simple *Ideas* to be put together, which makes the doubtfulness in the Names of mixed Modes; nor a supposed, but an unknown real Essence, with properties depending thereon, the precise number whereof are also unknown, which makes the difficulty in the Names of Substances. But on the contrary, in simple *Ideas* the whole signification of the Name is known at once, and consists not of parts, whereof more or less being put in, the *Idea* may be varied, and so the signification of its Name, be obscure, or uncertain.

§ 16. *Fifthly*, This farther may be observed, concerning *simple Ideas*, and their Names, that they *have but few Ascents in linea prædicamentali*, (as they call it,) *from the lowest Species, to the summum Genus.* The reason whereof is, that the lowest Species being but one simple *Idea*, nothing can be left out of it, that so the difference being taken away, it may agree with some other thing in one *Idea* common to them both; which having one Name, is the *Genus* of the other two: *v.g.* There is nothing can be left out of the *Idea* of White and Red, to make them agree in one common appearance, and so

§ 15. *Fourthly, Names of simple* Ideas *least doubtful.* § 16. *Fifthly, Simple* Ideas *have few Ascents* in linea prædicamentali.

(9) '§ 15.' *add.* **2–5** (33) in one *Idea*] **4–5** | in **3** | in one **1–2**

have one general name; as *Rationality* being left out of the complex *Idea* of *Man*, makes it agree with Brute, in the more general *Idea* and name of *Animal*. And therefore when to avoid unpleasant enumerations, Men would comprehend both *White* and *Red*, and several other such simple *Ideas*, under one general name; they have been fain to do it by a Word, which denotes only the way they get into the Mind. For when *White*, *Red*, and *Yellow*, are all comprehended under the *Genus* or name *Colour*, it signifies no more, but such *Ideas*, as are produced in the Mind only by the Sight, and have entrance only through the Eyes. And when they would frame yet a more general term, to comprehend both *Colours* and *Sounds*, and the like simple *Ideas*, they do it by a Word, that signifies all such as come into the Mind only by one Sense: And so the general term *Quality*, in its ordinary acception, comprehends Colours, Sounds, Tastes, Smells, and tangible Qualities, with distinction from Extension, Number, Motion, Pleasure, and Pain, which make impressions on the Mind, and introduce their *Ideas* by more Senses than one.

§ 17. *Sixthly*, The Names of simple *Ideas*, Substances, and mixed Modes, have also this difference; That those *of mixed Modes* stand for *Ideas* perfectly *arbitrary*: Those *of Substances*, are not perfectly so; but *referr to a pattern, though with some latitude: and those of simple* Ideas *are* perfectly taken from the existence of things, and are *not arbitrary at all*. Which what difference it makes in the significations of their Names, we shall see in the following Chapters.

The Names of simple Modes, differ little from those of simple *Ideas*.

CHAPTER V

Of the Names of mixed Modes and Relations.

§ 1. THE Names of mixed Modes being general, they stand, as has been shewn, for sorts or Species of Things, each of which has its peculiar Essence. The Essences of these Species also, as has been shewed, are nothing but the abstract *Ideas* in the Mind, to which the Name is annexed. Thus far the Names and Essences of mixed

§ 17. *Sixthly, Names of simple* Ideas *stand for* Ideas *not at all arbitrary.*
§ 1. *They stand for abstract* Ideas, *as other general Names.*

Modes, have nothing but what is common to them, with other *Ideas*: But if we take a little nearer survey of them, we shall find, that they have something peculiar, which, perhaps, may deserve our attention.

§ 2. The first Particularity I shall observe in them is, that the abstract *Ideas*, or, if you please, the Essences of the several Species *of mixed Modes are made by the Understanding*, wherein they differ from those of simple *Ideas*: in which sort, the Mind has no power to make any one, but only receives such as are presented to it, by the real Existence of Things operating upon it.

§ 3. In the next place, these *Essences of the Species of mixed Modes, are* not only *made* by the Mind, but made *very arbitrarily*, made without Patterns, or reference to any real Existence. Wherein they differ from those of Substances, which carry with them the Supposition of some real Being, from which they are taken, and to which they are conformable. But in its complex *Ideas* of mixed Modes, the Mind takes a liberty not to follow the Existence of Things exactly. It unites and retains certain Collections, as so many distinct specifick *Ideas*, whilst others, that as often occurr in Nature, and are as plainly suggested by outward Things, pass neglected without particular Names or Specifications. Nor does the Mind, in these of mixed Modes, as in the complex *Ideas* of Substances, examine them by the real Existence of Things; or verifie them by Patterns, containing such peculiar Compositions in Nature. To know whether his *Idea* of *Adultery*, or *Incest*, be right, will a Man seek it any where amongst Things existing? Or is it true, because any one has been Witness to such an Action? No: but it suffices here, that Men have put together such a Collection into one complex *Idea*, that makes the *Archetype*, and specifick *Idea*, whether ever any such Action were committed *in rerum natura*, or no.

§ 4. To understand this aright, we must consider *wherein this making of these complex* Ideas *consists*; and that is not in the making any new *Idea*, but putting together those which the Mind had before. Wherein the Mind does these three things: First, It chuses a certain Number. Secondly, It gives them connexion, and makes them into one *Idea*. Thirdly, It ties them together by a Name. If we

§ 2. *First, the* Ideas *they stand for, are made by the Understanding.* § 3. *Secondly, Made arbitrarily, and without Patterns.* § 4. *How this is done.*

(3) perhaps,] **1–3, 5** | perhaps **4** (32) is] **1T.er, 2–5** | it is **1** (33) but] **1–4** | by **5**

examine how the Mind proceeds in these, and what liberty it takes in them, we shall easily observe, how these essences of the Species of mixed Modes, are the Workmanship of the Mind; and consequently, that the Species themselves are of Men's making.

§ 5. No body can doubt, but that these *Ideas* of mixed Modes, are made by a voluntary Collection of *Ideas* put together in the Mind, independent from any original Patterns in Nature, who will but reflect, that this sort of complex *Ideas* may be made, abstracted, and have names given them, and so a Species be constituted, before any one individual of that Species ever existed. Who can doubt, but the *Ideas* of *Sacrilege*, or *Adultery*, might be framed in the Mind of Men, and have names given them; and so these Species of mixed Modes be constituted, before either of them was ever committed; and might be as well discoursed of, and reasoned about, and as certain Truths discovered of them, whilst yet they had no being but in the Understanding, as well as now, that they have but too frequently a real Existence? Whereby it is plain, how much *the sorts of mixed Modes are the Creatures of the Understanding*, where they have a being as subservient to all the ends of real Truth and Knowledge, as when they really exist: And we cannot doubt, but Law-makers have often made Laws about Species of Actions, which were only the Creatures of their own Understanding; Beings that had no other existence, but in their own Minds. And, I think, no body can deny, but that the *Resurrection* was a Species of mixed Modes in the Mind, before it really existed.

§ 6. To see *how arbitrarily these Essences of mixed Modes are made* by the Mind, we need but take a view of almost any of them. A little looking into them, will satisfie us, that 'tis the Mind, that combines several scattered independent *Ideas*, into one complex one; and by the common name it gives them, makes them the Essence of a certain Species, without regulating it self by any connexion they have in Nature. For what greater connexion in Nature, has the *Idea* of a Man, than the *Idea* of a Sheep with Killing, that this is made a particular Species of Action, signified by the word *Murder*, and the other not? Or what Union is there in Nature, between the *Idea* of

§ 5. *Evidently arbitrary, in that the* Idea *is often before the Existence.* § 6. *Instances Murther, Incest, Stabbing.*

(19) Truth] **2–5** | Truths **1** (22) Understanding] **1–4** | Understandings **5**
(35) is there] **1–4** | there is **5** (*l. below* 35: § 5.) *in*] **2–4**; *om.* **5**

the Relation of a Father, with Killing, than that of a Son, or Neighbour; that those are combined into one complex *Idea*, and thereby made the Essence of the distinct Species *Parricide*, whilst the other make no distinct Species at all? But though they have made killing a Man's Father, or Mother, a distinct Species from killing his Son, or Daughter; yet in some other cases, Son and Daughter are taken in too, as well as Father and Mother; and they are all equally comprehended in the same Species, as in that of *Incest*. Thus the Mind in mixed Modes arbitrarily unites into complex *Ideas*, such as it finds convenient; whilst others that have altogether as much union in Nature, are left loose, and never combined into one *Idea*, because they have no need of one name. 'Tis evident then, that the Mind, by its free choice, gives a connexion to a certain number of *Ideas*; which in Nature have no more union with one another, than others that it leaves out: Why else is the part of the Weapon, the beginning of the Wound is made with, taken notice of, to make the distinct Species call'd *Stabbing*, and the Figure and Matter of the Weapon left out? I do not say, this is done without Reason, as we shall see more by and by; but this I say, that it is done by the free choice of the Mind, pursuing its own ends; and that therefore these Species of mixed Modes, are the workmanship of the Understanding: And there is nothing more evident, than that for the most part, in the framing these *Ideas*, the Mind searches not its Patterns in Nature, nor refers the *Ideas* it makes to the real existence of Things; but puts such together, as may best serve its own Purposes, without tying it self to a precise imitation of any thing that really exists.

§ 7. But though these complex *Ideas*, or *Essences of mixed Modes*, depend on the Mind, and are made by it with great liberty; yet they *are not made at random*, and jumbled together without any reason at all. Though these complex *Ideas* be not always copied from Nature, yet they are always suited to the end for which abstract *Ideas* are made: And though they be Combinations made of *Ideas*, that are loose enough, and have as little union in themselves, as several other, to which the Mind never gives a connexion that combines them into one *Idea*; yet they are always made for the

§ 7. *But still subservient to the end of Language.*

(2) those] **2–5** | these **1** (3) other] **2–5** | others **1** (17) *Stabbing*] **Coste** *adds a linguistic footnote.* (26) imitation] **2–5** | intimation **1** (29) Mind,] **1–3, 5** | Mind. **4** (35) never] *add.* **1T.er, 2–5**

convenience of Communication, which is the chief end of Language. The Use of Language is, by short Sounds to signifie with ease and dispatch general Conceptions; wherein not only abundance of particulars may be contained, but also a great variety of independent *Ideas*, collected into one complex one. In the making therefore of the Species of mixed Modes, Men have had regard only to such Combinations, as they had occasion to mention one to another. Those they have combined into distinct complex *Ideas*, and given Names to; whilst others that in Nature have as near an union, are left loose and unregarded. For to go no farther than humane Actions themselves, if they would make distinct abstract *Ideas*, of all the Varieties might be observed in them, the Number must be infinite, and the Memory confounded with the Plenty, as well as overcharged to little purpose. It suffices, that Men make and name so many complex *Ideas* of these mixed Modes, as they find they have occasion to have names for, in the ordinary occurrence of their Affairs. If they join to the *Idea* of Killing, the *Idea* of Father, or Mother, and so make a distinct Species from killing a Man's Son, or Neighbour, it is because of the different heinousness of the Crime, and the distinct punishment is due to the murthering a Man's Father or Mother different from what ought to be inflicted on the Murther of a Son or Neighbour; and therefore they find it necessary to mention it by a distinct Name, which is the end of making that distinct Combination. But though the *Ideas* of Mother and Daughter, are so differently treated, in reference to the *Idea* of Killing, that the one is joined with it, to make a distinct abstract *Idea* with a name, and so a distinct Species, and the other not; yet in respect of carnal Knowledge, they are both taken in under *Incest*; and that still for the same convenience of expressing under one name, and reckoning of one Species, such unclean mixtures, as have a peculiar turpitude beyond others; and this to avoid Circumlocutions, and tedious Descriptions.

§ 8. A moderate skill *in different Languages*, will easily satisfie one of the truth of this, it being so obvious to observe great store of *Words in one* Language, *which have not any that answer them in another.* Which plainly shews, that those of one Country, by their customs

§ 8. *Whereof the intranslatable Words of divers Languages are a proof.*

(19–22) different . . . Neighbour] **2–5** | distinct punishment, the one deserves different from the other [other **1er** | other, **1**] Murther **1**

and manner of Life, have found occasion to make several complex *Ideas*, and give names to them, which others never collected into specifick *Ideas*. This could not have happened, if these Species were the steady Workmanship of Nature; and not Collections made and abstracted by the Mind, in order to naming, and for the convenience of Communication. The terms of our Law, which are not empty Sounds, will hardly find Words that answer them in the Spanish, or Italian, no scanty Languages; much less, I think, could any one translate them into the *Caribee*, or *Westoe* Tongues: And the *Versura* of the *Romans*, or *Corban* of the *Jews*, have no Words in other Languages to answer them: The reason whereof is plain, from what has been said. Nay, if we will look a little more nearly into this matter, and exactly compare different Languages, we shall find, that though they have Words, which in Translations and Dictionaries, are supposed to answer one another; yet there is scarce one of ten, amongst the names of complex *Ideas*, especially of mixed Modes, that stands for the same precise *Idea*, which the Word does that in Dictionaries it is rendred by. There are no *Ideas* more common, and less compounded, than the measures of Time, Extension, and Weight, and the Latin Names *Hora*, *Pes*, *Libra*, are, without difficulty, rendred by the *English* names, *Hour*, *Foot*, and *Pound*: But yet there is nothing more evident, than that the *Ideas* a *Roman* annexed to these Latin Names, were very far different from those which an *English*-man expresses by those English ones. And if either of these should make use of the measures that those of the other Language design'd by their Names, he would be quite out in his account. These are too sensible proofs to be doubted; and we shall find this much more so, in the names of more abstract and compounded *Ideas*; such as are the greatest part of those which make up Moral Discourses: Whose Names, when Men come curiously to compare, with those they are translated into, in other Languages, they will find very few of them exactly to correspond in the whole extent of their Significations.

§ 9. The reason why I take so particular Notice of this, is, that we may not be mistaken about *Genera*, and *Species*, and their *Essences*, as if they were Things regularly and constantly made by Nature,

§ 9. *This shews Species to be made for Communication.*

(14) Translations] **Coste** *adds a marginal note, remarking that* 'cette Traduction en est une preuve'. (20) Extension] **1–3** | Extention **4–5** (35) their] *add.* **2–5**

and had a real Existence in Things; when they appear, upon a more wary survey, to be nothing else but an Artifice of the Understanding, for the easier signifying such Collections of *Ideas*, as it should often have occasion to communicate by one general term; under which, divers particulars, as far forth as they agreed to that abstract *Idea*, might be comprehended. And if the doubtful signification of the word *Species*, may make it sound harsh to some, that I say, that the *Species* of mixed Modes are made by the Understanding; yet, I think, it can by no body be denied, that 'tis the Mind makes those abstract complex *Ideas*, to which specifick names are given. And if it be true, as it is, that the Mind makes the Patterns, for sorting and naming of Things, I leave it to be considered, who makes the Boundaries of the sort, or *Species*; since with me, *Species* and *Sort* have no other difference, than that of a Latin and English *Idiom*.

§ 10. *The near relation* that there is *between Species, Essences, and* their *general Names*, at least in *mixed Modes*, will farther appear, when we consider, that it is the Name that seems to preserve those *Essences*, and give them their lasting duration. For the connexion between the loose parts of those complex *Ideas*, being made by the Mind, this union, which has no particular foundation in Nature, would cease again, were there not something that did, as it were, hold it together, and keep the parts from scattering. Though therefore it be the Mind that makes the Collection, 'tis the Name which is, as it were the Knot, that ties them fast together. What a vast variety of different *Ideas*, does the word *Triumphus* hold together, and deliver to us as one *Species*! Had this Name been never made, or quite lost, we might, no doubt, have had descriptions of what passed in that Solemnity: But yet, I think, that which holds those different parts together, in the unity of one complex *Idea*, is that very word annexed to it: without which, the several parts of that, would no more be thought to make one thing, than any other shew, which having never been made but once, had never been united into one complex *Idea*, under one denomination. How much therefore, in mixed Modes, the unity necessary to any Essence, depends on the Mind; and how much the continuation and fixing of that Unity, depends on the Name in common use annexed to it, I leave

§§ 10, 11. *In mixed Modes 'tis the Name that ties the Combination together, and makes it a Species.*

---

(11) [*2nd*] the] **5** | these **1–4** (16) *Names*] **1–4** | *Name* **5**

to be considered by those, who look upon *Essences* and *Species*, as real established Things in Nature.

§ 11. Suitable to this, we find, that *Men speaking of mixed Modes, seldom* imagine or *take any other for Species of them, but such as are set out by name*: Because they being of Man's making only, in order to naming, no such *Species* are taken notice of, or supposed to be, unless a *Name* be joined to it, as the sign of Man's having combined into one *Idea* several loose ones; and by that *Name*, giving a lasting Union to the Parts, which would otherwise cease to have any, as soon as the Mind laid by that abstract *Idea*, and ceased actually to think on it. But when a Name is once annexed to it, wherein the parts of that complex *Idea* have a settled and permanent Union; then is the *Essence*, as it were established, and the *Species* look'd on as compleat. For to what purpose should the Memory charge it self with such Compositions, unless it were by Abstraction to make them general? And to what purpose make them general, unless it were, that they might have general *Names*, for the convenience of Discourse, and Communication? Thus we see, that killing a Man with a Sword, or a Hatchet, are looked on as no distinct species of Action: But if the Point of the Sword first enter the Body, it passes for a distinct *Species*, where it has a distinct *Name*, as in *England*, in whose Language it is called *Stabbing*: But in another Country, where it has not happened to be specified under a peculiar *Name*, it passes not for a distinct *Species*. But in the *Species* of corporeal Substances, though it be the Mind that makes the nominal Essence: yet since those *Ideas*, which are combined in it, are supposed to have an Union in Nature, whether the Mind joins them or no, therefore those are looked on as distinct *Species*, without any operation of the Mind, either abstracting, or giving a *Name* to that complex *Idea*.

§ 12. Conformable also to what has been said, concerning the *Essences* of the *Species* of *mixed Modes*, that they are the Creatures of the Understanding, rather than the Works of Nature: Conformable, I say, to this, we find, that *their Names lead our Thoughts to the Mind, and no farther*. When we speak of *Justice*, or *Gratitude*, we frame to our selves no Imagination of any thing existing, which we would conceive; but our Thoughts terminate in the abstract *Ideas* of those

§ 12. *For the Originals of mixed Modes, we look no farther than the Mind, which also shews them to be the Workmanship of the Understanding.*

---

(5) *name*] **5** | *names* **1–4** (22) *Stabbing*] **Coste** *adds a linguistic marginal note.*

Vertues, and look not farther; as they do, when we speak of a *Horse*, or *Iron*, whose specifick *Ideas* we consider not, as barely in the Mind, but as in Things themselves, which afford the original Patterns of those *Ideas*. But in mixed Modes, at least the most considerable parts of them, which are moral Beings, we consider the original Patterns, as being in the Mind; and to those we referr for the distinguishing of particular Beings under Names. And hence I think it is, That these *Essences* of the *Species* of mixed Modes, are by a more particular Name called *Notions*; as by a peculiar Right, appertaining to the Understanding.

§ 13. Hence likewise we may learn, *Why the complex* Ideas *of mixed Modes, are commonly more compounded, and decompounded, than those of natural Substances.* Because they being the Workmanship of the Understanding, pursuing only its own ends, and the conveniency of expressing in short those *Ideas* it would make known to another, does with great liberty unite often into one abstract *Idea* Things that in their Nature have no coherence; and so under one Term, bundle together a great variety of compounded, and decompounded *Ideas*. Thus the Name of *Procession*, what a great mixture of independant *Ideas* of Persons, Habits, Tapers, Orders, Motions, Sounds, does it contain in that complex one, which the Mind of Man has arbitrarily put together, to express by that one Name? Whereas the complex *Ideas* of the sorts of Substances, are usually made up of only a small number of simple ones; and in the *Species* of Animals, these two, *viz.* Shape and Voice, commonly make the whole nominal Essence.

§ 14. Another thing we may observe from what has been said, is, That *the Names of mixed Modes always signifie* (when they have any determined Signification) *the real Essences of their Species.* For these abstract *Ideas*, being the Workmanship of the Mind, and not referred to the real Existence of Things, there is no supposition of any thing more signified by that Name, but barely that complex *Idea*, the Mind it self has formed, which is all it would have express'd by it; and is that, on which all the properties of the *Species* depend, and

§ 13. *Their being made by the Understanding without Patterns, shews the reason why they are so compounded.* § 14. *Names of mixed Modes stand always for their real Essences.*

(1) a] **4–5** | an **1–3** (4) parts] **4–5** | part **1–3** (9) *Notions*] **Coste** *adds a marginal note*: 'On dit, *la Notion de la justice*, *de la temperance*; mais on ne dit point, *la notion d'un Cheval*, *d'une pierre*, etc.' (11) Hence . . . learn] **2–5** | This also shews us the Reason **1** (25) these] **2er, 4–5** | those **1–3** (29) determined] **5** (*likewise* **Coste**) | distinct **1–4**

from which alone they all flow: and so in these the *real* and *nominal Essence* is the same; which of what Concernment it is to the certain Knowledge of general Truths, we shall see hereafter.

§ 15. This also may shew us the Reason, *Why for the most part the Names of mixed Modes are got, before the* Ideas *they stand for are perfectly known*. Because there being no *Species* of these ordinarily taken notice of, but what have Names; and those *Species*, or rather their Essences, being abstract complex *Ideas* made arbitrarily by the Mind, it is convenient, if not necessary, to know the Names, before one endeavour to frame these complex *Ideas*: unless a Man will fill his Head with a Company of abstract complex *Ideas*, which others having no Names for, he has nothing to do with, but to lay by, and forget again. I confess, that in the beginning of Languages, it was necessary to have the *Idea*, before one gave it the Name: And so it is still, where making a new complex *Idea*, one also, by giving it a new Name, makes a new Word. But this concerns not Languages made, which have generally pretty well provided for *Ideas*, which Men have frequent Occasion to have, and communicate: And in such, I ask, whether it be not the ordinary Method, that Children learn the Names of mixed Modes, before they have their *Ideas*? What one of a thousand ever frames the abstract *Idea* of *Glory* or *Ambition*, before he has heard the Names of them. In simple *Ideas* and Substances, I grant it is otherwise; which being such *Ideas*, as have a real Existence and Union in Nature, the *Ideas*, or Names, are got one before the other, as it happens.

§ 16. What has been said here of mixed Modes, is with very little difference applicable also to Relations; which since every Man himself may observe, I may spare my self the Pains to enlarge on: Especially, since what I have here said concerning Words in this Third Book, will possibly be thought by some to be much more than what so slight a Subject required. I allow, it might be brought into a narrower Compass: but I was willing to stay my Reader on an Argument, that appears to me new, and a little out of the way, (I am sure 'tis one, I thought not of, when I began to write,) That by searching it to the bottom, and turning it on every side, some part

§ 15. *Why their Names are usually got before their* Ideas. § 16. *Reason of my being so large on this Subject.*

(3) Truths] **1–4** | Truth **5** (14) gave] **1–2, 4–5** | give **3** (23) grant] **2–5** | confess **1** (24) got] **2–5** | gotten **1** (26) *The section index* '§ 16.' *add.* **2–5**

or other might meet with every one's Thoughts, and give occasion to the most averse, or negligent, to reflect on a general Miscarriage; which, though of great consequence, is little taken notice of. When it is considered, what a pudder is made about *Essences*, and how much all sorts of Knowledge, Discourse, and Conversation, are pester'd and disorder'd by the careless, and confused Use and Application of Words, it will, perhaps, be thought worth while throughly to lay it open. And I shall be pardon'd, if I have dwelt long on an Argument, which I think therefore needs to be inculcated; because the Faults, Men are usually guilty of in this kind, are not only the greatest hinderances of true Knowledge; but are so well thought of, as to pass for it. Men would often see what a small pittance of Reason and Truth, or possibly none at all, is mixed with those huffing Opinions they are swell'd with; if they would but look beyond fashionable Sounds, and observe what *Ideas* are, or are not comprehended under those Words, with which they are so armed at all points, and with which they so confidently lay about them. I shall imagine I have done some Service to Truth, Peace, and Learning, if, by any enlargement on this Subject, I can make Men reflect on their own Use of Language; and give them Reason to suspect, that since it is frequent for others, it may also be possible for them, to have sometimes very good and approved Words in their Mouths, and Writings, with very uncertain, little, or no signification. And therefore it is not unreasonable for them to be wary herein themselves, and not to be unwilling to have them examined by others. With this design therefore, I shall go on with what I have farther to say, concerning this matter.

CHAPTER VI

Of the Names of Substances.

§ 1. THE *common Names of Substances*, as well as other general Terms, *stand for Sorts*: which is nothing else but the being made signs of such complex *Ideas*, wherein several particular Substances

§ 1. *The common names of Substances stand for sorts.*

(5) , and] **1–3, 5** | and **4** (7) perhaps,] **1–3, 5** | perhaps **4** (18) Learning] **Coste** 'la veritable Science'

do, or might agree, by virtue of which, they are capable to be comprehended in one common Conception, and be signified by one Name. I say, do or might agree: for though there be but one Sun existing in the World, yet the *Idea* of it being abstracted, so that more Substances (if there were several) might each agree in it; it is as much a Sort, as if there were as many Suns, as there are Stars. They want not their Reasons, who think there are, and that each fixed Star, would answer the *Idea* the name *Sun* stands for, to one who were placed in a due distance; which, by the way, may shew us how much the Sorts, or, if you please, *Genera* and *Species* of Things (for those Latin Terms signify to me, no more than the English word *Sort*) depend on such Collections of *Ideas*, as Men have made; and not on the real Nature of Things: since 'tis not impossible, but that in propriety of Speech, that might be a Sun to one, which is a Star to another.

§ 2. The measure and boundary of each Sort, or *Species*, whereby it is constituted that particular Sort, and distinguished from others, is that we call its *Essence*, which *is* nothing but that *abstract* Idea *to which the Name is annexed*: So that every thing contained in that *Idea*, is essential to that Sort. This, though it be all the *Essence* of natural Substances, that we know, or by which we distinguish them into Sorts; yet I call it by a peculiar name, the *nominal Essence*, to distinguish it from that real Constitution of Substances, upon which depends this *nominal Essence*, and all the Properties of that Sort; which therefore, as has been said, may be called the *real Essence*: *v.g.* the *nominal Essence* of *Gold*, is that complex *Idea* the word *Gold* stands for, let it be, for instance, a Body yellow, of a certain weight, malleable, fusible, and fixed. But the *real Essence* is the constitution of the insensible parts of that Body, on which those Qualities, and all the other Properties of *Gold* depend. How far these two are different, though they are both called *Essence*, is obvious, at first sight, to discover.

§ 3. For though, perhaps, voluntary Motion, with Sense and Reason, join'd to a Body of a certain shape, be the complex *Idea*, to which I, and others, annex the name *Man*; and so be the *nominal Essence* of the *Species* so called: yet no body will say, that that

§ 2. *The Essence of each sort is the abstract* Idea. § 3. *The nominal and real Essence different.*

(1) to be] **1–4** | of being **5** (2) be] **1–5**; *om.* **W** (4) so] **5** | so as **1–4**

complex *Idea* is the *real Essence* and Source of all those Operations, which are to be found in any Individual of that Sort. The foundation of all those Qualities, which are the Ingredients of our complex *Idea*, is something quite different: And had we such a Knowledge of that Constitution of *Man*, from which his Faculties of Moving, Sensation, and Reasoning, and other Powers flow; and on which his so regular shape depends, as 'tis possible Angels have, and 'tis certain his Maker has, we should have a quite other *Idea* of his *Essence*, than what now is contained in our Definition of that *Species*, be it what it will: And our *Idea* of any individual *Man* would be as far different from what it now is, as is his, who knows all the Springs and Wheels, and other contrivances within, of the famous Clock at *Strasburg*, from that which a gazing Country-man has of it, who barely sees the motion of the Hand, and hears the Clock strike, and observes only some of the outward appearances.

§ 4. That *Essence*, in the ordinary use of the word, relates to *Sorts*, and that it is considered in particular Beings, no farther than as they are ranked into *Sorts*, appears from hence: That take but away the abstract *Ideas*, by which we sort Individuals, and rank them under common Names, and then the thought of any thing *essential* to any of them, instantly vanishes: we have no notion of the one, without the other: which plainly shews their relation. 'Tis necessary for me to be as I am; GOD and Nature has made me so: But there is nothing I have, is essential to me. An Accident, or Disease, may very much alter my Colour, or Shape; a Fever, or Fall, may take away my Reason, or Memory, or both; and an Apoplexy leave neither Sense, nor Understanding, no nor Life. Other Creatures of my shape, may be made with more, and better, or fewer, and worse Faculties than I have: and others may have Reason, and Sense, in a shape and body very different from mine. None of these are essential to the one, or the other, or to any Individual whatsoever, till the Mind refers it to some Sort or *Species* of things; and then presently, according to the abstract *Idea* of that sort, something is found *essential*. Let any one examine his own Thoughts, and he will find, that as soon as he supposes or speaks of *Essential*, the consideration of some *Species*, or the complex *Idea*, signified by some

§§ 4–6. *Nothing essential to Individuals.*

(2) which] *add.* **4–5** (13) from] **1er–5** | is from **1** (16) That *Essence*] **4–5** | How much Essence [*Essence* **2–3**] **1–3** (26) Apoplexy] **4–5** | Apoplex **1–3**

general name, comes into his Mind: And 'tis in reference to that, that this or that Quality is said to be *essential*. So that if it be asked, whether it be *essential* to me, or any other particular corporeal Being to have Reason? I say no; no more than it is *essential* to this white thing I write on, to have words in it. But if that particular Being, be to be counted of the sort *Man*, and to have the name *Man* given it, then Reason is *essential* to it, supposing Reason to be a part of the complex *Idea* the name *Man* stands for: as it is *essential* to this thing I write on, to contain words, if I will give it the name *Treatise*, and rank it under that *Species*. So that *essential, and not essential, relate only to our abstract Ideas, and the names annexed to them*; which amounts to no more but this, That whatever particular Thing, has not in it those Qualities, which are contained in the abstract *Idea*, which any general Term stands for, cannot be ranked under that *Species*, nor be called by that name, since that abstract *Idea* is the very *Essence* of that *Species*.

§ 5. Thus if the *Idea* of *Body*, with some People, be bare Extension, or Space, then Solidity is not *essential* to Body: If others make the *Idea*, to which they give the name *Body*, to be Solidity and Extension, then Solidity is essential to *Body*. That therefore, and *that alone is* considered as *essential, which makes a part of the complex* Idea *the name of a Sort stands for*, without which, no particular Thing can be reckoned of that Sort, nor be intituled to that name. Should there be found a parcel of Matter, that had all the other Qualities that are in *Iron*, but wanted Obedience to the Load-stone; and would neither be drawn by it, nor receive Direction from it, Would any one question, whether it wanted any thing *essential*? It would be absurd to ask, Whether a thing really existing, wanted any thing *essential* to it. Or could it be demanded, Whether this made an *essential* or *specifick* difference, or no; since we have no other measure of *essential* or *specifick*, but our abstract *Ideas*? And to talk of specifick Differences in Nature, without reference to general *Ideas* and Names, is to talk unintelligibly. For I would ask any one, What is sufficient to make an *essential* difference in Nature, between any two particular Beings, without any regard had to some abstract *Idea*, which is looked upon as the Essence and Standard of a *Species*? All such Patterns and Standards, being quite laid aside, particular Beings, considered barely in themselves, will be found to have all their Qualities equally

(4) [*2nd*] no] **1er–5** | nor **1** (6) [*2nd*] the] **1er–5** | that **1** (20) to] **5** (*likewise* **Coste**) | also to **1–4**

essential; and every thing, in each Individual, will be *essential* to it, or, which is more true, nothing at all. For though it may be reasonable to ask, Whether obeying the Magnet, be *essential* to *Iron*? yet, I think, it is very improper and insignificant to ask, Whether it be *essential* to the particular parcel of Matter I cut my Pen with, without considering it under the name *Iron*, or as being of a certain *Species*? And if, as has been said, our abstract *Ideas*, which have names annexed to them, are the Boundaries of *Species*, nothing can be *essential* but what is contained in those *Ideas*.

§ 6. 'Tis true, I have often mentioned a *real Essence*, distinct in Substances, from those abstract *Ideas* of them, which I call their *nominal Essence*. By this *real Essence*, I mean, that real constitution of any Thing, which is the foundation of all those Properties, that are combined in, and are constantly found to co-exist with the *nominal Essence*; that particular constitution, which every Thing has within it self, without any relation to any thing without it. But *Essence*, even in this sense, *relates to a Sort*, and supposes a *Species*: For being that real Constitution, on which the Properties depend, it necessarily supposes a sort of Things, Properties belonging only to *Species*, and not to Individuals; *v.g.* Supposing the nominal Essence of *Gold*, to be Body of such a peculiar Colour and Weight, with Malleability and Fusibility, the real Essence is that Constitution of the parts of Matter, on which these Qualities, and their Union, depend; and is also the foundation of its Solubility in *Aqua Regia*, and other Properties accompanying that complex *Idea*. Here are *Essences* and *Properties*, but all upon supposition of a Sort, or general abstract *Idea*, which is considered as immutable: but there is no individual parcel of Matter, to which any of these Qualities are so annexed, as to be *essential* to it, or inseparable from it. That which is *essential*, belongs to it as a Condition, whereby it is of this or that Sort: But take away the consideration of its being ranked under the name of some abstract *Idea*, and then there is nothing necessary to it, nothing inseparable from it. Indeed, as to the *real Essences* of Substances, we only suppose their Being, without precisely knowing what they are: But that which annexes them still to the *Species*, is the nominal Essence, of which they are the supposed foundation and cause.

(2–3) be reasonable to ask] **5** | reasonably be asked **1–4**. (**Coste** 'quoy qu'on puisse demander raisonnablement') (5) the] **5** | that **1–4** (12) [*1st*] *Essence*] **5** | *Essences* **1–4** (21) Body] **5** | a Body **1–4** (32) then] *add.* **2–5**

§ 7. The next thing to be considered is, by which of those Essences it is, that *Substances are determined into* Sorts, or *Species*; and that 'tis evident, is *by the nominal Essence*. For 'tis that alone, that the name, which is the mark of the Sort, signifies. 'Tis impossible therefore, that any thing should determine the Sorts of Things, which we rank under general Names, but that *Idea*, which that Name is design'd as a mark for; which is that, as has been shewn, which we call the *Nominal Essence*. Why do we say, This is a *Horse*, and that a *Mule*; this is an *Animal*, that an *Herb*? How comes any particular Thing to be of this or that *Sort*, but because it has that nominal Essence, Or, which is all one, agrees to that abstract *Idea*, that name is annexed to? And I desire any one but to reflect on his own Thoughts, when he hears or speaks any of those, or other Names of Substances, to know what sort of *Essences* they stand for.

§ 8. And that the *Species of Things to us, are nothing but the ranking them under distinct Names, according to the complex* Ideas *in us*; and not according to precise, distinct, real *Essences* in them, is plain from hence; That we find many of the Individuals that are ranked into one Sort, called by one common Name, and so received as being of one *Species*, have yet Qualities depending on their real Constitutions, as far different one from another, as from others, from which they are accounted to differ *specifically*. This, as it is easy to be observed by all, who have to do with natural Bodies; so Chymists especially are often, by sad Experience, convinced of it, when they, sometimes in vain, seek for the same Qualities in one parcel of Sulphur, Antimony, or Vitriol, which they have found in others. For though they are Bodies of the same *Species*, having the same nominal *Essence*, under the same Name; yet do they often, upon severe ways of examination, betray Qualities so different one from another, as to frustrate the Expectation and Labour of very wary Chymists. But if Things were distinguished into *Species*, according to their real Essences, it would be as impossible to find different Properties in any two individual Substances of the same *Species*, as it is to find different Properties in two Circles, or two equilateral Triangles. That is properly the *Essence* to us, which determines every particular to this or that *Classis*; or, which is the same Thing,

§§ 7, 8. *The nominal essence bounds the Species.*

(8) a] **4–5** | an **1–3** (24) Experience,] **1–3, 5** | Experience / **4**

to this or that general Name: And what can that be else, but that abstract *Idea*, to which that name is annexed? and so has, in truth, a reference, not so much to the being of particular Things, as to their general Denominations.

§ 9. Nor indeed *can we* rank, and *sort Things*, and consequently (which is the end of sorting) denominate them *by their real Essences*, because we know them not. Our Faculties carry us no farther towards the knowledge and distinction of Substances, than a Collection of those sensible *Ideas*, which we observe in them; which however made with the greatest diligence and exactness, we are capable of, yet is more remote from the true internal Constitution, from which those Qualities flow, than, as I said, a Countryman's *Idea* is from the inward contrivance of that famous Clock at *Strasburg*, whereof he only sees the outward Figure and Motions. There is not so contemptible a Plant or Animal, that does not confound the most inlarged Understanding. Though the familiar use of Things about us, take off our Wonder; yet it cures not our Ignorance. When we come to examine the Stones, we tread on; or the Iron, we daily handle, we presently find, we know not their Make; and can give no Reason, of the different Qualities we find in them. 'Tis evident the internal Constitution, whereon their Properties depend, is unknown to us. For to go no farther than the grossest and most obvious we can imagine amongst them, What is that Texture of Parts, that real *Essence*, that makes Lead, and Antimony fusible; Wood, and Stones not? What makes Lead, and Iron malleable; Antimony, and Stones not? And yet how infinitely these come short, of the fine Contrivances, and unconceivable *real Essences* of Plants and Animals, every one knows. The Workmanship of the All-wise, and Powerful God, in the great Fabrick of the Universe, and every part thereof, farther exceeds the Capacity and Comprehension of the most inquisitive and intelligent Man, than the best contrivance of the most ingenious Man, doth the Conceptions of the most ignorant of rational Creatures. Therefore we in vain pretend to range Things into sorts, and dispose them into certain Classes, under Names, by their *real Essences*, that are so far from our discovery or comprehension. A blind Man may as soon

§ 9. *Not the real Essence which we know not.*

(11) , yet] **2–5** | ; yet our complex *Idea* **1** (28) and] **1–4** | or **5** (36) discovery or comprehension] **2–5** | Comprehensions **1**

sort Things by their Colours, and he that has lost his Smell, as well distinguish a Lily and a Rose by their Odors, as by those internal Constitutions which he knows not. He that thinks he can distinguish Sheep and Goats by their real Essences, that are unknown to him, may be pleased to try his Skill in those *Species*, called *Cassiowary*, and *Querechinchio*; and by their internal real Essences, determine the boundaries of those *Species*, without knowing the complex *Idea* of sensible Qualities, that each of those Names stands for, in the Countries where those Animals are to be found.

§ 10. Those therefore who have been taught, that the several *Species* of Substances had their distinct internal *substantial Forms*; and that it was those *Forms*, which made the distinction of Substances into their true *Species* and *Genera*, were led yet farther out of the way, by having their Minds set upon fruitless Enquiries after *substantial Forms*, wholly unintelligible, and whereof we have scarce so much as any obscure, or confused Conception in general.

§ 11. That our *ranking, and distinguishing natural Substances into Species consists in the Nominal Essences* the Mind makes, and not in the real Essences to be found in the Things themselves, is farther evident from our *Ideas* of *Spirits*. For the Mind getting, only by reflecting on its own Operations, those simple *Ideas* which it attributes to *Spirits*, it hath, or can have no other Notion of *Spirit*, but by attributing all those Operations, it finds in it self, to a sort of Beings, without Consideration of Matter. And even the most advanced Notion we have of God, is but attributing the same simple *Ideas* which we have got from Reflection on what we find in our selves, and which we conceive to have more Perfection in them, than would be in their absence, attributing, I say, those simple *Ideas* to him in an unlimited degree. Thus having got from reflecting on our selves, the *Idea* of Existence, Knowledge, Power, and Pleasure, each of which we find it better to have than to want; and the more we have of each, the better; joyning all these together, with infinity to each of them, we have the complex *Idea* of an eternal, omniscient, omnipotent, infinitely wise, and happy Being. And though we are told, that there are different *Species of Angels*; yet we know not how to frame distinct specifick *Ideas* of them; not out of any Conceit,

§ 10. *Not substantial forms which we know less.* § 11. *That the nominal Essence is that whereby we distinguish Species, farther evident from Spirits.*

---

(3) which] *add.* **4–5** (8) stands] **1–4** | stand **5** (26) which] *add.* **4–5**

that the Existence of more *Species* than one of *Spirits*, is impossible; But because having no more simple *Ideas* (nor being able to frame more) applicable to such Beings, but only those few, taken from our selves, and from the Actions of our own Minds in thinking, and being delighted, and moving several parts of our Bodies; we can no otherwise distinguish in our Conceptions the several *Species of Spirits*, one from another, but by attributing those Operations and Powers, we find in our selves, to them in a higher or lower degree; and so have no very distinct specifick *Ideas* of *Spirits*, except only of GOD, to whom we attribute both Duration, and all those other *Ideas* with Infinity; to the other *Spirits*, with limitation: Nor, as I humbly conceive do we, between GOD and them in our *Ideas*, put any difference by any number of simple *Ideas*, which we have of one, and not of the other, but only that of Infinity. All the particular *Ideas* of Existence, Knowledge, Will, Power, and Motion, *etc.* being *Ideas* derived from the Operations of our Minds, we attribute all of them to all sorts of *Spirits*, with the difference only of degrees, to the utmost we can imagine, even Infinity, when we would frame, as well as we can, an *Idea* of the first Being; who yet, 'tis certain, is infinitely more remote in the real Excellency of his Nature, from the highest and perfectest of all created Beings, than the greatest Man, nay, purest Seraphim, is from the most contemptible part of Matter; and consequently must infinitely exceed what our narrow Understandings can conceive of him.

§ 12. It is not impossible to conceive, nor repugnant to reason, that there may be many *Species of Spirits*, as much separated and diversified one from another by distinct Properties, whereof we have no *Ideas*, as the *Species* of sensible Things are distinguished one from another, by Qualities, which we know, and observe in them. That there should be more *Species* of intelligent Creatures above us, than there are of sensible and material below us, is probable to me from hence; That in all the visible corporeal World, we see no Chasms, or Gaps. All quite down from us, the descent is by easy steps, and a continued series of Things, that in each remove, differ

§ 12. *Whereof there are probably numberless Species.*

(9) no very] **2–5** | neither **1** (11) limitation] **2–5** | limitation, amongst which [**1er** | which, **1**] we make no distinction **1** (11–12) as I humbly conceive] *add.* **2–5** (21–4) than . . . him.] **4–5** | much more from what our narrow Understandings can conceive of Him, than the greatest Man, nay, purest Seraphim, is from the most contemptible part of Matter. **1–3**

very little one from the other. There are Fishes that have Wings, and are not Strangers to the airy Region: and there are some Birds, that are Inhabitants of the Water; whose Blood is cold as Fishes, and their Flesh so like in taste, that the scrupulous are allow'd them on Fish-days. There are Animals so near of kin both to Birds and Beasts, that they are in the middle between both: Amphibious Animals link the Terrestrial and Aquatique together; Seals live at Land and at Sea, and Porpoises have the warm Blood and Entrails of a Hog, not to mention what is confidently reported of Mermaids, or Sea-men. There are some Brutes, that seem to have as much Knowledge and Reason, as some that are called Men: and the Animal and Vegetable Kingdoms, are so nearly join'd, that if you will take the lowest of one, and the highest of the other, there will scarce be perceived any great difference between them; and so on till we come to the lowest and the most inorganical parts of Matter, we shall find every-where, that the several *Species* are linked together, and differ but in almost insensible degrees. And when we consider the infinite Power and Wisdom of the Maker, we have reason to think, that it is suitable to the magnificent Harmony of the Universe, and the great Design and infinite Goodness of the Architect, that the *Species* of Creatures should also, by gentle degrees, ascend upward from us toward his infinite Perfection, as we see they gradually descend from us downwards: Which if it be probable, we have reason then to be perswaded, that there are far more *Species* of Creatures above us, than there are beneath; we being in degrees of Perfection much more remote from the infinite Being of GOD, than we are from the lowest state of Being, and that which approaches nearest to nothing. And yet of all those distinct *Species*, for the reasons above-said, we have no clear distinct *Ideas*.

§ 13. But to return to the *Species* of corporeal Substances. If I should ask any one, whether *Ice* and *Water* were two distinct *Species* of Things, I doubt not but I should be answered in the affirmative: And it cannot be denied, but he that says they are two distinct *Species*, is in the right. But if an *English-man*, bred in *Jamaica*, who, perhaps, had never seen nor heard of *Ice*, coming into *England* in the Winter, find, the Water he put in his Bason at night, in a great part frozen in the morning; and not knowing any peculiar

§ 13. *The nominal Essence that of the Species, proved from Water and Ice.*

(4) so like in taste] **2–5** | in taste so near akin **1**　(9) a] **4–5** | an **1–3**
(22) toward] **3–5** | towards **1–2**　(29) clear] *add.* **2–5**

name it had, should call it harden'd Water; I ask, Whether this would be a new *Species* to him, different from Water? And, I think, it would be answered here, It would not to him be a new *Species*, no more than congealed Gelly, when it is cold, is a distinct *Species*, from the same Gelly fluid and warm; or than liquid Gold, in the Fornace, is a distinct *Species* from hard Gold in the Hands of a Workman. And if this be so, 'tis plain, that our *distinct Species, are nothing but distinct complex* Ideas, *with distinct Names annexed to them*. 'Tis true, every Substance that exists, has its peculiar Constitution, whereon depend those sensible Qualities, and Powers, we observe in it: But the ranking of Things into *Species*, which is nothing but sorting them under several Titles, is done by us, according to the *Ideas* that we have of them: Which tho' sufficient to distinguish them by Names; so that we may be able to discourse of them, when we have them not present before us: yet if we suppose it to be done by their real internal Constitutions, and that Things existing are distinguished by Nature into Species, by real Essences, according as we distinguish them into *Species* by Names, we shall be liable to great Mistakes.

§ 14. To distinguish substantial Beings into *Species*, according to the usual supposition, that there are certain precise *Essences* or *Forms* of Things, whereby all the Individuals existing, are, by Nature, distinguished into *Species*, these Things are necessary:

§ 15. *First*, To be assured, that Nature, in the production of Things, always designs them to partake of certain regulated established *Essences*, which are to be the Models of all Things to be produced. This, in that crude sense, it is usually proposed, would need some better explication, before it can fully be assented to.

§ 16. *Secondly*, It would be necessary to know, whether Nature always attains that *Essence*, it designs in the production of Things. The irregular and monstrous Births, that in divers sorts of Animals have been observed, will always give us reason to doubt of one, or both of these.

§ 17. *Thirdly*, It ought to be determined, whether those we call *Monsters*, be really a distinct *Species*, according to the scholastick notion of the word *Species*; since it is certain, that every thing that exists, has its particular Constitution: And yet we find, that some

§§ 14–18. *Difficulties against a certain number of real Essences.*

---

(3) *Species* [Species **1**] ,] **1–3, 5** | *Species* / **4**

of these monstrous Productions, have few or none of those Qualities, which are supposed to result from, and accompany the *Essence* of that *Species*, from whence they derive their Originals, and to which, by their descent, they seem to belong.

§ 18. *Fourthly*, The *real Essences* of those Things, which we distinguish into *Species*, and as so distinguished we name, ought to be known; *i.e.* we ought to have *Ideas* of them. But since we are ignorant in these four points, *the supposed real Essences of Things, stand us not in stead for the distinguishing Substances into Species.*

§ 19. *Fifthly*, The only imaginable help in this case would be, that having framed perfect complex *Ideas* of the *Properties* of things, flowing from their different real Essences, we should thereby distinguish them into *Species*. But neither can this be done: for being ignorant of the real Essence it self, it is impossible to know all those Properties, that flow from it, and are so annexed to it, that any one of them being away, we may certainly conclude, that that Essence is not there, and so the Thing is not of that *Species*. We can never know what are the precise number of Properties depending on the real Essence of *Gold*, any one of which failing, the real Essence of Gold, and consequently Gold, would not be there, unless we knew the real Essence of Gold it self, and by that determined that *Species*. By the Word *Gold* here, I must be understood to design a particular piece of Matter; *v.g.* the last Guinea that was coin'd. For if it should stand here in its ordinary Signification for that complex *Idea*, which I, or any one else calls Gold; *i.e.* for the nominal Essence of Gold, it would be *Jargon*: so hard is it, to shew the various meaning and imperfection of Words, when we have nothing else but Words to do it by.

§ 20. By all which it is clear, That our *distinguishing Substances into Species* by Names, *is not* at all *founded on their real Essences*; nor can we pretend to range, and determine them exactly into Species, according to internal essential differences.

§ 21. But since, as has been remarked, we have need of general Words, tho' we know not the real Essences of Things; all we can do, is to collect such a number of simple *Ideas*, as by Examination, we find to be united together in Things existing, and thereof to make

§§ 19, 20. *Our nominal Essences of Substances, not perfect Collections of Properties.* § 21. *But such a Collection as our Name stands for.*

(33) has been remarked] **4–5** | is aforesaid **1–3** (*l. below* 36: §§ 19, 20.) *In* **5** *this summary is applied to* §§ *18–20.*

one complex *Idea*. Which though it be not the real Essence of any Substance that exists, is yet *the specifick Essence*, to which our Name belongs, and is convertible with it; by which we may at least try the Truth of these nominal Essences. For Example, there be that say, that the Essence of *Body* is extension: If it be so, we can never mistake in putting the Essence of any thing for the Thing it self. Let us then in Discourse, put *Extension* for *Body*; and when we would say, that Body moves, let us say, that Extension moves, and see how it will look. He that should say, that one Extension, by impulse moves another extension, would, by the bare Expression, sufficiently shew the absurdity of such a Notion. The *Essence* of any thing, in respect of us, is the whole complex *Idea*, comprehended and marked by that Name; and in Substances, besides the several distinct simple *Ideas* that make them up, the confused one of Substance, or of an unknown Support and Cause of their Union, is always a part: And therefore the Essence of Body is not bare Extension, but an extended solid thing; and so to say, an extended solid thing moves, or impels another, is all one, and as intelligible, as to say, *Body* moves, or impels. Likewise, to say, that a rational Animal is capable of Conversation, is all one, as to say, a *Man*. But no one will say, That Rationality is capable of Conversation, because it makes not the whole Essence, to which we give the Name Man.

§ 22. There are Creatures in the World, that have shapes like ours, but are hairy, and want Language, and Reason. There are Naturals amongst us, that have perfectly our shape, but want Reason, and some of them Language too. There are Creatures, as 'tis said, (*sit fides penes Authorem*, but there appears no contradiction, that there should be such) that with Language, and Reason, and a shape in other Things agreeing with ours, have hairy Tails; others where the Males have no Beards, and others where the Females have. If it be asked, whether these be all *Men*, or no, all of humane *Species*; 'tis plain, the Question refers only to the nominal Essence: For those of them to whom the definition of the Word *Man*, or the complex *Idea* signified by that Name, agrees are *Men*, and the other not. But if the Enquiry be made concerning the supposed real Essence; and whether the internal Constitution and Frame of these

§ 22. *Our abstract* Ideas *are to us the measures of Species, instance in that of Man.*

(9) . He] **2–5** | : And he **1** (21) Rationality] **Coste** '*Raisonnabilité*', *and a footnote about his (and Locke's) coinings of words is added.* (33) of them] *add.* **4–5** (34) that] **1–4**; *om.* **5** are *Men*] **4–5** | , they are *Men* **2–3** | , they are Men **1**

several Creatures be specifically different, it is wholly impossible for us to answer, no part of that going into our specifick *Idea*: only we have Reason to think, that where the Faculties, or outward Frame so much differs, the internal Constitution is not exactly the same: But, what difference in the internal real Constitution makes a specifick difference, it is in vain to enquire; whilst *our measures of Species* be, as they *are*, *only our abstract* Ideas, which we know; and not that internal Constitution, which makes no part of them. Shall the difference of Hair only on the Skin, be a mark of a different internal specifick Constitution between a Changeling and a Drill, when they agree in Shape, and want of Reason, and Speech? And shall not the want of Reason and Speech, be a sign to us of different real Constitutions and *Species*, between a Changeling, and a reasonable Man? And so of the rest, if we pretend, that the distinction of *Species* or Sorts is fixedly established by the real Frame, and secret Constitutions of Things.

§ 23. Nor let any one say, that the power of propagation in animals by the mixture of Male and Female, and in Plants by Seeds, keeps the supposed real *Species* distinct and entire. For granting this to be true, it would help us in the distinction of the *Species* of things no farther than the Tribes of Animals and Vegetables. What must we do for the rest? But in those too it is not sufficient: for if History lie not, Women have conceived by Drills; and what real *Species*, by that measure, such a Production will be in Nature, will be a new Question; and we have Reason to think this not impossible, since Mules and Gimars, the one from the mixture of an Ass and a Mare, the other from the mixture of a Bull and a Mare, are so frequent in the World. I once saw a Creature, that was the Issue of a Cat and a Rat, and had the plain Marks of both about it; wherein Nature appear'd to have followed the Pattern of neither sort alone, but to have jumbled them both together. To which, he that shall add the monstrous Productions, that are so frequently to be met with in

§ 23. *Species not distinguished by Generation.*

(6) it] *add.* **2–5** (14) of] **1–2, 4–5** | to **3** (15) or Sorts] *add.* **4–5.** (*Not in* **Coste**) (17–21) power . . . Tribes] **2–5** | real *Species of Animals*, are *distinguished by* a Power of *Propagation*, by the mixture of Male and Female, and Plants by Seeds, for this would help us no farther, than in the distinction of the Species **1** (21) Animals] **1–3, 5** | animals **4** (22) But . . . is [was **3**] not sufficient] **2–5** | Nor is it sufficient in them **1** (26) Gimars] **1–4** | Jumarts **5.** (**Coste** 'Jumarts', *and a marginal note is added.*) Ass and a Mare] **2–5** | Horse, and an Ass **1** (31)–452(8) To . . . Tea?] *add.* **2–5**

Nature, will find it hard, even in the race of Animals to determine by the Pedigree of what *Species* every Animal's Issue is; and be at a loss about the real Essence, which he thinks certainly conveyed by Generation, and has alone a right to the specifick name. But farther, if the *Species* of Animals and Plants are to be distinguished only by propagation, must I go to the *Indies* to see the Sire and Dam of the one, and the Plant from which the Seed was gather'd, that produced the other, to know whether this be a Tiger or that Tea?

§ 24. Upon the whole matter, 'tis evident, that 'tis their own Collections of sensible Qualities, that Men make the Essences of their several sorts of Substances; and that their real internal Structures, are not considered by the greatest part of Men, in the sorting them. Much less were any *substantial Forms* ever thought on by any, but those who have in this one part of the World, learned the Language of the Schools: and yet those ignorant Men, who pretend not any insight into the real Essences, nor trouble themselves about substantial Forms, but are content with knowing Things one from another, by their sensible Qualities, are often better acquainted with their Differences; can more nicely distinguish them from their uses; and better know what they may expect from each, than those learned quick-sighted Men, who look so deep into them, and talk so confidently of something more hidden and essential.

§ 25. But supposing that the *real Essences* of Substances were discoverable, by those, that would severely apply themselves to that Enquiry; yet we could not reasonably think, that the *ranking of things under general Names, was regulated by* those internal real Constitutions, or any thing else but *their obvious appearances.* Since Languages, in all Countries, have been established long before Sciences. So that they have not been Philosophers, or Logicians, or such who have troubled themselves about *Forms* and *Essences,* that have made the general Names, that are in use amongst the several Nations of Men: But those, more or less comprehensive terms, have, for the most part, in all Languages, received their Birth and Signification, from ignorant and illiterate People, who sorted and

§ 24. *Not by substantial forms.* § 25. *The specifick Essences are made by the Mind.*

(7) produced] **2, 4–5** | produce **3.** (**Coste** 'qui produit') (8) *v.* 451(31), n. (13) . Much . . . *Forms*] **4–5** | ; much less any *substantial Forms* were **1–3** (16) pretend] **1–2, 4–5** | pretended **3** (20) from] **4–5** | for **1–3** (*likewise* **Coste**) (21) quick-sighted] **1–3** | quick sighted **4–5**

denominated Things, by those sensible Qualities they found in them, thereby to signify them, when absent, to others, whether they had an occasion to mention a Sort, or a particular Thing.

§ 26. Since then it is evident, that we sort and name Substances by their *nominal*, and not by their real *Essences*, the next thing to be considered is, how, and by whom these *Essences* come to be made. As to the latter, 'tis evident they *are made by the Mind*, and not by Nature: For were they Nature's Workmanship, they could not be so various and different in several Men, as experience tells us they are. For if we will examine it, we shall not find the nominal Essence of any one *Species* of Substances, in all Men the same; no not of that, which of all others we are the most intimately acquainted with. It could not possibly be, that the abstract *Idea*, to which the name *Man* is given, should be different in several Men, if it were of Nature's making; and that to one it should be *Animal rationale*, and to another *Animal implume bipes latis unguibus*. He that annexes the name *Man*, to a complex *Idea*, made up of Sense and spontaneous Motion, join'd to a Body of such a shape, has thereby one Essence of the *Species Man*: And he that, upon farther examination, adds rationality, has another Essence of the *Species* he calls *Man*: By which means, the same individual will be a true *Man* to the one, which is not so to the other. I think, there is scarce any one will allow this upright Figure, so well known, to be the essential difference of the *Species Man*; and yet how far Men determine of the sorts of Animals, rather by their Shape, than Descent, is very visible; since it has been more than once debated, whether several humane *Fœtus* should be preserved, or received to Baptism, or no, only because of the difference of their outward Configuration, from the ordinary Make of Children, without knowing whether they were not as capable of Reason, as Infants cast in another Mould: Some whereof, though of an approved shape, are never capable of as much appearance of Reason, all their Lives, as is to be found in an Ape, or an Elephant; and never give any signs of being acted by a rational Soul. Whereby it is evident, that the outward Figure, which only was found wanting, and not the Faculty of Reason, which no body could know would be wanting in its due Season, was made essential to the

§§ 26, 27. *Therefore very various and uncertain.*

(2) absent,] **2–5** | absent **1** (4) *In* **1**, *this section is also numbered* '25'. §§ *26, . . ., 51 in* **2–5** *correspond respectively to* §§ *25 [bis], . . ., 50 in* **1**. (9) experience tells us] **5** | 'tis evident **1–4**

humane *Species*. The learned Divine and Lawyer, must, on such occasions, renounce his sacred Definition of *Animal Rationale*, and substitute some other Essence of the humane *Species*. Monsieur *Menage* furnishes us with an Example worth the taking notice of on this occasion. *When the Abbot of St. Martin*, says he, *was born, he had so little of the Figure of a Man, that it bespake him rather a Monster. 'Twas for some time under Deliberation, whether he should be baptized or no. However, he was baptized and declared a Man provisionally* [till time should shew what he would prove.] *Nature had moulded him so untowardly, that he was called all his Life the Abbot Malotru*, i.e. Ill shaped. *He was of* Caen. Menagiana $\frac{278}{430}$. This Child we see was very near being excluded out of the *Species* of *Man*, barely by his Shape. He escaped very narrowly as he was, and 'tis certain a Figure a little more odly turn'd had cast him, and he had been executed as a thing not to be allowed to pass for a Man. And yet there can be no Reason given, why if the Lineaments of his Face had been a little alter'd, a rational Soul could not have been lodg'd in him; why a Visage somewhat longer, or a Nose flatter, or a wider Mouth could not have consisted, as well as the rest of his ill Figure, with such a Soul, such Parts, as made him, disfigured as he was, capable to be a Dignitary in the Church.

§ 27. Wherein then, would I gladly know, consists the precise and *unmovable Boundaries of* that *Species*? 'Tis plain, if we examine, there is *no* such thing *made by Nature*, and established by Her amongst Men. The real Essence of that, or any other sort of Substances, 'tis evident we know not; and therefore are so undetermined in our nominal Essences, which we make our selves, that if several Men were to be asked, concerning some odly-shaped *Fœtus*, as soon as born, whether it were a *Man*, or no, 'tis past doubt, one should meet with different Answers. Which could not happen, if the nominal Essences, whereby we limit and distinguish the *Species* of Substances, were not made by Man, with some liberty; but were exactly copied from precise Boundaries set by Nature, whereby it distinguish'd all Substances into certain *Species*. Who would undertake to resolve, what *Species* that Monster was of, which is mentioned by *Licetus*, *lib.* I. *c.* 3. with a Man's Head and Hog's

(3–21) Monsieur ... Church.] *add.* **4–5** (8–9) [till ... prove.] **4–5** (22) 27] **2–5** | 26 **1**. *Also, in* **2–3**, *many of the marginal summaries for §§ 27–45 are misplaced; I have not annotated these errors, which are correlated with the entries for the sections so numbered in the Table of Contents in* **1**. *See p. 31, n. 3 and 453(4), n.* (29) no,] **4–5** | no; **1–3** (35) would] **1–2, 4–5** | would not **3**

Body? Or those other, which to the Bodies of Men, had the Heads of Beasts, as Dogs, Horses, *etc.* If any of these Creatures had lived, and could have spoke, it would have increased the difficulty. Had the upper part, to the middle, been of humane shape, and all below Swine; Had it been Murther to destroy it? Or must the Bishop have been consulted, whether it were Man enough to be admitted to the Font, or no? As I have been told, it happen'd in *France* some Years since, in somewhat a like case. So uncertain are the Boundaries of *Species* of Animals to us, who have no other Measures, than the complex *Ideas* of our own collecting: And so far are we from certainly knowing what a *Man* is; though, perhaps, it will be judged great Ignorance to make any doubt about it. And yet, I think, I may say, that the certain Boundaries of that *Species*, are so far from being determined, and the precise number of simple *Ideas*, which make the nominal Essence, so far from being setled, and perfectly known, that very material Doubts may still arise about it: And I imagine, none of the Definitions of the word *Man*, which we yet have, nor Descriptions of that sort of Animal, are so perfect and exact, as to satisfie a considerate inquisitive Person; much less to obtain a general Consent, and to be that which Men would every where stick by, in the Decision of Cases, and determining of Life and Death, Baptism or no Baptism, in Productions that might happen.

§ 28. But though these *nominal Essences of Substances* are made by the Mind, they are *not* yet *made so arbitrarily, as those of mixed Modes.* To the making of any nominal Essence, it is necessary, *First,* That the *Ideas* whereof it consists, have such an Union as to make but one *Idea*, how compounded soever. *Secondly,* That the particular *Ideas* so united, be exactly the same, neither more nor less. For if two abstract complex *Ideas*, differ either in number, or sorts, of their component parts, they make two different, and not one and the same Essence. In the first of these, the Mind, in making its complex *Ideas* of Substances, only follows Nature; and puts none together, which are not supposed to have an union in Nature. No body joins the Voice of a Sheep, with the Shape of a Horse; nor the Colour of Lead, with the Weight and Fixedness of Gold, to be the complex *Ideas* of any real Substances; unless he has a mind to fill his Head

§ 28. *But not so arbitrary as mixed Modes.*

(14) [*2nd*] the] **5** (*likewise* **Coste**) | that **1–4** (17) which] *add.* **4–5** (18) are] *add.* **4–5** (23) 28] **2–5** | 27 **1** (34) [*2nd*] a] **4–5** | an **1–3**

with *Chimæra's*, and his Discourse with unintelligible Words. Men, observing certain Qualities always join'd and existing together, therein copied Nature; and of *Ideas* so united, made their complex ones of Substances. For though Men may make what complex *Ideas* they please, and give what Names to them they will; yet if they will be understood, when they speak of Things really existing, they must, in some degree, conform their *Ideas* to the Things they would speak of: Or else Men's Language will be like that of *Babel*; and every Man's Words, being intelligible only to himself, would no longer serve to Conversation, and the ordinary Affairs of Life, if the *Ideas* they stand for, be not some way answering the common appearances and agreement of Substances, as they really exist.

§ 29. *Secondly*, Though the Mind of Man, *in making* its *complex Ideas of Substances*, never puts any together that do not really, or are not supposed to co-exist; and so it truly borrows that Union from Nature: Yet *the number* it combines, *depends upon the various Care, Industry, or Fancy of him that makes it*. Men generally content themselves with some few sensible obvious Qualities; and often, if not always, leave out others as material, and as firmly united, as those that they take. Of sensible Substances there are two sorts; one of organiz'd Bodies, which are propagated by Seed; and in these, the Shape is that, which to us is the leading Quality, and most characteristical Part, that determines the *Species*: And therefore in Vegetables and Animals, an extended solid Substance of such a certain Figure usually serves the turn. For however some Men seem to prize their Definition of *Animal Rationale*, yet should there a Creature be found, that had Language and Reason, but partaked not of the usual shape of a Man, I believe it would hardly pass for a *Man*, how much soever it were *Animal Rationale*. And if *Baalam*'s Ass had, all his Life, discoursed as rationally as he did once with his Master, I doubt yet, whether any one would have thought him worthy the name *Man*, or allow'd him to be of the same *Species* with himself. As in Vegetables and Animals 'tis the Shape, so in most other Bodies, not propagated by Seed, 'tis the Colour we most fix on, and are most led by. Thus where we find the Colour of Gold, we are apt to imagine all the other Qualities, comprehended in our complex *Idea*, to be there also: and we commonly take these two obvious Qualities,

§ 29. *Though very imperfect.*

(13) 29] **2–5** | 28 **1**   (21) Seed] **2–5** | Seeds **1**   (24) such] **4–5** | such, **1–3**

viz. Shape and Colour, for so presumptive *Ideas* of several *Species*, that in a good Picture, we readily say, this is a Lion, and that a Rose; this is a Gold, and that a Silver Goblet, only by the different Figures and Colours, represented to the Eye by the Pencil.

§ 30. But though this serves well enough for gross and confused Conceptions, and unaccurate ways of Talking and Thinking; yet *Men are far enough from having agreed on the precise number of simple* Ideas, or Qualities, *belonging to any sort of Things, signified by its name.* Nor is it a wonder, since it requires much time, pains, and skill, strict enquiry, and long examination, to find out what, and how many those simple *Ideas* are, which are constantly and inseparably united in Nature, and are always to be found together in the same Subject. Most Men, wanting either Time, Inclination, or Industry enough for this, even to some tolerable degree, content themselves with some few obvious, and outward appearances of Things, thereby readily to distinguish and sort them for the common Affairs of Life: And so, without farther examination, give them names, or take up the Names already in use. Which, though in common Conversation they pass well enough for the signs of some few obvious Qualities co-existing, are yet far enough from comprehending, in a setled signification, a precise number of simple *Ideas*; much less all those, which are united in Nature. He that shall consider, after so much stir, about *Genus* and *Species*, and such a deal of talk of specifick Differences, how few Words we have yet setled Definitions of, may, with Reason, imagine, that those *Forms*, which there hath been so much noise made about, are only *Chimæra's*; which give us no light into the specifick Natures of Things. And he that shall consider, how far the names of Substances are from having Significations, wherein all who use them do agree, will have reason to conclude, that though the nominal Essences of Substances, are all supposed to be copied from Nature; yet they are all, or most of them, very imperfect. Since the Composition of those complex *Ideas*, are, in several Men, very different: and therefore, that these Boundaries of *Species*, are as Men, and not as Nature makes them, if at least there are in Nature any such prefixed Bounds. 'Tis true, that many particular Substances are so made by Nature, that they have agreement and likeness one with another, and so afford a

§ 30. *Which yet serve for common Converse.*

(5) 30] **2–4** | 20 **5** (16) and] **4–5** | , and **1–3** (25) which] *add.* **4–5**
(*l. below* 37) *serve*] **4–5** | *serves* **2–3**

Foundation of being ranked into sorts. But the sorting of Things by us, or the making of determinate *Species*, being in order to naming and comprehending them under general terms, I cannot see how it can be properly said, that Nature sets the Boundaries of the *Species* of Things: Or if it be so, our Boundaries of *Species*, are not exactly conformable to those in Nature. For we, having need of general names for present use, stay not for a perfect discovery of all those Qualities, which would best shew us their most material differences and agreements; but we our selves divide them, by certain obvious appearances, into *Species*, that we may the easier, under general names, communicate our thoughts about them. For having no other Knowledge of any Substance, but of the simple *Ideas*, that are united in it; and observing several particular Things to agree with others, in several of those simple *Ideas*, we make that collection our specifick *Idea*, and give it a general name; that in recording our own Thoughts and in our Discourse with others, we may in one short word, design all the Individuals that agree in that complex *Idea*, without enumerating the simple *Ideas*, that make it up; and so not waste our Time and Breath in tedious Descriptions: which we see they are fain to do, who would discourse of any new sort of things, they have not yet a Name for.

§ 31. But however, these *Species* of Substances pass well enough in ordinary Conversation, it is plain, that this complex *Idea*, wherein they observe several Individuals to agree, is, by different Men, made very differently; by some more, and others less accurately. In some, this complex *Idea* contains a greater, and in others a smaller number of Qualities; and so is apparently such as the Mind makes it. The yellow shining Colour, makes *Gold* to Children; others add Weight, Malleableness, and Fusibility; and others yet other Qualities, which they find joined with that yellow Colour, as constantly as its Weight and Fusibility: For in all these, and the like Qualities, one has as good a right to be put into the complex *Idea* of that Substance, wherein they are all join'd, as another. And therefore *different Men* leaving out, or putting in several simple *Ideas*, which others do not, according to their various Examination,

§ 31. *Essences of Species under the same name very different.*

---

(11) our thoughts] *add.* **2–5** (16) and] **4–5** | , and **1–3** in our] *add.* **5** (*likewise* **Coste**) (22) 31] **2–5** | 30 **1** (23) plain] **4–5** | plain enough **1–3** (30) which] *add.* **4–5** (31) [*1st*] and] **5** | or **1–4** : For] **5** | . For **1–4** (*l. below* 35) *New summary in* **4–5** (*cf. p. 31*).

Skill, or Observation of that subject, *have different Essences of Gold*; which must therefore be of their own, and not of Nature's making.

§ 32. If the *number of simple* Ideas, *that make the nominal Essence* of the lowest *Species*, or first sorting of Individuals, *depends on the Mind* of Man, variously collecting them, it is much more evident, that they do so, in the more comprehensive *Classes*, which, by the Masters of Logick are called *Genera*. These are complex *Ideas* designedly imperfect: And 'tis visible at first sight, that several of those Qualities, that are to be found in the Things themselves, are purposely left out of *generical Ideas*. For as the Mind, to make general *Ideas*, comprehending several particulars, leaves out those of Time, and Place, and such other, that make them incommunicable to more than one Individual, so to make other yet more general *Ideas*, that may comprehend different sorts, it leaves out those Qualities that distinguish them, and puts into its new Collection, only such *Ideas*, as are common to several sorts. The same Convenience that made Men express several parcels of yellow Matter coming from *Guiny* and *Peru*, under one name, sets them also upon making of one name, that may comprehend both Gold, and Silver, and some other Bodies of different sorts. This is done by leaving out those Qualities, which are peculiar to each sort; and retaining a complex *Idea*, made up of those, that are common to them all. To which the name *Metal* being annexed, there is a *Genus* constituted; the Essence whereof being that abstract *Idea*, containing only Malleableness and Fusibility, with certain degrees of Weight and Fixedness, wherein some Bodies of several Kinds agree, leaves out the Colour, and other Qualities peculiar to Gold, and Silver, and the other sorts comprehended under the name *Metal*. Whereby it is plain, that Men follow not exactly the Patterns set them by Nature, when they make their general *Ideas* of Substances; since there is no Body to be found, which has barely Malleableness and Fusibility in it, without other Qualities as inseparable as those. But Men, in making their general *Ideas*, seeking more the convenience of Language and quick dispatch,

§ 32. *The more general our* Ideas *are, the more incomplete and partial they are.*

---

(1) Observation] **1–3** | observation **4–5** (3) 32] **2–5** | 31 **1** (4) *depends*] **4–5** | *depend* **1–3** (6) *Classes*] **1–4** | *Classis* **5** (7) . These] **4–5** | , which **1–3** (8) : And . . . that] **4–5** | ; out of which, are purposely left out **1–3** (9–10) , are . . . [*1st*] *Ideas*] *add.* **4–5** (10) as] **1–4** | as to **5** (20) . This . . . by] **4–5** | , which it does by the same way of **1–3** (22) them all.] **4–5** | each Species [*Species* **2–3**]: **1–3**. (**Coste** 'à toutes ces Especes') (26) some] *add.* **4–5**

by short and comprehensive signs, than the true and precise Nature of Things, as they exist, have, in the framing their abstract *Ideas*, chiefly pursued that end, which was, to be furnished with store of general, and variously comprehensive Names. So that in this whole business of *Genera* and *Species*, the *Genus*, or more comprehensive, is but a partial Conception of what is in the *Species*, and the *Species*, but a partial *Idea* of what is to be found in each individual. If therefore any one will think, that a *Man*, and a *Horse*, and an Animal, and a Plant, *etc.* are distinguished by real Essences made by Nature, he must think Nature to be very liberal of these real Essences, making one for Body, another for an Animal, and another for a Horse; and all these Essences liberally bestowed upon *Bucephalus*. But if we would rightly consider what is done, in all these *Genera* and *Species*, or Sorts, we should find, that there is no new Thing made, but only more or less comprehensive signs whereby we may be enabled to express, in a few syllables, great numbers of particular Things, as they agree in more or less general conceptions, which we have framed to that purpose. In all which, we may observe, that the more general term, is always the name of a less complex *Idea*; and that each *Genus* is but a partial conception of the *Species* comprehended under it. So that if these abstract general *Ideas* be thought to be complete, it can only be in respect of a certain established relation, between them and certain names, which are made use of to signifie them; and not in respect of any thing existing, as made by Nature.

§ 33. *This* is *adjusted to the true end of Speech*, which is to be the easiest and shortest way of communicating our Notions. For thus he, that would make and discourse of Things, as they agreed in the complex *Idea* of Extension and Solidity, needed but use the word *Body*, to denote all such. He that, to these, would join others, signified by the words Life, Sense, and spontaneous Motion, needed but use the word *Animal*, to signify all which partaked of those *Ideas*: and he that had made a complex *Idea* of a Body, with Life, Sense, and Motion, with the Faculty of Reasoning, and a certain Shape joined to it, needed but use the short monosyllable *Man*, to express all particulars that correspond to that complex *Idea*. This

§ 33. *This all accommodated to the end of Speech.*

---

(3) was,] **1T.er, 2–5** | was **1** (8) [*2nd*] a] **4–5** | an **1–3** (12) a] **4–5** | an **1–3** (15) signs] **4–5** | signs; **1–3** (16) numbers] **2–5** | number **1** (36) correspond] **4–5** | corresponded **1–3**

is the proper business of *Genus* and *Species*: and this Men do, without any consideration of *real Essences*, or *substantial Forms*, which come not within the reach of our Knowledge, when we think of those things; nor within the signification of our Words, when we discourse with others.

§ 34. Were I to talk with any one, of a Sort of Birds, I lately saw in St. *James*'s Park, about three or four Foot high, with a Covering of something between Feathers and Hair, of a dark brown colour, without Wings, but in the place thereof, two or three little Branches, coming down like sprigs of Spanish Broom; long great Legs, with Feet only of three Claws, and without a Tail; I must make this Description of it, and so may make others understand me: But when I am told, that the name of it is *Cassuaris*, I may then use that word to stand in discourse for all my complex *Idea* mentioned in that description; though by that word, which is now become a specifick name, I know no more of the real Essence, or Constitution of that sort of Animals, than I did before; and knew probably as much of the nature of that *Species* of Birds, before I learn'd the name, as many *English*-men do of Swans, or Herons, which are specifick names, very well known of sorts of Birds common in *England*.

§ 35. From what has been said, 'tis evident, that *Men make sorts of Things*. For it being different Essences alone, that make different *Species*, 'tis plain, that they who make those abstract *Ideas*, which are the nominal Essences, do thereby make the *Species*, or Sort. Should there be a Body found, having all the other Qualities of Gold, except Malleableness, 'twould, no doubt, be made a question whether it were Gold or no; *i.e.* whether it were of that *Species*. This could be determined only by that abstract *Idea*, to which every one annexed the name *Gold*: so that it would be true Gold to him, and belong to that *Species*, who included not Malleableness in his nominal Essence, signified by the Sound *Gold*; and on the other side, it would not be true Gold, or of that *Species* to him, who included Malleableness in his specifick *Idea*. And who, I pray, is it, that makes these divers *Species*, even under one and the same name, but Men that make two different abstract *Ideas*, consisting not exactly of the same collection of Qualities? Nor is it a mere Supposition to imagine, that a Body may exist, wherein the other obvious Qualities

§ 34. *Instance in Cassuaries.* § 35. *Men determine the sorts.*

---

(21) 35] **2–5** | 34 **1** (27) *i.e.*] add. **4–5** (*l. below* 37: § 34.) *Cassuaries*] **2–4** | *Contraries* **5** (§ 35.) *New summary in* **4–5** (*cf. p. 32*).

of Gold may be without Malleableness; since it is certain, that Gold it self will be sometimes so eager, (as Artists call it) that it will as little endure the Hammer, as Glass it self. What we have said, of the putting in, or leaving out of Malleableness out of the complex *Idea*, the name *Gold* is, by any one, annexed to, may be said of its peculiar Weight, Fixedness, and several other the like Qualities: For whatsoever is left out, or put in, 'tis still the complex *Idea*, to which that name is annexed, that makes the *Species*: and as any particular parcel of Matter answers that *Idea*, so the name of the sort belongs truly to it; and it is of that *Species*. And thus any thing is true *Gold*, perfect *Metal*. All which determination of the *Species*, 'tis plain, depends on the Understanding of Man, making this or that complex *Idea*.

§ 36. This then, in short, is the case: *Nature makes many particular Things, which do agree* one with another, in many sensible Qualities, and probably too, in their internal frame and Constitution: but 'tis not this real Essence that distinguishes them into *Species*; 'tis *Men*, who, taking occasion from the Qualities they find united in them, and wherein, they observe often several individuals to agree, *range them into Sorts, in order to their naming*, for the convenience of comprehensive signs; under which individuals, according to their conformity to this or that abstract *Idea*, come to be ranked as under Ensigns: so that this is of the Blue, that the Red Regiment; this is a Man, that a Drill: And in this, I think, consists the whole business of *Genus* and *Species*.

§ 37. I do not deny, but Nature, in the constant production of particular Beings, makes them not always new and various, but very much alike and of kin one to another: But I think it is nevertheless true, that *the boundaries of the Species, whereby Men sort them, are made by Men*; since the Essences of the *Species*, distinguished by different Names, are, as has been proved, of Man's making, and seldom adequate to the internal Nature of the Things they are taken from. So that we may truly say, such a manner of sorting of Things, is the Workmanship of Men.

§ 38. One thing, I doubt not, but will seem very strange in this

§§ 36, 37. *Nature makes the Similitude.* § 38. *Each abstract* Idea *is an Essence.*

(6–7) whatsoever] **5** | whatever **1–4** (14) 36] **2–5** | 35 **1** (21) which individuals] **1T.er, 2–5** | which particular, Individuals **1** (26) 37] **2–5** | 36 **1** (28) is] **1–4**; *om.* **5** (35) 38] **2–5** | 37 **1** (*l. below* 35: §§ 36, 37.) *cf. p. 32.*

Doctrine; which is, that from what hath been said, it will follow, that *each abstract* Idea, *with a name to it, makes a distinct Species*. But who can help it, if Truth will have it so? For so it must remain, till some body can shew us the *Species* of Things, limited and distinguished by something else; and let us see, that general terms signify not our abstract *Ideas*, but something different from them. I would fain know, why a Shock and a Hound, are not as distinct *Species*, as a Spaniel and an Elephant. We have no other *Idea* of the different Essence of an Elephant and a Spaniel, than we have of the different Essence of a Shock and a Hound; all the essential difference, whereby we know and distinguish them one from another, consisting only in the different Collection of simple *Ideas*, to which we have given those different names.

§ 39. How much *the making of* Species *and* Genera *is in order to general names*, and how much general Names are necessary, if not to the Being, yet at least to the completing of a *Species*, and making it pass for such, will appear, besides what has been said above concerning Ice and Water, in a very familiar Example. A silent and a striking *Watch*, are but one *Species*, to those who have but one name for them: but he that has the name *Watch* for one, and *Clock* for the other, and distinct complex *Ideas*, to which those names belong, to him they are different *Species*. It will be said, perhaps, that the inward contrivance and constitution is different between these two, which the Watch-maker has a clear *Idea* of. And yet, 'tis plain, they are but one *Species* to him, when he has but one name for them. For what is sufficient in the inward Contrivance, to make a new *Species*? There are some *Watches*, that are made with four Wheels, others with five: Is this a specifick difference to the Workman? Some have Strings and Physies, and others none; some have the Balance loose, and others regulated by a spiral Spring, and others by Hogs Bristles: Are any, or all of these enough to make a specifick difference to the Workman, that knows each of these, and several other different contrivances, in the internal Constitutions of *Watches*? 'Tis certain, each of these hath a real difference from the rest: But whether it be an essential, a specifick difference or no, relates only to the complex *Idea*, to which the name *Watch* is given: as long as

§ 39. Genera *and* Species *are in order to naming.*

(10) [*2nd*] a] **4–5** | an **1–3** (14) 39] **2–5** | 38 **1** (17) above] **Coste** *adds a marginal reference to* § 13. (22) It . . . that] **4–5** | But it will be said, **1–3** (*l. below* 36) *cf. p.* 32.

they all agree in the *Idea* which that name stands for, and that name does not as a generical name comprehend different *Species* under it, they are not essentially nor specifically different. But if any one will make minuter Divisions from Differences, that he knows in the internal frame of Watches; and to such precise complex *Ideas*, give Names, that shall prevail, they will then be new *Species* to them, who have those *Ideas* with names to them; and can, by those differences, distinguish Watches into these several sorts, and then *Watch* will be a generical name. But yet they would be no distinct *Species* to Men, ignorant of Clock-work, and the inward Contrivances of Watches, who had no other *Idea*, but the outward shape and Bulk, with the marking of the Hours by the Hand. For to them, all those other Names would be but synonymous Terms for the same *Idea*, and signifie no more, nor no other thing but a *Watch*. Just thus, I think, it is in natural Things. No body will doubt, that the Wheels, or Springs (if I may so say) within, are different in a *rational Man*, and a *Changeling*, no more than that there is a difference in the frame between a *Drill* and a *Changeling*. But whether one, or both these differences be essential, or specifical, is only to be known to us, by their agreement, or disagreement with the complex *Idea* that the name *Man* stands for: For by that alone can it be determined, whether one, or both, or neither of those be a Man, or no.

§ 40. From what has been before said, we may see the reason, *why, in the Species of artificial Things, there is generally less confusion and uncertainty, than in natural*. Because an *artificial* Thing being a production of Man, which the Artificer design'd, and therefore well knows the *Idea* of, the name of it is supposed to stand for no other *Idea*, nor to import any other Essence, than what is certainly to be known, and easy enough to be apprehended. For the *Idea*, or Essence, of the several sorts of *artificial* Things, consisting, for the most part, in nothing but the determinate Figure of sensible Parts; and sometimes Motion depending thereon, which the Artificer fashions in Matter, such as he finds for his Turn, it is not beyond the reach of our Faculties to attain a certain *Idea* thereof; and so settle the signification of the Names, whereby the Species of

§ 40. *Species of artificial things less confused than natural.*

(1–2) which . . . *Species*] **4–5** | that belongs to that name, which has no Species [*Species* **2–3**] **1–3** (7) *Ideas*] **4–5** | *Ideas*, **1–3** differences,] **1–3**, **5** | differences **4** (8) *Watch*] **1T.er, 2–5** | Watches **1** (23) 40] **2–5** | 39 **1** (24) *Species*] **1–3, 5** | *species* **4**

artificial Things are distinguished, with less Doubt, Obscurity, and Equivocation, than we can in Things natural, whose differences and Operations depend upon Contrivances, beyond the reach of our Discoveries.

§ 41. I must be excused here, if I think, *artificial Things are of distinct Species*, as well as natural: Since I find they are as plainly and orderly ranked into sorts, by different abstract *Ideas*, with general names annexed to them, as distinct one from another as those of natural Substances. For why should we not think a Watch, and Pistol, as distinct Species one from another, as a Horse, and a Dog, they being expressed in our Minds by distinct *Ideas*, and to others, by distinct Appellations?

§ 42. This is farther to be observed concerning *Substances*, that they *alone* of all our several sorts of *Ideas*, *have* particular, or *proper Names*, whereby one only particular Thing is signified. Because in simple *Ideas*, Modes, and Relations, it seldom happens, that Men have occasion to mention often this, or that particular, when it is absent. Besides the greatest part of mixed Modes, being Actions, which perish in their Birth, are not capable of a lasting Duration, as Substances, which are the Actors; and wherein the simple *Ideas* that make up the complex *Ideas* designed by the Name, have a lasting Union.

§ 43. I must beg pardon of my Reader, for having dwelt so long upon this Subject, and perhaps, with some Obscurity. But I desire, it may be considered, how *difficult* it is, *to lead another by Words into the Thoughts of Things, stripp'd of those specifical differences* we give them: Which Things, if I name not, I say nothing; and if I do name them, I thereby rank them into some sort, or other, and suggest to the Mind the usual abstract *Idea* of that *Species*; and so cross my purpose. For to talk of a *Man*, and to lay by, at the same time, the ordinary signification of the Name Man, which is our complex *Idea*, usually annexed to it; and bid the Reader consider *Man*, as he is in himself, and as he is really distinguished from others, in his

§ 41. *Artificial things of distinct Species.* § 42. *Substances alone have proper Names.* § 43. *Difficulty to treat of Words.*

(5) 41] **2–5** | 40 **1** (6) plainly] **2–5** | plain, **1** (7) by different abstract] **2–5** | and have distinct complex **1** (7–8) with . . . them] **2–5** | to which we give general Names **1** (8) [*1st*] as] **2–5** | as much **1** those of] *add.* **2–5** (13) 42] **2–5** | 41 **1** (20–1) [*2nd*] the . . . up] *add.* **4–5** (21) [*2nd*] the] **4–5** | that **1–3**. (**Coste** 'un nom particulier') (23) 43] **2–5** | 42 **1** (24) upon] **2–5** | up-/ **1** (25) it is] **1T.er, 2–5** | is is **1** (33) as] **2–5** | whereby **1** (*2 ll. below* 33) *cf. p. 32.*

internal Constitution, or real Essence, that is, by something, he knows not what, looks like trifling: and yet thus one must do, who would speak of the supposed real Essences and *Species* of Things, as thought to be made by Nature, if it be but only to make it understood, that there is no such thing signified by the general Names, which Substances are called by. But because it is difficult by known familiar Names to do this, give me leave to endeavour by an Example, to make the different Consideration, the Mind has of specifick Names and *Ideas*, a little more clear; and to shew how the complex *Ideas* of Modes, are referred sometimes to Archetypes in the Minds of other intelligent Beings; or which is the same, to the signification annexed by others to their received Names; and sometimes to no Archetypes at all. Give me leave also to shew how the Mind always refers its *Ideas* of Substances, either to the Substances themselves, or to the signification of their Names, as to the *Archetypes*; and also to make plain the Nature of *Species*, or sorting of Things, as apprehended, and made use of by us; and of the Essences belonging to those *Species*, which is, perhaps, of more Moment, to discover the Extent and Certainty of our Knowledge, than we at first imagine.

§ 44. Let us suppose *Adam* in the State of a grown Man, with a good Understanding, but in a strange Country, with all Things new, and unknown about him; and no other Faculties, to attain the Knowledge of them, but what one of this Age has now. He observes *Lamech* more melancholy than usual, and imagines it to be from a suspicion he has of his Wife *Adah* (whom he most ardently loved) that she had too much Kindness for another Man. *Adam* discourses these his Thoughts to *Eve*, and desires her to take care that *Adah* commit not folly: And in these Discourses with *Eve*, he makes use of these two new Words, *Kinneah* and *Niouph*. In time, *Adam*'s mistake appears, for he finds *Lamech*'s Trouble proceeded from having kill'd a Man: But yet the two Names, *Kinneah* and *Niouph*; the one standing for suspicion, in a Husband, of his Wife's Disloyalty to him, and the other, for the Act of Committing Disloyalty, lost not their distinct significations. It is plain then, that

§§ 44–5. *Instance of mixed Modes in* Kinneah *and* Niouph.

---

(6) which] *add.* **2–5** (12) others . . . received] **1er–5** | others, to their receive/ **1** (15–16) the *Archetypes*] **4–5** | their Archetypes **1–3** (*likewise* **Coste**) (21) 44] **2–5** | 43 **1** (35) , lost . . . significations] *add.* **2–5**

here were two distinct complex *Ideas* of mixed Modes, with Names to them, two distinct Species of Actions essentially different, I ask wherein consisted the Essences of these two distinct Species of Actions, and 'tis plain, it consisted in a precise combination of simple *Ideas*, different in one from the other. I ask, whether the complex *Idea* in *Adam*'s Mind, which he call'd *Kinneah*, were adequate, or no? And it is plain it was, for it being a Combination of simple *Ideas*, which he without any regard to any Archetype, without respect to any thing as a Pattern, voluntarily put together, abstracted and gave the Name *Kinneah* to, to express in short to others, by that one sound, all the simple *Ideas* contain'd and united in that complex one, it must necessarily follow, that it was an adequate *Idea*. His own choice having made that Combination, it had all in it he intended it should, and so could not but be perfect, could not but be adequate, it being referr'd to no other Archetype, which it was supposed to represent.

§ 45. These Words, *Kinneah* and *Niouph*, by degrees grew into common use; and then the case was somewhat alter'd. *Adam*'s Children had the same Faculties, and thereby the same Power that he had, to make what complex *Ideas* of mixed Modes they pleased in their own Minds; to abstract them, and make what Sounds, they pleased, the signs of them: But the use of Names being to make our *Ideas* within us known to others, that cannot be done, but when the same Sign stands for the same *Idea* in two, who would communicate their Thoughts, and Discourse together. Those therefore of *Adam*'s Children, that found these two Words, *Kinneah* and *Niouph*, in familiar use, could not take them for insignificant sounds: but must needs conclude, they stood for something, for certain *Ideas*, abstract *Ideas*, they being general Names, which abstract *Ideas* were the Essences of the Species distinguished by those Names. If therefore they would use these Words, as Names of Species already establish'd and agreed on, they were obliged to conform the *Ideas*, in their Minds, signified by these Names, to the *Ideas*, that they stood for in other Men's Minds, as to their Patterns and *Archetypes*; and then indeed their *Ideas* of these complex Modes were liable to be inadequate, as being very apt (especially those that consisted of Combinations of many simple *Ideas*) not to be exactly conformable to the *Ideas* in other Men's Minds, using the same

(3) consisted] **2–5** | consist **1** (8) [*1st*] any] *add.* **4–5**. (*Not in* **Coste**) (17) 45] **2–5** | 44 **1** (31) Species] **2–5** | Species, **1** (34) Minds,] **2–5** | Minds, and to conform their *Ideas* to them, **1**

Names; though for this, there be usually a Remedy at Hand, which is, to ask the meaning of any word, we understand not, of him that uses it: it being as impossible, to know certainly, what the Words Jealousy and Adultery (which I think answer קנאה and נאוף) stand for in another Man's Mind, with whom I would discourse about them; as it was impossible, in the beginning of Language, to know what *Kinneah* and *Niouph* stood for in another Man's Mind, without Explication, they being voluntary Signs in every one.

§ 46. Let us now also consider after the same manner, the Names of Substances, in their first Application. One of *Adam*'s Children, roving in the Mountains, lights on a glittering Substance, which pleases his Eye; Home he carries it to *Adam*, who, upon consideration of it, finds it to be hard, to have a bright yellow Colour, and an exceeding great Weight. These, perhaps at first, are all the Qualities, he takes notice of in it, and abstracting this complex *Idea*, consisting of a Substance having that peculiar bright Yellowness, and a Weight very great in proportion to its Bulk, he gives it the Name *Zahab*, to denominate and mark all Substances, that have these sensible Qualities in them. 'Tis evident now that, in this Case, *Adam* acts quite differently, from what he did before in forming those *Ideas* of mixed Modes, to which he gave the Name *Kinneah* and *Niouph*. For there he put *Ideas* together, only by his own Imagination, not taken from the Existence of any thing; and to them he gave Names to denominate all Things, that should happen to agree to those his abstract *Ideas*, without considering whether any such thing did exist, or no: the Standard there was of his own making. But in the forming his *Idea* of this new Substance he takes the quite contrary Course; here he has a Standard made by Nature; and therefore being to represent that to himself, by the *Idea* he has of it, even when it is absent, he puts in no simple *Idea* into his complex one, but what he has the Perception of from the thing it self. He takes Care that his *Idea* be conformable to this *Archetype*, and intends the Name should stand for an *Idea* so conformable.

§ 47. This piece of Matter, thus denominated *Zahab* by *Adam*, being quite different from any he had seen before, no Body, I think, will deny to be a distinct Species, and to have its peculiar

§§ 46, 47. *Instance of Substances in* Zahab.

(4) נאוף] **1–3** | נאוךּ **4–5**. (*Hebrew not in* **Coste**) (9) 46] **2–5** | 45 **1** (12) Eye;] **2–4** (*upper stop in* ';' *in* **4** *hardly visible*) | Eye, **5** | Eyes; **1**. (**Coste** 'la veûë.') (20) acts] **1–3, 5** | Acts **4** (26) no:] **1–3** | no, **4** | no; **5**. (**Coste** 'non.') (28) a] **1–4**; *om.* **5** (34) 47] **2–5** | 46 **1**

Essence; and that the Name *Zahab* is the mark of the Species, and a Name belonging to all Things partaking in that Essence. But here it is plain, the Essence, *Adam* made the Name *Zahab* stand for, was nothing but a Body hard, shining, yellow, and very heavy. But the inquisitive Mind of Man, not content with the Knowledge of these, as I may say, superficial Qualities, puts *Adam* upon farther Examination of this Matter. He therefore knocks, and beats it with Flints, to see what was discoverable in the inside: He finds it yield to Blows, but not easily separate into pieces: he finds it will bend without breaking. Is not now Ductility to be added to his former *Idea*, and made part of the Essence of the Species, that Name *Zahab* stands for? Farther Trials discover Fusibility, and Fixedness. Are not they also, by the same Reason, that any of the others were, to be put into the complex *Idea*, signified by the Name *Zahab*? If not, What Reason will there be shewn more for the one than the other? If these must, then all the other Properties, which any farther Trials shall discover in this Matter, ought by the same Reason to make a part of the Ingredients of the complex *Idea*, which the Name *Zahab* stands for, and so be the Essence of the Species, marked by that Name. Which Properties, because they are endless, it is plain, that the *Idea* made after this fashion by this *Archetype*, will be always inadequate.

§ 48. But this is not all, it would also follow, that the *Names of Substances* would not only have, (as in truth they have) but would also be supposed to *have different Significations, as used by different Men*, which would very much cumber the use of Language. For if every distinct Quality, that were discovered in any Matter by any one, were supposed to make a necessary part of the complex *Idea*, signified by the common Name given it, it must follow, that Men must suppose the same Word to signify different Things in different Men: since they cannot doubt, but different Men may have discovered several Qualities in Substances of the same Denomination, which others know nothing of.

§ 49. To avoid this therefore, they have *supposed a real Essence belonging to every Species*, from which these Properties all flow, and

§ 48. *Their* Ideas *imperfect, and therefore various.* § 49. *Therefore to fix their Species, a real Essence is supposed.*

(3) Essence, *Adam*] **2–5** | Essence *Adam* signified, and **1** (11) made part of] *add.* **2–5** (15) shewn] **2–5** | shewed **1** (23) 48] **2–5** | 47 **1** (34) 49] **2–5** | 48 **1**

would have their name of the Species stand for that. But they not having any *Idea* of that real Essence in Substances, and their Words signifying nothing but the *Ideas* they have, that which is done by this Attempt, is only to put the name or sound, in the place and stead of the thing having that real Essence, without knowing what the real Essence is; and this is that which Men do, when they speak of Species of Things, as supposing them made by Nature, and distinguished by real Essences.

§ 50. For let us consider, when we affirm, that all *Gold* is fixed, either it means that Fixedness is a part of the Definition, part of the nominal Essence the Word *Gold* stands for; and so this Affirmation, *all Gold is fixed*, contains nothing but the signification of the Term *Gold*. Or else it means, that Fixedness not being a part of the definition of the Word *Gold*, is a Property of that Substance it self: in which case, it is plain, that the Word *Gold* stands in the place of a Substance, having the real Essence of a Species of Things, made by Nature. In which way of Substitution, it has so confused and uncertain a signification, that though this Proposition, *Gold is fixed*, be in that sense an Affirmation of something real; yet 'tis a Truth will always fail us in its particular Application, and so is of no real Use nor Certainty. For let it be never so true, that all *Gold*, *i.e.* all that has the real Essence of *Gold*, is fixed, What serves this for, whilst we know not in this sense, what is or is not *Gold*? For if we know not the real Essence of *Gold*, 'tis impossible we should know what parcel of Matter has that Essence, and so whether it be true *Gold* or no.

§ 51. To conclude; what liberty *Adam* had at first to make any complex *Ideas* of mixed Modes, by no other Pattern, but by his own Thoughts, the same have all Men ever since had. And the same necessity of conforming his *Ideas* of Substances to Things without him, as to *Archetypes* made by Nature, that *Adam* was under, if he would not wilfully impose upon himself, the same are all Men ever since under too. The same Liberty also, that *Adam* had of affixing any new name to any *Idea*; the same has any one still, (especially the beginners of Languages, if we can imagine any such,) but only with this difference, that in Places, where Men in Society have

§ 50. *Which supposition is of no use.* § 51. *Conclusion.*

(6) the] **5** | that **1–4** (9) 50] **2–5** | 49 **1** (21) *Gold*] **2–5** | God **1**
(27) 51] **2–5** | 50 **1**

already established a Language amongst them, the signification of Words are very warily and sparingly to be alter'd. Because Men being furnished already with Names for their *Ideas*, and common Use having appropriated known names to certain *Ideas*, an affected misapplication of them cannot but be very ridiculous. He that hath new Notions, will, perhaps, venture sometimes on the coining new Terms to express them: But Men think it a Boldness, and 'tis uncertain, whether common Use will ever make them pass for currant. But in Communication with others, it is necessary, that we conform the *Ideas* we make the vulgar Words of any Language stand for, to their known proper Significations, (which I have explain'd at large already,) or else to make known that new Signification, we apply them to.

CHAPTER VII

Of Particles.

§ 1. BESIDES Words, which are names of *Ideas* in the Mind, there are a great many others that are made use of, to signify the *connexion* that the Mind gives to *Ideas, or Propositions, one with another*. The Mind, in communicating its thought to others, does not only need signs of the *Ideas* it has then before it, but others also, to shew or intimate some particular action of its own, at that time, relating to those *Ideas*. This it does several ways; as, *Is*, and *Is not*, are the general marks of the Mind, affirming or denying. But besides affirmation, or negation, without which, there is in Words no Truth or Falshood, the Mind does, in declaring its Sentiments to others, connect, not only the parts of Propositions, but whole Sentences one to another, with their several Relations and Dependencies, to make a coherent Discourse.

§ 2. The Words, whereby it signifies what connection it gives to the several Affirmations and Negations, that it unites in one continued Reasoning or Narration, are generally call'd *Particles*: and 'tis in the right use of these, that more particularly consists the

§ 1. *Particles connect Parts, or whole Sentences together.* § 2. *In them consists the art of well speaking.*

(7) But] *add.* **1er–5** (17) its thought to] **2–5** | with **1**

clearness and beauty of a good Stile. To think well, it is not enough, that a Man has *Ideas* clear and distinct in his Thoughts, nor that he observes the agreement, or disagreement of some of them; but he must think in train, and observe the dependence of his Thoughts and Reasonings, one upon another: And to express well such methodical and rational Thoughts, he must have words to *shew* what *Connexion*, *Restriction*, *Distinction*, *Opposition*, *Emphasis*, etc. he gives to each respective *part of his Discourse*. To mistake in any of these, is to puzzle, instead of informing, his Hearer: and therefore it is, that those words, which are not truly, by themselves, the names of any *Ideas*, are of such constant and indispensible use in Language, and do so much contribute to Men's well expressing themselves.

§ 3. This part of Grammar has been, perhaps, as much neglected, as some others over-diligently cultivated. 'Tis easy for Men to write, one after another, of *Cases* and *Genders*, *Moods* and *Tenses*, *Gerunds* and *Supines*: In these and the like, there has been great diligence used; and Particles themselves, in some Languages, have been, with great shew of exactness, ranked into their several Orders. But though *Prepositions* and *Conjunctions*, etc. are names well known in Grammar, and the Particles contained under them carefully ranked into their distinct subdivisions; yet he who would shew the right use of Particles, and what significancy and force they have, must take a little more pains, enter into his own Thoughts, and observe nicely the several Postures of his Mind in discoursing.

§ 4. Neither is it enough, for the explaining of these Words, to render them, as is usually in Dictionaries, by Words of another Tongue which came nearest to their signification: For what is meant by them, is commonly as hard to be understood in one, as another Language. They are all *marks of some Action, or Intimation of the Mind*; and therefore to understand them rightly, the several views, postures, stands, turns, limitations, and exceptions, and several other Thoughts of the Mind, for which we have either none, or very deficient Names, are diligently to be studied. Of these, there are a great variety, much exceeding the number of Particles, that most Languages have, to express them by: and therefore it is not to be wondred, that most of these Particles have divers, and sometimes almost opposite significations. In the Hebrew Tongue,

§§ 3, 4. *They shew what Relation the Mind gives to its own Thoughts.*

(4) dependence] **2–5** | dependency **1** (9), his] **2–5** | his **1** (12) so] **1–4**; *om.* **5** (13) Grammar] **1–3** | Grammer **4–5** (35) have,] **2–5** | have **1**

there is a Particle consisting but of one single Letter, of which there are reckoned up, as I remember, seventy, I am sure above fifty several significations.

§ 5. *BUT* is a Particle, none more familiar in our Language: and he that says it is a discretive Conjunction, and that it answers *Sed* in Latin, or *Mais* in French, thinks he has sufficiently explained it. But yet it seems to me to intimate several relations, the Mind gives to the several Propositions or Parts of them, which it joins by this monosyllable.

First, *BUT to say no more*: Here it intimates a stop of the Mind, in the course it was going, before it came to the end of it.

Secondly, *I saw BUT two Planets*: Here it shews, that the Mind limits the sense to what is expressed, with a negation of all other.

Thirdly, *You pray; BUT it is not that GOD would bring you to the true Religion.*

Fourthly, *BUT that he would confirm you in your own*: The first of these *BUTS*, intimates a supposition in the Mind, of something otherwise than it should be; the latter shews, that the Mind makes a direct opposition between that, and what goes before it.

Fifthly, *All Animals have sense; BUT a Dog is an Animal*: Here it signifies little more, but that the latter Proposition is joined to the former, as the *Minor* of a Syllogism.

§ 6. To these, I doubt not, might be added a great many other significations of this Particle, if it were my business to examine it in its full latitude, and consider it in all the places it is to be found: which if one should do, I doubt, whether in all those manners it is made use of, it would deserve the title of *Discretive*, which Grammarians give to it. But I intend not here a full explication of this sort of Signs. The instances I have given in this one, may give occasion to reflect upon their use and force in Language, and lead us into the contemplation of several Actions of our Minds in discoursing, which it has found a way to intimate to others by these Particles, some whereof constantly, and others in certain constructions, have the sense of a whole Sentence contain'd in them.

§ 5. *Instance in* But. § 6. *This Matter but lightly touched here.*

---

(4) **Coste** *adds a linguistic footnote.* (7) yet] **1–4**; *om.* **5** (10) First] *The remainder of this section, apart from the paragraphs beginning* 'Thirdly' *and* 'Fourthly', *is different in* **Coste** (*where the two latter paragraphs are numbered* IV. *and* V., *with another paragraph following*). (12) *Planets*] **1–4** | *Plants* **5**

CHAPTER VIII

Of Abstract and Concrete Terms.

§ 1. THE ordinary Words of Language, and our common use of them, would have given us light into the nature of our *Ideas*, if they had been but considered with attention. The Mind, as has been shewn, has a power to abstract its *Ideas*, and so they become Essences, general Essences, whereby the Sorts of Things are distinguished. Now each abstract *Idea* being distinct, so that of any two the one can never be the other, the Mind will, by its intuitive Knowledge, perceive their difference; and therefore in Propositions, no two whole *Ideas* can ever be affirmed one of another. This we see in the common use of Language, which permits *not any two abstract Words, or Names of abstract Ideas*, to be *affirmed one of another*. For how near of kin soever they may seem to be, and how certain soever it is, that Man is an Animal, or rational, or white, yet every one, at first hearing, perceives the falshood of these Propositions; *Humanity is Animality*, or *Rationality*, or *Whiteness*: And this is as evident, as any of the most allow'd Maxims. All our Affirmations then are only in concrete, which is the affirming, not one abstract *Idea* to be another, but one abstract *Idea* to be join'd to another; which abstract *Ideas*, in Substances, may be of any sort; in all the rest, are little else but of Relations; and in Substances, the most frequent are of Powers; *v.g. a Man is White*, signifies, that the thing that has the Essence of a Man, has also in it the Essence of Whiteness, which is nothing but a power to produce the *Idea* of Whiteness in one, whose Eyes can discover ordinary Objects; or *a Man is rational*, signifies, that the same thing, that hath the Essence of a Man, hath also in it the Essence of Rationality, *i.e.* a power of Reasoning.

§ 2. This distinction of Names, shews us also the difference of our *Ideas*: For if we observe them, we shall find, that our *simple Ideas have all abstract, as well as concrete Names*: The one whereof is (to speak the Language of Grammarians) a Substantive, the other an Adjective; as Whiteness, White; Sweetness, Sweet. The like also holds in our *Ideas* of *Modes* and Relations; as Justice, Just; Equality, Equal; only with this difference, That some of the concrete Names of Relations,

§ 1. *Abstract Terms not predicable one of another, and why.* § 2. *They shew the difference of our* Ideas.

(6–7) of any two] *add.* **2er–5** (18) [*1st*] to] *add.* **1er–5**

amongst Men chiefly, are Substantives; as *Paternitas*, *Pater*; whereof it were easy to render a Reason. But as to our *Ideas* of *Substances*, we have very few or *no abstract Names* at all. For though the Schools have introduced *Animalitas*, *Humanitas*, *Corporietas*, and some others; yet they hold no proportion with that infinite number of Names of Substances, to which they never were ridiculous enough to attempt the coining of abstract ones: and those few that the Schools forged, and put into the mouths of their Scholars, could never yet get admittance into common use, or obtain the license of publick approbation. Which seems to me at least to intimate the confession of all Mankind, that they have no *Ideas* of the real Essences of Substances, since they have not Names for such *Ideas*: which no doubt they would have had, had not their consciousness to themselves of their ignorance of them, kept them from so idle an attempt. And therefore though they had *Ideas* enough to distinguish Gold from a Stone, and Metal from Wood; yet they but timorously ventured on such terms, as *Aurietas* and *Saxietas*, *Metallietas* and *Lignietas*, or the like names, which should pretend to signify the real Essences of those Substances, whereof they knew they had no *Ideas*. And indeed, it was only the Doctrine of *substantial Forms*, and the confidence of mistaken Pretenders to a knowledge that they had not, which first coined, and then introduced *Animalitas*, and *Humanitas*, and the like; which yet went very little farther than their own Schools, and could never get to be current amongst understanding Men. Indeed, *Humanitas* was a Word familiar amongst the *Romans*; but in a far different sense, and stood not for the abstract Essence of any Substance; but was the abstract Name of a Mode, and its concrete *Humanus*, not *Homo*.

CHAPTER IX

Of the Imperfection of Words.

§ 1. FROM what has been said in the foregoing Chapters, it is easy to perceive, what imperfection there is in Language, and how the

§ 1. *Words are used for recording and communicating our Thoughts.*

(6) they] **Coste** 'les Scholastiques' (17) *Lignietas*] **Coste** *adds a marginal linguistic note.* (19) *Ideas*] **2–5** | *Idea* **1** (21) mistaken] **1er–5** | shameless **1** (27) Name] **Coste** *adds a marginal linguistic note.*

very nature of Words, makes it almost unavoidable, for many of them to be doubtful and uncertain in their significations. To examine the perfection, or imperfection of Words, it is necessary first to consider their use and end: For as they are more or less fitted to attain that, so are they more or less perfect. We have, in the former part of this Discourse, often, upon occasion, mentioned *a double use of Words.*

First, One for the recording of our own Thoughts.

Secondly, The other for the communicating of our Thoughts to others.

§ 2. As to the first of these, *for the recording our own Thoughts* for the help of our own Memories, whereby, as it were, we talk to our selves, any Words will serve the turn. For since Sounds are voluntary and indifferent signs of any *Ideas*, a Man may use what Words he pleases, to signify his own *Ideas* to himself: and there will be no imperfection in them, if he constantly use the same sign for the same *Idea*: for then he cannot fail of having his meaning understood, wherein consists the right use and perfection of Language.

§ 3. *Secondly,* As to *communication by Words,* that too *has a double use.*

I. *Civil.*

II. *Philosophical.*

First, By their *civil Use,* I mean such a communication of Thoughts and *Ideas* by Words, as may serve for the upholding common Conversation and Commerce, about the ordinary Affairs and Conveniencies of civil Life, in the Societies of Men, one amongst another.

Secondly, By the *Philosophical Use* of Words, I mean such an use of them, as may serve to convey the precise Notions of Things, and to express, in general Propositions, certain and undoubted Truths, which the Mind may rest upon, and be satisfied with, in its search after true Knowledge. These two Uses are very distinct; and a great deal less exactness will serve in the one, than in the other, as we shall see in what follows.

§ 4. The chief End of Language in Communication being to be understood, Words serve not well for that end, neither in civil, nor philosophical Discourse, when any Word does not excite in the

§ 2. *Any Words will serve for recording.* § 3. *Communication by Words, Civil or Philosophical.* § 4. *The Imperfection of Words is the doubtfulness of their Signification.*

---

(15) pleases] **2–5** | please **1** (19) *by*] **1–4** | *of* **5** (26) By] **1–3, 5** | by **4** (*l. below* 35: § 3.) *Words,*] **2–3** | *Words* **4–5** (*2 ll. below* 35: § 4.) *Imperfection*] **2–4** | *Imperfections* **5**

Hearer, the same *Idea* which it stands for in the Mind of the Speaker. Now since Sounds have no natural connexion with our *Ideas*, but have all their signification from the arbitrary imposition of Men, the *doubtfulness* and uncertainty *of their signification*, which *is the imperfection* we here are speaking of, has its cause more in the *Ideas* they stand for, than in any incapacity there is in one Sound, more than in another, to signify any *Idea*: For in that regard, they are all equally perfect.

That then which makes doubtfulness and uncertainty in the signification of some more than other Words, is the difference of *Ideas* they stand for.

§ 5. Words having naturally no signification, the *Idea* which each stands for, must be learned and retained by those, who would exchange Thoughts, and hold intelligible Discourse with others, in any Language. But this is hardest to be done, where,

First, The *Ideas* they stand for, are very complex, and made up of a great number of *Ideas* put together.

Secondly, Where the *Ideas* they stand for, have no certain connexion in Nature; and so no settled Standard, any where in Nature existing, to rectify and adjust them by.

Thirdly, Where the signification of the Word is referred to a Standard, which Standard is not easy to be known.

Fourthly, Where the signification of the Word, and the real Essence of the Thing, are not exactly the same.

These are difficulties that attend the signification of several Words that are intelligible. Those which are not intelligible at all, such as Names standing for any simple *Ideas*, which another has not Organs or Faculties to attain; as the Names of Colours to a blind Man, or Sounds to a deaf Man, need not here be mentioned.

In all these cases, we shall find an imperfection in Words; which I shall more at large explain, in their particular application to our several sorts of *Ideas*: For if we examine them, we shall find, that the *Names of mixed Modes are most liable to doubtfulness and imperfection, for the two first of these Reasons; and the Names of Substances chiefly for the two latter.*

§ 6. *First*, The Names of *mixed Modes*, are many of them liable to great uncertainty and obscurity in their signification.

§ 5. *Causes of their Imperfection.* § 6. *The Names of mixed Modes doubtful.*

---

(10) other Words] **2–5** | others **1** (12) *Idea*] **2–5** | *Ideas* **1** (16) The] **1–3** | the **4–5** (25) *Paragraph-break in* **4–5**, *not in* **1–3**.

I. *Because of* that *great Composition*, these complex *Ideas* are often made up of. To make Words serviceable to the end of Communication, it is necessary, (as has been said) that they excite, in the Hearer, exactly the same *Idea*, they stand for in the Mind of the Speaker. Without this, Men fill one another's Heads with noise and sounds; but convey not thereby their Thoughts, and lay not before one another their *Ideas*, which is the end of Discourse and Language. But when a word stands for a very complex *Idea*, that is compounded and decompounded, it is not easy for Men to form and retain that *Idea* so exactly, as to make the Name in common use, stand for the same precise *Idea*, without any the least variation. Hence it comes to pass, that Men's Names, of very compound *Ideas*, such as for the most part are moral Words, have seldom, in two different Men, the same precise signification; since one Man's complex *Idea* seldom agrees with anothers, and often differs from his own, from that which he had yesterday, or will have to morrow.

§ 7. II. *Because the names of mixed Modes*, for the most part, *want Standards* in Nature, whereby Men may rectify and adjust their significations; therefore they are very various and doubtful. They are assemblages of *Ideas* put together at the pleasure of the Mind, pursuing its own ends of Discourse, and suited to its own Notions; whereby it designs not to copy any thing really existing, but to denominate and rank Things, as they come to agree, with those Archetypes or Forms it has made. He that first brought the word *Sham*, *Wheedle*, or *Banter* in use, put together, as he thought fit, those *Ideas* he made it stand for: And as it is with any new Names of Modes, that are now brought into any Language; so was it with the old ones, when they were first made use of. Names therefore, that stand for Collections of *Ideas*, which the Mind makes at pleasure, must needs be of doubtful signification, when such Collections are no-where to be found constantly united in Nature, nor any Patterns to be shewn whereby Men may adjust them. What the word *Murther*, or *Sacriledge*, *etc.* signifies, can never be known from Things themselves: There be many of the parts of those complex *Ideas*, which are not visible in the Action it self, the intention of the Mind, or the Relation of holy Things, which make a part of

§ 6(1). *First, Because the* Ideas *they stand for, are so complex.* § 7. *Secondly, Because they have no Standards.*

(3) it] *add.* **1er–5** (25) *Banter*] **Coste** *adds a linguistic footnote.* (31) any] **4–5** | no **1–3** (32) . What] **1er–5** | , what **1** (33) signifies] **2–5** | signifie **1**

Murther, or *Sacrilege*, have no necessary connexion with the outward and visible Action of him that commits either: and the pulling the Trigger of the Gun, with which the Murther is committed, and is all the Action, that, perhaps, is visible, has no natural connexion with those other *Ideas*, that make up the complex one, named *Murther*. They have their union and combination only from the Understanding which unites them under one Name: but uniting them without any Rule, or Pattern, it cannot be, but that the signification of the Name, that stands for such voluntary Collections, should be often various in the Minds of different Men, who have scarce any standing Rule to regulate themselves, and their Notions by, in such arbitrary *Ideas*.

§ 8. 'Tis true, *common Use*, that is the Rule of Propriety, may be supposed here to afford some aid, to settle the signification of Language; and it cannot be denied, but that in some measure it does. Common use *regulates the meaning of Words* pretty well for common Conversation; but no body having an Authority to establish the precise signification of Words, nor determine to what *Ideas* any one shall annex them, common Use is not sufficient to adjust them to philosophical Discourses; there being scarce any Name, of any very complex *Idea*, (to say nothing of others,) which, in common Use, has not a great latitude, and which keeping within the bounds of Propriety, may not be made the sign of far different *Ideas*. Besides, the rule and measure of Propriety it self being no where established, it is often matter of dispute, whether this or that way of using a Word, be propriety of Speech, or no. From all which, it is evident, that the Names of such kind of very complex *Ideas*, are naturally liable to this imperfection, to be of doubtful and uncertain signification; and even in Men, that have a Mind to understand one another, do not always stand for the same *Idea* in Speaker and Hearer. Though the Names *Glory* and *Gratitude* be the same in every Man's mouth, through a whole Country, yet the complex collective *Idea*, which every one thinks on, or intends by that name, is apparently very different in Men using the same Language.

§ 9. *The way* also *wherein the names of mixed Modes are ordinarily learned, does* not a little *contribute to the doubtfulness of their signification.* For if we will observe how Children learn Languages, we shall find,

§ 8. *Propriety not a sufficient Remedy.* § 9. *The way of Learning these Names contributes also to their Doubtfulness.*

(12) by . . . *Ideas*] **4–5** | of such arbitrary *Ideas* by **1–3** (34) in] **2–5** | by **1**

that to make them understand what the names of simple *Ideas*, or Substances, stand for, People ordinarily shew them the thing, whereof they would have them have the *Idea*; and then repeat to them the name that stands for it, as *White*, *Sweet*, *Milk*, *Sugar*, *Cat*, *Dog*. But as for mixed Modes, especially the most material of them, moral Words, the Sounds are usually learn'd first, and then to know what complex *Ideas* they stand for, they are either beholden to the explication of others, or (which happens for the most part) are left to their own Observation and industry; which being little laid out in the search of the true and precise meaning of Names, these moral Words are, in most Men's mouths, little more than bare Sounds; or when they have any, 'tis for the most part but a very loose and undetermined, and consequently obscure and confused signification. And even those themselves, who have with more attention settled their Notions, do yet hardly avoid the inconvenience, to have them stand for complex *Ideas*, different from those which other, even intelligent and studious Men, make them the signs of. Where shall one find any, either *controversial Debate*, or *familiar Discourse*, concerning *Honour*, *Faith*, *Grace*, *Religion*, *Church*, etc. wherein it is not easy to observe the different Notions Men have of them; which is nothing but this, that they are not agreed in the signification of those Words; nor have in their minds the same complex *Ideas* which they make them stand for: and so all the contests that follow thereupon, are only about the meaning of a Sound. And hence we see, that in the interpretation of Laws, whether Divine, or Humane, there is no end; Comments beget Comments, and Explications make new matter for Explications: And of limiting, distinguishing, varying the signification of these moral Words, there is no end. These *Ideas* of Men's making, are, by Men still having the same Power, multiplied *in infinitum*. Many a Man, who was pretty well satisfied of the meaning of a Text of Scripture, or Clause in the Code, at first reading, has by consulting Commentators, quite lost the sense of it, and, by those Elucidations, given rise or increase to his Doubts, and drawn obscurity upon the place. I say not this, that I think Commentaries needless; but to shew how uncertain the Names of mixed Modes naturally are, even in the mouths of those, who had both the Intention and the Faculty of Speaking as clearly, as Language was capable to express their Thoughts.

(12–13) loose . . . consequently] *add.* **4–5** (22) ; nor . . . minds] **4–5** | , have not **1–3** (23) which] *add.* **4–5** (32) consulting] **1–3, 5** | Consulting **4** (37) those] **1er–5** | these **1**

§ 10. What obscurity this has unavoidably brought upon the Writings of Men, who have lived in remote Ages, and different Countries, it will be needless to take notice. Since the numerous Volumes of learned Men, employing their Thoughts that way, are proofs more than enough, to shew what Attention, Study, Sagacity, and Reasoning is required, to find out the true meaning *of ancient Authors*. But there being no Writings we have any great concernment to be very sollicitous about the meaning of, but those that contain either Truths we are required to believe, or Laws we are to obey, and draw inconveniences on us, when we mistake or transgress, we may be less anxious about the sense of other Authors; who Writing but their own Opinions, we are under no greater necessity to know them, than they to know ours. Our good or evil depending not on their Decrees, we may safely be ignorant of their Notions: And therefore in the reading of them, if they do not use their Words with a due clearness and perspicuity, we may lay them aside, and without any injury done them, resolve thus with our selves,

*Si non vis intelligi, debes negligi.**

§ 11. If the signification of the Names of mixed Modes are uncertain, because there be no real Standards existing in Nature, to which those *Ideas* are referred, and by which they may be adjusted, the *Names of Substances are of a doubtful signification*, for a contrary reason, *viz. because* the *Ideas*, they stand for, are supposed conformable to the reality of Things, and are *referred to Standards* made by Nature. In our *Ideas* of Substances we have not the liberty as in mixed Modes, to frame what Combinations we think fit, to be the characteristical Notes, to rank and denominate Things by. In these we must follow Nature, suit our complex *Ideas* to real Existences, and regulate the signification of their Names by the Things themselves, if we will have our Names to be the signs of them, and stand for them. Here, 'tis true, we have Patterns to follow; but Patterns, that will make the signification of their names very uncertain: For Names must be of a very unsteady and various meaning, if the *Ideas*

§§ 10, 11. *Hence unavoidable Obscurity in ancient Authors.*

(5) Attention] **1–3, 5** | attention **4** (10) inconveniences] **4–5** | Inconveniencies **1–3**

* (*Source untraced*)

they stand for, be referred to Standards without us, *that either cannot be known at all, or can be known but imperfectly and uncertainly.*

§ 12. The *Names of Substances have*, as has been shewed, a double *reference* in their ordinary use.

First, Sometimes they are made to stand for, and so their signification is supposed to agree to, *The real Constitution of Things*, from which all their Properties flow, and in which they all centre. But this real Constitution, or (as it is apt to be called) Essence, being utterly unknown to us, any Sound that is put to stand for it, must be very uncertain in its application; and it will be impossible to know, what Things are, or ought to be called an *Horse*, or *Antimony*, when those Words are put for real Essences, that we have no *Ideas* of at all. And therefore in this supposition, the Names of Substances being referred to Standards that cannot be known, their significations can never be adjusted and established by those Standards.

§ 13. *Secondly*, The *simple Ideas* that are found to *co-exist in Substances*, being that which their Names immediately signify, these, as united in the several Sorts of Things, *are* the proper *Standards* to which their Names are referred, and by which their Significations may best be rectified. But neither will these *Archetypes* so well serve to this purpose, as to leave these Names without very various and uncertain significations. Because these simple *Ideas* that co-exist, and are united in the same Subject, being very numerous, and having all an equal right to go into the complex specifick *Idea*, which the specifick Name is to stand for, Men, though they propose to themselves the very same Subject to consider, yet frame very different *Ideas* about it; and so the Name they use for it, unavoidably comes to have, in several Men, very different significations. The simple Qualities which make up the complex *Ideas*, being most of them Powers, in relation to Changes, which they are apt to make in, or receive from other Bodies, are almost infinite. He that shall but observe, what a great variety of alterations any one of the baser Metals is apt to receive, from the different application only of Fire; and how much a greater number of Changes any of them will receive in the Hands of a Chymist, by the application of other Bodies, will not think it strange, that I count the

§ 12. *Names of Substances referr'd, First, To real Essences that cannot be known.* §§ 13, 14. *Secondly, To co-existing Qualities, which are known but imperfectly.*

(12) *Ideas*] **4–5** | *Idea* **1–3**. (**Coste** 'aucune idée') (25–6) propose] **2–5** purpose **1** (30) , which] *add.* **4–5** (35) a] **1–4**; *om.* **5**

Properties of any sort of Bodies not easy to be collected, and completely known by the ways of enquiry, which our Faculties are capable of. They being therefore at least so many, that no Man can know the precise and definite number, they are differently discovered by different Men, according to their various skill, attention, and ways of handling; who therefore cannot chuse but have different *Ideas* of the same Substance, and therefore make the signification of its common Name very various and uncertain. For the complex *Ideas* of Substances, being made up of such simple ones as are supposed to co-exist in Nature, every one has a right to put into his complex *Idea*, those Qualities he has found to be united together. For though in the Substance *Gold*, one satisfies himself with Colour and Weight, yet another thinks Solubility in *Aqua Regia*, as necessary to be joined with that Colour in his *Idea* of Gold, as any one does its Fusibility; Solubility in *Aqua Regia*, being a Quality as constantly join'd with its Colour and Weight, as Fusibility, or any other; others put in its Ductility or Fixedness, *etc.* as they have been taught by Tradition, or Experience. Who of all these, has establish'd the right signification of the Word *Gold*? Or who shall be the Judge to determine? Each has his Standard in Nature, which he appeals to, and with Reason thinks he has the same right to put into his complex *Idea*, signified by the word *Gold*, those Qualities, which upon Trial he has found united; as another, who has not so well examined, has to leave them out; or a third, who has made other Trials, has to put in others. For the Union in Nature of these Qualities, being the true Ground of their Union in one complex *Idea*, Who can say, one of them has more reason to be put in, or left out, than another? From whence it will always unavoidably follow, that the complex *Ideas* of Substances, in Men using the same Name for them, will be very various; and so the significations of those names, very uncertain.

§ 14. Besides, there is scarce any particular thing existing, which, in some of its simple *Ideas*, does not communicate with a greater, and in others with a less number of particular Beings: Who shall determine in this Case, which are those that are to make up the precise Collection, that is to be signified by the specifick Name; or can with any just Authority prescribe, which obvious or common Qualities are to be left out; or which more secret, or more particular, are to be put into the signification of the name of any Substance?

(36) that] **2–5** | which **1**

All *which* together, seldom or never fail to *produce* that various and *doubtful Signification in the names of Substances*, which causes such Uncertainty, Disputes, or Mistakes, when we come to a Philosophical Use of them.

§ 15. 'Tis true, as *to civil and common Conversation*, the general *names of Substances*, regulated in their ordinary Signification by some obvious Qualities, (as by the Shape and Figure in Things of known seminal Propagation, and in other Substances, for the most part by Colour, join'd with some other sensible Qualities,) *do well enough*, to design the Things Men would be understood to speak of: And so they usually conceive well enough the Substances meant by the Word *Gold*, or *Apple*, to distinguish the one from the other. *But in Philosophical Enquiries and Debates*, where general Truths *are* to be establish'd, and Consequences drawn from Positions laid down, there the precise signification of the names of Substances will be found, not only *not* to be *well established*, but also very hard to be so. For Example, he that shall make Malleableness, or a certain degree of Fixedness, a part of his complex *Idea* of *Gold*, may make Propositions concerning Gold, and draw Consequences from them, that will truly and clearly follow from *Gold*, taken in such a signification: But yet such as another Man can never be forced to admit, nor be convinced of their Truth, who makes not Malleableness, or the same degree of Fixedness, part of that complex *Idea*, that the name *Gold*, in his use of it, stands for.

§ 16. This is a natural, and almost unavoidable Imperfection in almost all the names of Substances, in all Languages whatsoever, which Men will easily find, when once passing from confused or loose Notions, they come to more strict and close Enquiries. For then they will be convinced, how doubtful and obscure those Words are in their Signification, which in ordinary use appeared very clear and determined. I was once in a Meeting of very learned and ingenious Physicians, where by chance there arose a Question, whether any Liquor passed through the Filaments of the Nerves. The Debate having been managed a good while, by variety of Arguments on both sides, I (who had been used to suspect, that the

§ 15. *With this imperfection, they may serve for Civil, but not well for Philosophical use.*
§ 16. *Instance Liquor.*

(10) Men] **2–5** | they **1** (11) they] **2–5** | Men **1** (17) Malleableness] **5** | Malleability **1–4** (*2 ll. below* 35) *Instance Liquor.*] **4–5** | *Instance Liquor of Nerves.* **2–3**. (**Coste** '*Exemple remarquable sur cela.*')

greatest part of Disputes were more about the signification of Words, than a real difference in the Conception of Things) desired, That before they went any farther on in this Dispute, they would first examine, and establish amongst them, what the Word *Liquor* signified. They at first were a little surprised at the Proposal; and had they been Persons less ingenuous, they might perhaps have taken it for a very frivolous or extravagant one: Since there was no one there, that thought not himself to understand very perfectly, what the Word *Liquor* stood for; which, I think too, none of the most perplexed names of Substances. However, they were pleased to comply with my Motion, and upon Examination found, that the signification of that Word, was not so settled and certain, as they had all imagined; but that each of them made it a sign of a different complex *Idea*. This made them perceive, that the Main of their Dispute was about the signification of that Term; and that they differed very little in their Opinions, concerning some fluid and subtile Matter, passing through the Conduits of the Nerves; though it was not so easy to agree whether it was to be called *Liquor*, or no, a thing which when each considered, he thought it not worth the contending about.

§ 17. How much this is the Case in the greatest part of Disputes, that Men are engaged so hotly in, I shall, perhaps, have an occasion in another place to take notice. Let us only here consider a little more exactly the fore-mentioned instance of the Word *Gold*, and we shall see how hard it is precisely to determine its Signification. I think all agree, to make it stand for a Body of a certain yellow shining Colour; which being the *Idea* to which Children have annexed that name, the shining yellow part of a Peacock's Tail, is properly to them Gold. Others finding Fusibility join'd with that yellow Colour in certain parcels of Matter, make of that combination a complex *Idea* to which they give the name *Gold* to denote a sort of Substances; And so exclude from being *Gold* all such yellow shining Bodies, as by Fire will be reduced to ashes, and admit to be of that

§ 17. *Instance Gold.*

---

(6) ingenuous] **2–4** | ingenious **1, 5**. (**Coste** 'honnêtes') (9) *Liquor*] *edit.* (*likewise* **Coste**) | Liquor **1–5** (21) in] **2–5** | of **1** (26) I . . . for] **4–5** | Almost all agree, that it should signifie **1–3** (30)–486(2) certain . . . fire] **4–5** | Gold, think the other which contain'd nothing but the *Idea* of Body with that Colour not truly to represent Gold, but to be an imperfect *Idea* of that sort of Substance: And therefore the Word Gold, as referr'd to that sort of Substances, does of right signifie a Body of that yellow Colour, which by the Fire will **1–3**

Species, or to be comprehended under that name *Gold* only such Substances as having that shining yellow Colour will by fire be reduced to Fusion, and not to Ashes. Another by the same Reason adds, the Weight, which being a Quality, as straitly join'd with that Colour, as its Fusibility, he thinks has the same Reason to be join'd in its *Idea*, and to be signified by its name: And therefore the other made up of Body, of such a Colour and Fusibility, to be imperfect; and so on of all the rest: Wherein no one can shew a Reason, why some of the inseparable Qualities, that are always united in nature, should be put into the nominal Essence, and others left out: Or why the Word *Gold*, signifying that sort of Body the Ring on his Finger is made of, should determine that sort, rather by its Colour, Weight, and Fusibility; than by its Colour, Weight, and Solubility in *Aqua Regia*: Since the dissolving it by that Liquor, is as inseparable from it, as the Fusion by Fire; and they are both of them nothing, but the relation which that Substance has to two other Bodies, which have a Power to operate differently upon it. For by what right is it, that Fusibility comes to be a part of the Essence, signified by the Word *Gold*, and Solubility but a property of it? Or why is its Colour part of the Essence, and its Malleableness but a property? That which I mean, is this, That these being all but Properties, depending on its real Constitution; and nothing but Powers, either active or passive, in reference to other Bodies, no one has Authority to determine the signification of the Word *Gold*, (as referr'd to such a Body existing in Nature) more to one Collection of *Ideas* to be found in that Body, than to another: Whereby the signification of that name must unavoidably be very uncertain. Since, as has been said, several People observe several Properties in the same Substance; and, I think, I may say no body all. And therefore we have but very imperfect descriptions of Things, and Words have very uncertain Significations.

§ 18. From what has been said, it is easy to observe, what has been before remarked, *viz.* That the *Names of simple* Ideas *are*, of all others the *least liable to Mistakes*, and that for these reasons. *First*,

§ 18. *The Names of simple* Ideas *the least doubtful.*

(2) *v.* 485(30), n. (13) Fusibility;] **1–3, 5** | Fusibility: **4** (14) *Aqua Regia*] *edit.* | *aq. Regia* **4–5** | *aq. regia* **1–3** (16) which] *add.* **4–5** (17) differently] **1–2, 4–5** | indifferently **3** (*likewise* **Coste**) (28) [*2nd*] several] *add.* **1er–5** (29) all] **1–4** | at all **5** (32) From] **2–5** | By **1** said] **2–5** | before said **1** (32–3) [*2nd*] what . . . *viz.*] *add.* **2–5** (34) , and . . . reasons] *add.* **2–5**

Because the *Ideas* they stand for, being each but one single perception, are much easier got, and more clearly retain'd, than the more complex ones, and therefore are not liable to the uncertainty, which usually attends those compounded ones of *Substances and mixed Modes*, in which the precise number of simple *Ideas*, that make them up, are not easily agreed, nor so readily kept in mind. And *Secondly*, because they are never referr'd to any other Essence, but barely that Perception they immediately signify: Which reference is that, which renders the signification of the names of Substances naturally so perplexed, and gives occasion to so many Disputes. Men that do not perversly use their Words, or on purpose set themselves to cavil, seldom mistake in any Language, which they are acquainted with, the Use and Signification of the names of simple *Ideas*, *White* and *Sweet*, *Yellow* and *Bitter*, carry a very obvious meaning with them, which every one precisely comprehends, or easily perceives he is ignorant of, and seeks to be informed. But what precise Collection of simple *Ideas*, *Modesty* or *Frugality* stand for in another's use, is not so certainly known. And however we are apt to think, we well enough know, what is meant by *Gold* or *Iron*; yet the precise complex *Idea*, others make them the signs of, is not so certain: And I believe it is very seldom that in Speaker and Hearer, they stand for exactly the same Collection. Which must needs produce Mistakes and Disputes, when they are made use of in Discourses, wherein Men have to do with universal Propositions, and would settle in their Minds universal Truths, and consider the Consequences, that follow from them.

§ 19. By the same Rule, the *names of simple Modes are next to those of simple* Ideas, *least liable to Doubt or Uncertainty*, especially those of Figure and Number, of which Men have so clear and distinct *Ideas*. Who ever, that had a Mind to understand them, mistook the ordinary meaning of *Seven*, or *a Triangle*? And in general the least compounded *Ideas* in every kind have the least dubious names.

§ 19. *And next to them simple Modes.*

(1–2) being . . . perception,] *add.* **2–5** (2) the] **2–5** | those of **1** (3) are] **2–5** | they are **1** (3–6), which . . . mind.] **2–5** | or inconvenience of those very compounded mixed Modes; **1** (6) nor] **2–4** | and **5** (11) set] **1–2, 4–5** | to set **3** (12) which] *add.* **4–5** (17) in] **1–2, 4–5**; *om.* **3** (27–8) *those of simple* Ideas,] **2–5** | *simple Ideas*, those that are **1** (28) *or*] **1–4** | *and* **5** (29) *Ideas.*] **4–5** | *Ideas:* **2–3** | *Ideas*, and amongst them, those that are least compounded, and least removed from simple ones. **1** (31–2) And . . . names.] *add.* **2–5**

§ 20. Mixed Modes therefore, that are made up but of a few and obvious simple *Ideas*, have usually names of no very uncertain Signification. But the names of *mixed Modes*, which comprehend a great number of simple *Ideas*, are commonly of a very doubtful, and undetermined meaning, as has been shewn. The names of Substances, being annexed to *Ideas*, that are neither the real Essences, nor exact Representations of the patterns they are referred to, are liable yet to greater Imperfection and Uncertainty, especially when we come to a philosophical use of them.

§ 21. The great disorder that happens in our Names of Substances, proceeding for the most part from our want of Knowledge, and Inability to penetrate into their real Constitutions, it may probably be wondered, *Why I charge this as an Imperfection*, rather *upon our Words* than Understandings. This Exception, has so much appearance of Justice, that I think my self obliged to give a Reason, why I have followed this Method. I must confess then, that when I first began this Discourse of the Understanding, and a good while after, I had not the least Thought, that any Consideration of Words was at all necessary to it. But when having passed over the Original and Composition of our *Ideas*, I began to examine the Extent and Certainty of our Knowledge, I found it had so near a connexion with Words, that unless their force and manner of Signification were first well observed, there could be very little said clearly and pertinently concerning Knowledge: which being conversant about Truth, had constantly to do with Propositions. And though it terminated in Things, yet it was for the most part so much by the intervention of Words, that they seem'd scarce separable from our general Knowledge. At least they interpose themselves so much between our Understandings, and the Truth, which it would contemplate and apprehend, that like the *Medium* through which visible Objects pass, their Obscurity and Disorder does not seldom cast a mist before our Eyes, and impose upon our Understandings. If we consider, in the Fallacies, Men put upon themselves, as well as others, and the Mistakes in Men's Disputes and Notions, how great a part is owing to Words, and their uncertain or mistaken

§ 20. *The most doubtful are the Names of very compounded mixed Modes and Substances.*
§ 21. *Why this imperfection charged upon Words.*

(1) therefore] **2–5** | also **1** (2) uncertain] **2–5** | doubtful **1** (5) meaning . . . shewn] **2–5** | Signification, as has been shewed **1** (6) , being] **2–5** | being **1** (29) which] *add.* **4–5**

Significations, we shall have reason to think this no small obstacle in the way to Knowledge, which, I conclude we are the more carefully to be warned of, because it has been so far from being taken notice of as an Inconvenience, that the Arts of improving it have been made the business of Men's study; and obtained the Reputation of Learning and Subtilty, as we shall see in the following Chapter. But I am apt to imagine, that were the imperfections of Language, as the Instrument of Knowledge, more throughly weighed, a great many of the Controversies that make such a noise in the World, would of themselves cease; and the way to Knowledge, and, perhaps, Peace too, lie a great deal opener than it does.

§ 22. Sure I am, that the signification of Words, in all Languages, depending very much on the Thoughts, Notions, and *Ideas* of him that uses them, must unavoidably be of great uncertainty, to Men of the same Language and Country. This is so evident in the Greek Authors, that he, that shall peruse their Writings, will find, in almost every one of them, a distinct Language, though the same Words. But when to this natural difficulty in every Country, there shall be added different Countries, and remote Ages, wherein the Speakers and Writers had very different Notions, Tempers, Customs, Ornaments, and Figures of Speech, *etc.* every one of which, influenced the signification of their Words then, though to us now they are lost and unknown, *it would become us to be charitable one to another in our Interpretations or Misunderstandings of* those *ancient Writings*, which though of great concernment to us to be understood, are liable to the unavoidable difficulties of Speech, which, (if we except the Names of simple *Ideas*, and some very obvious Things) is not capable, without a constant defining the terms, of conveying the sense and intention of the Speaker, without any manner of doubt and uncertainty, to the Hearer. And in Discourses of Religion, Law, and Morality, as they are matters of the highest concernment, so there will be the greatest difficulty.

§ 23. The Volumes of Interpreters, and Commentators on the Old and New Testament, are but too manifest proofs of this. Though every thing said in the Text be infallibly true, yet the Reader may

§§ 22, 23. *This should teach us Moderation, in imposing our own Sense of old Authors.*

(2–3) carefully] **4–5** | careful **1–3** (5) obtained] **3–5** | attained **1–2** (24) *Misunderstandings*] **1–4** | *Misunderstanding* **5** (28) terms,] **1–3** | terms **4–5**

be, nay cannot chuse but be very fallible in the understanding of it. Nor is it to be wondred, that the Will of GOD, when cloathed in Words, should be liable to that doubt and uncertainty, which unavoidably attends that sort of Conveyance, when even his Son, whilst cloathed in Flesh, was subject to all the Frailties and Inconveniencies of humane Nature, Sin excepted. And we ought to magnify his Goodness, that he hath spread before all the World, such legible Characters of his Works and Providence, and given all Mankind so sufficient a light of Reason, that they to whom this written Word never came, could not (when-ever they set themselves to search) either doubt of the Being of a GOD, or of the Obedience due to Him. Since then the Precepts of Natural Religion are plain, and very intelligible to all Mankind, and seldom come to be controverted; and other revealed Truths, which are conveyed to us by Books and Languages, are liable to the common and natural obscurities and difficulties incident to Words, methinks it would become us to be more careful and diligent in observing the former, and less magisterial, positive, and imperious, in imposing our own sense and interpretations of the latter.

CHAPTER X

Of the Abuse of Words.

§ 1. BESIDES the Imperfection that is naturally in Language, and the obscurity and confusion that is so hard to be avoided in the Use of Words, there are several *wilful Faults and Neglects*, which Men are guilty of, in this way of Communication, whereby they render these signs less clear and distinct in their signification, than naturally they need to be.

§ 2. *First*, In this kind, the first and most palpable abuse is, the using of Words, without clear and distinct *Ideas*; or, which is worse, signs without any thing signified. Of these there are two sorts:

I. One may observe, in all Languages, certain Words, that if they be examined, will be found, in their first Original, and their appropriated Use, not to stand for any clear and distinct *Ideas*. These, for

§ 1. *Abuse of Words.* §§ 2, 3. *First, Words without any, or without clear* Ideas.

(23) this] **1er–5** | the **1**

the most part, the several *Sects* of Philosophy and Religion have introduced. For their Authors, or Promoters, either affecting something singular, and out of the way of common apprehensions, or to support some strange Opinions, or cover some Weakness of their Hypothesis, seldom fail to *coin* new Words, and such as, when they come to be examined, may justly be called *insignificant Terms.* For having either had no determinate Collection of *Ideas* annexed to them, when they were first invented; or at least such as, if well examined, will be found inconsistent, 'tis no wonder if afterwards, in the vulgar use of the same party, they remain empty Sounds, with little or no signification, amongst those who think it enough to have them often in their Mouths, as the distinguishing Characters of their Church, or School, without much troubling their Heads to examine, what are the precise *Ideas* they stand for. I shall not need here to heap up Instances, every one's reading and conversation will sufficiently furnish him: Or if he wants to be better stored, the great Mint-Masters of these kind of Terms, I mean the Schoolmen and Metaphysicians, (under which, I think, the disputing natural and moral Philosophers of these latter Ages, may be comprehended,) have wherewithal abundantly to content him.

§ 3. II. Others there be, who extend this abuse yet farther, who take so little care to lay by Words, which in their primary notation have scarce any clear and distinct *Ideas* which they are annexed to, that by an unpardonable negligence, they familiarly *use Words*, which the Propriety of Language has affixed to very important *Ideas*, *without any distinct meaning* at all. *Wisdom*, *Glory*, *Grace*, etc. are Words frequent enough in every Man's Mouth; but if a great many of those who use them, should be asked, what they mean by them? they would be at a stand, and not know what to answer: A plain proof, that though they have learned those Sounds, and have them ready at their Tongues end, yet there are no determined *Ideas* laid up in their Minds, which are to be expressed to others by them.

§ 4. *Men*, having been *accustomed* from their Cradles *to learn Words*, which are easily got and retained, *before they knew*, or had framed *the complex Ideas*, to which they were annexed, or which

§ 4. *Occasioned by learning Names before the* Ideas *they belong to.*

---

(4) Weakness] **1–2, 4–5** | Weaknesses **3** (7) determinate] **2–5** | determinable **1** (23) which] *add.* **4–5** (25) *Ideas*,] **2–5** | *Ideas*, they use them, I say, **1** (31) end] **5** | ends **1–4** determined] **4–5** | clear and distinct **1–3**

were to be found in the things *they* were thought to *stand* for, they *usually continue to do so* all their Lives, and without taking the pains necessary to settle in their Minds determined *Ideas*, they use their Words for such unsteady and confused Notions as they have, contenting themselves with the same Words other People use; as if their very sound necessarily carried with it constantly the same meaning. This, though Men make a shift with, in the ordinary Occurrences of Life, where they find it necessary to be understood, and therefore they make signs till they are so; Yet this insignificancy in their Words, when they come to Reason concerning either their Tenents or Interest, manifestly fills their Discourse with abundance of empty unintelligible noise and jargon, especially in moral Matters, where the Words, for the most part, standing for arbitrary and numerous Collections of *Ideas*, not regularly and permanently united in Nature, their bare Sounds are often only thought on, or at least very obscure and uncertain Notions annexed to them. Men take the Words they find in use amongst their Neighbours; and that they may not seem ignorant what they stand for, use them confidently, without much troubling their heads about a certain fixed meaning; whereby, besides the ease of it, they obtain this advantage, That as in such Discourses they seldom are in the right, so they are as seldom to be convinced, that they are in the wrong; it being all one to go about to draw those Men out of their Mistakes, who have no setled Notions, as to dispossess a Vagrant of his Habitation, who has no setled abode. This I guess to be so; and every one may observe in himself and others, whether it be, or no.

§ 5. *Secondly*, Another great abuse of Words is, *Inconstancy* in the use of them. It is hard to find a Discourse written of any Subject, especially of Controversie, wherein one shall not observe, if he read with attention, the same Words (and those commonly the most material in the Discourse, and upon which the Argument turns) used sometimes for one Collection of simple *Ideas*, and sometimes for another, which is a perfect abuse of Language, Words being intended for signs of my *Ideas*, to make them known to others, not by any natural signification, but by a voluntary imposition, 'tis plain cheat and abuse, when I make them stand sometimes for one thing, and sometimes for another; the wilful doing whereof, can be imputed to

§ 5. *Secondly, Unsteady Application of them.*

(3) determined] **4–5** | clear and distinct **1–3** (7) the] **2–5** | their **1**

nothing but great Folly, or greater dishonesty. And a Man, in his Accompts with another, may, with as much fairness, make the Characters of Numbers stand sometimes for one, and sometimes for another Collection of Unites: *v.g.* this Character 3, stand sometimes for three, sometimes for four, and sometimes for eight; as in his Discourse, or Reasoning, make the same Words stand for different Collections of simple *Ideas*. If Men should do so in their Reckonings, I wonder who would have to do with them? One who would speak thus, in the Affairs and Business of the World, and call 8 sometimes seven, and sometimes nine, as best served his Advantage, would presently have clapp'd upon him one of the two Names Men constantly are disgusted with. And yet in Arguings, and learned Contests, the same sort of proceeding passes commonly for Wit and Learning: but to me it appears a greater dishonesty, than the misplacing of Counters, in the casting up a Debt; and the cheat the greater, by how much Truth is of greater concernment and value, than money.

§ 6. *Thirdly*, Another abuse of Language is, an *affected Obscurity*, by either applying old Words, to new and unusual Significations; or introducing new and ambiguous Terms, without defining either; or else putting them so together, as may confound their ordinary meaning. Though the Peripatetick Philosophy has been most eminent in this way, yet other Sects have not been wholly clear of it. There is scarce any of them that are not cumbred with some Difficulties, (such is the imperfection of Humane Knowledge,) which they have been fain to cover with Obscurity of Terms, and to confound the Signification of Words, which, like a Mist before Peoples Eyes, might hinder their weak parts from being discovered. That *Body* and *Extension*, in common use, stand for two distinct *Ideas*, is plain to any one that will but reflect a little. For were their Signification precisely the same, it would be as proper, and as intelligible to say, the *Body of an Extension*, as *the Extension of a Body*; and yet there are those who find it necessary to confound their signification. To this abuse, and the mischiefs of confounding the

§ 6. *Thirdly, Affected Obscurity by wrong Application.*

---

(4) stand] **2, 4–5** | stands **1, 3** (8) [*2nd*] would] **5** | should **1–4**. (**Coste** 'parleroit') (9) thus,] **1–3, 5** | thus; **4** of] **1er–5** | in **1** (10) and] *add.* **4–5** (11) **Coste** 'seroit regardé comme un fou ou un méchant homme.' (12) with.] **4** | with it. **5** | with; **1–3** (14) but] **4–5** | but yet, **1–3** (30–2) For . . . *Body*;] *om.* **Coste** (31) [*1st*] as] **1–4**; *om.* **5**

Signification of Words, Logick, and the liberal Sciences, as they have been handled in the Schools, have given Reputation; and the admired Art of Disputing, hath added much to the natural imperfection of Languages, whilst it has been made use of, and fitted, to perplex the signification of Words, more than to discover the Knowledge and Truth of Things: And he that will look into that sort of learned Writings, will find the Words there much more obscure, uncertain, and undetermined in their Meaning, than they are in ordinary Conversation.

§ 7. This is unavoidably to be so, where Men's Parts and Learning, are estimated by their Skill in *Disputing*. And if Reputation and Reward shall attend these Conquests, which depend mostly on the fineness and niceties of Words, 'tis no Wonder if the Wit of Man so employ'd, should perplex, involve, and subtilize the signification of Sounds, so as never to want something to say, in opposing or defending any Question; the Victory being adjudged not to him who had Truth on his side, but the last word in the Dispute.

§ 8. This, though a very useless Skill, and that which I think the direct opposite to the ways of Knowledge, hath yet passed hitherto under the laudable and esteemed Names of *Subtlety* and *Acuteness*; and has had the applause of the Schools, and encouragement of one part of the learned Men of the World. And no wonder, since the Philosophers of old, (the disputing and wrangling Philosophers I mean, such as *Lucian* wittily, and with reason taxes,)* and the Schoolmen since, aiming at Glory and Esteem, for their great and universal Knowledge, easier a great deal to be pretended to, than really acquired, found this a good Expedient to cover their Ignorance, with a curious and unexplicable Web of perplexed Words, and procure to themselves the admiration of others, by unintelligible Terms, the apter to produce wonder, because they could not be understood: whilst it appears in all History, that these profound Doctors were no wiser, nor more useful than their Neighbours; and brought but small advantage to humane Life, or the Societies, wherein they lived: Unless the coining of new Words, where they produced no new Things to apply them to, or the perplexing or

§ 7. *Logick and Dispute has much contributed to this.* § 8. *Calling it Subtlety.*

(16) adjudged] **2er–5** | adjusted **1–2**

* Lucian, (e.g.) *Bis accusatus, Vitarum auctio, Convivium.*

obscuring the signification of old ones, and so bringing all things into question and dispute, were a thing profitable to the Life of Man, or worthy Commendation and Reward.

§ 9. For, notwithstanding these learned Disputants, these all-knowing Doctors, it was to the unscholastick Statesman, that the Governments of the World owed their Peace, Defence, and Liberties; and from the illiterate and contemned Mechanick, (a Name of Disgrace) that they received the improvements of useful Arts. Nevertheless, this artificial Ignorance, and *learned Gibberish*, prevailed mightily in these last Ages, by the Interest and Artifice of those, who found no easier way to that pitch of Authority and Dominion they have attained, than by amusing the Men of Business, and Ignorant, with hard Words, or imploying the Ingenious and Idle in intricate Disputes, about unintelligible Terms, and holding them perpetually entangled in that endless Labyrinth. Besides, there is no such way to gain admittance, or give defence to strange and absurd Doctrines, as to guard them round about with Legions of obscure, doubtful, and undefined Words. Which yet make these Retreats, more like the Dens of Robbers, or Holes of Foxes, than the Fortresses of fair Warriours: which if it be hard to get them out of, it is not for the strength that is in them, but the Briars and Thorns, and the Obscurity of the Thickets they are beset with. For Untruth being unacceptable to the Mind of Man, there is no other defence left for Absurdity, but Obscurity.

§ 10. Thus learned Ignorance, and this Art of keeping, even inquisitive Men, from true Knowledge, hath been propagated in the World, and hath much perplexed, whilst it pretended to inform the Understanding. For we see, that other well-meaning and wise Men, whose Education and Parts had not acquired that *acuteness*, could intelligibly express themselves to one another; and in its plain use, make a benefit of Language. But though unlearned Men well enough understood the Words *White* and *Black*, *etc.* and had constant Notions of the *Ideas* signified by those Words; yet there were Philosophers found, who had learning and *subtlety* enough to prove, that *Snow* was *black*; *i.e.* to prove, that *White* was *Black*. Whereby they had the Advantage to destroy the Instruments and Means of Discourse, Conversation, Instruction, and Society; whilst with great Art and *Subtlety* they did no more but perplex and confound the

§ 9. *This Learning very little benefits Society.* § 10. *But destroys the Instruments of Knowledge and Communication.*

(29) acquired] **2–5** | attained **1**

signification of Words, and thereby render Language less useful, than the real Defects of it had made it, a Gift, which the illiterate had not attained to.

§ 11. These learned Men did equally instruct Men's Understandings, and profit their Lives, as he who should alter the signification of known Characters, and, by a subtle Device of Learning, far surpassing the Capacity of the Illiterate, Dull, and Vulgar, should, in his Writing, shew, that he could put *A.* for *B.* and *D.* for *E*, *etc.* to the no small admiration and benefit of his Reader. It being as sensless to put *Black*, which is a Word agreed on to stand for one sensible *Idea*, to put it, I say, for another, or the contrary *Idea*, *i.e.* to call *Snow Black*, as to put this mark *A.* which is a Character agreed on to stand for one modification of Sound, made by a certain motion of the Organs of Speech, for *B.* which is agreed on to stand for another Modification of Sound, made by another certain motion of the Organs of Speech.

§ 12. Nor hath this mischief stopped in logical Niceties, or curious empty Speculations; it hath invaded the great Concernments of Humane Life and Society; obscured and perplexed the material Truths of Law and Divinity; brought Confusion, Disorder, and Uncertainty into the Affairs of Mankind; and if not destroyed, yet in great measure rendred useless, those two great Rules, Religion and Justice. What have the greatest part of the Comments and Disputes, upon the Laws of GOD and Man served for, but to make the meaning more doubtful, and perplex the sense? What have been the effect of those multiplied curious Distinctions, and acute Niceties, but Obscurity and Uncertainty, leaving the Words more unintelligible, and the Reader more at a loss? How else comes it to pass, that Princes, speaking or writing to their Servants, in their ordinary Commands, are easily understood; speaking to their People, in their Laws, are not so? And, as I remarked before, doth it not often happen, that a Man of an ordinary Capacity, very well understands a Text, or a Law, that he reads, till he consults an Expositor, or goes to Council; who by that time he hath done explaining them, makes the Words signifie either nothing at all, or what he pleases.

§ 11. *As useful as to confound the sound of the Letters.* § 12. *This Art has perplexed Religion and Justice.*

(20) Disorder,] **1–3** | Disorder **4–5** (21) Uncertainty] **1–3, 5** | uncertainty **4**

§ 13. Whether any by Interests of these Professions have occasioned this, I will not here examine; but I leave it to be considered, whether it would not be well for Mankind, whose concernment it is to know Things as they are, and to do what they ought; and not to spend their Lives in talking about them, or tossing Words to and fro; Whether it would not be well, I say, that the Use of Words were made plain and direct; and that Language, which was given us for the improvement of Knowledge, and bond of Society, should not be employ'd to darken Truth, and unsettle Peoples Rights; to raise Mists, and render unintelligible both Morality and Religion? Or that at least, if this will happen, it should not be thought Learning or Knowledge to do so?

§ 14. *Fourthly*, Another great *abuse of Words is, the taking them for Things*. This, though it, in some degree, concerns all Names in general; yet more particularly affects those of Substances. To this Abuse, those Men are most subject, who confine their Thoughts to any one System, and give themselves up into a firm belief of the Perfection of any received Hypothesis: whereby they come to be persuaded, that the Terms of that Sect, are so suited to the Nature of Things, that they perfectly correspond with their real Existence. Who is there, that has been bred up in the Peripatetick Philosophy, who does not think the Ten Names, under which are ranked the Ten Predicaments, to be exactly conformable to the Nature of Things? Who is there, of that School, that is not persuaded, that *substantial Forms*, *vegetative Souls*, *abhorrence of a Vacuum*, *intentional Species*, etc. are something real? These Words Men have learned from their very entrance upon Knowledge, and have found their Masters and Systems lay great Stress upon them: and therefore they cannot quit the Opinion, that they are conformable to Nature, and are the Representations of something that really exists. The *Platonists* have their *Soul of the World*, and the *Epicureans* their *endeavour towards Motion* in their Atoms, when at rest. There is scarce any Sect in Philosophy has not a distinct set of Terms, that others understand not. But yet this Gibberish, which in the weakness of Humane Understanding, serves so well to palliate Men's Ignorance, and cover their Errours, comes by familiar use amongst those of the same Tribe, to seem the most important part of

§ 13. *And ought not to pass for Learning.* § 14. *Fourthly, taking them for Things.*

(15) . To] **4–5** | : And to **1–3** (16) those] **1T-er, 2–5** | these **1**

Language, and of all other the Terms the most significant: And should *Aërial* and *Ætherial Vehicles* come once, by the prevalency of that Doctrine, to be generally received any where, no doubt those Terms would make impressions on Men's Minds, so as to establish them in the persuasion of the reality of such Things, as much as *peripatetick Forms*, and *intentional Species* have heretofore done.

§ 15. How much *names taken for Things*, are apt to *mislead the Understanding*, the attentive reading of philosophical Writers would abundantly discover; and that, perhaps, in Words little suspected of any such misuse. I shall instance in one only, and that a very familiar one. How many intricate Disputes have there been about *Matter*, as if there were some such thing really in Nature, distinct from *Body*; as 'tis evident, the Word *Matter* stands for an *Idea* distinct from the *Idea* of Body? For if the *Ideas* these two Terms stood for, were precisely the same, they might indifferently in all places be put one for another. But we see, that tho' it be proper to say, There is *one Matter of all Bodies*, one cannot say, There is *one Body of all Matters*: We familiarly say, one *Body* is bigger than another, but it sounds harsh (and I think is never used) to say, one *Matter* is bigger than another. Whence comes this then? *Viz.* from hence, that though *Matter* and *Body*, be not really distinct, but where-ever there is the one, there is the other; Yet *Matter* and *Body*, stand for two different Conceptions, whereof the one is incomplete, and but a part of the other. For *Body* stands for a solid extended figured Substance, whereof *Matter* is but a partial and more confused Conception, it seeming to me to be used for the Substance and Solidity of Body, without taking in its Extension and Figure: And therefore it is that speaking of *Matter*, we speak of it always as one, because in truth, it expresly contains nothing but the *Idea* of a solid Substance, which is every where the same, every where uniform. This being our *Idea* of *Matter*, we no more conceive, or speak of different *Matters* in the World, than we do of different Solidities; though we both conceive, and speak of different Bodies, because Extension and Figure are capable of variation. But since Solidity cannot exist without Extension, and Figure, the taking *Matter* to be

§ 15. *Instance in Matter.*

---

(1) other] **2–5** | others **1** (6) *peripatetick Forms*, and *intentional Species*] **4–5** | that peripatetick Forms **1–3** (16) another.] **5** | the other. **4** | the other: **1–3** (22) [*1st*] the] *add.* **5** (*likewise* **Coste**) (31) . This . . . *Matter*,] **4–5** | : And therefore **1–3**

the name of something really existing under that Precision, has no doubt produced those obscure and unintelligible Discourses and Disputes, which have filled the Heads and Books of Philosophers concerning *Materia prima*; which Imperfection or Abuse, how far it may concern a great many other general Terms, I leave to be considered. This, I think, I may at least say, that we should have a great many fewer Disputes in the World, if Words were taken for what they are, the Signs of our *Ideas* only, and not for Things themselves. For when we argue about *Matter*, or any the like Term, we truly argue only about the *Idea* we express by that Sound, whether that precise *Idea* agree to any thing really existing in Nature, or no. And if Men would tell, what *Ideas* they make their Words stand for, there could not be half that Obscurity or Wrangling, in the search or support of Truth, that there is.

§ 16. But whatever inconvenience follows from this mistake of Words, this I am sure, that by constant and familiar use, they charm Men into Notions far remote from the Truth of Things. 'Twould be a hard Matter, to persuade any one, that the Words which his Father or Schoolmaster, the Parson of the Parish, or such a Reverend Doctor used, signified nothing that really existed in Nature: Which, perhaps, is *none of the least Causes, that Men are so hardly drawn to quit their Mistakes*, even in Opinions purely Philosophical, and where they have no other Interest but Truth. For the Words, they have a long time been used to, remaining firm in their Minds, 'tis no wonder, that the wrong Notions annexed to them, should not be removed.

§ 17. *Fifthly*, Another *Abuse of Words, is the setting them in the place of Things, which they do or can by no means signify*. We may observe, that in the general names of Substances, whereof the nominal Essences are only known to us, when we put them into Propositions, and affirm or deny any thing about them, we do most commonly tacitly suppose, or intend, they should stand for the real Essence of a certain sort of Substances. For when a Man says *Gold is Malleable*, he means and would insinuate something more than this, that *what I call Gold is malleable*, (though truly it amounts to no more) but would have this understood, *viz.* that *Gold*; i.e. *what has the real Essence of Gold is malleable*, which amounts to thus much, that

§ 16. *This makes Errors lasting.* § 17. *Fifthly, setting them for what they cannot signifie.*

(35) though] **1, 3, 5** | tho'/ **4** | tho / **2**

Malleableness depends on, and is inseparable from the real Essence of Gold. But a Man, not knowing wherein that real Essence consists, the connexion in his Mind of Malleableness, is not truly with an Essence he knows not, but only with the Sound Gold he puts for it. Thus when we say, that *Animal rationale* is, and *Animal implume bipes latis unguibus*, is not a good definition of a Man; 'tis plain, we suppose the Name *Man* in this case to stand for the real Essence of a Species, and would signifie, that a *rational Animal* better described that real Essence, than *a two-leg'd Animal with broad Nails, and without Feathers*. For else, why might not *Plato* as properly make the Word ἄνθρωπος or *Man* stand for his complex *Idea*, made up of the *Ideas* of a Body, distinguished from others by a certain shape and other outward appearances, as *Aristotle*, make the complex *Idea*, to which he gave the Name ἄνθρωπος or *Man*, of Body, and the Faculty of reasoning join'd together; unless the Name ἄνθρωπος or *Man*, were supposed to stand for something else, than what it signifies; and to be put in the place of some other thing, than the *Idea* a Man professes he would express by it?

§ 18. 'Tis true, the names of Substances would be much more useful, and Propositions made in them much more certain, were the real Essences of Substances the *Ideas* in our Minds, which those words signified. And 'tis for want of those real Essences, that our Words convey so little Knowledge or Certainty in our Discourses about them: And therefore the Mind, to remove that Imperfection as much as it can, makes them, by a secret Supposition, to stand for a Thing, having that real Essence, as if thereby it made some nearer approaches to it. For though the Word *Man* or *Gold*, signify nothing truly but a complex *Idea* of Properties, united together in one sort of Substances: Yet there is scarce any Body in the use of these Words, but often supposes each of those names to stand for a thing having the real Essence, on which those Properties depend. Which is so far from diminishing the Imperfection of our Words, that by a plain Abuse, it adds to it, when we would make them stand for something, which not being in our complex *Idea*, the name we use, can no ways be the sign of.

§ 19. This shews us the Reason, Why in *mixed Modes* any of the *Ideas* that make the Composition of the complex one, being left out,

§ 18. *V.g. Putting them for the real Essences of Substances.* § 19. *Hence we think every change of our* Idea *in Substances, not to change the Species.*

(17) to . . . than] *add.* **2–5** (to *not in* **2–3**)

or changed, it is allowed to be another thing, *i.e.* to be of another Species, as is plain in *Chance-medly*, *Man-slaughter*, *Murther*, *Parricide*, etc. The Reason whereof is, because the complex *Idea* signified by that name, is the real, as well as nominal Essence; and there is no secret reference of that name to any other Essence, but that. But in *Substances* it is not so. For though in that called *Gold*, one puts into his complex *Idea*, what another leaves out; and *Vice Versâ*: yet Men do not usually think, that therefore the Species is changed: Because they secretly in their Minds referr that name, and suppose it annexed to a real immutable Essence of a thing existing, on which those Properties depend. He that adds to his complex *Idea* of *Gold*, that of Fixedness or Solubility in *Aqua Regia*, which he put not in it before, is not thought to have changed the Species; but only to have a more perfect *Idea*, by adding another simple *Idea*, which is always in fact, joined with those other, of which his former complex *Idea* consisted. But this reference of the name to a thing, whereof we have not the *Idea*, is so far from helping at all, that it only serves the more to involve us in Difficulties. For by this tacit reference to the real Essence of that Species of Bodies, the Word *Gold* (which by standing for a more or less perfect Collection of simple *Ideas*, serves to design that sort of Body well enough in civil Discourse) comes to have no signification at all, being put for somewhat, whereof we have no *Idea* at all, and so can signify nothing at all, when the Body it self is away. For however it may be thought all one; yet, if well considered, it will be found a quite different thing, to argue about *Gold* in name, and about a parcel of the Body it self, *v.g.* a piece of *Leaf-Gold* laid before us; though in Discourse we are fain to substitute the name for the thing.

§ 20. That which, I think, very much disposes Men to substitute their names for the real Essences of *Species*, is the supposition before mentioned, that Nature works regularly in the Production of Things, and sets the Boundaries to each of those *Species*, by giving exactly the same real internal Constitution to each individual, which we rank under one general name. Whereas any one who observes their different Qualities can hardly doubt, that many of the

§ 20. *The Cause of this Abuse, a Supposition of Nature's working always regularly.*

(2) **Coste** *gives different italicized instances from some of these, and adds an explanatory linguistic footnote.* (12) Fixedness] **5** | fixedness **4** | Fixedness, **1–3** (14–15) simple . . . fact] **4–5** | , which is always in *rerum natura* **1–3** (29) think,] **1–3** | think **4–5** (*l. below* 35) *this*] **2–4** | *the* **5**

Individuals, called by the same name, are, in their internal Constitution, as different one from another, as several of those which are ranked under different specifick Names. *This supposition*, however *that the same precise internal Constitution goes always with the same specifick name*, *makes Men forward to take* those *names for the Representatives* of those real *Essences*, though indeed they signify nothing but the complex *Ideas* they have in their Minds when they use them. So that, if I may so say, signifying one thing, and being supposed for, or put in the place of another, they cannot but, in such a kind of use, cause a great deal of Uncertainty in Men's Discourses; especially in those, who have throughly imbibed the Doctrine of *substantial Forms*, whereby they firmly imagine the several Species of Things to be determined and distinguished.

§ 21. But however preposterous and absurd it be, to make our names stand for *Ideas* we have not, or (which is all one) Essences that we know not, it being in effect to make our Words the signs of nothing; yet 'tis evident to any one, whoever so little reflects on the use Men make of their Words, that there is nothing more familiar. When a Man asks, whether this or that thing he sees, let it be a Drill, or a monstrous *Fœtus*, be a *Man*, or no; 'tis evident, the Question is not, Whether that particular thing agree to his complex *Idea*, expressed by the name *Man*: But whether it has in it the real Essence of a Species of Things, which he supposes his name *Man* to stand for. In which way of using the names of Substances, there are these false suppositions contained.

First, That there are certain precise Essences, according to which Nature makes all particular Things, and by which they are distinguished into *Species*. That every Thing has a real Constitution, whereby it is what it is, and on which its sensible Qualities depend, is past doubt: But I think it has been proved, that this makes not the distinction of *Species*, as we rank them; nor the boundaries of their names.

Secondly, This tacitly also insinuates, as if we had *Ideas* of these proposed Essences. For to what purpose else is it, to enquire whether this or that thing have the real Essence of the Species *Man*, if we did not suppose that there were such a specifick Essence known? Which yet is utterly false: And therefore such Application of names, as would make them stand for *Ideas* which we have not,

§ 21. *This Abuse contains two false suppositions.*

(38) which] *add.* **4–5**

must needs cause great Disorder in Discourses and Reasonings about them, and be a great inconvenience in our Communication by Words.

§ 22. *Sixthly*, There remains yet another more general, though, perhaps, less observed *Abuse of Words*; and that is, that Men having by a long and familiar use annexed to them certain *Ideas*, they are apt *to imagine so near and necessary a connexion between the names and the signification* they use them in, that they forwardly suppose one cannot but understand what their meaning is; and therefore one ought to acquiesce in the Words delivered, as if it were past doubt, that in the use of those common received sounds, the Speaker and Hearer had necessarily the same precise *Ideas*. Whence presuming, that when they have in Discourse used any Term, they have thereby, as it were, set before others the very thing they talk of. And so likewise taking the Words of others, as naturally standing for just what they themselves have been accustomed to apply them to, they never trouble themselves to explain their own, or understand clearly others meaning. From whence commonly proceeds Noise, and Wrangling, without Improvement or Information; whilst Men take Words to be the constant regular marks of agreed Notions, which in truth are no more but the voluntary and unsteady signs of their own *Ideas*. And yet Men think it strange, if in Discourse, or (where it is often absolutely necessary) in Dispute, one sometimes asks the meaning of their Terms: Though the Arguings one may every day observe in Conversation, make it evident, that there are few names of complex *Ideas*, which any two Men use for the same just precise Collection. 'Tis hard to name a Word, which will not be a clear instance of this. *Life* is a Term, none more familiar. Any one almost would take it for an Affront, to be asked what he meant by it. And yet if it comes in Question, whether a Plant, that lies ready formed in the Seed, have Life; whether the Embrio in an Egg before Incubation, or a Man in a Swound without Sense or Motion, be alive, or no, it is easy to perceive, that a clear distinct settled *Idea* does not always accompany the Use of so known a Word, as that of *Life* is. Some gross and confused Conceptions Men indeed ordinarily have, to which they apply the common Words of their Language, and such a loose use of their words serves them well enough in their

§ 22. *Sixthly, a Supposition that Words have a certain and evident signification.*

(8) them in] **1er–5** | in them **1** (18) Noise] **1–3, 5** | noise **4** (37) such . . . words] **4–5** | that **1–3**

ordinary Discourses and Affairs. But this is not sufficient for philosophical Enquiries. Knowledge and Reasoning require precise determinate *Ideas.* And though Men will not be so importunately dull, as not to understand what others say, without demanding an explication of their Terms; nor so troublesomely critical, as to correct others in the use of the Words they receive from them: yet where Truth and Knowledge are concerned in the Case, I know not what Fault it can be to desire the explication of Words, whose Sense seems dubious; or why a Man should be ashamed to own his Ignorance, in what Sense another Man uses his Words, since he has no other way of certainly knowing it, but by being informed. This Abuse of taking Words upon Trust, has no where spread so far, nor with so ill Effects, as amongst Men of Letters. The multiplication and obstinacy of Disputes, which has so laid waste the intellectual World, is owing to nothing more, than to this ill use of Words. For though it be generally believed, that there is great diversity of Opinions in the Volumes and Variety of Controversies, the World is distracted with; yet the most I can find, that the contending learned Men of different Parties do, in their Arguings one with another, is, that they speak different Languages. For I am apt to imagine, that when any of them quitting Terms, think upon Things, and know what they think, they think all the same: Though perhaps, what they would have, be different.

§ 23. To conclude this Consideration of the Imperfection, and Abuse of Language; the *ends of Language in our Discourse with others,* being chiefly these three: *First, To make known* one Man's Thoughts or *Ideas* to another. *Secondly,* To do it *with* as much ease and *quickness,* as is possible; and *Thirdly,* Thereby *to convey* the *Knowledge* of Things. Language is either abused, or deficient, when it fails in any of these Three.

First, Words fail in the first of these Ends, and lay not open one Man's *Ideas* to anothers view. *First,* When Men have names in their Mouths without any determined *Ideas* in their Minds, whereof they are the signs: or *Secondly,* When they apply the common received names of any Language to *Ideas,* to which the common use of that Language does not apply them: or *Thirdly,* When they apply them

§ 23. *The Ends of Language, First, To convey our* Ideas.

(1) and] **1–4** | or **5** (29) in] **1–4** | of **5** (33) determined] **4–5** clear and distinct **1–3**

very unsteadily, making them stand now for one, and by and by for another *Idea*.

§ 24. *Secondly*, Men fail of conveying their Thoughts, with all the quickness and ease that may be, when they have complex *Ideas*, without having distinct names for them. This is sometimes the Fault of the Language it self, which has not in it a Sound yet apply'd to such a Signification: and sometimes the Fault of the Man, who has not yet learn'd the name for that *Idea* he would shew another.

§ 25. *Thirdly*, There is no Knowledge of Things conveyed by Men's Words, when their *Ideas* agree not to the Reality of Things. Though it be a Defect, that has its Original in our *Ideas*, which are not so conformable to the Nature of Things, as Attention, Study, and Application might make them: Yet it fails not to extend it self to our Words too, when we use them as Signs of real Beings, which yet never had any Reality or Existence.

§ 26. *First*, He that hath Words of any Language, without distinct *Ideas* in his Mind, to which he applies them, does, so far as he uses them in Discourse, only make a noise without any Sense or Signification; and how learned soever he may seem by the use of hard Words, or learned Terms, is not much more advanced thereby in Knowledge, than he would be in Learning, who had nothing in his Study but the bare Titles of Books, without possessing the Contents of them. For all such Words, however put into Discourse, according to the right Construction of Grammatical Rules, or the Harmony of well turned Periods, do yet amount to nothing but bare Sounds, and nothing else.

§ 27. *Secondly*, He that has complex *Ideas*, without particular names for them, would be in no better a Case than a Bookseller, who had in his Ware-house Volumes, that lay there unbound, and without Titles; which he could therefore make known to others, only by shewing the loose Sheets, and communicate them only by Tale. This Man is hindred in his Discourse, for want of Words to communicate his complex *Ideas*, which he is therefore forced to make known by an enumeration of the simple ones that compose them; and so is fain often to use twenty Words, to express what another Man signifies in one.

§ 28. *Thirdly*, He that puts not constantly the same Sign for the

§ 24. *Secondly, to do it with quickness.* § 25. *Thirdly, Therewith to convey the Knowledge of Things.* §§ 26–31. *How Men's Words fail in all these.*

(29) Ware-house] **Coste** 'Boutique' (37) puts] **2–5** | uses **1** (*likewise* **Coste**)

same *Idea*, but uses the same Words sometimes in one, and sometimes in another Signification, ought to pass in the Schools and Conversation, for as fair a Man, as he does in the Market and Exchange, who sells several Things under the same Name.

§ 29. *Fourthly*, He that applies the Words of any Language to *Ideas*, different from those, to which the common use of that Country applies them, however his own Understanding may be fill'd with Truth and Light, will not by such Words be able to convey much of it to others, without defining his Terms. For however, the Sounds are such as are familiarly known, and easily enter the Ears of those who are accustomed to them; yet standing for other *Ideas* than those they usually are annexed to, and are wont to excite in the Mind of the Hearers, they cannot make known the Thoughts of him who thus uses them.

§ 30. *Fifthly*, He that hath imagined to himself Substances such as never have been, and fill'd his Head with *Ideas* which have not any correspondence with the real Nature of Things, to which yet he gives settled and defined Names, may fill his Discourse, and, perhaps, another Man's Head, with the fantastical Imaginations of his own Brain; but will be very far from advancing thereby one jot in real and true Knowledge.

§ 31. He that hath Names without *Ideas*, wants meaning in his Words, and speaks only empty Sounds. He that hath complex *Ideas* without Names for them, wants Liberty and Dispatch in his Expressions, and is necessitated to use Periphrases. He that uses his Words loosly and unsteadily, will either be not minded, or not understood. He that applies his Names to *Ideas*, different from their common use, wants Propriety in his Language, and speaks Gibberish. And he that hath *Ideas* of Substances, disagreeing with the real Existence of Things, so far wants the Materials of true Knowledge in his Understanding, and hath, instead thereof, *Chimæras*.

§ 32. In our Notions concerning Substances, we are liable to all the former Inconveniencies: *v.g.* 1. He that uses the word *Tarantula*, without having any Imagination or *Idea* of what it stands for, pro-

§ 32. *How in Substances.*

(8) much] **2–5** | one jot **1** (9) his Terms] *add.* **2–5**. (**Coste** 'ces termes') (12–13) those . . . Hearers] **2–5** | they usually make them the signs of **1** (13–14) [*2nd*] the . . . thus] **4–5** | his Thoughts who **1–3** (15–16) imagined . . . not] **4–5** | *Ideas* of Substances, which never existed, nor have **1–3** (17) yet] *add.* **4–5** (33) 1.] **1–3** (*likewise* **Coste**); *om.* **4–5**

nounces a good Word; but so long means nothing at all by it. 2. He that, in a new-discovered Country, shall see several sorts of Animals and Vegetables, unknown to him before, may have as true *Ideas* of them, as of a Horse, or a Stag; but can speak of them only by a description, till he shall either take the Names the Natives call them by, or give them Names himself. 3. He that uses the word *Body* sometimes for pure Extension, and sometimes for Extension and Solidity together, will talk very fallaciously. 4. He that gives the Name *Horse*, to that *Idea* which common usage calls *Mule*, talks improperly, and will not be understood. 5. He that thinks the Name *Centaur* stands for some real Being, imposes on himself, and mistakes Words for Things.

§ 33. In Modes and Relations generally, we are liable only to the four first of these Inconveniencies, (*viz.*) 1. I may have in my Memory the Names of Modes, as *Gratitude*, or *Charity*, and yet not have any precise *Ideas* annexed in my Thoughts to those Names. 2. I may have *Ideas*, and not know the Names that belong to them; *v.g.* I may have the *Idea* of a Man's drinking, till his Colour and Humour be altered, till his Tongue trips, and his Eyes look red, and his Feet fail him; and yet not know, that it is to be called *Drunkenness*. 3. I may have the *Ideas* of Vertues, or Vices, and Names also, but apply them amiss: *v.g.* When I apply the Name *Frugality* to that *Idea* which others call and signify by this sound, *Covetousness*. 4. I may use any of those names with inconstancy. 5. But in Modes and Relations, I cannot have *Ideas* disagreeing to the Existence of Things: for Modes being complex *Ideas*, made by the Mind at pleasure; and Relation being but my way of considering, or comparing two Things together, and so also an *Idea* of my own making, these *Ideas* can scarce be found to disagree with any Thing existing; since they are not in the Mind, as the Copies of Things regularly made by Nature, nor as Properties inseparably flowing from the internal Constitution or Essence of any Substance; but, as it were, Patterns lodg'd in my Memory, with names annexed to them, to denominate Actions and Relations by, as they come to exist. But the mistake is commonly in my giving a wrong name to my Conceptions; and so using Words in a different sense from other People, I am not understood, but am thought to have wrong *Ideas* of them,

§ 33. *How in Modes and Relations.*

(5) Names] **3–5** | Name **1–2** (6) Names] **4–5** | one **1–3**

when I give wrong Names to them. Only if I put in my *Ideas* of mixed Modes or Relations, any inconsistent *Ideas* together, I fill my Head also with *Chimæras*; since such *Ideas*, if well examined, cannot so much as exist in the Mind, much less any real Being, be ever denominated from them.

§ 34. Since Wit and Fancy finds easier entertainment in the World, than dry Truth and real Knowledge, *figurative Speeches*, and allusion in Language, will hardly be admitted, as *an* imperfection or *abuse* of it. I confess, in Discourses, where we seek rather Pleasure and Delight, than Information and Improvement, such Ornaments as are borrowed from them, can scarce pass for Faults. But yet, if we would speak of Things as they are, we must allow, that all the Art of Rhetorick, besides Order and Clearness, all the artificial and figurative application of Words Eloquence hath invented, are for nothing else but to insinuate wrong *Ideas*, move the Passions, and thereby mislead the Judgment; and so indeed are perfect cheat: And therefore however laudable or allowable Oratory may render them in Harangues and popular Addresses, they are certainly, in all Discourses that pretend to inform or instruct, wholly to be avoided; and where Truth and Knowledge are concerned, cannot but be thought a great fault, either of the Language or Person that makes use of them. What, and how various they are, will be superfluous here to take notice; the Books of Rhetorick which abound in the world, will instruct those, who want to be informed: Only I cannot but observe, how little the preservation and improvement of Truth and Knowledge, is the Care and Concern of Mankind; since the Arts of Fallacy are endow'd and preferred. 'Tis evident how much Men love to deceive, and be deceived, since Rhetorick, that powerful instrument of Error and Deceit, has its established Professors, is publickly taught, and has always been had in great Reputation: And, I doubt not, but it will be thought great boldness, if not brutality in me, to have said thus much against it. *Eloquence*, like the fair Sex, has too prevailing Beauties in it, to suffer it self ever to be spoken against. And 'tis in vain to find fault with those Arts of Deceiving, wherein Men find pleasure to be Deceived.

§ 34. *Seventhly, Figurative Speech also an Abuse of Language.*

(19) or] **5** | and **1–4** (22–3) will be superfluous here] **4–5** | I shall not trouble my self **1–3** (24) instruct] **2–5** | inform **1** (27). 'Tis evident] **4–5** | ; and 'tis plain **1–3** (28–9) Rhetorick . . . Deceit] **2–5** | the great Art of Deceit and Errour, Rhetorick I mean **1** (*l. below* 35) *an*] **2, 4–5** | *in* **3**

CHAPTER XI

Of the Remedies of the foregoing Imperfections and Abuses.

§ 1. THE natural and improved Imperfections of Language, we have seen above at large: and Speech being the great Bond that holds Society together, and the common Conduit, whereby the Improvements of Knowledge are conveyed from one Man, and one Generation to another, it would well deserve our most serious Thoughts, to consider what *Remedies* are to be found *for these Inconveniences* above-mentioned.

§ 2. I am not so vain to think, that any one can pretend to attempt the perfect *Reforming* the *Languages* of the world, no not so much as that of his own Country, without rendring himself ridiculous. To require that Men should use their words constantly in the same sense, and for none but determined and uniform *Ideas*, would be to think, that all Men should have the same Notions, and should talk of nothing but what they have clear and distinct *Ideas* of. Which is not to be expected by any one, who hath not vanity enough to imagine he can prevail with Men, to be very knowing, or very silent. And he must be very little skill'd in the world, who thinks that a voluble Tongue, shall accompany only a good Understanding; or that Men's talking much or little, shall hold proportion only to their Knowledge.

§ 3. But though the Market and Exchange must be left to their own ways of Talking, and Gossippings not be robb'd of their ancient Privilege: though the Schools, and Men of Argument would perhaps take it amiss to have any thing offered, to abate the length, or lessen the number of their Disputes; yet, methinks those, *who* pretend *seriously* to *search after*, or maintain *Truth*, should think themselves obliged to study, how they might deliver themselves without Obscurity, Doubtfulness, or Equivocation, to which Men's Words are naturally liable, if care be not taken.

§ 4. For he that shall well consider the *Errors* and Obscurity, the Mistakes and Confusion, that is *spread in the World by an ill use of*

§ 1. *They are worth seeking.* § 2. *Are not easy.* § 3. *But yet necessary to Philosophy.* § 4. *Misuse of Words the cause of great Errors.*

(11) constantly] **4–5** | , all **1–3** (12) none but determined] **4–5** | clear, distinct, **1** (17) very] *add.* **5** (*likewise* **Coste**) (22) Gossippings not be] **2–5** | Gossippings, not **1**

Words, will find some reason to doubt, whether Language, as it has been employ'd, has contributed more to the improvement or hindrance of Knowledge amongst Mankind. How many are there, that when they would think on Things, fix their Thoughts only on Words, especially when they would apply their Minds to Moral Matters? And who then can wonder, if the result of such Contemplations and Reasonings, about little more than Sounds, whilst the *Ideas* they annexed to them, are very confused, or very unsteady, or perhaps none at all; who can wonder, I say, that such Thoughts and Reasonings, end in nothing but Obscurity and Mistake, without any clear Judgment or Knowledge?

§ 5. This Inconvenience, in an ill use of Words, Men suffer in their own private Meditations: but much more manifest are the Disorders which follow from it, in Conversation, Discourse, and Arguings with others. For Language being the great Conduit, whereby Men convey their Discoveries, Reasonings, and Knowledge, from one to another, he that makes an ill use of it, though he does not corrupt the Fountains of Knowledge, which are in Things themselves; yet he does, as much as in him lies, break or stop the Pipes, whereby it is distributed to the publick use and advantage of Mankind. He that uses Words without any clear and steady meaning, What does he but lead himself and others into Errors? And he that designedly does it, ought to be looked on as an Enemy to Truth and Knowledge. And yet, who can wonder, that all the Sciences and Parts of Knowledge, have been so over-charged with obscure and equivocal Terms, and insignificant and doubtful Expressions, capable to make the most attentive or quick-sighted, very little, or not at all the more Knowing or Orthodox; since Subtilty, in those who make Profession to teach or defend Truth, hath passed so much for a Vertue: A Vertue, indeed, which consisting, for the most part, in nothing but the fallacious and illusory use of *obscure* or *deceitful Terms*, is only fit to *make Men* more *conceited* in their Ignorance, and *obstinate* in their Errors.

§ 6. Let us look into the Books of Controversy of any kind, there we shall see, that the effect of obscure, unsteady, or equivocal Terms, is nothing but noise and wrangling about Sounds, without convincing or bettering a Man's Understanding. For if the *Idea* be

§ 5. *Obstinacy*. § 6. *And Wrangling*.

(34) Controversy] **2–5**| Controversies **1**

not agreed on, betwixt the Speaker and Hearer, for which the Words stand, the Argument is not about Things, but Names. As often as such a Word, whose Signification is not ascertained betwixt them, comes in use, their Understandings have no other Object wherein they agree, but barely the Sound, the Things, that they think on at that time as expressed by that Word, being quite different.

§ 7. Whether a *Bat* be a *Bird*, or no, is not a question, whether a Bat be another Thing than indeed it is, or have other Qualities than indeed it has, for that would be extremely absurd to doubt of: But the question is, 1. Either between those that acknowledged themselves to have but imperfect *Ideas* of one or both of those sorts of Things, for which these Names are supposed to stand; and then it is a real Enquiry, concerning the Nature of a *Bird*, or a *Bat*, to make their yet imperfect *Ideas* of it more complete, by examining, whether all the simple *Ideas*, to which combined together, they both give the name *Bird*, be all to be found in a *Bat*: But this is a question only of Enquirers, (not Disputers,) who neither affirm, nor deny, but examine: Or, 2. It is a question between Disputants; whereof the one affirms, and the other denies, that a *Bat* is a *Bird*. And then the Question is barely about the signification of one, or both these Words; in that they not having both the same complex *Ideas*, to which they give these two Names, one holds, and t'other denies, that these two names may be affirmed one of another. Were they agreed in the Signification of these two Names, it were impossible they should dispute about them. For they would presently and clearly see, (were that adjusted between them,) whether all the simple *Ideas*, of the more general name *Bird*, were found in the complex *Idea* of a *Bat*, or no; and so there could be no doubt, whether a *Bat* were a *Bird*, or no. And here I desire it may be considered, and carefully examined, whether the greatest part of the Disputes in the World, are not meerly Verbal, and about the Signification of Words; and whether if the terms they are made in, were defined, and reduced in their Signification (as they must be, where they signify any thing) to determined Collections of the simple *Ideas* they do or should stand for, those Disputes would not

§ 7. *Instance Bat and Bird.*

---

(10) acknowledged] **1–2, 4–5** | acknowledge **3** (*likewise* **Coste**) (32) whether] **4–5** | that **1–3** (34) determined Collections of] *add.* **4–5** (35) do or should] *add.* **4–5.** (*Not in* **Coste**) not] **1–2, 4–5**; *om.* **3**

end of themselves, and immediately vanish. I leave it then to be considered, what the learning of Disputation is, and how well they are employed for the advantage of themselves, or others, whose business is only the vain ostentation of Sounds; *i.e.* those who spend their Lives in Disputes and Controversies. When I shall see any of those Combatants, strip all his Terms of Ambiguity and Obscurity, (which every one may do in the Words he uses himself) I shall think him a Champion for Knowledge, Truth, and Peace, and not the Slave of Vain-glory, Ambition, or a Party.

§ 8. *To remedy the Defects of Speech* before-mentioned, to some degree, and to prevent the Inconveniencies that follow from them, I imagine, the observation of these following Rules may be of use, till some body better able shall judge it worth his while, to think more maturely on this Matter, and oblige the World with his Thoughts on it.

First, A Man should take care *to use no word without a signification*, no Name without an *Idea* for which he makes it stand. This Rule will not seem altogether needless, to any one who shall take the pains to recollect how often he has met with such Words; as *Instinct*, *Sympathy*, and *Antipathy*, etc. in the Discourse of others, so made use of, as he might easily conclude, that those that used them, had no *Ideas* in their Minds to which they applied them; but spoke them only as Sounds, which usually served instead of Reasons, on the like occasions. Not but that these Words, and the like, have very proper Significations in which they may be used; but there being no natural connexion between any Words, and any *Ideas*, these, and any other, may be learn'd by rote, and pronounced or writ by Men, who have no *Ideas* in their Minds, to which they have annexed them, and for which they make them stand; which is necessary they should, if Men would speak intelligibly even to themselves alone.

§ 9. *Secondly*, 'Tis not enough a Man *uses* his *Words as signs of* some *Ideas*; those *Ideas* he annexes them to, if they be *simple* must be

§ 8. *First, Remedy to use no Word without an* Idea. § 9. *Secondly, to have distinct* Ideas *annexed to them in Modes.*

---

(7) himself)] **4–5** | himself, as far as he has clear and distinct Notions to which he applies them,) **1–3** (11) Inconveniencies] **1–2, 4** | Inconveniences **3, 5** (24–5) very . . . used] **2–5** | and may be used, in very proper Significations **1** (26) connexion] **2er–5** | connexions **1–2** (30) would] **2–5** | should **1** (33) if they be *simple*] *add.* **4–5**

clear and distinct; if *complex* must be *determinate*, *i.e.* the precise Collection of simple *Ideas* settled in the Mind, with that Sound annexed to it, as the sign of that precise determined Collection, and no other. This is very necessary in Names of Modes, and especially moral Words; which having no settled Objects in Nature, from whence their *Ideas* are taken, as from their Original, are apt to be very confused. *Justice* is a Word in every Man's Mouth, but most commonly with a very undetermined loose signification: Which will always be so, unless a Man has in his Mind a distinct comprehension of the component parts, that complex *Idea* consists of; and if it be decompounded, must be able to resolve it still on, till he at last comes to the simple *Ideas*, that make it up: And unless this be done, a Man makes an ill use of the Word, let it be *Justice*, for example, or any other. I do not say, a Man needs stand to recollect, and make this Analysis at large, every time the word *Justice* comes in his way: But this, at least, is necessary, that he have so examined the signification of that Name, and settled the *Idea* of all its Parts in his Mind, that he can do it when he pleases. If one, who makes his complex *Idea* of *Justice*, to be such a treatment of the Person or Goods of another, as is according to Law, hath not a clear and distinct *Idea* what *Law* is, which makes a part of his complex *Idea* of Justice, 'tis plain, his *Idea* of Justice it self, will be confused and imperfect. This exactness will, perhaps, be judged very troublesome: and therefore most Men will think, they may be excused from settling the complex *Ideas* of mixed Modes so precisely in their Minds. But yet I must say, till this be done, it must not be wondred, that they have a great deal of Obscurity and Confusion in their own Minds, and a great deal of wrangling in their Discourses with others.

§ 10. In the Names of *Substances*, for a right use of them, something more is required than barely *determined Ideas*: In these *the Names must also be conformable to Things*, as they exist: But of this, I shall have occasion to speak more at large by and by. This Exactness is absolutely necessary in Enquiries after philosophical

§ 10. *And conformable in Substances.*

(1–4) clear . . . other.] **4–5** | *clear and distinct:* which in complex *Ideas*, is the knowing the particular ones that make that composition, of which, if any one be again complex, 'tis the knowing also the precise Collection, that is united in each, and so till we come to simple ones. **1–3** (6) Original] **5** | Originals **1–4** (27) that] *add.* **4–5** (29) the . . . them] **4–5** | *Substances* **1–3** (30–1) barely . . . *Names*] **4–5** | the distinct *Ideas* their Names stand for, they **1–3** (*l. below* 33) *And*] **4–5** | *And distinct and* **2–3** (*likewise* **Coste**)

Knowledge, and in Controversies about Truth. And though it would be well too, if it extended it self to common Conversation, and the ordinary Affairs of Life; yet I think, that is scarce to be expected. Vulgar Notions suit vulgar Discourses: and both, though confused enough, yet serve pretty well the Market, and the Wake. Merchants and Lovers, Cooks and Taylors, have Words wherewithal to dispatch their ordinary Affairs; and so, I think, might Philosophers and Disputants too, if they had a Mind to understand, and to be clearly understood.

§ 11. *Thirdly*, 'Tis not enough that Men have *Ideas*, determined *Ideas*, for which they make these signs stand; but they *must* also take care to *apply their Words*, as near as may be, *to such* Ideas *as common use has annexed them to*. For Words, especially of Languages already framed, being no Man's private possession, but the common measure of Commerce and Communication, 'tis not for any one, at pleasure, to change the Stamp they are current in; nor alter the *Ideas* they are affixed to; or at least when there is a necessity to do so, he is bound to give notice of it. Men's Intentions in speaking are, or at least should be, to be understood; which cannot be without frequent Explanations, Demands, and other the like incommodious Interruptions, where Men do not follow common Use. Propriety of Speech, is that which gives our Thoughts entrance into other Men's Minds with the greatest ease and advantage: and therefore deserves some part of our Care and Study, especially in the names of moral Words. The proper signification and use of Terms is best to be learned from those, who in their Writings and Discourses, appear to have had the clearest Notions, and apply'd to them their Terms with the exactest choice and fitness. This way of using a Man's Words, according to the Propriety of the Language, though it have not always the good Fortune to be understood: Yet most commonly leaves the blame of it on him, who is so unskilful in the Language he speaks, as not to understand it, when made use of, as it ought to be.

§ 12. *Fourthly*. But because common use has not so visibly annexed any signification to Words, as to make Men know always

§ 11. *Thirdly, Propriety.* § 12. *Fourthly, To make known their meaning.*

---

(1) in] *add.* **2–5** (10) determined] **4–5** | clear and distinct **1–3** (20) frequent] **2–5** | the frequent **1** (25–6) . The . . . learned] **4–5** | , whose proper use is to be learn'd **1–3** (26–7) Discourses,] **1–3, 5** | Discourses; **4** (28) exactest] **4–5** | best **1–3** fitness] **4–5** | Clearness **1–3**

certainly what they precisely stand for: And because Men in the Improvement of their Knowledge, come to have *Ideas* different from the vulgar and ordinary received ones, for which they must either make new Words, (which Men seldom venture to do, for fear of being thought guilty of Affectation, or Novelty,) or else *must* use old ones, in a new Signification. Therefore after the Observation of the foregoing Rules, it is sometimes necessary for the ascertaining the signification of Words, to *declare their Meaning*; where either common Use has left it uncertain and loose; (as it has in most Names of very complex *Ideas*) or where a Man uses them in a Sense any way peculiar to himself; or where the Term, being very material in the Discourse, and that upon which it chiefly turns, is liable to any Doubtfulness, or Mistake.

§ 13. As the *Ideas*, Men's Words stand for, are of different sorts: so the way of making known the *Ideas*, they stand for, when there is Occasion, is also different. For though defining be thought the proper *way, to make known the proper signification of Words*; yet there be some Words, that will not be defined, as there be others, whose precise Meaning cannot be made known, but by Definition: and, perhaps, a third, which partake somewhat of both the other, as we shall see in the names of simple *Ideas*, Modes, and Substances.

§ 14. *First*, When a Man makes use of the *name* of *any simple* Idea, which he perceives is not understood, or is in danger to be mistaken, he is obliged by the Laws of Ingenuity, and the end of Speech, to declare his Meaning, and make known what *Idea* he makes it stand for. This, as has been shewn, cannot be done by Definition: and therefore, when a synonymous Word fails to do it, there is but one of these ways left. *First*, Sometimes the *naming the Subject, wherein that simple* Idea *is* to be found, will make its name be understood by those, who are acquainted with that Subject, and know it by that name. So to make a Country-man understand what *Feuillemorte* Colour signifies, it may suffice to tell him, 'tis the Colour of wither'd Leaves falling in *Autumn*. *Secondly*, But the only sure way of making known the signification of the name of any simple *Idea*, is *by presenting to his Senses that Subject, which may produce it in his Mind*, and make him actually have the *Idea*, that Word stands for.

§ 13. *And that three ways.* § 14. *First, In simple* Ideas *by synonymous terms or shewing.*

(10–11) or . . . himself;] **1–4**; *om.* **5** (25) his] **5** | its **1–4** (26) shewn] **2–5** | shewed **1**. (**Coste** *adds marginal reference to III. iv. 6–11.*)

§ 15. *Secondly, Mixed Modes*, especially those belonging to Morality, being most of them such Combinations of *Ideas*, as the Mind puts together of its own choice; and whereof there are not always standing Patterns to be found existing, the signification of their Names cannot be made known, as those of simple *Ideas*, by any shewing: but in recompence thereof, may be perfectly and exactly *defined*. For they being Combinations of several *Ideas*, that the Mind of Man has arbitrarily put together, without reference to any Archetypes, Men may, if they please, exactly know the *Ideas*, that go to each Composition, and so both use these Words in a certain and undoubted Signification, and perfectly declare, when there is Occasion, what they stand for. This, if well considered, would lay great blame on those, who make not their Discourses about moral things very clear and distinct. For since the precise signification of the names of mixed Modes, or which is all one, the real Essence of each Species, is to be known, they being not of Nature's, but Man's making, it is a great Negligence and Perverseness, to discourse of moral Things with Uncertainty and Obscurity, which is much more pardonable in treating of natural Substances, where doubtful Terms are hardly to be avoided, for a quite contrary Reason, as we shall see by and by.

§ 16. Upon this ground it is, that I am bold to think, that *Morality is capable of Demonstration*, as well as Mathematicks: Since the precise real Essence of the Things moral Words stand for, may be perfectly known; and so the Congruity, or Incongruity of the Things themselves, be certainly discovered, in which consists perfect Knowledge. Nor let any one object, that the names of Substances are often to be made use of in Morality, as well as those of Modes, from which will arise Obscurity. For as to Substances, when concerned in moral Discourses, their divers Natures are not so much enquir'd into, as supposed; *v.g.* when we say that *Man is subject to Law*: We mean nothing by *Man*, but a corporeal rational Creature: What the real Essence or other Qualities of that Creature are in this Case, is no way considered. And therefore, whether a Child or Changeling be a *Man* in a physical Sense, may amongst the Naturalists be as disputable as it will, it concerns not at all the *moral Man*, as I may call him, which is this immoveable unchange-

§ 15. *Secondly, in mixed Modes by definition.* § 16. *Morality capable of Demonstration.*

---

(3) there] **2–5** | they **1** (10) Composition] **1–4** | Compositions **5** (11) , when] **2–5** | when **1** (18) much more] **1–4** | / more **5** (24) , or] **1–3, 5** | or, **4**

able *Idea, a corporeal rational Being*. For were there a Monkey, or any other Creature to be found, that had the use of Reason, to such a degree, as to be able to understand general Signs, and to deduce Consequences about general *Ideas*, he would no doubt be subject to Law, and, in that Sense, be a *Man*, how much soever he differ'd in Shape from others of that Name. The Names of Substances, if they be used in them, as they should, can no more disturb Moral, than they do Mathematical Discourses: Where, if the Mathematicians speak of a *Cube* or *Globe* of *Gold*, or any other Body, he has his clear setled *Idea*, which varies not, though it may, by mistake, be applied to a particular Body, to which it belongs not.

§ 17. This I have here mentioned by the bye, to shew of what Consequence it is for Men, in their names of mixed Modes, and consequently, in all their moral Discourses, to define their Words when there is Occasion: Since thereby moral Knowledge may be brought, to so great Clearness and Certainty. And it must be great want of Ingenuity, (to say no worse of it) to refuse to do it: Since a *Definition is the only way, whereby the precise Meaning of moral Words can be known*; and yet a way, whereby their Meaning may be known *certainly*, and without leaving any room for any contest about it. And therefore the Negligence or Perverseness of Mankind, cannot be excused, if their Discourses in Morality be not much more clear, than those in natural Philosophy: since they are about *Ideas* in the Mind, which are none of them false or disproportionate; they having no external Beings for *Archetypes* which they are referr'd to, and must correspond with. It is far easier for Men to frame in their Minds an *Idea*, which shall be the Standard to which they will give the Name *Justice*, with which Pattern so made, all Actions that agree shall pass under that denomination, than, having seen *Aristides*, to frame an *Idea*, that shall in all things be exactly like him, who is as he is, let Men make what *Idea*, they please of him. For the one, they need but know the combination of *Ideas*, that are put together within in their own Minds; for the other, they must enquire into the whole Nature, and abstruse hidden Constitution, and various Qualities of a Thing existing without them.

§ 17. *Definitions can make moral Discourses clear.*

---

(10) mistake,] **1–3** | mistake **4–5** (24) or] **5** | nor **1–4** (29) than, . . ., to] **2–5** | than . . . to **1** (31) *Idea*] **2–5** | Notion, or *Idea* **1** (32–3) combination . . . Minds;] **2–5** | *Ideas* they frame within themselves: **1** (34) various] *add.* **2–5**

§ 18. Another Reason that makes the *defining of mixed Modes* so necessary, *especially of moral Words*, is what I mentioned a little before, *viz.* That it is *the only way whereby the signification of the most of* them can be known with certainty. For the *Ideas* they stand for, being for the most part such, whose component Parts no where exist together, but scattered and mingled with others, it is the Mind alone that collects them, and gives them the Union of one *Idea*: and it is only by Words, enumerating the several simple *Ideas* which the Mind has united, that we can make known to others, what their Names stand for; the assistance of the senses in this case not helping us, by the proposal of sensible Objects, to shew the *Ideas*, which our names of this kind stand for, as it does often in the names of sensible simple *Ideas*, and also to some degree in those of Substances.

§ 19. *Thirdly*, *For the explaining* the signification of *the Names of Substances* as they stand for the *Ideas* we have of their distinct Species, both the fore-mentioned ways, *viz.* of *shewing and defining*, *are requisite*, in many cases, to be made use of. For there being ordinarily in each Sort some leading Qualities, to which we suppose the other *Ideas*, which make up our complex *Idea* of that Species, annexed, we forwardly give the specifick Name to that thing, wherein that characteristical Mark is found, which we take to be the most distinguishing *Idea* of that Species. These leading or characteristical (as I may so call them) *Ideas*, in the sorts of Animals and Vegetables, is (as has been before remarked, *Ch.* VI. § 29. and *Ch.* IX. § 15.) mostly Figure, and in inanimate Bodies Colour, and in some both together. Now,

§ 20. These *leading sensible Qualities* are those, which make *the chief Ingredients of our Specifick Ideas*, and consequently the most observable and unvariable part in the Definitions of our specifick Names, as attributed to Sorts *of Substances* coming under our Knowledge. For though the Sound *Man*, in its own Nature, be as apt to signifie a complex *Idea* made up of Animality and Rationality, united

§ 18. *And is the only way.* § 19. *Thirdly, in Substances, by shewing and defining.* § 20. Ideas *of the leading Qualities of Substances, are best got by shewing.*

---

(3) , *viz.*] **4–5** | ; and that is **1–3**. (**Coste** 'que c'est') (10–13) [*1st*] the . . . of] **2–5** | and not by any application to the Senses, as we can do in **1** (13–14) those of] *add.* **2–5** (20) *Ideas*] *add.* **4–5** make] **4–5** | makes **1–3** (21–2) forwardly . . . which] **4–5** | give the Name to some Quality, or *Idea*, which is the most observable, and **1–3** (25) , *Ch.* VI . . . § 15.] *add.* **4–5**. (*In* **Coste**, *this is added in a marginal note.*) (29–30) most . . . the] **2–5** | best **1**

in the same Subject, as to signify any other combination; yet used as a mark to stand for a sort of Creatures we count of our own kind, perhaps the outward shape is as necessary to be taken into our complex *Idea*, signified by the word *Man*, as any other we find in it. And therefore why *Plato*'s *Animal implume Bipes latis unguibus*, should not be as good a Definition of the Name *Man*, standing for that sort of Creatures, will not be easy to shew: for 'tis the Shape, as the leading Quality, that seems more to determine that Species, than a Faculty of Reasoning, which appears not at first, and in some never. And if this be not allow'd to be so, I do not know how they can be excused from Murther, who kill monstrous Births, (as we call them,) because of an unordinary Shape, without knowing whether they have a Rational Soul, or no; which can be no more discerned in a well-formed, than ill-shaped Infant, as soon as born. And who is it has informed us, that a Rational Soul can inhabit no Tenement, unless it has just such a sort of Frontispiece, or can join it self to, and inform no sort of Body, but one that is just of such an outward Structure?

§ 21. Now *these leading Qualities, are best made known by shewing*, and can hardly be made known otherwise. For the shape of an *Horse*, or *Cassuary*, will be but rudely and imperfectly imprinted on the Mind by Words, the sight of the Animals doth it a thousand times better: And the *Idea* of the particular Colour of *Gold*, is not to be got by any description of it, but only by the frequent exercise of the Eyes about it; as is evident in those who are used to this Metal, who will frequently distinguish true from counterfeit, pure from adulterate, by the sight, where others, (who have as good Eyes, but yet, by use, have not got the precise nice *Idea* of that peculiar Yellow) shall not perceive any difference. The like may be said of those other simple *Ideas*, peculiar in their kind to any Substance; for which precise *Ideas*, there are no peculiar Names. The particular ringing sound there is in *Gold*, distinct from the sound of other Bodies, has no particular Name annexed to it, no more than the particular Yellow, that belongs to that Metal.

§ 22. But because many of the simple *Ideas* that make up our specifick *Ideas* of Substances, are Powers, which lie not obvious to

§ 21. Ideas *of the leading Qualities of Substances, are best got by shewing.* § 22. *The* Ideas *of their Powers best by Definition.*

(3) the] **2–5** | , the **1** (18) Structure?] **1–3** (*likewise* **Coste**) | Structure. **4–5**
(25) ; as is evident] **1–3** (*likewise* **Coste**) | , as is evident; **4–5**

our Senses in the Things as they ordinarily appear; therefore, *in the signification of our Names of Substances, some part of the signification will be better made known, by enumerating those simple* Ideas, *than in shewing the Substance it self.* For he that, to the yellow shining Colour of *Gold* got by sight, shall, from my enumerating them, have the *Ideas* of great Ductility, Fusibility, Fixedness, and Solubility, in *Aqua Regia*, will have a perfecter *Idea* of *Gold*, than he can have by seeing a piece of *Gold*, and thereby imprinting in his Mind only its obvious Qualities. But if the formal Constitution of this shining, heavy, ductil Thing (from whence all these its Properties flow) lay open to our Senses, as the formal Constitution, or Essence of a Triangle does, the signification of the word *Gold*, might as easily be ascertained, as that of *Triangle*.

§ 23. Hence we may take notice, how much the Foundation of all *our Knowledge of corporeal Things, lies in our Senses*. For how Spirits, separate from Bodies, (whose Knowledge and *Ideas* of these Things, is certainly much more perfect than ours) know them, we have no Notion, no *Idea* at all. The whole extent of our Knowledge, or Imagination, reaches not beyond our own *Ideas*, limited to our ways of Perception. Though yet it be not to be doubted, that Spirits of a higher rank than those immersed in Flesh, may have as clear *Ideas* of the radical Constitution of Substances, as we have of a Triangle, and so perceive how all their Properties and Operations flow from thence: but the manner how they come by that Knowledge, exceeds our Conceptions.

§ 24. But though Definitions will serve to explain the Names of Substances, as they stand for our *Ideas*; yet they leave them not without great imperfection, as they stand for Things. For our Names of Substances being not put barely for our *Ideas*, but being made use of ultimately to represent Things, and so are put in their place, their signification must agree with the Truth of Things, as well as with Men's *Ideas*. And therefore in Substances, we are not always to rest in the ordinary complex *Idea*, commonly received as the signification of that Word, but must go a little farther, and enquire into the Nature and Properties of the Things themselves, and thereby perfect, as much as we can, our *Ideas* of their distinct

§ 23. *A Reflection on the Knowledge of Spirits.* § 24. Ideas *also of Substances must be conformable to Things.*

(34) must] **4–5** | to **1–3**

Species; or else learn them from such as are used to that sort of Things, and are experienced in them. For since 'tis intended their Names should stand for such Collections of simple *Ideas*, as do really exist in Things themselves, as well as for the complex *Idea* in other Men's Minds, which in their ordinary acceptation they stand for: therefore *to define their Names right, natural History is to be enquired into*; and their Properties are, with care and examination, to be found out. For it is not enough, for the avoiding Inconveniencies in Discourses and Arguings about natural Bodies and substantial Things, to have learned, from the Propriety of the Language, the common but confused, or very imperfect *Idea*, to which each Word is applied, and to keep them to that *Idea* in our use of them: but we must, by acquainting our selves with the History of that sort of Things, rectify and settle our complex *Idea*, belonging to each specifick Name; and in discourse with others, (if we find them mistake us) we ought to tell, what the complex *Idea* is, that we make such a Name stand for. This is the more necessary to be done by all those, who search after Knowledge, and philosophical Verity, in that Children being taught Words whilst they have but imperfect Notions of Things, apply them at random, and without much thinking, and seldom frame determined *Ideas* to be signified by them. Which Custom, (it being easy, and serving well enough for the ordinary Affairs of Life and Conversation) they are apt to continue, when they are Men: And so begin at the wrong end, learning Words first, and perfectly, but make the Notions, to which they apply those Words afterwards, very overtly. By this means it comes to pass, that Men speaking the proper Language of their Country, *i.e.* according to Grammar-Rules of that Language, do yet speak very improperly of Things themselves; and by their arguing one with another, make but small progress in the discoveries of useful Truths, and the Knowledge of Things, as they are to be found in themselves, and not in our Imaginations; and it matters not much, for the improvement of our Knowledge, how they are call'd.

§ 25. It were therefore to be wished, That Men, versed in physical Enquiries, and acquainted with the several sorts of natural

§ 25. *Not easy to be made so.*

---

(14) Things,] **1–3** | things **4–5** (21–2) , and . . . them.] **4–5** | or framing clear distinct *Ideas*; **1–3**

Bodies, would set down those simple *Ideas*, wherein they observe the Individuals of each sort constantly to agree. This would remedy a great deal of that confusion, which comes from several Persons, applying the same Name to a Collection of a smaller, or greater number of sensible Qualities, proportionably as they have been more or less acquainted with, or accurate in examining the Qualities of any sort of Things, which come under one denomination. But a Dictionary of this sort, containing, as it were, a Natural History, requires too many hands, as well as too much time, cost, pains, and sagacity, ever to be hoped for; and till that be done, we must content our selves with such Definitions of the Names of Substances, as explain the sense Men use them in. And 'twould be well, where there is occasion, if they would afford us so much. This yet is not usually done; but Men talk to one another, and dispute in Words, whose meaning is not agreed between them, out of a mistake, that the signification of common Words, are certainly established, and the precise *Ideas*, they stand for, perfectly known; and that it is a shame to be ignorant of them. Both which Suppositions are false: no Names of complex *Ideas* having so setled determined Significations, that they are constantly used for the same precise *Ideas*. Nor is it a shame for a Man not to have a certain Knowledge of any thing, but by the necessary ways of attaining it; and so it is no discredit not to know, what precise *Idea* any Sound stands for in another Man's Mind, without he declare it to me, by some other way than barely using that Sound, there being no other way, without such a Declaration, certainly to know it. Indeed, the necessity of Communication by Language, brings Men to an agreement in the signification of common Words, within some tolerable latitude, that may serve for ordinary Conversation: and so a Man cannot be supposed wholly ignorant of the *Ideas*, which are annexed to Words by common Use, in a Language familiar to him. But common Use, being but a very uncertain Rule, which reduces it self at last to the *Ideas* of particular Men, proves often but a very variable Standard. But though such a Dictionary, as I have above mentioned, will require too much time, cost, and pains, to be hoped for in this Age; yet, methinks, it is not unreasonable to propose, that Words standing for Things, which are known and distinguished by their outward shapes, should be expressed by little Draughts and Prints made of them. A Vocabulary made after this fashion, would,

(35) cost,] **1–3** | cost **4–5**

perhaps with more ease, and in less time, teach the true signification of many Terms, especially in Languages of remote Countries or Ages, and settle truer *Ideas* in Men's Minds of several Things, whereof we read the Names in ancient Authors, than all the large and laborious Comments of learned Criticks. Naturalists, that treat of Plants and Animals, have found the benefit of this way: And he that has had occasion to consult them, will have reason to confess, that he has a clearer *Idea* of *Apium*, or *Ibex* from a little Print of that Herb, or Beast, than he could have from a long Definition of the Names of either of them. And so, no doubt, he would have of *Strigil* and *Sistrum*, if instead of a *Curry-comb*, and *Cymbal*, which are the English Names Dictionaries render them by, he could see stamp'd in the Margin, small Pictures of these Instruments, as they were in use amongst the Ancients. *Toga*, *Tunica*, *Pallium*, are Words easily translated by *Gown*, *Coat*, and *Cloak*: but we have thereby no more true *Ideas* of the Fashion of those Habits amongst the *Romans*, than we have of the Faces of the Taylors who made them. Such things as these, which the Eye distinguishes by their shapes, would be best let into the Mind by Draughts made of them, and more determine the signification of such Words, than any other Words set for them, or made use of to define them. But this only by the bye.

§ 26. *Fifthly*, If Men will not be at the pains to declare the meaning of their Words, and Definitions of their Terms are not to be had; yet this is the least that can be expected, that in all Discourses, wherein one Man pretends to instruct or convince another, he should *use the same Word constantly in the same sense*: If this were done, (which no body can refuse, without great disingenuity) many of the Books extant might be spared; many of the Controversies in Dispute would be at an end; several of those great Volumes, swollen with ambiguous Words, now used in one sense, and by and by in another, would shrink into a very narrow compass; and many of the Philosophers (to mention no other,) as well as Poets Works, might be contained in a Nut-shell.

§ 27. But after all, the provision of Words is so scanty in respect of that infinite variety of Thoughts, than Men, wanting Terms to

§ 26. *Fifthly, by Constancy in their signification.* § 27. *When the variation is to be explain'd.*

(8) clearer] **1–4** | clear **5** (25) [*1st*] that] **1–4**; *om.* **5** (33) other] **2–5** | others **1** (35) the . . . is] **2–5** | Words are **1** (36) of Thoughts] **2–5** | is in Mens Thoughts **1**

suit their precise Notions, will, notwithstanding their utmost caution, be forced often to use the same Word, in somewhat different Senses. And though in the continuation of a Discourse, or the pursuit of an Argument, there be hardly room to digress into a particular Definition, as often as a Man varies the signification of any Term; yet the import of the Discourse will, for the most part, if there be no designed fallacy, sufficiently lead candid and intelligent Readers, into the true meaning of it: but where that is not sufficient to guide the Reader, there it concerns the Writer to explain his meaning, and shew in what sense he there uses that Term.

(1) Notions] **1–4, W** | Notion **5**

BOOK IV

CHAPTER I

Of Knowledge in General.

§ 1. SINCE *the Mind*, in all its Thoughts and Reasonings, hath no other immediate Object but its own *Ideas*, which it alone does or can contemplate, it is evident, that our Knowledge is only conversant about them.

§ 2. *Knowledge* then seems to me to be nothing but *the perception of the connexion and agreement, or disagreement and repugnancy of any of our Ideas.* In this alone it consists. Where this Perception is, there is Knowledge, and where it is not, there, though we may fancy, guess, or believe, yet we always come short of Knowledge. For when we know that *White is not Black*, what do we else but perceive, that these two *Ideas* do not agree? When we possess our selves with the utmost security of the Demonstration, that *the three Angles of a Triangle are equal to two right ones*, What do we more but perceive, that Equality to two right ones, does necessarily agree to, and is inseparable from the three Angles of a Triangle?

§ 3. But to understand a little more distinctly, wherein this agreement or disagreement consists, I think we may reduce it all to these four sorts:

1. *Identity*, or *Diversity*.
2. *Relation.*
3. *Co-existence*, or *necessary connexion.*
4. *Real Existence.*

§ 4. *First*, As to the first sort of Agreement or Disagreement, *viz. Identity*, or *Diversity*. 'Tis the first Act of the Mind, when it has any

§ 1. *Our Knowledge conversant about our* Ideas. § 2. *Knowledge is the Perception of the Agreement or Disagreement of two* Ideas. § 3. *This Agreement fourfold.* § 4. *First, of Identity or Diversity.*

(14) necessarily] **1–4** | necessary **5** (15) Triangle?] **5** *adds, in a footnote, a quotation from Locke's* Second Letter to the Bishop of Worcester, *pp. 83, etc.*; *prefaced by* 'The placing of Certainty, as Mr. *Locke* does in the Perception of the Agreement or Disagreement of our Ideas, the Bishop of *Worcester* suspects may be of dangerous Consequence to that Article of Faith, which he has endeavoured to defend; to which Mr. *Locke* answers,'.

Sentiments or *Ideas* at all, to perceive its *Ideas*, and so far as it perceives them, to know each what it is, and thereby also to perceive their difference, and that one is not another. This is so absolutely necessary, that without it there could be no Knowledge, no Reasoning, no Imagination, no distinct Thoughts at all. By this the Mind clearly and infallibly perceives each *Idea* to agree with it self, and to be what it is; and all distinct *Ideas* to disagree, *i.e.* the one not to be the other: And this it does without any pains, labour, or deduction; but at first view, by its natural power of Perception and Distinction. And though Men of Art have reduced this into those general Rules, *What is, is; and it is impossible for the same thing to be, and not to be*, for ready application in all cases, wherein there may be occasion to reflect on it; yet it is certain, that the first exercise of this Faculty, is about particular *Ideas*. A Man infallibly knows, as soon as ever he has them in his Mind that the *Ideas* he calls *White* and *Round*, are the very *Ideas* they are, and that they are not other *Ideas* which he calls *Red* or *Square*. Nor can any Maxim or Proposition in the World make him know it clearer or surer than he did before, and without any such general Rule. This then is the first agreement, or disagreement, which the Mind perceives in its *Ideas*; which it always perceives at first sight: And if there ever happen any doubt about it, 'twill always be found to be about the Names, and not the *Ideas* themselves, whose Identity and Diversity will always be perceived, as soon and as clearly as the *Ideas* themselves are, nor can it possibly be otherwise.

§ 5. *Secondly*, The next sort of Agreement, or Disagreement, the Mind perceives in any of its *Ideas*, may, I think, be called *Relative*, and is nothing but *the Perception of the Relation between any two Ideas*, of what kind soever, whether Substances, Modes, or any other. For since all distinct *Ideas* must eternally be known not to be the same, and so be universally and constantly denied one of another, there could be no room for any positive Knowledge at all, if we could not perceive any Relation between our *Ideas*, and find out the Agreement or Disagreement, they have one with another, in several ways the Mind takes of comparing them.

§ 6. *Thirdly*, The third sort of Agreement, or Disagreement to be found in our *Ideas*, which the Perception of the Mind is employ'd

§ 5. *Secondly, Relative.* § 6. *Thirdly, of Co-existence.*

(8) any] **1–4**; *om.* **5** (19) and] **2–5** | or **1**

about, is *Co-existence*, or *Non-co-existence* in the same Subject; and this belongs particularly to Substances. Thus when we pronounce concerning *Gold*, that it is fixed, our Knowledge of this Truth amounts to no more but this, that fixedness, or a power to remain in the Fire unconsumed, is an *Idea*, that always accompanies, and is join'd with that particular sort of Yellowness, Weight, Fusibility, Malleableness, and Solubility in *Aqua Regia*, which make our complex *Idea*, signified by the word *Gold.*

§ 7. *Fourthly*, The fourth and last sort is, that of *actual real Existence* agreeing to any *Idea*. Within these four sorts of Agreement or Disagreement, is, I suppose contained all the Knowledge we have, or are capable of: For all the Enquiries that we can make, concerning any of our *Ideas*, all that we know, or can affirm concerning any of them, is, That it is, or is not the same with some other; that it does, or does not always co-exist with some other *Idea* in the same Subject; that it has this or that Relation to some other *Idea*; or that it has a real existence without the Mind. Thus *Blue is not Yellow*, is of Identity. *Two Triangles upon equal Basis, between two Parallels are equal*, is of Relation. *Iron is susceptible of magnetical Impressions*, is of Co-existence, *GOD is*, is of real Existence. Though Identity and Co-existence are truly nothing but Relations, yet they are so peculiar ways of Agreement, or Disagreement of our *Ideas*, that they deserve well to be considered as distinct Heads, and not under Relation in general; since they are so different grounds of Affirmation and Negation, as will easily appear to any one, who will but reflect on what is said in several places of this Essay. I should now proceed to examine the several degrees of our Knowledge, but that it is necessary first, to consider the different acceptations of the word *Knowledge*.

§ 8. There are several ways wherein the Mind is possessed of Truth; each of which is called *Knowledge*.

1. There is *actual Knowledge*, which is the present view the Mind has of the Agreement, or Disagreement of any of its *Ideas*, or of the Relation they have one to another.

2. A Man is said to know any Proposition, which having been once laid before his Thoughts, he evidently perceived the Agreement,

§ 7. *Fourthly, of real Existence.* § 8. *Knowledge actual or habitual.*

(6) that] **1–2, 4–5** | the **3**

or Disagreement of the *Ideas* whereof it consists; and so lodg'd it in his Memory, that whenever that Proposition comes again to be reflected on, he, without doubt or hesitation, embraces the right side, assents to, and is certain of the Truth of it. This, I think, one may call *habitual Knowledge*: And thus a Man may be said to know all those Truths, which are lodg'd in his Memory, by a foregoing clear and full perception, whereof the Mind is assured past doubt, as often as it has occasion to reflect on them. For our finite Understandings being able to think, clearly and distinctly, but on one thing at once, if Men had no Knowledge of any more than what they actually thought on, they would all be very ignorant: And he that knew most, would know but one Truth, that being all he was able to think on at one time.

§ 9. Of habitual Knowledge, there are also, vulgarly speaking, two degrees:

First, The one is of *such Truths laid up in the Memory, as whenever they occur to the Mind, it actually perceives the Relation is between those Ideas*. And this is in all those Truths, whereof we have an *intuitive Knowledge*, where the *Ideas* themselves, by an immediate view, discover their Agreement or Disagreement one with another.

Secondly, The other is of *such Truths, whereof the Mind having been convinced, it retains the Memory of the Conviction, without the Proofs*. Thus a Man that remembers certainly, that he once perceived the Demonstration, that the three Angles of a Triangle are equal to two right ones, is certain that he knows it, because he cannot doubt of the truth of it. In his adherence to a Truth, where the Demonstration, by which it was at first known, is forgot, though a Man may be thought rather to believe his Memory, than really to know, and this way of entertaining a Truth seem'd formerly to me like something between Opinion and Knowledge, a sort of Assurance which exceeds bare Belief, for that relies on the Testimony of another; Yet upon a due examination I find it comes not short of

§ 9. *Habitual Knowledge two-fold.*

(14) speaking,] **1–3, 5** | speaking **4** (25) certain that he knows] **4–5** | commonly allow'd to know **1–3** (26–9) In . . . like] **4–5** | But yet having forgot the Demonstration, strictly speaking, he rather believes his Memory, than knows the thing; or rather it is **1–3** (26) his] **5** | this **4**. (**Coste** 'en adherant') (31) which] **4–5** | that **1–3** for that] **4–5** | which **1–3** (*likewise* **Coste**) (32)–530(19); Yet . . . shews,] **4–5** | , and yet comes short of perfect Knowledge. For Knowledge consisting in a clear Perception of the Relation of any two *Ideas*, either by an immediate *juxta*-Position, as in intuitive Knowledge; or by the intervention of other *Ideas*, which do immediately discover their Relation one to another, as in

perfect certainty, and is in effect true Knowledge. That which is apt to mislead our first Thoughts into a mistake in this Matter is, that the Agreement or Disagreement of the *Ideas* in this Case is not perceived, as it was at first, by an actual view of all the intermediate *Ideas* whereby the Agreement or Disagreement of those in the Proposition was at first perceived; but by other intermediate *Ideas*, that shew the Agreement or Disagreement of the *Ideas* contained in the Proposition whose certainty we remember. For Example in this Proposition, that the three Angles of a Triangle are equal to two right ones, one, who has seen and clearly perceived the Demonstration of this Truth, knows it to be true, when that Demonstration is gone out of his Mind; so that at present it is not actually in view, and possibly cannot be recollected: But he knows it in a different way, from what he did before. The Agreement of the two *Ideas* join'd in that Proposition is perceived, but it is by the intervention of other *Ideas* than those which at first produced that Perception. He remembers, *i.e.* he knows (for remembrance is but the reviving of some past knowledge) that he was once certain of the truth of this Proposition, that the three Angles of a Triangle are equal to two right ones. The immutability of the same relations between the same immutable things, is now the *Idea* that shews him, that if the three Angles of a Triangle were once equal to two right ones, they will always be equal to two right ones. And hence he comes to be certain, that what was once true in the case is always true; what *Ideas* once agreed will always agree; and consequently what he once knew to be true he will always know to be true, as long as he can remember that he once knew it. Upon this ground it is, that particular demonstrations in Mathematicks afford general Knowledge. If then the Perception that the same *Ideas* will eternally have the same Habitudes and Relations be not a sufficient ground of Knowledge, there could be no knowledge of general Propositions in Mathematicks, for no mathematical Demonstration would be any other than particular: And when a man had demonstrated any Proposition concerning one Triangle or Circle, his Knowledge would not reach beyond that particular

Demonstration, the Mind cannot, in strictness, be said to have so much as an habitual Knowledge, where it has not an habitual View of the Proofs; where it has not such a Memory of the Demonstration, that it can, when that Proposition is again recall'd to the Mind, perceive the connexion of those *Ideas*, by the intervention of such other *Ideas*, whose immediate connexion, or relation one to [one to **1–2** | to one **3**] another, shew the relation of the Extremes. And hence it is, **1–3**

Diagram. If he would extend it farther, he must renew his Demonstration in another instance, before he could know it to be true in another like Triangle, and so on: by which means one could never come to the knowledge of any general Propositions. No Body, I think, can deny that Mr. *Newton* certainly knows any Proposition, that he now at any time reads in his Book, to be true, though he has not in actual view that admirable Chain of intermediate *Ideas*, whereby he at first discovered it to be true. Such a Memory as that, able to retain such a train of Particulars, may be well thought beyond the reach of humane Faculties. When the very Discovery, Perception, and laying together that wonderful connection of *Ideas* is found to surpass most Readers Comprehension. But yet 'tis evident, the Author himself knows the Proposition to be true, remembring he once saw the connection of those *Ideas*, as certainly as he knows such a Man wounded another, remembring that he saw him run him through. But because the Memory is not always so clear as actual Perception, and does in all Men more or less decay in length of time, this amongst other Differences is one, which shews, that *demonstrative Knowledge*, is much more imperfect than *intuitive*, as we shall see in the following Chapter.

CHAPTER II

Of the Degrees of our Knowledge.

§ 1. ALL our Knowledge consisting, as I have said, in the view the Mind has of its own *Ideas*, which is the utmost Light and greatest Certainty, we with our Faculties, and in our way of Knowledge are capable of, it may not be amiss, to consider a little the degrees of its Evidence. The different clearness of our Knowledge seems to me to lie in the different way of Perception, the Mind has of the Agreement, or Disagreement of any of its *Ideas*. For if we will reflect on our own ways of Thinking, we shall find, that sometimes the Mind perceives the Agreement or Disagreement of two *Ideas* immediately

§ 1. *Intuitive.*

(1) farther,] **5** | farther/ **4** (5) think,] **5** | think **4** (6) Book] **Coste$_2$** *adds in a note* 'Intitulé *Principia Mathematica Philosophiae Naturalis.*' (11) Perception,] **5** | Perception/ **4** (19) *v.* 528(32), n.

by themselves, without the intervention of any other: And this, I think, we may call *intuitive Knowledge*. For in this, the Mind is at no pains of proving or examining, but perceives the Truth, as the Eye doth light, only by being directed toward it. Thus the Mind perceives, that *White* is not *Black*, That a *Circle* is not a *Triangle*, That *Three* are more than *Two*, and equal to *One* and *Two*. Such kind of Truths, the Mind perceives at the first sight of the *Ideas* together, by bare *Intuition*, without the intervention of any other *Idea*; and this kind of Knowledge is the clearest, and most certain, that humane Frailty is capable of. This part of Knowledge is irresistible, and like the bright Sun-shine, forces it self immediately to be perceived, as soon as ever the Mind turns its view that way; and leaves no room for Hesitation, Doubt, or Examination, but the Mind is presently filled with the clear Light of it. 'Tis on this *Intuition*, that depends all the Certainty and Evidence of all our Knowledge, which Certainty every one finds to be so great, that he cannot imagine, and therefore not require a greater: For a Man cannot conceive himself capable of a greater Certainty, than to know that any *Idea* in his Mind is such, as he perceives it to be; and that two *Ideas*, wherein he perceives a difference, are different, and not precisely the same. He that demands a greater Certainty than this, demands he knows not what, and shews only that he has a Mind to be a Sceptick, without being able to be so. Certainty depends so wholly on this Intuition, that in the next degree of *Knowledge*, which I call *Demonstrative*, this intuition is necessary in all the Connexions of the intermediate *Ideas*, without which we cannot attain Knowledge and Certainty.

§ 2. The next degree of Knowledge is, where the Mind perceives the Agreement or Disagreement of any *Ideas*, but not immediately. Though where-ever the Mind perceives the Agreement or Disagreement of any of its *Ideas*, there be certain Knowledge; Yet it does not always happen, that the Mind sees that Agreement or Disagreement, which there is between them, even where it is discoverable; and in that case, remains in Ignorance, and at most, gets no farther than a probable conjecture. The Reason why the Mind cannot always perceive presently the Agreement or Disagreement of two *Ideas* is, because those *Ideas*, concerning whose Agreement or

§ 2. *Demonstrative.*

(11) the] **1–4**; *om.* **5** (34) [*2nd*] and] **4–5** | or **1–3** (*likewise* **Coste**)

Disagreement the Enquiry is made, cannot by the Mind be so put together, as to shew it. In this Case then, when the Mind cannot so bring its *Ideas* together, as by their immediate Comparison, and as it were Juxta-position, or application one to another, to perceive their Agreement or Disagreement, it is fain, by the Intervention of other *Ideas* (one or more, as it happens) to discover the Agreement or Disagreement, which it searches; and this is that which we call *Reasoning*. Thus the Mind being willing to know the Agreement or Disagreement in bigness, between the three Angles of a Triangle, and two right ones, cannot by an immediate view and comparing them, do it: Because the three Angles of a Triangle cannot be brought at once, and be compared with any other one, or two Angles; and so of this the Mind has no immediate, no intuitive Knowledge. In this Case the Mind is fain to find out some other Angles, to which the three Angles of a Triangle have an Equality; and finding those equal to two right ones, comes to know their Equality to two right ones.

§ 3. Those intervening *Ideas*, which serve to shew the Agreement of any two others, are called *Proofs*; and where the Agreement or Disagreement is by this means plainly and clearly perceived, it is called *Demonstration*, it being *shewn* to the Understanding, and the Mind made see that it is so. A quickness in the Mind to find out these intermediate *Ideas*, (that shall discover the Agreement or Disagreement of any other,) and to apply them right, is, I suppose, that which is called *Sagacity*.

§ 4. *This Knowledge by intervening Proofs*, though it be certain, yet the evidence of it is *not* altogether *so clear* and bright, nor the assent so ready, *as* in *intuitive* Knowledge. For though in *Demonstration*, the Mind does at last perceive the Agreement or Disagreement of the *Ideas* it considers; yet 'tis not without pains and attention: There must be more than one transient view to find it. A steddy application and pursuit is required to this Discovery: And there must be a Progression by steps and degrees, before the Mind can in this way arrive at Certainty, and come to perceive the Agreement or Repugnancy between two *Ideas* that need Proofs and the Use of Reason to shew it.

§ 5. *Another difference between intuitive and demonstrative Knowledge*, is, that though in the latter all doubt be removed, when by the

§ 3. *Depends on Proofs.* § 4. *But not so easy.* § 5. *Not without precedent doubt.*

(12) other] **1–4**; *om.* **5**

Intervention of the intermediate *Ideas*, the Agreement or Disagreement is perceived; yet before the Demonstration there was a doubt, which in intuitive Knowledge cannot happen to the Mind that has its Faculty of Perception left to a degree capable of distinct *Ideas*, no more than it can be a doubt to the Eye, (that can distinctly see White and Black,) Whether this Ink, and this Paper be all of a Colour. If there be Sight in the Eyes, it will at first glimpse, without Hesitation, perceive the Words printed on this Paper, different from the Colour of the Paper: And so if the Mind have the Faculty of distinct Perception, it will perceive the Agreement or Disagreement of those *Ideas* that produce intuitive Knowledge. If the Eyes have lost the Faculty of seeing, or the Mind of perceiving, we in vain enquire after the quickness of Sight in one, or clearness of Perception in the other.

§ 6. 'Tis true, the Perception, produced by *Demonstration*, is also very clear; yet it is often with a great abatement of that evident lustre and full assurance, that always accompany that which I call *intuitive*; like a Face reflected by several Mirrors one to another, where as long as it retains the similitude and agreement with the Object, it produces a Knowledge; but 'tis still in every successive reflection with a lessening of that perfect Clearness and Distinctness, which is in the first, till at last, after many removes, it has a great mixture of Dimness, and is not at first Sight so knowable, especially to weak Eyes. Thus it is with Knowledge, made out by a long train of Proofs.

§ 7. Now, *in every step Reason makes in demonstrative Knowledge, there is an intuitive Knowledge* of that Agreement or Disagreement, it seeks, with the next intermediate *Idea*, which it uses as a Proof: For if it were not so, that yet would need a Proof. Since without the Perception of such Agreement or Disagreement, there is no Knowledge produced: If it be perceived by it self, it is intuitive Knowledge: If it cannot be perceived by it self, there is need of some intervening *Idea*, as a common measure to shew their Agreement or Disagreement. By which it is plain, that every step in Reasoning, that produces Knowledge, has intuitive Certainty; which when the

§ 6. *Not so clear.* § 7. *Each step must have intuitive Evidence.*

(14) Perception] **Coste** *adds in a footnote*: 'Ce mot se prend ici pour une Faculté, et c'est dans ce sens qu'on l'a pris au Liv. II. Ch. IXme. intitulé, *De la Perception.*' (16) yet] **5** | but yet **1–4**. (**Coste** 'mais') it] **1–2, 4–5**; *om.* **3** (20) in every successive] **2–5** | every **1** (22) , till at last, after] **2–5** | ; till in **1** (34) . By] **2–5** | , by **1**

Mind perceives, there is no more required, but to remember it to make the Agreement or Disagreement of the *Ideas*, concerning which we enquire, visible and certain. So that to make any thing a *Demonstration*, it is necessary to perceive the immediate Agreement of the intervening *Ideas*, whereby the Agreement or Disagreement of the two *Ideas* under Examination (whereof the one is always the first, and the other the last in the Account) is found. This intuitive Perception of the Agreement or Disagreement of the intermediate *Ideas*, in each Step and Progression of the *Demonstration*, must also be carried exactly in the Mind, and a Man must be sure that no part is left out; which because in long Deductions, and the use of many Proofs, the Memory does not always so readily and exactly retain: therefore it comes to pass, that this is more imperfect than intuitive Knowledge, and Men embrace often Falshoods for Demonstrations.

§ 8. The necessity of this intuitive Knowledge, in each step of scientifical or demonstrative Reasoning, gave occasion, I imagine, to that *mistaken Axiom, that all Reasoning was ex præcognitis et præconcessis*; which how far it is mistaken, I shall have occasion to shew more at large, where I come to consider Propositions, and particularly those Propositions, which are called Maxims; and to shew that 'tis by a mistake, that they are supposed to be the foundations of all our Knowledge and Reasonings.

§ 9. It has been generally taken for granted, that Mathematicks alone are capable of demonstrative certainty: But to have such an agreement or disagreement, as may intuitively be perceived, being, as I imagine, not the privilege of the *Ideas* of *Number*, *Extension*, and *Figure* alone, it may possibly be the want of due method, and application in us; and not of sufficient evidence in things, that Demonstration has been thought to have so little to do in other parts of Knowledge, and been scarce so much as aim'd at by any but Mathematicians. For whatever *Ideas* we have, wherein the Mind can perceive the immediate agreement or disagreement that is between them, there the Mind is capable of intuitive Knowledge;

§ 8. *Hence the mistake*, ex præcognitis, et præconcessis. § 9. *Demonstration not limited to quantity.*

---

(14) Falshoods] **1–4** | Falshood **5** (18) mistaken] **5** | a mistake **1–4**. (**Coste** 'de faux') (23–31) It . . . Mathematicians.] **2–5** (. . . Mathematicians: **2–3**) | It is *not* only Mathematicks, or the *Ideas alone of Number*, *Extension*, *and Figure*, that are *capable of Demonstration*, no more than it is these *Ideas* alone, and their Modes, that are capable of Intuition: **1** (25) agreement] **2–3** | Agreement **4–5**

and where it can perceive the agreement or disagreement of any two *Ideas*, by an intuitive perception of the agreement or disagreement they have with any intermediate *Ideas*, there the Mind is capable of Demonstration, which is not limited to *Ideas* of Extension, Figure, Number, and their Modes.

§ 10. The Reason why it has been generally sought for, and supposed to be only in those, I imagine, has been, not only the general usefulness of those Sciences; But because, in comparing their Equality or Excess, the Modes of Numbers have every the least difference very clear and perceivable: and though in Extension, every the least Excess is not so perceptible; yet the Mind has found out ways, to examine and discover demonstratively the just equality of two Angles, or Extensions, or Figures, and both these, *i.e.* Numbers and Figures, can be set down, by visible and lasting marks, wherein the *Ideas* under consideration are perfectly determined, which for the most part they are not, where they are marked only by Names and Words.

§ 11. But in other simple *Ideas*, whose Modes and Differences are made, and counted by degrees, and not quantity, we have not so nice and accurate a distinction of their differences, as to perceive, or find ways to measure their just Equality or the least Differences. For those other simple *Ideas*, being appearances or sensations, produced in us, by the Size, Figure, Number, and Motion of minute Corpuscles singly insensible, their different degrees also depend upon the variation of some, or all of those Causes; which since it cannot be observed by us in Particles of Matter, whereof each is too subtile to be perceived, it is impossible for us to have any exact Measures of the different degrees of these simple *Ideas*. For supposing the Sensation or *Idea* we name *Whiteness*, be produced in us by a certain number of Globules, which having a verticity about their own Centres, strike upon the *Retina* of the Eye, with a certain degree of Rotation, as well as progressive Swiftness; it will hence easily follow, that the more the superficial parts of any Body are so ordered, as to reflect the greater number of Globules of light, and to give them that proper Rotation, which is fit to produce this Sensation of White in us, the more White will that Body appear,

§§ 10–13. *Why it has been so thought.*

(4–5) Figure, Number, and] **2–5** | or Figure, or Number, or **1** (15–17) , wherein . . . Words] *add.* **4–5** (17) only by] **5** | by only **4** (21) or] **1–4, W** | of **5**

that, from an equal space sends to the *Retina* the greater number of such Corpuscles, with that peculiar sort of Motion. I do not say, that the nature of Light consists in very small round Globules, nor of Whiteness, in such a texture of parts as gives a certain Rotation to these Globules, when it reflects them; for I am not now treating physically of Light, or Colours: But this, I think, I may say, that I cannot (and I would be glad any one would make intelligible that he did) conceive how Bodies without us, can any ways affect our Senses, but by the immediate contact of the sensible Bodies themselves, as in Tasting and Feeling, or the impulse of some insensible Particles coming from them, as in Seeing, Hearing, and Smelling; by the different impulse of which Parts, caused by their different Size, Figure, and Motion, the variety of Sensations is produced in us.

§ 12. Whether then they be Globules, or no; or whether they have a Verticity about their own Centres, that produce the *Idea* of *Whiteness* in us, this is certain, that the more Particles of Light are reflected from a Body, fitted to give them that peculiar Motion, which produces the Sensation of Whiteness in us; and possibly too, the quicker that peculiar Motion is, the whiter does the Body appear, from which the greater number are reflected, as is evident in the same piece of Paper put in the Sun-beams, in the Shade, and in a dark Hole; in each of which, it will produce in us the *Idea* of Whiteness in far different degrees.

§ 13. Not knowing therefore what number of Particles, nor what Motion of them is fit to produce any precise degree of *Whiteness*, we cannot demonstrate the certain Equality of any two degrees of *Whiteness*, because we have no certain Standard to measure them by, nor Means to distinguish every the least real difference, the only help we have being from our Senses, which in this point fail us. But where the difference is so great, as to produce in the Mind clearly distinct *Ideas*, whose differences can be perfectly retained, there these *Ideas* of Colours, as we see in different kinds, as Blue and Red, are as capable of Demonstration, as *Ideas* of Number and Extension. What I have here said of *Whiteness* and Colours, I think, holds true in all secondary Qualities and their Modes.

§ 14. These two, (*viz.*) Intuition and Demonstration, are the degrees of our Knowledge; whatever comes short of one of these,

§ 14. *Sensitive Knowledge of particular Existence.*

(15) Centres] **1–3** | Centers **4–5** (19) that] **2–5** | the **1** (35) secondary] **2–5** | secundaries **1**

with what assurance soever embraced, is but Faith, or Opinion, but not Knowledge, at least in all general Truths. There is, indeed, another *Perception* of the Mind, employ'd about *the particular existence of finite Beings* without us; which going beyond bare probability, and yet not reaching perfectly to either of the foregoing degrees of certainty, passes under the name of Knowledge. There can be nothing more certain, than that the *Idea* we receive from an external Object is in our Minds; this is intuitive Knowledge. But whether there be any thing more than barely that *Idea* in our Minds, whether we can thence certainly inferr the existence of any thing without us, which corresponds to that *Idea*, is that, whereof some Men think there may be a question made, because Men may have such *Ideas* in their Minds, when no such Thing exists, no such Object affects their Senses. But yet here, I think, we are provided with an Evidence, that puts us past doubting: For I ask any one, Whether he be not invincibly conscious to himself of a different Perception, when he looks on the Sun by day, and thinks on it by night; when he actually tastes Wormwood, or smells a Rose, or only thinks on that Savour, or Odour? We as plainly find the difference there is between any *Idea* revived in our Minds by our own Memory, and actually coming into our Minds by our Senses, as we do between any two distinct *Ideas*. If any one say, a Dream may do the same thing, and all these *Ideas* may be produced in us, without any external Objects, he may please to dream that I make him this Answer, 1. That 'tis no great matter, whether I remove his Scruple, or no: Where all is but Dream, Reasoning and Arguments are of no use, Truth and Knowledge nothing. 2. That I believe he will allow a very manifest difference between dreaming of being in the Fire, and being actually in it. But yet if he be resolved to appear so sceptical, as to maintain, that what I call being actually in the Fire, is nothing but a Dream; and that we cannot thereby certainly know, that any such thing as Fire actually exists without us: I answer, That we certainly finding, that Pleasure or Pain follows upon the application of certain Objects to us, whose Existence we perceive, or dream that we perceive, by our Senses, this certainty is as great as our Happiness, or Misery, beyond which, we have no concernment to know, or to be. So that, I think, we may add to the two former sorts of *Knowledge*, this also, of the existence of particular

(4) bare] **1–2, 4–5** | her **3** (26) is] **1–4** | this **5** Reasoning] **1–3, 5** | reasoning **4** (29) the] **5** | a **1–4** (36) Misery,] **4–5** | Misery; **1–3**

external Objects, by that perception and Consciousness we have of the actual entrance of *Ideas* from them, and allow these *three degrees of Knowledge*, viz. *Intuitive*, *Demonstrative*, *and Sensitive*: in each of which, there are different degrees and ways of Evidence and Certainty.

§ 15. But since our Knowledge is founded on, and employ'd about our *Ideas* only, will it not follow from thence, that it is conformable to our *Ideas*; and that where our *Ideas* are clear and distinct, or obscure and confused, our Knowledge will be so too? To which I answer, No: For our Knowledge consisting in the perception of the Agreement, or Disagreement of any two *Ideas*, its clearness or obscurity, consists in the clearness or obscurity of that Perception, and not in the clearness or obscurity of the *Ideas* themselves: *v.g.* a Man that has as clear *Ideas* of the Angles of a Triangle, and of Equality to two right ones, as any Mathematician in the World, may yet have but a very obscure Perception of their Agreement, and so have but a very obscure Knowledge of it. But *Ideas*, which by reason of their Obscurity or otherwise, are confused, cannot produce any clear or distinct Knowledge; because as far as any *Ideas* are confused, so far the Mind cannot perceive clearly, whether they agree or disagree. Or to express the same thing in a way less apt to be misunderstood. He that hath not determined the *Ideas* to the Words he uses, cannot make Propositions of them, of whose Truth he can be certain.

CHAPTER III

Of the Extent of Humane Knowledge.

§ 1. KNOWLEDGE, as has been said, lying in the Perception of the Agreement, or Disagreement, of any of our *Ideas*, it follows from hence, That,

First, We can have *Knowledge* no farther than we have *Ideas*.

§ 15. *Knowledge not always clear, where the* Ideas *are so.*
§ 1(28). *First, No farther than we have* Ideas.

(7) our *Ideas* only] **2–5** | only our *Ideas* **1** obscure and confused *Ideas*, can never **1–3** obscure, **1–3** cannot] **4–5** | can never **1–3** (18–19) *Ideas* . . . cannot] **4–5** | (20) confused,] **4–5** | confused, or (21–4) Or . . . certain.] *add.* **4–5** (22) the] *add.* **5** (28) *Knowledge*] **1–2, 4–5** | no *Knowledge* **3**

§ 2. *Secondly,* That we can have no *Knowledge* farther, than we can have Perception of that Agreement, or Disagreement: Which Perception being, 1. Either by *Intuition,* or the immediate comparing any two *Ideas*; or, 2. By *Reason,* examining the Agreement, or Disagreement of two *Ideas,* by the Intervention of some others: Or, 3. By *Sensation,* perceiving the Existence of particular Things. Hence it also follows,

§ 3. *Thirdly,* That we cannot have an *intuitive Knowledge,* that shall extend it self to all our *Ideas,* and all that we would know about them; because we cannot examine and perceive all the Relations they have one to another by *juxta*-position, or an immediate comparison one with another. Thus having the *Ideas* of an obtuse, and an acute angled Triangle, both drawn from equal Bases, and between Parallels, I can by intuitive Knowledge, perceive the one not to be the other; but cannot that way know, whether they be equal, or no; because their Agreement, or Disagreement in equality, can never be perceived by an immediate comparing them: The difference of Figure makes their parts uncapable of an exact immediate application; and therefore there is need of some intervening Quantities to measure them by, which is Demonstration, or rational Knowledge.

§ 4. *Fourthly,* It follows also, from what is above observed, that our *rational Knowledge,* cannot reach to the whole extent of our *Ideas.* Because between two different *Ideas* we would examine, we cannot always find such *Mediums,* as we can connect one to another with an intuitive Knowledge, in all the parts of the Deduction; and whereever that fails, we come short of Knowledge and Demonstration.

§ 5. *Fifthly, Sensitive Knowledge* reaching no farther than the Existence of Things actually present to our Senses, is yet much narrower than either of the former.

§ 6. From all which it is evident, that *the extent of our Knowledge* comes not only short of the reality of Things, but even of the extent of our own *Ideas.* Though our Knowledge be limited to our *Ideas,* and cannot exceed them either in extent, or perfection; and though these be very narrow bounds, in respect of the extent of

§ 2. *Secondly, No farther than we can perceive their Agreement or Disagreement.* § 3. *Thirdly, Intuitive Knowledge extends it self not to all the Relations of all our* Ideas. § 4. *Fourthly, Nor demonstrative Knowledge.* § 5. *Fifthly, Sensitive Knowledge narrower than either.* § 6. *Sixthly, Our Knowledge therefore narrower than our* Ideas.

(8) 3.] **1–3** (*likewise* **Coste**) | 2. **4–5**

Allbeing, and far short of what we may justly imagine to be in some even created understandings, not tied down to the dull and narrow Information, is to be received from some few, and not very acute ways of Perception, such as are our Senses; yet it would be well with us, if our Knowledge were but as large as our *Ideas*, and there were not many Doubts and Enquiries concerning the *Ideas* we have, whereof we are not, nor I believe ever shall be in this World, resolved. Nevertheless, I do not question, but that Humane Knowledge, under the present Circumstances of our Beings and Constitutions may be carried much farther, than it hitherto has been, if Men would sincerely, and with freedom of Mind, employ all that Industry and Labour of Thought, in improving the means of discovering Truth, which they do for the colouring or support of Falshood, to maintain a System, Interest, or Party, they are once engaged in. But yet after all, I think I may, without Injury to humane Perfection, be confident, that our Knowledge would never reach to all we might desire to know concerning those *Ideas* we have; nor be able to surmount all the Difficulties, and resolve all the Questions might arise concerning any of them. We have the *Ideas* of a *Square*, a *Circle*, and *Equality*; and yet, perhaps, shall never be able to find a Circle equal to a Square, and certainly know that it is so. We have the *Ideas* of *Matter* and *Thinking*, but possibly shall never be able to know, whether any mere material Being thinks, or no; it being impossible for us, by the contemplation of our own *Ideas*, without revelation, to discover, whether Omnipotency has not given to some Systems of Matter fitly disposed, a power to perceive and think, or else joined and fixed to Matter so disposed, a

(3) to] **1–4**; *om.* **5** (4) Senses] **1–3, 5** | senses **4** (8) not] **4–5** | not yet **1–3** (22) *Thinking*] **5** *contains, in a footnote, quotations from Locke's* First Letter to the Bishop of Worcester, *pp. 64, etc., and his* Third Letter, *pp. 396, etc.*; *prefaced by* 'Against that Assertion of Mr. *Locke*, *That possibly we shall never be able to know whether any material Being* [*edit.* | *Beings* **5**] *thinks or not*, etc. The Bishop of *Worcester* argues thus: *If this be true, then for all that we can know by our Ideas of* Matter *and* Thinking, *Matter may have a Power of Thinking: And if this hold, then it is impossible to prove a spiritual Substance in us, from the* Idea *of* Thinking: *For how can we be assured by our Ideas, that God hath not given such a power of Thinking, to Matter so disposed as our Bodies are? Especially since it is said* (B.4 C.3.§6), "That in respect of our Notions, it is not much more remote from our Comprehension to conceive that God can, if he pleases, super-add to our Idea of Matter a Faculty of Thinking, than that he should super-add to it another Substance, with a Faculty of Thinking. *Whoever asserts this, can never prove a spiritual Substance in us from a Faculty of Thinking*; *because he cannot know from the Idea of Matter and Thinking, that Matter so disposed cannot think. And he cannot be certain, that God hath not framed the Matter of our Bodies so as to be capable of it.* [*paragraph*] To which Mr. *Locke* answers thus:' (23) any . . . Being] **2–5** | Matter **1** (26) not] *add.* **2–5** some Systems of] *add.* **2–5**

thinking immaterial Substance: It being, in respect of our Notions, not much more remote from our Comprehension to conceive, that GOD can, if he pleases, superadd to Matter a Faculty of Thinking, than that he should superadd to it another Substance, with a Faculty of Thinking; since we know not wherein Thinking consists, nor to what sort of Substances the Almighty has been pleased to give that Power, which cannot be in any created Being, but merely by the good pleasure and Bounty of the Creator. For I see no contradiction in it, that the first eternal thinking Being should, if he pleased, give to certain Systems of created sensless matter, put together as he thinks fit, some degrees of sense, perception, and thought: Though, as I think, I have proved, *Lib.* 4. *c.* 10*th*. it is no less than a contradiction to suppose matter (which is evidently in its own nature void of sense and thought) should be that Eternal first thinking Being. What certainty of Knowledge can any one have that some perceptions, such as *v.g.* pleasure and pain, should not be in some bodies themselves, after a certain manner modified and moved, as well as that they should be in an immaterial Substance, upon the Motion of the parts of Body: Body as far as we can conceive being able only to strike and affect body; and Motion, according to the utmost reach of our *Ideas*, being able to produce nothing but Motion, so that when we allow it to produce pleasure or pain, or the *Idea* of a Colour, or Sound, we are fain to quit our Reason, go beyond our *Ideas*, and attribute it wholly to the good Pleasure of our Maker. For since we must allow he has annexed Effects to Motion, which we can no way conceive Motion able to produce, what reason have we to conclude, that he could not order them as well to be produced in a Subject we cannot conceive capable of them, as well as in a Subject we cannot conceive the motion of Matter can any way operate upon? I say not this, that I would any way lessen the belief of the Soul's Immateriality: I am not here speaking of Probability, but Knowledge; and I think not only, that it becomes the Modesty of Philosophy, not to pronounce Magisterially, where we want that Evidence that can produce

(1) being] **2–5** | being equally easie **1** (2) not . . . Comprehension] *add.* **2–5** (3) Matter] **4–5** | our *Idea* of Matter **1–3** (4) than] **2–5** | as **1** (8–15) I . . . Being.] *add.* **2–5** (9) Being] **5** | Being or omnipotent Spirit **2–4** (11) sense, perception,] **3, 5** | sense, perception **4** | sense perception **2** (12) is] *add.* **5** (*likewise* **Coste**) (15) What] **2–5** | For what **1** certainty] **2–5** | assurance **1** (16) some perceptions] **2–5** | certain Thoughts **1** (17) some bodies themselves] **2–5** | Body it self **1** (18) they] **2–5** | it **1** (19–20) Body . . . [*2nd*] and] *add.* **2–5** (24) our] **4–5** | our own **1–3** (*likewise* **Coste**)

Knowledge; but also, that it is of use to us, to discern how far our Knowledge does reach; for the state we are at present in, not being that of Vision, we must, in many Things, content our selves with Faith and Probability: and in the present Question, about the immateriality of the Soul, if our Faculties cannot arrive at demonstrative Certainty, we need not think it strange. All the great Ends of Morality and Religion, are well enough secured, without philosophical Proofs of the Soul's Immateriality; since it is evident, that he who made us at first begin to subsist here, sensible intelligent Beings, and for several years continued us in such a state, can and will restore us to the like state of Sensibility in another World, and make us capable there to receive the Retribution he has designed to Men, according to their doings in this Life. And therefore 'tis not of such mighty necessity to determine one way or t'other, as some over zealous for, or against the Immateriality of the Soul, have been forward to make the World believe. Who, either on the one side, indulging too much to their Thoughts immersed altogether in Matter, can allow no existence to what is not material: Or, who on the other side, finding not *Cogitation* within the natural Powers of Matter, examined over and over again, by the utmost Intention of Mind, have the confidence to conclude, that Omnipotency it self, cannot give Perception and Thought to a Substance, which has the Modification of Solidity. He that considers how hardly Sensation is, in our Thoughts, reconcilable to extended Matter; or Existence to any thing that hath no Extension at all, will confess, that he is very far from certainly knowing what his Soul is. 'Tis a Point, which seems to me, to be put out of the reach of our Knowledge: And he who will give himself leave to consider freely, and look into the dark and intricate part of each Hypothesis, will scarce find his Reason able to determine him fixedly for, or against the Soul's Materiality. Since on which side soever he views it, either as an unextended Substance, or as a thinking extended Matter; the difficulty to conceive either, will, whilst either alone is in his Thoughts, still drive him to the contrary side. An unfair way which some Men take with themselves: who, because of the unconceivableness of something they find in one, throw themselves violently into the contrary Hypothesis, though altogether as unintelligible to an unbiassed Understanding. This serves, not only to shew the Weakness and the Scantiness of our Knowledge, but the insignificant

(13)–543(27) And . . . Knowledge.] *add.* **4–5** (17) to] **4**; *om.* **5** ('much/ their')

Triumph of such sort of Arguments, which, drawn from our own Views, may satisfy us that we can find no certainty on one side of the Question; but do not at all thereby help us to Truth, by running into the opposite Opinion, which, on examination, will be found clogg'd with equal difficulties. For what Safety, what Advantage to any one is it, for the avoiding the seeming Absurdities, and, to him, unsurmountable Rubs he meets with in one Opinion, to take refuge in the contrary, which is built on something altogether as inexplicable, and as far remote from his Comprehension? 'Tis past controversy, that we have in us something that thinks, our very Doubts about what it is, confirm the certainty of its being, though we must content our selves in the Ignorance of what kind of *Being* it is: And 'tis in vain to go about to be sceptical in this, as it is unreasonable in most other cases to be positive against the being of any thing, because we cannot comprehend its Nature. For I would fain know what Substance exists that has not something in it, which manifestly baffles our Understandings. Other Spirits, who see and know the Nature and inward Constitution of things, how much must they exceed us in Knowledge? To which if we add larger Comprehension, which enables them at one Glance to see the Connexion and Agreement of very many *Ideas*, and readily supplys to them the intermediate Proofs, which we by single and slow Steps, and long poring in the dark, hardly at last find out, and are often ready to forget one before we have hunted out another, we may guess at some part of the Happiness of superior Ranks of Spirits, who have a quicker and more penetrating Sight, as well as a larger Field of Knowledge. But to return to the Argument in hand, our *Knowledge*, I say, is not only limited to the Paucity and Imperfections of the *Ideas* we have, and which we employ it about, but even comes short of that too: But how far it reaches, let us now enquire.

§ 7. The affirmations or negations we make concerning the *Ideas* we have, may, as I have before intimated in general, be reduced to these four sorts, *viz.* Identity, Co-existence, Relation, and real Existence. I shall examine how far our Knowledge extends in each of these:

§ 8. *First*, *As to Identity and Diversity*, in this way of the Agreement, or Disagreement of our *Ideas*, *our intuitive Knowledge is as far*

§ 7. *How far our Knowledge reaches.* § 8. *First, Our Knowledge of Identity and Diversity, as far as our* Ideas.

(27) *v.* 542(13), n. (30) , let] **1–3** | let **4–5** (33) Existence] **1–3, 5** | existence **4**

extended as our Ideas themselves: and there can be no *Idea* in the Mind, which it does not presently, by an intuitive Knowledge, perceive to be what it is, and to be different from any other.

§ 9. *Secondly*, *As to* the second sort, which is the *Agreement, or Disagreement* of our *Ideas in Co-existence*, in this our Knowledge is very short, though in this consists the greatest and most material part of our Knowledge concerning Substances. For our *Ideas* of the Species of Substances, being, as I have shewed, nothing but certain Collections of simple *Ideas* united in one Subject, and so co-existing together: *v.g.* Our *Idea* of *Flame* is a Body hot, luminous, and moving upward; of *Gold*, a Body heavy to a certain degree, yellow, malleable, and fusible. These or some such complex *Ideas* as these in Men's Minds, do these two names of the different Substances, *Flame* and *Gold*, stand for. When we would know any thing farther concerning these, or any other sort of Substances, what do we enquire but what other Qualities, or Powers, these Substances have, or have not? which is nothing else but to know, what other simple *Ideas* do, or do not co-exist with those that make up that complex *Idea*.

§ 10. This, how weighty and considerable a part soever of Humane Science, is yet very narrow, and scarce any at all. The reason whereof is, that the simple *Ideas* whereof our complex *Ideas* of Substances are made up, are, for the most part such, as carry with them, in their own Nature, no visible necessary connexion, or inconsistency with any other simple *Ideas*, whose *co-existence* with them we would inform our selves about.

§ 11. The *Ideas*, that our complex ones of Substances are made up of, and about which our Knowledge, concerning Substances, is most employ'd, are those of their *secondary Qualities*; which depending all (as has been shewn) upon the primary Qualities of their minute and insensible parts; or if not upon them, upon something yet more remote from our Comprehension, 'tis impossible we should know, which have a necessary union or inconsistency one with another:

§ 9. *Secondly, Of Co-existence a very little way.* § 10. *Because the connexion between most simple* Ideas *is unknown.* § 11. *Especially of Secondary Qualities.*

---

(11) upward;] **1–3, 5** | upward, **4** (12) . These] **4er–5** | : for these **1–4**. (**Coste** '; ces') (13) the] *add.* **2–5** (17) what other] **1er–5** | whether **1** (19) *Idea.*] **1** | *Idea?* **1–5**. (**Coste** 'Et lorsque . . ., nos recherches ne tendent qu'à savoir quelles . . ., c'est à dire, . . . nôtre idée complexe.') (30) shewn] **2–5** | shewed **1**. (**Coste** *adds a marginal reference to Book II, Chap. viii.*)

For not knowing the Root they spring from, not knowing what size, figure, and texture of Parts they are, on which depend and from which result those Qualities which make our complex *Idea* of Gold, 'tis impossible we should know what other Qualities result from, or are incompatible with the same Constitution of the insensible parts of *Gold*; and so consequently must always *co-exist* with that complex *Idea* we have of it, or else are *inconsistent* with it.

§ 12. Besides this Ignorance of the primary Qualities of the insensible Parts of Bodies, on which depend all their secondary Qualities, there is yet another and more incurable part of Ignorance, which sets us more remote from a certain Knowledge of the *Co-existence*, or *Inco-existence* (if I may so say) of different *Ideas* in the same Subject; and that is, that there is no discoverable connection between any *secondary Quality, and those primary Qualities* that it depends on.

§ 13. That the size, figure, and motion of one Body should cause a change in the size, figure, and motion of another Body, is not beyond our Conception; the separation of the Parts of one Body, upon the intrusion of another; and the change from rest to motion, upon impulse; these, and the like, seem to us to have some *connexion* one with another. And if we knew these primary Qualities of Bodies, we might have reason to hope, we might be able to know a great deal more of these Operations of them one upon another: But our Minds not being able to discover any *connexion* betwixt these primary qualities of Bodies, and the sensations that are produced in us by them, we can never be able to establish certain and undoubted Rules, of the Consequence or *Co-existence* of any secondary Qualities, though we could discover the size, figure, or motion of those invisible Parts, which immediately produce them. We are so far from knowing what figure, size, or motion of parts produce a yellow Colour, a sweet Taste, or a sharp Sound, that we can by no means conceive how any *size, figure, or motion* of any Particles, can possibly produce in us the *Idea* of any *Colour, Taste,* or *Sound* whatsoever; there is no conceivable *connexion* betwixt the one and the other.

§ 14. In vain therefore shall we endeavour to discover by our *Ideas,* (the only true way of certain and universal Knowledge,) what

§§ 12–14. *Because all connexion between any secondary and primary Qualities is undiscoverable.*

(4–5) , or . . . with] *add.* **4–5** (16) figure,] **1–3** | figure **4–5** (17) figure,] **1–3** | figure **4–5** (29) invisible] **2–5** | in- / sible **1**

other *Ideas* are to be found constantly joined with that of our complex *Idea* of any Substance: since we neither know the real Constitution of the minute Parts, on which their Qualities do depend; nor, did we know them, could we discover any necessary *connexion* between them, and any of the *secondary Qualities*: which is necessary to be done, before we can certainly know their *necessary co-existence*. So that let our complex *Idea* of any Species of Substances, be what it will, we can hardly, from the simple *Ideas* contained in it, certainly determine the *necessary co-existence* of any other Quality whatsoever. Our Knowledge in all these Enquiries, reaches very little farther than our Experience. Indeed, some few of the primary Qualities have a necessary dependence, and visible connexion one with another, as Figure necessarily supposes Extension, receiving or communicating Motion by impulse, supposes Solidity. But though these, and perhaps some others of our *Ideas* have: yet there are so *few* of them, that have a *visible Connexion* one with another, that we can by Intuition or Demonstration, discover the co-existence of very few of the Qualities are to be found united in Substances: and we are left only to the assistance of our Senses, to make known to us, what Qualities they contain. For of all the Qualities that are *co-existent* in any Subject, without this dependence and evident connexion of their *Ideas* one with another, we cannot know certainly any two to *co-exist* any farther, than Experience, by our Senses, informs us. Thus though we see the yellow Colour, and upon trial find the Weight, Malleableness, Fusibility, and Fixedness, that are united in a piece of Gold; yet because no one of these *Ideas* has any evident *dependence*, or necessary connexion with the other, we cannot certainly know, that where any four of these are, the fifth will be there also, how highly probable soever it may be: Because the highest Probability, amounts not to Certainty; without which, there can be no true Knowledge. For this *co-existence* can be no farther known, than it is perceived; and it cannot be perceived but either in particular Subjects, by the observation of our Senses, or in general, by the necessary *connexion* of the *Ideas* themselves.

§ 15. *As to incompatibility or repugnancy to co-existence*, we may know, that any Subject can have of each sort of primary Qualities,

§ 15. *Of Repugnancy to co-exist larger.*

---

(4) nor,] **1–3, 5** | nor **4** (13) Figure] **1–3, 5** | figure **4** (15) so] **1er–5** | some **1** (20) of] *add.* **4–5** (23) any two] *add.* **4–5**

but one particular at once, *v.g.* each particular Extension, Figure, number of Parts, Motion, excludes all other of each kind. The like also is certain of all sensible *Ideas* peculiar to each Sense; for whatever of each kind is present in any Subject, excludes all other of that sort; *v.g.* no one Subject can have two Smells, or two Colours, at the same time. To this, perhaps, will be said, has not an *Opall*, or the infusion of *Lignum Nephriticum*, two Colours at the same time? To which I answer, that these Bodies, to Eyes differently placed, may at the same time afford different Colours: But I take Liberty also to say, that to Eyes differently placed, 'tis different parts of the object, that reflect the Particles of Light: And therefore 'tis not the same part of the Object, and so not the very same Subject, which at the same time appears both yellow and azure. For 'tis as impossible that the very same Particle of any Body, should at the same time differently modify, or reflect the Rays of Light, as that it should have two different Figures and Textures at the same time.

§ 16. But *as to the Powers of Substances* to change the sensible Qualities of other Bodies, which make a great part of our Enquiries about them, and is no inconsiderable branch of our Knowledge; I doubt, as to these, whether *our Knowledge reaches* much farther than our Experience; or whether we can come to the discovery of most of these Powers, and be certain that they are in any Subject by the connexion with any of those *Ideas*, which to us make its Essence. Because the Active and Passive Powers of Bodies, and their ways of operating, consisting in a Texture and Motion of Parts, which we cannot by any means come to discover: 'Tis but in very few Cases, we can be able to perceive their dependence on, or repugnance to any of those *Ideas*, which make our complex one of that sort of Things. I have here instanced in the corpuscularian Hypothesis, as that which is thought to go farthest in an intelligible Explication of the Qualities of Bodies; and I fear the Weakness of humane Understanding is scarce able to substitute another, which will afford us a fuller and clearer discovery of the necessary Connexion, and *Co-existence*, of the Powers, which are to be observed united in several

§ 16. *Of the Co-existence of Powers a very little way.*

---

(17) *Powers*] **1–2, 4–5** | *Power* **3** (*likewise* **Coste**) (19) inconsiderable] **1–4** | considerable **5** (29) corpuscularian Hypothesis] **Coste** 'l'hypothese des Philosophes *Materialistes*', *adding in a marginal note* 'Qui expliquent les effets de la nature par la seule consideration de la grosseur, de la figure, et du mouvement des parties de la Matiere.'

sorts of them. This at least is certain, that which ever Hypothesis be clearest and truest, (for of that it is not my business to determine,) our Knowledge concerning corporeal Substances, will be very little advanced by any of them, till we are made see, what Qualities and Powers of Bodies have a *necessary Connexion or Repugnancy* one with another; which in the present State of Philosophy, I think, we know but to a very small degree: And, I doubt, whether with those Faculties we have, we shall ever be able to carry our general Knowledge (I say not particular Experience) in this part much farther. Experience is that, which in this part we must depend on. And it were to be wish'd, that it were more improved. We find the advantages some Men's generous pains have this way brought to the stock of natural Knowledge. And if others, especially the Philosophers by fire, who pretend to it, had been so wary in their observations, and sincere in their reports, as those who call themselves Philosophers ought to have been, our acquaintance with the bodies here about us, and our insight into their Powers and Operations had been yet much greater.

§ 17. If we are at this loss in respect of the Powers, and Operations of Bodies, I think it is easy to conclude, *we are much more in the dark in reference to Spirits*; whereof we naturally have no *Ideas*, but what we draw from that of our own, by reflecting on the Operations of our own Souls within us, as far as they can come within our Observation. But how inconsiderable a rank the Spirits that inhabit our Bodies hold amongst those various, and possibly innumerable, kinds of nobler Beings; and how far short they come of the Endowments and Perfections of Cherubims, and Seraphims, and infinite sorts of Spirits above us, is what by a transient hint, in another place, I have offered to my Reader's Consideration.

§ 18. As to the third sort of our Knowledge, *viz.* the *Agreement or Disagreement of any of our* Ideas *in any other Relation*: This, as it is the largest Field of our Knowledge, so it is hard to determine how far it may extend: Because the Advances that are made in this part of Knowledge, depending on our Sagacity, in finding intermediate *Ideas*, that may shew the *Relations* and *Habitudes* of *Ideas*, whose Coexistence is not considered, 'tis a hard Matter to tell, when we are

§ 17. *Of Spirits yet narrower.* § 18. *Thirdly, Of other Relations it is not easy to say how far.*

(10–18) Experience . . . greater.] *add.* **2–5** (21–2) *Spirits*; . . . own,] **4–5** | *Spirits*, . . . own; **1–3** (28–9) is . . . Consideration] **4–5** | we have in another Place made some Reflection upon **1–3** (33) are] **5** | are to be **1–4** (36) a] **4–5** | an **1–3**

at an end of such Discoveries; and when Reason has all the helps it is capable of, for the finding of Proofs, or examining the Agreement or Disagreement of remote *Ideas*. They that are ignorant of *Algebra* cannot imagine the Wonders in this kind are to be done by it: and what farther Improvements and Helps, advantageous to other parts of Knowledge, the sagacious Mind of Man may yet find out, 'tis not easy to determine. This at least I believe, that the *Ideas* of Quantity are not those alone that are capable of Demonstration and Knowledge; and that other, and perhaps more useful parts of Contemplation, would afford us Certainty, if Vices, Passions, and domineering Interest did not oppose, or menace such Endeavours.

The *Idea* of a supreme Being, infinite in Power, Goodness, and Wisdom, whose Workmanship we are, and on whom we depend; and the *Idea* of our selves, as understanding, rational Beings, being such as are clear in us, would, I suppose, if duly considered, and pursued, afford such Foundations of our Duty and Rules of Action, as might place *Morality amongst the Sciences capable of Demonstration*: wherein I doubt not, but from self-evident Propositions, by necessary Consequences, as incontestable as those in Mathematicks, the measures of right and wrong might be made out, to any one that will apply himself with the same Indifferency and Attention to the one, as he does to the other of these Sciences. The *Relation* of other *Modes* may certainly be perceived, as well as those of Number and Extension: and I cannot see, why they should not also be capable of Demonstration, if due Methods were thought on to examine, or pursue their Agreement or Disagreement. *Where there is no Property, there is no Injustice*, is a Proposition as certain as any Demonstration in *Euclid*: For the *Idea* of *Property*, being a right to any thing; and the *Idea* to which the Name *Injustice* is given, being the Invasion or Violation of that right; it is evident, that these *Ideas* being thus established, and these Names annexed to them, I can as certainly know this Proposition to be true, as that a Triangle has three

§ 18(12). *Morality capable of Demonstration.*

---

(2) or] **4–5** | and **1–3** (*likewise* **Coste**) (10–11) Interest] **4–5** | Interests **1–3** (*likewise* **Coste**) (12) , Goodness,] *add.* **2–5** (14) Beings] **5** | Creatures **1–4** (18–19) self-evident . . . Consequences] **4–5** | Principles **1–3** (19) in Mathematicks,] **4–5** | of the Mathematicks, by necessary Consequences, **1–3** (26) *Property*] **2–5** | *Propriety* **1** (*l. below* 32) *This summary is placed, in* **5**, *at the beginning of the second paragraph of* § *18; in* **4**, *near the end of the first paragraph of* § *18; and in* **2–3** (*and* **Coste**), *immediately after the first summary for* § *18.*

Angles equal to two right ones. Again, *No Government allows absolute Liberty*: The *Idea* of Government being the establishment of Society upon certain Rules or Laws, which require Conformity to them; and the *Idea* of absolute Liberty being for any one to do whatever he pleases; I am as capable of being certain of the Truth of this Proposition, as of any in Mathematicks.

§ 19. That which in this respect has given the advantage to the *Ideas* of Quantity, and made them thought more capable of Certainty and Demonstration, is,

First, That they can be set down, and represented by sensible marks, which have a greater and nearer Correspondence with them than any Words or Sounds whatsoever. Diagrams drawn on Paper are Copies of the *Ideas* in the Mind, and not liable to the Uncertainty that Words carry in their Signification. An Angle, Circle, or Square, drawn in Lines, lies open to the view, and cannot be mistaken: It remains unchangeable, and may at leisure be considered, and examined, and the Demonstration be revised, and all the parts of it may be gone over more than once, without any danger of the least change in the *Ideas*. This cannot be thus done in *moral Ideas*, we have no sensible marks that resemble them, whereby we can set them down; we have nothing but Words to express them by: which though, when written, they remain the same, yet the *Ideas* they stand for, may change in the same Man; and 'tis very seldom, that they are not different in different Persons.

Secondly, Another thing that makes the greater difficulty in *Ethicks*, is, That *moral Ideas* are commonly more complex than those of the Figures ordinarily considered in Mathematicks. From whence these two Inconveniencies follow. *First*, That their names are of more uncertain Signification, the precise Collection of simple *Ideas* they stand for not being so easily agreed on, and so the Sign, that is used for them in Communication always, and in Thinking often, does not steadily carry with it the same *Idea*. Upon which the same Disorder, Confusion, and Error follows, as would if a Man, going to demonstrate something of an *Heptagon*, should in the Diagram he took to do it, leave out one of the Angles, or by over-sight make the

§ 19. *Two Things have made moral* Ideas *thought uncapable of Demonstration. Their Complexedness, and want of sensible Representations.*

(16) unchangeable] **1T.er, 2–5** | unchangeably **1** (28) Inconveniencies] **2–5** | Inconveniences **1** (32) steadily] **1er–5** | always **1** (34) the] **1–2, 4–5** | a **3** (35) or] **1T.er, 2–5** | and **1**

Figure with one Angle more than the Name ordinarily imported, or he intended it should, when at first he thought of his Demonstration. This often happens, and is hardly avoidable in very complex moral *Ideas*, where the same name being retained, one Angle, *i.e.* one simple *Idea* is left out or put in, in the complex one, (still called by the same name) more at one time than another. *Secondly*, From the Complexedness of these moral *Ideas* there follows another Inconvenience, (*viz.*) that the Mind cannot easily retain those precise Combinations, so exactly and perfectly, as is necessary in the Examination of the Habitudes and Correspondencies, Agreements or Disagreements, of several of them one with another; especially where it is to be judg'd of by long Deductions, and the Intervention of several other complex *Ideas*, to shew the Agreement or Disagreement of two remote ones.

The great help against this, which Mathematicians find in Diagrams and Figures, which remain unalterable in their Draughts, is very apparent, and the memory would often have great difficulty otherwise to retain them so exactly, whilst the Mind went over the parts of them, step by step, to examine their several Correspondencies: And though in casting up a long Sum, either in *Addition*, *Multiplication*, or *Division*, every part be only a Progression of the Mind, taking a view of its own *Ideas*, and considering their Agreement or Disagreement; and the Resolution of the Question be nothing but the Result of the whole, made up of such particulars, whereof the Mind has a clear Perception: yet without setting down the several Parts by marks, whose precise Significations are known, and by marks, that last and remain in view, when the memory had let them go, it would be almost impossible to carry so many different *Ideas* in Mind, without confounding, or letting slip some parts of the Reckoning, and thereby making all our Reasonings about it useless. In which Case, the Cyphers or Marks help not the Mind at all to perceive the Agreement of any two, or more Numbers, their Equalities or Proportions: That the Mind has only by Intuition of its own *Ideas* of the Numbers themselves. But the numerical Characters are helps to the memory, to record and retain the several *Ideas* about which the Demonstration is made, whereby a Man may know how far his intuitive Knowledge, in surveying several of the particulars, has proceeded; that so he may without Confusion go on

(1) more] **1T.er, 2–5** | less **1** (3) very] **1–2, 4–5** | every **3** (*likewise* **Coste**)
(9) exactly] **1–3** | exact **4–5** (33) : That] **2–5** | . That **1**

to what is yet unknown; and, at last, have in one view before him the Result of all his Perceptions and Reasonings.

§ 20. One part of *these Disadvantages*, in moral *Ideas*, which has made them be thought not capable of Demonstration, may in a good measure be *remedied* by Definitions, setting down that Collection of simple *Ideas*, which every Term shall stand for; and then using the Terms steadily and constantly for that precise Collection. And what methods *Algebra*, or something of that kind, may hereafter suggest, to remove the other difficulties, is not easy to fore-tell. Confident I am, that if Men would in the same method, and with the same indifferency, search after moral, as they do mathematical Truths, they would find them to have a stronger Connection one with another, and a more necessary Consequence from our clear and distinct *Ideas*, and to come nearer perfect Demonstration, than is commonly imagined. But much of this is not to be expected, whilst the desire of Esteem, Riches, or Power, makes Men espouse the well endowed Opinions in Fashion, and then seek Arguments, either to make good their Beauty, or varnish over, and cover their Deformity. Nothing being so beautiful to the Eye, as Truth is to the Mind; nothing so deformed and irreconcilable to the Understanding, as a Lye. For though many a Man can with satisfaction enough own a no very handsome Wife in his Bosom; yet who is bold enough openly to avow, that he has espoused a Falshood, and received into his Breast so ugly a thing as a Lye? Whilst the Parties of Men, cram their Tenets down all Men's Throats, whom they can get into their Power, without permitting them to examine their Truth or Falshood; and will not let Truth have fair play in the World, nor Men the Liberty to search after it; What Improvements can be expected of this kind? What greater Light can be hoped for in the moral Sciences? The Subject part of Mankind, in most Places, might, instead thereof, with *Ægyptian* Bondage, expect *Ægyptian* Darkness, were not the Candle of the Lord set up by himself in Men's minds, which it is impossible for the Breath or Power of Man wholly to extinguish.

§ 21. As to the fourth sort of our Knowledge, *viz. of* the *real, actual, Existence* of Things, we have an intuitive Knowledge of our

§ 20. *Remedies of those Difficulties.* § 21. *Fourthly, of real Existence we have an intuitive Knowledge of our own, demonstrative of God's, sensible of some few other Things.*

---

(7) Collection] **1–3, 5** | Collexion **4** (25) Men,] **4–5** | Men, I say, **1–3** Tenets] **4** | Tenents **1–3, 5** (34) Power] **1–3, 5** | power **4** (36) Things] **2–5** | Things without us **1**

own *Existence*; a demonstrative Knowledge of the *Existence* of a God; of the *Existence* of any thing else, we have no other but a sensitive Knowledge, which extends not beyond the Objects present to our Senses.

§ 22. Our Knowledge being so narrow, as I have shew'd, it will, perhaps, give us some Light into the present State of our minds, if we look a little into the dark side, and take a view of *our Ignorance*: which being infinitely larger than our Knowledge, may serve much to the quieting of Disputes, and Improvement of useful Knowledge; if discovering how far we have clear and distinct *Ideas*, we confine our Thoughts within the Contemplation of those Things, that are within the reach of our Understandings, and lanch not out into that Abyss of Darkness (where we have not Eyes to see, nor Faculties to perceive any thing,) out of a Presumption, that nothing is beyond our Comprehension. But to be satisfied of the Folly of such a Conceit, we need not go far. He that knows any thing, knows this in the first place, that he need not seek long for Instances of his Ignorance. The meanest, and most obvious Things that come in our way, have dark sides, that the quickest Sight cannot penetrate into. The clearest, and most enlarged Understandings of thinking Men find themselves puzzled, and at a loss, in every Particle of Matter. We shall the less wonder to find it so, when we consider the *Causes of our Ignorance*, which, from what has been said, I suppose, will be found to be chiefly these three:

First, Want of *Ideas.*

Secondly, Want of a discoverable Connexion between the *Ideas* we have.

Thirdly, Want of tracing, and examining our *Ideas.*

§ 23. *First*, There are some Things, and those not a few, that we are ignorant of for *want of Ideas.*

First, All the simple *Ideas* we have are confined (as I have shewn) to those we receive from corporeal Objects by *Sensation*, and from the Operations of our own Minds as the Objects of *Reflection.* But how much these few and narrow Inlets are disproportionate

§ 22. *Our Ignorance great.* § 23. *First, one cause of it want of* Ideas, *either such as we have no Conception of, or such as particularly we have not.*

---

(5) 22] **1–3, 5** | 21 **4**   (22) . We] **4–5** | ; which we **1–3**   to find it so **4–5** | at **1–3** (*likewise* **Coste**)   (31) [*1st*] have] **1–4, W**; *om.* **5**   (32) those] . . . *Sensation*] **5** | the Observation of our Senses **1–4**   [*2nd*] from] *add.* **5**   (33) as . . . *Reflection*] **5** | , that we are conscious of in our selves **1–4**

to the vast whole Extent of all Beings, will not be hard to persuade those, who are not so foolish, as to think their span the measure of all Things. What other simple *Ideas* 'tis possible the Creatures in other parts of the Universe may have, by the Assistance of Senses and Faculties more or perfecter, than we have, or different from ours, 'tis not for us to determine. But to say, or think there are no such, because we conceive nothing of them, is no better an argument, than if a blind Man should be positive in it, that there was no such thing as Sight and Colours, because he had no manner of *Idea*, of any such thing, nor could by any means frame to himself any Notions about Seeing. The Ignorance, and Darkness that is in us, no more hinders, nor confines the Knowledge, that is in others, than the blindness of a Mole is an Argument against the quick-sightedness of an Eagle. He that will consider the Infinite Power, Wisdom, and Goodness of the Creator of all Things, will find Reason to think, it was not all laid out upon so inconsiderable, mean, and impotent a Creature, as he will find Man to be; who in all probability, is one of the lowest of all intellectual Beings. What Faculties therefore other Species of Creatures have to penetrate into the Nature, and inmost Constitutions of Things; what *Ideas* they may receive of them, far different from ours, we know not. This we know, and certainly find, that we want several other views of them, besides those we have, to make Discoveries of them more perfect. And we may be convinced that the *Ideas*, we can attain to by our Faculties, are very disproportionate to Things themselves, when a positive clear distinct one of Substance it self, which is the Foundation of all the rest, is concealed from us. But want of *Ideas* of this kind being a Part, as well as Cause of our Ignorance, cannot be described. Only this, I think, I may confidently say of it, that the intellectual and sensible World, are in this perfectly alike; That that part, which we see of either of them, holds no proportion with what we see not; And whatsoever we can reach with our Eyes, or our Thoughts of either of them, is but a point, almost nothing, in comparison of the rest.

§ 24. *Secondly*, Another great Cause of Ignorance, is the *want of* Ideas *we are capable of*. As the want of *Ideas*, which our faculties are not able to give us, shuts us wholly from those views of Things,

§ 24. *Because of their Remoteness, or,*

(12) nor] **1–5** | or **1er** (21) from] **1–4, W** | of **5** (37) [*2nd*] us] **1–2, 4–5**; *om.* **3**

which 'tis reasonable to think other Beings, perfecter than we, have, of which we know nothing; so the want of *Ideas*, I now speak of, keeps us in ignorance of Things, we conceive capable of being known to us. *Bulk*, *Figure*, and *Motion*, we have *Ideas* of. But though we are not without *Ideas* of these primary qualities of Bodies in general, yet not knowing what is the particular *Bulk*, *Figure*, and *Motion*, of the greatest part of the Bodies of the Universe, we are ignorant of the several Powers, Efficacies, and Ways of Operation, whereby the Effects, which we daily see, are produced. These are hid from us in some Things, by being *too remote*; *and* in others, by being too *minute*. When we consider the vast distance of the known and visible parts of the World, and the Reasons we have to think, that what lies within our Ken, is but a small part of the immense Universe, we shall then discover an huge Abyss of Ignorance. What are the particular Fabricks of the great Masses of Matter, which make up the whole stupendious frame of Corporeal Beings; how far they are extended; what is their Motion, and how continued, or communicated; and what Influence they have one upon another, are Contemplations, that at first glimpse our Thoughts lose themselves in. If we narrow our Contemplation, and confine our Thoughts to this little Canton, I mean this System of our Sun, and the grosser Masses of Matter, that visibly move about it, what several sorts of Vegetables, Animals, and intellectual corporeal Beings, infinitely different from those of our little spot of Earth, may there probably be in the other Planets, to the Knowledge of which, even of their outward Figures and Parts, we can no way attain, whilst we are confined to this Earth, there being no natural Means, either by Sensation or Reflection, to convey their certain *Ideas* into our Minds? They are out of the reach of those Inlets of all our Knowledge: and what sorts of Furniture and Inhabitants those Mansions contain in them, we cannot so much as guess, much less have clear, and distinct *Ideas* of them.

§ 25. If a great, nay far the greatest part of the several ranks of *Bodies* in the Universe, scape our notice by their remoteness, there are others that are no less concealed from us by their *Minuteness*. These insensible Corpuscles, being the active parts of Matter, and

§ 25. *Because of their Minuteness.*

---

(1) Beings . . . we,] **2–5** | perfecter Beings than we **1** (9) , which] *add.* **4–5** (17) their] **1–2, 4–5** | there **3** (24) there] *add.* **4–5** (29) Minds?] **1er, 4–5** | Minds. **1–3** (33) 25.] **1–4** | 23. **5** far] **1er–5** | for **1**

the great Instruments of Nature, on which depend not only all their secondary Qualities, but also most of their natural Operations, our want of precise distinct *Ideas* of their primary Qualities, keeps us in an uncurable Ignorance of what we desire to know about them. I doubt not but if we could discover the Figure, Size, Texture, and Motion of the minute Constituent parts of any two Bodies, we should know without Trial several of their Operations one upon another, as we do now the Properties of a Square, or a Triangle. Did we know the Mechanical affections of the Particles of *Rhubarb*, *Hemlock*, *Opium*, and a *Man*, as a Watchmaker does those of a Watch, whereby it performs its Operations, and of a File which by rubbing on them will alter the Figure of any of the Wheels, we should be able to tell before Hand, that *Rhubarb* will purge, *Hemlock* kill, and *Opium* make a Man sleep; as well as a Watch-maker can, that a little piece of Paper laid on the Balance, will keep the Watch from going, till it be removed; or that some small part of it, being rubb'd by a File, the Machin would quite lose its Motion, and the Watch go no more. The dissolving of Silver in *aqua fortis*, and Gold in *aqua Regia*, and not *vice versa*, would be then, perhaps, no more difficult to know, than it is to a Smith to understand, why the turning of one Key will open a Lock, and not the turning of another. But whilst we are destitute of Senses acute enough, to discover the minute Particles of Bodies, and to give us *Ideas* of their mechanical Affections, we must be content to be ignorant of their properties and ways of Operation; nor can we be assured about them any farther, than some few Trials we make, are able to reach. But whether they will succeed again another time, we cannot be certain. This hinders our certain Knowledge of universal Truths concerning natural Bodies: and our Reason carries us herein very little beyond particular matter of Fact.

§ 26. And therefore I am apt to doubt that, how far soever humane Industry may advance useful and *experimental* Philosophy *in physical Things*, *scientifical* will still be out of our reach: because we want perfect and adequate *Ideas* of those very Bodies, which are

§ 26. *Hence no Science of Bodies.*

---

(2) Operations] **1–2, 4–5** | Operation **3** (5) Texture] **2–5** | Connexion **1** (8–18) . Did . . . more.] **2–5** | : And [**1er** | ; and **1**] we should be able to tell before Hand, . . ., and the Watch go no more, did [**1er** | . Did **1**] we know . . . of any of the Wheels. [**1er** | Wheels; **1**] **1** (11) its] **2–5** | all its **1** (13) will] **4–5** | would **1–3** (14) can,] **2–5** | does **1**

nearest to us, and most under our Command. Those which we have ranked into Classes under names, and we think our selves best acquainted with, we have but very imperfect, and incompleat *Ideas* of. Distinct *Ideas* of the several sorts of Bodies, that fall under the Examination of our Senses, perhaps, we may have: but adequate *Ideas*, I suspect, we have not of any one amongst them. And though the former of these will serve us for common Use and Discourse: yet whilst we want the latter, we are not capable of *scientifical Knowledge*; nor shall ever be able to discover general, instructive, unquestionable Truths concerning them. *Certainty* and *Demonstration*, are Things we must not, in these Matters, pretend to. By the Colour, Figure, Taste, and Smell, and other sensible qualities, we have as clear, and distinct *Ideas* of Sage and Hemlock, as we have of a Circle and a Triangle: But having no *Ideas* of the particular primary Qualities of the minute parts of either of these Plants, nor of other Bodies which we would apply them to, we cannot tell what effects they will produce; Nor when we see those Effects, can we so much as guess, much less know, their manner of production. Thus having no *Ideas* of the particular mechanical Affections of the minute parts of Bodies, that are within our view and reach, we are ignorant of their Constitutions, Powers, and Operations: and of Bodies more remote, we are yet more ignorant not knowing so much as their very outward Shapes or the sensible and grosser parts of their Constitutions.

§ 27. This, at first sight, will shew us how disproportionate our Knowledge is to the whole extent even of material Beings; to which, if we add the Consideration of that infinite number of *Spirits* that may be, and probably are, which are yet more remote from our Knowledge, whereof we have no cognizance, nor can frame to our selves any distinct *Ideas* of their several ranks and sorts, we shall find this cause of Ignorance conceal from us, in an impenetrable obscurity, almost the whole intellectual World; a greater certainly, and more beautiful World, than the material. For bating some very few, and those, if I may so call them, superficial

§ 27. *Much less of Spirits.*

---

(3) incompleat] **1–2, 4–5** | compleat **3** (9–10) , unquestionable] *add.* **2–5** (16) which] *add.* **4–5** (22) yet more] *add.* **2–5** (22–4) not . . . Constitutions] **4–5** | not knowing so much as their very outward Shapes and Beings **2–3** | of their very outward Shapes and Beings **1** (33) certainly] **1–2, 4–5** | certainty **3**

Ideas of Spirit, which by reflection we get of our own, and from thence, the best we can, collect, of the Father of all Spirits, the eternal independent Author of them and us and all Things, we have no certain information, so much as of the Existence of other Spirits, but by revelation. Angels of all sorts are naturally beyond our discovery: And all those intelligences, whereof 'tis likely there are more Orders than of corporeal Substances, are Things, whereof our natural Faculties give us no certain account at all. That there are Minds, and thinking Beings in other Men as well as himself, every Man has a reason, from their Words and Actions, to be satisfied: And the Knowledge of his own Mind cannot suffer a Man, that considers, to be ignorant, that there is a GOD. But that there are degrees of Spiritual Beings between us and the great GOD, who is there, that by his own search and ability can come to know? Much less have we distinct *Ideas* of their different Natures, Conditions, States, Powers, and several Constitutions, wherein they agree or differ from one another, and from us. And therefore in what concerns their different Species and Properties, we are under an absolute ignorance.

§ 28. *Secondly*, What a small part of the substantial Beings, that are in the Universe, the want of *Ideas* leave open to our Knowledge, we have seen. In the next place, another cause of Ignorance, of no less moment, is a want of *a discoverable Connection* between those *Ideas* which we have. For wherever we want that, we are utterly uncapable of universal and certain Knowledge; and are, as in the former case, left only to Observation and Experiment: which how narrow and confined it is, how far from general Knowledge, we need not be told. I shall give some few instances of this cause of our Ignorance and so leave it. 'Tis evident that the bulk, figure, and motion of several Bodies about us, produce in us several Sensations, as of Colours, Sounds, Tastes, Smells, Pleasure and Pain, *etc.* These mechanical Affections of Bodies, having no affinity at all with those

§ 28. *Secondly, want of a discoverable connexion between* Ideas *we have.*

(1) [*1st*] of . . . we] **2–5** | , which Spirit, [*all om.* **1er**] we, by reflection, **1** (1–2) from . . . collect, [collect **2–3**]] *add.* **2–5** (4) the . . . Spirits] **2–5** | their Existence **1** (11–12) And . . . GOD.] *add.* **2–5** (12–14) [*2nd*] that . . . know?] **2–5** | between us and the Great GOD, we can have no certain knowledge of the Existence of any Spirits, but by revelation; **1** (23) a] **4–5** | the **1–3**. (**Coste** 'nous ne saurions trouver') (24) which] *add.* **4–5** (31) Smells] **5** | or Smells **1–4** These] **2er–5** | those **1–2** (Those **2**) (32) those] **2er–5** | these **1–2**

Ideas, they produce in us, (there being no conceivable connexion between any impulse of any sort of Body, and any perception of a Colour, or Smell, which we find in our Minds) we can have no distinct knowledge of such Operations beyond our Experience; and can reason no otherwise about them, than as effects produced by the appointment of an infinitely Wise Agent, which perfectly surpass our Comprehensions. As the *Ideas* of sensible secondary Qualities, which we have in our Minds, can, by us, be no way deduced from bodily Causes, nor any correspondence or connexion be found between them and those primary Qualities which (Experience shews us) produce them in us; so on the other side, the Operation of our Minds upon our Bodies is as unconceivable. How any thought should produce a motion in Body is as remote from the nature of our *Ideas*, as how any Body should produce any Thought in the Mind. That it is so, if Experience did not convince us, the Consideration of the Things themselves would never be able, in the least, to discover to us. These, and the like, though they have a constant and regular connexion, in the ordinary course of Things: yet that connexion being not discoverable in the *Ideas* themselves, which appearing to have no necessary dependance one on another, we can attribute their connexion to nothing else, but the arbitrary Determination of that All-wise Agent, who has made them to be, and to operate as they do, in a way wholly above our weak Understandings to conceive.

§ 29. In some of our *Ideas* there are certain Relations, Habitudes, and Connexions, so visibly included in the Nature of the *Ideas* themselves, that we cannot conceive them separable from them, by any Power whatsoever. And in these only, we are capable of certain and universal Knowledge. Thus the *Idea* of a right-lined Triangle necessarily carries with it an equality of its Angles to two right ones. Nor can we conceive this Relation, this connexion of these two *Ideas*, to be possibly mutable, or to depend on any arbitrary Power, which of choice made it thus, or could make it otherwise. But the coherence and continuity of the parts of Matter; the production of Sensation in us of Colours and Sounds, *etc.* by impulse

§ 29. *Instances.*

---

(3) which] *add.* **1er–5** (5–6) effects . . . the] **4–5** | the effects or **1–3** (8) , which] *add.* **4–5** (11) Operation] **2–5** | Operations **1** (15) Consideration] **2–5** | Considerations **1** (23) wholly] **2–5** | utterly **1** Understandings] **4–5** | Understanding **1–3** (*likewise* **Coste**) (32) [*2nd*] to] *add.* **2–5**

and motion; nay, the original Rules and Communication of Motion being such, wherein we can discover no natural connexion with any *Ideas* we have, we cannot but ascribe them to the arbitrary Will and good Pleasure of the Wise Architect. I need not, I think, here mention the Resurrection of the dead, the future state of this Globe of Earth, and such other Things, which are by every one acknowledged to depend wholly on the Determination of a free Agent. The Things that, as far as our Observation reaches, we constantly find to proceed regularly, we may conclude, do act by a Law set them; but yet by a Law, that we know not: whereby, though Causes work steadily, and Effects constantly flow from them, yet their *Connexions* and *Dependancies* being not discoverable in our *Ideas*, we can have but an experimental Knowledge of them. From all which 'tis easy to perceive, what a darkness we are involved in, how little 'tis of Being, and the things that are, that we are capable to know. And therefore we shall do no injury to our Knowledge when we modestly think with our selves, that we are so far from being able to comprehend the whole nature of the Universe, and all the things contained in it, that we are not capable of a philosophical *Knowledge* of the Bodies that are about us, and make a part of us: Concerning their secondary Qualities, Powers, and Operations, we can have no universal certainty. Several effects come every day within the notice of our Senses, of which we have so far *sensitive Knowledge*: but the causes, manner, and certainty of their production, for the two foregoing Reasons, we must be content to be ignorant of. In these we can go no farther than particular Experience informs us of matter of fact, and by Analogy to guess what Effects the like Bodies are, upon other tryals, like to produce. But as to a perfect *Science* of natural Bodies, (not to mention spiritual Beings,) we are, I think, so far from being capable of any such thing, that I conclude it lost labour to seek after it.

§ 30. *Thirdly*, Where we have adequate *Ideas*, and where there is a certain and discoverable connexion between them, yet we are often ignorant, for want of *tracing* those *Ideas* which we have, or may have; and for want of finding out those intermediate *Ideas*, which may shew us, what habitude of agreement or disagreement they have

§ 30. *Thirdly, want of tracing our* Ideas.

---

(5) the dead] **4–5** | our Bodies **1–3** (10) by] *add.* **2–5** (13) Knowledge] **1–3, 5** | Knowledge, /**4** (34) which] *add.* **4–5** (35) for want of] *add.* **4–5**

one with another. And thus many are ignorant of mathematical Truths, not out of any imperfection of their Faculties, or uncertainty in the Things themselves; but for want of application in acquiring, examining, and by due ways comparing those *Ideas*. That which has most contributed to hinder the due *tracing* of our *Ideas*, and finding out their Relations, and Agreements or Disagreements one with another, has been, I suppose, the ill use of *Words*. It is impossible that Men should ever truly seek, or certainly discover the Agreement or Disagreement of *Ideas* themselves, whilst their Thoughts flutter about, or stick only in Sounds of doubtful and uncertain significations. Mathematicians abstracting their Thoughts from Names, and accustoming themselves to set before their Minds, the *Ideas* themselves, that they would consider, and not Sounds instead of them, have avoided thereby a great part of that perplexity, puddering, and confusion, which has so much hindred Mens progress in other parts of Knowledge. For whilst they stick in Words of undetermined and uncertain signification, they are unable to distinguish True from False, Certain from Probable, Consistent from Inconsistent, in their own Opinions. This having been the fate or misfortune of a great part of the men of Letters, the increase brought into the Stock of real Knowledge, has been very little, in proportion to the Schools, Disputes, and Writings, the World has been fill'd with; whilst Students, being lost in the great Wood of Words, knew not whereabout they were, how far their Discoveries were advanced, or what was wanting in their own, or the general Stock of Knowledge. Had Men, in the discoveries of the material, done, as they have in those of the intellectual World, involved all in the obscurity of uncertain and doubtful ways of talking, Volumes writ of Navigation and Voyages, Theories and Stories of Zones and Tydes multiplied and disputed; nay, Ships built, and Fleets set out, would never have taught us the way beyond the Line; and the Antipodes would be still as much unknown, as when it was declared Heresy to hold there were any. But having spoken sufficiently of Words, and the ill or careless use, that is commonly made of them, I shall not say any thing more of it here.

(16) . For . . . stick] **4–5** | ; who sticking **1–3** (17) they are] **4–5** | were **1–3** (19–20) . This . . . Letters,] **4–5** | : Whereby **1–3** (22) Schools,] **1–3, 5** | Schools **4** (23) Students] **4–5** | Men **1–3** (26) [*2nd*] the] **5** | their **1–4** (28) ways] **4–5** | terms and ways **1–3** (*likewise* **Coste**) (30) Tydes] **1–4** | Tydes, **5** (32) be still] **1–2, 4–5** | still be **3**

§ 31. Hitherto we have examined the *extent* of our Knowledge, in respect of the several sorts of Beings that are. There is another *extent of it, in respect of universality*, which will also deserve to be considered: and in this regard, our Knowledge follows the Nature of our *Ideas*. If the *Ideas* are abstract, whose agreement or disagreement we perceive, our Knowledge is universal. For what is known of such general *Ideas*, will be true of every particular thing, in whom that Essence, *i.e.* that abstract *Idea* is to be found: and what is once known of such *Ideas*, will be perpetually, and for ever true. So that as to all general Knowledge, we must search and find it only in our own Minds, and 'tis only the examining of our own *Ideas*, that furnisheth us with that. Truths belonging to Essences of Things, (that is, to abstract *Ideas*) are eternal, and are to be found out by the contemplation only of those Essences: as the Existence of Things is to be known only from Experience. But having more to say of this in the Chapters, where I shall speak of general and real Knowledge, this may here suffice, as to the Universality of our Knowledge in general.

CHAPTER IV

Of the Reality of our Knowledge.

§ 1. I Doubt not but my Reader, by this time, may be apt to think, that I have been all this while only building a Castle in the Air; and be ready to say to me, To what purpose all this stir? Knowledge, say you, is only the perception of the agreement or disagreement of our own *Ideas*: but who knows what those *Ideas* may be? Is there any thing so extravagant, as the Imaginations of Men's Brains? Where is the Head that has no *Chimeras* in it? Or if there be a sober and a wise Man, what difference will there be, by your Rules, between his Knowledge, and that of the most extravagant Fancy in the World? They both have their *Ideas*, and perceive their agreement and disagreement one with another. If there be any difference between them, the advantage will be on the warm-headed Man's side, as having the more *Ideas*, and the more lively.

§ 31. *Extent in respect of Universality.*
§ 1. *Objection, Knowledge placed in* Ideas *may be all bare vision.*

(15) say] *add.* **1T.er, 2–5** (29) their] **1–2, 4–5** | the **3** (*likewise* **Coste**)

And so, by your Rules, he will be the more knowing. If it be true, that all Knowledge lies only in the perception of the agreement or disagreement of our own *Ideas*, the Visions of an Enthusiast, and the Reasonings of a sober Man, will be equally certain. 'Tis no matter how Things are: so a Man observe but the agreement of his own Imaginations, and talk conformably, it is all Truth, all Certainty. Such Castles in the Air, will be as strong Holds of Truth, as the Demonstrations of *Euclid*. That an Harpy is not a Centaur, is by this way as certain knowledge, and as much a Truth, as that a Square is not a Circle.

But *of what use is all this* fine *Knowledge of Men's own Imaginations*, to a Man that enquires after the reality of Things? It matters not what Men's Fancies are, 'tis the Knowledge of things that is only to be prized: 'tis this alone gives a value to our Reasonings, and preference to one Man's Knowledge over another's, that it is of Things as they really are, and not of Dreams and Fancies.

§ 2. To which I answer, That if our Knowledge of our *Ideas* terminate in them, and reach no farther, where there is something farther intended, our most serious Thoughts will be of little more use, than the Reveries of a crazy Brain; and the Truths built thereon of no more weight, than the Discourses of a Man, who sees Things clearly in a Dream, and with great assurance utters them. But, I hope, before I have done, to make it evident, that this way of certainty, by the Knowledge of our own *Ideas*, goes a little farther than bare Imagination: and, I believe it will appear, that all the certainty of general Truths a Man has, lies in nothing else.

§ 3. 'Tis evident, the Mind knows not Things immediately, but only by the intervention of the *Ideas* it has of them. *Our Knowledge* therefore is *real*, only so far as there is a conformity between our *Ideas* and the reality of Things. But what shall be here the Criterion? How shall the Mind, when it perceives nothing but its own *Ideas*, know that they agree with Things themselves? This, though it seems not to want difficulty, yet, I think there be two sorts of *Ideas*, that, we may be assured, agree with Things.

§ 4. *First*, The first are simple *Ideas*, which since the Mind, as has been shewed, can by no means make to it self, must necessarily be

§§ 2, 3. *Answer, Not so, where* Ideas *agree with Things.* § 4. *As, First, All simple* Ideas *do.*

(19) will] **4–5** | would **1–3** (20) Reveries] **1, 4–5** (Resveries **1**) | Reserves **2–3** (33) seems] **4–5** | seem **1–3**

the product of Things operating on the Mind in a natural way, and producing therein those Perceptions which by the Wisdom and Will of our Maker they are ordained and adapted to. From whence it follows, that *simple* Ideas *are not fictions* of our Fancies, but the natural and regular productions of Things without us, really operating upon us; and so carry with them all the conformity which is intended; or which our state requires: For they represent to us Things under those appearances which they are fitted to produce in us: whereby we are enabled to distinguish the sorts of particular Substances, to discern the states they are in, and so to take them for our Necessities, and apply them to our Uses. Thus the *Idea* of Whiteness, or Bitterness, as it is in the Mind, exactly answering that Power which is in any Body to produce it there, has all the real conformity it can, or ought to have, with Things without us. And this conformity between our simple *Ideas*, and the existence of Things, is sufficient for real Knowledge.

§ 5. *Secondly, All our complex* Ideas, *except those of Substances*, being *Archetypes* of the Mind's own making, not intended to be the Copies of any thing, nor referred to the existence of any thing, as to their Originals, *cannot want any conformity necessary to real Knowledge*. For that which is not designed to represent any thing but it self, can never be capable of a wrong representation, nor mislead us from the true apprehension of any thing, by its dislikeness to it: and such, excepting those of Substances, are all our complex *Ideas*. Which, as I have shewed in another place, are Combinations of *Ideas*, which the Mind, by its free choice, puts together, without considering any connexion they have in Nature. And hence it is, that in all these sorts the *Ideas* themselves are considered as the *Archetypes*, and Things no otherwise regarded, but as they are conformable to them. So that we cannot but be infallibly certain, that all the Knowledge we attain concerning these *Ideas* is real, and reaches Things themselves. Because in all our Thoughts, Reasonings, and Discourses of this kind, we intend Things no farther, than as they are conformable to our *Ideas*. So that in these, we cannot miss of a certain undoubted reality.

§ 5. *Secondly, All complex* Ideas, *except of Substances.*

---

(7) which . . . which] *add.* **4–5** (7–8) : For . . . us] **4–5** | , which is to represent **1–3** (8) which] *add.* **4–5** (9–11) are . . . Necessities] **4–5** | may distinguish the Substances they are in **1–3**

§ 6. I doubt not but it will be easily granted, that the *Knowledge* we may have *of Mathematical Truths, is* not only certain, but *real Knowledge*; and not the bare empty Vision of vain insignificant *Chimeras* of the Brain: And yet, if we will consider, we shall find that it is only of our own *Ideas*. The Mathematician considers the Truth and Properties belonging to a Rectangle, or Circle, only as they are in *Idea* in his own Mind. For 'tis possible he never found either of them existing mathematically, *i.e.* precisely true, in his Life. But yet the knowledge he has of any Truths or Properties belonging to a Circle, or any other mathematical Figure, are nevertheless true and certain, even of real Things existing: because real Things are no farther concerned, nor intended to be meant by any such Propositions, than as Things really agree to those *Archetypes* in his Mind. Is it true of the *Idea* of a *Triangle*, that its three Angles are equal to two right ones? It is true also of a *Triangle*, where-ever it really exists. Whatever other Figure exists, that is not exactly answerable to that *Idea* of a *Triangle* in his Mind, is not at all concerned in that Proposition. And therefore he is certain all his Knowledge concerning such *Ideas*, is real Knowledge: because intending Things no farther than they agree with those his *Ideas*, he is sure what he knows concerning those Figures, when they have barely *an Ideal Existence* in his Mind, will hold true of them also, when they have a real existence in Matter; his consideration being barely of those Figures, which are the same, where-ever, or however they exist.

§ 7. And hence it follows, that *moral Knowledge is as capable of real Certainty*, as Mathematicks. For Certainty being but the Perception of the Agreement, or Disagreement of our *Ideas*; and Demonstration nothing but the Perception of such Agreement, by the Intervention of other *Ideas*, or Mediums, our *moral Ideas*, as well as mathematical, being *Archetypes* themselves, and so adequate, and complete *Ideas*, all the Agreement, or Disagreement, which we shall find in them, will produce real Knowledge, as well as in mathematical Figures.

§ 8. For the attaining of *Knowledge* and Certainty it is requisite, that we have determined *Ideas*: and to make our Knowledge *real*, it is requisite, that the *Ideas* answer their *Archetypes*. Nor let it be

§ 6. *Hence the Reality of mathematical Knowledge.* § 7. *And of moral.* § 8. *Existence not required to make it real.*

(3–4) and . . . Brain] **4–5** | not idle *Chimeras* of Men's Brains **1–3** (24) where-ever] *v. Register ad. loc.* (31) , which] *add.* **4–5** (33–5) For . . . *Ideas*] **4–5** | That which is requisite to make our Knowledge certain, is the Clearness of our *Ideas*; and that which is required to make it real [*real* **2–3**], is, that they **1–3**

wondred, that I place the Certainty of our Knowledge in the Consideration of our *Ideas*, with so little Care and Regard (as it may seem) to the real Existence of Things: Since most of those Discourses, which take up the Thoughts and engage the Disputes of those who pretend to make it their Business to enquire after Truth and Certainty, will, I presume, upon Examination be found to be *general Propositions*, and Notions in which Existence is not at all concerned. All the Discourses of the Mathematicians about the squaring of a Circle, conick Sections, or any other part of Mathematicks, *concern not* the *Existence* of any of those Figures: but their Demonstrations, which depend on their *Ideas*, are the same, whether there be any Square or Circle existing in the World, or no. In the same manner, the Truth and Certainty of *moral* Discourses abstracts from the Lives of Men, and the Existence of those Vertues in the World, whereof they treat: Nor are *Tully*'s Offices less true, because there is no Body in the World that exactly practises his Rules, and lives up to that pattern of a vertuous Man, which he has given us, and which existed no where, when he writ, but in *Idea*. If it be true in Speculation, *i.e.* in *Idea*, that *Murther deserves Death*, it will also be true in Reality of any Action that exists conformable to that *Idea* of *Murther*. As for other Actions, the Truth of that Proposition concerns them not. And thus it is of all other Species of Things, which have no other Essences, but those *Ideas*, which are in the Minds of Men.

§ 9. But it will here be said, that if *moral Knowledge* be placed in the Contemplation of our own *moral Ideas*, and those, as other Modes, be of our own making, What strange Notions will there be of *Justice* and *Temperance*? What confusion of Vertues and Vices, if every one may make what *Ideas* of them he pleases? No confusion nor disorder in the Things themselves, nor the Reasonings about them; no more than (in Mathematicks) there would be a Disturbance in the Demonstration, or a change in the Properties of Figures, and their Relations one to another, if a Man should make a Triangle with four Corners, or a *Trapezium* with four right Angles: that is, in plain *English*, change the Names of the Figures, and call that by one Name, which Mathematicians call'd ordinarily by another. For let a Man make to himself the *Idea* of a Figure with three Angles,

§ 9. *Nor will it be less true or certain, because moral* Ideas *are of our own making and naming.*

---

(15) are] **4–5** | is **1–3**   (18) where, . . . writ,] **4–5** | where . . . writ **1–3**

whereof one is a right one, and call it, if he please, *Equilaterum* or *Trapezium*, or any thing else, the Properties of, and Demonstrations about that *Idea*, will be the same, as if he call'd it a *Rectangular-Triangle*. I confess, the change of the Name, by the impropriety of Speech, will at first disturb him, who knows not what *Idea* it stands for: but as soon as the Figure is drawn, the Consequences and Demonstration are plain and clear. Just the same is it in *moral* Knowledge, let a Man have the *Idea* of taking from others, without their Consent, what their honest Industry has possessed them of, and call this *Justice*, if he please. He that takes the Name here without the *Idea* put to it, will be mistaken, by joining another *Idea* of his own to that Name: But strip the *Idea* of that Name, or take it such as it is in the Speaker's Mind, and the same Things will agree to it, as if you call'd it *Injustice*. Indeed, wrong Names in moral Discourses, breed usually more disorder, because they are not so easily rectified, as in Mathematicks, where the Figure once drawn and seen, makes the Name useless and of no force. For what need of a Sign, when the Thing signified is present and in view? But in moral Names, that cannot be so easily and shortly done, because of the many decompositions that go to the making up the complex *Ideas* of those Modes. But yet for all this the *miscalling of* any of those *Ideas*, contrary to the usual signification of the Words of that Language, hinders not, but that we may have certain and demonstrative Knowledge of their several Agreements and Disagreements, if we will carefully, as in Mathematicks, keep to the same precise *Ideas*, and trace them in their several Relations one to another, without being led away by their Names. If we but separate the *Idea* under consideration from the Sign that stands for it, our Knowledge goes equally on in the discovery of real Truth and Certainty, whatever Sounds we make use of.

§ 10. One thing more we are to take notice of, That where GOD, or any other Law-maker, hath defined any Moral Names, there they have made the Essence of that Species to which that Name belongs; and there it is not safe to apply or use them otherwise: But in other cases 'tis bare impropriety of Speech to apply them contrary to the

§ 10. *Mis-naming disturbs not the Certainty of the Knowledge.*

---

(6) drawn,] **1–3** | drawn/ **4–5** [*2nd*] the] **1–2, 4–5** | and **3** (7) Just] **2–5** | And just **1** (19) shortly] **2–5** | shorty **1** (21) this] **1–4**; *om.* **5** (23) that] *add.* **4–5**

common usage of the Country. But yet even this too disturbs not the certainty of that Knowledge, which is still to be had by a due contemplation and comparing of those even nick-nam'd *Ideas*.

§ 11. *Thirdly*, There is another sort of *complex Ideas*, which being referred to *Archetypes* without us, may differ from them, and so our Knowledge about them, may come short of being real. Such are our *Ideas* of Substances, which consisting of a Collection of simple *Ideas*, supposed taken from the Works of Nature, may yet vary from them, by having more or different *Ideas* united in them, than are to be found united in the things themselves: From whence it comes to pass, that they may, and often do fail of being exactly conformable to Things themselves.

§ 12. I say then, that to have *Ideas* of *Substances*, which, by being conformable to Things, may afford us *real* Knowledge, it is not enough, as in Modes, to put together such *Ideas* as have no inconsistence, though they did never before so exist. *V.g.* the *Ideas* of *Sacrilege* or *Perjury*, *etc.* were as real and true *Ideas* before, as after the existence of any such fact. But *our Ideas of Substances* being supposed Copies, and referred to *Archetypes* without us, must still be taken from something that does or has existed; they must not consist of *Ideas* put together at the pleasure of our Thoughts, without any real pattern they were taken from, though we can perceive no inconsistence in such a Combination. The reason whereof is, because we knowing not what real Constitution it is of Substances, whereon our simple *Ideas* depend, and which really is the cause of the strict union of some of them one with another, and the exclusion of others; there are very few of them, that we can be sure are, or are not inconsistent in Nature, any farther than Experience and sensible Observation reaches. Herein therefore is founded the *reality* of our Knowledge concerning *Substances*, that all our complex *Ideas* of them must be such, and such only, as are made up of such simple ones, as have been discovered to co-exist in Nature. And our *Ideas* being thus true, though not, perhaps, very exact Copies, are yet the Subjects of *real* (as far as we have any) *Knowledge* of them. Which (as has been already shewed) will not be found to reach very far: But so far as it does, it will still be *real Knowledge*. Whatever *Ideas* we have, the

§ 11. Ideas *of Substances have their Archetypes without us.* § 12. *So far as they agree with those, so far our Knowledge concerning them is real.*

(6) . Such] **4–5** | ; and these **1–3** (15–16) inconsistence] **4–5** | inconsistency **1–3**
(27, 31, 34) are, . . . only, . . . them.] **4–5** | are . . . only . . . them; **1–3**

Agreement we find they have with others, will still be knowledge. If those *Ideas* be abstract, it will be general Knowledge. But to make it *real* concerning Substances, the *Ideas* must be taken from the real existence of things. Whatever simple *Ideas* have been found to co-exist in any Substance, these we may with confidence join together again, and so make abstract *Ideas* of Substances. For whatever have once had an union in Nature, may be united again.

§ 13. This, if we rightly consider, and *confine not our Thoughts* and abstract *Ideas* to Names, as if there were, *or* could be no other *Sorts* of Things, than what known Names had already determined, and as it were set out, we should think of Things with greater freedom and less confusion, than perhaps we do. 'Twould possibly be thought a bold Paradox, if not a very dangerous Falshood, if I should say, that some *Changelings*, who have lived forty years together, without any appearance of Reason, are something between a Man and a Beast: Which prejudice is founded upon nothing else but a false Supposition, that these two Names, *Man* and *Beast*, stand for distinct Species so set out by real Essences, that there can come no other Species between them: Whereas if we will abstract from those Names, and the Supposition of such specifick Essences made by Nature, wherein all Things of the same Denominations did exactly and equally partake; if we would not fansy, that there were a certain number of these Essences, wherein all Things, as in Molds, were cast and formed, we should find that the *Idea* of the Shape, Motion, and Life of a Man without Reason, is as much a distinct *Idea*, and makes as much a distinct *sort* of Things from Man and Beast, as the *Idea* of the Shape of an *Ass* with Reason, would be different from either that of Man or Beast, and be a Species of an Animal between, or distinct from both.

§ 14. Here every body will be ready to ask, if *Changelings* may be supposed something between Man and Beast, 'Pray what are they? I answer, *Changelings*, which is as good a Word to signify something different from the signification of *MAN or BEAST*, as the Names Man and Beast are to have significations different one from the other. This, well considered, would resolve this matter, and shew

§ 13. *In our Enquiries about Substances, we must consider* Ideas, *and not confine our Thoughts to Names or Species supposed set out by Names.* §§ 14, 15. *Objection against a Changeling, being something between Man and Beast, answered.*

(28) Man] **1–2, 4–5** | a Man **3** (*3 ll. below* 35) *Man*] **2–4** | *a Man* **5**

my meaning without any more ado. But I am not so unacquainted with the Zeal of some Men, which enables them to spin Consequences, and to see Religion threatned, whenever any one ventures to quit their Forms of Speaking, as not to foresee, what Names such a Proposition as this is like to be charged with: And without doubt it will be asked, If *Changelings* are something between Man and Beast, what will become of them in the other World? To which I answer, 1. It concerns me not to know or enquire. To their own Master they stand or fall.* It will make their state neither better nor worse, whether we determine any thing of it, or no. They are in the hands of a faithful Creator and a bountiful Father, who disposes not of his Creatures according to our narrow Thoughts or Opinions, nor distinguishes them according to Names and Species of our Contrivance. And we that know so little of this present World we are in, may, I think, content our selves without being peremptory in defining the different states, which Creatures shall come into, when they go off this Stage. It may suffice us, that he hath made known to all those, who are capable of Instruction, Discourse, and Reasoning, that they shall come to an account, and receive according to what they have done in this Body.**

§ 15. But, *Secondly*, I answer, The force of these Men's Question, (*viz.* will you deprive *Changelings* of a future state?) is founded on one of two Suppositions, which are both false. The first is, That all Things that have the outward Shape and Appearance of a Man, must necessarily be designed to an immortal future Being, after this Life. Or, secondly, that whatever is of humane Birth, must be so. Take away these Imaginations, and such Questions will be groundless and ridiculous. I desire then those, who think there is no more but an accidental difference between themselves and *Changelings*, the Essence in both being exactly the same, to consider, whether they can imagine Immortality annexed to any outward shape of the Body; the very proposing it, is, I suppose, enough to make them disown it. No one yet, that ever I heard of, how much soever immersed in Matter, allow'd that Excellency to any Figure of the gross sensible outward parts, as to affirm eternal Life due to it, or necessary consequence of it; or that any mass of Matter should,

(15) in] **4–5** | , in **1–3** (16) states, which] **4–5** | states **2–3** | state **1**

* Cf. Rom. 14: 4.
** Cf. 2 Cor. 5: 10.

after its dissolution here, be again restored hereafter to an everlasting state of Sense, Perception, and Knowledge, only because it was molded into this or that Figure, and had such a particular frame of its visible parts. Such an Opinion as this, placing Immortality in a certain superficial Figure, turns out of doors all consideration of Soul or Spirit, upon whose account alone some corporeal Beings have hitherto been concluded immortal, and others not. This is to attribute more to the outside, than inside of Things; to place the Excellency of a Man, more in the external Shape of his Body, than internal Perfections of his Soul: which is but little better than to annex the great and inestimable advantage of Immortality and Life everlasting, which he has above other material Beings, to annex it, I say, to the Cut of his Beard, or the Fashion of his Coat. For this or that outward Make of our Bodies, no more carries with it the hopes of an eternal Duration, than the Fashion of a Man's Suit gives him reasonable grounds to imagine it will never wear out, or that it will make him immortal. 'Twill perhaps be said, that no Body thinks that the Shape makes any thing immortal, but 'tis the Shape is the sign of a rational Soul within, which is immortal. I wonder who made it the sign of any such Thing: for barely saying it, will not make it so. It would require some Proofs to persuade one of it. No Figure that I know speaks any such Language. For it may as rationally be concluded, that the dead Body of a Man, wherein there is to be found no more appearance or action of Life, than there is in a Statue, has yet nevertheless a living Soul in it, because of its shape; as that there is a rational Soul in a *Changeling*, because he has the outside of a rational Creature, when his Actions carry far less marks of Reason with them, in the whole course of his Life, than what are to be found in many a Beast.

§ 16. But 'tis the issue of rational Parents, and must therefore be concluded to have a rational Soul. I know not by what Logick you must so conclude. I am sure this is a Conclusion, that Men no where allow of. For if they did, they would not make bold, as everywhere they do, to destroy ill-formed and mis-shaped productions. Ay, but these are *Monsters*. Let them be so; What will your drivling, unintelligent, intractable *Changeling* be? Shall a defect in the Body

§ 16. *Monsters.*

---

(6) Spirit, upon] **1er–5** | Spirit; and upon **1** (32) so conclude] **4–5** | conclude so **1–3** (*l. below* 36) *Monsters.*] *add.* **4–5**

make a *Monster*; a defect in the Mind, (the far more Noble, and, in the common phrase, the far more Essential Part) not? Shall the want of a Nose, or a Neck, make a *Monster*, and put such Issue out of the rank of Men; the want of Reason and Understanding, not? This is to bring all back again, to what was exploded just now: This is to place all in the Shape, and to take the measure of a Man only by his out-side. To shew that according to the ordinary way of Reasoning in this Matter, People do lay the whole stress on the Figure, and resolve the whole Essence of the Species of Man (as they make it) into the outward Shape, how unreasonable soever it be, and how much soever they disown it, we need but trace their Thoughts and Practice a little farther, and then it will plainly appear. The well-shaped *Changeling* is a Man, has a rational Soul, though it appear not; this is past doubt, say you. Make the Ears a little longer, and more pointed, and the Nose a little flatter than ordinary, and then you begin to boggle: Make the Face yet narrower, flatter, and longer, and then you are at a stand: Add still more and more of the likeness of a Brute to it, and let the Head be perfectly that of some other Animal, then presently 'tis a *Monster*; and 'tis demonstration with you, that it hath no rational Soul, and must be destroy'd. Where now (I ask) shall be the just measure; which the utmost Bounds of that Shape, that carries with it a rational Soul? For since there has been humane *Fœtus*'s produced, half Beast, and half Man; and others three parts one, and one part t'other; and so it is possible they may be in all the variety of approaches to the one or the other Shape, and may have several degrees of mixture of the likeness of a Man, or a Brute, I would gladly know what are those precise Lineaments, which according to this Hypothesis, are, or are not capable of a rational Soul to be joined to them. What sort of outside is the certain sign that there is, or is not such an Inhabitant within? For till that be done, we talk at random of *Man*: and shall always, I fear, do so, as long as we give our selves up to certain Sounds, and the Imaginations of setled and fixed Species in Nature, we know not what. But after all, I desire it may be considered, that those who think they have answered the difficulty, by telling us, that a mis-shaped *Fœtus* is a *Monster*, run into the same Fault they are arguing against, by constituting a Species between Man and Beast. For what

(2–4)) not . . ., not] **2er–5** | , not . . .,) not **1–2** (10–11) it . . . soever] **1–4**; *om.* **5** (17) are at a stand] **2–5** | begin to doubt **1** (24) parts] **2–5** | part **1** (25–6) [*2nd*] the . . . Shape] **4–5** | one shape or the other **1–3** (27) , I] **4–5** | . I **1–3**

else, I pray, is their Monster in the case, (if the word *Monster* signifies any thing at all) but something neither Man nor Beast, but partaking somewhat of either: And just so is the *Changeling* before-mentioned. So necessary is it to quit the common notion of Species and Essences, if we will truly look into the Nature of Things, and examine them, by what our Faculties can discover in them as they exist, and not by groundless Fancies, that have been taken up about them.

§ 17. I have mentioned this here, because I think we cannot be too cautious, that *Words* and *Species*, in the ordinary Notions which we have been used to of them, impose not on us. For I am apt to think, therein lies one great obstacle to our clear and distinct Knowledge, especially in reference to Substances; and from thence has rose a great part of the Difficulties about Truth and Certainty. Would we accustom our selves to separate our Contemplations and Reasonings from Words, we might, in a great measure, remedy this Inconvenience within our own Thoughts: But yet it would still disturb us in our Discourse with others, as long as we retained the Opinion, that *Species* and their Essences were any thing else but our abstract *Ideas*, (such as they are) with Names annexed to them, to be the signs of them.

§ 18. Where-ever we perceive the Agreement or Disagreement of any of our *Ideas* there is certain Knowledge: and where-ever we are sure those *Ideas* agree with the reality of Things, there is certain real Knowledge. Of which Agreement of our *Ideas* with the reality of Things, having here given the marks, I think I have shewn wherein it is, that *Certainty*, *real Certainty*, consists. Which whatever it was to others, was, I confess, to me heretofore, one of those *Desiderata* which I found great want of.

§ 17. *Words and Species.* § 18. *Recapitulation.*

(1–2) signifies] **4–5** | signifie **1–3** (7) , that] *add.* **4–5** (10) which] *add.* **4–5** (20) the] **1–2, 4–5**; *om.* **3** (*l. below* 29: § 17.) *Words and Species.*] **4–5** | *Objection against a Changeling, being something between Man and Beast* [*Beast,* **3**] *answered.* **2–3**

CHAPTER V

Of Truth in general.

§ 1. WHAT is *Truth*, was an Enquiry many Ages since; and it being that which all Mankind either do, or pretend to search after, it cannot but be worth our while carefully to examine wherein it consists; and so acquaint our selves with the Nature of it, as to observe how the Mind distinguishes it from Falshood.

§ 2. *Truth* then seems to me, in the proper import of the Word, to signify nothing but *the joining or separating of Signs, as the Things signified by them, do agree or disagree one with another*. The *joining* or *separating* of signs here meant is what by another name, we call Proposition. So that Truth properly belongs only to Propositions: whereof there are two sorts, *viz.* Mental and Verbal; as there are two sorts of Signs commonly made use of, *viz. Ideas* and Words.

§ 3. To form a clear Notion of *Truth*, it is very necessary to consider *Truth* of Thought, and *Truth* of Words, distinctly one from another: but yet it is very difficult to treat of them asunder. Because it is unavoidable, in treating of mental Propositions, to make use of Words: and then the Instances given of *Mental Propositions*, cease immediately to be barely Mental, *and* become *Verbal*. For a *mental Proposition* being nothing but a bare consideration of the *Ideas*, as they are in our Minds stripp'd of Names, they lose the Nature of purely *mental Propositions*, as soon as they are put into Words.

§ 4. And that which makes it yet *harder to treat of mental* and verbal *Propositions separately*, is, That most Men, if not all, in their Thinking and Reasonings within themselves, make use of Words instead of *Ideas*; at least when the subject of their Meditation contains in it complex *Ideas*. Which is a great evidence of the imperfection and uncertainty of our *Ideas* of that kind, and may, if attentively made use of, serve for a mark to shew us, what are those Things, we have clear and perfect established *Ideas* of, and what not. For if we will curiously observe the way our Mind takes in Thinking and

§ 1. *What Truth is.* § 2. *A right joining, or separating of Signs*; i.e. Ideas *or Words*. § 3. *Which make mental or verbal Propositions.* § 4. *Mental Propositions are very hard to be treated of.*

(8–9) . The . . . *separating*] **2–5** | ; which way of joining or separating **1**
(9) here . . . name] *add.* **2–5**

Reasoning, we shall find, I suppose, that when we make any Propositions within our own Thoughts, about *White* or *Black*, *Sweet* or *Bitter*, a *Triangle* or a *Circle*, we can and often do frame in our Minds the *Ideas* themselves, without reflecting on the Names. But when we would consider, or make Propositions about the more complex *Ideas*, as of a *Man*, *Vitriol*, *Fortitude*, *Glory*, we usually put the Name for the *Idea*: Because the *Ideas* these Names stand for, being for the most part imperfect, confused, and undetermined, we reflect on the *Names* themselves, because they are more clear, certain, and distinct, and readier occurr to our Thoughts, than the pure *Ideas*: and so we make use of these Words instead of the *Ideas* themselves, even when we would meditate and reason within our selves, and make tacit mental Propositions. In *Substances*, as has been already noted, this is occasioned by the imperfection of our *Ideas*: we making the Name stand for the real Essence, of which we have no *Idea* at all. In *Modes*, it is occasioned by the great number of simple *Ideas*, that go to the making them up. For many of them being very much compounded, the *Name* occurs much easier, than the complex *Idea* it self, which requires time and attention to be recollected, and exactly represented to the Mind, even in those Men, who have formerly been at the pains to do it; and is utterly impossible to be done by those, who though they have ready in their Memory, the greatest part of the common Words of their Language, yet perhaps never troubled themselves in all their Lives, to consider what precise *Ideas* the most of them stood for. Some confused or obscure Notions have served their turns; and many who talk very much of *Religion* and *Conscience*, of *Church* and *Faith*, of *Power* and *Right*, of *Obstructions* and *Humours*, *Melancholy* and *Choler*, would, perhaps, have little left in their Thoughts and Meditations, if one should desire them to think only of the Things themselves, and lay by those Words, with which they so often confound others, and not seldom themselves also.

§ 5. But to return to the consideration of Truth. We must, I say, observe two sorts of Propositions, that we are capable of making.

First, *Mental*, *wherein* the *Ideas* in our Understandings *are* without the use of Words *put together*, *or separated* by the Mind, perceiving, or judging of their Agreement, or Disagreement.

§ 5. *Being nothing but the joining, or separating* Ideas *without Words.*

(18) very much] **1–4**; *om.* **5**. (**Coste** 'la plûpart d'entr'eux étant extremement complexes')

Secondly, *Verbal Propositions*, which *are Words* the signs of our *Ideas put together or separated in affirmative or negative Sentences*. By which way of affirming or denying, these Signs, made by Sounds, are as it were put together or separated one from another. So that Proposition consists in joining, or separating Signs, and Truth consists in the putting together, or separating these Signs, according as the Things, which they stand for, agree or disagree.

§ 6. Every one's Experience will satisfie him, that the Mind, either by perceiving or supposing the Agreement or Disagreement of any of its *Ideas*, does tacitly within it self put them into a kind of Proposition affirmative or negative, which I have endeavoured to express by the terms *Putting together* and *Separating*. But this Action of the Mind, which is so familiar to every thinking and reasoning Man, is easier to be conceived by reflecting on what passes in us, when we affirm or deny, than to be explained by Words. When a Man has in his Mind the *Idea* of two Lines, *viz.* the *Side* and *Diagonal* of a Square, whereof the Diagonal is an Inch long, he may have the *Idea* also of the division of that Line, into a certain number of equal parts; *v.g.* into Five, Ten, an Hundred, a Thousand, or any other Number, and may have the *Idea* of that Inch Line, being divisible or not divisible, into such equal parts, as a certain number of them will be equal to the Side-line. Now whenever he perceives, believes, or supposes such a kind of Divisibility to agree or disagree to his *Idea* of that Line, he, as it were, *joins* or *separates* those two *Ideas*, *viz.* the *Idea* of that Line, and the *Idea* of that kind of Divisibility, and so makes a mental Proposition, which is true or false, according as such a kind of Divisibility, a Divisibility into such *aliquot* parts, does really agree to that Line, or no. When *Ideas* are so put together, or separated in the Mind, as they, or the Things they stand for do agree, or not, that is, as I may call it, *mental Truth*. But *Truth of Words* is something more, and that is the affirming or denying of Words one of another, as the *Ideas* they stand for agree or disagree: And this again is twofold. Either *purely Verbal*, and trifling, which I shall speak of, *Chap.* 10. *or Real* and instructive; which is the Object of that real Knowledge, which we have spoken of already.

§ 6. *When mental Propositions contain real Truth, and when verbal.*

---

(2) *negative*] **1–3** | *Negative* **4–5** (5) Signs,] **4–5** | Signs; **1–3** (*likewise* **Coste**) (7) , which] *add.* **4–5** (15) affirm or deny] **2–5** | reason, judge, or suppose **1** (28) . When] **4–5** | : And when **1–3**. (**Coste** 'Ligne. Et quand') (35) which] **1–3** | which, **4–5**

§ 7. But here again will be apt to occurr the same doubt about Truth, that did about Knowledge: And it will be objected, That if Truth be nothing but the joining or separating of Words in Propositions, as the *Ideas* they stand for agree or disagree in Men's Minds, the Knowledge of *Truth is not so valuable a Thing*, as it is taken to be; nor worth the Pains and Time Men imploy in the search of it: since *by this account*, it amounts to no more than the conformity of Words, to the *Chimæras* of Men's Brains. Who knows not what odd Notions many Men's Heads are fill'd with, and what strange *Ideas* all Men's Brains are capable of? But if we rest here, we know the Truth of nothing by this Rule, but of the visionary World in our own Imaginations; nor have other Truth, but what as much concerns *Harpies* and *Centaurs*, as Men and Horses. For those, and the like, may be *Ideas* in our Heads, and have their agreement and disagreement there, as well as the *Ideas* of real Beings, and so have as true Propositions made about them. And 'twill be altogether as true a Proposition, to say *all Centaurs are Animals*, as that *all Men are Animals*; and the certainty of one, as great as the other. For in both the Propositions, the Words are put together according to the agreement of the *Ideas* in our Minds: And the agreement of the *Idea* of *Animal*, with that of *Centaur*, is as clear and visible to the Mind, as the agreement of the *Idea* of *Animal*, with that of *Man*; and so these two Propositions are equally true, equally certain. But of what use is all such Truth to us?

§ 8. Though what has been said in the fore-going Chapter, to distinguish real from imaginary Knowledge, might suffice here, in answer to this Doubt, to distinguish *real Truth* from *chimerical*, or (if you please,) *barely nominal*, they depending both on the same foundation; yet it may not be amiss here again to consider, that though our Words signifie nothing but our *Ideas*, yet being designed by them to signifie Things, the *Truth* they contain, when put into Propositions, will be only *Verbal*, when they stand for *Ideas* in the Mind, that have not an agreement with the reality of Things. And therefore Truth, as well as Knowledge, may well come under the distinction of *Verbal* and *Real*; that being only *verbal Truth*, wherein Terms are joined according to the agreement or disagreement of the

§ 7. *Objection against verbal Truth, that thus it may all be chimerical.* § 8. *Answered, real Truth is about* Ideas *agreeing to Things.*

(4) Minds] **2–5** | Mind **1** (6) in] **1–4** | to **5** (17) [*1st*] *all*] *edit.* | all **1–5**

Ideas they stand for, without regarding whether our *Ideas* are such, as really have, or are capable of having an Existence in Nature. But then it is they contain *real Truth*, when these signs are joined, as our *Ideas* agree; and when our *Ideas* are such, as we know are capable of having an Existence in Nature: which in Substances we cannot know, but by knowing that such have existed.

§ 9. *Truth* is the marking down in Words, the agreement or disagreement of *Ideas* as it is. *Falshood* is the marking down in Words, the agreement or disagreement of *Ideas* otherwise than it is. And so far as these *Ideas*, thus marked by Sounds, agree to their Archetypes, so far only is the *Truth real*. The knowledge of this Truth, consists in knowing what *Ideas* the Words stand for, and the perception of the agreement or disagreement of those *Ideas*, according as it is marked by those Words.

§ 10. But because Words are looked on as the great Conduits of Truth and Knowledge, and that in conveying and receiving of Truth, and commonly in reasoning about it, we make use of Words and Propositions, I shall more at large enquire, wherein the certainty of real Truths, contained in Propositions, consists, and where it is to be had; and endeavour to shew in what sort of universal Propositions we are capable of being *certain* of their real Truth, or Falshood.

I shall begin with general Propositions, as those which most employ our Thoughts, and exercise our Contemplation. *General Truths* are most looked after by the Mind, as those that most enlarge our Knowledge; and by their comprehensiveness, satisfying us at once of many particulars, enlarge our view, and shorten our way to Knowledge.

§ 11. Besides Truth taken in the first sense before-mentioned, there are other sorts of Truths; as, 1. *Moral Truth*, which is speaking Things according to the perswasion of our own Minds, though the Proposition we speak agree not to the reality of Things. 2. *Metaphysical Truth*, which is nothing but the real Existence of Things, conformable to the *Ideas* to which we have annexed their names. This, though it seems to consist in the very Beings of Things, yet when considered a little nearly, will appear to include a tacit

§ 9. *Falshood is the joining of Names otherwise than their* Ideas *agree.* § 10. *General Propositions to be treated of more at large.* § 11. *Moral and metaphysical Truth.*

---

(5) : which] **2–5** | ; which **1** we] **1–4** | she **5** (14) those] **2–5** | these **1** (28) Besides] **1–3** | Besides, **4–5** (*2 ll. below* 35: § 10.) *more at large*] **2–3, 5** | *mo at largo* **4**

Proposition, whereby the Mind joins that particular Thing, to the *Idea* it had before settled with a name to it. But these Considerations of Truth, either having been before taken notice of, or not being much to our present purpose, it may suffice here only to have mentioned them.

CHAPTER VI

Of Universal Propositions, their Truth and Certainty.

§ 1. THOUGH the examining and judging of *Ideas* by themselves, their Names being quite laid aside, be the best and surest way to clear and distinct Knowledge: yet through the prevailing custom of using Sounds for *Ideas*, I think it is very seldom practised. Every one may observe how common it is for Names to be made use of, instead of the *Ideas* themselves, even when Men think and reason within their own Breasts; especially if the *Ideas* be very complex, and made up of a great Collection of simple ones. This makes *the consideration of Words and Propositions*, so *necessary a part of the Treatise of Knowledge*, that 'tis very hard to speak intelligibly of the one, without explaining the other.

§ 2. All the Knowledge we have, being only of particular or *general Truths*, 'tis evident, that whatever may be done in the former of these, the latter, which is that which with Reason is most sought after, can never be well made known, and is very *seldom apprehended, but as conceived and expressed in Words*. It is not therefore out of our way, in the Examination of our Knowledge, to enquire into the Truth and Certainty of universal Propositions.

§ 3. But that we may not be mis-led in this case, by that which is the danger every-where, I mean by the doubtfulness of Terms, 'tis fit to observe, that Certainty is twofold; *Certainty of Truth*, and *Certainty of Knowledge. Certainty of Truth* is, when Words are so put together in Propositions, as exactly to express the agreement or disagreement of the *Ideas* they stand for, as really it is. *Certainty of Knowledge* is, to perceive the agreement or disagreement of *Ideas*, as

§ 1. *Treating of Words necessary to Knowledge.* § 2. *General Truths hardly to be understood, but in verbal Propositions.* § 3. *Certainty twofold, of Truth and of Knowledge.*

(9) . Every] **4–5** | ; and every **1–3**. (**Coste** '. Et chacun')

expressed in any Proposition. This we usually call knowing, or being certain of the Truth of any Proposition.

§ 4. Now because *we cannot be certain of the Truth of any general Proposition, unless we know the precise bounds and extent of the Species its Terms stand for*, it is necessary we should know the Essence of each *Species*, which is that which constitutes and bounds it. This, in all simple *Ideas* and Modes, is not hard to do. For in these, the real and nominal Essence being the same; or which is all one, the abstract *Idea*, which the general Term stands for, being the sole Essence and Boundary, that is or can be supposed, of the *Species*, there can be no doubt, how far the *Species* extends, or what Things are comprehended under each Term: which, 'tis evident, are all, that have an exact conformity with the *Idea* it stands for, and no other. But in Substances, wherein a real Essence, distinct from the nominal, is supposed to constitute, determine, and bound the Species, the extent of the general Word is very uncertain: because not knowing this real Essence, we cannot know what is, or is not of that *Species*; and consequently what may, or may not with certainty be affirmed of it. And thus speaking of a *Man*, or *Gold*, or any other *Species* of natural Substances, as supposed constituted by a precise real Essence, which Nature regularly imparts to every individual of that Kind, whereby it is made to be of that Species, we cannot be certain of the truth of any Affirmation of Negation made of it. For *Man*, or *Gold*, taken in this sense, and used for *Species* of Things, constituted by real Essences, different from the complex *Idea* in the Mind of the Speaker, stand for we know not what: and the extent of these Species, with such Boundaries, are so unknown and undetermined, that it is impossible, with any certainty, to affirm, that all Men are rational, or that all Gold is yellow. But where the nominal Essence is kept to, as the Boundary of each Species, and Men extend the application of any general Term no farther than to the particular Things, in which the complex *Idea* it stands for is to be found, there they are in no danger to mistake the bounds of each *Species*, nor can be in doubt, on this account, whether any Proposition be true, or no. I have chose to explain this uncertainty of Propositions

§ 4. *No Proposition can be known to be true, where the Essence of each Species mentioned is not known.*

---

(9) which] *add.* **2–5** (14) wherein] **2–5** | where **1** (15) [*2nd*] the] **2–5** | there the **1** (20–2) constituted . . . of] **2–5** | made by Nature, and partaking of that real Essence, which is supposed to constitute **1** (34) nor can] **4–5** | or **1–3**

in this scholastick way, and have made use of the Terms of *Essences* and *Species*, on purpose to shew the absurdity and inconvenience there is to think of them, as of any other sort of Realities, than barely abstract *Ideas* with Names to them. To suppose, that the *Species* of Things are any thing, but the sorting of them under general Names, according as they agree to several abstract *Ideas*, of which we make those Names the Signs, is to confound Truth, and introduce Uncertainty into all general Propositions, that can be made about them. Though therefore these Things might, to People not possessed with scholastick Learning, be perhaps treated of, in a better and clearer way: yet those wrong Notions of *Essences* and *Species*, having got root in most Peoples Minds, who have received any tincture from the Learning, which has prevailed in this part of the World, are to be discovered and removed, to make way for that use of Words, which should convey certainty with it.

§ 5. *The Names of Substances* then, *whenever made to stand for Species, which are supposed to be constituted by real Essences*, which we know not, *are not capable to convey Certainty to the Understanding*: Of the Truth of general Propositions made up of such Terms we cannot be sure. The reason whereof is plain. For how can we be sure that this or that quality is in *Gold*, when we know not what is or is not *Gold*. Since in this way of speaking nothing is *Gold*, but what partakes of an Essence, which we not knowing, cannot know where it is, or is not, and so cannot be sure, that any parcel of Matter in the World is or is not in this sense *Gold*; being incurably ignorant, whether it has or has not that which makes any thing to be called *Gold*, *i.e.* that real Essence of *Gold* whereof we have no *Idea* at all. This being as impossible for us to know, as it is for a blind Man to tell in what Flower the Colour of a *pansie* is, or is not to be found, whilst he has no *Idea* of the Colour of a *pansie* at all. Or if we could (which is impossible) certainly know where a real Essence, which we know not, is, *v.g.* in what parcels of matter the real Essence of *Gold* is, yet could we not be sure, that this or that quality could with truth be affirm'd of *Gold*; since it is impossible for us to know, that this or

§ 5. *This more particularly concerns Substances.*

---

(12) and] **1–4** | or **5** (18) *Essences*] **1–4, W** | *Essence* **5** (21)–582(3) The . . . constitute.] *add.* **2–5** (30) *pansie*] **Coste** *adds a marginal linguistic note.* (35) it is] **4–5** | 'tis **2–3**

that quality or *Idea* has a necessary connexion with a real Essence, of which we have no *Idea* at all, whatever Species that supposed real Essence may be imagined to constitute.

§ 6. On the other side, the *Names of Substances*, when made use of as they should be, for the *Ideas* Men have in their Minds, though they carry a clear and determinate signification with them, *will not* yet *serve us to make many universal Propositions, of whose Truth we can be certain.* Not because in this use of them we are uncertain what Things are signified by them, but because the complex *Ideas* they stand for, are such Combinations of simple ones, as carry not with them any discoverable connexion or repugnancy, but with a very few other *Ideas.*

§ 7. The complex *Ideas*, that our Names of the Species of Substances properly stand for, are Collections of such Qualities, as have been observed to co-exist in an unknown *Substratum* which we call *Substance*; but what other Qualities necessarily co-exist with such Combinations, we cannot certainly know, unless we can discover their natural dependence; which in their primary Qualities, we can go but a very little way in; and in all their secondary Qualities, we can discover no connexion at all, for the Reasons mentioned, *Chap.* 3. *viz.* 1. Because we know not the real Constitutions of Substances, on which each *secondary Quality* particularly depends. 2. Did we know that, it would serve us only for experimental (not universal) Knowledge; and reach with certainty no farther, than that bare instance. Because our Understandings can discover no conceivable connexion between any *secondary Quality*, and any modification whatsoever of any of the *primary* ones. And therefore there are very few general Propositions to be made concerning Substances, which can carry with them *undoubted Certainty.*

§ 8. *All Gold is fixed*, is a Proposition whose Truth we cannot be certain of, how universally soever it be believed. For if, according to the useless Imagination of the Schools, any one supposes the term *Gold* to stand for a Species of Things set out by Nature, by a real Essence belonging to it, 'tis evident he knows not what particular Substances are of that Species; and so cannot, with certainty,

§ 6. *The Truth of few universal Propositions concerning Substances, is to be known.* § 7. *Because Co-existence of* Ideas *in few Cases to be known.* §§ 8, 9. *Instance in Gold.*

---

(2) *Idea*] **2, 4–5** | *Ideas* **3** (3) *v.* 581(21), n. (13) of the Species] *add.* **4–5** (15–16) in . . . *Substance*] *add.* **4–5** (25) . Because] **4–5** | : because **1–3**

affirm any thing universally of *Gold*. But if he makes *Gold* stand for a Species, determined by its nominal Essence, let the nominal Essence, for example, be the complex *Idea* of a *Body*, of a certain *yellow* colour, *malleable*, *fusible*, and *heavier* than any other known; in this proper use of the word *Gold*, there is no difficulty to know what is, or is not *Gold*. But yet no other Quality can with certainty be universally affirmed or denied of *Gold*, but what hath a discoverable connexion, or inconsistency with that nominal Essence. *Fixedness*, for example, having no necessary connexion, that we can discover, with the Colour, Weight, or any other simple *Idea* of our complex one, or with the whole Combination together; it is impossible that we should certainly know the Truth of this Proposition, That *all Gold is fixed.*

§ 9. As there is no discoverable connexion between *Fixedness*, and the Colour, Weight, and other simple *Ideas* of that nominal Essence of *Gold*; so if we make our complex *Idea* of *Gold*, a *Body yellow*, *fusible*, *ductile*, *weighty*, and *fixed*, we shall be at the same uncertainty concerning *Solubility* in *Aqua regia*; and for the same reason. Since we can never, from consideration of the *Ideas* themselves, with certainty affirm or deny, of a Body, whose complex *Idea* is made up of yellow, very weighty, ductile, fusible, and fixed, that it is soluble in *Aqua regia*: And so on of the rest of its Qualities. I would gladly meet with one general Affirmation, concerning any Quality of *Gold*, that any one can certainly know is true. It will, no doubt, be presently objected, Is not this an universal certain Proposition, *All Gold is malleable*? To which I answer, It is a very certain Proposition, if *Malleableness* be a part of the complex *Idea* the word *Gold* stands for. But then here is nothing affirmed of *Gold*, but that that Sound stands for an *Idea* in which *Malleableness* is contained: And such a sort of Truth and Certainty as this, it is to say *a Centaur is four-footed.* But if *Malleableness* makes not a part of the specifick Essence the name *Gold* stands for, 'tis plain, *All Gold is Malleable*, is not a certain Proposition. Because let the complex *Idea* of *Gold*, be made up of which soever of its other Qualities you please, *Malleableness* will not appear to depend on that complex *Idea*; nor follow from any simple one contained in it. The connexion that *Malleableness* has (if it has any) with those other Qualities, being only by the intervention of the real Constitution of its insensible parts, which, since we know not, 'tis impossible we should perceive that connexion, unless we could discover that which ties them together.

(1, 30) makes] **4–5** | make **1–3** (3) *Body*,] **4–5** | Body **1–3** (*Body* **2–3**)

§ 10. The more, indeed, of these co-existing Qualities we unite into one complex *Idea*, under one name, the more precise and determinate we make the signification of that Word; But yet never make it thereby more capable of *universal Certainty*, in respect of other Qualities, not contained in our complex *Idea*; since we perceive not their connexion, or dependence one on another; being ignorant both of that real Constitution in which they are all founded; and also how they flow from it. For the chief part of our Knowledge concerning Substances is not, as in other Things, barely of the relation of two *Ideas*, that may exist separately; but is of the necessary connexion and co-existence of several distinct *Ideas* in the same Subject, or of their repugnancy so to co-exist. Could we begin at the other end, and discover what it was, wherein that Colour consisted, what made a Body lighter or heavier, what texture of Parts made it malleable, fusible, and fixed, and fit to be dissolved in this sort of Liquor, and not in another; if (I say) we had such an *Idea* as this of Bodies, and could perceive wherein all sensible Qualities originally consist, and how they are produced; we might frame such abstract *Ideas* of them, as would furnish us with matter of more general Knowledge, and enable us to make universal Propositions, that should carry *general Truth* and *Certainty* with them. But whilst our complex *Ideas* of the sorts of Substances, are so remote from that internal real Constitution, on which their sensible Qualities depend; and are made up of nothing but an imperfect Collection of those apparent Qualities our Senses can discover, there can be very few general Propositions concerning Substances, of whose real Truth we can be *certainly* assured; since there are but few simple *Ideas*, of whose connexion and necessary co-existence, we can have certain and undoubted Knowledge. I imagine, amongst all the *secondary Qualities* of Substances, and the Powers relating to them, there cannot any two be named, whose necessary co-existence, or repugnance to co-exist, can certainly be known, unless in those of the same sense, which necessarily exclude one another, as I have elsewhere shewed. No one, I think, by the Colour that is in any Body, can certainly know what Smell, Taste, Sound, or tangible Qualities it has, nor what Alterations it is

§ 10. *As far as any such Co-existence can be known, so far universal Propositions may be certain. But this will go but a little way, because,*

(4) thereby] *add.* **2–5** (7) all] **1–2, 4–5**; *om.* **3** (*likewise* **Coste**) (10) is] *add.* **4–5.** (*Not in* **Coste**) (14) made] **1–2, 4–5** | makes **3**

capable to make, or receive, on, or from other Bodies. The same may be said of the Sound, or Taste, *etc.* Our specifick Names of Substances standing for any Collections of such *Ideas*, 'tis not to be wondred, that we can, with them, make very few general Propositions of *undoubted real certainty*. But yet so far as any complex *Idea*, of any sort of Substances, contains in it any simple *Idea*, whose necessary co-existence with any other may be discovered, so far *universal Propositions* may *with certainty* be made concerning it: *v.g.* Could any one discover a necessary connexion between *Malleableness*, and the *Colour* or *Weight* of *Gold*, or any other part of the complex *Idea* signified by that Name, he might make a *certain* universal Proposition concerning *Gold* in this respect; and the real Truth of this Proposition, That *all Gold is malleable*, would be as *certain* as of this, *The three Angles of all right-lined Triangles, are equal to two right ones.*

§ 11. Had we such *Ideas* of Substances, as to know what real Constitutions produce those sensible Qualities we find in them, and how those Qualities flowed from thence, we could, by the specifick *Ideas* of their real Essences in our own Minds, more certainly find out their Properties, and discover what Qualities they had, or had not, than we can now by our Senses: and to know the Properties of *Gold*, it would be no more necessary, that *Gold* should exist, and that we should make Experiments upon it, than it is necessary for the knowing the Properties of a Triangle, that a Triangle should exist in any Matter, the *Idea* in our Minds would serve for the one, as well as the other. But we are so far from being admitted into the Secrets of Nature, that we scarce so much as ever approach the first entrance towards them. For we are wont to consider the Substances we meet with, each of them, as an entire thing by it self, having all its Qualities in it self, and independent of other Things; overlooking, for the most part, the Operations of those invisible Fluids, they are encompassed with; and upon whose Motions and operations depend the greatest part of those qualities which are taken notice of in them, and are made by us the inherent marks of Distinction, whereby we know and denominate them. Put a piece of *Gold* any where by it self, separate from the reach and influence

§§ 11, 12. *The Qualities which make our complex* Ideas *of Substances, depend mostly on external, remote, and unperceived Causes.*

---

(2) *etc.*] **1–3** | etc. **4–5** (3) standing for] **2–5** | signifying **1** (5) *Idea*,] **1–3, W** | *Idea*; **4–5** (15) we] **1–2, 4–5** | he **3** (29) it] **1–2, 4–5** | its **3** (34) Put] **1–2, 4–5** | But **3** (*likewise* **Coste**) (35)–586(1) separate . . . bodies] **4–5** | separate from all other bodies **2–3** | let no other Body encompass it **1**

of all other bodies, it will immediately lose all its Colour and Weight, and perhaps Malleableness too; which, for ought I know, would be changed into a perfect Friability. *Water*, in which to us *Fluidity* is an essential Quality, left to it self, would cease to be fluid. But if inanimate Bodies owe so much of their present state to other Bodies without them, that they would not be what they appear to us, were those Bodies that environ them removed, it is yet more so in *Vegetables*, which are nourished, grow, and produce Leaves, Flowers, and Seeds, in a constant Succession. And if we look a little nearer into the state of *Animals*, we shall find, that their Dependence, as to Life, Motion, and the most considerable Qualities to be observed in them, is so wholly on extrinsecal Causes and Qualities of other Bodies, that make no part of them, that they cannot subsist a moment without them: though yet those Bodies on which they depend, are little taken notice of, and make no part of the complex *Ideas*, we frame of those Animals. Take the Air but a minute from the greatest part of Living Creatures, and they presently lose Sense, Life, and Motion. This the necessity of breathing has forced into our Knowledge. But how many other extrinsecal, and possibly very remote Bodies, do the Springs of those admirable Machines depend on, which are not vulgarly observed, or so much as thought on; and how many are there, which the severest Enquiry can never discover? The Inhabitants of this spot of the Universe, though removed so many millions of Miles from the Sun, yet depend so much on the duly tempered motion of Particles coming from, or agitated by it, that were this Earth removed, but a small part of that distance, out of its present situation, and placed a little farther or nearer that Source of Heat, 'tis more than probable, that the greatest part of the Animals in it, would immediately perish: since we find them so often destroyed by an excess or defect of the Sun's warmth, which an accidental position, in some parts of this our little Globe, exposes them to. The Qualities observed in a *Load-stone*, must needs have their Source far beyond the Confines of that Body; and the ravage made often on several sorts of Animals, by invisible Causes, the certain death (as we are told) of some of them, by barely passing the Line, or, as 'tis certain of others, by being removed into a Neighbouring Country, evidently shew, that the Concurrence and Operation of several Bodies, with which, they are seldom thought, to have any thing to do, is absolutely necessary to

(1) *v.* 585(35), n. (23) Universe,] **1, 4–5** | Universe; **2–3**

make them be, what they appear to us, and to preserve those Qualities, by which we know, and distinguish them. We are then quite out of the way, when we think, that Things contain within themselves the Qualities, that appear to us in them: And we in vain search for that Constitution within the Body of a Fly, or an Elephant, upon which depend those Qualities and Powers we observe in them. For which, perhaps, to understand them aright, we ought to look, not only beyond this our Earth and Atmosphere, but even beyond the Sun, or remotest Star our Eyes have yet discovered. For how much the Being and Operation of particular Substances in this our Globe, depend on Causes utterly beyond our view, is impossible for us to determine. We see and perceive some of the Motions and grosser Operations of Things here about us; but whence the Streams come that keep all these curious Machines in motion and repair, how conveyed and modified, is beyond our notice and apprehension; and the great Parts and Wheels, as I may so say, of this stupendious Structure of the Universe, may, for ought we know, have such a connexion and dependence in their Influences and Operations one upon another, that, perhaps, Things in this our Mansion, would put on quite another face, and cease to be what they are, if some one of the Stars, or great Bodies incomprehensibly remote from us, should cease to be, or move as it does. This is certain, Things, however absolute and entire they seem in themselves, are but Retainers to other parts of Nature, for that which they are most taken notice of by us. Their observable Qualities, Actions, and Powers, are owing to something without them; and there is not so complete and perfect a part, that we know, of Nature, which does not owe the Being it has, and the Excellencies of it, to its Neighbours; and we must not confine our thoughts within the surface of any body, but look a great deal farther, to comprehend perfectly those Qualities that are in it.

§ 12. If this be so, it is not to be wondred, that *we have very imperfect* Ideas *of Substances*; and that the real Essences, on which depend their Properties and Operations, are unknown to us. We cannot discover so much as that *size*, *figure*, and *texture* of their minute and active Parts, which is really in them; much less the

(2) , by . . . them] **4–5** | we know, and distinguish them by **1–3** (19) our] **1–2, 4–5** | our own **3** (29–30) not . . . farther] **2–5** | *look a great deal farther than the Surface of any Body* **1** (32) is] **1–4, W**; *om.* **5** (35) much] **1–2, 4–5** | much, and how, 3. (*This reading in* **3** *stems from a misprinted line-number* ('4' *for* 40') *in* **2er**; *cf.* 589(2), n.) that] **2–5** | the **1**

different Motions and Impulses made in and upon them by Bodies from without, upon which depends, and by which is formed the greatest and most remarkable part of those Qualities we observe in them, and of which our complex *Ideas* of them are made up. This consideration alone is enough to put an end to all our hopes of ever having the *Ideas* of their real Essences; which, whilst we want, the nominal Essences, we make use of instead of them, will be able to furnish us but very sparingly with any *general Knowledge*, or universal Propositions capable of real *Certainty*.

§ 13. We are not therefore to wonder, if *Certainty* be to be found in very few general Propositions made concerning Substances: Our Knowledge of their Qualities and Properties go very seldom farther than our Senses reach and inform us. Possibly inquisitive and observing Men may, by strength of *Judgment*, penetrate farther, and on Probabilities taken from wary Observation, and Hints well laid together, often guess right at what Experience has not yet discovered to them. But this is but guessing still; it amounts only to Opinion, and has not that *certainty*, which is requisite to Knowledge. For all *general Knowledge* lies only in our own Thoughts, and consists barely in the contemplation of our own abstract *Ideas*. Where-ever we perceive any agreement or disagreement amongst them, there we have *general Knowledge*; and by putting the Names of those *Ideas* together accordingly in Propositions, can with certainty pronounce *general Truths*. But because the abstract *Ideas* of Substances, for which their specifick Names stand, whenever they have any distinct and determinate signification, have a discoverable connexion or inconsistency with but a very few other *Ideas*, the *certainty of universal Propositions concerning Substances*, is very narrow and scanty in that part, which is our principal enquiry concerning them; and there is scarce any of the Names of Substances, let the *Idea* it is applied to be what it will, of which we can generally, and with certainty pronounce, that it has or has not this or that other Quality belonging to it, and constantly co-existing or inconsistent with that *Idea*, where-ever it is to be found.

§ 14. Before we can have any tolerable knowledge of this kind, we

§ 13. *Judgment may reach farther, but that is not Knowledge.* § 14. *What is requisite for our Knowledge of Substances.*

(2) without,] **2–5** | without, and the Effects of them, **1** depends] **2–5** | depend **1** (5) is . . . ever] **2–5** | may set us at rest, as to all hopes of our **1** (6) want,] **2–5** | want **1** (27) but] *add.* **4er–5**

must first know what Changes the *primary Qualities* of one Body, do regularly produce in the *primary Qualities* of another, and how. Secondly, we must know what *primary Qualities* of any Body, produce certain Sensations or *Ideas* in us. This is in truth, no less than to know all the Effects of Matter, under its divers modifications of Bulk, Figure, Cohesion of Parts, Motion, and Rest. Which, I think, every body will allow, is utterly impossible to be known by us, without revelation. Nor if it were revealed to us, what sort of Figure, Bulk, and Motion of Corpuscles, would produce in us the Sensation of a *yellow* Colour, and what sort of Figure, Bulk, and Texture of Parts in the superficies of any Body, were fit to give such Corpuscles their due motion to produce that Colour, Would that be enough to make *universal* Propositions with *certainty*, concerning the several sorts of them, unless we had Faculties acute enough to perceive the precise Bulk, Figure, Texture, and Motion of Bodies in those minute Parts, by which they operate on our Senses, that so we might by those frame our abstract *Ideas* of them. I have mentioned here only *corporeal* Substances, whose Operations seem to lie more level to our Understandings: For as to the *Operations of Spirits*, both their thinking and moving of Bodies, we at first sight find our selves at a loss; though perhaps, when we have applied our Thoughts a little nearer to the consideration of Bodies, and their Operations, and examined how far our Notions, even in these, reach, with any clearness, beyond sensible matter of fact, we shall be bound to confess, that even in these too, our Discoveries amount to very little beyond perfect Ignorance and Incapacity.

§ 15. This is evident, *the abstract complex* Ideas *of Substances*, for which their general Names stand, not comprehending their real Constitutions, *can afford us but very little universal Certainty*. Because our *Ideas* of them are not made up of that, on which those Qualities we observe in them, and would inform our selves about, do depend, or with which they have any certain connexion. *V.g.* Let the *Idea* to which we give the name *Man*, be, as it commonly is, a Body of the ordinary shape, with Sense, voluntary Motion, and Reason join'd

§ 15. *Whilst our* Ideas *of Substances contain not their real Constitutions, we can make but few general Propositions concerning them.*

---

(2) and how] **1, 2er, 4–5** | and know **2–3** (4–5) . This . . . than] **4–5** |; which is [is *add.* **1er–3**], in truth, **1–3** (5) its] **1–4, W** | it **5** (6) . Which,] **4–5** | ; which, **2–3** | ; which **1er** | ; which is, **1** (12) Colour,] **1–4** | Colour. **5** (15) precise] *add.* **4–5** (17) that so we might] **4–5** | and so could **1–3** (29–30) . Because . . . that,] **4–5** | ; they not being that **1–3**

to it. This being the abstract *Idea*, and consequently the Essence of our Species *Man*, we can make but very few general certain Propositions concerning *Man*, standing for such an *Idea*. Because not knowing the real Constitution on which Sensation, power of Motion, and Reasoning, with that peculiar Shape, depend, and whereby they are united together in the same Subject, there are very few other Qualities, with which we can perceive them to have a necessary connexion: and therefore we cannot with Certainty affirm, That *all Men sleep by intervals*; That *no Man can be nourished by Wood or Stones*; That *all Men will be poisoned by Hemlock*: because these *Ideas* have no connexion nor repugnancy with this our nominal Essence of *Man*, with this abstract *Idea* that Name stands for. We must in these and the like appeal to trial in particular Subjects, which can reach but a little way. We must content our selves with Probability in the rest: but can have no general Certainty, whilst our specifick *Idea* of *Man*, contains not that real Constitution, which is the root, wherein all his inseparable Qualities are united, and from whence they flow. Whilst our *Idea*, the word *Man* stands for, is only an imperfect Collection of some sensible Qualities and Powers in him, there is no discernible connexion or repugnance between our specifick *Idea*, and the Operation of either the Parts of Hemlock or Stones, upon his Constitution. There are Animals that safely eat Hemlock, and others that are nourished by Wood and Stones: But as long as we want *Ideas* of those real Constitutions of different sorts of Animals, whereon these, and the like Qualities and Powers depend, we must not hope to reach *Certainty* in universal Propositions concerning them. Those few *Ideas* only, which have a discernible connexion with our nominal Essence, or any part of it, can afford us such Propositions. But these are so few, and of so little moment, that we may justly look on our certain *general Knowledge of Substances*, as almost none at all.

§ 16. To conclude, *General Propositions*, of what kind soever, are then only capable of *Certainty*, when the Terms used in them, stand for such *Ideas*, whose agreement or disagreement, as there expressed, is capable to be discovered by us. And we are then certain of their Truth or Falshood, when we perceive the *Ideas* the Terms stand for, to agree or not agree, according as they are affirmed or denied one

§ 16. *Wherein lies the general Certainty of Propositions.*

---

(25) different sorts of] *add.* **2–5** (36) the Terms] **5** | they **1–4**

of another. Whence we may take notice, that *general Certainty* is never to be found but in our *Ideas*. Whenever we go to seek it elsewhere in Experiment, or Observations without us, our Knowledge goes not beyond particulars. 'Tis the contemplation of our own abstract *Ideas*, that alone is able to afford us *general Knowledge*.

CHAPTER VII

Of Maxims.

§ 1. THERE are a sort of Propositions, which under the name of *Maxims* and *Axioms*, have passed for Principles of Science: and because they are *self-evident*, have been supposed innate, without that any Body (that I know) ever went about to shew the reason and foundation of their clearness or cogency. It may however be worth while, to enquire into the reason of their evidence, and see whether it be peculiar to them alone, and also examine how far they influence and govern our other Knowledge.

§ 2. *Knowledge*, as has been shewn, consists in the perception of the agreement or disagreement of *Ideas*: Now where that agreement or disagreement is perceived immediately by it self, without the intervention or help of any other, there our *Knowledge is self-evident*. This will appear to be so to any one, who will but consider any of those Propositions, which, without any proof, he assents to at first sight: for in all of them he will find, that the reason of his Assent, is from that agreement or disagreement, which the Mind, by an immediate comparing them, finds in those *Ideas* answering the Affirmation or Negation in the Proposition.

§ 3. This being so, in the next place let us consider, whether this *Self-evidence* be peculiar only to those Propositions, which commonly pass under the Name of Maxims, and have the dignity of Axioms allowed them. And here 'tis plain, that several other Truths, not allow'd to be Axioms, partake equally with them in this *Self-evidence*.

§ 1. *They are self-evident.* § 2. *Wherein that Self-evidence consists.* § 3. *Self-evidence not peculiar to received Axioms.*

---

(3) Experiment] **4–5** | Experiments **1–3**. (**Coste** 'Experiences') (18) those] **2–5** | these **1** (20) of them] **2–5** | these **1** (21) , which] *add.* **2–5** (25) *Self-evidence*] **2–5** | Self-evident **1**. (**Coste** *adds a linguistic footnote.*) those] **2–5** | these **1** (25–6) commonly . . . [*1st*] of] **4–5** | are received for **1–3** (*l. above* 6) **Coste** '*Des Propositions qu'on nomme* Maximes *ou* Axiomes.'

This we shall see, if we go over those several sorts of agreement or disagreement of *Ideas*, which I havė above-mentioned, *viz.* Identity, Relation, Co-existence, and real Existence; which will discover to us, that not only those few Propositions, which have had the credit of *Maxims*, are self-evident, but a great many, even almost an infinite number of *other Propositions* are such.

§ 4. For, *First*, the immediate perception of the agreement or disagreement of *Identity*, being founded in the Mind's having distinct *Ideas*, this affords us as many *self-evident* Propositions, as we have distinct *Ideas*. Every one that has any Knowledge at all, has, as the Foundation of it, various and distinct *Ideas*: And it is the first act of the Mind, (without which, it can never be capable of any Knowledge,) to know every one of its *Ideas* by it self, and distinguish it from others. Every one finds in himself, that he knows the *Ideas* he has; That he knows also, when any one is in his Understanding, and what it is; And that when more than one are there, he knows them distinctly and unconfusedly one from another. Which always being so, (it being impossible but that he should perceive what he perceives,) he can never be in doubt when any *Idea* is in his Mind, that it is there, and is that *Idea* it is; and that two distinct *Ideas*, when they are in his Mind, are there, and are not one and the same *Idea*. So that all such Affirmations, and Negations, are made without any possibility of doubt, uncertainty, or hesitation, and must necessarily be assented to, as soon as understood; that is, as soon as we have, in our Minds, determined *Ideas*, which the Terms in the Proposition stand for. And therefore where-ever the mind with attention considers any proposition, so as to perceive the two *Ideas*, signified by the terms and affirmed or denyed one of the other, to be the same or different; it is presently and infallibly certain of the truth of such a proposition, and this equally whether these propositions be in terms standing for more general *Ideas* or such as are less so, *v.g.* whether the general *Idea* of *Being* be affirmed of it self, as in this proposition *whatsoever is, is*; or a more particular *Idea* be affirmed of it self, as *a man is a man*, or *whatsoever is white is white*. Or whether the *Idea* of *Being* in general be denied of *not Being*,

§ 4. *First, As to Identity and Diversity, all Propositions are equally self-evident.*

(1) those] **5** | these **1–4** (14–15) Every . . . That] **2–5** | This is that which every one finds in himself, that the *Ideas* he has he knows; **1** (16) that] *add.* **2–5** (17) another.] **4–5** | another: **1–3** (25) determined *Ideas*] **4–5** | the *Ideas* clear and distinct **1–3** (26)–593(12) And . . . comprehensive.] *add.* **4–5** (26) where-ever] *edit.* | whereever **4** | wherever **5** (35) *Being*,] **5** | *Being* **4**

which is the only (if I may so call it) *Idea* different from it, as in this other Proposition, *It is impossible for the same to be and not to be*; or any *Idea* of any particular being be denied of another different from it, as *a man is not a horse*; *Red is not Blew*. The difference of the *Ideas* as soon as the Terms are understood, makes the truth of the proposition presently visible, and that with an equal certainty and easiness in the less as well as the more general propositions, and all for the same reason, *viz.* Because the mind perceives in any *Ideas*, that it has the same *Idea* to be the same with it self; And two different *Ideas* to be different and not the same. And this it is equally certain of, whether these *Ideas* be more or less general, abstract, and comprehensive. It is not therefore alone to these two general Propositions, *Whatsoever is, is*; and, *It is impossible for the same Thing to be, and not to be*, that this Self-evidence belongs by any peculiar right. The perception of being, or not being, belongs no more to these vague *Ideas*, signified by the terms *Whatsoever*, and *Thing*, than it does to any other *Ideas*. These two general Maxims amounting to no more in short but this, that *the same is the same*, and *the same is not different*, are truths known in more particular instances, as well as in these general Maxims, and known also in particular instances, before these general Maxims are ever thought on, and draw all their force from the discernment of the mind employed about particular *Ideas*. There is nothing more visible, than that the Mind, without the help of any Proof, or Reflection on either of these general Propositions perceives so clearly, and knows so certainly, that the *Idea* of *White*, is the *Idea* of White, and not the *Idea* of Blue; and that the *Idea* of White, when it is in the Mind, is there, and is not absent, that the consideration of these Axioms can add nothing to the Evidence or certainty of its Knowledge. Just so it is (as every one may experiment in himself) in all the *Ideas* a man has in his Mind: He knows each to be it self, and not to be another; and to be in his Mind, and not away when it is there, with a certainty that cannot be greater, and therefore the truth of no general Proposition can be known with a greater certainty, nor add any thing to this. So that in respect of Identity, our intuitive Knowledge reaches as far

(9) [*1st*] same] **5** | Samc **4** be] **4**; *om.* **5** (12) *v.* 592 (26), n. (15) to] **1er–5** | no **1** (17–23) These . . . that] *add.* **2–5** (18) [*3rd*] *the*] **2–4**; *om.* **5** (18–19, 21, 23), are . . . in more . . . on, [**5** | on **4**] and . . . There] **4–5** | (which are . . . in . . . on) . . . And there **2–3** (24–5) or . . . Propositions] *add.* **2–5** (25) [*1st*] so] **2–5** | as **1** so] **2–5** | as **1** (27–34) , that [**2er** | . That **2**] . . . this.] **2–5** | ; and so a *Triangle*, *Motion*, a *Man*, or any other *Ideas* whatsoever. **1** (29) Just so] **4–5** | And the same **2–3** (30) a man has in] **4–5** | of **2–3**

as our *Ideas*. And we are capable of making as many self-evident Propositions, as we have names for distinct *Ideas*. And I appeal to every one's own Mind, whether this Proposition, *A Circle is a Circle*, be not as self-evident a Proposition, as that consisting of more general terms, *Whatsoever is, is*: And again, whether this Proposition, *Blue is not Red*, be not a Proposition that the Mind can no more doubt of, as soon as it understands the Words, than it does of that Axiom, *It is impossible for the same thing to be, and not to be*? and so of all the like.

§ 5. *Secondly*, As to *Co-existence*, or such a necessary connexion between two *Ideas*, that in the Subject where one of them is supposed, there the other must necessarily be also: Of such agreement, or disagreement as this, the Mind has an immediate perception but in very few of them. And therefore in this sort, we have but very little intuitive Knowledge: nor are there to be found very many Propositions that are self-evident, though some there are; *v.g.* the *Idea* of filling of a place equal to the Contents of its superficies, being annexed to our *Idea* of Body, I think it is a self-evident Proposition, *That two Bodies cannot be in the same place*.

§ 6. *Thirdly*, As to the *Relations* of Modes, Mathematicians have framed many Axioms concerning that one Relation of Equality. As *Equals taken from Equals, the remainder will be Equals*; which, with the rest of that kind, however they are received for Maxims by the Mathematicians, and are unquestionable Truths; yet, I think, that any one who considers them, will not find, that they have a clearer self-evidence than these, that *one and one, are equal to two*; that *if you take from the five Fingers of one Hand two, and from the five Fingers of the other Hand two, the remaining numbers will be equal*. These, and a thousand other such Propositions, may be found in Numbers, which, at very first hearing, force the assent, and carry with them an equal, if not greater clearness, than those mathematical Axioms.

§ 7. *Fourthly*, As to *real Existence*, since that has no connexion with any other of our *Ideas*, but that of our selves, and of a first Being, we have in that, concerning the real existence of all other Beings, not so much as demonstrative, much less a self-evident Knowledge: And therefore concerning those there are no Maxims.

§ 5. *Secondly, In Co-existence we have few self-evident Propositions.* § 6. *Thirdly, In other Relations we may have.* § 7. *Fourthly, Concerning real Existence we have none.*

(1) . And] **4–5** | : And so **1–3** (3) every] **2–5** | ever **1** (20) many] **1–3**, **5** (*likewise* **Coste**) | may **4** (27) *numbers*] **4–5** | number **1–3** (*likewise* **Coste**)

§ 8. In the next place let us consider, what *influence* these received *Maxims* have, upon the other parts of our Knowledge. The Rules established in the Schools, that all Reasonings are *ex præcognitis, et præconcessis*, seem to lay the foundation of all other Knowledge, in these Maxims, and to suppose them to be *præcognita*; whereby, I think, is meant these two things: First, That these Axioms, are those Truths that are first known to the Mind; and, secondly, That upon them, the other parts of our Knowledge depend.

§ 9. *First*, That they are not the *Truths first known* to the Mind, is evident to Experience, as we have shewn in another place, *B.*I. *Ch.*II. Who perceives not, that a Child certainly knows, that a Stranger is not its Mother; that its Sucking-bottle is not the Rod, long before he knows, that *'tis impossible for the same thing to be, and not to be*? And how many Truths are there about Numbers, which it is obvious to observe, that the Mind is perfectly acquainted with, and fully convinced of, before it ever thought on these general Maxims, to which Mathematicians, in their Arguings, do sometimes referr them? Whereof the reason is very plain: For that which makes the Mind assent to such Propositions, being nothing else but the perception it has of the agreement, or disagreement of its *Ideas*, according as it finds them affirmed or denied one of another, in Words it understands; and every *Idea* being known to be what it is, and every two distinct *Ideas* being known not to be the same, it must necessarily follow, that such self-evident Truths, must be *first* known, which consist of *Ideas* that are *first* in the Mind: and the *Ideas first* in the Mind, 'tis evident, are those of particular Things, from whence, by slow degrees, the Understanding proceeds to some few general ones; which being taken from the ordinary and familiar Objects of Sense, are settled in the Mind, with general Names to them. Thus particular *Ideas* are *first* received and distinguished, and so Knowledge got about them: and next to them, the less general, or specifick, which are next to particular. For abstract *Ideas* are not so obvious or easie to Children, or the yet unexercised Mind, as particular ones. If they seem so to grown Men, 'tis only because by constant and

§ 8. *These Axioms do not much influence our other Knowledge.* § 9. *Because they are not the Truths the first known.*

---

(1) these] **2–5** | those **1** (10) , as . . . place [, **5** | . **2–4**]] *add.* **2–5** (10) *B.*I. *Ch.*II] *add.* **4–5** (22) understands;] **1–3** | understands, **4–5** (23) being known] *add.* **4–5** the] *add.* **1T.er, 2–5** (27) some few] **1–2, 4–5** | these two **3** (29) Mind] **1–4, W** | Minds **5** (34) grown] **1–4** | grow **5** (2 *ll. below* 34) *the first known*] **2–4** | *we first knew* **5**

familiar use they are made so. For when we nicely reflect upon them, we shall find, that general *Ideas* are Fictions and Contrivances of the Mind, that carry difficulty with them, and do not so easily offer themselves, as we are apt to imagine. For example, Does it not require some pains and skill to form the *general Idea* of a *Triangle*, (which is yet none of the most abstract, comprehensive, and difficult,) for it must be neither Oblique, nor Rectangle, neither Equilateral, Equicrural, nor Scalenon; but all and none of these at once. In effect, it is something imperfect, that cannot exist; an *Idea* wherein some parts of several different and inconsistent *Ideas* are put together. 'Tis true, the Mind in this imperfect state, has need of such *Ideas*, and makes all the haste to them it can, for the conveniency of Communication, and Enlargement of Knowledge; to both which, it is naturally very much enclined. But yet one has reason to suspect such *Ideas* are marks of our Imperfection; at least, this is enough to shew, that the most abstract and general *Ideas*, are not those that the Mind is *first* and most easily acquainted with, nor such as its earliest Knowledge is conversant about.

§ 10. *Secondly*, From what has been said, it plainly follows, that these magnified *Maxims*, are not the Principles and *Foundations* of all our other *Knowledge*. For if there be a great many other Truths, which have as much self-evidence as they, and a great many that we know before them, it is impossible they should be the *Principles*, from which we deduce all other Truths. Is it impossible to know that *One* and *Two* are equal to *Three*, but by virtue of this, or some such Axiom, *viz. the Whole is equal to all its Parts taken together*? Many a one knows that *One* and *Two* are equal to *Three*, without having heard, or thought on that, or any other Axiom, by which it might be proved; and knows it as certainly, as any other Man knows, that the *Whole is equal to all its Parts*, or any other Maxim; and all from the same Reason of self-evidence; the Equality of those *Ideas*, being as visible and certain to him without that, or any other Axiom, as with it, it needing no proof to make it perceived. Nor after the Knowledge, *That the Whole is equal to all its parts*, does he know that *one and two are equal to three*, better, or more certainly

§ 10. *Because on them the other parts of our Knowledge do not depend.*

---

(24) Is it] **1–3, 5** (*likewise* **Coste**) | It is **4** (*l. below* 35) *Because . . . depend.*] **4er–5** | *Because they are not the Truths the first known.* **2–4**

than he did before. For if there be any odds in those *Ideas*, the *Whole* and *Parts* are more obscure, or at least more difficult to be settled in the Mind, than those of *One*, *Two*, and *Three*. And indeed, I think, I may ask these Men, who will needs have all Knowledge besides those general Principles themselves, to *depend* on general, innate, and self-evident Principles, What Principle is requisite to prove, that *One* and *One* are *Two*, that *Two* and *Two* are *Four*, that *Three* times *Two* are *Six*? Which being known without any proof, do evince, That either all Knowledge does not *depend* on certain *Præcognita* or general Maxims, called Principles; or else that these are Principles: and if these are to be counted Principles, a great part of Numeration will be so. To which if we add all the self-evident Propositions, which may be made about all our distinct *Ideas*, Principles will be almost infinite, at least innumerable, which Men arrive to the Knowledge of, at different Ages; and a great many of these innate Principles, they never come to know all their Lives. But whether they come in view of the Mind, earlier or later, this is true of them, that they are all known by their native Evidence, are wholly independent, receive no Light, nor are capable of any proof one from another; much less the more particular, from the more general; or the more simple, from the more compounded: the more simple, and less abstract, being the most familiar, and the easier and earlier apprehended. But which ever be the clearest *Ideas*, the Evidence and *Certainty* of all such Propositions is in this, That a Man sees the same *Idea* to be the same *Idea*, and infallibly perceives two different *Ideas* to be different *Ideas*. For when a Man has in his Understanding, the *Ideas* of *one* and of *two*, the *Idea* of *Yellow* and the *Idea* of *Blue*, he cannot but certainly know, that the *Idea* of One is the *Idea* of One, and not the *Idea* of Two; and that the *Idea* of Yellow is the *Idea* of Yellow, and not the *Idea* of Blue. For a Man cannot confound the *Ideas* in his Mind, which he has distinct: That would be to have them confused and distinct at the same time, which is a contradiction: And to have none distinct, is to have no use of our Faculties, to have no Knowledge at all. And therefore what *Idea* soever is affirmed of it self; or whatsoever two entire distinct *Ideas* are denied one of another, the Mind cannot but assent to such a Proposition, as infallibly true, as soon as it understands the Terms, without Hesitation or need of Proof, or regarding those made in more general Terms, and called Maxims.

(12) [*2nd*] which] *add.* **4–5**

§ 11. What shall we then say. Are these *general Maxims* of no use? By no means, Though perhaps their use is not that, which it is commonly taken to be. But since doubting in the least of what hath been by some Men ascribed to these *Maxims* may be apt to be cried out against, as overturning the Foundations of all the Sciences; it may be worth while to consider them, with respect to other parts of our Knowledge, and examine more particularly to what Purposes they serve, and to what not.

1. It is evident from what has been already said, that they are of no use to prove or confirm less general self-evident Propositions.

2. 'Tis as plain that they are not, nor have been the Foundations whereon any Science hath been built. There is, I know, a great deal of Talk, propagated from Scholastick Men, of Sciences and the *Maxims* on which they are built: But it has been my ill luck, never to meet with any such Sciences; much less any one built upon these two *Maxims*, *What is, is*; and *It is impossible for the same to be and not to be*. And I would be glad to be shewn where any such Science erected upon these, or any other general *Axioms* is to be found: and should be obliged to any one who would lay before me the Frame and System of any Science so built on these, or any such like *Maxims*, that could not be shewn to stand as firm without any Consideration of them. I ask, Whether these general *Maxims* have not the same use in the Study of Divinity, and in Theological Questions, that they have in the other Sciences? They serve here too, to silence Wranglers, and put an end to dispute. But I think that no body will therefore say, that the *Christian* Religion is built on these *Maxims*, or that the Knowledge we have of it, is derived from these *Principles*. 'Tis from Revelation we have received it, and without Revelation these *Maxims* had never been able to help us to it. When we find out an *Idea*, by whose Intervention we discover the Connexion of two others, this is a Revelation from God to us, by the Voice of Reason. For we then come to know a Truth that we did not know before. When God declares any Truth to us, this is a Revelation to us by the Voice of his Spirit, and we are advanced in our Knowledge. But in neither of these do we receive our Light or Knowledge from *Maxims*. But in the one the things themselves afford it, and we see the Truth in them by perceiving their Agreement or Disagree-

§ 11. *What use these general Maxims have.*

(2)–601(34) By . . . Knowledge.] *add.* **4–5**

ment. In the other, God himself affords it immediately to us, and we see the Truth of what he says in his unerring Veracity.

3. They are not of use to help Men forwards in the Advancement of Sciences, or new Discoveries of yet unknown Truths. Mr. *Newton*, in his never enough to be admired Book, has demonstrated several Propositions, which are so many new Truths, before unknown to the World, and are farther Advances in Mathematical Knowledge: But for the Discovery of these, it was not the general *Maxims*, *What is, is*; or *The whole is bigger than a part*, or the like, that help'd him. These were not the Clues that lead him into the Discovery of the Truth and Certainty of those Propositions. Nor was it by them that he got the Knowledge of those Demonstrations; but by finding out intermediate *Ideas*, that shew'd the Agreement or Disagreement of the *Ideas*, as expressed in the Propositions he demonstrated. This is the great Exercise and Improvement of Humane Understanding in the enlarging of Knowledge, and advancing the Sciences; wherein they are far enough from receiving any Help from the Contemplation of these, or the like magnified *Maxims*. Would those who have this Traditional Admiration of these Propositions, that they think no Step can be made in Knowledge without the support of an *Axiom*, no Stone laid in the building of the Sciences without a general *Maxim*, but distinguish between the Method of acquiring Knowledge, and of communicating it; between the Method of raising any Science, and that of teaching it to others as far as it is advanced, they would see that those general *Maxims* were not the Foundations on which the first Discoverers raised their admirable Structures, nor the Keys that unlocked and opened those Secrets of Knowledge. Though afterwards, when Schools were erected, and Sciences had their Professors to teach what others had found out, they often made use of *Maxims*, *i.e.* laid down certain Propositions which were self-evident, or to be received for true, which being setled in the Minds of their Scholars as unquestionable Verities, they on occasion made use of, to convince them of Truths in particular Instances, that were not so familiar to their Minds as those general *Axioms* which had before been inculcated to them and carefully setled in their Minds. Though these particular Instances, when well reflected on, are no less self-evident to the Understanding than the general *Maxims* brought to confirm them: And it was in

(5) Book] **Coste** *adds a marginal note* 'Intitulé, *Philosophiae Naturalis Principia Mathematica.*' (23) it;] **4**; *om.* **5**

those particular Instances, that the first Discoverer found the Truth, without the help of the general *Maxims*: And so may any one else do, who with Attention considers them.

To come therefore to the use that is made of *Maxims*.

1. They are of use, as has been observed, in the ordinary Methods of teaching Sciences as far as they are advanced: But of little or none in advancing them farther.

2. They are of use in Disputes, for the silencing of obstinate Wranglers, and bringing those Contests to some Conclusion. Whether a need of them to that end, came not in, in the manner following, I crave leave to enquire. The Schools having made Disputation the Touchstone of Mens Abilities, and the *Criterion* of Knowledge, adjudg'd Victory to him that kept the Field: and he that had the last Word was concluded to have the better of the Argument, if not of the Cause. But because by this means there was like to be no Decision between skilful Combatants, whilst one never fail'd of a *medius terminus* to prove any Proposition; and the other could as constantly, without, or with a Distinction, deny the *Major* or *Minor*; To prevent, as much as could be, the running out of Disputes into an endless train of Syllogisms, certain general Propositions, most of them indeed self-evident, were introduced into the Schools, which being such as all Men allowed and agreed in, were look'd on as general Measures of Truth, and serv'd instead of Principles, (where the Disputants had not laid down any other between them) beyond which there was no going, and which must not be receded from by either side. And thus these *Maxims* getting the name of *Principles*, beyond which Men in dispute could not retreat, were by mistake taken to be the Originals and Sources, from whence all Knowledge began, and the Foundations whereon the Sciences were built. Because when in their Disputes they came to any of these, they stopped there, and went no farther, the Matter was determined. But how much this is a mistake hath been already shewn.

This Method of the Schools, which have been thought the Fountains of Knowledge, introduced as I suppose the like use of these Maxims, into a great part of Conversation out of the Schools, to stop the Mouths of Cavillers, whom any one is excused from

(15) Cause.] **5** | Cause, **4** (31) stopped] *edit.* | stopp'd **4–5**. *From here to the end of IV. viii. 5 I have substituted* 'e' *for the apostrophe in verbs and participles, and* 'though' *for* 'tho'', *wherever the apostrophized forms occurred in* **4** (*in gathering with signature* Aaa) *and not in* **1–2**; *the compositor of these pages in* **4** *regularly used such apostrophized forms.*

arguing any longer with, when they deny these general self-evident Principles received by all reasonable Men, who have once thought of them: But yet their use herein, is but to put an end to wrangling. They in truth, when urged in such cases, teach nothing: That is already done by the intermediate *Ideas* made use of in the Debate, whose Connexion may be seen without the help of those Maxims, and so the truth known before the Maxim is produced, and the Argument brought to a first Principle. Men would give off a wrong Argument before it came to that, if in their Disputes they proposed to themselves the finding and imbracing of Truth, and not a Contest for Victory. And thus Maxims have their use to put a stop to their perverseness, whose Ingenuity should have yielded sooner. But the Method of the Schools, having allowed and encouraged Men to oppose and resist evident Truth, till they are baffled, *i.e.* till they are reduced to contradict themselves, or some established Principle; 'tis no wonder that they should not in civil Conversation be ashamed of that, which in the Schools is counted a Vertue and a Glory; *viz.* obstinately to maintain that side of the Question they have chosen, whether true or false, to the last extremity; even after Conviction. A strange way to attain Truth and Knowledge: And that which I think the rational part of Mankind not corrupted by Education, could scarce believe should ever be admitted amongst the Lovers of Truth, and Students of Religion or Nature; or introduced into the Seminaries of those who are to propagate the Truths of Religion or Philosophy, amongst the Ignorant and Unconvinced. How much such a way of Learning is likely to turn young Men's Minds from the sincere Search and Love of Truth; nay, and to make them doubt whether there is any such thing, or at least worth the adhering to, I shall not now enquire. This, I think, that bating those places, which brought the *Peripatetick* Philosophy into their Schools, where it continued many Ages, without teaching the World any thing but the Art of Wrangling; these Maxims were no where thought the Foundations on which the Sciences were built, nor the great helps to the Advancement of Knowledge.

As to these *General Maxims* therefore, they are as I have said of great *Use* in Disputes, *to stop the Mouths of Wranglers*; but not of much *Use* to the Discovery of unknown Truths, or to help the Mind

§ 11(35). *What Use these General Maxims have.*

---

(6) be] **5** | bee **4** (8) Principle.] **5** | Principle **4** (34) *v.* 598(2), n.
(35) As . . . said] **4–5** | Yes, they *are* **1–3** [*not new paragraph*]

forwards, in its Search after Knowledge. For whoever began to build his Knowledge on this General Proposition, *What is, is*: or, *It is impossible for the same thing to be, and not to be*: and from either of these, as from a Principle of Science, deduced a *System* of Useful Knowledge? Wrong Opinions often involving Contradictions, one of these Maxims, as a Touch-stone, may *serve* well to shew whither they lead. But yet, however fit, to lay open the Absurdity or Mistake of a Man's Reasoning or Opinion, they are of very little *Use* for enlightning the Understanding: And it will not be found, that the Mind receives much help from them in its Progress in Knowledge; which would be neither less, nor less certain, were these two *General Propositions* never thought on. 'Tis true, as I have said, they sometimes *serve* in Argumentation to stop a Wrangler's Mouth, by shewing the Absurdity of what he saith, and by exposing him to the shame of contradicting what all the World knows, and he himself cannot but own to be true. But it is one thing, to shew a Man that he is in an Error; and another, to put him in possession of Truth: and I would fain know what Truths these two Propositions are able to teach, and by their Influence make us know, which we did not know before, or could not know without them. Let us reason from them, as well as we can, they are only about Identical Predications, and *Influence*, if any at all, none but such. Each particular Proposition concerning Identity or Diversity, is as clearly and certainly known in it self, if attended to, as either of these general ones: Only these general ones, as serving in all cases, are therefore more inculcated and insisted on. As to other less general Maxims, many of them are no more than bare verbal Propositions, and teach us nothing but the Respect and Import of Names one to another. *The Whole is equal to all its Parts*; What real Truth, I beseech you, does it teach us? What more is contained in that Maxim, than what the Signification of the word *Totum*, or the *Whole*, does of it self import? And he that knows that the word *Whole*, stands for what is made up of all its Parts, knows very little less, than that the *Whole* is equal to all its *Parts*. And upon the same ground, I think that this Proposition, *A Hill is higher than a Valley*, and several

(3) *is*] **1–4**; *om.* **5** (5) often] **4–5** | , often **1–3** (6) whither] **1–4** | whether **5** (8) Mistake] **1–3, 5** | mistake **4** (14–16) what . . . true] **4–5** | his Opinion **1–3** (18) two] *add.* **4–5**. (*Not in* **Coste**) (19) , and] **4–5** | ; and **1–3** (21) Identical] **Coste** *adds a linguistic footnote.* (25–6) Only . . . on] **4–5** | and there is nothing more certain, then that by these Maxims alone we cannot evidence to our selves the Truth of any one thing really existing **1–3**

the like, may also pass for Maxims. But yet Masters of *Mathematicks*, when they would, as Teachers of what they know, initiate others in that Science, do not without Reason place this, and some other such Maxims, at the entrance of their *Systems*; that their Scholars, having in the beginning perfectly acquainted their Thoughts with these Propositions, made in such general Terms, may be used to make such Reflections, and have these more general Propositions, as formed Rules and Sayings, ready to apply to all particular Cases. Not that if they be equally weighed, they are more clear and evident than the particular Instances they are brought to confirm; but that being more familiar to the Mind, the very naming them, is enough to satisfy the Understanding. But this, I say, is more from our Custom of using them, and the establishment they have got in our Minds, by our often thinking of them, than from the different Evidence of the Things. But before Custom has settled Methods of Thinking and Reasoning in our Minds, I am apt to imagine it is quite otherwise; and that the Child, when a part of his Apple is taken away, knows it better in that particular Instance, than by this General Proposition, *The Whole is equal to all its Parts*; and that if one of these have need to be confirmed to him by the other, the general has more need to be let into his Mind by the particular, than the particular by the general. For in particulars, our Knowledge begins, and so spreads it self, by degrees, to generals. Though afterwards, the Mind takes the quite contrary course, and having drawn its Knowledge into as general Propositions as it can, makes those familiar to its Thoughts, and accustoms it self to have recourse to them, as to the Standards of Truth and Falshood. By which familiar *Use* of them, as Rules to measure the Truth of other Propositions, it comes in time to be thought, that more particular Propositions have their Truth and Evidence from their Conformity to these more general ones, which in Discourse and Argumentation, are so frequently urged, and constantly admitted. And this, I think, to be the Reason why amongst so many Self-evident Propositions, the most general only have had the Title of Maxims.

§ 12. One thing farther, I think, it may not be amiss to observe

§ 12. *Maxims, if care be not taken in the Use of Words, may prove Contradictions.*

(1–3) Masters . . . Science,] **4–5** | Mathematicians **1–3** (4) Maxims . . . *Systems*;] **4–5** | , amongst their Maxims, **1–3** (5) beginning] **4–5** | entrance **1–3** (6–8) be . . . Sayings,] **4–5** | have them **1–3** (13–14) and . . . them,] *add.* **4–5** (14) from] *add.* **4–5** (16) imagine] **1–3, 5** | imagin **4** (18) this] **4–5** | that **1–3** (23) it] **1–3, 5** | its **4**

concerning these general Maxims, That they are so far from improving or establishing our Minds in true Knowledge, that if our Notions be wrong, loose, or unsteady, and we resign up our Thoughts to the sound of Words, rather than fix them on settled determined *Ideas* of Things; I say, these *General Maxims* will *serve* to confirm us in Mistakes; and in such a way of use of Words, which is most common, will *serve* to prove Contradictions: *v.g.* He that with *Des-Cartes*, shall frame in his Mind an *Idea* of what he calls *Body*, to be nothing but Extension, may easily demonstrate, that there is no *Vacuum*; *i.e.* no Space void of Body, by this Maxim, *What is, is*. For the *Idea* to which he annexes the name *Body*, being bare Extension, his Knowledge, that Space cannot be without Body, is certain. For he knows his own *Idea* of Extension clearly and distinctly, and knows that it is *what it is*, and not another *Idea*, though it be called by these three names, *Extension*, *Body*, *Space*. Which three Words standing for one and the same *Idea*, may no doubt, with the same evidence and certainty, be affirmed one of another, as each of it self: And it is as certain, that whilst I use them all to stand for one and the same *Idea*, this Predication is as true and identical in its signification, *That Space is Body*, as this Predication is true and identical, *that Body is Body*, both in signification and sound.

§ 13. But if another shall come, and make to himself another *Idea*, different from *Des-Cartes*'s of the thing, which yet, with *Des-Cartes* he calls by the same name *Body*, and make his *Idea*, which he expresses by the word *Body*, to be of a thing that hath both *Extension* and *Solidity* together, he will as easily demonstrate, that there may be a *Vacuum*, or Space without a Body, as *Des-Cartes* demonstrated the contrary. Because the *Idea* to which he gives the name *Space*, being barely the simple one of *Extension*; and the *Idea*, to which he gives the name *Body*, being the complex *Idea* of *Extension* and *Resistibility*, or *Solidity* together in the same subject, these two *Ideas* are not exactly one and the same, but in the Understanding as distinct as the *Ideas* of One and Two, White and Black, or as of *Corporeity* and *Humanity*, if I may use those barbarous Terms: And

§ 13. *Instance in* Vacuum.

(4–5) to . . . determined] **4–5** | rather to the sound of Words, than to setled, clear, distinct **1–3** (8, 28) *Des-Cartes*] **4–5** | *Cartes* **1–3** (24) *Des-Cartes*'s] **4–5** | *Cartes*, **1–3** (24–5) *Des-Cartes*] **4–5** | *Cartes*, **1–3** (26) be . . . both] **4–5** | consist of **1–3** (28) Space] **4–5** | Space, **1–3** (30) barely . . . *Extension*;] **4–5** | bare Extension [*Extension* **2–3**], **1–3** (32) together . . . subject,] **4–5** | together; **1–3** therefore the Predication of them in our Minds, or in Words standing for them is not identical, but the Negation of them one of another; *viz.* this Proposition Extension or *Space is not Body*, is as true and evidently certain, as this Maxim, *It is impossible for the same thing to be, and not to be*, can make any Proposition.

§ 14. But yet though both these Propositions (as you see) may be equally demonstrated, *viz.* That there may be a *Vacuum*, and that there cannot be a *Vacuum*, by these two certain Principles, (*viz.*) *What is, is*, and *The same thing cannot be, and not be*: yet neither of these Principles will serve to prove to us, that any, or what Bodies do exist: For that we are left to our Senses, to discover to us as far as they can. Those Universal and Self-evident Principles, being only our constant, clear, and distinct Knowledge of our own *Ideas*, more general or comprehensive, can assure us of nothing that passes without the Mind, their certainty is founded only upon the Knowledge we have of each *Idea* by it self, and of its Distinction from others; about which, we cannot be mistaken whilst they are in our Minds, though we may, and often are mistaken, when we retain the Names without the *Ideas*; or use them confusedly sometimes for one, and sometimes for another *Idea*. In which cases, the force of these *Axioms* reaching only to the Sound, and not the Signification of the Words, *serves* only to lead us into Confusion, Mistake, and Errour. 'Tis to shew Men, that these Maxims, however cry'd up for the great guards to Truth, will not secure them from Errour in a careless loose use of their Words, that I have made this Remark. In all that is here suggested concerning their little use for the Improvement of Knowledge, or dangerous use in undetermined *Ideas*, I have been far enough from saying or intending they should be *laid aside*, as some have been too forward to charge me. I affirm them to be Truths, Self-evident Truths; and so cannot be *laid aside*. As far as their influence will reach, 'tis in vain to endeavour, nor would I attempt to abridge it. But yet without any injury to Truth or Knowledge, I may have reason to think their use is not answerable to the great Stress which seems to be laid on them, and I may warn Men not to make an ill use of them, for the confirming themselves in Errours.

§ 14. *They prove not the Existence of Things without us.*

(3–5) ; *viz.* . . . Proposition.] **4–5** | , as certain and evident, as *that it is impossible for the same thing to be, and not to be.* **1–3** (9) *not*] **1–3** (*likewise* **Coste**); *om.* **4–5** (14) *Ideas*,] **4–5** | *Ideas* **1–3** (16) it] **4–5** | its **1–3** (23–36) 'Tis . . . Errours.] *add.* **4–5** (29) *laid aside*] **Coste** *adds a linguistic footnote.*

§ 15. But let them be of what *Use* they will in verbal Propositions, they cannot discover or prove to us the least Knowledge of the Nature of Substances, as they are found and exist without us, any farther than grounded on Experience. And though the Consequence of these two Propositions, called Principles, be very clear, and their *Use* not dangerous, or hurtful, in the Probation of such Things, wherein there is no need at all of them for Proof, but such as are clear by themselves without them, *viz.* where our *Ideas* are determined, and known by the Names that stand for them: yet when these Principles, *viz. What is, is*; and, *It is impossible for the same thing to be, and not to be*, are made use of in the Probation of Propositions, wherein are Words standing for complex *Ideas, v.g. Man, Horse, Gold, Vertue*; there they are of infinite danger, and most commonly make Men receive and retain Falshood for manifest Truth, and Uncertainty for Demonstration: upon which follows Errour, Obstinacy, and all the Mischiefs that can happen from wrong Reasoning. The reason whereof is not, that these Principles are less true, or of less force in proving Propositions made of Terms standing for complex *Ideas*, than where the Propositions are about simple *Ideas*. But because Men mistake generally, thinking that where the same Terms are preserved, the Propositions are about the same things, though the *Ideas* they stand for are in truth different. Therefore these Maxims are made use of to support those, which in sound and appearance are contradictory Propositions; as is clear in the Demonstrations above-mentioned about a *Vacuum*. So that whilst Men take Words for Things, as usually they do, these Maximes may and do commonly serve to prove contradictory Propositions. As shall yet be farther made manifest.

§ 16. For Instance: Let *Man* be that, concerning which you would by these first Principles demonstrate any thing, and we shall see, that so far as Demonstration is by these Principles, it is only verbal, and gives us no certain universal true Proposition, or knowledge of any Being existing without us. First, a Child having

§ 15. *Their Application dangerous about complex* Ideas. §§ 16–18. *Instance in Man.*

(6) dangerous] **4–5** | very dangerous **1–3** (9) determined] **4–5** | clear and distinct **1–3** (16) from] **1–4** | for **5** (18) , or . . . Terms] **4–5** | in such Propositions, consisting of Words **1–3** (19) where . . . about] **4–5** | in those of **1–3** (20–8) that . . . manifest.] **4–5** | such Propositions to be about the reality of Things, and not the bare signification of Words, when indeed they are, for the most part, nothing else, as is clear in the [*om.* **3**] demonstration of *Vacuum*, where the word *Body*, sometimes stands for one *Idea*, and sometimes for another: But shall be yet made more manifest. **1–3** (29) For] **4–5** | As for **1–3**

framed the *Idea* of a *Man*, it is probable, that his *Idea* is just like that Picture, which the Painter makes of the visible Appearances joyned together; and such a Complication of *Ideas* together in his Understanding, makes up the single complex *Idea* which he calls *Man*, whereof White or Flesh-colour in *England* being one, the Child can demonstrate to you, that *a Negro is not a Man*, because White-colour was one of the constant simple *Ideas* of the complex *Idea* he calls *Man*: And therefore he can demonstrate by the Principle, *It is impossible for the same Thing to be, and not to be*, that *a Negro is not a Man*; the foundation of his Certainty being not that universal Proposition, which, perhaps, he never heard nor thought of, but the clear distinct Perception he hath of his own simple *Ideas* of Black and White, which he cannot be persuaded to take, nor can ever mistake one for another, whether he knows that Maxim or no: And to this Child, or any one who hath such an *Idea*, which he calls *Man*, Can you never demonstrate that a *Man* hath a Soul, because his *Idea* of Man includes no such Notion or *Idea* in it. And therefore to him, the Principle of *What is, is*, proves not this matter; but it depends upon Collection and Observation, by which he is to make his complex *Idea* called *Man*.

§ 17. *Secondly*, Another that hath gone farther in framing and collecting the *Idea* he calls *Man*, and to the outward shape adds *Laughter*, and *Rational Discourse*, may demonstrate, that Infants, and Changelings are no Men, by this Maxim, *It is impossible for the same Thing to be, and not to be*: And I have discoursed with very Rational Men, who have actually denied that they are *Men*.

§ 18. *Thirdly*, Perhaps, another makes up the complex *Idea* which he calls *Man*, only out of the *Ideas* of Body in general, and the Powers of Language and Reason, and leaves out the Shape wholly: This Man is able to demonstrate, that a Man may have no Hands, but be *Quadrupes*, neither of those being included in his *Idea* of *Man*; and in whatever Body or Shape he found *Speech* and *Reason* joyn'd, that was a *Man*: because having a clear Knowledge of such a complex *Idea*, it is certain, that *What is, is*.

§ 19. So that, if rightly considered, I think we may say, That where our *Ideas* are determined in our Minds, and have annexed to

§ 19. *Little Use of these Maxims in Proofs where we have clear and distinct* Ideas.

(3) Complication] **4–5** | complexion **1–3** (17) it.] **4–5** | it? **1–3** (27) up] **2–5** | us **1** (36)–608(2) where... Determinations] **4–5** | *where our Ideas are clear and distinct, and the Names agreed on*, that shall stand for each clear and distinct *Idea* **1–3** (where ... *Ideas* ... [rom.] *Idea* **2–3**) (*l. below* 36) *Proofs*] **4–5** | *Proofs*, **2–3**

them by us known and steady, Names under those settled Determinations, there is *little need*, or *no use* at all of these *Maxims*, to prove the Agreement, or Disagreement of any of them. He that cannot discern the Truth or Falshood of such Propositions, without the help of these, and the like Maxims, will not be *helped* by these Maxims to do it: since he cannot be supposed to know the Truth of these Maxims themselves without proof, if he cannot know the Truth of others without proof, which are as self-evident as these. Upon this ground it is, that intuitive Knowledge neither requires, nor admits any proof, one part of it more than another. He that will suppose it does, takes away the foundation of all Knowledge, and Certainty: And he that needs any proof to make him certain, and give his Assent to this Proposition, that *Two are equal to Two*, will also have need of a proof to make him admit, that *What is, is.* He that needs a probation to convince him, that *Two are not Three*, that *White is not Black*, that *a Triangle is not a Circle, etc.* or any other two determined distinct *Ideas* are not one and the same, will need also a Demonstration to convince him, that *it is impossible for the same thing to be, and not to be.*

§ 20. And as these Maxims are of *little use*, where we have determined *Ideas*, so they are, as I have shewed, of *dangerous use*, where our *Ideas* are not determined; and where we use Words that are not annexed to determined *Ideas*, but such as are of a loose and wandering signification sometimes standing for one, and sometimes for another *Idea*; from which follows Mistake and Errour, which these Maxims (brought as proofs to establish Propositions, wherein the terms stand for undetermined *Ideas*) do by their Authority confirm and rivet.

§ 20. *Their Use dangerous, where our* Ideas *are confused.*

---

(2) *v.* 607(36), n. (9) Upon . . . that] **2–5** | And upon the very same grounds, **1** (11) does, takes] **2–5** | , does take **1** (13) *are*] **2–5** | is **1** (15) *are*] **2–5** | is **1** (16) [*2nd*] that] **1–3** (*likewise* **Coste**) | *that* **4–5** (17) determined] **4–5** | clear **1–3** (18) *it is impossible*] **1–3** (*likewise* **Coste**) | it is impossible **4–5** (19) *be*,] **1–3** | *be* **4–5** (20–1) determined] **4–5** | clear and distinct **1–3** (22) determined] **4–5** | clear and distinct **1–3** (23) determined] **4–5** | clear and distinct **1–3** such] **4–5** | to such **1–3** (27) undetermined] **4–5** | confused or uncertain **1–3**

CHAPTER VIII

Of Trifling Propositions.

§ 1. WHETHER the Maxims treated of in the fore-going Chapter, be of that use to real Knowledge, as is generally supposed, I leave to be considered. This, I think, may confidently be affirmed, That there are Universal Propositions; that though they be certainly true, yet they add no Light to our Understandings, bring no increase to our Knowledge. Such are,

§ 2. *First, All purely identical Propositions.* These obviously, and at first blush, appear to contain no Instruction in them. For when we affirm the same Term of it self, whether it be barely verbal, or whether it contains any clear and real *Idea*, it shews us nothing, but what we must certainly know before, whether such a Proposition be either made by, or proposed to us. Indeed, that most general one, *What is, is*, may serve sometimes to shew a Man the absurdity he is guilty of, when by circumlocution, or equivocal terms, he would, in particular Instances, deny the same thing of it self; because no body will so openly bid defiance to common Sense, as to affirm visible and direct Contradictions in plain Words: Or if he does, a Man is excused if he breaks off any farther Discourse with him. But yet, I think, I may say, that neither that received Maxim, nor any other identical Proposition teaches us any thing: And though in such kind of Propositions, this great and magnified Maxim, boasted to be the foundation of Demonstration, may be, and often is made use of to confirm them, yet all it proves, amounts to no more than this, That the same Word may with great certainty be affirmed of it self, without any doubt of the Truth of any such Proposition; and let me add also, without any real Knowledge.

§ 3. For at this rate, any very ignorant Person, who can but make a Proposition, and knows what he means when he says, *Ay*, or *No*, may make a million of Propositions, of whose truth he may be infallibly certain, and yet not know one thing in the World thereby;

§ 1. *Some Propositions bring no increase to our Knowledge.* §§ 2, 3. *As First, Identical Propositions.*

---

(9) same] **1–3** (*likewise* **Coste**) | said **4–5** (18) breaks] **4–5** | break **1–3**
(29) truth] **1–4** (Truth **1–3**) | Truths **5**

v.g. what is a Soul, is a Soul; or *a Soul is a Soul*; *a Spirit is a Spirit*; *a Fetiche is a Fetiche, etc.* These all being equivalent to this Proposition, *viz. What is, is*, i.e. *what hath Existence, hath Existence*; or, *who hath a Soul, hath a Soul.* What is this more than trifling with Words? It is but like a Monkey shifting his Oyster from one hand to the other; and had he had but Words, might, no doubt, have said, Oyster in right hand is *Subject*, and Oyster in left hand is *Predicate*: and so might have made a self-evident Proposition of Oyster, *i.e. Oyster is Oyster*; and yet, with all this, not have been one whit the wiser, or more knowing: and that way of handling the matter, would much at one have satisfied the Monkey's Hunger, or a Man's Understanding; and they two would have improved in Knowledge and Bulk together.

I know there are some, who because *Identical Propositions* are self-evident, shew a great concern for them, and think they do great service to Philosophy by crying them up, as if in them was contained all Knowledge, and the Understanding were led into all Truth by them only. I grant as forwardly as any one, that they are all true and self-evident. I grant farther, that the foundation of all our Knowledge lies in the Faculty we have of perceiving the same *Idea* to be the same, and of discerning it, from those that are different, as I have shewn in the fore-going Chapter. But how that vindicates the making use of *Identical Propositions*, for the Improvement of Knowledge, from the imputation of Trifling, I do not see. Let any one repeat as often as he pleases, that *the Will is the Will*, or lay what stress on it he thinks fit; of what use is this, and an infinite the like Propositions, for the enlarging our Knowledge? Let a Man abound as much as the plenty of Words, which he has, will permit him in such Propositions as these. *A Law is a Law*, and *Obligation is Obligation*: *Right is Right*, and *Wrong is Wrong*, will these and the like ever help him to an acquaintance with *Ethicks*? or instruct him or others, in the Knowledge of *Morality*? Those who know not, nor perhaps ever will know, what is *Right*, and what is *Wrong*; nor the measures of them, can with as much assurance make, and infallibly know the truth of these and all such Propositions, as he that is best instructed in *Morality*, can do. But what advance do such Propositions give in the Knowledge of any thing necessary, or useful for their conduct?

(12) two] **5er** (*likewise* **Coste**) | who **4–5**; *not in* **1–3**, **W** (14)–612(12) I . . . *Identical.*] *add.* **4–5**

He would be thought to do little less than Trifle, who for the enlightning the Understanding in any part of Knowledge, should be busie with *Identical Propositions*, and insist on such Maxims as these. *Substance is Substance*, and *Body is Body*; *a Vacuum is a Vacuum*, and *a Vortex is a Vortex*: A *Centaure is a Centaure*, and a *Chimæra is a Chimæra*, *etc.* For these, and all such are equally true, equally certain, and equally self-evident. But yet they cannot but be counted trifling, when made use of as Principles of Instruction, and stress laid on them, as helps to Knowledge: since they teach nothing but what every one, who is capable of Discourse, knows without being told: *viz.* That the same Term is the same Term, and the same *Idea* the same *Idea*. And upon this Account it was that I formerly did, and do still think, the offering and inculcating such Propositions, in order to give the Understanding any new light, or inlet into the Knowledge of things, no better than trifling.

Instruction lies in something very different, and he that would enlarge his own, or another's Mind, to Truths he does not yet know, must find out intermediate *Ideas*, and then lay them in such order one by another, that the Understanding may see the agreement, or disagreement of those in question. Propositions that do this, are instructive: But they are far from such as affirm the same Term of it self, which is no way to advance ones self or others, in any sort of Knowledge. It no more helps to that, than it would help any one in his Learning to read, to have such Propositions as these inculcated to him, *an A is an A*, and *a B is a B*; which a Man may know as well as any School-Master, and yet never be able to read a word as long as he lives. Nor do these, or any such Identical Propositions help him one jot forwards in the skill of Reading, let him make what use of them he can.

If those who blame my calling them *Trifling Propositions*, had but read, and been at the pains to understand what I had above writ in very plain *English*, they could not but have seen that by *Identical Propositions*, I mean only such, wherein the same Term importing the same *Idea*, is affirmed of it self: which I take to be the proper signification of *Identical Proposition*; and concerning all such, I think I may continue safely to say, That to propose them as instructive, is no better than trifling. For no one who has the use of Reason can

(11–12) *Idea . . . Idea*] *edit.* | Idea the same Idea **4–5** (14) light,] **4** | Light **5** (22) ones] **5** | one **4** (26) [*2nd*] as] **4er–5** | to **4** School-Master] **5** |School/ Master **4** (28) forwards] **5** | forwards, **4**

miss them, where it is necessary they should be taken notice of; nor doubt of their truth, when he does take notice of them.

But if Men will call Propositions *Identical*, wherein the same Term is not affirmed of it self, whether they speak more properly than I, others must judge: This is certain, all that they say of Propositions that are not *Identical*, in my sense, concerns not me, nor what I have said; all that I have said relating to those Propositions, wherein the same Term is affirmed of it self. And I would fain see an Instance, wherein any such can be made use of, to the Advantage and Improvement of any one's Knowledge. Instances of other kinds, whatever use may be made of them, concern not me, as not being such as I call *Identical*.

§ 4. *Secondly*, Another sort of Trifling Propositions is, *when a part of the complex* Idea *is predicated of the Name of the whole*; a part of the Definition of the Word defined. Such are all Propositions wherein the *Genus* is predicated of the *Species*, or more comprehensive of less comprehensive Terms: For what Information, what Knowledge carries this Proposition in it, *viz. Lead is a Metal*, to a Man, who knows the complex *Idea* the name *Lead* stands for. All the simple *Ideas* that go to the complex one signified by the Term *Metal*, being nothing but what he before comprehended, and signified by the name *Lead*. Indeed, to a Man that knows the Signification of the word *Metal*, and not of the word *Lead*, it is a shorter way to explain the Signification of the word *Lead*, by saying it is a *Metal*, which at once expresses several of its simple *Ideas*, than to enumerate them one by one, telling him it is a Body very *heavy*, *fusible*, and *malleable*.

§ 5. Alike trifling it is, *to predicate any other part of the Definition of the Term defined*, or to affirm any one of the simple *Ideas* of a complex one, of the Name of the whole complex *Idea*; as *All Gold is fusible*. For *Fusibility* being one of the simple *Ideas* that goes to the making up the complex one the sound *Gold* stands for, what can it be but playing with Sounds, to affirm that of the name *Gold*, which is comprehended in its received Signification? 'Twould be thought little better than ridiculous, to affirm gravely as a Truth of moment, That *Gold is yellow*; and I see not how it is any jot more material to

§ 4. *Secondly, When a part of any complex* Idea *is predicated of the whole.* § 5. *As part of the Definition of the defined.*

---

(8) self.] **5** | self, **4** (12) *v.* 610(14), n. (28) Alike] **1–2, 4** | A like **3, 5**
(33) to affirm] **2–5** | by affirming **1** (*l. below* 36: § 4.) *Secondly*,] **2–3, 5** | *Secondly* **4**

say, *It is fusible*, unless that Quality be left out of the complex *Idea*, of which the Sound *Gold* is the mark in ordinary Speech. What Instruction can it carry with it, to tell one that which he hath been told already, or he is supposed to know before? For I am supposed to know the Signification of the word another uses to me, or else he is to tell me. And if I know that the name *Gold* stands for this complex *Idea* of *Body*, *Yellow*, *Heavy*, *Fusible*, *Malleable*, 'twill not much instruct me to put it solemnly afterwards in a Proposition, and gravely say, *All Gold is fusible*. Such Propositions can only serve to shew the Disingenuity of one, who will go from the Definition of his own Terms, by re-minding him sometimes of it; but carry no Knowledge with them, but of the Signification of Words, however certain they be.

§ 6. *Every* Man *is an Animal*, or living Body, is as certain a Proposition as can be; but no more conducing to the Knowledge of Things, than to say, *A Palfry is an ambling Horse*, or a neighing ambling *Animal*, both being only about the signification of Words, and make me know but this; That *Body*, *Sense*, and *Motion*, or power of Sensation and Moving, are three of those *Ideas*, that I always comprehend and signify by the word *Man*; and where they are not to be found together, the name *Man* belongs not to that Thing: And so of the other, that *Body*, *Sense*, and *a certain way of going*, with *a certain kind of Voice*, are some of those *Ideas* which I always comprehend, and signify by the word *Palfry*; and when they are not to be found together, the name *Palfry* belongs not to that thing. 'Tis just the same, and to the same purpose, when any term standing for any one or more of the simple *Ideas*, that altogether make up that complex *Idea* which is called a *Man*, is affirmed of the term *Man*: *v.g.* suppose a *Roman*, signified by the word *Homo*: all these distinct *Ideas* united in one subject, *Corporeitas*, *Sensibilitas*, *Potentia se movendi*, *Rationalitas*, *Risibilitas*, he might, no doubt, with great certainty, universally affirm one, more, or all of these together of the word *Homo*, but did no more than say, that the word *Homo*, in his Country, comprehended in its signification, all these *Ideas*. Much like a *Romance* Knight, who by the word *Palfry*, signified these *Ideas*; *Body of a certain figure*, *fourlegg'd*, *with sense*, *motion*, *ambling*, *neighing*, *white*, *used to have a Woman on his back*, might with the same certainty,

§ 6. *Instance Man and Palfry.*

(4) before ?] **4–5** | before: **1–3** (19) *Ideas*,] **2–5** | simple *Ideas* **1** (23) *Ideas*] **2–5** | simple *Ideas* **1** (32) , more,] **1er–5** | more, **1**

universally affirm also any, or all of these of the word *Palfry*: but did thereby teach no more, but that the word *Palfry*, in his, or Romance Language, stood for all these, and was not to be applied to any thing, where any of these was wanting. But he that shall tell me, that in whatever thing *Sense*, *Motion*, *Reason*, and *Laughter*, were united, that Thing had actually a notion of GOD, or would be cast into a sleep by *Opium*, made indeed an instructive Proposition: because neither *having the notion of GOD*, nor *being cast into sleep by Opium*, being contained in the *Idea* signified by the Word *Man*, we are by such Propositions taught something more than barely what the word *Man* stands for: And therefore the Knowledge contained in it, is more than *verbal*.

§ 7. Before a Man makes any Proposition, he is supposed to understand the terms he uses in it, or else he talks like a Parrot, only making a noise by imitation, and framing certain Sounds, which he has learnt of others; but not, as a rational Creature, using them for signs of *Ideas*, which he has in his Mind. The Hearer also is supposed to understand the Terms as the Speaker uses them, or else he talks jargon, and makes an unintelligible noise. And therefore he trifles with Words, who makes such a Proposition, which when it is made, contains no more than one of the Terms does, and which a Man was supposed to know before: *v.g. a Triangle hath three sides*, or *Saffron is yellow*. And this is no farther tolerable, than where a Man goes to explain his Terms, to one who is supposed or declares himself not to understand him: and then *it teaches only the signification of that Word*, and the use of that Sign.

§ 8. We can know then the Truth of two sorts of Propositions, with perfect *certainty*; the one is, of those trifling Propositions, which have a certainty in them, but 'tis but a *verbal Certainty*, but not instructive. And, secondly, we can know the Truth, and so may be *certain* in Propositions, which affirm something of another, which is a necessary consequence of its precise complex *Idea*, but not contained in it. As that *the external Angle of all Triangles, is bigger than either of the opposite internal Angles*; which relation of the outward Angle, to either of the opposite internal Angles, making no part of the complex *Idea*, signified by the name Triangle, this is a real Truth, and conveys with it instructive *real Knowledge*.

§ 7. *For this teaches but the signification of Words.* § 8. *But no real Knowledge.*

(15) , which] *add.* **4–5** (17) , which] *add.* **4–5** (',' **2–5**)

§ 9. We having little or no knowledge of what Combinations there be of simple *Ideas* existing together in Substances, but by our Senses, we cannot make any universal *certain* Propositions concerning them, any farther than our nominal Essences lead us: which being to a very few and inconsiderable Truths, in respect of those which depend on their real Constitutions, the general *Propositions* that are made *about Substances*, *if they are certain*, *are for the most part but trifling*; and if they are instructive, are uncertain, and such as we can have no knowledge of their real Truth, how much soever constant Observation and Analogy may assist our Judgments in guessing. Hence it comes to pass, that one may often meet with very clear and coherent Discourses, that amount yet to nothing. For 'tis plain, that Names of substantial Beings, as well as others, as far as they have relative Significations affixed to them, may, with great Truth, be joined negatively and affirmatively in Propositions, as their relative Definitions make them fit to be so joined; and Propositions consisting of such Terms, may, with the same clearness, be deduced one from another, as those that convey the most real Truths; and all this, without any knowledge of the Nature or Reality of Things existing without us. By this method, one may make Demonstrations and undoubted Propositions in Words, and yet thereby advance not one jot in the Knowledge of the Truth of Things; *v.g.* he that having learnt these following Words, with their ordinary mutually relative Acceptations annexed to them; *v.g. Substance*, *Man*, *Animal*, *Form*, *Soul*, *Vegetative*, *Sensitive*, *Rational*, may make several undoubted Propositions about the Soul, without knowing at all what the Soul really is; and of this sort, a Man may find an infinite number of Propositions, Reasonings, and Conclusions, in Books of Metaphysicks, School-Divinity, and some sort of natural Philosophy; and after all, know as little of GOD, *Spirits*, or *Bodies*, as he did before he set out.

§ 10. He that hath liberty to define, *i.e.* determine the signification of his Names of Substances, (as certainly every one does in effect, who makes them stand for his own *Ideas*,) and makes their Significations at a venture, taking them from his own or other Men's Fancies, and not from an Examination or Enquiry into the Nature of

§ 9. *General Propositions concerning Substances are often trifling.* § 10. *And why.*

(1) little or] *add.* **2–5** (13–14) [*3rd*] as . . . relative] **4–5** | having constant and setled **1–3** (16) relative] *add.* **4–5** (24) mutually relative] *add.* **4–5** (26) Propositions] **1–3**, **5** | Propositions,/ **4** (36) or] **5** and **1–4**. (**Coste** 'un serieux examen')

Things themselves, may, with little Trouble, demonstrate them one of another, according to those several Respects, and mutual Relations he has given them one to another; wherein, however Things agree, or disagree, in their own Nature, he needs mind nothing but his own Notions, with the Names he hath bestowed upon them: but thereby no more increases his own Knowledge, than he does his Riches, who taking a Bag of Counters, calls one in a certain place a *Pound*, another in another place, a *Shilling*, and a third in a third place, a *Penny*; and so proceeding, may undoubtedly reckon right, and cast up a great Sum, according to his Counters so placed, and standing for more or less as he pleases, without being one jot the richer, or without even knowing how much a Pound, Shilling, or Penny is, but only that one is contained in the other twenty times, and contains the other twelve; which a Man may also do in the signification of Words, by making them in respect of one another, more, or less, or equally comprehensive.

§ 11. Though yet concerning most Words used in Discourses, especially Argumentative and Controversial, there is this more to be complained of, which is the worst sort of *Trifling*, and which sets us yet farther from the certainty of Knowledge we hope to attain by them, or find in them, *viz.* that most Writers are so far from instructing us in the Nature and Knowledge of Things, that they *use their Words loosly* and uncertainly, and do not, by using them constantly and steadily in the same significations, make plain and clear deductions of Words one from another, and make their Discourses coherent and clear, (how little soever it were instructive,) which were not difficult to do, did they not find it convenient to shelter their Ignorance or Obstinacy, under the Obscurity and perplexedness of their Terms; to which, perhaps, Inadvertency, and ill Custom does in many Men much contribute.

§ 12. To conclude, *barely verbal Propositions* may be known by these following *Marks*:

First, All Propositions, wherein two abstract Terms are affirmed one of another, are barely about the signification of Sounds. For since no abstract *Idea* can be the same with any other but it self,

§ 11. *Thirdly, Using Words variously, is trifling with them.* § 12. *Marks of verbal Propositions, First, Predication in abstract.*

(2–3) , according . . . another] *add.* **4–5** (4) needs] **4–5** | need **1–3** (24) significations] **5** | signification **4** (26) instructive,)] **1–3, 5** | instructive, **4** (35) it] **3–5** | its **1–2**

when its abstract Name is affirmed of any other Term, it can signify no more but this, that it may, or ought to be called by that Name; or that these two Names signify the same *Idea*. Thus should any one say, that *Parsimony is Frugality*, that *Gratitude is Justice*; that this or that Action is, or is not *Temperance*: However specious these and the like Propositions may at first sight seem, yet when we come to press them, and examine nicely what they contain, we shall find, that it all amounts to nothing, but the signification of those Terms.

§ 13. *Secondly*, All *Propositions*, *wherein a part of the complex* Idea, which any Term stands for, *is predicated of that Term*, *are only* verbal, *v.g.* to say, *that Gold is a Metal*, or *heavy*. And thus all Propositions, wherein more comprehensive Words, called *Genera*, are *affirmed* of subordinate, or less comprehensive, called *Species*, *or Individuals*, are barely verbal.

When by these two Rules, we have examined the Propositions, that make up the Discourses we ordinarily meet with, both in and out of Books, we shall, perhaps, find that a greater part of them, than is usually suspected, are purely about the signification of Words, and contain nothing in them, but the Use and Application of these Signs.

This, I think, I may lay down for an infallible Rule, that where-ever the distinct *Idea* any Word stands for, is not known and considered, and something not contained in the *Idea*, is not affirmed, or denied of it, there our Thoughts stick wholly in Sounds, and are able to attain no real Truth or Falshood. This, perhaps, if well heeded, might save us a great deal of useless Amusement and Dispute; and very much shorten our Trouble, and wandring in the search of real and true Knowledge.

§ 13. *Secondly, A part of the Definition predicated of any term.*

(2) or] **1–3, 5** | or or **4** (23) Word stands] **2–5** | Words stand **1** (24) the] **4–5** | that **1–3** (*likewise* **Coste**)

CHAPTER IX

Of our Knowledge of Existence.

§ 1. HITHERTO we have only considered the Essences of Things, which being only abstract *Ideas*, and thereby removed in our Thoughts from particular Existence, (that being the proper Operation of the Mind, in Abstraction, to consider an *Idea* under no other Existence, but what it has in the Understanding,) gives us no Knowledge of real Existence at all. Where by the way we may take notice, that *universal Propositions*, of whose Truth or Falshood we can have certain Knowledge, concern not *Existence*; and farther, that all *particular Affirmations or Negations*, that would not be certain if they were made general, are only concerning *Existence*; they declaring only the accidental Union or Separation of *Ideas* in Things existing, which in their abstract Natures, have no known necessary Union or Repugnancy.

§ 2. But leaving the Nature of Propositions, and different ways of Predication to be considered more at large in another place, Let us proceed now to enquire concerning our Knowledge of the *Existence* of Things, and how we come by it. I say then, that we have the Knowledge of *our own Existence* by Intuition; of the *Existence of* GOD by Demonstration; and of other Things by Sensation.

§ 3. As for *our own Existence*, we perceive it so plainly, and so certainly, that it neither needs, nor is capable of any proof. For nothing can be more evident to us, than our own Existence. *I think, I reason, I feel Pleasure and Pain*; Can any of these be more evident to me, than my own Existence? If I doubt of all other Things, that very doubt makes me perceive my own *Existence*, and will not suffer me to doubt of that. For if I know *I feel Pain*, it is evident, I have as certain a Perception of my own Existence, as of the Existence of the Pain I feel: Or if I know *I doubt*, I have as certain a Perception of the Existence of the thing doubting, as of that Thought, which I call *doubt*. Experience then convinces us, that *we have an intuitive Knowledge of our own Existence*, and an internal infallible Perception that

§ 1. *General certain Propositions concern not Existence.* § 2. *A threefold Knowledge of Existence.* § 3. *Our Knowledge of our own Existence is intuitive.*

(6) may] *add.* **1T.er, 2–5** (28) a] **1–4**; *om.* **5**

we are. In every Act of Sensation, Reasoning, or Thinking, we are conscious to our selves of our own Being; and, in this Matter, come not short of the highest degree of *Certainty*.

CHAPTER X

Of our Knowledge of the Existence of a GOD.

§ 1. THOUGH GOD has given us no innate *Ideas* of himself; though he has stamped no original Characters on our Minds, wherein we may read his Being: yet having furnished us with those Faculties, our Minds are endowed with, he hath not left himself without witness: since we have Sense, Perception, and Reason, and cannot want a clear proof of him, as long as we carry our selves about us. Nor can we justly complain of our Ignorance in this great Point, since he has so plentifully provided us with the means to discover, and know him, so far as is necessary to the end of our Being, and the great concernment of our Happiness. But though this be the most obvious Truth that Reason discovers; and though its Evidence be (if I mistake not) equal to mathematical Certainty: yet it requires Thought and Attention; and the Mind must apply it self to a regular deduction of it from some part of our intuitive Knowledge, or else we shall be as uncertain, and ignorant of this, as of other Propositions, which are in themselves capable of clear Demonstration. To shew therefore, that we are capable of *knowing*, i.e. *being certain that there is a* GOD, and how we may come by this certainty, I think we need go no farther than our selves, and that undoubted Knowledge we have of our own Existence.

§ 2. I think it is beyond Question, that *Man has a clear Perception of his own Being*; he knows certainly, that he exists, and that he is something. He that can doubt, whether he be any thing, or no, I speak not to, no more than I would argue with pure nothing, or endeavour to convince Non-entity, that it were something. If any one pretends to be so sceptical, as to deny his own Existence, (for

§ 1. *We are capable of knowing certainly that there is a GOD.* § 2. *Man knows that he himself is.*

---

(1) Reasoning,] *edit.* | Reasoning **1–5** (5) on] **2–5** | in **1** (16) it] **3–5** | its **1–2** (17) part . . . intuitive] **2–5** | unquestionable parts of our **1** (20) we . . . *certain*] **2–5** | *we are capable of knowing, certainly* knowing **1** (21) may] *add.* **2–5** this certainty] **2–5** | it **1** (22) go] **2–5** | look **1** (29) pretends] **4–5** | pretend **1–3**

really to doubt of it, is manifestly impossible,) let him for me enjoy his beloved Happiness of being nothing, until Hunger, or some other Pain convince him of the contrary. This then, I think, I may take for a Truth, which every ones certain Knowledge assures him of, beyond the liberty of doubting, *viz.* that he is something that actually exists.

§ 3. In the next place, Man knows by an intuitive Certainty, that bare *nothing can no more produce any real Being, than it can be equal to two right Angles.* If a Man knows not that Non-entity, or the Absence of all Being cannot be equal to two right Angles, it is impossible he should know any demonstration in *Euclid.* If therefore we know there is some real Being, and that Non-entity cannot produce any real Being, it is an evident demonstration, that from Eternity there has been something; Since what was not from Eternity, had a Beginning; and what had a Beginning, must be produced by something else.

§ 4. Next, it is evident, that what had its Being and Beginning from another, must also have all that which is in, and belongs to its Being from another too. All the Powers it has, must be owing to, and received from the same Source. This eternal Source then of all being must also be the Source and Original of all Power; and so *this eternal Being must be also the most powerful.*

§ 5. Again, a Man finds in himself *Perception*, and *Knowledge*. We have then got one step farther; and we are certain now, that there is not only some Being, but some knowing intelligent Being in the World.

There was a time then, when there was no knowing Being, and when Knowledge began to be; or else, there has been also *a knowing Being from Eternity.* If it be said, there was a time when no Being had any Knowledge, when that eternal Being was void of all Understanding. I reply, that then it was impossible there should ever have been any Knowledge. It being as impossible, that Things wholly void of Knowledge, and operating blindly, and without any Perception, should produce a knowing Being, as it is impossible, that a Triangle should make it self three Angles bigger than two right ones. For it is as repugnant to the *Idea* of senseless Matter,

§ 3. *He knows also, that Nothing cannot produce a Being, therefore something eternal.* § 4. *That eternal Being must be most powerful.* § 5. *And most knowing.*

---

(9) not] **1–3** (*likewise* **Coste**); *om.* **4–5** (14) ; Since] **4–5** | . Since **1–3**

that it should put into it self Sense, Perception, and Knowledge, as it is repugnant to the *Idea* of a Triangle, that it should put into it self greater Angles than two right ones.

§ 6. Thus from the Consideration of our selves, and what we infallibly find in our own Constitutions, our Reason leads us to the Knowledge of this certain and evident Truth, That *there is an eternal, most powerful, and most knowing Being*; which whether any one will please to call *God*, it matters not. The thing is evident, and from this *Idea* duly considered, will easily be deduced all those other Attributes, which we ought to ascribe to this eternal Being. If nevertheless any one should be found so senslesly arrogant, as to suppose Man alone knowing and wise, but yet the product of mere ignorance and chance; and that all the rest of the Universe acted only by that blind hap-hazard: I shall leave with him that very Rational and Emphatical rebuke of *Tully* l. 2. *de leg.* to be considered at his leisure. "What can be more sillily arrogant and misbecoming, than for a Man to think that he has a Mind and Understanding in him, but yet in all the Universe beside, there is no such thing? Or that those things, which with the utmost stretch of his Reason he can scarce comprehend, should be moved and managed without any Reason at all?" *Quid est enim verius, quam neminem esse oportere tam stultè arrogantem, ut in se mentem et rationem putet inesse, in cœlo mundoque non putet? Aut ea quæ vix summâ ingenii ratione comprehendat, nullâ ratione moveri putet?*

From what has been said, it is plain to me, we have a more certain Knowledge of the Existence of a GOD, than of any thing our Senses have not immediately discovered to us. Nay, I presume I may say, that we more certainly know that there is a GOD, than that there is any thing else without us. When I say we *know*, I mean there is such a Knowledge within our reach, which we cannot miss, if we will but apply our Minds to that, as we do to several other Enquiries.

§ 7. *How far the* Idea *of a most perfect Being*, which a Man may frame in his Mind, does, or does not prove the *Existence of a* GOD, I will not here examine. For in the different Make of Men's Tempers, and Application of their Thoughts, some Arguments prevail more

§ 6. *And therefore GOD.* § 7. *Our* Idea *of a most perfect Being not the sole proof of a GOD.*

(10) which] *add.* **4–5** (11–16) If . . . leisure.] *add.* **2–5** (16–21) "What . . . all?"] *add.* **4–5** (21–4) *Quid . . . putet?*] *add.* **2–5** (32) Idea] **2–5** | Ideas **1**

on one, and some on another, for the Confirmation of the same Truth. But yet, I think, this I may say, that it is an ill way of establishing this Truth, and silencing Atheists, to lay the whole stress of so important a Point, as this, upon that sole Foundation: And take some Men's having that *Idea* of GOD in their Minds, (for 'tis evident, some Men have none, and some worse than none, and the most very different,) for the only proof of a Deity; and out of an over-fondness of that Darling Invention, cashier, or at least endeavour to invalidate all other Arguments, and forbid us to hearken to those proofs, as being weak, or fallacious, which our own Existence, and the sensible parts of the Universe, offer so clearly, and cogently to our Thoughts, that I deem it impossible for a considering Man to withstand them. For I judge it as certain and clear a Truth, as can any where be delivered, That *the invisible Things of GOD are clearly seen from the Creation of the World, being understood by the Things that are made, even his Eternal Power, and God-head.** Though our own Being furnishes us, as I have shewn, with an evident, and incontestable proof of a Deity; And I believe no Body can avoid the Cogency of it, who will but as carefully attend to it, as to any other Demonstration of so many parts: Yet this being so fundamental a Truth, and of that Consequence, that all Religion and genuine Morality depend thereon, I doubt not but I shall be forgiven by my Reader, if I go over some parts of this Argument again, and enlarge a little more upon them.

§ 8. There is no Truth more evident, than that *something* must be *from Eternity*. I never yet heard of any one so unreasonable, or that could suppose so manifest a Contradiction, as a Time, wherein there was perfectly nothing. This being of all Absurdities the greatest, to imagine that pure nothing, the perfect Negation and Absence of all Beings, should ever produce any real Existence.

It being then unavoidable for all rational Creatures, to conclude, that something has existed from Eternity; Let us next see what kind of thing that must be.

§ 9. There are but two sorts of Beings in the World, that Man knows or conceives.

§ 8. *Something from Eternity.* § 9. *Two sorts of Beings, Cogitative and Incogitative.*

(7) different] **1–2**, **4–5** | indifferent **3**. (**Coste** 'une idée telle quelle')

* Rom. 1: 20.

First, Such as are purely material, without Sense, Perception, or Thought, as the clippings of our Beards, and paring of our Nails.

Secondly, Sensible, thinking, perceiving Beings, such as we find our selves to be, which if you please, we will hereafter call *cogitative and incogitative* Beings; which to our present purpose, if for nothing else, are, perhaps, better Terms, than material and immaterial.

§ 10. If then there must be something eternal, let us see what sort of Being it must be. And to that, it is very obvious to Reason, that it must necessarily be a *cogitative* Being. For it is as impossible to conceive, that ever bare incogitative Matter should produce a thinking intelligent Being, as that nothing should of it self produce Matter. Let us suppose any parcel of Matter eternal, great or small, we shall find it, in it self, able to produce nothing. For Example; let us suppose the Matter of the next Pebble, we meet with, eternal, closely united, and the parts firmly at rest together, if there were no other Being in the World, Must it not eternally remain so, a dead inactive Lump? Is it possible to conceive it can add Motion to it self, being purely Matter, or produce any thing? Matter then, by its own Strength, cannot produce in it self so much as Motion: the Motion it has, must also be from Eternity, or else be produced, and added to Matter by some other Being more powerful than Matter; Matter, as is evident, having not Power to produce Motion in it self. But let us suppose Motion eternal too; yet Matter, *incogitative Matter* and Motion, whatever changes it might produce of Figure and Bulk, *could never produce Thought*: Knowledge will still be as far beyond the Power of Motion and Matter to produce, as Matter is beyond the Power of *nothing*, or *non-entity* to produce. And I appeal to every one's own Thoughts, whether he cannot as easily conceive Matter produced by *nothing*, as Thought to be produced by pure Matter, when before there was no such thing as Thought, or an intelligent Being existing. Divide Matter into as minute parts as you will, (which we are apt to imagine a sort of spiritualizing, or making a thinking thing of it,) vary the Figure and Motion of it, as much as you please, a Globe, Cube, Cone, Prism, Cylinder, *etc.* whose Diameters are but 1000000th part of a

§ 10. *Incogitative Being cannot produce a Cogitative.*

(13) parcel] **2–5** | part **1**. (**Coste** 'une partie') (28–9) *nothing*, or *non-entity*] **4–5** | nothing **1–3** (*likewise* **Coste**)

Gry (a) will operate no otherwise upon other Bodies of proportionable Bulk, than those of an inch or foot Diameter; and you may as rationally expect to produce Sense, Thought, and Knowledge, by putting together in a certain Figure and Motion, gross Particles of Matter, as by those that are the very minutest, that do any where exist. They knock, impell, and resist one another, just as the greater do, and that is all they can do. So that if we will suppose nothing first, or eternal; *Matter* can never begin to be: If we suppose bare Matter, without Motion, eternal; *Motion* can never begin to be: If we suppose only Matter and Motion first, or eternal; *Thought* can never begin to be. For it is impossible to conceive that Matter either with or without Motion could have originally in and from it self Sense, Perception, and Knowledge, as is evident from hence, that then Sense, Perception, and Knowledge must be a property eternally inseparable from Matter and every Particle of it. Not to add, that though our general or specifick conception of Matter makes us speak of it as one thing, yet really all Matter is not one individual thing, neither is there any such thing existing as one material Being or one single Body that we know or can conceive. And therefore if Matter were the eternal first cogitative Being, there would not be one eternal infinite cogitative Being, but an infinite number of eternal finite cogitative Beings, independent one of another, of limited force, and distinct thoughts, which could never produce that order, harmony, and beauty which is to be found in Nature. Since therefore whatsoever is the first eternal *Being* must necessarily be cogitative; And whatsoever is first of all Things, must necessarily contain in it, and actually have, at least, all the Perfections that can ever after exist; nor can it ever give to another any perfection that it hath not, either actually in it self, or at least in a higher degree; It necessarily follows, that the first eternal Being cannot be Matter.

(a) *A Gry is $\frac{1}{10}$ of a line, a line $\frac{1}{10}$ of an inch, an inch $\frac{1}{10}$ of a philosophical foot, a philosophical foot $\frac{1}{3}$ of a pendulum, whose Diadroms, in the latitude of 45 degrees, are each equal to one Second of time, or $\frac{1}{60}$ of a minute. I have affectedly made use of this measure here, and the parts of it, under a decimal division with names to them; because, I think, it would be of general convenience, that this should be the common measure in the Commonwealth of Letters.*

(8, 9, 10) eternal;] **4–5** | eternal, **1–3** (11–25) For . . . Nature.] *add.* **2–5** (14) then] **2er–5** | the **2** (23) [*1st*] of] **2er, 4–5** | with **2–3** (24) be] **2–4**; *om.* **5** (25–6) Since . . . And] **2–5** | Whatsoever therefore is eternal, must be a cogitative Being, a Spirit: **1** (30–1) It . . . Matter.] *add.* **2–5** (*l. below* 31: (a)) **Coste** *adds, at the end of the note on* '*Gry*', 'Cette Note est de Mr. *Locke*. Le mot *Gry* est de sa façon. Il l'a inventé pour exprimer $\frac{1}{10}$ de Ligne, mesure qui jusqu'ici n'a point eû de nom, et qu'on peut aussi bien désigner par ce mot que par quelque autre que ce soit.'

§ 11. *If* therefore it be evident, that *something* necessarily must *exist from Eternity*, 'tis also as evident, that *that Something must* necessarily *be a cogitative Being*: For it is as impossible, that incogitative Matter should produce a cogitative Being, as that nothing, or the negation of all Being, should produce a positive Being or Matter.

§ 12. Though this discovery of the *necessary Existence of an eternal Mind*, does sufficiently lead us into the Knowledge of GOD; since it will hence follow, that all other knowing Beings that have a beginning, must depend on him, and have no other ways of knowledge, or extent of Power, than what he gives them; And therefore if he made those, he made also the less-excellent pieces of this Universe, all inanimate Beings, whereby his *Omniscience*, *Power*, and *Providence*, will be established, and all his other Attributes necessarily follow: Yet to clear up this a little farther, we will see what Doubts can be raised against it.

§ 13. *First*, Perhaps it will be said, that though it be as clear as demonstration can make it, that there must be an eternal Being, and that Being must also be knowing: yet it does not follow, but that thinking Being may also be material. Let it be so; it equally still follows, that there is a GOD. For if there be an Eternal, Omniscient, Omnipotent Being, it is certain, that there is a GOD, whether you imagine that Being to be material, or no. But, herein, I suppose, lies the danger and deceit of that Supposition: There being no way to avoid the demonstration, that there is an eternal knowing Being, Men, devoted to Matter, would willingly have it granted, that this knowing Being is material; and then letting slide out of their Minds, or the Discourse, the demonstration whereby an eternal knowing Being was proved necessarily to exist, would argue all to be Matter, and so deny a GOD, that is, an eternal cogitative Being: whereby they are so far from establishing, that they destroy their own Hypothesis. For if there can be, in their Opinion, eternal Matter, without any eternal cogitative Being, they manifestly separate Matter and Thinking, and suppose no necessary connexion of the one with the other, and so establish the necessity of an eternal Spirit, but not of Matter; since it has been proved already, that an eternal cogitative Being is unavoidably to be granted. Now if

§§ 11, 12. *Therefore there has been an eternal Wisdom.* § 13. *Whether material or no.*

(8) does] **4–5** | do **1–3** Knowledge] **1–3, 5** | Knowledg **4** GOD] **2–5** | a GOD **1** (19) it] **2–5** | is **1** (33) any] **2–5** | an **1**

Thinking and Matter may be separated, *the eternal Existence of Matter, will not follow from the eternal Existence of a cogitative Being*, and they suppose it to no purpose.

§ 14. But now let us see how they can satisfie themselves, or others, that this *eternal thinking Being* is *material.*

First, I would ask them, whether they imagine, that all Matter, *every particle of Matter, thinks*? This, I suppose, they will scarce say; since then there would be as many eternal thinking Beings, as there are Particles of Matter, and so an infinity of Gods. And yet if they will not allow Matter as Matter, that is, every Particle of Matter to be as well cogitative, as extended, they will have as hard a task to make out to their own Reasons, a cogitative Being out of incogitative Particles, as an extended Being, out of unextended Parts, if I may so speak.

§ 15. *Secondly*, If all Matter does not think, I next ask, whether it be *only one Atom that does so*? This has as many Absurdities as the other; for then this Atom of Matter must be alone eternal, or not. If this alone be eternal, then this alone, by its powerful Thought, or Will, made all the rest of Matter. And so we have the creation of Matter by a powerful Thought, which is that the Materialists stick at. For if they suppose one single thinking Atom, to have produced all the rest of Matter, they cannot ascribe that Preeminency to it upon any other account, than that of its Thinking, the only supposed difference. But allow it to be by some other way, which is above our conception, it must be still Creation; and these Men must give up their great Maxim, *Ex nihilo nil fit.** If it be said, that all the rest of Matter is equally eternal, as that thinking Atom, it will be to say any thing at pleasure, though never so absurd: For to suppose all matter eternal, and yet one small particle in Knowledge and Power infinitely above all the rest, is without any the least appearance of Reason to frame any Hypothesis. Every particle of Matter, as Matter, is capable of all the same Figures and Motions of any other; and I challenge any one in his Thoughts, to add any Thing else to one above another.

§ 14. *Not material, First, because every particle of Matter is not cogitative.* § 15. *Secondly, One particle alone of Matter cannot be cogitative.*

(1) and] **1–4**; *om.* **5** (5) this] **1, 3** | this, **2, 4–5** (12) a] *add.* **1T.er, 2–5** (15) does] **4–5** | do **1–3**

* Cf. Lucretius, *De Rerum Natura*, I, 150 ff.

§ 16. *Thirdly*, If then neither one peculiar Atom alone, can be this eternal thinking Being; nor all Matter, as Matter; *i.e.* every particle of Matter can be it, it only remains, that it is *some certain System of Matter* duly put together, that is this *thinking eternal Being*. This is that, which, I imagine, is that Notion, which Men are aptest to have of GOD, who would have him a material Being, as most readily suggested to them, by the ordinary conceit they have of themselves, and other Men, which they take to be material thinking Beings. But this Imagination, however more natural, is no less absurd than the other: For to suppose the eternal thinking Being, to be nothing else but a composition of Particles of Matter, each whereof is incogitative, is to ascribe all the Wisdom and Knowledge of that eternal Being, only to the *juxta*-position of parts; than which, nothing can be more absurd. For unthinking Particles of Matter, however put together, can have nothing thereby added to them, but a new relation of Position, which 'tis impossible should give thought and knowledge to them.

§ 17. But farther, this *corporeal System* either has all its parts at rest, or it is a certain motion of the parts wherein its Thinking consists. If it be perfectly at rest, it is but one lump, and so can have no priviledges above one Atom.

If it be the motion of its parts, on which its Thinking depends, all the Thoughts there must be unavoidably accidental, and limited; since all the Particles that by Motion cause Thought, being each of them in it self without any Thought, cannot regulate its own Motions, much less be regulated by the Thought of the whole; since that Thought is not the cause of Motion, (for then it must be antecedent to it, and so without it,) but the consequence of it, whereby Freedom, Power, Choice, and all rational and wise thinking or acting will be quite taken away: So that such a thinking Being will be no better nor wiser, than pure blind Matter; since to resolve all into the accidental unguided motions of blind Matter, or into Thought depending on unguided motions of blind Matter, is the same thing; not to mention the narrowness of such Thoughts and Knowledge, that must depend on the motion of such parts. But there needs no enumeration of any more Absurdities and Impossibilities in this Hypothesis, (however full of them it be,) than that before-mentioned; since let this thinking System be all, or a

§ 16. *Thirdly, a System of incogitative Matter, cannot be cogitative.* § 17. *Whether in motion, or at rest.*

part of the Matter of the Universe, it is impossible that any one Particle, should either know its own, or the motion of any other Particle, or the Whole know the motion of every Particular; and so regulate its own Thoughts or Motions, or indeed have any Thought resulting from such Motion.

§ 18. Others would have *Matter* to be *eternal*, notwithstanding that they allow an eternal, cogitative, immaterial Being. This, tho' it take not away the Being of a GOD, yet since it denies one and the first great piece of his Workmanship, the Creation, let us consider it a little. *Matter* must be allowed eternal: Why? Because you cannot conceive how it can be made out of nothing; why do you not also think your self eternal? You will answer, perhaps, Because about twenty or forty Years since, you began to be. But if I ask you what that *You* is, which began then to be, you can scarce tell me. The Matter whereof you are made, began not then to be: for if it did, then it is not eternal: But it began to be put together in such a fashion and frame, as makes up your Body; but yet that frame of Particles, is not You, it makes not that thinking Thing You are; (for I have now to do with one, who allows an eternal, immaterial, thinking Being, but would have unthinking Matter eternal too;) therefore when did that thinking Thing begin to be? If it did never begin to be, then have you always been a thinking Thing from Eternity; the absurdity whereof I need not confute, till I meet with one, who is so void of Understanding, as to own it. If therefore you can allow a thinking Thing, to be made out of nothing, (as all Things that are not eternal must be,) why also can you not allow it possible, for a material Being to be made out of nothing, by an equal Power, but that you have the experience of the one in view, and not of the other? Though, when well considered, Creation of a Spirit will be found to require no less Power, than the Creation of Matter. Nay possibly, if we would emancipate our selves from vulgar Notions, and raise our Thoughts, as far as they would reach, to a closer contemplation of things, we might be able to aim at some dim and seeming conception how Matter might at first be made, and begin to exist by the power of that

§§ 18, 19. *Matter not co-eternal with an eternal Mind.*

---

(11) ; why] **2–5** | , why **1** (14) then] *add.* **2–5** (30)–629(9) a Spirit . . . that] **2–5** | one, as well as t'other, requires an equal Power: And we have no more reason to boggle at the effect of that Power in one, than in the other; because the manner of it in both, is equally beyond our comprehension. For **1** (33) , to] **4–5** | to **2–3**

eternal first being: But to give beginning and being to a Spirit, would be found a more inconceivable effect of omnipotent Power. But this being what would perhaps lead us too far from the Notions, on which the Philosophy now in the World is built, it would not be pardonable to deviate so far from them; or to enquire, so far as Grammar it self would authorize, if the common setled Opinion opposes it: Especially in this place, where the received Doctrine serves well enough to our present purpose, and leaves this past doubt, that the Creation or Beginning of any one SUBSTANCE out of nothing, being once admitted, the Creation of all other, but the CREATOR himself, may, with the same ease, be supposed.

§ 19. But you will say, Is it not impossible to admit of the *making any thing out of nothing*, since we cannot possibly conceive it? I answer, No: 1. Because it is not reasonable to deny the power of an infinite Being, because we cannot comprehend its Operations. We do not deny other effects upon this ground, because we cannot possibly conceive the manner of their Production. We cannot conceive how any thing but impulse of Body can move Body; and yet that is not a Reason sufficient to make us deny it possible, against the constant Experience, we have of it in our selves, in all our voluntary Motions, which are produced in us only by the free Action or Thought of our own Minds; and are not, nor can be the effects of the impulse or determination of the Motion of blind Matter, in or upon our Bodies; for then it could not be in our power or choice to alter it. For example: My right Hand writes, whilst my left Hand is still: What causes rest in one, and motion in the other? Nothing but my Will, a Thought of my Mind; my Thought only changing, the right Hand rests, and the left Hand moves. This is matter of fact, which cannot be denied: Explain this, and make it intelligible, and then the next step will be to understand Creation. For the giving a new determination to the motion of the animal Spirits (which some make use of to explain voluntary motion) clears not the difficulty one jot. To alter the determination of motion, being in this case no easier nor less, than to give motion it self: Since the new determination given to the animal Spirits must be either immediately by thought, or by some other body put in their way by thought, which was not in their way before, and

(9) *v.* 628(30), n. or] **2–5** | , or **1** SUBSTANCE] **2–5** | thing **1** (10) all other] **2–5** | every thing else **1** (17) the manner of] *add.* **2–5** (18) any . . . [*1st*] Body] **4–5** | Thought (or any thing but motion in Body) **1–3** (22) Action or Thought] **4–5** | Thoughts **1–3** can] **2–5** | cannot **1** (31)–630(2) For . . . before.] *add.* **2–5**

so must owe its motion to thought; either of which leaves voluntary motion as unintelligible as it was before. In the mean time, 'tis an overvaluing our selves, to reduce all to the narrow measure of our Capacities; and to conclude, all things impossible to be done, whose manner of doing exceeds our Comprehension. This is to make our Comprehension infinite, or GOD finite, when what he can do, is limitted to what we can conceive of it. If you do not understand the Operations of your own finite Mind, that thinking Thing within you, do not deem it strange, that you cannot comprehend the Operations of that eternal infinite Mind, who made and governs all Things, and whom the Heaven of Heavens cannot contain.

CHAPTER XI

Of our Knowledge of the Existence of other Things.

§ 1. THE Knowledge of our own Being, we have by intuition. The Existence of a GOD, Reason clearly makes known to us, as has been shewn.

The *Knowledge of the Existence* of any other thing we can have only by *Sensation*: For there being no necessary connexion of *real Existence*, with any *Idea* a Man hath in his Memory, nor of any other Existence but that of GOD, with the Existence of any particular Man; no particular Man can know the *Existence* of any other Being, but only when by actual operating upon him, it makes it self perceived by him. For the having the *Idea* of any thing in our Mind, no more proves the Existence of that Thing, than the picture of a Man evidences his being in the World, or the Visions of a Dream make thereby a true History.

§ 2. 'Tis therefore the actual receiving of *Ideas* from without, that gives us notice of the *Existence* of other Things, and makes us know, that something doth exist at that time without us, which causes that *Idea* in us, though perhaps we neither know nor consider how it does it: For it takes not from the certainty of our Senses, and the *Ideas* we receive by them, that we know not the manner wherein

§ 1. *Is to be had only by Sensation.* § 2. *Instance whiteness of this Paper.*

(1) owe] **2, 4–5** | own **3** (2) *v.* 629(31), n. In the mean time] **1–5; Coste** '2. D'ailleurs' (26) makes] **1–4, W** | make **5**

they are produced: *v.g.* whilst I write this, I have, by the Paper affecting my Eyes, that *Idea* produced in my Mind, which whatever Object causes, I call *White*; by which I know, that that Quality or Accident (*i.e.* whose appearance before my Eyes, always causes that *Idea*) doth really exist, and hath a Being without me. And of this, the greatest assurance I can possibly have, and to which my Faculties can attain, is the Testimony of my Eyes, which are the proper and sole Judges of this thing, whose Testimony I have reason to rely on, as so certain, that I can no more doubt, whilst I write this, that I see White and Black, and that something really exists, that causes that Sensation in me, than that I write or move my Hand; which is a Certainty as great, as humane Nature is capable of, concerning the Existence of any thing, but a Man's self alone, and of GOD.

§ 3. *The notice we have by our Senses, of the existing of Things without* us, though it be not altogether so certain, as our intuitive Knowledge, or the Deductions of our Reason, employ'd about the clear abstract *Ideas* of our own Minds; yet it is an assurance that *deserves the name of Knowledge.* If we persuade our selves, that our Faculties act and inform us right, concerning the existence of those Objects that affect them, it cannot pass for an ill-grounded confidence: For I think no body can, in earnest, be so sceptical, as to be uncertain of the Existence of those Things which he sees and feels. At least, he that can doubt so far, (whatever he may have with his own Thoughts) will never have any Controversie with me; since he can never be sure I say any thing contrary to his Opinion. As to my self, I think GOD has given me assurance enough of the Existence of Things without me: since by their different application, I can produce in my self both Pleasure and Pain, which is one great Concernment of my present state. This is certain, the confidence that our Faculties do not herein deceive us, is the greatest assurance we are capable of, concerning the Existence of material Beings. For we cannot act any thing, but by our Faculties; nor talk of Knowledge it self, but by the help of those Faculties, which are fitted to apprehend even what Knowledge is. But besides the assurance we have from our

§ 3. *This though not so certain as demonstration, yet may be called Knowledge, and proves the existence of things without us.*

---

(8) whose] **2–5** | and whose **1** (18) . If] **2–5** | , if **1** (22) which] *add.* **4–5** (24) Controversie] **1T.er, 2–5** | Controversies **1** (26) GOD] **1–3, 5** | God **4** (34)–632(1) we . . . themselves] **2–5** | our Senses themselves give us **1** (*l. below* 34) *demonstration*] **2, 4–5** | *demonstrations* **3** (*likewise* **Coste**)

Senses themselves, that they do not err in the Information they give us, of the Existence of Things without us, when they are affected by them, we are farther confirmed in this assurance, by other concurrent Reasons.

§ 4. *First*, 'Tis plain, those Perceptions are produced in us by exteriour Causes affecting our Senses: Because *those that want the Organs of any Sense, never can have the* Ideas *belonging to that Sense* produced in their Minds. This is too evident to be doubted: and therefore we cannot but be assured, that they come in by the Organs of that Sense, and no other way. The Organs themselves, 'tis plain, do not produce them: for then the Eyes of a Man in the dark, would produce Colours, and his Nose smell Roses in the Winter: but we see no body gets the relish of a Pine-apple, till he goes to the *Indies*, where it is, and tastes it.

§ 5. *Secondly*, Because *sometimes I find, that I cannot avoid the having those* Ideas *produced in my Mind.* For though when my Eyes are shut, or Windows fast, I can at Pleasure re-call to my Mind the *Ideas* of *Light*, or the *Sun*, which former Sensations had lodg'd in my Memory; so I can at pleasure lay by that *Idea*, and take into my view that of the *smell* of a Rose, or *taste* of Sugar. But if I turn my Eyes at noon towards the Sun, I cannot avoid the *Ideas*, which the Light, or Sun, then produces in me. So that there is a manifest difference, between the *Ideas* laid up in my Memory; (over which, if they were there only, I should have constantly the same power to dispose of them, and lay them by at pleasure) and those which force themselves upon me, and I cannot avoid having. And therefore it must needs be some exteriour cause, and the brisk acting of some Objects without me, whose efficacy I cannot resist, that produces those *Ideas* in my Mind, whether I will, or no. Besides, there is no body who doth not perceive the difference in himself, between contemplating the Sun, as he hath the *Idea* of it in his Memory, and actually looking upon it: Of which two, his perception is so distinct, that few of his *Ideas* are more distinguishable one from another. And therefore he hath certain knowledge, that they are not both Memory, or the Actions of his Mind, and Fancies only within him; but that actual seeing hath a Cause without.

§ 4. *First, Because we cannot have them but by the inlet of the Senses.* § 5. *Because an* Idea *from actual Sensation, and another from Memory, are very distinct Perceptions.*

(1) *v.* 631(34), n. (18) Sensations] **2–5** | Experience **1**

§ 6. *Thirdly*, Add to this, that *many of those* Ideas *are produced in us with pain, which afterwards we remember without the least offence.* Thus the pain of Heat or Cold, when the *Idea* of it is revived in our Minds, gives us no disturbance; which, when felt, was very troublesome, and is again, when actually repeated: which is occasioned by the disorder the external Object causes in our Bodies, when applied to it: And we remember the pain of *Hunger*, *Thirst*, or the *Head-ach*, without any pain at all; which would either never disturb us, or else constantly do it, as often as we thought of it, were there nothing more but *Ideas* floating in our Minds, and appearances entertaining our Fancies, without the real Existence of Things affecting us from abroad. The same may be said of Pleasure, accompanying several actual Sensations: And though mathematical demonstrations depend not upon sense, yet the examining them by Diagrams, gives great credit to the Evidence of our Sight, and seems to give it a Certainty approaching to that of the Demonstration it self. For it would be very strange, that a Man should allow it for an undeniable Truth, that two Angles of a Figure, which he measures by Lines and Angles of a Diagram, should be bigger one than the other; and yet doubt of the Existence of those Lines and Angles, which by looking on, he makes use of to measure that by.

§ 7. *Fourthly*, Our *Senses*, in many cases bear *witness* to the Truth of each other's report, concerning the Existence of sensible Things without us. He that sees a *Fire*, may, if he doubt whether it be any thing more than a bare Fancy, feel it too; and be convinced, by putting his Hand in it. Which certainly could never be put into such exquisite pain, by a bare *Idea* or Phantom, unless that the pain be a fancy too: Which yet he cannot, when the Burn is well, by raising the *Idea* of it, bring upon himself again.

Thus I see, whilst I write this, I can change the Appearance of the Paper; and by designing the Letters, tell before-hand what new *Idea* it shall exhibit the very next moment, barely by drawing my Pen over it: which will neither appear (let me fancy as much as I will) if my Hand stands still; or though I move my Pen, if my Eyes

§ 6. *Thirdly, Pleasure or Pain, which accompanies actual Sensation, accompanies not the returning of those* Ideas *without the external Objects.* § 7. *Fourthly, Our Senses assist one anothers Testimony of the Existence of outward Things.*

(12–13) The . . . Sensations:] *add.* **4–5** (14) demonstrations depend] **1–3** (*likewise* **Coste**) | Demonstration depends **4–5** (32) drawing my] **2–5** | my drawing the **1** (34) stands] **4–5** | stand **1–3**

be shut: Nor when those Characters are once made on the Paper, can I chuse afterwards but see them as they are; that is, have the *Ideas* of such Letters as I have made. Whence it is manifest, that they are not barely the Sport and Play of my own Imagination, when I find, that the Characters, that were made at the pleasure of my own Thoughts, do not obey them; nor yet cease to be, whenever I shall fancy it, but continue to affect my Senses constantly and regularly, according to the Figures I made them. To which if we will add, that the sight of those shall, from another Man, draw such Sounds, as I before-hand design they shall stand for, there will be little reason left to doubt, that those Words, I write, do really exist without me, when they cause a long series of regular Sounds to affect my Ears, which could not be the effect of my Imagination, nor could my Memory retain them in that order.

§ 8. But yet, if after all this, any one will be so sceptical, as to distrust his Senses, and to affirm, that all we see and hear, feel and taste, think and do, during our whole Being, is but the series and deluding appearances of a long Dream, whereof there is no reality; and therefore will question the Existence of all Things, or our Knowledge of any thing: I must desire him to consider, that if all be a Dream, then he doth but dream, that he makes the Question; and so it is not much matter, that a waking Man should answer him. But yet, if he pleases, he may dream that I make him this answer, That *the certainty of* Things existing *in rerum Naturâ*, when we have *the testimony of our Senses* for it, is not only *as great* as our frame can attain to, but *as our Condition needs*. For our Faculties being suited not to the full extent of Being, nor to a perfect, clear, comprehensive Knowledge of things free from all doubt and scruple; but to the preservation of us, in whom they are; and accommodated to the use of Life: they serve to our purpose well enough, if they will but give us certain notice of those Things, which are convenient or inconvenient to us. For he that sees a Candle burning, and hath experimented the force of its Flame, by putting his Finger in it, will little doubt, that this is something existing without him, which does him harm, and puts him to great pain: which is assurance enough, when no Man requires greater certainty to govern his

§ 8. *This Certainty is as great as our Condition needs.*

(22) waking] *add.* **1er–5** him] *add.* **1er–5** (23) pleases] **4–5** | please **1–3** him] *add.* **5** (*likewise* **Coste**) (28) free] **4–5** | , free **1–3** (35) pain:] **4–5** | pain; **1–3**

Actions by, than what is as certain as his Actions themselves. And if our Dreamer pleases to try, whether the glowing heat of a glass Furnace, be barely a wandring Imagination in a drowsy Man's Fancy, by putting his Hand into it, he may perhaps be wakened into a certainty greater than he could wish, that it is something more than bare Imagination. So that this Evidence is as great, as we can desire, being as certain to us, as our Pleasure or Pain; *i.e.* Happiness or Misery; beyond which we have no concernment, either of Knowing or Being. Such an assurance of the Existence of Things without us, is sufficient to direct us in the attaining the Good and avoiding the Evil, which is caused by them, which is the important concernment we have of being made acquainted with them.

§ 9. In fine then, when our Senses do actually convey into our Understandings any *Idea*, we cannot but be satisfied, that there doth something at that time really exist without us, which doth affect our Senses, and by them give notice of it self to our apprehensive Faculties, and actually produce that *Idea*, which we then perceive: and we cannot so far distrust their Testimony, as to doubt, that such Collections of simple *Ideas*, as we have observed by our Senses to be united together, do really exist together. But *this Knowledge extends as far as the present Testimony of our Senses*, employ'd about particular Objects, that do then affect them, *and no farther*. For if I saw such a Collection of simple *Ideas*, as is wont to be called *Man*, existing together one minute since, and am now alone, I cannot be certain, that the same Man exists now, since there is no necessary connexion of his Existence a minute since, with his Existence now: by a thousand ways he may cease to be, since I had the Testimony of my Senses for his Existence. And if I cannot be certain, that the Man I saw last to day, is now in Being, I can less be certain, that he is so, who hath been longer removed from my Senses, and I have not seen since yesterday, or since the last year: and much less can I be certain of the Existence of Men, that I never saw. And therefore though it be highly probable, that Millions of Men do now exist, yet whilst I am alone writing this, I have not that Certainty of it, which we strictly call Knowledge; though the

§ 9. *But reaches no farther than actual Sensation.*

---

(10) Good] **4** | Good, **1–3, 5** (11) Evil,] **2–5** | Evil **1** (14) cannot but be satisfied,] **4–5** | are well assured **1–3** (16) it] **4–5** | its **1–3** (25) certain,] **4–5** | sure **1–3**. (**Coste** 'assûré') (29) certain] **4–5** | sure **1–3**. (**Coste** 'certain') (29–30) less be certain,] **4–5** | be less sure **1–3** (34) this] **2–5** | of this **1** (34–5) not . . . Knowledge] **5** | I have no unquestionable Knowledge of it **1–4**

great likelihood of it puts me past doubt, and it be reasonable for me to do several things upon the confidence, that there are Men (and Men also of my acquaintance, with whom I have to do) now in the World: But this is but probability, not Knowledge.

§ 10. Whereby yet we may observe, how foolish and vain a thing it is, for a Man of narrow Knowledge, who having Reason given him to judge of the different evidence and probability of Things, and to be sway'd accordingly; how *vain*, I say, it is *to expect Demonstration* and Certainty *in things not capable of it*; and refuse Assent to very rational Propositions, and act contrary to very plain and clear Truths, because they cannot be made out so evident, as to surmount every the least (I will not say Reason, but) pretence of doubting. He that in the ordinary Affairs of Life, would admit of nothing but direct plain Demonstration, would be sure of nothing, in this World, but of perishing quickly. The wholesomness of his Meat or Drink would not give him reason to venture on it: And I would fain know, what 'tis he could do upon such grounds, as were capable of no Doubt, no Objection.

§ 11. As when our Senses are actually employ'd about any Object, we do know that it does exist; so *by our Memory* we may be assured, that heretofore Things, that affected our Senses, have existed. And thus *we have knowledge of the past Existence* of several Things, whereof our Senses having informed us, our Memories still retain the *Ideas*; and of this we are past all doubt, so long as we remember well. But this Knowledge also reaches no farther than our Senses have formerly assured us. Thus seeing Water at this instant, 'tis an unquestionable Truth to me, that Water doth exist: and remembring that I saw it yesterday, it will also be always true; and as long as my Memory retains it, always an undoubted Proposition to me, that Water did exist 10th. *July*, 1688. as it will also be equally true, that a certain number of very fine Colours did exist, which, at the same time, I saw upon a Bubble of that Water: But being now quite out of the sight both of the Water and Bubbles too, it is no more certainly known to me, that the Water doth now exist,

§ 10. *Folly to expect demonstration in every thing.* § 11. *Past Existence is known by Memory.*

---

(6) for a Man] **1–5** | for man **1er** of] **1–4** | of a **5** (13) the] *add.* **4–5** (15) [*1st*] of] *add.* **2–5** (16) would not] **4–5** | , would be scarce capable of certainty enough to **1–3** (18) Objection] **2er–5** | Objections **1–2** (27) Water] **1–3** | Water, **4–5** (30) [*date*]] **Coste** *adds a marginal note* 'C'est en ce temps-là que Mr. *Locke* ecrivoit ceci.' (34) now] *add.* **2–5**

than that the Bubbles or Colours therein do so; it being no more necessary that Water should exist to day, because it existed yesterday, than that the Colours or Bubbles exist to day, because they existed yesterday, though it be exceedingly much more probable, because Water hath been observed to continue long in Existence, but Bubbles, and the Colours on them quickly cease to be.

§ 12. What *Ideas* we have of Spirits, and how we come by them, I have already shewn. But though we have those *Ideas* in our Minds, and know we have them there, the having the *Ideas* of Spirits does not make us *know*, that any such Things do exist without us, or *that there are any finite Spirits*, or any other spiritual Beings, but the Eternal GOD. We have ground from revelation, and several other Reasons, to believe with assurance, that there are such Creatures: but our Senses not being able to discover them, we want the means of knowing their particular Existences. For we can no more know, that there are finite Spirits really existing, by the *Idea* we have of such Beings in our Minds, than by the *Ideas* any one has of Fairies, or Centaurs, he can come to know, that Things answering those *Ideas*, do really exist.

And therefore concerning the Existence of finite Spirits, as well as several other Things, we must content our selves with the Evidence of Faith; but universal certain Propositions concerning this matter are beyond our reach. For however true it may be, *v.g.* that all the intelligent Spirits that GOD ever created, do still exist; yet it can never make a part of our certain Knowledge. These and the like Propositions, we may assent to, as highly probable, but are not, I fear, in this state, capable of knowing. We are not then to put others upon demonstrating, nor our selves upon search of universal Certainty in all those matters, wherein we are not capable of any other Knowledge, but what our Senses give us in this or that particular.

§ 13. By which it appears, that there are two sorts of *Propositions.* 1°. There is one sort of Propositions *concerning* the *Existence* of any thing answerable to such an *Idea*: as having the *Idea* of an *Elephant*, *Phœnix*, *Motion*, or an *Angel*, in my Mind, the first and natural enquiry is, Whether such a thing does any where exist? And this

§ 12. *The Existence of Spirits not knowable.* § 13. *Particular Propositions concerning Existence are knowable.*

(1) do so] *add.* **2–5** (2) it] **1–2, 4–5** | they **3** (32–3) . 1°. . . . Propositions] **4–5** | ; one **1–3**

Knowledge is only of *Particulars.* No existence of any thing without us, but only of GOD, can certainly be known farther than our Senses inform us. 2°. There is another sort of *Propositions*, wherein is expressed the Agreement, or Disagreement of our abstract *Ideas*, and their dependence one on another. Such Propositions may be *universal* and certain. So having the *Idea* of GOD and my self, of Fear and Obedience, I cannot but be sure that GOD is to be feared and obeyed by me: And this Proposition will be certain, concerning *Man* in general, if I have made an abstract *Idea* of such a Species, whereof I am one particular. But yet this Proposition, how certain soever, That Men ought to fear and obey GOD, proves not to me the Existence of Men in the World, but will be true of all such Creatures, whenever they do exist: Which *certainty* of such general Propositions, depends on the Agreement or Disagreement is to be discovered in those abstract *Ideas.*

§ 14. In the former case, our Knowledge is the consequence of the Existence of Things producing *Ideas* in our Minds by our Senses: in the latter, Knowledge is the consequence of the *Ideas* (be they what they will) that are in our Minds producing there general certain Propositions. Many of these are called *æternæ veritates*, and all of them indeed are so; not from being written all or any of them in the Minds of all Men, or that they were any of them Propositions in any ones Mind, till he, having got the abstract *Ideas*, joyn'd or separated them by affirmation or negation. But wheresoever we can suppose such a creature as *Man* is, endowed with such faculties, and thereby furnished with such *Ideas*, as we have, we must conclude, he must needs, when he applies his thoughts to the consideration of his *Ideas*, know the truth of certain Propositions, that will arise from the Agreement or Disagreement, which he will perceive in his own *Ideas.* Such Propositions are therefore called *Eternal Truths*, not because they are Eternal Propositions actually formed, and antecedent to the Understanding, that at any time makes them; nor because they are imprinted on the Mind from any patterns, that

§ 14. *And general Propositions concerning abstract* Ideas.

(3) 2°.] *add.* **4–5** (5) . Such] **4–5** | ; and such **1–3** (11) GOD,] **2–5** | , GOD **1** (17) : in] **4–5** | ; in **1–3** (18–19) (be . . . will)] *add.* **2–5** (19) Minds producing there] **2–5** | Minds whatsoever they are, and produce **1** (20) . Many of these] **4–5** | , many whereof **1–3** (20–1) , and . . . are] **2–5** | ; and are indeed **1** (21) all . . . them] *add.* **2–5** (22–4) [*1st*] any . . . negation.] **2–5** (negation: **2–3**) | before the World: **1** (25) is,] **2–5** is **1** (29) which] *add.* **4–5** (29–30) in . . . *Ideas*] **2–5** | amongst them **1** (30)–639(5) Such . . . true.] *add.* **2–5** (30) Such] **4–5** | Which **2–3**.

are any where of them out of the Mind, and existed before: But because being once made, about abstract *Ideas*, so as to be true, they will, whenever they can be supposed to be made again at any time past or to come, by a Mind having those *Ideas*, always actually be true. For Names being supposed to stand perpetually for the same *Ideas*; and the same *Ideas* having immutably the same Habitudes one to another, Propositions, concerning any abstract *Ideas*, that are once true, must needs be *eternal Verities*.

CHAPTER XII

Of the Improvement of our Knowledge.

§ 1. It having been the common received Opinion amongst Men of Letters, that *Maxims* were the foundations of all Knowledge; and that the Sciences were each of them built upon certain *præcognita*, from whence the Understanding was to take its rise, and by which it was to conduct it self, in its enquiries into the matters belonging to that Science; the beaten Road of the Schools has been, to lay down in the beginning one or more general Propositions, as Foundations whereon to build the Knowledge that was to be had of that Subject. These Doctrines thus laid down for Foundations of any Science, were called *Principles*, as the beginnings from which we must set out, and look no farther backwards in our Enquiries, as we have already observed.

§ 2. One Thing, which might probably give an occasion to this way of proceeding in other Sciences, was (as I suppose) the good success it seemed to have in *Mathematicks*, wherein Men, being observed to attain a great certainty of Knowledge, these Sciences came by pre-eminence to be called Μαθήματα, and Μάθησις, Learning, or things learn'd, throughly learn'd, as having of all others the greatest certainty, clearness, and evidence in them.

§ 1. *Knowledge is not from Maxims.* § 2. (*The occasion of that Opinion.*)

(4) always] **4–5** | alway **2–3** (5) *v.* 638(30), n. (7) *Ideas*,] **2–5** | *Ideas* **1** (13) was] **1–4, W** | is was **5** (16) [*1st*] that] *add.* **4–5** (19–20) as . . . observed] **4–5** | but take these for certain and unquestionable Truths, and established Principles **1–3** (21) One . . . an] **4–5** | That which gave **1–3** (27) others] **4–5** | other **1–3**

§ 3. But if any one will consider, he will (I guess) find, that *the great advancement* and certainty of *real Knowledge*, which Men arrived to in these Sciences, was not owing to the influence of these Principles, nor derived from any peculiar advantage they received from two or three general Maxims laid down in the beginning; but *from* the *clear*, *distinct*, *complete Ideas* their Thoughts were employ'd about, and the relation of Equality and Excess so clear between some of them, that they had an intuitive Knowledge, and by that, a way to discover it in others, and this without the help of those *Maxims*. For I ask, Is it not possible for a young Lad to know, that his whole Body is bigger than his little Finger, but by virtue of this Axiom, that *the whole is bigger than a part*; nor be assured of it, till he has learned that *Maxim*? Or cannot a Country-Wench know, that having received a Shilling from one that owes her three, and a Shilling also from another that owes her three, that the remaining Debts in each of their Hands are equal? cannot she know this, I say, without she fetch the certainty of it from this Maxim, That *if you take Equals from Equals, the remainder will be Equals*, a Maxim which possibly she never heard or thought of? I desire any one to consider, from what has been elsewhere said, which is known first and clearest by most People, the particular instance, or the general Rule; and which it is that gives Life and Birth to the other. These general Rules are but the comparing our more general and abstract *Ideas*, which are the Workmanship of the Mind, made, and Names given to them, for the easier dispatch in its Reasonings, and drawing into comprehensive Terms, and short Rules, its various and multiplied Observations. But Knowledge began in the Mind, and was founded on particulars; though afterwards, perhaps, no notice be taken thereof: it being natural for the Mind (forward still to enlarge its Knowledge) most attentively to lay up those general Notions, and make the proper use of them, which is to disburden the Memory of the cumbersome load of Particulars. For I desire it may be considered what more certainty there is to a Child, or any one, that his Body, Little-Finger and all, is bigger than his Little-Finger alone, after you have given to his Body the Name *whole*, and to his Little-Finger the Name

§ 3. *But from the comparing clear and distinct* Ideas.

---

(2) , which] *add.* **4–5** (3) [*2nd*] these] **2–5** | their **1** (19–20) , from . . . said,] *add.* **2–5** (31) disburden] **4–5** | disburthen **1–3** (32)–641(19) For . . . please.] *add.* **4–5**

part, than he could have had before; or what new Knowledge concerning his Body, can these two relative Terms give him, which he could not have without them? Could he not know that his Body was bigger than his Little-Finger, if his Language were yet so imperfect, that he had no such relative Terms as *whole* and *part*? I ask farther when he has got these Names, how is he more certain that his Body is a *whole*, and his Little-Finger a *part*, than he was or might be certain before, he learnt those Terms, that his Body was bigger than his Little-Finger? Any one may as reasonably doubt or deny that his Little-Finger is a part of his Body, as that it is less than his Body. And he that can doubt whether it be less, will as certainly doubt whether it be a Part. So that the Maxim, *The whole is bigger than a part*, can never be made use of to prove the Little-Finger less than the Body, but when it is useless, by being brought to convince one of a truth which he knows already. For he that does not certainly know that any parcel of matter, with another parcel of matter joyn'd to it, is bigger than either of them alone, will never be able to know it by the help of these two relative Terms *whole* and *part*, make of them what Maxim you please.

§ 4. But be it in the Mathematicks as it will, whether it be clearer, that taking an Inch from a black Line of two Inches, and an Inch from a red Line of two Inches, the remaining parts of the two Lines will be equal, or that *if you take equals from equals, the remainder will be equals*: Which, I say, of these two, is the clearer and first known, I leave to any one to determine, it not being material to my present occasion. That which I have here to do, is to enquire, whether if it be the readiest way to Knowledge, to begin with general Maxims, and build upon them, it be yet a safe way to take the *Principles*, which are laid down in any other Science, as unquestionable Truths; and so receive them without examination, and adhere to them, without suffering them to be doubted of, because Mathematicians have been so happy, or so fair, to use none but self-evident and undeniable. If this be so, I know not what may not pass for Truth in Morality, what may not be introduced and proved in Natural Philosophy.

Let that Principle of some of the old Philosophers, That all is Matter, and that there is nothing else, be received for certain and indubitable,

§ 4. *Dangerous to build upon precarious Principles.*

(19) *v.* 640(32), n. (31) them] **1–4**; *om.* **5** (34) proved] **1er–5** | improved **1**
(36) old] **1–4**; *om.* **5**

and it will be easy to be seen by the Writings of some that have revived it again in our days, what consequences it will lead us into. Let any one, with *Polemo*, take the World; or, with the *Stoicks*, the *Æther*, or the Sun; or, with *Anaximenes*, the Air, to be *God*; and what a Divinity, Religion, and Worship must we needs have! *Nothing* can be *so dangerous, as Principles* thus *taken up without questioning or examination*; especially if they be such as concern Morality, which influence Men's Lives, and give a biass to all their Actions. Who might not justly expect another kind of Life in *Aristippus*, who placed Happiness in bodily Pleasure; and in *Antisthenes*, who made Virtue sufficient to Felicity? And he who, with *Plato*, shall place Beatitude in the Knowledge of GOD, will have his Thoughts raised to other Contemplations, than those who look not beyond this spot of Earth, and those perishing Things which are to be had in it. He that, with *Archelaus*, shall lay it down as a Principle, That Right and Wrong, Honest and Dishonest, are defined only by Laws, and not by Nature, will have other measures of moral Rectitude and Pravity, than those who take it for granted, that we are under Obligations antecedent to all humane Constitutions.

§ 5. If therefore those that pass for *Principles*, are *not certain*, (which we must have some way to know, that we may be able to distinguish them from those that are doubtful,) but are only made so to us by our blind assent, we are liable to be misled by them; and instead of being guided into Truth, we shall, by Principles, be only confirmed in Mistake and Errour.

§ 6. But since the Knowledge of the Certainty of Principles, as well as of all other Truths, depends only upon the perception, we have, of the Agreement, or Disagreement of our *Ideas*, *the way to improve our Knowledge*, is not, I am sure, blindly, and with an implicit Faith, to receive and swallow Principles; but is, I think, *to* get and *fix in our Minds clear*, *distinct*, *and complete* Ideas, as far as they are to be had, *and annex to them proper and constant Names*. And thus, perhaps, without any other Principles, but barely considering those *Ideas*, and by *comparing them one with another*, finding their Agreement, and Disagreement, and their several Relations and Habitudes; we shall get more true and clear Knowledge, by the conduct of this one

§ 5. *This is no certain way to Truth.* § 6. *But to compare clear complete* Ideas *under steady Names.*

(2) days] **1–2, 4–5** | day **3** (14) which] *add.* **4–5** (30) Faith,] **2–5** | Faith **1** (33) *Ideas*] **5** (*likewise* **Coste**) | perfect *Ideas* **1–4**

Rule, than by taking up Principles, and thereby putting our Minds into the disposal of others.

§ 7. *We must* therefore, if we will proceed, as Reason advises, *adapt our methods of Enquiry to the nature of the* Ideas *we examine*, and the Truth we search after. General and certain Truths, are only founded in the Habitudes and Relations of abstract *Ideas*. A sagacious and methodical application of our Thoughts, for the finding out these Relations, is the only way to discover all, that can be put, with Truth and Certainty concerning them, into general Propositions. By what steps we are to proceed in these, is to be learned in the Schools of the Mathematicians, who from very plain and easy beginnings, by gentle degrees, and a continued Chain of Reasonings, proceed to the discovery and demonstration of Truths, that appear at first sight beyond humane Capacity. The Art of finding Proofs, and the admirable Methods they have invented for the singling out, and laying in order those intermediate *Ideas*, that demonstratively shew the equality or inequality of unapplicable quantities, is that which has carried them so far, and produced such wonderful and unexpected discoveries: but whether something like this, in respect of other *Ideas*, as well as those of magnitude, may not in time be found out, I will not determine. This, I think, I may say, that if other *Ideas*, that are the real, as well as nominal Essences of their Species, were pursued in the way familiar to Mathematicians, they would carry our Thoughts farther, and with greater evidence and clearness, than possibly we are apt to imagine.

§ 8. This gave me the confidence to advance that Conjecture, which I suggest, *Chap.* 3. viz. That *Morality is capable of Demonstration*, as well as Mathematicks. For the *Ideas* that Ethicks are conversant about, being all real Essences, and such as, I imagine, have a discoverable connexion and agreement one with another; so far as we can find their Habitudes and Relations, so far we shall be possessed of certain, real, and general Truths: and I doubt not, but if a right method were taken, a great part of Morality might be made out with that clearness, that could leave, to a considering Man, no more reason to doubt, than he could have to doubt of the Truth

§ 7. *The true method of advancing Knowledge, is by considering our abstract* Ideas. § 8. *By which Morality also may be made clearer.*

(9) Certainty] **1–3** | certainty **4–5** (10) in these] *add.* **2–5** (14) humane] **1–3** | human **4–5** (15–16) admirable . . . *Ideas*,] **2–5** | *Ideas* **1** (17) shew] **1–2, 4–5** | know **3** (17–19) that . . . discoveries] **2–5** | , I confess, of great help to them **1** (27) *Chap.* 3.] **Coste** *adds in a marginal note* '§. 18. *etc.*'

of Propositions in Mathematicks, which have been demonstrated to him.

§ 9. In our search after the Knowledge of *Substances*, our want of *Ideas*, that are suitable to such a way of proceeding, obliges us to a quite different method. We advance not here, as in the other (where our abstract *Ideas* are real as well as nominal Essences) by contemplating our *Ideas*, and considering their Relations and Correspondencies; that helps us very little, for the Reasons, that in another place we have at large set down. By which, I think, it is evident, that Substances afford Matter of very little general Knowledge; and the bare Contemplation of their abstract *Ideas*, will carry us but a very little way in the search of Truth and Certainty. What then are we to do for the improvement of our *Knowledge in substantial Beings*? Here we are to take a quite contrary Course, the want of *Ideas* of their real *Essences* sends us from our own Thoughts, to the Things themselves, as they exist. *Experience here must teach me*, what Reason cannot: and 'tis by trying alone, that I can certainly know, what other Qualities co-exist with those of my complex *Idea*, *v.g.* whether that *yellow*, *heavy*, *fusible* Body, I call *Gold*, be *malleable*, or no; which Experience (which way ever it prove, in that particular Body, I examine) makes me not certain, that it is so, in all, or any other *yellow*, *heavy*, *fusible* Bodies, but that which I have tried. Because it is no Consequence one way or t'other from my complex *Idea*; the Necessity or Inconsistence of *Malleability*, hath no visible connexion with the Combination of that *Colour*, *Weight*, and *Fusibility* in any body. What I have said here of the nominal Essence of *Gold*, supposed to consist of a Body of such a determinate *Colour*, *Weight*, and *Fusibility*, will hold true, if *Malleableness*, *Fixedness*, and *Solubility* in *Aqua Regia* be added to it. Our Reasonings from these *Ideas* will carry us but a little way in the certain discovery of the other Properties in those Masses of Matter, wherein all these are to be found. Because the other Properties of such Bodies, depending not on these, but on that unknown real Essence, on which these also depend, we cannot by them discover the rest; we can go no farther than the simple *Ideas* of our nominal Essence will carry us, which is

§ 9. *But Knowledge of Bodies is to be improved only by Experience.*

---

(8) ; that] **4–5** | , that **1–3** (9) set down] **2–5** | shewed **1** (15) Thoughts,] **2–5** | Thoughts, from contemplating, and drawing Consequences from our own *Ideas*, **1** (16) *here*] *add.* **2–5** (17) 'tis . . . alone,] **2–5** | and by trying, 'tis alone **1** (22) Bodies] **2–5** | Body **1** (24) Inconsistence] **1–3, 5** | inconsistence **4**

very little beyond themselves; and so afford us but very sparingly any certain, universal, and useful Truths. For upon Trial, having found that particular piece (and all others of that Colour, Weight, and Fusibility, that I ever tried) *malleable*, that also makes now perhaps, a part of my complex *Idea*, part of my nominal Essence of *Gold*: Whereby though I make my complex *Idea*, to which I affix the Name *Gold*, to consist of more simple *Ideas* than before: yet still, it not containing the real Essence of any Species of Bodies, it helps me not certainly to know (I say to know, perhaps, it may to conjecture) the other remaining Properties of that Body, farther than they have a visible connexion, with some or all of the simple *Ideas*, that make up my nominal Essence. For Example, I cannot be certain from this complex *Idea*, whether *Gold* be fixed, or no: Because, as before, there is no necessary connexion, or inconsistence to be discovered betwixt a complex *Idea* of a Body, *yellow*, *heavy*, *fusible*, *malleable*, betwixt these, I say, and *Fixedness*, so that I may certainly know, that in whatsoever Body these are found, there *Fixedness* is sure to be. Here again for assurance, I must apply my self to *Experience*; as far as that reaches, I may have certain Knowledge, but no farther.

§ 10. I deny not, but a Man accustomed to rational and regular Experiments shall be able to see farther into the Nature of Bodies, and guess righter at their yet unknown Properties, than one, that is a Stranger to them: But yet, as I have said, this is but Judgment and Opinion, not Knowledge and Certainty. This *way* of getting, and *improving our Knowledge in Substances only by Experience* and History, which is all that the weakness of our Faculties in this State of *Mediocrity*, which we are in in this World, can attain to, makes me suspect, that natural Philosophy is not capable of being made a Science. We are able, I imagine, to reach very little general Knowledge concerning the Species of Bodies, and their several Properties. Experiments and Historical Observations we may have, from which we may draw Advantages of Ease and Health, and thereby increase our stock of Conveniences for this Life: but beyond this, I fear our Talents reach not, nor are our Faculties, as I guess, able to advance.

§ 10. *This may procure us convenience, not Science.*

---

(17) these] **2–5** | those **1** (18) ; as] **4–5** | , as **1–3** (24) getting] **2–5** | attaining **1** (26) which . . . that] **2–5** | to which **1** (27) , which] *add.* **4–5** can attain to,] *add.* **2–5** (30) Properties.] **4–5** | Properties, **1–3** (33) I fear] *add.* **2–5** (34–5) nor . . . advance] **2–5** | our Faculties cannot attain **1**

§ 11. From whence it is obvious to conclude, that since our Faculties are not fitted to penetrate into the internal Fabrick and real Essences of Bodies; but yet plainly discover to us the Being of a GOD, and the Knowledge of our selves, enough to lead us into a full and clear discovery of our Duty, and great Concernment, it will become us, as rational Creatures, to imploy those Faculties we have about what they are most adapted to, and follow the direction of Nature, where it seems to point us out the way. For 'tis rational to conclude, that our proper Imployment lies in those Enquiries, and in that sort of Knowledge, which is most suited to our natural Capacities, and carries in it our greatest interest, *i.e.* the Condition of our eternal Estate. Hence I think I may conclude, that *Morality* is *the proper Science, and Business of Mankind in general*; (who are both concerned, and fitted to search out their *Summum Bonum*,) as several Arts, conversant about several parts of Nature, are the Lot and private Talent of particular Men, for the common use of humane Life, and their own particular Subsistence in this World. Of what Consequence the discovery of one natural Body, and its Properties may be to humane Life, the whole great Continent of *America* is a convincing instance: whose Ignorance in useful Arts, and want of the greatest part of the Conveniences of Life, in a Country that abounded with all sorts of natural Plenty, I think, may be attributed to their Ignorance, of what was to be found in a very ordinary despicable Stone, I mean the Mineral of *Iron*. And whatever we think of our Parts or Improvements in this part of the World, where Knowledge and Plenty seem to vie each with other; yet to any one, that will seriously reflect on it, I suppose, it will appear past doubt, that were the use of *Iron* lost among us, we should in a few Ages be unavoidably reduced to the Wants and Ignorance of the ancient savage *Americans*, whose natural Endowments and Provisions come no way short of those of the most flourishing and polite Nations. So that he who first made known the use of that one contemptible Mineral, may be truly styled the Father of Arts, and Author of Plenty.

§ 11. *We are fitted for moral Knowledge, and natural Improvements.*

(6–7) those . . . have] **2–5** | our Faculties **1** (12) . Hence I think I may conclude] **4–5** | : and therefore it is, I think **1–3** (16) use] **2–5** | Convenience **1** (21) Conveniences] **2–5** | Conveniencies **1** (29) unavoidably] **1–2, 4–5** | unavoidable **3** (31) Nations] **2–5** | Notions **1**

§ 12. I would *not therefore* be thought to dis-esteem, or *dissuade the Study of Nature.* I readily agree the Contemplation of his Works gives us occasion to admire, revere, and glorify their Author: and if rightly directed, may be of greater benefit to Mankind, than the Monuments of exemplary Charity, that have at so great Charge been raised, by the Founders of Hospitals and Alms-houses. He that first invented Printing; discovered the Use of the Compass; or made publick the Virtue and right Use of *Kin Kina*, did more for the propagation of Knowledge; for the supplying and increase of useful commodities; and saved more from the Grave, than those who built Colleges, Work-houses, and Hospitals. All that I would say, is, that we should not be too forwardly possessed with the Opinion, or Expectation of Knowledge, where it is not to be had; or by ways, that will not attain it: That we should not take doubtful Systems, for complete Sciences; nor unintelligible Notions, for scientifical Demonstrations. In the Knowledge of Bodies, we must be content to glean, what we can, from particular Experiments: since we cannot from a Discovery of their real Essences, grasp at a time whole Sheaves; and in bundles, comprehend the Nature and Properties of whole Species together. Where our Enquiry is concerning Co-existence, or Repugnancy to co-exist, which by Contemplation of our *Ideas*, we cannot discover; there Experience, Observation, and natural History, must give us by our Senses, and by retail, an insight into corporeal Substances. The Knowledge of Bodies we must get by our Senses, warily employed in taking notice of their Qualities, and Operations on one another: And what we hope to know of separate Spirits in this World, we must, I think, expect only from Revelation. He that shall consider, *how little general Maxims, precarious Principles, and Hypotheses laid down at Pleasure, have promoted true Knowledge*, or helped to satisfy the Enquiries of rational Men after real Improvements; How little, I say, the setting out at that end, has for many Ages together advanced Men's Progress towards the Knowledge of natural Philosophy, will think, we have Reason to thank those, who in this latter Age have taken another Course, and have trod out to us, though not an easier way to learned Ignorance, yet a surer way to profitable Knowledge.

§ 12. *But must beware of Hypotheses and wrong Principles.*

(9–10) ; for . . . commodities] **2–5** | , for the acquisition of Conveniencies of Life **1** (11) Work-houses] **Coste** 'Manufactures', *adding a marginal linguistic note.* (27) separate] **2–5** | separated **1** (32) that] **1er–5** | the **1** (34) those] **2–5** | those Men **1**

§ 13. Not that we may not, to explain any *Phænomena* of Nature, make use of any probable *Hypothesis* whatsoever: *Hypotheses*, if they are well made, are at least great helps to the Memory, and often direct us to new discoveries. But my Meaning is, that we should *not take up any one too hastily*, (which the Mind, that would always penetrate into the Causes of Things, and have Principles to rest on, is very apt to do,) till we have very well examined Particulars, and made several Experiments, in that thing which we would explain by our Hypothesis, and see whether it will agree to them all; whether our Principles will carry us quite through, and not be as inconsistent with one *Phænomenon* of Nature, as they seem to accommodate, and explain another. And at least, that we take care, that the Name of *Principles* deceive us not, nor impose on us, by making us receive that for an unquestionable Truth, which is really, at best, but a very doubtful conjecture, such as are most (I had almost said all) of the *Hypotheses* in natural Philosophy.

§ 14. But whether natural Philosophy be capable of Certainty, or no, the *ways to enlarge our Knowledge*, as far as we are capable, seem to me, in short, to be these two:

First, The *First* is *to get and settle in our Minds* determined *Ideas* of those Things, whereof we have general or specific Names; at least of so many of them as we would consider and improve our Knowledge in, or reason about. And if they be *specific* Ideas of *Substances*, we should endeavour also to make them as complete as we can, whereby I mean, that we should put together as many simple Ideas, as being constantly observed to co-exist, may perfectly determine the *Species*: And each of those simple Ideas, which are the ingredients of our Complex one, should be clear and distinct in our Minds. For it being evident, that our Knowledge cannot exceed our *Ideas*; as far as they are either imperfect, confused, or obscure, we cannot expect to have certain, perfect, or clear Knowledge.

Secondly, The other is the Art of *finding out* those *Intermediate Ideas*, which may shew us the Agreement, or Repugnancy of other *Ideas*, which cannot be immediately compared.

§ 13. *The true use of Hypotheses.* § 14. *Clear and distinct* Ideas *with settled Names, and the finding of those which shew their agreement, or disagreement, are the ways to enlarge our Knowledge.*

(8) which] *add.* **4–5** (20) determined] **4–5** | , as far as we can, *clear*, *distinct*, *and constant* **1–3** (21–9) , whereof . . . Minds] **4–5** | we would consider and know **1–3** (28) Complex one,] *edit.* (complex ones, **W**) | Complex, one/ **4–5** (30) ; as far as] **4–5** |, where **1–3** confused,] *add.* **2–5** (31) perfect, or clear] **2–5** | and perfect **1**

§ 15. That these two (and not the relying on Maxims, and drawing Consequences from some general Propositions) are the right Method of improving our Knowledge in the *Ideas* of other Modes besides those of quantity, the Consideration of Mathematical Knowledge will easily inform us. Where first we shall find, that he, that has not a perfect, and clear *Idea* of those Angles, or Figures of which he desires to know any thing, is utterly thereby uncapable of any Knowledge about them. Suppose but a Man, not to have a perfect exact *Idea* of a *right Angle*, a *Scalenum*, or *Trapezium*; and there is nothing more certain than, that he will in vain seek any Demonstration about them. Farther it is evident, that it was not the influence of those Maxims, which are taken for Principles in Mathematicks, that hath led the Masters of that Science into those wonderful Discoveries they have made. Let a Man of good Parts know all the Maxims generally made use of in Mathematicks never so perfectly, and contemplate their Extent and Consequences, as much as he pleases, he will by their Assistance, I suppose, scarce ever come to know that *the square of the Hypotenuse in a right angled Triangle, is equal to the squares of the two other sides*. The Knowledge, that *the Whole is equal to all its Parts*, and *if you take Equals from Equals, the remainder will be Equal*, etc. helped him not, I presume, to this Demonstration: And a Man may, I think, pore long enough on those Axioms, without ever seeing one jot the more of mathematical Truths. They have been discovered by the Thoughts otherways applied: The Mind had other Objects, other Views before it, far different from those Maxims, when it first got the Knowledge of such kind of Truths in Mathematicks, which Men well enough acquainted with those received Axioms, but ignorant of their Method, who first made these Demonstrations, can never sufficiently admire. And who knows what Methods, to enlarge our Knowledge in other parts of Science, may hereafter be invented, answering that of *Algebra* in Mathematicks, which so readily finds out *Ideas* of Quantities to measure others by, whose Equality or Proportion we could otherwise very hardly, or, perhaps, never come to know?

§ 15. *Mathematicks an instance of it.*

(3–4) the . . . quantity] **2–5** | other *Ideas* of Modes **1** (10) certain than] **4–5** | clear **1–3** (11) Farther] **4–5** | And farther **1–3** (18) *Hypotenuse*] **4–5** | *Hypotieneuse* **2–3** | Hypotieneuson **1** (20–1) *Equals from Equals*] **4–5** | *Equal from Equal* **1–3** (22) think,] **1–3, 5** | think **4** (30–1) , to . . . answering] **2–5** | may hereafter be found out to enlarge our Knowledge in other Things, as well as **1**

CHAPTER XIII

Some farther Considerations concerning our Knowledge.

§ 1. *OUR Knowledge*, as in other Things, so in this, has a great Conformity with our Sight, that it is *neither wholly necessary, nor wholly voluntary*. If our Knowledge were altogether necessary, all Men's Knowledge would not only be alike, but every Man would know all that is knowable: and if it were wholly voluntary, some Men so little regard or value it, that they would have extreme little, or none at all. Men that have Senses, cannot chuse but receive some *Ideas* by them; and if they have Memory, they cannot but retain some of them; and if they have any distinguishing Faculty, cannot but perceive the Agreement, or Disagreement of some of them one with another: As he that has Eyes, if he will open them by day, cannot but see some Objects, and perceive a difference in them. But though a Man with his Eyes open in the Light, cannot but see; yet there be certain Objects, which he may chuse whether he will turn his Eyes to; there may be in his reach a Book containing Pictures, and Discourses, capable to delight, or instruct him, which yet he may never have the Will to open, never take the Pains to look into.

§ 2. There is also another thing in a Man's Power, and that is, though he turns his Eyes sometimes towards an Object, yet he may chuse whether he will curiously survey it, and with an intent application, endeavour to observe accurately all that is visible in it. But yet what he does see, he cannot see otherwise than he does. It depends not on his Will to see that *Black*, which appears *Yellow*; nor to persuade himself, that what actually *scalds* him, feels *cold*: The Earth will not appear painted with Flowers, nor the Fields covered with Verdure, whenever he has a Mind to it: in the cold Winter, he cannot help seeing it white and hoary, if he will look abroad. Just thus is it with our Understanding, all that is *voluntary* in our Knowledge, is the *employing*, or with-holding any of *our Faculties* from this or that sort of Objects, and a more, or less accurate survey of them: But they being employed, *our Will hath no Power to determine*

§ 1. *Our Knowledge partly necessary, partly voluntary.* § 2. *The application voluntary; but we know as things are, not as we please.*

(19) turns] **4–5** | turn **1–3** (20) curiously] **2–5** | intently **1** (20–1) intent application] **2–5** | accurate search **1** (21) accurately] *add.* **2–5**

the Knowledge of the Mind one way or other; that is done only by the Objects themselves, as far as they are clearly discovered. And therefore, as far as Men's Senses are conversant about external Objects, the Mind cannot but receive those *Ideas*, which are presented by them, and be informed of the Existence of Things without: and so far as Men's Thoughts converse with their own determined *Ideas*, they cannot but, in some measure, observe the Agreement, and Disagreement that is to be found amongst some of them, which is so far Knowledge: and if they have Names for those *Ideas* which they have thus considered, they must needs be assured of the Truth of those Propositions, which express that Agreement, or Disagreement, they perceive in them, and be undoubtedly convinced of those Truths. For what a Man sees, he cannot but see; and what he perceives, he cannot but know that he perceives.

§ 3. Thus he that has got the *Ideas* of Numbers, and hath taken the Pains to compare *One*, *Two*, and *Three*, to *Six*, cannot chuse but know that they are equal: He that hath got the *Idea* of a Triangle, and found the ways to measure its Angles, and their Magnitudes, is certain that its three Angles are equal to two right ones. And can as little doubt of that, as of this Truth, that *it is impossible for the same to be, and not to be*.

He also that hath the *Idea* of an intelligent, but frail and weak Being, made by and depending on another, who is eternal, omnipotent, perfectly wise and good, will as certainly know that Man is to honour, fear, and obey GOD, as that the Sun shines when he sees it. For if he hath but the *Ideas* of two such Beings in his mind, and will turn his Thoughts that way, and consider them, he will as certainly find that the Inferior, Finite, and Dependent, is under an Obligation to obey the Supreme and Infinite, as he is certain to find, that *Three*, *Four*, and *Seven*, are less than *Fifteen*, if he will consider, and compute those Numbers; nor can he be surer in a clear Morning that the Sun is risen, if he will but open his Eyes, and turn them that way. But yet these Truths, being never so certain, never so clear, he may be ignorant of either, or all of them, who will never take the Pains to employ his Faculties, as he should, to inform himself about them.

§ 3. *Instance in Numbers.* § 3(22). *In Natural Religion.*

---

(6) determined] **4–5** | clear and distinct **1–3** (9) *Ideas* which] **4–5** | *Ideas*, **1–3** (19) certain] **4–5** | as certain **1–3** (19–20) . And . . . Truth,] **4–5** | , as **1–3** (30) *Four*] **1er–5** | *Five* **1** (*l. below* 35: § 3.) *Instance*] **4–5** | Instances **2–3** (*l. below* 35: § 3(22).) *In Natural Religion.*] *add.* **4–5**

CHAPTER XIV

Of Judgment.

§ 1. THE Understanding Faculties being given to Man, not barely for Speculation, but also for the Conduct of his Life, Man would be at a great loss, if he had nothing to direct him, but what has the Certainty of true *Knowledge*. For that being very short and scanty, as we have seen, he would be often utterly in the dark, and in most of the Actions of his Life, perfectly at a stand, had he nothing to guide him in the absence of clear and certain Knowledge. He that will not eat, till he has Demonstration that it will nourish him; he that will not stir, till he infallibly knows the Business he goes about will succeed, will have little else to do, but sit still and perish.

§ 2. Therefore as God has set some Things in broad day-light; as he has given us some certain Knowledge, though limited to a few Things in comparison, probably, as a Taste of what intellectual Creatures are capable of, to excite in us a Desire and Endeavour after a better State: So in the greatest part of our Concernment, he has afforded us only the twilight, as I may so say, of *Probability*, suitable, I presume, to that State of Mediocrity and Probationership, he has been pleased to place us in here; wherein to check our over-confidence and presumption, we might by every day's Experience be made sensible of our short-sightedness and liableness to Error; the Sense whereof might be a constant Admonition to us, to spend the days of this our Pilgrimage with Industry and Care, in the search, and following of that way, which might lead us to a State of greater Perfection. It being highly rational to think, even were Revelation silent in the Case, That as Men employ those Talents, God has given them here, they shall accordingly receive their Rewards at the close of the day, when their Sun shall set, and Night shall put an end to their Labours.

§ 1. *Our Knowledge being short, we want something else.* § 2. *What use to be made of this twilight State.*

---

(7) He] **4–5** | For he **1–3** (19) us in] **1er–5** | in us **1** (19–20) to . . . we] **4–5** | we might not be over confident, and presume; but **1–3** (22) the Sense whereof] **4–5** | which **1–3** (26) were . . . silent] **1er–5** | where . . . is silent **1** (27) here] **2–5** | , here **1** (*2 ll. below* 29) *State*] **4–5** | *Estate* **2–3**. (**Coste** 'Monde')

§ 3. The Faculty, which God has given Man to supply the want of clear and certain Knowledge in Cases where that cannot be had, is *Judgment*: whereby the Mind takes its *Ideas* to agree, or disagree; or which is the same, any Proposition to be true, or false, without perceiving a demonstrative Evidence in the Proofs. The Mind sometimes exercises this *Judgment* out of necessity, where demonstrative Proofs, and certain Knowledge are not to be had; and sometimes out of Laziness, Unskilfulness, or Haste, even where demonstrative and certain Proofs are to be had. Men often stay not warily to examine the Agreement or Disagreement of two *Ideas*, which they are desirous, or concerned to know; but either incapable of such Attention, as is requisite in a long Train of Gradations, or impatient of delay, lightly cast their Eyes on, or wholly pass by the Proofs; and so without making out the Demonstration, determine of the Agreement or Disagreement of two *Ideas*, as it were by a view of them as they are at a distance, and take it to be the one or the other, as seems most likely to them upon such a loose survey. This Faculty of the Mind, when it is exercised immediately about Things, is called *Judgment*; when about Truths delivered in Words, is most commonly called *Assent* or *Dissent*: which being the most usual way, wherein the Mind has occasion to employ this Faculty, I shall under these Terms treat of it, as least liable in our Language to Equivocation.

§ 4. Thus the Mind has two Faculties, conversant about Truth and Falshood.

First, *Knowledge*, whereby it certainly perceives, and is undoubtedly satisfied of the Agreement or Disagreement of any *Ideas*.

Secondly, *Judgment*, which is the putting *Ideas* together, or separating them from one another in the Mind, when their certain Agreement or Disagreement is not perceived, but *presumed* to be so; which is, as the Word imports, taken to be so before it certainly appears. And if it so unites, or separates them, as in Reality Things are, it is *right Judgment*.

§ 3. *Judgment supplies the want of Knowledge.* § 4. *Judgment is the presuming things to be so without perceiving it.*

(1–2) supply . . . of] **4–5** | enlighten him, next to **1–3** (2) in . . . had] *add.* **4–5** (2–3) , is] **1–3, 5** | is **4** (13) cast . . . on] **2–5** | survey **1** (14) by]**2–5** | over **1** (16) them] **1T.er, 2–5** | them, **1**

CHAPTER XV

Of Probability.

§ 1. As Demonstration is the shewing the Agreement, or Disagreement of two *Ideas*, by the intervention of one or more Proofs, which have a constant, immutable, and visible connexion one with another: so *Probability* is nothing but the appearance of such an Agreement, or Disagreement, by the intervention of Proofs, whose connexion is not constant and immutable, or at least is not perceived to be so, but is, or appears for the most part to be so, and is enough to induce the Mind to *judge* the Proposition to be true, or false, rather than the contrary. For example: In the demonstration of it, a Man perceives the certain immutable connexion there is of Equality, between the three Angles of a *Triangle*, and those intermediate ones, which are made use of to shew their Equality to two right ones: and so by an intuitive Knowledge of the Agreement, or Disagreement of the intermediate *Ideas* in each step of the progress, the whole Series is continued with an evidence, which clearly shews the Agreement, or Disagreement, of those three Angles, in equality to two right ones: And thus he has certain Knowledge that it is so. But another Man who never took the pains to observe the Demonstration, hearing a Mathematician, a Man of credit, affirm the three Angles of a Triangle, to be equal to two right ones, *assents* to it; *i.e.* receives it for true. In which case, the foundation of his Assent is the Probability of the thing, the Proof being such, as for the most part carries Truth with it: The Man, on whose Testimony he receives it, not being wont to affirm any thing contrary to, or besides his Knowledge, especially in matters of this kind. So that that which causes his Assent to this Proposition, that the three Angles of a Triangle are equal to two right ones, that which makes him take these *Ideas* to agree, without knowing them to do so, is the wonted Veracity of the Speaker in other cases, or his supposed Veracity in this.

§ 2. Our Knowledge, as has been shewn, being very narrow, and we not happy enough to find certain Truth in every thing which we

§ 1. *Probability is the appearance of agreement upon fallible proofs.* § 2. *It is to supply the want of Knowledge.*

(32) thing which] **4–5** | thing, **1–3**

have occasion to consider; most of the Propositions we think, reason, discourse, nay act upon, are such, as we cannot have undoubted Knowledge of their Truth: yet some of them border so near upon Certainty, that we make no doubt at all about them; but *assent* to them as firmly, and act, according to that Assent, as resolutely, as if they were infallibly demonstrated, and that our Knowledge of them was perfect and certain. But there being degrees herein, from the very neighbourhood of Certainty and Demonstration, quite down to Improbability and Unlikeliness, even to the Confines of Impossibility; and also degrees of *Assent* from full *Assurance* and Confidence, quite down to *Conjecture*, *Doubt*, and *Distrust*. I shall come now, (having, as I think, found out the bounds of humane Knowledge and Certainty,) in the next place to consider *the several degrees and grounds of Probability, and Assent or Faith.*

§ 3. *Probability* is likeliness to be true, the very notation of the Word signifying such a Proposition, for which there be Arguments or Proofs, to make it pass or be received for true. The entertainment the Mind gives this sort of Propositions, is called *Belief*, *Assent*, or *Opinion*, which is the admitting or receiving any Proposition for true, upon Arguments or Proofs that are found to perswade us to receive it as true, without certain Knowledge that it is so. And herein lies the *difference between Probability* and *Certainty*, *Faith* and *Knowledge*, that in all the parts of Knowledge, there is intuition; each immediate *Idea*, each step has its visible and certain connexion; in belief not so. That which makes me believe, is something extraneous to the thing I believe; something not evidently joined on both sides to, and so not manifestly shewing the Agreement, or Disagreement of those *Ideas*, that are under consideration.

§ 4. *Probability* then, being to supply the defect of our Knowledge, and to guide us where that fails, is always conversant about Propositions, whereof we have no certainty, but only some inducements to

§ 3. *Being that which makes us presume things to be true, before we know them to be so.* § 4. *The grounds of Probability are two; conformity with our own Experience, or the Testimony of others Experience.*

(5) resolutely] **2–5** | vigorously **1** (10) from] **5** (*likewise* **Coste**) | from certain Knowledge, and what is next it, **1–4** (11) and *Distrust*] **5** (*likewise* **Coste**) | *Distrust*, and *Disbelief* **1–4** (12–13) (having . . . Certainty,)] **5** (*likewise* **Coste**) | as having (as I think) found out the bounds of humane Knowledge and Certainty, **1–4** (14) *Assent*] **1–3, 5** | *assent* **4** (15) *Probability*] **2–5** | *Probability* then **1** (18) Propositions] **1–2, 4–5** | Proposition **3** (29) then,] **2–5** | then **1** (30) is] **2–5** | it is **1** (30–1) Propositions] **3–5** | things **1–2** (31)–656(1) whereof . . . true] **1–2, 4–5** | which we have some Inducements to receive for true, without certain Knowledge that they are so **3** (*likewise* **Coste**)

receive them for true. The *grounds of it* are, in short, these *two* following:

First, The conformity of any thing with our own Knowledge, Observation, and Experience.

Secondly, The Testimony of others, vouching their Observation and Experience. In the Testimony of others, is to be considered, 1. The Number. 2. The Integrity. 3. The Skill of the Witnesses. 4. The Design of the Author, where it is a Testimony out of a Book cited. 5. The Consistency of the Parts, and Circumstances of the Relation. 6. Contrary Testimonies.

§ 5. Probability wanting that intuitive Evidence, which infallibly determines the Understanding, and produces certain Knowledge, *the Mind if it will proceed rationally, ought to examine all the grounds of Probability*, and see how they make more or less, *for or against* any probable Proposition, before it assents to or dissents from it, and upon a due ballancing the whole, reject, or receive it, with a more or less firm assent, proportionably to the preponderancy of the greater grounds of Probability on one side or the other. For example:

If I my self see a Man walk on the Ice, it is past *Probability*, 'tis Knowledge: but if another tells me he saw a Man in *England* in the midst of a sharp Winter, walk upon Water harden'd with cold; this has so great conformity with what is usually observed to happen, that I am disposed by the nature of the thing it self to assent to it, unless some manifest suspicion attend the Relation of that matter of fact. But if the same thing be told to one born between the Tropicks, who never saw nor heard of any such Thing before, there the whole Probability relies on Testimony: And as the Relators are more in number, and of more Credit, and have no Interest to speak contrary to the Truth; so that matter of Fact is like to find more or less belief. Though to a Man, whose Experience has been always quite contrary, and has never heard of any thing like it, the most untainted Credit of a Witness will scarce be able to find belief. And as it happened to a *Dutch* Ambassa-

§ 5. *In this all the agreements* pro *and* con *ought to be examined, before we come to a Judgment.*

---

(1) them] **4–5** | it **1–2** (1) *v.* 655(31), n. (11) Probability] **2–5** | Now Probability **1** (13) *if . . . rationally*] **3–5** (rationally **3**) | , *before it* rationally *assents or dissents* to any probable Proposition **1–2** *examine*] **1–3, 5** | *examin* **4** (14–15) any . . . from] *add.* **3–5** (assent . . . dissent **3**) (33) belief.] **1–3, 5** | belief, **4** And as] **5** | As **1–4** *Dutch*] **3, 5** (*likewise* **Coste**) | Dutch **1–2, 4**

dor, who entertaining the King of *Siam* with the particularities of *Holland*, which he was inquisitive after, amongst other things told him, that the Water in his Country, would sometimes, in cold weather, be so hard, that Men walked upon it, and that it would bear an Elephant, if he were there. To which the King replied, *Hitherto I have believed the strange Things you have told me, because I look upon you as a sober fair man, but now I am sure you lye.*

§ 6. Upon these grounds depends the *Probability* of any Proposition: And as the conformity of our Knowledge, as the certainty of Observations, as the frequency and constancy of Experience, and the number and credibility of Testimonies, do more or less agree, or disagree with it, so is any Proposition in it self, more or less probable. There is another, I confess, which though by it self it be no true ground of *Probability*, yet is often made use of for one, by which Men most commonly regulate their Assent, and upon which they pin their Faith more than any thing else, and, that is, *the Opinion of others*; though there cannot be a more dangerous thing to rely on, nor more likely to mislead one; since there is much more Falshood and Errour amongst Men, than Truth and Knowledge. And if the Opinions and Perswasions of others, whom we know and think well of, be a ground of Assent, Men have Reason to be Heathens in *Japan*, Mahumetans in *Turkey*, Papists in *Spain*, Protestants in *England*, and Lutherans in *Sueden*. But of this wrong ground of Assent, I shall have occasion to speak more at large in another place.

CHAPTER XVI

Of the Degrees of Assent.

§ 1. THE grounds of Probability, we have laid down in the foregoing Chapter, as they are the Foundations on which our *Assent* is built; so are they also the measure whereby its several degrees are, or ought to be *regulated*: only we are to take notice, that whatever grounds of Probability there may be, they yet operate no farther on the Mind, which searches after Truth, and endeavours to judge

§ 6. *They being capable of great variety.*
§ 1. *Our Assent ought to be regulated by the grounds of Probability.*

(16) , and,] **3–5** | ; and **1er–2** |; any, **1**   (19) amongst] **1–3** | among/ **4–5**

right, than they appear; at least in the first Judgment or Search that the Mind makes. I confess, in the Opinions Men have, and firmly stick to, in the World, their *Assent* is not always from an actual view of the Reasons that at first prevailed with them: It being in many cases almost impossible, and in most very hard, even for those who have very admirable Memories, to retain all the Proofs, which upon a due examination, made them embrace that side of the Question. It suffices, that they have once with care and fairness, sifted the Matter as far as they could; and that they have searched into all the Particulars, that they could imagine to give any light to the Question; and with the best of their Skill, cast up the account upon the whole Evidence: and thus having once found on which side the Probability appeared to them, after as full and exact an enquiry as they can make, they lay up the Conclusion in their Memories, as a Truth they have discovered; and for the future, they remain satisfied with the Testimony of their Memories, that this is the Opinion, that by the Proofs they have once seen of it, deserves such a *degree* of their *Assent* as they afford it.

§ 2. This is all that the greatest part of Men are capable of doing, in regulating their *Opinions* and Judgments; unless a Man will exact of them, either to retain distinctly in their Memories all the Proofs concerning any probable Truth, and that too in the same order, and regular deduction of Consequences, in which they have formerly placed or seen them; which sometimes is enough to fill a large Volume upon one single Question: Or else they must require a Man, for every Opinion that he embraces, every day to examine the Proofs: both which are impossible. It is unavoidable therefore, that the Memory be relied on in the case, and that *Men be perswaded of several Opinions, whereof the Proofs are not actually in their Thoughts*; nay, which perhaps they are not able actually to re-call. Without this, the greatest part of Men must be either very Scepticks, or change every Moment, and yield themselves up to whoever, having lately studied the Question, offers them Arguments; which for want of Memory, they are not able presently to answer.

§ 3. I cannot but own, that Men's *sticking to* their *past Judgment*, and adhering firmly to Conclusions formerly made, is often the

§ 2. *These cannot always be all actually in view, and then we must content our selves with the remembrance that we once saw ground for such a degree of Assent.* § 3. *The ill consequence of this, if our former Judgment were not rightly made.*

(8) sifted] **2–5** | examined **1** (*l. below* 36) *all*] **2–3** (*likewise* **Coste**); *om.* **4–5**

cause of great obstinacy in Errour and Mistake. But the fault is not that they rely on their Memories, for what they have before well judged; but because they judged before they had well examined. May we not find a great number (not to say the greatest part) of Men, that think they have formed right Judgments of several matters; and that for no other reason, but because they never thought otherwise? That imagine themselves to have judged right, only because they never questioned, never examined their own Opinions? Which is indeed to think they judged right, because they never judged at all: And yet these of all Men hold their Opinions with the greatest stiffness; those being generally the most fierce and firm in their Tenets, who have least examined them. What we once know, we are certain is so: and we may be secure, that there are no latent Proofs undiscovered, which may overturn our Knowledge, or bring it in doubt. But in matters of Probability, 'tis not in every case we can be sure, that we have all the Particulars before us, that any way concern the Question; and that there is no evidence behind, and yet unseen, which may cast the Probability on the other side, and out-weigh all, that at present seems to preponderate with us. Who almost is there, that hath the leisure, patience, and means, to collect together all the Proofs concerning most of the Opinions he has, so as safely to conclude, that he hath a clear and full view; and that there is no more to be alledged for his better information? And yet we are forced to determine our selves on the one side or other. The conduct of our Lives, and the management of our great Concerns, will not bear delay: for those depend, for the most part, on the determination of our Judgment in points, wherein we are not capable of certain and demonstrative Knowledge, and wherein it is necessary for us to embrace the one side, or the other.

§ 4. Since therefore it is unavoidable to the greatest part of Men, if not all, to have several *Opinions*, without certain and indubitable Proofs of their Truths; and it carries too great an imputation of ignorance, lightness, or folly, for Men to quit and renounce their former Tenets, presently upon the offer of an Argument, which they cannot immediately answer, and shew the insufficiency of: It would, methinks, become all Men to maintain *Peace*, and the common Offices of Humanity, *and Friendship, in the diversity of Opinions*,

§ 4. *The right use of it is mutual Charity and Forbearance.*

(16) [*1st*] we] **2–5** | that we **1** (*l. below* 37) *is*] **2–3** (*likewise* **Coste**); *om.* **4–5**

since we cannot reasonably expect, that any one should readily and obsequiously quit his own Opinion, and embrace ours with a blind resignation to an Authority, which the Understanding of Man acknowledges not. For however it may often mistake, it can own no other Guide but Reason, nor blindly submit to the Will and Dictates of another. If he, you would bring over to your Sentiments, be one that examines before he assents, you must give him leave, at his leisure, to go over the account again, and re-calling what is out of his Mind, examine all the Particulars, to see on which side the advantage lies: And if he will not think our Arguments of weight enough to engage him anew in so much pains, 'tis but what we do often our selves in the like case; and we should take it amiss, if others should prescribe to us what points we should study. And if he be one who takes his Opinions upon trust, How can we imagine that he should renounce those Tenets, which Time and Custom have so settled in his Mind, that he thinks them self-evident, and of an unquestionable Certainty; or which he takes to be impressions he has received from GOD Himself, or from Men sent by Him? How can we expect, I say, that Opinions thus settled, should be given up to the Arguments or Authority of a Stranger, or Adversary; especially if there be any suspicion of Interest, or Design, as there never fails to be, where Men find themselves ill treated? We should do well to commiserate our mutual Ignorance, and endeavour to remove it in all the gentle and fair ways of Information; and not instantly treat others ill, as obstinate and perverse, because they will not renounce their own, and receive our Opinions, or at least those we would force upon them, when 'tis more than probable, that we are no less obstinate in not embracing some of theirs. For where is the Man, that has uncontestable Evidence of the Truth of all that he holds, or of the Falshood of all he condemns; or can say, that he has examined, to the bottom, all his own, or other Men's Opinions? The necessity of believing, without Knowledge, nay, often upon very slight grounds, in this fleeting state of Action and Blindness we are in, should make us more busy and careful to inform our selves, than constrain others. At least those, who have not throughly examined to the bottom all their own Tenets, must confess, they are unfit to prescribe to others; and are unreasonable in imposing that as a Truth on other Men's Belief, which they themselves have not searched into, nor weighed the Arguments of

(20) [*1st*] or] **1–3** (*likewise* **Coste**) | of **4–5** (28) some of] *add.* **2–5**

Probability, on which they should receive or reject it. Those who have fairly and truly examined, and are thereby got past doubt in all the Doctrines they profess, and govern themselves by, would have a juster pretence to require others to follow them: But these are so few in number, and find so little reason to be magisterial in their Opinions, that nothing insolent and imperious is to be expected from them: And there is reason to think, that if Men were better instructed themselves, they would be less imposing on others.

§ 5. But to return to the grounds of Assent, and the several degrees of it, we are to take notice, that the Propositions we receive upon Inducements of *Probability*, are *of two sorts*; either concerning some particular Existence, or, as it is usually termed, matter of fact, which falling under Observation, is capable of humane Testimony, or else concerning Things, which being beyond the discovery of our Senses, are not capable of any such Testimony.

§ 6. Concerning the *first* of these, *viz. particular matter of fact*,

First, Where any particular thing, consonant to the constant Observation of our selves and others, in the like case, comes attested by the concurrent Reports of all that mention it, we receive it as easily, and build as firmly upon it, as if it were certain Knowledge; and we reason and act thereupon with as little doubt, as if it were perfect demonstration. Thus, if all *English*-men, who have occasion to mention it, should affirm, that it froze in *England* the last Winter, or that there were Swallows seen there in the Summer, I think a Man could almost as little doubt of it, as that Seven and Four are Eleven. The first therefore, and *highest degree of Probability*, is, when the general consent of all Men, in all Ages, as far as it can be known, concurrs with a Man's constant and never-failing Experience in like cases, to confirm the Truth of any particular matter of fact attested by fair Witnesses: such are all the stated Constitutions and Properties of Bodies, and the regular proceedings of Causes and Effects in the ordinary course of Nature. This we call an Argument from the nature of Things themselves. For what our own and other Men's constant Observation has found always to be after the same manner, that we with reason conclude to be the Effects of steady and regular Causes, though they come not within the reach of our

§ 5. *Probability is either of matter of fact or speculation.* § 6. *The concurrent experience of all other Men with ours, produces assurance approaching to Knowledge.*

(13) Observation] **2–5** | our Observation **1** Testimony,] **2–5** | Testimony; **1**
(19) by] **4–5** | with **1–3**

Knowledge. Thus, That Fire warmed a Man, made Lead fluid, and changed the colour or consistency in Wood or Charcoal: that Iron sunk in Water, and swam in Quicksilver: These and the like Propositions about particular facts, being agreeable to our constant Experience, as often as we have to do with these matters; and being generally spoke of, (when mentioned by others,) as things found constantly to be so, and therefore not so much as controverted by any body, we are put past doubt, that a relation affirming any such thing to have been, or any predication that it will happen again in the same manner, is very true. These *Probabilities* rise so near to *Certainty*, that they govern our Thoughts as absolutely, and influence all our Actions as fully, as the most evident demonstration: and in what concerns us, we make little or no difference between them and certain Knowledge: our Belief thus grounded, rises to *Assurance*.

§ 7. *Secondly*, *The next degree of Probability* is, when I find by my own Experience, and the Agreement of all others that mention it, a thing to be, for the most part, so; and that the particular instance of it is attested by many and undoubted Witnesses: *v.g.* History giving us such an account of Men in all Ages; and my own Experience, as far as I had an opportunity to observe, confirming it, that most Men preferr their private Advantage, to the publick. If all Historians that write of *Tiberius*, say that *Tiberius* did so, it is extremely probable. And in this case, our Assent has a sufficient foundation to raise it self to a degree, which we may call *Confidence*.

§ 8. *Thirdly*, In things that happen indifferently, as that a Bird should fly this or that way; that it should thunder on a Man's right or left Hand, *etc.* when any particular matter of fact is vouched by the concurrent Testimony of unsuspected Witnesses, there our Assent is also unavoidable. Thus: That there is such a City in *Italy* as *Rome*: That about 1700 years ago, there lived in it a Man, called *Julius Cæsar*; that he was a General, and that he won a Battel against another called *Pompey*. This, though in the nature of the thing, there be nothing for, nor against it, yet, being related by Historians of credit, and contradicted by no one Writer, a Man cannot avoid believing it, and can as little doubt of it, as he does of

§ 7. *Unquestionable Testimony and Experience for the most part produce Confidence.* § 8. *Fair Testimony, and the nature of the Thing indifferent, produces also confident belief.*

---

(14) : our] **4–5** | . And our **1–3** (27) is vouched] **4–5** | comes attested **1–3.** (**Coste** 'est attesté') (32) against] **2–5** | again **1**

the Being and Actions of his own Acquaintance, whereof he himself is a Witness.

§ 9. Thus far the matter goes easie enough. Probability upon such grounds carries so much evidence with it, that it naturally determines the Judgment, and leaves us as little liberty to believe, or disbelieve, as a Demonstration does, whether we will know, or be ignorant. The difficulty is, when Testimonies contradict common Experience, and the reports of History and Witnesses clash with the ordinary course of Nature, or with one another; there it is, where Diligence, Attention, and Exactness is required, to form a right Judgment, and to proportion the *Assent* to the different Evidence and Probability of the thing; which rises and falls, according as those two foundations of Credibility, *viz.* Common Observation in like cases, and particular Testimonies in that particular instance, favour or contradict it. These are liable to so great variety of contrary Observations, Circumstances, Reports, different Qualifications, Tempers, Designs, Over-sights, *etc.* of the Reporters, that 'tis impossible to reduce to precise Rules, the various degrees wherein Men give their Assent. This only may be said in general, That as the Arguments and Proofs, *pro* and *con*, upon due Examination, nicely weighing every particular Circumstance, shall to any one appear, upon the whole matter, in a greater or less degree, to preponderate on either side, so they are fitted to produce in the Mind such different Entertainment, as we call *Belief*, *Conjecture*, *Guess*, *Doubt*, *Wavering*, *Distrust*, *Disbelief*, etc.

§ 10. This is what concerns *Assent* in matters wherein Testimony is made use of: concerning which, I think, it may not be amiss to take notice of a Rule observed in the Law of *England*; which is, That though the attested Copy of a Record be good Proof, yet the Copy of a Copy never so well attested, and by never so credible Witnesses, will not be admitted as a proof in Judicature. This is so generally approved as reasonable, and suited to the Wisdom and Caution to be used in our Enquiry after material Truths, that I never yet heard of any one that blamed it. This practice, if it be allowable in the Decisions of Right and Wrong, carries this Observation along with it, *viz.* That any Testimony, the farther off it is from the

§ 9. *Experiences and Testimonies clashing, infinitely vary the degrees of Probability.*
§ 10. *Traditional Testimonies, the farther removed, the less their Proof.*

(5) liberty] **5** | at liberty **1–4** (8) reports] **2–5** | report **1** clash] **2–5** | clashes **1** (15) favour or contradict] **2–5** | favours or contradicts **1**

original Truth, the less force and proof it has. The Being and Existence of the thing it self, is what I call the original Truth. A credible Man vouching his Knowledge of it, is a good proof: But if another equally credible, do witness it from his Report, the Testimony is weaker; and a third that attests the Hear-say of an Hear-say, is yet less considerable. So that *in traditional Truths, each remove weakens the force of the proof*: And the more hands the Tradition has successively passed through, the less strength and evidence does it receive from them. This I thought necessary to be taken notice of: Because I find amongst some Men, the quite contrary commonly practised, who look on Opinions to gain force by growing older; and what a thousand years since would not, to a rational Man, contemporary with the first Voucher, have appeared at all probable, is now urged as certain beyond all question, only because several have since, from him, said it one after another. Upon this ground Propositions, evidently false or doubtful enough in their first beginning, come by an inverted Rule of Probability, to pass for authentick Truths; and those which found or deserved little credit from the Mouths of their first Authors, are thought to grow venerable by Age, and are urged as undeniable.

§ 11. I would not be thought here to lessen the Credit and use of *History*: 'tis all the light we have in many cases; and we receive from it a great part of the useful Truths we have, with a convincing evidence. I think nothing more valuable than the Records of Antiquity: I wish we had more of them, and more uncorrupted. But this, Truth it self forces me to say, That no *Probability* can arise higher than its first Original. What has no other Evidence than the single Testimony of one only Witness, must stand or fall by his only Testimony, whether good, bad, or indifferent; and though cited afterwards by hundreds of others, one after another, is so far from receiving any strength thereby, that it is only the weaker. Passion, Interest, Inadvertency, Mistake of his Meaning, and a thousand odd Reasons, or Caprichio's, Men's Minds are acted by, (impossible to be discovered,) may make one Man quote another Man's Words or Meaning wrong. He that has but ever so little examined the Citations of Writers, cannot doubt how little Credit the Quotations deserve, where the Originals are wanting; and consequently how

§ 11. *Yet History is of great use.*

---

(12) years] **3–5** | year **1–2**

much less Quotations of Quotations can be relied on. This is certain, that what in one Age was affirmed upon slight grounds, can never after come to be more valid in future Ages, by being often repeated. But the farther still it is from the Original, the less valid it is, and has always less force in the mouth, or writing of him that last made use of it, that in his from whom he received it.

§ 12. The Probabilities we have hitherto mentioned, are only such as concern matter of fact, and such Things as are capable of Observation and Testimony. There remains that other sort *concerning* which, Men entertain Opinions with variety of Assent, though the *Things* be such, that *falling not under the reach of our Senses, they are not capable of Testimony*. Such are, 1. The Existence, Nature, and Operations of finite immaterial Beings without us; as Spirits, Angels, Devils, *etc.* Or the Existence of material Beings; which either for their smallness in themselves, or remoteness from us, our Senses cannot take notice of, as whether there be any Plants, Animals, and intelligent Inhabitants in the Planets, and other Mansions of the vast Universe. 2. Concerning the manner of Operation in most parts of the Works of Nature: wherein though we see the sensible effects, yet their causes are unknown, and we perceive not the ways and manner how they are produced. We see Animals are generated, nourished, and move; the Load-stone draws Iron; and the parts of a Candle successively melting, turn into flame, and give us both light and heat. These and the like Effects we see and know: but the causes that operate, and the manner they are produced in, we can only guess, and probably conjecture. For these and the like coming not within the scrutiny of humane Senses, cannot be examined by them, or be attested by any body, and therefore can appear more or less probable, only as they more or less agree to Truths that are established in our Minds, and as they hold proportion to other parts of our Knowledge and Observation. *Analogy* in these matters is the only help we have, and 'tis from that alone we draw all our grounds of Probability. Thus observing that the bare rubbing of two Bodies violently one upon another, produces heat, and very often fire it self, we have reason to think, that what we call Heat and Fire,

§ 12. *In things which Sense cannot discover, Analogy is the great Rule of Probability.*

---

(11) *they*] *add.* **2–5** (12) . Such] **4–5** | ; and such **1–3** (14) Or] **2–5** | or **1**
(17) in] **2–5** | of **1** (18) Universe.] **1–3, 5** (*likewise* **Coste**) | Universe **4**
(19) Nature:] **4–5** | Nature; **1–3** (27) Senses,] **1–3, 5** | Senses **4**

consists in a violent agitation of the imperceptible minute parts of the burning matter: Observing likewise that the different refractions of pellucid Bodies produce in our Eyes the different appearances of several Colours; and also that the different ranging and laying the superficial parts of several Bodies, as of Velvet, watered Silk, *etc.* does the like, we think it probable that the Colour and shining of Bodies, is in them nothing but the different Arangement and Refraction of their minute and insensible parts. Thus finding in all parts of the Creation, that fall under humane Observation, that there is a gradual connexion of one with another, without any great or discernable gaps between, in all that great variety of Things we see in the World, which are so closely linked together, that, in the several ranks of Beings, it is not easy to discover the bounds betwixt them, we have reason to be perswaded, that by such gentle steps Things ascend upwards in degrees of Perfection. 'Tis an hard Matter to say where Sensible and Rational begin, and where Insensible and Irrational end: and who is there quick-sighted enough to determine precisely, which is the lowest Species of living Things, and which the first of those which have no Life? Things, as far as we can observe, lessen, and augment, as the quantity does in a regular Cone, where though there be a manifest odds betwixt the bigness of the Diameter at remote distance: yet the difference between the upper and under, where they touch one another, is hardly discernable. The difference is exceeding great between some Men, and some Animals: But if we will compare the Understanding and Abilities of some Men, and some Brutes, we shall find so little difference, that 'twill be hard to say, that that of the Man is either clearer or larger. Observing, I say, such gradual and gentle descents downwards in those parts of the Creation, that are beneath Man, the rule of Analogy may make it probable, that it is so also in Things above us, and our Observation; and that there are several ranks of intelligent Beings, excelling us in several degrees of Perfection, ascending upwards towards the infinite Perfection of the Creator, by gentle steps and differences, that are every one at no great distance from the next to it. This sort of Probability, which is the best conduct of rational Experiments, and the rise of Hypothesis, has also its Use and Influence; and a wary Reasoning from Analogy

(1) a] **4–5** | a certain **1–3** (*likewise* **Coste**) (9) parts] **4–5** | the parts **1–3** (*likewise* **Coste**) (14) by] **2–5** | in **1** (15) ascend . . . Perfection] **2–5** | in Perfection ascend upwards **1** (22) distance] **5** | distances **1–4** (36) Hypothesis,] ',' *add.* **4–5**

leads us often into the discovery of Truths, and useful Productions, which would otherwise lie concealed.

§ 13. Though the common Experience, and the ordinary Course of Things have justly a mighty Influence on the Minds of Men, to make them give or refuse Credit to any thing proposed to their Belief; yet there is one Case, wherein the strangeness of the Fact lessens not the Assent to a fair Testimony given of it. For where such supernatural Events are suitable to ends aim'd at by him, who has the Power to change the course of Nature, there, under such Circumstances, they may be the fitter to procure Belief, by how much the more they are beyond, or contrary to ordinary Observation. This is the proper Case of *Miracles*, which well attested, do not only find Credit themselves; but give it also to other Truths, which need such Confirmation.

§ 14. Besides those we have hitherto mentioned, there is one sort of Propositions that challenge the highest Degree of our Assent, upon bare Testimony, whether the thing proposed, agree or disagree with common Experience, and the ordinary course of Things, or no. The Reason whereof is, because the Testimony is of such an one, as cannot deceive, nor be deceived, and that is of God himself. This carries with it Assurance beyond Doubt, Evidence beyond Exception. This is called by a peculiar Name, *Revelation*, and our Assent to it, *Faith*: which as absolutely determines our Minds, and as perfectly excludes all wavering as our Knowledge it self; and we may as well doubt of our own Being, as we can, whether any Revelation from GOD be true. So that Faith is a setled and sure Principle of Assent and Assurance, and leaves no manner of room for Doubt or Hesitation. Only we must be sure, that it be a divine Revelation, and that we understand it right: else we shall expose our selves to all the Extravagancy of Enthusiasm, and all the Error of wrong Principles, if we have Faith and Assurance in what is not divine Revelation. And therefore in those Cases, our Assent can be rationally no higher than the Evidence of its being a Revelation, and that this is the meaning of the Expressions it is delivered in. If the Evidence of its being a Revelation, or that this its true Sense be

§ 13. *One case where contrary Experience lessens not the Testimony.* § 14. *The bare Testimony of Revelation is the highest certainty.*

---

(21) Assurance] **5** (*likewise* **Coste**) | Certainty **1–4** (23–4) as . . . wavering] **5** (*likewise* **Coste**) | has as much Certainty **1–4** (*2 ll. below* 35) *certainty.*] **2–3, 5** | *certain-|* **4**

only on probable Proofs, our Assent can reach no higher than an Assurance or Diffidence, arising from the more, or less apparent Probability of the Proofs. But of Faith, and the Precedency it ought to have before other Arguments of Perswasion, I shall speak more hereafter, where I treat of it, as it is ordinarily placed, in contradistinction to Reason; though in Truth, it be nothing else but an Assent founded on the highest Reason.

CHAPTER XVII

Of Reason.

§ 1. *THE Word Reason* in the *English* Language *has different Significations*: sometimes it is taken for true, and clear Principles: Sometimes for clear, and fair deductions from those Principles: and sometimes for the Cause, and particularly the final Cause. But the Consideration I shall have of it here, is in a Signification different from all these; and that is, as it stands for a Faculty in Man, That Faculty, whereby Man is supposed to be distinguished from Beasts, and wherein it is evident he much surpasses them.

§ 2. If general Knowledge, as has been shewn, consists in a Perception of the Agreement, or Disagreement of our own *Ideas*; and the Knowledge of the Existence of all Things without us (except only of a GOD whose existence every Man may certainly know and demonstrate to himself from his own existence) be had only by our Senses; What room then is there for the Exercise of any other Faculty, but outward Sense and inward Perception? What need is there of Reason? Very much; both for the enlargement of our Knowledge, and regulating our Assent: For it hath to do, both in Knowledge and Opinion, and is necessary, and assisting to all our other intellectual Faculties, and indeed contains two of them, *viz. Sagacity and Illation.* By the one, it finds out, and by the other, it so orders the intermediate *Ideas*, as to discover what connexion there is in each link of the Chain, whereby the Extremes are held together; and thereby, as it were, to draw into view the Truth sought for,

§ 1. *Various significations of the word Reason.* § 2. *Wherein Reasoning consists.*

(19–20) a . . . existence] **2–5** | GOD **1**

which is that we call *Illation* or *Inference*, and consists in nothing but the Perception of the connexion there is between the *Ideas*, in each step of the deduction, whereby the Mind comes to see, either the certain Agreement or Disagreement of any two *Ideas*, as in Demonstration, in which it arrives at Knowledge; or their probable connexion, on which it gives or with-holds its Assent, as in Opinion. Sense and Intuition reach but a very little way. The greatest part of our Knowledge depends upon Deductions and intermediate *Ideas*: And in those Cases, where we are fain to substitute Assent instead of Knowledge, and take Propositions for true, without being certain they are so, we have need to find out, examine, and compare the grounds of their Probability. In both these Cases, the Faculty which finds out the Means, and rightly applies them to discover Certainty in the one, and Probability in the other, is that which we call Reason. For as Reason perceives the necessary, and indubitable connexion of all the *Ideas* or Proofs one to another, in each step of any Demonstration that produces Knowledge: so it likewise perceives the probable connexion of all the *Ideas* or Proofs one to another, in every step of a Discourse, to which it will think Assent due. This is the lowest degree of that, which can be truly called Reason. For where the Mind does not perceive this probable connexion; where it does not discern, whether there be any such connexion, or no, there Men's Opinions are not the product of Judgment, or the Consequence of Reason; but the effects of Chance and Hazard, of a Mind floating at all Adventures, without choice, and without direction.

§ 3. So that we may in *Reason* consider these *four Degrees*; the first and highest, is the discovering, and finding out of Proofs; the second, the regular and methodical Disposition of them, and laying them in a clear and fit Order, to make their Connexion and Force be plainly and easily perceived; the third is the perceiving their Connexion; and the fourth, the making a right conclusion. These several degrees may be observed in any mathematical Demonstration: it being one thing to perceive the connexion of each part, as the Demonstration is made by another; another to perceive the dependence of the conclusion on all the parts; a third to make out a Demonstration clearly and neatly ones self, and something different from all these, to

§ 3. *Its four parts.*

(32) [*2nd*] the] **1–4** | a **5**. (**Coste** 'le quatriéme à tirer')

have first found out those intermediate *Ideas* or Proofs by which it is made.

§ 4. There is one thing more, which I shall desire to be considered concerning Reason; and that is, whether *Syllogism*, as is generally thought, be the proper instrument of it, and the usefullest way of exercising this Faculty. The Causes I have to doubt, are these.

First, Because Syllogism serves our Reason, but in one only of the forementioned parts of it; and that is, to shew the connexion of the Proofs in any one instance, and no more: but in this, it is of no great use, since the Mind can perceive such Connexion where it really is, as easily, nay, perhaps, better without it.

If we will observe the Actings of our own Minds, we shall find, that we reason best and clearest, when we only observe the connexion of the Proofs, without reducing our Thoughts to any Rule of Syllogism. And therefore we may take notice, that there are many Men that Reason exceeding clear and rightly, who know not how to make a Syllogism. He that will look into many parts of *Asia* and *America*, will find Men reason there, perhaps, as acutely as himself, who yet never heard of a Syllogism, nor can reduce any one Argument to those Forms: and I believe scarce any one ever makes Syllogisms in reasoning within himself. Indeed Syllogism is made use of on occasion to discover a Fallacy hid in a rhetorical Flourish, or cunningly wrapp'd up in a smooth Period; and stripping an Absurdity of the Cover of Wit, and good Language, shew it in its naked Deformity. But the weakness or fallacy of such a loose Discourse it shews, by the artificial Form it is put into, only to those who have throughly studied *Mode and Figure*, and have so examined the many Ways, that three Propositions may be put together, as to know which of them does certainly conclude right, and which not, and upon what grounds it is that they do so. All who have so far considered *Syllogism*, as to see the Reason, why, in three Propositions laid together in one Form, the Conclusion will be certainly right, but in another, not certainly so, I grant are certain of the Conclusion they draw from the Premisses in the allowed *Modes* and *Figures*: But they who have not so far looked into those Forms, are not sure by

§ 4. *Syllogism not the great Instrument of Reason.*

---

(14) Proofs] **1–4** | Proof **5** our Thoughts] **2–5** | it **1** (20–1) : and . . . himself] *add.* **2–5** (21–2) Syllogism . . . occasion] **4–5** | sometimes it may serve **1–3** (*likewise* **Coste**) (25)–671(24) the . . . Syllogizing:] *add.* **4–5**

Virtue of Syllogism, that the Conclusion certainly follows from the Premisses; They only take it to be so by an implicit Faith in their Teachers, and a Confidence in those Forms of Argumentation; but this is still but believing, not being certain. Now if of all Mankind, those who can make Syllogisms are extremely few in comparison of those who cannot, and if of those few who have been taught Logick, there is but a very small Number, who do any more than believe that Syllogisms in the allowed *Modes* and *Figures* do conclude right, without knowing certainly that they do so; If Syllogisms must be taken for the only proper instrument of reason and means of Knowledge, it will follow, that before *Aristotle* there was not one Man that did or could know any thing by Reason; and that since the invention of Syllogisms, there is not one of Ten Thousand that doth.

But God has not been so sparing to Men to make them barely two-legged Creatures, and left it to *Aristotle* to make them Rational, *i.e.* those few of them that he could get so to examine the Grounds of Syllogisms, as to see, that in above threescore ways, that three Propositions may be laid together, there are but about fourteen wherein one may be sure that the Conclusion is right, and upon what ground it is, that in these few the Conclusion is certain, and in the other not. God has been more bountiful to Mankind than so. He has given them a Mind that can reason without being instructed in Methods of Syllogizing: The Understanding is not taught to reason by these Rules; it has a native Faculty to perceive the Coherence, or Incoherence of its *Ideas*, and can range them right, without any such perplexing Repetitions. I say not this any way to lessen *Aristotle*, whom I look on as one of the greatest Men amongst the Antients; whose large Views, acuteness and penetration of Thought, and strength of Judgment, few have equalled: And who in this very invention of Forms of Argumentation, wherein the Conclusion may be shewn to be rightly inferred, did great service against those, who were not ashamed to deny any thing. And I readily own, that all right reasoning may be reduced to his Forms of Syllogism. But yet I think without any diminution to him I may truly say, that they are not the only, nor the best way of reasoning, for the leading of those into Truth who are willing to find it, and desire to make the best use they may of their Reason, for the

(24) *v.* 670(25), n. Understanding] **4–5** | Mind **1–3** (27)–672(4) I . . . *Ideas*.] *add.* **4–5** (30) Thought] **4er–5** | Thoughts **4**

attainment of Knowledge. And he himself it is plain, found out some Forms to be conclusive, and others not, not by the Forms themselves but by the original way of Knowledge, *i.e.* by the visible agreement of *Ideas*. Tell a Country Gentlewoman, that the Wind is South-West, and the Weather louring, and like to rain, and she will easily understand, 'tis not safe for her to go abroad thin clad, in such a day, after a Fever: she clearly sees the probable Connexion of all these, *viz.* South-West-Wind, and Clouds, Rain, wetting, taking Cold, Relapse, and danger of Death, without tying them together in those artificial and cumbersome Fetters of several Syllogisms, that clog and hinder the Mind, which proceeds from one part to another quicker and clearer without them: and the Probability which she easily perceives in Things thus in their native State, would be quite lost, if this Argument were managed learnedly, and proposed in Mode and Figure. For it very often confounds the connexion: and, I think, every one will perceive in mathematical Demonstrations, that the Knowledge gained thereby, comes shortest and clearest without Syllogism.

Inference is looked on as the great Act of the Rational Faculty, and so it is when it is rightly made; But the Mind, either very desirous to inlarge its Knowledge, or very apt to favour the Sentiments it has once imbibed, is very forward to make Inferences, and therefore often makes too much hast, before it perceives the connexion of the *Ideas* that must hold the Extremes together.

To infer is nothing but by virtue of one Proposition laid down as true, to draw in another as true, *i.e.* to see or suppose such a connexion of the two *Ideas*, of the inferr'd Proposition. *v.g.* Let this be the Proposition laid down, *Men shall be punished in another World*, and from thence be inferred this other, *then Men can determine themselves.* The Question now is to know, whether the Mind has made this Inference right or no; if it has made it by finding out the intermediate *Ideas*, and taking a view of the connexion of them, placed in a due order, it has proceeded rationally, and made a right Inference. If it has done it without such a View, it has not so much made an Inference that will hold, or an Inference of right Reason, as shewn a willingness to have it be, or be taken for such. But in neither Case is it *Syllogism* that discovered those *Ideas*, or shewed the connexion of them, for they must be both found out, and the connexion every

(4) *v.* 671(27), n. (19)–677(15) Inference . . . them.] *add.* **4–5** (27) two *Ideas*] **Coste** 'certaines Idées moyennes qui montrent la connexion de deux Idées'

where perceived, before they can rationally be made use of in *Syllogism*: unless it can be said, that any *Idea* without considering what connexion it hath with the two other, whose Agreement should be shewn by it, will do well enough in a *Syllogism*, and may be taken at a venture for the *Medius Terminus*, to prove any Conclusion. But this no body will say, because it is by vertue of the perceived Agreement of the intermediate *Idea* with the Extremes, that the Extremes are concluded to agree, and therefore each intermediate *Idea* must be such, as in the whole Chain hath a visible connexion with those two it is placed between, or else thereby, the Conclusion cannot be inferr'd or drawn in; for wherever any Link of the Chain is loose, and without connexion, there the whole strength of it is lost, and it hath no force to infer or draw in any thing. In the instance above mentioned, what is it shews the force of the Inference, and consequently the reasonableness of it, but a view of the connexion of all the intermediate *Ideas* that draw in the Conclusion, or Proposition inferr'd. *v.g. Men shall be punished,——God the punisher,——just Punishment,——the Punished guilty——could have done otherwise——Freedom——self-determination*, by which Chain of *Ideas* thus visibly link'd together in train, *i.e.* each intermediate *Idea* agreeing on each side with those two it is immediately placed between, the *Ideas* of Men and self-determination appear to be connected, *i.e.* this Proposition *Men can determine themselves* is drawn in, or inferr'd from this *that they shall be punished in the other World*. For here the Mind seeing the connexion there is between the *Idea of Men's Punishment in the other World*, and the *Idea of God punishing*, between *God punishing*, and *the Justice of the Punishment*; between *Justice of Punishment* and *Guilt*, between *Guilt* and a *Power to do otherwise*, between a *Power to do otherwise* and *Freedom*, and between *Freedom* and *self-determination*, sees the connexion between *Men*, and *self-determination*.

Now I ask whether the connexion of the Extremes be not more clearly seen in this simple and natural Disposition, than in the perplexed Repetitions, and Jumble of five or six *Syllogisms*. I must beg Pardon for calling it Jumble, till some Body shall put these *Ideas* into so many *Syllogisms*, and then say, that they are less jumbled, and their connexion more visible, when they are transposed and repeated, and spun out to a greater length in artificial Forms; than in that

(18) *could have done*] **Coste** '*Il auroit pû faire*' (22) connected,] **5** | connected. **4**

short natural plain order, they are laid down in here, wherein every one may see it; and wherein they must be seen, before they can be put into a Train of *Syllogisms*. For the natural order of the connecting *Ideas* must direct the order of the *Syllogisms*, and a Man must see the connexion of each intermediate *Idea* with those that it connects, before he can with Reason make use of it in a *Syllogism*. And when all those Syllogisms are made, neither those that are, nor those that are not Logicians will see the force of the Argumentation, *i.e.* the connexion of the Extremes one jot the better. [For those that are not Men of Art, not knowing the true Forms of *Syllogism*, nor the Reasons of them, cannot know whether they are made in right and conclusive *Modes* and *Figures* or no, and so are not at all helped by the Forms they are put into, though by them the natural order, wherein the Mind could judge of their respective connexion, being disturb'd renders the illation much more incertain than without them.] And as for Logicians themselves they see the connexion of each intermediate *Idea* with those it stands between (on which the Force of the inference depends) as well before as after the *Syllogism* is made, or else they do not see it at all. For a *Syllogism* neither shews nor strengthens the connexion of any two *Ideas* immediately put together, but only by the connexion seen in them shews what connexion the Extremes have one with another. But what connexion the intermediate has with either of the Extremes in that Syllogism, that no Syllogism does or can shew. That the Mind only doth, or can perceive as they stand there in that *juxta-position* only by its own view, to which the Syllogistical Form it happens to be in, gives no help or light at all; it only shews that if the intermediate *Idea* agrees with those it is on both sides immediately applied to, then those two remote ones, or as they are called *Extremes* do certainly agree, and therefore the immediate connexion of each *Idea* to that which it is applyed to on each side, on which the force of the reasoning depends, is as well seen before as after the *Syllogism* is made, or else he that makes the Syllogism could never see it at all. This as has been already observed, is seen only by the Eye or the perceptive Faculty of the Mind, taking a view of them laid together, in a *juxta-position*, which view of any two it has equally, whenever they are laid together in any Proposition, whether that Proposition be placed as a *Major*, or a *Minor*, in a *Syllogism* or no.

(8) Argumentation,] **5** | Argumentation. **4** (9–16) *Square brackets in* **4–5**; *no brackets in* **Coste.** (19) at] **4**; *om.* **5**

Of what use then are *Syllogisms*? I answer, Their chief and main use is in the Schools, where Men are allowed without Shame to deny the Agreement of *Ideas*, that do manifestly agree; or out of the Schools to those, who from thence have learned without shame to deny the connexion of *Ideas*, which even to themselves is visible. But to an ingenuous Searcher after Truth, who has no other aim, but to find it, there is no need of any such Form, to force the allowing of the Inference: the Truth and reasonableness of it is better seen in ranging of the *Ideas* in a simple and plain order; And hence it is, that Men in their own inquiries after Truth never use *Syllogisms* to convince themselves, (or in teaching others to instruct willing Learners). Because, before they can put them into a *Syllogism* they must see the connexion, that is between the intermediate *Idea*, and the two other *Ideas* it is set between, and applied to, to shew their Agreement, and when they see that, they see whether the inference be good or no, and so *Syllogism* comes too late to settle it. For to make use again of the former Instance; I ask whether the Mind considering the *Idea* of Justice, placed as an intermediate *Idea* between the *punishment* of Men, and the guilt of the punished, (and till it does so consider it, the Mind cannot make use of it as a *medius terminus*) does not as plainly see the force and strength of the Inference, as when it is formed into Syllogism. To shew it in a very plain and easy Example; let *Animal* be the intermediate *Idea* or *medius terminus* that the Mind makes use of to shew the connexion of *Homo* and *vivens*: I ask whether the Mind does not more readily and plainly see that connexion, in the simple and proper Position of the connecting *Idea* in the middle; thus,

Homo—Animal—vivens,

Than in this perplexed one,

Animal—vivens—Homo—Animal.

Which is the Position these *Ideas* have in a Syllogism, to shew the connexion between *Homo* and *vivens* by the intervention of *Animal*.

Indeed Syllogism is thought to be of necessary use, even to the Lovers of Truth, to shew them the Fallacies, that are often concealed in florid, witty, or involved Discourses. But that this is a mistake will appear, if we consider, that the Reason why sometimes Men, who sincerely aim at Truth, are imposed upon by such loose,

(10) own] *add.* **5** (*likewise* **Coste**) (11) , (or . . . Learners)] *add.* **5** (*likewise* **Coste**). (*Here square brackets are used in* **5**, *but no brackets in* **Coste**.) (24): I] **5** | ; I **4** (35) , or] *edit.* | or **4–5**

and as they are called Rhetorical Discourses, is that their Phancies being struck with some lively metaphorical Representations, they neglect to observe, or do not easily perceive what are the true *Ideas*, upon which the Inference depends. Now to shew such Men the weakness of such an Argumentation, there needs no more but to strip it of the superfluous *Ideas*, which blended and confounded with those on which the Inference depends, seem to shew a connexion, where there is none; or at least do hinder the discovery of the want of it; and then to lay the naked *Ideas* on which the force of the Argumentation depends, in their due order, in which Position the Mind taking a view of them, sees what connexion they have, and so is able to judge of the Inference, without any need of a Syllogism at all.

I grant that *Mode* and *Figure* is commonly made use of in such Cases, as if the detection of the incoherence of such loose Discourses, were wholly owing to the Syllogistical Form; and so I my self formerly thought, till upon a stricter Examination, I now find that laying the intermediate *Ideas* naked in their due order, shews the incoherence of the Argumentation better, than Syllogism; not only as subjecting each Link of the Chain, to the immediate view of the Mind in its proper place, whereby its connexion is best observed; But also because Syllogism shews the incoherence only to those (who are not one of Ten Thousand) who perfectly understand *Mode* and *Figure*, and the Reason upon which those Forms are established; whereas a due and orderly placing of the *Ideas*, upon which the Inference is made, makes every one both Logician or not Logician, who understands the Terms, and hath the Faculty to perceive the Agreement, or Disagreement of such *Ideas* (without which, in or out of Syllogism, he cannot perceive the strength or weakness, coherence or incoherence of the Discourse) see the want of Connexion in the Argumentation, and the absurdity of the Inference.

And thus I have known a Man unskilful in Syllogism, who at first hearing could perceive the weakness and inconclusiveness of a long artificial and plausible Discourse, wherewith others better skill'd in Syllogism have been misled. And I believe there are few of my Readers who do not know such. And indeed if it were not so, the Debates of most Princes Councels, and the Business of Assemblies would be in danger to be mismanaged, since those who are relied upon, and have usually a great stroke in them, are not always such, who have the good luck to be perfectly knowing in the Forms of

(13) grant] **5** | Grant **4** (32) inconclusiveness] **4** | Inclusiveness **5**

Syllogism, or expert at *Mode* and *Figure*. And if Syllogism were the only, or so much as the surest way to detect the Fallacies of artificial Discourses; I do not think that all Mankind, even Princes in Matters that concern their Crowns and Dignities, are so much in Love with Falshood and Mistake, that they would every where have neglected to bring Syllogism into the debates of Moment; or thought it ridiculous, so much as to offer them in affairs of Consequence; a plain Evidence to me, that Men of Parts and Penetration who were not idly to dispute at their Ease, but were to act according to the result of their debates, and often pay for their mistakes with their Heads or Fortunes, found those scholastique Forms were of little use to discover Truth or Fallacy, whilst both the one and the other might be shewn, and better shewn without them, to those, who would not refuse to see, what was visibly shewn them.

Secondly, Another reason that makes me doubt whether Syllogism be the only proper Instrument of Reason in the discovery of Truth, is, that of whatever use *Mode* and *Figure* is pretended to be in the laying open of Fallacy (which has been above consider'd) those scholastique Forms of Discourse, are not less liable to Fallacies, than the plainer ways of Argumentation: And for this I appeal to common observation, which has always found these artificial Methods of reasoning more adapted to catch and intangle the Mind, that to instruct and inform the Understanding. And hence it is, that Men even when they are bafled and silenced in this Scholastique way, are seldom or never convinced, and so brought over to the conquering side; they perhaps acknowledge their Adversary to be the more skilful Disputant; but rest nevertheless perswaded of the truth on their side; and go away, worsted as they are, with the same Opinion they brought with them, which they could not do, if this way of Argumentation carryed Light and Conviction with it, and made Men see where the truth lay. And therefore Syllogism has been thought more proper for the attaining Victory in dispute,

(1) at] **4** | in **5**. (**Coste** *lacks* 'or expert . . . *Figure*'.) (6) into] **5** (*likewise* **Coste**) | into to **4** (15) *v.* 672(19), n. (16) *Secondly*] **1–3** | Secondly **4–5** (16)–678(4) Another . . . them.] **4–5** | Because though Syllogism serves to shew the Force or Fallacy of an Argument, made use of in the usual way of discoursing, by supplying the absent Proposition, and so setting it before the view in a clear Light; yet it no less engages the Mind in the perplexity of obscure, equivocal, and fallacious Terms, wherewith this artificial way of Reasoning always abounds: it being adapted more to the attaining of Victory in Dispute, than the discovery or confirmation of Truth in fair Enquiries. **1–3** (25) even] **4er–5** | ever **4** (28) be the] **4er–5** | the be **4**

than for the Discovery or Confirmation of Truth, in fair Enquiries. And if it be certain, that Fallacy can be couch'd in Syllogisms, as it cannot be denied, it must be something else, and not Syllogism that must discover them.

I have had Experience, how ready some Men are, when all the use which they have been wont to ascribe to any thing, is not allow'd, to cry out, that I am for laying it wholly aside. But to prevent such unjust and groundless Imputations, I tell them, that I am not for taking away any helps to the Understanding, in the attainment of Knowledge. And if Men skill'd in, and used to Syllogisms, find them assisting to their Reason in the discovery of Truth, I think they ought to make use of them. All that I aim at is, that they should not ascribe more to these Forms than belongs to them; And think that Men have no use, or not so full a use of their reasoning Faculty without them. Some Eyes want Spectacles to see things clearly and distinctly; but let not those that use them therefore say, no body can see clearly without them: Those who do so, will be thought in favour of Art (which perhaps they are beholding to) a little too much to depress and discredit Nature. Reason by its own Penetration where it is strong, and exercised, usually sees, quicker and clearer without Syllogism. If use of those Spectacles has so dimmed its Sight, that it cannot without them see consequences or inconsequences in Argumentation, I am not so unreasonable as to be against the using them. Every one knows what best fits his own Sight. But let him not thence conclude all in the dark, who use not just the same Helps that he finds a need of.

§ 5. But however it be in Knowledge, I think I may truly say, it is of *far* less, or *no use* at all *in Probabilities*. For the Assent there, being to be determined by the preponderancy, after a due weighing of all the Proofs, with all Circumstances on both sides, nothing is so unfit to assist the Mind in that, as Syllogism; which running away with one assumed Probability, or one topical Argument, pursues that till it has led the Mind quite out of sight of the thing under Consideration; and forcing it upon some remote Difficulty, holds it fast there, intangled perhaps, and as it were, manacled in the Chain of Syllogisms, without allowing it the liberty, much less affording

§ 5. *Helps little in Demonstration, less in Probability.*

---

(4) *v.* 677(16), n. (5–26) I . . . of.] *add.* **4–5** (18) of] **4** | with **5** (20) exercised,] **5** | exercised **4** (24) one] **4er–5** | own **4**

it the Helps requisite to shew on which side, all Things considered, is the greater Probability.

§ 6. But let it help us (as, perhaps, may be said) in convincing Men of their Errors and Mistakes: (and yet I would fain see the Man, that was forced out of his Opinion by dint of *Syllogism*,) yet still it *fails our Reason in* that part, which if not its highest Perfection, is yet certainly its hardest Task, and that which we most need its help in; and that is *the finding out of Proofs, and making new Discoveries*. The Rules of *Syllogism* serve not to furnish the Mind with those intermediate *Ideas*, that may shew the connexion of remote ones. This way of reasoning discovers no new Proofs, but is the Art of marshalling, and ranging the old ones we have already. The 47th. Proposition of the First Book of *Euclid* is very true; but the discovery of it, I think, not owing to any Rules of common Logick. A Man knows first, and then he is able to prove syllogistically. So that *Syllogism* comes after Knowledge, and then a Man has little or no need of it. But 'tis chiefly by the finding out those *Ideas* that shew the connexion of distant ones, that our stock of Knowledge is increased, and that useful Arts and Sciences are advanced. *Syllogism*, at best, is but the Art of fencing with the little Knowledge we have, without making any Addition to it. And if a Man should employ his Reason all this way, he will not do much otherwise, than he, who having got some Iron out of the Bowels of the Earth, should have it beaten up all into Swords, and put it into his Servants Hands to fence with, and bang one another. Had the King of *Spain* imployed the Hands of his People, and his *Spanish* Iron so, he had brought to Light but little of that Treasure, that lay so long hid in the dark Entrails of *America*. And I am apt to think, that he who shall employ all the force of his Reason only in brandishing of *Syllogisms*, will discover very little of that Mass of Knowledge, which lies yet concealed in the secret recesses of Nature; and which I am apt to think, native rustick Reason (as it formerly has done) is likelier to open a way to, and add to the common stock of Mankind, rather than any scholastick Proceeding by the strict Rules of Mode and Figure.

§ 7. I doubt not nevertheless, but there are ways to be found to assist our Reason in this most useful part; and this the judicious

§ 6. *Serves not to increase our Knowledge, but fence with it.* § 7. *Other helps should be sought.*

(3) , may] **1–3** | may **4–5** (4) and] **4–5** | or **1–3** (*likewise* **Coste**) (5) Opinion] **5** | Opinions **1–4** (*l. below* 36: § 6.) *In* **Coste**, *this marginal summary is applied to* §§ *6 and 7.*

Hooker encourages me to say, who in his *Eccl. Pol. l.* 1. §. 6. speaks thus: *If there might be added the right helps of true Art and Learning, (which helps I must plainly confess, this Age of the World carrying the Name of a learned Age, doth neither much know, nor generally regard,) there would undoubtedly be almost as much difference in Maturity of Judgment between Men therewith inured, and that which now Men are, as between Men that are now, and Innocents.* I do not pretend to have found, or discovered here any of those *right helps of Art*, this great Man of deep Thought mentions: but this is plain, that *Syllogism*, and the Logick now in Use, which were as well known in his days, can be none of those he means. It is sufficient for me, if by a Discourse, perhaps, something out of the way, I am sure as to me wholly new, and unborrowed, I shall have given Occasion to others, to cast about for new Discoveries, and to seek in their own Thoughts, for those *right Helps of Art*, which will scarce be found, I fear, by those who servilely confine themselves to the Rules and Dictates of others. For beaten Tracts lead these sort of Cattel, (as an observing *Roman* calls them,) whose Thoughts reach only to Imitation, *non quo eundum est, sed quo itur.** But I can be bold to say, that this Age is adorned with some Men of that Strength of Judgment, and Largeness of Comprehension, that if they would employ their Thoughts on this Subject, could open new and undiscovered Ways to the Advancement of Knowledge.

§ 8. Having here had an occasion to speak of *Syllogism* in general, and the Use of it, in Reasoning, and the Improvement of our Knowledge, 'tis fit, before I leave this Subject, to take notice of one manifest Mistake in the Rules of *Syllogism*; *viz.* That no Syllogistical Reasoning can be right and conclusive, but what has, at least, one general Proposition in it. As if we could not *reason*, and have Knowledge *about Particulars*. Whereas, in truth, the Matter rightly considered, the immediate Object of all our Reasoning and Knowledge, is nothing but Particulars. Every Man's Reasoning and Knowledge, is only about the *Ideas* existing in his own Mind, which are truly, every one of them, particular Existences: and our Knowledge and Reasoning about other Things, is only as they correspond with those

§ 8. *We reason about Particulars.*

---

(9) Thought] **5** | Thoughts **1–4**. (**Coste** 'avoit l'Esprit si pénétrant') (24) an] *add.* **5**

* Horace, *Epistles*, I, 19.

our particular *Ideas*. So that the Perception of the Agreement, or Disagreement of our particular *Ideas*, is the whole and utmost of all our Knowledge. Universality is but accidental to it, and consists only in this, That the particular *Ideas*, about which it is, are such, as more than one particular Thing can correspond with, and be represented by. But the Perception of the Agreement, or Disagreement of any two *Ideas*, and consequently, our Knowledge, is equally clear and certain, whether either, or both, or neither of those *Ideas* be capable of representing more real Beings than one, or no. One thing more I crave leave to offer about Syllogism, before I leave it, *viz*. May one not upon just Ground enquire whether the Form Syllogism now has, is that which in Reason it ought to have? For the *Medius Terminus* being to joyn the Extremes, *i.e.* the intermediate *Ideas* by its Intervention, to shew the Agreement or Disagreement of the two in Question, would not the Position of the *Medius Terminus* be more natural, and shew the Agreement or Disagreement of the Extremes clearer and better, if it were placed in the Middle between them? Which might be easily done by transposing the Propositions, and making the *Medius Terminus* the predicate of the First, and the Subject of the Second. As thus,

Omnis Homo est Animal,
Omne Animal est vivens,
Ergo omnis Homo est vivens.

Omne corpus est extensum et solidum,
Nullum extensum et solidum est pura extensio,
Ergo corpus non est pura extensio.

I need not trouble my Reader with Instances in *Syllogisms*, whose conclusions are particular. The same Reason holds for the same form in them, as well as in the general.

§ 9. *Reason*, Though it penetrates into the Depths of the Sea and Earth, elevates our Thoughts as high as the Stars, and leads us through the vast Spaces, and large Rooms of this mighty Fabrick, yet it comes far short of the real Extent of even corporeal Being; and there are many Instances wherein it *fails us*: As,

§ 9. *First, Reason fails us for want of* Ideas.

(9–29) One . . . general.] *add.* **4–5**

First, It perfectly fails us, *where our* Ideas *fail*. It neither does, nor can extend it self farther than they do. And therefore, where-ever we have no *Ideas*, our Reasoning stops, and we are at an End of our Reckoning: And if at any time we reason about Words, which do not stand for any *Ideas*, 'tis only about those Sounds, and nothing else.

§ 10. *Secondly*, Our Reason is often puzled, and at a loss, *because of the obscurity, Confusion, or Imperfection of the* Ideas *it is employed about*; and there we are involved in Difficulties and Contradictions. Thus, not having any perfect *Idea* of the least Extension of Matter, nor of Infinity, we are at a loss about the Divisibility of Matter; but having perfect, clear, and distinct *Ideas* of Number, our Reason meets with none of those inextricable Difficulties in Numbers, nor finds it self involved in any Contradictions about them. Thus, we having but imperfect *Ideas* of the Operations of our Minds, and of the Beginning of Motion or Thought how the Mind produces either of them in us, and much imperfecter yet, of the Operation of GOD, run into great Difficulties about free created Agents, which Reason cannot well extricate it self out of.

§ 11. *Thirdly*, Our Reason is often at a stand, *because it perceives not those* Ideas, *which could serve to shew the certain or probable Agreement, or Disagreement of any two other* Ideas: and in this, some Men's Faculties far out-go others. Till *Algebra*, that great Instrument and Instance of Humane Sagacity, was discovered, Men, with Amazement, looked on several of the Demonstrations of ancient Mathematicians, and could scarce forbear to think the finding several of those Proofs to be something more than humane.

§ 12. *Fourthly*, The Mind *by proceeding upon false Principles* is often engaged in Absurdities and Difficulties, brought into Straits and Contradictions, without knowing how to free it self: And in that case it is in vain to implore the help of Reason, unless it be to discover the falshood, and reject the influence of those wrong Principles. Reason is so far from clearing the Difficulties which the

§ 10. *Secondly, Because of obscure and imperfect* Ideas. § 11. *Thirdly, For want of intermediate* Ideas. § 12. *Fourthly, Because of wrong Principles.*

---

(14) Minds,] **2–5** (';' **2–3**) | Minds upon our Bodies or Thoughts; **1** (15) Motion] **2–5** | either Motion **1** how . . . them] *add.* **2–5** (25) several] **4–5** | some **1–3** (26) to be something more] **4–5** | , more **1–3** (27) The . . . *Principles*] **4–5** | Reason **1–3** (29–32) self . . . Reason] **4–5** | self, *by proceeding upon false Principles*; which, being followed, lead Men into Contradictions to themselves, and Inconsistency in their own Thoughts; which their Reason **1–3** (32)–683(1) [*1st*] the . . . into] *add.* **4–5**

building upon false foundations brings a Man into, that if he will pursue it, it entangles him the more, and engages him deeper in Perplexities.

§ 13. *Fifthly*, As obscure and imperfect *Ideas* often involve our Reason, so, upon the same Ground, do *dubious Words*, and uncertain Signs, *often*, in Discourses and Arguings, when not warily attended to, *puzzle Men's Reason*, and bring them to a *Non-plus*. But these two latter are our Fault, and not the Fault of Reason. But yet, the Consequences of them are nevertheless obvious; and the Perplexities, or Errors, they fill Men's Minds with, are every where observable.

§ 14. Some of the *Ideas* that are in the Mind, are so there, that they can be, by themselves, immediately compared, one with another: And in these, the Mind is able to perceive, that they agree or disagree, as clearly, as that it has them. Thus the Mind perceives, that an Arch of a Circle is less than the whole Circle, as clearly as it does the *Idea* of a Circle: And this, therefore, as has been said, I call *Intuitive Knowledge*; which is certain, beyond all Doubt, and needs no Probation, nor can have any; this being the highest of all Humane Certainty. In this consists the Evidence of all those *Maxims*, which no Body has any Doubt about, but every Man (does not, as is said, only assent to, but) knows to be true, as soon as ever they are proposed to his Understanding. In the Discovery of, and Assent to these Truths, there is no Use of the discursive Faculty, *no need of Reasoning*, but they are known by a superior, and higher Degree of Evidence. And such, if I may guess at Things unknown, I am apt to think, that Angels have now, and the Spirits of just Men made perfect, shall have, in a future State, of Thousands of Things, which now, either wholly escape our Apprehensions, or which, our short-sighted Reason having got some faint Glimpse of, we, in the Dark, grope after.

§ 15. But though we have, here and there, a little of this clear Light, some Sparks of bright Knowledge: yet the greatest part of our *Ideas* are such, that we cannot discern their Agreement, or Disagreement, by an immediate Comparing them. And in all these, we have *Need of Reasoning*, and must, by Discourse and Inference,

§ 13. *Fifthly, Because of doubtful terms.* § 14. *Our highest degree of Knowledge is intuitive, without reasoning.* § 15. *The next is Demonstration by reasoning.*

(1) *v.* 682(32), n. he] **4–5** | they **1–3** (2) [*1st*] him] **4–5** | them **1–3** [*2nd*] him] **4–5** | them **1–3** (10) are] **4–5** | is **1–3** (17) Doubt] **1–3** | doubt **4–5** (19) *Maxims*] **2–5** | *Æternæ Veritates* **1** (24) *Reasoning*,] **4–5** | *Reason*; **1–3** (35) *Reasoning*,] **4–5** | our *Reason*; **1–3** (',' **3**)

make our Discoveries. Now of these, there are two sorts, which I shall take the liberty to mention here again.

First, Those whose Agreement, or Disagreement, though it cannot be seen by an immediate putting them together, yet may be examined by the Intervention of other *Ideas*, which can be compared with them. In this case when the Agreement, or Disagreement of the intermediate *Idea*, on both sides with those which we would compare, is plainly discerned, there it amounts to Demonstration, whereby Knowledge is produced, which though it be certain, yet it is not so easy, nor altogether so clear, as *Intuitive Knowledge*. Because in that there is barely one simple Intuition, wherein there is no room for any the least mistake or doubt: the Truth is seen all perfectly at once. In demonstration, 'tis true, there is Intuition too, but not altogether at once; for there must be a Remembrance of the Intuition of the Agreement of the *Medium*, or intermediate *Idea*, with that we compared it with before, when we compare it with the other: and where there be many *Mediums*, there the danger of the Mistake is the greater. For each Agreement, or Disagreement of the *Ideas* must be observed and seen in each step of the whole train, and retained in the Memory, just as it is, and the Mind must be sure that no part of what is necessary to make up the Demonstration is omitted, or overlooked. This makes some Demonstrations long and perplex'd, and too hard for those who have not strength of Parts distinctly to perceive, and exactly carry so many particulars orderly in their Heads. And even those, who are able to master such intricate Speculations, are fain sometimes to go over them again, and there is need of more than one review before they can arrive at Certainty. But yet where the Mind clearly retains the Intuition it had of the Agreement of any *Idea* with another, and that with a third, and that with a fourth, *etc.* there the Agreement of the first and the fourth is a Demonstration, and produces certain Knowledge, which may be called *Rational Knowledge*, as the other is *Intuitive*.

(6–14) . In . . . once;] **4–5** | ; wherein, if the Agreement, or Disagreement, be plainly discerned, of the intermediate *Ideas* on both sides, with those we would compare, there it is *Demonstration*; and it produces certain Knowledge, though not altogether so evident as the former: Because there is in the former, bare Intuition, but in these there is Intuition indeed, but not altogether at once; **1–3** (7) of the intermediate *Idea*] **Coste** 'des Idées moyennes' (15) or intermediate *Idea*,] *add.* **4–5** (18–28) . For . . . Certainty.] **4–5** | , and consequently it may be liable to the greater uncertainty. **1–3** (22) Demonstrations] **4** | Demonstration **5**

§ 16. *Secondly*, There are other *Ideas*, whose Agreement, or Disagreement, can no otherwise be judged of, but by the intervention of others, which have not a certain Agreement with the Extremes, but an usual or likely one: And in these it is, that the *Judgment* is properly exercised, which is the acquiescing of the Mind, that any *Ideas* do agree, by comparing them with such probable *Mediums*. This, though it never amounts to Knowledge, no not to that which is the lowest degree of it: yet sometimes the intermediate *Ideas* tie the Extremes so firmly together, and the Probability is so clear and strong, that Assent as necessarily follows it, as Knowledge does Demonstration. The great Excellency and Use of the Judgment, is to observe Right, and take a true estimate of the force and weight of each Probability; and then casting them up all right together, chuse that side, which has the over-balance.

§ 17. *Intuitive Knowledge*, is the perception of the certain Agreement, or Disagreement of two *Ideas* immediately compared together.

Rational Knowledge, is the perception of the certain Agreement, or Disagreement of any two *Ideas*, by the intervention of one or more other *Ideas*.

Judgment, is the thinking or taking two *Ideas* to agree, or disagree, by the intervention of one or more *Ideas*, whose certain Agreement, or Disagreement with them it does not perceive, but hath observed to be frequent and usual.

§ 18. Though the deducing one Proposition from another, or making *Inferences in Words*, be a great part of Reason, and that which it is usually employ'd about: yet the principal Act of Ratiocination is the finding the Agreement, or Disagreement of two *Ideas* one with another, by the intervention of a third. As a Man, by a Yard, finds two Houses to be of the same length, which could not be brought together to measure their Equality by *juxta*-position. Words have their Consequences, as the signs of such *Ideas*: and Things agree or disagree, as really they are; but we observe it only by our *Ideas*.

§ 19. Before we quit this Subject, it may be worth our while a little to reflect on *four sorts of Arguments*, that Men in their Reasonings

§ 16. *To supply the narrowness of this, we have nothing but Judgment upon probable reasoning.* § 17. *Intuition, Demonstration, Judgment.* § 18. *Consequences of Words, and Consequences of* Ideas. § 19. *Four sorts of Arguments. First,* Ad Verecundiam.

---

(7) This] **4–5** | And this **1–3** (9) together,] **4–5** | together; **1–3**

with others do ordinarily make use of, to prevail on their Assent; or at least so to awe them, as to silence their Opposition.

First, The first is, to alledge the Opinions of Men, whose Parts, Learning, Eminency, Power, or some other cause has gained a name, and settled their Reputation in the common esteem with some kind of Authority. When Men are established in any kind of Dignity, 'tis thought a breach of Modesty for others to derogate any way from it, and question the Authority of Men, who are in possession of it. This is apt to be censured, as carrying with it too much of Pride, when a Man does not readily yield to the Determination of approved Authors, which is wont to be received with respect and submission by others: and 'tis looked upon as insolence, for a Man to set up, and adhere to his own Opinion, against the current Stream of Antiquity; or to put it in the balance against that of some learned Doctor, or otherwise approved Writer. Whoever backs his Tenets with such Authorities, thinks he ought thereby to carry the Cause, and is ready to style it Impudence in any one, who shall stand out against them. This, I think, may be called *Argumentum ad Verecundiam*.

§ 20. *Secondly*, Another way that Men ordinarily use to drive others, and force them to submit their Judgments, and receive the Opinion in debate, is to require the Adversary to admit what they alledge as a Proof, or to assign a better. And this I call *Argumentum ad Ignorantiam*.

§ 21. *Thirdly*, A third way is, to press a Man with Consequences drawn from his own Principles, or Concessions. This is already known under the Name of *Argumentum ad Hominem*.

§ 22. *Fourthly*, The fourth is, the using of Proofs drawn from any of the Foundations of Knowledge, or Probability. This I call *Argumentum ad Judicium*. This alone of all the four, brings true Instruction with it, and advances us in our way to Knowledge. For, 1. It argues not another Man's Opinion to be right, because I out of respect, or any other consideration, but that of conviction, will not contradict him. 2. It proves not another Man to be in the right way, nor that I ought to take the same with him, because I know

§ 20. *Secondly*, Ad Ignorantiam. § 21. *Thirdly*, Ad Hominem. § 22. *Fourthly*, Ad Judicium.

---

(5) name . . . Reputation] **2–5** | Reputation to, and setled **1** (10) yield] **4–5** | veil **2–3** | vail **1** (10–11) Determination] **2–5** | Opinions **1** (11) is wont to be] **2–5** | have been **1** (20) § 20. *Secondly*,] **2–5** | *Secondly*, § 20. **1**

not a better. 3. Nor does it follow, that another Man is in the right way, because he has shewn me, that I am in the wrong. I may be modest, and therefore not oppose another Man's Persuasion: I may be ignorant, and not be able to produce a better: I may be in an Errour, and another may shew me that I am so. This may dispose me, perhaps, for the reception of Truth, but helps me not to it; That must come from Proofs, and Arguments, and Light arising from the nature of Things themselves, and not from my Shamefacedness, Ignorance, or Errour.

§ 23. By what has been before said of *Reason*, we may be able to make some guess at the distinction of Things, into those that are according to, above, and contrary to Reason. 1. *According to Reason* are such Propositions, whose Truth we can discover, by examining and tracing those *Ideas* we have from *Sensation* and *Reflexion*; and by natural deduction, find to be true, or probable. 2. *Above Reason* are such Propositions, whose Truth or Probability we cannot by Reason derive from those Principles. 3. *Contrary to Reason* are such Propositions, as are inconsistent with, or irreconcilable to our clear and distinct *Ideas*. Thus the Existence of one GOD is according to Reason; the Existence of more than one GOD, contrary to Reason; the Resurrection of the Dead, above Reason. Farther, as *Above Reason* may be taken in a double Sense, *viz.* either as signifying above Probability, or above Certainty: so in that large Sense also, Contrary to Reason, is, I suppose, sometimes taken.

§ 24. There is another use of the Word *Reason*, wherein it is *opposed to Faith*; which though it be in it self a very improper way of speaking, yet common Use has so authorized it, that it would be folly either to oppose or hope to remedy it: Only I think it may not be amiss to take notice, that however *Faith* be opposed to Reason, *Faith* is nothing but a firm Assent of the Mind: which if it be regulated, as is our Duty, cannot be afforded to any thing, but upon good Reason; and so cannot be opposite to it. He that believes, without having any Reason for believing, may be in love with his own Fancies; but neither seeks Truth as he ought, nor pays the Obedience due to his Maker, who would have him use those discerning

§ 23. *Above, contrary, and according to Reason.* § 24. *Reason and Faith not opposite.*

---

(21) Dead] **4–5** | Body after death **1–3** (21–3) Farther . . . so] **5** (*likewise* **Coste**) | Above Reason also may be taken in a double Sense, *viz.* Above Probability, or above Certainty: [; **1–3**] And **1–4** (30) Mind:] **4–5** | Mind; **1–3**

Faculties he has given him, to keep him out of Mistake and Errour. He that does not this to the best of his Power, however he sometimes lights on Truth, is in the right but by chance; and I know not whether the luckiness of the Accident will excuse the irregularity of his proceeding. This at least is certain, that he must be accountable for whatever Mistakes he runs into: whereas he that makes use of the Light and Faculties GOD has given him, and seeks sincerely to discover Truth, by those Helps and Abilities he has, may have this satisfaction in doing his Duty as a rational Creature, that though he should miss Truth, he will not miss the Reward of it. For he governs his Assent right, and places it as he should, who in any Case or Matter whatsoever, believes or disbelieves, according as Reason directs him. He that does otherwise, transgresses against his own Light, and misuses those Faculties, which were given him to no other end, but to search and follow the clearer Evidence, and greater Probability. But since Reason and Faith are by some Men opposed, we will so consider them in the following Chapter.

CHAPTER XVIII

Of Faith and Reason, and their distinct Provinces.

§ 1. IT has been above shewn, 1. That we are of necessity ignorant, and want Knowledge of all sorts, where we want *Ideas*. 2. That we are ignorant, and want rational Knowledge, where we want Proofs. 3. That we want general Knowledge and Certainty, as far as we want clear and determined specifick *Ideas*. 4. That we want Probability to direct our Assent in Matters where we have neither Knowledge of our own, nor Testimony of other Men to bottom our Reason upon.

From these Things thus premised, I think we may come to lay down the Measures and *Boundaries between Faith and Reason*: the want whereof, may possibly have been the cause, if not of great Disorders, yet at least of great Disputes, and perhaps Mistakes in the World. For till it be resolved, how far we are to be guided by Reason, and

§ 1. *Necessary to know their Boundaries.*

---

(14) those] **4–5** | the **1–3** (27) *Reason*:] **4–5** | *Reason*; **1–3**

how far by Faith, we shall in vain dispute, and endeavour to convince one another in Matters of Religion.

§ 2. I find every Sect, as far as Reason will help them, make use of it gladly: and where it fails them, they cry out, *'Tis matter of Faith, and above Reason.* And I do not see how they can argue with any one, or ever convince a Gainsayer, who makes use of the same Plea, without setting down strict Boundaries between *Faith* and *Reason*; which ought to be the first Point established in all Questions, where *Faith* has any thing to do.

Reason therefore here, as contradistinguished to *Faith*, I take to be the discovery of the Certainty or Probability of such Propositions or Truths, which the Mind arrives at by Deductions made from such *Ideas*, which it has got by the use of its natural Faculties, *viz.* by Sensation or Reflection.

Faith, on the other side, is the Assent to any Proposition, not thus made out by the Deductions of Reason; but upon the Credit of the Proposer, as coming from GOD, in some extraordinary way of Communication. This way of discovering Truths to Men we call *Revelation.*

§ 3. *First*, Then, I say, That *no Man inspired by GOD, can by any Revelation communicate to others any new simple Ideas* which they had not before from Sensation or Reflexion. For whatsoever Impressions he himself may have from the immediate hand of GOD, this Revelation, if it be of new simple *Ideas*, cannot be conveyed to another, either by Words, or any other signs. Because Words, by their immediate Operation on us, cause no other *Ideas*, but of their natural Sounds: and 'tis by the Custom of using them for Signs, that they excite, and revive in our Minds latent *Ideas*; but yet only such *Ideas*, as were there before. For Words seen or heard, re-call to our Thoughts those *Ideas* only, which to us they have been wont to be Signs of: But cannot introduce any perfectly new, and formerly unknown simple *Ideas*. The same holds in all other Signs, which cannot signify to us Things, of which we have before never had any *Idea* at all.

§ 2. *Faith and Reason what, as contradistinguished.* § 3. *No new simple* Idea *can be conveyed by Traditional Revelation.*

(5–6) argue . . . Gainsayer] **2–5** | ever be convinced by any **1** (12) Deductions] **1–4** | Deduction **5** (16) Reason;] **4–5** | Reason, **1–3** (17–19) from . . . *Revelation.*] **4–5** | immediately from GOD; which we call Revelation. **1–3** (31–2) , and . . . *Ideas*] **2–5** | simple *Ideas*, which were never there before **1** (34) *Idea*] **2, 4–5** | *Ideas* **1, 3** (*l. below* 34: § 3.) Idea] **3** | *Idea* **1–2, 4–5**

Thus whatever Things were discovered to St. *Paul*, when he was rapp'd up into the Third Heaven; whatever new *Ideas* his Mind there received, all the description he can make to others of that Place, is only this, That there are such Things, *as Eye hath not seen, nor Ear heard, nor hath it entred into the Heart of Man to conceive.** And, supposing GOD should discover to any one, supernaturally, a Species of Creatures inhabiting, For Example, *Jupiter*, or *Saturn* (for that it is possible there may be such, no body can deny) which had six Senses; and imprint on his Mind the *Ideas* convey'd to theirs by that sixth Sense, he could no more, by Words, produce in the Minds of other Men those *Ideas*, imprinted by that sixth Sense, than one of us could convey the *Idea* of any Colour, by the sound of Words into a Man, who having the other four Senses perfect, had always totally wanted the fifth of Seeing. For our simple *Ideas* then, which are the Foundation, and sole Matter of all our Notions, and Knowledge, we must depend wholly on our Reason, I mean, our natural Faculties; and can by no means receive them, or any of them, from *Traditional Revelation.* I say, *Traditional Revelation*, in distinction to *Original Revelation.* By the one, I mean that first Impression, which is made immediately by GOD, on the Mind of any Man, to which we cannot set any Bounds; and by the other, those Impressions delivered over to others in Words, and the ordinary ways of conveying our Conceptions one to another.

§ 4. *Secondly*, I say, that *the same Truths may be discovered, and conveyed down from Revelation, which are discoverable to us by Reason*, and by those *Ideas* we naturally may have. So GOD might, by Revelation, discover the Truth of any Proposition in *Euclid*; as well as Men, by the natural use of their Faculties, come to make the discovery themselves. In all Things of this Kind, there is little need or use of *Revelation*, GOD having furnished us with natural, and surer means to arrive at the Knowledge of them. For whatsoever Truth we come to the clear discovery of, from the Knowledge and Contemplation of our own *Ideas*, will always be certainer to us, than those

§ 4. *Traditional Revelation may make us know Propositions knowable also by Reason, but not with the same certainty that Reason doth.*

---

(12) sound] **1–4** | Sounds **5** (21) we cannot] **2–5** | , I pretend not to **1** (25) *Revelation*] **1–3, 5** | *revelation* **4** (25–6) and . . . have] *not in* **Coste** by those] **4–5** | those clear **1–3** (26) naturally] *add.* **2–5** (27) *Euclid*;] **4–5** | *Euclid*, **1–3** (29) Kind] **2–5** | Nature **1** (32) clear] *add.* **4–5** (33) *Ideas*] **4–5** | clear *Ideas* **1–3**

---

* 1 Cor. 2: 9.

which are conveyed to us by *Traditional Revelation*. For the Knowledge, we have, that this *Revelation* came at first from GOD, can never be so sure, as the Knowledge we have from the clear and distinct Perception of the Agreement, or Disagreement of our own *Ideas*, *v.g.* If it were revealed some Ages since, That the three Angles of a Triangle were equal to two right ones, I might assent to the Truth of that Proposition, upon the Credit of the Tradition, that it was revealed: But that would never amount to so great a Certainty, as the Knowledge of it, upon the comparing and measuring my own *Ideas* of two right Angles, and the three Angles of a Triangle. The like holds in matter of Fact, knowable by our Senses, *v.g.* the History of the Deluge is conveyed to us by Writings, which had their Original from Revelation: And yet no Body, I think, will say, he has as certain and clear a Knowledge of the Flood, as *Noah* that saw it; or that he himself would have had, had he then been alive, and seen it. For he has no greater an assurance than that of his Senses, that it is writ in the Book supposed writ by *Moses* inspired: But he has not so great an assurance, that *Moses* writ that Book, as if he had seen *Moses* write it. So that the assurance of its being a Revelation, is less still than the assurance of his Senses.

§ 5. In Propositions then, whose Certainty is built upon the clear Perception of the Agreement, or Disagreement of our *Ideas* attained either by immediate intuition, as in self-evident Propositions, or by evident deductions of Reason, in demonstrations, we need not the assistance of *Revelation*, as necessary to gain our Assent, and introduce them into our Minds. Because the natural ways of Knowledge could settle them there, or had done it already, which is the greatest assurance we can possibly have of any thing, unless where GOD immediately reveals it to us: And there too our Assurance can be no greater, than our Knowledge is, that it is a *Revelation* from GOD. But yet nothing, I think, can, under that Title, shake or over-rule plain Knowledge; or rationally prevail with any Man, to admit it for true, in a direct contradiction to the clear Evidence of his own Understanding. For since no evidence of our Faculties, by which we receive such *Revelations*, can exceed, if equal, the certainty

§ 5. *Revelation cannot be admitted against the clear evidence of Reason.*

(3–5) [*2nd*] the . . . If] **4–5** | our own clear and distinct *Ideas*. As if **1–3** (10) *Ideas*] **4–5** | clear *Ideas* **1–3** (11) knowable] **1–4** | knowably **5** (17) inspired] *add.* **2–5** (19) it.] **4–5** | it; **1–3** (21–4) the . . . demonstrations] **4–5** | clear, and perfect *Ideas*, and evident Deductions of Reason **1–3** (32) ; or] **2–5** | , nor **1** of our intuitive Knowledge, we can never receive for a Truth any thing, that is directly contrary to our clear and distinct Knowledge, *v.g.* The *Ideas* of one Body, and one Place, do so clearly agree; and the Mind has so evident a Perception of their Agreement, that we can never assent to a Proposition, that affirms the same Body to be in two distant Places at once, however it should pretend to the Authority of a divine *Revelation*: Since the Evidence, *First*, That we deceive not our selves in ascribing it to GOD; *Secondly*, That we understand it right, can never be so great, as the Evidence of our own intuitive Knowledge, whereby we discern it impossible, for the same Body to be in two Places at once. And therefore, *no Proposition can be received for Divine Revelation*, or obtain the Assent due to all such, *if it be contradictory to our clear intuitive Knowledge.* Because this would be to subvert the Principles, and Foundations of all Knowledge, Evidence, and Assent whatsoever: And there would be left no difference between Truth and Falshood, no measures of Credible and Incredible in the World, if doubtful Propositions shall take place before self-evident; and what we certainly know, give way to what we may possibly be mistaken in. In Propositions therefore contrary to the clear Perception of the Agreement or Disagreement of any of our *Ideas*, 'twill be in vain to urge them as Matters of *Faith*. They cannot move our Assent under that, or any other Title whatsoever. For *Faith* can never convince us of any Thing, that contradicts our Knowledge. Because though *Faith* be founded on the Testimony of GOD (who cannot lye) revealing any Proposition to us: yet we cannot have an assurance of the Truth of its being a divine Revelation, greater than our own Knowledge. Since the whole strength of the Certainty depends upon our Knowledge, that GOD revealed it, which in this Case, where the Proposition supposed revealed contradicts our Knowledge or Reason, will always have this Objection hanging to it, (*viz.*) that we cannot tell how to conceive that to come from GOD, the bountiful Author of our Being, which if received for true, must overturn all the Principles and

(3–7) *v.g.* . . . *Revelation*:] *not in* **Coste** (3) *Ideas*] **2–5** | *Idea* **1** do] **2–5** | does **1** (4) their Agreement] **2–5** | it **1** (7) : Since the Evidence,] **2–5** | , since the Evidence; **1** (10–11) for . . . once.] **Coste** 'que deux Idées dont nous voyons intuitivement la disconvenance, doivent être regardées ou admises comme ayant une parfaite convenance entr'elles.' (14) Because] **2–5** | Since **1** (15–16) : And . . . left] **2–5** | ; and leave **1** (16) , no] **2–5** | ; no **1** (17) , if] **1, 4–5** | ; if **2–3** (20–1) [*1st*] the . . . our] **4–5** | our distinct and clear **1–3** (25–6) (who . . . us:] **2–5** (';' **2–3**) | , (revealing any Proposition to us,) who cannot lie; **1** (33) the] **2–5** | our **1**

Foundations of Knowledge he has given us; render all our Faculties useless; wholly destroy the most excellent Part of his Workmanship, our Understandings; and put a Man in a Condition, wherein he will have less Light, less Conduct than the Beast that perisheth. For if the Mind of Man can never have a clearer (and, perhaps, not so clear) Evidence of any thing to be a divine *Revelation*, as it has of the Principles of its own Reason, it can never have a ground to quit the clear Evidence of its Reason, to give place to a Proposition, whose *Revelation* has not a greater Evidence, than those Principles have.

§ 6. Thus far a Man has use of Reason, and ought to hearken to it, even in immediate and original *Revelation*, where it is supposed to be made to himself: But to all those who pretend not to immediate *Revelation*, but are required to pay Obedience, and to receive the Truths revealed to others, which, by the Tradition of Writings, or Word of Mouth, are conveyed down to them, Reason has a great deal more to do, and is that only which can induce us to receive them. For Matter of Faith being only Divine Revelation, and nothing else, *Faith*, as we use the Word, (called commonly, *Divine Faith*) has to do with no Propositions, but those which are supposed to be divinely revealed. So that I do not see how those, who make Revelation alone the sole Object of *Faith*, can say, That it is a Matter of *Faith*, and not of *Reason*, to believe, That such or such a Proposition, to be found in such or such a Book, is of Divine Inspiration; unless it be revealed, That that Proposition, or all in that Book, was communicated by Divine Inspiration. Without such a *Revelation*, the believing, or not believing that Proposition, or Book, to be of Divine Authority, can never be Matter of *Faith*, but Matter of Reason; and such, as I must come to an Assent to, only by the use of my Reason, which can never require or enable me to believe that, which is contrary to it self: It being impossible for Reason, ever to procure any Assent to that, which to it self appears unreasonable.

In all Things therefore, where we have clear Evidence from our *Ideas*, and those Principles of Knowledge, I have above mentioned, *Reason* is the proper Judge; and *Revelation*, though it may in consenting with it, confirm its Dictates, yet cannot in such Cases, invalidate

§ 6. *Traditional Revelation much less.*

---

(1) he has given us] *add.* **2–5** (6) Evidence] **2–5** | an Evidence **1** (9–10) , than those Principles have] *add.* **2–5** (12) supposed to be] **2–5** | supposedly **1** (34) above mentioned] **1–3** | abovementioned **4** (*hyphened* **5**)

its Decrees: *Nor can we be obliged, where we have the clear and evident Sentence of Reason, to quit it, for the contrary Opinion, under a Pretence that it is Matter of Faith*; which can have no Authority against the plain and clear Dictates of *Reason.*

§ 7. But *Thirdly*, There being many Things, wherein we have very imperfect Notions, or none at all; and other Things, of whose past, present, or future Existence, by the natural Use of our Faculties, we can have no Knowledge at all; these, as being beyond the Discovery of our natural Faculties, and above *Reason*, are, when revealed, *the proper Matter of Faith*. Thus that part of the Angels rebelled against GOD, and thereby lost their first happy state: And that the dead shall rise, and live again: These, and the like, being beyond the Discovery of *Reason*, are purely Matters of *Faith*; with which *Reason* has, directly, nothing to do.

§ 8. But since GOD in giving us the light of *Reason* has not thereby tied up his own Hands from affording us, when he thinks fit, the light of *Revelation* in any of those Matters, wherein our natural Faculties are able to give a probable Determination, *Revelation*, where God has been pleased to give it, *must carry it, against the probable Conjectures of Reason*. Because the Mind, not being certain of the Truth of that it does not evidently know, but only yielding to the Probability that appears in it, is bound to give up its Assent to such a Testimony, which, it is satisfied, comes from one, who cannot err, and will not deceive. But yet, it still belongs to *Reason*, to judge of the Truth of its being a Revelation, and of the signification of the Words, wherein it is delivered. Indeed, if any thing shall be thought *Revelation*, which is contrary to the plain Principles of Reason, and the evident Knowledge the Mind has of its own clear and distinct *Ideas*; there *Reason* must be hearkned to, as to a Matter within its Province. Since a Man can never have so certain a Knowledge, that a Proposition which contradicts the clear Principles and Evidence of his own Knowledge, was divinely revealed, or that he understands the Words rightly, wherein it is delivered, as he has, that

§ 7. *Things above Reason.* § 8. *Or not contrary to Reason, if revealed, are matter of Faith.*

(3–4) ; which . . . *Reason*] *add.* **2–5** (12) dead] **4–5** | Bodies of Men **1–3** (13) , are] **1–3, 5** | are **4** (15–19) But . . . it,] **4–5** | But since all Things that are under the Character of Divine Revelation, are esteemed Matter of Faith; and there are amongst them, several Things, that fall under the *Examen* of Reason; and are such as we could judge of by our natural Faculties, without a Supernatural Revelation. In these, *Revelation* **1–3** (21–2) only . . . it] **4–5** | is only probably convinced of **1–3** (30) . Since] **4–5** | : since **1–3** the contrary is true, and so is bound to consider and judge of it as a Matter of Reason, and not swallow it, without Examination, as a Matter of *Faith*.

§ 9. *First*, Whatever Proposition is revealed, of whose Truth our Mind, by its natural Faculties and Notions, cannot judge, that is purely *Matter of Faith*, and above Reason.

Secondly, All Propositions, whereof the Mind, by the use of its natural Faculties, can come to determine and judge, from naturally acquired *Ideas*, are *Matter of Reason*; with this difference still, that in those, concerning which it has but an uncertain Evidence, and so is perswaded of their Truth, only upon probable Grounds, which still admit a Possibility of the contrary to be true, without doing violence to the certain Evidence of its own Knowledge, and overturning the Principles of all Reason, in such probable Propositions, I say, an evident *Revelation* ought to determine our Assent even against Probability. For where the Principles of Reason have not evidenced a Proposition to be certainly true or false, there clear *Revelation*, as another Principle of Truth, and Ground of Assent, may determine; and so it may be Matter of *Faith*, and be also above *Reason*. Because *Reason*, in that particular Matter, being able to reach no higher than Probability, *Faith* gave the Determination, where *Reason* came short; and *Revelation* discovered on which side the Truth lay.

§ 10. Thus far the Dominion of *Faith* reaches, and that without any violence, or hindrance to *Reason*; which is not injured, or disturbed, but assisted and improved, by new Discoveries of Truth, coming from the Eternal Fountain of all Knowledge. Whatever GOD hath revealed, is certainly true; no Doubt can be made of it. This is the proper Object of *Faith*: But whether it be a divine Revelation, or no, *Reason* must judge; which can never permit the Mind to reject a greater Evidence to embrace what is less evident, nor allow it to entertain Probability in opposition to Knowledge and Certainty. There can be no evidence, that any traditional Revelation is of divine Original, in the Words we receive it, and in the Sense we understand it, so clear, and so certain, as that of the

§ 9. *Revelation in Matters where Reason cannot judge, or but probably, ought to be hearkened to.* § 10. *In matters where Reason can afford certain knowledge that is to be hearkened to.*

(4) *First*] **2–5** | The Summ of all is, / *First* **1** (8) naturally] **4–5** | natural **1–3** (14) , in] **4–5** | : In **1–3** (17) evidenced] **2–5** | determined **1** (32–3) allow . . . Certainty] **4–5** | prefer less Certainty to the greater **1–3** (35) that] **5** (*likewise* **Coste**) | those **1–4**

Principles of Reason: And therefore, *Nothing that is contrary to, and inconsistent with the clear and self-evident Dictates of Reason, has a Right to be urged, or assented to, as a Matter of Faith, wherein Reason hath nothing to do.* Whatsoever is divine *Revelation*, ought to over-rule all our Opinions, Prejudices, and Interests, and hath a right to be received with full Assent: Such a Submission as this of our *Reason* to *Faith*, takes not away the Land-marks of Knowledge: This shakes not the Foundations of Reason, but leaves us that Use of our Faculties, for which they were given us.

§ 11. *If the Provinces of Faith and Reason are not kept distinct by these Boundaries*, there will, in matter of Religion, be no room for *Reason* at all; and those extravagant Opinions and Ceremonies, that are to be found in the several Religions of the World, will not deserve to be blamed. For, to this crying up of *Faith*, in opposition to *Reason*, we may, I think, in good measure, ascribe those Absurdities, that fill almost all the Religions which possess and divide Mankind. For Men having been principled with an Opinion, that they must not consult *Reason* in the Things of Religion, however apparently contradictory to common Sense, and the very Principles of all their Knowledge, have let loose their Fancies, and natural Superstition; and have been, by them, led into so strange Opinions, and extravagant Practices in Religion, that a considerate Man cannot but stand amazed at their Follies, and judge them so far from being acceptable to the great and wise GOD, that he cannot avoid thinking them ridiculous, and offensive to a sober, good Man. So that, in effect Religion which should most distinguish us from Beasts, and ought most peculiarly to elevate us, as rational Creatures, above Brutes, is that wherein Men often appear most irrational, and more senseless than Beasts themselves. *Credo, quia impossibile est*: *I believe, because it is impossible*,* might, in a good Man, pass for a Sally of Zeal; but would prove a very ill Rule for Men to chuse their Opinions, or Religion by.

§ 11. *If the boundaries be not set between Faith and Reason, no Enthusiasm, or extravagancy in Religion can be contradicted.*

(6) full] **5** | a full **1–4** (11) room] **1er–5** | more **1** (14) . For] **4–5** | : For **1–3** (20) Superstition;] **4–5** | Superstition, **1–3** (26–7) Religion . . . us] **4–5** | , that which most properly ought to distinguish us from Beasts, that wherein we are elevated **1–3** (27–8) , is . . . often] **4–5** | ; in that we **1–3**

* Cf. Tertullian, *De Carne Christi*, V.

CHAPTER XIX[1]

Of Enthusiasm.

§ 1. HE that would seriously set upon the search of Truth, ought in the first Place to prepare his Mind with a Love of it. For he that Loves it not, will not take much Pains to get it; nor be much concerned when he misses it. There is no Body in the Commonwealth of Learning, who does not profess himself a lover of Truth: and there is not a rational Creature that would not take it amiss to be thought otherwise of. And yet for all this one may truly say, there are very few lovers of Truth for Truths sake, even amongst those, who perswade themselves that they are so. How a Man may know whether he be so in earnest is worth enquiry: And I think there is this one unerring mark of it, *viz.* The not entertaining any Proposition with greater assurance than the Proofs it is built upon will warrant. Whoever goes beyond this measure of Assent, 'tis plain receives not Truth in the Love of it; loves not Truth for Truths sake, but for some other bye end. For the evidence that any Proposition is true (except such as are self-evident) lying only in the Proofs a Man has of it, whatsoever degrees of Assent he affords it beyond the degrees of that Evidence, 'tis plain all that surplusage of assurance is owing to some other Affection, and not to the Love of Truth: It being as impossible, that the Love of Truth should carry my Assent above the Evidence, that there is to me, that it is true, As that the Love of Truth should make me assent to any Proposition, for the sake of that Evidence, which it has not, that it is true: which is in effect to Love it as a Truth, because it is possible or probable that it may not be true. In any Truth that gets not possession of our Minds by the irresistible Light of Self-evidence, or by the force of Demonstration, the Arguments that gain it Assent, are the vouchers and gage of its Probability to us; and we can receive it for no other than such as they deliver it to our Understandings. Whatsoever Credit or Authority we give to any Proposition more than it receives from the Principles and Proofs it supports it self upon, is

§ 1. *Love of Truth necessary.*

[1] *The whole of this chapter xix add.* **4–5**, *with a consequent re-numbering, in* **4–5**, *of the chapters numbered xix and xx in* **1–3**.

owing to our Inclinations that way, and is so far a Derogation from the Love of Truth as such: which as it can receive no Evidence from our Passions or Interests, so it should receive no Tincture from them.

§ 2. The assuming an Authority of Dictating to others, and a forwardness to prescribe to their Opinions, is a constant concomitant of this bias and corruption of our Judgments. For how almost can it be otherwise, but that he should be ready to impose on others Belief, who has already imposed on his own? Who can reasonably expect Arguments and Conviction from him, in dealing with others, whose Understanding is not accustomed to them in his dealing with himself? Who does Violence to his own Faculties, Tyrannizes over his own Mind, and usurps the Prerogative that belongs to Truth alone, which is to command Assent by only its own Authority, *i.e.* by and in proportion to that Evidence which it carries with it.

§ 3. Upon this occasion I shall take the Liberty to consider a third Ground of Assent, which with some Men has the same Authority, and is as confidently relied on as either *Faith* or *Reason*, I mean *Enthusiasm*. Which laying by Reason would set up Revelation without it. Whereby in effect it takes away both Reason and Revelation, and substitutes in the room of it, the ungrounded Fancies of a Man's own Brain, and assumes them for a Foundation both of Opinion and Conduct.

§ 4. *Reason* is natural *Revelation*, whereby the eternal Father of Light, and Fountain of all Knowledge communicates to Mankind that portion of Truth, which he has laid within the reach of their natural Faculties: *Revelation* is natural *Reason* enlarged by a new set of Discoveries communicated by GOD immediately, which *Reason* vouches the Truth of, by the Testimony and Proofs it gives, that they come from GOD. So that he that takes away *Reason*, to make way for *Revelation*, puts out the Light of both, and does much what the same, as if he would perswade a Man to put out his Eyes the better to receive the remote Light of an invisible Star by a Telescope.

§ 5. Immediate *Revelation* being a much easier way for Men to establish their Opinions, and regulate their Conduct, than the

§ 2. *A forwardness to dictate from whence.* § 3. *Force of Enthusiasm.* § 4. *Reason and Revelation.* § 5. *Rise of Enthusiasm.*

(33) would] **5** | should **4** (*l. below* 37: § 2.) *whence.*] **W** | *whence:* **4–5**

tedious and not always successful Labour of strict Reasoning, it is no wonder, that some have been very apt to pretend to Revelation, and to perswade themselves, that they are under the peculiar guidance of Heaven in their Actions and Opinions, especially in those of them, which they cannot account for by the ordinary Methods of Knowledge, and Principles of Reason. Hence we see, that in all Ages, Men, in whom Melancholy has mixed with Devotion, or whose conceit of themselves has raised them into an Opinion of a greater familiarity with GOD, and a nearer admittance to his Favour than is afforded to others, have often flatter'd themselves with a perswasion of an immediate intercourse with the Deity, and frequent communications from the divine Spirit. GOD I own cannot be denied to be able to enlighten the Understanding by a Ray darted into the Mind immediately from the Fountain of Light: This they understand he has promised to do, and who then has so good a title to expect it, as those who are his peculiar People, chosen by him and depending on him?

§ 6. Their Minds being thus prepared, whatever groundless Opinion comes to settle it self strongly upon their Fancies, is an Illumination from the Spirit of GOD, and presently of divine Authority: And whatsoever odd Action they find in themselves a strong Inclination to do, that impulse is concluded to be a call or direction from Heaven, and must be obeyed; 'tis a Commission from above, and they cannot err in executing it.

§ 7. This I take to be properly Enthusiasm, which though founded neither on Reason, nor Divine Revelation, but rising from the Conceits of a warmed or over-weening Brain, works yet, where it once gets footing, more powerfully on the Perswasions and Actions of Men, than either of those two, or both together: Men being most forwardly obedient to the impulses they receive from themselves; And the whole Man is sure to act more vigorously, where the whole Man is carried by a natural Motion. For strong conceit like a new Principle carries all easily with it, when got above common Sense, and freed from all restraint of Reason, and check of Reflection, it is heightened into a Divine Authority, in concurrence with our own Temper and Inclination.

§ 8. Though the odd Opinions and extravagant Actions, *Enthusiasm* has run Men into, were enough to warn them against this wrong

§§ 6, 7. *Enthusiasm.* §§ 8, 9. *Enthusiasm mistaken for seeing and feeling.*

(31) more] **5** (*likewise* **Coste**) | most **4**

Principle so apt to misguide them both in their Belief and Conduct: yet the Love of something extraordinary, the Ease and Glory it is to be inspired and be above the common and natural ways of Knowledge so flatters many Men's Laziness, Ignorance, and Vanity, that when once they are got into this way of immediate Revelation; of Illumination without search; and of certainty without Proof, and without Examination, 'tis a hard matter to get them out of it. Reason is lost upon them, they are above it: they see the Light infused into their Understandings, and cannot be mistaken; 'tis clear and visible there; like the Light of bright Sunshine, shews it self, and needs no other Proof, but its own Evidence: they feel the Hand of GOD moving them within, and the impulses of the Spirit, and cannot be mistaken in what they feel. Thus they support themselves, and are sure Reason hath nothing to do with what they see and feel in themselves: what they have a sensible Experience of admits no doubt, needs no probation. Would he not be ridiculous who should require to have it proved to him, that the Light shines, and that he sees it? It is its own Proof, and can have no other. When the Spirit brings Light into our Minds, it dispels Darkness. We see it, as we do that of the Sun at Noon, and need not the twilight of Reason to shew it us. This Light from Heaven is strong, clear, and pure, carries its own Demonstration with it, and we may as rationally take a Glow-worme to assist us to discover the Sun, as to examine the celestial Ray by our dim Candle, Reason.

§ 9. This is the way of talking of these Men: they are sure, because they are sure: and their Perswasions are right, only because they are strong in them. For, when what they say is strip'd of the Metaphor of seeing and feeling, this is all it amounts to: and yet these Similes so impose on them, that they serve them for certainty in themselves, and demonstration to others.

§ 10. But to examine a little soberly this internal Light, and this feeling on which they build so much. These Men have, they say, clear Light, and they see; They have an awaken'd Sense, and they feel: This cannot, they are sure, be disputed them. For when a Man says he sees or he feels, no Body can deny it him, that he does so. But here let me ask: This seeing is it the perception of the Truth of

§ 10. *Enthusiasm how to be discover'd.*

(4), and] **5** | and **4** (5) Revelation;] **5** | *Revelation*, **4** (6) ; and] **5** | , and **4** (8–24) them . . . Reason.] **Coste** 'eux. "Ils . . . lumignon."'

the Proposition, or of this, that it is a Revelation from GOD? This feeling is it a perception of an Inclination or Fancy to do something, or of the Spirit of GOD moving that Inclination? These are two very different Perceptions, and must be carefully distinguish'd, if we would not impose upon our selves. I may perceive the Truth of a Proposition, and yet not perceive, that it is an immediate Revelation from GOD. I may perceive the Truth of a Proposition in *Euclid*, without its being, or my perceiving it to be, a Revelation: Nay I may perceive I came not by this Knowledge in a natural way, and so may conclude it revealed, without perceiving that it is a Revelation from GOD. Because there be Spirits, which, without being divinely commissioned, may excite those *Ideas* in me, and lay them in such order before my Mind, that I may perceive their Connexion. So that the Knowledge of any Proposition coming into my Mind, I know not how, is not a Perception that it is from GOD. Much less is a strong Perswasion, that it is true, a Perception that it is from GOD, or so much as true. But however it be called light and seeing; I suppose, it is at most but Belief, and Assurance: and the Proposition taken for a Revelation is not such, as they know, to be true, but take to be true. For where a Proposition is known to be true, Revelation is needless: And it is hard to conceive how there can be a Revelation to any one of what he knows already. If therefore it be a Proposition which they are perswaded, but do not know, to be true, whatever they may call it, it is not seeing, but believing. For these are two ways, whereby Truth comes into the Mind, wholly distinct, so that one is not the other. What I see I know to be so by the Evidence of the thing it self: what I believe I take to be so upon the Testimony of another: But this Testimony I must know to be given, or else what ground have I of believing? I must see that it is GOD that reveals this to me, or else I see nothing. The question then here is, How do I know that GOD is the Revealer of this to me; that this Impression is made upon my Mind by his holy Spirit, and that therefore I ought to obey it? If I know not this, how great soever the Assurance is, that I am possess'd with, it is groundless; whatever Light I pretend to, it is but *Enthusiasm*. For whether the Proposition supposed to be revealed, be in it self evidently true, or visibly probable, or by the natural ways of Knowledge uncertain, the Proposition that must be well grounded, and manifested to be true is this, that GOD is the Revealer of it, and that what I take to

(6) it] **4**; *om.* **5**   (21) there] **5** | these **4er** | that **4**   (31) is,] **5** | is. **4**

be a Revelation is certainly put into my Mind by him, and is not an Illusion drop'd in by some other Spirit, or raised by my own phancy. For if I mistake not, these Men receive it for true, because they presume GOD revealed it. Does it not then stand them upon, to examine upon what Grounds they presume it to be a Revelation from GOD? or else all their Confidence is mere Presumption: and this Light, they are so dazled with, is nothing, but an *ignis fatuus* that leads them continually round in this Circle. *It is a Revelation, because they firmly believe it*, and *they believe it*, *because it is a Revelation.*

§ 11. In all that is of Divine *Revelation* there is need of no other Proof but that it is an Inspiration from GOD: For he can neither deceive nor be deceived. But how shall it be known, that any Proposition in our Minds is a Truth infused by God; a Truth that is reveal'd to us by him, which he declares to us, and therefore we ought to believe? Here it is that *Enthusiasm* fails of the Evidence it pretends to. For Men thus possessed boast of a Light whereby they say, they are enlightened, and brought into the Knowledge of this or that Truth. But if they know it to be a Truth, they must know it to be so either by its own self-evidence to natural Reason; or by the rational Proofs that make it out to be so. If they see and know it to be a Truth, either of these two ways, they in vain suppose it to be a Revelation: For they know it to be true by the same way, that any other Man naturally may know, that it is so without the help of Revelation. For thus all the Truths of what kind soever, that Men uninspired are enlightened with, came into their Minds, and are established there. If they say they know it to be true, because it is a *Revelation* from GOD, the reason is good: but then it will be demanded, how they know it to be a Revelation from GOD. If they say by the Light it brings with it, which shines bright in their Minds, and they cannot resist; I beseech them to consider, whether this be any more, than what we have taken notice of already, *viz.* that it is a Revelation because they strongly believe it to be true. For all the Light they speak of is but a strong, though ungrounded perswasion of their own Minds that it is a Truth. For rational Grounds from Proofs that it is a Truth they must acknowledge to have none, for then it is not received as a *Revelation*, but upon the ordinary Grounds, that other Truths are received: And if they believe

§ 11. *Enthusiasm fails of Evidence, that the Proposition is from GOD.*

---

(20) out] **4** | ought **5** (30) resist;] *edit.* | resist. **4–5.** (**Coste** 'resister,')

it to be true, because it is a *Revelation*, and have no other reason for its being a *Revelation*, but because they are fully perswaded without any other reason that it is true, they believe it to be a Revelation only because they strongly believe it to be a Revelation, which is a very unsafe ground to proceed on, either in our Tenets, or Actions: And what readier way can there be to run our selves into the most extravagant Errors and Miscarriages than thus to set up phancy for our supreme and sole Guide, and to believe any Proposition to be true, any Action to be right, only because we believe it to be so? The strength of our Perswasions are no Evidence at all of their own rectitude: Crooked things may be as stiff and unflexible as streight: and Men may be as positive and peremptory in Error as in Truth. How come else the untractable Zealots in different and opposite Parties? For if the Light, which every one thinks he has in his Mind, which in this Case is nothing but the strength of his own Perswasion, be an Evidence that it is from GOD, contrary Opinions may have the same title to be inspirations; and GOD will be not only the Father of Lights, but of opposite and contradictory Lights, leading Men contrary ways; and contradictory Propositions will be divine Truths, if an ungrounded strength of Assurance be an Evidence, that any Proposition is a Divine Revelation.

§ 12. This cannot be otherwise, whilst firmness of Perswasion is made the cause of Believing, and confidence of being in the Right, is made an Argument of Truth; St. *Paul* himself believed he did well, and that he had a call to it, when he persecuted the Christians, whom he confidently thought in the Wrong: But yet it was he, and not they, who were mistaken. Good Men are Men still, liable to Mistakes, and are sometimes warmly engaged in Errors, which they take for divine Truths, shining in their Minds with the clearest Light.

§ 13. Light, true Light in the Mind is, or can be nothing else but the Evidence of the Truth of any Proposition; and if it be not a self-evident Proposition, all the Light it has, or can have, is from the clearness and validity of those Proofs, upon which it is received. To talk of any other light in the Understanding is to put our selves in the dark, or in the power of the Prince of Darkness, and by our own consent, to give ourselves up to Delusion to believe a Lie. For if strength of Perswasion be the Light, which must guide us; I ask

§ 12. *Firmness of Perswasion no Proof that any Proposition is from GOD.* § 13. *Light in the Mind, what.*

how shall any one distinguish between the delusions of Satan, and the inspirations of the Holy Ghost? He can transform himself into an Angel of Light. And they who are led by this Son of the Morning are as fully satisfied of the Illumination, *i.e.* are as strongly perswaded, that they are enlightned by the Spirit of God, as any one who is so: They acquiesce and rejoyce in it, are acted by it: and no body can be more sure, nor more in the right (if their own strong belief may be judge) than they.

§ 14. He therefore that will not give himself up to all the Extravagancies of Delusion and Error must bring this Guide of his *Light within* to the Tryal. God when he makes the Prophet does not unmake the Man. He leaves all his Faculties in their natural State, to enable him to judge of his Inspirations, whether they be of divine Original or no. When he illuminates the Mind with supernatural Light, he does not extinguish that which is natural. If he would have us assent to the Truth of any Proposition, he either evidences that Truth by the usual Methods of natural Reason, or else makes it known to be a Truth, which he would have us assent to, by his Authority, and convinces us that it is from him, by some Marks which Reason cannot be mistaken in. *Reason* must be our last Judge and Guide in every Thing. I do not mean, that we must consult Reason, and examine whether a Proposition revealed from God can be made out by natural Principles, and if it cannot, that then we may reject it: But consult it we must, and by it examine, whether it be a *Revelation* from God or no: And if *Reason* finds it to be revealed from GOD, *Reason* then declares for it, as much as for any other Truth, and makes it one of her Dictates. Every Conceit that throughly warms our Fancies must pass for an Inspiration, if there be nothing but the Strength of our Perswasions, whereby to judge of our Perswasions: If *Reason* must not examine their Truth by something extrinsical to the Perswasions themselves; Inspirations and Delusions, Truth and Falshood will have the same Measure, and will not be possible to be distinguished.

§ 15. If this internal Light, or any Proposition which under that Title we take for inspired, be conformable to the Principles of Reason or to the Word of GOD, which is attested Revelation, *Reason* warrants it, and we may safely receive it for true, and be

§ 14. *Revelation must be judged of by Reason.* §§ 15, 16. *Belief no Proof of Revelation.*

(5) enlightned] **5** | enlightend **4**

guided by it in our Belief and Actions: If it receive no Testimony nor Evidence from either of these Rules, we cannot take it for a *Revelation*, or so much as for true, till we have some other Mark that it is a *Revelation*, besides our believing that it is so. Thus we see the holy Men of old, who had *Revelations* from GOD, had something else besides that internal Light of assurance in their own Minds, to testify to them, that it was from GOD. They were not left to their own Perswasions alone, that those Perswasions were from GOD; But had outward Signs to convince them of the Author of those Revelations. And when they were to convince others, they had a Power given them to justify the Truth of their Commission from Heaven; and by visible Signs to assert the divine Authority of the Message they were sent with. *Moses* saw the Bush burn without being consumed, and heard a Voice out of it. This was something besides finding an impulse upon his Mind to go to *Pharaoh*, that he might bring his Brethren out of *Egypt*: and yet he thought not this enough to authorise him to go with that Message, till GOD by another Miracle, of his Rod turned into a Serpent, had assured him of a Power to testify his Mission by the same Miracle repeated before them, whom he was sent to. *Gideon* was sent by an Angel to deliver *Israel* from the *Mideanites*, and yet he desired a Sign to convince him, that this Commission was from GOD. These and several the like Instances to be found among the Prophets of old, are enough to shew, that they thought not an inward seeing or perswasion of their own Minds without any other Proof a sufficient Evidence, that it was from GOD, though the Scripture does not every where mention their demanding or having such Proofs.

§ 16. In what I have said I am far from denying, that GOD can, or doth sometimes enlighten Mens Minds in the apprehending of certain Truths, or excite them to Good Actions by the immediate influence and assistance of the Holy Spirit, without any extraordinary Signs accompanying it. But in such Cases too we have Reason and the Scripture, unerring Rules to know whether it be from GOD or no. Where the Truth imbraced is consonant to the *Revelation* in the written word of GOD; or the Action conformable to the dictates of right *Reason* or Holy Writ, we may be assured that we run no risque in entertaining it as such, because though perhaps it be not an immediate Revelation from GOD, extraordinarily

(5) of old] **4er–5** | of GOD **4**. (*Not in* **Coste**) (12) [*2nd*] the] **4** (*likewise* **Coste, Coste**$_2$) | a **5** (28) 16] **5** (*likewise* **Coste**) | 15 **4**

operating on our Minds, yet we are sure it is warranted by that Revelation which he has given us of Truth. But it is not the strength of our private perswasion within our selves, that can warrant it to be a Light or Motion from Heaven: Nothing can do that but the written Word of GOD without us, or that Standard of Reason which is common to us with all Men. Where Reason or Scripture is express for any Opinion or Action, we may receive it as of divine Authority: But 'tis not the strength of our own Perswasions which can by it self give it that Stamp. The bent of our own Minds may favour it as much as we please; That may shew it to be a Fondling of our own, but will by no means prove it to be an Offspring of Heaven, and of divine Original.

CHAPTER XX

Of wrong Assent, or Errour.

§ 1. KNOWLEDGE being to be had only of visible certain Truth, *Errour* is not a Fault of our Knowledge, but a Mistake of our Judgment giving Assent to that, which is not true.

But if Assent be grounded on Likelihood, if the proper Object and Motive of our Assent be Probability, and that Probability consists in what is laid down in the foregoing Chapters, it will be demanded, how Men come to give their Assents contrary to Probability. For there is nothing more common, than Contrariety of Opinions; nothing more obvious, than that one Man wholly disbelieves what another only doubts of, and a third stedfastly believes, and firmly adheres to. The Reasons whereof, though they may be very various, yet, I suppose, may all be reduced to these four.

1. *Want of Proofs.*
2. *Want of Ability to use them.*
3. *Want of Will to use them.*
4. *Wrong Measures of Probability.*

§ 2. *First*, By *Want of Proofs*: I do not mean, only the Want of those Proofs which are no where extant, and so are no where to be

§ 1. *Causes of Errour.* § 2. *First, Want of Proofs.*

(9) [*1st*] it] **4**; *om.* **5** (*l. below* 12) *This chapter is numbered xx in* **4–5**, *but xix in* **1–3**. (*2 ll. below* 12) *Assent*,] **1–3, 5** | *Assent* **4** (17) consists] **4–5** | consist **1–3** (30) and so] **2–5** | which **1**

had; but the Want even of those Proofs which are in Being, or might be procured. And thus Men want Proofs, who have not the Convenience, or Opportunity to make Experiments and Observations themselves, tending to the Proof of any Proposition; nor likewise the Convenience to enquire into, and collect the Testimonies of others: And in this State are the greatest part of Mankind, who are given up to Labour, and enslaved to the Necessity of their mean Condition; whose Lives are worn out, only in the Provisions for Living. These Men's Opportunity of Knowledge and Enquiry, are commonly as narrow as their Fortunes; and their Understandings are but little instructed, when all their whole Time and Pains is laid out, to still the Croaking of their own Bellies, or the Cries of their Children. 'Tis not to be expected, that a Man, who drudges on, all his Life, in a laborious Trade, should be more knowing in the variety of Things done in the World, than a Pack-horse, who is driven constantly forwards and backwards, in a narrow Lane, and dirty Road, only to Market, should be skilled in the Geography of the Country. Nor is it at all more possible, that he who wants Leisure, Books, and Languages, and the Opportunity of Conversing with variety of Men, should be in a Condition to collect those Testimonies and Observations, which are in Being, and are necessary to make out many, nay most of the Propositions, that, in the Societies of Men, are judged of the greatest Moment; or to find out Grounds of Assurance so great, as the Belief of the points he would build on them, is thought necessary. So that a great part of Mankind are, by the natural and unalterable State of Things in this World, and the Constitution of humane Affairs, unavoidably given over to invincible Ignorance of those Proofs, on which others build, and which are necessary to establish those Opinions: The greatest part of Men, having much to do to get the Means of Living, are not in a Condition to look after those of learned and laborious Enquiries.

§ 3. What shall we say then? Are the greatest part of Mankind, by the necessity of their Condition, subjected to unavoidable Ignorance in those Things, which are of greatest Importance to them? (for of those, 'tis obvious to enquire.) Have the Bulk of Mankind no other Guide, but Accident, and blind Chance, to

§ 3. Obj. *What shall become of those who want them, answered.*

---

(23) Men] **4er–5** (*likewise* **Coste**) | Man **1–4** (*l. below* 37) *those*] **2–4** | *these* **5**

conduct them to their Happiness, or Misery? Are the current Opinions, and licensed Guides of every Country sufficient Evidence and Security to every Man, to venture his greatest Concernments on; nay, his everlasting Happiness, or Misery? Or can those be the certain and infallible Oracles and Standards of Truth, which teach one Thing in *Christendom*, and another in *Turkey*? Or shall a poor Country-man be eternally happy, for having the Chance to be born in *Italy*; or a Day-Labourer be unavoidably lost, because he had the ill Luck to be born in *England*? How ready some Men may be to say some of these Things, I will not here examine: but this I am sure, that Men must allow one or other of these to be true, (let them chuse which they please;) or else grant, That GOD has furnished Men with Faculties sufficient to direct them in the Way they should take, if they will but seriously employ them that Way, when their ordinary Vocations allow them the Leisure. No Man is so wholly taken up with the Attendance on the Means of Living, as to have no spare Time at all to think of his Soul, and inform himself in Matters of Religion. Were Men as intent upon this, as they are on Things of lower Concernment, there are none so enslaved to the Necessities of Life, who might not find many Vacancies, that might be husbanded to this Advantage of their Knowledge.

§ 4. Besides those, whose Improvements and informations are straitned by the narrowness of their Fortunes, there are others, whose largeness of Fortune would plentifully enough supply Books, and other Requisites for clearing of Doubts, and discovering of Truth: But they are *cooped in* close, *by the Laws* of their Countries, and the strict guards of those, whose Interest it is to keep them ignorant, lest, knowing more, they should believe the less in them. These are as far, nay farther *from the Liberty and Opportunities of a fair Enquiry*, than those poor and wretched Labourers, we before spoke of. And, however they may seem high and great, are confined to narrowness of Thought, and enslaved in that which should be the freest part of Man, their Understandings. This is generally the

§ 4. *People hindred from enquiry.*

---

(17) of] **5** | on **1–4** (20) Necessities] **4–5** | Necessity **1–3** (*likewise* **Coste**) (25) Requisites for] **5** (*likewise* **Coste**) | Opportunities of **1–4** (26) Truth:] *In* **Coste** *and* **Coste**$_2$ *the remainder of this section runs* 'mais ils sont détournez de cela par des obstacles pleins d'artifice qu'il est assez facile d'appercevoir, sans qu'il soit nécessaire de les étaler en cet endroit.' (29) . These] **2–5** | , that they **1** *Liberty* | **2–5** | *Liberties* **1** (31) And] **2–5** | These Men **1** (*l. below* 33) *In* **Coste**, § *4 comes under the same marginal summary as* § *3*.

Case of all those, who live in Places where Care is taken to propagate Truth, without Knowledge; where Men are forced, at a venture, to be of the Religion of the Country; and must therefore swallow down Opinions, as silly People do Empiricks Pills, without knowing what they are made of, or how they will work, and have nothing to do, but believe that they will do the Cure: but in this, are much more miserable than they, in that they are not at liberty to refuse swallowing, what perhaps they had rather let alone; or to chuse the Physician, to whose Conduct they would trust themselves.

§ 5. *Secondly*, Those who *want skill to use those Evidences they have* of Probabilities; who cannot carry a train of Consequences in their Heads, nor weigh exactly the preponderancy of contrary Proofs and Testimonies, making every Circumstance its due allowance, may be easily misled to assent to Positions that are not probable. There are some Men of one, some but of two Syllogisms, and no more; and others that can but advance one step farther. These cannot always discern that side on which the strongest Proofs lie; cannot constantly follow that which in it self is the more probable Opinion. Now that there is such a difference between Men, in respect of their Understandings, I think no body, who has had any Conversation with his Neighbours, will question: though he never was at *Westminster-hall*, or the *Exchange* on the one hand; nor at *Alms-Houses*, or *Bedlam* on the other. Which great difference in Men's Intellectuals, whether it rises from any defect in the Organs of the Body, particularly adapted to Thinking; or in the dulness or untractableness of those Faculties, for want of use; or, as some think, in the natural differences of Men's Souls themselves; or some, or all of these together, it matters not here to examine: Only this is evident, that there is a difference of degrees in Men's Understandings, Apprehensions, and Reasonings, to so great a latitude, that one may, without doing injury to Mankind, affirm, that there is a greater distance between some Men, and others, in this respect, than between some Men and some Beasts. But how this comes about, is a Speculation, though of great consequence, yet not necessary to our present purpose.

§ 5. *Secondly, want of skill to use them.*

---

(10) who] **4–5** | that **1–3** (11) ; who] **4–5** | , that **1–3** (13) its] **1**, **4–5** | is **2–3** (18) it] **4–5** | its **1–3** (20–1) , who . . . question:] **2–5** | will question, who has had any Conversation with his Neighbours, **1** (27) ; or] **2–5** | , or **1**

§ 6. *Thirdly*, There are another sort of People that *want Proofs*, not because they are out of their reach, but *because they will not use them*: Who though they have Riches and Leisure enough, and want neither Parts nor other helps, are yet never the better for them. Their hot pursuit of pleasure, or constant drudgery in business engages some Men's thoughts elsewhere: Laziness and Oscitancy in general, or a particular aversion for Books, Study, and Meditation keep others from any serious thoughts at all: And some out of fear, that an impartial enquiry would not favour those Opinions, which best suit their Prejudices, Lives, and Designs, content themselves without examination, to take upon trust, what they find convenient, and in fashion. Thus most Men, even of those that might do otherwise, pass their Lives without an acquaintance with, much less a rational assent to Probabilities, they are concerned to know, tho they lie so much within their view, that to be convinced of them, they need but turn their Eyes that way. But we know some Men will not read a Letter, which is supposed to bring ill news; and many Men forbear to cast up their Accompts, or so much as think upon their Estates, who have reason to fear their Affairs are in no very good posture. How Men, whose plentiful Fortunes allow them leisure to improve their Understandings, can satisfy themselves with a lazy Ignorance, I cannot tell: But methinks they have a low Opinion of their Souls, who lay out all their Incomes in Provisions for the Body, and employ none of it to procure the Means and Helps of Knowledge; who take great care to appear always in a neat and splendid outside, and would think themselves miserable in coarse Cloaths, or a patched Coat, and yet contentedly suffer their Minds to appear abroad in a pie-bald Livery of coarse Patches, and borrowed Shreds, such as it has pleased Chance, or their Country-Tailor, (I mean the common Opinion of those they have conversed with,) to cloath them in. I will not here mention how unreasonable this is for Men that ever think of a future state, and their concernment in it, which no rational Man can avoid to do sometimes: nor shall I take notice what a shame and confusion it is, to the greatest

§ 6. *Thirdly, want of Will to use them.*

(1) There] **1–3** | there **4–5** (4–15) other . . . they] **2–5** | Learning, may, yet through their hot pursuit of Pleasure, or Business, or else out of laziness or fear, that the Doctrines, whose Truth they should enquire into, would not suit well with their Opinions, Lives, or Designs, may never come to the knowledge of, nor give their Assent to those Probabilities which **1** (12) . Thus] **4–5** | : And so **2–3** those] **4–5** | these **2–3** (19) in no] **2–5** | not in a **1** (31) in] *add.* **1T.er, 2–5**

Contemners of Knowledge, to be found ignorant in Things they are concerned to know. But this, at least, is worth the consideration of those who call themselves Gentlemen, That however they may think Credit, Respect, Power, and Authority the Concomitants of their Birth and Fortune, yet they will find all these still carried away from them, by Men of lower Condition who surpass them in Knowledge. They who are blind, will always be led by those that see, or else fall into the Ditch:* and he is certainly the most subjected, the most enslaved, who is so in his Understanding. In the foregoing instances, some of the Causes have been shewn of wrong Assent, and how it comes to pass, that probable Doctrines are not always received with an Assent proportionable to the Reasons, which are to be had for their Probability: but hitherto we have considered only such Probabilities, whose Proofs do exist, but do not appear to him that embraces the Errour.

§ 7. *Fourthly*, There remains yet the last sort, who, even where the real Probabilities appear, and are plainly laid before them, do not admit of the conviction, nor yield unto manifest Reasons, but do either ἐπέχειν, suspend their Assent, or give it to the less probable Opinion. And to this danger are those exposed, who have taken up *wrong measures of Probability*, which are,

1. *Propositions that are not in themselves certain and evident, but doubtful and false, taken up for Principles.*
2. *Received Hypotheses.*
3. *Predominant Passions or Inclinations.*
4. *Authority.*

§ 8. *First*, The first and firmest ground of Probability, is the conformity any thing has to our own Knowledge; especially that part of our Knowledge which we have embraced, and continue to look on as *Principles*. These have so great an influence upon our Opinions, that 'tis usually by them we judge of Truth, and measure Probability, to that degree, that what is inconsistent with our *Principles*, is so far from passing for probable with us, that it will not be allowed possible. The reverence is born to these *Principles* is so great, and

§ 7. *Fourthly, Wrong measures of Probability, whereof.* §§ 8–10. *First, Doubtful Propositions taken for Principles.*

(6) Condition] **4–5** | Condition, **1–3** (13–14) we have considered only] **4–5** | it has been only of **1–3** (14) [*1st*] do] **4–5** | do only **1–3** (17) do] **4–5** | yet do **1–3** (*likewise* **Coste**) (31–2) , and . . . , to] **4–5** | ; and . . . to **1–3** (34) [*1st*] is] **1–4**; *om.* **5**

* Cf. Matt. 15: 14; Luke 6: 39

their Authority so paramount to all other, that the Testimony not only of other Men, but the Evidence of our own Senses are often rejected, when they offer to vouch any thing contrary to these established Rules. How much the Doctrine of innate *Principles*, and that *Principles* are not to be proved or questioned, has contributed to this, I will not here examine. This I readily grant, that one Truth cannot contradict another: but withal I take leave also to say, that every one ought very carefully to beware what he admits for a *Principle*, to examine it strictly, and see whether he certainly knows it to be true of it self by its own Evidence, or whether he does only with assurance believe it to be so, upon the Authority of others. For he hath a strong biass put into his Understanding, which will unavoidably misguide his Assent, who hath imbibed *wrong Principles*, and has blindly given himself up to the Authority of any Opinion in it self not evidently true.

§ 9. There is nothing more ordinary, than that *Children* should receive into their Minds Propositions (especially about Matters of Religion) from their Parents, Nurses, or those about them: which being insinuated into their unwary, as well as unbiass'd Understandings, and fastened by degrees, are at last (equally, whether true or false) riveted there by long Custom and Education beyond all possibility of being pull'd out again. For Men, when they are grown up, reflecting upon their Opinions, and finding those of this sort to be as ancient in their Minds as their very Memories, not having observed their early Insinuation, nor by what means they got them, they are apt to reverence them as sacred Things, and not to suffer them to be prophaned, touched, or questioned: They look on them as the *Urim* and *Thummim* set up in their Minds immediately by GOD Himself, to be the great and unerring Deciders of Truth and Falshood, and the Judges to which they are to appeal in all manner of Controversies.

§ 10. This Opinion of his *Principles* (let them be what they will) being *once established in any one's Mind*, it is easy to be imagined, what reception any Proposition shall find, how clearly soever proved, that shall invalidate their Authority, or at all thwart with these internal Oracles; whereas the grossest Absurdities and Improbabilities, being but agreeable to such Principles, go down glibly, and are easily digested. The great obstinacy, that is to be found in Men firmly believing quite contrary Opinions, though many times

(26) and] *add.* **2–5** (27) : They] **4–5** | , but **1–3** (*likewise* **Coste**)

equally absurd, in the various Religions of Mankind, are as evident a Proof, as they are an unavoidable consequence of this way of Reasoning from received traditional Principles. So that Men will disbelieve their own Eyes, renounce the Evidence of their Senses, and give their own Experience the lye, rather than admit of any thing disagreeing with these sacred Tenets. Take an intelligent *Romanist*, that from the very first dawning of any Notions in his Understanding, hath had this Principle constantly inculcated, *viz.* That he must believe as the Church (*i.e.* those of his Communion) believes, or that the Pope is Infallible; and this he never so much as heard questioned, till at forty or fifty years old he met with one of other Principles; How is he prepared easily to swallow, not only against all Probability, but even the clear Evidence of his Senses, the Doctrine of *Transubstantiation*? This Principle has such an influence on his Mind that he will believe that to be Flesh, which he sees to be Bread. And what way will you take to convince a Man of any improbable Opinion he holds, who with some Philosophers, hath laid down this as a foundation of Reasoning, That he must believe his Reason (for so Men improperly call Arguments drawn from their Principles) against their Senses? Let an *Enthusiast* be principled, that he or his Teacher is inspired, and acted by an immediate Communication of the Divine Spirit, and you in vain bring the Evidence of clear Reasons against his Doctrines. Whoever therefore have imbibed wrong *Principles*, are not, in Things inconsistent with these Principles, to be moved by the most apparent and convincing Probabilities, till they are so candid and ingenuous to themselves, as to be persuaded to examine even those very *Principles*, which many never suffer themselves to do.

§ 11. *Secondly*, Next to these, are Men whose Understandings are cast into a Mold, and fashioned just to the size of a *received Hypothesis*. The difference between these and the former, is, that they will

§ 11. *Secondly, Received Hypothesis.*

(7) *Romanist*] **Coste** '*Lutherien*' dawning] **5** | dawnings **1–4**. (**Coste** '(dès que son Entendement a commencé de recevoir quelques notions')) (9) (*i.e.* . . . Communion)] *add.* **4–5** (10) or . . . Infallible] *Not in* **Coste** (14–16) *?* This . . . he] **4–5** | , and **1–3** **Coste** *turns* '*Transubstantiation* . . . Bread.' *into* '*Consubstantiation*, non seulement contre toute probabilité, mais même contre l'évidence manifeste de ses propres Sens? Ce Principe a une telle influence sur son Esprit qu'il croira qu'une chose est Chair et Pain tout à la fois, quoy qu'il soit impossible qu'elle soit autre chose que l'un des deux:' (18) a] **1–4**; *om.* **5**. (23) Doctrines] **1–4** | Doctrine **5**

admit of Matter of Fact, and agree with Dissenters in that; but differ only in assigning of Reasons, and explaining the manner of Operation. These are not at that open defiance with their Senses, as the former: they can endure to hearken to their information a little more patiently; but will by no means admit of their Reports, in the Explanation of Things; nor be prevailed on by Probabilities, which would convince them, that Things are not brought about just after the same manner, that they have decreed within themselves, that they are. Would it not be an insufferable thing for a learned Professor, and that which his Scarlet would blush at, to have his Authority of forty years standing wrought out of hard Rock Greek and Latin, with no small expence of Time and Candle, and confirmed by general Tradition, and a reverend Beard, in an instant overturned by an upstart Novelist? Can any one expect that he should be made to confess, That what he taught his Scholars thirty years ago, was all Errour and Mistake; and that he sold them hard Words and Ignorance at a very dear rate? What Probabilities, I say, are sufficient to prevail in such a Case? And who ever by the most cogent Arguments will be prevailed with, to disrobe himself at once of all his old Opinions, and Pretences to Knowledge and Learning, which with hard Study, he hath all his Time been labouring for; and turn himself out stark naked, in quest a-fresh of new Notions? All the Arguments can be used, will be as little able to prevail, as the Wind did with the Traveller, to part with his Cloak, which he held only the faster. To this of wrong Hypothesis, may be reduced the Errors, that may be occasioned by a true *Hypothesis*, or right Principles, but not rightly understood. There is nothing more familiar than this. The Instances of Men, contending for different Opinions, which they all derive from the infallible Truth of the Scripture, are an undeniable Proof of it. All that call themselves Christians, allow the Text, that says, μετανοεῖτε, to carry in it the Obligation to a very weighty Duty. But yet however erroneous will one of their Practices be, who understanding nothing but the *French*, take this Rule with one Translation to be *repentez vous*, repent; or with the other, *faitez Penitence*, do Penance.

§ 12. *Thirdly*, Probabilities, which cross Men's Appetites, and

§ 12. *Thirdly, predominant Passions.*

(4) information] **2–5** | Intelligence **1** (9) thing] **2–5** | a thing **1** (10) at] **2–5** | for **1** (14) ? Can . . . be] **4–5** | ; and he **1–3** (29) derive] **1–3, 5er** | drive **4–5** (32) however] **4–5** | how **1–3** (35) *faitez*] **1–3** (*likewise* **Coste**), **5er** | *fatiez* **4–5**

prevailing Passions, run the same Fate. Let never so much Probability hang on one side of a covetous Man's Reasoning, and Money on the other; and it is easie to foresee which will out-weigh. Earthly Minds, like Mud-Walls, resist the strongest Batteries: and though, perhaps, sometimes the force of a clear Argument may make some Impression, yet they nevertheless stand firm, keep out the Enemy Truth, that would captivate, or disturb them. Tell a Man, passionately in Love, that he is jilted; bring a score of Witnesses of the Falshood of his Mistress, 'tis ten to one but three kind Words of hers, shall invalidate all their Testimonies. *Quod volumus, facilè credimus*;* *what suits our Wishes, is forwardly believed*, is, I suppose, what every one hath more than once experimented: and though Men cannot always openly gain-say, or resist the force of manifest Probabilities, that make against them; yet yield they not to the Argument. Not but that it is the Nature of the Understanding constantly to close with the more probable side, but yet a Man hath a Power to suspend and restrain its Enquiries, and not permit a full and satisfactory Examination, as far as the matter in Question is capable, and will bear it to be made. Until that be done, there will be always these *two ways left of evading the most apparent Probabilities*.

§ 13. *First*, That the Arguments being (as for the most part they are) brought in Words, *there may be a Fallacy látent* in them: and the Consequences being, perhaps, many in Train, they may be some of them incoherent. There be very few Discourses, are so short, clear, and consistent, to which most Men may not, with satisfaction enough to themselves, raise this doubt; and from whose *conviction* they may not, without reproach of Disingenuity or Unreasonableness, set themselves free with the old Reply, *Non persuadebis, etiamsi persuaseris*;** *though I cannot answer, I will not yield.*

§ 14. *Secondly*, Manifest Probabilities may be evaded, and the Assent withheld upon this Suggestion, That *I know not yet all that may be said on the contrary side*. And therefore though I be beaten, 'tis not necessary I should yield, not knowing what Forces there are in reserve behind. This is a refuge against *Conviction* so open and so

§ 13. *The means of evading Probabilities*, 1st. *Supposed fallacy*. § 14. 2ly. *Supposed Arguments for the contrary.*

(24) clear,] **5** | clear **1–4** (32, 33) I] **4–5** | he **1–3**

* *Cf.* Caesar, *De Bello Civili*, II, 27; *De Bello Gallico*, III, 18; and Bacon, *Novum Organum*, I, 49.
** *Cf.* Erasmus, *Adagia*, II. vii. 61.

wide, that it is hard to determine, when a Man is quite out of the Verge of it.

§ 15. But yet there is some end of it, and a Man having carefully enquired into all the grounds of Probability and Unlikeliness; done his utmost to inform himself in all Particulars fairly; and cast up the Summ total on both sides, may in most Cases come to acknowledge, upon the whole Matter, on which side the Probability rests: wherein some Proofs in Matter of Reason, being suppositions upon universal Experience, are so cogent and clear; and some Testimonies in Matter of Fact so universal, that he cannot refuse his Assent. So that, I think, we may conclude, that in Propositions, where though the Proofs in view are of most Moment, yet there are sufficient grounds, to suspect that there is either Fallacy in Words, or certain Proofs, as considerable, to be produced on the contrary side, there Assent, Suspense, or Dissent, are often voluntary Actions: But *where* the Proofs are such as make it highly probable and there is not sufficient ground to suspect, that there is either Fallacy of Words, (which sober and serious Consideration may discover,) nor equally valid Proofs yet undiscovered latent on the other side, (which also the Nature of the Thing, may, in some Cases, make plain to a considerate Man,) there, I think, *a Man*, who has weighed them, *can scarce refuse his Assent* to the side, on which the greater Probability appears. Whether it be probable, that a promiscuous jumble of printing Letters should often fall into a Method and Order, which should stamp on Paper a coherent Discourse; or that a blind fortuitous concourse of Atoms, not guided by an understanding Agent, should frequently constitute the Bodies of any Species of Animals: in these and the like Cases, I think, no Body that considers them, can be one jot at a stand which side to take, nor at all waver in his Assent. Lastly, when there can be no Supposition, (the thing in its own nature indifferent, and wholly depending upon the Testimony of Witnesses,) that there is as fair Testimony against, as for the Matter of Fact attested; which by Enquiry, is to be learned, *v.g.* whether there was 1700 years agone such a Man at *Rome* as *Julius Cæsar*: In all such Cases, I say, I think it is not

§ 15. *What Probabilities determine the Assent.*

---

(6) Summ total] **2–5** | whole Summ **1** (8, 10) Matter] **2–5** | Matters **1** (*likewise* **Coste**) (8) being suppositions] **2–5** | which are suppositious **1** (25) on] **2–5** | in **1**

in any rational Man's Power to refuse his Assent; but that it necessarily follows, and closes with such Probabilities. In other less clear Cases, I think, it is in a Man's Power to suspend his Assent; and, perhaps, content himself with the Proofs he has, if they favour the Opinion that suits with his Inclination, or Interest, and so stop from farther search. But that a Man should afford his Assent to that side, on which the less Probability appears to him, seems to me utterly impracticable, and as impossible, as it is to believe the same thing probable and improbable at the same time.

§ 16. As Knowledge, is no more arbitrary than Perception: so, I think, Assent is no more in our Power than Knowledge. When the Agreement of any two *Ideas* appears to our Minds, whether immediately, or by the Assistance of Reason, I can no more refuse to perceive, no more avoid knowing it, than I can avoid seeing those Objects, which I turn my Eyes to, and look on in day-light: And what upon full Examination I find the most probable, I cannot deny my Assent to. But though we cannot hinder our Knowledge, where the Agreement is once perceived; nor our Assent, where the Probability manifestly appears upon due Consideration of all the Measures of it: Yet *we can hinder both Knowledge and Assent, by stopping our Enquiry*, and not imploying our Faculties in the search of any Truth. If it were not so, Ignorance, Error, or Infidelity could not in any Case be a Fault. Thus in some Cases, we can prevent or suspend our Assent: But can a Man, versed in modern or ancient History, doubt whether there be such a Place as *Rome*, or whether there was such a Man as *Julius Cæsar*? Indeed there are millions of Truths, that a Man is not, or may not think himself concerned to know; as whether our King *Richard* the Third was crook-back'd, or no; or whether *Roger Bacon* was a Mathematician, or a Magician. In these and such like Cases, where the Assent one way or other, is of no Importance to the Interest of any one, no Action, no Concernment of his following, or depending thereon, there 'tis not strange, that the Mind should give it self up to the common Opinion, or render it self to the first Comer. These and the like Opinions, are of so

§ 16. *Where it is in our power to suspend it.*

---

(12) appears] **2–5** | appear **1** (18) perceived] **2–5** | perceived by our Minds **1** (21) Truth.] **2–5** | Truth: **1** (28) our King] *add.* **2–5.** (*In* **Coste**, 'si *Richard* III.', *with a marginal note* 'Roy d'Angleterre.') the Third] **1–2, 4–5** | III. **3** (*likewise* **Coste**) (*l. below* 34) *Where*] **2, 4–5** | *Wherein* **3**

little weight and moment, that like Motes in the Sun, their Tendencies are very rarely taken notice of. They are there, as it were, by Chance, and the Mind lets them float at liberty. But where the Mind judges that the Proposition has concernment in it; where the Assent, or not Assenting is thought to draw Consequences of Moment after it, and Good or Evil to depend on chusing, or refusing the right side, and the Mind sets it self seriously to enquire, and examine the Probability: there, I think, it is not in our Choice, to take which side we please, if manifest odds appear on either. The greater Probability, I think, in that Case, will determine the Assent: and a Man can no more avoid assenting, or taking it to be true, where he perceives the greater Probability, than he can avoid knowing it to be true, where he perceives the Agreement or Disagreement of any two *Ideas*.

If this be so, the Foundation of Errour will lie in wrong Measures of Probability; as the Foundation of Vice in wrong Measures of Good.

§ 17. *Fourthly*, The fourth and last *wrong Measure of Probability* I shall take notice of, and which keeps in Ignorance, or Errour, more People than all the other together, is that which I have mentioned in the fore-going Chapter, I mean, the *giving up our Assent to the common received Opinions*, either of our Friends, or Party; Neighbourhood, or Country. How many Men have no other ground for their Tenets, than the supposed Honesty, or Learning, or Number of those of the same Profession? As if honest, or bookish Men could not err; or Truth were to be established by the Vote of the Multitude: yet this with most Men serves the Turn. The Tenet has had the attestation of reverend Antiquity, it comes to me with the Pass-port of former Ages, and therefore I am secure in the Reception I give it: other Men have been, and are of the same Opinion, (for that is all is said,) and therefore it is reasonable for me to embrace it. A Man may more justifiably throw up Cross and Pile for his Opinions, than take them up by such Measures. All Men are liable to Errour, and most Men are in many Points, by Passion or Interest, under Temptation to it. If we could but see the secret motives, that influenced the Men of Name and Learning in the World, and the

§ 17. *Fourthly, Authority.*

---

(4) judges that] **2–5** | judges, **1** (6) of Moment after it] **2–5** | after it of moment **1** (8) : there] **4–5** | ; there **1–3** (23) , or] **1–3** | or **4–5** (26–8) : yet . . . , it] **4–5** | ; yet . . . ; it **1–3**

Leaders of Parties, we should not always find, that it was the embracing of Truth for its own sake, that made them espouse the Doctrines, they owned and maintained. This at least is certain, there is not an Opinion so absurd, which a Man may not receive upon this ground. There is no Errour to be named, which has not had its Professors: And a Man shall never want crooked Paths to walk in, if he thinks that he is in the right way, where-ever he has the Foot-steps of others to follow.

§ 18. But notwithstanding the great Noise is made in the World about Errours and Opinions, I must do Mankind that Right, as to say, *There are not so many Men in Errours, and wrong Opinions, as is commonly supposed.* Not that I think they embrace the Truth; but indeed, because, concerning those Doctrines they keep such a stir about, they have no Thought, no Opinion at all. For if any one should a little catechize the greatest part of the Partisans of most of the Sects in the World, he would not find, concerning those Matters they are so zealous for, that they have any Opinions of their own: much less would he have Reason to think, that they took them upon the Examination of Arguments, and Appearance of Probability. They are resolved to stick to a Party, that Education or Interest has engaged them in; and there, like the common Soldiers of an Army, shew their Courage and Warmth, as their Leaders direct, without ever examining, or so much as knowing the Cause they contend for. If a Man's Life shews, that he has no serious Regard to Religion; for what Reason should we think, that he beats his Head about the Opinions of his Church, and troubles himself to examine the grounds of this or that Doctrine? 'Tis enough for him to obey his Leaders, to have his Hand and his Tongue ready for the support of the common Cause, and thereby approve himself to those, who can give him Credit, Preferment, or Protection in that Society. Thus Men become Professors of, and Combatants for those Opinions, they were never convinced of, nor Proselytes to; no, nor ever had so much as floating in their Heads: And though one cannot say, there are fewer improbable or erroneous Opinions in the World than there are; yet this is certain, there are fewer, that actually assent to them, and mistake them for truths, than is imagined.

§ 18. *Men not in so many Errours as is imagined.*

---

(2) its] **1–3, 5** | it's **4** (7) that] *add.* **2–5** (24) to] **1–4** | for **5**
(34) or erroneous] *add.* **2–5** (36) , and . . . truths,] *add.* **2–5**

CHAPTER XXI

Of the Division of the Sciences.

§ 1. ALL that can fall within the compass of Humane Understanding, being either, *First*, The Nature of Things, as they are in themselves, their Relations, and their manner of Operation: Or, *Secondly*, That which Man himself ought to do, as a rational and voluntary Agent, for the Attainment of any End, especially Happiness: Or, *Thirdly*, The ways and means, whereby the Knowledge of both the one and the other of these, are attained and communicated; I think, *Science* may be divided properly into these *Three sorts.*

§ 2. *First*, The Knowledge of Things, as they are in their own proper Beings, their Constitutions, Properties, and Operations, whereby I mean not only Matter, and Body, but Spirits also, which have their proper Natures, Constitutions, and Operations as well as Bodies. This in a little more enlarged Sense of the Word, I call φυσική, *or natural Philosophy*. The end of this, is bare speculative Truth, and whatsoever can afford the Mind of Man any such, falls under this branch, whether it be God himself, Angels, Spirits, Bodies, or any of their Affections, as Number, and Figure, *etc.*

§ 3. *Secondly*, *Πρακτική*, The Skill of Right applying our own Powers and Actions, for the Attainment of Things good and useful. The most considerable under this Head, is *Ethicks*, which is the seeking out those Rules, and Measures of humane Actions, which lead to Happiness, and the Means to practise them. The end of this is not bare Speculation, and the Knowledge of Truth; but Right, and a Conduct suitable to it.

§ 4. *Thirdly*, The Third Branch may be called σημειωτική, or *the Doctrine of Signs*, the most usual whereof being Words, it is aptly enough termed also λογική, Logick; the business whereof, is to consider the Nature of Signs, the Mind makes use of for the understanding of Things, or conveying its Knowledge to others. For since the Things, the Mind contemplates, are none of them, besides

§ 1. *Three sorts.* § 2. *First*, Physica. § 3. *Secondly*, Practica. § 4. *Thirdly*, Σημειωτική.

(2 *ll. above* 1) XXI] **2–5** | XX **1** (1) Humane] **1–3** (humane **1**) | Human **4–5** (5) End] **2–5** | Ends **1** (14, 18, 25, 27, 2 *ll. below* 30) *Greek accents and spellings amended edit.* (17) any] **2–5** | any other **1** (30) , are] **1–3** | are **4–5**

it self, present to the Understanding, 'tis necessary that something else, as a Sign or Representation of the thing it considers, should be present to it: And these are *Ideas*. And because the Scene of *Ideas* that makes one Man's Thoughts, cannot be laid open to the immediate view of another, nor laid up any where but in the Memory, a no very sure Repository: Therefore to communicate our Thoughts to one another, as well as record them for our own use, Signs of our *Ideas* are also necessary. Those which Men have found most convenient, and therefore generally make use of, are articulate Sounds. The Consideration then of *Ideas* and *Words*, as the great Instruments of Knowledge, makes no despicable part of their Contemplation, who would take a view of humane Knowledge in the whole Extent of it. And, perhaps, if they were distinctly weighed, and duly considered, they would afford us another sort of Logick and Critick, than what we have been hitherto acquainted with.

§ 5. *This* seems to me *the first and most general*, *as well as natural division* of the Objects of our Understanding. For a Man can employ his Thoughts about nothing, but either the Contemplation of *Things* themselves for the discovery of Truth; Or about the Things in his own Power, which are his own *Actions*, for the Attainment of his own Ends; Or the *Signs* the Mind makes use of, both in the one and the other, and the right ordering of them for its clearer Information. All which three, *viz. Things* as they are in themselves knowable; *Actions* as they depend on us, in order to Happiness; and the right use of *Signs* in order to Knowledge, being *toto cælo* different, they seemed to me to be the three great Provinces of the intellectual World, wholly separate and distinct one from another.

§ 5. *This is the first Division of the Objects of Knowledge.*

FINIS

(3–5) Scene . . . nor] **4–5** | *Ideas* of one Man's Mind cannot immediately be laid open to the view of another; nor be themselves **1–3** (6) a . . . Repository] **4–5** | which is apt to let them go and lose them **1–3** (6–7) Thoughts to one] **4–5** | *Ideas* one to **1–3** (11) makes] **1er–5** | make **1** (17) For] **2–5** | For since **1**

INDEX[1]

[1] *The Index add.* **2–5**. *The page numbers in the copy-text have been altered by adaption to the present edition.* [2] ABBOT . . . § 26.] *add.* **4–5** [3] What,] **3, 5** | What **2, 4**. *Page number given follows* **2–3**; *page number* (347) *that is in both* **4** *and* **5** *entails reference to IV. vi. 1, and III. ii. 1, respectively.* [4] Abstraction . . . § 1.] *add.* **4–5** [5] 385–6] *Page number given follows* **2–3**; *page numbers in* **4–5** *entail reference to II. xxxi instead of to II. xxxii.* [6] ACCIDENT,] **3, 5** | ACCIDENT **2, 4** [7] § 69.] **2–3, 5** | § 69 **4** [8] 1, 2.] *add.* **4–5** [9] 525–7 . . . § 7.] *add.* **4–5**. *In* **4**, *the page number* (*adapted in* **5**) *is printed* 341 *instead of* 314. [10] § 12.] *edit.* | § 13. **2–5** [11] ANTIPATHY . . . § 7.] *add.* **4–5** [12] Natural . . . Caus'd . . . *ibid.*] **4**; *not in* **2–3, 5** [13] 686. § 21. . . . 686. § 22. . . . *ibid.* § 22.] *edit.* | ib. 21. . . . ib. 22. . . . ib. 22. **2–5** ([*2nd*] 22. *is* 22 *in* **4**) [14] Enthusiasm . . . § 3.] **4**; *not in* **2–3, 5**. *In* **4**, *the section number is* 27. [15] What . . . § 3.] **2–4**; *not in* **5**. *Page numbers given follow* **2–3**; *in* **4**, *the page numbers wrongly repeat those given in* **2–3**.

[1] Often . . . 2.] **2–4**; *not in* **5**. *Page number given follows* **2–3**; *reading in* **4** *is* '*ib.* § 1, 2.', *which entails reference to IV. xv instead of to IV. xvi.* [2] Dissent . . . § 15.] **2–4** (§ 15, 16. **2–3**); *not in* **5** [3] *This entry, and the following entries under* ASSOCIATION of Ideas, *add.* **4–5** [4] *This entry om.* **5** [5] what] **2–3, 5**, | *what* **4** [6] AXIOMS . . . § 1.] **4**; *not in* **2–3, 5** [7] Being] **4–5** | *B.* **2–3** [8] § 10.] **5** | *ibid.* **4** | § 9. **2–3** [9] B.] **2–4** | Be **5** [10] BODY.] *In* **2–5**, *these entries under* 'BODY' *followed the two entries under* 'BRUTES' *given below.* [11] no] **2–4**; *om.* **5** [12] *In* **2–4**, § *17 occurs on p. 62, but they cite* '64'. [13] § *11 occurs on p. 61 in* **4** *and on p. 75 in* **5**; *but* **4** *cites* '60' *and* **5** *cites* '71'. [14] § 11.] **4–5** | § 12. **2–3** (*which wrongly cite* '48' *as the page number*) [15] *The reference given in* **2–3** ('126. §. 11.') *and the first of the two references given in* **4** ('126. §. 11. 176. §. 1.') *are wrong.* [16] *ibid.*] **4–5** | 175. **2–3**

D[11]

[1] § 3.] **2–4**; *om.* **5** [2] Of Knowledge, *ibid.*] **2–4** (**2–3** ', 333. §. 3.'); *om.* **5** [3] and . . . § 15.] **2–4** (**4** *wrongly repeats page number given in* **2–3**); *om.* **5** [4] CHANGELINGS] **5** | CHANGLINGS **2–4** [5] *This entry om.* **5** [6] **4** *cites wrong page number* ('79' *instead of* '75'), *adapted by* **5**. [7] § 5, 6, 7.] **2–3, 5** | 5, 6, 7. **4** [8] § 8.] **5** | § 18. **2–4** [9] § 1.] **5** | § 7. **2–4** [10] § 16.] *edit.* | § 15. **2–4**. *The whole entry om.* **5** [11] D] **2–3, 5** | C **4** [12] Genus] **2–3** | Genius **4–5** [13] *This entry om.* **5**

[1] § 58.] **2–4** | § 38. **5** (*but cites correct page number*) [2] DESPAIR] **4–5** | DISPAIR **2–3**. *In* **2–5**, *this entry follows that under* DISCOURSE *below.* [3] *Wrong page number* ('297' *instead of* '279') *cited in* **2–3**; *wrong page numbers* ('202, 203' *instead of* '292, 293') *cited in* **4** (*adapted in* **5**). [4] § 10, 11.] **2–3** (*likewise* **Coste**) | § 10, 15. **4–5** [5] **4** *wrongly cites same page number* ('168' *instead of* '169') *as* **2–3**. [6] *Section numbers have been editorially altered; see* 192(3), *n.* [7] § 9.] **2–3** | *Se* 9. **4**. *This whole entry om.* **5** [8] EDUCATION . . . § 3.] *add.* **4–5** [9] **4** *cites wrong page number* ('420' *instead of* '422'). [10] *This entry, and the following entries under* ENTHUSIASM, *add.* **4–5**

[1] Enthusiasm] *edit.* | *Enth.* **4–5** [2] what] **2–3, 5** | *what* **4** [3] *This entry, and the following entries under* ERROR, *in* **4** *wrongly cite the same page numbers as in* **2–3**. [4] 711.] *Page number given follows* **2–3**; *page number cited in* **4** *is* '401' (*as in* **2–3**) *instead of* '431', *while that in* **5** *wrongly entails reference to IV. v. 7.* [5] Real and Nominal] **2–3, 5** | *Real and Nominal* **4** [6] § 4, 5, 6.] **2–4**; *om.* **5** [7] *Wrong page number cited in* **5.** [8] 2.] **4–5**; *not in* **2–3** [9] Essences] **5** | *Essences* **2–4** [10] 455.] *Page number given follows* **2–3, 5**; *page number cited in* **4** *is* '255' (*as in* **2–3**) *instead of* '267'. [11] in several] **4–5** | or indifferent **2–3** [12] 453. § 26.] *Page and section numbers given follow* **2–3** *instead of* **4–5**, *which entail reference to p. 455, § 28.* [13] Es.] **5** | *Es.* **2–4**. [14] Idea] **5** | *Idea* **2–4** [15] 416.] *edit.* (*following* **2–3, 5**)| ib. 230. **4**. (*Instead of* '230' (*as in* **2–3**), '242' *should be cited in* **4**.) [16] Es.] **5** | *Es.* **2–4** [17] Idea] **5** | *Idea* **2–4** [18] E.] **5** | *E.* **2–4** [19] § 27.] *Section number has been editorially altered; see 192(3), n.*

[1] § 3.] **2–4** | § 2. **5** [2] § 3.] **5** | § 2. **2–4** [3] § 11.] **5** | § 1. **2–4**
[4] Should] *edit.* | should **4–5** [5] Should . . . § 26.] *add.* **4–5** [6] § 3.] **2–4** | § 2. **5** [7] § 11.] **5** | § 12. **2–4** [8] 179. § 26.] *add.* **4–5** [9] , 654. § 2.] *Reference follows* **5**; **2–4** *read* ', 2.' [10] 688.] *Reference follows* **5**; *wrong page number* ('293') *cited in* **2–4**. [11] contra-distinguish'd] **2–3, 5** | contra distinguish'd **4**
[12] 691–4] **4** *cites* '419. *etc.*', **5** *similarly*; **2–3** *cite* '395.' [13] 168.] *Reference follows* **5**; *wrong page number* ('89' *instead of* '82') *cited in* **2–4**. [14] § 6.] **2–3** | § 9. **4**. *The whole entry om.* **5** [15] 452. § 24.] *edit.*; **2–3** *cite* '244. § 10' *and* **5** *cites* '353. § 10', *which entail reference to* III. iii. 10; **4** *copies reference in* **2–3**. [16] 263.] *Wrong page number cited in* **5**. [17] made, . . . § 9.] *edit.* | made . . . Sect. 9. **4** | made . . . § 9. **5**
[18] GENERAL Ideas . . . § 31.] **4–5** | GENERAL Knowledge what, [562]. § 31. **2–3**

H

[1] 159. § 9.] **4**; *not in* **2–3, 5** [2] *In* **2–5**, *this entry follows the entries under* GENUS *below*. [3] not] **2–3**; *om.* **4–5** [4] § 9.] **2–4** | § 10. **5** [5] § 1.] **2–4** | § 8. **5** [6] 89–90.] *Page numbers given follow* **5**; **2–4** *wrongly cite* '3' *instead of* '30'. [7] Being] **2–3, 5** | being **4** [8] § 50.] **2–3, 5** | § 54. **4** [9] HABIT,] **2–3, 5** | HABIT. **4**

[1] HISTORY,] **5** | HISTORY **2–4** [2] § 13.] **4–5** | § 113. **2–3** [3] *This entry om.* **5**; **4** *wrongly copies page number cited in* **2–3**. [4] *This entry om.* **5**; **4** *wrongly cites* '257' *instead of* '357'. [5] *This entry om.* **5**. [6] *First page reference om.* **5**. [7] 117.] *Page number given follows* **5**; **2–4** *wrongly cite* '39' *instead of* '49'. [8] [Ch. v.]] *edit.* | *S.* 1. **2–5** [9] § 7.] *add.* **5** [10] 286.] *Page number given follows* **2–3**, **5**; **4** *wrongly cites* '151' *instead of* '153', *copying (correct) page number in* **2–3**. [11] God] **3–5** | God, **2** [12] Infinity] *edit.* | infinitely **2–5** [13] 364.] *Page number given follows* **2–3**, **5**; **4** *wrongly cites* '207' *instead of* '201'. [14] adequate,] **2–3**, **5** | Adequate. **4**

[1] § 4, 5.] *edit.* | 4, 5. **2–5** [2] § 3.] **2–4** | § 11. **5** [3] § 13.] *edit.* | 13. **2–5** [4] § 14.] *edit.* | 14. **2–5** [5] reference,] **2–3, 5** | reference. **4** [6] least . . . false,] **2–3** | lest . . . false **4–5** [7] false,] **5** | false **2–4** [8] resemblances, *ibid.*] **2–4** | Resemblances. **5** [9] § 18.] **2–3** | § 26. **4–5.** *Page number given follows* **2–3.** [10] or] **2–3** | of **4–5** [11] made;] *edit.* | made **2–5** [12] Substances,] *edit.* | Substances **2–5** [13] *Zahab*, 468. § 47.] **4–5** | *Zahab.* **2–3** [14] names, 474. § 1.] **4–5** | names. **2–3** [15] § 2.] *add.* **4–5** [16] privative] **2–3** | private **4–5** [17] nothing,] **2–3, 5** | nothing **4** [18] *This entry not in* **2–3, 5.** [19] What] *edit.* | what **4**

[1] *Page number cited in* **5** *is* '22' *instead of* '222'. [2] 337. § 11.] *This follows* **2–3**; *om.* **4–5** [3] *Page number cited in* **5** *is* '325' *instead of* '225'. [4] *No page number cited in* **5**. [5] *ibid.*] **4–5** | [553]. § 23. **2–3** [6] 123.] *A citation of* '§ 1.' *add.* **5**; *but on the page it cites, there are two sections so numbered, belonging to different chapters.* [7] 49.] *A citation of* '§ 5.' *add.* **5** [8] 672–3.] *Page numbers given follow* **2–4**; **5** *adds citation of* '§ 2, 3, 4.' [9] 369. § 15.] *This entry om.* **5**; **2–4** *wrongly cite* '103' *instead of* '205'. [10] 370.] *Wrong page number* ('204' *instead of* '205') *cited in* **4**.

[1] 210. § 3.] *edit.* | *ib. S.* **2–5** [2] I.] **5** | *I.* **2–4**. [3] § 5.] *edit.* | § 4. **2–4**. *The whole entry om.* **5**. [4] **5** *adds the entry* 'INVENTION, wherein it consists, 7.' *immediately before* JOY; *this insertion refers to an excerpt from Locke's* Reply to the Bishop of Worcester. [5] § 2.] *edit.* | § 10. **2–4** [6] wherein . . . Men's] **2–4**; *om.* **5**. [7] Judgments] **5** | *Judgments* **2–4** [8] 652.] *om.* **5**. *Page number given follows* **2–3**; **4** *cites* '39' *instead of* '393'. [9] J.] **5** | *J.* **2–4** [10] 653.] *edit.* | 37. 5. **2–5**. ('375' *would be correct reference in* **2–3**, *but not in* **4–5**.) [11] 685. § 16.] *Reference given follows* **2–3**; **4** *cites* '411. §. 5.' *which entails reference to IV. xvi. 5*; **5** *omits* '§ 16.' [12] Knowledge] **4–5** | *K.* **2–3**. [13] 302.] **4** *wrongly cites* '161' *instead of* '162'. [14] *This entry om.* **5** [15] K.] **5** | *K.* **2–4** [16] Ideas] **5** | *Ideas* **2–4**. (*Likewise at second entry below.*)

L

[1] *In* **2–3**, *an entry* 'Our *K.* of Identity and Diversity, as large as our *Ideas*, 311. § 8.' *intervenes before the next entry in* **4–5** 'Of . . . § 11.'; *cf. the entry* 'Of Identity and Diversity . . .' *below.* [2] K.] **5** | *K.* **2–4** [3] 543. § 8.] *add.* **4–5** [4] 603.] *Page number cited in* **4–5** *refers to the beginning, and not to the most relevant portion, of the section.* [5] § 2, 3.] *edit.* | § 2. **4–5** | § 3. **2–3** [6] Sensible . . . *etc.*] **2–4**; *om.* **5**. (*Page number cited in* **4** *is* '390'—*and* **4** *has two pages so numbered.*) [7] 640.] *Page number is wrongly cited in* **5** ('444' *instead of* '544'). [8] § 9.] **2–3** | § 7. **4–5** [9] necessary,] **5** | necessary **2–4** [10] 402.] *Page numbers cited in* **2–5** *wrongly entail reference to II. xx. 1–3 instead of to III. i. 1–3.* [11] *In* **2–5** *this entry is repeated immediately following the next entry.*

[1] 509.] *Wrong page number is cited in* **2–3**. [2] Idea] **5** | *Idea* **2–4** [3] 515.] *Page number given follows* **2–3**; **4** *cites* '395' *instead of* '305'. [4] Making . . . § 12.] **2–4**; *om.* **5** [5] 515.] *Page number given follows* **2–3**; **4** *cites* '293' (*as in* **2–3**) *instead of* '305'. [6] Meaning . . . § 13.] **2–4**; *om.* **5** [7] *This entry om.* **5**. [8] *This entry om.* **5**. [9] tho'] **3, 5** | tho **2, 4** [10] [241.] § 15.] *add.* **4–5** [11] Mind,] **5** | Mind **4** [12] *This entry add.* **4–5**. [13] 494–5.] *A citation of* '§ 7.' *add.* **5** [14] MADNESS . . . § 4.] *add.* **4–5** [15] shape,] **2–3, 5** | shape. **4** [16] 453. § 26.] **4**; *not in* **2–3, 5**. *Page number wrongly cited in* **4** ('254' *instead of* '266'). [17] § 27.] **4–5** | § 26. **2–3** [18] 308–11 and 313.] *edit.* | p. 166. and p. 169. **4** | 454. § 6. **5** | 310. § 6. **2–3**

[1] in us] *add.* **4–5** [2] *ibid.*] **4–5** | [623]. § 10. **2–3** [3] *Page numbers given follow* **2–3, 5**; **4** *wrongly cites same page numbers* ('341, 346') *as in* **2–3**. [4] self-evident] **2–3, 5** | self evident **4** [5] *Page number given follows* **2–3, 5**; **4** *wrongly cites same page number as in* **2–3**. [6] *This entry om.* **5**. *Page number wrongly cited in* **2–4**; *in* **2–3** *it is misprinted* '267' *instead of* '367'; **4** *wrongly copies* '267'. [7] *Page number given follows* **2–3, 5**; **4** *wrongly cites same page number* ('344') *as in* **2–3**. [8] *Page number given follows* **2–3**; **4** *wrongly cites same page number* ('389') *as in* **2–3**; **5** *wrongly cites* '550' *instead of* '577'. [9] 598–601.] **5** *adds citation of* '§ 11, 12.' [10] Maxims . . . § 11.] **4**; *not in* **2–3, 5** [11] The . . . 598–601.] **4**; *not in* **2–3, 5** [12] only] **4–5** | only, **2–3** [13] § 12, 20.] **4–5** | § 12–20. **2–3** [14] known,] **2–4**; *om.* **5** [15] MIND,] **5** | MIND **2–4**

[1] Ms.] **5** | *Ms.* **2–4** [2] 165. § 5.] *This reference om.* **5**. *Page number is misprinted in* **2–4** ('p. 8' *for* 'p. 80'). [3] M.] **5** | *M.* **2–4** [4] M.] **5** | *M.* **2–4** [5] if] **2–3** | of **4–5** [6] § 16.] **4–5** | § 16. and **2–3** [7] § 15.] **2–3, 5** | § 15 **4** [8] to] **2–3, 5** | to to **4** [9] M.] **5** | *M.* **2–4** [10] reconciled] **2–3, 5** | reeonciled **4** [11] 9,] *add.* **4–5** [12] *Page number cited in* **4** *is* '340' *instead of* '339'; *citations in* **2–3, 5** *are correct.* [13] *Page number cited in* **4** *is* '349' *instead of* '348'; *citations in* **2–3, 5** *are correct.* [14] Ns.] **5** | *Ns* **4** | *Ns.* **2–3** [15] Ns.] **5** | *Ns.* **2–4** [16] § 2.] *edit.* | § 1. 2. [17] And . . . § 3.] *The arrangement of this entry as subsidiary to the preceding follows* **2**. useless] **5** | useful **2–4** § 3.] *edit.* | 2. **2–5** [18] Ns.] **5** | *Ns.* **2–4** [19] [417].] **2–3, 5** | 243 [417] **4** [20] Ideas] **5** | *Ideas* **2–4** [21] [420].] **4**; **5** *adds citation of* '§ 2.'; **2–3** *add* 'S.' (*without a section number*).

[1] 421.] **4** *cites* '*ibid.*'; **2–3, 5** *cite pagination.* [2] § 3.] *edit.* | 3. **2–5** [3] § 7.] **5** | 7. **2–4** [4] *in linea predicamentali*,] *edit.* | in *linea predicamentali* **4**. (*Slightly different forms also in* **2–3, 5**.) [5] § 16.] *edit.* | 16. **2–5** [6] § 2.] **4–5** | § 2, 3. **2–3** [7] Ns.] **5** | *Ns.* **2–4** [8] 47.] **2–3, 5** | 47 **4** [9] § 9.] **2–3** | § 3. **4**. *The whole entry om.* **5**. [10] § 17.] *edit.* | § 16. **2–5** [11] Names,] **2–3** | Names **4–5** [12] 133.] **4** *wrongly cites* 'p. 60' *instead of* 'p. 59'. [13] Mr. . . . § 11.] *add.* **4–5**. **4** *wrongly cites page number as* '360' *instead of* '359'.

[1] *ibid.*] **2–4**; **5** *adds citation of* '§ 9.' [2] 217. § 13.] *om.* **5**. *Page number given follows* **2–3**; **4** *wrongly cites* '12' *instead of* '112'. [3] examined,] **2–3** | examined **4–5** [4] Os.] **5** | *Os.* **2–4** [5] 658.] *Page number given follows* **2–3**; **4** *wrongly copies* '379' *cited in* **2–3.** [6] Often . . . § 3.] **2–4**; *om.* **5** [7] Organs] **5** | *Organs* **2–4** [8] **4** *wrongly cites same page number* '161' *as in* **2–3**. [9] strongly] **2–3** | presently **4–5** [10] PARROT . . . *ibid.*] *add.* **4–5** [11] PASCAL,] **5** | PASCAL **2–4** [12] 714.] *Page number given follows* **2–3**; **4** *wrongly copies* '403' *cited in* **2–3.** [13] Ps.] **5** | *Ps.* **2–4** [14] § 39.] **2–4** | § 59. **5** [15] *This entry is an independent one, and not subsidiary to* PASSIONS, *in* **2–3**. [16] P.] **5** | *P.* **2–4** [17] Ideas] **5** | *Ideas* **2–4** [18] PERSON] **2–3, 5** | REASON **4** [19] P.] **5** | *P.* **2–4** [20] 340–1.] *Page number given follows* **2–3**; **4** *wrongly cites* '148' *instead of* '186', *and* **5** *wrongly cites* '152' *instead of* '226'. [21] *etc.*] **5** | etc. **2–4** [22] personal] **5** | *personal* **2–4** [23] 341.] **4** *wrongly copies page number cited in* **2–3.**

[1] 170.] *Wrong page number* ('82' *instead* of '83') *cited in* **2–4**. [2] 232.] *Wrong page number* ('p. 122.' *instead of* 'p. 123.') *cited in* **4**. [3] Idea] **5** | *Idea* **2–4** [4] 299. § 7.] **5**; **4** *wrongly copies correct page number* ('159') *and incorrect section number* ('§. 2.') *cited in* **2–3**. [5] 300.] *Wrong page number* ('168' *instead of* '161') *cited in* **4**. [6] 661.] *edit.*; *page numbers cited in* **2–5** *entail reference to IV. xv. 6 instead of to IV. xvi. 6.* [7] § 13, 14.] *edit.* | § 13. **2–5** [8] 382.] **4** *wrongly copies page number cited in* **2–3**. [9] 617.] *edit.* | *ib.* **2–5**

[1] 617.] *Page number is misprinted* ('253' *for* '353') *in* **2–3**. [2] are particular,] **2–3** | are particular **4** | , are particular **5** [3] 574 . . . § 5.] **2–3, 5**; *in* **4**, *these references are preceded by a reproduction of them but with the page numbers cited in* **2–3**. [4] QUALITY.] *edit.* | QUALITY **2–4** | QUALITY, **5** [5] § 12, 13.] **2–3, 5** | 12, 13. **4** [6] could] **2–4** | would **5** [7] Primary,] **2–3** | Primary **4–5** [8] 140–2.] **4** *cites* 'p. 64, 65.' *while* **2–3** *cite* 'p. 64.' (*likewise* **5**). [9] § 25.] **4–5** | § 27. **2–3** [10] § 11.] *edit.* | § 12. **2–5** [11] *This entry add.* **4–5**. [12] judge of] **5** | judge **4** [13] *This entry add.* **4–5** [14] § 3.] **2–3**; *om.* **4–5**

[1] to,] **2–3** | to **4** [2] *Page number in* **4** *is misprinted* ('410' *for* '416'). [3] According . . . § 23.] **2–4**; *om.* **5** [4] 696.] *Page number given follows* **2–3**; *that cited in* **4** *entails reference to IV. xx. 11 instead of IV. xviii. 11.* [5] To . . . § 11.] **2–4**; *om.* **5** [6] Terms,] **5** | Terms **2–4** [7] R.] **5** | *R.* **2–4** [8] 349.] **4** *wrongly cites same page number as in* **2–3**. [9] 360. § 18] *edit.* | *ibid.* **4–5** | [360]. § 17 **2–3** [10] 360.] *add.* **4–5** [11] Rs.] **5** | *Rs.* **2–4** [12] § 5.] **4–5** | § 55. **2–3** [13] R.] **5** | *R.* **2–4** [14] § 7.] **2–3** | § 6. **4–5** [15] R.] **5** | *R.* **2–4** [16] 319.] **4** *wrongly copies same page numbers as in* **2–3**, *thereby entailing reference to II. xxiv. 1 instead of to II. xxv. 1.* [17] R.] **5** | *R.* **2–4** [18] § 2.] **2–3** | § 1. **4–5** [19] Rs.] **5** | *Rs.* **2–4** [20] 327.] *Page number given follows that cited in* **2–3** ('177'); **4** *wrongly cites* '171'; *page number cited in* **5** *wrongly entails reference to II. xxv. 6 instead of to II. xxvi. 6.* [21] RELIGION,] *edit.* | RELIGION **2–5** [22] R.] *edit.* | *R.* **2–4** [23] 490.] *Wrong page number cited in* **4**. [24] The . . . § 23.] **2–4**; *om.* **5** [25] 356.] **4** *wrongly copies same page number as in* **2–3**. [26] § 13.] **2–3** | § 14. **4–5** [27] Belief . . . § 15.] *add.* **4–5** [28] R.] *edit.* | *R.* **2–5** [29] 689.] *Page number is misprinted in* **4** ('411' *for* '417'). [30] R.] *edit.* | *R.* **2–5**

[1] Eye,] **5** | Eye **2–4** [2] 344–5.] *Page number is misprinted in* **4** ('199' *for* '189'). [3] needed] **4–5** | need **2–3** [4] 139–40.] **5** *adds citation of* '§ 21.'. [5] Ss.] *edit.* | *Ss.* **2–4** | S. **5** [6] contact] **2–3** | contract **4** [7] Cannot . . . § 11.] **2–4**; *om.* **5** [8] § 11, 12.] *edit.* | § 11. **2–5** [9] S.] **5** | *S.* **2–4** [10] Power . . . § 1.] *add.* **4–5** [11] § 19.] **2–3, 5** | § 1 . [*sic*] **4** [12] 620.] **4** *wrongly cites* '372' *instead of* '373'. [13] 622.] **4** *wrongly copies page number cited in* **2–3** ('356' *instead of* '375').

[1] S's.] **5** | *Ss.* **2–4** [2] SOUND,] **5** | SOUND **2–4** [3] § 13.] *edit.* | § 12. **2–5** [4] 173.] *Wrong page numbers cited in* **2–5** ('65' *instead of* '85' *in* **2–4**; '76' *instead of* '103' *in* **5**). [5] § 21.] *edit.* | § 20. **2–5** [6] S.] *edit.* | *S.* **2–4** | Soul **5** [7] 203.] **2–4** *wrongly cite* 'p. 102' *instead of* 'p. 103'. [8] S.] *edit.* | *S.* **2–4** | Soul **5** [9] S.] *edit.* | *S.* **2–4** | S **5** [10] 518.] *Page number given follows* **2–3**; *page numbers cited in* **4–5** *wrongly entail reference to III. x. 19–20 instead of to III. xi. 19–20 (see also entry* 'Of Animals . . . § 29.' *below*). [11] [*1st*] 443 . . . 13.] *These references are grouped somewhat differently in* **5**. [12] § 25.] **2–4** | § 35. **5** [13] Of Man . . . § 26.] *add.* **4–5** [14] Instance . . . 454.] *add.* **4–5** [15] § 36, 37.] **4–5** | § 35. **2–3** [16] S.] *edit.* | *S.* **2–4** | S **5**

[1] Ss.] *edit.* | *Ss.* **2–4** | Ss **5** [2] § 28.] **4–5** | § 32. **2–3** [3] Ss.] *edit.* | *Ss.* **2–4** | Ss **5** [4] 295.] **4** *wrongly copies page number cited in* **2–3**. [5] Ss.] *edit.* | *Ss.* **4** | Ss **5** [6] The . . . § 21.] *add.* **4–5** [7] In] **3** | in **2, 4–5** [8] Ss.] *edit.* | *Ss.* **2–4** | Ss **5**. (*Thus in all subsequent entries under* SUBSTANCE *which contain* 'Ss.'.) [9] perfectest] **2–3** | perfect **4–5** [10] S.] *edit.* | *S.* **2–4** | S **5** [11] § 6.] **2–4** | § 9. **5** [12] Connections . . . 672–5.] **4**; *not in* **2–3, 5** [13] S.] **5** | *S.* **2–4** [14] Whether . . . § 8.] *add.* **4–5**

[1] smells,] *edit.* | smells **2–4** | Smells, **5** [2] § 3, 4.] *edit.* | § 34. **2–4** [3] THINKING . . . § 3, 4.] **2–4** | THINKING. **5** [4] 664.] *Page number is misprinted in* **4** ('407' *for* '401'). [5] 578. § 11.] **2–4**; *om.* **5** [6] Love . . . § 1.] *add.* **4–5** [7] *ibid.*] *edit.* | ib. **4–5** [8] How . . . *ibid.*] *add.* **4–5** [9] 353–4.] *Page number given follows* **2–3**; *no page numbers cited in* **4–5**. [10] *In* **2–5** *another entry under* VERTUE *is included*: 'Wholly passive in the reception of simple Ideas, p. 49. § 25.'; *this belongs under* UNDERSTANDING *and is also the final entry under the latter in* **2–5**. [11] § 5, 6.] **4–5** | § 5. **2–3** [12] 164.] *Page number* ('56') *cited in* **2–4** *entails reference to II. vii. 2 instead of to II. xii. 2.* [13] Is . . . § 2.] **2–4**; *om.* **5** [14] Three . . . § 5.] *add.* **4–5** [15] 249, *etc.*] *In* **2–3**, *page number is misprinted* ('123' *for* '133'). [16] 131.] *Page number is misprinted in* **5**.

[1] UNIVERSALS,] **5** | UNIVERSALS **2–4** [2] is is,] **5** | is, **2–4** [3] 599.] *Page number given follows* **2–3**; *wrong page numbers cited in* **4–5**. (*See also* 602–3.) [4] W.] **5** | *W.* **2–4** [5] Is the . . . § 2.] **2–4**; *om.* **5** [6] Ws.] **5** | *Ws.* **2–4**. (*Thus in all subsequent entries under* WORDS *which contain* 'Ws.'.) [7] 492.] *No page number cited in* **2–3**. [8] Inconstancy] **3–5** | In constancy **2** [9] Words] *edit.* | *Words* **2–4** | Ws. **5** [10] Words] **5** | *Words* **2–4**. (*Thus in the two subsequent entries under* WORDS *which contain* 'Words'.) [11] 510.] *No page number is cited in* **2–5**. [12] another] **2–4** | and another **5** [13] § 14.] *edit.* | § 13. **2–5**.

FINIS

[1] 522.] *Page number is misprinted in* **4** ('409' *for* '309'). [2] 2. . . . § 5.] *In* **2–5** *this is printed as a main entry under* WORDS, *and not as a sub-entry.* [3] 290.] **4** *wrongly copies page number cited in* **2–3**. [4] W.] **5** | *W.* **2–4** [5] § 22.] **2–3** | § 23. **4–5**. (*Page cited in* **4** *does not contain any part of* § *23.*)